The
Crossword
Finisher

The Crossword Finisher

Compiled by
John Griffiths

St. Martin's Press
New York

Library of Congress Catalog Card Number: 77-92803
First published in the United States of America in 1978

Library of Congress Cataloging in Publication Data

Griffiths, John, 1942–
   The crossword finisher.

   1. Crossword puzzles—Glossaries, vocabularies, etc.
I. Title.
GV1507.C7G7   793.7'32'014   77-92803
ISBN 0-312-17687-2

Introduction

The case for a crossword finisher
'A 5-letter word, second letter "A" and fourth letter "A"!'
How many times have your crossword endeavours come to a
halt when faced with this kind of problem, especially when
there are no more letters to be filled in from unsolved clues?
Galling enough when there is more of the crossword still to
solve, but exasperating when this mere five-letter word, two-
fifths completed, is the very last problem to be surmounted.
There are only two alternatives: admit defeat and wait irritably
for the solution in tomorrow's newspaper, or work laboriously
through hundreds of dictionary pages in the hope of spotting
a word of the suitable length and meaning.

But here is a third alternative: a book designed specifically
to help you solve crossword puzzles, and in particular to enable
you, simply and effectively, to track down that last elusive clue
in which one or more letters are known. Let us take the example
of the missing 5-letter word. There are 4,000 5-letter words of
current crossword usage listed in this book. If the second letter
of the word is known to be 'A' the list of possible solutions
shortens to 620; and if the fourth letter is also known to
be 'A' the number of alternatives is dramatically reduced to 40.
It then becomes a simple matter of choice to isolate the correct
word.

How to use this book
The five chapters in this book deal with words of 3, 4, 5, 6 and
7 letters respectively, and each is further divided into sections
listing words alphabetically according to the known letter or
letters within the word. So for a 5-letter word where the
second letter is known the order will be as follows:

     — A — — — etc.
     — B — — — etc.
     — C — — — etc.
     — D — — — and so on.

Where two letters are known—say the third and the fifth—the order will be as follows:

    __ __ A __ A etc.
    __ __ A __ B etc.
    __ __ A __ C etc.
    . . . .
    __ __ B __ A and so on.

The procedure when searching for a word is as follows:

If one letter is known
1) select chapter appropriate for length of word;
2) find section where appropriate letter in word (second, fourth, etc.) is shown in bold type (e.g. **A**)
3) proceed through this section until appropriate letter in word changes to known letter.

If two letters are known
1) select chapter appropriate for length of word;
2) find section where appropriate letters in word are both indicated by an 'A';
3) proceed through this section until appropriate bold-type letter changes to known letter;
4) proceed further until the other letter (shown in italic at the top of the page) changes to second known letter.
(NB All pairs of even letters and most pairs of odd letters are listed. These constitute the combinations of letter pairs most frequently encountered in crossword puzzles.)

Following a change of the primary letter (in bold type) there will be a line space, and following a change of the secondary letter (in italics) a full-stop.

The vocabulary

The word-list represents a crossword user's vocabulary of over 21,000 words of 3, 4, 5, 6 and 7 letters. Of these, some 750 are geographical proper names marked with an (*), and some 1,000 are personal proper names marked with a (+). These proper names include first names, mythological names and a selection of surnames of, amongst others, artists, writers, composers and statesmen. A word which can serve as both a common word and a proper name is only entered once, e.g. *HARROW, +JASMINE. Of the plural noun forms only some of the irregular ones are included, e.g. RADII, LOAVES. Where a word may end in -ED or -ER, usually only one of the alternatives is listed, e.g. GAMBLER but not GAMBLED.

The value of this book does not necessarily cease when words of 8 letters or more are required; if the one or two known letters fall within the first 7 letters of the word, the stem of the word may be unearthed, e.g. ENGAGE.MENT, NATURAL.LY.

The word-list is selected to cover all but the most esoteric of crosswords. As no meanings are given, the presence of a large number of rare words would probably hinder rather than help the user. However, this book will be found invaluable as an aid for solving all kinds of crosswords.

The author and publishers have sought the help of the very latest computer techniques in the word-arrangement of this book. In this way human error, which would seriously prejudice the effectiveness of this work, has, it is hoped, been avoided.

Acknowledgements
The author and publishers wish to thank Valerie Brooks and
H. J. Smith of Computer Posting Ltd., 46 Oxford Street,
London W1N 9FJ, for their co-operation in the production of
this book.

This book is dedicated to Amanda and Samantha.

Contents

ABB	AYE	CAY.	DUG	FEW	GOY.	ICE	+KIM
+ABE	*AYR	CHI.	DUN	FEY	GUM	ICY.	KIN
ABY.		+CID.	DUO	*FEZ.	GUN	IDE	KIP
ACE	BAA	COB	DUX.	FIB	GUP	IDO.	+KIT
ACT.	BAD	COD	DYE	FID	+GUS	*IFE.	
+ADA	BAG	COG		FIE	GUT	ILK	LAB
ADD	BAN	CON	EAR	FIG	+GUY.	ILL.	LAC
ADO.	BAP	COO	EAT.	FIN	GYM	IMP.	LAD
AFT.	BAR	*COP	EBB.	FIR	GYP	INK	LAG
AGA	BAT	COR	EEL	FIT		INN.	LAH
AGE	BAY.	*COS	EEN	FIX.	HAD	ION	LAM
AGO.	BED	COT	EER.	+FLO	HAE	IOU.	LAP
AHA.	BEE	COW	EFT.	FLU	HAG	IRE	LAR
AID	BEG	COX	EGG	FLY.	HAH	IRK.	LAW
AIL	BEL	COY.	EGO.	FOB	HAM	+ISA	LAX
AIM	+BEN	CRY.	EKE.	FOE	HAP	ISM.	LAY.
AIN	BET.	CUB	ELF	FOG	HAS	ITS.	*LEA
AIR	BIB	CUD	ELK	FOP	HAT	IVE	LED
AIT.	BID	CUE	ELL	FOR	HAW	IVY	+LEE
ALB	BIG	CUP	ELM	FOX.	HAY.		LEG
ALE	BIN	CUR	*ELY.	FRO	HED	JAB	LEM
+ALF	BIS	CUT	EMU.	+FRY.	HEM	JAG	+LEN
ALL	BIT.		+ENA	FUG	HEN	JAH	+LEO
*ALN	BOA	DAB	END.	FUN	HEP	JAM	LET
ALP	+BOB	DAD	EON	FUR	HER	JAP	+LEW.
ALT.	BOG	DAM	+EOS.		HES	JAR	LID
+AMY.	BOO	+DAN	ERA	GAB	HEW	JAW	LIE
AND	BOT	DAW	ERE	GAD	HEX	JAY.	LIP
ANE	BOW	DAY.	ERG	GAG	HEY.	JET	LIT
+ANN	BOX	DEB	ERR.	GAL	HID	JEW.	+LIZ.
ANT	BOY.	DEW	*ESK	GAM	HIM	JIB	LOB
ANY.	BRA.	DEY.	ESQ.	GAP	HIP	JIG	LOG
APE	BUD	DID	ETA	GAR	HIS	+JIM.	LOO
APT.	BUG	DIE	ETC.	GAS	HIT.	+JOB	LOP
ARC	BUM	DIG	+EVA	+GAY.	HOB	+JOE	LOT
ARE	BUN	DIM	+EVE.	GEE	HOD	JOG	LOW.
ARK	BUR	DIN	EWE.	GEL	HOE	JOT	LSD.
ARM	BUS	DIP.	*EXE.	GEM	HOG	+JOY.	LUG
ART.	BUT	DOE	EYE	GEN	HOP	JUG	LUR
ASH	BUY.	DOG		GET.	HOT	JUT	LUX.
ASK	BYE	DOH	FAB	GIB	HOW		LYE
ASP		DOM	FAD	GIG	*HOY.	KAW	
ASS.	CAB	*DON	FAG	GIN.	HUB	+KAY.	MAC
+ATE.	CAD	+DOT.	FAN	GNU.	HUE	KEA	MAD
AUK.	CAM	DRY.	FAR	GOB	HUG	KEG	MAG
AVE.	CAN	DUB	FAT	GOD	HUM	+KEN	MAN
AWE	CAP	DUD	+FAY.	+GOG	HUN	KEX	+MAO
AWL	CAR	DUE	FED	GOO	HUT	KEY.	MAP
AWN.	CAT		FEE	GOT		KID	MAR
AXE.	CAW	DUE	FEN	GOV	+IAN.		MAT

MAW		PIT.	ROD	SOW.	TUG	WOO	PAD
+MAX	OAF	PLY.	ROE	SPA	TUN	WOW.	RAD
+MAY.	OAK	POA	ROT	SPY.	TUP	WRY.	SAD
+MEG	OAR	POD	ROW	STY.	TUT.	*WYE	WAD.
MEN	OAT.	+POE	+ROY.	SUB	TWA		HAE
MET	OBI.	POP	RUB	+SUE	TWO	YAK	+RAE.
MEW.	ODD	POT	RUE	SUM		YAM	OAF.
MHO.	ODE.	POX.	RUG	SUN	UGH.	YAP	BAG
MID	OER.	PRY.	RUM	SUP	+ULM	YAW.	FAG
MIL	OFF	PSI.	RUN		ULT.	YEA	GAG
MIX.	OFT.	PUB	RUT.	TAB	+UNA.	YEN	HAG
MOA	OHM	PUD	RYE	TAG	URN.	YES	JAG
MOB	OHO.	PUG		+TAM	USE	YET	LAG
MOD	OIL.	PUN	SAC	TAN	*USK	YEW.	MAG
MOO	OLD.	PUP	SAD	TAP		YOD	NAG
MOP	ONE.	PUS	SAG	TAR	VAC	YON	RAG
MOW.	OPT.	PUT.	SAL	+VAL	YOU	SAG
MRS.	ORB	PYX	+SAM	TAU	VAN		TAG
MUD	ORC		SAP	TAW	VAS	ZAX.	WAG.
MUG	ORE.	QUA	SAT	TAX	VAT.	ZED	HAH
MUM	OUR		SAW	*TAY.	VET	ZEE	JAH
	OUT.	+RAB	SAX	TEA	VEX.	ZEL	LAH
NAB	OVA.	RAD	SAY.	TEC	VIA	ZEN.	RAH.
NAG	OWE	+RAE	SEA	+TED	VIE	ZIP.	RAJ.
NAP	OWL	RAG	SEC	TEE	VIM	+ZOE	OAK
+NAT	OWN	RAH	SEE	TEN	VIZ.	ZOO	YAK.
NAY.		RAJ	SET	TER.	VOE		GAL
NEB	PAD	RAM	SEW	THE	VOW		PAL
+NED	PAL	RAN	SEX.	THO		BAA.	SAL
NEE	+PAM	RAP	SHE	THY.	WAD	CAB	+VAL.
NEF	PAN	RAT	SHY.	TIC	WAG	DAB	CAM
NET	PAP	RAW	SIC	TIE	WAN	FAB	DAM
NEW.	PAR	+RAY.	+SID	TIG	WAR	GAB	GAM
NIB	PAS	RED	SIN	+TIM	WAS	JAB	HAM
NIL	+PAT	REE	SIP	TIN	WAX	LAB	JAM
NIP	PAW	REF	SIR	TIP	WAY.	NAB	LAM
*NIS	PAX	+REG	SIS	TIS	WEB	+RAB	+PAM
NIT	PAY.	REM	SIT	TIT.	WED	TAB.	RAM
NIX.	PEA	REP	SIX.	TOD	WEE	LAC	+SAM
NOB	+PEG	REV	SKI	TOE	WEN	MAC	+TAM
NOD	PEN	+REX.	SKY.	+TOM	WET	SAC	YAM.
NOG	PEP	RHO.	SLY.	TON	WEY.	VAC.	BAN
NOR	PER	+RIA	SOB	TOO	WHO	BAD	CAN
NOT	PET	RIB	SOC	TOP	WHY.	CAD	+DAN
NOW	PEW.	RID	SOD	TOR	WIG	DAD	FAN
+NOX.	PHI.	RIG	SOL	TOT	WIN	FAD	+IAN
NUB	PIE	RIM	SON	TOW	WIT.	GAD	+JAN
NUN	PIG	RIP.	SOP	TOY.	WOE	HAD	MAN
NUT.	PIN	ROB	SOT	TRY.	WON	LAD	PAN
+NYE	PIP	ROC	SOU	TUB		MAD	RAN

TAN	HAW	ADO	+BEN	SEX	+CID	NIP	ALP.
VAN	JAW	IDO	DEN	VEX.	DID	PIP	ALT
WAN.	KAW		EEN	DEY	FID	RIP	ULT.
+MAO.	LAW	KEA	FEN	FEY	HID	SIP	FLU.
BAP	MAW	*LEA	GEN	HEY	KID	TIP	*ELY
CAP	PAW	PEA	HEN	KEY	LID	ZIP.	FLY
GAP	RAW	SEA	+KEN	WEY.	MID	AIR	PLY
HAP	SAW	TEA	+LEN		RID	FIR	SLY
JAP	TAW	YEA.	MEN	*FEZ	+SID.	SIR.	
LAP	YAW.	DEB	PEN		DIE	BIS	IMP.
MAP	LAX	NEB	TEN	*IFE.	FIE	HIS	EMU.
NAP	+MAX	WEB.	WEN	OFF.	LIE	*NIS	+AMY
PAP	PAX	SEC	YEN	AFT	PIE	SIS	
RAP	SAX	TEC.	ZEN.	EFT	TIE	TIS.	+ENA
SAP	TAX	BED	+LEO.	OFT	VIE.	AIT	+UNA.
TAP	WAX	FED	HEP		BIG	BIT	AND
YAP.	ZAX.	HED	PEP	AGA.	DIG	FIT	END.
BAR	BAY	LED	REP.	AGE.	FIG	HIT	ANE
CAR	CAY	+NED	EER	EGG.	GIG	+KIT	ONE.
EAR	DAY	RED	HER	UGH.	JIG	LIT	INK.
FAR	+FAY	+TED	OER	AGO	PIG	NIT	+ANN
GAR	+GAY	WED	PER	EGO	RIG	PIT	INN.
JAR	HAY	ZED.	TER.	AHA.	TIG	SIT	ANT.
LAR	JAY	BEE	HES	SHE	WIG.	TIT	GNU.
MAR	+KAY	*DEE	YES.	THE.	AIL	WIT.	ANY
OAR	LAY	FEE	BET	CHI	MIL	FIX	
PAR	+MAY	GEE	GET	PHI.	NIL	MIX	BOA
TAR	NAY	+LEE	JET	OHM.	OIL.	NIX	MOA
WAR.	PAY	NEE	LET	MHO	AIM	SIX.	POA.
GAS	+RAY	REE	MET	OHO	DIM	+LIZ	+BOB
HAS	SAY	SEE	NET	RHO	HIM	VIZ	COB
PAS	*TAY	TEE	PET	THO	+JIM		FOB
VAS	WAY	WEE	SET	WHO.	+KIM	EKE.	GOB
WAS.		ZEE.	VET	SHY	RIM	SKI.	HOB
BAT	ABB	NEF	WET	THY	+TIM	SKY	+JOB
CAT	EBB.	REF.	YET.	WHY	VIM.		LOB
EAT	+ABE	BEG	REV.		AIN	ALB.	MOB
FAT	OBI.	KEG	DEW	+RIA	BIN	OLD.	NOB
HAT	ABY	LEG	FEW	VIA.	DIN	ALE.	ROB
MAT		+MEG	HEW	BIB	FIN	+ALF	SOB.
+NAT	ACE	+PEG	JEW	FIB	GIN	ELF.	ROC
OAT	ICE.	+REG.	MEW	GIB	KIN	ELK	SOC.
+PAT	ACT.	BEL	+LEW	JIB	PIN	ILK.	COD
RAT	ICY	EEL	NEW	NIB	SIN	ALL	GOD
SAT		GEL	PEW	RIB.	TIN	ELL	HOD
TAT	+ADA.	ZEL.	SEW	SIC	WIN.	ILL.	MOD
VAT.	ADD	GEM	YEW.	TIC	DIP	ELM	NOD
TAU.	ODD.	HEM	HEX	+VIC.	HIP	*ULM.	POD
CAW	IDE	LEM	KEX	AID	KIP	*ALN.	ROD
DAW	ODE.	REM.	+REX	BID	LIP	+FLO.	SOD

TOD	FOR		PUB	LUR	*AYR.	JAB	DID
YOD.	NOR	BRA	RUB	OUR.	PYX	JIB	DUD.
DOE	TOR.	ERA.	SUB	BUS		+JOB.	END.
FOE	*COS	ORB.	TUB.	+GUS		LAB	FAD
HOE	+EOS.	ARC	PUS.	+ADA	LOB.	FED	
+JOE	BOT	ORC.	CUD	BUT	AGA	MOB.	FID
+POE	COT	ARE	DUD	CUT	AHA.	NAB	GAD
ROE	+DOT	ERE	MUD	GUT	BAA	NEB	GOD.
TOE	GOT	IRE	PUD.	HUT	BOA	NIB	HAD
VOE	HOT	ORE.	CUE	JUT	BRA.	NOB	HED
WOE	JOT	ERG.	DUE	NUT	+ENA	NUB.	HID
+ZOE.	LOT	ARK	HUE	OUT	ERA	ORB.	HOD.
BOG	NOT	IRK.	RUE	PUT	ETA	PUB.	KID.
COG	POT	ARM.	+SUE.	RUT	+EVA.	+RAB	LAD
DOG	ROT	URN.	BUG	TUT.	+ISA.	RIB	LED
FOG	SOT	FRO.	DUG	DUX	KEA.	ROB	LID
+GOG	TOT.	ERR.	FUG	LUX.	*LEA.	RUB.	LSD.
HOG	IOU	MRS.	HUG	BUY	MOA.	SOB	MAD
JOG	SOU	ART.	JUG	+GUY	OVA.	SUB.	MID
LOG	YOU.	CRY	LUG		PEA	TAB	MOD
NOG.	GOV.	DRY	MUG	+EVA	POA.	TUB.	MUD.
DOH.	BOW	+FRY	PUG	OVA.	QUA.	WEB	+NED
SOL.	COW	PRY	RUG	AVE	+RIA.		NOD.
DOM	HOW	TRY	TUG.	+EVE	SEA	ARC.	ODD
+TOM.	LOW	WRY	AUK.	IVE.	SPA.	ETC.	OLD.
CON	MOW		BUM	IVY	TEA	LAC.	PAD
*DON	NOW	+ISA.	GUM		TWA.	MAC.	POD
EON	ROW	LSD.	HUM	TWA.	+UNA.	ORC.	PUD.
ION	SOW	USE.	MUM	AWE	VIA.	ROC.	RAD
SON	TOW	ASH.	RUM	EWE	YEA	SAC	RED
TON	VOW	PSI.	SUM.	OWE.		SEC	RID
WON	WOW.	ASK	BUN	AWL	ABB	SIC	ROD.
YON.	BOX	*ESK	DUN	OWL.	ALB.	SOC.	SAD
BOO	COX	*USK.	FUN	AWN	BIB	TEC	+SID
COO	FOX	ISM.	GUN	OWN.	+BOB.	TIC.	SOD.
GOO	+NOX	ASP.	HUN	TWO	CAB	VAC	+TED
LOO	POX.	ESQ.	NUN		COB	+VIC	TOD.
MOO	BOY	ASS	PUN	AXE	CUB.		WAD
TOO	COY		RUN	*EXE	DAB	ADD	WED.
WOO	GOY	ETA.	SUN		DEB	AID	YOD.
ZOO.	*HOY	ETC.	TUN.	AYE	DUB.	AND.	ZED
*COP	+JOY	+ATE.	DUO.	BYE	EBB	BAD	
FOP	+ROY	ITS.	CUP	DYE	FAB	BED	+ABE
HOP	TOY	STY	GUP	EYE	FIB	BID	ACE
LOP			PUP	LYE	FOB.	BUD.	AGE
MOP	SPA.	QUA.	SUP	+NYE	GAB	CAD	ALE
POP	APE.	CUB	TUP.	RYE	GIB	+CID	ANE
SOP	APT	DUB	BUR	*WYE.	GOB.	COD	APE
TOP.	OPT.	HUB	CUR	GYM.	HOB	CUD.	ARE
COR	SPY	NUB	FUR	GYP.	HUB.	DAD	+ATE

AVE	TEE	MAG	BEL.	*ULM.	TAN	HAP	HER.
AWE	THE	+MEG.	EEL	VIM.	TEN	HEP	JAR.
AXE	TIE	MUG.	ELL.	YAM	TIN	HIP	LAR
AYE.	TOE.	NAG	GAL		TON	HOP.	LUR.
BEE	USE.	NOG.	GEL.	AIN	TUN.	IMP.	MAR.
BYE.	VIE	+PEG	ILL.	*ALN	URN.	JAP.	NOR.
CUE.	VOE.	PIG	MIL.	+ANN.	VAN.	KIP.	OAR
*DEE	WEE	PUG.	NIL.	AWN.	WAN	LAP	OER
DIE	WOE	RAG	OIL	BAN	WEN	LIP	OUR.
DOE	*WYE.	+REG.	OWL.	+BEN.	WIN	LOP.	PAR
DUE	ZEE	RIG	PAL.	BIN	WON.	MAP	PER.
DYE.	+ZOE	RUG.	SAL	BUN.	YEN	MOP.	SIR.
EKE		SAG	SOL.	CAN	YON.	NAP	TAR
ERE	+ALF.	TAG	+VAL.	CON.	ZEN	NIP.	TER
+EVE	ELF.	TIG	ZEL	+DAN		PAP	TOR.
EWE	NEF.	TUG.		DEN	ADO	PEP	WAR
*EXE	OAF.	WAG	AIM	DIN	AGO.	PIP	
EYE.	OFF.	WIG	ARM.	*DON.	BOO.	POP	ASS.
FEE	REF		BUM.	DUN.	COO.	PUP.	BIS
FIE		ASH.	CAM.	EEN	DUO.	RAP	BUS.
FOE.	BAG	DOH.	DAM	EON.	EGO.	REP	*COS.
GEE.	BEG	HAH.	DIM.	FAN	+FLO	RIP.	+EOS.
HAE	BIG	JAH.	DOM.	FEN	FRO.	SAP	GAS
HOE	BOG	LAH.	ELM.	FIN	GOO.	SIP	+GUS.
HUE.	BUG.	RAH.	GAM	FUN.	IDO.	SOP	HAS
ICE	COG.	UGH	GEM	GEN	+LEO	SUP.	HES
IDE	DIG		GUM	GIN	LOO.	TAP	HIS.
*IFE	DOG	CHI.	GYM.	GUN.	+MAO	TIP	ITS.
IRE	DUG.	OBI.	HAM	HEN	MHO	TOP	MRS.
IVE.	EGG	PHI	HEM	HUN.	MOO.	TUP.	*NIS.
+JOE.	ERG.	PSI.	HIM	+IAN	OHO.	YAP	PAS
+LEE	FAG	SKI	HUM.	INN	RHO.	ZIP	PUS.
LIE	FIG		ISM.	ION.	THO		SIS.
LYE.	FOG	RAJ	JAM	+JAN.	TOO.	ESQ	TIS.
NEE	FUG.		+JIM.	+KEN.	TWO.		VAS.
+NYE.	GAG	ARK	+KIM.	KIN.	WHO	AIR	WAS.
ODE	GIG	ASK	LAM	+LEN.	WOO.	*AYR.	YES
ONE	+GOG.	AUK.	LEM.	MAN	ZOO	BAR	
ORE	HAG	ELK	MUM.	MEN.		BUR.	ACT
OWE.	HOG	*ESK.	OHM.	NUN.	ALP	CAR	AFT
PIE	HUG.	ILK	+PAM.	OWN.	ASP.	COR	AIT
+POE.	JAG	INK	RAM	PAN	BAP.	CUR.	ALT
+RAE	JIG	IRK.	REM	PEN	CAP	EAR	ANT
REE	JOG	OAK.	RIM	PIN	*COP	EER	APT
ROE	JUG.	*USK.	RUM.	PUN.	CUP.	ERR.	ART.
RUE	KEG.	YAK	+SAM	RAN	DIP.	FAR	BAT
RYE.	LAG		SUM.	RUN.	FOP.	FIR	BET
SEE	LEG	AIL	+TAM	SIN	GAP	FOR	BIT
SHE	LOG	ALL	+TIM.	SON	GUP	FUR.	BOT
+SUE.	LUG.	AWL.	+TOM.	SUN.	GYP.	GAR.	BUT

CAT	VAT		IVY.
COT	VET.	BOX.	JAY
CUT.	WET	COX.	+JOY.
+DOT.	WIT.	DUX.	+KAY
EAT	YET	FIX	KEY.
EFT.		FOX.	LAY.
FAT	EMU.	HEX.	+MAY.
FIT.	FLU.	KEX.	NAY.
GET	GNU.	LAX	PAY
GOT	IOU.	LUX.	PLY
GUT.	SOU.	+MAX	PRY.
HAT	TAU.	MIX.	+RAY
HIT	YOU	NIX	+ROY.
HOT		+NOX.	SAY
HUT.	GOV.	PAX	SHY
JET	REV	POX	SKY
JOT		PYX.	SLY
JUT.	BOW.	+REX.	SPY
+KIT.	CAW	SAX	STY.
LET	COW.	SEX	*TAY
LIT	DAW	SIX.	THY
LOT.	DEW.	TAX.	TOY
MAT	FEW.	VEX.	TRY.
MET.	HAW	WAX.	WAY
+NAT	HEW	ZAX	WEY
NET	HOW.		WHY
NIT	JAW	ABY	WRY
NOT	JEW.	+AMY	
NUT.	KAW.	ANY.	*FEZ.
OAT	LAW	BAY	+LIZ.
OFT	+LEW.	BOY	VIZ
OPT	LOW.	BUY.	
OUT.	MAW	CAY	
+PAT	MEW	COY	
PET	MOW.	CRY.	
PIT	NEW.	DAY	
POT	NOW.	DEY	
PUT.	PAW	DRY.	
RAT	PEW.	*ELY.	
ROT	RAW	+FAY	
RUT.	ROW.	FEY	
SAT	SAW	FLY	
SET	SEW	+FRY.	
SIT	SOW.	+GAY	
SOT.	TAW	GOY	
TAT	TOW.	+GUY.	
TIT	VOW.	HAY	
TOT	WOW.	HEY	
TUT.	YAW	*HOY.	
ULT.	YEW	ICY	

6

+ADAM	AGIO	AIRY	BIDE	BULL.	BIRO	CHAT
ADAR	AKIN	AURA	BODE	BEMA	BORA	CHAW
AFAR	AMID	AWRY.	BODY	BOMB	BORE	CHAY
AGAR	AMIR	ALSO	*BUDE.	BUMF	+BORN	CLAD
+AHAB	+AMIS	APSE.	BEEF	BUMP.	BORT	CLAM
AJAR	ANIL	ALTO	BEEN	BAND	BURL	CLAP
+AJAX	+APIS	ANTE	BEEP	BANE	BURN	CLAW
+ALAN	ARIA	ANTI	BEER	BANG	BURP	CLAY
ALAR	ARID	ARTS	BEET	BANK	BURR	COAL
ALAS	*ASIA	ARTY.	BIER	BANT	BURY	COAT
AMAH	AVID	ABUT	BLEB	BEND	BYRE.	COAX
ANAL	AXIL	AGUE	BLED	BENT	BASE	CRAB
ARAB	AXIS.	ALUM	BLEW	BIND	BASH	CRAG
ARAR	ANKH.	ANUS	BOER	BINE	BASK	CRAM
AWAY	ABLE	AQUA.	BRED	BING	BASS	CRAN
AYAH.	ABLY	AMYL.	BREN	BOND	+BESS	CRAP
ABBA	ALLY	ADZE	BREW.	BONE	BEST	CRAW
ABBE	AXLE.		BIFF	*BONN	BISE	CZAR.
AMBO.	ACME	BAAL	BUFF.	*BRNO	BISK	*CEBU
ARCH	+ALMA	BEAD	+BOHR	BUNA	BOSH	*CUBA
ASCI.	ALMS	BEAK	BUHL.	BUND	BOSK	CUBE.
*ALDE	AMMO	BEAM	BAIL	BUNG	BOSS	COCA
+ANDY.	ARMS	BEAN	BAIT	BUNK	BUSH	COCK
ABED	ARMY.	BEAR	BLIP	BUNT.	BUSK	COCO.
+ABEL	ACNE	BEAT	BOIL	BLOB	BUSS	CADE
ABET	AINT	BEAU	BRIE	BLOC	BUST	CADI
ACER	+ANNA	BIAS	BRIG	BLOT	BUSY.	CEDE
*ADEN	+ANNE	BLAB	BRIM	BLOW	BATE	CODA
AGED	ARNI	BOAR	BRIO.	*BATH	CODE.
AHEM	*ARNO	BOAT	BAKE	BOOB	BETA	*CAEN
AKEE	AUNT.	BRAD	*BAKU	BOOK	+BETH	CHEF
ALEE	AEON	BRAE	BIKE.	BOOM	BITE	CHEW
AMEN	AGOG	BRAG	*BALA	BOON	BITT	CIEL
ANEW	AHOY	BRAN	BALD	BOOR	BOTH	CLEF
APED	ALOE	BRAT	BALE	BOOT	BOTT	CLEG
APEX	ALOW	BRAW	*BALI	BROW	*BUTE	CLEM
AREA	AMOK	BRAY.	BALK	BUOY.	BUTT.	+CLEO
+ARES	+AMOS	BABE	BALL	BARB	BLUB	CLEW
AVER	*AMOY	+BABS	BALM	BARD	BLUE	CO-ED
AWED	ANON	BABU	+BELL	BARE	BLUR	CREW.
AXED	ATOM	BABY	BELT	*BARI	BOUT.	CAFE
AYES.	ATOP	BUBO.	BILE	BARK	BEVY.	CUFF.
ALFA.	*AVON	+BACH	BILK	BARM	BAWD	CAGE.
ALGA.	AVOW	BACK	+BILL	BARN	BAWL	CEIL
ACHE	AXON.	BECK	BOLD	+BART	BOWL.	CHIC
ASHY.	*ALPS.	BICE	BOLE	BERE	BUZZ	CHID
ABIB	ACRE	BOCK	BOLL	BERG		CHIN
ACID	ADRY	BUCK.	BOLT	BERM	*CHAD	CHIP
+ACIS	AERY	BADE	BULB	+BERT	CHAP	CHIT
ADIT	*AGRA	+BEDE	BULK	BIRD	CHAR	+CLIO

CLIP	COOT	CLUB	DIEB	DUMP.	DUTY.	EPIC
COIF	CROP	CLUE	DIED	DANE	DAUB	+ERIC
COIL	CROW.	COUP	DIET	DANK	DOUR	*ERIE
COIN	CAPA	CRUX.	DOER	DENE	DRUB	EVIL
COIR	CAPE	CAVE	DOES	DENT	DRUG	EXIT.
CRIB.	COPE	CAVY	DREW	DENY	DRUM.	+ELLA.
CAKE	COPT	CIVE	DREY	DINE	+DAVE	+ELMA
COKE.	COPY.	COVE.	DUEL	DING	+DAVY	ELMO
CALF	CARD	COWL.	DUET	DINT	DEVA	ELMY
CALK	CARE	COXA.	DYED	DONE	DIVA	+EMMA.
CALL	CARK	+CUYP	DYER.	DONT	DIVE	+EDNA
CALM	+CARL		DAFF	DUNE	DIVI	ERNE
CALP	CARP	D-DAY	DAFT	DUNG	DOVE.	*ETNA.
CALX	CART	DEAD	DEFT	DUNK	+DAWN	EBON
CELL	CERE	DEAF	DEFY	DUNT	DEWY	ENOW
CELT	CERT	*DEAL	DOFF	DYNE.	DOWN.	EPOS
COLA	CIRC	DEAN	DUFF	DHOW	DOXY.	+EROS
COLD	CORD	DEAR	+DUFY.	DOOL	DAZE	*ETON
COLE	CORE	DHAK	DAGO	DOOM	DOZE	EXON
*COLL	CORF	DHAL	DIGS	DOOR.	DOZY	EYOT.
COLT	*CORK	DIAL	DOGE.	DOPE		ESPY.
CULL	CORM	DOAB	DAIL	DUPE.	*EDAM	EARL
CULM	CORN	DRAB	DAIS	DARE	EGAD	EARN
CULT.	CURB	DRAG	DOIT	DARK	*ELAN	ECRU
CAME	CURD	DRAM	DRIP.	DARN	+EVAN	EERY
CAMP	CURE	DRAT	DEJA.	DART	+EWAN	*EYRE
COMA	CURL	DRAW	DIKE	DERM	EXAM	+EZRA.
COMB	CURT.	DRAY	DUKE	DERV	EYAS.	EASE
COME	CASE	DUAL	DYKE.	DIRE	*ELBA	EAST
*COMO	CASH	DYAD	DALE	+DIRK	*ELBE.	EASY
CYMA	CASK	DYAK.	+DALI	DIRT	EACH	+ELSA
CYME.	CAST	DEBT	DELE	+DORA	ETCH.	ELSE
CANE	CESS	DIBS.	DELF	DORP	EDDA	ERSE
CANT	CIST	DACE	DELI	DORR	EDDY.	ERST.
CENT	COSH	DECK	DELL	DORY.	*EDEN	ELUL
CINE	COST	DICE	DILL	DASH	EKED	ETUI.
CONE	COSY	+DICK	DOLE	DESK	EVEN	ENVY
CONK	CUSP	DOCK	DOLL	DISC	EVER	
CONY.	CUSS	DUCE	DOLT	DISH	EWER	FEAR
CHOP	CYST.	DUCK	DULL	DISK	EYED.	FEAT
CHOW	CATE	DUCT.	DULY.	DISS	EDGE	FIAT
CLOD	CITE	DADA	DAME	DISS	EDGY	FLAG
CLOG	CITY	DADO	DAMN	DOSE	*EIGG	FLAK
CLOP	COTE	+DIDO	DAMP	DOSS	ERGO.	FLAM
CLOT	CUTE.	DODO	DEME	DOST	ECHO	FLAN
CLOY	CAUK	DUDE.	DEMI	DUSK	EPHA.	FLAP
+COOK	CAUL	DEED	DEMY	DUST.	EDIT	FLAT
COOL	CHUB	DEEM	DIME	DATA	EMIR	FLAW
COON	CHUG	DEEP	DOME	DATE	EMIT	FLAX
CO-OP	CHUM	DEER	DUMB	DOTE	+ENID	FLAY

FOAL	FEND	FIZZ	GALL	GAUR	HAIR	HOPI
FOAM	FENT	FUZZ	GELD	GEUM	HEIR.	HYPO.
FRAU	FIND		GILD	GLUE	HAKE	HARD
FRAY.	FINE	GEAN	+GILL	GLUM	HIKE.	HARE
FACE	FINK	GEAR	GILT	GLUT	HALE	HARK
FACT	FOND	GHAT	GOLD	GOUT	HALF	HARL
FICO	FONT	GLAD	GOLF	GRUB.	HALL	HARM
FOCI.	FUND	G-MAN	GULF	GAVE	HALM	HARP
FADE.	FUNK.	GNAT	GULL	GIVE	HALO	HART
FEED	FLOE	GNAW	GULP	GYVE.	+HALS	+HERA
FEEL	FLOG	GOAD	GYLE.	GAWK	HALT	HERB
FEET	FLOP	GOAL	GAME	GOWK	HELD	HERD
FIEF	FLOW	GOAT	GAMP	GOWN.	HELL	HERE
FLEA	FOOD	GRAB	GAMY	+GOYA	HELM	HERM
FLED	FOOL	GRAM	GIMP.	*GWYN.	HELP	+HERO
FLEE	FOOT	GRAY	GANG	GAZE	HILL	HERR
FLEW	FROG	*GUAM	+GENE		HILT	HERS
FLEX	FROM.	GYAL.	GENT	HEAD	HOLD	HIRE
+FRED	FARE	GABY	GONE	HEAL	HOLE	HORN
FREE	FARM	GIBE	GONG	HEAP	HOLM	HURL
FRET	FARO	*GOBI	GONK.	HEAR	HOLS	HURT.
FUEL.	FERN	GO-BY	GAOL	HEAT	+HOLT	HASH
*FIFE.	FIRE	GYBE.	GLOW	HOAR	HOLY	HASP
FOGY.	FIRM	+GIDE.	GOOD	HOAX.	HULA	HAST
FOHN.	FORD	GAEL	GOOF	+HEBE	HULK	HEST
FAIL	FORE	GLEE	GOON	HOBO.	*HULL.	HISS
FAIN	FORK	GLEN	GROG	HACK	HAME	HOSE
FAIR	FORM	GOER	GROW.	HECK	HEMP	HOST
FLIP	FORT	GREW	GAPE.	HICK	HOME	HUSH
FLIT	FURL	GREY	GARB	HOCK.	HOMO	HUSK.
FOIL	FURY.	+GWEN.	*GARY	HADE	HOMY	HATE
FRIT.	FASH	GAFF	GERM	HADJ	+HUME	HATH.
*FIJI	FAST	GIFT	GIRD	HIDE	HUMP	HAUL
*FUJI.	FISH	GUFF.	GIRL	*HYDE.	HYMN.	HAUM
FAKE.	FIST	GAGA	GIRT	HEED	HAND	HOUR.
FALL	FOSS	GAGE	GORE	HEEL	HANG	HAVE
FELL	FUSE	+GOGH	GORY	HIED	HANK	HIVE
FELT	FUSS.	GO-GO.	GURU	HOED.	HIND	*HOVE.
FILE	FATE	+GAIL	GYRE	HAFT	HINT	HAWK
FILL	FETE.	GAIN	GYRO.	HEFT	HONE	HEWN
FILM	FAUN	GAIT	GASH	HI-FI	HONK	HOWE
FOLD	FEUD	GLIB	GASP	HUFF.	HUNG	HOWL.
FOLK	FLUE	GRID	GEST	HIGH	HUNK	HAZE
FULL.	FLUX	GRIG	GIST	HOGG	HUNT.	HAZY
FAMA	FOUL	GRIM	GOSH	HUGE	HOOD	
FAME	FOUR.	GRIN	GUSH	+HUGH	HOOF	IMAM
FUME	FIVE.	GRIP	GUST.	+HUGO.	HOOK	IMAN
FUMY.	FAWN	GRIT.	GATE	HA-HA.	HOOP	*IRAN
FANE	FOWL.	GALA	GOTH.	HAIK	HOOT.	*IRAQ
FANG	FOXY.	GALE	GAUD	HAIL	HOPE	+IVAN.

9

INCA	JEEP	KECK	KISS	LIEU	LING	LUTE.
INCH	JEER.	KICK.	KIST.	LUES.	LINK	LAUD
ITCH.	+JEFF	KADI	+KATE	LEFT	LINN	LOUD
IBEX	JIFF.	KUDU.	KITE	LIFE	LINO	LOUR
ICED	JEHU	KEEK	KITH.	LIFT	LINT	LOUT.
IDEA	+JOHN.	KEEL	KNUR.	LOFT	LONE	LAVA
IDEM	JAIL	KEEN	KAVA.	LUFF.	LONG	LAVE
IDES	JAIN	KEEP	KIWI.	LOGE	+LUNA	LEVI
ILEX	JOIN.	*KIEL	KAYO	LUGE.	LUNG	LEVY
ITEM.	JU-JU.	*KIEV		LAIC	LUNT	LIVE
INFO.	JOKE.	+KLEE	LEAD	LAID	+LYNN	LOVE.
+IAIN	JELL	KNEE	LEAF	LAIN	LYNX.	LAWN
IBID	+JILL	KNEW.	LEAK	LAIR	*LAOS	LEWD.
IBIS	JILT	KOHL.	LEAL	LOIN	LION	LUXE.
+IRIS	JOLT	KAIL	LEAN	LOIR.	LOOK	LAZE
+ISIS	JULY.	KNIT	LEAP	LAKE	LOOM	LAZY
IXIA.	JAMB	KRIS.	+LEAR	LAKH	LOON	
ILKA	JUMP.	KAKA.	LIAR	LAKY	LOOP	MAAM
INKY.	+JANE	KALE	LIAS	LIKE	LOOT.	MEAD
IDLE	*JENA	KALI	LOAD	+LOKI	LAPP	MEAL
IDLY	JINK	KELP	LOAF	+LUKE	LOPE.	MEAN
INLY	JINN	KELT	LOAM	LYKE.	LARD	MEAT
ISLE.	JINX	KILL	LOAN.	LILT	LARK	MOAN
IAMB.	+JUNE	KILN	LOBE	+LILY	LIRA	MOAT.
*IFNI	JUNK	KILO	LUBE.	+LOLA	LIRE	MACE
*IONA	+JUNO.	KILT	LACE	LOLL	LORD	MACH
ISNT.	JAPE.	KOLA	LACK	LULL	LORE	MICA
ICON	JARL	KYLE.	LACY	LULU.	LORN	MICE
IDOL	JERK	KAME	LICE	LAMA	LORY	+MICK
IKON	*JURA	KEMP.	LICH	+LAMB	LURE	MOCK
IRON	JURY.	+KANT	LICK	LAME	LURK	MUCH
+IVOR.	JESS	*KENT	LOCH	LAMP	LYRE.	MUCK.
IMPI.	JEST	KIND	LOCI	*LIMA	LASH	MADE
INRO.	JOSH	KINE	LOCK	LIMB	LASS	MODE.
INST.	JOSS	KING	LOCO	LIME	LAST	MEEK
INTO	JUST.	KINK	LUCE	LIMN	LESS	MEET
IOTA.	JOTA	KINO.	LUCK	LIMP	LEST	MIEN.
*IOWA	JUTE.	KAON	+LUCY.	LIMY	+LISA	MIFF
	*JAVA	KNOB	LADE	LUMP	LISP	MUFF.
+JEAN	JIVE	KNOP	LADY	*LYME.	LIST	MAGI
+JOAN	JOVE.	KNOT	+LEDA	LAND	LOSE	MEGA.
+JUAN.	JOWL.	KNOW	LIDO	LANE	LOSS	MAID
JIBE	JAZZ	+KNOX.	LODE	LANG	LOST	MAIL
JUBA		KEPI	LUDO.	LANK	LUSH	MAIM
JUBE.	KHAN	KEPT.	LEEK	+LENA	LUST.	MAIN
+JACK	KNAG	+KARL	LEER	LEND	LATE	MOIL.
+JOCK.	KNAP	KERB	LEES	LENO	LATH	MAKE
JADE	KNAR	KERF	LIED	LENS	+LETO	+MIKE.
JUDO	KVAS.	KIRK.	LIEF	LENT	LITH	MALE
+JUDY.	KIBE.	KISH	LIEN	LINE	LOTH	MALL

MALM	MORN	NUDE.	NEXT.	*OISE	PREP	PUNY.
MALT	MURK	NEED	*NAZE	*OMSK	PREY.	PEON
MELD	+MYRA.	NEER	NAZI	*OUSE	PUFF.	PHON
MELT	MASH	+NOEL		OUST.	PAGE	PHOT
MILD	MASK	NOES.	*OBAN	OATH	POGO.	PION
MILE	MASS	NIGH	ODAL	ONTO	PAID	PLOD
MILK	MAST	NO-GO.	OGAM	ORTS.	PAIL	PLOP
+MILL	MESH	NAIK	OKAY	ONUS	PAIN	PLOT
MILT	MESS	NAIL	+OLAF	OPUS	PAIR	PLOY
MOLE	MISS	+NEIL	OPAL	OVUM.	+PHIL	POOH
MOLL	MIST	NOIL.	ORAL	ONYX	PRIG	POOL
MULE	MOSS	+NELL	*ORAN	ORYX.	PRIM.	POOP
*MULL.	MOST	*NILE	OVAL.	OOZE	PIKE	POOR
MEMO	MUSE	NULL.	ONCE	OOZY	POKE	PROA
MIME.	MUSH	NAME	OUCH.		POKY	PROD
MANA	MUSK	NOME	ODDS.	PEAK	PUKE.	PROF
MANE	MUSS	NUMB.	OBEY	PEAL	PALE	PROM
+MANN	MUST.	*NENE	*ODER	PEAR	PALI	PROP
MANX	MATE	+NINA	OGEE	PEAT	PALL	PROW.
MANY	+MATT	NINE	OMEN	+PIAF	PALM	PAPA
MEND	META	NONE.	ONER	PLAN	PALP	PIPE
MENU	METE	NEON	OPEN	PLAT	+PELE	+POPE
MIND	MITE	NOOK	OVEN	PLAY	PELT	PUPA.
MINE	MITT	NOON.	OWED	PRAM	PILE	PARA
MINI	MOTE	NAPE	+OWEN	PRAY.	PILL	PARD
MINK	MOTH	NOPE.	OXEN	PACA	POLE	PARE
MINT	MUTE	NARD	OYER	PACE	POLL	PARK
MINX	MUTT	NARK	OYEZ.	PACK	+POLO	PART
+MONA	MYTH.	NARY	+OLGA	PACO	PULE	PERI
MONK	+MAUD	+NERO	ORGY.	PACT	PULL	PERK
MONO	MAUL	NORM	OBIT	PECK	PULP.	PERM
*MONS.	MOUE.	NORN.	+ODIN	PICA	PIMP	PERN
MOOD	MOVE.	+NASH	*OHIO	PICK	POME	PERT
MOON	MEWS	*NESS	OLIO	PICO	POMP	*PERU
MOOR	MOWN.	NEST	OMIT	PICT	PUMA	PIRN
MOOT	MAXI.	NISI	+OVID.	POCK	PUMP.	PORE
MUON.	MAYA	NOSE	OGLE	PUCE	PANE	PORK
MOPE.	*MAYO.	NOSH	OILY	PUCK.	PANG	PORT
MARE	MAZE	NOSY.	OLLA	PEEK	PANT	PURE
+MARK	MAZY	NETT	ONLY	+PEEL	PENT	PURL
MARL		NOTE.	ORLE	PEEN	PINE	PURR
+MARS	+NEAL	NEUM	*OSLO.	PEEP	PINK	PYRE.
MART	NEAP	NOUN	OBOE	PEER	PINT	PASH
+MARX	NEAR	NOUS.	OBOL.	PHEW	PINY	PASS
+MARY	NEAT.	NAVE	OGPU.	PIED	POND	PAST
MERE	NECK	NAVY	OGRE	PIER	PONE	PESO
MIRE	*NICE	NOVA.	OKRA	PLEA	PONG	PEST
+MIRO	+NICK	NEWS	OURS.	PLEB	PONY	*PISA
MIRY	NOCK.	NEWT	OAST	POEM	PUNK	POSE
MORE	NODE	NOWT.		POET	PUNT	POSH

POST	RECK	*RENO	ROUX.	SWAM	*SOHO.	SENT
POSY	RICE	RENT	RAVE	SWAN	SAID	*SIND
PUSH	RICH	RIND	RIVE	SWAP	SAIL	SINE
PUSS.	+RICK	RINE	ROVE.	SWAT	SHIM	SING
PATE	ROCK	RING	*RHYL	SWAY.	SHIN	SINK
PATH	RUCK.	RINK	+RHYS.	SACK	SHIP	SONG
+PETE	REDE	*RONA	RAZE	SECT	SKID	SUNG
PITH	RIDE	RUNE	RAZZ	SICK	SKIM	SUNK
+PITT	RODE	RUNG		SOCK	SKIN	SYNE.
PITY	RUDE.	RUNT.	*SAAR	SUCH	SKIP	SCOT
PUTT.	REED	RIOT	SCAB	SUCK	SKIT	SCOW
+PAUL	REEF	ROOD	SCAN	SYCE.	SLID	SHOD
PHUT	REEK	ROOF	SCAR	SODA	SLIM	SHOE
PLUG	REEL	ROOK	SCAT	SUDD	SLIP	SHOO
PLUM	+RHEA	ROOM	SEAL	SUDS.	SLIT	SHOP
PLUS	RUED.	ROOP	SEAM	SEED	SNIP	SHOT
POUF	RAFT	ROOT	+SEAN	SEEK	SOIL	SHOW
POUR	REFT	RYOT.	SEAR	SEEM	SPIN	SLOB
POUT.	RIFE	RAPE	SEAT	SEEN	SPIT	SLOE
PAVE.	RIFF	RAPT	SHAD	SEEP	SPIV	SLOG
PAWL	RIFT	REPP	SHAG	SEER	STIR	SLOP
PAWN.	RUFF.	RIPE	SHAH	SHEA	SUIT	SLOT
PIXY.	RAGE	ROPE	SHAM	SHED	SWIG	SLOW
PAYE	*RIGA.	ROPY.	+SHAW	SHES	SWIM.	SMOG
	*RUHR.	RARE	SHAY	SHEW	SAKE	SNOB
QUAD	RAID	+RORY.	SLAB	SKEP	+SAKI	SNOG
QUAG	RAIL	RASH	SLAG	SKEW	SIKH	SNOT
QUAY.	RAIN	RASP	SLAM	SLED	SOKE.	+SNOW
QUID	REIN	REST	SLAP	SLEW	SALE	SOON
QUIP	RUIN.	RISE	SLAT	SMEE	SALT	SOOT
QUIT	RAJA.	RISK	SLAV	SPEC	SELF	SPOT
QUIZ.	RAKE.	+ROSE	SLAW	SPED	SELL	STOA
QUOD	RELY	*ROSS	SLAY	SPEW	SILK	STOP
	RILE	ROSY	SNAG	STEM	SILL	STOW
READ	RILL	RUSE	SNAP	STEP	SILO	SWOP
REAL	ROLE	RUSH	SOAK	STET	SILT	SWOT.
REAM	ROLL	RUSK	SOAP	STEW	SOLD	SEPT.
REAP	RULE.	RUSS	SOAR	SUED	SOLE	SARD
REAR	RAMP	RUST.	SPAM	SUET	SOLO	SARI
ROAD	RIME	RATA	SPAN	*SUEZ.	SULK.	*SARK
ROAM	RIMY	RATE	SPAR	SAFE	SAME	SCRY
ROAN	*ROME	+RITA	SPAT	SIFT	SEMI	SERE
ROAR.	ROMP	RITE	SPAY	SOFA	SOME	SERF
ROBE	RUMP.	ROTA	STAB	SOFT.	SUMP.	SIRE
RUBE	RAND	ROTE	STAG	SAGA	SAND	SORE
+RUBY.	RANG	+RUTH.	+STAN	SAGE	SANE	SORN
RACA	RANK	*RHUM	STAR	SAGO	SANG	SORT
RACE	RANT	ROUE	STAY	SIGH	SANK	SPRY
RACK	REND	ROUP	SWAB	SIGN.	SANS	SURD
RACY	+RENE	ROUT	SWAG		SEND	SURE

SURF.	TEAK	TOGS.	TOOK	*URAL	VERB	WALE
SASH	TEAL	TAIL	TOOL	*UTAH.	VERT	WALK
SO-SO	TEAM	TEIL	TOOT	UMBO.	VERY.	WALL
SUSS.	TEAR	THIN	TROD	UNCO.	VASA	+WALT
SATE	TEAT	THIS	TROT	UNDO	VASE	WELD
SATI	THAN	TOIL	*TROY.	URDU.	VAST	WELL
SETA	THAT	TRIG	TAPE	UREA	VEST	WELT
SETT	THAW	TRIM	TOPE	USED	VISA	WILD
SITE.	TOAD	TRIO	TOPI	USER	VISE.	WILE
+SAUL	TRAD	TRIP	TYPE.	UVEA.	VETO	+WILL
SCUD	TRAM	TWIG	TARE	URGE.	VOTE.	WILT
SCUM	TRAP	TWIN	TARN	UNIT	VIVA	WILY
SCUT	TRAY	TWIT.	TART	URIC.		WOLD
SHUN	TSAR	TAKE	TERM	UGLY.	WEAK	WOLF.
SHUT	TWAS	TIKE	TERN	ULNA.	WEAL	WOMB.
SKUA	TZAR.	TIKI	THRU	UPON.	WEAN	WAND
SLUB	TABU	TYKE.	TIRE	*UIST	WEAR	WANE
SLUG	+TOBY	TALC	TORE	*UNST.	WHAT	WANT
SLUM	TUBA	TALE	TORI	UNTO.	WOAD	WEND
SLUR	TUBE.	TALK	TORN	URUS	WRAP.	WENT
SLUT	TACK	TALL	TORT		WICK.	WIND
SMUG	TACT	TELE	TORY	VEAL	WADD	WINE
SMUT	TICK	TELL	TURF	VIAL.	WADE	WING
SNUB	TUCK.	TILE	TURK	VICE.	WADI	WINK
SNUG	TIDE	TILL	TURN	VEDA	WIDE.	WINY
SOUL	TIDY	TILT	TYRE	VIDE.	WEED	WONT.
SOUP	TO-DO.	TOLD	TYRO.	VEER	WEEK	WHOA
SOUR	TAEL	TOLL	TASK	VIED	WEEP	WHOM
SPUD	TEED	TOLU.	TASS	VIEW	WHEN	WOOD
SPUE	TEEM	TAME	TEST	VLEI.	WHET	WOOF
SPUN	*TEES	TAMP	TOSS	VEGA.	WHEW	WOOL.
SPUR	THEE	TIME	TUSH	VAIL	WHEY	WEPT
STUB	THEM	TOMB	TUSK.	VAIN	WREN.	WIPE.
STUD	THEN	TOME	TETE	VEIL	WAFT	WARD
STUM	+THEO	TUMP.	+TITO	VEIN	WEFT	*WARE
STUN	THEY	TANG	TOTE	VOID.	WIFE.	WARM
SWUM.	TIED	TANK	TUTU.	VALE	WAGE.	WARN
SAVE.	TIER	TEND	TAUT	VELD	WAIF	WARP
SAWN	TOED	TENT	THUD	VILE	WAIL	WART
SEWN	TREE	TINE	THUG	VOLA	WAIT	WARY
SOWN.	TREK	TING	THUS	VOLE	WEIR	WERE
SAXE	TRET	TINT	TOUR	VOLT.	WHIG	WERT
SEXT	TREY.	TINY	TOUT	VAMP.	WHIM	WIRE
SEXY.	+TAFT	TONE	TRUE	VANE	WHIN	WIRY
*SKYE	TIFF	+TONY	TRUG.	VEND	WHIP	WORD
SOYA	TOFF	TUNA	TOWN.	VENT	WHIT	WORE
STYX.	TUFA	TUNE	TAXI	VINE.	WHIZ	WORK
SIZE	TUFT.	*TYNE.	TEXT	VIOL.	WRIT.	WORM
	TOGA	+THOR		VARY	WAKE	WORN.
TAAL	*TOGO	THOU	UPAS	+VERA	WOKE.	WASH

13

WASP	+ZOLA	CARD	FACE	PALE	RANG	DANK
WAST	ZULU.	GAUD	FADE	PANE	SANG	DARK
WEST	ZEME.	HAND	FAKE	PARE	TANG.	GAWK
WISE	ZANY	HARD	FAME	PATE	+BACH	HACK
WISH	ZEND	LAID	FANE	PAVE	BASH	HAIK
WISP	ZINC	LAND	FARE	PAYE	*BATH	HANK
WIST.	ZONE.	LARD	FATE	RACE	CASH	HARK
WATT	ZION	LAUD	GAGE	RAGE	DASH	HAWK
WITH.	ZOOM.	MAID	GALE	RAKE	EACH	+JACK
WAVE	ZERO.	+MAUD	GAME	RAPE	FASH	LACK
WAVY	ZEST.	NARD	GAPE	RARE	GASH	LANK
WEVE	ZETA.	PAID	GATE	RATE	HASH	LARK
WIVE	+ZEUS	PARD	GAVE	RAVE	HATH	+MARK
WOVE.		RAID	GAZE	RAZE	LAKH	MASK
WAXY		RAND	HADE	SAFE	LASH	NAIK
	*BALA	SAID	HAKE	SAGE	LATH	NARK
XMAS	CAPA	SAND	HALE	SAKE	MACH	PACK
X-RAY.	DADA	SARD	HAME	SALE	MASH	PARK
XEME	DATA	WADD	HARE	SAME	+NASH	RACK
	FAMA	WAND	HATE	SANE	OATH	RANK
YEAH	GAGA	WARD	HAVE	SATE	PASH	SACK
YEAR.	GALA	YARD.	HAZE	SAVE	PATH	SANK
+YVES.	HA-HA	BABE	JADE	SAXE	RASH	*SARK
YOGA	*JAVA	BADE	+JANE	TAKE	SASH	TACK
YOGH	KAKA	BAKE	JAPE	TALE	WASH.	TALK
YOGI.	KAVA	BALE	KALE	TAME	*BALI	TANK
YOKE.	LAMA	BANE	KAME	TAPE	*BARI	TASK
YALE	LAVA	BARE	+KATE	TARE	CADI	WALK
YELL	MANA	BASE	LACE	VALE	+DALI	YANK.
YELP	MAYA	BATE	LADE	VANE	KADI	BAAL
YOLK	PACA	CADE	LAKE	VASE	KALI	BAIL
YULE.	PAPA	CAFE	LAME	WADE	MAGI	BALL
YANK.	PARA	CAGE	LANE	WAGE	MAXI	BAWL
YAPP.	RACA	CAKE	LATE	WAKE	NAZI	CALL
YARD	RAJA	CAME	LAVE	WALE	PALI	+CARL
YARN	RATA	CANE	LAZE	WANE	+SAKI	CAUL
YORE	SAGA	CAPE	MACE	*WARE	SARI	DAIL
*YORK.	VASA.	CARE	MADE	WAVE	SATI	EARL
YETI.	BARB	CASE	MAKE	YALE.	TAXI	FAIL
YOUD	DAUB	CATE	MALE	CALF	WADI.	FALL
YOUR.	GARB	CAVE	MANE	DAFF	HADJ.	GAEL
YAWL	IAMB	DACE	MARE	GAFF	BACK	+GAIL
YAWN	JAMB	DALE	MATE	HALF	BALK	GALL
YAWS	+LAMB.	DAME	MAZE	WAIF.	BANK	GAOL
YOWL.	LAIC	DANE	NAME	BANG	BARK	HAIL
YO-YO	TALC.	DARE	NAPE	FANG	BASK	HALL
	BALD	DATE	NAVE	GANG	CALK	HARL
ZEAL.	BAND	+DAVE	*NAZE	HANG	CARK	HAUL
ZEBU.	BARD	DAZE	PACE	LANG	CASK	JAIL
ZOIC.	BAWD	EASE	PAGE	PANG	CAUK	JARL

KAIL	+MANN	PASS	CALX	ICED	+HERA	DELE
+KARL	PAIN	SANS	MANX	SCUD.	*JENA	DEME
MAIL	PAWN	TASS	+MARX.	ACHE	+LEDA	DENE
MALL	RAIN	YAWS.	BABY	ACME	+LENA	FETE
MARL	SAWN	BAIT	CAVY	ACNE	MEGA	+GENE
MAUL	TARN	BANT	+DAVY	ACRE.	META	+HEBE
NAIL	VAIN	+BART	EASY	SCUM.	SETA	HERE
PAIL	WARN	CANT	GABY	ICON	VEDA	MERE
PALL	YARN	CART	GAMY	SCAN.	VEGA	METE
+PAUL	YAWN.	CAST	*GARY	ECHO.	+VERA	*NENE
PAWL	DADO	DAFT	HAZY	ACER	ZETA.	+PELE
RAIL	DAGO	DART	LACY	SCAR.	HERB	+PETE
SAIL	FARO	EAST	LADY	+ACIS.	KERB	REDE
+SAUL	HALO	FACT	LAKY	SCAT	BEAD	+RENE
TAAL	KAYO	FAST	LAZY	VERB.	BEND	SERE
TAEL	*MAYO	GAIT	MANY	SCOT	DEAD	TELE
TAIL	PACO	HAFT	+MARY	SCUT.	DEED	TETE
TALL	SAGO.	HALT	MAZY	ECRU.	FEED	WERE
VAIL	CALP	HART	NARY	SCOW.	FEND	WEVE
WAIL	CAMP	HAST	NAVY	SCRY	FEUD	XEME
WALL	CARP	+KANT	RACY		GELD	ZEME.
YAWL.	DAMP	LAST	VARY	EDDA	HEAD	BEEF
BALM	GAMP	MALT	WARY	+EDNA	HEED	DEAF
BARM	GASP	MART	WAVY	IDEA.	HELD	DELF
CALM	HARP	MAST	WAXY	ADZE	HERD	+JEFF
FARM	HASP	+MATT	ZANY.	EDGE	LEAD	KERF
HALM	LAMP	OAST	JAZZ	IDLE.	LEND	LEAF
HARM	LAPP	PACT	RAZZ	IDOL	LEWD	REEF
HAUM	PALP	PANT		ODAL.	MEAD	SELF
MAAM	RAMP	PART	ABBA.	+ADAM	MELD	SERF.
MAIM	RASP	PAST	ABIB.	*EDAM	MEND	BERG
MALM	TAMP	RAFT	ABED	IDEM.	NEED	+BETH
PALM	VAMP	RANT	IBID.	*ADEN	READ	MESH
WARM.	WARP	RAPT	ABBE	*EDEN	REED	YEAH.
BARN	WASP	SALT	ABLE	+ODIN.	REND	DELI
*CAEN	YAPP.	TACT	OBOE.	ADAR	SEED	DEMI
DAMN	FAIR	+TAFT	+ABEL	*ODER.	SEND	KEPI
DARN	GAUR	TART	OBOL.	IDES	TEED	LEVI
+DAWN	HAIR	TAUT	EBON	ODDS.	TEND	PERI
EARN	LAIR	VAST	*OBAN.	ADIT	VELD	SEMI
FAIN	PAIR	WAFT	IBIS.	EDIT.	VEND	YETI.
FAUN	*SAAR.	WAIT	ABET	ADRY	WEED	BEAK
FAWN	+BABS	+WALT	ABUT	D-DAY	WELD	BECK
GAIN	BASS	WANT	OBIT.	EDDY	WEND	DECK
IAIN	DAIS	WART	IBEX.	EDGY	ZEND.	DESK
JAIN	+HALS	WAST	ABLY	IDLY		HECK
KAON	*LAOS	WATT.	OBEY		BEHA	+BEDE	JERK
LAIN	LASS	BABU		BETA	BERE	KECK
LAWN	+MARS	*BAKU	SCAB.	DEJA	CEDE	KEEK
MAIN	MASS	TABU.	ACID	DEVA	CERE	LEAK

15

LEEK	GEUM	KEMP	+BERT	VENT	CHUB.	SHES
MEEK	HELM	LEAP	BEST	VERT	CHIC.	THIS
NECK	HERM	NEAP	CELT	VEST	*CHAD	THUS.
PEAK	NEUM	PEEP	CENT	WEFT	CHID	CHAT
PECK	PERM	REAP	CERT	WELT	SHAD	CHIT
PEEK	REAM	REPP	DEBT	WENT	SHED	GHAT
PERK	SEAM	SEEP	DEFT	WEPT	SHOD	PHOT
RECK	SEEM	WEEP	DENT	WERT	THUD.	PHUT
REEK	TEAM	YELP.	FEAT	WEST	SHOE	SHOT
SEEK	TEEM	BEAR	FEET	ZEST.	THEE.	SHUT
TEAK	TERM.	BEER	FELT	BEAU	CHEF.	THAT
WEAK	AEON	DEAR	FENT	*CEBU	CHUG	WHAT
WEEK.	BEAN	DEER	GENT	JEHU	SHAG	WHET
+BELL	BEEN	FEAR	GEST	MENU	THUG	WHIT.
CEIL	DEAN	GEAR	HEAT	*PERU	WHIG.	THOU
CELL	FERN	HEAR	HEFT	ZEBU.	SHAH.	THRU.
*DEAL	GEAN	HEIR	HEST	DERV.	DHAK.	CHAW
DELL	HEWN	HERR	JEST	AERY	DHAL	CHEW
FEEL	+JEAN	JEER	KELT	BEVY	+PHIL	CHOW
FELL	KEEN	+LEAR	*KENT	DEFY	*RHYL.	DHOW
HEAL	LEAN	LEER	KEPT	DEMY	AHEM	PHEW
HEEL	MEAN	NEAR	LEFT	DENY	CHUM	+SHAW
HELL	NEON	NEER	LENT	DEWY	*RHUM	SHEW
JELL	PEEN	PEAR	LEST	EERY	SHAM	SHOW
KEEL	PEON	PEER	MEAT	LEVY	SHIM	THAW
LEAL	PERN	REAR	MEET	RELY	THEM	WHEW.
MEAL	REIN	SEAR	MELT	SEXY	WHIM	AHOY
+NEAL	+SEAN	SEER	NEAT	VERY	WHOM.	CHAY
+NEIL	SEEN	TEAR	NEST		CHIN	SHAY
+NELL	SEWN	VEER	NETT	*IFNI.	KHAN	THEY
PEAL	TERN	WEAR	NEWT	AFAR	PHON	WHEY.
+PEEL	VEIN	WEIR	NEXT		SHIN	WHIZ
REAL	WEAN.	YEAR.	PEAT	*AGRA.	SHUN	
REEL	+HERO	+BESS	PELT	AGED	THAN	DIVA
SEAL	LENO	CESS	PENT	EGAD.	THEN	*LIMA
SELL	+LETO	HERS	PERT	AGUE	THIN	LIRA
TEAL	MEMO	JESS	PEST	OGEE	WHEN	+LISA
TEIL	+NERO	LEES	REFT	OGLE	WHIN.	MICA
TELL	PESO	LENS	RENT	OGRE.	*OHIO	+NINA
VEAL	*RENO	LESS	REST	AGOG.	SHOO	PICA
VEIL	VETO	MESS	SEAT	OGAM.	+THEO.	*PISA
WEAL	ZERO.	MEWS	SECT	AGIO.	CHAP	+RIGA
WELL	BEEP	*NESS	SENT	AGAR.	CHIP	+RITA
YELL	DEEP	NEWS	SEPT	OGPU.	CHOP	VISA
ZEAL.	HEAP	*TEES	SETT	UGLY	SHIP	VIVA.
BEAM	HELP	+ZEUS.	SEXT		SHOP	DIEB
BERM	HEMP	BEAT	TEAT	+RHEA	WHIP.	LIMB.
DEEM	JEEP	BEET	TENT	SHEA	CHAR	CIRC
DERM	KEEP	BELT	TEST	WHOA.	+THOR.	DISC
GERM	KELP	BENT	TEXT	+AHAB	+RHYS	ZINC

BIND	KINE	WIDE	DISK	LION	KIST	AKEE
BIRD	KITE	WIFE	FINK	MIEN	LIFT	*SKYE.
DIED	LICE	WILE	HICK	PION	LILT	SKIM.
FIND	LIFE	WINE	JINK	PIRN	LINT	AKIN
GILD	LIKE	WIPE	KICK	SIGN	LIST	IKON
GIRD	LIME	WIRE	KINK	ZION.	MILT	SKIN.
HIED	LINE	WISE	KIRK	BIRO	MINT	SKEP
HIND	LIRE	WIVE.	LICK	+DIDO	MIST	SKIP.
KIND	LIVE	BIFF	LINK	FICO	MITT	SKIT.
LIED	MICE	FIEF	+MICK	KILO	PICT	SKEW.
MILD	+MIKE	JIFF	MILK	KINO	PINT	OKAY
MIND	MILE	LIEF	MINK	LIDO	+PITT	
PIED	MIME	MIFF	+NICK	LINO	RIFT	ALFA
RIND	MINE	RIFF	PICK	+MIRO	RIOT	ALGA
*SIND	MIRE	RIFF	PINK	PICO	SIFT	+ALMA
TIED	MITE	TIFF.	+RICK	SILO	SILT	*ELBA
VIED	*NICE	BING	RINK	+TITO.	TILT	+ELLA
WILD	*NILE	DING	RISK	GIMP	TINT	+ELMA
WIND.	NINE	*EIGG	SICK	LIMP	*UIST	+ELSA
BICE	*OISE	KING	SILK	LISP	WILT	FLEA
BIDE	PIKE	LING	SINK	PIMP	WIST.	ILKA
BIKE	PILE	RING	TICK	WISP.	LIEU.	+OLGA
BILE	PINE	SING	WICK	BIER	*KIEV.	OLLA
BINE	PIPE	TING	WINK.	LIAR	VIEW.	PLEA
BISE	RICE	WING.	+BILL	PIER	JINX	ULNA.
BITE	RIDE	DISH	CIEL	TIER.	MINX.	BLAB
CINE	RIFE	FISH	DIAL	BIAS	AIRY	BLEB
CITE	RILE	HIGH	DILL	DIBS	CITY	BLOB
CIVE	RIME	KISH	FILL	DIGS	+LILY	BLUB
DICE	RINE	KITH	+GILL	DISS	LIMY	CLUB
DIKE	RIPE	LICH	GIRL	HISS	MIRY	GLIB
DIME	RISE	LITH	HILL	KISS	OILY	PLEB
DINE	RITE	NIGH	+JILL	LIAS	PINY	SLAB
DIRE	RIVE	PITH	*KIEL	MISS.	PITY	SLOB
DIVE	SIDE	RICH	KILL	AINT	PIXY	SLUB.
*FIFE	SINE	SIGH	+MILL	BITT	RIMY	BLOC.
FILE	SIRE	SIKH	PILL	CIST	TIDY	BLED
FINE	SITE	WISH	RILL	DIET	TINY	CLAD
FIRE	SIZE	WITH.	SILL	DINT	WILY	CLOD
FIVE	TIDE	DIVI	TILL	DIRT	WINY	FLED
GIBE	TIKE	*FIJI	VIAL	FIAT	WIRY.	GLAD
+GIDE	TILE	HI-FI	VIOL	FIST	FIZZ	PLOD
GIVE	TIME	KIWI	+WILL.	GIFT		SLED
HIDE	TINE	MINI	FILM	GILT	AJAR.	SLID.
HIKE	TIRE	NISI	FIRM.	GIRT	+AJAX	*ALOE
HIRE	VICE	TIKI.	JINN	GIST		ALEE
HIVE	VIDE	BILK	KILN	HILT	OKRA	ALOE
JIBE	VILE	BISK	LIEN	HINT	SKUA.	BLUE
JIVE	VINE	+DICK	LIMN	JILT	EKED	CLUE
KIBE	VISE	+DIRK	LINN	KILT	SKID.	*ELBE

17

ELSE	SLIP	SMUG.	UNTO.	SOFA	COKE	OOZE
FLEE	SLOP.	AMAH.	KNAP	SOYA	COLE	POKE
FLOE	ALAR	IMPI.	KNOP	TOGA	COME	POLE
FLUE	BLUR	AMOK	SNAP	VOLA	CONE	POME
GLEE	SLUR.	*OMSK.	SNIP.	YOGA	COPE	PONE
GLUE	ALAS	AMYL.	KNAR	+ZOLA.	CORE	+POPE
+KLEE	ALMS	IMAM.	KNUR	BOMB	COTE	PORE
SLOE.	*ALPS	AMEN	ONER.	BOOB	COVE	POSE
CLEF	PLUS.	G-MAN	ANUS	COMB	DOGE	ROBE
+OLAF.	BLOT	IMAN	ONUS.	DOAB	DOLE	RODE
CLEG	CLOT	OMEN.	GNAT	TOMB	DOME	ROLE
CLOG	FLAT	AMBO	INST	WOMB.	DONE	*ROME
FLAG	FLIT	AMMO	KNIT	ZOIC.	DOPE	ROPE
FLOG	GLUT	UMBO.	KNOT	BOLD	DOSE	+ROSE
PLUG	PLAT	AMIR	SNOT	BOND	DOTE	ROTE
SLAG	PLOT	EMIR.	UNIT	CO-ED	DOVE	ROUE
SLOG	SLAT	+AMIS	*UNST.	COLD	DOZE	ROVE
SLUG.	SLIT	+AMOS	ANEW	CORD	FORE	SOKE
VLEI.	SLOT	XMAS.	ENOW	FOLD	GONE	SOLE
FLAK.	SLUT.	EMIT	GNAW	FOND	GORE	SOME
ELUL.	SLAV.	OMIT	KNEW	FOOD	HOLE	SORE
ALUM	ALOW	SMUT.	KNOW	FORD	HOME	TOME
CLAM	BLEW	*AMOY	+SNOW.	GOAD	HONE	TONE
CLEM	BLOW		+KNOX	GOLD	HOPE	TOPE
FLAM	CLAW	+ANNA	ONYX.	GOOD	HOSE	TORE
GLUM	CLEW	INCA.	+ANDY	HOED	*HOVE	TOTE
PLUM	FLAW	KNOB	ENVY	HOLD	HOWE	VOLE
SLAM	FLEW	SNOB	INKY	HOOD	JOKE	VOTE
SLIM	FLOW	SNUB.	INLY	LOAD	JOVE	WOKE
SLUM.	GLOW	+ENID.	ONLY	LORD	LOBE	WORE
+ALAN	SLAW	+ANNE		LOUD	LODE	WOVE
*ELAN	SLEW	ANTE	BORA	MOOD	LOGE	YOKE
FLAN	SLOW.	KNEE	COCA	POND	LONE	YORE
GLEN	FLAX	ONCE.	CODA	ROAD	LOPE	ZONE.
PLAN.	FLEX	KNAG	COLA	ROOD	LORE	COIF
ALSO	FLUX	SNAG	COMA	SOLD	LOSE	CORF
ALTO	ILEX.	SNOG	COXA	TOAD	LOVE	DOFF
+CLEO	ALLY	SNUG.	+DORA	TOED	MODE	GOLF
+CLIO	CLAY	ANKH	+GOYA	TOLD	MOLE	GOOF
ELMO	CLOY	INCH.	*IONA	VOID	MOPE	HOOF
OLIO.	ELMY	ANTI.	IOTA	WOAD	MORE	LOAF
BLIP	FLAY	ANAL	*IOWA	WOLD	MOTE	POUF
CLAP	PLAY	ANIL	JOTA	WOOD	MOUE	ROOF
CLIP	PLOY	ANON.	KOLA	WORD	MOVE	TOFF
CLOP	SLAY	INFO	+LOLA	YOUD.	NODE	WOLF
FLAP		INRO	+MONA	BODE	NOME	WOOF
FLIP	+EMMA.	INTO	NOVA	BOLE	NONE	GONG
FLOP	AMID.	ONTO	*RONA	BONE	NOPE	HOGG
PLOP	SMEE.	UNCO	ROTA	BORE	NOSE	LONG
SLAP	SMOG	UNDO	SODA	CODE	NOTE	PONG

BIND	KINE	WIDE	DISK	LION	KIST	AKEE
BIRD	KITE	WIFE	FINK	MIEN	LIFT	*SKYE.
DIED	LICE	WILE	HICK	PION	LILT	SKIM.
FIND	LIFE	WINE	JINK	PIRN	LINT	AKIN
GILD	LIKE	WIPE	KICK	SIGN	LIST	IKON
GIRD	LIME	WIRE	KINK	ZION	MILT	SKIN.
HIED	LINE	WISE	KIRK	BIRO	MINT	SKEP
HIND	LIRE	WIVE.	LICK	+DIDO	MIST	SKIP.
KIND	LIVE	BIFF	LINK	FICO	MITT	SKIT.
LIED	MICE	FIEF	+MICK	KILO	PICT	SKEW.
MILD	+MIKE	JIFF	MILK	KINO	PINT	OKAY
MIND	MILE	LIEF	MINK	LIDO	+PITT	
PIED	MIME	MIFF	+NICK	LINO	RIFT	ALFA
RIND	MINE	+PIAF	PICK	+MIRO	RIOT	ALGA
*SIND	MIRE	RIFF	PINK	PICO	SIFT	+ALMA
TIED	MITE	TIFF.	+RICK	SILO	SILT	*ELBA
VIED	*NICE	BING	RINK	+TITO.	TILT	+ELLA
WILD	*NILE	DING	RISK	GIMP	TINT	+ELMA
WIND.	NINE	*EIGG	SICK	LIMP	*UIST	+ELSA
BICE	*OISE	KING	SILK	LISP	WILT	FLEA
BIDE	PIKE	LING	SINK	PIMP	WIST.	ILKA
BIKE	PILE	RING	TICK	WISP.	LIEU.	+OLGA
BILE	PINE	SING	WICK	BIER	VIEW.	OLLA
BINE	PIPE	TING	WINK.	LIAR	JINX	PLEA
BISE	RICE	WING.	+BILL	PIER	MINX.	ULNA.
BITE	RIDE	DISH	CIEL	TIER.	AIRY	BLAB
CINE	RIFE	FISH	DIAL	BIAS	CITY	BLEB
CITE	RILE	HIGH	DILL	DIBS	+LILY	BLOB
CIVE	RIME	KISH	FILL	DIGS	LIMY	BLUB
DICE	RINE	KITH	+GILL	DISS	MIRY	CLUB
DIKE	RIPE	LICH	GIRL	HISS	OILY	GLIB
DIME	RISE	LITH	HILL	KISS	PINY	PLEB
DINE	RITE	NIGH	+JILL	LIAS	PITY	SLAB
DIRE	RIVE	PITH	*KIEL	MISS.	PIXY	SLOB
DIVE	SIDE	RICH	KILL	AINT	RIMY	SLUB.
*FIFE	SINE	SIGH	+MILL	BITT	TIDY	BLOC.
FILE	SIRE	SIKH	PILL	CIST	TINY	BLED
FINE	SITE	WISH	RILL	DIET	WILY	CLAD
FIRE	SIZE	WITH.	SILL	DINT	WINY	CLOD
FIVE	TIDE	DIVI	TILL	DIRT	WIRY.	FLED
GIBE	TIKE	*FIJI	VIAL	FIAT	FIZZ	GLAD
+GIDE	TILE	HI-FI	VIOL	FIST		PLOD
GIVE	TIME	KIWI	+WILL.	GIFT		SLED
HIDE	TINE	MINI	FILM	GILT	AJAR.	SLID.
HIKE	TIRE	NISI	FIRM.	GIRT	+AJAX	*ALOE
HIRE	VICE	TIKI.	JINN	GIST		ALEE
HIVE	VIDE	BILK	KILN	HILT	OKRA	ALOE
JIBE	VILE	BISK	LIEN	HINT	SKUA.	BLUE
JIVE	VINE	+DICK	LIMN	JILT	EKED	CLUE
KIBE	VISE	+DIRK	LINN	KILT	SKID.	*ELBE

ELSE	SLIP	SMUG.	UNTO.	SOFA	COKE	OOZE
FLEE	SLOP.	AMAH.	KNAP	SOYA	COLE	POKE
FLOE	ALAR	IMPI.	KNOP	TOGA	COME	POLE
FLUE	BLUR	AMOK	SNAP	VOLA	CONE	POME
GLEE	SLUR.	*OMSK.	SNIP.	YOGA	COPE	PONE
GLUE	ALAS	AMYL.	KNAR	+ZOLA.	CORE	+POPE
+KLEE	ALMS	IMAM.	KNUR	BOMB	COTE	PORE
SLOE.	*ALPS	AMEN	ONER.	BOOB	COVE	POSE
CLEF	PLUS.	G-MAN	ANUS	COMB	DOGE	ROBE
+OLAF.	BLOT	IMAN	ONUS.	DOAB	DOLE	RODE
CLEG	CLOT	OMEN.	GNAT	TOMB	DOME	ROLE
CLOG	FLAT	AMBO	INST	WOMB.	DONE	*ROME
FLAG	FLIT	AMMO	KNIT	ZOIC.	DOPE	ROPE
FLOG	GLUT	UMBO.	KNOT	BOLD	DOSE	+ROSE
PLUG	PLAT	AMIR	SNOT	BOND	DOTE	ROTE
SLAG	PLOT	EMIR.	UNIT	CO-ED	DOVE	ROUE
SLOG	SLAT	+AMIS	*UNST.	COLD	OOZE	ROVE
SLUG.	SLIT	+AMOS	ANEW	CORD	FORE	SOKE
VLEI.	SLOT	XMAS.	ENOW	FOLD	GONE	SOLE
FLAK.	SLUT.	EMIT	GNAW	FOND	GORE	SOME
ELUL.	SLAV.	OMIT.	KNEW	FOOD	HOLE	SORE
ALUM	ALOW	SMUT.	KNOW	FORD	HOME	TOME
CLAM	BLEW	*AMOY	+SNOW.	GOAD	HONE	TONE
CLEM	BLOW		+KNOX	GOLD	HOPE	TOPE
FLAM	CLAW	+ANNA	ONYX.	GOOD	HOSE	TORE
GLUM	CLEW	INCA.	+ANDY	HOED	*HOVE	TOTE
PLUM	FLAW	KNOB	ENVY	HOLD	HOWE	VOLE
SLAM	FLEW	SNOB	INKY	HOOD	JOKE	VOTE
SLIM	FLOW	SNUB.	INLY	LOAD	JOVE	WOKE
SLUM.	GLOW	+ENID.	ONLY	LORD	LOBE	WORE
+ALAN	SLAW	+ANNE		LOUD	LODE	WOVE
*ELAN	SLEW	ANTE	BORA	MOOD	LOGE	YOKE
FLAN	SLOW.	KNEE	COCA	POND	LONE	YORE
GLEN	FLAX	ONCE.	CODA	ROAD	LOPE	ZONE.
PLAN.	FLEX	KNAG	COLA	ROOD	LORE	COIF
ALSO	FLUX	SNAG	COMA	SOLD	LOSE	CORF
ALTO	ILEX.	SNOG	COXA	TOAD	LOVE	DOFF
+CLEO	ALLY	SNUG.	+DORA	TOED	MODE	GOLF
+CLIO	CLAY	ANKH	+GOYA	TOLD	MOLE	GOOF
ELMO	CLOY	INCH.	*IONA	VOID	MOPE	HOOF
OLIO.	ELMY	ANTI.	IOTA	WOAD	MORE	LOAF
BLIP	FLAY	ANAL	*IOWA	WOLD	MOTE	POUF
CLAP	PLAY	ANIL.	JOTA	WOOD	MOUE	ROOF
CLIP	PLOY	ANON.	KOLA	WORD	MOVE	TOFF
CLOP	SLAY	INFO	+LOLA	YOUD.	NODE	WOLF
FLAP		INRO	+MONA	BODE	NOME	WOOF
FLIP	+EMMA.	INTO	NOVA	BOLE	NONE	GONG
FLOP	AMID.	ONTO	*RONA	BONE	NOPE	HOGG
PLOP	SMEE.	UNCO	ROTA	BORE	NOSE	LONG
SLAP	SMOG	UNDO	SODA	CODE	NOTE	PONG

SONG.	SOAK	ROAM	TO-DO	TOGS	HOAX	SPAT
BOSH	SOCK	ROOM	*TOGO	TOSS.	ROUX.	SPIT
BOTH	TOOK	WORM	YO-YO.	BOAT	BODY	SPOT.
COSH	WORK	ZOOM.	CO-OP	BOLT	BONY	SPIV.
DOTH	YOLK	*BONN	COUP	BOOT	CONY	SPEW.
+GOGH	*YORK.	BOON	DORP	BORT	COPY	APEX.
GOSH	BOIL	+BORN	HOOP	BOTT	COSY	SPAY
GOTH	BOLL	COIN	LOOP	BOUT	DORY	SPRY
JOSH	BOWL	COON	POMP	COAT	DOXY	
LOCH	COAL	CORN	POOP	COLT	DOZY	AQUA
LOTH	COIL	DOWN	ROMP	COOT	FOGY	
MOTH	COOL	FOHN	ROOP	COPT	FOXY	AREA
NOSH	COWL	GOON	ROUP	COST	GO-BY	ARIA
POOH	DOLL	GOWN	SOAP	DOIT	GORY	PROA
POSH	DOOL	HORN	SOUP.	DOLT	HOLY	UREA.
YOGH.	FOAL	+JOAN	BOAR	DONT	HOMY	ARAB
FOCI	FOIL	+JOHN	BOER	DOST	LORY	CRAB
*GOBI	FOOL	JOIN	BOOR	FONT	NOSY	CRIB
HOPI	FOUL	LOAN	COIR	FOOT	OOZY	DRAB
LOCI	FOWL	LOIN	DOER	FORT	POKY	DRUB
+LOKI	GOAL	LOON	DOOR	GOAT	PONY	GRAB
TOPI	HOWL	LORN	DORR	GOUT	POSY	GRUB.
TORI	JOWL	MOAN	DOUR	+HOLT	ROPY	+ERIC
YOGI.	KOHL	MOON	FOUR	HOOT	+RORY	URIC.
BOCK	LOLL	MORN	GOER	HOST	ROSY	ARID
BOOK	MOIL	MOWN	HOAR	JOLT	+TOBY	BRAD
BOSK	MOLL	NOON	HOUR	LOFT	+TONY	BRED
COCK	+NOEL	NORN	LOIR	LOOT	TORY	+FRED
CONK	NOIL	NOUN	LOUR	LOST		GRID
+COOK	POLL	ROAN	MOOR	LOUT	EPHA.	PROD
*CORK	POOL	SOON	POOR	MOAT	EPIC	TRAD
DOCK	ROLL	SORN	POUR	MOOT	SPEC.	TROD.
FOLK	SOIL	SOWN	ROAR	MOST	APED	BRAE
FORK	SOUL	TORN	SOAR	NOWT	SPED	BRIE
GONK	TOIL	TOWN	SOUR	POET	SPUD.	*ERIE
GOWK	TOLL	WORN.	TOUR	PORT	APSE	ERNE
HOCK	TOOL	COCO	YOUR.	POST	SPUE.	ERSE
HONK	WOOL	*COMO	BOSS	POUT	OPAL.	FREE
HOOK	YOWL.	DODO	DOES	ROOT	SPAM.	ORLE
JOCK	BOOM	GO-GO	DOSS	ROUT	OPEN	TREE
LOCK	CORM	HOBO	FOSS	SOFT	SPAN	TRUE
LOOK	DOOM	HOMO	HOLS	SOOT	SPIN	URGE.
MOCK	FOAM	LOCO	JOSS	SORT	SPUN	PROF.
MONK	FORM	MONO	LOSS	TOOT	UPON.	BRAG
NOCK	HOLM	NO-GO	*MONS	TORT	SPAR	BRIG
NOOK	LOAM	POGO	MOSS	TOUT	SPUR.	CRAG
POCK	LOOM	+POLO	NOES	VOLT	+APIS	DRAG
PORK	NORM	*SOHO	NOUS	WONT.	EPOS	DRUG
ROCK	POEM	SOLO	*ROSS	TOLU.	OPUS	FROG
ROOK		SO-SO		COAX	UPAS.	GRIG

19

GROG	KRIS	+ISIS.	CURD	YULE.	MURK	JUMP
PRIG	ORTS	ISNT.	FUND	BUFF	MUSK	LUMP
TRIG	URUS.	ASHY	QUAD	BUMF	PUCK	PULP
TRUG.	BRAT	ESPY	QUID	CUFF	PUNK	PUMP
ARCH.	DRAT		QUOD	DUFF	RUCK	QUIP
ARNI.	ERST	*ETNA	RUED	GUFF	RUSK	RUMP
TREK.	FRET	STOA.	SUDD	GULF	SUCK	SUMP.
ORAL	FRIT	STAB	SUED	HUFF	SULK	BURR
*URAL.	GRIT	STUB.	SURD.	LUFF	SUNK	PURR
BRIM	TRET	STUD.	*BUDE	MUFF	TUCK	*RUHR
CRAM	TROT	STAG.	*BUTE	PUFF	TURK	BUSS
DRAM	WRIT.	ETCH	CUBE	RUFF	TUSK.	CUSS
DRUM	FRAU	ITCH	CURE	SURF	BUHL	FUSS
FROM	URDU.	*UTAH.	CUTE	TURF.	BULL	LUES
GRAM	BRAW	ETUI.	DUCE	BUNG	BURL	MUSS
GRIM	BREW	ATOM	DUDE	DUNG	CULL	OURS
PRAM	BROW	ITEM	DUKE	HUNG	CURL	PUSS
PRIM	CRAW	STEM	DUNE	LUNG	DUAL	RUSS
PROM	CREW	STUM.	DUPE	QUAG	DUEL	SUDS
TRAM	CROW	*ETON	FUME	RUNG	DULL	SUSS.
TRIM.	DRAW	+STAN	FUSE	SUNG.	FUEL	AUNT
BRAN	DREW	STUN.	HUGE	BUSH	FULL	BUNT
BREN	GREW	ATOP	+HUME	GUSH	FURL	BUST
CRAN	GROW	STEP	JUBE	+HUGH	GULL	BUTT
GRIN	PROW.	STOP.	+JUNE	HUSH	*HULL	CULT
*IRAN	CRUX	STAR	JUTE	LUSH	HURL	CURT
IRON	ORYX.	STIR.	LUBE	MUCH	LULL	DUCT
*ORAN	ARMY	STET.	LUCE	MUSH	*MULL	DUET
WREN.	ARTY	STEW	LUGE	OUCH	NULL	DUNT
*ARNO	BRAY	STOW.	+LUKE	PUSH	PULL	DUST
BRIO	DRAY	STYX.	LURE	RUSH	PURL.	GUST
*BRNO	DREY	STAY	LUTE	+RUTH	CULM	HUNT
ERGO	FRAY		LUXE	SUCH	*GUAM.	HURT
TRIO.	GRAY	AURA	MULE	TUSH.	BURN	JUST
CRAP	GREY	BUNA	MUSE	*FUJI.	+JUAN	LUNT
CROP	ORGY	*CUBA	MUTE	BUCK	MUON	LUST
DRIP	PRAY	HULA	NUDE	BULK	RUIN	MUST
GRIP	PREY	JUBA	*OUSE	BUNK	TURN.	MUTT
PREP	TRAY	*JURA	PUCE	BUSK	BUBO	OUST
PROP	TREY	+LUNA	PUKE	DUCK	+HUGO	PUNT
TRAP	*TROY	PUMA	PULE	DUNK	JUDO	PUTT
TRIP	X-RAY	PUPA	PURE	DUSK	+JUNO	QUIT
WRAP.	*ASIA.	TUBA	RUBE	FUNK	LUDO.	RUNT
*IRAQ.	USED.	TUFA	RUDE	HULK	BUMP	RUST
ARAR.	ISLE.	TUNA.	RULE	HUNK	BURP	SUET
+ARES	ASCI.	BULB	RUNE	HUSK	CUSP	SUIT
ARMS	*OSLO.	CURB	RUSE	JUNK	+CUYP	TUFT.
ARTS	TSAR	DUMB	SURE	LUCK	DUMP	GURU
+EROS	USER.	NUMB.	TUBE	LURK	GULP	JU-J
+IRIS		BUND	TUNE	MUCK	HUMP	

KUDU	SWIM	SYCE	HEAD	GOAL	*ELAN	BEAR
LULU	SWUM.	SYNE	LEAD	GYAL	+EVAN	BOAR
TUTU	+EWAN	TYKE	LOAD	HEAL	+EWAN	CHAR
ZULU.	+GWEN	*TYNE	MEAD	LEAL	FLAN	CZAR
BUOY	+GWYN	TYPE	QUAD	MEAL	GEAN	DEAR
BURY	+OWEN	TYRE.	READ	+NEAL	G-MAN	FEAR
BUSY	SWAN	AYAH	ROAD	ODAL	IMAN	GEAR
+DUFY	TWIN.	MYTH.	SHAD	OPAL	*IRAN	HEAR
DULY	SWAP	DYAK.	TOAD	ORAL	+IVAN	HOAR
DUTY	SWOP.	GYAL.	TRAD	OVAL	+JEAN	KNAR
FUMY	EWER.	HYMN	WOAD.	PEAL	+JOAN	+LEAR
FURY	TWAS.	+LYNN.	BRAE.	REAL	+JUAN	LIAR
+JUDY	SWAT	GYRO	DEAF	SEAL	KHAN	NEAR
JULY	SWOT	HYPO	LEAF	TAAL	LEAN	PEAR
JURY	TWIT.	TYRO.	LOAF	TEAL	LOAN	REAR
+LUCY	AWAY	DYER	+OLAF	*URAL	MEAN	ROAR
PUNY	AWRY	OYER.	+PIAF.	VEAL	MOAN	*SAAR
QUAY	SWAY	AYES	BRAG	VIAL	*OBAN	SCAR
+RUBY.		EYAS.	CRAG	WEAL	*ORAN	SEAR
BUZZ	IXIA.	CYST	DRAG	ZEAL.	PLAN	SOAR
FUZZ	AXED.	EYOT	FLAG	+ADAM	ROAN	SPAR
QUIZ	AXLE.	RYOT.	KNAG	BEAM	SCAN	STAR
*SUEZ	AXIL.	LYNX.	QUAG	CLAM	+SEAN	TEAR
	EXAM.	OYEZ	SHAG	CRAM	SPAN	TSAR
UVEA.	AXON		SLAG	DRAM	+STAN	TZAR
AVID	EXON	+EZRA.	SNAG	*EDAM	SWAN	WEAR
+OVID.	OXEN.	CZAR	STAG	EXAM	THAN	YEAR.
EVIL	AXIS.	TZAR	SWAG.	FLAM	WEAN.	ALAS
OVAL.	EXIT		AMAH	FOAM	CHAP	BIAS
OVUM.			AYAH	GRAM	CLAP	EYAS
*AVON	CYMA	+AHAB	SHAH	*GUAM	CRAP	KVAS
+EVAN	+MYRA.	ARAB	*UTAH	IMAM	FLAP	LIAS
EVEN	DYAD	BLAB	YEAH.	LOAM	HEAP	TWAS
+IVAN	DYED	CRAB	BEAK	MAAM	KNAP	UPAS
OVEN.	EYED.	DOAB	DHAK	OGAM	LEAP	XMAS.
AVER	BYRE	DRAB	DYAK	PRAM	NEAP	BEAT
EVER	CYME	GRAB	FLAK	REAM	REAP	BOAT
+IVOR	DYKE	SCAB	LEAK	ROAM	SLAP	BRAT
OVER.	DYNE	SLAB	PEAK	SEAM	SNAP	CHAT
KVAS	*EYRE	STAB	SOAK	SHAM	SOAP	COAT
+YVES.	GYBE	SWAB.	TEAK	SLAM	SWAP	DRAT
AVOW	GYLE	BEAD	WEAK.	SPAM	TRAP	FEAT
	GYRE	BRAD	ANAL	SWAM	WRAP.	FIAT
SWAB.	GYVE	*CHAD	BAAL	TEAM	*IRAQ.	FLAT
AWED	*HYDE	CLAD	COAL	TRAM.	ADAR	GHAT
OWED.	KYLE	DEAD	*DEAL	+ALAN	AFAR	GNAT
SWAG	LYKE	DYAD	DHAL	BEAN	AGAR	GOAT
SWIG	*LYME	EGAD	DIAL	BRAN	AJAR	HEAT
TWIG.	LYRE	GLAD	DUAL	CRAN	ALAR	MEAT
SWAM	PYRE	GOAD	FOAL	DEAN	ARAR	MOAT

21

NEAT	*CUBA	LUCE	MUCK	BODE	AREA	ALEE
PEAT	*ELBA	MACE	NECK	*BUDE	FLEA	FLEE
PLAT	JUBA	MICE	+NICK	CADE	IDEA	FREE
SCAT	TUBA.	*NICE	NOCK	CEDE	PLEA	GLEE
SEAT	ABBE	ONCE	PACK	CODE	+RHEA	+KLEE
SLAT	BABE	PACE	PECK	DUDE	SHEA	KNEE
SPAT	CUBE	PUCE	PICK	FADE	UREA	OGEE
SWAT	*ELBE	RACE	POCK	+GIDE	UVEA.	SMEE
TEAT	GIBE	RICE	PUCK	HADE	BLEB	THEE
THAT	GYBE	SYCE	RACK	HIDE	DIEB	TREE.
WHAT.	+HEBE	VICE.	RECK	*HYDE	PLEB.	BEEF
BEAU	JIBE	ARCH	+RICK	JADE	SPEC.	CHEF
FRAU.	JUBE	+BACH	ROCK	LADE	ABED	CLEF
SLAV.	KIBE	EACH	RUCK	LODE	AGED	FIEF
BRAW	LOBE	ETCH	SACK	MADE	APED	LIEF
CHAW	LUBE	INCH	SICK	MODE	AWED	REEF.
CLAW	ROBE	ITCH	SOCK	NODE	AXED	CLEG.
CRAW	RUBE	LICH	SUCK	NUDE	BLED	VLEI.
DRAW	TUBE.	LOCH	TACK	REDE	BRED	KEEK
FLAW	*GOBI.	MACH	TICK	RIDE	CO-ED	LEEK
GNAW	AMBO	MUCH	TUCK	RODE	DEED	MEEK
+SHAW	BUBO	OUCH	WICK.	RUDE	DIED	PEEK
SLAW	HOBO	RICH	COCO	SIDE	DYED	REEK
THAW.	UMBO.	SUCH.	FICO	TIDE	EKED	SEEK
+AJAX	+BABS	ASCI	LOCO	VIDE	EYED	TREK
COAX	DIBS.	FOCI	PACO	WADE	FEED	WEEK.
FLAX	DEBT.	LOCI.	PICO	WIDE.	FLED	+ABEL
HOAX.	BABU	BACK	UNCO.	CADI	+FRED	CIEL
AWAY	*CEBU	BECK	DUCT	KADI	HEED	DUEL
BRAY	TABU	BOCK	FACT	WADI.	HIED	FEEL
CHAY	ZEBU.	BUCK	PACT	HADJ.	HOED	FUEL
CLAY	BABY	COCK	PICT	DADO	ICED	GAEL
D-DAY	GABY	DECK	SECT	+DIDO	LIED	HEEL
DRAY	GO-BY	+DICK	TACT.	DODO	NEED	KEEL
FLAY	+RUBY	DOCK	LACY	JUDO	OWED	*KIEL
FRAY	+TOBY	DUCK	+LUCY	LIDO	PIED	+NOEL
GRAY		HACK	RACY	LUDO	REED	+PEEL
OKAY	COCA	HECK		TO-DO	RUED	REEL
PLAY	INCA	HICK	CODA	UNDO.	SEED	TAEL.
PRAY	MICA	HOCK	DADA	ODDS	SHED	AHEM
QUAY	PACA	+JACK	EDDA	SUDS.	SLED	CLEM
SHAY	PICA	+JOCK	+LEDA	KUDU	SPED	DEEM
SLAY	RACA.	KECK	SODA	URDU.	SUED	IDEM
SPAY	BICE	KICK	VEDA.	+ANDY	TEED	ITEM
STAY	DACE	LACK	SUDD	BODY	TIED	POEM
SWAY	DICE	LICK	WADD.	EDDY	TOED	SEEM
TRAY	DUCE	LOCK	*ALDE	+JUDY	USED	STEM
X-RAY	FACE	LUCK	BADE	LADY	VIED	TEEM
	LACE	+MICK	+BEDE	TIDY	WEED.	THEM
ABBA	LICE	MOCK	BIDE		AKEE	*ADEN

AMEN	OYER	FLEX	LOFT	POGO	SKID	SHIM
BEEN	PEER	IBEX	RAFT	SAGO	SLID	SKIM
BREN	PIER	ILEX.	REFT	*TOGO.	VOID.	SLIM
*CAEN	SEER	DREY	RIFT	DIGS	BRIE	SWIM
*EDEN	TIER	GREY	SIFT	TOGS.	*ERIE.	TRIM
EVEN	USER	OBEY	SOFT	EDGY	COIF	WHIM.
GLEN	VEER.	PREY	+TAFT	FOGY	WAIF.	AKIN
+GWEN	+ARES	THEY	TUFT	ORGY	BRIG	CHIN
KEEN	AYES	TREY	WAFT		GRIG	COIN
LIEN	DOES	WHEY.	WEFT.	EPHA	PRIG	FAIN
MIEN	IDES	OYEZ	DEFY	HA-HA.	SWIG	GAIN
OMEN	LEES	*SUEZ	+DUFY	ACHE.	TRIG	GRIN
OPEN	LUES			BUHL	TWIG	+IAIN
OVEN	NOES	ALFA	ALGA	KOHL.	WHIG.	JAIN
+OWEN	SHES	SOFA	GAGA	FOHN	HAIK	JOIN
OXEN	*TEES	TUFA.	MEGA	+JOHN.	NAIK.	LAIN
PEEN	+YVES.	CAFE	+OLGA	ECHO	ANIL	LOIN
SEEN	ABET	*FIFE	*RIGA	*SOHO.	AXIL	MAIN
THEN	BEET	LIFE	SAGA	+BOHR	BAIL	+ODIN
WHEN	DIET	RIFE	TOGA	*RUHR.	BOIL	PAIN
WREN.	DUET	SAFE	VEGA	JEHU.	CEIL	RAIN
+CLEO	FEET	WIFE.	YOGA.	ASHY	COIL	REIN
+THEO.	FRET	BIFF	CAGE		DAIL	RUIN
BEEP	MEET	BUFF	DOGE	ARIA	EVIL	SHIN
DEEP	POET	CUFF	EDGE	*ASIA	FAIL	SKIN
JEEP	STET	DAFF	GAGE	IXIA.	FOIL	SPIN
KEEP	SUET	DOFF	HUGE	ABIB	+GAIL	THIN
PEEP	TRET	DUFF	LOGE	CRIB	HAIL	TWIN
PREP	WHET.	GAFF	LUGE	GLIB.	JAIL	VAIN
SEEP	LIEU.	GUFF	PAGE	CHIC	KAIL	VEIN
SKEP	*KIEV.	HUFF	RAGE	EPIC	MAIL	WHIN.
STEP	ANEW	+JEFF	SAGE	+ERIC	MOIL	AGIO
WEEP	BLEW	JIFF	URGE	LAIC	NAIL	BRIO
ACER	BREW	LUFF	WAGE.	URIC	+NEIL	+CLIO
AVER	CHEW	MIFF	*EIGG	ZOIC.	NOIL	*OHIO
BEER	CLEW	MUFF	HOGG.	ACID	PAIL	OLIO
BIER	CREW	PUFF	+GOGH	AMID	+PHIL	TRIO.
BOER	DREW	RIFF	HIGH	ARID	RAIL	BLIP
DEER	FLEW	RUFF	+HUGH	AVID	SAIL	CHIP
DOER	GREW	TIFF	NIGH	CHID	SOIL	CLIP
DYER	KNEW	TOFF.	SIGH	+ENID	TAIL	DRIP
EVER	PHEW	HI-FI.	YOGH.	GRID	TEIL	FLIP
EWER	SHEW	INFO.	MAGI	IBID	TOIL	GRIP
GOER	SKEW	DAFT	YOGI.	LAID	VAIL	QUIP
JEER	SLEW	DEFT	SIGN.	MAID	VEIL	SHIP
LEER	SPEW	GIFT	DAGO	+OVID	WAIL.	SKIP
NEER	STEW	HAFT	ERGO	PAID	BRIM	SLIP
ODER	VIEW	HEFT	GO-GO	QUID	GRIM	SNIP
ONER	WHEW.	LEFT	+HUGO	RAID	MAIM	TRIP
OVER	APEX	LIFT	NO-GO	SAID	PRIM	WHIP

AMIR	RAJA.	GALA	ORLE	CALL	HALM	ZULU.
COIR	*FIJI	HULA	PALE	CELL	HELM	CALX.
EMIR	*FUJI.	KOLA	+PELE	*COLL	HOLM	ABLY
FAIR	JU-JU	+LOLA	PILE	CULL	MALM	ALLY
HAIR		OLLA	POLE	DELL	PALM.	DULY
HEIR	ILKA	VOLA	PULE	DILL	KILN.	HOLY
LAIR	KAKA.	+ZOLA.	RILE	DOLL	HALO	IDLY
LOIR	BAKE	BULB.	ROLE	DULL	KILO	INLY
PAIR	BIKE	TALC.	RULE	FALL	*OSLO	JULY
STIR	CAKE	BALD	SALE	FELL	+POLO	+LILY
WEIR.	COKE	BOLD	SOLE	FILL	SILO	OILY
+ACIS	DIKE	COLD	TALE	FULL	SOLO.	ONLY
+AMIS	DUKE	FOLD	TELE	GALL	CALP	RELY
+APIS	DYKE	GELD	TILE	+GILL	GULP	UGLY
AXIS	FAKE	GILD	VALE	GULL	HELP	WILY
DAIS	HAKE	GOLD	VILE	HALL	KELP	
IBIS	HIKE	HELD	VOLE	HELL	PALP	+ALMA
+IRIS	JOKE	HOLD	WALE	HILL	PULP	BEMA
+ISIS	LAKE	MELD	WILE	*HULL	YELP.	COMA
KRIS	LIKE	MILD	YALE	JELL	+HALS	CYMA
THIS.	+LUKE	SOLD	YULE.	+JILL	HOLS.	+ELMA
ADIT	LYKE	TOLD	CALF	KILL	BELT	+EMMA
BAIT	MAKE	VELD	DELF	LOLL	BOLT	FAMA
CHIT	+MIKE	WELD	GOLF	LULL	CELT	LAMA
DOIT	PIKE	WILD	GULF	MALL	COLT	*LIMA
EDIT	POKE	WOLD.	HALF	+MILL	CULT	PUMA.
EMIT	PUKE	ABLE	SELF	MOLL	DOLT	BOMB
EXIT	RAKE	AXLE	WOLF.	*MULL	FELT	COMB
FLIT	SAKE	BALE	*BALI	+NELL	GILT	DUMB
FRIT	SOKE	BILE	+DALI	NULL	HALT	IAMB
GAIT	TAKE	BOLE	DELI	PALL	HILT	JAMB
GRIT	TIKE	COLE	KALI	PILL	+HOLT	+LAMB
KNIT	TYKE	DALE	PALI.	POLL	JILT	LIMB
OBIT	WAKE	DELE	BALK	PULL	JOLT	NUMB
OMIT	WOKE	DOLE	BILK	RILL	KELT	TOMB
QUIT	YOKE.	FILE	BULK	ROLL	KILT	WOMB.
SKIT	ANKH	GALE	CALK	SELL	LILT	ACME
SLIT	LAKH	GYLE	FOLK	SILL	MALT	CAME
SPIT	SIKH.	HALE	HULK	TALL	MELT	COME
SUIT	+LOKI	HOLE	MILK	TELL	MILT	CYME
TWIT	+SAKI	IDLE	SILK	TILL	PELT	DAME
UNIT	TIKI.	ISLE	SULK	TOLL	SALT	DEME
WAIT	*BAKU.	KALE	TALK	WALL	SILT	DIME
WHIT	INKY	KYLE	WALK	WELL	TILT	DOME
WRIT.	LAKY	MALE	YOLK.	+WILL	VOLT	FAME
SPIV.	POKY	MILE	BALL	YELL.	+WALT	FUME
QUIZ		MOLE	+BELL	BALM	WELT	GAME
WHIZ	*BALA	MULE	+BILL	CALM	WILT.	HAME
	COLA	*NILE	BOLL	CULM	LULU	HOME
DEJA	+ELLA	OGLE	BULL	FILM	TOLU	+HUME

24

KAME	VAMP.	TEND	VANE	LINK	LUNT	ROOD
LAME	ALMS	VEND	VINE	MINK	MINT	SHOD
LIME	ARMS.	WAND	WANE	MONK	PANT	TROD
*LYME	ARMY	WEND	WINE	PINK	PENT	WOOD.
MIME	DEMY	WIND	ZONE.	PUNK	PINT	ALOE
NAME	ELMY	ZEND.	BANG	RANK	PUNT	FLOE
NOME	FUMY	ACNE	BING	RINK	RANT	OBOE
POME	GAMY	+ANNE	BUNG	SANK	RENT	SHOE
RIME	HOMY	BANE	DING	SINK	RUNT	SLOE.
*ROME	LIMY	BINE	DUNG	SUNK	SENT	GOOF
SAME	RIMY	BONE	FANG	TANK	TENT	HOOF
SOME		CANE	GANG	WINK	TINT	PROF
TAME	+ANNA	CINE	GONG	YANK.	VENT	ROOF
TIME	BUNA	CONE	HANG	*BONN	WANT	WOOF.
TOME	+EDNA	DANE	HUNG	JINN	WENT	AGOG
XEME	*ETNA	DENE	KING	LINN	WONT.	CLOG
ZEME.	*IONA	DINE	LANG	+LYNN	MENU.	FLOG
BUMF.	*JENA	DONE	LING	+MANN.	JINX	FROG
DEMI	+LENA	DUNE	LONG	*ARNO	LYNX	GROG
SEMI.	+LUNA	DYNE	LUNG	*BRNO	MANX	SLOG
DAMN	MANA	ERNE	PANG	+JUNO	MINX.	SMOG
HYMN	+MONA	FANE	PONG	KINO	BONY	SNOG.
LIMN.	+NINA	FINE	RANG	LENO	CONY	POOH.
AMMO	*RONA	+GENE	RING	LINO	DENY	AMOK
*COMO	TUNA	GONE	RUNG	MONO	MANY	BOOK
ELMO	ULNA.	HONE	SANG	*RENO.	PINY	+COOK
HOMO	ZINC.	+JANE	SING	LENS	PONY	HOOK
MEMO.	BAND	+JUNE	SONG	*MONS	PUNY	LOOK
BUMP	BEND	KINE	SUNG	SANS.	TINY	NOOK
CAMP	BIND	LANE	TANG	AINT	+TONY	ROOK
DAMP	BOND	LINE	TING	AUNT	WINY	TOOK.
DUMP	BUND	LONE	WING.	BANT	ZANY	COOL
GAMP	FEND	MANE	ARNI	BENT		DOOL
GIMP	FIND	MINE	*IFNI	BUNT	PROA	FOOL
HEMP	FOND	*NENE	MINI.	CANT	STOA	GAOL
HUMP	FUND	NINE	BANK	CENT	WHOA.	IDOL
JUMP	HAND	NONE	BUNK	DENT	BLOB	OBOL
KEMP	HIND	PANE	CONK	DINT	BOOB	POOL
LAMP	KIND	PINE	DANK	DONT	KNOB	TOOL
LIMP	LAND	PONE	DUNK	DUNT	SLOB	VIOL
LUMP	LEND	+RENE	FINK	FENT	SNOB.	WOOL.
PIMP	MEND	RINE	FUNK	FONT	BLOC.	ATOM
POMP	MIND	RUNE	GONK	GENT	CLOD	BOOM
PUMP	POND	SANE	HANK	HINT	FOOD	DOOM
RAMP	RAND	SINE	HONK	HUNT	GOOD	FROM
ROMP	REND	SYNE	HUNK	ISNT	HOOD	LOOM
RUMP	RIND	TINE	JINK	+KANT	MOOD	PROM
SUMP	SAND	TONE	JUNK	*KENT	PLOD	ROOM
TAMP	SEND	TUNE	KINK	LENT	PROD	WHOM
TUMP	*SIND	*TYNE	LANK	LINT	QUOD	ZOOM

25

AEON	+AMOS	BUOY	+DORA	GYRE	LARK	PERN
ANON	EPOS	CLOY	+EZRA	HARE	LURK	PIRN
*AVON	+EROS	PLOY	+HERA	HERE	+MARK	SORN
AXON	*LAOS.	*TROY	*JURA	HIRE	MURK	TARN
BOON	BLOT		LIRA	LIRE	NARK	TERN
COON	BOOT	CAPA	+MYRA	LORE	PARK	TORN
EBON	CLOT	PAPA	OKRA	LURE	PERK	TURN
*ETON	COOT	PUPA.	PARA	LYRE	PORK	WARN
EXON	EYOT	CAPE	+VERA.	MARE	*SARK	WORN
GOON	FOOT	COPE	BARB	MERE	TURK	YARN.
ICON	HOOT	DOPE	CURB	MIRE	WORK	BIRO
IKON	KNOT	DUPE	GARB	MORE	*YORK.	FARO
IRON	LOOT	GAPE	HERB	OGRE	BURL	GYRO
KAON	MOOT	HOPE	KERB	PARE	+CARL	+HERO
LION	PHOT	JAPE	VERB.	PORE	CURL	INRO
LOON	PLOT	LOPE	CIRC.	PURE	EARL	+MIRO
MOON	RIOT	MOPE	BARD	PYRE	FURL	+NERO
MUON	ROOT	NAPE	BIRD	RARE	GIRL	TYRO
NEON	RYOT	NOPE	CARD	SERE	HARL	ZERO.
NOON	SCOT	PIPE	CORD	SIRE	HURL	BURP
PEON	SHOT	+POPE	CURD	SORE	JARL	CARP
PHON	SLOT	RAPE	FORD	SURE	+KARL	DORP
PION	SNOT	RIPE	GIRD	TARE	MARL	HARP
SOON	SOOT	ROPE	HARD	TIRE	PURL.	WARP.
UPON	SPOT	TAPE	HERD	TORE	BARM	BURR
ZION.	SWOT	TOPE	LARD	TYRE	BERM	DORR
SHOO.	TOOT	TYPE	LORD	*WARE	CORM	HERR
ATOP	TROT.	WIPE.	NARD	WERE	DERM	PURR.
CHOP	THOU.	HOPI	PARD	WIRE	FARM	HERS
CLOP	ALOW	IMPI	SARD	WORE	FIRM	+MARS
CO-OP	AVOW	KEPI	SURD	YORE.	FORM	OURS.
CROP	BLOW	TOPI.	WARD	CORF	GERM	+BART
FLOP	BROW	HYPO.	WORD	KERF	HARM	+BERT
HOOP	CHOW	LAPP	YARD.	SERF	HERM	BORT
KNOP	CROW	REPP	ACRE	SURF	NORM	CART
LOOP	DHOW	YAPP.	BARE	TURF.	PERM	CERT
PLOP	ENOW	*ALPS.	BERE	BERG.	TERM	CURT
POOP	FLOW	COPT	BORE	*BARI	WARM	DART
PROP	GLOW	KEPT	BYRE	PERI	WORM.	DIRT
ROOP	GROW	RAPT	CARE	SARI	BARN	FORT
SHOP	KNOW	SEPT	CERE	TORI.	+BORN	GIRT
SLOP	PROW	WEPT.	CORE	BARK	BURN	HART
STOP	SCOW	OGPU.	CURE	CARK	CORN	HURT
SWOP.	SHOW	COPY	DARE	*CORK	DARN	MART
BOOR	SLOW	ESPY	DIRE	DARK	EARN	PART
DOOR	+SNOW	ROPY	*EYRE	+DIRK	FERN	PERT
+IVOR	STOW.		FARE	FORK	HORN	PORT
MOOR	+KNOX.	*AGRA	FIRE	HARK	LORN	SORT
POOR	AHOY	AURA	FORE	JERK	MORN	TART
+THOR.	*AMOY	BORA	GORE	KIRK	NORN	TORT

VERT	MUSE	DISK	BEST	EASY	*BATH	CLUB
WART	NOSE	DUSK	BUST	NOSY	+BETH	DAUB
WERT.	*OISE	HUSK	CAST	POSY	BOTH	DRUB
ECRU	*OUSE	MASK	CIST	ROSY	DOTH	GRUB
GURU	POSE	MUSK	COST		GOTH	SLUB
*PERU	RISE	*OMSK	CYST	BETA	HATH	SNUB
THRU.	+ROSE	RISK	DOST	DATA	KITH	STUB.
DERV.	RUSE	RUSK	DUST	IOTA	LATH	FEUD
+MARX.	VASE	TASK	EAST	JOTA	LITH	GAUD
ADRY	VISE	TUSK.	ERST	META	LOTH	LAUD
AERY	WISE.	ALSO	FAST	RATA	MOTH	LOUD
AIRY	BASH	PESO	FIST	+RITA	MYTH	+MAUD
AWRY	BOSH	SO-SO.	GEST	ROTA	OATH	SCUD
BURY	BUSH	CUSP	GIST	SETA	PATH	SPUD
DORY	CASH	GASP	GUST	ZETA.	PITH	STUD
EERY	COSH	HASP	HAST	ANTE	+RUTH	THUD
FURY	DASH	LISP	HEST	BATE	WITH.	YOUD.
*GARY	DISH	RASP	HOST	BITE	ANTI	AGUE
GORY	FASH	WASP	INST	*BUTE	SATI	BLUE
JURY	FISH	WISP.	JEST	CATE	YETI	CLUE
LORY	GASH	BASS	JUST	CITE	ALTO	FLUE
+MARY	GOSH	+BESS	KIST	COTE	INTO	GLUE
MIRY	GUSH	BOSS	LAST	CUTE	+LETO	MOUE
NARY	HASH	BUSS	LEST	DATE	ONTO	ROUE
+RORY	HUSH	CESS	LIST	DOTE	+TITO	SPUE
SCRY	JOSH	CUSS	LOST	FATE	UNTO	TRUE.
SPRY	KISH	DISS	LUST	FETE	VETO.	POUF.
TORY	LASH	DOSS	MAST	GATE	ARTS	CHUG
VARY	LUSH	FOSS	MIST	HATE	ORTS.	DRUG
VERY	MASH	FUSS	MOST	JUTE	BITT	PLUG
WARY	MESH	HISS	MUST	+KATE	BOTT	SLUG
WIRY	MUSH	JESS	NEST	KITE	BUTT	SMUG
	+NASH	JOSS	OAST	LATE	+MATT	SNUG
+ELSA	NOSH	KISS	OUST	LUTE	MITT	THUG
+LISA	PASH	LASS	PAST	MATE	MUTT	TRUG.
*PISA	POSH	LESS	PEST	METE	NETT	ETUI.
VASA	PUSH	LOSS	POST	MITE	+PITT	CAUK.
VISA.	RASH	MASS	REST	MOTE	PUTT	CAUL
DISC.	RUSH	MESS	RUST	MUTE	SETT	ELUL
APSE	SASH	MISS	TEST	NOTE	WATT.	FOUL
BASE	TUSH	MOSS	*UIST	PATE	TUTU.	HAUL
BISE	WASH	MUSS	*UNST	+PETE	ARTY	MAUL
CASE	WISH.	*NESS	VAST	RATE	CITY	+PAUL
DOSE	NISI.	PASS	VEST	RITE	DUTY	+SAUL
EASE	BASK	PUSS	WAST	ROTE	PITY	SOUL.
ELSE	BISK	*ROSS	WEST	SATE		ALUM
ERSE	BOSK	RUSS	WIST	SITE	AQUA	CHUM
FUSE	BUSK	SUSS	ZEST.	TETE	SKUA.	DRUM
HOSE	CASK	TASS	BUSY	TOTE	BLUB	GEUM
LOSE	DESK	TOSS.	COSY	VOTE.	CHUB	GLUM

HAUM	TAUT	WAVY	SEXY	AQUA	*JENA	SOFA
NEUM	TOUT.		WAXY	AREA	JOTA	SOYA
OVUM	CRUX	*IOWA.		ARIA	JUBA	STOA.
PLUM	FLUX	BAWD	+GOYA	*ASIA	*JURA.	TOGA
*RHUM	ROUX	LEWD.	MAYA	AURA.	KAKA	TUBA
SCUM		HOWE.	SOYA.	*BALA	KAVA	TUFA
SLUM	DEVA	KIWI.	PAYE	BEMA	KOLA	TUNA.
STUM	DIVA	GAWK	*SKYE.	BETA	LAMA	ULNA
SWUM.	*JAVA	GOWK	AMYL	BORA	LAVA	UREA
FAUN	KAVA	HAWK.	*RHYL.	BUNA.	+LEDA	UVEA.
NOUN	LAVA	BAWL	+GWYN.	CAPA	+LENA	VASA
SHUN	NOVA	BOWL	KAYO	COCA	*LIMA	VEDA
SPUN	VIVA.	COWL	*MAYO	CODA	LIRA	VEGA
STUN.	CAVE	FOWL	YO-YO.	COLA	*LISA	+VERA
COUP	CIVE	HOWL		COMA	+LOLA	VISA
ROUP	COVE	JOWL	ONYX	COXA	+LUNA.	VIVA
SOUP.	+DAVE	PAWL	ORYX	*CUBA	MANA	VOLA.
BLUR	DIVE	YAWL	STYX	CYMA.	MAYA	WHOA.
DOUR	DOVE	YOWL.		DADA	MEGA	YOGA.
FOUR	FIVE	+DAWN		DATA	META	ZETA
GAUR	GAVE	DOWN	ADZE	DEJA	MICA	+ZOLA
HOUR	GIVE	FAWN	DAZE	DEVA	+MONA	
KNUR	GYVE	GOWN	DOZE	DIVA	+MYRA.	ABIB
LOUR	HAVE	HEWN	GAZE	+DORA.	+NINA	+AHAB
POUR	HIVE	LAWN	HAZE	EDDA	NOVA.	ARAB.
SLUR	*HOVE	MOWN	LAZE	+EDNA	OKRA	BARB
SOUR	JIVE	PAWN	MAZE	*ELBA	+OLGA	BLAB
SPUR	JOVE	SAWN	*NAZE	+ELLA	OLLA.	BLEB
TOUR	LAVE	SEWN	OOZE	+ELMA	PACA	BLOB
YOUR.	LIVE	SOWN	RAZE	+ELSA	PAPA	BLUB
ANUS	LOVE	TOWN	SIZE.	+EMMA	PARA	BOMB
NOUS	MOVE	YAWN.	NAZI.	EPHA	PICA	BOOB
ONUS	NAVE	MEWS	DOZY	*ETNA	*PISA	BULB.
OPUS	PAVE	NEWS	HAZY	+EZRA.	PLEA	CHUB
PLUS	RAVE	YAWS.	LAZY	FAMA	PROA	CLUB
THUS	RIVE	NEWT	MAZY	FLEA.	PUMA	COMB
URUS	ROVE	NOWT.	OOZY.	GAGA	PUPA.	CRAB
+ZEUS.	SAVE	DEWY	BUZZ	GALA	RACA	CRIB
ABUT	WAVE		FIZZ	+GOYA	RAJA	CURB.
BOUT	WEVE	COXA.	FUZZ	HA-HA	RATA	DAUB
GLUT	WIVE	LUXE	JAZZ	+HERA	+RHEA	DIEB
GOUT	WOVE.	SAXE.	RAZZ	HULA.	*RIGA	DOAB
LOUT	DIVI	MAXI		IDEA	+RITA	DRAB
PHUT	LEVI.	TAXI.		ILKA	*RONA	DRUB
POUT	BEVY	NEXT	ABBA	INCA	ROTA.	DUMB.
ROUT	CAVY	SEXT	*AGRA	*IONA	SAGA	GARB
SCUT	+DAVY	TEXT.	ALFA	IOTA	SETA	GLIB
SHUT	ENVY	DOXY	ALGA	*IOWA	SHEA	GRAB
SLUT	LEVY	FOXY	+ALMA	IXIA.	SKUA	GRUB.
SMUT	NAVY	PIXY	+ANNA	*JAVA	SODA	HERB

28

IAMB.	BIRD	HERD	SAID	ABBE	CARE	DUDE
JAMB.	BLED	HIED	SAND	ABLE	CASE	DUKE
KERB	BOLD	HIND	SARD	ACHE	CATE	DUNE
KNOB.	BOND	HOED	SCUD	ACME	CAVE	DUPE
+LAMB	BRAD	HOLD	SEED	ACNE	CEDE	DYKE
LIMB.	BRED	HOOD.	SEND	ACRE	CERE	DYNE.
NUMB.	BUND.	IBID	SHAD	ADZE	CINE	EASE
PLEB.	CARD	ICED.	SHED	AGUE	CITE	EDGE
SCAB	*CHAD	KIND.	SHOD	AKEE	CIVE	*ELBE
SLAB	CHID	LAID	*SIND	*ALDE	CLUE	ELSE
SLOB	CLAD	LAND	SKID	ALEE	CODE	*ERIE
SLUB	CLOD	LARD	SLED	ALOE	COKE	ERNE
SNOB	CO-ED	LAUD	SLID	+ANNE	COLE	ERSE
SNUB	COLD	LEAD	SOLD	ANTE	COME	*EYRE.
STAB	CORD	LEND	SPED	APSE	CONE	FACE
STUB	CURD.	LEWD	SPUD	AXLE.	COPE	FADE
SWAB.	DEAD	LIED	STUD	BABE	CORE	FAKE
TOMB.	DEED	LOAD	SUDD	BADE	COTE	FAME
VERB.	DIED	LORD	SUED	BAKE	COVE	FANE
WOMB	DYAD	LOUD.	SURD.	BALE	CUBE	FARE
	DYED.	MAID	TEED	BANE	CURE	FATE
BLOC.	EGAD	+MAUD	TEND	BARE	CUTE	FETE
CHIC	EKED	MEAD	THUD	BASE	CYME.	*FIFE
CIRC.	+ENID	MELD	TIED	BATE	DACE	FILE
DISC.	EYED.	MEND	TOAD	*BEDE	DALE	FINE
EPIC	FEED	MILD	TOED	BERE	DAME	FIRE
+ERIC.	FEND	MIND	TOLD	BICE	DANE	FIVE
LAIC.	FEUD	MOOD.	TRAD	BIDE	DARE	FLEE
SPEC.	FIND	NARD	TROD.	BIKE	DATE	FLOE
TALC.	FLED	NEED.	USED.	BILE	+DAVE	FLUE
URIC.	FOLD	+OVID	VELD	BINE	DAZE	FORE
ZINC	FOND	OWED.	VEND	BISE	DELE	FREE
ZOIC	FOOD	PAID	VIED	BITE	DEME	FUME
	FORD	PARD	VOID.	BLUE	DENE	FUSE.
ABED	+FRED	PIED	WADD	BODE	DICE	GAGE
ACID	FUND.	PLOD	WAND	BOLE	DIKE	GALE
AGED	GAUD	POND	WARD	BONE	DIME	GAME
AMID	GELD	PROD.	WEED	BORE	DINE	GAPE
APED	GILD	QUAD	WELD	BRAE	DIRE	GATE
ARID	GIRD	QUID	WEND	BRIE	DIVE	GAVE
AVID	GLAD	QUOD.	WILD	*BUDE	DOGE	GAZE
AWED	GOAD	RAID	WIND	*BUTE	DOLE	+GENE
AXED.	GOLD	RAND	WOAD	BYRE.	DOME	GIBE
BALD	GOOD	READ	WOLD	CADE	DONE	+GIDE
BAND	GRID.	REED	WOOD	CAFE	DOPE	GIVE
BARD	HAND	REND	WORD.	CAGE	DOSE	GLEE
BAWD	HARD	RIND	YARD	CAKE	DOTE	GLUE
BEAD	HEAD	ROAD	YOUD.	CAME	DOVE	GONE
BEND	HEED	ROOD	ZEND	CANE	DOZE	GORE
BIND	HELD	RUED.		CAPE	DUCE	GYBE

GYLE	LAKE	MOPE	+POPE	SAXE	VICE	FIEF.
GYRE	LAME	MORE	PORE	SERE	VIDE	GAFF
GYVE.	LANE	MOTE	POSE	SHOE	VILE	GOLF
HADE	LATE	MOUE	PUCE	SIDE	VINE	GOOF
HAKE	LAVE	MOVE	PUKE	SINE	VISE	GUFF
HALE	LAZE	MULE	PULE	SIRE	VOLE	GULF.
HAME	LICE	MUSE	PURE	SITE	VOTE.	HALF
HARE	LIFE	MUTE.	PYRE.	SIZE	WADE	HOOF
HATE	LIKE	NAME	RACE	*SKYE	WAGE	HUFF.
HAVE	LIME	NAPE	RAGE	SLOE	WAKE	+JEFF
HAZE	LINE	NAVE	RAKE	SMEE	WALE	JIFF
+HEBE	LIRE	*NAZE	RAPE	SOKE	WANE	KERF.
HERE	LIVE	*NENE	RARE	SOLE	*WARE	LEAF
HIDE	LOBE	*NICE	RATE	SOME	WAVE	LIEF
HIKE	LODE	*NILE	RAVE	SORE	WERE	LOAF
HIRE	LOGE	NINE	RAZE	SPUE	WEVE	LUFF.
HIVE	LONE	NODE	REDE	SURE	WIDE	MIFF
HOLE	LOPE	NOME	+RENE	SYCE	WIFE	MUFF.
HOME	LORE	NONE	RICE	SYNE.	WILE	+OLAF
HONE	LOSE	NOPE	RIDE	TAKE	WINE	+PIAF
HOPE	LOVE	NOSE	RIFE	TALE	WIPE	POUF
HOSE	LUBE	NOTE	RILE	TAME	WIRE	PROF
*HOVE	LUCE	NUDE.	RIME	TAPE	WISE	PUFF.
HOWE	LUGE	OBOE	RINE	TARE	WIVE	REEF
HUGE	+LUKE	OGEE	RIPE	TELE	WOKE	RIFF
+HUME	LURE	OGLE	RISE	TETE	WORE	ROOF
*HYDE.	LUTE	OGRE	RITE	THEE	WOVE.	RUFF.
IDLE	LUXE	*OISE	RIVE	TIDE	XEME.	SELF
ISLE.	LYKE	ONCE	ROBE	TIKE	YALE	SERF
JADE	*LYME	OOZE	RODE	TILE	YOKE	SURF.
+JANE	LYRE.	ORLE	ROLE	TIME	YORE	TIFF
JAPE	MACE	*OUSE.	*ROME	TINE	YULE.	TOFF
JIBE	MADE	PACE	ROPE	TIRE	ZEME	TURF.
JIVE	MAKE	PAGE	+ROSE	TOME	ZONE	WAIF
JOKE	MALE	PALE	ROTE	TONE		WOLF
JOVE	MANE	PANE	ROUE	TOPE		WOOF
JUBE	MARE	PARE	ROVE	TORE	BEEF	
+JUNE	MATE	PATE	RUBE	TOTE	BIFF	
JUTE.	MAZE	PAVE	RUDE	TREE	BUFF	AGOG.
KALE	MERE	PAYE	RULE	TRUE	BUMF.	BANG
KAME	METE	+PELE	RUNE	TUBE	CALF	BERG
+KATE	MICE	+PETE	RUSE.	TUNE	CHEF	BING
KIBE	+MIKE	PIKE	SAFE	TYKE	CLEF	BRAG
KINE	MILE	PILE	SAGE	*TYNE	COIF	BRIG
KITE	MIME	PINE	SAKE	TYPE	CORF	BUNG.
+KLEE	MINE	PIPE	SALE	TYRE.	CUFF.	CHUG
KNEE	MIRE	POKE	SAME	URGE.	DAFF	CLEG
KYLE.	MITE	POLE	SANE	VALE	DEAF	CLOG
LACE	MODE	POME	SATE	VANE	DELF	CRAG.
LADE	MOLE	PONE	SAVE	VASE	DOFF	DING
					DUFF.	DRAG

DRUG	WHIG	MUCH	KADI	COCK	LARK	SACK
DUNG.	WING	MUSH	KALI	CONK	LEAK	SANK
*EIGG.		MYTH.	KEPI.	+COOK	LEEK	*SARK
FANG	AMAH	+NASH	KIWI.	*CORK.	LICK	SEEK
FLAG	ANKH	NIGH	LEVI.	DANK	LINK	SICK
FLOG	ARCH	NOSH.	LOCI	DARK	LOCK	SILK
FROG.	AYAH.	OATH	+LOKI.	DECK	LOOK	SINK
GANG	+BACH	OUCH.	MAGI	DESK	LUCK	SOAK
GONG	BASH	PASH	MAXI	DHAK.	LURK.	SOCK
GRIG	*BATH	PATH	MINI.	+DICK	+MARK	SUCK
GROG.	+BETH	PITH	NAZI	+DIRK	MASK	SULK
HANG	BOSH	POOH	NISI.	DISK	MEEK	SUNK.
HOGG	BOTH	POSH	PALI	DOCK	+MICK	TACK
HUNG.	BUSH.	PUSH.	PERI.	DUCK	MILK	TALK
KING	CASH	RASH	+SAKI	DUNK	MINK	TANK
KNAG.	COSH.	RICH	SARI	DUSK	MOCK	TASK
LANG	DASH	RUSH	SATI	DYAK.	MONK	TEAK
LING	DISH	+RUTH.	SEMI.	FINK	MUCK	TICK
LONG	DOTH.	SASH	TAXI	FLAK	MURK	TOOK
LUNG.	EACH	SHAH	TIKI	FOLK	MUSK.	TREK
PANG	ETCH.	SIGH	TOPI	FORK	NAIK	TUCK
PLUG	FASH	SIKH	TORI.	FUNK.	NARK	TURK
PONG	FISH.	SUCH.	VLEI.	GAWK	NECK	TUSK.
PRIG.	GASH	TUSH.	WADI.	GONK	+NICK	WALK
QUAG.	+GOGH	*UTAH.	YETI	GOWK.	NOCK	WEAK
RANG	GOSH	WASH	YOGI	HACK	NOOK.	WEEK
RING	GOTH	WISH		HAIK	*OMSK.	WICK
RUNG.	GUSH.	WITH.	HADJ	HANK	PACK	WINK
SANG	HASH	YEAH		HARK	PARK	WORK.
SHAG	HATH	YOGH	AMOK.	HAWK	PEAK	YANK
SING	HIGH		BACK	HECK	PECK	YOLK
SLAG	+HUGH	ANTI	BALK	HICK	PEEK	*YORK
SLOG	HUSH.	ARNI	BANK	HOCK	PERK	
SLUG	INCH	ASCI.	BARK	HONK	PICK	+ABEL
SMOG	ITCH.	*BALI	BASK	HOOK	PINK	AMYL
SMUG	JOSH.	*BARI.	BEAK	HULK	POCK	ANAL
SNAG	KISH	CADI	BECK	HUNK	PORK	ANIL
SNOG	KITH.	+DALI	BILK	HUSK.	PUCK	AXIL.
SNUG	LAKH	DELI	BISK	+JACK	PUNK.	BAAL
SONG	LASH	DEMI	BOCK	JERK	RACK	BAIL
STAG	LATH	DIVI.	BOOK	JINK	RANK	BALL
SUNG	LICH	ETUI.	BOSK	+JOCK	RECK	BAWL
SWAG	LITH	*FIJI	BUCK	JUNK.	REEK	+BELL
SWIG.	LOCH	FOCI	BULK	KECK	+RICK	+BILL
TANG	LOTH	*FUJI.	BUNK	KEEK	RINK	BOIL
THUG	LUSH.	*GOBI.	BUSK.	KICK	RISK	BOLL
TING	MACH	HI-FI	CALK	KINK	ROCK	BOWL
TRIG	MASH	HOPI.	CARK	KIRK.	ROOK	BUHL
TRUG	MESH	*IFNI	CASK	LACK	RUCK	BULL
TWIG.	MOTH	IMPI.	CAUK	LANK	RUSK.	BURL

CALL	HALL	PEAL	AHEM	NEUM	BARN	IMAN
+CARL	HARL	+PEEL	ALUM	NORM.	BEAN	*IRAN
CAUL	HAUL	+PHIL	ATOM.	OGAM	BEEN	IRON
CEIL	HEAL	PILL	BALM	OVUM.	*BONN	+IVAN
CELL	HEEL	POLL	BARM	PALM	BOON	JAIN
CIEL	HELL	POOL	BEAM	PERM	+BORN	+JEAN
COAL	HILL	PULL	BERM	PLUM	BRAN	JINN
COIL	HOWL	PURL.	BOOM	POEM	BREN	+JOAN
*COLL	*HULL	RAIL	BRIM.	PRAM	BURN.	+JOHN
COOL	HURL.	REAL	CALM	PRIM	*CAEN	JOIN
COWL	IDOL.	REEL	CHUM	PROM.	CHIN	+JUAN.
CULL	JAIL	*RHYL	CLAM	REAM	COIN	KAON
CURL.	JARL	RILL	CLEM	*RHUM	COON	KEEN
DAIL	JELL	ROLL.	CORM	ROAM	CORN	KHAN
*DEAL	+JILL	SAIL	CRAM	ROOM.	CRAN.	KILN.
DELL	JOWL.	+SAUL	CULM.	SCUM	DAMN	LAIN
DHAL	KAIL	SEAL	DEEM	SEAM	DARN	LAWN
DIAL	+KARL	SELL	DERM	SEEM	+DAWN	LEAN
DILL	KEEL	SILL	DOOM	SHAM	DEAN	LIEN
DOLL	*KIEL	SOIL	DRAM	SHIM	DOWN.	LIMN
DOOL	KILL	SOUL.	DRUM.	SKIM	EARN	LINN
DUAL	KOHL.	TAAL	*EDAM	SLAM	EBON	LION
DUEL	LEAL	TAEL	EXAM.	SLIM	*EDEN	LOAN
DULL.	LOLL	TAIL	FARM	SLUM	*ELAN	LOIN
EARL	LULL.	TALL	FILM	SPAM	*ETON	LOON
ELUL	MAIL	TEAL	FIRM	STEM	+EVAN	LORN
EVIL.	MALL	TEIL	FLAM	STUM	EVEN	+LYNN.
FAIL	MARL	TELL	FOAM	SWAM	+EWAN	MAIN
FALL	MAUL	TILL	FORM	SWIM	EXON.	+MANN
FEEL	MEAL	TOIL	FROM.	SWUM.	FAIN	MEAN
FELL	+MILL	TOLL	GERM	TEAM	FAUN	MIEN
FILL	MOIL	TOOL.	GEUM	TEEM	FAWN	MOAN
FOAL	MOLL	*URAL.	GLUM	TERM	FERN	MOON
FOIL	*MULL.	VAIL	GRAM	THEM	FLAN	MORN
FOOL	NAIL	VEAL	GRIM	TRAM	FOHN.	MOWN
FOUL	+NEAL	VEIL	*GUAM.	TRIM.	GAIN	MUON-
FOWL	+NEIL	VIAL	HALM	WARM	GEAN	NEON
FUEL	+NELL	VIOL.	HARM	WHIM	GLEN	NOON
FULL	+NOEL	WAIL	HAUM	WHOM	G-MAN	NORN
FURL.	NOIL	WALL	HELM	WORM.	GOON	NOUN-
GAEL	NULL.	WEAL	HERM	ZOOM	GOWN	*OBAN
+GAIL	OBOL	WELL	HOLM.		GRIN	+ODIN
GALL	ODAL	+WILL	IDEM	*ADEN	+GWEN	OMEN
GAOL	OPAL	WOOL.	IMAM	AEON	+GWYN.	OPEN
+GILL	ORAL	YAWL	ITEM.	AKIN	HEWN	*ORAN
GIRL	OVAL.	YELL	LOAM	+ALAN	HORN	OVEN
GOAL	PAIL	YOWL.	LOOM.	AMEN	HYMN.	+OWEN
GULL	PALL	ZEAL	MAAM	ANON	+IAIN	OXEN
GYAL.	+PAUL		MAIM	*AVON	ICON	PAIN
HAIL	PAWL	+ADAM	MALM.	AXON.	IKON	PAWN

PEEN		+NERO	CUSP	REAP	BIER	PEAR
PEON	AGIO	NO-GO.	+CUYP.	REPP	BLUR	PEER
PERN	ALSO	*OHIO	DAMP	ROMP	BOAR	PIER
PHON	ALTO	OLIO	DEEP	ROOP	BOER	POOR
PION	AMBO	ONTO	DORP	ROUP	+BOHR	POUR
PIRN	AMMO	*OSLO.	DRIP	RUMP.	BOOR	PURR.
PLAN.	*ARNO.	PACO	DUMP.	SEEP	BURR.	REAR
RAIN	BIRO	PESO	FLAP	SHIP	CHAR	ROAR
REIN	BRIO	PICO	FLIP	SHOP	COIR	*RUHR.
ROAN	*BRNO.	POGO	FLOP.	SKEP	CZAR.	*SAAR
RUIN.	BUBO.	+POLO.	GAMP	SKIP	DEAR	SCAR
SAWN	+CLEO	*RENO.	GASP	SLAP	DEER	SEAR
SCAN	+CLIO	SAGO	GIMP	SLIP	DOER	SEER
+SEAN	COCO	SHOO	GRIP	SLOP	DOOR	SLUR
SEEN	*COMO.	SILO	GULP.	SNAP	DORR	SOAR
SEWN	DADO	*SOHO	HARP	SNIP	DOUR	SOUR
SHIN	DAGO	SOLO	HASP	SOAP	DYER.	SPAR
SHUN	+DIDO	SO-SO.	HEAP	SOUP	EMIR	SPUR
SIGN	DODO.	+THEO	HELP	STEP	EVER	STAR
SKIN	ECHO	+TITO	HEMP	STOP	EWER.	STIR.
SOON	ELMO	TO-DO	HOOP	SUMP	FAIR	TEAR
SORN	ERGO.	*TOGO	HUMP.	SWAP	FEAR	+THOR
SOWN	FARO	TRIO	JEEP	SWOP.	FOUR.	TIER
SPAN	FICO.	TYRO.	JUMP.	TAMP	GAUR	TOUR
SPIN	GO-GO	UMBO	KEEP	TRAP	GEAR	TSAR
SPUN	GYRO.	UNCO	KELP	TRIP	GOER.	TZAR.
+STAN	HALO	UNDO	KEMP	TUMP.	HAIR	USER.
STUN	+HERO	UNTO.	KNAP	VAMP.	HEAR	VEER.
SWAN.	HOBO	VETO.	KNOP.	WARP	HEIR	WEAR
TARN	HOMO	YO-YO.	LAMP	WASP	HERR	WEIR.
TERN	+HUGO	ZERO	LAPP	WEEP	HOAR	YEAR
THAN	HYPO.		LEAP	WHIP	HOUR.	YOUR
THEN	INFO	ATOP.	LIMP	WISP	+IVOR.	
THIN	INRO	BEEP	LISP	WRAP		+ACIS
TORN	INTO.	BLIP	LOOP	YAPP	JEER.	ALAS
TOWN	JUDO	BUMP.	LUMP.	YELP	KNAR	ALMS
TURN	+JUNO.	BURP.	NEAP.		KNUR.	*ALPS
TWIN.	KAYO	CALP	PALP	*IRAQ	LAIR	+AMIS
UPON.	KILO	CAMP	PEEP		LEER	+AMOS
VAIN	KINO.	CARP	PIMP	ACER	LIAR	ANUS
VEIN.	LENO	CHAP	PLOP	ADAR	LOIR	+APIS
WARN	+LETO	CHIP	POMP	AFAR	LOUR.	+ARES
WEAN	LIDO	CHOP	POOP	AGAR	MOOR.	ARMS
WHEN	LINO	CLAP	PREP	AJAR	NEAR	ARTS
WHIN	LOCO	CLIP	PROP	ALAR	NEER.	AXIS
WORN	LUDO.	CLOP	PULP	AMIR	*ODER	AYES.
WREN.	*MAYO	CO-OP	PUMP.	ARAR	ONER	+BABS
YARN	MEMO	COUP	QUIP.	AVER.	OVER	BASS
YAWN.	+MIRO	CRAP	RAMP	BEAR	OYER.	+BESS
ZION	MONO.	CROP	RASP	BEER	PAIR	BIAS

BOSS	OPUS	BUNT	FIAT	KNOT.	PHOT	SORT
BUSS.	ORTS	BUST	FIST	LAST	PHUT	SPAT
CESS	OURS.	BUTT.	FLAT	LEFT	PICT	SPIT
CUSS.	PASS	CANT	FLIT	LENT	PINT	SPOT
DAIS	PLUS	CART	FONT	LEST	+PITT	STET
DIBS	PUSS.	CAST	FOOT	LIFT	PLAT	SUET
DIGS	+RHYS	CELT	FORT	LILT	PLOT	SUIT
DISS	*ROSS	CENT	FRET	LINT	POET	SWAT
DOES	RUSS.	CERT	FRIT.	LIST	PORT	SWOT.
DOSS.	SANS	CHAT	GAIT	LOFT	POST	TACT
EPOS	SHES	CHIT	GENT	LOOT	POUT	+TAFT
+EROS	SUDS	CIST	GEST	LOST	PUNT	TART
EYAS	SUSS.	CLOT	GHAT	LOUT	PUTT.	TAUT
FOSS	TASS	COAT	GIFT	LUNT	QUIT.	TEAT
FUSS.	*TEES	COLT	GILT	LUST.	RAFT	TENT
+HALS	THIS	COOT	GIRT	MALT	RANT	TEST
HERS	THUS	COPT	GIST	MART	RAPT	TEXT
HISS	TOGS	COST	GLUT	MAST	REFT	THAT
HOLS.	TOSS	CULT	GNAT	+MATT	RENT	TILT
IBIS	TWAS.	CURT	GOAT	MEAT	REST	TINT
IDES	UPAS	CYST.	GOUT	MEET	RIFT	TOOT
+IRIS	URUS.	DAFT	GRIT	MELT	RIOT	TORT
+ISIS.	XMAS.	DART	GUST.	MILT	ROOT	TOUT
JESS	YAWS	DEBT	HAFT	MINT	ROUT	TRET
JOSS.	+YVES.	DEFT	HALT	MIST	RUNT	TROT
KISS	+ZEUS	DENT	HART	MITT	RUST	TUFT
KRIS		DIET	HAST	MOAT	RYOT.	TWIT.
KVAS.		DINT	HEAT	MOOT	SALT	*UIST
*LAOS	ABET	DIRT	HEFT	MOST	SCAT	UNIT
LASS	ABUT	DOIT	HEST	MUST	SCOT	*UNST.
LEES	ADIT	DOLT	HILT	MUTT.	SCUT	VAST
LENS	AINT	DONT	HINT	NEAT	SEAT	VENT
LESS	AUNT.	DOST	+HOLT	NEST	SECT	VERT
LIAS	BAIT	DRAT	HOOT	NETT	SENT	VEST
LOSS	BANT	DUCT	HOST	NEWT	SEPT	VOLT.
LUES.	+BART	DUET	HUNT	NEXT	SETT	WAFT
+MARS	BEAT	DUNT	HURT.	NOWT.	SEXT	WAIT
MASS	BEET	DUST.	INST	OAST	SHOT	+WALT
MESS	BELT	EAST	ISNT.	OBIT	SHUT	WANT
MEWS	BENT	EDIT	JEST	OMIT	SIFT	WART
MISS	+BERT	EMIT	JILT	OUST.	SILT	WAST
*MONS	BEST	ERST	JOLT	PACT	SKIT	WATT
MOSS	BITT	EXIT	JUST.	PANT	SLAT	WEFT
NUSS.	BLOT	EYOT.	+KANT	PART	SLIT	WELT
*NESS	BOAT	FACT	KELT	PAST	SLOT	WENT
NEWS	BOLT	FAST	*KENT	PEAT	SLUT	WEPT
NOES	BOOT	FEAT	KEPT	PELT	SMUT	WERT
NOUS.	BORT	FEET	KILT	PENT	SNOT	WEST
ODDS	BOTT	FELT	KIST	PERT	SOFT	WHAT
ONUS	BRAT	FENT	KNIT	PEST	SOOT	WHET

WHIT	CREW	ONYX	EDGY	PITY	FUZZ.
WILT	CROW.	ORYX.	EERY	PIXY	JAZZ.
WIST	OHOW	ROUX.	ELMY	PLAY	OYEZ.
WONT	DRAW	STYX	ENVY	PLOY	QUIZ.
WRIT.	DREW.		ESPY.	POKY	RAZZ.
ZEST	ENOW.	ABLY	FLAY	PONY	*SUEZ.
	FLAW	ADRY	FOGY	POSY	WHIZ
BABU	FLEW	AERY	FOXY	PRAY	
*BAKU	FLOW.	AHOY	FRAY	PREY	
BEAU.	GLOW	AIRY	FUMY	PUNY.	
*CEBU.	GNAW	ALLY	FURY.	QUAY.	
ECRU.	GREW	*AMOY	GABY	RACY	
FRAU.	GROW.	+ANDY	GAMY	RELY	
GURU.	KNEW	ARMY	*GARY	RIMY	
JEHU	KNOW.	ARTY	GO-BY	ROPY	
JU-JU.	PHEW	ASHY	GORY	+RORY	
KUDU.	PROW.	AWAY	GRAY	ROSY	
LIEU	SCOW	AWRY.	GREY.	+RUBY.	
LULU.	+SHAW	BABY	HAZY	SCRY	
MENU.	SHEW	BEVY	HOLY	SEXY	
OGPU.	SHOW	BODY	HOMY.	SHAY	
*PERU.	SKEW	BONY	IDLY	SLAY	
TABU	SLAW	BRAY	INKY	SPAY	
THOU	SLEW	BUOY	INLY.	SPRY	
THRU	SLOW	BURY.	+JUDY	STAY	
TOLU	+SNOW	BUSY.	JULY	SWAY.	
TUTU.	SPEW	CAVY	JURY.	THEY	
URDU.	STEW	CHAY	LACY	TIDY	
ZEBU	STOW	CITY	LADY	TINY	
ZULU	THAW	CLAY	LAKY	+TOBY	
	VIEW.	CLOY	LAZY	+TONY	
DERV.	WHEW	CONY	LEVY	TORY	
*KIEV.		COPY	+LILY	TRAY	
SLAV	+AJAX	COSY.	LIMY	TREY	
SPIV	APEX.	+DAVY	LORY	*TROY.	
	CALX	D-DAY	+LUCY.	UGLY.	
ALOW	COAX	DEFY	MANY	VARY	
ANEW	CRUX.	DEMY	+MARY	VERY.	
AVOW.	FLAX	DENY	MAZY	WARY	
BLEW	FLEX	DEWY	MIRY.	WAVY	
BLOW	FLUX.	DORY	NARY	WAXY	
BRAW	HOAX.	DOXY	NAVY	WHEY	
BREW	IBEX	DOZY	NOSY.	WILY	
BROW.	ILEX.	DRAY	OBEY	WINY	
CHAW	JINX.	DREY	OILY	WIRY.	
CHEW	+KNOX.	+DUFY	OKAY	X-RAY.	
CHOW	LYNX.	DULY	ONLY	ZANY	
CLAW	MANX	DUTY.	OOZY		
CLEW	+MARX	EASY	ORGY.	BUZZ.	
CRAW	MINX.	EDDY	PINY	FIZZ	

35

ABACK	+AUDEN	ACINI	ADMAN	APPAL	AMUSE
ABAFT	AUDIT.	ADIEU	ADMIT	APPLE	AZURE.
ABASE	ABEAM	*ADIGE	ADMIX	APPLY	ANVIL.
ABASH	ABELE	AFIRE	AIMED	APPUI	*ASWAN.
ABATE	ADEEM	AGILE	*AMMAN	ASPEN	ABYSS
ADAGE	+ADELE	ALIAS	+AMMON	ASPIC.	ARYAN
+ADAMS	ADEPT	ALIBI	ARMED.	+AARON	AZYME.
ADAPT	AGENT	+ALICE	+ABNER	ACRID	ANZAC
AGAIN	AHEAD	ALIEN	+AGNES	AERIE	
AGAMA	ALERT	ALIGN	ANNAL	AGREE	BEACH
AGAPE	AMEER	ALIKE	ANNEX	AIRED	BEADY
AGATE	AMEND	ALIVE	ANNOY	AIRER	BE-ALL
AGAVE	ANELE	AMICE	ANNUL	*AKRON	BEANO
ALACK	ANENT	AMINO	AWNED.	AORTA	BEARD
ALARM	APEAK	AMISS	ABODE	+APRIL	BEAST
ALATE	APERY	AMITY	ABOIL	APRON	BEAUX
AMAIN	AREAL	ANIMA	A-BOMB	*ARRAN	BHANG
AMASS	ARENA	ANION	ABORT	*ARRAS	BLACK
AMATE	ARENT	ANISE	ABOUT	ARRAY	BLADE
AMAZE	ARETE	+ANITA	ABOVE	ARRIS	BLAIN
APACE	AVERT.	APIAN	ACORN	ARROW	+BLAKE
APART	AFFIX	APING	ADOBE	AURAL	BLAME
*AQABA	+ALFIE	APISH	ADOPT	AURIC	BLAND
AVAIL	AWFUL.	ARIAN	ADORE	+AVRIL.	BLANK
AVAST	AEGIS	ARIEL	ADORN	+AESOP	BLARE
AWAIT	AGGER	ARIES	AFOOT	AISLE	BLASE
AWAKE	ALGAE	+ARION	AFORE	APSIS	BLAST
AWARD	ALGAL	ARISE	AGONY	ARSIS	BLAZE
AWARE	ALGID	ASIAN	AGORA	ARSON	BOARD
AWASH.	ALGUM	ASIDE	ALOFT	ASSAI	BOAST
ABBEY	ANGEL	AVIAN	ALONE	*ASSAM	BRACE
+ABBIE	ANGER	AWING	ALONG	ASSAY	BRACT
ABBOT	ANGLE	AXIAL	ALOOF	ASSET.	+BRAGG
ALBUM	ANGRY	AXILE	ALOUD	ACTED	BRAID
AMBER	ANGST	AXIOM.	AMONG	ACTOR	BRAIN
AMBIT	*ANGUS	*ANJOU.	AMOUR	AFTER	BRAKE
AMBLE	ARGIL	ANKLE	ANODE	ALTAR	BRAND
AMBRY	ARGOL	ASKED	ANOMY	ALTER	BRANT
ARBOR.	ARGON	ASKEW.	ANONA	ANTIC	BRASH
*ACCRA	ARGOT	AGLET	AROMA	APTLY	BRASS
ARCED	ARGUE	AGLOW	AROSE	ARTIC	BRAVE
*ASCOT.	+ARGUS	ALLAH	ATOLL	ASTER	BRAVO
ADDAX	AUGER	ALLAY	ATONE	ASTIR	BRAWL
ADDED	AUGHT	ALLEY	AVOID	ATTAR	BRAWN
ADDER	AUGUR.	ALL-IN	AWOKE	ATTIC	BRAZE
ADDLE	ABHOR	*ALLOA	AZOIC	AZTEC.	BWANA.
AIDED	ACHED	ALLOT	AZOTE.	ABUSE	BABEL
ALDER	APHIS	ALLOW	ALPHA	ACUTE	BABOO
*ANDES	ASHEN.	ALLOY	AMPLE	ADULT	BABUL
ASDIC	ABIDE	*ATLAS.	AMPLY	AMUCK	BEBOP

BIBLE	BOGIE	BULGE	BARED	BATED	CEASE
+BOBBY	BOGLE	BULKY	BARGE	BATHE	CHAFE
BUBAL.	BOGUS	BULLY	BARMY	BATIK	CHAFF
+BACON	BUGGY	BY-LAW.	BARON	BATON	CHAIN
*BACUP	BUGLE.	BOMBE	*BARRA	BATTY	CHAIR
BOCHE	+BEHAN	BUMBO	+BARRY	BETEL	CHALK
BUCKO.	BOHEA.	BUMPH	BERET	+BETSY	CHAMP
BADGE	BAIRN	BUMPY.	+BERIA	+BETTY	CHANT
BADLY	BAIZE	BANAL	*BERNE	BITCH	+CHAOS
BEDEW	BEIGE	BANDY	BERRY	BITTS	CHAPE
BEDIM	BEING	*BANFF	BERTH	BOTCH	*CHARD
BIDED	*BEIRA	BANJO	+BERYL	BOTHY	CHARM
BIDET	BLIMP	BANNS	BIRCH	BUTCH	CHART
BODED	BLIND	BENCH	BIRTH	BUTTE.	CHARY
BUDDY	BLINK	BENDS	BORAX	BAULK	CHASE
BUDGE	+BLISS	+BENNY	BORED	BLUES	CHASM
BUDGY.	BLITZ	BINGE	BORER	BLUFF	CLACK
BEECH	+BRIAN	BINGO	BORIC	BLUNT	CLAIM
BEEFY	BRIAR	BONED	BORNE	BLURB	CLAMP
BEERY	BRIBE	BONGO	BORON	BLURT	CLANG
BLEAK	BRICK	BONNY	BURGH	BLUSH	CLANK
BLEAR	BRIDE	BONUS	BURIN	BOUGH	+CLARE
BLEAT	BRIEF	BONZE	BURKE	BOULE	CLARY
BLEED	BRILL	BUNCH	BURLY	BOUND	CLASH
BLEEP	BRINE	BUNCO	*BURMA	BOURN	CLASP
BLEND	BRING	BUNNY.	+BURNS	+BRUCE	CLASS
BLESS	BRINK	BLOAT	BURNT	BRUIN	COACH
BLEST	BRINY	BLOCK	BURRO	BRUIT	COALY
BREAD	BRISK	BLOKE	BURST	BRUME	COAST
BREAK	BUILD	BLOND	+BYRON.	BRUNT	COATI
BREAM	BUILT.	BLOOD	BASAL	BRUSH	CRACK
BREED	BIJOU.	BLOOM	BASED	BRUTE.	CRAFT
*BRENT	BAKED	BLOWN	BASIC	+BEVAN	CRAKE
*BREST	BAKER.	BOOBY	+BASIL	BEVEL.	CRAMP
BREVE.	BALAS	BOOST	BASIN	BAWDY	CRANE
BEFIT	BALED	+BOOTH	BASIS	BOWER	CRANK
BEFOG	BALER	BOOTY	BASON	BOWIE	CRAPE
BIFID.	BALMY	BOOZE	*BASRA	BOWLS	CRAPS
BAGGY	BALSA	BOOZY	BASTE	BY-WAY.	CRASH
BEGAD	BELAY	BROAD	BESET	BOXED	CRASS
BEGAN	BELCH	BROCK	BESOM	BOXER	CRATE
BEGET	BELIE	BROIL	BISON	BUXOM.	CRAVE
BEGIN	BELLE	BROKE	+BOSCH	BAYED	CRAWL
BEGOT	BELLY	BROOD	BOSKY	BAYOU	CRAZE
BEGUM	BELOW	BROOK	BOSOM	*BLYTH	CRAZY.
BEGUN	BILBO	BROOM	BOSON	+BOYLE	CABAL
BIGHT	BILGE	BROSE	BOSSY	BUYER.	CABBY
BIGOT	BILLY	BROTH	BUSBY	BEZEL	CABER
BOGEY	BOLAS	BROWN.	BUSHY.	+BIZET	CABIN
BOGGY	BOLUS	BIPED.	BATCH		CABLE

CABOB	CREEP	CALYX	CLOTH	CORNY	COURT
COBLE	+CREON	+CELIA	CLOUD	+COROT	COUTH
COBRA	CREPE	CELLO	CLOUT	CORPS	CRUDE
CUBBY	CREPT	+CHLOE	CLOVE	CURDY	CRUEL
CUBEB	CRESS	CILIA	CLOWN	CURED	CRUET
CUBED	CREST	COLIC	COOED	CURER	CRUMB
CUBIC	*CRETE	+COLIN	COOMB	CURIA	CRUMP
CUBIT.	*CREWE.	*COLNE	CO-OPT	CURIE	CRUSE
CACAO	CAGED	COLON	CROAK	CURIO	CRUSH
CACHE	CAGEY	COLZA	CROCK	CURLY	CRUST.
CACTI	CIGAR.	CULEX.	CROFT	CURRY	*CAVAN
+CACUS	CAIRN	CAMEL	CRONE	CURSE	CAVED
+CECIL	*CAIRO	CAMEO	CRONY	CURVE	CAVIL
COCCI	CHIAN	+CAMUS	CROOK	+CYRIL	CIVET
COCKY	CHICK	COMET	CROON	+CYRUS.	CIVIC
COCOA	CHIDE	COMFY	CRORE	CASED	CIVIL
CYCLE.	CHIEF	COMIC	CROSS	CASTE	COVEN
CADDY	CHILD	COMMA	CROUP	CISSY	COVER
CADET	*CHILE	COMPO	CROWD	CUSEC	COVET
CADGE	CHILI	+COMUS	CROWN.	CUSHY.	COVEY.
*CADIZ	CHILL	CUMIN	CAPER	CATCH	COWED
CADRE	CHIME	CYMAR	CAPON	CATER	COWER
CEDAR	CHIMP	*CYMRU.	*CAPRI	CATES	*COWES.
CEDED	*CHINA	CANAL	COPAL	+CATHY	*CLYDE
CIDER	CHINE	CANDY	COPED	CATTY	COYLY
CODED	CHINK	CANED	COPER	CETIC	COYPU
CODEX	*CHIOS	*CANNA	COPRA	CETIN	CRYPT.
CUDDY.	CHIRP	CANNY	COPSE	CITED	COZEN
CHEAP	CHIRR	CANOE	+CUPID.	COTTA	
CHEAT	CHIVE	CANON	CARAT	CUTIE	DEALT
CHECK	CLICK	CANTO	CARET	CUTIS	DEARY
CHEEK	+CLIFF	CENSE	CARGO	CUTTY.	DEATH
CHEEP	CLIMB	CINCH	CARIB	CAULK	+DIANA
CHEER	CLIME	CONCH	CAROB	CAUSE	DIARY
CHELA	CLING	CONGA	+CAROL	*CEUTA	DRAFF
CHERT	CLINK	CONGE	CARRY	CHUCK	DRAFT
CHESS	CLINT	*CONGO	CARTE	CHUMP	DRAIL
CHEST	+CLIVE	CONIC	CARVE	CHUNK	DRAIN
CLEAN	COIGN	CYNIC.	+CERES	CHURL	+DRAKE
CLEAR	CRICK	CHOCK	+CHRIS	CHURN	DRAMA
CLEAT	CRIED	CHOIR	CIRCA	CHUTE	DRANK
CLEEK	CRIER	CHOKE	+CIRCE	CLUCK	DRAPE
CLEFT	CRIME	CHOKY	CORAL	CLUED	DRAWL
CLERK	CRIMP	CHORD	*CORBY	CLUMP	DRAWN
CREAK	CRISP.	CHORE	CORED	CLUNG	DWARF.
CREAM	CAKED	CHOSE	CORER	COUCH	DEBAG
CREDO	COKEY.	CLOAK	*CORFE	COUGH	DEBAR
CREED	CALIF	CLOCK	*CORFU	COULD	DEBIT
CREEK	CALIX	CLONE	CORGI	COUNT	DEBUT
CREEL	CALVE	CLOSE	CORKY	COUPE	*DUBAI

*DACCA	DYING.	DHOTI	DOUSE	ENDOW	ENJOY.
DECAL	*DIJON.	DIODE	DRUID	ENDUE.	ECLAT
DECAY	*DAKAR.	DROIT	DRUNK	EDEMA	+ELLEN
DECOR	DALAI	DROLL	DRUPE.	EGEST	+ELLIS.
DECOY	DALLY	DROME	+DAVID	EJECT	+EAMON
DECRY	DELAY	DRONE	DAVIT	ELECT	+ELMER.
DICED	*DELFT	DROOL	DEVIL	ELEGY	ENNUI
DICEY	*DELHI	DROOP	*DEVON	ELEMI	+ERNIE.
DICKY	*DELOS	DROSS	DIVAN	EMEND	EBONY
DICTA	DELTA	DROVE	DIVED	EMERY	ELOPE
DUCAL	DELVE	DROWN.	DIVER	ENEMA	EMOTE
DUCAT	DILDO	DEPOT	DIVOT	ENEMY	+ENOCH
DUCHY	+DILYS	DEPTH	DIVVY	ERECT	EPOCH
DUCKY.	DOLCE	DIPUS	*DOVER.	EVENT	EPODE
DADDY	DOLLY	DOPED	DOWDY	EVERT	EPOXY
DIDNT	DULLY	DOPEY	DOWEL	EVERY	ERODE
DODGE	DULSE	DUPED	DOWER	EXEAT	EVOKE.
DODGY.	+DYLAN.	DUPLE.	DOWNY	EXERT.	EMPTY
DIENE	DEMOB	DARED	DOWRY	ELFIN.	EXPEL.
DREAD	DEMON	DARKY	DOWSE.	EAGER	EARLY
DREAM	DEMOS	*DERBY	DIXIE.	EAGLE	EARTH
DREAR	DEMUR	+DEREK	DOYEN	EAGRE	EERIE
DREGS	DIMER	DERMA	+DOYLE	+EDGAR	EGRET
DRESS	DIMLY	DIRGE	DRYAD	EDGED	ENROL
DWELL	DOMED	DIRTY	DRYER	EGGER	ERRED
DWELT.	+DUMAS	DORIC	DRYLY.	EIGHT	+ERROL
DAFFY	DUMMY	+DORIS	DAZED	+ELGAR	ERROR
DEFER	DUMPY.	DORMY	DIZZY	*ELGIN	EYRIE.
+DEFOE.	DANCE	+DURER	DOZED	ERGOT.	EASED
+DEGAS	DANDY	DURST.	DOZEN	*EGHAM	EASEL
DIGIT	+DANNY	DISHY	DOZER	EPHOD	+ELSIE
DOGGY	+DANTE	DOSED		*ESHER	ENSUE
DOGMA.	DENIM	DUSKY	ELAND	+ETHEL	*EPSOM
DAILY	+DENIS	DUSTY.	ELATE	ETHER	ESSAY
DAIRY	DENSE	DATAL	ENACT	ETHIC	*ESSEN
+DAISY	+DINAH	DATED	EPACT	ETHOS	*ESSEX.
DE-ICE	DINAR	DATUM	ERASE	ETHYL.	EATEN
DEIFY	DINED	DETER	EVADE	EDICT	EATER
DEIGN	DINER	DITCH	EXACT	EDIFY	ENTER
DEISM	DINGO	DITTO	EXALT.	+EDITH	ENTRY
DEIST	DINGY	DITTY	EBBED	ELIDE	ESTER
DEITY	DINKY	DOTED	ELBOW	+ELIOT	EXTOL
DOILY	DONEE	DOTER	EMBAY	ELITE	EXTRA.
DOING	+DONNA	DOTTY	EMBED	+ELIZA	EDUCE
DRIED	+DONNE	DUTCH.	EMBER	+EMILY	ELUDE
DRIER	DONOR	DAUNT	EMBUS.	+ERICA	EQUAL
DRIFT	DUNCE	DEUCE	EXCEL.	*ERITH	EQUIP
DRILL	DUNGY.	DOUBT	EIDER	EVICT	ERUCT
DRINK	DHOBI	DOUGH	ELDER	EXILE	ERUPT
DRIVE	DHOLE	*DOURO	ENDED	EXIST.	EXUDE

EXULT.	FREAK	FAMED	FORBY	FRUIT	GIBED
EAVES	+FREDA	FEMUR	FORCE	FRUMP.	GIBUS
ELVAN	FREED	FUMED.	FOREL	FAVUS	GYBED.
ELVER	FRESH	FANCY	FORGE	FEVER	GECKO.
ELVES	+FREUD	+FANNY	FORGO	FIVER	GIDDY
ENVOY.	+FREYA.	FANON	FORME	FIVES	GODLY.
+EDWIN	FIFER	FENCE	FORTE	FOVEA.	GEESE
	FIFTH	FENNY	*FORTH	FEWER.	*GHENT
FEAST	FIFTY.	FINAL	FORTY	FIXED	GLEAM
FLAIL	FIGHT	FINCH	FORUM	FIXER	GLEAN
FLAIR	FOGEY	FINER	FURRY	FOXED.	GLEBE
FLAKE	FOGGY	FINIS	FURZE	FLYER	GLEET
FLAKY	FUGAL	FINNY	FURZY.	FOYER	GREAT
FLAME	FUGGY	FUNGI	FESSE	FRYER.	GREBE
FLAMY	FUGUE.	FUNKY	FISHY	FIZZY	GREED
FLANK	FAINT	FUNNY.	FOSSA	FUZZY	GREEK
FLARE	FAIRY	+FIONA	FOSSE		GREEN
FLASH	+FAITH	FIORD	FUSED	*GHANA	GREET
FLASK	FEIGN	FJORD	FUSEE	GIANT	+GRETA
FOAMY	FEINT	FLOAT	FUSEL	GLACE	GUESS
FRAIL	FLICK	FLOCK	FUSSY	GLADE	GUEST.
FRAME	FLIES	FLONG	FUSTY.	GLAIR	GAFFE
FRANC	FLING	FLOOD	FATAL	GLAND	GOFER.
+FRANK	FLINT	FLOOR	FATED	GLARE	GIGOT
FRASS	FLIRT	+FLORA	FATTY	GLASS	GIGUE.
FRAUD.	FLITE	FLOSS	FETCH	GLAZE	GAILY
FABLE	FOIST	FLOUR	FETED	GNARL	GLIDE
FIBRE	FRIAR	FLOUT	FETID	GNASH	GLINT
FUBSY.	FRILL	FLOWN	FETOR	+GRACE	GOING
FACED	FRISK	FROCK	FETUS	GRADE	GRIDE
FACER	FRITH	*FROME	FITCH	GRAFT	GRIEF
FACET	FRIZZ.	FROND	FITLY.	GRAIL	GRILL
FACIA	FAKED	FRONT	FAULT	GRAIN	GRIME
FICHU	FAKER	+FROST	FAUNA	GRAND	+GRIMM
FOCAL	FAKIR.	FROTH	+FAUST	+GRANT	GRIMY
FOCUS	FALSE	FROWN	*FIUME	GRAPE	GRIND
FUCUS.	FELID	FROZE.	FLUFF	GRAPH	GRIPE
FADDY	+FELIX	FARAD	FLUID	GRAPY	GRIST
FADED	FELLY	FARCE	FLUKE	GRASP	GUIDE
FUDGE.	FELON	FARCY	FLUKY	+GRASS	GUILD
FEEZE	FILAR	FARED	FLUME	GRATE	GUILE
FIELD	FILCH	FERAL	FLUMP	GRAVE	GUILT
FIEND	FILER	FERIA	FLUNG	GRAVY	GUISE.
FIERY	FILET	FERNY	FLUNK	GRAZE	GALOP
FLEAM	FILLY	FERRY	FLUOR	GUANA	GELID
FLECK	FILMY	FIRED	FLUSH	GUANO	+GILES
FLEER	FILTH	FIRRY	FLUTE	GUARD	GOLLY
FLEET	FOLIO	FIRST	FLUTY	GUAVA.	GULCH
FLESH	FOLLY	FIRTH	FOUND	GABLE	GULES
FOEHN	FULLY.	FORAY	FOUNT	*GABON	GULLY

GAMED	GYPSY.	HOARD	HOMEY	+HORUS	IRATE
GAMIN	+GARBO	HOARY.	HUMAN	*HURON	+ISAAC
GAMMA	+GARTH	HABIT	HUMID	HURRY	*ITALY
GAMMY	GIRTH	HOBBY	HUMPH	HURST	IZARD.
GAMUT	GORED	HUBBY.	HUMPY	HYRAX.	IMBUE.
GEMMA	GORGE	HOCUS.	HUMUS	HASNT	INCUR
GEMMY	GORSE	HADES	HYMEN.	HASTE	INCUS
GUMBO	GORSY	HADJI	HANDY	HASTY	ITCHY.
GUMMA	GYRAL.	HADNT	HANKY	+HESSE	INDEX
GUMMY.	GASSY	HEDGE	*HANOI	HOSED	*INDIA
+GENET	GESSO	*HYDRA	HANSE	HUSKY	INDRI
GENIC	GUSTO	HYDRO.	HENCE	HUSSY	*INDUS.
GENIE	GUSTY.	HYENA.	HENNA	HYSON.	IDEAL
*GENOA	GATED	HEFTY	+HENRY	HATCH	ILEUM
GENRE	GET-UP.	HUFFY.	HINDI	HATED	INEPT
GENUS	GAUDY	*HAGUE.	HINDU	HATER	INERT
GONAD	GAUGE	*HAIFA	HINGE	HITCH	+IRENE
GONER	GAULT	HAIRY	HINNY	HOTEL	*ISERE.
GUNNY.	GAUNT	*HAITI	HONED	HOTLY	INFER
+GEOFF	GAUSS	HEIGH	HONEY	HUTCH	INFIX
GHOST	GAUZE	HEIST	HONKY	*HYTHE.	INFRA.
GHOUL	GAUZY	HOICK	HUNCH.	HAULM	INGLE
GLOAT	GLUED	HOIST.	H-BOMB	HAUNT	INGOT.
GLOBE	GLUEY	HAKIM	HAUNT	HOUGH	ICHOR.
GLOOM	*GOUDA	HIKER	HOOCH	HOUND	*IBIZA
GLORY	GOUGE	HOKUM.	HOOEY	HOURI	ICILY
GLOSS	GOURD	HALED	HOOVE	HOUSE.	ICING
GLOVE	GOUTY	HALLO	HYOID.	HAVEN	IDIOM
GLOZE	GRUEL	HALMA	HAPLY	HAVER	IDIOT
GNOME	GRUFF	HALVE	HAPPY	HAVOC	ILIAC
GOODY	GRUNT.	HIPPO	HIPPÓ	HIVED	ILIAD
GOOEY	GAVEL	+HELEN	HIPPY	HIVES	ILIUM
GOOFY	+GAVIN	+HELGA	HOPED	HOVEL	+INIGO
*GOOLE	GIVEN	HELIX	HYPER.	HOVER.	IRISH
GOOSE	GYVED.	+HELLE	+HARDY	HAWED	IVIED.
GROAN	GAWKY	HELLO	HARED	HAWSE	INKED
GROAT	GOWAN	HELOT	HAREM	HEWED	IRKED.
GROIN	*GOWER.	HELVE	HARPY	HEWER	IDLED
GROOK	GHYLL	+HILDA	+HARRY	HOWDY.	IDLER
GROOM	GLYPH	HILLY	HARSH	HEXAD.	IGLOO
GROPE	GOYIM	HILUM	+HEROD	+HAYDN	IN-LAW
GROSS	GUYED.	HOLED	HERON	HAYED.	INLAY
GROUP	GAZED	HOLEY	HERTZ	HAZED	INLET
GROUT		HOLLY	HIRED	+HAZEL	ISLAM
GROVE		+HOLST	HIRER		*ISLAY
GROWL	HEADY	HYLIC.	+HORAE		ISLET.
GROWN.	HEARD	HAMES	HORAL	*IDAHO	*IZMIR.
GAPED	HEART	HAMMY	HORDE	IMAGE	INNER
GIPSY	+HEATH	HE-MAN	HORNY	IMAGO	IONIC.
GUPPY	HEAVE	HOMED	HORSE	INANE	IRONY
	HEAVY	+HOMER	HORSY	INAPT	

IVORY.	JINGO	*KELSO	LOAMY	+LEILA	LUPUS.
IMPED	+JONAH	KULAK	LOATH.	*LEITH	LARCH
IMPEL	JUNKY	KYLOE.	LABEL	*LOIRE	LARDY
IMPLY	JUNTA	KUMIS.	LIBEL	+LIBBY	LARES
IMPOT	JUNTO.	*KANDY	LIBRA	LYING.	LARGE
INPUT.	*JAPAN	*KENYA	*LIBYA	LAKEY	LARGO
+IBSEN	JAPED	KINKY.	LOBAR	LIKED	LARKY
INSET	JUPON.	KIOSK	LOBBY	LIKEN.	+LARRY
ISSUE.	JERKY	KNOCK	LOBED	LILAC	LARVA
ICTUS	+JERRY	KNOLL	LUBRA.	*LILLE	LORIS
INTER	JORUM	KNOUT	LACED	LOLLY.	+LORNA
ISTLE.	JUROR.	KNOWN	LICIT	LAMED	LORRY
INURE	+JASON	KOOKY	LOCAL	LAMIA	LURCH
INURN.	+JESSE	KRONE	+LOCKE	LEMON	LURED
INVAR.	+JESUS.	*KYOTO.	LOCUM	LEMUR	LURID
IDYLL	JETON	KAPOK	LOCUS	LIMBO	LYRIC.
	JETTY.	KAPPA	+LUCIA	LIMED	LASER
JEANS.	JAUNT	KAPUT	LUCID	LIMEY	LASSO
JABOT	JOULE	KOPEC	LUCKY	LIMIT	LISLE
JIBED.	JOUST.	KOPJE.	LUCRE	LUMEN	+LISZT
JACKS	JIVED.	+KAREN	LYCEE.	LUMPY	LOSER
+JACOB	JAWED	KARMA	+LANCE	LYMPH.	LUSTY
JOCKO.	JEWEL	KAROO	LADDY	LANKY	LYSOL.
JADED	JEWRY.	*KERRY	LADED	+LENIN	LATCH
+JUDAS	JUXTA.	KORAN	LADEN	+LENNY	LATER
JUDGE.	+JOYCE.	*KOREA	LADLE	+LINDA	LATEX
*JAFFA	JAZZY	KYRIE.	LEDGE	LINED	LATHE
JIFFY.		KETCH	LODGE	LINEN	LATIN
JUGAL.	KAAMA	+KITTY.	+LYDIA.	LINER	LETHE
JIHAD.	+KEATS	KNURL	LEECH	LINGO	LITHE
JOINT	KHAKI	KNURR.	*LEEDS	LINKS	LITRE
JOIST	KNACK	KEVEL	LEERY	LONER	LOTTO
JUICE	KNAVE	+KEVIN.	LIEGE	LUNAR	LOTUS
JUICY.	KOALA	KAYAK	LIE-IN	LUNCH	LUTED
JOKED	KRAAL	KEYED	LOESS.	*LUNDY	*LUTON.
JOKER.	KRAIT.		LIFER	LUNGE	LAUGH
JALAP	*KABUL.	LEACH	LOFTY.	LUNIK	+LAURA
JELLY	KEDGE	LEADY	LAGAN	LYNCH.	LOUGH
JOLLY	KIDDY	LEAFY	LAGER	+LLOYD	+LOUIS
JULEP	KUDOS.	LEAKY	*LAGOS	LOONY	LOUSE
+JULIE.	KNEAD	LEANT	LEGAL	LOOPY	LOUSY.
+JAMES	KNEED	LEAPT	LEGGY	LOOSE	LAVER
JAMMY	KNEEL	LEARN	LEGIT	*LYONS.	LEVEE
JEMMY	KNELL	LEASE	LIGHT	LAPEL	LEVEL
+JIMMY	KNELT.	LEASH	LOGAN	LAPIS	LEVER
JUMBO	KAFIR	LEAST	LOGIC	LAPSE	LIVED
JUMPY.	+KAFKA.	LEAVE	LOGOS.	LEPER	LIVEN
+JANET	+KEITH	*LHASA	LAHAR.	LIPID	LIVER
+JANUS	KNIFE.	LIANA	LAIRD	LOPED	LIVES
+JENNY	KUKRI.	LLAMA	LAITY	LUPIN	LIVID

42

LOVED	MOGUL	MINUS	MOSSY	MAYST.	+NIOBE
LOVER.	MUGGY.	MONAD	MUSED	MAZER	NOOSE.
*LEWES	*MAINE	+MONET	MUSHY	MEZZO	NAPPY
*LEWIS	MAIZE	MONEY	MUSIC	MIZEN	*NEPAL
LOWED	+MOIRA	MONTH	MUSKY	MUZAK	NIPPY
LOWER	MOIRE	+MUNCH.	MUSTY.	MUZZY	NOPAL.
LOWLY.	MOIST.	MAORI	MATCH		NARES
LAXLY.	MAJOR	MOOCH	MATED	NAAFI	NARKY
LAYBY	MUJIK.	MOODY	MATER	*NEATH	NERVE
LAYER	MAKER.	MOOED	MATHS	*NYASA.	NERVY
LOYAL.	*MALMO	MOONY	METAL	NABOB	+NORMA
LAZAR	*MALTA	+MOORE	METED	+NOBEL	NORSE
LAZED	MELON	MOOSE.	METER	NOBLE	NORTH
	*MILAN	MAPLE	METHS	NOBLY.	NURSE.
MEALY	MILCH	MOPED.	METOL	NACRE	NASAL
MEANT	MILER	MARCH	METRE	NICER	NASTY
MEATY	+MILES	MARGE	METRO	NICHE.	NOSED
*MIAMI	MILKY	+MARGO	MITRE	NADIR	NOSEY.
MIAOW.	+MILNE	+MARIA	+MITZI	NODAL	*NATAL
*MABEL.	MOLAR	*MARNE	MOTEL	NODUS	NATTY
*MACAO	+MOLLY	MARRY	MOTET	NUDGE.	NITRE
MACAW	MULCH	MARSH	MOTIF	NEEDY	NOTCH
MACED	MULCT	MERCY	MOTOR	NIECE.	NOTED
*MACON	MULTI.	MERGE	MOTTO	NIFTY.	NUTTY.
*MECCA	MAMBA	MERIT	MUTED.	NEGRO	NEUME.
MICRO	MAMMA	+MERLE	+MAUDE	NEGUS	NAVAL
MOCHA	MIMED	MERRY	MAUVE	+NIGEL	NAVEL
MUCKY	MIMIC	MIRED	*MEUSE	*NIGER	NAVVY
MUCUS.	MUMMY	MIRTH	MOULD	NIGHT.	NEVER
MADAM	MUMPS.	+MORAG	MOULT	+NEHRU.	*NEVIS
MADLY	MANES	MORAL	MOUND	NAIAD	NOVEL.
+MADOC	+MANET	*MORAY	MOUNT	*NAIRN	NEWEL
MEDAL	MANGE	MOREL	MOURN	NAIVE	NEWER
+MEDEA	MANGO	MORES	MOUSE	NEIGH	NEWLY
MEDIA	MANGY	MORON	MOUSY	NOISE	NEWSY
*MEDOC	MANIA	MORSE	MOUTH.	NOISY.	NOWAY.
+MIDAS	MANIC	MURAL	+MAVIS	NAKED.	NEXUS
MIDGE	MANLY	MUREX	MOVED	NYLON.	NIXIE
MIDST	MANNA	MURKY	MOVER	NAMED	+NIXON.
MODAL	MANOR	+MYRNA	MOVIE.	*NIMES	+NOYES
MODEL	MANSE	MYRRH.	MEWED	NOMAD	
MODUS	*MENAI	MASER	MOWED	NYMPH.	OKAPI
MUDDY.	MINCE	MASON	MOWER.	+NANCY	*OMAGH
MAFIA	MINED	MASSY	MAXIM	NANNA	*OMAHA
MUFTI.	MINER	MESNE	MIXED	NANNY	OP-ART
MAGIC	MINGY	MESON	MIXER	NINNY	ORATE
MAGMA	MINIM	MESSY	MIX-UP.	NINTH	*OSAKA
+MAGOG	MINOR	MISER	MAYBE	NONCE	OVARY
MAGUS	+MINOS	MISTY	MAYNT	NONES.	OVATE
MIGHT	*MINSK	+MOSES	MAYOR	+NAOMI	*OZARK

O - B - -			P - U - -		
OMBRE	OOMPH	+PLATO	PRICK	+PENNY	PARRY
ORBED	ORMER.	PLAZA	PRIDE	PINCH	PARSE
ORBIT	OUNCE	POACH	PRIED	PINED	PARTY
OXBOW.	OWNED	PRANG	PRIMA	PINKY	PERCH
OCCUR	OWNER.	PRANK	PRIME	PINNA	+PERCY
+ORCZY	ODOUR	PRASE	PRIMP	PINNY	PERDU
+OSCAR.	OVOID	PRATE	PRINK	PIN-UP	PERIL
ODDER	OZONE.	PRAWN	PRINT	PONCE	PERKY
ODDLY	ORPIN.	PSALM.	PRIOR	PUNCH	PERNE
OLDEN	OARED	PUBES	PRISE	PUNTY.	+PERON
OLDER	ORRIS.	PUBIC	PRISM	PEONY	+PERRY
ORDER.	OASES	PUBIS.	PRIVY	PHONE	PERSE
OBEAH	OASIS	PACED	PRIZE.	PHONO	*PERTH
OBELI	ONSET	PECAN	PEKOE	PHONY	PORCH
OBESE	+ORSON	PICOT	POKED	PHOTO	PORED
OCEAN	OUSEL.	POCKY.	POKER	PIOUS	PORGE
OLEIC	OATEN	+PADDY	PUKED	PLONK	PORKY
OLEIN	OCTAD	PADRE	PUKKA.	POOCH	PUREE
OMEGA	OCTET	*PADUA	PALED	*POOLE	PURER
OPERA	OFTEN	PEDAL	PALER	PROBE	PURGE
OVERT.	OPTED	PODGY	PALLY	PROEM	PURSE
OFFAL	OPTIC	PODIA	*PALMA	PROLE	PURSY.
OFFER.	OTTER	PUDGY	PALMY	PRONE	PASHA
ORGAN	OUTDO	PUDSY.	PALSY	PRONG	PASSE
OUGHT.	OUTER	+PAEAN	PHLOX	PROOF	PASTA
OCHRE	OUTGO	PEEVE	PILCH	PROPS	PASTE
OGHAM	OUTRE.	PIECE	PILED	PROSE	PASTY
OTHER.	OVULE.	PIETA	PILOT	PROSY	PESKY
ODIUM	OOZED	PIETY	POLAR	PROUD	POSED
OGIVE	OUZEL	PIEZO	POLED	PROVE	POSER
OLIVE		PLEAD	POLIO	PROWL	POSIT
ONION	PEACE	PLEAT	POLKA	PROXY.	POSSE
OPINE	PEACH	POESY	+POLLY	PAPAL	PUSSY.
OPIUM	PEAKY	PREEN	POLYP	PAPAW	PATCH
ORIEL	+PEARL	PRESS.	PULED	PAPER	PATEN
+ORION	PEASE	PUFFY.	PULPY	*PAPUA	PATER
OSIER	PEATY	PAGAN	PULSE	PEPPY	PATIO
OUIJA	PHAGE	PAGED	PYLON.	+PEPYS	*PATNA
OVINE	PHASE	+PEGGY	POMMY.	PIPED	+PATTY
OWING	PIANO	PIGGY	PANDA	PIPER	PETAL
OXIDE.	PLACE	PIGMY	PANED	PIPIT	+PETER
OAKEN	PLAID	PYGAL	PANEL	POPPY	PETTY
OAKUM.	PLAIN	PYGMY.	PANIC	POPSY	PITCH
OGLED	PLAIT	PAINT	PANNE	PUPIL	PITHY
OILED	PLANE	PHIAL	PANSY	PUPPY.	PITOT
ORLOP	PLANK	PLIED	PANTO	PIQUE.	POTTO
OWLET	PLANT	POINT	PANTS	PARCH	POTTY
OXLIP.	PLASH	POISE	PENAL	PARED	PUTTO
OGMIC	PLASM	+PRIAM	PENCE	*PARIS	PUTTY.
OHMIC	PLATE	PRICE	PENIS	PARKY	+PAULA

44

PAUSE	QUILT	RUDER.	RONDO	RAVED	SHANK
PLUCK	QUINS	REEDY	RUNIC	RAVEL	SHANT
PLUMB	QUINT	REEKY	RUNNY.	RAVEN	SHAPE
PLUME	QUIRE	REEST	+RHODA	REVEL	SHARD
PLUMP	QUIRK	REEVE	RHOMB	REVET	SHARE
PLUMY	QUIRT	RHEUM.	*RHONE	REVUE	SHARK
PLUNK	QUITE	REFER	ROOKY	RIVAL	SHARP
PLUSH	*QUITO	REFIT	ROOMY	RIVED	SHAVE
+PLUTO	QUITS.	RIFLE	ROOST.	RIVEN	SHAWL
POUCH	QUOIN	+RUFUS.	RAPED	RIVER	SHAWM
POULP	QUOIT	REGAL	RAPID	RIVET	SKALD
POULT	QUOTA	RIGHT	REPAY	ROVED	SKATE
+POUND	QUOTE	RIGID	REPEL	ROVEN	SLACK
PRUDE	QUOTH.	RIGOR	REPLY	ROVER.	SLAIN
PRUNE.	*QATAR	+ROGER	REPOT	RAWLY	SLAKE
PAVAN		ROGUE	RIPEN	ROWAN	SLANG
PIVOT.	REACH	*RUGBY.	RIPER	ROWDY	SLANT
PAWED	REACT	RAINY	*RIPON	ROWED	SLASH
PAWKY	READY	RAISE	ROPED	ROWEL	SLATE
PEWIT	REALM	REICH	ROPEY	ROWER.	SLATY
POWER.	REARM	REIGN	RUPEE.	RAYED	SLAVE
PIXIE	ROACH	*RHINE	RARER	RAYON	SMACK
PYXED	ROAST.	RHINO	RORAL	RHYME	SMALL
PYXIS.	*RABAT	RUING.	RORIC	ROYAL.	SMALT
PAYED	RABBI	RAJAH.	RURAL.	RAZED	SMART
PAYEE	RABID	RAKED.	RESET	RAZOR	SMASH
PHYLA	REBEC	RALLY	RESIN		SNACK
PHYLE	REBEL	+RALPH	RISEN	SCALD	SNAFU
	REBUS	RELAX	RISER	SCALE	SNAIL
QUACK	REBUT	RELAY	RISKY	SCALP	SNAKE
QUAFF	ROBED	RELIC	ROSIN	SCALY	SNAKY
QUAIL	+ROBIN	RILED	RUSHY	SCAMP	SNARE
QUAKE	ROBOT.	RILLE	RUSTY.	SCANT	SNARL
QUALM	RACED	RULED	RATAL	*SCAPA	SOAPY
QUANT	RACER	RULER.	RATCH	SCAPE	SPACE
QUARK	RECAP	REMIT	RATED	SCARE	SPADE
QUART	RECTO	+REMUS	RATIO	SCARF	SPAHI
QUASH.	RECUR	ROMAN	RATTY	SCARP	*SPAIN
QUEAN	ROCKY	RUMBA	RETCH	SCART	SPAKE
QUEEN	RUCHE.	RUMLY	RETRY	SEAMY	SPANK
QUEER	RADAR	RUMMY.	RITZY	SHACK	SPARE
QUELL	RADII	RANCE	ROTOR	SHADE	SPARK
QUERN	RADIO	RANCH	RUTTY.	SHADY	SPASM
QUERY	RADIX	RANDY	RHUMB	SHAFT	SPATE
QUEST	RADON	RANEE	ROUGE	SHAKE	SPAWN
QUEUE.	RIDER	RANGE	ROUGH	SHAKO	STACK
QUICK	RIDGE	RANGY	ROUND	SHAKY	STAFF
QUIET	RODEO	RENAL	ROUSE	SHALE	STAGE
QUIFF	+RODIN	RENEW	ROUST	SHALY	STAGY
QUILL	RUDDY	RINSE	ROUTE.	SHAME	STAID

STAIN	SIEGE	SIGMA	SPINE	SAMBA	SHOUT
STAIR	SIEVE	SOGGY	SPINY	SAMBO	SHOVE
STAKE	SKEET	SUGAR.	SPIRE	*SAMOA	SHOWN
STALE	SKEIN	SAHIB.	SPIRT	SEMEN	SHOWY
STALK	*SLEAT	SAINT	SPIRY	+SIMON	SIOUX
STALL	SLEEK	SCION	SPITE	*SOMME.	SLOOP
STAMP	SLEEP	*SEINE	STICH	+SANDY	SLOPE
STAND	SLEET	SEISE	STICK	SANER	SLOSH
STANK	SMEAR	SEIZE	STIFF	SANTA	SLOTH
STARE	SMELL	SHIED	STILE	SENNA	SMOCK
STARK	SMELT	SHIFT	STILL	SENOR	SMOKE
START	SNEAK	SHINE	STILT	SENSE	SMOKY
STASH	SNEER	SHINY	STING	*SINAI	SMOTE
STATE	SNELL	SHIRE	STINK	SINCE	SNOOD
STAVE	SPEAK	SHIRK	STINT	SINEW	SNOOK
SUAVE	SPEAR	SHIRR	SUING	SINGE	SNOOP
SWAIN	SPECK	SHIRT	SUITE	+SINON	SNORE
SWAMP	SPECS	SKIED	+SWIFT	SINUS	SNORT
SWANK	SPEED	SKIER	SWILL	SONAR	SNOUT
SWARD	SPELL	SKIFF	SWINE	+SONIA	SNOWY
SWARM	SPELT	SKILL	SWING	SONIC	SOOTH
SWASH	SPEND	SKIMP	SWIPE	SONNY	SOOTY
SWATH.	SPENT	SKINT	SWIRL	SONSY	SPODE
SABLE	SPERM	SKIRL	SWISH	SUNNY	SPOIL
SABOT	STEAD	SKIRT	SWISS.	SUN-UP	SPOKE
SABRE	STEAK	SKIVE	SAKER.	SYNOD.	SPOOF
SOBER	STEAL	SLICE	SALAD	*SAONE	SPOOK
+SYBIL.	STEAM	SLICK	SALEP	SCOBS	SPOOL
SOCLE	STEAN	SLIDE	SALIC	SCOFF	SPOON
SYCEE.	STEED	*SLIGO	SALIX	SCOLD	SPOOR
+SADIE	STEEL	SLIME	+SALLY	SCONE	SPORE
SADLY	STEEN	SLIMY	SALMI	SCOOP	SPORT
SEDAN	STEEP	SLING	SALON	SCOOT	SPOUT
SEDGE	STEER	SLINK	SALSE	SCOPE	STOAT
SIDED	STERE	SMILE	SALTY	SCORE	STOCK
SIDLE	STERN	SMIRK	SALVE	SCORN	STOIC
*SUDAN.	+STEVE	SMITE	SALVO	SCOTS	STOKE
SCENA	SUEDE	SMITH	SELAH	+SCOTT	STOLE
SCENE	SUETY	SNICK	SILEX	SCOUR	STOMA
SCENT	SWEAR	SNIDE	SILKY	SCOUT	STONE
SEEDY	SWEAT	SNIFF	SILLY	SCOWL	STONY
SHEAF	SWEDE	SNIPE	SOLAR	*SEOUL	STOOD
SHEAR	SWEEP	SPICE	SOLED	SHOAL	STOOK
SHEEN	SWEET	SPICY	SOLID	SHOCK	STOOL
SHEEP	SWELL	SPIED	SOLVE	SHONE	STOOP
SHEER	SWEPT.	SPIEL	SPLAY	SHOOK	STORE
SHEET	SAFER	SPIKE	*SPLIT	SHOOT	STORK
SHELF	*SOFIA.	SPIKY	SULKY	SHORE	STORM
SHELL	+SAGAN	SPILL	SULLY	SHORN	STORY
SHEOL	SIGHT	SPILT	SYLPH.	SHORT	STOUP

*STOUR	STRIP	SPUNK	TRACK	TRESS	+TYLER.
STOUT	STROP	SPURN	TRACT	TREWS	TAMED
STOVE	STRUM	SPURT	+TRACY	TWEAK	TAMER
SWOON	STRUT	SQUAB	TRADE	*TWEED	TAMIL
SWOOP	SURER	SQUAD	TRAIL	TWEEN	TAMIS
SWORD	SURGE	SQUAT	TRAIN	TWEET	TAMMY
SWORE	SURLY	SQUAW	TRAIT	TWERE	*TAMPA
SWORN.	*SYRIA	SQUIB	TRAMP	TWERP.	TEMPO
SAPID	*SYROS	SQUID	TRASH	TAFFY.	TEMPT
SAPPY	SYRUP.	STUCK	TRAWL	TIGER	TIMED
SEPAL	SISAL	STUDY	+TWAIN	TIGHT.	TIMER
SEPIA	SISSY	STUFF	TWANG.	TAINT	TIMID
SEPOY	+SUSAN.	STUMP	TABBY	THICK	*TIMOR
SOPPY	SATAN	STUNG	TABES	THIEF	+TOMMY
SUPER.	SATED	STUNK	TABLE	THIGH	TUMID
SARKY	SATIN	STUNT	TABOO	THINE	TUMMY.
SCRAG	SATYR	STUPE	TABOR	THING	TANGO
SCRAM	SET-TO	SWUNG.	*TIBER	THIRD	TANGY
SCRAP	SET-UP	SAVED	*TIBET	TRIAD	TANSY
SCREE	SITED	SAVER	TIBIA	TRIAL	+TANYA
SCREW	SIT-IN	SAVOY	TUBAL	TRIBE	*TENBY
SCRIM	SOTTO.	SAVVY	TUBBY	TRICE	TENCH
SCRIP	SAUCE	SEVEN	TUBER.	TRICK	TENET
SCRUB	SAUCY	SEVER.	TACIT	TRIED	TENON
SCRUM	SAUNA	SAWED	TACKY.	TRIER	TENOR
SERAC	SAUTE	SEWED	+TEDDY	TRILL	TENSE
SERAI	SCUFF	SEWER	TIDAL	TRINE	TENTH
SERGE	SCULL	SOWED	TIDED	TRIPE	TINCT
SERIF	SCULP	SOWER.	TODAY	TRITE	TINGE
SERUM	SCURF	SAXON	TODDY	TWICE	TINNY
SERVE	SHUCK	SEXED	TUDOR.	TWILL	TONAL
SHRED	SHUNT	SEXTO	TEENS	TWINE	TONED
SHREW	SHUSH	SIXTH	TEENY	TWIRL	*TONGA
SHRUB	+SHUTE	SIXTY.	TEETH	TWIST	TONGS
SHRUG	SKULK	SAY-SO	THECA	TWIXT.	TONIC
SIRED	SKULL	SHYLY	THEFT	TAKEN	TONNE
SIREN	SKUNK	SLYLY	THEIR	TAKER	TONUS
SORER	SLUMP	SLYPE	THEME	TOKAY	TUNED
SORRY	SLUNG	STYLE.	THERE	TOKEN	TUNER
SPRAG	SLUNK	SIZAR	THERM	*TOKYO.	TUNIC
SPRAT	SLUSH	SIZED	THESE	TALLY	*TUNIS
SPRAY	SNUFF		THETA	TALON	TUNNY.
SPREE	SOUGH	TEACH	THEWS	TALUS	THOLE
SPRIG	SOUND	TEASE	THEWY	TELEX	THONG
SPRIT	SOUPY	THANE	TIE-UP	TELLY	THORN
STRAP	+SOUSA	THANK	TREAD	TILDE	THORP
STRAW	SOUSE	TIARA	TREAT	TILED	THOSE
STRAY	SOUTH	TOADY	TREED	TILTH	TOOTH
STREW	SPUME	TOAST	TREND	TULIP	TROLL
STRIA	SPUMY	TRACE	*TRENT	TULLE	TRONC

TROOP	TOTAL	UNCLE	VAGUE	VETCH	WAIST
TROPE	TOTED	UNCUT.	VIGIL	VITAL	WAIVE
TROTH	TOTEM	UDDER	VOGUE.	VOTED	WEIGH
TROUT.	TUTOR	UNDER	VOICE	VOTER.	WEIRD
TAPED	TUTTY.	UNDID	VOILE	VAULT	WHICH
TAPER	TAUNT	UNDUE.	VYING.	VAUNT	WHIFF
TAPIR	THUMB	UP—END.	VALET	VOUCH.	WHILE
TAPIS	THUMP	UNFIT	VALID	VIVID.	WHINE
TEPEE	TOUCH	UNFIX.	VALUE	VOWED	WHIRL
TEPID	TOUGH	URGED.	VALVE	VOWEL.	WHIRR
TIPSY	TRUCE	USHER.	VELAR	VEXED	WHISK
TOPAZ	TRUCK	UMIAK	VELDT	VIXEN	WHIST
TOPEE	TRUER	UNIAT	VELUM		WHITE
TOPER	TRULL	UNIFY	VILER	*WEALD	WRICK
TOPIC	TRULY	UNION	VILLA	WEARY	WRING
TYPED.	TRUMP	UNITE	VILLI	WEAVE	WRIST
TOQUE.	TRUNK	UNITY	VOLED	WHACK	WRITE.
TARDO	*TRURO	URINE	VOLET	WHALE	WAKED
TARDY	TRUSS	USING.	*VOLGA	WHARF	WAKEN
TAROT	TRUST	UHLAN.	*VOLTA	WHAUP	WOKEN.
TARRY	TRUTH.	UNMAN.	VOLTE	WRACK	*WALES
TARTY	TAWED	ULNAR.	VULVA.	WRATH.	WALLA
TERRA	TAWNY	U—BOAT.	VOMIT.	WACKY.	WALTZ
+TERRY	TAWSE	UNPEG	VENAL	WADDY	WELCH
TERSE	TOWED	UNPEN	VENOM	WADED	+WELLS
THREE	TOWEL	UNPIN	VENUE	WADER	WELSH
THREW	TOWER.	UPPER.	+VENUS	WEDGE	+WILDE
THROB	TAXED	UNRIG	VINIC	WIDEN	WILED.
THROE	TAXIN	UNRIP.	VINYL.	WIDER	WOMAN
THROW	TAXIS	UNSAY	+VIOLA.	WIDOW	WOMEN.
THRUM	*TEXAS	UNSEX	VAPID	WIDTH	+WANDA
TIRED	TOXIC	UPSET.	VIPER.	+WODEN.	WANED
*TIREE	TOXIN.	ULTRA	VAREC	WEEDY	WANLY
TORAH	THYME	UNTIE	VARIX	WEENY	WENCH
TORAN	TOYED	UNTIL	+VERDI	WEEPY	+WENDY
TORCH	TRY—ON	UTTER.	VERGE	WHEAT	WINCE
TORSO	TRYST.	USUAL	+VERNE	WHEEL	WINCH
TORUS	TIZZY	USURP	VERSE	WHELK	WINDY
TURBO		USURY	VERSO	WHELP	WINED.
TURFY	UKASE	UVULA.	VERST	WHERE	WHOLE
*TURIN	UNAPT	UNWED.	VERVE	WIELD	WHOOP
TURPS	UNARM	UNZIP	VIRGO	WREAK	WHORE
*TYROL.	USAGE.		VIRTU	WRECK	WHORL
TASTE	UMBEL	VICAR	VIRUS.	WREST.	WHOSE
TASTY	UMBER	+VICKY	VASAL	WAFER.	WHOSO
TESTY.	UMBRA	VOCAL.	+VESTA	WAGED	WOODY
TATTY	UNBAR	VEDIC	VISIT	WAGER	WOOER
TITAN	URBAN.	+VIDAL	VISOR	WAGON	+WOOLF
TITHE	ULCER	VIDEO	VISTA.	*WIGAN	WRONG
TITLE	UNCAP	VODKA.	VATIC	*WIGHT.	WROTE

WROTH.	YOGIN.	NAIAD	BAWDY	EASEL	LAYER
WIPED	YAHOO.	NASAL	CADDY	EATEN	LAZED
WIPER.	YOKED	*NATAL	CANDY	EATER	+MABEL
WARTY	YOKEL	NAVAL	DADDY	EAVES	MACED
WIRED	*YUKON.	+PAEAN	FADDY	FACED	MAKER
WORDY	YOLKY.	PAGAN	FADDY	FACER	MANES
WORLD	*YEMEN.	PAPAL	GAUDY	FACET	+MANET
WORMY	YAPON.	PAPAW	HANDY	FADED	MASER
WORRY	*YPRES.	PAVAN	+HARDY	FAKED	MATED
WORSE	YOULL	*QATAR	+HAYDN	FAKER	MATER
WORST	YOUNG	*RABAT	*KANDY	FAMED	MAZER
WORTH.	YOURE	RADAR	LADDY	FARED	NAKED
WASHY	YOURS	RAJAH	LARDY	FATED	NAMED
WASNT	YOUTH	RATAL	+MAUDE	GAMED	NARES
WASTE	YOUVE.	+SAGAN	+PADDY	GAPED	NAVEL
WISER	YAWED	SALAD	PANDA	GATED	OAKEN
WISPY.		SATAN	RANDY	GAVEL	OARED
WATCH	ZEBRA	VASAL.	TARDO	GAZED	OASES
WATER	ZIBET.	CABBY	TARDY	HADES	OATEN
WETLY	*ZAIRE.	+GARBO	WADDY	HALED	PACED
WITCH	ZOMBI.	LAYBY	+WANDA.	HAMES	PAGED
WITHE	ZONAL	MAMBA	BABEL	HARED	PALED
WITHY	ZONED.	MAYBE	BAKED	HAREM	PALER
WITTY.	ZOOID.	RABBI	BAKER	HATED	PANED
+WAUGH	ZIPPY.	SAMBA	BALED	HATER	PANEL
WOULD	ZORIL	SAMBO	BALER	HAVEN	PAPER
WOUND		TABBY.	BARED	HAVER	PARED
WRUNG.		BATCH	BASED	HAWED	PATEN
WAVED	BALAS	CATCH	BATED	HAYED	PATER
WAVER	BANAL	*DACCA	BAYED	HAZED	PAWED
WIVED	BASAL	DANCE	CABER	+HAZEL	PAYED
WIVES	CABAL	FANCY	CADET	JADED	PAYEE
WOVEN.	CACAO	FARCE	CAGED	+JAMES	RACED
WAXED	CANAL	FARCY	CAGEY	+JANET	RACER
WAXEN.	CARAT	HATCH	CAKED	JAPED	RAKED
WRYLY.	*CAVAN	+LANCE	CAMEL	JAWED	RANEE
WIZEN	*DAKAR	LARCH	CAMEO	+KAREN	RAPED
	DALAI	LATCH	CANED	LABEL	RARER
	DATAL	MARCH	CAPER	LACED	RATED
XEBEC.	FARAD	MATCH	CARET	LADED	RAVED
XYLEM.	FATAL	+NANCY	CASED	LADEN	RAVEL
XENIA	JALAP	PARCH	CATER	LAGER	RAVEN
XENON	*JAPAN	PATCH	CATES	LAKEY	RAYED
	KAYAK	RANCE	CAVED	LAMED	RAZED
YEARN	LAGAN	RANCH	DARED	LAPEL	SAFER
YEAST	LAHAR	RATCH	DATED	LARES	SAKER
+YEATS.	LAZAR	SAUCE	DAZED	LASER	SALEP
YACHT	*MACAO	SAUCY	EAGER	LATER	SANER
YUCCA.	MACAW	WATCH.	EASED	LATEX	SATED
YODEL.	MADAM	BANDY	EASEL	LAVER	SAVED
YIELD.					

SAVER	RANGY	RADIX	HAULM	*MARNE	RAYON
SAWED	TANGO	RAPID	LADLE	MAYNT	RAZOR
TABES	TANGY	RATIO	LAXLY	NANNA	SABOT
TAKEN	+WAUGH.	+SADIE	MADLY	NANNY	SALON
TAKER	BATHE	SAHIB	MANLY	PAINT	*SAMOA
TAMED	CACHE	SALIC	MAPLE	PANNE	SAVOY
TAMER	+CATHY	SALIX	PALLY	*PATNA	SAXON
TAPED	LATHE	SAPID	+PAULA	RAINY	TABOO
TAPER	MATHS	SATIN	RALLY	SAINT	TABOR
TAWED	PASHA	TACIT	RAWLY	*SAONE	TALON
TAXED	WASHY	TAMIL	SABLE	SAUNA	TAROT
VALET	YACHT.	TAMIS	SADLY	TAINT	WAGON
VAREC	BASIC	TAPIR	TABLE	TAUNT	YAHOO
WADED	+BASIL	TAPIS	TALLY	TAWNY	YAPON.
WADER	BASIN	TAXIN	VAULT	VAUNT	HAPPY
WAFER	BASIS	TAXIS	WALLA	WASNT.	HARPY
WAGED	BATIK	VALID	WANLY.	+AARON	KAPPA
WAGER	CABIN	VAPID	BALMY	BABOO	NAPPY
WAKED	*CADIZ	VARIX	BARMY	+BACON	+RALPH
WAKEN	CALIF	VATIC.	GAMMA	BARON	SAPPY
*WALES	CALIX	BANJO	GAMMY	BASON	*TAMPA.
WANED	CARIB	HADJI.	HALMA	BATON	BAIRN
WATER	CAVIL	DARKY	HAMMY	BAYOU	*BARRA
WAVED	+DAVID	GAWKY	JAMMY	CABOB	+BARRY
WAVER	DAVIT	HANKY	KAAMA	CANOE	*BASRA
WAXED	FACIA	JACKS	KARMA	CANON	CADRE
WAXEN	FAKIR	+KAFKA	MAGMA	CAPON	CAIRN
YAWED.	GAMIN	LANKY	*MALMO	CAROB	*CAIRO
*BANFF	+GAVIN	LARKY	MAMMA	+CAROL	*CAPRI
DAFFY	HABIT	NARKY	+NAOMI	+EAMON	CARRY
GAFFE	HAKIM	PARKY	*PALMA	FANON	DAIRY
*HAIFA	KAFIR	PAWKY	PALMY	*GABON	EAGRE
*JAFFA	LAMIA	SARKY	SALMI	GALOP	FAIRY
NAAFI	LAPIS	TACKY	TAMMY.	*HANOI	HAIRY
TAFFY.	LATIN	WACKY.	BANNS	HAVOC	+HARRY
BADGE	MAFIA	BADLY	*CANNA	JABOT	LAIRD
BAGGY	MAGIC	BAULK	CANNY	+JACOB	+LARRY
BARGE	MANIA	CABLE	+DANNY	+JASON	+LAURA
CADGE	MANIC	CAULK	DAUNT	KAPOK	MAORI
CARGO	+MARIA	DAILY	FAINT	KAROO	MARRY
GAUGE	+MAVIS	DALLY	+FANNY	*LAGOS	NACRE
LARGE	MAXIM	EAGLE	FAUNA	*MACON	*NAIRN
LARGO	NADIR	EARLY	GAUNT	+MADOC	PADRE
LAUGH	OASIS	FABLE	HADNT	+MAGOG	PARRY
MANGE	PANIC	FAULT	HASNT	MAJOR	SABRE
MANGO	*PARIS	GABLE	HAUNT	MANOR	TARRY
MANGY	PATIO	GAILY	JAUNT	MASON	*ZAIRE
MARGE	RABID	GAULT	*MAINE	MAYOR	BALSA
+MARGO	RADII	HALLO	MANNA	NABOB	CAUSE
RANGE	RADIO	HAPLY	MANNA	RADON	+DAISY

FALSE	RATTY	ABEAM	SCALE	ADDED	MEDAL
+FAUST	SALTY	OBEAH	SCALP	ADDER	*MENAI
GASSY	SANTA	U-BOAT.	SCALY	ADEEM	METAL
GAUSS	SAUTE	ABACK.	SCOLD	ADIEU	*NEPAL
HANSE	TARTY	ABIDE	SCULL	EDGED	PECAN
HARSH	TASTE	ABODE.	SCULP.	IDLED	PEDAL
HAWSE	TASTY	ABBEY	SCAMP.	IDLER	PENAL
LAPSE	TATTY	+ABNER	ACINI	ODDER	PETAL
LASSO	WALTZ	EBBED	ICING	UDDER.	RECAP
MANSE	WARTY	+IBSEN.	SCANT	EDIFY.	REGAL
MARSH	WASTE.	ABAFT.	SCENA	ADAGE	RELAX
MASSY	BABUL	+ABBIE	SCENE	*ADIGE.	RELAY
MAYST	*BACUP	ABOIL.	SCENT	*IDAHO.	RENAL
PALSY	+CACUS	ABELE	SCONE.	ADMIT	REPAY
PANSY	+CAMUS	OBELI.	ACTOR	ADMIX	SEDAN
PARSE	DATUM	A-BOMB	ICHOR	+EDWIN.	SELAH
PASSE	FAVUS	H-BOMB.	SCION	ADDLE	SEPAL
PAUSE	GAMUT	EBONY.	SCOOP	+ADELE	SERAC
RAISE	*HAGUE	ABBOT	SCOOT.	ADULT	SERAI
SALSE	+JANUS	ABHOR.	*SCAPA	IDYLL	*TEXAS
SAY-SO	*KABUL	ABORT.	SCAPE	ODDLY.	VELAR
TANSY	KAPUT	ABASE	SCOPE.	+ADAMS	VENAL.
TAWSE	MAGUS	ABASH	*ACCRA	EDEMA.	*DERBY
WAIST.	OAKUM	ABUSE	ACORN	IDIOM	*TENBY.
BASTE	*PADUA	ABYSS	OCHRE	IDIOT.	BEACH
BATTY	*PAPUA	OBESE.	SCARE	ADAPT	BEECH
CACTI	TALUS	ABATE.	SCARF	ADEPT	BELCH
CANTO	VAGUE	ABOUT.	SCARP	ADOPT.	BENCH
CARTE	VALUE.	ABOVE.	SCART	ADORE	DE-ICE
CASTE	CALVE	*IBIZA	SCORE	ADORN.	DEUCE
CATTY	CARVE		SCORN	+EDITH.	FENCE
+DANTE	HALVE	ECLAT	SCURF.	ODIUM	FETCH
EARTH	LARVA	OCEAN	ACUTE	ODOUR	HENCE
+FAITH	MAUVE	OCTAD	SCOTS		KETCH
FATTY	NAIVE	SCRAG	+SCOTT.	BEGAD	LEACH
+GARTH	NAVVY	SCRAM	ICTUS	BEGAN	LEECH
*HAITI	SALVE	SCRAP.	OCCUR	+BEHAN	*MECCA
HASTE	SALVO	SCOBS.	SCOUR	BELAY	MERCY
HASTY	SAVVY	ACHED	SCOUT	+BEVAN	PEACE
LAITY	VALVE	ACTED	SCRUB	CEDAR	PEACH
*MALTA	WAIVE.	OCTET	SCRUM.	DEBAG	PENCE
NASTY	CALYX	SCREE	SCOWL	DEBAR	PERCH
NATTY	SATYR	SCREW.		DECAL	+PERCY
PANTO	+TANYA.	SCOFF	ADDAX	DECAY	REACH
PANTS	BAIZE	SCUFF.	ADMAN	+DEGAS	REACT
PARTY	GAUZE	ACRID	+EDGAR	DELAY	REICH
PASTA	GAUZY	SCRIM	IDEAL.	FERAL	RETCH
PASTE	JAZZY	SCRIP.	ADOBE.	HE-MAN	TEACH
PASTY	MAIZE	ICILY	EDICT	HEXAD	TENCH
PATTY		SCALD	EDUCE.	LEGAL	VETCH

WELCH	NEWER	BEDIM	BELLY	BELOW	*KERRY
WENCH.	+PETER	BEFIT	CELLO	BESOM	LEARN
BEADY	REBEC	BEGIN	DEALT	DECOR	LEERY
BENDS	REBEL	BELIE	FELLY	DECOY	MERRY
HEADY	REFER	+BERIA	+HELLE	+DEFOE	METRE
LEADY	RENEW	+CECIL	HELLO	*DELOS	METRO
*LEEDS	REPEL	+CELIA	JELLY	DEMOB	NEGRO
NEEDY	RESET	CETIC	+LEILA	DEMON	+NEHRU
PERDU	REVEL	CETIN	MEALY	DEMOS	+PEARL
READY	REVET	DEBIT	+MERLE	DEPOT	+PERRY
REEDY	SEMEN	DENIM	NEWLY	*DEVON	REARM
SEEDY	SEVEN	+DENIS	REALM	FELON	RETRY
+TEDDY	SEVER	DEVIL	REPLY	FETOR	TERRA
VELDT	SEWED	EERIE	TELLY	*GENOA	+TERRY
+VERDI	SEWER	FELID	*WEALD	HELOT	WEARY
WEEDY	SEXED	+FELIX	+WELLS	+HEROD	WEIRD
+WENDY.	TELEX	FERIA	WETLY.	HERON	YEARN
BEDEW	TENET	FETID	DERMA	JETON	ZEBRA.
BEGET	TEPEE	GELID	GEMMA	LEMON	BEAST
BERET	VEXED	GENIC	GEMMY	*MEDOC	+BETSY
BESET	XEBEC	GENIE	JEMMY	MELON	CEASE
BETEL	*YEMEN.	HELIX	NEUME	MESON	CENSE
BEVEL	BEEFY	+KEVIN	SEAMY.	METOL	DEISM
BEZEL	DEIFY	LEGIT	BEANO	PEKOE	DEIST
CEDED	*DELFT	+LENIN	BEING	+PERON	DENSE
+CERES	+GEOFF	*LEWIS	+BENNY	REPOT	FEAST
DEFER	LEAFY.	MEDIA	*BERNE	SENOR	FESSE
+DEREK	BEIGE	MERIT	FEINT	SEPOY	GEESE
DETER	DEIGN	*NEVIS	FENNY	TENON	GESSO
FETED	FEIGN	PENIS	FERNY	TENOR	HEIST
FEVER	HEDGE	PERIL	HENNA	VENOM	+HESSE
FEWER	HEIGH	PEWIT	JEANS	XENON.	+JESSE
+GENET	+HELGA	REFIT	+JENNY	LEAPT	*KELSO
+HELEN	KEDGE	RELIC	LEANT	PEPPY	LEASE
HEWED	LEDGE	REMIT	+LENNY	TEMPO	LEASH
HEWER	LEGGY	RESIN	MEANT	TEMPT	LEAST
JEWEL	MERGE	SEPIA	MESNE	WEEPY.	MESSY
KEVEL	NEIGH	SERIF	+PENNY	BEARD	*MEUSE
KEYED	+PEGGY	TEPID	PEONY	BEERY	NEWSY
LEPER	REIGN	VEDIC	PERNE	*BEIRA	PEASE
LEVEE	SEDGE	XENIA.	*SEINE	BERRY	PERSE
LEVEL	SERGE	GECKO	SENNA	DEARY	REEST
LEVER	VERGE	JERKY	TEENS	DECRY	SEISE
*LEWES	WEDGE	LEAKY	TEENY	FERRY	SENSE
+MEDEA	WEIGH.	PEAKY	+VERNE	GENRE	TEASE
METED	*DELHI	PERKY	WEENY.	HEARD	TENSE
METER	LETHE	PESKY	+AESOP	HEART	TERSE
MEWED	METHS.	REEKY.	BEBOP	+HENRY	VERSE
NEVER	AEGIS	BE-ALL	BEFOG	+JERRY	VERSO
NEWEL	AERIE	BELLE	BEGOT	JEWRY	VERST

WELSH	VELUM	EGEST.	THEFT	CHANT	SHARE
YEAST.	VENUE	AGATE.	WHIFF.	*CHINA	SHARK
BERTH	+VENUS.	AGAVE	PHAGE	CHINE	SHARP
+BETTY	DELVE	OGIVE	THIGH.	CHINK	SHIRE
*CEUTA	HEAVE		CHAIN	CHUNK	SHIRK
DEATH	HEAVY	AHEAD	CHAIR	*GHANA	SHIRR
DEITY	HELVE	CHEAP	CHOIR	*GHENT	SHIRT
DELTA	LEAVE	CHEAT	+CHRIS	PHONE	SHORE
DEPTH	NERVE	CHIAN	OHMIC	PHONO	SHORN
+HEATH	NERVY	PHIAL	THEIR.	PHONY	SHORT
HEFTY	PEEVE	SHEAF	CHOKE	*RHINE	THERE
HERTZ	REEVE	SHEAR	CHOKY	RHINO	THERM
JETTY	SERVE	SHOAL	KHAKI	*RHONE	THIRD
+KEATS	VERVE	UHLAN	SHAKE	SHANK	THORN
+KEITH	WEAVE.	WHEAT.	SHAKO	SHANT	THORP
*LEITH	+BERYL	DHOBI.	SHAKY.	SHINE	WHARF
MEATY	*KENYA	CHECK	CHALK	SHINY	WHERE
*NEATH	+PEPYS.	CHICK	CHELA	SHONE	WHIRL
PEATY	FEEZE	CHOCK	CHILD	SHUNT	WHIRR
*PERTH	MEZZO	CHUCK	*CHILE	THANE	WHORE
PETTY	SEIZE	SHACK	CHILI	THANK	WHORL.
RECTO		SHOCK	CHILL	THINE	CHASE
SET-TO	OFFAL.	SHUCK	DHOLE	THING	CHASM
SEXTO	AFTER	THECA	GHYLL	THONG	CHESS
TEETH	OFFER	THICK	PHYLA	WHINE.	CHEST
TENTH	OFTEN.	WHACK	PHYLE	+CHAOS	CHOSE
TESTY	AFFIX.	WHICH.	SHALE	*CHIOS	GHOST
+VESTA	AFOOT.	CHIDE	SHALY	+CHLOE	*LHASA
+YEATS.	AFIRE	+RHODA	SHELF	PHLOX	PHASE
BEAUX	AFORE	SHADE	SHELL	SHEOL	SHUSH
BEGUM		SHADY.	SHYLY	SHOOK	THESE
BEGUN	*EGHAM	CHEEK	THOLE	SHOOT	THOSE
DEBUT	OGHAM.	CHEEP	WHALE	THROB	WHISK
DEMUR	AGGER	CHEER	WHELK	THROE	WHIST
FEMUR	AGLET	CHIEF	WHELP	THROW	WHOSE
FETUS	+AGNES	SHEEN	WHILE	WHOOP.	WHOSO.
GENUS	AGREE	SHEEP	WHOLE.	CHAPE	CHUTE
GET-UP	EGGER	SHEER	CHAMP	SHAPE.	DHOTI
+JESUS	EGRET	SHEET	CHIME	*CHARD	PHOTO
LEMUR	OGLED.	SHIED	CHIMP	CHARM	+SHUTE
NEGUS	AGAIN	SHRED	CHUMP	CHART	THETA
NEXUS	OGMIC.	SHREW	RHOMB	CHARY	WHITE.
REBUS	AGILE.	THIEF	RHUMB	CHERT	GHOUL
REBUT	AGAMA.	THREE	RHYME	CHIRP	RHEUM
RECUR	AGENT	THREW	SHAME	CHIRR	SHOUT
+REMUS	AGONY.	WHEEL.	THEME	CHORD	SHRUB
REVUE	AGLOW	CHAFE	THUMB	CHORE	SHRUG
*SEOUL	IGLOO.	CHAFF	THUMP	CHURL	THRUM
SERUM	AGAPE.	SHAFT	THYME.	CHURN	WHAUP.
SET-UP	AGORA.	SHIFT	BHANG	SHARD	CHIVE

SHAVE	SINCE	HIVED	SIREN	FICHU	AISLE
SHOVE.	TINCT	HIVES	SITED	FIGHT	BIBLE
SHAWL	WINCE	JIBED	SIZED	FISHY	BILLY
SHAWM	WINCH	JIVED	*TIBER	LIGHT	DIMLY
SHOWN	WITCH.	LIBEL	*TIBET	LITHE	FIELD
SHOWY	DILDO	LIFER	TIDED	MIGHT	FILLY
THEWS	DIODE	LIKED	TIGER	NICHE	FITLY
THEWY	GIDDY	LIKEN	TILED	NIGHT	HILLY
	+HILDA	LIMED	TIMED	PITHY	*LILLE
CIGAR	HINDI	LIMEY	TIMER	RIGHT	LISLE
+DINAH	HINDU	LINED	TIRED	SIGHT	RIFLE
DINAR	KIDDY	LINEN	*TIREE	TIGHT	RILLE
DIVAN	+LINDA	LINER	VIDEO	TITHE	SIDLE
FILAR	TILDE	LIVED	VILER	*WIGHT	SILLY
FINAL	+WILDE	LIVEN	VIPER	WITHE	TITLE
JIHAD	WINDY.	LIVER	VIXEN	WITHY.	VILLA
LILAC	AIDED	LIVES	WIDEN	BIFID	VILLI
+MIDAS	AIMED	MILER	WIDER	CILIA	+VIOLA
*MILAN	AIRED	+MILES	WILED	CIVIC	WIELD
RIVAL	AIRER	MIMED	WINED	CIVIL	YIELD.
*SINAI	BIDED	MINED	WIPED	DIGIT	FILMY
SISAL	BIDET	MINER	WIPER	DIXIE	*FIUME
SIZAR	BIPED	MIRED	WIRED	FINIS	+JIMMY
TIDAL	+BIZET	MISER	WISER	LICIT	*MIAMI
TITAN	CIDER	MIXED	WIVED	LIE-IN	PIGMY
VICAR	CITED	MIXER	WIVES	LIMIT	SIGMA.
+VIDAL	CIVET	MIZEN	WIZEN	LIPID	+DIANA
VITAL	DICED	NICER	ZIBET.	LIVID	DIDNT
*WIGAN.	DICEY	+NIGEL	JIFFY.	MIMIC	DIENE
BILBO	DIMER	*NIGER	BILGE	MINIM	FIEND
+LIBBY	DINED	*NIMES	BINGE	NIXIE	FINNY
LIMBO	DINER	OILED	BINGO	PIPIT	+FIONA
+NIOBE.	DIVED	PILED	DINGO	PIXIE	GIANT
BIRCH	DIVER	PINED	DINGY	RIGID	HINNY
BITCH	EIDER	PIPED	DIRGE	SIT-IN	LIANA
CINCH	FIFER	PIPER	HINGE	TIBIA	+MILNE
CIRCA	FILER	RIDER	JINGO	TIMID	NINNY
+CIRCE	FILET	RILED	LIEGE	VIGIL	PIANO
DITCH	FINER	RIPEN	LINGO	VINIC	PINNA
FILCH	FIRED	RIPER	MIDGE	VISIT	PINNY
FINCH	FIVER	RISEN	MINGY	VIVID.	TINNY
FITCH	FIVES	RISER	PIGGY	DICKY	BIGOT
HITCH	FIXED	RIVED	RIDGE	DINKY	BIJOU
MILCH	FIXER	RIVEN	SIEGE	KINKY	BISON
MINCE	GIBED	RIVER	SINGE	LINKS	*DIJON
NIECE	+GILES	RIVET	TINGE	MILKY	DIVOT
PIECE	GIVEN	SIDED	VIRGO.	PINKY	GIGOT
PILCH	HIKER	SILEX	BIGHT	RISKY	MIAOW
PINCH	HIRED	SINEW	DISHY	SILKY	MINOR
PITCH	HIRER	SIRED	EIGHT	+VICKY.	*MINOS

+NIXON	MISTY	SKIMP.	FLECK	ELEGY	ALONE
PICOT	NIFTY	SKINT	FLICK	*SLIGO.	ALONG
PILOT	NINTH	SKUNK.	FLOCK	ALPHA.	BLAND
PITOT	PIETA	*AKRON.	GLACE	+ALFIE	BLANK
PIVOT	PIETY	OKAPI.	PLACE	ALGID	BLEND
RIGOR	SIXTH	SKIRL	PLUCK	ALL-IN	BLIND
*RIPON	SIXTY	SKIRT.	SLACK	BLAIN	BLINK
+SIMON	TILTH	UKASE.	SLICE	CLAIM	BLOND
+SINON	VIRTU	SKATE.	SLICK.	ELFIN	BLUNT
*TIMOR	VISTA	SKIVE	BLADE	*ELGIN	CLANG
VISOR	WIDTH		*CLYDE	+ELLIS	CLANK
WIDOW.	WITTY.	ALGAE	ELIDE	+ELSIE	CLING
HIPPO	DIPUS	ALGAL	ELUDE	FLAIL	CLINK
HIPPY	GIBUS	ALIAS	GLADE	FLAIR	CLINT
NIPPY	GIGUE	ALLAH	GLIDE	FLUID	CLONE
WISPY	HILUM	ALLAY	SLIDE.	GLAIR	CLUNG
ZIPPY.	MINUS	ALTAR	ALDER	OLEIC	ELAND
DIARY	MIX-UP	BLEAK	ALIEN	OLEIN	FLANK
FIBRE	PIN-UP	BLEAR	ALLEY	PLAID	FLING
FIERY	PIOUS	BLEAT	ALTER	PLAIN	FLINT
FIORD	PIQUE	BLOAT	BLEED	PLAIT	FLONG
FIRRY	SINUS	CLEAN	BLEEP	SLAIN.	FLUNG
LIBRA	SIOUX	CLEAR	BLUES	ALIKE	FLUNK
LITRE	TIE-UP	CLEAT	CLEEK	+BLAKE	GLAND
MICRO	VIRUS.	CLOAK	CLUED	BLOKE	GLINT
MITRE	DIVVY	+ELGAR	ELDER	FLAKE	PLANE
NITRE	SIEVE.	ELVAN	+ELLEN	FLAKY	PLANK
TIARA.	+DILYS	FLEAM	+ELMER	FLUKE	PLANT
CISSY	*LIBYA	FLOAT	ELVER	FLUKY	PLONK
FIRST	VINYL.	GLEAM	ELVES	SLAKE.	PLUNK
GIPSY	DIZZY	GLEAN	FLEER	SLYLY.	SLANG
KIOSK	FIZZY	GLOAT	FLEET	BLAME	SLANT
MIDST	+LISZT	ILIAC	FLIES	BLIMP	SLING
*MINSK	+MITZI	ILIAD	FLYER	CLAMP	SLINK
RINSE	PIEZO	PLEAD	GLEET	CLIMB	SLUNG
SISSY	RITZY	PLEAT	GLUED	CLIME	SLUNK.
TIPSY.	TIZZY	*SLEAT	GLUEY	CLUMP	*ALLOA
BIRTH		ULNAR.	OLDEN	ELEMI	ALLOT
BITTS	EJECT.	ALIBI	OLDER	FLAME	ALLOW
DICTA	FJORD	GLEBE	PLIED	FLAMY	ALLOY
DIRTY		GLOBE.	SLEEK	FLUME	ALOOF
DITTO	SKEET	ALACK	SLEEP	FLUMP	BLOOD
DITTY	SKIED	+ALICE	SLEET	LLAMA	BLOOM
FIFTH	SKIER.	BLACK	ULCER.	PLUMB	ELBOW
FIFTY	SKIFF.	BLOCK	ALOFT	PLUME	+ELIOT
FILTH	SKEIN.	CLACK	BLUFF	PLUMP	FLOOD
FIRTH	SKALD	CLICK	CLEFT	PLUMY	FLOOR
GIRTH	SKILL	CLOCK	+CLIFF	SLIME	FLUOR
KITTY	SKULK	CLUCK	FLUFF.	SLIMY	GLOOM
MIRTH	SKULL.	ELECT	ALIGN	SLUMP.	SLOOP

ELOPE	PLATE	OMEGA.	SNEAK	UNPIN	KNURL
GLYPH	+PLATO	*OMAHA.	UNBAR	UNRIG	KNURR
SLOPE	+PLUTO	AMAIN	UNCAP	UNRIP	SNARE
SLYPE.	SLATE	AMBIT.	UNIAT	UNTIE	SNARL
ALARM	SLATY	SMOKE	UNMAN	UNTIL	SNORE
ALERT	SLOTH.	SMOKY.	UNSAY.	UNZIP.	SNORT
BLARE	ALBUM	AMBLE	ENACT	SNAKE	UNARM
BLURB	ALGUM	AMPLE	+ENOCH	SNAKY.	ANGST
BLURT	ALOUD	AMPLY	KNACK	ANELE	ANISE
+CLARE	CLOUD	+EMILY	KNOCK	ANGLE	GNASH.
CLARY	CLOUT	IMPLY	SNACK	ANKLE	+ANITA
CLERK	FLOUR	SMALL	SNICK.	INGLE	UNITE
FLARE	FLOUT	SMALT	ANODE	KNELL	UNITY.
FLIRT	ILEUM	SMELL	SNIDE.	KNELT	*ANGUS
+FLORA	ILIUM.	SMELT	*ANDES	KNOLL	ANNUL
GLARE	ALIVE	SMILE.	ANGEL	SNELL	ENDUE
GLORY	+CLIVE	AMEND	ANGER	UNCLE.	ENNUI
ULTRA.	CLOVE	AMINO	ANNEX	ANIMA	ENSUE
BLASE	GLOVE	AMONG	ENDED	ANOMY	INCUR
BLAST	OLIVE	EMEND.	ENTER	ENEMA	INCUS
BLESS	SLAVE.	+AMMON	INDEX	ENEMY	*INDUS
BLEST	BLOWN	IMPOT.	INFER	GNOME.	INPUT
+BLISS	CLOWN	AMBRY	INKED	ANENT	KNOUT
BLUSH	FLOWN.	EMERY	INLET	ANONA	SNOUT
CLASH	+LLOYD.	OMBRE	INNER	INANE.	UNCUT
CLASP	BLAZE	SMART	INSET	ANION	UNDUE.
CLASS	+ELIZA	SMIRK	INTER	*ANJOU	KNAVE.
CLOSE	GLAZE	UMBRA.	KNEED	ANNOY	KNOWN
FLASH	GLOZE	AMASS	KNEEL	ENDOW	SNOWY
FLASK	PLAZA	AMISS	ONSET	ENJOY	
FLESH		AMUSE	SNEER	ENROL	BOLAS
FLOSS	*AMMAN	SMASH.	UNDER	ENVOY	BORAX
FLUSH	EMBAY	AMATE	UNPEG	INGOT	COPAL
GLASS	SMEAR	AMITY	UNPEN	ONION	CORAL
GLOSS	UMIAK.	EMOTE	UNSEX	SNOOD	FOCAL
PLASH	AMICE	EMPTY	UNWED.	SNOOK	FORAY
PLASM	AMUCK	SMITE	KNIFE	SNOOP	GONAD
PLUSH	SMACK	SMITH	SNAFU	UNION.	GOWAN
SLASH	SMOCK.	SMOTE.	SNIFF	INAPT	+HORAE
SLOSH	AMBER	AMOUR	SNUFF	INEPT	HORAL
SLUSH.	AMEER	EMBUS	UNIFY.	SNIPE	+JONAH
ALATE	EMBED	IMBUE.	+INIGO.	UNAPT.	KORAN
BLITZ	EMBER	AMAZE	ANTIC	ANGRY	LOBAR
*BLYTH	IMPED		ANVIL	ENTRY	LOCAL
CLOTH	IMPEL	ANNAL	*INDIA	GNARL	LOGAN
ELATE	UMBEL	ANZAC	INFIX	INDRI	LOYAL
ELITE	UMBER.	IN-LAW	SNAIL	INERT	MODAL
FLITE	IMAGE	INLAY	UNDID	INFRA	MOLAR
FLUTE	IMAGO	INVAR	UNFIT	INURE	MONAD
FLUTY	*OMAGH	KNEAD	UNFIX	INURN	+MORAG

MORAL	POUCH	DOTER	+MOSES	VOTED	FOEHN
*MORAY	ROACH	*DOVER	MOTEL	VOTER	MOCHA.
NODAL	TORCH	DOWEL	MOTET	VOWED	BOGIE
NOMAD	TOUCH	DOWER	MOVED	VOWEL	BORIC
NOPAL	VOICE	DOYEN	MOVER	+WODEN	BOWIE
NOWAY	VOUCH.	DOZED	MOWED	WOKEN	COLIC
POLAR	DOWDY	DOZEN	MOWER	WOMEN	+COLIN
ROMAN	GOODY	DOZER	+NOBEL	WOOER	COMIC
RORAL	*GOUDA	FOGEY	NONES	WOVEN	CONIC
ROWAN	HORDE	FOREL	NOSED	YODEL	DORIC
ROYAL	HOWDY	FOVEA	NOSEY	YOKED	+DORIS
SOLAR	MOODY	FOXED	NOTED	YOKEL	FOLIO
SONAR	RONDO	FOYER	NOVEL	ZONED.	GOYIM
TODAY	ROWDY	GOFER	+NOYES	COMFY	IONIC
TOKAY	TOADY	GONER	OOZED	*CORFE	LOGIC
TONAL	TODDY	GOOEY	POKED	*CORFU	LORIS
TOPAZ	WOODY	GORED	POKER	GOOFY.	+LOUIS
TORAH	WORDY.	*GOWER	POLED	BOGGY	MOTIF
TORAN	BODED	HOLED	PORED	BONGO	MOVIE
TOTAL	BOGEY	HOLEY	POSED	BOUGH	PODIA
VOCAL	BOHEA	HOMED	POSER	COIGN	POLIO
WOMAN	BONED	+HOMER	POWER	CONGA	POSIT
ZONAL.	BORED	HOMEY	ROBED	CONGE	+ROBIN
+BOBBY	BORER	HONED	RODEO	*CONGO	+RODIN
BOMBE	BOWER	HONEY	+ROGER	CORGI	RORIC
BOOBY	BOXED	HOOEY	ROPED	COUGH	ROSIN
*CORBY	BOXER	HOPED	ROPEY	DODGE	*SOFIA
DOUBT	CODED	HOSED	ROVED	DODGY	SOLID
FORBY	CODEX	HOTEL	ROVEN	DOGGY	+SONIA
HOBBY	COKEY	HOVEL	ROVER	DOUGH	SONIC
LOBBY	COMET	HOVER	ROWED	FOGGY	TONIC
ZOMBI.	COOED	JOKED	ROWEL	FORGE	TOPIC
+BOSCH	COPED	JOKER	ROWER	FORGO	TOXIC
BOTCH	COPER	KOPEC	SOBER	GORGE	TOXIN
COACH	CORED	*KOREA	SOLED	GOUGE	VOMIT
COCCI	CORER	LOBED	SORER	HOUGH	YOGIN
CONCH	COVEN	LONER	SOWED	LODGE	ZOOID
COUCH	COVER	LOPED	SOWER	LOUGH	ZORIL.
DOLCE	COVET	LOSER	TOKEN	PODGY	KOPJE.
FORCE	COVEY	LOVED	TONED	PORGE	BOSKY
HOICK	COWED	LOVER	TOPEE	ROUGE	COCKY
HOOCH	COWER	LOWED	TOPER	ROUGH	CORKY
+JOYCE	*COWES	LOWER	TOTED	SOGGY	HONKY
MOOCH	COZEN	MODEL	TOTEM	SOUGH	JOCKO
NONCE	DOMED	+MONET	TOWED	*TONGA	KOOKY
NOTCH	DONEE	MONEY	TOWEL	TONGS	+LOCKE
POACH	DOPED	MOOED	TOWER	TOUGH	POCKY
PONCE	DOPEY	MOPED	TOYED	*VOLGA.	POLKA
POOCH	DOSED	MOREL	VOLED	BOCHE	PORKY
PORCH	DOTED	MORES	VOLET	BOTHY	ROCKY

ROOKY	*SOMME	OOMPH	MOIST	TOOTH	SPECS
VODKA	+TOMMY	POPPY	MOOSE	*VOLTA	SPICE
YOLKY.	WORMY.	SOAPY	MORSE	VOLTE	SPICY.
BOGLE	BONNY	SOPPY	MOSSY	WORTH	EPODE
BOULE	BORNE	SOUPY.	MOUSE	YOUTH.	SPADE
BOWLS	BOUND	BOARD	MOUSY	BOGUS	SPODE.
+BOYLE	*COLNE	BOURN	NOISE	BOLUS	OPTED
COALY	CORNY	COBRA	NOISY	BONUS	SPEED
COBLE	COUNT	COPRA	NOOSE	+COMUS	SPIED
COULD	DOING	COURT	NORSE	FOCUS	SPIEL
COYLY	+DONNA	*DOURO	POESY	FORUM	SPREE
DOILY	+DONNE	DOWRY	POISE	HOCUS	UPPER
DOLLY	DOWNY	GOURD	POPSY	HOKUM	UPSET
+DOYLE	FOUND	HOARD	POSSE	+HORUS	*YPRES.
FOLLY	FOUNT	HOARY	ROAST	JORUM	SPAHI.
GODLY	GOING	HOURI	ROOST	LOCUM	APHIS
GOLLY	HORNY	*LOIRE	ROUSE	LOCUS	+APRIL
*GOOLE	HOUND	LORRY	ROUST	LOTUS	APSIS
HOLLY	JOINT	+MOIRA	SONSY	MODUS	OPTIC
HOTLY	LOONY	MOIRE	SOUSE	MOGUL	*SPAIN
JOLLY	+LORNA	*MOORE	TOAST	NODUS	*SPLIT
JOULE	MOONY	MOURN	TORSO	ROGUE	SPOIL
KOALA	MOUND	SORRY	WORSE	TONUS	SPRIG
LOLLY	MOUNT	WORRY	WORST.	TOQUE	SPRIT.
LOWLY	POINT	YOURE	AORTA	TORUS	SPAKE
+MOLLY	+POUND	YOURS.	+BOOTH	VOGUE.	SPIKE
MOULD	ROUND	BOAST	BOOTY	HOOVE	SPIKY
MOULT	SONNY	BOOST	COATI	SOLVE	SPOKE.
NOBLE	SOUND	BOSSY	COTTA	YOUVE.	APPLE
NOBLY	TONNE	COAST	COUTH	POLYP	APPLY
+POLLY	WOUND	COPSE	DOTTY	*TOKYO.	APTLY
*POOLE	YOUNG.	DOUSE	FORTE	BONZE	SPELL
POULP	BORON	DOWSE	*FORTH	BOOZE	SPELT
POULT	BOSOM	FOIST	FORTY	BOOZY	SPILL
SOCLE	BOSON	FOSSA	GOUTY	COLZA	SPILT.
VOILE	COCOA	FOSSE	LOATH		SPUME
+WOOLF	COLON	GOOSE	LOFTY	APEAK	SPUMY.
WORLD	+COROT	GORSE	LOTTO	APIAN	APING
WOULD	DONOR	GORSY	MONTH	APPAL	OPINE
YOULL.	LOGOS	HOIST	MOTTO	SPEAK	SPANK
COMMA	MORON	+HOLST	MOUTH	SPEAR	SPEND
COOMB	MOTOR	HORSE	NORTH	SPLAY	SPENT
DOGMA	ROBOT	HORSY	POTTO	SPRAG	SPINE
DORMY	ROTOR.	HOUSE	POTTY	SPRAT	SPINY
FOAMY	COMPO	JOIST	ROUTE	SPRAY.	SPUNK
FORME	CO-OPT	JOUST	SOOTH	APACE	UP-EN
LOAMY	CORPS	LOESS	SOOTY	EPACT	APRON
+NORMA	COUPE	LOOSE	SOTTO	EPOCH	EPHOD
POMMY	COYPU	LOUSE	SOUTH	SPACE	*EPSOM
ROOMY	LOOPY	LOUSY	SOUTH	SPECK	SPOOF

SPOOK	CREAK	WRICK.	CRAFT	WRYLY.	PRANG
SPOOL	CREAM	BRIDE	CROFT	AROMA	PRANK
SPOON	CROAK	CREDO	DRAFF	BRUME	PRINK
SPOOR.	DREAD	CRUDE	DRAFT	CRAMP	PRINT
APART	DREAM	ERODE	DRIFT	CRIME	PRONE
APERY	DREAR	+FREDA	GRAFT	CRIMP	PRONG
OP-ART	DRYAD	GRADE	GRUFF.	CRUMB	PRUNE
OPERA	FREAK	GRIDE	+BRAGG	CRUMP	TREND
SPARE	FRIAR	PRIDE	DREGS.	DRAMA	*TRENT
SPARK	GREAT	PRUDE	ARGIL	DROME	TRINE
SPERM	GROAN	TRADE.	ARRIS	FRAME	TRONC
SPIRE	GROAT	ARCED	ARSIS	*FROME	TRUNK
SPIRT	KRAAL	ARIEL	ARTIC	FRUMP	URINE
SPIRY	ORGAN	ARIES	BRAID	GRIME	WRING
SPORE	+PRIAM	ARMED	BRAIN	+GRIMM	WRONG
SPORT	TREAD	BREED	BROIL	GRIMY	WRUNG.
SPURN	TREAT	BRIEF	BRUIN	PRIMA	ARBOR
SPURT.	TRIAD	CREED	BRUIT	PRIME	ARGOL
APISH	TRIAL	CREEK	DRAIL	PRIMP	ARGON
SPASM.	URBAN	CREEL	DRAIN	TRAMP	ARGOT
SPATE	WREAK.	CREEP	DROIT	TRUMP.	+ARION
SPITE.	BRIBE	CRIED	DRUID	ARENA	ARROW
APPUI	GREBE	CRIER	+ERNIE	ARENT	ARSON
OPIUM	PROBE	CRUEL	FRAIL	BRAND	BROOD
SPOUT.	TRIBE.	CRUET	FRUIT	BRANT	BROOK
SPAWN.	BRACE	DRIED	GRAIL	*BRENT	BROOM
EPOXY	BRACT	DRIER	GRAIN	BRINE	+CREON
	BRICK	DRYER	GROIN	BRING	CROOK
EQUAL	BROCK	ERRED	KRAIT	BRINK	CROON
SQUAB	+BRUCE	FREED	ORBIT	BRINY	DROOL
SQUAD	CRACK	FRYER	ORPIN	BRUNT	DROOP
SQUAT	CRICK	GREED	ORRIS	CRANE	ERGOT
SQUAW.	CROCK	GREEK	TRAIL	CRANK	+ERROL
*AQABA.	ERECT	GREEN	TRAIN	CRONE	ERROR
EQUIP	+ERICA	GREET	TRAIT.	CRONY	GROOK
SQUIB	ERUCT	GRIEF	BRAKE	DRANK	GROOM
SQUID	FROCK	GRUEL	BROKE	DRINK	+ORION
	+GRACE	IRKED	CRAKE	DRONE	ORLOP
AREAL	PRICE	ORBED	+DRAKE.	DRUNK	+ORSON
ARIAN	PRICK	ORDER	BRILL	FRANC	PRIOR
*ARRAN	TRACE	ORIEL	DRILL	+FRANK	PROOF
*ARRAS	TRACK	ORMER	DROLL	FROND	TROOP
ARRAY	TRACT	PREEN	DRYLY	FRONT	TRY-ON.
ARYAN	+TRACY	PRIED	FRILL	GRAND	CRAPE
BREAD	TRICE	PROEM	GRILL	+GRANT	CRAPS
BREAK	TRICK	TREED	PROLE	GRIND	CREPE
BREAM	TRUCE	TRIED	TRILL	GRUNT	CREPT
+BRIAN	TRUCK	TRIER	TROLL	+IRENE	CRYPT
BRIAR	WRACK	TRUER	TRULL	IRONY	DRAPE
BROAD	WRECK	URGED.	TRULY	KRONE	DRUPE

ERUPT	TRYST	DRAWL	*OSAKA.	STRIA	STRUT.
GRAPE	WREST	DRAWN	ISTLE	STRIP.	STAVE
GRAPH	WRIST.	DROWN	PSALM.	STAKE	+STEVE
GRAPY	ARETE	FROWN	USING.	STOKE.	STOVE.
GRIPE	BROTH	GROWL	*ASCOT.	ATOLL	ETHYL
GROPE	BRUTE	GROWN	*ISERE	*ITALY	
PROPS	CRATE	PRAWN	USURP	STALE	AURAL
TRIPE	*CRETE	PROWL	USURY.	STALK	BUBAL
TROPE.	*ERITH	TRAWL	ISSUE	STALL	*DUBAI
CRORE	FRITH	TREWS.		STILE	DUCAL
*TRURO.	FROTH	PROXY.	*ATLAS	STILL	DUCAT
ARISE	GRATE	+FREYA.	ATTAR	STILT	+DUMAS
AROSE	+GRETA	BRAZE	STEAD	STOLE	FUGAL
BRASH	IRATE	CRAZE	STEAK	STYLE.	HUMAN
BRASS	ORATE	CRAZY	STEAL	STAMP	+JUDAS
*BREST	PRATE	FRIZZ	STEAM	STOMA	JUGAL
BRISK	TRITE	FROZE	STEAN	STUMP.	KULAK
BROSE	TROTH	GRAZE	STOAT	ATONE	LUNAR
BRUSH	TRUTH	+ORCZY	STRAP	STAND	MURAL
CRASH	WRATH	PRIZE	STRAW	STANK	MUZAK
CRASS	WRITE		STRAY.	STING	QUEAN
CRESS	WROTE	ASIAN	STACK	STINK	RURAL
CREST	WROTH.	ASSAI	STICH	STINT	*SUDAN
CRISP	ARGUE	*ASSAM	STICK	STONE	SUGAR
CROSS	+ARGUS	ASSAY	STOCK	STONY	+SUSAN
CRUSE	CROUP	*ASWAN	STUCK.	STUNG	TUBAL.
CRUSH	FRAUD	ESSAY	STUDY.	STUNK	BUMBO
CRUST	+FREUD	+ISAAC	+ETHEL	STUNT.	BUSBY
DRESS	GROUP	ISLAM	ETHER	ETHOS	CUBBY
DROSS	GROUT	*ISLAY	OTHER	STOOD	GUMBO
ERASE	PROUD	+OSCAR	OTTER	STOOK	HUBBY
FRASS	TROUT.	USUAL.	STEED	STOOL	JUMBO
FRESH	BRAVE	ASIDE.	STEEL	STOOP	*RUGBY
FRISK	BRAVO	ASHEN	STEEN	STROP.	RUMBA
+FROST	BREVE	ASKED	STEEP	STUPE.	TUBBY
GRASP	CRAVE	ASKEW	STEER	STARE	TURBO.
+GRASS	DRIVE	ASPEN	STREW	STARK	BUNCH
GRIST	DROVE	ASSET	UTTER.	START	BUNCO
GROSS	GRAVE	ASTER	STAFF	STERE	BUTCH
IRISH	GRAVY	*ESHER	STIFF	STERN	DUNCE
PRASE	GROVE	*ESSEN	STUFF.	STORE	DUTCH
PRESS	PRIVY	*ESSEX	STAGE	STORK	GULCH
PRISE	PROVE.	ESTER	STAGY.	STORM	HUNCH
PRISM	BRAWL	ISLET	ITCHY.	STORY.	HUTCH
PROSE	BRAWN	OSIER	ATTIC	STASH.	JUICE
PROSY	BROWN	USHER.	ETHIC	STATE.	JUICY
TRASH	CRAWL	USAGE.	STAID	STOUP	LUNCH
TRESS	*CREWE	ASDIC	STAIN	*STOUR	LURCH
TRUSS	CROWD	ASPIC	STAIR	STOUT	MULCH
TRUST	CROWN	ASTIR.	STOIC	STRUM	MULCT

+MUNCH	RUDER	CUTIS	GUILT	PULPY	MUSTY
OUNCE	RULED	HUMID	GULLY	PUPPY	NUTTY
PUNCH	RULER	+JULIE	QUALM	TURPS.	PUNTY
QUACK	RUPEE	KUMIS	QUELL	BURRO	PUTTO
QUICK	SUPER	+LUCIA	QUILL	CURRY	PUTTY
YUCCA.	SURER	LUCID	QUILT	FURRY	QUITE
BUDDY	TUBER	LUNIK	RUMLY	GUARD	*QUITO
CUDDY	TUNED	LUPIN	SULLY	HURRY	QUITS
CURDY	TUNER.	LURID	SURLY	KUKRI	QUOTA
GUIDE	HUFFY	MUJIK	TULLE.	LUBRA	QUOTE
*LUNDY	PUFFY	MUSIC	*BURMA	LUCRE	QUOTH
MUDDY	QUAFF	PUBIC	DUMMY	OUTRE	RUSTY
OUTDO	QUIFF	PUBIS	GUMMA	QUARK	RUTTY
RUDDY	TURFY.	PUPIL	GUMMY	QUART	SUETY
SUEDE.	BUDGE	QUAIL	MUMMY	QUERN	SUITE
+AUDEN	BUDGY	QUOIN	RUMMY	QUERY	TUTTY.
AUGER	BUGGY	QUOIT	TUMMY.	QUIRE	AUGUR
BUYER	BULGE	RUNIC	BUNNY	QUIRK	FUCUS
CUBEB	BURGH	TULIP	+BURNS	QUIRT.	FUGUE
CUBED	DUNGY	TUMID	BURNT	BURST	HUMUS
CULEX	FUDGE	TUNIC	FUNNY	CURSE	LUPUS
CURED	FUGGY	*TUNIS	GUANA	DULSE	MUCUS
CURER	FUNGI	*TURIN.	GUANO	DURST	QUEUE
CUSEC	JUDGE	OUIJA.	GUNNY	FUBSY	+RUFUS
DUPED	LUNGE	BUCKO	QUANT	FUSSY	SUN-UP.
+DURER	MUGGY	BULKY	QUINS	GUESS	CURVE
FUMED	NUDGE	BURKE	QUINT	GUEST	GUAVA
FUSED	OUTGO	DUCKY	RUING	GUISE	SUAVE
FUSEE	PUDGY	DUSKY	RUNNY	HURST	VULVA.
FUSEL	PURGE	FUNKY	SUING	HUSSY	FURZE
GULES	SURGE.	HUSKY	SUNNY	NURSE	FURZY
GUYED	AUGHT	JUNKY	TUNNY.	PUDSY	FUZZY
JULEP	BUSHY	LUCKY	BUXOM	PULSE	MUZZY
LUMEN	CUSHY	MUCKY	*HURON	PURSE	
LURED	DUCHY	MURKY	JUPON	PURSY	AVIAN.
LUTED	MUSHY	MUSKY	JUROR	PUSSY	EVICT.
MUREX	OUGHT	PUKKA	KUDOS	QUASH	EVADE.
MUSED	RUCHE	QUAKE	*LUTON	QUEST.	IVIED.
MUTED	RUSHY.	SULKY.	TUDOR	BUTTE	AVAIL
OUSEL	AUDIT	BUGLE	TUTOR	CUTTY	AVOID
OUTER	AURIC	BUILD	*YUKON.	DUSTY	+AVRIL
OUZEL	BURIN	BUILT	BUMPH	FUSTY	OVOID.
PUBES	CUBIC	BULLY	BUMPY	GUSTO	EVOKE.
PUKED	CUBIT	BURLY	DUMPY	GUSTY	OVULE
PULED	CUMIN	CURLY	GUPPY	JUNTA	UVULA.
PUREE	+CUPID	DULLY	HUMPH	JUNTO	EVENT
PURER	CURIA	DUPLE	HUMPY	JUXTA	OVINE.
QUEEN	CURIE	FULLY	JUMPY	LUSTY	AVERT
QUEER	CURIO	GUILD	LUMPY	MUFTI	EVERT
QUIET	CUTIE	GUILE	MUMPS	MULTI	EVERY

IVORY	SWIRL	+TYLER	AZURE	ABASE	GRAVE
OVARY	SWORD	TYPED	IZARD	ABATE	GRAZE
OVERT.	SWORE	XYLEM.	*OZARK.	ADAGE	HEAVE
AVAST.	SWORN	*HYTHE.	AZOTE	AGAPE	IMAGE
OVATE	TWERE	CYNIC		AGATE	INANE
	TWERP	+CYRIL		AGAVE	IRATE
SWEAR	TWIRL.	EYRIE	AGAMA	ALATE	KNAVE
SWEAT	AWASH	HYLIC	*AQABA	AMATE	LEASE
TWEAK.	SWASH	HYOID	BWANA	AMAZE	LEAVE
TWICE.	SWISH	KYRIE	+DIANA	APACE	ORATE
SWEDE.	SWISS	+LYDIA	DRAMA	AWAKE	OVATE
AWNED	TWIST.	LYRIC	*GHANA	AWARE	PEACE
OWLET	SWATH.	PYXIS	GUANA	BLADE	PEASE
OWNED	AWFUL.	+SYBIL	GUAVA	+BLAKE	PHAGE
OWNER	TWIXT	*SYRIA.	KAAMA	BLAME	PHASE
SWEEP		CYCLE.	KOALA	BLARE	PLACE
SWEET	AXIAL	PYGMY.	*LHASA	BLASE	PLANE
*TWEED	EXEAT.	DYING	LIANA	BLAZE	PLATE
TWEEN	EXACT.	HYENA	LLAMA	BRACE	PRASE
TWEET.	EXUDE	LYING	*NYASA	BRAKE	PRATE
+SWIFT.	OXIDE.	*LYONS	*OMAHA	BRAVE	QUAKE
AWAIT	EXCEL	+MYRNA	*OSAKA	BRAZE	SCALE
SWAIN	EXPEL.	VYING.	PLAZA	CEASE	SCAPE
+TWAIN.	OXLIP.	+BYRON	*SCAPA	CHAFE	SCARE
AWAKE	AXILE	HYSON	TIARA.	CHAPE	SHADE
AWOKE.	EXALT	KYLOE	FRANC	CHASE	SHAKE
DWELL	EXILE	LYSOL	+ISAAC.	+CLARE	SHALE
DWELT	EXULT.	NYLON	AWARD	CRAKE	SHAME
SWELL	AXIOM	PYLON	BEARD	CRANE	SHAPE
SWILL	EXTOL	SYNOD	BLAND	CRAPE	SHARE
TWILL.	OXBOW.	*SYROS	BOARD	CRATE	SHAVE
SWAMP.	EXERT	*TYROL.	BRAID	CRAVE	SKATE
AWING	EXTRA.	LYMPH	BRAND	CRAZE	SLAKE
BWANA	EXIST	NYMPH	*CHARD	+DRAKE	SLATE
OWING		SYLPH.	ELAND	DRAPE	SLAVE
SWANK	BY-LAW	*CYMRU	FRAUD	ELATE	SNAKE
SWINE	BY-WAY	*HYDRA	GLAND	ERASE	SNARE
SWING	CYMAR	HYDRO	GRAND	EVADE	SPACE
SWUNG	+DYLAN	MYRRH.	GUARD	FLAKE	SPADE
TWANG	GYRAL	GYPSY	HEARD	FLAME	SPAKE
TWINE.	HYRAX	*NYASA.	HOARD	FLARE	SPARE
SWOON	PYGAL.	*KYOTO.	IZARD	FRAME	SPATE
SWOOP.	LYNCH.	+CYRUS	PLAID	GLACE	STAGE
SWEPT	GYBED	SYRUP	SCALD	GLADE	STAKE
SWIPE.	GYVED		SHARD	GLARE	STALE
AWARD	HYMEN	AZTEC.	SKALD	GLAZE	STARE
AWARE	HYPER	AZOIC	STAID	+GRACE	STATE
DWARF	LYCEE	*IZMIR.	STAND	GRADE	STAVE
SWARD	PYXED	AZYME.	SWARD	GRAPE	SUAVE
SWARM	SYCEE	OZONE.	*WEALD.	GRATE	TEASE

THANE	WRATH.	FRAIL	IMAGO	ENACT	HEADY
TRACE	COATI	GNARL	PIANO	EPACT	HEAVY
TRADE	KHAKI	GRAIL	+PLATO	EXACT	HOARY
UKASE	*MIAMI	KRAAL	SHAKO.	EXALT	*ITALY
USAGE	NAAFI	+PEARL	CHAMP	FEAST	LEADY
WEAVE	OKAPI	QUAIL	CLAMP	GIANT	LEAFY
WHALE.	SPAHI.	SHAWL	CLASP	GRAFT	LEAKY
CHAFF	ABACK	SMALL	CRAMP	+GRANT	LOAMY
DRAFF	ALACK	SNAIL	GRASP	HEART	MEALY
DWARF	BLACK	SNARL	SCALP	INAPT	MEATY
QUAFF	BLANK	STALL	SCAMP	KRAIT	OVARY
SCARF	CHALK	TRAIL	SCARP	LEANT	PEAKY
STAFF	CLACK	TRAWL.	SHARP	LEAPT	PEATY
WHARF.	CLANK	ALARM	STAMP	LEAST	READY
BHANG	CRACK	CHARM	SWAMP	MEANT	SCALY
+BRAGG	CRANK	CHASM	TRAMP	OP-ART	SEAMY
CLANG	DRANK	CLAIM	WHAUP.	PLAIT	SHADY
PRANG	FLANK	PLASM	CHAIR	PLANT	SHAKY
SLANG	FLASK	PSALM	FLAIR	QUANT	SHALY
TWANG.	+FRANK	QUALM	GLAIR	QUART	SLATY
ABASH	KNACK	REALM	STAIR.	REACT	SNAKY
AWASH	*OZARK	REARM	+ADAMS	ROAST	SOAPY
BEACH	PLANK	SHAWM	AMASS	SCANT	STAGY
BRASH	PRANK	SPASM	BRASS	SCART	TOADY
CLASH	QUACK	SWARM	+CHAOS	SHAFT	+TRACY
COACH	QUARK	UNARM.	CLASS	SHANT	WEARY
CRASH	SHACK	AGAIN	CRAPS	SLANT	
DEATH	SHANK	AMAIN	CRASS	SMALT	COBRA
FLASH	SHARK	BLAIN	FRASS	SMART	LIBRA
GNASH	SLACK	BRAIN	GLASS	START	*LIBYA
GRAPH	SMACK	BRAWN	+GRASS	TOAST	LUBRA
+HEATH	SNACK	CHAIN	JEANS	TRACT	TIBIA
LEACH	SPANK	DRAIN	+KEATS	TRAIT	UMBRA
LEASH	SPARK	DRAWN	+YEATS.	UNAPT	ZEBRA.
LOATH	STACK	GRAIN	ABAFT	YEAST.	CABOB
*NEATH	STALK	LEARN	ADAPT	SNAFU.	CUBEB
*OMAGH	STANK	PLAIN	APART	MIAOW.	NABOB.
PEACH	STARK	PRAWN	AVAST	BEAUX.	CUBIC
PLASH	SWANK	SLAIN	AWAIT	BEADY	PUBIC
POACH	THANK	*SPAIN	BEAST	CHARY	REBEC
QUASH	TRACK	SPAWN	BLAST	CLARY	XEBEC.
REACH	WHACK	STAIN	BOAST	COALY	CUBED
ROACH	WRACK.	SWAIN	BRACT	CRAZY	EBBED
SLASH	AVAIL	TRAIN	BRANT	DEARY	EMBED
SMASH	BE-ALL	+TWAIN	CHANT	DIARY	GIBED
STASH	BRAWL	YEARN.	CHART	FLAKY	GYBED
SWASH	CRAWL	BEANO	COAST	FLAMY	JIBED
SWATH	DRAIL	BRAVO	CRAFT	FOAMY	LOBED
TEACH	DRAWL	GUANO	DEALT	GRAPY	ORBED
TRASH	FLAIL	*IDAHO	DRAFT	GRAVY	RABID

ROBED.	UNBAR.	FACED	VICAR.	AIDED	+AUDEN
+ABBIE	EMBUS	LACED	+CACUS	BIDED	LADEN
AMBLE	GIBUS	LUCID	FOCUS	BODED	OLDEN
BIBLE	PUBES	MACED	FUCUS	CEDED	RADON
CABLE	PUBIS	PACED	HOCUS	CODED	+RODIN
COBLE	REBUS	RACED.	INCUS	ENDED	SEDAN
FABLE	TABES.	BOCHE	JACKS	FADED	*SUDAN
FIBRE	ABBOT	CACHE	LOCUS	JADED	WIDEN
GABLE	AMBIT	CYCLE	MUCUS.	LADED	+WODEN.
IMBUE	CUBIT	+LOCKE	*ASCOT	SIDED	HYDRO
NOBLE	DEBIT	LUCRE	DUCAT	TIDED	RADIO
OMBRE	DEBUT	LYCEE	FACET	UNDID	RODEO
SABLE	HABIT	NACRE	LICIT	WADED.	VIDEO.
SABRE	JABOT	NICHE	PICOT	ADDLE	ADDER
TABLE.	ORBIT	RUCHE	TACIT	BADGE	ALDER
DEBAG.	*RABAT	SOCLE	UNCUT	BUDGE	CEDAR
*DUBAI	REBUT	SYCEE	YACHT.	CADGE	CIDER
RABBI.	ROBOT	UNCLE.	FICHU.	CADRE	EIDER
BABEL	SABOT	CACTI	MACAW.	DODGE	ELDER
BABUL	*TIBET	COCCI.	COCKY	ENDUE	NADIR
BUBAL	ZIBET.	+CECIL	DECAY	FUDGE	ODDER
CABAL	ELBOW	DECAL	DECOY	HEDGE	OLDER
*KABUL	OXBOW.	DUCAL	DECRY	JUDGE	ORDER
LABEL	ABBEY	EXCEL	DICEY	KEDGE	RADAR
LIBEL	AMBRY	FOCAL	DICKY	LADLE	RIDER
+MABEL	+BOBBY	LOCAL	DUCHY	LEDGE	RUDER
+NOBEL	CABBY	VOCAL.	DUCKY	LODGE	TUDOR
REBEL	CUBBY	LOCUM.	ITCHY	MIDGE	UDDER
+SYBIL	EMBAY	+BACON	LUCKY	NUDGE	UNDER
TUBAL	FUBSY	*MACON	MUCKY	PADRE	WADER
UMBEL.	HOBBY	PECAN.	+ORCZY	RIDGE	WIDER.
ALBUM.	HUBBY	BUCKO	POCKY	+SADIE	*ANDES
CABIN	+LIBBY	CACAO	ROCKY	SEDGE	HADES
*GABON	LOBBY	GECKO	TACKY	SIDLE	*INDUS
+ROBIN	NOBLY	JOCKO	+VICKY	UNDUE	+JUDAS
URBAN.	TABBY	*MACAO	WACKY	WEDGE.	KUDOS
BABOO	TUBBY	MICRO		WIDTH.	+MIDAS
TABOO.		RECTO.	*HYDRA	HADJI	MODUS
BEBOP.	*ACCRA	*BACUP	*INDIA	INDRI	NODUS.
AMBER	COCOA	RECAP	+LYDIA	RADII.	AUDIT
ARBOR	*DACCA	UNCAP.	+MEDEA	MEDAL	BIDET
CABER	DICTA	DECOR	MEDIA	MODAL	CADET
DEBAR	FACIA	FACER	*PADUA	MODEL	DIDNT
EMBER	+LUCIA	INCUR	PODIA	NODAL	HADNT
LOBAR	*MECCA	NICER	VODKA.	PEDAL	MIDST.
SOBER	MOCHA	OCCUR	ASDIC	TIDAL	BEDEW
TABOR	YUCCA.	+OSCAR	+MADOC	+VIDAL	ENDOW
*TIBER	+JACOB.	RACER	*MEDOC	YODEL.	WIDOW.
TUBER	ARCED	RECUR	VEDIC.	BEDIM	ADDAX
UMBER	DICED	ULCER	ADDED	MADAM.	CODEX

INDEX	CREED	SWEDE	STEEL	CLEAR	EXEAT
RADIX.	DREAD	THEME	SWELL	DREAR	EXERT
BADLY	EMEND	THERE	WHEEL.	FLEER	FLEET
BUDDY	FIELD	THESE	ABEAM	QUEER	*GHENT
BUDGY	FIEND	TWERE	ADEEM	SHEAR	GLEET
CADDY	FREED	WHERE.	BREAM	SHEER	GREAT
CUDDY	+FREUD	SHEAF	CREAM	SMEAR	GREET
DADDY	GREED	SHELF.	DREAM	SNEER	GUEST
DODGY	KNEAD	BEECH	FLEAM	SPEAR	INEPT
FADDY	KNEED	FLESH	GLEAM	STEER	INERT
GIDDY	PLEAD	FRESH	ILEUM	SWEAR	KNELT
GODLY	SPEED	LEECH	RHEUM	THEIR.	OVERT
KIDDY	SPEND	OBEAH	SPERM	BLESS	PLEAT
LADDY	STEAD	TEETH.	STEAM	CHESS	QUEST
MADLY	STEED	ELEMI	THERM.	CRESS	REEST
MUDDY	TREAD	OBELI.	CLEAN	DREGS	SCENT
ODDLY	TREED	APEAK	+CREON	DRESS	SHEET
+PADDY	TREND	BLEAK	FOEHN	GUESS	SKEET
PODGY	*TWEED	BREAK	GLEAN	*LEEDS	*SLEAT
PUDGY	UP-END	CHECK	GREEN	LOESS	SLEET
PUDSY	WIELD	CHEEK	LIE-IN	PRESS	SMELT
RUDDY	YIELD.	CLEEK	OCEAN	SPECS	SPELT
SADLY	ABELE	CLERK	OLEIN	TEENS	SPENT
+TEDDY	+ADELE	CREAK	+PAEAN	THEWS	SWEAT
TODAY	ANELE	CREEK	PREEN	TRESS	SWEET
TODDY	ARETE	FLECK	QUEAN	TREWS.	SWEPT
WADDY.	BREVE	FREAK	QUEEN	ADEPT	THEFT
*CADIZ	CREPE	GREEK	QUERN	AGENT	TREAT
	*CRETE	SLEEK	SHEEN	ALERT	*TRENT
ARENA	*CREWE	SNEAK	SKEIN	ANENT	TWEET
CHELA	DIENE	SPEAK	STEAN	ARENT	WHEAT
EDEMA	FEEZE	SPECK	STEEN	AVERT	WREST.
ENEMA	GEESE	STEAK	STERN	BLEAT	APERY
+FREDA	GLEBE	TWEAK	TWEEN.	BLEST	BEEFY
+FREYA	GREBE	WHELK	CREDO	*BRENT	BEERY
+GRETA	+IRENE	WREAK	PIEZO.	*BREST	ELEGY
HYENA	*ISERE	WRECK.	BLEEP	CHEAT	EMERY
OMEGA	LIEGE	AREAL	CHEAP	CHERT	ENEMY
OPERA	NIECE	CREEL	CHEEP	CHEST	EVERY
PIETA	OBESE	DWELL	CREEP	CLEAT	FIERY
SCENA	PEEVE	IDEAL	SHEEP	CLEFT	LEERY
THECA	PIECE	KNEEL	SLEEP	CREPT	NEEDY
THETA.	QUEUE	KNELL	STEEP	CREST	PIETY
OLEIC.	REEVE	QUELL	SWEEP	DWELT	POESY
AHEAD	SCENE	SHELL	TIE-UP	EGEST	QUERY
AMEND	SIEGE	SHEOL	TWERP	EJECT	REEDY
BLEED	SIEVE	SMELL	WHELP.	ELECT	REEKY
BLEND	STERE	SNELL	AMEER	ERECT	SEEDY
BREAD	+STEVE	SPELL	BLEAR	EVENT	SUETY
BREED	SUEDE	STEAL	CHEER	EVERT	TEENY

THEWY	SIGMA.	+SAGAN	TIGHT	+ELIZA	CHINE
WEEDY	LOGIC	WAGON	*WIGHT.	+ERICA	CHIVE
WEENY	MAGIC.	*WIGAN	ANGRY	*HAIFA	CLIME
WEEPY	ALGID	ANGRY	BAGGY	+IBIZA	+CLIVE
	BEGAD	YOGIN.	BOGEY	+LEILA	CRIME
INFRA	CAGED	NEGRO.	BOGGY	+MOIRA	DE-ICE
*JAFFA	EDGED	AGGER	BUGGY	OUIJA	DRIVE
+KAFKA	PAGED	ANGER	CAGEY	PRIMA.	ELIDE
MAFIA	RIGID	AUGER	DOGGY	CLIMB.	ELITE
*SOFIA.	URGED	AUGUR	FOGEY	ILIAC.	EXILE
BIFID.	WAGED.	CIGAR	FOGGY	BLIND	FLITE
+ALFIE	ALGAE	EAGER	FUGGY	BUILD	GLIDE
+DEFOE	ANGLE	+EDGAR	LEGGY	CHILD	GRIDE
GAFFE	ARGUE	EGGER	MUGGY	CRIED	GRIME
RIFLE.	BOGIE	+ELGAR	+PEGGY	DRIED	GRIPE
BEFOG.	BOGLE	LAGER	PIGGY	GRIND	GUIDE
FIFTH.	BUGLE	*NIGER	PIGMY	GUILD	GUILE
MUFTI.	EAGLE	RIGOR	PYGMY	ILIAD	GUISE
AWFUL	EAGRE	+ROGER	*RUGBY	IVIED	JUICE
OFFAL.	FUGUE	SUGAR	SOGGY	LAIRD	KNIFE
ELFIN.	GIGUE	TIGER		NAIAD	*LOIRE
DEFER	*HAGUE	WAGER.	BOHEA.	PLIED	*MAINE
FIFER	INGLE	AEGIS	SAHIB.	PRIED	MAIZE
GOFER	ROGUE	*ANGUS	ETHIC.	SHIED	MOIRE
INFER	VAGUE	+ARGUS	ACHED	SKIED	NAIVE
KAFIR	VOGUE.	BOGUS	EPHOD	SPIED	NOISE
LIFER	+MAGOG.	+DEGAS	JIHAD.	THIRD	OGIVE
OFFER	ALGAL	*LAGOS	OCHRE.	TRIAD	OLIVE
REFER	ANGEL	LOGOS	+ETHEL	TRIED	OPINE
SAFER	ARGIL	MAGUS	ETHYL.	WEIRD.	OVINE
WAFER.	ARGOL	NEGUS.	*EGHAM	ABIDE	OXIDE
+RUFUS.	FUGAL	ANGST	OGHAM.	*ADIGE	POISE
BEFIT	JUGAL	ARGOT	ASHEN	AFIRE	PRICE
REFIT	LEGAL	AUGHT	+BEHAN.	AGILE	PRIDE
UNFIT.	MOGUL	BEGET	YAHOO.	+ALICE	PRIME
AFFIX	+NIGEL	BEGOT	ABHOR	ALIKE	PRISE
INFIX	PYGAL	BIGHT	*ESHER	ALIVE	PRIZE
UNFIX.	REGAL	BIGOT	ETHER	AMICE	QUIRE
DAFFY	VIGIL.	DIGIT	ICHOR	ANISE	QUITE
FIFTY	ALGUM	EIGHT	LAHAR	ARISE	RAISE
HEFTY	BEGUM.	ERGOT	OTHER	ASIDE	*RHINE
HUFFY	ARGON	FIGHT	USHER.	AXILE	*SEINE
JIFFY	BEGAN	GIGOT	APHIS	BAIZE	SEISE
LOFTY	BEGIN	INGOT	ETHOS.	BEIGE	SEIZE
NIFTY	BEGUN	LEGIT	+NEHRU	BRIBE	SHINE
PUFFY	*ELGIN	LIGHT		BRIDE	SHIRE
TAFFY	LAGAN	MIGHT	ANIMA	BRINE	SKIVE
	LOGAN	NIGHT	+ANITA	CHIDE	SLICE
DOGMA	ORGAN	OUGHT	*BEIRA	*CHILE	SLIDE
MAGMA	PAGAN	RIGHT	*CHINA	CHIME	SLIME
		SIGHT			

SMILE	ICING	SHIRK	AVIAN	DRIFT	DEITY
SMITE	LYING	SLICK	BAIRN	EDICT	DOILY
SNIDE	OWING	SLINK	+BRIAN	+ELIOT	EDIFY
SNIPE	RUING	SMIRK	CAIRN	EVICT	+EMILY
SPICE	SLING	SNICK	CHIAN	EXIST	FAIRY
SPIKE	STING	STICK	COIGN	FAINT	GAILY
SPINE	SUING	STINK	DEIGN	FEINT	GRIMY
SPIRE	SWING	THICK	FEIGN	FLINT	HAIRY
SPITE	THING	TRICK	*NAIRN	FLIRT	ICILY
STILE	USING	UMIAK	ONION	FOIST	JUICY
SUITE	VYING	WHISK	+ORION	GLINT	LAITY
SWINE	WRING.	WRICK.	REIGN	GRIST	NOISY
SWIPE	APISH	ARIEL	SCION	GUILT	PRIVY
THINE	+EDITH	AXIAL	UNION	HEIST	RAINY
TRIBE	*ERITH	BRILL	AMINO	HOIST	SHINY
TRICE	+FAITH	CHILL	*CAIRO	IDIOT	SLIMY
TRINE	FRITH	DRILL	+INIGO	JOINT	SPICY
TRIPE	HEIGH	FRILL	*QUITO	JOIST	SPIKY
TRITE	IRISH	GRILL	RHINO	MOIST	SPINY
TWICE	+KEITH	ORIEL	*SLIGO.	PAINT	SPIRY
TWINE	*LEITH	PHIAL	BLIMP	POINT	UNIFY
UNITE	NEIGH	QUILL	CHIMP	PRINT	UNITY.
URINE	REICH	SKILL	CHIRP	QUIET	BLITZ
VOICE	SMITH	SKIRL	CRIMP	QUILT	FRIZZ
VOILE	STICH	SPIEL	CRISP	QUINT	
WAIVE	SWISH	SPILL	PRIMP	QUIRT	RAJAH.
WHILE	THIGH	STILL	SKIMP.	SAINT	MUJIK.
WHINE	WEIGH	SWILL	BRIAR	SHIFT	*DIJON.
WHITE	WHICH.	SWIRL	CHIRR	SHIRT	MAJOR.
WRITE	ACINI	TRIAL	CRIER	SKINT	*ANJOU
*ZAIRE.	ALIBI	TRILL	DRIER	SKIRT	BIJOU.
BRIEF	CHILI	TWILL	FRIAR	SPILT	ENJOY
CHIEF	*HAITI.	TWIRL	OSIER	SPIRT	
+CLIFF	BLINK	WHIRL.	PRIOR	STILT	PUKKA.
GRIEF	BRICK	AXIOM	SHIRR	STINT	ASKED
QUIFF	BRINK	DEISM	SKIER	+SWIFT	BAKED
SKIFF	BRISK	+GRIMM	TRIER	TAINT	CAKED
SNIFF	CHICK	IDIOM	WHIRR.	TWIST	FAKED
STIFF	CHINK	ILIUM	ALIAS	TWIXT	INKED
THIEF	CLICK	ODIUM	AMISS	UNIAT	IRKED
WHIFF.	CLINK	OPIUM	ARIES	WAIST	JOKED
APING	CRICK	+PRIAM	+BLISS	WHIST	LIKED
AWING	DRINK	PRISM.	*CHIOS	WRIST.	NAKED
BEING	FLICK	ALIEN	FLIES	ADIEU.	POKED
BRING	FRISK	ALIGN	QUINS	AMITY	PUKED
CLING	HOICK	ANION	QUITS	BRINY	RAKED
DOING	PRICK	APIAN	SWISS.	DAILY	WAKED
DYING	PRINK	ARIAN	BUILT	DAIRY	YOKED.
FLING	QUICK	+ARION	CLINT	+DAISY	ANKLE
GOING	QUIRK	ASIAN	DEIST	DEIFY	PEKOE

67

KUKRI.	BALED	CALIF.	GALOP	AGLOW	RALLY
YOKEL.	FELID	ALLAH	JALAP	ALLOW	RELAY
HAKIM	GELID	BELCH	JULEP	BELOW	+SALLY
HOKUM	HALED	FILCH	ORLOP	BY-LAW	SALTY
OAKUM.	HOLED	FILTH	OXLIP	IN-LAW.	SILKY
LIKEN	IDLED	GULCH	POLYP	CALIX	SILLY
OAKEN	OGLED	MILCH	SALEP	CALYX	SPLAY
TAKEN	OILED	MULCH	TULIP.	CULEX	SULKY
TOKEN	PALED	PILCH	BALER	+FELIX	SULLY
WAKEN	PILED	+RALPH	FILAR	HELIX	TALLY
WOKEN	POLED	SELAH	FILER	PHLOX	TELLY
*YUKON.	PULED	SYLPH	IDLER	RELAX	YOLKY.
*TOKYO.	RILED	TILTH	MILER	SALIX	WALTZ
BAKER	RULED	WELCH	MOLAR	SILEX	
*DAKAR	SALAD	WELSH.	PALER	TELEX.	COMMA
FAKER	SOLED	DALAI	POLAR	ALLAY	GAMMA
FAKIR	SOLID	*DELHI	RULER	ALLEY	GEMMA
HIKER	TILED	MULTI	SOLAR	ALLOY	GUMMA
JOKER	VALID	SALMI	+TYLER	BALMY	LAMIA
MAKER	VOLED	VILLI.	VELAR	BELAY	MAMBA
POKER	WILED.	KULAK.	VILER.	BELLY	MAMMA
SAKER	BELIE	HILUM	*ATLAS	BILLY	RUMBA
TAKER.	BELLE	ISLAM	BALAS	BULKY	SAMBA
ASKEW.	BILGE	VELUM	BOLAS	BULLY	*SAMOA
COKEY	BULGE	XYLEM.	BOLUS	DALLY	*TAMPA.
LAKEY	CALVE	ALL-IN	*DELOS	DELAY	DEMOB.
TOKAY	+CHLOE	+COLIN	+DILYS	DOLLY	COMIC
	*COLNE	COLON	+ELLIS	DULLY	MIMIC
*ALLOA	DELVE	+DYLAN	+GILES	FELLY	OGMIC
BALSA	DOLCE	+ELLEN	GULES	FILLY	OHMIC.
+CELIA	DULSE	FELON	+MILES	FILMY	AIMED
CILIA	FALSE	+HELEN	TALUS	FOLLY	ARMED
COLZA	HALVE	MELON.	*WALES	FULLY	DOMED
DELTA	+HELLE	*MILAN	+WELLS.	GOLLY	FAMED
HALMA	HELVE	NYLON	AGLET	GULLY	FUMED
+HELGA	+JULIE	PYLON	ALLOT	HILLY	GAMED
+HILDA	KYLOE	SALON	*DELFT	HOLEY	HOMED
*MALTA	*LILLE	TALON	ECLAT	HOLLY	HUMID
*PALMA	+MILNE	UHLAN.	FILET	INLAY	LAMED
POLKA	PULSE	BILBO	HELOT	*ISLAY	LIMED
VILLA	RILLE	CELLO	+HOLST	JELLY	MIMED
*VOLGA	SALSE	DILDO	INLET	JOLLY	NAMED
*VOLTA	SALVE	FOLIO	ISLET	LOLLY	NOMAD
VULVA	SOLVE	HALLO	MULCT	MILKY	TAMED
WALLA.	TILDE	HELLO	OWLET	+MOLLY	TIMED
COLIC	TULLE	IGLOO	PILOT	PALLY	TIMID
HYLIC	VALUE	*KELSO	*SPLIT	PALMY	TUMID.
LILAC	VALVE	*MALMO	VALET	PALSY	BOMBE
RELIC	VOLTE	POLIO	VELDT	+POLLY	*SOMME.
SALIC.	+WILDE.	SALVO.	VOLET.	PULPY	BUMPH

HUMPH	HAMES	MANIA	+DONNE	WENCH	DINER
LYMPH	HUMUS	MANNA	OUNCE	WINCH.	DONOR
NYMPH	+JAMES	NANNA	+ERNIE	ENNUI	FINER
OOMPH.	KUMIS	PANDA	FENCE	FUNGI	GONER
ZOMBI.	MUMPS	PINNA	GENIE	*HANOI	INNER
CAMEL	*NIMES	SANTA	GENRE	HINDI	LINER
TAMIL.	+REMUS	SENNA	HANSE	*MENAI	LONER
ADMAN	TAMIS.	+SONIA	HENCE	*SINAI.	LUNAR
*AMMAN	ADMIT	+TANYA	HINGE	LUNIK	MANOR
+AMMON	COMET	*TONGA	+LANCE	*MINSK.	MINER
CUMIN	GAMUT	+WANDA	LUNGE	ANNAL	MINOR
DEMON	LIMIT	XENIA.	MANGE	ANNUL	OWNER
+EAMON	REMIT	CONIC	MANSE	BANAL	SANER
GAMIN	TEMPT	CYNIC	MINCE	CANAL	SENOR
HE-MAN	VOMIT.	GENIC	NONCE	FINAL	SONAR
HUMAN	*CYMRU.	IONIC	OUNCE	PANEL	TENOR
HYMEN	ADMIX.	MANIC	PANNE	PENAL	TUNER
LEMON	BUMPY	PANIC	PENCE	RENAL	ULNAR.
LUMEN	COMFY	RUNIC	PONCE	TONAL	+AGNES
ROMAN	DIMLY	SONIC	RANCE	VENAL	BANNS
SEMEN	DUMMY	TONIC	RANEE	VINYL	BENDS
+SIMON	DUMPY	TUNIC	RANGE	ZONAL.	BONUS
UNMAN	GAMMY	VINIC.	RINSE	DENIM	+DENIS
WOMAN	GEMMY	AWNED	SENSE	MINIM	FINIS
WOMEN	GUMMY	BONED	SINCE	VENOM.	GENUS
*YEMEN.	HAMMY	CANED	SINGE	CANON	+JANUS
BUMBO	HOMEY	DINED	TENSE	FANON	LINKS
CAMEO	HUMPY	GONAD	TINGE	+LENIN	MANES
COMPO	JAMMY	HONED	TONNE	LINEN	+MINOS
GUMBO	JEMMY	LINED	VENUE	+SINON	MINUS
JUMBO	+JIMMY	MINED	WINCE.	TENON	NONES
LIMBO	JUMPY	MONAD	*BANFF.	XENON.	PANTS
SAMBO	LIMEY	OWNED	BENCH	BANJO	PENIS
TEMPO.	LUMPY	PANED	BUNCH	BINGO	SINUS
CYMAR	MUMMY	PINED	CINCH	BONGO	TONGS
DEMUR	POMMY	SYNOD	CONCH	BUNCO	TONUS
DIMER	RUMLY	TONED	+DINAH	CANTO	*TUNIS
+ELMER	RUMMY	TUNED	FINCH	*CONGO	+VENUS.
FEMUR	TAMMY	WANED	HUNCH	DINGO	+GENET
+HOMER	+TOMMY	WINED	+JONAH	JINGO	+JANET
*IZMIR	TUMMY	ZONED.	LUNCH	JUNTO	+MANET
LEMUR		BINGE	LYNCH	LINGO	+MONET
ORMER	*CANNA	BONZE	MONTH	MANGO	TENET
TAMER	CONGA	CANOE	+MUNCH	PANTO	TINCT.
TIMER	+DONNA	CENSE	NINTH	RONDO	HINDU.
*TIMOR.	*GENOA	CONGE	PINCH	TANGO.	RENEW
+CAMUS	HENNA	DANCE	PUNCH	PIN-UP	SINEW.
+COMUS	JUNTA	+DANTE	RANCH	SUN-UP.	ANNEX.
DEMOS	*KENYA	DENSE	TENCH	+ABNER	ANNOY
+DUMAS	+LINDA	DONEE	TENTH	DINAR	BANDY

+BENNY	TANSY	ADOBE	*POOLE	+ENOCH	*SEOUL
BONNY	*TENBY	ADORE	PROBE	EPOCH	SHOAL
BUNNY	TINNY	AFORE	PROLE	FROTH	SPOIL
CANDY	TUNNY	ALONE	PRONE	HOOCH	SPOOL
CANNY	WANLY	ANODE	PROSE	MOOCH	STOOL
DANDY	+WENDY	AROSE	PROVE	POOCH	TROLL
+DANNY	WINDY	ATONE	QUOTE	QUOTH	WHORL.
DINGY		AWOKE	*RHONE	SLOSH	BLOOM
DINKY	AGORA	AZOTE	*SAONE	SLOTH	BROOM
DUNGY	ANONA	BLOKE	SCONE	SOOTH	GLOOM
FANCY	AROMA	BOOZE	SCOPE	TOOTH	GROOM
+FANNY	+FIONA	BROKE	SCORE	TROTH	PROEM
FENNY	+FLORA	BROSE	SHONE	WROTH.	STORM.
FINNY	QUOTA	CHOKE	SHORE	DHOBI	ACORN
FUNKY	+RHODA	CHORE	SHOVE	DHOTI	ADORN
FUNNY	STOMA	CHOSE	SLOPE	MAORI	BLOWN
GUNNY	+VIOLA.	CLONE	SMOKE	+NAOMI.	BROWN
HANDY	A-BOMB	CLOSE	SMOTE	BLOCK	CLOWN
HANKY	COOMB	CLOVE	SNORE	BROCK	CROON
+HENRY	H-BOMB	CRONE	SPODE	BROOK	CROWN
HINNY	RHOMB.	CRORE	SPOKE	CHOCK	DROWN
HONEY	AZOIC	DHOLE	SPORE	CLOAK	FLOWN
HONKY	STOIC	DIODE	STOKE	CLOCK	FROWN
+JENNY	TRONC.	DROME	STOLE	CROAK	GROAN
JUNKY	ALOUD	DRONE	STONE	CROCK	GROIN
*KANDY	AVOID	DROVE	STORE	CROOK	GROWN
KINKY	BLOND	ELOPE	STOVE	FLOCK	KNOWN
LANKY	BLOOD	EMOTE	SWORE	FROCK	QUOIN
+LENNY	BROAD	EPODE	THOLE	GROOK	SCORN
*LUNDY	BROOD	ERODE	THOSE	KIOSK	SHORN
MANGY	CHORD	EVOKE	TROPE	KNOCK	SHOWN
MANLY	CLOUD	*FROME	WHOLE	PLONK	SPOON
MINGY	COOED	FROZE	WHORE	SHOCK	SWOON
MONEY	CROWD	GLOBE	WHOSE	SHOOK	SWORN
+NANCY	FIORD	GLOVE	WROTE.	SMOCK	THORN.
NANNY	FJORD	GLOZE	ALOOF	SNOOK	*KYOTO
NINNY	FLOOD	GNOME	+GEOFF	SPOOK	PHONO
PANSY	FROND	*GOOLE	PROOF	STOCK	PHOTO
+PENNY	HYOID	GOOSE	SCOFF	STOOK	WHOSO.
PINKY	+LLOYD	GROPE	SPOOF	STORK.	CROUP
PINNY	MOOED	GROVE	+WOOLF.	ABOIL	DROOP
PUNTY	OVOID	HOOVE	ALONG	ATOLL	GROUP
RANDY	PROUD	KRONE	AMONG	BROIL	SCOOP
RANGY	SCOLD	LOOSE	FLONG	DROLL	SLOOP
RUNNY	SNOOD	+MOORE	PRONG	DROOL	SNOOP
+SANDY	STOOD	MOOSE	THONG	GHOUL	STOOP
SONNY	SWORD	+NIOBE	WRONG.	GROWL	STOUP
SONSY	ZOOID.	NOOSE	+BOOTH	KNOLL	SWOOP
SUNNY	ABODE	OZONE	BROTH	PROWL	THORP
TANGY	ABOVE	PHONE	CLOTH	SCOWL	TROOP

70

WHOOP.	SPORT	BIPED	*JAPAN	POPPY	CORED
AMOUR	SPOUT	COPED	JUPON	POPSY	CURED
CHOIR	STOAT	+CUPID	LUPIN	PUPPY	DARED
FLOOR	STOUT	DOPED	ORPIN	REPAY	ERRED
FLOUR	TROUT	DUPED	RIPEN	REPLY	FARAD
ODOUR	U-BOAT.	GAPED	*RIPON	ROPEY	FARED
SCOUR	SIOUX.	HOPED	UNPEN	SAPPY	FIRED
SPOOR	AGONY	IMPED	UNPIN	SEPOY	GORED
*STOUR	ANOMY	JAPED	YAPON.	SOPPY	HARED
WOOER.	BOOBY	LIPID	HIPPO.	TIPSY	+HEROD
CROSS	BOOTY	LOPED	CAPER	ZIPPY.	HIRED
DROSS	BOOZY	MOPED	COPER	TOPAZ	LURED
FLOSS	CHOKY	PIPED	HYPER		LURID
GLOSS	CRONY	RAPED	LEPER	PIQUE	MIRED
GROSS	EBONY	RAPID	PAPER	TOQUE	OARED
*LYONS	EPOXY	ROPED	PIPER		PARED
PIOUS	GLORY	SAPID	RIPER	AORTA	PORED
PROPS	GOODY	TAPED	SUPER	*BARRA	SHRED
SCOBS	GOOEY	TEPID	TAPER	+BERIA	SIRED
SCOTS.	GOOFY	TYPED	TAPIR	*BURMA	TIRED
ABORT	HOOEY	VAPID	TOPER	CIRCA	WIRED
ABOUT	IRONY	WIPED.	UPPER	CURIA	WORLD.
ADOPT	IVORY	AMPLE	VIPER	DERMA	AERIE
AFOOT	KOOKY	APPLE	WIPER.	FERIA	AGREE
ALOFT	LOONY	COPSE	DIPUS	KARMA	BARGE
BLOAT	LOOPY	DUPLE	LAPIS	*KOREA	*BERNE
BOOST	MOODY	KOPJE	LUPUS	LARVA	BORNE
CLOUT	MOONY	LAPSE	*PEPYS	+LORNA	BURKE
CO-OPT	PEONY	MAPLE	TAPIS.	+MARIA	CARTE
CROFT	PHONY	RUPEE	DEPOT	+MYRNA	CARVE
DROIT	PROSY	TEPEE	IMPOT	+NORMA	+CIRCE
FLOAT	PROXY	TOPEE.	INPUT	STRIA	*CORFE
FLOUT	ROOKY	UNPEG.	KAPUT	*SYRIA	CURIE
FRONT	ROOMY	DEPTH.	PIPIT	TERRA.	CURSE
+FROST	SHOWY	APPUI	REPOT.	CARIB	CURVE
GHOST	SMOKY	*CAPRI.	PAPAW.	CAROB	DIRGE
GLOAT	SNOWY	KAPOK.	AMPLY	SCRUB	EERIE
GROAT	SOOTY	APPAL	APPLY	SHRUB	EYRIE
GROUT	STONY	COPAL	DOPEY	THROB.	FARCE
KNOUT	STORY	EXPEL	EMPTY	AURIC	FORCE
QUOIT	WOODY	IMPEL	GIPSY	BORIC	FORGE
ROOST		LAPEL	GUPPY	DORIC	FORME
SCOOT	ALPHA	*NEPAL	GYPSY	LYRIC	FORTE
+SCOTT	COPRA	NOPAL	HAPLY	RORIC	FURZE
SCOUT	KAPPA	PAPAL	HAPPY	SERAC	GORGE
SHOOT	*PAPUA	PUPIL	HIPPY	VAREC.	GORSE
SHORT	SEPIA.	REPEL	IMPLY	ACRID	+HORAE
SHOUT	ASPIC	SEPAL.	NAPPY	AIRED	HORDE
SNORT	KOPEC	ASPEN	NIPPY	BARED	HORSE
SNOUT	TOPIC.	CAPON	PEPPY	BORED	KYRIE

71

LARGE	MARSH	BORON	+CYRUS	CARRY	SARKY
MARGE	MIRTH	BURIN	+DORIS	*CORBY	SORRY
*MARNE	MYRRH	+BYRON	+HORUS	CORKY	SPRAY
MERGE	NORTH	HERON	LARES	CORNY	STRAY
+MERLE	PARCH	*HURON	LORIS	CURDY	SURLY
MORSE	PERCH	+KAREN	MORES	CURLY	TARDY
NERVE	*PERTH	KORAN	NARES	CURRY	TARRY
NORSE	PORCH	MORON	ORRIS	DARKY	TARTY
NURSE	TORAH	+PERON	*PARIS	*DERBY	+TERRY
?ARSE	TORCH	SIREN	*SYROS	DIRTY	TURFY
PERNE	WORTH.	TORAN	TORUS	DORMY	WARTY
PERSE	CORGI	*TURIN.	TURPS	EARLY	WORDY
PORGE	SERAI	BURRO	VIRUS	FARCY	WORMY
PUREE	+VERDI.	CARGO	*YPRES.	FERNY	WORRY.
PURGE	+DEREK.	CURIO	BERET	FERRY	HERTZ
PURSE	+APRIL	FORGO	BURNT	FIRRY	
SCREE	AURAL	+GARBO	BURST	FORAY	*BASRA
SERGE	+AVRIL	KAROO	CARAT	FORBY	FOSSA
SERVE	+BERYL	LARGO	CARET	FORTY	PASHA
SPREE	+CAROL	*MARGO	*COROT	FURRY	PASTA
SURGE	CORAL	TARDO	DURST	FURZY	+VESTA
TERSE	+CYRIL	TORSO	EGRET	GORSY	VISTA.
THREE	ENROL	TURBO	FIRST	+HARDY	BASIC
THROE	+ERROL	VERSO	HURST	HARPY	CUSEC
*TIREE	FERAL	VIRGO.	MERIT	+HARRY	MUSIC.
VERGE	FOREL	SCRAP	SPRAT	HORNY	BASED
+VERNE	GYRAL	SCRIP	SPRIT	HORSY	CASED
VERSE	HORAL	STRAP	STRUT	HURRY	DOSED
VERVE	MORAL	STRIP	TAROT	JERKY	EASED
WORSE.	MOREL	STROP	VERST	+JERRY	FUSED
SERIF.	MURAL	SYRUP	WORST.	*KERRY	HOSED
+MORAG	PERIL	UNRIP.	*CORFU	LARDY	MUSED
SCRAG	RORAL	AIRER	PERDU	LARKY	NOSED
SHRUG	RURAL	BORER	VIRTU.	+LARRY	POSED.
SPRAG	*TYROL	CORER	ARROW	LORRY	AISLE
SPRIG	ZORIL.	CURER	SCREW	MARRY	BASTE
UNRIG.	FORUM	+DURER	SHREW	MERCY	CASTE
BERTH	HAREM	ERROR	STRAW	MERRY	+ELSIE
BIRCH	JORUM	HIRER	STREW	*MORAY	ENSUE
BIRTH	SCRAM	JUROR	THREW	MURKY	FESSE
BURGH	SCRIM	PURER	THROW.	NARKY	FOSSE
EARTH	SCRUM	RARER	BORAX	NERVY	FUSEE
FIRTH	SERUM	SORER	HYRAX	PARKY	HASTE
*FORTH	STRUM	SURER.	MUREX	PARRY	+HESSE
+GARTH	THRUM.	*ARRAS	VARIX.	PARTY	ISSUE
GIRTH	+AARON	ARRIS	ARRAY	+PERCY	+JESSE
HARSH	*AKRON	+BURNS	BARMY	PERKY	LISLE
LARCH	APRON	+CERES	+BARRY	+PERRY	MESNE
LURCH	*ARRAN	+CHRIS	BERRY	PORKY	PASSE
MARCH	BARON	CORPS	BURLY	PURSY	PASTE

72

POSSE	+MOSES	RUSTY	METRE	BATON	+PETER
TASTE	OASES	SISSY	MITRE	CETIN	*QATAR
WASTE.	OASIS.	TASTY	NITRE	EATEN	ROTOR
+BOSCH.	ASSET	TESTY	OUTRE	JETON	SATYR
ASSAI.	BESET	UNSAY	TITHE	LATIN	TUTOR
BASAL	HASNT	WASHY	TITLE	*LUTON	UTTER
+BASIL	INSET	WISPY	UNTIE	OATEN	VOTER
EASEL	+LISZT		WITHE.	OFTEN	WATER.
FUSEL	ONSET	COTTA	MOTIF.	PATEN	BITTS
LYSOL	POSIT	EXTRA	BATCH	SATAN	CATES
NASAL	RESET	*PATNA	BITCH	SATIN	CUTIS
OUSEL	UPSET	ULTRA.	BOTCH	SIT-IN	FETUS
SISAL	VISIT	ANTIC	BUTCH	TITAN.	ICTUS
VASAL.	WASNT.	ARTIC	CATCH	DITTO	LOTUS
*ASSAM	*ESSEX	ATTIC	DITCH	LOTTO	MATHS
BESOM	UNSEX.	AZTEC	DUTCH	METRO	METHS.
BOSOM	ASSAY	CETIC	FETCH	MOTTO	MOTET
*EPSOM.	BOSKY	OPTIC	FITCH	OUTDO	OCTET
ARSON	BOSSY	VATIC.	HATCH	OUTGO	PITOT.
BASIN	BUSBY	ACTED	HITCH	PATIO	LATEX.
BASON	BUSHY	BATED	HUTCH	POTTO	APTLY
BISON	CISSY	CITED	KETCH	PUTTO	BATTY
BOSON	CUSHY	DATED	LATCH	RATIO	+BETSY
*ESSEN	DISHY	DOTED	MATCH	SET-TO	+BETTY
HYSON	DUSKY	FATED	NOTCH	SOTTO.	BOTHY
+IBSEN	DUSTY	FETED	PATCH	GET-UP	+CATHY
+JASON	ESSAY	FETID	PITCH	SET-UP.	CATTY
MASON	FISHY	GATED	RATCH	ACTOR	CUTTY
MESON	FUSSY	HATED	RETCH	AFTER	DITTY
+ORSON	FUSTY	LUTED	VETCH	ALTAR	DOTTY
RESIN	GASSY	MATED	WATCH	ALTER	ENTRY
RISEN	GUSTY	METED	WITCH.	ASTER	FATTY
ROSIN	HASTY	MUTED	+MITZI.	ASTIR	FITLY
+SUSAN.	HUSKY	NOTED	BATIK.	ATTAR	HOTLY
GESSO	HUSSY	OCTAD	BETEL	CATER	JETTY
GUSTO	LUSTY	OPTED	DATAL	DETER	+KITTY
LASSO.	MASSY	RATED	EXTOL	DOTER	NATTY
+AESOP.	MESSY	SATED	FATAL	EATER	NUTTY
LASER	MISTY	SITED	HOTEL	ENTER	+PATTY
LOSER	MOSSY	TOTED	METAL	ESTER	PETTY
MASER	MUSHY	VOTED.	METOL	FETOR	PITHY
MISER	MUSKY	BATHE	MOTEL	HATER	POTTY
POSER	MUSTY	BUTTE	*NATAL	INTER	PUTTY
RISER	NASTY	CUTIE	PETAL	LATER	RATTY
VISOR	NOSEY	*HYTHE	RATAL	MATER	RETRY
WISER.	PASTY	ISTLE	TOTAL	METER	RITZY
APSIS	PESKY	LATHE	UNTIL	MOTOR	RUTTY
ARSIS	PUSSY	LETHE	VITAL.	OTTER	TATTY
BASIS	RISKY	LITHE	DATUM	OUTER	TUTTY
+JESUS	RUSHY	LITRE	TOTEM.	PATER	WETLY

73

WITHY	DOUSE	WRUNG	EQUAL	DOUBT	HIVED
WITTY	DRUPE	YOUNG.	GRUEL	ERUCT	JIVED
	EDUCE	BLUSH	KNURL	ERUPT	LIVED
*CEUTA	ELUDE	BOUGH	SCULL	EXULT	LIVID
FAUNA	EXUDE	BRUSH	SKULL	FAULT	LOVED
*GOUDA	*FIUME	COUCH	TRULL	►FAUST	MOVED
►LAURA	FLUKE	COUGH	USUAL	FOUNT	RAVED
►PAULA	FLUME	COUTH	YOULL.	FRUIT	RIVED
SAUNA	FLUTE	CRUSH	HAULM.	GAULT	ROVED
►SOUSA	GAUGE	DOUGH	BOURN	GAUNT	SAVED
UVULA.	GAUZE	FLUSH	BRUIN	GRUNT	VIVID
BLURB	GOUGE	HOUGH	CHURN	HAUNT	WAVED
CRUMB	HOUSE	LAUGH	INURN	JAUNT	WIVED.
PLUMB	INURE	LOUGH	MOURN	JOUST	LEVEE
RHUMB	JOULE	MOUTH	SPURN.	MOULT	MOVIE
SQUAB	LOUSE	PLUSH	*DOURO	MOUNT	REVUE.
SQUIB	►MAUDE	POUCH	►PLUTO	POULT	ANVIL
THUMB.	MAUVE	ROUGH	*TRURO.	ROUST	BEVEL
BOUND	*MEUSE	SHUSH	CHUMP	SHUNT	CAVIL
CLUED	MOUSE	SLUSH	CLUMP	SPURT	CIVIL
COULD	NEUME	SOUGH	CRUMP	SQUAT	DEVIL
DRUID	OVULE	SOUTH	EQUIP	STUNT	GAVEL
FLUID	PAUSE	TOUCH	FLUMP	TAUNT	HOVEL
FOUND	PLUME	TOUGH	FRUMP	TRUST	KEVEL
GLUED	PRUDE	TRUTH	PLUMP	VAULT	LEVEL
GOURD	PRUNE	VOUCH	POULP	VAUNT.	NAVAL
HOUND	ROUGE	YOUTH.	SCULP	SQUAW.	NAVEL
MOULD	ROUSE	HOURI.	SLUMP	FLUKY	NOVEL
MOUND	ROUTE	AMUCK	STUMP	FLUTY	RAVEL
►POUND	SAUCE	BAULK	THUMP	GAUDY	REVEL
ROUND	SAUTE	CAULK	TRUMP	GAUZY	RIVAL.
SOUND	►SHUTE	CHUCK	USURP.	GLUEY	►BEVAN
SQUAD	SOUSE	CHUNK	FLUOR	GOUTY	*CAVAN
SQUID	SPUME	CLUCK	KNURR	LOUSY	COVEN
WOULD	STUPE	DRUNK	TRUER.	MOUSY	*DEVON
WOUND.	TRUCE	FLUNK	BLUES	PLUMY	DIVAN
ABUSE	YOURE	PLUCK	GAUSS	SAUCY	ELVAN
ACUTE	YOUVE.	PLUNK	►LOUIS	SOUPY	►GAVIN
AMUSE	BLUFF	SHUCK	TRUSS	SPUMY	GIVEN
AZURE	FLUFF	SKULK	YOURS.	STUDY	HAVEN
BOULE	GRUFF	SKUNK	ADULT	TRULY	►KEVIN
►BRUCE	SCUFF	SLUNK	BLUNT	USURY	LIVEN
BRUME	SCURF	SPUNK	BLURT		PAVAN
BRUTE	SNUFF	STUCK	BRUIT	FOVEA.	RAVEN
CAUSE	STUFF.	STUNK	BRUNT	CIVIC	RIVEN
CHUTE	CLUNG	TRUCK	COUNT	HAVOC.	ROVEN
COUPE	FLUNG	TRUNK.	COURT	CAVED	SEVEN
CRUDE	SLUNG	CHURL	CRUET	►DAVID	WOVEN.
CRUSE	STUNG	CRUEL	CRUST	DIVED	COVER
DEUCE	SWUNG		DAUNT	GYVED	DIVER

*DOVER	SAWED	NEWLY	PAYED		AREAL
ELVER	SEWED	NEWSY	RAYED	ANZAC.	ARIAN
FEVER	SOWED	NOWAY	TOYED.	DAZED	*ARRAN
FIVER	TAWED	PAWKY	AZYME	DOZED	*ARRAS
HAVER	TOWED	RAWLY	+BOYLE	GAZED	ARRAY
HOVER	UNWED	ROWDY	*CLYDE	HAZED	ARYAN
INVAR	VOWED	TAWNY	+DOYLE	LAZED	ASIAN
LAVER	YAWED.		+JOYCE	OOZED	ASSAI
LEVER	BOWIE	JUXTA.	MAYBE	RAZED	*ASSAM
LIVER	DOWSE	TOXIC.	PAYEE	SIZED	ASSAY
LOVER	HAWSE	BOXED	PHYLE	MUZAK.	*ASWAN
MOVER	TAWSE.	FIXED	RHYME	BEZEL	*ATLAS
NEVER	DOWEL	FOXED	SLYPE	+HAZEL	ATTAR
RIVER	JEWEL	HEXAD	STYLE	OUZEL.	AURAL
ROVER	NEWEL	MIXED	THYME.	COZEN	AVIAN
SAVER	ROWEL	PYXED	*BLYTH	DOZEN	AXIAL.
SEVER	TOWEL	SEXED	GLYPH.	MIZEN	BALAS
WAVER.	VOWEL.	TAXED	KAYAK.	WIZEN	BANAL
EAVES	*ASWAN	VEXED	GHYLL	MEZZO.	BASAL
ELVES	+EDWIN	WAXED.	IDYLL	UNZIP.	BEGAD
FAVUS	GOWAN	DIXIE	LOYAL	DOZER	BEGAN
FIVES	ROWAN.	NIXIE	ROYAL.	LAZAR	+BEHAN
HIVES	BOWER	PIXIE.	GOYIM.	MAZER	BELAY
LIVES	COWER	SIXTH.	ARYAN	RAZOR	+BEVAN
+MAVIS	DOWER	BUXOM	DOYEN	SIZAR.	BLEAK
*NEVIS	FEWER	MAXIM.	+HAYDN	+BIZET.	BLEAR
WIVES.	*GOWER	+NIXON	RAYON	DIZZY	BLEAT
CIVET	HEWER	SAXON	TRY-ON.	FIZZY	BLOAT
COVET	LOWER	TAXIN	SAY-SO.	FUZZY	BOLAS
DAVIT	MOWER	TOXIN	BUYER	JAZZY	BORAX
DIVOT	NEWER	VIXEN	DRYER	MUZZY	BREAD
PIVOT	POWER	WAXEN.	FLYER	TIZZY	BREAK
REVET	ROWER	SEXTO.	FOYER		BREAM
RIVET.	SEWER	MIX-UP.	FRYER		+BRIAN
COVEY	SOWER	BOXER	LAYER	ABEAM	BRIAR
DIVVY	TOWER.	FIXER	MAYOR.	ADDAX	BROAD
ENVOY	BOWLS	MIXER.	ABYSS	ADMAN	BUBAL
NAVVY	*COWES	NEXUS	+NOYES.	AHEAD	BY-LAW
SAVOY	*LEWES	PYXIS	CRYPT	ALGAE	BY-WAY.
SAVVY	*LEWIS.	TAXIS	MAYNT	ALGAL	CABAL
	PEWIT.	*TEXAS.	MAYST	ALIAS	CACAO
COWED	BAWDY	LAXLY	TRYST.	ALLAH	CANAL
HAWED	BY-WAY	SIXTY	BAYOU	ALLAY	CARAT
HEWED	DOWDY		COYPU.	ALTAR	*CAVAN
JAWED	DOWNY	PHYLA.	COYLY	*AMMAN	CEDAR
LOWED	DOWRY	BAYED	DRYLY	ANNAL	CHEAP
MEWED	GAWKY	DRYAD	LAYBY	ANZAC	CHEAT
MOWED	HOWDY	GUYED	SHYLY	APEAK	CHIAN
PAWED	JEWRY	HAYED	SLYLY	APIAN	CIGAR
ROWED	LOWLY	KEYED	WRYLY	APPAL	CLEAN

75

CLEAR	FUGAL.	*MENAI	REGAL	STRAW	BILBO
CLEAT	GLEAM	METAL	RELAX	STRAY	+BOBBY
CLOAK	GLEAN	+MIDAS	RELAY	*SUDAN	BOMBE
COPAL	GLOAT	*MILAN	RENAL	SUGAR	BOOBY
CORAL	GONAD	MODAL	REPAY	SUSAN	+SUSAN → BRIBE
CREAK	GOWAN	MOLAR	RIVAL	SWEAR	BUMBO
CREAM	GREAT	MONAD	ROMAN	SWEAT.	BUSBY.
CROAK	GROAN	+MORAG	RORAL	*TEXAS	CABBY
CYMAR.	GROAT	MORAL	ROWAN	TIDAL	*CORBY
*DAKAR	GYRAL.	*MORAY	ROYAL	TITAN	CUBBY
DALAI	HE-MAN	MURAL	RURAL.	TODAY	*DERBY
DATAL	HEXAD	MUZAK.	+SAGAN	TOKAY	DHOBI
DEBAG	+HORAE	NAIAD	SALAD	TONAL	DOUBT.
DEBAR	HORAL	NASAL	SATAN	TOPAZ	FORBY.
DECAL	HUMAN	*NATAL	SCRAG	TORAH	+GARBO
DECAY	HYRAX.	NAVAL	SCRAM	TORAN	GLEBE
+DEGAS	IDEAL	*NEPAL	SCRAP	TOTAL	GLOBE
DELAY	ILIAC	NODAL	SEDAN	TREAD	GREBE
+DINAH	ILIAD	NOMAD	SELAH	TREAT	GUMBO.
DINAR	IN-LAW	NOPAL	SEPAL	TRIAD	HOBBY
DIVAN	INLAY	NOWAY.	SERAC	TRIAL	HUBBY.
DREAD	INVAR	OBEAH	SERAI	TUBAL	JUMBO.
DREAM	+ISAAC	OCEAN	SHEAF	TWEAK.	LAYBY
DREAR	ISLAM	OCTAD	SHEAR	U-BOAT	+LIBBY
DRYAD	*ISLAY.	OFFAL	SHOAL	UHLAN	LIMBO
*DUBAI	JALAP	OGHAM	*SINAI	ULNAR	LOBBY.
DUCAL	*JAPAN	ORGAN	SISAL	UMIAK	MAMBA
DUCAT	JIHAD	+OSCAR.	SIZAR	UNBAR	MAYBE.
+DUMAS	+JONAH	+PAEAN	*SLEAT	UNCAP	+NIOBE.
+DYLAN.	+JUDAS	PAGAN	SMEAR	UNIAT	PROBE.
ECLAT	JUGAL.	PAPAL	SNEAK	UNMAN	RABBI
+EDGAR	KAYAK	PAPAW	SOLAR	UNSAY	*RUGBY
*EGHAM	KNEAD	PAVAN	SONAR	URBAN	RUMBA.
+ELGAR	KORAN	PECAN	SPEAK	USUAL.	SAMBA
ELVAN	KRAAL	PEDAL	SPEAR	VASAL	SAMBO
EMBAY	KULAK.	PENAL	SPLAY	VELAR	SCOBS.
EQUAL	LAGAN	PETAL	SPRAG	VENAL	TABBY
ESSAY	LAHAR	PHIAL	SPRAT	VICAR	*TENBY
EXEAT.	LAZAR	PLEAD	SPRAY	+VIDAL	TRIBE
FARAD	LEGAL	PLEAT	SQUAB	VITAL	TUBBY
FATAL	LILAC	POLAR	SQUAD	VOCAL.	TURBO.
FERAL	LOBAR	+PRIAM	SQUAT	WHEAT	ZOMBI
FILAR	LOCAL	PYGAL.	SQUAW	*WIGAN	
FINAL	LOGAN	*QATAR	STEAD	WOMAN	ABACK
FLEAM	LOYAL	QUEAN.	STEAK	WREAK.	ALACK
FLOAT	LUNAR.	*RABAT	STEAL	ZONAL	+ALICE
FOCAL	*MACAO	RADAR	STEAM		AMICE
FORAY	MACAW	RAJAH	STEAN	ADOBE	AMUCK
FREAK	MADAM	RATAL	STOAT	ALIBI	APACE.
FRIAR	MEDAL	RECAP	STRAP	*AQABA.	BATCH

76

BEACH	+ENOCH	MINCE	SMACK	BANDY	LEADY
BEECH	EPACT	MOOCH	SMOCK	BAWDY	*LEEDS
BELCH	EPOCH	MULCH	SNACK	BEADY	+LINDA
BENCH	ERECT	MULCT	SNICK	BENDS	+LUNDY
BIRCH	+ERICA	+MUNCH.	SPACE	BLADE	+MAUDE
BITCH	ERUCT	+NANCY	SPECK	BRIDE	MOODY
BLACK	EVICT	NIECE	SPECS	BUDDY.	MUDDY.
BLOCK	EXACT.	NONCE	SPICE	CADDY	NEEDY.
+BOSCH	FANCY	NOTCH.	SPICY	CANDY	OUTDO
BOTCH	FARCE	OUNCE.	STACK	CHIDE	OXIDE.
BRACE	FARCY	PARCH	STICH	*CLYDE	+PADDY
BRACT	FENCE	PATCH	STICK	CREDO	PANDA
BRICK	FETCH	PEACE	STOCK	CRUDE	PERDU
BROCK	FILCH	PEACH	STUCK.	CUDDY	PRIDE
+BRUCE	FINCH	PENCE	TEACH	CURDY.	PRUDE.
BUNCH	FITCH	PERCH	TENCH	DADDY	RANDY
BUNCO	FLECK	+PERCY	THECA	DANDY	READY
BUTCH.	FLICK	PIECE	THICK	DILDO	REEDY
CATCH	FLOCK	PILCH	TINCT	DIODE	+RHODA
CHECK	FORCE	PINCH	TORCH	DOWDY.	RONDO
CHICK	FROCK.	PITCH	TOUCH	ELIDE	ROWDY
CHOCK	GLACE	PLACE	TRACE	ELUDE	RUDDY.
CHUCK	+GRACE	PLUCK	TRACK	EPODE	+SANDY
CINCH	GULCH.	POACH	TRACT	ERODE	SEEDY
CIRCA	HATCH	PONCE	+TRACY	EVADE	SHADE
+CIRCE	HENCE	POOCH	TRICE	EXUDE.	SHADY
CLACK	HITCH	PORCH	TRICK	FADDY	SLIDE
CLICK	HOICK	POUCH	TRUCE	+FREDA.	SNIDE
CLOCK	HOOCH	PRICE	TRUCK	GAUDY	SPADE
CLUCK	HUNCH	PRICK	TWICE.	GIDDY	SPODE
COACH	HUTCH.	PUNCH.	VETCH	GLADE	STUDY
COCCI	+JOYCE	QUACK	VOICE	GLIDE	SUEDE
CONCH	JUICE	QUICK.	VOUCH.	GOODY	SWEDE.
COUCH	JUICY.	RANCE	WATCH	*GOUDA	TARDO
CRACK	KETCH	RANCH	WELCH	GRADE	TARDY
CRICK	KNACK	RATCH	WENCH	GRIDE	+TEDDY
CROCK.	KNOCK.	REACH	WHACK	GUIDE.	TILDE
*DACCA	+LANCE	REACT	WHICH	HANDY	TOADY
DANCE	LARCH	REICH	WINCE	+HARDY	TODDY
DE-ICE	LATCH	RETCH	WINCH	+HAYDN	TRADE.
DEUCE	LEACH	ROACH.	WITCH	HEADY	VELDT
DITCH	LEECH	SAUCE	WRACK	+HILDA	+VERDI.
DOLCE	LUNCH	SAUCY	WRECK	HINDI	WADDY
DUNCE	LURCH	SHACK	WRICK.	HINDU	+WANDA
DUTCH.	LYNCH.	SHOCK	YUCCA	HORDE	WEEDY
EDICT	MARCH	SHUCK		HOWDY.	+WENDY
EDUCE	MATCH	SINCE	ABIDE	*KANDY	+WILDE
EJECT	*MECCA	SLACK	ABODE	KIDDY.	WINDY
ELECT	MERCY	SLICE	ANODE	LADDY	WOODY
ENACT	MILCH	SLICK	ASIDE.	LARDY	WORDY

77

ABBEY	BEDEW	CLUED	DOTED	FARED	GRIEF
+ABNER	BEGET	CODED	DOTER	FATED	GRUEL
ACHED	BERET	CODEX	*DOVER	FETED	GULES
ACTED	BESET	COKEY	DOWEL	FEVER	GUYED
ADDED	BETEL	COMET	DOWER	FEWER	GYBED
ADDER	BEVEL	COOED	DOYEN	FIFER	GYVED.
ADEEM	BEZEL	COPED	DOZED	FILER	HADES
ADIEU	BIDED	COPER	DOZEN	FILET	HALED
AFTER	BIDET	CORED	DOZER	FINER	HAMES
AGGER	BIPED	CORER	DRIED	FIRED	HARED
AGLET	+BIZET	COVEN	DRIER	FIVER	HAREM
+AGNES	BLEED	COVER	DRYER	FIVES	HATED
AGREE	BLEEP	COVET	DUPED	FIXED	HATER
AIDED	BLUES	COVEY	EAGER	FIXER	HAVEN
AIMED	BODED	COWED	EASED	FLEER	HAVER
AIRED	BOGEY	COWER	EASEL	FLEET	HAWED
AIRER	BOHEA	*COWES	EATEN	FLIES	HAYED
ALDER	BONED	COZEN	EATER	FLYER	HAZED
ALIEN	BORED	CREED	EAVES	FOGEY	+HAZEL
ALLEY	BORER	CREEK	EBBED	FOREL	+HELEN
ALTER	BOWER	CREEL	EDGED	FOVEA	HEWED
AMBER	BOXED	CREEP	EGGER	FOXED	HEWER
AMEER	BOXER	CRIED	EGRET	FOYER	HIKER
*ANDES	BREED	CRIER	EIDER	FREED	HIRED
ANGEL	BRIEF	CRUEL	ELDER	FRYER	HIRER
ANGER	BUYER.	CRUET	+ELLEN	FUMED	HIVED
ANNEX	CABER	CUBEB	+ELMER	FUSED	HIVES
ARCED	CADET	CUBED	ELVER	FUSEE	HOLED
ARIEL	CAGED	CULEX	ELVES	FUSEL.	HOLEY
ARIES	CAGEY	CURED	EMBED	GAMED	HOMED
ARMED	CAKED	CURER	EMBER	GAPED	+HOMER
ASHEN	CAMEL	CUSEC.	ENDED	GATED	HOMEY
ASKED	CAMEO	DARED	ENTER	GAVEL	HONED
ASKEW	CANED	DATED	ERRED	GAZED	HONEY
ASPEN	CAPER	DAZED	*ESHER	+GENET	HOOEY
ASSET	CARET	DEFER	*ESSEN	GIBED	HOPED
ASTER	CASED	+DEREK	*ESSEX	+GILES	HOSED
+AUDEN	CATER	DETER	ESTER	GIVEN	HOTEL
AUGER	CATES	DICED	+ETHEL	GLEET	HOVEL
AWNED	CAVED	DICEY	ETHER	GLUED	HOVER
AZTEC.	CEDED	DIMER	EXCEL	GLUEY	HYMEN
BABEL	+CERES	DINED	EXPEL.	GOFER	HYPER.
BAKED	CHEEK	DINER	FACED	GONER	+IBSEN
BAKER	CHEEP	DIVED	FACER	GOOEY	IDLED
BALED	CHEER	DIVER	FACET	GORED	IDLER
BALER	CHIEF	DOMED	FADED	*GOWER	IMPED
BARED	CIDER	DONEE	FAKED	GREED	IMPEL
BASED	CITED	DOPED	FAKER	GREEK	INDEX
BATED	CIVET	DOPEY	FAMED	GREEN	INFER
BAYED	CLEEK	DOSED	FAMED	GREET	INKED

INLET	LIMEY	+MOSES	OUSEL	RATED	SEVEN
INNER	LINED	MOTEL	OUTER	RAVED	SEVER
INSET	LINEN	MOTET	OUZEL	RAVEL	SEWED
INTER	LINER	MOVED	OWLET	RAVEN	SEWER
IRKED	LIVED	MOVER	OWNED	RAYED	SEXED
ISLET	LIVEN	MOWED	OWNER.	RAZED	SHEEN
IVIED.	LIVER	MOWER	PACED	REBEC	SHEEP
JADED	LIVES	MUREX	PAGED	REBEL	SHEER
+JAMES	LOBED	MUSED	PALED	REFER	SHEET
+JANET	LONER	MUTED.	PALER	RENEW	SHIED
JAPED	LOPED	NAKED	PANED	REPEL	SHRED
JAWED	LOSER	NAMED	PANEL	RESET	SHREW
JEWEL	LOVED	NARES	PAPER	REVEL	SIDED
JIBED	LOVER	NAVEL	PARED	REVET	SILEX
JIVED	LOWED	NEVER	PATEN	RIDER	SINEW
JOKED	LOWER	NEWEL	PATER	RILED	SIRED
JOKER	LUMEN	NEWER	PAWED	RIPEN	SIREN
JULEP.	LURED	NICER	PAYED	RIPER	SITED
+KAREN	LUTED	+NIGEL	PAYEE	RISEN	SIZED
KEVEL	LYCEE.	*NIGER	+PETER	RISER	SKEET
KEYED	+MABEL	*NIMES	PILED	RIVED	SKIED
KNEED	MACED	+NOBEL	PINED	RIVEN	SKIER
KNEEL	MAKER	NONES	PIPED	RIVER	SLEEK
KOPEC	MANES	NOSED	PIPER	RIVET	SLEEP
*KOREA.	+MANET	NOSEY	PLIED	ROBED	SLEET
LABEL	MASER	NOTED	POKED	RODEO	SNEER
LACED	MATED	NOVEL	POKER	+ROGER	SOBER
LADED	MATER	+NOYES.	POLED	ROPED	SOLED
LADEN	MAZER	OAKEN	PORED	ROPEY	SORER
LAGER	+MEDEA	OARED	POSED	ROVED	SOWED
LAKEY	METED	OASES	POSER	ROVEN	SOWER
LAMED	METER	OATEN	POWER	ROVER	SPEED
LAPEL	MEWED	OCTET	PREEN	ROWED	SPIED
LARES	MILER	ODDER	PRIED	ROWEL	SPIEL
LASER	+MILES	OFFER	PROEM	ROWER	SPREE
LATER	MIMED	OFTEN	PUBES	RUDER	STEED
LATEX	MINED	OGLED	PUKED	RULED	STEEL
LAVER	MINER	OILED	PULED	RULER	STEEN
LAYER	MIRED	OLDEN	PUREE	RUPEE.	STEEP
LAZED	MISER	OLDER	PURER	SAFER	STEER
LEPER	MIXED	ONSET	PYXED.	SAKER	STREW
LEVEE	MIXER	OOZED	QUEEN	SALEP	SUPER
LEVEL	MIZEN	OPTED	QUEER	SANER	SURER
LEVER	MODEL	ORBED	QUIET.	SATED	SWEEP
*LEWES	+MONET	ORDER	RACED	SAVED	SWEET
LIBEL	MONEY	ORIEL	RACER	SAVER	SYCEE.
LIFER	MOOED	ORMER	RAKED	SAWED	TABES
LIKED	MOPED	OSIER	RANEE	SCREE	TAKEN
LIKEN	MOREL	OTHER	RAPED	SCREW	TAKER
LIMED	MORES	OTTER	RARER	SEMEN	TAMED

79

TAMER	UNWED	XEBEC	SHAFT	DOUGH	PHAGE
TAPED	UPPER	XYLEM.	SHIFT	DREGS	PIGGY
TAPER	UPSET	YAWED	SKIFF	DUNGY.	PODGY
TAWED	URGED	*YEMEN	SNAFU	ELEGY.	PORGE
TAXED	USHER	YODEL	SNIFF	FEIGN	PUDGY
TELEX	UTTER.	YOKED	SNUFF	FOGGY	PURGE.
TENET	VALET	YOKEL	STAFF	FORGE	RANGE
TEPEE	VAREC	*YPRES.	STIFF	FORGO	RANGY
THIEF	VEXED	ZIBET	STUFF	FUDGE	REIGN
THREE	VIDEO	ZONED	+SWIFT.	FUGGY	RIDGE
THREW	VILER		TAFFY	FUNGI.	ROUGE
*TIBER	VIPER	ABAFT	THEFT	GAUGE	ROUGH.
*TIBET	VIXEN	ALOFT.	TURFY.	GORGE	SEDGE
TIDED	VOLED	*BANFF	UNIFY.	GOUGE.	SERGE
TIGER	VOLET	BEEFY	WHIFF	HEDGE	SIEGE
TILED	VOTED	BLUFF.		HEIGH	SINGE
TIMED	VOTER	CHAFE	ADAGE	+HELGA	*SLIGO
TIMER	VOWED	CHAFF	*ADIGE	HINGE	SOGGY
TIRED	VOWEL.	CLEFT	ALIGN.	HOUGH.	SOUGH
*TIREE	WADED	+CLIFF	BADGE	IMAGE	STAGE
TOKEN	WADER	COMFY	BAGGY	IMAGO	STAGY
TONED	WAFER	*CORFE	BARGE	+INIGO.	SURGE.
TOPEE	WAGED	*CORFU	BEIGE	JINGO	TANGO
TOPER	WAGER	CRAFT	BILGE	JUDGE.	TANGY
TOTED	WAKED	CROFT.	BINGE	KEDGE.	THIGH
TOTEM	WAKEN	DAFFY	BINGO	LARGE	TINGE
TOWED	*WALES	DEIFY	BOGGY	LARGO	*TONGA
TOWEL	WANED	*DELFT	BONGO	LAUGH	TONGS
TOWER	WATER	DRAFF	BOUGH	LEDGE	TOUGH.
TOYED	WAVED	DRAFT	+BRAGG	LEGGY	USAGE.
TREED	WAVER	DRIFT.	BUDGE	LIEGE	VERGE
TRIED	WAXED	EDIFY.	BUDGY	LINGO	VIRGO
TRIER	WAXEN	FLUFF.	BUGGY	LODGE	*VOLGA.
TRUER	WHEEL	GAFFE	BULGE	LOUGH	+WAUGH
TUBER	WIDEN	+GEOFF	BURGH.	LUNGE.	WEDGE
TUNED	WIDER	GOOFY	CADGE	MANGE	WEIGH
TUNER	WILED	GRAFT	CARGO	MANGO	
*TWEED	WINED	GRUFF.	COIGN	MANGY	ALPHA
TWEEN	WIPED	*HAIFA	CONGA	MARGE	AUGHT.
TWEET	WIPER	HUFFY.	CONGE	+MARGO	BATHE
+TYLER	WIRED	*JAFFA	*CONGO	MERGE	BIGHT
TYPED.	WISER	JIFFY.	CORGI	MIDGE	BOCHE
UDDER	WIVED	KNIFE.	COUGH.	MINGY	BOTHY
ULCER	WIVES	LEAFY.	DEIGN	MUGGY.	BUSHY.
UMBEL	WIZEN	NAAFI.	DINGO	NEIGH	CACHE
UMBER	+WODEN	PUFFY.	DINGY	NUDGE.	+CATHY
UNDER	WOKEN	QUAFF	DIRGE	*OMAGH	CUSHY.
UNPEG	WOMEN	QUIFF.	DODGE	OMEGA	*DELHI
UNPEN	WOOER	SCOFF	DODGY	OUTGO.	DISHY
UNSEX	WOVEN.	SCUFF	DOGGY	+PEGGY	DUCHY

80

EIGHT.	ANTIC	CETIN	FELID	+LOUIS	POSIT
FICHU	ANVIL	CHAIN	+FELIX	+LUCIA	PUBIC
FIGHT	APHIS	CHAIR	FERIA	LUCID	PUBIS
FISHY	+APRIL	CHOIR	FETID	LUNIK	PUPIL
FOEHN.	APSIS	+CHRIS	FINIS	LUPIN	PYXIS.
*HYTHE.	ARGIL	CILIA	FLAIL	LURID	QUAIL
*IDAHO	ARRIS	CIVIC	FLAIR	+LYDIA	QUOIN
ITCHY.	ARSIS	CIVIL	FLUID	LYRIC.	QUOIT.
LATHE	ARTIC	CLAIM	FOLIO	MAFIA	RABID
LETHE	ASDIC	COLIC	FRAIL	MAGIC	RADII
LIGHT	ASPIC	+COLIN	FRUIT.	MANIA	RADIO
LITHE.	ASTIR	COMIC	GAMIN	MANIC	RADIX
MATHS	ATTIC	CONIC	+GAVIN	MAXIM	RAPID
METHS	AUDIT	CUBIC	GELID	MEDIA	RATIO
MIGHT	AURIC	CUBIT	GENIC	MERIT	REFIT
MOCHA	AVAIL	CUMIN	GENIE	MIMIC	RELIC
MUSHY.	AVOID	+CUPID	GLAIR	MINIM	REMIT
NICHE	+AVRIL	CURIA	GOYIM	MOTIF	RESIN
NIGHT.	AWAIT	CURIE	GRAIL	MOVIE	RIGID
*OMAHA	AZOIC.	CURIO	GRAIN	MUJIK	+ROBIN
OUGHT.	BASIC	CUTIE	GROIN.	MUSIC.	+RODIN
PASHA	+BASIL	CUTIS	HABIT	NADIR	RORIC
PITHY.	BASIN	CYNIC	HAKIM	*NEVIS	ROSIN
RIGHT	BASIS	+CYRIL.	HELIX	NIXIE.	RUNIC.
RUCHE	BATIK	+DAVID	HUMID	OASIS	+SADIE
RUSHY.	BEDIM	DAVIT	HYLIC	OGMIC	SAHIB
SIGHT	BEFIT	DEBIT	HYOID.	OHMIC	SALIC
SPAHI.	BEGIN	DENIM	*INDIA	OLEIC	SALIX
TIGHT	BELIE	+DENIS	INFIX	OLEIN	SAPID
TITHE.	+BERIA	DEVIL	IONIC	OPTIC	SATIN
WASHY	BIFID	DIGIT	*IZMIR.	ORBIT	SCRIM
*WIGHT	BLAIN	DIXIE	+JULIE.	ORPIN	SCRIP
WITHE	BOGIE	DORIC	KAFIR	ORRIS	SEPIA
WITHY.	BORIC	+DORIS	+KEVIN	OVOID	SERIF
YACHT	BOWIE	DRAIL	KRAIT	OXLIP.	SIT-IN
	BRAID	DRAIN	KUMIS	PANIC	SKEIN
+ABBIE	BRAIN	DROIT	KYRIE.	*PARIS	SLAIN
ABOIL	BROIL	DRUID.	LAMIA	PATIO	SNAIL
ACRID	BRUIN	+EDWIN	LAPIS	PENIS	*SOFIA
ADMIT	BRUIT	EERIE	LATIN	PERIL	SOLID
ADMIX	BURIN.	ELFIN	LEGIT	PEWIT	+SONIA
AEGIS	CABIN	*ELGIN	+LENIN	PIPIT	SONIC
AERIE	*CADIZ	+ELLIS	*LEWIS	PIXIE	*SPAIN
AFFIX	CALIF	+ELSIE	LICIT	PLAID	*SPLIT
AGAIN	CALIX	EQUIP	LIE-IN	PLAIN	SPOIL
+ALFIE	CARIB	+ERNIE	LIMIT	PLAIT	SPRIG
ALGID	CAVIL	ETHIC	LIPID	PODIA	SPRIT
ALL-IN	+CECIL	EYRIE.	LIVID	POLIO	SQUIB
AMAIN	+CELIA	FACIA	LOGIC		SQUID
AMBIT	CETIC	FAKIR	LORIS		STAID

S--I				R--L	
STAIN	VOMIT.	KINKY	YOLKY	CYCLE.	HOTLY.
STAIR	XENIA.	KOOKY.		DAILY	ICILY
STOIC	YOGIN.	LANKY	ABELE	DALLY	IDYLL
STRIA	ZOOID	LARKY	ADDLE	DEALT	IMPLY
STRIP	ZORIL	LEAKY	+ADELE	DHOLE	INGLE
SWAIN		LINKS	ADULT	DIMLY	ISTLE
+SYBIL	BANJO.	+LOCKE	AGILE	DOILY	*ITALY.
*SYRIA.	HADJI.	LUCKY.	AISLE	DOLLY	JELLY
TACIT	KOPJE.	MILKY	AMBLE	+DOYLE	JOLLY
TAMIL	OUIJA	MUCKY	AMPLE	DRILL	JOULE.
TAMIS		MURKY	AMPLY	DROLL	KNELL
TAPIR	ALIKE	MUSKY.	ANELE	DRYLY	KNELT
TAPIS	AWAKE	NARKY	ANGLE	DULLY	KNOLL
TAXIN	AWOKE.	*OSAKA.	ANKLE	DUPLE	KOALA.
TAXIS	+BLAKE	PARKY	APPLE	DWELL	LADLE
TEPID	BLOKE	PAWKY	APPLY	DWELT.	LAXLY
THEIR	BOSKY	PEAKY	APTLY	EAGLE	+LEILA
TIBIA	BRAKE	PERKY	ATOLL	EARLY	*LILLE
TIMID	BROKE	PESKY	AXILE.	+EMILY	LISLE
TONIC	BUCKO	PINKY	BADLY	EXALT	LOLLY
TOPIC	BULKY	POCKY	BAULK	EXILE	LOWLY.
TOXIC	BURKE.	POLKA	BE-ALL	EXULT.	MADLY
TOXIN	CHOKE	PORKY	BELLE	FABLE	MANLY
TRAIL	CHOKY	PUKKA.	BELLY	FAULT	MAPLE
TRAIN	COCKY	QUAKE.	BIBLE	FELLY	MEALY
TRAIT	CORKY	REEKY	BILLY	FIELD	+MERLE
TULIP	CRAKE.	RISKY	BOGLE	FILLY	+MOLLY
TUMID	DARKY	ROCKY	BOULE	FITLY	MOULD
TUNIC	DICKY	ROOKY.	BOWLS	FOLLY	MOULT.
*TUNIS	DINKY	SARKY	+BOYLE	FRILL	NEWLY
*TURIN	+DRAKE	SHAKE	BRILL	FULLY.	NOBLE
+TWAIN.	DUCKY	SHAKO	BUGLE	GABLE	NOBLY.
UNDID	DUSKY.	SHAKY	BUILD	GAILY	OBELI
UNFIT	EVOKE.	SILKY	BUILT	GAULT	ODDLY
UNFIX	FLAKE	SLAKE	BULLY	GHYLL	OVULE.
UNPIN	FLAKY	SMOKE	BURLY.	GODLY	PALLY
UNRIG	FLUKE	SMOKY	CABLE	GOLLY	+PAULA
UNRIP	FLUKY	SNAKE	CAULK	*GOOLE	PHYLA
UNTIE	FUNKY.	SNAKY	CELLO	GRILL	PHYLE
UNTIL	GAWKY	SPAKE	CHALK	GUILD	+POLLY
UNZIP.	GECKO.	SPIKE	CHELA	GUILE	*POOLE
VALID	HANKY	SPIKY	CHILD	GUILT	POULP
VAPID	HONKY	SPOKE	*CHILE	GULLY.	POULT
VARIX	HUSKY.	STAKE	CHILI	HALLO	PROLE
VATIC	JACKS	STOKE	CHILL	HAPLY	PSALM.
VEDIC	JERKY	SULKY.	COALY	HAULM	QUALM
VIGIL	JOCKO	TACKY.	COBLE	+HELLE	QUELL
VINIC	JUNKY.	+VICKY	COULD	HELLO	QUILL
VISIT	+KAFKA	VODKA.	COYLY	HILLY	QUILT.
VIVID	KHAKI	WACKY.	CURLY	HOLLY	RALLY

R - - L -		F - - N -			
RAWLY	SWILL.	CHAMP	JEMMY	THUMP	BWANA.
REALM	TABLE	CHIME	+JIMMY.	THYME	*CANNA
REPLY	TALLY	CHIMP	KAAMA	+TOMMY	CANNY
RIFLE	TELLY	CHUMP	KARMA.	TRAMP	CHANT
RILLE	THOLE	CLAMP	LLAMA	TRUMP	*CHINA
RUMLY.	TITLE	CLIMB	LOAMY.	TUMMY.	CHINE
SABLE	TRILL	CLIME	MAGMA	WORMY	CHINK
SADLY	TROLL	CLUMP	*MALMO		CHUNK
+SALLY	TRULL	COMMA	MAMMA	ACINI	CLANG
SCALD	TRULY	COOMB	*MIAMI	AGENT	CLANK
SCALE	TULLE	CRAMP	MUMMY.	AGONY	CLING
SCALP	TWILL.	CRIME	+NAOMI	ALONE	CLINK
SCALY	UNCLE	CRIMP	NEUME	ALONG	CLONE
SCOLD	UVULA.	CRUMB	+NORMA.	AMEND	CLUNG
SCULL	VAULT	CRUMP.	*PALMA	AMINO	*COLNE
SCULP	VILLA	DERMA	PALMY	AMONG	CORNY
SHALE	VILLI	DOGMA	PIGMY	ANENT	COUNT
SHALY	+VIOLA	DORMY	PLUMB	ANONA	CRANE
SHELF	VOILE.	DRAMA	PLUME	APING	CRANK
SHELL	WALLA	DROME	PLUMP	ARENA	CRONE
SHYLY	WANLY	DUMMY.	PLUMY	ARENT	CRONY.
SIDLE	*WEALD	EDEMA	POMMY	ATONE	+DANNY
SILLY	+WELLS	ELEMI	PRIMA	AWING.	DAUNT
SKALD	WETLY	ENEMA	PRIME	BANNS	+DIANA
SKILL	WHALE	ENEMY.	PRIMP	BEANO	DIDNT
SKULK	WHELK	FILMY	PYGMY.	BEING	DIENE
SKULL	WHELP	*FIUME	RHOMB	+BENNY	DOING
SLYLY	WHILE	FLAME	RHUMB	*BERNE	+DONNA
SMALL	WHOLE	FLAMY	RHYME	BHANG	+DONNE
SMALT	WIELD	FLUME	ROOMY	BLAND	DOWNY
SMELL	+WOOLF	FLUMP	RUMMY.	BLANK	DRANK
SMELT	WORLD	FOAMY	SALMI	BLEND	DRINK
SMILE	WOULD	FORME	SCAMP	BLIND	DRONE
SNELL	WRYLY.	FRAME	SEAMY	BLINK	DRUNK
SOCLE	YIELD	*FROME	SHAME	BLOND	DYING.
SPELL	YOULL	FRUMP.	SIGMA	BLUNT	EBONY
SPELT		GAMMA	SKIMP	BONNY	ELAND
SPILL	A-BOMB	GAMMY	SLIME	BORNE	EMEND
SPILT	+ADAMS	GEMMA	SLIMY	BOUND	EVENT.
STALE	AGAMA	GEMMY	SLUMP	BRAND	FAINT
STALK	ANIMA	GNOME	*SOMME	BRANT	+FANNY
STALL	ANOMY	GRIME	SPUME	*BRENT	FAUNA
STILE	AROMA	+GRIMM	SPUMY	BRINE	FEINT
STILL	AZYME.	GRIMY	STAMP	BRING	FENNY
STILT	BALMY	GUMMA	STOMA	BRINK	FERNY
STOLE	BARMY	GUMMY.	STUMP	BRINY	FIEND
STYLE	BLAME	HALMA	SWAMP.	BRUNT	FINNY
SULLY	BLIMP	HAMMY	TAMMY	BUNNY	+FIONA
SURLY	BRUME	H-BOMB.	THEME	+BURNS	FLANK
SWELL	*BURMA.	JAMMY	THUMB	BURNT	FLANK

FLING	*MAINE	*RHONE	SWING	+AMMON	+CREON
FLINT	MANNA	ROUND	SWUNG.	ANION	CROOK
FLONG	*MARNE	RUING	TAINT	*ANJOU	CROON.
FLUNG	MAYNT	RUNNY.	TAUNT	ANNOY	DECOR
FLUNK	MEANT	SAINT	TAWNY	APRON	DECOY
FOUND	MESNE	*SAONE	TEENS	ARBOR	+DEFOE
FOUNT	+MILNE	SAUNA	TEENY	ARGOL	*DELOS
FRANC	MOONY	SCANT	THANE	ARGON	DEMOB
+FRANK	MOUND	SCENA	THANK	ARGOT	DEMON
FROND	MOUNT	SCENE	THINE	+ARION	DEMOS
FRONT	+MYRNA.	SCENT	THING	ARROW	DEPOT
FUNNY.	NANNA	SCONE	THONG	ARSON	*DEVON
GAUNT	NANNY	*SEINE	TINNY	*ASCOT	*DIJON
*GHANA	NINNY.	SENNA	TONNE	AXIOM.	DIVOT
*GHENT	OPINE	SHANK	TREND	BABOO	DONOR
GIANT	OVINE	SHANT	*TRENT	+BACON	DROOL
GLAND	OWING	SHINE	TRINE	BARON	DROOP.
GLINT	OZONE.	SHINY	TRONC	BASON	+EAMON
GOING	PAINT	SHONE	TRUNK	BATON	ELBOW
GRAND	PANNE	SHUNT	TUNNY	BAYOU	+ELIOT
+GRANT	*PATNA	SKINT	TWANG	BEBOP	ENDOW
GRIND	+PENNY	SKUNK	TWINE.	BEFOG	ENJOY
GRUNT	PEONY	SLANG	UP-END	BEGOT	ENROL
GUANA	PERNE	SLANT	URINE	BELOW	ENVOY
GUANO	PHONE	SLING	USING.	BESOM	EPHOD
GUNNY.	PHONO	SLINK	VAUNT	BIGOT	*EPSOM
HADNT	PHONY	SLUNG	+VERNE	BIJOU	ERGOT
HASNT	PIANO	SLUNK	VYING.	BISON	+ERROL
HAUNT	PINNA	SONNY	WASNT	BLOOD	ERROR
HENNA	PINNY	SOUND	WEENY	BLOOM	ETHOS
HINNY	PLANE	SPANK	WHINE	BORON	EXTOL.
HORNY	PLANK	SPEND	WOUND	BOSOM	FANON
HOUND	PLANT	SPENT	WRING	BOSON	FELON
HYENA.	PLONK	SPINE	WRONG	BROOD	FETOR
ICING	PLUNK	SPINY	WRUNG.	BROOK	FLOOD
INANE	POINT	SPUNK	YOUNG	BROOM	FLOOR
+IRENE	+POUND	STAND		BUXOM	FLUOR.
IRONY.	PRANG	STANK	+AARON	+BYRON.	*GABON
JAUNT	PRANK	STING	ABBOT	CABOB	GALOP
JEANS	PRINK	STINK	ABHOR	CANOE	*GENOA
+JENNY	PRINT	STINT	ACTOR	CANON	GIGOT
JOINT.	PRONE	STONE	+AESOP	CAPON	GLOOM
KRONE.	PRONG	STONY	AFOOT	CAROB	GROOK
LEANT	PRUNE.	STUNG	AGLOW	+CAROL	GROOM.
+LENNY	QUANT	STUNK	*AKRON	*CHAOS	*HANOI
LIANA	QUINS	STUNT	*ALLOA	*CHIOS	HAVOC
LOONY	QUINT.	SUING	ALLOT	+CHLOE	HELOT
+LORNA	RAINY	SUNNY	ALLOW	COCOA	+HEROD
LYING	*RHINE	SWANK	ALLOY	COLON	HERON
*LYONS.	RHINO	SWINE	ALOOF	+COROT	*HURON

R - - L -				F - - N -	
RAWLY	SWILL.	CHAMP	JEMMY	THUMP	BWANA.
REALM	TABLE	CHIME	+JIMMY.	THYME	*CANNA
REPLY	TALLY	CHIMP	KAAMA	+TOMMY	CANNY
RIFLE	TELLY	CHUMP	KARMA.	TRAMP	CHANT
RILLE	THOLE	CLAMP	LLAMA	TRUMP	*CHINA
RUMLY.	TITLE	CLIMB	LOAMY.	TUMMY.	CHINE
SABLE	TRILL	CLIME	MAGMA	WORMY	CHINK
SADLY	TROLL	CLUMP	*MALMO		CHUNK
+SALLY	TRULL	COMMA	MAMMA	ACINI	CLANG
SCALD	TRULY	COOMB	*MIAMI	AGENT	CLANK
SCALE	TULLE	CRAMP	MUMMY.	AGONY	CLING
SCALP	TWILL.	CRIME	+NAOMI	ALONE	CLINK
SCALY	UNCLE	CRIMP	NEUME	ALONG	CLINT
SCOLD	UVULA.	CRUMB	+NORMA.	AMEND	CLONE
SCULL	VAULT	CRUMP.	*PALMA	AMINO	CLUNG
SCULP	VILLA	DERMA	PALMY	AMONG	*COLNE
SHALE	VILLI	DOGMA	PIGMY	ANENT	CORNY
SHALY	+VIOLA	DORMY	PLUMB	ANONA	COUNT
SHELF	VOILE.	DRAMA	PLUME	APING	CRANE
SHELL	WALLA	DROME	PLUMP	ARENA	CRANK
SHYLY	WANLY	DUMMY.	PLUMY	ARENT	CRONE
SIDLE	*WEALD	EDEMA	POMMY	ATONE	CRONY.
SILLY	+WELLS	ELEMI	PRIMA	AWING.	+DANNY
SKALD	WETLY	ENEMA	PRIME	BANNS	DAUNT
SKILL	WHALE	ENEMY.	PRIMP	BEANO	+DIANA
SKULK	WHELK	FILMY	PYGMY.	BEING	DIDNT
SKULL	WHELP	*FIUME	RHOMB	+BENNY	DIENE
SLYLY	WHILE	FLAME	RHUMB	*BERNE	DOING
SMALL	WHOLE	FLAMY	RHYME	BHANG	+DONNA
SMALT	WIELD	FLUME	ROOMY	BLAND	+DONNE
SMELL	+WOOLF	FLUMP	RUMMY.	BLANK	DOWNY
SMELT	WORLD	FOAMY	SALMI	BLEND	DRANK
SMILE	WOULD	FORME	SCAMP	BLIND	DRINK
SNELL	WRYLY.	FRAME	SEAMY	BLINK	DRONE
SOCLE	YIELD	*FROME	SHAME	BLOND	DRUNK
SPELL	YOULL	FRUMP.	SIGMA	BLUNT	DYING.
SPELT		GAMMA	SKIMP	BONNY	EBONY
SPILL	A-BOMB	GAMMY	SLIME	BORNE	ELAND
SPILT	+ADAMS	GEMMA	SLIMY	BOUND	EMEND
STALE	AGAMA	GEMMY	SLUMP	BRAND	EVENT.
STALK	ANIMA	GNOME	*SOMME	BRANT	FAINT
STALL	ANOMY	GRIME	SPUME	*BRENT	+FANNY
STILE	AROMA	+GRIMM	SPUMY	BRINE	FAUNA
STILL	AZYME.	GRIMY	STAMP	BRING	FEINT
STILT	BALMY	GUMMA	STOMA	BRINK	FENNY
STOLE	BARMY	GUMMY.	STUMP	BRINY	FERNY
STYLE	BLAME	HALMA	SWAMP.	BRUNT	FIEND
SULLY	BLIMP	HAMMY	TAMMY	BUNNY	FINNY
SURLY	BRUME	H-BOMB.	THEME	+BURNS	+FIONA
SWELL	*BURMA.	JAMMY	THUMB	BURNT	FLANK

FLING	*MAINE	*RHONE	SWING	+AMMON	+CREON
FLINT	MANNA	ROUND	SWUNG.	ANION	CROOK
FLONG	*MARNE	RUING	TAINT	*ANJOU	CROON.
FLUNG	MAYNT	RUNNY.	TAUNT	ANNOY	DECOR
FLUNK	MEANT	SAINT	TAWNY	APRON	DECOY
FOUND	MESNE	*SAONE	TEENS	ARBOR	+DEFOE
FOUNT	+MILNE	SAUNA	TEENY	ARGOL	*DELOS
FRANC	MOONY	SCANT	THANE	ARGON	DEMOB
+FRANK	MOUND	SCENA	THANK	ARGOT	DEMON
FROND	MOUNT	SCENE	THINE	+ARION	DEMOS
FRONT	+MYRNA.	SCENT	THING	ARROW	DEPOT
FUNNY.	NANNA	SCONE	THONG	ARSON	*DEVON
GAUNT	NANNY	*SEINE	TINNY	*ASCOT	*DIJON
*GHANA	NINNY.	SENNA	TONNE	AXIOM.	DIVOT
*GHENT	OPINE	SHANK	TREND	BABOO	DONOR
GIANT	OVINE	SHANT	*TRENT	BARON	DROOL
GLAND	OWING	SHINE	TRINE	BASON	DROOP.
GLINT	OZONE.	SHINY	TRONC	BATON	+EAMON
GOING	PAINT	SHONE	TRUNK	BAYOU	ELBOW
GRAND	PANNE	SHUNT	TUNNY	BEBOP	+ELIOT
+GRANT	*PATNA	SKINT	TWANG	BEFOG	ENDOW
GRIND	+PENNY	SKUNK	TWINE.	BEGOT	ENJOY
GRUNT	PEONY	SLANG	UP-END	BELOW	ENROL
GUANA	PERNE	SLANT	URINE	BESOM	ENVOY
GUANO	PHONE	SLING	USING.	BIGOT	EPHOD
GUNNY.	PHONO	SLINK	VAUNT	BIJOU	*EPSOM
HADNT	PHONY	SLUNG	+VERNE	BISON	ERGOT
HASNT	PIANO	SLUNK	VYING.	BLOOD	+ERROL
HAUNT	PINNA	SONNY	WASNT	BLOOM	ERROR
HENNA	PINNY	SOUND	WEENY	BORON	ETHOS
HINNY	PLANE	SPANK	WHINE	BOSOM	EXTOL.
HORNY	PLANK	SPEND	WOUND	BOSON	FANON
HOUND	PLANT	SPENT	WRING	BROOD	FELON
HYENA.	PLONK	SPINE	WRONG	BROOK	FETOR
ICING	PLUNK	SPINY	WRUNG.	BROOM	FLOOD
INANE	POINT	SPUNK	YOUNG	BUXOM	FLOOR
+IRENE	+POUND	STAND			FLUOR.
IRONY.	PRANG	STANK	+AARON	+BYRON.	*GABON
JAUNT	PRANK	STING	ABBOT	CABOB	GALOP
JEANS	PRINK	STINK	ABHOR	CANOE	*GENOA
+JENNY	PRINT	STINT	ACTOR	CANON	GIGOT
JOINT.	PRONE	STONE	*AESOP	CAPON	GLOOM
KRONE.	PRONG	STONY	AFOOT	CAROB	GROOK
LEANT	PRUNE.	STUNG	AGLOW	+CAROL	GROOM.
+LENNY	QUANT	STUNK	*AKRON	*CHAOS	*HANOI
LIANA	QUINS	STUNT	*ALLOA	*CHIOS	HAVOC
LOONY	QUINT.	SUING	ALLOT	+CHLOE	HELOT
+LORNA	RAINY	SUNNY	ALLOW	COCOA	+HEROD
LYING	*RHINE	SWANK	ALLOY	COLON	HERON
*LYONS.	RHINO	SWINE	ALOOF	+COROT	*HURON

HYSON.	PILOT	TAROT	GROPE	WEEPY	CHURL
ICHOR	PITOT	TENON	GUPPY.	WISPY.	CHURN
IDIOM	PIVOT	TENOR	HAPPY	ZIPPY	+CLARE
IDIOT	PRIOR	THROB	HARPY		CLARY
IGLOO	PROOF	THROE	HIPPO	ABORT	CLERK
IMPOT	PYLON.	THROW	HIPPY	*ACCRA	COBRA
INGOT.	RADON	*TIMOR	HUMPH	ACORN	COPRA
JABOT	RAYON	TROOP	HUMPY.	ADORE	COURT
+JACOB	RAZOR	TRY-ON	INAPT	ADORN	CRORE
+JASON	REPOT	TUDOR	INEPT.	AFIRE	CURRY
JETON	RIGOR	TUTOR	JUMPY.	AFORE	*CYMRU.
JUPON	*RIPON	*TYROL.	KAPPA.	AGORA	DAIRY
JUROR.	ROBOT	UNION.	LEAPT	ALARM	DEARY
KAPOK	ROTOR.	VENOM	LOOPY	ALERT	DECRY
KAROO	SABOT	VISOR.	LUMPY	AMBRY	DIARY
KUDOS	SALON	WAGON	LYMPH.	ANGRY	*DOURO
KYLOE.	*SAMOA	WHOOP	MUMPS.	APART	DOWRY
*LAGOS	SAVOY	WIDOW.	NAPPY	APERY	DWARF.
LEMON	SAXON	XENON	NIPPY	AVERT	EAGRE
LOGOS	SCION	YAHOO	NYMPH.	AWARD	EMERY
*LUTON	SCOOP	YAPON	OKAPI	AWARE	ENTRY
LYSOL.	SCOOT	*YUKON	OOMPH.	AZURE.	EVERT
*MACON	SENOR		PEPPY	BAIRN	EVERY
+MADOC	SEPOY	ADAPT	POPPY	*BARRA	EXERT
+MAGOG	SHEOL	ADEPT	PROPS	+BARRY	EXTRA.
MAJOR	SHOOK	ADOPT	PULPY	*BASRA	FAIRY
MANOR	SHOOT	AGAPE.	PUPPY.	BEARD	FERRY
MASON	+SIMON	BUMPH.	+RALPH.	BEERY	FIBRE
MAYOR	+SINON	BUMPY.	SAPPY	*BEIRA	FIERY
*MEDOC	SLOOP	CHAPE	*SCAPA	BERRY	FIORD
MELON	SNOOD	COMPO	SCAPE	BLARE	FIRRY
MESON	SNOOK	CO-OPT	SCOPE	BLURB	FJORD
METOL	SNOOP	CORPS	SHAPE	BLURT	FLARE
MIAOW	SPOOF	COUPE	SLOPE	BOARD	FLIRT
MINOR	SPOOK	COYPU	SLYPE	BOURN	+FLORA
+MINOS	SPOOL	CRAPE	SNIPE	BURRO.	FURRY.
MORON	SPOON	CRAPS	SOAPY	CADRE	GENRE
MOTOR.	SPOOR	CREPE	SOPPY	CAIRN	GLARE
NABOB	STOOD	CREPT	SOUPY	*CAIRO	GLORY
+NIXON	STOOK	CRYPT.	STUPE	*CAPRI	GNARL
NYLON.	STOOL	DRAPE	SWEPT	CARRY	GOURD
ONION	STOOP	DRUPE	SWIPE	*CHARD	GUARD.
+ORION	STROP	DUMPY.	SYLPH.	CHARM	HAIRY
ORLOP	SWOON	ELOPE	*TAMPA	CHART	+HARRY
+ORSON	SWOOP	ERUPT.	TEMPO	CHARY	HEARD
OXBOW.	SYNOD	GLYPH	TEMPT	CHERT	HEART
PEKOE	*SYROS.	GRAPE	TRIPE	CHIRP	+HENRY
+PERON	TABOO	GRAPH	TROPE	CHIRR	HOARD
PHLOX	TABOR	GRAPY	TURPS.	CHORD	HOARY
PICOT	TALON	GRIPE	UNAPT.	CHORE	HOURI

85

HURRY	OVARY	SPORE	ZEBRA	CRASH	GNASH
*HYDRA	OVERT	SPORT		CRASS	GOOSE
HYDRO.	*OZARK.	SPURN	ABASE	CRESS	GORSE
INDRI	PADRE	SPURT	ABASH	CREST	GORSY
INERT	PARRY	STARE	ABUSE	CRISP	GRASP
INFRA	+PEARL	STARK	ABYSS	CROSS	+GRASS
INURE	+PERRY.	START	AMASS	CRUSE	GRIST
INURN	QUARK	STERE	AMISS	CRUSH	GROSS
*ISERE	QUART	STERN	AMUSE	CRUST	GUESS
IVORY	QUERN	STORE	ANGST	CURSE.	GUEST
IZARD.	QUERY	STORK	ANISE	+DAISY	GUISE
+JERRY	QUIRE	STORM	APISH	DEISM	GYPSY.
JEWRY.	QUIRK	STORY	ARISE	DEIST	HANSE
*KERRY	QUIRT.	SWARD	AROSE	DENSE	HARSH
KNURL	REARM	SWARM	AVAST	DOUSE	HAWSE
KNURR	RETRY.	SWIRL	AWASH.	DOWSE	HEIST
KUKRI.	SABRE	SWORD	BALSA	DRESS	+HESSE
LAIRD	SCARE	SWORE	BEAST	DROSS	HOIST
+LARRY	SCARF	SWORN.	+BETSY	DULSE	+HOLST
+LAURA	SCARP	TARRY	BLASE	DURST.	HORSE
LEARN	SCART	TERRA	BLAST	EGEST	HORSY
LEERY	SCORE	+TERRY	BLESS	ERASE	HOUSE
LIBRA	SCORN	THERE	BLEST	EXIST.	HURST
LITRE	SCURF	THERM	+BLISS	FALSE	HUSSY.
*LOIRE	SHARD	THIRD	BLUSH	+FAUST	IRISH.
LORRY	SHARE	THORN	BOAST	FEAST	+JESSE
LUBRA	SHARK	THORP	BOOST	FESSE	JOIST
LUCRE.	SHARP	TIARA	BOSSY	FIRST	JOUST.
MAORI	SHIRE	*TRURO	BRASH	FLASH	*KELSO
MARRY	SHIRK	TWERE	BRASS	FLASK	KIOSK.
MERRY	SHIRR	TWERP	*BREST	FLESH	LAPSE
METRE	SHIRT	TWIRL.	BRISK	FLOSS	LASSO
METRO	SHORE	ULTRA	BROSE	FLUSH	LEASE
MICRO	SHORN	UMBRA	BRUSH	FOIST	LEASH
MITRE	SHORT	UNARM	BURST.	FOSSA	LEAST
+MOIRA	SKIRL	USURP	CAUSE	FOSSE	*LHASA
MOIRE	SKIRT	USURY.	CEASE	FRASS	LOESS
+MOORE	SMART	WEARY	CENSE	FRESH	LOOSE
MOURN	SMIRK	WEIRD	CHASE	FRISK	LOUSE
MYRRH.	SNARE	WHARF	CHASM	+FROST	LOUSY.
NACRE	SNARL	WHERE	CHESS	FUBSY	MANSE
*NAIRN	SNORE	WHIRL	CHEST	FUSSY.	MARSH
NEGRO	SNORT	WHIRR	CHOSE	GASSY	MASSY
+NEHRU	SORRY	WHORE	CISSY	GAUSS	MAYST
NITRE.	SPARE	WHORL	CLASH	GEESE	MESSY
OCHRE	SPARK	WORRY.	CLASP	GESSO	*MEUSE
OMBRE	SPERM	YEARN	CLASS	GHOST	MIDST
OP-ART	SPIRE	YOURE	CLOSE	GIPSY	*MINSK
OPERA	SPIRT	YOURS.	COAST	GLASS	MOIST
OUTRE	SPIRY	*ZAIRE	COPSE	GLOSS	MOOSE

MORSE	SENSE	ALATE	EMOTE	MONTH	SAUTE
MOSSY	SHUSH	AMATE	EMPTY	MOTTO	SCOTS
MOUSE	SISSY	AMITY	*ERITH.	MOUTH	+SCOTT
MOUSY.	SLASH	+ANITA	+FAITH	MUFTI	SET-TO
NEWSY	SLOSH	AORTA	FATTY	MULTI	SEXTO
NOISE	SLUSH	ARETE	FIFTH	MUSTY.	+SHUTE
NOISY	SMASH	AZOTE.	FIFTY	NASTY	SIXTH
NOOSE	SONSY	BASTE	FILTH	NATTY	SIXTY
NORSE	+SOUSA	BATTY	FIRTH	*NEATH	SKATE
NURSE	SOUSE	BERTH	FLITE	NIFTY	SLATE
*NYASA.	SPASM	+BETTY	FLUTE	NINTH	SLATY
OBESE.	STASH	BIRTH	FLUTY	NORTH	SLOTH
PALSY	SWASH	BITTS	FORTE	NUTTY.	SMITE
PANSY	SWISH	BLITZ	*FORTH	ORATE	SMITH
PARSE	SWISS.	*BLYTH	FORTY	OVATE.	SMOTE
PASSE	TANSY	+BOOTH	FRITH	PANTO	SOOTH
PAUSE	TAWSE	BOOTY	FROTH	PANTS	SOOTY
PEASE	TEASE	BROTH	FUSTY.	PARTY	SOTTO
PERSE	TENSE	BRUTE	+GARTH	PASTA	SOUTH
PHASE	TERSE	BUTTE.	GIRTH	PASTE	SPATE
PLASH	THESE	CACTI	GOUTY	PASTY	SPITE
PLASM	THOSE	CANTO	GRATE	+PATTY	STATE
PLUSH	TIPSY	CARTE	+GRETA	PEATY	SUETY
POESY	TOAST	CASTE	GUSTO	*PERTH	SUITE
POISE	TORSO	CATTY	GUSTY.	PETTY	SWATH.
POPSY	TRASH	*CEUTA	*HAITI	PHOTO	TARTY
POSSE	TRESS	CHUTE	HASTE	PIETA	TASTE
PRASE	TRUSS	CLOTH	HASTY	PIETY	TASTY
PRESS	TRUST	COATI	+HEATH	PLATE	TATTY
PRISE	TRYST	COTTA	HEFTY	+PLATO	TEETH
PRISM	TWIST.	COUTH	HERTZ.	+PLUTO	TENTH
PROSE	UKASE.	CRATE	IRATE	POTTO	TESTY
PROSY	VERSE	*CRETE	JETTY	POTTY	THETA
PUDSY	VERSO	CUTTY.	JUNTA	PRATE	TILTH
PULSE	VERST.	+DANTE	JUNTO	PUNTY	TOOTH
PURSE	WAIST	DEATH	JUXTA.	PUTTO	TRITE
PURSY	WELSH	DEITY	+KEATS	PUTTY.	TROTH
PUSSY.	WHISK	DELTA	+KEITH	QUITE	TRUTH
QUASH	WHIST	DEPTH	+KITTY	*QUITO	TUTTY.
QUEST.	WHOSE	DHOTI	*KYOTO.	QUITS	UNITE
RAISE	WHOSO	DICTA	LAITY	QUOTA	UNITY.
REEST	WORSE	DIRTY	*LEITH	QUOTE	+VESTA
RINSE	WORST	DITTO	LOATH	QUOTH.	VIRTU
ROAST	WREST	DITTY	LOFTY	RATTY	VISTA
ROOST	WRIST.	DOTTY	LOTTO	RECTO	*VOLTA
ROUSE	YEAST	DUSTY.	LUSTY.	ROUTE	VOLTE.
ROUST.		EARTH	*MALTA	RUSTY	WALTZ
SALSE	ABATE	+EDITH	MEATY	RUTTY.	WARTY
SAY-SO	ACUTE	ELATE	MIRTH	SALTY	WASTE
SEISE	AGATE	ELITE	MISTY	SANTA	WHITE

87

WIDTH	FOCUS	OCCUR	VALUE	SALVO	
WITTY	FORUM	ODIUM	VELUM	SAVVY	EPOXY.
WORTH	FRAUD	ODOUR	VENUE	SERVE	PROXY.
WRATH	+FREUD	OPIUM.	+VENUS	SHAVE	TWIXT
WRITE	FUCUS	*PADUA	VIRUS	SHOVE	
WROTE	FUGUE.	*PAPUA	VOGUE.	SIEVE	+BERYL.
WROTH.	GAMUT	PIN-UP	WHAUP	SKIVE	CALYX.
+YEATS	GENUS	PIOUS		SLAVE	+DILYS.
YOUTH	GET-UP	PIQUE	ABOVE	SOLVE	ETHYL.
	GHOUL	PROUD.	AGAVE	STAVE	+FREYA.
ABOUT	GIBUS	QUEUE.	ALIVE.	+STEVE	*KENYA.
ALBUM	GIGUE	REBUS	BRAVE	STOVE	*LIBYA
ALGUM	GROUP	REBUT	BRAVO	SUAVE.	+LLOYD.
ALOUD	GROUT.	RECUR	BREVE.	VALVE	+PEPYS
AMOUR	*HAGUE	+REMUS	CALVE	VERVE	POLYP.
*ANGUS	HILUM	REVUE	CARVE	VULVA.	SATYR.
ANNUL	HOCUS	RHEUM	CHIVE	WAIVE	+TANYA
APPUI	HOKUM	ROGUE	+CLIVE	WEAVE.	*TOKYO.
ARGUE	+HORUS	+RUFUS.	CLOVE	YOUVE	VINYL
+ARGUS	HUMUS.	SCOUR	CRAVE		
AUGUR	ICTUS	SCOUT	CURVE.	BLOWN	AMAZE.
AWFUL.	ILEUM	SCRUB	DELVE	BRAWL	BAIZE
BABUL	ILIUM	SCRUM	DIVVY	BRAWN	BLAZE
*BACUP	IMBUE	*SEOUL	DRIVE	BROWN.	BONZE
BEAUX	INCUR	SERUM	DROVE.	CLOWN	BOOZE
BEGUM	INCUS	SET-UP	GLOVE	CRAWL	BOOZY
BEGUN	*INDUS	SHOUT	GRAVE	*CREWE	BRAZE.
BOGUS	INPUT	SHRUB	GRAVY	CROWD	COLZA
BOLUS	ISSUE.	SHRUG	GROVE	CROWN.	CRAZE
BONUS.	+JANUS	SINUS	GUAVA.	DRAWL	CRAZY.
+CACUS	+JESUS	SIOUX	HALVE	DRAWN	DIZZY.
+CAMUS	JORUM.	SNOUT	HEAVE	DROWN.	+ELIZA.
CLOUD	*KABUL	SPOUT	HEAVY	FLOWN	FEEZE
CLOUT	KAPUT	STOUP	HELVE	FROWN.	FIZZY
+COMUS	KNOUT.	*STOUR	HOOVE.	GROWL	FRIZZ
CROUP	LEMUR	STOUT	KNAVE.	GROWN.	FROZE
+CYRUS.	LOCUM	STRUM	LARVA	KNOWN.	FURZE
DATUM	LOCUS	STRUT	LEAVE.	PRAWN	FURZY
DEBUT	LOTUS	SUN-UP	MAUVE.	PROWL.	FUZZY
DEMUR	LUPUS.	SYRUP.	NAIVE	SCOWL	GAUZE
DIPUS.	MAGUS	TALUS	NAVVY	SHAWL	GAUZY
EMBUS	MINUS	THRUM	NERVE	SHAWM	GLAZE
ENDUE	MIX-UP	TIE-UP	NERVY.	SHOWN	GLOZE
ENNUI	MODUS	TONUS	OGIVE	SHOWY	GRAZE
ENSUE.	MOGUL	TOQUE	OLIVE.	SNOWY	*IBIZA
FAVUS	MUCUS.	TORUS	PEEVE	SPAWN.	JAZZY
FEMUR	NEGUS	TROUT.	PRIVY	THEWS	+LISZT
FETUS	NEXUS	UNCUT	PROVE.	THEWY	MAIZE
FLOUR	NODUS.	UNDUE.	REEVE.	TRAWL	MEZZO
FLOUT	OAKUM	VAGUE	SALVE	TREWS	+MITZI

88

MUZZY.	DOGMA	*LHASA	RUMBA.	DEMOB.	*MEDOC
+ORCZY.	+DONNA	LIANA	SAMBA	H-BOMB.	MIMIC
PIEZO	DRAMA.	LIBRA	*SAMOA	+JACOB.	MUSIC.
PLAZA	EDEMA	*LIBYA	SANTA	NABOB.	OGMIC
PRIZE.	+ELIZA	+LINDA	SAUNA	PLUMB.	OHMIC
RITZY.	ENEMA	LLAMA	*SCAPA	RHOMB	OLEIC
SEIZE.	+ERICA	+LORNA	SCENA	RHUMB.	OPTIC.
TIZZY	EXTRA.	LUBRA	SENNA	SAHIB	PANIC
	FACIA	+LUCIA	SEPIA	SCRUB	PUBIC.
	FAUNA	+LYDIA.	SIGMA	SHRUB	REBEC
*ACCRA	FERIA	MAFIA	*SOFIA	SQUAB	RELIC
AGAMA	+FIONA	MAGMA	+SONIA	SQUIB.	RORIC
AGORA	+FLORA	*MALTA	+SOUSA	THROB	RUNIC.
*ALLOA	FOSSA	MAMBA	STOMA	THUMB	SALIC
ALPHA	FOVEA	MAMMA	STRIA		SERAC
ANIMA	+FREDA	MANIA	*SYRIA.	ANTIC	SONIC
+ANITA	+FREYA.	MANNA	*TAMPA	ANZAC	STOIC.
ANONA	GAMMA	+MARIA	+TANYA	ARTIC	TONIC
AORTA	GEMMA	*MECCA	TERRA	ASDIC	TOPIC
*AQABA	*GENOA	+MEDEA	THECA	ASPIC	TOXIC
ARENA	*GHANA	MEDIA	THETA	ATTIC	TRONC
AROMA.	*GOUDA	MOCHA	TIARA	AURIC	TUNIC.
BALSA	+GRETA	+MOIRA	TIBIA	AZOIC	VAREC
*BARRA	GUANA	+MYRNA.	*TONGA.	AZTEC.	VATIC
*BASRA	GUAVA	NANNA	ULTRA	BASIC	VEDIC
*BEIRA	GUMMA.	+NORMA	UMBRA	BORIC.	VINIC.
+BERIA	*HAIFA	*NYASA.	UVULA.	CETIC	XEBEC
BOHEA	HALMA	*OMAHA	+VESTA	CIVIC	
*BURMA	+HELGA	OMEGA	VILLA	COLIC	ACHED
BWANA.	HENNA	OPERA	+VIOLA	COMIC	ACRID
*CANNA	+HILDA	*OSAKA	VISTA	CONIC	ACTED
+CELIA	*HYDRA	OUIJA.	VODKA	CUBIC	ADDED
*CEUTA	HYENA.	*PADUA	*VOLGA	CUSEC	AHEAD
CHELA	*IBIZA	*PALMA	*VOLTA	CYNIC.	AIDED
*CHINA	*INDIA	PANDA	VULVA.	DORIC.	AIMED
CILIA	INFRA.	*PAPUA	WALLA	ETHIC.	AIRED
CIRCA	*JAFFA	PASHA	+WANDA.	FRANC.	ALGID
COBRA	JUNTA	PASTA	XENIA	GENIC.	ALOUD
COCOA	JUXTA.	*PATNA	YUCCA.	HAVOC	AMEND
COLZA	KAAMA	+PAULA	ZEBRA	HYLIC.	ARCED
COMMA	+KAFKA	PHYLA		ILIAC	ARMED
CONGA	KAPPA	PIETA	A-BOMB.	IONIC	ASKED
COPRA	KARMA	PINNA	BLURB.	+ISAAC.	AVOID
COTTA	*KENYA	PLAZA	CABOB	KOPEC.	AWARD
CURIA	KOALA	PODIA	CARIB	LILAC	AWNED.
*DACCA	*KOREA.	POLKA	CAROB	LOGIC	BAKED
DELTA	LAMIA	PRIMA	CLIMB	LYRIC.	BALED
DERMA	LARVA	PUKKA.	COOMB	+MADOC	BARED
+DIANA	+LAURA	QUOTA.	CRUMB	MAGIC	BASED
DICTA	+LEILA	+RHODA	CUBEB.	MANIC	BATED

BAYED	DATED	FUSED.	JAWED	NOTED.	RULED.
BEARD	+DAVID	GAMED	JIBED	OARED	SALAD
BEGAD	DAZED	GAPED	JIHAD	OCTAD	SAPID
BIDED	DICED	GATED	JIVED	OGLED	SATED
BIFID	DINED	GAZED	JOKED.	OILED	SAVED
BIPED	DIVED	GELID	KEYED	OOZED	SAWED
BLAND	DOMED	GIBED	KNEAD	OPTED	SCALD
BLEED	DOPED	GLAND	KNEED.	ORBED	SCOLD
BLEND	DOSED	GLUED	LACED	OVOID	SEWED
BLIND	DOTED	GONAD	LADED	OWNED.	SEXED
BLOND	DOZED	GORED	LAIRD	PACED	SHARD
BLOOD	DREAD	GOURD	LAMED	PAGED	SHIED
BOARD	DRIED	GRAND	LAZED	PALED	SHRED
BODED	DRUID	GREED	LIKED	PANED	SIDED
BONED	DRYAD	GRIND	LIMED	PARED	SIRED
BORED	DUPED.	GUARD	LINED	PAWED	SITED
BOUND	EASED	GUILD	LIPID	PAYED	SIZED
BOXED	EBBED	GUYED	LIVED	PILED	SKALD
BRAID	EDGED	GYBED	LIVID	PINED	SKIED
BRAND	ELAND	GYVED.	+LLOYD	PIPED	SNOOD
BREAD	EMBED	HALED	LOBED	PLAID	SOLED
BREED	EMEND	HARED	LOPED	PLEAD	SOLID
BROAD	ENDED	HATED	LOVED	PLIED	SOUND
BROOD	EPHOD	HAWED	LOWED	POKED	SOWED
BUILD.	ERRED.	HAYED	LUCID	POLED	SPEED
CAGED	FACED	HAZED	LURED	PORED	SPEND
CAKED	FADED	HEARD	LURID	POSED	SPIED
CANED	FAKED	+HEROD	LUTED.	+POUND	SQUAD
CASED	FAMED	HEWED	MACED	PRIED	SQUID
CAVED	FARAD	HEXAD	MATED	PROUD	STAID
CEDED	FARED	HIRED	METED	PUKED	STAND
*CHARD	FATED	HIVED	MEWED	PULED	STEAD
CHILD	FELID	HOARD	MIMED	PYXED.	STEED
CHORD	FETED	HOLED	MINED	RABID	STOOD
CITED	FETID	HOMED	MIRED	RACED	SWARD
CLOUD	FIELD	HONED	MIXED	RAKED	SWORD
CLUED	FIEND	HOPED	MONAD	RAPED	SYNOD.
CODED	FIORD	HOSED	MOOED	RAPID	TAMED
COOED	FIRED	HOUND	MOPED	RATED	TAPED
COPED	FIXED	HUMID	MOULD	RAVED	TAWED
CORED	FJORD	HYOID.	MOUND	RAYED	TAXED
COULD	FLOOD	IDLED	MOVED	RAZED	TEPID
COWED	FLUID	ILIAD	MOWED	RIGID	THIRD
CREED	FOUND	IMPED	MUSED	RILED	TIDED
CRIED	FOXED	INKED	MUTED.	RIVED	TILED
CROWD	FRAUD	IRKED	NAIAD	ROBED	TIMED
CUBED	FREED	IVIED	NAKED	ROPED	TIMID
+CUPID	+FREUD	IZARD.	NAMED	ROUND	TIRED
CURED.	FROND	JADED	NOMAD	ROVED	TONED
DARED	FUMED	JAPED	NOSED	ROWED	TOTED

90

TOWED	ABODE	AZURE	CACHE	CRUDE	ERASE
TOYED	ABOVE	AZYME.	CADGE	CRUSE	+ERNIE
TREAD	ABUSE	BADGE	CADRE	CURIE	ERODE
TREED	ACUTE	BAIZE	CALVE	CURSE	EVADE
TREND	ADAGE	BARGE	CANOE	CURVE	EVOKE
TRIAD	ADDLE	BASTE	CARTE	CUTIE	EXILE
TRIED	+ADELE	BATHE	CARVE	CYCLE.	EXUDE
TUMID	*ADIGE	BEIGE	CASTE	DANCE	EYRIE.
TUNED	ADOBE	BELIE	CAUSE	+DANTE	FABLE
*TWEED	ADORE	BELLE	CEASE	+DEFOE	FALSE
TYPED.	AERIE	*BERNE	CENSE	DE-ICE	FARCE
UNDID	AFIRE	BIBLE	CHAFE	DELVE	FEEZE
UNWED	AFORE	BILGE	CHAPE	DENSE	FENCE
UP-END	AGAPE	BINGE	CHASE	DEUCE	FESSE
URGED.	AGATE	BLADE	CHIDE	DHOLE	FIBRE
VALID	AGAVE	+BLAKE	*CHILE	DIENE	*FIUME
VAPID	AGILE	BLAME	CHIME	DIODE	FLAKE
VEXED	AGREE	BLARE	CHINE	DIRGE	FLAME
VIVID	AISLE	BLASE	CHIVE	DIXIE	FLARE
VOLED	ALATE	BLAZE	+CHLOE	DODGE	FLITE
VOTED	+ALFIE	BLOKE	CHOKE	DOLCE	FLUKE
VOWED.	ALGAE	BOCHE	CHORE	DONEE	FLUME
WADED	+ALICE	BOGIE	CHOSE	+DONNE	FLUTE
WAGED	ALIKE	BOGLE	CHUTE	DOUSE	FORCE
WAKED	ALIVE	BOMBE	+CIRCE	DOWSE	FORGE
WANED	ALONE	BONZE	+CLARE	+DOYLE	FORME
WAVED	AMATE	BOOZE	CLIME	+DRAKE	FORTE
WAXED	AMAZE	BORNE	+CLIVE	DRAPE	FOSSE
*WEALD	AMBLE	BOULE	CLONE	DRIVE	FRAME
WEIRD	AMICE	BOWIE	CLOSE	DROME	*FROME
WIELD	AMPLE	+BOYLE	CLOVE	DRONE	FROZE
WILED	AMUSE	BRACE	*CLYDE	DROVE	FUDGE
WINED	ANELE	BRAKE	COBLE	DRUPE	FUGUE
WIPED	ANGLE	BRAVE	*COLNE	DULSE	FURZE
WIRED	ANISE	BRAZE	CONGE	DUNCE	FUSEE.
WIVED	ANKLE	BREVE	COPSE	DUPLE.	GABLE
WORLD	ANODE	BRIBE	*CORFE	EAGLE	GAFFE
WOULD	APACE	BRIDE	COUPE	EAGRE	GAUGE
WOUND.	APPLE	BRINE	CRAKE	EDUCE	GAUZE
YAWED	ARETE	BROKE	CRANE	EERIE	GEESE
YIELD	ARGUE	BROSE	CRAPE	ELATE	GENIE
YOKED.	ARISE	+BRUCE	CRATE	ELIDE	GENRE
ZONED	AROSE	BRUME	CRAVE	ELITE	GIGUE
ZOOID	ASIDE	BRUTE	CRAZE	ELOPE	GLACE
	ATONE	BUDGE	CREPE	+ELSIE	GLADE
ABASE	AWAKE	BUGLE	*CRETE	ELUDE	GLARE
ABATE	AWARE	BULGE	*CREWE	EMOTE	GLAZE
*ABBIE	AWOKE	BURKE	CRIME	ENDUE	GLEBE
ABELE	AXILE	BUTTE.	CRONE	ENSUE	GLIDE
ABIDE	AZOTE	CABLE	CRORE	EPODE	GLOBE

91

GLOVE	ISTLE.	METRE	PEASE	REVUE	SIDLE
GLOZE	+JESSE	*MEUSE	PEEVE	*RHINE	SIEGE
GNOME	JOULE	MIDGE	PEKOE	*RHONE	SIEVE
*GOOLE	+JOYCE	+MILNE	PENCE	RHYME	SINCE
GOOSE	JUDGE	MINCE	PERNE	RIDGE	SINGE
GORGE	JUICE	MITRE	PERSE	RIFLE	SKATE
GORSE	+JULIE.	MOIRE	PHAGE	RILLE	SKIVE
GOUGE	KEDGE	+MOORE	PHASE	RINSE	SLAKE
+GRACE	KNAVE	MOOSE	PHONE	ROGUE	SLATE
GRADE	KNIFE	MORSE	PHYLE	ROUGE	SLAVE
GRAPE	KOPJE	MOUSE	PIECE	ROUSE	SLICE
GRATE	KRONE	MOVIE.	PIQUE	ROUTE	SLIDE
GRAVE	KYLOE	NACRE	PIXIE	RUCHE	SLIME
GRAZE	KYRIE.	NAIVE	PLACE	RUPEE.	SLOPE
GREBE	LADLE	NERVE	PLANE	SABLE	SLYPE
GRIDE	+LANCE	NEUME	PLATE	SABRE	SMILE
GRIME	LAPSE	NICHE	PLUME	+SADIE	SMITE
GRIPE	LARGE	NIECE	POISE	SALSE	SMOKE
GROPE	LATHE	+NIOBE	PONCE	SALVE	SMOTE
GROVE	LEASE	NITRE	*POOLE	*SAONE	SNAKE
GUIDE	LEAVE	NIXIE	PORGE	SAUCE	SNARE
GUILE	LEDGE	NOBLE	POSSE	SAUTE	SNIDE
GUISE.	LETHE	NOISE	PRASE	SCALE	SNIPE
*HAGUE	LEVEE	NONCE	PRATE	SCAPE	SNORE
HALVE	LIEGE	NOOSE	PRICE	SCARE	SOCLE
HANSE	*LILLE	NORSE	PRIDE	SCENE	SOLVE
HASTE	LISLE	NUDGE	PRIME	SCONE	*SOMME
HAWSE	LITHE	NURSE.	PRISE	SCOPE	SOUSE
HEAVE	LITRE	OBESE	PRIZE	SCORE	SPACE
HEDGE	+LOCKE	OCHRE	PROBE	SCREE	SPADE
+HELLE	LODGE	OGIVE	PROLE	SEDGE	SPAKE
HELVE	*LOIRE	OLIVE	PRONE	*SEINE	SPARE
HENCE	LOOSE	OMBRE	PROSE	SEISE	SPATE
+HESSE	LOUSE	OPINE	PROVE	SEIZE	SPICE
HINGE	LUCRE	ORATE	PRUDE	SENSE	SPIKE
HOOVE	LUNGE	OUNCE	PRUNE	SERGE	SPINE
+HORAE	LYCEE.	OUTRE	PULSE	SERVE	SPIRE
HORDE	*MAINE	OVATE	PUREE	SHADE	SPITE
HORSE	MAIZE	OVINE	PURGE	SHAKE	SPODE
HOUSE	MANGE	OVULE	PURSE.	SHALE	SPOKE
*HYTHE.	MANSE	OXIDE	QUAKE	SHAME	SPORE
IMAGE	MAPLE	OZONE.	QUEUE	SHAPE	SPREE
IMBUE	MARGE	PADRE	QUIRE	SHARE	SPUME
INANE	*MARNE	PANNE	QUITE	SHAVE	STAGE
INGLE	+MAUDE	PARSE	QUOTE.	SHINE	STAKE
INURE	MAUVE	PASSE	RAISE	SHIRE	STALE
IRATE	MAYBE	PASTE	RANCE	SHONE	STARE
+IRENE	MERGE	PAUSE	RANEE	SHORE	STATE
*ISERE	+MERLE	PAYEE	RANGE	SHOVE	STAVE
ISSUE	MESNE	PEACE	REEVE	+SHUTE	STERE

+STEVE	TROPE	BRIEF.	FLONG	+BOOTH	GLYPH
STILE	TRUCE	CALIF	FLUNG.	+BOSCH	GNASH
STOKE	TULLE	CHAFF	GOING.	BOTCH	GRAPH
STOLE	TWERE	CHIEF	ICING.	BOUGH	GULCH.
STONE	TWICE	+CLIFF.	LYING.	BRASH	HARSH
STORE	TWINE.	DRAFF	+MAGOG	BROTH	HATCH
STOVE	UKASE	DWARF.	+MORAG.	BRUSH	+HEATH
STUPE	UNCLE	FLUFF.	OWING.	BUMPH	HEIGH
STYLE	UNDUE	+GEOFF	PRANG	BUNCH	HITCH
SUAVE	UNITE	GRIEF	PRONG.	BURGH	HOOCH
SUEDE	UNTIE	GRUFF.	RUING.	BUTCH.	HOUGH
SUITE	URINE	MOTIF.	SCRAG	CATCH	HUMPH
SURGE	USAGE.	PROOF.	SHRUG	CINCH	HUNCH
SWEDE	VAGUE	QUAFF	SLANG	CLASH	HUTCH.
SWINE	VALUE	QUIFF.	SLING	CLOTH	IRISH.
SWIPE	VALVE	SCARF	SLUNG.	COACH	+JONAH.
SWORE	VENUE	SCOFF	SPRAG	CONCH	+KEITH
SYCEE.	VERGE	SCUFF	SPRIG	COUCH	KETCH.
TABLE	+VERNE	SCURF	STING	COUGH	LARCH
TASTE	VERSE	SERIF	STUNG	COUTH	LATCH
TAWSE	VERVE	SHEAF	SUING.	CRASH	LAUGH
TEASE	VOGUE	SHELF	SWING	CRUSH.	LEACH
TENSE	VOICE	SKIFF	SWUNG.	DEATH	LEASH
TEPEE	VOILE	SNIFF	THING	DEPTH	LEECH
TERSE	VOLTE.	SNUFF	THONG	+DINAH	*LEITH
THANE	WAIVE	SPOOF	TWANG.	DITCH	LOATH
THEME	WASTE	STAFF	UNPEG	DOUGH	LOUGH
THERE	WEAVE	STIFF	UNRIG	DUTCH.	LUNCH
THESE	WEDGE	STUFF.	USING.	EARTH	LURCH
THINE	WHALE	THIEF.	VYING.	+EDITH	LYMPH
THOLE	WHERE	WHARF	WRING	+ENOCH	LYNCH.
THOSE	WHILE	WHIFF	WRONG	EPOCH	MARCH
THREE	WHINE	+WOOLF	WRUNG.	*ERITH.	MARSH
THROE	WHITE		YOUNG	+FAITH	MATCH
THYME	WHOLE	ALONG		FETCH	MILCH
TILDE	WHORE	AMONG	ABASH	FIFTH	MIRTH
TINGE	WHOSE	APING	ALLAH	FILCH	MONTH
*TIREE	+WILDE	AWING.	APISH	FILTH	MOOCH
TITHE	WINCE	BEFOG	AWASH.	FINCH	MOUTH
TITLE	WITHE	BEING	BATCH	FIRTH	MULCH
TONNE	WORSE	BHANG	BEACH	FITCH	+MUNCH
TOPEE	WRITE	+BRAGG	BEECH	FLASH	MYRRH.
TOQUE	WROTE.	BRING.	BELCH	FLESH	*NEATH
TRACE	YOURE	CLANG	BENCH	FLUSH	NEIGH
TRADE	YOUVE.	CLING	BERTH	*FORTH	NINTH
TRIBE	*ZAIRE	CLUNG.	BIRCH	FRESH	NORTH
TRICE		DEBAG	BIRTH	FRITH	NOTCH
TRINE	ALOOF.	DOING	BITCH	FROTH.	NYMPH.
TRIPE	*BANFF	DYING.	BLUSH	+GARTH	OBEAH
TRITE	BLUFF	FLING	*BLYTH	GIRTH	*OMAGH

93

OOMPH.	TILTH	KHAKI	CLEEK	QUACK	TWEAK.
PARCH	TOOTH	KUKRI.	CLERK	QUARK	UMIAK.
PATCH	TORAH	MAORI	CLICK	QUICK	WHACK
PEACH	TORCH	*MENAI	CLINK	QUIRK.	WHELK
PERCH	TOUCH	*MIAMI	CLOAK	SHACK	WHISK
*PERTH	TOUGH	+MITZI	CLOCK	SHANK	WRACK
PILCH	TRASH	MUFTI	CLUCK	SHARK	WREAK
PINCH	TROTH	MULTI.	CRACK	SHIRK	WRECK
PITCH	TRUTH.	NAAFI	CRANK	SHOCK	WRICK
PLASH	VETCH	+NAOMI.	CREAK	SHOOK	
PLUSH	VOUCH.	OBELI	CREEK	SHUCK	ABOIL
POACH	WATCH	OKAPI.	CRICK	SKULK	ALGAL
POOCH	+WAUGH	RABBI	CROAK	SKUNK	ANGEL
PORCH	WEIGH	RADII.	CROCK	SLACK	ANNAL
POUCH	WELCH	SALMI	CROOK.	SLICK	ANNUL
PUNCH.	WELSH	SERAI	+DEREK	SLINK	ANVIL
QUASH	WENCH	*SINAI	DRANK	SLUNK	APPAL
QUOTH.	WHICH	SPAHI.	DRINK	SMACK	+APRIL
RAJAH	WIDTH	+VERDI	DRUNK.	SMIRK	AREAL
+RALPH	WINCH	VILLI.	FLANK	SMOCK	ARGIL
RANCH	WITCH	ZOMBI	FLASK	SNACK	ARGOL
RATCH	WORTH		FLECK	SNEAK	ARIEL
REACH	WRATH	ABACK	FLICK	SNICK	ATOLL
REICH	WROTH.	ALACK	FLOCK	SNOOK	AURAL
RETCH	YOUTH	AMUCK	FLUNK	SPANK	AVAIL
ROACH		APEAK.	+FRANK	SPARK	+AVRIL
ROUGH.	ACINI	BATIK	FREAK	SPEAK	AWFUL
SELAH	ALIBI	BAULK	FRISK	SPECK	AXIAL.
SHUSH	APPUI	BLACK	FROCK.	SPOOK	BABEL
SIXTH	ASSAI.	BLANK	GREEK	SPUNK	BABUL
SLASH	CACTI	BLEAK	GROOK.	STACK	BANAL
SLOSH	*CAPRI	BLINK	HOICK.	STALK	BASAL
SLOTH	CHILI	BLOCK	KAPOK	STANK	+BASIL
SLUSH	COATI	BREAK	KAYAK	STARK	BE-ALL
SMASH	COCCI	BRICK	KIOSK	STEAK	+BERYL
SMITH	CORGI.	BRINK	KNACK	STICK	BETEL
SOOTH	DALAI	BRISK	KNOCK	STINK	BEVEL
SOUGH	*DELHI	BROCK	KULAK.	STOCK	BEZEL
SOUTH	DHOBI	BROOK.	LUNIK.	STOOK	BRAWL
STASH	DHOTI	CAULK	*MINSK	STORK	BRILL
STICH	*DUBAI.	CHALK	MUJIK	STUCK	BROIL
SWASH	ELEMI	CHECK	MUZAK.	STUNK	BUBAL.
SWATH	ENNUI.	CHEEK	*OZARK.	SWANK.	CABAL
SWISH	FUNGI.	CHICK	PLANK	THANK	CAMEL
SYLPH.	HADJI	CHINK	PLONK	THICK	CANAL
TEACH	*HAITI	CHOCK	PLUCK	TRACK	+CAROL
TEETH	*HANOI	CHUCK	PLUNK	TRICK	CAVIL
TENCH	HINDI	CHUNK	PRANK	TRUCK	+CECIL
TENTH	HOURI.	CLACK	PRICK	TRUNK	CHILL
THIGH	INDRI.	CLANK	PRINK.		CHURL

CIVIL	IDEAL	PENAL	SWILL	BREAM	SERUM
COPAL	IDYLL	PERIL	SWIRL	BROOM	SHAWM
CORAL	IMPEL.	PETAL	+SYBIL.	BUXOM.	SPASM
CRAWL	JEWEL	PHIAL	TAMIL	CHARM	SPERM
CREEL	JUGAL.	PROWL	TIDAL	CHASM	STEAM
CRUEL	*KABUL	PUPIL	TONAL	CLAIM	STORM
+CYRIL.	KEVEL	PYGAL.	TOTAL	CREAM.	STRUM
DATAL	KNEEL	QUAIL	TOWEL	DATUM	SWARM.
DECAL	KNELL	QUELL	TRAIL	DEISM	THERM
DEVIL	KNOLL	QUILL.	TRAWL	DENIM	THRUM
DOWEL	KNURL	RATAL	TRIAL	DREAM.	TOTEM.
DRAIL	KRAAL.	RAVEL	TRILL	*EGHAM	UNARM.
DRAWL	LABEL	REBEL	TROLL	*EPSOM.	VELUM
DRILL	LAPEL	REGAL	TRULL	FLEAM	VENOM.
DROLL	LEGAL	RENAL	TUBAL	FORUM.	XYLEM
DROOL	LEVEL	REPEL	TWILL	GLEAM	
DUCAL	LIBEL	REVEL	TWIRL	GLOOM	+AARON
DWELL.	LOCAL	RIVAL	*TYROL.	GOYIM	ACORN
EASEL	LOYAL	RORAL	UMBEL	+GRIMM	ADMAN
ENROL	LYSOL.	ROWEL	UNTIL	GROOM.	ADORN
EQUAL	+MABEL	ROYAL	USUAL.	HAKIM	AGAIN
+ERROL	MEDAL	RURAL.	VASAL	HAREM	*AKRON
+ETHEL	METAL	SCOWL	VENAL	HAULM	ALIEN
ETHYL	METOL	SCULL	+VIDAL	HILUM	ALIGN
EXCEL	MODAL	*SEOUL	VIGIL	HOKUM.	ALL-IN
EXPEL	MODEL	SEPAL	VINYL	IDIOM	AMAIN
EXTOL.	MOGUL	SHAWL	VITAL	ILEUM	*AMMAN
FATAL	MORAL	SHELL	VOCAL	ILIUM	+AMMON
FERAL	MOREL	SHEOL	VOWEL.	ISLAM.	ANION
FINAL	MOTEL	SHOAL	WHEEL	JORUM.	APIAN
FLAIL	MURAL.	SISAL	WHIRL	LOCUM.	APRON
FOCAL	NASAL	SKILL	WHORL.	MADAM	ARGON
FOREL	*NATAL	SKIRL	YODEL	MAXIM	ARIAN
FRAIL	NAVAL	SKULL	YOKEL	MINIM.	+ARION
FRILL	NAVEL	SMALL	YOULL.	OAKUM	*ARRAN
FUGAL	*NEPAL	SMELL	ZONAL	ODIUM	ARSON
FUSEL.	NEWEL	SNAIL	ZORIL	OGHAM	ARYAN
GAVEL	+NIGEL	SNARL		OPIUM.	ASHEN
GHOUL	+NOBEL	SNELL	ABEAM	PLASM	ASIAN
GHYLL	NODAL	SPELL	ADEEM	+PRIAM	ASPEN
GNARL	NOPAL	SPIEL	ALARM	PRISM	*ASWAN
GRAIL	NOVEL.	SPILL	ALBUM	PROEM	+AUDEN
GRILL	OFFAL	SPOIL	ALGUM	PSALM.	AVIAN.
GROWL	ORIEL	SPOOL	*ASSAM	QUALM.	+BACON
GRUEL	OUSEL	STALL	AXIOM.	REALM	BAIRN
GYRAL.	OUZEL.	STEAL	BEDIM	REARM	BARON
+HAZEL	PANEL	STEEL	BEGUM	RHEUM.	BASIN
HORAL	PAPAL	STILL	BESOM	SCRAM	BASON
HOTEL	+PEARL	STOOL	BLOOM	SCRIM	BATON
HOVEL.	PEDAL	SWELL	BOSOM	SCRUM	BEGAN

BEGIN	+EDWIN	LINEN	RIVEN	*TURIN	DILDO
BEGUN	ELFIN	LIVEN	+ROBIN	*TWAIN	DINGO
+BEHAN	*ELGIN	LOGAN	+RODIN	TWEEN.	DITTO
+BEVAN	+ELLEN	LUMEN	ROMAN	UHLAN	*DOURO.
BISON	ELVAN	LUPIN	ROSIN	UNION	FOLIO
BLAIN	*ESSEN.	*LUTON.	ROVEN	UNMAN	FORGO.
BLOWN	FANON	*MACON	ROWAN.	UNPEN	+GARBO
BORON	FEIGN	MASON	+SAGAN	UNPIN	GECKO
BOSON	FELON	MELON	SALON	URBAN.	GESSO
BOURN	FLOWN	MESON	SATAN	VIXEN.	GUANO
BRAIN	FOEHN	*MILAN	SATIN	WAGON	GUMBO
BRAWN	FROWN.	MIZEN	SAXON	WAKEN	GUSTO.
+BRIAN	*GABON	MORON	SCION	WAXEN	HALLO
BROWN	GAMIN	MOURN.	SCORN	WIDEN	HELLO
BRUIN	+GAVIN	*NAIRN	SEDAN	*WIGAN	HIPPO
BURIN	GIVEN	+NIXON	SEMEN	WIZEN	HYDRO.
+BYRON.	GLEAN	NYLON.	SEVEN	+WODEN	*IDAHO
CABIN	GOWAN	OAKEN	SHEEN	WOKEN	IGLOO
CAIRN	GRAIN	OATEN	SHORN	WOMAN	IMAGO
CANON	GREEN	OCEAN	SHOWN	WOMEN	+INIGO.
CAPON	GROAN	OFTEN	+SIMON	WOVEN.	JINGO
*CAVAN	GROIN	OLDEN	+SINON	XENON.	JOCKO
CETIN	GROWN.	OLEIN	SIREN	YAPON	JUMBO
CHAIN	HAVEN	ONION	SIT-IN	YEARN	JUNTO.
CHIAN	+HAYDN	ORGAN	SKEIN	*YEMEN	KAROO
CHURN	+HELEN	+ORION	SLAIN	YOGIN	*KELSO
CLEAN	HE-MAN	ORPIN	*SPAIN	*YUKON	*KYOTO.
CLOWN	HERON	+ORSON.	SPAWN		LARGO
COIGN	HUMAN	+PAEAN	SPOON	AMINO.	LASSO
+COLIN	*HURON	PAGAN	SPURN	BABOO	LIMBO
COLON	HYMEN	PATEN	STAIN	BANJO	LINGO
COVEN	HYSON.	PAVAN	STEAN	BEANO	LOTTO.
COZEN	+IBSEN	PECAN	STEEN	BILBO	*MACAO
+CREON	INURN.	+PERON	STERN	BINGO	*MALMO
CROON	*JAPAN	PLAIN	*SUDAN	BONGO	MANGO
CROWN	+JASON	PRAWN	+SUSAN	BRAVO	+MARGO
CUMIN.	JETON	PREEN	SWAIN	BUCKO	METRO
DEIGN	JUPON.	PYLON.	SWOON	BUMBO	MEZZO
DEMON	+KAREN	QUEAN	SWORN.	BUNCO	MICRO
*DEVON	+KEVIN	QUEEN	TAKEN	BURRO.	MOTTO.
*DIJON	KNOWN	QUERN	TALON	CACAO	NEGRO.
DIVAN	KORAN.	QUOIN.	TAXIN	*CAIRO	OUTDO
DOYEN	LADEN	RADON	TENON	CAMEO	OUTGO.
DOZEN	LAGAN	RAVEN	THORN	CANTO	PANTO
DRAIN	LATIN	RAYON	TITAN	CARGO	PATIO
DRAWN	LEARN	REIGN	TOKEN	CELLO	PHONO
DROWN	LEMON	RESIN	TORAN	COMPO	PHOTO
+DYLAN.	+LENIN	RIPEN	TOXIN	*CONGO	PIANO
+EAMON	LIE-IN	*RIPON	TRAIN	CREDO	PIEZO
EATEN	LIKEN	RISEN	TRY-ON	CURIO.	+PLATO

+PLUTO	CRISP	SYRUP.	CHEER	FEMUR	LEMUR
POLIO	CROUP	THORP	CHIRR	FETOR	LEPER
POTTO	CRUMP.	THUMP	CHOIR	FEVER	LEVER
PUTTO.	DROOP.	TIE-UP	CIDER	FEWER	LIFER
*QUITO.	EQUIP.	TRAMP	CIGAR	FIFER	LINER
RADIO	FLUMP	TROOP	CLEAR	FILAR	LIVER
RATIO	FRUMP.	TRUMP	COPER	FILER	LOBAR
RECTO	GALOP	TULIP	CORER	FINER	LONER
RHINO	GET-UP	TWERP.	COVER	FIVER	LOSER
RODEO	GRASP	UNCAP	COWER	FIXER	LOVER
RONDO.	GROUP.	UNRIP	CRIER	FLAIR	LOWER
SALVO	JALAP	UNZIP	CURER	FLEER	LUNAR.
SAMBO	JULEP.	USURP.	CYMAR.	FLOOR	MAJOR
SAY-SO	MIX-UP.	WHAUP	*DAKAR	FLOUR	MAKER
SET-TO	ORLOP	WHELP	DEBAR	FLUOR	MANOR
SEXTO	OXLIP.	WHOOP	DECOR	FLYER	MASER
SHAKO	PIN-UP		DEFER	FOYER	MATER
*SLIGO	PLUMP	ABHOR	DEMUR	FRIAR	MAYOR
SOTTO.	POLYP	+ABNER	DETER	FRYER.	MAZER
TABOO	POULP	ACTOR	DIMER	GLAIR	METER
TANGO	PRIMP.	ADDER	DINAR	GOFER	MILER
TARDO	RECAP.	AFTER	DINER	GONER	MINER
TEMPO	SALEP	AGGER	DIVER	*GOWER.	MINOR
*TOKYO	SCALP	AIRER	DONOR	HATER	MISER
TORSO	SCAMP	ALDER	DOTER	HAVER	MIXER
*TRURO	SCARP	ALTAR	*DOVER	HEWER	MOLAR
TURBO.	SCOOP	ALTER	DOWER	HIKER	MOTOR
VERSO	SCRAP	AMBER	DOZER	HIRER	MOVER
VIDEO	SCRIP	AMEER	OREAR	HOVER	MOWER.
VIRGO.	SCULP	AMOUR	DRIER	+HOMER	NADIR
WHOSO.	SET-UP	ANGER	DRYER	HYPER.	NEVER
YAHOO	SHARP	ARBOR	+DURER.	ICHOR	NEWER
	SHEEP	ASTER	EAGER	IDLER	NICER
+AESOP.	SKIMP	ASTIR	EATER	INCUR	*NIGER.
*BACUP	SLEEP	ATTAR	+EDGAR	INFER	OCCUR
BEBOP	SLOOP	AUGER	EGGER	INNER	ODDER
BLEEP	SLUMP	AUGUR.	EIDER	INTER	ODOUR
BLIMP.	SNOOP	BAKER	ELDER	INVAR	OFFER
CHAMP	STAMP	BALER	+ELGAR	*IZMIR.	OLDER
CHEAP	STEEP	BLEAR	+ELMER	JOKER	ORDER
CHEEP	STOOP	BORER	ELVER	JUROR.	ORMER
CHIMP	STOUP	BOWER	EMBER	KAFIR	+OSCAR
CHIRP	STRAP	BOXER	ENTER	KNURR.	OSIER
CHUMP	STRIP	BRIAR	ERROR	LAGER	OTHER
CLAMP	STROP	BUYER.	*ESHER	LAHAR	OTTER
CLASP	STUMP	CABER	ESTER	LASER	OUTER
CLUMP	SUN-UP	CAPER	ETHER.	LATER	OWNER.
CRAMP	SWAMP	CATER	FACER	LAVER	PALER
CREEP	SWEEP	CEDAR	FAKER	LAYER	PAPER
CRIMP	SWOOP	CHAIR	FAKIR	LAZAR	PATER

+PETER	STAIR		CROSS	JEANS	+PEPYS
PIPER	STEER		CUTIS	+JESUS	PIOUS
POKER	*STOUR		+CYRUS.	+JUDAS.	PRESS
POLAR	SUGAR	ABYSS	+DEGAS	+KEATS	PROPS
POSER	SUPER	+ADAMS	*DELOS	KUDOS	PUBES
POWER	SURER	AEGIS	DEMOS	KUMIS.	PUBIS
PRIOR	SWEAR.	+AGNES	+DENIS	*LAGOS	PYXIS.
PURER.	TABOR	ALIAS	+DILYS	LAPIS	QUINS
+QATAR	TAKER	AMASS	DIPUS	LARES	QUITS.
QUEER.	TAMER	AMISS	+DORIS	*LEEDS	REBUS
RACER	TAPER	*ANDES	DREGS	*LEWES	+REMUS
RADAR	TAPIR	*ANGUS	DRESS	*LEWIS	+RUFUS.
RARER	TENOR	APHIS	DROSS	LINKS	SCOBS
RAZOR	THEIR	APSIS	+DUMAS.	LIVES	SCOTS
RECUR	*TIBER	+ARGUS	EAVES	LOCUS	SINUS
REFER	TIGER	ARIES	+ELLIS	LOESS	SPECS
RIDER	TIMER	*ARRAS	ELVES	LOGOS	SWISS
RIGOR	*TIMOR	ARRIS	EMBUS	LORIS	*SYROS.
RIPER	TOPER	ARSIS	ETHOS.	LOTUS	TABES
RISER	TOWER	*ATLAS.	FAVUS	+LOUIS	TALUS
RIVER	TRIER	BALAS	FETUS	LUPUS	TAMIS
+ROGER	TRUER	BANNS	FINIS	*LYONS.	TAPIS
ROTOR	TUBER	BASIS	FIVES	MAGUS	TAXIS
ROVER	TUDOR	BENDS	FLIES	MANES	TEENS
ROWER	TUNER	BITTS	FLOSS	MATHS	*TEXAS
RUDER	TUTOR	BLESS	FOCUS	+MAVIS	THEWS
RULER.	+TYLER.	+BLISS	FRASS	METHS	TONGS
SAFER	UDDER	BLUES	FUCUS.	+MIDAS	TONUS
SAKER	ULCER	BOGUS	GAUSS	+MILES	TORUS
SANER	ULNAR	BOLAS	GENUS	+MINOS	TRESS
SATYR	UMBER	BOLUS	GIBUS	MINUS	TREWS
SAVER	UNBAR	BONUS	+GILES	MODUS	TRUSS
SCOUR	UNDER	BOWLS	GLASS	MORES	*TUNIS
SENOR	UPPER	BRASS	GLOSS	+MOSES	TURPS.
SEVER	USHER	+BURNS.	+GRASS	MUCUS	+VENUS
SEWER	UTTER.	+CACUS	GROSS	MUMPS.	VIRUS.
SHEAR	VELAR	+CAMUS	GUESS	NARES	*WALES
SHEER	VICAR	CATES	GULES.	NEGUS	+WELLS
SHIRR	VILER	+CERES	HADES	*NEVIS	WIVES.
SIZAR	VIPER	+CHAOS	HAMES	NEXUS	+YEATS
SKIER	VISOR	CHESS	HIVES	*NIMES	YOURS
SMEAR	VOTER.	*CHIOS	HOCUS	NODUS	*YPRES
SNEER	WADER	+CHRIS	+HORUS	NONES	
SOBER	WAFER	CLASS	HUMUS.	+NOYES.	ABAFT
SOLAR	WAGER	+COMUS	ICTUS	OASES	ABBOT
SONAR	WATER	CORPS	INCUS	OASIS	ABORT
SORER	WAVER	*COWES	*INDUS.	ORRIS.	ABOUT
SOWER	WHIRR	CRAPS	JACKS	PANTS	ADAPT
SPEAR	WIDER	CRASS	+JAMES	*PARIS	ADEPT
SPOOR	WIPER	CRESS	+JANUS	PENIS	ADMIT

ADOPT	CARET	ELECT	GREET	MIDST	ROBOT
ADULT	CHANT	+ELIOT	GRIST	MIGHT	ROOST
AFOOT	CHART	ENACT	GROAT	MOIST	ROUST.
AGENT	CHEAT	EPACT	GROUT	+MONET	SABOT
AGLET	CHERT	ERECT	GRUNT	MOTET	SAINT
ALERT	CHEST	ERGOT	GUEST	MOULT	SCANT
ALLOT	CIVET	ERUCT	GUILT.	MOUNT	SCART
ALOFT	CLEAT	ERUPT	HABIT	MULCT.	SCENT
AMBIT	CLEFT	EVENT	HADNT	NIGHT.	SCOOT
ANENT	CLINT	EVERT	HASNT	OCTET	+SCOTT
ANGST	CLOUT	EVICT	HAUNT	ONSET	SCOUT
APART	COAST	EXACT	HEART	OP-ART	SHAFT
ARENT	COMET	EXALT	HEIST	ORBIT	SHANT
ARGOT	CO-OPT	EXEAT	HELOT	OUGHT	SHEET
*ASCOT	+COROT	EXERT	HOIST	OVERT	SHIFT
ASSET	COUNT	EXIST	+HOLST	OWLET.	SHIRT
AUDIT	COURT	EXULT.	HURST.	PAINT	SHOOT
AUGHT	COVET	FACET	IDIOT	PEWIT	SHORT
AVAST	CRAFT	FAINT	IMPOT	PICOT	SHOUT
AVERT	CREPT	FAULT	INAPT	PILOT	SHUNT
AWAIT.	CREST	+FAUST	INEPT	PIPIT	SIGHT
BEAST	CROFT	FEAST	INERT	PITOT	SKEET
BEFIT	CRUET	FEINT	INGOT	PIVOT	SKINT
BEGET	CRUST	FIGHT	INLET	PLAIT	SKIRT
BEGOT	CRYPT	FILET	INPUT	PLANT	SLANT
BERET	CUBIT.	FIRST	INSET	PLEAT	*SLEAT
BESET	DAUNT	FLEET	ISLET.	PCINT	SLEET
BIDET	DAVIT	FLINT	JABOT	POULT	SMALT
BIGHT	DEALT	FLIRT	+JANET	POSIT	SMART
BIGOT	DEBIT	FLOAT	JAUNT	PRINT.	SMELT
+BIZET	DEBUT	FLOUT	JOINT	QUANT	SNORT
BLAST	DEIST	FOIST	JOIST	QUART	SNOUT
BLEAT	*DELFT	FOUNT	JOUST.	QUEST	SPELT
BLEST	DEPOT	FRONT	KAPUT	QUIET	SPENT
BLOAT	DIDNT	+FROST	KNELT	QUILT	SPILT
BLUNT	DIGIT	FRUIT.	KNOUT	QUINT	SPIRT
BLURT	DIVOT	GAMUT	KRAIT.	QUIRT	*SPLIT
BOAST	DOUBT	GAULT	LEANT	QUOIT.	SPORT
BOOST	DRAFT	GAUNT	LEAPT	*RABAT	SPOUT
BRACT	DRIFT	+GENET	LEAST	REACT	SPRAT
BRANT	DROIT	*GHENT	LEGIT	REBUT	SPRIT
*BRENT	DUCAT	GHOST	LICIT	REEST	SPURT
*BREST	DURST	GIANT	LIGHT	REFIT	SQUAT
BRUIT	DWELT.	GIGOT	LIMIT	REMIT	START
BRUNT	ECLAT	GLEET	+LISZT.	REPOT	STILT
BUILT	EDICT	GLINT	+MANET	RESET	STINT
BURNT	EGEST	GLOAT	MAYNT	REVET	STOAT
BURST.	EGRET	GRAFT	MAYST	RIGHT	STOUT
CADET	EIGHT	+GRANT	MEANT	RIVET	STRUT
CARAT	EJECT	GREAT	MERIT	ROAST	STUNT

99

SWEAT		*ESSEX.	+BETSY	CURDY	DUSKY
SWEET	ADIEU	+FELIX.	+BETTY	CURLY	DUSTY.
SWEPT	*ANJOU.	HELIX	BILLY	CURRY	EARLY
+SWIFT.	BAYOU	HYRAX.	+BOBBY	CUSHY	EBONY
TACIT	BIJOU.	INDEX	BOGEY	CUTTY.	EDIFY
TAINT	*CORFU	INFIX.	BOGGY	DADDY	ELEGY
TAROT	COYPU	LATEX.	BONNY	DAFFY	EMBAY
TAUNT	*CYMRU.	MUREX.	BOOBY	DAILY	EMERY
TEMPT	FICHU.	PHLOX.	BOOTY	DAIRY	+EMILY
TENET	HINDU.	RADIX	BOOZY	+DAISY	EMPTY
THEFT	+NEHRU.	RELAX.	BOSKY	DALLY	ENEMY
*TIBET	PERDU.	SALIX	BOSSY	DANDY	ENJOY
TIGHT	SNAFU.	SILEX	BOTHY	+DANNY	ENTRY
TINCT	VIRTU	SIOUX.	BRINY	DARKY	ENVOY
TOAST		TELEX.	BUDDY	DEARY	EPOXY
TRACT	AGLOW	UNFIX	BUDGY	DECAY	ESSAY
TRAIT	ALLOW	UNSEX.	BUGGY	DECOY	EVERY.
TREAT	ARROW	VARIX	BULKY	DECRY	FADDY
*TRENT	ASKEW.		BULLY	DEIFY	FAIRY
TROUT	BEDEW	ABBEY	BUMPY	DEITY	FANCY
TRUST	BELOW	AGONY	BUNNY	DELAY	+FANNY
TRYST	BY-LAW.	ALLAY	BURLY	*DERBY	FARCY
TWEET	ELBOW	ALLEY	BUSBY	DIARY	FATTY
TWIST	ENDOW.	ALLOY	BUSHY	DICEY	FELLY
TWIXT.	IN-LAW.	AMBRY	BY-WAY.	DICKY	FENNY
U-BOAT	MACAW	AMITY	CABBY	DIMLY	FERNY
UNAPT	MIAOW.	AMPLY	CADDY	DINGY	FERRY
UNCUT	OXBOW.	ANGRY	CAGEY	DINKY	FIERY
UNFIT	PAPAW.	ANNOY	CANDY	DIRTY	FIFTY
UNIAT	RENEW.	ANOMY	CANNY	DISHY	FILLY
UPSET.	SCREW	APERY	CARRY	DITTY	FILMY
VALET	SHREW	APPLY	+CATHY	DIVVY	FINNY
VAULT	SINEW	APTLY	CATTY	DIZZY	FIRRY
VAUNT	SQUAW	ARRAY	CHARY	DODGY	FISHY
VELDT	STRAW	ASSAY.	CHOKY	DOGGY	FITLY
VERST	STREW.	BADLY	CISSY	DOILY	FIZZY
VISIT	THREW	BAGGY	CLARY	DOLLY	FLAKY
VOLET	THROW.	BALMY	COALY	DOPEY	FLAMY
VOMIT.	WIDOW	BANDY	COCKY	DORMY	FLUKY
WAIST		BARMY	COKEY	DOTTY	FLUTY
WASNT	ADDAX	+BARRY	COMFY	DOWDY	FOAMY
WHEAT	ADMIX	BATTY	*CORBY	DOWNY	FOGEY
WHIST	AFFIX	BAWDY	CORKY	DOWRY	FOGGY
*WIGHT	ANNEX.	BEADY	CORNY	DRYLY	FOLLY
WORST	BEAUX	BEEFY	COVEY	DUCHY	FORAY
WREST	BORAX.	BEERY	COYLY	DUCKY	FORBY
WRIST.	CALIX	BELAY	CRAZY	DULLY	FORTY
YACHT	CALYX	BELLY	CRONY	DUMMY	FUBSY
YEAST.	CODEX	+BENNY	CUBBY	DUMPY	FUGGY
ZIBET	CULEX.	BERRY	CUDDY	DUNGY	FULLY

FUNKY	HIPPY	LAKEY	MUGGY	PETTY	ROPEY
FUNNY	HOARY	LANKY	MUMMY	PHONY	ROWDY
FURRY	HOBBY	LARDY	MURKY	PIETY	RUDDY
FURZY	HOLEY	LARKY	MUSHY	PIGGY	*RUGBY
FUSSY	HOLLY	+LARRY	MUSKY	PIGMY	RUMLY
FUSTY	HOMEY	LAXLY	MUSTY	PINKY	RUMMY
FUZZY.	HONEY	LAYBY	MUZZY.	PINNY	RUNNY
GAILY	HONKY	LEADY	+NANCY	PITHY	RUSHY
GAMMY	HOOEY	LEAFY	NANNY	PLUMY	RUSTY
GASSY	HORNY	LEAKY	NAPPY	POCKY	RUTTY.
GAUDY	HORSY	LEERY	NARKY	PODGY	SADLY
GAUZY	HOTLY	LEGGY	NASTY	POESY	+SALLY
GAWKY	HOWDY	+LENNY	NATTY	+POLLY	SALTY
GEMMY	HUBBY	+LIBBY	NAVVY	POMMY	+SANDY
GIDDY	HUFFY	LIMEY	NEEDY	POPPY	SAPPY
GIPSY	HUMPY	LOAMY	NERVY	POPSY	SARKY
GLORY	HURRY	LOBBY	NEWLY	PORKY	SAUCY
GLUEY	HUSKY	LOFTY	NEWSY	POTTY	SAVOY
GODLY	HUSSY.	LOLLY	NIFTY	PRIVY	SAVVY
GOLLY	ICILY	LOONY	NINNY	PROSY	SCALY
GOODY	IMPLY	LOOPY	NIPPY	PROXY	SEAMY
GOOEY	INLAY	LORRY	NOBLY	PUDGY	SEEDY
GOOFY	IRONY	LOUSY	NOISY	PUDSY	SEPOY
GORSY	*ISLAY	LOWLY	NOSEY	PUFFY	SHADY
GOUTY	*ITALY	LUCKY	NOWAY	PULPY	SHAKY
GRAPY	ITCHY	LUMPY	NUTTY.	PUNTY	SHALY
GRAVY	IVORY.	*LUNDY	ODDLY	PUPPY	SHINY
GRIMY	JAMMY	LUSTY.	+ORCZY	PURSY	SHOWY
GULLY	JAZZY	MADLY	OVARY.	PUSSY	SHYLY
GUMMY	JELLY	MANGY	+PADDY	PUTTY	SILKY
GUNNY	JEMMY	MANLY	PALLY	PYGMY.	SILLY
GUPPY	+JENNY	MARRY	PALMY	QUERY	SISSY
GUSTY	JERKY	MASSY	PALSY	RAINY	SIXTY
GYPSY.	+JERRY	MEALY	PANSY	RALLY	SLATY
HAIRY	JETTY	MEATY	PARKY	RANDY	SLIMY
HAMMY	JEWRY	MERCY	PARRY	RANGY	SLYLY
HANDY	JIFFY	MERRY	PARTY	RATTY	SMOKY
HANKY	+JIMMY	MESSY	PASTY	RAWLY	SNAKY
HAPLY	JOLLY	MILKY	+PATTY	READY	SNOWY
HAPPY	JUICY	MINGY	PAWKY	REEDY	SOAPY
+HARDY	JUMPY	MISTY	PEAKY	REEKY	SOGGY
HARPY	JUNKY.	+MOLLY	PEATY	RELAY	SONNY
+HARRY	*KANDY	MONEY	+PEGGY	REPAY	SONSY
HASTY	*KERRY	MOODY	+PENNY	REPLY	SOOTY
HEADY	KIDDY	MOONY	PEONY	RETRY	SOPPY
HEAVY	KINKY	*MORAY	PEPPY	RISKY	SORRY
HEFTY	+KITTY	MOSSY	+PERCY	RITZY	SOUPY
+HENRY	KOOKY.	MOUSY	+PERRY	ROCKY	SPICY
HILLY	LADDY	MUCKY	PERKY	ROOKY	SPIKY
HINNY	LAITY	MUDDY	PESKY	ROOMY	SPINY

SPIRY	UNITY
SPLAY	UNSAY
SPRAY	USURY.
SPUMY	+VICKY.
STAGY	WACKY
STONY	WADDY
STORY	WANLY
STRAY	WARTY
STUDY	WASHY
SUETY	WEARY
SULKY	WEEDY
SULLY	WEENY
SUNNY	WEEPY
SURLY.	+WENDY
TABBY	WETLY
TACKY	WINDY
TAFFY	WISPY
TALLY	WITHY
TAMMY	WITTY
TANGY	WOODY
TANSY	WORDY
TARDY	WORMY
TARRY	WORRY
TARTY	WRYLY.
TASTY	YOLKY.
TATTY	ZIPPY
TAWNY	
+TEDDY	BLITZ.
TEENY	*CADIZ.
TELLY	FRIZZ.
*TENBY	HERTZ.
+TERRY	TOPAZ.
TESTY	WALTZ
THEWY	
TINNY	
TIPSY	
TIZZY	
TOADY	
TODAY	
TODDY	
TOKAY	
+TOMMY	
+TRACY	
TRULY	
TUBBY	
TUMMY	
TUNNY	
TURFY	
TUTTY.	
UNIFY	

102

ABACUS	ACCEPT	AVENUE	AKIMBO	ALMOST
*ABADAN	ACCESS	AVERSE	+ALICIA	ARMADA
ABASED	ACCORD	AWEARY	ALIGHT	*ARMAGH
ABATED	ACCOST	AWEIGH.	+ALISON	ARMFUL
ABATIS	ACCRUE	AFFAIR	AMIDST	ARMING
ACACIA	ACCUSE	AFFECT	*AMIENS	ARMLET
*ACADIA	+ALCOTT	AFFIRM	ANIMAL	ARMOUR
ACAJOU	ALCOVE	AFFLUX	ANIMUS	ARMPIT.
ACANTH	ANCHOR	AFFORD	APIARY	ADNOUN
ADAGIO	ARCADE	AFFRAY	APICAL	+AENEAS
AGAMIC	ARCANA	+ALFRED.	APICES	AGNAIL
AGARIC	ARCANE	*AEGEAN	APIECE	AGNATE
+AGATHA	ARCHED	+AEGEUS	ARIDLY	AMNION
ALALIA	ARCHER	ALGOID	ARIGHT	ANNEAL
ALARUM	+ARCHIE	ALGOUS	ARIOSO	ANNEXE
*ALASKA	ARCHIL	ANGARY	ARISEN	ANNUAL
+AMANDA	ARCHLY	+ANGELA	+ASIMOV	ARNICA
AMATOL	ARCHON	ANGINA	AVIARY	+ARNOLD
AMAZED	ARCING	ANGLED	AVIATE	AUNTIE
AMAZON	*ARCTIC	ANGLER	AVIDLY.	AWNING.
ANABAS	ASCEND	*ANGOLA	ABJECT	ABOARD
ANADEM	ASCENT.	ANGORA	ABJURE	ABOUND
ANANAS	ABDUCT	ARGALA	ADJECT	+ADONIS
APACHE	ADDICT	ARGENT	ADJOIN	ADORER
APATHY	ADDING	ARGIVE	ADJURE	+AEOLUS
*ARABIA	ADDLED	ARGOSY	ADJUST.	AGONIC
ARABIC	ADDUCE	ARGUED	ALKALI	AGOUTI
ARABLE	AEDILE	*ARGYLL	ALKANE	AMOEBA
*ARARAT	AIDING	AUGEAN	ALKENE	AMORAL
ATAXIA	+ALDOUS	AUGURY	*ANKARA	AMOUNT
AVATAR	+ANDREW	AUGUST.	ANKLET	ANOINT
AVAUNT	ARDENT.	ACHENE	ASKING.	ANOMIA
AWAKEN	ARDOUR	ACHING	ABLAUT	ANONYM
AZALEA.	AUDILE	ADHERE	ABLAZE	ANORAK
ABBACY	+AUDREY.	AGHAST	AFLAME	APODAL
ABBESS	ACERIC	APHONY	AFLOAT	APOGEE
*ALBANY	ACETIC	APHTHA	+AILEEN	+APOLLO
ALBATA	AGENCY	ASH-CAN	AILING	AROUND
ALBEIT	AGENDA	ASHLAR	ALLEGE	AROUSE
+ALBERT	AGE-OLD	ASHORE	ALLIED	ATOMIC
ALBINO	ALEVIN	+ATHENA	ALLIES	ATONAL
ALBITE	ALEXIA	+ATHENE	ALL-OUT	ATONED
AMBLED	+ALEXIS	*ATHENS	ALLUDE	ATONIC
AMBUSH	+AMELIA	AWHEEL	ALLURE	AVOCET
ARBOUR	AMENDS	AWHILE.	APLOMB	AVOSET
AUBADE	AMERCE	ABIDED	ASLANT	AVOUCH
AUBURN.	APE-MAN	ACIDIC	ASLEEP	AVOWAL
*AACHEN	APEPSY	ACIDLY	ASLOPE.	AVOWED
ACCEDE	AREOLA	ACINUS	ADMIRE	AWOKEN
ACCENT	AVENGE	AFIELD	ALMOND	*AZORES

ALPACA	ASSAIL	ACUITY	BRANDY	BUDGET.
ALPHOS	ASSENT	ACUMEN	+BRAQUE	BEECHY
ALPINE	ASSERT	AGUISH	BRASHY	BEETLE
AMPERE	ASSESS	ALUMNI	BRASSY	BLEACH
APPEAL	ASSETS	AMULET	BRAVED	BLEARY
APPEAR	ASSIGN	AMUSED	BRAVER	BLENCH
APPEND	*ASSISI	+ANUBIS.	BRAWNY	BLENDE
APPORT	ASSIST	ADVENT	BRAYED	BREACH
ASPECT	ASSIZE	ADVERB	BRAZEN	BREAST
ASPIRE.	ASSORT	ADVERT	*BRAZIL.	BREATH
ACQUIT.	ASSUME	ADVICE	BABBLE	+BRECHT
ABRADE	ASSURE	ADVISE	BABOON	*BRECON
ABROAD	+AUSTEN	ALVINE.	BOBBED	BREECH
ABRUPT	*AUSTIN.	ALWAYS.	BOBBIN	BREEKS
ACRITA	ACTING	AUXINS.	BOBCAT	BREEZE
ACROSS	ACTION	ADYTUM	BUBBLE	BREEZY
+ADRIAN	ACTIVE	ANYHOW	BUBBLY.	+BRENDA
ADRIFT	ACTUAL	ANYONE	BACKED	BRETON
ADROIT	AETHER	ASYLUM	BACKER	BREVET
AERATE	ANTHEM		BACONY	BREWER.
AERIAL	ANTHER	BEACON	BECALM	*BAFFIN
AERIFY	ANTIAR	BEADLE	BECAME	BAFFLE
AFRAID	ANTLER	BEAGLE	BECKON	BEFALL
AFRESH	+ANTONY	BEAKED	BECOME	BEFELL
*AFRICA	*ANTRIM	BEAKER	BICEPS	BEFOOL
AGREED	ANTRUM	BEAMED	BICKER	BEFORE
AIR-BED	ARTERY	BEARER	BUCCAL	BEFOUL
AIR-GUN	ARTFUL	BEATEN	*BUCHAN	BIFFIN
AIRILY	+ARTHUR	BEATER	BUCKET	BOFFIN
AIRING	ARTILY	*BEAUNE	BUCKLE	BOFORS
AIRMAN	ARTIST	BEAUTY	BUCKRA.	BUFFER
AIR-SAC	ASTERN	BEAVER	BADGER	BUFFET.
AIRWAY	ASTHMA	*BIAFRA	BEDAUB	BAGGED
AORIST	ASTRAL	BIASED	BEDDED	BAGMAN
ARRANT	ASTRAY	BLADED	BEDECK	BAGNIO
ARREAR	+ASTRID	BLAGUE	BEDLAM	BEGGAR
ARREST	ASTUTE	BLAMED	BED-PAN	BEGGED
ARRIVE	ATTACH	BLANCH	BED-SIT	BEGONE
ARROWY	ATTACK	BLARED	BIDDER	BIGAMY
ARRUYO	ATTAIN	BLAZED	BIDING	BIGGER
+ATREUS	ATTEND	BLAZER	BODEGA	BIGWIG
AURIST	ATTEST	BLAZON	BODICE	BOGGED
AURORA	+ATTILA	BOATER	BODIED	BOGGLE
AUROUS.	ATTIRE	BRACER	BODILY	BOG-OAK
ABSENT	+ATTLEE	+BRAHMS	BODING	*BOGOTA
ABSORB	ATTUNE	BRAINY	BODKIN	BUGGED
ABSURD	AUTHOR	BRAISE	*BODMIN	BUGGER
ADSORB	AUTISM	BRAKED	BUDDED	BUGLER
ANSWER	AUTUMN.	BRANCH	+BUDDHA	BYGONE.
ARSINE	ABUSED	+BRANDT	BUDGED	*BAHAMA

BEHALF	BELTED	BINDER	+BROOKE	BURDEN
BEHAVE	*BILBAO	BONBON	BROWSE	BUREAU
BEHEAD	BILKER	BONDED	BUOYED.	BURGEE
BEHELD	BILLED	BONDER	BY-PASS	BURGLE
BEHEST	BILLET	BONING	BYPATH.	BURIAL
BEHIND	BILLOW	BONITO	BARBED	BURIED
BEHOLD	BOLDER	BONNET	BARBEL	BURLAP
BEHOVE.	BOLDLY	BUNCHY	BARBER	BURNED
BAILEE	BOLERO	BUNDLE	BARBET	BURNER
BAILER	+BOLEYN	BUNGED	BARDIC	BURNET
BAILEY	BOLIDE	BUNGLE	BARELY	BURPED
BAITED	BOLTED	BUNION	BARGEE	BURROW
*BEIRUT	*BOLTON	BUNKER	BARING	BURSAR
BLIGHT	BULBED	BUNKUM	BARIUM	*BURTON
BLIMEY	BULBIL	BUNSEN	BARKER	BY-ROAD
BLITHE	BULBUL	+BUNYAN	BARLEY	BASALT
BOILED	BULGER	BUNYIP	BARMAN	BASELY
BOILER	BULLET	BYNAME.	*BARNET	BASEST
BRIBED	BY-LINE.	BAOBAB	BARONY	BASHED
BRIDAL	BAMBOO	BIOPSY	BARQUE	BASIAL
BRIDGE	BEMOAN	BIOTIC	BARRED	BASKED
BRIDLE	BEMUSE	BIOTIN	BARREL	BASKET
BRIGHT	*BOMBAY	BLONDE	BARREN	BASQUE
BRITON.	BOMBED	BLOODY	+BARRIE	BASSET
BAKERY	BOMBER	BLOTCH	*BARROW	BASTED
BAKING	BOMBIC	BLOUSE	BARTER	BESEEM
BIKINI.	BUMPED	BLOWER	+BARTOK	BESIDE
BALATA	BUMPER.	BLOW-UP	BARTON	BESTED
*BALBOA	BANANA	BOODLE	BARYON	BESTIR
+BALDER	BANDED	BOOKED	BARYTA	BESTOW
BALDLY	BANDIT	BOOKIE	BERATE	BISECT
BALEEN	BANGED	BOOMED	BERBER	BISHOP
BALING	BANGLE	BOOMER	BEREFT	BISQUE
*BALKAN	*BANGOR	BOOTED	*BERGEN	BISTRE
BALKED	BANIAN	BOOTEE	*BERING	*BOSTON
BALLAD	BANISH	*BOOTLE	*BERLIN	BUSHED
BALLET	BANKED	BOOZED	+BERTHA	BUSHEL
BALLOT	BANKER	BOOZER	BIRDIE	*BUSHEY
BALSAM	BANNED	BROACH	BIREME	BUSIED
*BALTIC	BANNER	BROCHE	BORAGE	BUSILY
+BALZAC	BANTAM	BROGUE	BORATE	BUSKER
BELDAM	BANTER	BROKEN	BORDER	BUSKIN
BELFRY	BANYAN	BROKER	BOREAL	BUSMAN
BELIAL	BENDED	BROLLY	BORING	BUSTLE
BELIEF	*BENGAL	BROMIC	*BORNEO	BYSSUS.
BELIKE	BENIGN	BRONCO	BORROW	BATHER
+BELLOC	BENUMB	+BRONTE	BORSCH	BATHOS
+BELLOW	BENZOL	BRONZE	BORZOI	BATING
BELONG	BINARY	BROOCH	BURBLE	BATMAN
*BELPAR	BINATE	BROODY	BURBOT	BATTED

105

BATTEN	BOWING	CRABBY	COCK-UP	CRETON
BATTER	BOW-LEG	CRADLE	COCOON	CREWEL.
BATTLE	BOWLER	CRAFTY	CUCKOO	CAFTAN
BATTUE	BOWMAN	CRAGGY	CYCLED	COFFEE
BETAKE	BOW-SAW	CRAMBO	CYCLIC.	COFFER
BETHEL	BOW-TIE	CRANED	CADDIS	COFFIN
BETIDE	BOW-WOW	CRANKY	CADGER	COFFLE
BETONY	BYWORD.	CRANNY	+CADMUS	CUFFED.
BETOOK	BOXING	CRASIS	CEDING	CAGILY
BETRAY	*BUXTON.	CRATCH	CODDER	CAGING
BETTED	BAYING	CRATED	CODDLE	COGENT
BETTER	BEYOND	CRATER	CODGER	COGGED
BITCHY	BOYISH	CRATUR	CODIFY	COGNAC
BITING	+BRYONY	CRAVAT	CODING	CYGNET.
BITTEN	BUYING.	CRAVED	CUDDLE	CAHOOT
BITTER	BAZAAR	CRAVEN	CUDDLY	COHEIR
BOTANY	BEZANT	CRAWLY	CUDGEL.	COHERE
BOTCHY	BUZZER	CRAYON	CAECUM	COHORT.
BOTFLY		CRAZED	+CAESAR	CAIQUE
BOTHER	CEASED	CYANIC.	CHEEKY	CHIBUK
BOTTLE	CHAFED	CABALA	CHEERY	CHICHI
BOTTOM	CHAFFY	CABMAN	CHEESE	CHICLE
BUTANE	CHAISE	COBALT	CHEESY	CHICLY
BUTLER	CHALET	COBBER	CHEQUE	CHIDED
BUTTER	CHALKY	COBBLE	+CHERRY	CHILLI
BUTTON.	CHANCE	COBBLY	CHERUB	CHILLY
BAUBLE	CHANCY	COBNUT	CHESIL	CHIMED
*BHUTAN	CHANGE	COBURG	CHESTY	CHINTZ
BLUISH	CHAPEL	COBWEB	CHEVIN	CHIPPY
BOUGHT	CHARGE	CUBAGE	CHEVVY	+CHIRON
BOUGIE	+CHARON	CUBBED	CHEWED	CHIRPY
BOUNCE	CHASED	CUBING	CLEAVE	CHISEL
BOUNCY	CHASER	CUBISM	CLENCH	CHITIN
BOUNTY	CHASSE	CUBOID	CLERGY	CHITON
BOURSE	CHASTE	+CYBELE.	CLERIC	CHIVVY
BRUISE	CHATTY	CACHET	CLEVER	CLICHE
BRUMAL	+CLAIRE	CACHOU	CLEVIS	CLIENT
BRUNCH	CLAMMY	CACKLE	CLEWED	CLIMAX
*BRUNEI	CLAQUE	CACTUS	COERCE	CLINCH
+BRUNEL	CLARET	CECITY	COEVAL	CLINGY
BRUSHY	CLASSY	CICADA	CREAMY	CLINIC
BRUTAL	+CLAUDE	CICALA	CREASE	CLIQUE
+BRUTUS.	CLAUSE	CICELY	CREATE	COILED
BOVATE	CLAWED	+CICERO	CRECHE	COINER
BOVINE.	CLAYEY	COCCUS	CREDAL	COITAL
BAWLED	COAITA	COCCYX	CREDIT	COITUS
BEWAIL	COALER	*COCHIN	CREEPY	CRIKEY
BEWARE	COARSE	COCKED	CREOLE	*CRIMEA
BOWELS	COATEE	COCKER	CRESOL	CRIMPY
BOWERY	COAXED	COCKLE	CRETIN	CRINGE

CRISIS	COMBER	CONCHA	COOLIE	CARNAL
CRISPY	COMEDY	CONCUR	COOLLY	CARPAL
CRITIC.	COMELY	CONDOM	COOPED	CARPED
CAJOLE.	COMFIT	CONDOR	COOPER	CARPEL
CAKING.	COMING	CONFAB	CROAKY	CARPET
*CALAIS	COMITY	CONFER	CROCKY	CARPUS
CALASH	COMMIE	CONGER	CROCUS	CARREL
CALCAR	COMMIT	CONKED	*CROMER	CARROT
CALICO	COMMON	CONKER	+CRONOS	CARTED
CALIPH	COMOSE	CON-MAN	CROSSE	CARTEL
CALKIN	COMPEL	CONNED	CROTCH	CARTON
*CALLAO	COMPLY	CONOID	CROUCH	+CARUSO
CALLED	CUMBER	+CONRAD	CROUPY	CERATE
CALLER	CYMBAL	CONSUL	CROWED.	CERIPH
CALLOW	CYMRIC.	CONTRA	+CAPONE	CERISE
CALL-UP	*CANADA	CONVEX	+CAPOTE	CERIUM
CALLUS	CANARD	CONVEY	CAPPED	CERMET
CALMED	CANARY	CONVOY	CAPTOR	CERTES
CALMER	CAN-CAN	*CONWAY.	CIPHER	CERVIX
CALMLY	CANCEL	CHOICE	COPECK	CHRISM
CALVED	CANCER	CHOKED	COPIED	+CHRIST
CALVES	*CANDIA	CHOKER	COPIER	CHROME
+CALVIN	CANDID	CHOLER	COPING	CIRCLE
CELERY	CANDLE	CHOOSE	COP-OUT	CIRCUM
CELLAR	CANINE	CHOOSY	COPPED	CIRCUS
CELTIC	CANING	+CHOPIN	COPPER	CIRQUE
CILICE	CANKER	CHOPPY	COPTIC	CIRRUS
CILIUM	CANNED	CHORAL	COPULA	CORBAN
COLDER	CANNER	CHOREA	CUPFUL	CORBEL
COLDLY	*CANNES	CHORIC	CUPOLA	CORBIE
COLLAR	CANNON	CHORUS	CUPPED	CORDED
COLLET	CANNOT	CHOSEN	CUPPER	CORDON
COLLIE	CANOPY	CHOUGH	CUPRIC	CORING
COLLOP	CANTAB	CLOACA	CUP-TIE	CORIUM
COLONY	CANTED	CLOCHE	CYPHER	CORKED
COLOUR	CANTER	CLOSED	*CYPRUS.	CORKER
COLUMN	*CANTON	CLOSET	COQUET.	CORNEA
CULLED	CANTOR	CLOTHE	CARAFE	CORNED
CULTUS	+CANUTE	+CLOTHO	CARBON	CORNEL
CULVER.	CANVAS	CLOUDY	CARBOY	CORNER
CAMBER	*CANVEY	CLOUGH	CAREEN	CORNET
*CAMDEN	CANYON	CLOVEN	CAREER	CORONA
CAMERA	CENSOR	CLOVER	CARESS	COROZO
CAMION	CENSUS	CLOYED	CARFAX	CORPSE
CAMPED	CENTAL	COOING	CARIES	CORPUS
CAMPER	CENTRE	COOKED	CARING	CORRAL
CAMPUS	CINDER	COOKER	*CARLOW	CORRIE
CEMENT	CINEMA	COOKIE	CARMAN	CORSET
COMBAT	CINGLE	COOLED	*CARMEL	CORTEX
COMBED	CINQUE	COOLER	+CARMEN	+CORTEZ

CORVES	CUSSED	CAVERN	DIBBER	DIESIS
CORYMB	CUSTOM	CAVIAR	DIBBLE	DIETAL
CORYZA	CYSTIC.	CAVING	DOBBIN	DIETED
CURACY	CATCHY	CAVITY	DUBBED	DOESNT
CURARE	CATGUT	CAVORT	DUBBIN	DREAMT
CURATE	CATION	COVERT	*DUBLIN	DREAMY
CURBED	CATKIN	COVING.	DYBBUK.	DREARY
CURDED	CAT-NAP	COWARD	DACOIT	DREDGE
CURDLE	CATTLE	COWBOY	DACRON	DRENCH
CURFEW	CETANE	COWING	DACTYL	DRESSY
CURING	CITING	COWMAN	DECADE	DUENNA
CURIUM	CITRIC	COW-POX	DECAMP	DYEING.
CURLED	CITRON	COWRIE.	DECANT	DEFACE
CURLER	CITRUS	+CAXTON.	DECEIT	DEFAME
CURLEW	COTTAR	*CAYMAN	DECENT	DEFEAT
CURSED	COTTER	*CEYLON	DECIDE	DEFECT
CURSOR	COTTON	COYOTE	DECKED	DEFEND
CURTLY	CUTELY	CRYING	DECKER	DEFIED
CURTSY	CUTLER		DECKLE	DEFILE
CURVED	CUTLET	DEACON	DECOCT	DEFINE
CURVET.	CUT-OFF	DEADEN	DECODE	DEFORM
+CASALS	CUT-OUT	DEADLY	DECOKE	DEFRAY
CASEIN	CUTTER.	DEAFEN	DECREE	DEFTLY
CASHED	CAUCUS	DEALER	DICING	DEFUSE
CASHEW	CAUDAL	DEARER	DICKER	DIFFER
CASING	CAUDLE	DEARLY	DICKEY	DOFFED
CASINO	CAUGHT	DEARTH	DICTUM	DUFFED
CASKET	CAUSAL	DHARMA	DOCILE	DUFFEL
CASQUE	CAUSED	DIADEM	DOCKED	DUFFER
CASSIA	CAUTER	DIAPER	DOCKER	DUFFLE.
CASTER	CHUBBY	DIATOM	DOCKET	DAGGER
CASTLE	CHUMMY	DRABLY	DOCTOR	DAGGLE
CASTOR	CHUNKY	DRACHM	DUCKED	DEGREE
+CASTRO	CHURCH	DRAFFY	DUCKER.	DIGEST
CASUAL	CLUMSY	DRAGON	DEDUCE	DIGGED
CISTUS	CLUTCH	DRAPED	DEDUCT	DIGGER
COSHER	COUGAR	DRAPER	*DIDCOT	DIGLOT
COSILY	COUNTY	DRAWEE	DIDDLE	DOGATE
COSINE	COUPLE	DRAWER	DODDER	DOG-FOX
COSMIC	COUPON	DYADIC.	DODGED	DOGGED
COSMOS	COURSE	DABBED	DODGER	DOGGER
COSSET	COUSIN	DABBER	*DUDLEY.	DUGONG
COSTAL	CRUISE	DABBLE	DAEDAL	DUGOUT.
CO-STAR	CRUMBY	DEBARK	DAEMON	DAHLIA.
COSTED	CRUMMY	DEBASE	DEEMED	DAINTY
COSTER	CRUNCH	DEBATE	DEEPEN	DE-ICER
COSTLY	CRURAL	+DEBBIE	DEEPER	DOITED
CUSCUS	CRUSTY	DEBRIS	DEEPLY	DRIEST
CUSHAT	CRUTCH.	DEBTOR	*DIEPPE	DRIVEL
CUSPED	CAVEAT	DEBUNK	DIESEL	DRIVEN

DRIVER	DOMAIN	DOOMED	DORIAN	DITONE
DUIKER	DOMINO	DROGUE	DORMER	DOTAGE
+DWIGHT.	DUMBLY	DRONED	DORSAL	DOTARD
DEJECT.	DUMDUM	DROPSY	*DORSET	DOTING
*DAKOTA	DUMPED	DROSSY	DORSUM	DOTTED
DIK-DIK.	DUMPER	DROUTH	*DURBAN	DOTTLE.
*DALLAS	DUMPTY.	DROVER	DURBAR	DAUBED
+DALTON	DANCER	DROWSE	DURESS	+DAUDET
DELATE	DANDER	DROWSY	*DURHAM	DEUCED
DELETE	DANDLE	+DVORAK.	DURING.	DOUANE
*DELPHI	DANGER	+DAPHNE	DASHED	DOUBLE
DELUDE	DANGLE	DAPPER	DASHER	DOUBLY
DELUGE	+DANIEL	DAPPLE	DESCRY	DOUCHE
DELVED	DANISH	DEPART	DESERT	+DOUGAL
DILATE	*DANUBE	DEPEND	DESIGN	DOUGHY
DILUTE	*DANZIG	DEPICT	DESIRE	DOURLY
DOLLAR	DENARY	DEPLOY	DESIST	DOUSED
DOLLED	DENGUE	DEPONE	DESPOT	DRUDGE
DOLLOP	DENIAL	DEPORT	DISARM	DRUPEL.
DOLMAN	DENIED	DEPOSE	DISBAR	DEVICE
DOLMEN	DENIER	DEPUTE	DISBUD	DEVISE
DOLOSE	+DENISE	DEPUTY	DISCAL	DEVOID
DOLOUR	DENOTE	DIPOLE	DISCUS	DEVOTE
DULCET	DENSER	DIPPED	DISEUR	DEVOUR
DULLED	DENTAL	DIPPER	DISHED	DEVOUT
DULLER	DENTED	DOPING	DISMAL	DIVERS
+DULLES.	DENTIL	DOPTRE	DISMAY	DIVERT
DAMAGE	DENUDE	DUPING	+DISNEY	DIVEST
DAMASK	*DENVER	DUPLET	DISOWN	DIVIDE
DAMMAR	DINGHY	DUPLEX.	DISPEL	DIVINE
DAMMED	DINGLE	DARING	DISTAL	DIVING.
DAMNED	DINING	DARKEN	DISTIL	DAWDLE
DAMPEN	DINKUM	DARKER	DISUSE	DAWNED
DAMPER	DINNED	DARKLY	DOSAGE	DEWLAP
DAMPLY	DINNER	DARNED	DOSSAL	DOWLAS
DAMSEL	+DONALD	DARNEL	DOSSED	DOWNED
DAMSON	DONATE	DARNER	DOSSER	DOWSED
DEMAND	DONJON	DARTED	DOSSIL	DOWSER.
DEMEAN	DONKEY	*DARWIN	DUSTED	DEXTER
DEMENT	DONNED	DERAIL	DUSTER.	DEXTRO.
DEMISE	*DUNBAR	DERATE	DATING	DAY-BED
DEMODE	+DUNCAN	DERIDE	DATIVE	DAY-BOY
DEMOTE	*DUNDEE	DERIVE	DETACH	DRY-FLY
DEMURE	DUNKED	DERMIS	DETAIL	DRY-ICE
DIMITY	DUNLIN	DERRIS	DETAIN	DRYING
DIMMED	DUNNED	DIRECT	DETECT	DRYISH
DIMMER	DYNAMO	DIRELY	DETENT	DRY-ROT
DIMPLE	DYNAST.	DIRNDL	DETEST	DAZING
DIMPLY	DEODAR	DORADO	DETOUR	DAZZLE
DIMWIT	DOODLE	+DOREEN	DITHER	DOZING

ECARTE	EDENIC	ELIDED	EXPIRY	EQUINE
+ELAINE	EKEING	+ELINOR	EXPORT	EQUITY
ELAPSE	ELEVEN	ELIXIR	EXPOSE.	EXUDED.
ELATED	EMERGE	EMIGRE	EARING	ENVIED.
ELATER	EMETIC	ENIGMA	EARNED	+EDWARD
ENABLE	ENERGY	EPICAL	EARTHY	+EDWINA
ENAMEL	*EREBUS	+ERINYS	EARWAX	ENWRAP.
ERASED	+EVELYN	EVILLY	EARWIG	ETYMON.
EVADED	EVENED	EVINCE	EERILY	ECZEMA
EXARCH.	EVENLY	EXILED	EGRESS	ENZYME
EBBING	EXEMPT	EXILIC	ENRAGE	
EMBALM	*EXETER	EXITED.	ENRAPT	FEALTY
EMBANK	EXEUNT	ENJOIN.	ENRICH	FEARED
EMBARK	EYEFUL	ESKIMO.	ENROBE	FIACRE
EMBLEM	EYEING	*EALING	ERRAND	FIANCE
EMBODY	EYELET	ECLAIR	ERRANT	FIASCO
EMBOSS	EYELID.	+EILEEN	ERRATA	FLABBY
EMBRYO	EFFACE	ENLACE	ERRING	FLAGGY
ERBIUM.	EFFECT	ENLIST	EUREKA	FLAGON
*ECCLES	EFFETE	EOLITH	+EUROPA	FLAKED
ENCAGE	EFFIGY	EULOGY.	*EUROPE.	FLAMED
ENCAMP	EFFLUX	+EDMUND	EASIER	FLAMEN
ENCASE	EFFORT	ENMESH	EASILY	FLANCH
ENCASH	EFFUSE	ENMITY	EASING	FLANGE
ENCORE	+EIFFEL	ERMINE.	*EASTER	FLARED
ENCYST	ELFISH	+ERNEST	ENSIGN	FLASHY
EOCENE	ENFACE	+EUNICE	ENSILE	FLATLY
ESCAPE	ENFOLD.	EUNUCH.	ENSUED	FLATUS
ESCHAR	EAGLET	EGOISM	ENSURE	FLAUNT
ESCHEW	EDGING	EGOIST	ERSATZ.	FLAVIN
ESCORT	EGG-CUP	ELOPED	EATING	FLAWED
ESCUDO	EGG-NOG	ENOSIS	ECTYPE	FLAXEN
ETCHED	EIGHTH	ENOUGH	EITHER	FLAYED
EUCHRE	EIGHTY	EPONYM	ENTAIL	FOALED
+EUCLID	ENGAGE	ERODED	ENTICE	FOAMED
EXCEED	ENGINE	EROTIC	ENTIRE	FRACAS
EXCEPT	ENGULF	EVOKED	ENTITY	FRAISE
EXCESS	+EUGENE.	EVOLVE	ENTOMB	FRAMED
EXCISE	ECHOED	EXODUS	ENTRAP	FRAMER
EXCITE	ECHOIC	EXOTIC.	ENTREE	*FRANCE
EXCUSE.	ETHANE	EMPIRE	ESTATE	FRAPPE
EDDAIC	ETHNIC	EMPLOY	ESTEEM	FRAYED
EDDIED	EXHALE	*EPPING	+ESTHER	FRAZIL.
EDDISH	EXHORT	ESPIAL	EXTANT	FABIAN
ELDEST	EXHUME.	ESPIED	EXTEND	FABLED
END-ALL	EDIBLE	EXPAND	EXTENT	FABRIC
ENDEAR	+EDISON	EXPECT	EXTORT.	FIBBED
ENDING	EDITED	EXPEND	EDUCED	FIBBER
ENDIVE	EDITOR	EXPERT	ELUDED	FIBRIL
ENDURE.	ELICIT	EXPIRE	EQUATE	FIBRIN

FIBULA	FUHRER.	FOLIAR	FLORET	FORMER
FOBBED.	FAILED	FOLKSY	FLORID	FORMIC
FACADE	FAILLE	FOLLOW	FLORIN	FURFUR
FACIAL	FAIRLY	FULFIL	FLOSSY	FURLED
FACILE	FLIGHT	FULLER	FLOURY	FURORE
FACING	FLIMSY	FULMAR	FLOWED	FURRED
FACTOR	FLINCH	FYLFOT.	FLOWER	FURROW.
FACTUM	FLINTY	FAMILY	FOOLED	FASCES
FACULA	FLIRTY	FAMINE	FOOTED	FASCIA
FECUND	FLITCH	FAMISH	FOOTER	FASTEN
FICKLE.	FOIBLE	FAMOUS	FOOZLE	FASTER
FADING	FOILED	FEMALE	FROLIC	FESCUE
FEDORA	FRIARY	FOMENT	FROSTY	FESTAL
FIDDLE	FRIDAY	FUMADE	FROTHY	FESTER
FIDGET	FRIDGE	FUMBLE	FROWST	FISCAL
FODDER	FRIEND	FUMING	FROWZY	FISHER
FUDDLE.	FRIEZE	FUMOUS.	FROZEN.	FISTED
FAECAL	+FRIGGA	FANGED	FARINA	FISTIC
FAECES	FRIGHT	FAN-JET	FARING	FOSSIL
FAERIE	FRIGID	FANNED	FARMER	FOSTER
*FAEROE	FRILLY	FENCED	FAR-OFF	FUSING
FEEBLE	FRINGE	FENCER	FARROW	FUSION
FEEBLY	FRISKY	FENDED	FERIAL	FUSSED
FEEDER	FRIVOL	FENDER	FERINE	FUSTIC.
FEELER	FRIZZY.	FENIAN	FERITY	FATHER
FIERCE	FAKING.	FENNEC	FERRET	FATHOM
FIESTA	FALCON	FENNEL	FERRIC	FATTED
FLECHE	FALLEN	FINALE	FERRIS	FATTEN
FLEDGE	FALLOW	FINDER	FERULA	FATTER
FLEECE	FALTER	FINELY	FERULE	FETIAL
FLEECY	FELINE	FINERY	FERVID	FETISH
FLENCH	FELLAH	FINEST	FIRING	FETTER
FLESHY	FELLER	FINGER	FIRKIN	FETTLE
FLETCH	FELLOE	FINIAL	FIRMAN	FITFUL
FLEXED	FELLOW	FINING	FIRMER	FITTED
FLEXOR	FELONY	FINISH	FIRMLY	FITTER
FOEMAN	FELTED	FINITE	FORAGE	FUTILE
FOETAL	FILIAL	FINNAN	FORBID	FUTURE.
FOETID	FILING	FINNER	FORCED	FAUCAL
FOETUS	FILLED	FINNIC	FORDED	FAUCET
FREELY	FILLER	FINNOC	FOREGO	FAULTY
FREEZE	FILLET	FONDLE	FOREST	FEUDAL
FRENCH	FILL-IN	FONDLY	FORGED	FEUDED
FRENZY	FILLIP	FONTAL	FORGER	FLUENT
FRESCO.	FILMED	FUNDED	FORGET	FLUFFY
FAG-END	FILMIC	FUNGUS	FORGOT	FLUKED
FAGGED	FILTER	FUNNEL.	FORKED	FLURRY
FAGGOT	FILTHY	FLOOZY	FORMAL	FLUTED
FIGURE	FOLDED	FLOPPY	FORMAT	FOUGHT
FOGGED.	FOLDER	FLORAL	FORMED	FOULED

FOULLY	GRATER	GAGGLE	GULPED.	GNOMIC
FOURTH	GRATIN	GIGGLE	*GAMBIA	GNOMON
FRUGAL	GRATIS	GIGOLO	GAMBIT	GNOSIS
FRUITY	GRAVEL	GOGGLE	GAMBLE	GOODLY
FRUMPY	GRAVER	GOGLET.	GAMBOL	GOOGLY
FRUTEX.	+GRAVES	GAIETY	GAMELY	GROCER
FAVOUR.	GRAVID	GAINED	GAMETE	GROGGY
*FAWLEY	GRAZED.	GAITER	GAMING	GROOVE
FAWNED	GABBED	GEIGER	GAMMED	GROOVY
FAWNER	GABBLE	GEISHA	GAMMER	GROPED
FEWEST	GABION	GLIBLY	GAMMON	GROTTO
FOWLER.	GABLED	GLIDER	GEMINI	GROTTY
FIXATE	GIBBER	GOITRE	GEMMED	GROUCH
FIXING	GIBBET	GRIDED	GIMLET	GROUND
FIXITY	GIBBON	GRIEVE	GUMMED	GROUSE
FOXING.	GIBING	GRILLE	GANDER	GROVEL
FLYING	GIBLET	GRILSE	+GANDHI	GROWER
FLYMAN.	GOBANG	GRIMLY	GANGED	GROWTH
FIZGIG	GOBBET	GRIPED	GANGER	GROYNE.
FIZZED	GOBBLE	GRIPPE	*GANGES	GAPING
FIZZER	GOBLET	GRISLY	GANGUE	GOPHER
FIZZLE	GOBLIN	GRISON	GANNET	GYPSUM.
	GYBING.	GRITTY	GANOID	GARAGE
	GO-CART.	GUIDED	GANTRY	GARBED
*GDANSK	GADDED	GUIDON	GENDER	GARBLE
GEARED	GADFLY	GUILTY	GENERA	GARDEN
GIAOUR	GADGET	*GUINEA	*GENEVA	GARGLE
GLACIS	+GIDEON	GUISER	GENIAL	GARISH
GLADLY	GODDAM	GUITAR.	GENIUS	GARLIC
+GLADYS	+GODIVA	GO-KART.	GENTLE	GARNER
*GLAMIS	GODSON	GALAXY	GENTLY	GARNET
GLANCE	GODWIT.	GALENA	GENTRY	GARRET
GLARED	GAELIC	GALLED	GINGER	GARTER
GLASSY	GEEZER	GALLEY	GINGKO	+GERALD
GLAZED	GHETTO	GALLIC	GUNITE	GERMAN
GLAZER	GNEISS	GALLON	GUNMAN	GERMEN
GNAWED	+GOETHE	GALLOP	GUNNED	GERMON
GNAWER	GREASE	GALLUP	GUNNER	GERUND
GOADED	GREASY	GALORE	GUN-SHY	GIRDED
GOALIE	*GREECE	GALOSH	GUNTER.	GIRDER
GOATEE	GREEDY	*GALWAY	GAOLER	GIRDLE
GRACED	+GREENE	GELDED	+GEORGE	+GORDON
GRADED	+GRETEL	GELLED	GLOBAL	GORGED
GRADIN	*GRETNA.	GILDED	GLOOMY	GORGET
GRADUS	GAFFED	GILLIE	+GLORIA	+GORGON
+GRAHAM	GAFFER	GOLDEN	GLOSSY	GORING
GRAINY	GIFTED	GOLFER	GLOVED	GURGLE
GRAMME	GOFFER	GOLOSH	GLOVER	GYRATE.
GRANGE	GUFFAW.	GULLED	GLOWED	GAS-BAG
GRANNY	GAGGED	GULLET	GLOWER	GASHED

GASIFY	HEARSE	HIGHER	HOMILY	HOOTER
GAS-JET	HEARTH	HIGHLY	HOMING	HOOVED
GASKET	HEARTY	HOGGED	HOMINY	+HOOVER
GASMAN	HEATED	HOGGET	HUMANE	HOOVES.
GASPED	HEATER	HUGELY	*HUMBER	HAPPED
GASPER	HEATHY	HUGGED	HUMBLE	HAPPEN
GASSED	HEAVED	+HYGEIA.	HUMBLY	HEPTAD
GOSPEL	HEAVEN	HAILED	HUMBUG	HIPPED
GOSSIP	HEAVER	HAIR-DO	HUMIFY	HOPING
GUSHER	HIATUS	HEIFER	HUMMED	HOPPED
GUSSET.	HOARSE	HEIGHT.	HUMOUR	HOPPER
GATEAU	HOAXER.	HIJACK.	HUMPED	HOPPLE
.GATHER	HABEAS	HIKING.	HUMPTY	HYPHEN.
GATING	HEBREW	HALIDE	HYMNAL.	HARASS
GETTER	*HOBART	HALING	HANDED	HARDEN
GOTHIC	HOBBLE	HALLOO	+HANDEL	HARDER
GOTTEN	HOBNOB	HALLOW	HANDLE	HARDLY
GUTTED	HUBBUB	HALLUX	HANGAR	HARING
GUTTER.	+HUBERT	HALOED	HANGED	HARKEN
GAUCHE	HUBRIS	HALOID	HANGER	HARLOT
GAUCHO	HYBRID.	HALTED	HANG-UP	*HARLOW
GAUGED	HACKED	HALTER	HANKER	HARMED
GAUGER	HACKLE	HALVED	+HANNAH	+HAROLD
+GAULLE	+HECATE	+HELIOS	HANSOM	HARPED
GLUMLY	HECKLE	HELIUM	*HENDON	HARPER
GLUTEN	HECTIC	HELMED	*HENLEY	*HARRIS
GOUGED	+HECTOR	HELMET	HINDER	*HARROW
GRUBBY	HICCUP	HELPED	HINGED	+HARVEY
GRUDGE	HOCKED	HELPER	HINTED	HERALD
GRUMPY.	HOCKEY.	HELTER	HONEST	HERBAL
GIVING	HEDDLE	+HILARY	HONING	HERDED
GOVERN	HEDGER	HOLDER	HONKED	HEREAT
GYVING.	HIDDEN	HOLD-UP	HONOUR	HEREBY
GEWGAW.	HIDING	HOLIER	HUNGER	HEREIN
*GDYNIA	HODDEN	HOLILY	HUNGRY	HEREOF
GEYSER	HODMAN	HOLING	HUNTED	HERESY
GLYCOL	HUDDLE	HOLISM	HUNTER.	HERETO
*GUYANA	*HUDSON	HOLLER	HOODED	HERIOT
GUYING.	HYDRIC.	HOLLOW	HOODOO	+HERMES
GAZEBO	HAEMAL	HULLED.	HOOFED	HERMIT
GAZING	HEEDED	HAMITE	HOOKAH	HERNIA
GUZZLE	HEELED	HAMLET	HOOKED	HEROIC
	HOEING.	HAMMED	HOOKER	HEROIN
HEADED	HAFTED	HAMMER	HOOKEY	HERPES
HEADER	HEFTED	HAMOSE	HOOKUP	HIRING
HEALED	HUFFED.	HAMPER	HOOPED	+HORACE
HEALER	HAGGED	HEMMED	HOOP-LA	HORARY
HEALTH	HAGGIS	HEMPEN	HOOPOE	HORDED
HEAPED	HAGGLE	HOMAGE	HOORAY	HORNED
HEARER	HIGGLE	HOMELY	HOOTED	HORNET

113

HORRID	HAWSER	INDUCE	IAMBUS	ITSELF.
HORROR	HEWING	INDUCT	IMMESH	INTACT
HORSED	+HOWARD	INDULT	IMMUNE	INTAKE
HURDLE	HOWDAH	IODIDE	IMMURE	INTEND
HURLER	HOWLED	IODINE	INMATE	INTENT
HURLEY	HOWLER.	IODISM	INMOST.	INTERN
HURRAH	HEXANE	IODIZE.	IGNITE	INTONE.
HURRAY	HEXOSE	ICE-AXE	IGNORE	IGUANA
HURTLE.	+HUXLEY.	ICEBOX	INNATE	INURED.
HASHED	HAYBOX	ICE-CAP	IONIAN	INVADE
HASPED	HAYING	ICEMAN	IONIZE.	INVENT
HASTED	HEYDAY	IREFUL	ICONIC	INVERT
HASTEN	HOYDEN.	IRENIC.	IDOLUM	INVEST
HISPID	HAZARD	*ILFORD	+IMOGEN	INVITE
HISSED	HAZILY	INFAMY	IRONED	INVOKE
HOSIER	HAZING	INFANT	IRONIC	+IRVING.
HOSING		INFECT	ISOBAR	INWARD
HOSTEL	*IBADAN	INFEST	+ISOLDE	INWOVE
HUSHED	+ICARUS	INFIRM	ISOMER	
HUSKED	IMAGED	INFLOW	ISOPOD.	+JOANNA.
HUSSAR	INARCH	INFLUX	IMPACT	JABBED
HUSTLE	+ISABEL	INFORM	IMPAIR	JABBER
HYSSOP.	+ISAIAH	INFUSE.	IMPALE	JABIRU
HATING	ISATIN	INGEST	IMPART	JIBBED
HATPIN	ITALIC.	+INGRID.	IMPAWN	JIBING
HATRED	IMBIBE	INHALE	IMPEDE	JOBBED
HATTED	IMBREX	INHERE	IMPEND	JOBBER.
HATTER	IMBRUE	INHUME	IMPING	JACKAL
HETMAN	IMBUED	*ITHACA.	IMPISH	JACKED
HITHER	INBAND	IBIDEM	IMPORT	JACKET
+HITLER	INBORN	ICICLE	IMPOSE	JOCKEY
HITTER	INBRED.	IDIOCY	IMPOST	JOCOSE
HOTBED	INCEPT	IRISED	IMPUGN	JOCUND.
HOTPOT	INCEST	IRITIS.	IMPURE	JADING
HOT-ROD	INCHED	INJECT	IMPUTE.	JUDAIC
HOTTED	INCISE	IN-JOKE	INROAD	JUDGED
HOTTER	INCITE	INJURE	INRUSH	+JUDITH.
HUTTED.	INCOME	INJURY.	*ISRAEL.	JEERED.
HAULED	INCUSE	*ILKLEY	INSANE	JAGGED
HAUNCH	*ISCHIA	INKING	INSECT	JAGUAR
HOURLY	ITCHED.	INK-POT	INSERT	JIGGED
HOUSED.	INDABA	IRKING.	INSIDE	JIGGER
*HAVANA	INDEED	IDLING	INSIST	JIGGLE
HAVENT	INDENT	ILL-USE	INSOLE	JIGSAW
HAVING	INDIAN	INLAID	INSPAN	JOGGED
HIVING.	INDICT	INLAND	INSTEP	JOGGLE
*HAWAII	INDIGO	INLIER	INSTIL	JUGATE
HAW-HAW	INDITE	IOLITE	INSULT	JUGFUL
HAWING	INDIUM	ISLAND.	INSURE	JUGGED
HAWKER	INDOOR	IAMBIC	ISSUED	JUGGLE

114

JAILED	JESTED	KAFFIR	KITTED	LECHER
JAILER	JESTER	KAFTAN.	KITTEN	LICHEN
JOINED	JESUIT	KAISER	KITTLE.	LICKED
JOINER.	+JOSEPH	KNIFED	KOWTOW	LICTOR
JEJUNE	JOSHED	KNIGHT	*KUWAIT.	LOCALE
JUJUBE.	+JOSHUA	KNIVES.	KAYOED	LOCATE
JOKING.	+JOSIAH	KALMIA	KEYING	LOCKED
JALOPY	JOSTLE	KELPIE	+KEYNES	LOCKER
JELLED	+JUSTIN	KELSON	*KHYBER	LOCKET
JILTED	JUSTLY.	KELTIC		LOCK-UP
JOLTED	JETSAM	KILLED	LAAGER	LOCUST
+JULIAN	JETTED	KILLER	LEADED	LUCENT
+JULIET	JETTON	KILTED.	LEADEN	+LUCIUS
+JULIUS.	JITTER	KIMONO	LEADER	LYCEUM.
JAMBOK	JOTTED	KUMMEL.	LEAD-IN	LADDER
JAM-JAR	JOTTER	KANAKA	LEAFED	LADDIE
JAMMED	JUTTED.	*KANSAS	LEAGUE	LADING
+JEMIMA	JAUNTY	*KENDAL	LEAKED	LADLED
JIMINY	JOUNCE.	KENNED	LEANED	LEDGER
JUMBAL	JIVING	KENNEL	LEAN-TO	LIDDED
JUMBLE	JOVIAL	KINDER	LEAPED	LODGED
JUMPED	JOVIAN.	KINDLE	LEARNT	LODGER
JUMPER.	JAWING	KINDLY	LEASED	*LUDLOW.
JANGLE	JEWESS	KINGED	LEAVED	LEERED
+JANICE	JEWISH.	KINGLY	LEAVEN	LEEWAY
JENNET	JOYFUL	KINKED	LEAVES	+LIEBIG
JINGLE	JOYOUS.	KINKLE.	LIABLE	LUETIC.
JINGLY	JAZZED	KAOLIN	LIAISE	LIFTED
JINKED		KNOBBY	LIASED	LIFTER
JINNEE	KLAXON	KNOTTY.	LOADED	LOFTED
JUNGLE	KRAKEN.	+KEPLER	LOADER	LOFTER.
JUNGLY	KIBBLE	KIPPED	LOAFER	LAGGED
JUNIOR	KIBLAH	KIPPER	LOAMED	LAGOON
JUNKED	KOBOLD.	KOPECK.	LOANED	LEGACY
JUNKER	KECKED	KARATE	LOATHE	LEGATE
JUNKET.	KECKLE	KERBED	LOAVES.	LEGATO
JAPING.	KICKED	KERMES	LABIAL	LEGEND
JARGON	KEDGED	KERMIS	LABILE	LEGGED
JARRED	KIDDED	KERNEL	LABOUR	LEGION
*JARROW	KIDDIE	KERRIE	LIBIDO	LEGIST
JERBOA	KIDDLE	KERSEY	LOBATE	LEGUME
+JEREMY	KIDNAP	KIRSCH	LOBBED	LIGNUM
JERKED	KIDNEY	KIRTLE.	LOBULE	LOGGED
JERKIN	*KODIAK.	KISMET	LUBBER.	LOGGER
+JEROME	KEELED	KISSED	LACHES	LOGGIA
*JERSEY	KEENED	KISSER	LACING	LUGGED
*JORDAN	KEENER	KOSHER.	LACKED	LUGGER.
JURIST.	KEENLY	KETONE	LACKEY	*LAHORE.
+JASPER	KEEPER	KETTLE	LACTIC	LAICAL
+JESSIE	KOEDOE.	KIT-BAG	LACUNA	LOITER

LIKELY	LINING	LASHER	LOUVRE.	MADAME
LIKING.	LINKED	LASSIE	LAVISH	MADCAP
+LILIAN	LINNET	LASTED	LEVANT	MADDED
LILTED	LINTEL	LASTLY	LEVIED	MADDEN
LOLIGO	*LONDON	*LESBOS	LEVITE	MADDER
+LOLITA	LONELY	LESION	LEVITY	MADMAN
LOLLED	LONGED	+LESLEY	LIVELY	*MADRAS
LOLLOP	LONGER	LESSEE	LIVERY	*MADRID
LULLED.	LUNACY	LESSEN	LIVING	MEDDLE
LAMBDA	LUNATE	LESSER	LOVE-IN	MEDIAL
LAMBED	LUNGED.	LESSON	LOVELY	MEDIAN
LAMELY	+LIONEL	LESSOR	LOVING.	+MEDICI
LAMENT	LOOFAH	+LESTER	LAWFUL	MEDICO
LAMINA	LOOKED	*LISBON	LAWYER	MEDIUM
LAMING	LOOKER	LISPED	LEWDLY	MEDLAR
LAMMAS	LOOK-IN	LISSOM	LOWEST	MEDLEY
LAMMED	LOOMED	LISTED	LOWING.	+MEDUSA
LIMBED	LOOPED	LISTEN	LAXITY	*MEDWAY
LIMBER	LOOPER	+LISTER	LUXATE	MIDDAY
LIMING	LOOSED	LOSING	LUXURY.	MIDDEN
LIMNER	LOOSEN	LUSTED	LAYING	MIDDLE
LIMPED	LOOSER	LUSTRE.	LAYMAN	MIDGET
LIMPET	LOOTER.	LATEEN	LAY-OFF	MIDWAY
LIMPID	LAPDOG	LATELY	LAYOUT	MODERN
LIMPLY	LAPPED	LATENT	*LEYDEN.	MODEST
*LOMOND	LAPPET	LATEST	LAZILY	MODIFY
LUMBAR	LAPSED	LATHER	LAZING	MODISH
LUMBER.	LEPTON	LATTEN	LIZARD	MODULE
LANATE	LIPPED	LATTER		MUDDLE.
LANCED	LOPING	LETHAL	MEADOW	MAENAD
LANCER	LOPPED.	LETTER	MEAGRE	MEEKER
LANCET	LIQUID	LITANY	MEALIE	MEEKLY.
LANDAU	LIQUOR	LITCHI	MEASLY	MUFFED
LANDED	LOQUAT.	LITMUS	MIASMA	MUFFIN
LANDES	LARDED	LITTER	MOANED	MUFFLE.
LANGUR	LARDER	LITTLE	MOATED.	MAGGOT
LANNER	LARGER	LOTION	MOBBED	MAGNET
LENDER	LARIAT	+LUTHER	MOBILE.	MAGNOX
LENGTH	LARKED	LUTING	MACKLE	MAGNUM
LENITY	LARRUP	*LYTHAM.	MACRON	MAGPIE
LENTEN	LARVAE	LAUDED	MACULA	MAGYAR
LENTIL	LARVAL	LAUNCE	MICKEY	MEGRIM
LINAGE	LARYNX	LAUNCH	MICKLE	MIGHTY
LINDEN	LORDED	LAUREL	MICRON	MUGGED.
LINEAL	LORDLY	+LAURIE	MOCKED	+MAHLER
LINEAR	LURING	LOUDER	MOCKER	MAHOUT
LINE-UP	LURKER	LOUDLY	MOCK-UP	MOHAIR
LINGAM	LYRIST.	+LOUISE	MUCKED	MOHAWK
LINGER	LASCAR	LOUNGE	MUCKLE	MOHOLE.
LINGUA	LASHED	LOUVER	MUCOUS.	MAIDEN

MAILED	MUMMED	MOOING	MORMON	MUSING
+MAILER	MUMMER.	MOONED	MOROSE	MUSKET
MAIMED	MANAGE	MOORED	+MORRIS	MUSK-OX
MAINLY	MANFUL	MOOTED	MORROW	MUSLIM
MOIETY.	MANGER	MYOPIA	MORSEL	MUSLIN
MAKE-UP	MANGLE	MYOPIC.	MORTAL	MUSSEL
MAKING	MANIAC	MAPPED	MORTAR	MUSTER
MIKADO.	*MANILA	MOPING	MURDER	MUSTNT
MALADY	MANIOC	MOPPED	+MURIEL	MYSELF
*MALAGA	MANNED	MOPPET.	MURINE	MYSTIC.
*MALAWI	MANNER	MAQUIS.	MURMUR	MATING
*MALAYA	MANQUE	MARAUD	*MURRAY	MATINS
MALICE	MANTEL	MARBLE	MYRIAD	MATRIC
MALIGN	MANTIC	+MARCIA	+MYRTLE.	MATRIX
MALLET	MANTIS	MARGIN	MASCOT	MATRON
MALLOW	MANTLE	+MARIAN	MASHED	MATTED
MALTED	MANUAL	+MARINA	MASHIE	MATTER
MALTHA	+MANUEL	MARINE	MASKED	MATURE
MELDED	MANURE	MARKED	MASKER	METEOR
MELLOW	MENACE	MARKER	MASQUE	METHOD
MELODY	MENDED	MARKET	MASSED	METHYL
MELTED	+MENDEL	MARLED	MASSIF	METING
+MELVYN	*MENDIP	*MARLOW	MASTED	METRIC
MILADY	MENHIR	MARMOT	MASTER	METTLE
MILDER	MENIAL	MAROON	MASTIC	MITRED
MILDEW	MENSES	MARRED	MESCAL	MITTEN
MILDLY	MENTAL	MARROW	MESHED	MOTHER
MILIEU	MENTOR	MARSHY	+MESMER	MOTION
MILKED	MINCED	MARTEN	MESSED	MOTIVE
MILKER	MINCER	+MARTHA	MESSRS	MOTLEY
MILLED	MINDED	+MARTIN	MISERE	MOTTLE
+MILLER	MINGLE	MARTYR	MISERY	MUTANT
MILLET	MINIMA	MARVEL	MISFIT	MUTATE
MILTED	MINING	MERCER	MISHAP	MUTING
+MILTON	MINION	MERELY	MISLAY	MUTINY
MOLEST	MINNOW	MERGED	MISLED	MUTISM
MOLOCH	MINOAN	MERGER	MISSAL	MUTTER
MOLTEN	MINTED	MERINO	MISSED	MUTTON
MULISH	MINUET	*MERLIN	MISSEL	MUTUAL
MULLED	MINUTE	MERMAN	MISSUS	MYTHIC.
MULLET.	*MONACO	*MERSEY	MISTED	MAULED
MAMMAL	MONDAY	MIRAGE	MISTER	MAUNDY
MAMMON	MONGER	+MIRIAM	MISTLE	MAUSER
MEMBER	MONGOL	MIRING	MISUSE	MOULDY
MEMOIR	+MONICA	MIRROR	MOSAIC	MOUNTY
MEMORY	MONISM	MORALE	MOSLEM	MOUSER
MIMING·	MONIST	MORASS	MOSQUE	MOUSSE.
MIMOSA	MONKEY	MORBID	*MUSCAT	MOVING.
MOMENT	MONODY	+MORGAN	MUSCLE	MEWING
MUMBLE	+MONROE.	MORGUE	MUSEUM	MOWING

117

MAXIMA	NEEDED	NESTED	OXALIC.	OBITER
+MAXINE	NEEDLE	NESTLE	ORBING	ODIOUS
*MEXICO	NIELLO	NOSHED	+OSBERT.	OGIVAL
MIXING.	+NOELLE.	NOSING.	OCCULT	+OLIVER
MAYBUG	NAGGED	NATANT	OCCUPY	ONIONY
MAYEST	NAGGER	+NATHAN	ONCOST	OPIATE
MAYFLY	NEGATE	NATION	OOCYTE	OPINED
MAYHEM	NIGGER	NATIVE	ORCHID	ORIENT
MAYING.	NIGGLE	NATTER	ORCHIS.	ORIGIN
MIZZLE	NIGHTY	NATURE	ODDEST	ORIOLE
+MOZART	NOGGIN	NETHER	ODDITY	ORISON
MUZZLE	NO-GOOD	NETTED	ODD-JOB	+OSIRIS
	NUGGET.	NETTLE	ODDS-ON	OTIOSE
NEARBY	NAILED.	NITRIC	OEDEMA	OTITIS.
NEARED	+NELSON	NITWIT	OLDEST	OBJECT.
NEARER	NILGAI.	NOTARY	*OLDHAM	*ORKNEY.
NEARLY	NAMELY	NOTICE	OODLES	OBLATE
NEATEN	NAMING	NOTIFY	ORDAIN	OBLIGE
NEATLY	NIMBLE	NOTING	ORDEAL	OBLONG
NUANCE.	NIMBLY	NOTION	ORDURE.	OCLOCK
NABBED	NIMBUS	NUTMEG	OBELUS	OGLING
NEBULA	NUMBED	NUTRIA	+OBERON	OIL-CAN
NIBBLE	NUMBER	NUTTER.	OBEYED	OILING
NO-BALL	NUMBLY	NAUGHT	OCELLI	ON-LINE
NOBBED	NYMPHO.	NAUSEA	OCELOT	OOLITE
NOBBLE	NINETY	NAUTCH	*ODESSA	OWLISH.
NOBLER	NONAGE	NEURAL	+ODETTE	ORMOLU.
NOBODY	NONARY	NEURON	OLEFIN	OMNIUM
NUBILE.	NUNCIO.	NEUTER	OMELET	ORNATE
NECKED	NIOBIC	NOUGAT	ONE-OFF	*OUNDLE
NECTAR	NOODLE	NOUGHT.	ONE-WAY	OWNING.
NICELY	NOOSED.	*NEVADA	OPENER	*OPORTO.
NICENE	NAPALM	NOVENA	OPENLY	OEPEMA
NICEST	NAPKIN	NOVICE.	*OREGAN	OPPOSE
NICETY	*NAPLES	*NEWARK	OREIDE	ORPHAN
NICKED	NAPPED	NEWEST	OVERDO	ORPHIC
NICKEL	NEPHEW	+NEWTON	OVERLY	ORPINE
NICKER	NIPPED	NOWAYS	OX-EYED.	OSPREY.
+NICOLE	NIPPER	NOWISE.	OAFISH	OARING
NOCKED	NIPPLE.	NAZISM	OFF-DAY	OGRESS
NUCLEI.	NARKED	NOZZLE	OFFEND	OGRISH
+NADINE	NARROW	NUZZLE	OFFICE	ONRUSH
NODDED	NEREID		OFFING	ORRERY.
NOODLE	NERVED	ONAGER	OFFISH	OBSESS
NODOSE	NORDIC	OPAQUE	OFFSET	OSSIFY
NODULE	NORMAL	ORACLE	ONFALL	OUSTED
NUDGED	+NORMAN	ORALLY	*ORFORD	OYSTER.
NUDISM	*NORWAY	ORANGE	*OXFORD.	OBTAIN
NUDIST	NURSED.	ORATED	ORGASM.	OBTUSE
NUDITY.	*NASSAU	ORATOR	OX-HIDE.	OCTANE

O - T - - -				P -N - - -
OCTAVE	PLAQUE	PEELED	PLIERS	+PILATE
OCTAVO	PLASHY	PEELER	PLIGHT	PILE-UP
OPTANT	PLASMA	PEEPER	PLINTH	PILFER
OPTICS	PLATAN	PEERED	POISED	PILING
OPTING	PLATED	PEEVED	POISON	PILLAR
OPTION	PLATEN	PEEWIT	PRICED	PILLOW
*OSTEND	PLATER	PHENOL	PRIDED	PILOSE
OSTLER	PLAYED	PIECED	PRIEST	PILOUS
*OTTAWA	PLAYER	PIERCE	PRIMAL	PILULE
OUTBID	*PRAGUE	PLEASE	PRIMED	POLACK
OUTCRY	PRAISE	PLEBBY	PRIMER	*POLAND
OUTDID	PRANCE	PLEDGE	PRIMLY	POLDER
OUTFIT	PRATED	PLENTY	PRIMUS	POLICE
OUTING	PRATIE	PLENUM	PRINCE	POLICY
OUTLAW	PRAXIS	PLEURA	PRIORY	POLING
OUTLAY	PRAYED	PLEXUS	PRISON	POLISH
OUTLET	PRAYER.	POETIC	PRISSY	POLITE
OUTPUT	PEBBLE	POETRY	PRIVET	POLITY
OUTRAN	PEBBLY	PREACH	PRIZED	POLLED
OUTRUN	PUBLIC.	PRECIS	PUISNE.	POLLEN
OUTSET	PACIFY	PREFAB	PYJAMA.	POLLEX
OUTWIT.	PACING	PREFER	*PEKING	POLONY
OCULAR.	PACKED	PREFIX	POKING	PULING
ONWARD	PACKER	PRELIM	PUKING.	PULLED
*ORWELL	PACKET	PREPAY	PALACE	PULLER
+OSWALD.	PECKED	PRESTO	PALAIS	PULLET
OXYGEN.	PECKER	PRETTY	PALATE	PULLEY
OOZILY	PECTEN	PRE-WAR	PALELY	PULL-IN
OOZING	PECTIC	PREYED	PALEST	PULPER
	PECTIN	PSEUDO	PALING	PULPIT
PEAHEN	PICKAX	PUEBLO.	PALLED	PULQUE
PEAKED	PICKED	PIFFLE	PALLET	PULSAR
PEALED	PICKER	PUFFED	PALLID	PULSED.
PEANUT	PICKET	PUFFER	PALLOR	+PAMELA
PEARLY	PICKLE	PUFFIN.	PALMAR	PAMPAS
PHANON	PICNIC	PAGING	PALMED	PAMPER
PHAROS	POCKET	PAGODA	PALMER	PIMPED
PHASED	PUCKER.	PEGGED	PALPED	PIMPLE
PHASIC	PADDED	PEG-LEG	PALTER	PIMPLY
PIAZZA	PADDLE	PIGEON	PALTRY	POMACE
PLACED	PEDALO	PIGGED	PELLET	POMADE
PLACER	PEDANT	PIGLET	PELMET	POMMEL
PLACET	PEDDLE	PIGNUT	+PELOPS	POMPOM
PLACID	PEDLAR	PIGSTY	PELOTA	POMPON
PLAGUE	PIDGIN	POGROM	PELTED	PUMICE
PLAICE	PODDED	PUGGED.	PELVIC	PUMMEL
PLAINT	PODIUM	PAINED	PELVIS	PUMPED.
PLANCH	PUDDLE.	PAIRED	PHLEGM	*PANAMA
PLANED	PAEONY	+PHILIP	PHLOEM	PANDER
PLANET	PEEKED	PLIANT	PILAFF	PANNED

119

PANTED	PROPEL	PARSED	PASTRY	PUTLOG
PANTRY	PROPER	PARSEE	PESETA	PUTRID
PANZER	PROSER	PARSON	PESTER	PUTSCH
PENCIL	PROSIT	PARTED	PESTLE	PUTTEE
PENIAL	PROTON	PARTLY	PISCES	PUTTER
PENNED	+PROUST	PARVIS	PISTIL	PYTHON.
PENNON	PROVED	PERIOD	PISTOL	RAUNCH
PENTAD	PROVEN.	PERISH	PISTON	PAUPER
PENURY	PAPACY	PERKED	POSEUR	PAUSED
PINEAL	PAPAIN	PERMED	POSHLY	PLUCKY
PINING	PAPIST	PERMIT	POSING	PLUG-IN
PINION	PEPLUM	PERRON	POSSET	PLUMED
PINKED	PEPPED	PERSON	POSSUM	PLUMMY
PINNED	PEPPER	PERTLY	POSTAL	PLUNGE
*PINNER	PEPSIN	PERUKE	POSTED	PLURAL
PINOLE	PEPTIC	PERUSE	POSTER	PLUSHY
+PINTER	PIPING	PHRASE	PUSHED	POUNCE
PINTLE	PIPKIN	PIRACY	PUSHER	POURER
PONCHO	PIPPED	PIRATE	PUSHTU.	POUTED
PONDER	PIPPIN	PORING	PATCHY	POUTER
PONGEE	POPERY	PORKER	PATENT	PRUNED
PUNDIT	POPGUN	POROUS	PATHAN	PRUNUS.
PUNILY	POPISH	PORTAL	PATHIC	PAVANE
PUNISH	POPLAR	PORTED	PATHOS	+PAVLOV.
*PUNJAB	POPLIN	PORTER	PATINA	PAWING
PUNNED	POPPED	PORTLY	PATOIS	PAWNED
PUNNET	POPPET	PURDAH	PATROL	PEWTER
PUNTED	PUPATE	PURELY	PATRON	POWDER
PUNTER.	PUPPED	PUREST	PATTED	POW-WO
PEOPLE	PUPPET.	PURGED	PATTEN	PYXING
PHOBIA	PIQUED	PURIFY	PATTER	PAYING
PHOBIC	PIQUET.	PURISM	PETITE	PAYNIM
+PHOEBE	PARADE	PURITY	PETREL	PEYOTE
PHONED	PARAPH	PURLED	PETROL	PHYLUM
PHONEY	PARCEL	PURLER	PETTED	PHYSIC
PHONIC	PARDON	PURLIN	+PETULA	PLYING
PHOTON	PARENT	PURPLE	PITCHY	PRYING
PIOLET	PARGET	PURRED	PITIED	+PSYCHE
PLOUGH	PARIAH	PURSED	PITMAN	PSYCHO
PLOVER	PARIAN	PURSER	PITTED	PUZZLE
POODLE	PARING	PURSUE	POTAGE	
POOGYE	PARISH	PURVEY	POT-ALE	QUAGGA
POOLED	PARITY	PYROPE.	POTASH	QUAGGY
POORER	PARKED	+PASCAL	POTATO	QUAINT
POORLY	PARKIN	PASSED	POTEEN	QUAKED
PROBED	PARLEY	PASSER	POTENT	QUAKER
PROFIT	PARODY	PASSIM	POTION	QUANT.
PROLIX	PAROLE	PASTED	POTMAN	QUARRY
PROMPT	PARROT	PASTEL	POTTED	QUARTE
PRONTO	PARSEC	PASTOR	POTTER	QUART

QUASAR	RUBBLE	REDDLE	RAGING	RAMIFY
QUAVER.	+RUBENS	REDEEM	RAGLAN	RAMJET
QUEASY	RUBRIC.	RED-GUM	RAGMAN	RAMMED
*QUEBEC	RACEME	REDUCE	RAGOUT	RAMMER
QUENCH	+RACHEL	RIDDEN	REGAIN	RAMPED
QUEUED.	RACIAL	RIDDLE	REGALE	RAMROD
QUINCE	RACIER	RIDGED	REGARD	REMADE
QUINSY	RACILY	RIDING	REGENT	REMAIN
QUITCH	RACING	RODENT	REGIME	REMAKE
QUIVER.	RACISM	+RODNEY	+REGINA	REMAND
QUORUM	RACIST	RUDDER	REGION	REMARK
QUOTER	RACKED	RUDDLE	REGIUS	REMEDY
QUOTHA	RACKET	RUDELY	REGNAL	REMIND
	RACOON	RUDEST.	REGRET	REMISS
*RAASAY	RECALL	REEDED	RIGGED	REMORA
READER	RECANT	RE-EDIT	RIGOUR	REMOTE
REALLY	RECAST	REEFER	ROGUED	REMOVE
REALTY	RECEDE	REEKED	RUGGED	RIMMED
REAMER	RECENT	REELED	RUGGER.	RIMOSE
REAPER	RECESS	REEVED	REHASH.	RIMOUS
REARED	RECIPE	RHESUS	RAIDER	ROMANY
REASON	RECITE	RHEUMY	RAILED	ROMISH
ROAMER	RECKON	RUEFUL	RAINED	+ROMMEL
ROARED	RECOIL	RUEING.	RAISED	*ROMNEY
ROARER	RECORD	RAFFIA	RAISIN	ROMPED
*RWANDA.	RECOUP	RAFFLE	REINED	RUMBLE
RABBET	RECTAL	RAFTED	RHINAL	RUMOUR
RABBIN	RECTOR	RAFTER	RHIZIC	RUMPLE
RABBIT	RECTUM	REFACE	RUINED.	RUMPUS.
RABBLE	RICHER	REFILL	RAJPUT	RANCID
RABIES	RICHLY	REFINE	REJECT	RANDAN
REBATE	RICKED	REFLEX	REJOIN.	RANDOM
REBECK	RICTUS	REFLUX	RAKING	RANGED
REBORE	ROCHET	REFOOT	RAKISH.	RANGER
REBORN	ROCKED	REFORM	RELAID	RANKED
REBUFF	ROCKER	REFUEL	RELATE	RANKER
REBUKE	ROCKET	REFUGE	RELENT	RANKLE
RIBALD	ROCOCO	REFUND	RELICT	RANKLY
RIBAND	RUCKED.	REFUSE	RELIED	RANSOM
RIBBED	RADDLE	REFUTE	RELIEF	RENDER
RIBBON	RADIAL	RIFFLE	RELINE	RENNET
RIBOSE	RADIAN	RIFLED	RELISH	+RENOIR
ROBBED	RADISH	RIFLER	RELIVE	RENOWN
ROBBER	RADIUM	RIFTED	RILING	RENTAL
ROBERT	RADIUS	RUFFED	+ROLAND	RENTED
ROBING	*RADNOR	RUFFLE	ROLLED	RENTER
ROBUST	REDACT	RUFOUS.	ROLLER	RINGED
RUBATO	REDCAP	RAG-BAG	ROLL-UP	RINGER
RUBBED	REDDEN	RAG-DAY	RULING.	RINKED
RUBBER	REDDER	RAGGED	RAMBLE	RINSED

+RONALD	RESEAT	ROTTEN	SEA-DOG	SPARED
RUNNEL	RESENT	ROTTER	SEALED	SPARSE
RUNNER	RESIDE	ROTULA	SEALER	*SPARTA
RUNWAY.	RESIGN	ROTUND	SEAMAN	SPAVIN
REOPEN	RESILE	RUTILE	SEAMED	SPAYED
*RHODES	RESIST	RUTTED.	SEAMEN	STABLE
RIOTER	RESORB	+REUBEN	SEANCE	STABLY
ROOFED	RESORT	ROUBLE	SEARCH	STACTE
ROOKED	RESTED	ROUGED	SEARED	*STAFFA
ROOKIE	RESULT	ROUSER	SEASON	STAGER
ROOMED	RESUME	ROUTED	SEATED	STAITH
ROOTED	RISING	*RYUKYU.	SEA-WAY	STAKED
ROOTLE.	RISKED	RAVAGE	SHABBY	STALER
RAPIER	RISQUE	RAVINE	SHADED	+STALIN
RAPINE	ROSARY	RAVING	SHADOW	STAMEN
RAPING	ROSEAL	RAVISH	SHAGGY	STANCE
RAPIST	ROSIER	REVEAL	SHAKEN	STANCH
RAPPED	ROSILY	REVERE	SHAKER	STANZA
RAPTLY	ROSTER	REVERS	SHAMAN	STAPES
RAPTOR	ROSTRA	REVERT	SHAMED	STAPLE
REPAID	RUSHED	REVIEW	SHAMMY	STARCH
REPAIR	RUSHEN	REVILE	SHANDY	STARED
REPAST	+RUSKIN	REVISE	SHANTY	STARRY
REPEAL	RUSSET	REVIVE	SHAPED	STARVE
REPEAT	*RUSSIA	REVOKE	SHARED	STASIS
REPENT	RUSTED	REVOLT	SHAVED	STATED
REPINE	RUSTIC	REVVED	SHAVEN	STATER
REPLAY	RUSTLE.	RIVING	SHAVER	STATIC
REPORT	RATHER	ROVING.	SKATER	STATOR
REPOSE	RATIFY	REWARD	SLACKS	STATUE
REPUTE	RATING	+ROWENA	SLAKED	STATUS
RIPELY	RATION	ROWING.	SLANGY	STAVED
RIPEST	RATTAN	RAYING	SLAP-UP	STAYED
RIPPED	RATTED	RHYMED	SLATED	STAYER
RIPPLE	RATTER	RHYMER	SLATER	SWAMPY
RIPPLY	RATTLE	RHYTHM.	SLAVER	SWANKY
RIP-SAW	RETAIL	RAZING	SLAVIC	SWATHE
ROPING	RETAIN	RAZZIA	SLAYER	SWAYED.
+RUPERT.	RETAKE		SMARMY	+SABINA
ROQUET.	RETARD	SCABBY	SNAKED	SOBBED
RAREFY	RETINA	SCALAR	SNAPPY	SUBDUE
RARELY	RETIRE	SCALED	SNARED	SUBLET
RAREST	RETOOK	SCAMPI	SNATCH	SUBMIT
RARITY.	RETORT	SCANTY	SNAZZY	SUBORN
RASCAL	RETROD	SCARAB	SOAKED	SUBTLE
RASHER	RETURN	SCARCE	SOAKER	SUBTLY
RASHLY	RITUAL	SCARED	SOAPED	SUBURB
RASPED	ROTARY	SCATHE	SOARED	SUBWAY.
RASTER	ROTATE	SCATTY	SPACED	SACHET
RESCUE	ROTTED	SEA-COW	SPACER	SACKED

SACRAL	SHERRY	SIGNAL	SPICED	SILTED
SACRED	SIENNA	SIGNED	SPIDER	SILVER
SACRUM	SIERRA	SIGNET	SPIGOT	SOLACE
SECANT	SIESTA	SIGNOR	SPIKED	SOLDER
SECEDE	SIEVED	SUGARY.	SPINAL	SOLELY
SECOND	SKERRY	*SAHARA	SPINET	SOLEMN
SECRET	SKETCH	SCHEMA	SPIRAL	*SOLENT
SECTOR	SKEWED	SCHEME	SPIRED	SOLING
SECURE	SKEWER	SCHISM	SPIRIT	SOLUTE
*SICILY	SLEAZY	SCHIST	SPITED	SOLVED
SICKEN	SLEDGE	SCHIZO	STICKY	SPLASH
SICKER	SLEEPY	SCHOOL	STIFLE	SPLEEN
SICKLE	SLEEVE	SPHERE	STIGMA	SPLICE
SICKLY	SLEIGH	SPHINX.	STILLY	SPLINE
SOCAGE	SLEUTH	*SAIGON	STINGY	SPLINT
SOCCER	SLEWED	SAILED	STITCH	SULLEN
SOCIAL	SMELLY	SAILER	STIVER	SULTAN
SOCKET	SNEEZE	SAILOR	SUITED	SULTRY
SUCKED	SPECIE	*SCILLY	SUITOR	SYLVAN
SUCKER	SPEECH	SEISED	SWIPED	+SYLVIA.
SUCKLE.	SPEEDY	SEISIN	SWITCH	SAMITE
SADDEN	SPEWED	SEIZED	SWIVEL.	SAMPAN
SADDER	STEADY	SHIELD	*SIKKIM.	SAMPLE
SADDLE	STEAMY	SHIFTY	SALAAM	+SAMUEL
SADISM	STEELY	SHIMMY	SALAMI	SEMITE
SADIST	+STELLA	SHINDY	SALARY	SIMIAN
SEDATE	STENCH	SHINED	SALIFY	SIMILE
SEDUCE	STEPPE	SHINER	SALINE	SIMMER
*SIDCUP	STEREO	SHINTO	SALIVA	SIMNEL
SIDING	+STEVEN	SHIRTY	SALLOW	SIMONY
SIDLED	STEWED	SHIVER	SALMON	SIMOOM
SODDEN	SVELTE	SKIING	+SALOME	SIMPER
SODIUM	SWEATY	SKILLY	SALOON	SIMPLE
SODOMY	*SWEDEN	SKIMPY	SALTED	SIMPLY
SUDDEN	SWEENY	SKINNY	SALTER	*SOMALI
*SYDNEY.	SWERVE.	SKIVER	SALUKI	SOMBRE
SCENIC	SAFARI	SKIVVY	SALUTE	SUMMED
SEEDED	SAFELY	SLICED	SALVED	SUMMER
SEEING	SAFEST	SLICER	SALVER	SUMMIT
SEEKER	SAFETY	SLIGHT	SALVIA	SUMMON
SEEMED	SIFTER	SLIMLY	SALVOR	SYMBOL.
SEEMLY	SOFTEN	SLINKY	SELDOM	SANDAL
SEEPED	SOFTER	SLIVER	SELECT	SANDED
SEETHE	SOFTLY	SMILED	SELLER	+SANDRA
SHEARS	SUFFER	SMIRCH	SELVES	SANELY
SHEATH	SUFFIX.	SMITHY	+SELWYN	SANEST
SHEENY	SAGELY	SNIPER	SILAGE	SANITY
SHEIKH	SAGGAR	SNIVEL	SILENT	SENATE
SHEKEL	SAGGED	SOILED	SILICA	SENDAL
SHELVE	SIGHED	SOIREE	SILKEN	SENDER

SENILE	SLOGAN	SOPPED	SORBET	SURELY
SENIOR	SLOPED	SUPERB	SORDID	SUREST
SENORA	SLOPPY	SUPINE	SORELY	SURETY
SENSED	SLOUCH	SUPPED	SOREST	SURFER
SENSOR	*SLOUGH	SUPPER	SORREL	SURGED
SENTRY	SLOVEN	SUPPLE	SORROW	*SURREY
SINEWY	SLOWER	SUPPLY	SORTED	SURTAX
SINFUL	SLOWLY	SYPHON.	SORTER	SURVEY
SINGED	SMOKED	SEQUEL	SORTIE	SYRINX
SINGER	SMOKER	SEQUIN.	SPRAIN	SYRUPY.
SINGLE	SMOOCH	SARONG	SPRANG	SESAME
SINGLY	SMOOTH	SARSEN	SPRAWL	SESTET
SINKER	SNOBBY	*SARTRE	SPREAD	SISKIN
SINNED	SNOOTY	SCRAPE	SPRING	SISTER
SINNER	SNOOZE	SCRAWL	SPRINT	SUSSED
SINTER	SNORED	SCREAM	SPRITE	*SUSSEX
SONANT	SNOTTY	SCREED	SPROUT	SYSTEM.
SONATA	SNOWED	SCREEN	SPRUCE	SATEEN
SONNET	SOONER	SCREWY	SPRUNG	SATING
SUNDAE	SOOTHE	SCRIBE	STRAFE	SATIRE
SUNDAY	SPOKEN	SCRIED	STRAIN	SATRAP
SUNDER	SPONGE	SCRIMP	STRAIT	+SATURN
SUNDEW	SPONGY	SCRIPT	STRAKE	SET-OFF
SUNDRY	SPOOKY	SCROLL	STRAND	SETOSE
SUN-GOD	SPORTY	SCROTA	STRATA	SET-OUT
SUN-HAT	SPOTTY	SCRUFF	STRATH	SETTEE
SUNKEN	SPOUSE	SERAPE	STRAWY	SETTER
SUNLIT	STOCKY	SERAPH	STREAK	SETTLE
SUNNED	STODGE	SERENE	STREAM	SITING
SUNSET	STODGY	SERIAL	STREET	SITTER
SUN-TAN	STOKER	SERIES	STRESS	SUTLER
SYNDIC	STOLEN	SERMON	STREWN	SUTTEE
SYNTAX.	STOLID	SEROUS	STRICT	*SUTTON
SCONCE	STONED	SERVED	STRIDE	SUTURE
SCORCH	STOOGE	SERVER	STRIFE	SAUCED
SCORED	STORED	SHRANK	STRIKE	SAUCER
SCORER	STOREY	SHREWD	STRING	SCULPT
SCORIA	STORMY	SHRIEK	STRIPE	SCUMMY
SCOTCH	STOWED.	SHRIFT	STRIPY	SCURFY
SCOTER	SAPPED	SHRIKE	STRIVE	SCURRY
SCOUSE	SAPPER	SHRILL	STROBE	SCURVY
SHODDY	SEPSIS	SHRIMP	STRODE	SLUDGE
SHOOED	SEPTAL	SHRINE	STROKE	SLUICE
SHORED	SEPTET	SHRINK	STROLL	SLUMMY
SHOULD	SEPTIC	SHRIVE	STROMA	SLURRY
SHOVED	SEPTUM	SHROUD	STRONG	SLUSHY
SHOVEL	SIPHON	SHROVE	*STROUD	SMUDGE
SHOWED	SIPPED	SHRUNK	STROVE	SMUDGY
SHOWER	SIPPET	SIRING	STRUCK	SMUGLY
*SKOPJE	+SOPHIA	SIRIUS	STRUNG	SMUTCH

SMUTTY	SOWING.	TABLED	TUFTED.	TELEDU
SNUGLY	*SAXONY	TABLET	TAGGED	TELFER
SOUGHT	SEXIER	*TOBAGO	TIGHTS	TELLER
SOUPED	SEXILY	TUBBED	*TIGRIS	TILING
SOURCE	SEXING	TUBING.	TOGGLE	TILLED
SOURED	SEXPOT	TACKED	TUGGED.	TILLER
SOURLY	SEXTET	TACKLE	*TAHITI.	TILTED
SOUSED	SEXTON	TICKED	TAILED	TOLLED.
SPUMED	SEXUAL.	TICKER	TAILOR	TAMELY
SPURGE	+SAYERS	TICKET	THIEVE	TAMING
SPUTUM	SAYING	TICKLE	THINLY	TAMPED
SQUALL	SCYTHE	TOCSIN	THIRST	TAMPER
SQUAMA	SHYING	TUCKED	THIRTY	TAMPON
SQUARE	SKYING	TUCKER	+THISBE	TEMPER
SQUASH	SPYING	TUCKET	TOILER	TEMPLE
SQUAWK	STYLED	TYCOON.	TOILET	TIMBAL
SQUEAK	STYLUS	TEDDER	TRIBAL	TIMBER
SQUEAL	STYMIE.	TEDIUM	TRICAR	TIMBRE
SQUILL	SIZING	TIDIER	TRICED	TIMELY
SQUINT	SIZZLE	TIDILY	TRICKY	TIMING
SQUIRE	SYZYGY	TIDING	TRICOT	TOMATO
SQUIRM		TODDLE.	TRIFID	TOMBOY
SQUIRT	TEA-BAG	TEEING	TRIFLE	TOM-CAT
SQUISH	TEACUP	TEEMED	TRILBY	TOMTOM
+STUART	TEAMED	TEETER	TRIMLY	TUMBLE
+STUBBS	TEAPOT	*THEBES	TRIODE	TUMEFY
STUBBY	TEAPOY	THEISM	TRIPLE	TUMOUR
STUCCO	TEASED	THEIST	TRIPOD	TUMULI
STUDIO	TEASEL	+THELMA	TRIPOS	TUMULT.
STUFFY	TEASER	THENCE	+TRITON	TANDEM
STUMPY	TEA-SET	THEORY	TRIUNE	TANGED
STUPID	TEA-URN	THESIS	TRIVET	TANGLE
STUPOR	THALER	THEWED	TRIVIA	TANGLY
STURDY.	+THALIA	TIE-PIN	TWIGGY	TANIST
SAVAGE	*THAMES	TIERCE	TWILIT	TANKER
SAVANT	THANKS	TOE-CAP	TWINED	TANNED
SAVATE	THATCH	TOEING	TWINGE	TANNER
SAVING	THAWED	TREATY	TWISTY	TANNIC
SAVORY	TRACED	TREBLE	TWITCH.	TANNIN
SAVOUR	TRACER	TREMOR	TAKING.	TENANT
SEVERE	TRADED	TRENCH	TALCUM	TENDED
SEVERN	TRADER	TRENDY	TALENT	TENDER
SOVIET.	TRAGIC	TREPAN	TALION	TENDON
SAW-FLY	TRANCE	+TREVOR	TALKED	TENNIS
SAWING	TRAPSE	TSETSE	TALKER	TENSED
SAWNEY	TRASHY	TWELVE	TALKIE	TENSOR
SAWYER	TRAUMA	TWENTY.	TALLER	TENTED
SEWAGE	TRAVEL.	TIFFIN	TALLOW	TENTER
SEWELL	TABARD	TOFFEE	TALMUD	TENURE
SEWING	TABBED	TUFFET	TELARY	TENUTO

125

TIN-CAN	TIPTOP	TORPOR	TOTING	UMBRAL
TINDER	TOP-HAT	TORQUE	*TOTNES	UNBEND
TINGED	TOPING	TORRID	TOTTED	UNBENT
TINGLE	TOPPED	TURBAN	TOTTER	UNBIND
TINIER	TOPPER	TURBID	TUTTED.	UNBOLT
TINILY	TOPPLE	TURBOT	TAUGHT	UNBORN
TINKER	TYPHUS	TUREEN	TAURUS	UPBEAT
TINKLE	TYPIFY	TURFED	TAUTEN	URBANE.
TINNED	TYPING	TURGID	TAUTER	UNCASE
TINPOT	TYPIST.	*TURKEY	TAUTLY	UNCATE
TINSEL	TARGET	TURNED	TAUTOG	UNCIAL
TONGUE	TARIFF	+TURNER	TEUTON	UNCOIL
TONING	TARMAC	TURNIP	*THURSO	UNCORD
TONITE	TARPAN	TURN-UP	THUSLY	UNCORK
TONSIL	TARRED	TURRET	TOUCAN	UPCAST
TUNDRA	TARSAL	TURTLE	TOUCHE	URCHIN.
TUNING	TARSIA	TURVES	TOUCHY	UNDIES
TUNNEL.	TARSUS	TYRANT	TOUPEE	+UNDINE
TAOISM	TARTAN	TYRIAN	TOURED	UNDONE
+THOMAS	TARTAR	*TYRONE.	TOURER	UNDULY
THORAX	TARTED	TASKED	TOUSLE	UP-DATE
THORNY	TARTLY	TASSEL	TOUTED	+UPDIKE.
THORPE	TERCET	TASSIE	TRUANT	UNEASY
THOUGH	TEREDO	TASTED	TRUDGE	UNEVEN
TOOLER	TERGAL	TASTER	TRUEST	URETER
TOOTED	TERMED	TESTED	TRUISM	URETIC
TOOTLE	TERNAL	TESTER	+TRUMAN	USEFUL
TROGON	TERROR	TESTES	TRUSTY.	UTERUS.
TROIKA	THRALL	TISANE	TAVERN.	UNFAIR
TROJAN	THRASH	TISSUE	TAWDRY	UNFOLD
TROPHY	THREAD	TOSSED	TAWING	UNFURL.
TROPIC	THREAT	TUSKED	THWACK	UNGIRD
TROPPO	THRESH	TUSKER	THWART	UNGIRT
TROUGH	THRICE	TUSSLE.	TOWAGE	UNGUAL
TROUPE	THRIFT	TATTED	TOWARD.	UNGULA
TROVER	THRILL	TATTER	TAXIED	URGENT
TROWEL	THRIPS	TATTLE	TAXING	URGING.
TWO-PLY	THRIVE	TATTOO	TUXEDO.	UNHAND
TWOULD	THROAT	TETCHY	THYMOL	UNHASP
TWO-WAY.	THRONE	TETHER	TOYING	UNHEWN
TAPING	THRONG	TETRAD	TRYING	UNHOLY
TAPPED	THROVE	TETTER	TRY-OUT	UNHOOK
TAPPET	THROWN	TITBIT		UNHURT
TIPCAT	THRUSH	TITFER	*UGANDA	UPHELD
TIP-OFF	THRUST	+TITIAN	UNABLE	UPHILL
TIPPED	TIRADE	TITLED	URAEUS	UPHOLD.
TIPPER	TIRING	TITTER	+URANUS	UNIPED
TIPPET	TORERO	TITTLE	USABLE	UNIQUE
TIPPLE	TOROID	TITTUP	USANCE.	UNISEX
TIPTOE	TORPID	TOTHER	UMBLES	UNISON

126

UNITED	UNSHOD	VAINLY	VARIED	VOYEUR.
URINAL.	UNSTOP	VEILED	VARLET	VIZIER
UNJUST.	UNSUNG	VEINED	VERBAL	
UNKIND	UNSURE	VOICED	VERGED	WEAKEN
UNKNIT	UPSHOT	VOIDED.	VERGER	WEAKER
UPKEEP.	UPSIDE	VIKING.	VERIFY	WEAKLY
UGLIER	URSINE	VALISE	VERILY	WEALTH
UGLIFY	+URSULA.	VALLEY	VERITY	WEANED
ULLAGE	ULTIMA	VALLUM	VERMIN	WEAPON
UMLAUT	ULTIMO	VALOUR	VERNAL	WEASEL
UNLADE	UNTACK	VALUED	*VERONA	WEAVER
UNLAID	UNTIDY	VALUER	VERSED	WHALER
UNLASH	UNTIED	VALUTA	VERSET	WRAITH.
UNLESS	UNTOLD	VALVED	VERSUS	WEBBED
UNLIKE	UNTRUE	VELETA	VERTEX	WOBBLE
UNLOAD	UPTAKE	VELLUM	VERVET	WOBBLY.
UNLOCK	UPTOWN	VELURE	VIRAGO	WICKED
UPLAND	UPTURN.	VELVET	+VIRGIL	WICKER
UPLIFT.	UNUSED	VILELY	*VIRGIN	WICKET.
UNMADE	USURER	VILEST	VIRILE	WADDED
UNMAKE	UVULAR.	VILIFY	VIRTUE	WADDLE
UNMASK	UNVEIL.	VILLUS	VORTEX	WADING
UNMEET	UNWARY	VOLING	*VYRNWY.	WEDDED
UNMOOR	UNWELL	VOLLEY	VASSAL	WEDGED
UPMOST	UNWEPT	VOLTED	VASTER	WIDELY
UTMOST.	UNWIND	VOLUME	VASTLY	WIDEST
UTOPIA.	UNWISE	VOLUTE	VESICA	*WIDNES.
UMPIRE	UNWORN	+VULCAN	+VESPER	WEEDED
UNPACK	UNWRAP	VULGAR	VESPID	WEEKLY
UNPICK	UPWARD.	VULVAR.	VESSEL	WEEPER
UNPLUG	UNYOKE	VAMOSE	VESTAL	WEEVIL
UPPISH		VAMPED.	VESTED	WHEEZE
UPPITY.	VIABLE	VANDAL	VESTRY	WHEEZY
UNREAD	VIANDS.	VANISH	VISAGE	WHENCE
UNREAL	VACANT	VANITY	VISARD	WHERRY
UNREEL	VACATE	VENDEE	VISCID	WOEFUL
UNREST	VACUUM	VENDER	VISION	WREATH
UNRIPE	VECTOR	VENDOR	VISUAL.	WRENCH
UNROBE	VICTIM	VENEER	VETOED	WRETCH.
UNROLL	+VICTOR	VENIAL	VETTED	WAFFLE
UNRULY	VICUNA.	*VENICE	VITALS	WAFTED
UPROAR	VIDUAL.	VENOSE	VOTARY	WIFELY.
UPROOT	VEERED	VENOUS	VOTING	WAGGED
UPRUSH.	*VIENNA	VENTED	VOTIVE.	WAGGLE
*ULSTER	VIEWER.	VINERY	VIVACE	WAGGON
UNSAFE	VAGARY	VINOUS.	+VIVIAN	WAGING
UNSAID	VAGINA	+VIOLET	VIVIFY.	+WAGNER
UNSEAL	VAGUER	VIOLIN	VOWING.	WIGGLE
UNSEAT	VIGOUR.	VOODOO.	VEXING.	WIGWAM.
UNSHIP	VAINER	VAPOUR.	VOYAGE	WAILED

127

WAITED	WOMBAT.	WIRING	YOKING.	
WAITER	WANDER	WORDED	YELLED	BAZAAR
WAIVED	WANGLE	WORKED	YELLOW	BASALT
WAIVER	WANING	WORKER	YELPED.	*BAHAMA
WEIGHT	WANTED	WORMED	YANKED	BANANA
WHILED	WANTON	WORSEN	YANKEE	BALATA
WHILST	WENDED	WORTHY.	YENNED	*CANADA
WHIMSY	WINCED	WASHED	YONDER.	CARAFE
WHINED	WINDED	WASHER	YAOURT	*CALAIS
WHINNY	WINDER	WASTED	YEOMAN	CABALA
WHIPPY	WINDOW	WASTER	*YEOVIL	+CASALS
WHISKY	WIND-UP	+WESLEY	+YVONNE.	CANARD
*WHITBY	WINGED	WISDOM	YAPPED.	CANARY
WHITEN	WINING	WISELY	YARROW	CALASH
WHITER	WINKED	WISEST	+YORICK	DAMAGE
WRITER	WINKLE	WISHED.	YORKER.	DAMASK
WRITHE.	WINNER	WATERY	YES-MAN.	FACADE
WAKING	WINNOW	WATTLE	YAWING	GARAGE
*WOKING.	WINTER	WETHER	YAWNED	GALAXY
WALING	WINTRY	WETTED	YOWLED	*HAWAII
WALKER	WONDER	WETTER		*HAVANA
WALLED	WONTED.	WITHAL	ZEALOT.	HAZARD
WALLET	WHOLLY	WITHER	ZODIAC.	HARASS
+WALLIS	WHOOSH	WITHIN.	ZAFFRE.	KANAKA
WALLOP	WHORED	WAVING	ZIGZAG	KARATE
WALLOW	WOODED	WYVERN.	ZYGOMA	LANATE
WALNUT	WOODEN	WAXING.	ZYGOTE.	MALADY
WALRUS	WOOFER	WAYLAY	*ZAMBIA	*MALAGA
+WALTER	WOOING	WAY-OUT.	ZOMBIE	MANAGE
+WALTON	WOOLLY.	WIZARD	ZYMASE.	MADAME
WELDER	WAPITI		ZENANA	MARAUD
WELKIN	WIPING.	X-RAYED.	ZENITH	*MALAWI
WELLED	WARBLE	XYLENE	ZINNIA	*MALAYA
WELTED	WARDED	XYLITE	ZONARY	NAPALM
WELTER	WARDEN	XYLOID	ZONATE	NATANT
*WELWYN	WARDER	XYLOSE.	ZONING.	PALACE
+WILBUR	+WARHOL	XANADU	ZOOMED.	PAPACY
WILDER	WARIER	XENIAL.	+ZAPATA	PARADE
WILDLY	WARILY	XYSTER.	ZEPHYR	PAPAIN
WILFUL	WARMED	+XAVIER	ZIPPED	PALAIS
WILILY	WARMER		ZIPPER.	*PANAMA
WILING	WARMLY	YEARLY	ZARIBA	PAVANE
WILLED	WARMTH	YEASTY.	ZEROED	PARAPH
WILLOW	WARNED	YABBER.	ZIRCON	PALATE
+WILSON	WARPED	YAFFLE.	*ZURICH.	RAVAGE
WILTED	WARRED	YOGURT.	ZITHER.	SALAAM
*WILTON	+WARREN	YAHWEH	ZEUGMA	SAVAGE
WOLFED	*WARSAW	+YEHUDI.	ZOUAVE	SALAMI
WOLVES.	WERENT	YOICKS.	ZOUNDS	SAVANT
WIMPLE	WIRILY	YAKKED		*SAHARA

SAFARI	RABBIT	CANDLE	WARDEN	SAFETY
SALARY	RAMBLE	CAUDLE	WARDER	TAMELY
SAVATE	RABBLE	DAEDAL	WANDER	TALENT
TABARD	TABBED	DANDER	WADDLE.	TAVERN
VACANT	WARBLE	+DAUDET	BALEEN	WATERY.
VAGARY	YABBER	DANDLE	BARELY	*BAFFIN
VACATE	*ZAMBIA.	DAWDLE	BASELY	BAFFLE
XANADU	CAN-CAN	GADDED	BAKERY	CARFAX
+ZAPATA.	CALCAR	GARDEN	BASEST	GAFFED
BAOBAB	CANCEL	GANDER	CAVEAT	GAFFER
BARBED	CANCER	+GANDHI	CAREEN	GADFLY
BARBEL	CATCHY	HANDED	CAREER	KAFFIR
BARBER	CAECUM	+HANDEL	CASEIN	LAWFUL
BARBET	CAUCUS	HARDEN	CAMERA	MAYFLY
BABBLE	DANCER	HARDER	CAVERN	MANFUL
BAUBLE	FAECAL	HANDLE	CARESS	RAFFIA
*BALBOA	FAUCAL	HARDLY	FAG-END	RAFFLE
BAMBOO	FAECES	LANDAU	GATEAU	SAW-FLY
CAMBER	FASCES	LANDED	GAZEBO	WAFFLE
CARBON	FAUCET	LARDED	GAMELY	YAFFLE
CARBOY	FASCIA	LAUDED	GALENA	ZAFFRE.
DAY-BED	FALCON	LADDER	GAMETE	BANGED
DABBED	GAUCHE	LARDER	GAIETY	BAGGED
DAUBED	GAUCHO	LANDES	HABEAS	BARGEE
DABBER	LAICAL	LADDIE	HAVENT	BADGER
DABBLE	LASCAR	LAPDOG	LATEEN	BANGLE
DAY-BOY	LANCED	MADDED	LATELY	*BANGOR
GAS-BAG	LANCER	MAIDEN	LAMELY	CADGER
GARBED	LANCET	MADDEN	LAMENT	CAUGHT
GABBED	MADCAP	MADDER	LATENT	CATGUT
*GAMBIA	+MARCIA	PADDED	LATEST	DANGER
GAMBIT	MASCOT	PANDER	MAYEST	DAGGER
GABBLE	+PASCAL	PADDLE	MAKE-UP	DANGLE
GARBLE	PARCEL	PARDON	NAMELY	DAGGLE
GAMBLE	PATCHY	RANDAN	+PAMELA	FANGED
GAMBOL	RASCAL	RAG-DAY	PALELY	FAGGED
HAYBOX	RANCID	RAIDER	PARENT	FAGGOT
IAMBIC	SAUCED	RADDLE	PATENT	GAGGED
IAMBUS	SAUCER	RANDOM	PALEST	GANGED
JABBED	TALCUM.	SANDAL	RAREFY	GAUGED
JABBER	BANDED	SANDED	RARELY	GAUGER
JAMBOK	+BALDER	SADDEN	RACEME	GANGER
LAMBDA	BARDIC	SADDER	RAREST	*GANGES
LAMBED	BANDIT	SADDLE	SATEEN	GADGET
MARBLE	BALDLY	+SANDRA	SANELY	GARGLE
MAYBUG	CAUDAL	TANDEM	SAGELY	GAGGLE
NABBED	*CAMDEN	TAWDRY	SAFELY	GANGUE
RAG-BAG	*CANDIA	VANDAL	+SAYERS	HANGAR
RABBET	CANDID	WADDED	SAFEST	HAGGED
RABBIN	CADDIS	WARDED	SANEST	HANGED

HANGER	HAW-HAW	DANISH	LAYING	RAYING
HAGGIS	HASHED	DATIVE	LAVISH	RACING
HAGGLE	LASHED	EASIER	LAXITY	RAVING
HANG-UP	LASHER	EASILY	MANIAC	RATING
JAGGED	LATHER	*EALING	+MARIAN	RAPING
JANGLE	LACHES	EASING	MALICE	RAKING
JARGON	MASHED	EATING	MALIGN	RAGING
LAGGED	MAYHEM	EARING	*MANILA	RATION
LARGER	MASHIE	FACIAL	MAXIMA	RADISH
LAAGER	+NATHAN	FABIAN	+MARINA	RAKISH
LANGUR	PATHAN	FACILE	+MAXINE	RAVISH
MANGER	PATHIC	FAMILY	MARINE	RACISM
MARGIN	PATHOS	FARINA	MAYING	RAPIST
MANGLE	+RACHEL	FAMINE	MAKING	RACIST
MAGGOT	RASHER	FAKING	MATING	RARITY
NAGGED	RATHER	FADING	MATINS	RADIUM
NAGGER	RASHLY	FARING	MANIOC	RADIUS
NAUGHT	SACHET	FACING	+NADINE	SALIFY
PARGET	WASHED	FAMISH	NAMING	+SABINA
RAGGED	WASHER	GASIFY	NATION	SALINE
RANGED	+WARHOL.	GATING	NAZISM	SAYING
RANGER	BASIAL	GAMING	NATIVE	SATING
SAGGAR	BANIAN	GAPING	OARING	SAVING
SAGGED	BAYING	GAZING	OAFISH	SAWING
*SAIGON	BALING	GABION	PARIAH	SATIRE
TAGGED	BAKING	GARISH	PARIAN	SADISM
TANGED	BATING	HALIDE	PACIFY	SADIST
TARGET	BARING	HAZILY	PATINA	SAMITE
TAUGHT	BANISH	HAYING	PAGING	SANITY
TANGLE	BARIUM	HARING	PARING	SALIVA
TANGLY	CAVIAR	HALING	PACING	TAXIED
WAGGED	CALICO	HATING	PALING	TARIFF
WANGLE	CARIES	HAVING	PAWING	TAWING
WAGGLE	CAGILY	HAWING	PAYING	TAKING
WAGGON.	CANINE	HAZING	PARISH	TAXING
*AACHEN	CASING	HAMITE	PAPIST	TAMING
BASHED	CAVING	+JANICE	PARITY	TAPING
BATHER	CARING	JAPING	RADIAL	TALION
BATHOS	CAKING	JADING	RACIAL	TAOISM
CASHED	CAGING	JAWING	RADIAN	TANIST
CACHET	CANING	JABIRU	RAPIER	*TAHITI
CASHEW	CASINO	LABIAL	RACIER	VARIED
CACHOU	CAMION	LARIAT	RABIES	VAGINA
DASHED	CATION	LABILE	RATIFY	VALISE
DASHER	CALIPH	LAZILY	RAMIFY	VANISH
+DAPHNE	CAVITY	LAMINA	RACILY	VANITY
FATHER	+DANIEL	LACING	RAVINE	WARIER
FATHOM	DARING	LADING	RAPINE	WARILY
GASHED	DAZING	LAMING	RAGING	WALING
GATHER	DATING	LAZING	RAZING	WAGING

WAXING	PACKED	GAOLER	VALLEY	TARMAC
WANING	PARKED	GALLEY	VALLUM	TALMUD
WAVING	PACKER	GARLIC	WAYLAY	WARMED
WADING	PACKET	GAELIC	WALLED	WARMER
WAKING	PARKIN	GALLIC	WAILED	WARMLY
WAPITI	RACKED	+GAULLE	WALLET	WARMTH.
+XAVIER	RANKED	GALLON	+WALLIS	BANNED
YAWING	RANKER	GALLOP	WALLOP	BANNER
ZARIBA.	RACKET	GALLUP	WALLOW.	*BARNET
FAN-JET	RANKLE	HAULED	BAGMAN	BAGNIO
GAS-JET	RANKLY	HAILED	BATMAN	CARNAL
JAM-JAR	SACKED	HAMLET	BARMAN	CAT-NAP
RAMJET.	TACKED	HALLOO	*CAYMAN	CANNED
*BALKAN	TASKED	HARLOT	CARMAN	CANNER
BASKED	TALKED	*HARLOW	CABMAN	*CANNES
BALKED	TALKER	HALLOW	CALMED	CANNON
BANKED	TANKER	HALLUX	*CARMEL	CANNOT
BACKED	TALKIE	JAILED	+CARMEN	DAMNED
BACKER	TACKLE	JAILER	CALMER	DARNED
BARKER	WALKER	KAOLIN	CALMLY	DAWNED
BANKER	YAKKED	LADLED	+CADMUS	DARNEL
BASKET	YANKED	MARLED	DAMMAR	DARNER
CANKER	YANKEE.	MAILED	DAMMED	DAINTY
CASKET	BALLAD	MAULED	DAEMON	EARNED
CALKIN	BAWLED	+MAHLER	FARMER	FAWNED
CATKIN	BAILEE	+MAILER	GASMAN	FANNED
CACKLE	BAILER	MALLET	GAMMED	FAWNER
DARKEN	BALLET	*MARLOW	GAMMER	GAINED
DARKER	BAILEY	MALLOW	GAMMON	GARNER
DARKLY	BARLEY	NAILED	HAEMAL	GANNET
GASKET	BALLOT	*NAPLES	HARMED	GARNET
HACKED	*CALLAO	PALLED	HAMMED	+HANNAH
HARKEN	CALLED	PALLET	HAMMER	HAUNCH
HANKER	CALLER	PARLEY	JAMMED	JAUNTY
HAWKER	*CARLOW	PALLID	KALMIA	LAUNCE
HACKLE	CALLOW	PALLOR	LAYMAN	LAUNCH
JACKAL	CALL-UP	+PAVLOV	LAMMAS	LANNER
JACKED	CALLUS	RAGLAN	LAMMED	MAENAD
JACKET	*DALLAS	RAILED	MAMMAL	MAUNDY
LACKED	DAHLIA	SAILED	MADMAN	MANNED
LARKED	EAGLET	SAILER	MAIMED	MANNER
LACKEY	FABLED	SAILOR	MAMMON	MAGNET
MASKED	FAILED	SALLOW	MARMOT	MAINLY
MARKED	FALLEN	TAILED	PALMAR	MAGNOX
MARKER	*FAWLEY	TABLED	PALMED	MAGNUM
MASKER	FAILLE	TALLER	PALMER	PAUNCH
MARKET	FALLOW	TABLET	RAGMAN	PAINED
MACKLE	FAULTY	TAILOR	RAMMED	PANNED
NARKED	GALLED	TALLOW	RAMMER	PAWNED
NAPKIN	GABLED	VARLET	SALMON	PAYNIM

RAINED	+SALOME	SAMPLE	PATRON	TASSIE
*RADNOR	SARONG	TARPAN	PARROT	TARSUS
SAWNEY	*SAXONY	TAPPED	RAMROD	VASSAL
TANNED	SALOON	TAMPED	SACRAL	*WARSAW.
TANNER	SAVORY	TAMPER	SATRAP	BANTAM
TANNIC	SAVOUR	TAPPET	SACRED	BATTED
TANNIN	VAMOSE	TAMPON	SACRUM	BAITED
VAINER	VALOUR	VAMPED	TARRED	BASTED
VAINLY	VAPOUR	WARPED	TAURUS	BATTEN
WARNED	WAY-OUT.	YAPPED.	WARRED	BANTER
+WAGNER	CARPAL	BASQUE	+WARREN	BARTER
WALNUT	CARPED	BARQUE	WALRUS	BATTER
YAWNED.	CAMPED	CAIQUE	YARROW.	*BALTIC
BARONY	CAPPED	CASQUE	BALSAM	BATTLE
BACONY	CARPEL	MANQUE	BASSET	+BARTOK
BABOON	CAMPER	MASQUE.	CAUSAL	BARTON
CAJOLE	CARPET	BARRED	+CAESAR	BATTUE
+CAPONE	CAMPUS	BARREL	CAUSED	CANTAB
CAHOOT	CARPUS	BARREN	CASSIA	CAFTAN
CANOPY	DAMPEN	+BARRIE	DAMSEL	CARTED
CAVORT	DAMPER	*BARROW	DAMSON	CANTED
+CAPOTE	DAPPER	CARREL	GASSED	CARTEL
DACOIT	DAPPLE	CARROT	HAWSER	CAUTER
*DAKOTA	DAMPLY	DACRON	HANSOM	CANTER
FAR-OFF	GASPED	FABRIC	*KANSAS	CASTER
FAVOUR	GASPER	FAERIE	KAISER	CASTLE
FAMOUS	HARPED	FAIRLY	LAPSED	CATTLE
GANOID	HAPPED	*FAEROE	LASSIE	*CANTON
GALORE	HASPED	FARROW	MASSED	+CAXTON
GALOSH	HAPPEN	GARRET	MAUSER	CANTON
HALOED	HAMPER	HAIR-DO	MARSHY	CARTON
HALOID	HARPER	HATRED	MASSIF	CANTOR
+HAROLD	HATPIN	*HARRIS	*NASSAU	CAPTOR
HAMOSE	+JASPER	*HARROW	NAUSEA	CASTOR
JALOPY	LAPPED	JARRED	PARSEC	+CASTRO
KAYOED	LAPPET	LAUREL	PASSED	CACTUS
LAY-OFF	MAPPED	+LAURIE	PARSED	DARTED
LAGOON	MAGPIE	LARRUP	PAUSED	+DALTON
*LAHORE	NAPPED	*MADRAS	PARSEE	DACTYL
LABOUR	PAMPAS	MARRED	PASSER	*EASTER
LAYOUT	PALPED	MATRIC	PASSIM	EARTHY
MAROON	PAUPER	MATRIX	PARSON	FATTED
MAHOUT	PAMPER	*MADRID	*RAASAY	FATTEN
PAGODA	RAMPED	MATRON	RAISED	FASTEN
PARODY	RASPED	RAISIN	RAISIN	FATTER
PATOIS	RAPPED	MACRON	RANSOM	FALTER
PAROLE	RAJPUT	MARROW	SARSEN	FASTER
PAEONY	SAMPAN	NARROW	TARSAL	FACTOR
RACOON	SAPPED	PAIRED	TASSEL	FACTUM
RAGOUT	SAPPER	PATROL	TARSIA	GARTER

132

GAITER	RAFTER	SALUTE	OBTAIN	ACCEPT
GANTRY	RATTLE	VALUED	OBLATE.	ACCESS
HATTED	RAPTLY	VAGUER	ABACUS.	ECZEMA
HALTED	RAPTOR	VALUER	*ABADAN	SCREAM
HAFTED	SALTED	VALUTA	ABIDED	SCREED
HASTED	SALTER	VACUUM	*IBADAN	SCREEN
HASTEN	+SARTRE	YAOURT.	IBIDEM.	SCHEMA
HATTER	TARTAN	CANVAS	ABJECT	SCHEME
HALTER	TARTAR	CALVED	ABSENT	SCREWY.
KAFTAN	TATTED	CALVES	ABBESS	ACHING
LASTED	TASTED	*CANVEY	OBJECT	ACTING
LATTEN	TARTED	+CALVIN	OBSESS.	ACTION
LATTER	TAUTEN	HALVED	EBBING	ACRITA
LACTIC	TATTER	+HARVEY	OBLIGE.	ACUITY
LASTLY	TAUTER	LARVAE	OBELUS.	ACTIVE
MATTED	TASTER	LARVAL	ABROAD	SCRIBE
MALTED	TATTLE	MARVEL	ABSORB	SCRIED
MASTED	TAUTLY	PARVIS	OBLONG.	SCRIMP
MANTEL	TARTLY	SALVED	+OBERON.	SCRIPT
MARTEN	TAUTOG	SALVER	ABASED	SCHISM
MASTER	TATTOO	SALVIA	ABUSED.	SCHIST
MATTER	VASTER	SALVOR	ABATED	SCHIZO.
+MARTHA	VASTLY	VALVED	ABATIS	ACAJOU.
MALTHA	WAFTED	WAIVED	OBITER.	*ECCLES
MANTIC	WASTED	WAIVER.	ABDUCT	OCULAR
MASTIC	WANTED	*DARWIN	ABOUND	OCELLI
+MARTIN	WAITED	EARWAX	ABRUPT	OCELOT
MANTIS	+WALTER	EARWIG	ABSURD	SCALAR
MANTLE	WAITER	*GALWAY	ABJURE	SCALED
MARTYR	WASTER	YAHWEH.	OBTUSE.	*SCILLY
NAUTCH	WATTLE	BANYAN	OBEYED	SCULPT.
NATTER	+WALTON	BARYON		ACUMEN
PASTED	WANTON.	BARYTA	ECLAIR	ICEMAN
PARTED	CASUAL	CANYON	ICE-AXE	SCUMMY
PATTED	+CARUSO	LAWYER	OCTANE	SCAMPI.
PANTED	+CANUTE	LARYNX	OCTAVE	ACANTH
PASTEL	*DANUBE	MAGYAR	OCTAVO	ACINUS
PATTEN	FACULA	SAWYER.	SCRAPE	ICONIC
PALTER	JAGUAR	+BALZAC	SCRAWL.	SCONCE
PATTER	LACUNA	*DANZIG	ICEBOX	SCENIC
PARTLY	MANUAL	DAZZLE	SCABBY.	SCANTY.
PASTOR	+MANUEL	JAZZED	ACACIA	ACCORD
PALTRY	MAQUIS	PANZER	ICE-CAP	ACROSS
PASTRY	MACULA	RAZZIA	ICICLE.	ACCOST
PANTRY	MATURE		*ACADIA	ECHOED
RATTAN	MANURE	ABBACY	ACIDIC	ECHOIC
RATTED	NATURE	ABRADE	ACIDLY.	OCLOCK
RAFTED	+SAMUEL	ABOARD	ACCEDE	SCROLL
RASTER	SALUKI	ABLAUT	ACHENE	SCHOOL
RATTER	+SATURN	ABLAZE	ACCENT	SCROTA

133

ACERIC	EDDISH	DECAMP	SEWAGE	FEUDAL
ACCRUE	IDLING	DEMAND	SESAME	FENDED
ECARTE	ODDITY.	DECANT	SECANT	FEUDED
+ICARUS	ODD-JOB.	DEBARK	SERAPE	FENDER
SCARAB	ADDLED	DEPART	SERAPH	FEEDER
SCARCE	IDOLUM.	DENARY	SENATE	GELDED
SCORCH	+ADONIS	DEBASE	SEDATE	GENDER
SCARED	EDENIC	DELATE	TENANT	HEYDAY
SCORED	+GDYNIA	DERATE	TELARY	HEADED
SCORER	*GDANSK.	DEBATE	ZENANA.	HEEDED
SCURFY	ADJOIN	FEMALE	BERBER	HERDED
SCORIA	ADROIT	+GERALD	+DEBBIE	HEADER
SCURRY	ADSORB	HERALD	FEEBLE	HEDDLE
SCURVY.	ADNOUN	HEXANE	FEEBLY	*HENDON
ACETIC	IDIOCY	+HECATE	HERBAL	*KENDAL
SCOTCH	ODIOUS.	LEGACY	JERBOA	LEADED
SCOTER	ADORER.	LEVANT	KERBED	*LEYDEN
SCATHE	+EDISON	LEGATE	*LESBOS	LEADEN
SCYTHE	ODDS-ON	LEGATO	MEMBER	LENDER
SCATTY.	*ODESSA.	MENACE	PEBBLE	LEADER
ACTUAL	ADYTUM	*NEVADA	PEBBLY	LEAD-IN
ACQUIT	EDITED	*NEWARK	+REUBEN	LEWDLY
ACCUSE	EDITOR	NEGATE	TEA-BAG	MENDED
OCCULT	+ODETTE.	PEDALO	VERBAL	MELDED
OCCUPY	ADDUCE	PEDANT	WEBBED.	+MENDEL
SCRUFF	ADJURE	REFACE	BEECHY	*MENDIP
SCOUSE.	ADJUST	REDACT	BEACON	MEDDLE
ECTYPE	+EDMUND	REMADE	DEUCED	MEADOW
		RELAID	DE-ICER	NEEDED
EDDAIC	AERATE	REPAID	DEACON	NEEDLE
+EDWARD.	BEWAIL	RETAIL	DESCRY	PEDDLE
EDIBLE.	BETAKE	REMAIN	FENCED	REEDED
EDUCED.	BEHALF	RETAIN	FENCER	REDDEN
ADJECT	BEFALL	REGAIN	FESCUE	RENDER
ADVENT	BECALM	REPAIR	MESCAL	REDDER
ADVERB	BECAME	REMAKE	MERCER	READER
ADHERE	BEZANT	RETAKE	PENCIL	RE-EDIT
ADVERT	BEWARE	REGALE	REDCAP	REDDLE
ODDEST.	BERATE	RECALL	RESCUE	SENDAL
ADAGIO.	BEDAUB	REMAND	SEA-COW	SEEDED
+ADRIAN	BEHAVE	RECANT	TERCET	SENDER
ADVICE	CETANE	REGARD	TETCHY	SEA-DOG
ADDICT	CERATE	REWARD	TEACUP.	SELDOM
ADRIFT	DEFACE	RETARD	BELDAM	TENDED
ADDING	DETACH	REMARK	BEDDED	TEDDER
ADMIRE	DECADE	REHASH	BENDED	TENDER
ADVISE	DERAIL	REPAST	BEADLE	TENDON
EDDIED	DETAIL	RECAST	DEODAR	VENDEE
+EDWINA	DETAIN	RELATE	DEADEN	VENDER
EDGING	DEFAME	REBATE	DEADLY	VENDOR

WEDDED	REVEAL	MERGER	DEFINE	RELIEF
WEEDED	REPEAT	MEAGRE	DESIRE	REVIEW
WENDED	RESEAT	PEGGED	+DENISE	RESIGN
WELDER.	REBECK	RED-GUM	DEMISE	REVILE
*AEGEAN	REJECT	TERGAL	DEVISE	RESILE
+AENEAS	RECEDE	VERGED	DESIST	REFILL
+AEGEUS	REMEDY	VERGER	DERIVE	REGIME
BEHEAD	REDEEM	WEDGED	EERILY	+REGINA
BEDECK	REPENT	WEIGHT	FERIAL	RETINA
BESEEM	RESENT	ZEUGMA.	FETIAL	REMIND
BEREFT	RECENT	AETHER	FENIAN	REFINE
BEHELD	RELENT	BETHEL	FERINE	RELINE
BEFELL	REGENT	LETHAL	FELINE	REPINE
BEHEST	REVERE	LECHER	FETISH	REGION
CEMENT	REVERS	MESHED	FERITY	RECIPE
CELERY	REVERT	MENHIR	GENIAL	RETIRE
DEMEAN	RECESS	METHOD	GEMINI	REVISE
DEFEAT	SELECT	METHYL	GENIUS	RELISH
DEFECT	SECEDE	NETHER	HEWING	REMISS
DETECT	+SEWELL	NEPHEW	+HELIOS	RESIST
DEJECT	SERENE	PEAHEN	HERIOT	RECITE
DECEIT	SEVERE	TETHER	HELIUM	REGIUS
DEPEND	SEVERN	WETHER	+JEMIMA	RELIVE
DEFEND	TEREDO	ZEPHYR.	JEWISH	REVIVE
DETENT	TELEDU	AERIAL	KEYING	SERIAL
DECENT	VENEER	AERIFY	LEVIED	SEXIER
DEMENT	VELETA	AEDILE	LEGION	SERIES
DESERT	WERENT.	BELIAL	LESION	SENILE
DETEST	BELFRY	BESIDE	LEGIST	SEXILY
DELETE	DEAFEN	BETIDE	LEVITE	SEEING
FEWEST	HEIFER	BELIEF	LENITY	SEXING
GENERA	LEAFED	BENIGN	LEVITY	SEWING
*GENEVA	REEFER	BELIKE	MENIAL	SENIOR
HEREAT	TELFER.	BEHIND	MEDIAL	SEMITE
HEREBY	*BENGAL	*BERING	MEDIAN	TEEING
HEREIN	BEGGAR	CEDING	+MEDICI	TEDIUM
HEREOF	BEGGED	CERIPH	*MEXICO	VENIAL
HERESY	*BERGEN	CERISE	MEDICO	VESICA
HERETO	BEAGLE	CECITY	METING	*VENICE
+JEREMY	DENGUE	CERIUM	MEWING	VERIFY
JEWESS	GEWGAW	DENIAL	MERINO	VERILY
LEGEND	GEIGER	DEVICE	MEDIUM	VEXING
MERELY	HEDGER	DEPICT	PENIAL	VERITY
METEOR	HEIGHT	DERIDE	*PEKING	XENIAL
NEREID	KEDGED	DECIDE	PERIOD	ZENITH.
NEWEST	LEGGED	DENIED	PERISH	BEAKED
OEPEMA	LEDGER	DEFIED	PETITE	BEAKER
OEDEMA	LENGTH	DENIER	RELICT	BECKON
PESETA	LEAGUE	DESIGN	RESIDE	DECKED
REPEAL	MERGED	DEFILE	RELIED	DECKER

DECKLE	MEDLEY	REAMER	BEHOVE	SET-OFF
HECKLE	MEALIE	SEAMAN	DECOCT	SECOND
JERKED	+MERLIN	SEAMED	DECODE	SENORA
JERKIN	MELLOW	SEEMED	DEMODE	SETOSE
KECKED	PEDLAR	SEAMEN	DEVOID	SEROUS
KECKLE	PEELED	SEEMLY	DECOKE	SET-OUT
LEAKED	PEALED	SERMON	DEPONE	¥ETOED
MEEKER	PEG-LEG	TERMED	DEFORM	*VERONA
MEEKLY	PEELER	TEAMED	DEPORT	VENOSE
NECKED	PELLET	TEEMED	DEPOSE	VENOUS
PECKED	PEPLUM	VERMIN	DEMOTE	ZEROED.
PEAKED	REPLAY	YES-MAN	DENOTE	BED-PAN
PEEKED	REELED	YEOMAN.	DEVOTE	*BELPAR
PERKED	REFLEX	FENNEC	DEVOUR	DEEPEN
PECKER	REALLY	FENNEL	DETOUR	DEEPER
REEKED	REALTY	HERNIA	DEVOUT	*DELPHI
RECKON	REFLUX	JENNET	FELONY	DEEPLY
SEEKER	SEALED	KEENED	FEDORA	DESPOT
WEAKEN	SELLER	KENNED	HEROIC	HEAPED
WEAKER	SEALER	KERNEL	HEROIN	HELPED
WELKIN	TELLER	KENNEL	HEXOSE	HEMPEN
WEAKLY	VEILED	KEENER	+JEROME	HELPER
WEEKLY.	VELLUM	+KEYNES	KETONE	HERPES
+AEOLUS	WELLED	KEENLY	MELODY	KEEPER
BEDLAM	+WESLEY	LEANED	MEMOIR	KELPIE
*BERLIN	WEALTH	LEAN-TO	MEMORY	LEAPED
+BELLOC	YELLED	PENNED	+PELOPS	PEPPED
+BELLOW	YELLOW	PENNON	PELOTA	PEPPER
CELLAR	ZEALOT.	PEANUT	PEYOTE	PEEPER
*CEYLON	BEAMED	REGNAL	RECOIL	PEOPLE
DEWLAP	CERMET	REINED	REJOIN	REOPEN
DEALER	DEEMED	RENNET	+RENOIR	REAPER
DEPLOY	DERMIS	SEANCE	REVOKE	SEEPED
FELLAH	GERMAN	TERNAL	REVOLT	SEXPOT
FELLER	GEMMED	TENNIS	RETOOK	TEMPER
FEELER	GERMEN	VERNAL	REFOOT	TEMPLE
FELLOE	GERMON	VEINED	REMORA	TEAPOT
FELLOW	HETMAN	WEANED	RESORB	TEAPOY
FEALTY	HEMMED	YENNED.	RECORD	+VESPER
GELLED	HELMED	BEMOAN	REBORE	VESPID
HEALED	+HERMES	BEHOLD	REFORM	WEEPER
HEELED	HELMET	BECOME	REBORN	WEAPON
HEALER	HERMIT	BEYOND	RETORT	YELPED.
*HENLEY	KERMES	BEGONE	REPORT	BETRAY
HEALTH	KERMIS	BELONG	RESORT	BEARER
JELLED	MERMAN	BETONY	REPOSE	*BEIRUT
KEELED	+MESMER	BETOOK	REMOTE	DEFRAY
+KEPLER	PERMED	BEFOOL	RECOUP	DECREE
+LESLEY	PELMET	BEFORE	REMOVE	DEGREE
MEDLAR	PERMIT	BEFOUL	RENOWN	DEARER

DEBRIS	*JERSEY	CENTRE	PELTED	BENUMB
DERRIS	+JESSIE	DENTAL	PETTED	*BEAUNE
DEARLY	KERSEY	DENTED	PECTEN	BEMUSE
DEARTH	KELSON	DEXTER	PEWTER	BEAUTY
FEARED	LEASED	DENTIL	PESTER	DEDUCE
FERRET	LESSEE	DEFTLY	PEPTIC	DEDUCT
FERRIC	LESSEN	DEBTOR	PECTIC	DENUDE
FERRIS	LESSER	DEXTRO	PECTIN	DELUDE
GEARED	LESSON	FESTAL	PESTLE	DELUGE
+GEORGE	LESSOR	FELTED	PERTLY	DEBUNK
HEARER	MESSED	FETTER	RECTAL	DEMURE
HEBREW	MENSES	FESTER	RENTAL	DEFUSE
HEARSE	*MERSEY	FETTLE	RESTED	DEPUTE
HEARTH	MEASLY	GETTER	RENTED	DEPUTY
HEARTY	MESSRS	GENTLE	RENTER	FERULA
JEERED	+NELSON	GENTLY	RECTOR	FERULE
KERRIE	PEPSIN	GENTRY	RECTUM	FECUND
LEERED	PERSON	HEPTAD	SEPTAL	GERUND
LEARNT	REASON	HEFTED	SEATED	JESUIT
METRIC	SEISED	HEATED	SETTEE	JEJUNE
MEGRIM	SENSED	HELTER	SETTER	LEGUME
NEURAL	SEISIN	HEATER	SESTET	+MEDUSA
NEARBY	SEPSIS	HEATHY	SEXTET	NEBULA
NEARED	SEASON	HECTIC	SEPTET	PERUKE
NEARER	SENSOR	+HECTOR	SEETHE	+PETULA
NEARLY	TENSED	JETTED	SEPTIC	PENURY
NEURON	TEASED	JESTED	SETTLE	PERUSE
PEERED	TEASEL	JESTER	SEXTON	REDUCE
PETREL	TEASER	JETTON	SECTOR	REFUEL
PEARLY	TEA-SET	KELTIC	SENTRY	REBUFF
PETROL	TENSOR	KETTLE	SEPTUM	REFUGE
PERRON	VERSED	LENTEN	TESTED	REBUKE
REARED	VESSEL	+LESTER	TENTED	RESULT
REGRET	VERSET	LETTER	TETTER	RESUME
RETROD	VERSUS	LENTIL	TEETER	REFUND
SEARCH	WEASEL	LEPTON	TENTER	RETURN
SEARED	YEASTY.	MENTAL	TESTER	REFUSE
SECRET	BESTED	MELTED	TESTES	REFUTE
TETRAD	BELTED	METTLE	TEUTON	REPUTE
TERROR	BETTED	MENTOR	VESTAL	SEXUAL
VEERED	BEATEN	NECTAR	VENTED	SEDUCE
YEARLY.	BEATER	NESTED	VETTED	SEQUEL
BED-SIT	BETTER	NETTED	VESTED	SEQUIN
CEASED	+BERTHA	NEATEN	VERTEX	SECURE
CENSOR	BESTIR	NEUTER	VECTOR	TENURE
CENSUS	BEETLE	NETTLE	VESTRY	TEA-URN
DENSER	BESTOW	NESTLE	WELTED	TENUTO
GEYSER	CENTAL	NEATLY	WETTED	VELURE
GEISHA	CERTES	+NEWTON	WELTER	+YEHUDI.
JETSAM	CELTIC	PENTAD	WETTER.	BEAVER

CERVIX	OFFING	*KHYBER	THEISM	SHINTO
DELVED	OFFISH.	PHOBIA	THEIST	SHANTY
*DENVER	AFFLUX	PHOBIC	THRIVE.	THENCE
FERVID	EFFLUX.	SHABBY	CHOKED	THANKS
HEAVED	AFLOAT	*THEBES.	CHOKER	THINLY
HEAVEN	AFFORD	CHICHI	SHEKEL	WHENCE
HEAVER	EFFORT.	CHICLE	SHAKEN	WHINED
LEAVED	AFFRAY	CHICLY.	SHAKER.	WHINNY.
LEAVEN	OFFSET.	CHIDED	CHOLER	CHROME
LEAVES	EFFUSE	*RHODES	CHALET	CHOOSE
+MELVYN		SHODDY	CHALKY	CHOOSY
NERVED	AGNAIL	SHADED	CHILLI	PHLOEM
PEEVED	AGHAST	SHADOW.	CHILLY	SHOOED
PELVIC	AGNATE	CHEEKY	+PHILIP	SHROUD
PELVIS	IGUANA.	CHEERY	PHYLUM	SHROVE
REVVED	EGG-CUP.	CHEESE	SHELVE	THROAT
REEVED	AGREED	CHEESY	THALER	THRONE
SERVED	EGRESS	+PHOEBE	+THALIA	THRONG
SERVER	OGRESS.	PHLEGM	+THELMA	THEORY
SELVES	AGUISH	SHIELD	WHILED	THROVE
VELVET	EGOISM	SHEENY	WHALER	THROWN
VERVET	EGOIST	SHREWD	WHOLLY	WHOOSH.
WEAVER	IGNITE	THREAD	WHILST.	CHAPEL
WEEVIL	OGLING	THREAT	CHIMED	+CHOPIN
*YEOVIL.	OGRISH	THRESH	CHUMMY	CHIPPY
LEEWAY	UGLIER	THIEVE	RHYMED	CHOPPY
*MEDWAY	UGLIFY.	WHEEZE	RHYMER	SHAPED
PEEWIT	AGAMIC.	WHEEZY.	SHAMAN	WHIPPY.
SEA-WAY	AGENCY	CHAFED	SHAMED	CHEQUE.
+SELWYN	AGENDA	CHAFFY	SHIMMY	CHORAL
*WELWYN.	AGONIC	SHIFTY.	SHAMMY	CHURCH
BENZOL	EGG-NOG	SHAGGY.	+THOMAS	CHOREA
GEEZER	*UGANDA.	CHOICE	*THAMES	CHARGE
SEIZED	AGE-OLD	CHAISE	THYMOL	CHORIC
	IGNORE.	CHRISM	WHIMSY.	+CHARON
AFRAID	AGARIC.	+CHRIST	CHANCE	+CHIRON
AFFAIR	+AGATHA.	SHRIEK	CHANCY	CHIRPY
AFLAME	AGOUTI.	SHRIFT	CHANGE	+CHERRY
EFFACE.	OGIVAL	SHRIKE	CHUNKY	CHERUB
OFF-DAY.		SHEIKH	CHINTZ	CHORUS
AFFECT	PHRASE	SHRILL	PHONED	DHARMA
AFIELD	SHRANK	SHRIMP	PHONEY	PHAROS
AFRESH	SHEARS	SHRINE	PHONIC	SHARED
EFFECT	SHEATH	SHYING	PHENOL	SHORED
EFFETE	THWACK	SHRINK	PHANON	SHERRY
OFFEND.	THRALL	SHRIVE	RHINAL	SHIRTY
*AFRICA	THWART	THRICE	SHINDY	THORAX
AFFIRM	THRASH.	THRIFT	SHANDY	THORNY
EFFIGY	CHUBBY	THRILL	SHINED	THORPE
OFFICE	CHIBUK	THRIPS	SHINER	*THURSO

THIRST	THAWED	LIMBED	GIRDED	LINEAL
THIRTY	THEWED.	LIMBER	GILDED	LINEAR
WHORED	RHIZIC	+LIEBIG	GIRDER	LIVELY
WHERRY.		LIABLE	GIRDLE	LIKELY
CHASED	BIGAMY	*LISBON	HIDDEN	LIVERY
CHISEL	BINARY	NIOBIC	HINDER	LINE-UP
CHOSEN	BINATE	NIBBLE	KIDDED	MISERE
CHASER	CICADA	NIMBLE	KINDER	MISERY
CHESIL	CICALA	NIMBLY	KIDDIE	NICELY
CHASSE	DISARM	NIMBUS	KIDDLE	NICENE
CHASTE	DILATE	RIBBED	KINDLE	NICEST
CHESTY	FINALE	RIBBON	KINDLY	NICETY
PHASED	FIXATE	TIMBAL	LIDDED	NINETY
PHASIC	HIJACK	TIMBER	LINDEN	PINEAL
PHYSIC	+HILARY	TITBIT	MIDDAY	PIGEON
RHESUS	LINAGE	TIMBRE	MINDED	PILE-UP
+THISBE	LITANY	VIABLE	MIDDEN	RIPELY
THESIS	LIZARD	+WILBUR.	MILDER	RIPEST
THUSLY	MIKADO	BITCHY	MILDEW	SILENT
WHISKY.	MILADY	CIRCLE	MIDDLE	SINEWY
*BHUTAN	MIRAGE	CIRCUM	MILDLY	TIMELY
CHITIN	PIRACY	CIRCUS	RIDDEN	VILELY
CHITON	PILAFF	DISCAL	RIDDLE	VINERY
CHATTY	+PILATE	*DIDCOT	TINDER	VILEST
GHETTO	PIRATE	DISCUS	WINDED	WISELY
PHOTON	RIBALD	FISCAL	WILDER	WIDELY
RHYTHM	RIBAND	FIACRE	WINDER	WIFELY
THATCH	SILAGE	HICCUP	WILDLY	WISEST
*WHITBY	TIRADE	LITCHI	WISDOM	WIDEST.
WHITEN	TISANE	MINCED	WINDOW	BIFFIN
WHITER.	VIVACE	MINCER	WIND-UP.	*BIAFRA
CHOUGH	VISAGE	OIL-CAN	+AILEEN	DIFFER
RHEUMY	VIRAGO	PIECED	BISECT	+EIFFEL
SHOULD	VITALS	PISCES	BIREME	FITFUL
SHRUNK	VISARD	PITCHY	BICEPS	MISFIT
THOUGH	WIZARD.	*SIDCUP	CICELY	PILFER
THRUSH	AIR-BED	TIN-CAN	CINEMA	PIFFLE
THRUST.	*BILBAO	TIPCAT	+CICERO	RIFFLE
CHEVIN	DISBAR	VISCID	DIRECT	SINFUL
CHEVVY	DIBBER	WINCED	DIRELY	TITFER
CHIVVY	DIBBLE	ZIRCON.	DIVERS	TIFFIN
SHAVED	DISBUD	BIDDER	DIVERT	WILFUL.
SHOVED	FIBBED	BINDER	DIVEST	AIR-GUN
SHOVEL	FIBBER	BIRDIE	DIGEST	BIGGER
SHAVEN	GIBBER	CINDER	DISEUR	CINGLE
SHIVER	GIBBET	DIADEM	+EILEEN	DIGGED
SHAVER.	GIBBON	DIK-DIK	FINELY	DIGGER
CHEWED	JIBBED	DIDDLE	FINERY	DINGHY
SHOWED	KIT-BAG	FINDER	FINEST	DINGLE
SHOWER	KIBBLE	FIDDLE	+GIDEON	FINGER

FIDGET	MISHAP	LIKING	WIRING	WICKET
FIZGIG	MIGHTY	LIVING	WILING	WINKLE.
GINGER	NIGHTY	LINING	WINING.	BILLED
GINGKO	RICHER	LIAISE	BICKER	BILLET
GIGGLE	RICHLY	+MIRIAM	BILKER	BILLOW
HINGED	SIGHED	MILIEU	DICKER	DIGLOT
HIGGLE	SIPHON	MINIMA	DICKEY	FILLED
JIGGED	TIGHTS	MIMING	DINKUM	FILLER
JIGGER	WITHAL	MIXING	FIRKIN	FILLET
JINGLE	WISHED	MINING	FICKLE	FILL-IN
JIGGLE	WITHER	MIRING	JINKED	FILLIP
JINGLY	WITHIN	MINION	KINKED	GIMLET
KINGED	ZITHER.	OILING	KICKED	GIBLET
KINGLY	AIRILY	PITIED	KINKLE	GILLIE
LINGAM	AIRING	PILING	LICKED	+HITLER
LINGER	AILING	PINING	LINKED	KIBLAH
LINGUA	AIDING	PIPING	MILKED	KILLED
MIDGET	BITING	PINION	MILKER	KILLER
MINGLE	BIDING	RIVING	MICKEY	MISLAY
NILGAI	BIKINI	RIDING	MICKLE	MILLED
NIGGER	CILICE	RISING	NICKED	MISLED
NIGGLE	CITING	RILING	NICKEL	+MILLER
PIGGED	CILIUM	SIMIAN	NICKER	MILLET
PIDGIN	DIVIDE	SILICA	PICKAX	NIELLO
RINGED	DIVINE	SIMILE	PICKED	PILLAR
RIGGED	DIVING	*SICILY	PINKED	PIGLET
RIDGED	DINING	SIDING	PICKER	PIGLET
RINGER	DICING	SIRING	PICKET	PILLOW
SINGED	DIMITY	SITING	PIPKIN	RIFLED
SINGER	FILIAL	SIZING	PICKLE	RIFLER
SINGLE	FINIAL	SIRIUS	RISKED	SIDLED
SINGLY	FILING	+TITIAN	RINKED	TITLED
TINGED	FIRING	TINIER	RICKED	TILLED
TINGLE	FINING	TIDIER	SICKEN	TILLER
+VIRGIL	FIXING	TINILY	SILKEN	+VIOLET
*VIRGIN	FINISH	TIDILY	SICKER	VIOLIN
WINGED	FINITE	TIRING	SINKER	VILLUS
WIGGLE.	FIXITY	TILING	*SIKKIM	WILLED
BISHOP	GIVING	TIMING	SISKIN	WILLOW.
CIPHER	GIBING	TIDING	SICKLE	AIRMAN
DISHED	HIRING	+VIVIAN	SICKLY	DISMAL
DITHER	HIVING	VIZIER	TICKED	DISMAY
EITHER	HIDING	VILIFY	TICKER	DIMMED
EIGHTH	HIKING	VIVIFY	TINKER	DIMMER
EIGHTY	JIBING	VIRILE	TICKET	FIRMAN
FISHER	JIVING	VIKING	TICKLE	FILMED
HIGHER	JIMINY	VISION	TINKLE	FIRMER
HITHER	+LILIAN	WILILY	WINKED	FILMIC
HIGHLY	LIBIDO	WIRILY	WICKED	FIRMLY
LICHEN	LIMING	WIPING	WICKER	KISMET

LITMUS	PILOSE	TINPOT	BIOTIC	RIFTED
PITMAN	PILOUS	WIMPLE	BIOTIN	RIOTER
RIMMED	RIBOSE	ZIPPED	BISTRE	RICTUS
SIMMER.	RIMOSE	ZIPPER.	CISTUS	SILTED
DIRNDL	RIGOUR	BISQUE	DISTAL	SIFTER
DINNED	RIMOUS	CIRQUE	DIETAL	SISTER
DINNER	SIMONY	CINQUE	DIETED	SITTER
+DISNEY	SIMOOM	RISQUE.	DISTIL	SINTER
FINNAN	TIP-OFF	CITRIC	DIATOM	TILTED
FIANCE	VIGOUR	CITRON	DICTUM	TITTER
FINNER	VINOUS.	CITRUS	FISTED	TITTLE
FINNIC	BIOPSY	CIRRUS	FITTED	TIPTOE
FINNOC	DIPPED	FIERCE	FILTER	TIPTOP
JINNEE	DISPEL	FIBRIL	FITTER	TITTUP
KIDNAP	DIAPER	FIBRIN	FILTHY	VICTIM
KIDNEY	DIPPER	MITRED	FISTIC	+VICTOR
+LIONEL	DIMPLE	MICRON	GIFTED	VIRTUE
LIMNER	DIMPLY	MIRROR	HINTED	WILTED
LINNET	*DIEPPE	NITRIC	HITTER	WINTER
LIGNUM	HIPPED	PIERCE	HIATUS	*WILTON
MINNOW	HISPID	SIERRA	JILTED	WINTRY.
PINNED	KIPPED	TIERCE	JITTER	DISUSE
*PINNER	KIPPER	*TIGRIS.	KITTED	DILUTE
PICNIC	LISPED	AIR-SAC	KILTED	FIBULA
PIGNUT	LIPPED	BIASED	KITTEN	FIGURE
SIGNAL	LIMPED	DIESEL	KIRTLE	LIQUID
SINNED	LIMPET	DIESIS	KITTLE	LIQUOR
SIGNED	LIMPID	FIASCO	LISTED	MINUET
SIMNEL	LIMPLY	FIESTA	LILTED	MISUSE
SINNER	NIPPED	HISSED	LIFTED	MINUTE
SIGNET	NIPPER	JIGSAW	LINTEL	PIQUED
SIENNA	NIPPLE	KIRSCH	LISTEN	PIQUET
SIGNOR	PIPPED	KISSED	+LISTER	PILULE
TINNED	PIMPED	KISSER	LIFTER	RITUAL
VIANDS	PIPPIN	LIASED	LITTER	VIDUAL
*VIENNA	PIMPLE	LISSOM	LITTLE	VISUAL
WINNER	PIMPLY	MISSAL	LICTOR	VICUNA.
*WIDNES	RIPPED	MISSED	MISTED	SIEVED
WINNOW	RIPPLE	MISSEL	MILTED	SILVER.
ZINNIA.	RIPPLY	MIASMA	MINTED	AIRWAY
DIPOLE	SIPPED	MISSUS	MITTEN	BIGWIG
DITONE	SIMPER	PIGSTY	MISTER	DIMWIT
DISOWN	SIPPET	RIP-SAW	MISTLE	MIDWAY
GIGOLO	SIMPLE	RINSED	+MILTON	NITWIT
GIAOUR	SIMPLY	SIESTA	PITTED	VIEWER
KIMONO	TIPPED	TINSEL	+PINTER	WIGWAM.
MINOAN	TIPPER	TISSUE	PISTIL	FIZZED
MIMOSA	TIPPET	+WILSON.	PINTLE	FIZZER
+NICOLE	TIE-PIN	BITTEN	PISTOL	FIZZLE
PINOLE	TIPPLE	BITTER	PISTON	MIZZLE

PIAZZA	SLICED	ELFISH	PLENTY	GLASSY
SIZZLE	SLICER	FLYING	PLENUM	GLOSSY
ZIGZAG	SLACKS.	PLAICE	SLANGY	PLASHY
	BLADED	PLYING	SLINKY.	PLUSHY
EKEING	ELIDED	PLAINT	ALGOID	PLASMA
SKIING	ELUDED	SLUICE	ALMOND	SLUSHY.
SKYING.	FLEDGE	SLEIGH	ALMOST	BLOTCH
SKILLY.	GLIDER	ULTIMA	+ALCOTT	BLITHE
AKIMBO	GLADLY	ULTIMO.	+ALDOUS	CLUTCH
SKIMPY.	+GLADYS	FLAKED	ALGOUS	CLOTHE
SKINNY.	PLEDGE	FLUKED	ALL-OUT	+CLOTHO
*SKOPJE.	SLUDGE	SLAKED.	ALCOVE	ELATED
SKERRY.	SLEDGE.	ALALIA	BLOODY	ELATER
SKETCH	ALLEGE	*ILKLEY.	FLOOZY	FLITCH
SKATER.	ALBEIT	ALUMNI	GLOOMY	FLETCH
SKIVER	ALKENE	BLAMED	*ILFORD.	FLUTED
SKIVVY.	+ALBERT	BLIMEY	ELOPED	FLATLY
SKEWED	CLIENT	CLIMAX	ELAPSE	FLATUS
SKEWER	ELDEST	CLAMMY	FLOPPY	GLUTEN
	FLEECE	CLUMSY	SLOPED	PLATAN
ALPACA	FLEECY	FLYMAN	SLOPPY	PLATED
ALKALI	FLUENT	FLAMED	SLAP-UP.	PLATEN
ALKANE	OLDEST	FLAMEN	CLAQUE	PLATER
*ALBANY	PLIERS	FLIMSY	CLIQUE	SLATED
ALBATA	SLEEPY	*GLAMIS	PLAQUE.	SLATER
ALWAYS	SLEEVE.	GLUMLY	+ALFRED	*ULSTER.
BLEACH	FLUFFY	PLUMED	ALARUM	ALLUDE
BLEARY	OLEFIN.	PLUMMY	BLARED	ALLURE
CLOACA	ALIGHT	SLIMLY	CLARET	BLOUSE
CLEAVE	BLIGHT	SLUMMY.	CLERGY	+CLAUDE
PLIANT	BLAGUE	BLENCH	CLERIC	CLOUDY
PLEASE	FLAGGY	BLANCH	FLORAL	CLOUGH
SLEAZY	FLIGHT	BLENDE	FLARED	CLAUSE
ULLAGE.	FLAGON	BLONDE	FLORET	FLAUNT
FLABBY	PLIGHT	CLINCH	FLORID	FLOURY
GLOBAL	PLUG-IN	CLENCH	FLORIN	ILL-USE
GLIBLY	PLAGUE	CLINGY	FLURRY	PLOUGH
PLEBBY.	SLOGAN	CLINIC	FLIRTY	PLEURA
+ALICIA	SLIGHT.	+ELINOR	GLARED	SLOUCH
CLOCHE	ALPHOS	FLINCH	+GLORIA	*SLOUGH
CLICHE	*OLDHAM.	FLENCH	PLURAL	SLEUTH.
ELICIT	ALLIED	FLANCH	SLURRY.	ALEVIN
FLECHE	ALLIES	FLANGE	*ALASKA	CLOVEN
GLACIS	ALPINE	FLINTY	+ALISON	CLEVER
GLYCOL	ALVINE	GLANCE	CLOSED	CLOVER
PLACED	ALBINO	PLANCH	CLOSET	CLEVIS
PLACER	ALBITE	PLANED	CLASSY	ELEVEN
PLACET	BLUISH	PLANET	FLASHY	FLAVIN
PLACID	+CLAIRE	PLUNGE	FLESHY	GLOVED
PLUCKY	+ELAINE	PLINTH	FLOSSY	GLOVER

+OLIVER	AMOEBA	SMITHY	UNMAKE	UNLESS
PLOVER	*AMIENS	SMUTTY.	UNHAND	UNREST
SLOVEN	AMPERE	AMOUNT	UNWARY	UNHEWN.
SLIVER	IMPEDE	AMBUSH	UNCASE	KNIFED.
SLAVER	IMPEND	IMBUED	UNLASH	ENIGMA
SLAVIC.	IMMESH.	IMPUGN	UNMASK	KNIGHT
BLOWER	EMIGRE	IMMUNE	UNHASP	ONAGER
BLOW-UP	IMAGED	IMMURE	UNEASY	SNUGLY.
CLAWED	+IMOGEN	IMPURE	UNCATE.	ANTHEM
CLEWED	SMUGLY.	IMPUTE.	ANABAS	ANTHER
FLAWED	AMNION	AMAZED	+ANUBIS	ANCHOR
FLOWED	EMPIRE	AMAZON	ENABLE	ANYHOW
FLOWER	IMBIBE		KNOBBY	INCHED
GLOWED	IMPING	*ANKARA	SNOBBY	UNSHIP
GLOWER	IMPISH	ANGARY	UNABLE.	UNSHOD.
SLEWED	OMNIUM	ENFACE	ANADEM.	ANTIAR
SLOWER	UMPIRE.	ENLACE	ANNEAL	ANGINA
SLOWLY.	SMOKED	ENGAGE	+ANGELA	ANOINT
ALEXIA	SMOKER.	ENRAGE	ANNEXE	ENTICE
+ALEXIS	AMBLED	ENCAGE	ENDEAR	ENRICH
ELIXIR	AMULET	ENTAIL	ENMESH	ENVIED
FLEXED	+AMELIA	END-ALL	INSECT	ENSIGN
FLAXEN	EMBLEM	ENCAMP	INFECT	ENSILE
FLEXOR	EMPLOY	ENRAPT	INJECT	ENGINE
KLAXON	OMELET	ENCASE	INDEED	ENDING
PLEXUS.	SMILED	ENCASH	INTEND	ENTIRE
CLOYED	SMELLY	INDABA	INTENT	ENLIST
CLAYEY	UMBLES.	INTACT	INDENT	ENMITY
FLAYED	+AMANDA	INVADE	INVENT	ENTITY
PLAYED	AMENDS.	INLAID	INCEPT	ENDIVE
PLAYER	EMBODY	INTAKE	INHERE	GNEISS
SLAYER.	EMBOSS	INHALE	INTERN	INDIAN
BLAZED	IMPORT	INFAMY	INSERT	INDICT
BLAZER	IMPOSE	INLAND	INVERT	INSIDE
BLAZON	IMPOST	INBAND	INGEST	INLIER
GLAZED	SMOOCH	INSANE	INCEST	INDIGO
GLAZER	SMOOTH.	INFANT	INVEST	INKING
	AMORAL	INWARD	INFEST	INFIRM
EMBALM	AMERCE	INMATE	SNEEZE	INCISE
EMBANK	EMERGE	INNATE	UNREAD	INSIST
EMBARK	EMBRYO	ONFALL	UNSEAL	INVITE
IMPACT	IMBREX	ONWARD	UNREAL	INDITE
IMPAIR	IMBRUE	UNPACK	UNSEAT	INCITE
IMPALE	SMIRCH	UNTACK	UNREEL	INDIUM
IMPART	SMARMY	UNMADE	UNMEET	ON-LINE
IMPAWN	UMBRAL.	UNLADE	UNVEIL	UNCIAL
UMLAUT.	AMUSED.	UNSAFE	UNWELL	UNPICK
AMIDST	AMATOL	UNSAID	UNBEND	UNTIDY
SMUDGE	EMETIC	UNLAID	UNBENT	UNTIED
SMUDGY.	SMUTCH	UNFAIR	UNWEPT	UNDIES

143

UNLIKE	SNOOZE	UNITED	DOMAIN	*TOBAGO
UNWIND	UNLOAD	UNSTOP.	+DONALD	TOWARD
UNBIND	UNROBE	ANNUAL	DOUANE	TOMATO
UNKIND	UNLOCK	ENSUED	DOTARD	VOYAGE
+UNDINE	UNCOIL	ENOUGH	DOGATE	VOTARY
UNRIPE	UNYOKE	ENGULF	DONATE	ZONARY
UNGIRD	UNFOLD	ENDURE	FORAGE	ZONATE
UNGIRT	UNTOLD	ENSURE	GOBANG	ZOUAVE.
UNWISE.	UNROLL	INDUCE	GO-KART	*BOMBAY
SNAKED.	UNBOLT	INDUCT	GO-CART	BOMBED
ANGLED	UNHOLY	INDULT	+HORACE	BOBBED
ANTLER	UNDONE	INSULT	HOMAGE	BOMBER
ANGLER	UNHOOK	INHUME	+HOWARD	BOMBIC
ANKLET	UNMOOR	INSURE	*HOBART	BOBBIN
INFLOW	UNCORD	INJURE	HORARY	BONBON
INFLUX	UNCORK	INJURY	LOCALE	CORBAN
UNPLUG.	UNWORN	INCUSE	LOCATE	COMBAT
ANIMAL	UNBORN.	INFUSE	LOBATE	COMBED
ANOMIA	INSPAN	INRUSH	*MONACO	CORBEL
ANIMUS	INK-POT	ONRUSH	MOSAIC	COMBER
ENAMEL	SNIPER	UNGUAL	MOHAIR	COBBER
GNOMIC	SNAPPY	UNGULA	MORALE	CORBIE
GNOMON.	UNIPED.	UNRULY	+MOZART	COBBLE
ANANAS	UNIQUE.	UNDULY	MORASS	COBBLY
ANONYM	ANORAK	UNSUNG	MOHAWK	COWBOY
UNKNIT.	+ANDREW	UNSURE	NONAGE	DOBBIN
*ANGOLA	*ANTRIM	UNFURL	NO-BALL	DOUBLE
ANYONE	ANTRUM	UNHURT	NONARY	DOUBLY
+ANTONY	ENTRAP	UNJUST.	NOTARY	FOBBED
ANGORA	ENWRAP	KNIVES	NOWAYS	FORBID
ENROBE	ENTREE	SNIVEL	POMACE	FOIBLE
ENJOIN	ENERGY	UNEVEN.	POLACK	GOBBET
ENFOLD	INARCH	ANSWER	POMADE	GOBBLE
ENTOMB	INBRED	GNAWED	POTAGE	HOTBED
ENCORE	INURED	GNAWER	POT-ALE	HOBBLE
INROAD	+INGRID	ONE-WAY	*POLAND	JOBBED
IN-JOKE	SNARED	SNOWED.	POTASH	JOBBER
INVOKE	SNORED	ENZYME	POTATO	LOBBED
INSOLE	UNWRAP	ENCYST.	+RONALD	MOBBED
INCOME	UNTRUE.	SNAZZY	+ROLAND	MORBID
INTONE	ENOSIS		ROMANY	NOBBED
INDOOR	GNOSIS	BORAGE	ROTARY	NOBBLE
INFORM	UNUSED	BOTANY	ROSARY	ROBBED
INBORN	UNISEX	BOVATE	ROTATE	ROBBER
INMOST	UNISON.	BORATE	SOLACE	ROUBLE
INWOVE	INSTEP	COBALT	SOCAGE	SOBBED
ONE-OFF	INSTIL	COWARD	*SOMALI	SORBET
ONIONY	KNOTTY	DORADO	SONANT	SOMBRE
ONCOST	SNATCH	DOSAGE	SONATA	TOMBOY
SNOOTY	SNOTTY	DOTAGE	TOWAGE	WOMBAT

WOBBLE	HODDEN	FOREGO	ROOFED	POPGUN
WOBBLY	HOYDEN	FOMENT	TOFFEE	POOGYE
ZOMBIE.	HOLDER	FOREST	WOLFED	ROUGED
BOBCAT	HOODOO	GOVERN	WOOFER	SOUGHT
BOTCHY	HOLD-UP	HOMELY	WOEFUL.	TOGGLE
CONCHA	*JORDAN	HONEST	BOGGED	TONGUE.
CONCUR	KOEDOE	+JOSEPH	BOUGHT	BOTHER
COCCUS	LOADED	KOPECK	BOUGIE	COSHER
COCCYX	LORDED	LOVE-IN	BOGGLE	*COCHIN
DOUCHE	LOUDER	LONELY	COUGAR	GOPHER
FORCED	LOADER	LOVELY	COGGED	GOTHIC
PONCHO	LOUDLY	LOWEST	CONGER	JOSHED
SOCCER	LORDLY	MOMENT	CODGER	+JOSHUA
TOUCAN	*LONDON	MODERN	+DOUGAL	KOSHER
TOE-CAP	MONDAY	MOLEST	DOGGED	MOTHER
TOM-CAT	NODDED	MODEST	DODGED	NOSHED
TOUCHE	NORDIC	MOIETY	DOGGER	POSHLY
TOUCHY	NOODLE	NOVENA	DODGER	ROCHET
VOICED	NOODLE	POTEEN	DOUGHY	+SOPHIA
YOICKS.	PODDED	POTENT	FOGGED	TOP-HAT
BONDED	POWDER	POPERY	FORGED	TOTHER.
BORDER	PONDER	POSEUR	FORGER	AORIST
BOLDER	POLDER	ROSEAL	FORGET	BODICE
BONDER	POODLE	+ROWENA	FOUGHT	BOLIDE
BOODLE	SODDEN	RODENT	FORGOT	BODIED
BOLDLY	SOLDER	+ROBERT	GORGED	BODILY
CORDED	SORDID	SOLELY	GOUGED	BOVINE
COLDER	TODDLE	SORELY	GORGET	BODING
CODDER	VOIDED	SOLEMN	GOGGLE	BOXING
CODDLE	VOODOO	*SOLENT	GOOGLY	BONING
COLDLY	WORDED	SOREST	+GORGON	BOWING
CONDOM	WOODED	TORERO	HOGGED	BORING
CORDON	WOODEN	VOYEUR.	HOGGET	BOYISH
CONDOR	WONDER	BOFFIN	JOGGED	BONITO
DODDER	YONDER.	BOTFLY	JOGGLE	COPIED
DOODLE	BOREAL	CONFAB	LOGGED	COPIER
FORDED	BODEGA	COFFEE	LONGED	CODIFY
FOLDED	BOWELS	COFFER	LODGED	COSILY
FOLDER	BOLERO	CONFER	LODGER	COSINE
FODDER	BOWERY	COFFIN	LONGER	COOING
FONDLE	+BOLEYN	COMFIT	LOGGER	CORING
FONDLY	COPECK	COFFLE	LOGGIA	COWING
GODDAM	COMEDY	DOFFED	+MORGAN	COPING
GOADED	COHEIR	DOG-FOX	MONGER	COVING
GOLDEN	COMELY	GOFFER	MONGOL	CODING
GOODLY	COGENT	GOLFER	MORGUE	COMING
+GORDON	COHERE	HOOFED	NOUGAT	COAITA
HOWDAH	COVERT	JOYFUL	NOUGHT	COMITY
HORDED	+DOREEN	LOOFAH	NOGGIN	CORIUM
HOODED	EOCENE	LOAFER	PONGEE	DORIAN

DOCILE	MODISH	+YORICK	ROCKER	POPLAR
DOZING	MONISM	YOKING	ROCKET	POOLED
DOPING	MONIST	ZODIAC	ROOKIE	POLLED
DOTING	MOTIVE	ZONING.	SOAKED	POLLEN
DOMINO	NOTICE	DONJON.	SOAKER	POLLEX
EOLITH	NOVICE	BOOKED	SOCKET	POPLIN
FOLIAR	NOTIFY	BOOKIE	WORKED	ROLLED
FOXING	NOTING	BODKIN	WORKER	ROLLER
GORING	NOSING	CONKED	YORKER.	ROLL-UP
+GODIVA	NOTION	COCKED	BOILED	SOILED
HOLIER	NOWISE	COOKED	BOW-LEG	TOLLED
HOSIER	OOZILY	CORKED	BOILER	TOILER
HOMILY	OOZING	COOKER	BOWLER	TOOLER
HOLILY	OOLITE	CONKER	COLLAR	TOILET
HOMING	POLICE	CORKER	COILED	VOLLEY
HOPING	POLICY	COCKER	COOLED	WOOLLY
HOEING	POSING	COOKIE	COALER	YOWLED.
HOSING	POLING	COCKLE	COOLER	BOWMAN
HONING	PORING	COCK-UP	COLLET	BOOMED
HOLING	POKING	DOCKED	COOLIE	BOOMER
HOMINY	POTION	DOCKER	COLLIE	*BODMIN
HOLISM	POPISH	DOCKET	COOLLY	CON-MAN
IONIAN	POLISH	DONKEY	COLLOP	COWMAN
IODIDE	POLITE	FORKED	DOLLAR	COSMIC
IODINE	POLITY	FOLKSY	DOWLAS	COMMIE
IODISM	PODIUM	HOOKAH	DOLLED	COMMIT
IOLITE	ROSIER	HOOKED	DOLLOP	COMMON
IONIZE	ROSILY	HOCKED	FOULED	COSMOS
IODIZE	ROBING	HONKED	FOOLED	DOLMAN
+JOSIAH	ROWING	HOOKER	FOILED	DOOMED
JOVIAL	ROPING	HOCKEY	FOALED	DOLMEN
JOVIAN	ROVING	HOOKEY	FOWLER	DORMER
JOKING	ROMISH	HOOKUP	FOULLY	FORMAL
*KODIAK	SOCIAL	JOCKEY	FOLLOW	FOEMAN
LOLIGO	SOVIET	LOCKED	GOBLET	FORMAT
LOSING	SOWING	LOOKED	GOGLET	FOAMED
LOPING	SOLING	LOCKER	GOALIE	FORMED
LOWING	SODIUM	LOOKER	GOBLIN	FORMER
LOVING	TOEING	LOCKET	HOWLED	FORMIC
LOTION	TOPING	LOOK-IN	HOLLER	HODMAN
+LOUISE	TOTING	LOCK-UP	HOWLER	LOAMED
+LOLITA	TOYING	MOCKED	HOLLOW	LOOMED
+MONICA	TONING	MOCKER	LOLLED	MORMON
MODIFY	TONITE	MONKEY	LOLLOP	NORMAL
MOBILE	VOWING	MOCK-UP	MOULOY	+NORMAN
MOWING	VOLING	NOCKED	MOSLEM	POTMAN
MOOING	VOTING	PORKER	MOTLEY	POMMEL
MOVING	VOTIVE	POCKET	NOBLER	ROOMED
MOPING	*WOKING	ROCKED	+NOELLE	+ROMMEL
MOTION	WOOING	ROOKED	OODLES	ROAMER

WORMED	COROZO	SOPPED	COSSET	CO-STAR
ZOOMED.	DOLOSE	SOUPED	CORSET	COTTAR
BOUNCE	DOLOUR	SOAPED	COUSIN	COSTED
BOUNCY	GOLOSH	TOPPED	CONSUL	COATEE
*BORNEO	HONOUR	TOUPEE	DOSSAL	COSTER
BONNET	JOCOSE	TOPPER	DORSAL	COTTER
BOUNTY	JOYOUS	TORPID	DOWSED	CORTEX
COGNAC	KOBOLD	TOPPLE	DOSSED	+CORTEZ
CORNEA	*LOMOND	TORPOR.	DOUSED	COPTIC
CONNED	MOLOCH	MOSQUE	DOWSER	COSTLY
CORNED	MONODY	TORQUE.	DOSSER	COTTON
CORNEL	MOHOLE	BORROW	*DORSET	CONTRA
COINER	MOROSE	BOURSE	DOSSIL	COITUS
CORNER	NOBODY	+CONRAD	DOESNT	DOTTED
CORNET	NO-GOOD	CORRAL	DORSUM	DOITED
COUNTY	NODOSE	COERCE	FOSSIL	DOTTLE
COBNUT	POLONY	COWRIE	GOSSIP	DOCTOR
DOWNED	POROUS	CORRIE	GODSON	DOPTRE
DONNED	ROCOCO	COURSE	HOUSED	FOETAL
HORNED	SODOMY	COARSE	HORSED	FONTAL
HORNET	TOROID.	DOURLY	LOOSED	FOOTED
HOBNOB	COOPED	FOURTH	\OOSEN	FOOTER
JOUNCE	COPPED	HOORAY	LOOSER	FOSTER
JOINED	COMPEL	HORRID	MORSEL	FOETID
JOINER	COPPER	HOURLY	MOUSER	FOETUS
+JOANNA	COOPER	HOT-ROD	MOUSSE	GOATEE
LOANED	COUPLE	HORROR	NOOSED	GOTTEN
LOUNGE	COMPLY	HOARSE	POISED	+GOETHE
MOANED	COUPON	MOORED	POSSET	GOITRE
MOONED	COW-POX	+MORRIS	POISON	HOOTED
MOUNTY	CORPSE	+MONROE	POSSUM	HOTTED
POUNCE	CORPUS	MORROW	ROUSER	HOSTEL
*ROMNEY	GOSPEL	POURER	SOUSED	HOOTER
+RODNEY	HOPPED	POORER	TOSSED	HOTTER
SOONER	HOOPED	POORLY	TONSIL	JOTTED
SONNET	HOPPER	POGROM	TOCSIN	JOLTED
*TOTNES	HOOP-LA	ROARED	TOUSLE	JOTTER
ZOUNDS.	HOPPLE	ROARER	WORSEN.	JOSTLE
BOG-OAK	HOOPOE	SOURCE	BOOTED	KOWTOW
BOFORS	HOTPOT	SOURED	BOLTED	LOFTED
*BOGOTA	LOOPED	SOARED	BOOTEE	LOOTER
CONOID	LOPPED	SOIREE	BOATER	LOITER
CORONA	LOOPER	SORREL	BOW-TIE	LOFTER
COLONY	MOPPED	SOURLY	*BOOTLE	LOATHE
COCOON	MOPPET	SORROW	BOTTLE	MORTAL
COHORT	POPPED	TOURED	BOTTOM	MORTAR
COMOSE	POPPET	TOURER	*BOLTON	MOATED
COYOTE	POMPOM	TORRID.	*BOSTON	MOOTED
COLOUR	POMPON	BOW-SAW	COITAL	MOLTEN
COP-OUT	ROMPED	BORSCH	COSTAL	MOTTLE

147

PORTAL	ROTULA	APICES	OPENLY	EQUITY
POSTAL	ROTUND	APACHE	SPINAL	SQUILL
POSTED	ROBUST	EPICAL	SPINET	SQUINT
POUTED	SOLUTE	SPACED	SPONGE	SQUIRE
POTTED	VOLUME	SPICED	SPONGY.	SQUIRM
PORTED	VOLUTE	SPACER	APLOMB	SQUIRT
POUTER	YOGURT.	SPECIE.	APHONY	SQUISH
PORTER	COEVAL	APODAL	APPORT	
POSTER	CORVES	SPIDER.	OPPOSE	ARMADA
POTTER	CONVEX	APPEAL	SPOOKY	ARCADE
POETIC	CONVEY	APPEAR	SPROUT	*ARMAGH
PORTLY	CONVOY	APIECE	UPROAR	ARGALA
POETRY	HOOVED	APPEND	UPHOLD	ARCANA
ROOTED	+HOOVER	SPREAD	UPROOT	ARCANE
ROTTED	HOOVES	SPEECH	UPMOST	ARRANT
ROUTED	LOUVER	SPEEDY	UPTOWN.	BREACH
ROTTEN	LOAVES	SPLEEN	APEPSY.	BROACH
ROTTER	LOUVRE	SPHERE	OPAQUE.	BREAST
ROSTER	SOLVED	UPBEAT	*OPORTO	BREATH
ROOTLE	WOLVES.	UPKEEP	SPIRAL	CROAKY
ROSTRA	BOW-WOW	UPHELD.	SPARED	CREAMY
SORTED	*CONWAY	APOGEE	SPIRED	CREASE
SOFTEN	COBWEB	SPIGOT.	SPURGE	CREATE
SOFTER	GODWIT	UPSHOT.	SPIRIT	DREAMT
SORTER	*NORWAY	*EPPING	SPARSE	DREAMY
SOOTHE	POW-WOW.	OPTICS	SPORTY.	DREARY
SORTIE	COAXED	OPTING	APHTHA	ERRAND
SOFTLY	HOAXER.	OPTION	APATHY	ERRANT
TOUTED	CORYMB	SPLICE	SPITED	ERRATA
TOTTED	CORYZA	SPLINE	SPOTTY	ERSATZ
TOOTED	OOCYTE.	SPYING	SPUTUM.	FRIARY
TOTTER	BOOZED	SPRING	SPRUCE	GREASE
TOOTLE	BOOZER	SPLINT	SPRUNG	GREASY
TOMTOM	BORZOI	SPRINT	SPOUSE	ORDAIN
VOLTED	FOOZLE	SPHINX	UPTURN	ORGASM
VORTEX	NOZZLE	SPRITE	UPRUSH.	ORNATE
WONTED		UPSIDE	SPAVIN.	PREACH
WORTHY.	APIARY	UPLIFT	SPEWED.	TRUANT
COQUET	OPTANT	+UPDIKE	SPAYED	TREATY
COPULA	OPIATE	UPHILL		URBANE
COLUMN	SPRAIN	UPPISH		WREATH.
COBURG	SPRANG	UPPITY.	EQUATE	*ARABIA
JOCUND	SPLASH	SPIKED	SQUALL	ARABIC
LOQUAT	SPRAWL	SPOKEN.	SQUAMA	ARABLE
LOBULE	UPTAKE	+APOLLO.	SQUARE	BRIBED
LOCUST	UPLAND	APE-MAN	SQUASH	CRABBY
MODULE	UPWARD	SPUMED.	SQUAWK.	DRABLY
NODULE	UPCAST	EPONYM	SQUEAK	*EREBUS
ROGUED	UP-DATE.	OPINED	SQUEAL.	GRUBBY
ROQUET	APICAL	OPENER	EQUINE	PROBED

TRIBAL	BREEZE	ARCHER	BROKEN	CRANKY
TREBLE.	BREEZY	+ARCHIE	BROKER	CRANNY
BRACER	CREEPY	ARCHIL	CRIKEY	+CRONOS
BROCHE	DRIEST	ARCHLY	KRAKEN.	DRENCH
+BRECHT	+ERNEST	ARCHON	ARMLET	DRONED
*BRECON	FREELY	+ARTHUR	BROLLY	+ERINYS
CRECHE	FRIEND	+BRAHMS	FROLIC	*FRANCE
CROCKY	FREEZE	+GRAHAM	FRILLY	FRENCH
CROCUS	FRIEZE	ORPHAN	GRILLE	FRINGE
DRACHM	*GREECE	ORPHIC	GRILSE	FRENZY
FRACAS	GREEDY	ORCHID	ORALLY	GRANGE
GRACED	+GREENE	ORCHIS	PRELIM	GRANNY
GROCER	GRIEVE	URCHIN.	PROLIX	IRONED
ORACLE	ORDEAL	ARNICA	TRILBY.	IRONIC
PRICED	*ORWELL	ARTILY	BRUMAL	IRENIC
PRECIS	ORIENT	ARSINE	BROMIC	*ORKNEY
TRICAR	ORRERY	ARCING	CRAMBO	ORANGE
TRICED	PRIEST	ARMING	CRUMBY	PRANCE
TRACED	TRUEST	ARTIST	*CRIMEA	PRINCE
TRACER	URGENT	ARGIVE	*CROMER	PRUNED
TRICKY	URAEUS.	ARRIVE	CRUMMY	PRONTO
TRICOT.	ARMFUL	BRAINY	CRIMPY	PRUNUS
ARIDLY	ARTFUL	BRUISE	FRAMED	TRANCE
BRIDAL	CRAFTY	BRAISE	FRAMER	TRENCH
BRIDGE	DRAFFY	CRYING	FRUMPY	TRENDY
BRIDLE	DRY-FLY	CRUISE	GRIMLY	URINAL
CREDAL	IREFUL	DRY-ICE	GRAMME	+URANUS
CREDIT	PREFAB	DRYING	GRUMPY	WRENCH.
CRADLE	PREFER	DRYISH	PRIMAL	AREOLA
DRUDGE	PROFIT	ERMINE	PRIMED	+ARNOLD
DREDGE	PREFIX	ERRING	PRIMER	ARIOSO
ERODED	TRIFID	ERBIUM	PRIMLY	ARGOSY
FRIDAY	TRIFLE.	FRAISE	PROMPT	ARMOUR
FRIDGE	ARIGHT	FRUITY	PRIMUS	ARDOUR
GRIDED	BRIGHT	GRAINY	+TRUMAN	ARBOUR
GRADED	BROGUE	+IRVING	TRIMLY	ARMOUR
GRUDGE	CRAGGY	IRKING	TREMOR.	ARROWY
GRADIN	DRAGON	OREIDE	BRUNCH	ARROYO
GRADUS	DROGUE	ORPINE	BRANCH	BROOCH
PRIDED	FRUGAL	ORBING	BRONCO	BROODY
TRADED	+FRIGGA	PRYING	+BRENDA	+BROOKE
TRADER	FRIGHT	PRAISE	+BRANDT	+BRYONY
TRUDGE.	FRIGID	TROIKA	BRANDY	CREOLE
ARREAR	GROGGY	TRYING	*BRUNEI	GROOVE
ARDENT	*OREGAN	TRUISM	+BRUNEL	GROOVY
ARGENT	ORIGIN	URSINE	+BRONTE	ORIOLE
ARTERY	*PRAGUE	URGING	BRONZE	ORMOLU
ARREST	TRAGIC	WRAITH.	CRUNCH	*ORFORD
BREECH	TROGON.	TROJAN.	CRANED	PRIORY
BREEKS	ARCHED	BRAKED	CRINGE	TRIODE

149

TRY-OUT.	PRESTO	ORDURE	CRAYON	*ASSISI
ARMPIT	TRASHY	+PROUST	FRAYED	ASSIST
DRAPED	TRUSTY.	TROUGH	GROYNE	ASSIZE
DRUPEL	*ARCTIC	TRAUMA	PREYED	ESPIAL
DRAPER	BRUTAL	TRIUNE	PRAYED	ESPIED
DROPSY	BRITON	TROUPE	PRAYER	ESKIMO
FRAPPE	BRETON	+URSULA.	X-RAYED.	+ISAIAH
GRIPED	+BRUTUS	BRAVED	BRAZEN	OSSIFY.
GROPED	CRUTCH	BRAVER	*BRAZIL	ASHLAR
GRIPPE	CROTCH	BREVET	CRAZED	ASYLUM
PREPAY	CRATCH	CRAVAT	FROZEN	+ISOLDE
PROPEL	CRATED	CRAVED	FRAZIL	OSTLER.
PROPER	CRATER	CRAVEN	FRIZZY	+ASIMOV
TREPAN	CRITIC	DRIVEL	GRAZED	ISOMER.
TROPHY	CRETIN	DRIVEN	PRIZED	USANCE.
TROPIC	CRETON	DROVER		ASLOPE
TRIPLE	CRATUR	DRIVER	ASSAIL	ASHORE
TRIPOD	EROTIC	FRIVOL	ASLANT	ASSORT
TRIPOS	FRUTEX	GROVEL	ESCAPE	ESCORT.
TROPPO	FROTHY	GRAVEL	ESTATE	ISOPOD.
TRAPSE.	+GRETEL	GRAVER	*ISRAEL	ASTRAL
+BRAQUE.	GRATER	+GRAVES	ISLAND	ASTRAY
*ARARAT	GRATIN	GRAVID	+OSWALD.	+ASTRID
CRURAL	GRATIS	PROVED	ISOBAR	OSPREY
DRY-ROT.	*GRETNA	PROVEN	+ISABEL	+OSIRIS
ARISEN	GROTTO	PRIVET	USABLE.	USURER.
BRASHY	GRITTY	TRAVEL	ASH-CAN	ISATIN
BRUSHY	GROTTY	TROVER	+PSYCHE	TSETSE.
BRASSY	IRITIS	TRIVET	PSYCHO.	ASSUME
CRASIS	ORATED	TRIVIA	ASPECT	ASSURE
CRISIS	ORATOR	+TREVOR.	ASLEEP	ASTUTE
CRESOL	PRATED	BREWER	ASCEND	ESCUDO
CRISPY	PRATIE	BRAWNY	ASCENT	ISSUED
CROSSE	PROTON	BROWSE	ASSENT	PSEUDO
CRUSTY	PRETTY	CROWED	ASTERN	
DRESSY	+TRITON	CREWEL	ASSERT	ATTACH
DROSSY	URETER	CRAWLY	ASSESS	ATTACK
ERASED	URETIC	DRAWEE	ASSETS	ATTAIN
FRESCO	WRETCH	DRAWER	ESTEEM	ETHANE
FRISKY	WRITER	DROWSE	*OSTEND	*ITHACA
FROSTY	WRITHE.	DROWSY	+OSBERT.	*OTTAWA
GRISLY	ARGUED	FROWST	USEFUL.	STEADY
GRISON	AROUND	FROWZY	ASTHMA	STRAFE
GRASSY	AROUSE	GROWER	ESCHAR	STRAIN
IRISED	CROUCH	GROWTH	+ESTHER	STRAIT
ORISON	CROUPY	PRE-WAR	ESCHEW	STRAKE
PROSER	DROUTH	TROWEL.	*ISCHIA.	STEAMY
PROSIT	GROUCH	PRAXIS.	ASSIGN	STRAND
PRISON	GROUND	*ARGYLL	ASKING	+STUART
PRISSY	GROUSE	BRAYED	ASPIRE	STRATA

STRATH	STALER	STITCH	*DURBAN	CUDDLY
STRAWY.	STOLID	STATED	*DUNBAR	*DUNDEE
+STUBBS	+STALIN	STATER	DURBAR	DUMDUM
STUBBY	+STELLA	STATIC	DUBBED	FUNDED
STABLE	STILLY	STATOR	DUBBIN	FUDDLE
STABLY.	STYLUS.	STATUE	DUMBLY	GUIDED
STUCCO	ATOMIC	STATUS.	FUMBLE	GUIDON
STOCKY	ETYMON	ATTUNE	*HUMBER	HURDLE
STICKY	STAMEN	STRUCK	HUMBLE	HUDDLE
STACTE.	STYMIE	STRUNG.	HUMBLY	MURDER
STODGE	STUMPY.	STAVED	HUBBUB	MUDDLE
STODGY	ATONAL	+STEVEN	HUMBUG	OUTDID
STUDIO.	ATONED	STIVER.	JUMBAL	*OUNDLE
+ATHENA	ATONIC	STEWED	JUMBLE	PURDAH
ATTEND	ETHNIC	STOWED.	LUMBAR	PUNDIT
+ATHENE	STANCE	ATAXIA.	LUBBER	PUDDLE
*ATHENS	STENCH	STAYED	LUMBER	RUDDER
ATTEST	STANCH	STAYER	MUMBLE	RUDDLE
+ATREUS	STONED		NUMBED	SUNDAE
ITSELF	STINGY	AUBADE	NUMBER	SUNDAY
STREAK	STANZA.	BUTANE	NUMBLY	SUDDEN
STREAM	OTIOSE	CURACY	OUTBID	SUNDER
STREET	STROBE	CUBAGE	PUEBLO	SUNDEW
STEELY	STRODE	CURARE	*QUEBEC	SUNDRY
STRESS	STOOGE	CURATE	RUBBED	SUBDUE
STREWN.	STROKE	FUMADE	RUBBER	TUNDRA.
*STAFFA	STROLL	*GUYANA	RUMBLE	AUGEAN
STUFFY	STROMA	HUMANE	RUBBLE	BUREAU
STIFLE.	STRONG	JUDAIC	TURBAN	CUTELY
STAGER	*STROUD	JUGATE	TUBBED	DURESS
STIGMA.	STROVE	*KUWAIT	TURBID	EUREKA
ETCHED	UTMOST.	LUNACY	TUMBLE	+EUGENE
ITCHED.	STAPES	LUNATE	TURBOT.	HUGELY
+ATTILA	STUPID	LUXATE	BUCCAL	+HUBERT
ATTIRE	STAPLE	MUTANT	BUNCHY	LUCENT
STRICT	STUPOR	MUTATE	CUSCUS	MUSEUM
STRIDE	STEPPE	PUPATE	+DUNCAN	PURELY
STRIFE	UTOPIA.	QUEASY	DULCET	PUREST
STRIKE	STARCH	RUBATO	*MUSCAT	RUDELY
STRING	STURDY	SUGARY.	MUSCLE	+RUBENS
STRIPE	STORED	BULBED	NUNCIO	+RUPERT
STRIPY	STARED	BULBIL	OUTCRY	RUDEST
STAITH	STEREO	BURBLE	+VULCAN.	SURELY
STRIVE.	STOREY	BUBBLE	BUDDED	SUPERB
STAKED	STORMY	BUBBLY	BURDEN	SUREST
STOKER.	STARRY	BURBOT	+BUDDHA	SURETY
ATTLEE	STARVE	BULBUL	BUNDLE	TUXEDO
ITALIC	UTERUS.	CUBBED	CURDED	TUREEN
STYLED	STASIS.	CURBED	CURDLE	TUMEFY.
STOLEN	OTITIS	CUMBER	CUDDLE	BUFFER

BUFFET	LUGGER	FUSING	BUNKUM	FULLER
CUFFED	MUGGED	FUMING	CUCKOO	GULLED
CURFEW	NUDGED	FUSION	DUNKED	GULLET
CUPFUL	NUGGET	GUYING	DUCKED	GUILTY
DUFFED	PURGED	GUNITE	DUCKER	HULLED
DUFFEL	PUGGED	HUMIFY	DUIKER	HURLER
DUFFER	QUAGGA	+JULIAN	HUSKED	+HUXLEY
DUFFLE	QUAGGY	+JULIET	JUNKED	HURLEY
FULFIL	RUGGED	JUNIOR	JUNKER	LULLED
FURFUR	RUGGER	JURIST	JUNKET	+LUDLOW
GUFFAW	SURGED	+JUDITH	LURKER	MULLED
HUFFED	SUN-GOD	+JULIUS	MUCKED	MULLET
JUGFUL	TUGGED	LUTING	MUSKET	MUSLIM
MUFFED	TURGID	LURING	MUCKLE	MUSLIN
MUFFIN	VULGAR.	+LUCIUS	MUSK-OX	NUCLEI
MUFFLE	AUTHOR	+MURIEL	PUCKER	OUTLAW
OUTFIT	*BUCHAN	MURINE	QUAKED	OUTLAY
PUFFED	BUSHED	MUTING	QUAKER	OUTLET
PUFFER	BUSHEL	MUSING	RUCKED	PULLED
PUFFIN	*BUSHEY	MUTINY	+RUSKIN	PURLED
RUFFED	CUSHAT	MULISH	SUCKED	PURLER
RUFFLE	*DURHAM	MUTISM	SUNKEN	PULLER
RUEFUL	EUCHRE	NUBILE	SUCKER	PULLET
SURFER	GUSHER	NUDISM	SUCKLE	PULLEY
SUFFER	HUSHED	NUDIST	TUCKED	PUBLIC
SUFFIX	+LUTHER	NUDITY	TUSKED	PULL-IN
TURFED	PUSHED	OUTING	TUCKER	PURLIN
TUFFET.	PUSHER	PUMICE	TUSKER	PUTLOG
BUNGED	PUSHTU	PURIFY	TUCKET	SULLEN
BUDGED	RUSHED	PUNILY	*TURKEY.	SUTLER
BUGGED	RUSHEN	PULING	BURLAP	SUBLET
BURGEE	SUN-HAT.	PUKING	BUTLER	SUNLIT.
BUGGER	AUDILE	PUNISH	BUGLER	BUSMAN
BULGER	AUXINS	PURISM	BULLET	FULMAR
BUDGET	AUTISM	PURITY	CULLED	GUNMAN
BUNGLE	AURIST	QUAINT	CURLED	GUMMED
BURGLE	BURIAL	RUTILE	CUTLER	HUMMED
CUDGEL	BUSIED	RUEING	CURLER	KUMMEL
FUNGUS	BURIED	RULING	CUTLET	MUMMED
GURGLE	BUSILY	SUPINE	CURLEW	MUMMER
HUGGED	BUYING	TUNING	DULLED	MURMUR
HUNGER	BUNION	TUBING	DULLER	NUTMEG
HUNGRY	CURING	*ZURICH.	+DULLES	PUMMEL
JUGGED	CUBING	*PUNJAB.	DUPLET	SUMMED
JUDGED	CUBISM	BUSKER	DUPLEX	SUMMER
JUGGLE	CURIUM	BUNKER	*DUDLEY	SUBMIT
JUNGLE	DUPING	BUCKET	*DUBLIN	SUMMIT
JUNGLY	DURING	BUSKIN	DUNLIN	SUMMON
LUNGED	+EUNICE	BUCKLE	+EUCLID	BURNED
LUGGED	FUTILE	BUCKRA	FURLED	BURNER

BURNET	DUMPTY	GUN-SHY	LUETIC	QUAVER
DUNNED	GULPED	HUSSAR	LUSTRE	QUIVER
DUENNA	HUMPED	*HUDSON	MUSTER	SURVEY
FUNNEL	HUMPTY	MUSSEL	MUTTER	TURVES
*GUINEA	JUMPED	NURSED	MUSTNT	VULVAR.
GUNNED	JUMPER	OUTSET	MUTTON	OUTWIT
GUNNER	OUTPUT	PULSAR	NUTTER	RUNWAY
NUANCE	PUMPED	PUTSCH	OUSTED	SUBWAY.
PUNNED	PUPPED	PURSED	PUNTED	+BUNYAN
PUNNET	PULPER	PULSED	PUTTEE	BUOYED
QUINCE	PUPPET	PURSER	PUTTER	BUNYIP.
QUENCH	PULPIT	PUISNE	PUNTER	BUZZER
QUINSY	PURPLE	PURSUE	QUITCH	GUZZLE
QUANTA	RUMPLE	QUASAR	QUOTER	MUZZLE
RUINED	RUMPUS	RUSSET	QUOTHA	NUZZLE
RUNNEL	SUPPED	*RUSSIA	RUSTED	PUZZLE
RUNNER	SUPPER	SUSSED	RUTTED	
SUNNED	SUPPLE	SUNSET	RUSTIC	AVIARY
TURNED	SUPPLY.	*SUSSEX	RUSTLE	AVIATE.
TUNNEL	PULQUE.	TUSSLE.	SUN-TAN	AVOCET.
+TURNER	+AUDREY	*AUSTEN	SULTAN	AVIDLY
TURNIP	BURROW	AUNTIE	SURTAX	EVADED.
TURN-UP.	CUPRIC	*AUSTIN	SUITED	EVOKED.
AURORA	FURRED	BUTTER	SUTTEE	EVILLY
AUROUS	FUHRER	BUSTLE	SUBTLE	EVOLVE
CUT-OFF	FURROW	*BUXTON	SUBTLY	+EVELYN
CUBOID	HURRAH	*BURTON	*SUTTON	SVELTE
CUPOLA	HURRAY	BUTTON	SUITOR	UVULAR.
CUT-OUT	HUBRIS	CUTTER	SULTRY	AVENGE
DUGONG	*MURRAY	CUP-TIE	TUTTED	AVENUE
DUGOUT	NUTRIA	CURTLY	TUFTED	EVINCE
EULOGY	OUTRAN	CUSTOM	TURTLE.	EVENED
+EUROPA	OUTRUN	CURTSY	AUTUMN	EVENLY
*EUROPE	PURRED	CULTUS	AUBURN	+YVONNE.
FURORE	PUTRID	DUSTED	AUGURY	AVERSE
FUMOUS	QUARRY	DUSTER	AUGUST	+DVORAK
HUMOUR	QUARTO	FUSTIC	EUNUCH	OVERDO
MUCOUS	QUARTZ	GUITAR	FUTURE	OVERLY.
RUMOUR	QUORUM	GUTTED	JUJUBE	AVOSET.
RUFOUS	RUBRIC	GUTTER	LUXURY	AVATAR.
SUBORN	*SURREY	GUNTER	MUTUAL	AVOUCH
TUMOUR.	TURRET.	HUNTED	QUEUED	AVAUNT.
BURPED	BURSAR	HUTTED	SUBURB	AVOWAL
BUMPED	BUNSEN	HUNTER	SUTURE	AVOWED
BUMPER	CUSSED	HUSTLE	TUMULI	
CUSPED	CURSED	HURTLE	TUMULT.	AWEARY
CUPPED	CURSOR	JUTTED	CURVED	SWEATY.
CUPPER	FUSSED	+JUSTIN	CULVER	*SWEDEN.
DUMPED	GUISER	JUSTLY	CURVET	AWHEEL
DUMPER	GUSSET	LUSTED	PURVEY	SWEENY

+DWIGHT	OXALIC.	LYRIST		STANCE
TWIGGY.	EXEMPT.	MYRIAD	AZALEA.	STANCH
AWEIGH	EXPORT	PYXING	*AZORES	STARCH
AWHILE	EXTORT	SYRINX		THATCH
AWNING	EXHORT	TYRIAN		TRANCE
OWNING	EXPOSE	TYPIFY	*ABADAN	USANCE.
OWLISH.	*OXFORD.	TYPING	ANABAS	+AMANDA
AWAKEN	EXARCH.	TYPIST	ANANAS	+BRANDT
AWOKEN.	EXITED	XYLITE.	*ARARAT	BRANDY
TWILIT	*EXETER	*RYUKYU.	AVATAR	+CLAUDE
TWELVE.	EXOTIC.	CYCLED	CRAVAT	*RWANDA
SWAMPY.	EXHUME	CYCLIC	FRACAS	SHANDY
*RWANDA	EXEUNT	EYELET	+GRAHAM	*UGANDA
SWANKY	EXCUSE.	EYELID.	*IBADAN	VIANDS.
TWINED	OX-EYED	CYGNET	+ISAIAH	ABASED
TWINGE		CYANIC	PLATAN	ABATED
TWENTY.	BYNAME	HYMNAL	QUASAR	AMAZED
SWIPED	BY-PASS	*SYDNEY	*RAASAY	ANADEM
TWO-PLY.	BYPATH	*VYRNWY.	SCALAR	AWAKEN
SWERVE.	DYNAMO	BY-ROAD	SCARAB	AZALEA
TWISTY.	DYNAST	BYGONE	SEAMAN	BEAKED
SWITCH	GYRATE	BYWORD	SEA-WAY	BEAKER
SWATHE	PYJAMA	PYROPE	SHAMAN	BEAMED
TWITCH.	TYRANT	*TYRONE	TEA-BAG.	BEARER
TWOULD.	ZYMASE.	TYCOON	CRABBY	BEATEN
SWIVEL.	CYMBAL	XYLOID	CRAMBO	BEATER
TWO-WAY.	DYBBUK	XYLOSE	FLABBY	BEAVER
SWAYED	SYMBOL.	ZYGOMA	NEARBY	BIASED
	DYADIC	ZYGOTE.	SCABBY	BLADED
EXHALE	SYNODIC.	MYOPIA	SHABBY.	BLAMED
EXPAND	+CYBELE	MYOPIC	BLANCH	BLARED
EXTANT.	+HYGEIA	NYMPHO.	BRANCH	BLAZED
EXUDED	LYCEUM	CYMRIC	CHANCE	BLAZER
EXODUS.	MYSELF	*CYPRUS	CHANCY	BOATER
EXPECT	WYVERN	HYDRIC	CRATCH	BRACER
EXCEED	XYLENE.	HYBRID.	EXARCH	BRAKED
EXTEND	EYEFUL	BYSSUS	FIANCE	BRAVED
EXPEND	FYLFOT.	GYPSUM	FIASCO	BRAVER
EXTENT	CYPHER	HYSSOP.	FLANCH	BRAYED
EXCEPT	HYPHEN	CYSTIC	*FRANCE	BRAZEN
EXPERT	*LYTHAM	MYSTIC	GLANCE	CEASED
EXCESS.	MYTHIC	+MYRTLE	INARCH	CHAFED
OXYGEN.	PYTHON	OYSTER	NUANCE	CHALET
EXPIRE	SYPHON	SYNTAX	PLAICE	CHAPEL
EXPIRY	TYPHUS.	SYSTEM	PLANCH	CHASED
EXCISE	BY-LINE	XYSTER.	PRANCE	CHASER
EXCITE	DYEING	SYRUPY.	SCARCE	CLARET
OX-HIDE.	EYEING	SYLVAN	SEANCE	CLAWED
EXILED	GYVING	+SYLVIA.	SEARCH	CLAYEY
EXILIC	GYBING	SYZYGY	SNATCH	COALER

COATEE	GRAZED	PLANET	SPARED	APATHY
COAXED	HEADED	PLATED	SPAYED	BRASHY
CRANED	HEADER	PLATEN	STAGER	DRACHM
CRATED	HEALED	PLATER	STAKED	FLASHY
CRATER	HEALER	PLAYED	STALER	HEATHY
CRAVED	HEAPED	PLAYER	STAMEN	LOATHE
CRAVEN	HEARER	PRATED	STAPES	PLASHY
CRAZED	HEATED	PRAYED	STARED	SCATHE
DEADEN	HEATER	PRAYER	STATED	SWATHE
DEAFEN	HEAVED	QUAKED	STATER	TRASHY.
DEALER	HEAVEN	QUAKER	STAVED	ABATIS
DEARER	HEAVER	QUAVER	STAYED	ACACIA
DIADEM	HOAXER	READER	STAYER	*ACADIA
DIAPER	IMAGED	REAMER	SWAYED	ADAGIO
DRAPED	+ISABEL	REAPER	TEAMED	AGAMIC
DRAPER	KRAKEN	REARED	TEASED	AGARIC
DRAWEE	LAAGER	ROAMER	TEASEL	ALALIA
DRAWER	LEADED	ROARED	TEASER	*ARABIA
ELATED	LEADEN	ROARER	TEA-SET	ARABIC
ELATER	LEADER	SCALED	THALER	ATAXIA
ENAMEL	LEAFED	SCARED	*THAMES	*BRAZIL
ERASED	LEAKED	SEALED	THAWED	CRASIS
EVADED	LEANED	SEALER	TRACED	CYANIC
FEARED	LEAPED	SEAMED	TRACER	DYADIC
FLAKED	LEASED	SEAMEN	TRADED	FLAVIN
FLAMED	LEAVED	SEARED	TRADER	FRAZIL
FLAMEN	LEAVEN	SEATED	TRAVEL	GLACIS
FLARED	LEAVES	SHADED	WEAKEN	*GLAMIS
FLAWED	LIASED	SHAKEN	WEAKER	GOALIE
FLAXEN	LOADED	SHAKER	WEANED	GRADIN
FLAYED	LOADER	SHAMED	WEASEL	GRATIN
FOALED	LOAFER	SHAPED	WEAVER	GRATIS
FOAMED	LOAMED	SHARED	WHALER	GRAVID
FRAMED	LOANED	SHAVED	X-RAYED.	ISATIN
FRAMER	LOAVES	SHAVEN	CHAFFY	ITALIC
FRAYED	MOANED	SHAVER	DRAFFY	LEAD-IN
GEARED	MOATED	SKATER	*STAFFA.	MEALIE
GLARED	NEARED	SLAKED	CHANGE	OXALIC
GLAZED	NEARER	SLATED	CHARGE	PHASIC
GLAZER	NEATEN	SLATER	CRAGGY	PLACID
GNAWED	ONAGER	SLAVER	FLAGGY	PRATIE
GNAWER	ORATED	SLAYER	FLANGE	PRAXIS
GOADED	PEAHEN	SNAKED	GRANGE	SLAVIC
GOATEE	PEAKED	SNARED	ORANGE	SPAVIN
GRACED	PEALED	SOAKED	QUAGGA	+STALIN
GRADED	PHASED	SOAKER	QUAGGY	STASIS
GRATER	PLACED	SOAPED	SHAGGY	STATIC
GRAVEL	PLACER	SOARED	SLANGY.	+THALIA
GRAVER	PLACET	SPACED	+AGATHA	TRAGIC.
GRAVES	PLANED	SPACER	APACHE	*ALASKA

155

CHALKY	+JOANNA	*GDANSK	PLAQUE	GOBLET
CRANKY	LEARNT	GLASSY	*PRAGUE	HEBREW
SLACKS	PLAINT	GRASSY	SLAP-UP	IMBREX
SWANKY	QUAINT.	HEARSE	STATUE	IMBUED
THANKS.	ACAJOU	HOARSE	STATUS	INBRED
ARABLE	AMATOL	LIAISE	TEACUP	JABBED
BEADLE	AMAZON	PRAISE	URAEUS	JABBER
BEAGLE	BEACON	SPARSE	+URANUS.	JIBBED
CRADLE	BLAZON	TRAPSE.	STARVE.	JOBBED
CRAWLY	+CHARON	ACANTH	+GLADYS.	JOBBER
DEADLY	CRAYON	BEAUTY	PIAZZA	LOBBED
DEARLY	DEACON	CHASTE	SNAZZY	LUBBER
DRABLY	DIATOM	CHATTY	STANZA	MOBBED
ENABLE	DRAGON	COAITA		NABBED
FLATLY	FLAGON	CRAFTY	BOBCAT	NOBBED
GLADLY	KLAXON	DEARTH	CABMAN	NOBLER
LIABLE	MEADOW	ECARTE	FABIAN	RABBET
MEASLY	ORATOR	FEALTY	HABEAS	RABIES
NEARLY	PHANON	HEALTH	KIBLAH	RIBBED
NEATLY	PHAROS	HEARTH	LABIAL	ROBBED
ORACLE	REASON	HEARTY	SUBWAY	ROBBER
ORALLY	SEA-COW	LEAN-TO	UMBRAL	RUBBED
PEARLY	SEA-DOG	QUANTA	UPBEAT.	RUBBER
REALLY	SEASON	QUARTO	IMBIBE.	SOBBED
STABLE	SHADOW	QUARTZ	ABBACY	SUBLET
STABLY	STATOR	REALTY	REBECK.	TABBED
STAPLE	TEAPOT	SCANTY	AUBADE	TABLED
UNABLE	TEAPOY	SCATTY	EMBODY	TABLET
USABLE	WEAPON	SHANTY	LIBIDO	TUBBED
VIABLE	ZEALOT.	*SPARTA	NOBODY.	UMBLES
WEAKLY	FRAPPE	STACTE	AMBLED	WEBBED
YEARLY.	SCAMPI	STAITH	BOBBED	YABBER.
+BRAHMS	SNAPPY	WEALTH	COBBER	REBUFF.
CLAMMY	SWAMPY.	WRAITH	COBWEB	CUBAGE
DHARMA	*BIAFRA	YEASTY.	CUBBED	*TOBAGO.
GRAMME	+CLAIRE	ABACUS	DABBED	ALBEIT
MIASMA	FIACRE	ALARUM	DABBER	BOBBIN
PLASMA	MEAGRE	BLAGUE	DIBBER	CUBOID
SHAMMY	QUARRY	+BRAQUE	DUBBED	+DEBBIE
SMARMY	STARRY	CLAQUE	EMBLEM	DEBRIS
TRAUMA.	TEA-URN.	CRATUR	FABLED	DOBBIN
AVAUNT	BRAISE	FLATUS	FIBBED	DUBBIN
*BEAUNE	BRASSY	GIAOUR	FIBBER	*DUBLIN
BRAINY	CHAISE	GRADUS	FOBBED	FABRIC
BRAWNY	CHASSE	HIATUS	GABBED	FIBRIL
CRANNY	CLASSY	+ICARUS	GABLED	FIBRIN
+ELAINE	CLAUSE	LEAGUE	GIBBER	GOBLIN
FLAUNT	COARSE	OPAQUE	GIBBET	HUBRIS
GRAINY	ELAPSE	PEANUT	GIBLET	HYBRID
GRANNY	FRAISE	PLAGUE	GOBBET	PUBLIC

RABBIN	JIBING	ERBIUM	DUCKED	RICHER
RABBIT	ORBING	HUBBUB	DUCKER	RICKED
RUBRIC	RIBAND	IMBRUE	*ECCLES	ROCHET
SUBMIT.	ROBING	LABOUR	ESCHEW	ROCKED
REBUKE.	+RUBENS	SUBDUE.	ETCHED	ROCKER
BABBLE	+SABINA	EMBRYO	EXCEED	ROCKET
BUBBLE'	TUBING		HACKED	RUCKED
BUBBLY	UNBEND	BUCCAL	HOCKED	SACHET
CABALA	UNBENT	*BUCHAN	HOCKEY	SACKED
COBALT	UNBIND	ESCHAR	INCHED	SACRED
COBBLE	URBANE.	FACIAL	ITCHED	SECRET
COBBLY	BABOON	JACKAL	JACKED	SICKEN
+CYBELE	DEBTOR	NECTAR	JACKET	SICKER
DABBLE	GABION	PICKAX	JOCKEY	SOCCER
DIBBLE	GIBBON	RACIAL	KECKED	SOCKET
EMBALM	HOBNOB	RECTAL	KICKED	SUCKED
FIBULA	RIBBON.	SACRAL	LACHES	SUCKER
GABBLE	+ALBERT	SOCIAL	LACKED	TACKED
GOBBLE	AUBURN	UNCIAL.	LACKEY	TICKED
HOBBLE	COBURG	DECOCT	LECHER	TICKER
KIBBLE	DEBARK	ROCOCO.	LICHEN	TICKET
KOBOLD	EMBARK	ACCEDE	LICKED	TUCKED
LABILE	*HOBART	ARCADE	LOCKED	TUCKER
LOBULE	+HUBERT	CICADA	LOCKER	TUCKE·T
MOBILE	INBORN	DECADE	LOCKET	WICKED
NEBULA	JABIRU	DECIDE	MICKEY	WICKER
NIBBLE	+OSBERT	DECODE	MOCKED	WICKET.
NO-BALL	REBORE	ESCUDO	MOCKER	PACIFY.
NOBBLE	REBORN	FACADE	MUCKED	ENCAGE
NUBILE	+ROBERT	RECEDE	NECKED	SOCAGE.
PEBBLE	SUBORN	SECEDE.	NICKED	+ARCHIE
PEBBLY	SUBURB	*AACHEN	NICKEL	ARCHIL
RABBLE	TABARD	ARCHED	NICKER	*ARCTIC
RIBALD	UNBORN.	ARCHER	NOCKED	*COCHIN
RUBBLE	ABBESS	BACKED	NUCLEI	CYCLIC
SUBTLE	AMBUSH	BACKER	PACKED	DACOIT
SUBTLY	CUBISM	BICKER	PACKER	DECEIT
UNBOLT	DEBASE	BUCKET	PACKET	+EUCLID
WOBBLE	EMBOSS	CACHET	PECKED	HECTIC
WOBBLY.	RIBOSE	COCKED	PECKER	*ISCHIA
*ALBANY	ROBUST.	COCKER	PECTEN	LACTIC
ALBINO	ALBATA	CYCLED	PICKED	ORCHID
CUBING	ALBITE	DECKED	PICKER	ORCHIS
DEBUNK	DEBATE	DECKER	PICKET	PECTIC
EBBING	LOBATE	DECREE	POCKET	PECTIN
EMBANK	REBATE	DICKER	PUCKER	PICNIC
GIBING	RUBATO.	DICKEY	+RACHEL	RECOIL
GOBANG	ARBOUR	DOCKED	RACIER	TOCSIN
GYBING	COBNUT	DOCKER	RACKED	UNCOIL
INBAND	DYBBUK	DOCKET	RACKET	URCHIN

VICTIM.	DICING	GO-CART	RECOUP	IODIDE.
DECOKE.	EOCENE	RECORD	RECTUM	ADDLED
ARCHLY	FACING	SECURE	RICTUS	+ANDREW
BECALM	FECUND	UNCORD	SACRUM	+AUDREY
BUCKLE	JOCUND	UNCORK.	VACUUM.	BADGER
CACKLE	LACING	ACCESS	ALCOVE.	BEDDED
CICALA	LACUNA	ACCOST	COCCYX	BIDDER
CICELY	LUCENT	ACCUSE	DACTYL	BODIED
COCKLE	NICENE	ENCASE		BUDDED
DECKLE	PACING	ENCASH	BEDLAM	BUDGED
DOCILE	RACING	ENCYST	BED-PAN	BUDGET
FACILE	RECANT	EXCESS	ENDEAR	CADGER
FACULA	RECENT	EXCISE	GODDAM	CODDER
FICKLE	SECANT	EXCUSE	HODMAN	CODGER
HACKLE	SECOND	INCEST	INDIAN	CUDGEL
HECKLE	VACANT	INCISE	KIDNAP	DODDER
KECKLE	VICUNA.	INCUSE	*KODIAK	DODGED
LOCALE	ANCHOR	JOCOSE	MADCAP	DODGER
MACKLE	ARCHON	LOCUST	MADMAN	*DUDLEY
MACULA	BECKON	NICEST	*MADRAS	EDDIED
MICKLE	CACHOU	ONCOST	MEDIAL	FIDGET
MUCKLE	COCOON	RACISM	MEDIAN	FODDER
NICELY	CUCKOO	RACIST	MEDLAR	GADDED
+NICOLE	DACRON	RECAST	*MEDWAY	GADGET
OCCULT	DOCTOR	RECESS	MIDDAY	HEDGER
PICKLE	FACTOR	UNCASE	MIDWAY	HIDDEN
RACILY	+HECTOR	UPCAST.	*OLDHAM	HODDEN
RECALL	LICTOR	CECITY	ORDEAL	INDEED
RICHLY	MACRON	CECITY	PEDLAR	JUDGED
*SICILY	MICRON	EXCITE	RADIAL	KEDGED
SICKLE	RACOON	+HECATE	RADIAN	KIDDED
SICKLY	RECKON	INCITE	REDCAP	KIDNEY
SUCKLE	RECTOR	LOCATE	VIDUAL	LADDER
TACKLE	SECTOR	NICETY	ZODIAC.	LADLED
TICKLE.	TYCOON	OOCYTE	INDABA.	LEDGER
BECAME	VECTOR	RECITE	ABDUCT	LIDDED
BECOME	+VICTOR.	UNCATE	ADDICT	LODGED
DECAMP	ACCEPT	VACATE.	ADDUCE	LODGER
ENCAMP	BICEPS	ACCRUE	BEDECK	MADDED
INCOME	ESCAPE	CACTUS	BODICE	MADDEN
RACEME.	EXCEPT	COCCUS	DEDUCE	MADDER
ACCENT	INCEPT	COCK-UP	DEDUCT	MEDLEY
ARCANA	OCCUPY	DICTUM	INDICT	MIDDEN
ARCANE	RECIPE.	FACTUM	INDUCE	MIDGET
ARCING	ACCORD	HICCUP	INDUCT	NODDED
ASCEND	BUCKRA	LOCK-UP	+MEDICI	NUDGED
ASCENT	+CICERO	+LUCIUS	MEDICO	OODLES
BACONY	ENCORE	LYCEUM	REDACT	PADDED
DECANT	ESCORT	MOCK-UP	REDUCE	PODDED
DECENT	EUCHRE	MUCOUS	SEDUCE.	REDDEN

REDDER	HUDDLE	*DIDCOT	IODIZE	WHENCE
REDEEM	INDULT	+GIDEON		WRENCH
RIDDEN	KIDDLE	GODSON	APE-MAN	WRETCH.
RIDGED	MEDDLE	*HUDSON	+CAESAR	AGENDA
+RODNEY	MIDDLE	INDOOR	COEVAL	AMENDS
RUDDER	MODULE	*LUDLOW	CREDAL	BLENDE
SADDEN	MUDDLE	ODD-JOB	DAEDAL	+BRENDA
SADDER	NODDLE	ODDS-ON	DIETAL	GREEDY
SIDLED	NODULE	*RADNOR.	FAECAL	OREIDE
SODDEN	PADDLE	ENDURE	FOEMAN	OVERDO
SUDDEN	PEDALO	FEDORA	FOETAL	PSEUDO
*SYDNEY	PEDDLE	MODERN	HAEMAL	SPEEDY
TEDDER	PUDDLE	ORDURE.	ICE-CAP	STEADY
TIDIER	RADDLE	EDDISH	ICEMAN	TRENDY.
UNDIES	REDDLE	ELDEST	LEEWAY	BREVET
WADDED	RIDDLE	IODISM	MAENAD	BREWER
WEDDED	RUDDLE	+MEDUSA	ONE-WAY	CHEWED
WEDGED	RUDELY	MODEST	*OREGAN	CLEVER
*WIDNES.	SADDLE	MODISH	PREFAB	CLEWED
CODIFY	TIDILY	NODOSE	PREPAY	CREWEL
MODIFY.	TODDLE	NUDISM	PRE-WAR	DEEMED
BODEGA	UNDULY	NUDIST	TOE-CAP	DEEPEN
INDIGO.	WADDLE	ODDEST	TREPAN.	DEEPER
+BUDDHA.	WIDELY.	OLDEST	PLEBBY.	DIESEL
BED-SIT	MADAME	RADISH	AGENCY	DIETED
BODKIN	OEDEMA	RUDEST	AMERCE	ELEVEN
*BODMIN	SODOMY.	SADISM	BLEACH	EVENED
CADDIS	ADDING	SADIST	BLENCH	*EXETER
EDDAIC	AIDING	WIDEST.	BREACH	EYELET
GODWIT	ARDENT	INDITE	BREECH	FAECES
HYDRIC	BIDING	+JUDITH	CLENCH	FEEDER
JUDAIC	BODING	NUDITY	COERCE	FEELER
KIDDIE	CEDING	ODDITY	DRENCH	FLEXED
LADDIE	CODING	SEDATE	FIERCE	GEEZER
*MADRID	ENDING	UP-DATE.	FLEECE	+GRETEL
ORDAIN	FADING	+ALDOUS	FLEECY	HEEDED
PIDGIN.	HIDING	ARDOUR	FLENCH	HEELED
+UPDIKE.	INDENT	BEDAUB	FLETCH	JEERED
AEDILE	IODINE	+CADMUS	FRENCH	KEELED
AUDILE	JADING	INDIUM	FRESCO	KEENED
BODILY	LADING	MEDIUM	*GREECE	KEENER
CODDLE	+NADINE	PODIUM	PIERCE	KEEPER
CUDDLE	PEDANT	RADIUM	PREACH	LEERED
CUDDLY	RIDING	RADIUS	QUENCH	MEEKER
DIDDLE	RODENT	RED-GUM	SKETCH	NEEDED
END-ALL	SIDING	*SIDCUP	SPEECH	OBEYED
FIDDLE	TIDING	SODIUM	STENCH	OMELET
FUDDLE	+UNDINE	TEDIUM.	THENCE	OPENER
GADFLY	UNDONE	ENDIVE	TIERCE	OX-EYED
HEDDLE	WADING.	+GODIVA.	TRENCH	PEEKED

PEELED	BEECHY	EVENLY	ICEBOX	PRETTY
PEELER	+BRECHT	FEEBLE	KOEDOE	SHEATH
PEEPER	CRECHE	FEEBLY	+OBERON	SIESTA
PEERED	FLECHE	FREELY	OCELOT	SLEUTH
PEEVED	FLESHY	KEENLY	PHENOL	SVELTE
PIECED	+GOETHE	MEEKLY	TREMOR	SWEATY
PREFER	SEETHE.	NEEDLE	+TREVOR.	TREATY
PREYED	ACERIC	NIELLO	CREEPY	TWENTY
*QUEBEC	ACETIC	+NOELLE	*DIEPPE.	WREATH.
QUEUED	ALEVIN	OCELLI	EXEMPT	AVENUE
REEDED	ALEXIA	OPENLY	SLEEPY	CAECUM
REEFER	+ALEXIS	OVERLY	STEPPE.	CHEQUE
REEKED	+AMELIA	PUEBLO	AWEARY	CHERUB
REELED	CHESIL	SEEMLY	BLEARY	*EREBUS
REEVED	CHEVIN	SMELLY	CHEERY	EYEFUL
SEEDED	CLERIC	STEELY	+CHERRY	FOETUS
SEEKER	CLEVIS	+STELLA	DREARY	IREFUL
SEEMED	CREDIT	TREBLE	PLEURA	OBELUS
SEEPED	CRETIN	WEEKLY.	POETRY	PLENUM
SHEKEL	DIESIS	CREAMY	SHEARS	PLEXUS
SIEVED	EDENIC	DREAMT	SHERRY	RHESUS
SKEWED	EMETIC	DREAMY	SIERRA	RUEFUL
SKEWER	EYELID	RHEUMY	SKERRY	USEFUL
SLEWED	FAERIE	STEAMY	THEORY	UTERUS
SPEWED	FOETID	+THELMA.	WHERRY.	WOEFUL.
STEREO	GAELIC	DOESNT	APEPSY	CHEVVY
+STEVEN	IRENIC	DUENNA	AVERSE	CLEAVE
STEWED	+LIEBIG	DYEING	BREAST	SHELVE
*SWEDEN	LUETIC	EKEING	CHEESE	SLEEVE
TEEMED	OLEFIN	EXEUNT	CHEESY	SWERVE
TEETER	PEEWIT	EYEING	CREASE	TWELVE.
*THEBES	POETIC	+GREENE	DRESSY	ICE-AXE
THEWED	PRECIS	*GRETNA	GNEISS	+EVELYN.
UNEVEN	PREFIX	HOEING	GREASE	BREEZE
URETER	PRELIM	PAEONY	GREASY	BREEZY
VEERED	RE-EDIT	RUEING	*ODESSA	FREEZE
VIEWER	SCENIC	SEEING	PLEASE	FRENZY
WEEDED	SPECIE	SHEENY	QUEASY	SLEAZY
WEEPER.	THESIS	SIENNA	THEISM	SNEEZE
ONE-OFF.	TIE-PIN	SWEENY	THEIST	WHEEZE
AVENGE	URETIC	TEEING	TSETSE	WHEEZY
AWEIGH	WEEVIL.	TOEING	UNEASY.	
CLERGY	BREEKS	*VIENNA.	BREATH	AFFRAY
DREDGE	CHEEKY	*BRECON	CHESTY	CAFTAN
EMERGE	SHEIKH.	BRETON	CREATE	DEFEAT
ENERGY	AGE-OLD	CRESOL	FIESTA	DEFRAY
FLEDGE	AREOLA	CRETON	GHETTO	GUFFAW
PLEDGE	BEETLE	DAEMON	+ODETTE	KAFTAN
SLEDGE	CREOLE	*FAEROE	PLENTY	OFF-DAY
SLEIGH.	DEEPLY	FLEXOR	PRESTO	AFFECT

DEFACE	TUFTED	AFFORD	WIGWAM	PEG-LEG
DEFECT	WAFTED.	BEFORE	ZIGZAG.	PIGGED
EFFACE	EFFIGY	BOFORS	LEGACY.	PIGLET
EFFECT	REFUGE.	DEFORM	PAGODA.	PUGGED
ENFACE	AFFAIR	EFFORT	ANGLED	RAGGED
INFECT	*BAFFIN	*ILFORD	ANGLER	REGRET
OFFICE	BIFFIN	INFIRM	ARGUED	RIGGED
REFACE.	BOFFIN	INFORM	BAGGED	ROGUED
+ALFRED	COFFIN	*ORFORD	BEGGED	RUGGED
BUFFER	KAFFIR	*OXFORD	BIGGER	RUGGER
BUFFET	MUFFIN	REFORM	BOGGED	SAGGED
COFFEE	PUFFIN	SAFARI	BUGGED	SIGHED
COFFER	RAFFIA	UNFURL	BUGGER	SIGNED
CUFFED	SUFFIX	ZAFFRE.	BUGLER	SIGNET
DEFIED	TIFFIN	DEFUSE	COGGED	TAGGED
DIFFER	UNFAIR.	EFFUSE	CYGNET	TUGGED
DOFFED	BAFFLE	ELFISH	DAGGER	VAGUER
DUFFED	BEFALL	INFEST	DEGREE	WAGGED
DUFFEL	BEFELL	INFUSE	DIGGED	+WAGNER.
DUFFER	COFFLE	OAFISH	DIGGER	ENGAGE.
+EIFFEL	DEFILE	OFFISH	DOGGED	ALGOID
GAFFED	DEFTLY	REFUSE	DOGGER	BAGNIO
GAFFER	DUFFLE	SAFEST.	EAGLET	BIGWIG
GIFTED	ENFOLD	EFFETE	FAGGED	HAGGIS
GOFFER	MUFFLE	REFUTE	FOGGED	*HYGEIA
HAFTED	ONFALL	SAFETY.	GAGGED	+INGRID
HEFTED	PIFFLE	AFFLUX	GOGLET	LOGGIA
HUFFED	RAFFLE	BEFOUL	HAGGED	MAGPIE
LIFTED	REFILL	EFFLUX	HIGHER	MEGRIM
LIFTER	RIFFLE	INFLUX	HOGGED	NOGGIN
LOFTED	RUFFLE	REFLUX	HOGGET	REGAIN
LOFTER	SAFELY	RUFOUS	HUGGED	*TIGRIS.
MUFFED	SOFTLY		JAGGED	+ANGELA
OFFSET	UNFOLD	*AEGEAN	JIGGED	*ANGOLA
PUFFED	WAFFLE	AUGEAN	JIGGER	ARGALA
PUFFER	WIFELY	BAGMAN	JOGGED	*ARGYLL
RAFTED	YAFFLE.	BEGGAR	JUGGED	BOGGLE
RAFTER	DEFAME	BOG-OAK	LAGGED	CAGILY
REFLEX	INFAMY.	COGNAC	LEGGED	DAGGLE
REFUEL	DEFEND	JAGUAR	LOGGED	ENGULF
RIFLED	DEFINE	JIGSAW	LOGGER	GAGGLE
RIFLER	INFANT	MAGYAR	LUGGED	GIGGLE
RIFTED	OFFEND	RAG-BAG	LUGGER	GIGOLO
RUFFED	OFFING	RAG-DAY	MAGNET	GOGGLE
SIFTER	REFINE	RAGLAN	MUGGED	HAGGLE
SOFTEN	REFUND.	RAGMAN	NAGGED	HIGGLE
SOFTER	BEFOOL	REGNAL	NAGGER	HIGHLY
SUFFER	INFLOW	SAGGAR	NIGGER	HUGELY
TOFFEE	REFOOT.	SIGNAL	NUGGET	JIGGLE
TUFFET	AFFIRM	UNGUAL	PEGGED	JOGGLE

161

- -G-L-		- -I-E-		
JUGGLE	REGARD	APHTHA.	UNHASP.	BAILER
NIGGLE	SUGARY	COHEIR	*TAHITI.	BAILEY
REGALE	UNGIRD	DAHLIA	MAHOUT.	BAITED
SAGELY	UNGIRT	ECHOIC	BEHAVE	BLIMEY
TOGGLE	VAGARY	ETHNIC	BEHOVE.	BOILED
UNGULA	YOGURT.	MOHAIR.	MOHAWK	BOILER
WAGGLE	ARGOSY	AWHILE	UNHEWN.	BRIBED
WIGGLE.	AUGUST	BEHALF	SCHIZO	CHIDED
BIGAMY	DIGEST	BEHELD		CHIMED
LEGUME	INGEST	BEHOLD	ANIMAL	CHISEL
REGIME	LEGIST	EXHALE	APICAL	COILED
ZYGOMA.	ORGASM.	INHALE	BRIDAL	COINER
ANGINA	*BOGOTA	MOHOLE	CLIMAX	CRIKEY
ARGENT	DOGATE	UNHOLY	COITAL	*CRIMEA
BEGONE	EIGHTH	UPHELD	EPICAL	DE-ICER
BYGONE	EIGHTY	UPHILL	FRIDAY	DOITED
CAGING	JUGATE	UPHOLD.	GUITAR	DRIVEL
COGENT	LEGATE	*BAHAMA	LAICAL	DRIVEN
DUGONG	LEGATO	EXHUME	OGIVAL	DRIVER
EDGING	MIGHTY	INHUME	PRIMAL	DUIKER
ENGINE	NEGATE	SCHEMA	RHINAL	EDITED
+EUGENE	NIGHTY	SCHEME.	SPINAL	ELIDED
FAG-END	PIGSTY	ACHENE	SPIRAL	EXILED
LEGEND	TIGHTS	ACHING	TRIBAL	EXITED
PAGING	ZYGOTE.	APHONY	TRICAR	FAILED
RAGING	+AEGEUS	+ATHENA	URINAL.	FOILED
REGENT	ALGOUS	+ATHENE	AKIMBO	GAINED
+REGINA	DUGOUT	*ATHENS	+THISBE	GAITER
URGENT	EGG-CUP	BEHIND	TRILBY	GEIGER
URGING	JUGFUL	ETHANE	*WHITBY.	GLIDER
VAGINA	LIGNUM	SPHINX	APIECE	GRIDED
WAGING.	MAGNUM	UNHAND.	CLINCH	GRIPED
DIGLOT	PIGNUT	CAHOOT	EVINCE	GUIDED
DOG-FOX	RAGOUT	SCHOOL	FLINCH	*GUINEA
EGG-NOG	REGIUS	UNHOOK.	FLITCH	GUISER
FAGGOT	RIGOUR	ADHERE	IDIOCY	HAILED
LAGOON	VIGOUR.	ASHORE	PRINCE	HEIFER
LEGION	ARGIVE	COHERE	QUINCE	IBIDEM
MAGGOT		COHORT	QUITCH	IRISED
MAGNOX	.ASH-CAN	EXHORT	SMIRCH	JAILED
NO-GOOD	ASHLAR	INHERE	STITCH	JAILER
PIGEON	BEHEAD.	*LAHORE	SWITCH	JOINED
POGROM	*ITHACA.	*SAHARA	TWITCH.	JOINER
REGION	OX-HIDE	SPHERE	HAIR-DO	KAISER
SIGNOR	+YEHUDI.	UNHURT.	SHINDY	KNIFED
WAGGON.	AWHEEL	AGHAST	TRIODE.	KNIVES
ANGARY	ECHOED	BEHEST	ABIDED	LOITER
ANGORA	FUHRER	REHASH	APICES	MAIDEN
AUGURY	+MAHLER	SCHISM	ARISEN	MAILED
FIGURE	YAHWEH.	SCHIST	BAILEE	+MAILER

--I-E-			--I-U-	
MAIMED	TRICED	CHITIN	SHIELD	CRIMPY
NAILED	TRIVET	CLINIC	SKILLY	CRISPY
OBITER	TWINED	CRISIS	SLIMLY	GRIPPE
+OLIVER	UNIPED	CRITIC	STIFLE	SKIMPY
OPINED	UNISEX	ELICIT	STILLY	WHIPPY.
PAINED	UNITED	ELIXIR	THINLY	APIARY
PAIRED	VAINER	EXILIC	TRIFLE	AVIARY
POISED	VEILED	FRIGID	TRIMLY	EMIGRE
PRICED	VEINED	IRITIS	TRIPLE	FRIARY
PRIDED	VOICED	ORIGIN	VAINLY.	GOITRE
PRIMED	VOIDED	+OSIRIS	ENIGMA	PLIERS
PRIMER	WAILED	OTITIS	SHIMMY	PRIORY.
PRIVET	WAITED	+PHILIP	STIGMA.	AMIDST
PRIZED	WAITER	RAISIN	*AMIENS	ARIOSO
QUIVER	WAIVED	RHIZIC	CLIENT	DRIEST
RAIDER	WAIVER	SEISIN	FRIEND	FLIMSY
RAILED	WHILED	SPIRIT	ONIONY	GRILSE
RAINED	WHINED	TRIFID	ORIENT	OTIOSE
RAISED	WHITEN	TRIVIA	PLIANT	PRIEST
REINED	WHITER	TWILIT.	PUISNE	PRISSY
RUINED	WRITER.	FRISKY	SKIING	QUINSY
SAILED	BRIDGE	SLINKY	SKINNY	THIRST
SAILER	CLINGY	STICKY	TRIUNE	WHILST
SEISED	CRINGE	TRICKY	WHINNY.	WHIMSY.
SEIZED	FRIDGE	WHISKY	+ALISON	AVIATE
SHINED	+FRIGGA	YOICKS.	+ASIMOV	CHINTZ
SHINER	FRINGE	ACIDLY	BRITON	DAINTY
SHIVER	STINGY	AFIELD	+CHIRON	FLINTY
SKIVER	TWIGGY	ARIDLY	CHITON	FLIRTY
SLICED	TWINGE.	AVIDLY	+EDISON	GAIETY
SLICER	ALIGHT	BRIDLE	EDITOR	GRITTY
SLIVER	ARIGHT	CHICLE	+ELINOR	GUILTY
SMILED	BLIGHT	CHICLY	FRIVOL	MOIETY
SNIPER	BLITHE	CHILLI	GRISON	OPIATE
SNIVEL	BRIGHT	CHILLY	GUIDON	PLINTH
SOILED	CHICHI	EDIBLE	ORISON	SHIFTY
SOIREE	CLICHE	EVILLY	POISON	SHINTO
SPICED	+DWIGHT	FAILLE	PRISON	SHIRTY
SPIDER	FLIGHT	FAIRLY	*SAIGON	THIRTY
SPIKED	FRIGHT	FOIBLE	SAILOR	TWISTY.
SPINET	GEISHA	FRILLY	SPIGOT	ACINUS
SPIRED	HEIGHT	GLIBLY	SUITOR	ANIMUS
SPITED	KNIGHT	GRILLE	TAILOR	*BEIRUT
STIVER	PLIGHT	GRIMLY	TRICOT	CAIQUE
SUITED	SLIGHT	GRISLY	TRIPOD	CHIBUK
SWIPED	SMITHY	ICICLE	TRIPOS	CLIQUE
SWIVEL	WEIGHT	MAINLY	+TRITON	COITUS
TAILED	WRITHE.	ORIOLE	UNISON.	ODIOUS
TOILER	ACIDIC	PRIMLY	CHIPPY	PRIMUS
TOILET	+ALICIA	*SCILLY	CHIRPY	UNIQUE

163

CHIVVY	HIKING	PILLAR	BULGER	HELTER
GRIEVE	INKING	PULSAR	BULLET	HOLDER
SKIVVY	IRKING	SALAAM	CALLED	HOLIER
THIEVE.	JOKING	SULTAN	CALLER	HOLLER
+ERINYS.	LIKING	SYLVAN	CALMED	HULLED
FRIEZE	MAKING	UNLOAD	CALMER	INLIER
FRIZZY	*PEKING	+VULCAN	CALVED	JELLED
	POKING	VULGAR	CALVES	JILTED
JUJUBE.	PUKING	VULVAR.	COLDER	JOLTED
ABJECT	RAKING	CALICO	COLLET	+JULIET
ADJECT	TAKING	CILICE	CULLED	KILLED
DEJECT	UNKIND	ENLACE	CULVER	KILLER
HIJACK	VIKING	MALICE	DELVED	KILTED
INJECT	WAKING	MOLOCH	DOLLED	LILTED
OBJECT	*WOKING	OCLOCK	DOLMEN	LOLLED
REJECT.	YOKING.	PALACE	DULCET	LULLED
ADJOIN	INK-POT.	POLACK	DULLED	MALLET
ENJOIN	*ANKARA	POLICE	DULLER	MALTED
REJOIN.	BAKERY	POLICY	+DULLES	MELDED
IN-JOKE.	GO-KART.	RELICT.	+EILEEN	MELTED
CAJOLE.	RAKISH.	SELECT	FALLEN	MILDER
PYJAMA.	*DAKOTA.	SILICA	FALTER	MILDEW
JEJUNE.	MAKE-UP	SOLACE	FELLER	MILIEU
ABJURE		SPLICE	FELTED	MILKED
ADJURE	AFLOAT	UNLOCK.	FILLED	MILKER
INJURE	*BALKAN	ALLUDE	FILLER	MILLED
INJURY.	BALLAD	BOLIDE	FILLET	+MILLER
ADJUST	BALSAM	DELUDE	FILMED	MILLET
UNJUST.	+BALZAC	HALIDE	FILTER	MILTED
RAJPUT	BELDAM	MALADY	FOLDED	MOLTEN
	BELIAL	MELODY	FOLDER	MULLED
MIKADO.	*BELPAR	MILADY	FULLER	MULLET.
ANKLET	*BILBAO	TELEDU	GALLED	PALLED
*ILKLEY	CALCAR	UNLADE.	GALLEY	PALLET
*ORKNEY	*CALLAO	+AILEEN	GELDED	PALMED
UPKEEP	CELLAR	ALLIED	GELLED	PALMER
YAKKED.	COLLAR	ALLIES	GILDED	PALPED
DIK-DIK	*DALLAS	ASLEEP	GOLDEN	PALTER
*SIKKIM	DOLLAR	+BALDER	GOLFER	PELLET
UNKNIT.	DOLMAN	BALEEN	GULLED	PELMET
ALKALI	FELLAH	BALKED	GULLET	PELTED
LIKELY.	FILIAL	BALLET	GULPED	PHLOEM
ESKIMO.	FOLIAR	BELIEF	HALOED	PILFER
ALKANE	FULMAR	BELTED	HALTED	POLDER
ALKENE	*GALWAY	BILKER	HALTER	POLLED
ASKING	+JULIAN	BILLED	HALVED	POLLEN
BAKING	+LILIAN	BILLET	HELMED	POLLEX
BIKINI	NILGAI	BOLDER	HELMET	PULLED
CAKING	OIL-CAN	BOLTED	HELPED	PULLER
FAKING	PALMAR	BULBED	HELPER	PULLET

PULLEY	YELLED	+WALLIS	PULING	SALMON
PULPER	YELPED.	WELKIN	RELENT	SALOON
PULSED	PILAFF	XYLOID.	RELINE	SALVOR
RELIED	SALIFY	BELIKE	RILING	SELDOM
RELIEF	UGLIFY	SALUKI	+ROLAND	TALION
ROLLED	UPLIFT	UNLIKE.	RULING	TALLOW
ROLLER	VILIFY.	BALDLY	SALINE	WALLOP
SALTED	ALLEGE	BOLDLY	SILENT	WALLOW
SALTER	DELUGE	CALMLY	*SOLENT	+WALTON
SALVED	EULOGY	COLDLY	SOLING	WILLOW
SALVER	LOLIGO	HOLILY	SPLINE	+WILSON
SELLER	*MALAGA	MILDLY	SPLINT	*WILTON
SELVES	MALIGN	PALELY	TALENT	YELLOW.
SILKEN	OBLIGE	PILULE	TILING	ASLOPE
SILTED	PHLEGM	SOLELY	UPLAND	CALIPH
SILVER	SILAGE	VILELY	VOLING	JALOPY
SOLDER	ULLAGE.	WILDLY	WALING	+PELOPS.
SOLVED	*DELPHI	WILILY.	WILING	ALLURE
SPLEEN	FILTHY	AFLAME	XYLENE.	BELFRY
SULLEN	MALTHA.	APLOMB	*BALBOA	BOLERO
TALKED	*BALTIC	COLUMN	BALLOT	CELERY
TALKER	BULBIL	SALAMI	+BELLOC	GALORE
TALLER	*CALAIS	+SALOME	*BELLOW	+HILARY
TELFER	CALKIN	SOLEMN	BILLOW	PALTRY
TELLER	+CALVIN	VOLUME.	*BOLTON	SALARY
TILLED	CELTIC	AILING	CALLOW	SULTRY
TILLER	COLLIE	ASLANT	COLLOP	TELARY
TILTED	ECLAIR	BALING	+DALTON	VELURE.
TOLLED	FILL-IN	BELONG	DOLLOP	CALASH
UGLIER	FILLIP	BY-LINE	FALCON	DOLOSE
VALLEY	FILMIC	COLONY	FALLOW	ENLIST
VALUED	FULFIL	*EALING	FELLOE	FOLKSY
VALUER	GALLIC	FELINE	FELLOW	GALOSH
VALVED	GILLIE	FELONY	FOLLOW	GOLOSH
VELVET	HALOID	FILING	FYLFOT	HOLISM
VOLLEY	INLAID	GALENA	GALLON	ILL-USE
VOLTED	KALMIA	HALING	GALLOP	MOLEST
WALKER	KELPIE	HOLING	HALLOO	MULISH
WALLED	KELTIC	IDLING	HALLOW	OWLISH
WALLET	PALAIS	INLAND	+HELIOS	PALEST
+WALTER	PALLID	ISLAND	HOLLOW	PILOSE
WELDER	PELVIC	OBLONG	KELSON	POLISH
WELLED	PELVIS	OGLING	LOLLOP	RELISH
WELTED	PULL-IN	OILING	MALLOW	SPLASH
WELTER	PULPIT	ON-LINE	MELLOW	UNLASH
WILDER	RELAID	PALING	+MILTON	UNLESS
WILLED	SALVIA	PILING	+NELSON	VALISE
WILTED	+SYLVIA	*POLAND	PALLOR	VILEST
WOLFED	TALKIE	POLING	PILLOW	XYLOSE.
WOLVES	UNLAID	POLONY	SALLOW	BALATA

165

DELATE	RELIVE	COMBER	RAMMER	FAMILY
DELETE	SALIVA.	COMPEL	RAMPED	FEMALE
DILATE	*MALAWI.	CUMBER	RIMMED	FUMBLE
DILUTE	GALAXY.	DAMMED	+ROMMEL	GAMBLE
EOLITH	+BOLEYN	DAMNED	*ROMNEY	GAMELY
IOLITE	*MALAYA	DAMPEN	ROMPED	HOMELY
+LOLITA	+MELVYN	DAMPER	+SAMUEL	HOMILY
OBLATE	+SELWYN	DAMSEL	SIMMER	HUMBLE
OOLITE	*WELWYN.	DIMMED	SIMNEL	HUMBLY
PALATE	ABLAZE	DIMMER	SIMPER	JUMBLE
PELOTA		DUMPED	SUMMED	LAMELY
+PILATE	BEMOAN	DUMPER	SUMMER	LIMPLY
POLITE	*BOMBAY	GAMMED	TAMPED	MUMBLE
POLITY	COMBAT	GAMMER	TAMPER	NAMELY
RELATE	CYMBAL	GEMMED	TEMPER	NIMBLE
SALUTE	DAMMAR	GIMLET	TIMBER	NIMBLY
SOLUTE	DEMEAN	GUMMED	UNMEET	NUMBLY
VALUTA	HYMNAL	HAMLET	VAMPED.	ORMOLU
VELETA	JAM-JAR	HAMMED	HUMIFY	+PAMELA
VOLUTE	JUMBAL	HAMMER	RAMIFY	PIMPLE
XYLITE.	LAMMAS	HAMPER	TUMEFY.	PIMPLY
ABLAUT	LUMBAR	HEMMED	*ARMAGH	RAMBLE
ALL-OUT	MAMMAL	HEMPEN	DAMAGE	RUMBLE
BULBUL	PAMPAS	*HUMBER	HOMAGE.	RUMPLE
CALL-UP	SAMPAN	HUMMED	NYMPHO.	SAMPLE
CALLUS	SIMIAN	HUMPED	ARMPIT	SIMILE
CILIUM	TIMBAL	JAMMED	BOMBIC	SIMPLE
COLOUR	TOM-CAT	JUMPED	COMFIT	SIMPLY
CULTUS	WOMBAT.	JUMPER	COMMIE	*SOMALI
DOLOUR	POMACE	KUMMEL	COMMIT	TAMELY
GALLUP	PUMICE.	LAMBED	CYMRIC	TEMPLE
HALLUX	ARMADA	LAMMED	DIMWIT	TIMELY
HELIUM	COMEDY	LIMBED	DOMAIN	TUMBLE
HOLD-UP	DEMODE	LIMBER	*GAMBIA	TUMULI
+JULIUS	FUMADE	LIMNER	GAMBIT	TUMULT
PILE-UP	LAMBDA	LIMPED	IAMBIC	WIMPLE.
PILOUS	POMADE	LIMPET	LIMPID	+JEMIMA.
PULQUE	REMADE	LUMBER	MEMOIR	ALMOND
ROLL-UP	REMEDY	MEMBER	REMAIN	ARMING
TALCUM	UNMADE.	MUMMED	SUMMIT	CEMENT
TALMUD	ARMLET	MUMMER	*ZAMBIA	COMING
UMLAUT	BOMBED	NUMBED	ZOMBIE.	DEMAND
VALLUM	BOMBER	NUMBER	REMAKE	DEMENT
VALOUR	BUMPED	PAMPER	UNMAKE.	DOMINO
VELLUM	BUMPER	PIMPED	COMELY	+EDMUND
VILLUS	CAMBER	POMMEL	COMPLY	ERMINE
WALNUT	*CAMDEN	PUMMEL	DAMPLY	FAMINE
WALRUS	CAMPED	PUMPED	DIMPLE	FOMENT
+WILBUR	CAMPER	RAMJET	DIMPLY	FUMING
WILFUL.	COMBED	RAMMED	DUMBLY	GAMING

166

GEMINI	COMOSE	BANTAM	SYNTAX	CONVEY
HOMING	DAMASK	BANYAN	TIN-CAN	DANCER
HOMINY	DEMISE	*BENGAL	VANDAL	DANDER
HUMANE	ENMESH	+BUNYAN	VENIAL	DANGER
IMMUNE	FAMISH	CAN-CAN	XENIAL.	+DANIEL
JIMINY	HAMOSE	CANTAB	*DANUBE.	DENIED
KIMONO	IMMESH	CANVAS	ARNICA	DENIER
LAMENT	INMOST	CENTAL	+EUNICE	DENSER
LAMINA	MIMOSA	CONFAB	EUNUCH	DENTED
LAMING	REMISS	CON-MAN	+JANICE	*DENVER
LIMING	RIMOSE	+CONRAD	LUNACY	DINNED
*LOMOND	ROMISH	*CONWAY	MENACE	DINNER
MIMING	UNMASK	DENIAL	*MONACO	DONKEY
MOMENT	UPMOST	DENTAL	+MONICA	DONNED
NAMING	UTMOST	*DUNBAR	*VENICE.	*DUNDEE
REMAND	VAMOSE	+DUNCAN	*CANADA	DUNKED
REMIND	ZYMASE.	FENIAN	DENUDE	DUNNED
ROMANY	COMITY	FINIAL	MONODY	FANGED
SIMONY	DEMOTE	FINNAN	XANADU.	FAN-JET
TAMING	DIMITY	FONTAL	BANDED	FANNED
TIMING.	DUMPTY	GENIAL	BANGED	FENCED
BAMBOO	ENMITY	GUNMAN	BANKED	FENCER
CAMION	GAMETE	HANGAR	BANKER	FENDED
COMMON	HAMITE	+HANNAH	BANNED	FENDER
DAMSON	HUMPTY	IONIAN	BANNER	FENNEC
GAMBOL	INMATE	*KANSAS	BANTER	FENNEL
GAMMON	REMOTE	*KENDAL	BENDED	FINDER
JAMBOK	SAMITE	LANDAU	BINDER	FINGER
MAMMON	SEMITE	LINEAL	BONDED	FINNER
POMPOM	TOMATO.	LINEAR	BONDER	FUNDED
POMPON	ARMFUL	LINGAM	BONNET	FUNNEL
RAMROD	ARMOUR	MANIAC	BUNGED	GANDER
SIMOOM	CAMPUS	MANUAL	BUNKER	GANGED
SUMMON	DUMDUM	MENIAL	BUNSEN	GANGER
SYMBOL	FAMOUS	MENTAL	CANCEL	*GANGES
TAMPON	FUMOUS	MINOAN	CANCER	GANNET
TOMBOY	HUMBUG	MONDAY	CANKER	GENDER
TOMTOM	HUMOUR	PENIAL	CANNED	GINGER
UNMOOR.	IAMBUS	PENTAD	CANNER	GUNNED
ADMIRE	NIMBUS	PINEAL	*CANNES	GUNNER
CAMERA	RIMOUS	*PUNJAB	CANTED	GUNTER
DEMURE	RUMOUR	RANDAN	CANTER	HANDED
IMMURE	RUMPUS	RENTAL	*CANVEY	+HANDEL
MEMORY	TUMOUR.	RUNWAY	CINDER	HANGED
REMARK	REMOVE	SANDAL	CONFER	HANGER
REMORA		SENDAL	CONGER	HANKER
SOMBRE	+AENEAS	SUNDAE	CONKED	*HENLEY
TIMBRE.	ANNEAL	SUNDAY	CONKER	HINDER
ALMOST	ANNUAL	SUN-HAT	CONNED	HINGED
BEMUSE	BANIAN	SUN-TAN	CONVEX	HINTED

HONKED	PENNED	TINDER	MANTIC	PINOLE
HUNGER	PINKED	TINGED	MANTIS	PINTLE
HUNTED	PINNED	TINIER	*MENDIP	PUNILY
HUNTER	*PINNER	TINKER	MENHIR	RANKLE
JENNET	+PINTER	TINNED	NUNCIO	RANKLY
JINKED	PONDER	TINSEL	PENCIL	+RONALD
JINNEE	PONGEE	TUNNEL	PUNDIT	SANELY
JUNKED	PUNNED	VENDEE	RANCID	SENILE
JUNKER	PUNNET	VENDER	+RENOIR	SINGLE
JUNKET	PUNTED	VENEER	SUNLIT	SINGLY
KENNED	PUNTER	VENTED	SYNDIC	TANGLE
KENNEL	RANGED	WANDER	TANNIC	TANGLY
KINDER	RANGER	WANTED	TANNIN	TINGLE
KINGED	RANKED	WENDED	TENNIS	TINILY
KINKED	RANKER	WINCED	TONSIL	TINKLE
LANCED	RENDER	WINDED	ZINNIA.	WANGLE
LANCER	RENNET	WINDER	GINGKO	WINKLE.
LANCET	RENTED	WINGED	KANAKA.	BENUMB
LANDED	RENTER	WINKED	+ARNOLD	BYNAME
LANDES	RINGED	WINNER	BANGLE	CINEMA
LANNER	RINGER	WINTER	BUNDLE	DYNAMO
LENDER	RINKED	WONDER	BUNGLE	MINIMA
LENTEN	RINSED	WONTED	CANDLE	*PANAMA.
LINDEN	RUNNEL	YANKED	CINGLE	AWNING
LINGER	RUNNER	YANKEE	DANDLE	BANANA
LINKED	SANDED	YENNED	DANGLE	BONING
LINNET	SENDER	YONDER.	DINGLE	CANINE
LINTEL	SENSED	BENIGN	+DONALD	CANING
LONGED	SINGED	LINAGE	FINALE	DINING
LONGER	SINGER	MANAGE	FINELY	FINING
LUNGED	SINKER	NONAGE.	FONDLE	HONING
MANGER	SINNED	BUNCHY	FONDLY	LINING
MANNED	SINNER	CONCHA	GENTLE	MINING
MANNER	SINTER	DINGHY	GENTLY	OWNING
MANTEL	SONNET	+GANDHI	HANDLE	PINING
+MANUEL	SUNDER	GUN-SHY	JANGLE	SONANT
MENDED	SUNDEW	PONCHO.	JINGLE	TENANT
+MENDEL	SUNKEN	AGNAIL	JINGLY	TONING
MENSES	SUNNED	AUNTIE	JUNGLE	TUNING
MINCED	SUNSET	BANDIT	JUNGLY	WANING
MINCER	TANDEM	BUNYIP	KINDLE	WINING
MINDED	TANGED	*CANDIA	KINDLY	ZENANA
MINTED	TANKER	CANDID	KINGLY	ZONING.
MINUET	TANNED	CONOID	KINKLE	AMNION
MONGER	TANNER	*DANZIG	LONELY	*BANGOR
MONKEY	TENDED	DENTIL	MANGLE	BENZOL
PANDER	TENDER	DUNLIN	*MANILA	BONBON
PANNED	TENSED	FINNIC	MANTLE	BUNION
PANTED	TENTED	GANOID	MINGLE	CANNON
PANZER	TENTER	LENTIL	*OUNDLE	CANNOT

*CANTON	+SANDRA	BUNKUM	AMOEBA	CLOSET
CANTOR	SENORA	CENSUS	KNOBBY	CLOVEN
CANYON	SENTRY	CINQUE	+PHOEBE	CLOVER
CENSOR	SUNDRY	CONCUR	SNOBBY.	CLOYED
CONDOM	TENURE	CONSUL	AVOUCH	COOKED
CONDOR	TUNDRA	DENGUE	BLOTCH	COOKER
CONVOY	VINERY	DINKUM	BROACH	COOLED
DONJON	WINTRY	FUNGUS	BRONCO	COOLER
FINNOC	ZONARY.	GANGUE	BROOCH	COOPED
HANSOM	BANISH	GENIUS	CHOICE	COOPER
*HENDON	DANISH	HANG-UP	CLOACA	*CROMER
JUNIOR	+DENISE	HONOUR	CROTCH	CROWED
*LONDON	DYNAST	LANGUR	CROUCH	DOOMED
MANIOC	+ERNEST	LINE-UP	GROUCH	DRONED
MENTOR	FINEST	LINGUA	SCONCE	DROVER
MINION	FINISH	MANFUL	SCORCH	ELOPED
MINNOW	HONEST	MANQUE	SCOTCH	ERODED
MONGOL	MONISM	OMNIUM	SLOUCH	EVOKED
+MONROE	MONIST	SINFUL.	SMOOCH.	FLORET
PENNON	PUNISH	TONGUE	BLONDE	FLOWED
PINION	SANEST	VENOUS	BLOODY	FLOWER
RANDOM	TANIST	VINOUS	BROODY	FOOLED
RANSOM	VANISH	WIND-UP.	CLOUDY	FOOTED
SENIOR	VENOSE.	*GENEVA.	+ISOLDE	FOOTER
SENSOR	AGNATE	RENOWN	SHOODY.	FROZEN
SUN-GOD	BINATE	SINEWY.	ADORER	GAOLER
TENDON	BONITO	ANNEXE.	APOGEE	GLOVED
TENSOR	+CANUTE	IONIZE	ATONED	GLOVER
TINPOT	DENOTE		AVOCET	GLOWED
VENDOR	DONATE	AMORAL	AVOSET	GLOWER
WANTON	FINITE	ANORAK	AVOWED	GROCER
WINDOW	GUNITE	APODAL	AWOKEN	GROPED
WINNOW.	IGNITE	ATONAL	*AZORES	GROVEL
CANOPY.	INNATE	AVOWAL	BLOWER	GROWER
BINARY	LANATE	BAOBAB	BOOKED	HOODED
CANARD	LENGTH	CHORAL	BOOMED	HOOFED
CANARY	LENITY	DEODAR	BOOMER	HOOKED
CENTRE	LUNATE	+DVORAK	BOOTED	HOOKER
CONTRA	MINUTE	FLORAL	BOOTEE	HOOKEY
DENARY	NINETY	GLOBAL	BOOZED	HOOPED
FINERY	ORNATE	HOOKAH	BOOZER	HOOTED
GANTRY	SANITY	HOORAY	BROKEN	HOOTER
GENERA	SENATE	ISOBAR	BROKER	HOOVED
GENTRY	SONATA	LOOFAH	BUOYED	+HOOVER
HUNGRY	TENUTO	SLOGAN	CHOKED	HOOVES
IGNORE	TONITE	+THOMAS	CHOKER	+IMOGEN
MANURE	VANITY	THORAX	CHOLER	IRONED
NONARY	ZENITH	TROJAN	CHOREA	ISOMER
PANTRY	ZONATE.	TWO-WAY	CHOSEN	+LIONEL
PENURY	ADNOUN	YEOMAN.	CLOSED	LOOKED

LOOKER	STOKER	COOLIE	POORLY	DROSSY
LOOMED	STOLEN	ENOSIS	ROOTLE	DROWSE
LOOPED	STONED	EROTIC	SHOULD	DROWSY
LOOPER	STORED	EXOTIC	SLOWLY	EGOISM
LOOSED	STOREY	FLORID	TOOTLE	EGOIST
LOOSEN	STOWED	FLORIN	TWO-PLY	FLOSSY
LOOSER	TOOLER	FROLIC	TWOULD	FROWST
LOOTER	TOOTED	+GLORIA	WHOLLY	GLOSSY
MOONED	TROVER	GNOMIC	WOOLLY.	GROUSE
MOORED	TROWEL	GNOSIS	GLOOMY	+PROUST
MOOTED	+VIOLET	ICONIC	STORMY.	SCOUSE
NOOSED	WHORED	IRONIC	ABOUND	SPOUSE
PHONED	WOODED	KAOLIN	AMOUNT	TAOISM
PHONEY	WOODEN	LOOK-IN	ANOINT	WHOOSH.
PIOLET	WOOFER	MYOPIA	AROUND	AGOUTI
PLOVER	ZOOMED.	MYOPIC	COOING	+BRONTE
POOLED	CHOUGH	NIOBIC	GROUND	DROUTH
POORER	CLOUGH	PHOBIA	GROYNE	FROSTY
PROBED	ENOUGH	PHOBIC	MOOING	GROTTO
PROPEL	+GEORGE	PHONIC	THORNY	GROTTY
PROPER	GROGGY	PROFIT	WOOING	GROWTH
PROSER	PLOUGH	PROLIX	+YVONNE.	KNOTTY
PROVED	*SLOUGH	PROSIT	+CRONOS	*OPORTO
PROVEN	SPONGE	ROOKIE	GNOMON	PRONTO
QUOTER	SPONGY	SCORIA	HOODOO	SMOOTH
REOPEN	STODGE	STOLID	HOOPOE	SNOOTY
*RHODES	STODGY	TROPIC	ISOPOD	SNOTTY
RIOTER	STOOGE	UTOPIA	PHOTON	SPORTY
ROOFED	THOUGH	VIOLIN	PROTON	SPOTTY.
ROOKED	TROUGH.	*YEOVIL.	TROGON	+AEOLUS
ROOMED	BROCHE	*SKOPJE.	VOODOO.	BLOW-UP
ROOTED	CLOCHE	+BROOKE	CHOPPY	BROGUE
SCORED	CLOTHE	CROAKY	CROUPY	CHORUS
SCORER	+CLOTHO	CROCKY	FLOPPY	CROCUS
SCOTER	FROTHY	SPOOKY	PROMPT	DROGUE
SHODED	QUOTHA	STOCKY	SLOPPY	EXODUS
SHORED	SOOTHE	TROIKA.	THORPE	HOOKUP
SHOVED	TROPHY.	+APOLLO	TROPPO	IDOLUM
SHOVEL	+ADONIS	BOODLE	TROUPE.	QUORUM.
SHOWED	AGONIC	*BOOTLE	ABOARD	EVOLVE
SHOWER	ANOMIA	BROLLY	FLOURY	GROOVE
SLOPED	ATOMIC	COOLLY	YAOURT.	GROOVY.
SLOVEN	ATONIC	DOODLE	AROUSE	ANONYM
SLOWER	BIOTIC	FOOZLE	BIOPSY	EPONYM
SMOKED	BIOTIN	GOODLY	BLOUSE	POOGYE.
SMOKER	BOOKIE	GOOGLY	BROWSE	BRONZE
SNORED	BROMIC	HOOP-LA	CHOOSE	FLOOZY
SNOWED	+CHOPIN	NOODLE	CHOOSY	FROWZY
SOONER	CHORIC	PEOPLE	CROSSE	SNOOZE
SPOKEN	COOKIE	POODLE	DROPSY	

APPEAL	LAPPET	PAPAIN	RAPING	REPOSE
APPEAR	LAPSED	PEPSIN	REPENT	RIPEST
ESPIAL	LIPPED	PEPTIC	REPINE	TYPIST
HEPTAD	LOPPED	PIPKIN	ROPING	UPPISH.
ORPHAN	MAPPED	PIPPIN	SUPINE	BYPATH
POPLAR	MOPPED	POPLIN	TAPING	+CAPOTE
REPEAL	MOPPET	REPAID	TOPING	DEPUTE
REPEAT	*NAPLES	REPAIR	TYPING	DEPUTY
REPLAY	NAPPED	SEPSIS	WIPING.	IMPUTE
RIP-SAW	NEPHEW	SEPTIC	ALPHOS	PUPATE
SEPTAL	NIPPED	+SOPHIA.	CAPTOR	REPUTE
TIPCAT	NIPPER	COPULA	DEPLOY	UPPITY
TOP-HAT.	OSPREY	CUPOLA	EMPLOY	WAPITI
ALPACA	PEPPED	DAPPLE	LAPDOG	+ZAPATA.
ASPECT	PEPPER	DIPOLE	LEPTON	COP-OUT
COPECK	PIPPED	HOPPLE	RAPTOR	CUPFUL
DEPICT	POPPED	IMPALE	SIPHON	*CYPRUS
EXPECT	POPPET	NAPALM	SYPHON	GYPSUM
IMPACT	PUPPED	NIPPLE	TIPTOE	PEPLUM
KOPECK	PUPPET	RAPTLY	TIPTOP.	POPGUN
PAPACY	RAPIER	RIPELY	AMPERE	SEPTUM
UNPACK	RAPPED	RIPPLE	APPORT	TYPHUS
UNPICK.	RIPPED	RIPPLY	ASPIRE	UNPLUG
IMPEDE.	SAPPED	SUPPLE	DEPART	VAPOUR.
CAPPED	SAPPER	SUPPLY	DEPORT	IMPAWN.
CIPHER	SEPTET	TIPPLE	DOPTRE	ZEPHYR
COPIED	SIPPED	TOPPLE.	EMPIRE	
COPIER	SIPPET	OEPEMA.	EXPERT	LOQUAT.
COPPED	SOPPED	ALPINE	EXPIRE	COQUET
COPPER	SUPPED	APPEND	EXPIRY	PIQUED
CUPPED	SUPPER	+CAPONE	EXPORT	PIQUET
CUPPER	TAPPED	COPING	IMPART	ROQUET
CYPHER	TAPPET	+DAPHNE	IMPORT	SEQUEL.
DAPPER	TIPPED	DEPEND	IMPURE	ACQUIT
DIPPED	TIPPER	DEPONE	POPERY	LIQUID
DIPPER	TIPPET	DOPING	REPORT	MAQUIS
DUPLET	TOPPED	DUPING	+RUPERT	SEQUIN.
DUPLEX	TOPPER	*EPPING	SUPERB	LIQUOR
ESPIED	YAPPED	EXPAND	UMPIRE.	
GOPHER	ZIPPED	EXPEND	BY-PASS	ABROAD
HAPPED	ZIPPER.	GAPING	DEPOSE	+ADRIAN
HAPPEN	TIP-OFF	HOPING	EXPOSE	AERIAL
HIPPED	TYPIFY.	IMPEND	IMPISH	AIRMAN
HOPPED	IMPUGN.	IMPING	IMPOSE	AIR-SAC
HOPPER	COPTIC	JAPING	IMPOST	AIRWAY
HYPHEN	CUPRIC	LOPING	OPPOSE	ARREAR
+KEPLER	CUP-TIE	MOPING	PAPIST	BARMAN
KIPPED	IMPAIR	ORPINE	POPISH	BOREAL
KIPPER	NAPKIN	PIPING	RAPIST	BUREAU
LAPPED	ORPHIC	RAPINE	REPAST	BURIAL

171

BURLAP	TARMAC	BARBED	CURDED	+HERMES
BURSAR	TARPAN	BARBEL	CURFEW	HERPES
BY-ROAD	TARSAL	BARBER	CURLED	HORDED
CARFAX	TARTAN	BARBET	CURLER	HORNED
CARMAN	TARTAR	BARGEE	CURLEW	HORNET
CARNAL	TERGAL	BARKER	CURSED	HORSED
CARPAL	TERNAL	BARLEY	CURVED	HURLER
CORBAN	THREAD	*BARNET	CURVET	HURLEY
CORRAL	THREAT	BARRED	DARKEN	*ISRAEL
DORIAN	THROAT	BARREL	DARKER	JARRED
DORSAL	TURBAN	BARREN	DARNED	JERKED
*DURBAN	TYRIAN	BARTER	DARNEL	*JERSEY
DURBAR	UNREAD	BERBER	DARNER	KERBED
*DURHAM	UNREAL	*BERGEN	DARTED	KERMES
EARWAX	UPROAR	BORDER	+DOREEN	KERNEL
FERIAL	VERBAL	*BORNEO	DORMER	KERSEY
FIRMAN	VERNAL	BURDEN	*DORSET	LARDED
FORMAL	*WARSAW.	BURGEE	EARNED	LARDER
FORMAT	ENROBE	BURIED	FARMER	LARGER
GERMAN	HEREBY	BURNED	FERRET	LARKED
HERBAL	SCRIBE	BURNER	FIRMER	LORDED
HEREAT	STROBE	BURNET	FORCED	LURKER
HURRAH	UNROBE	BURPED	FORDED	MARKED
HURRAY	ZARIBA.	CAREEN	FORGED	MARKER
INROAD	*AFRICA	CAREER	FORGER	MARKET
*JORDAN	BORSCH	CARIES	FORGET	MARLED
LARIAT	CURACY	*CARMEL	FORKED	MARRED
LARVAE	DIRECT	+CARMEN	FORMED	MARTEN
LARVAL	ENRICH	CARPED	FORMER	MARVEL
+MARIAN	+HORACE	CARPEL	FURLED	MERCER
MERMAN	KIRSCH	CARPET	FURRED	MERGED
+MIRIAM	PIRACY	CARREL	GARBED	MERGER
+MORGAN	SPRUCE	CARTED	GARDEN	*MERSEY
MORTAL	STRICT	CARTEL	GARNER	MORSEL
MORTAR	STRUCK	CERMET	GARNET	MURDER
*MURRAY	THRICE	CERTES	GARRET	+MURIEL
MYRIAD	+YORICK	CORBEL	GARTER	NARKED
NORMAL	*ZURICH.	CORDED	GERMEN	NERVED
+NORMAN	ABRADE	CORKED	GIRDED	NURSED
*NORWAY	DERIDE	CORKER	GIRDER	PARCEL
PARIAH	DIRNDL	CORNEA	GORGED	PARGET
PARIAN	DORADO	CORNED	GORGET	PARKED
PORTAL	PARADE	CORNEL	HARDEN	PARLEY
PURDAH	PARODY	CORNER	HARDER	PARSEC
SCREAM	STRIDE	CORNET	HARKEN	PARSED
SERIAL	STRODE	CORSET	HARMED	PARSEE
SPREAD	TEREDO	CORTEX	HARPED	PARTED
STREAK	TIRADE.	+CORTEZ	HARPER	PERKED
STREAM	AGREED	CORVES	+HARVEY	PERMED
SURTAX	AIR-BED	CURBED	HERDED	PORKER

172

PORTED	WARDER	*DARWIN	PERUKE	UNROLL
PORTER	WARIER	DERAIL	SHRIKE	UNRULY
PURGED	WARMED	DERMIS	STRAKE	VERILY
PURLED	WARMER	DERRIS	STRIKE	VIRILE
PURLER	WARNED	EARWIG	STROKE.	WARBLE
PURRED	WARPED	FERRIC	AIRILY	WARILY
PURSED	WARRED	FERRIS	BARELY	WARMLY
PURSER	+WARREN	FERVID	BURBLE	WIRILY.
PURVEY	WORDED	FIRKIN	BURGLE	BIREME
SARSEN	WORKED	FORBID	CIRCLE	CHROME
SCREED	WORKER	FORMIC	CURDLE	CORYMB
SCREEN	WORMED	GARLIC	CURTLY	+JEREMY
SCRIED	WORSEN	*HARRIS	DARKLY	+JEROME
SERIES	YORKER	HEREIN	DIRELY	SCRIMP
SERVED	ZEROED.	HERMIT	EERILY	SHRIMP
SERVER	ADRIFT	HERNIA	FERULA	STROMA.
SHRIEK	AERIFY	HEROIC	FERULE	AIRING
SORBET	BEREFT	HEROIN	FIRMLY	ARRANT
SORREL	CARAFE	HORRID	GARBLE	BARING
SORTED	FAR-OFF	JERKIN	GARGLE	BARONY
SORTER	PURIFY	KERMIS	+GERALD	*BERING
STREET	RAREFY	KERRIE	GIRDLE	BORING
SURFER	SCRUFF	+MARCIA	GURGLE	CARING
SURGED	SHRIFT	MARGIN	HARDLY	CORING
*SURREY	STRAFE	+MARTIN	+HAROLD	CORONA
SURVEY	STRIFE	+MERLIN	HERALD	CURING
TARGET	TARIFF	MORBID	HURDLE	DARING
TARRED	THRIFT	+MORRIS	HURTLE	DURING
TARTED	VERIFY.	NEREID	KIRTLE	EARING
TERCET	BORAGE	NORDIC	LORDLY	ERRAND
TERMED	ENRAGE	PARKIN	MARBLE	ERRANT
TUREEN	FORAGE	PARVIS	MERELY	ERRING
TURFED	FOREGO	PERMIT	MORALE	FARINA
*TURKEY	GARAGE	PURLIN	+MYRTLE	FARING
TURNED	MIRAGE	SORDID	PAROLE	FERINE
+TURNER	VIRAGO.	SORTIE	PARTLY	FIRING
TURRET	+BERTHA	SPRAIN	PERTLY	GERUND
TURVES	EARTHY	STRAIN	PORTLY	GORING
UNREEL	MARSHY	STRAIT	PURELY	HARING
VARIED	+MARTHA	TARSIA	PURPLE	HIRING
VARLET	WORTHY.	TOROID	RARELY	LARYNX
VERGED	ADROIT	TORPID	SCROLL	LURING
VERGER	AFRAID	TORRID	SHRILL	+MARINA
VERSED	BARDIC	TURBID	SORELY	MARINE
VERSET	+BARRIE	TURGID	STROLL	MERINO
VERTEX	*BERLIN	TURNIP	SURELY	MIRING
VERVET	BIRDIE	VERMIN	TARTLY	MURINE
VORTEX	CERVIX	+VIRGIL	THRALL	OARING
WARDED	CORBIE	*VIRGIN.	THRILL	PARENT
WARDEN	CORRIE	EUREKA	TURTLE	PARING

PORING	HEREOF	+SARTRE	CURATE	ARRIVE
SARONG	HERIOT	TORERO.	DERATE	DERIVE
SERENE	HORROR	ACROSS	ERRATA	SHRIVE
SHRANK	JARGON	AFRESH	FERITY	SHROVE
SHRINE	*JARROW	AORIST	GYRATE	STRIVE
SHRINK	JERBOA	ARREST	HERETO	STROVE
SHRUNK	*MARLOW	AURIST	KARATE	THRIVE
SIRING	MARMOT	CARESS	PARITY	THROVE.
SPRANG	MAROON	+CARUSO	PIRATE	ARROWY
SPRING	MARROW	CERISE	PURITY	SCRAWL
SPRINT	MIRROR	CHRISM	RARITY	SCREWY
SPRUNG	MORMON	+CHRIST	RARITY	SHREWD
STRAND	MORROW	CORPSE	SCROTA	SPRAWL
STRING	NARROW	CURTSY	SPRITE	STRAWY
STRONG	PARDON	DURESS	STRATA	STREWN
STRUNG	PARROT	EGRESS	STRATH	THROWN
SYRINX	PARSON	FOREST	SURETY	*VYRNWY.
THRONE	PERIOD	GARISH	VERITY	ARROYO
THRONG	PERRON	HARASS	WARMTH.	MARTYR.
TIRING	PERSON	HERESY	AIR-GUN	COROZO
TYRANT	SERMON	INRUSH	+ATREUS	CORYZA
*TYRONE	SORROW	JURIST	AUROUS	
*VERONA	TERROR	LYRIST	BARIUM	
WERENT	TORPOR	MORASS	BARQUE	BASIAL
WIRING.	TURBOT	MOROSE	CARPUS	BUSMAN
*BARROW	UPROOT	OGRESS	CERIUM	CASUAL
+BARTOK	+WARHOL	OGRISH	CIRCUM	COSTAL
BARTON	YARROW	ONRUSH	CIRCUS	CO-STAR
BARYON	ZIRCON.	PARISH	CIRQUE	CUSHAT
BORROW	ABRUPT	PERISH	CIRRUS	DISBAR
BORZOI	CERIPH	PERUSE	CORIUM	DISCAL
BURBOT	ENRAPT	PHRASE	CORPUS	DISMAL
BURROW	+EUROPA	PUREST.	CURIUM	DISMAY
*BURTON	*EUROPE	PURISM	DORSUM	DISTAL
CARBON	PARAPH	RAREST	FURFUR	DOSSAL
CARBOY	PYROPE	SOREST	LARRUP	FESTAL
*CARLOW	SCRAPE	STRESS	MARAUD	FISCAL
CARROT	SCRIPT	SUREST	MORGUE	GAS-BAG
CARTON	SERAPE	THRASH	MURMUR	GASMAN
CORDON	SERAPH	THRESH	POROUS	HUSSAR
CURSOR	STRIPE	THRUSH	PURSUE	INSPAN
FARROW	STRIPY	THRUST	SEROUS	+JOSIAH
FORGOT	SYRUPY	UNREST	SHROUD	LASCAR
FURROW	THRIPS	UPRUSH.	SIRIUS	MESCAL
GERMON	UNRIPE.	ACRITA	SPROUT	MISHAP
+GORDON	AURORA	AERATE	*STROUD	MISLAY
+GORGON	CURARE	BARYTA	TARSUS	MISSAL
HARLOT	FURORE	BERATE	TORQUE	*MUSCAT
*HARLOW	HORARY	BORATE	TURN-UP	*NASSAU
*HARROW	ORRERY	CERATE	VERSUS	+PASCAL
			VIRTUE.	POSTAL

174

RASCAL	*EASTER	LUSTED	TASKED	+JUSTIN
RESEAT	ENSUED	MASHED	TASSEL	LASSIE
ROSEAL	FASCES	MASKED	TASTED	MASHIE
UNSEAL	FASTEN	MASKER	TASTER	MASSIF
UNSEAT	FASTER	MASSED	TESTED	MASTIC
VASSAL	FESTER	MASTED	TESTER	MISFIT
VESTAL	FISHER	MASTER	TESTES	MOSAIC
VISUAL	FISTED	MESHED	TOSSED	MUSLIM
YES-MAN.	FOSTER	+MESMER	TUSKED	MUSLIN
BISECT	FUSSED	MESSED	TUSKER	MYSTIC
INSECT	GASHED	MISLED	*ULSTER	PASSIM
VESICA.	GAS-JET	MISSED	VASTER	PISTIL
BESIDE	GASKET	MISSEL	+VESPER	+RUSKIN
INSIDE	GASPED	MISTED	VESSEL	*RUSSIA
RESIDE	GASPER	MISTER	VESTED	RUSTIC
UPSIDE.	GASSED	MOSLEM	WASHED	SISKIN
ANSWER	GOSPEL	MUSKET	WASHER	TASSIE
+AUSTEN	GUSHER	MUSSEL	WASTED	UNSAID
BASHED	GUSSET	MUSTER	WASTER	UNSHIP
BASKED	HASHED	NESTED	+WESLEY	VESPID
BASKET	HASPED	NOSHED	WISHED	VISCID.
BASSET	HASTED	OUSTED	XYSTER.	BASALT
BASTED	HASTEN	OYSTER	GASIFY	BASELY
BESEEM	HISSED	PASSED	OSSIFY	BUSILY
BESTED	HOSIER	PASSER	UNSAFE.	BUSTLE
BUSHED	HOSTEL	PASTED	ASSIGN	+CASALS
BUSHEL	HUSHED	PASTEL	DESIGN	CASTLE
*BUSHEY	HUSKED	PESTER	DOSAGE	COSILY
BUSIED	INSTEP	PISCES	ENSIGN	COSTLY
BUSKER	ISSUED	POSSET	RESIGN	EASILY
CASHED	+JASPER	POSTED	VISAGE.	ENSILE
CASHEW	JESTED	POSTER	ASSAIL	HUSTLE
CASKET	JESTER	PUSHED	*AUSTIN	INSOLE
CASTER	JOSHED	PUSHER	BESTIR	INSULT
COSHER	KISMET	RASHER	BUSKIN	ITSELF
COSSET	KISSED	RASPED	CASEIN	JOSTLE
COSTED	KISSER	RASTER	CASSIA	JUSTLY
COSTER	KOSHER	RESTED	COSMIC	LASTLY
CUSPED	LASHED	RISKED	CYSTIC	MISTLE
CUSSED	LASHER	ROSIER	DISTIL	MUSCLE
DASHED	LASTED	ROSTER	DOSSIL	MYSELF
DASHER	+LESLEY	RUSHED	FASCIA	NESTLE
DISHED	LESSEE	RUSHEN	FISTIC	PESTLE
+DISNEY	LESSEN	RUSSET	FOSSIL	POSHLY
DISPEL	LESSER	RUSTED	FUSTIC	RASHLY
DOSSED	+LESTER	SESTET	GOSSIP	RESILE
DOSSER	LISPED	SISTER	HISPID	RESULT
DUSTED	LISTED	SUSSED	INSTIL	ROSILY
DUSTER	LISTEN	*SUSSEX	+JESSIE	RUSTLE
EASIER	+LISTER	SYSTEM	JESUIT	TUSSLE

+URSULA	WISDOM.	DISBUD	DETECT	HATTER
VASTLY	+JOSEPH.	DISCUS	ENTICE	HITHER
WISELY.	ABSORB	DISEUR	INTACT	+HITLER
ASSUME	ABSURD	FESCUE	NOTICE	HITTER
RESUME	ADSORB	+JOSHUA	OPTICS	HOTBED
SESAME.	ASSERT	MASQUE	PUTSCH	HOTTED
ABSENT	ASSORT	MISSUS	UNTACK.	HOTTER
ARSINE	ASSURE	MOSQUE	BETIDE	HUTTED
ASSENT	BISTRE	MUSEUM	UNTIDY.	JETTED
CASING	+CASTRO	POSEUR	AETHER	JITTER
CASINO	DESCRY	POSSUM	ANTHEM	JOTTED
COSINE	DESERT	RESCUE	ANTHER	JOTTER
EASING	DESIRE	RISQUE	ANTLER	JUTTED
FUSING	DISARM	TISSUE.	+ATTLEE	KITTED
HOSING	ENSURE	DISOWN.	BATHER	KITTEN
INSANE	INSERT	ASSIZE	BATTED	LATEEN
LOSING	INSURE		BATTEN	LATHER
MUSING	LUSTRE	ACTUAL	BATTER	LATTEN
MUSTNT	MESSRS	ANTIAR	BETHEL	LATTER
NOSING	MISERE	ASTRAL	BETTED	LETTER
POSING	MISERY	ASTRAY	BETTER	LITTER
RESENT	PASTRY	BATMAN	BITTEN	+LUTHER
RISING	RESORB	BETRAY	BITTER	MATTED
TISANE	RESORT	CAT-NAP	BOTHER	MATTER
UNSUNG	ROSARY	COTTAR	BUTLER	MITRED
URSINE.	ROSTRA	ENTRAP	BUTTER	MITTEN
BESTOW	UNSURE	FETIAL	COTTER	MOTHER
BISHOP	VESTRY	GATEAU	CUTLER	MOTLEY
*BOSTON	VISARD.	HETMAN	CUTLET	MUTTER
CASTOR	ASSESS	JETSAM	CUTTER	NATTER
COSMOS	*ASSISI	KIT-BAG	DITHER	NETHER
CUSTOM	ASSIST	LETHAL	DOTTED	NETTED
DESPOT	BASEST	*LYTHAM	EITHER	NUTMEG
FUSION	DESIST	MUTUAL	ENTREE	NUTTER
HYSSOP	DISUSE	+NATHAN	ESTEEM	OSTLER
*LESBOS	INSIST	OUTLAW	+ESTHER	OUTLET
LESION	MISUSE	OUTLAY	FATHER	OUTSET
LESSON	OBSESS	OUTRAN	FATTED	PATTED
LESSOR	RESIST	PATHAN	FATTEN	PATTEN
*LISBON	WISEST.	PITMAN	FATTER	PATTER
LISSOM	ASSETS	POTMAN	FETTER	PETREL
MASCOT	ERSATZ	RATTAN	FITTED	PETTED
MUSK-OX	PESETA	RITUAL	FITTER	PITIED
PASTOR	PUSHTU.	SATRAP	GATHER	PITTED
PISTOL	BASQUE	TETRAD	GETTER	POTEEN
PISTON	BISQUE	+TITIAN	GOTTEN	POTTED
UNSHOD	BYSSUS	WITHAL.	GUTTED	POTTER
UNSTOP	CASQUE	ATTACH	GUTTER	PUTTEE
UPSHOT	CISTUS	ATTACK	HATRED	PUTTER
VISION	CUSCUS	DETACH	HATTED	RATHER

RATTED	DETAIL	SETTLE	*OSTEND	DOTARD
RATTER	DETAIN	TATTLE	OUTING	ENTIRE
ROTTED	ENTAIL	TITTLE	PATENT	EXTORT
ROTTEN	GOTHIC	UNTOLD	PATINA	FUTURE
ROTTER	HATPIN	VITALS	POTENT	INTERN
RUTTED	MATRIC	WATTLE.	RATING	MATURE
SATEEN	MATRIX	ASTHMA	RETINA	NATURE
SETTEE	METRIC	AUTUMN	ROTUND	NOTARY
SETTER	MYTHIC	ENTOMB	SATING	OUTCRY
SITTER	NITRIC	ULTIMA	SITING	RETARD
SUTLER	NITWIT	ULTIMO.	TOTING	RETIRE
SUTTEE	NUTRIA	ACTING	VOTING.	RETORT
TATTED	OBTAIN	+ANTONY	ACTION	RETURN
TATTER	OUTBID	ATTEND	AUTHOR	ROTARY
TETHER	OUTDID	ATTUNE	BATHOS	SATIRE
TETTER	OUTFIT	BATING	BETOOK	+SATURN
TITFER	OUTWIT	BETONY	BOTTOM	SUTURE
TITLED	PATHIC	BITING	BUTTON	UPTURN
TITTER	PATOIS	BOTANY	CATION	VOTARY
TOTHER	PUTRID	BUTANE	CITRON	WATERY.
*TOTNES	RETAIL	CETANE	COTTON	ARTIST
TOTTED	RETAIN	CITING	FATHOM	ATTEST
TOTTER	TITBIT	DATING	HOTPOT	AUTISM
TUTTED	WITHIN.	DETENT	HOT-ROD	DETEST
UNTIED	BETAKE	DITONE	JETTON	FETISH
VETOED	INTAKE	DOTING	LOTION	LATEST
VETTED	RETAKE	EATING	MATRON	MUTISM
WETHER	UPTAKE.	EXTANT	METEOR	OBTUSE
WETTED	ARTILY	EXTEND	METHOD	POTASH
WETTER	+ATTILA	EXTENT	MOTION	SETOSE.
WITHER	BATTLE	GATING	MUTTON	ASTUTE
ZITHER.	BOTFLY	HATING	NATION	ENTITY
CUT-OFF	BOTTLE	INTEND	NOTION	ESTATE
NOTIFY	CATTLE	INTENT	OPTION	MUTATE
RATIFY	CUTELY	INTONE	PATHOS	PETITE
SET-OFF.	DOTTLE	KETONE	PATROL	POTATO
DOTAGE	FETTLE	LATENT	PATRON	ROTATE.
POTAGE.	FUTILE	LITANY	PETROL	ANTRUM
BITCHY	KETTLE	LUTING	POTION	ARTFUL
BOTCHY	KITTLE	MATING	PUTLOG	+ARTHUR
CATCHY	LATELY	MATINS	PYTHON	BATTUE
LITCHI	LITTLE	METING	RATION	CATGUT
PATCHY	METTLE	MUTANT	RETOOK	CITRUS
PITCHY	MOTTLE	MUTING	RETROD	CUT-OUT
TETCHY.	NETTLE	MUTINY	*SUTTON	DETOUR
*ANTRIM	+PETULA	NATANT	TATTOO.	FITFUL
+ASTRID	POT-ALE	NOTING	ECTYPE.	LITMUS
ATTAIN	RATTLE	OCTANE	ARTERY	OUTPUT
CATKIN	ROTULA	OPTANT	ASTERN	OUTRUN
CITRIC	RUTILE	OPTING	ATTIRE	SET-OUT

177

TITTUP	PAUNCH	PLUMED	TOUCHY.	GRUMPY
UNTRUE.	POUNCE	POURER	+ANUBIS	SCULPT
ACTIVE	SLUICE	POUTED	BOUGIE	STUMPY.
DATIVE	SMUTCH	POUTER	COUSIN	FLURRY
MOTIVE	SOURCE	PRUNED	+LAURIE	LOUVRE
NATIVE	STUCCO.	+REUBEN	PLUG-IN	SCURRY
OCTAVE	MAUNDY	ROUGED	STUDIO	SLURRY
OCTAVO	MOULDY	ROUSER	STUPID.	SQUARE
VOTIVE.	STURDY	ROUTED	CHUNKY	SQUIRE
*OTTAWA	ZOUNDS.	SAUCED	PLUCKY.	SQUIRM
UPTOWN.	ABUSED	SAUCER	BAUBLE	SQUIRT
METHYL	ACUMEN	SOUPED	CAUDLE	+STUART.
	AMULET	SOURED	COUPLE	AGUISH
*BHUTAN	AMUSED	SOUSED	DOUBLE	BLUISH
BRUMAL	*BRUNEI	SPUMED	DOUBLY	BOURSE
BRUTAL	+BRUNEL	TAUTEN	DOURLY	BRUISE
CAUDAL	CAUSED	TAUTER	FOULLY	CLUMSY
CAUSAL	CAUTER	TOUPEE	+GAULLE	COURSE
COUGAR	DAUBED	TOURED	GLUMLY	CRUISE
CRURAL	+DAUDET	TOURER	HOURLY	+LOUISE
+DOUGAL	DEUCED	TOUTED	LOUDLY	MOUSSE
FAUCAL	DOUSED	UNUSED	ROUBLE	SQUASH
FEUDAL	DRUPEL	USURER.	SMUGLY	SQUISH
FRUGAL	EDUCED	FLUFFY	SNUGLY	*THURSO
NEURAL	ELUDED	SCURFY	SOURLY	TRUEST
NOUGAT	EXUDED	STUFFY.	SQUALL	TPUISM.
OCULAR	FAUCET	DRUDGE	SQUILL	ACUITY
PLURAL	FEUDED	GRUDGE	TAUTLY	BOUNTY
SQUEAK	FLUKED	LOUNGE	THUSLY	COUNTY
SQUEAL	FLUTED	PLUNGE	TOUSLE.	CRUSTY
TOUCAN	FOULED	SLUDGE	CHUMMY	EQUATE
+TRUMAN	FRUTEX	SMUDGE	CRUMMY	EQUITY
UVULAR.	GAUGED	SMUDGY	PLUMMY	FAULTY
CHUBBY	GAUGER	SPURGE	SCUMMY	FOURTH
CRUMBY	GLUTEN	TRUDGE.	SLUMMY	FRUITY
GRUBBY	GOUGED	BOUGHT	SQUAMA	JAUNTY
+STUBBS	HAULED	BRUSHY	ZEUGMA.	MOUNTY
STUBBY.	HOUSED	CAUGHT	ALUMNI	SMUTTY
BOUNCE	INURED	DOUCHE	DOUANE	TRUSTY.
BOUNCY	LAUDED	DOUGHY	EQUINE	+BRUTUS
BRUNCH	LAUREL	FOUGHT	FLUENT	CAUCUS
CHURCH	LOUDER	GA'UCHE	IGUANA	PRUNUS
CLUTCH	LOUVER	GAUCHO	SQUINT	SPUTUM
CRUNCH	MAULED	NAUGHT	TRUANT.	TAURUS.
CRUTCH	MAUSER	NOUGHT	COUPON	SCURVY
HAUNCH	MOUSER	PLUSHY	NEURON	ZOUAVE.
JOUNCE	NAUSEA	SLUSHY	STUPOR	SQUAWK.
LAUNCE	NEUTER	SOUGHT	TAUTOG	*RYUKYU
LAUNCH	PAUPER	TAUGHT	TEUTON.	
NAUTCH	PAUSED	TOUCHE	FRUMPY	CAVEAT

CAVIAR	NOVENA	COWMAN	HAWING	
JOVIAL	PAVANE	DEWLAP	HEWING	SEXUAL.
JOVIAN	RAVINE	DOWLAS	JAWING	*MEXICO.
REVEAL	RAVING	ENWRAP	LOWING	TUXEDO.
+VIVIAN.	RIVING	GEWGAW	MEWING	DEXTER
ADVICE	ROVING	HAW-HAW	MOWING	+HUXLEY
DEVICE	SAVANT	HOWDAH	PAWING	SEXIER
NOVICE	SAVING	UNWRAP.	+ROWENA	SEXTET
VIVACE.	WAVING.	THWACK.	ROWING	TAXIED.
DIVIDE	+PAVLOV.	BAWLED	SAWING	SEXILY.
INVADE	ADVERB	BOW-LEG	SEWING	MAXIMA.
*NEVADA.	ADVERT	BOWLER	SOWING	AUXINS
ENVIED	CAVERN	DAWNED	TAWING	BOXING
LEVIED	CAVORT	DOWNED	UNWIND	FIXING
REVIEW	COVERT	DOWSED	VOWING	FOXING
REVVED	DIVERS	DOWSER	YAWING.	HEXANE
SOVIET	DIVERT	*FAWLEY	BOW-WOW	+MAXINE
+XAVIER.	GOVERN	FAWNED	COWBOY	MIXING
VIVIFY.	INVERT	FAWNER	COW-POX	PYXING
RAVAGE	LIVERY	FOWLER	KOWTOW	*SAXONY
SAVAGE.	REVERE	HAWKER	+NEWTON	SEXING
DEVOID	REVERS	HAWSER	POW-WOW.	TAXING
LOVE-IN	REVERT	HOWLED	UNWEPT.	VEXING
UNVEIL.	SAVORY	HOWLER	BEWARE	WAXING.
INVOKE	SEVERE	LAWYER	BOWERY	*BUXTON
REVOKE.	*SEVERN	PAWNED	BYWORD	+CAXTON
LIVELY	TAVERN	PEWTER	COWARD	SEXPOT
LOVELY	WYVERN.	POWDER	+EDWARD	SEXTON.
REVILE	ADVISE	SAWNEY	+HOWARD	DEXTRO
REVOLT.	DEVISE	SAWYER	INWARD	LUXURY.
ADVENT	DIVEST	YAWNED	*NEWARK	HEXOSE.
ALVINE	INVEST	YOWLED.	ONWARD	FIXATE
BOVINE	LAVISH	SEWAGE	REWARD	FIXITY
CAVING	RAVISH	TOWAGE.	TAWDRY	LAXITY
COVING	REVISE.	BEWAIL	THWART	LUXATE
DIVINE	BOVATE	BOW-TIE	TOWARD	
DIVING	CAVITY	COWRIE	UNWARY	*CAYMAN
GIVING	DEVOTE	*HAWAII	UNWORN	FLYMAN
GYVING	INVITE	*KUWAIT.	UPWARD.	HEYDAY
*HAVANA	LEVITE	BOWELS	FEWEST	LAYMAN
HAVENT	LEVITY	DAWDLE	JEWESS	WAYLAY.
HAVING	SAVATE.	LEWDLY	JEWISH	DRY-ICE
HIVING	DEVOUR	*ORWELL	LOWEST	DAY-BED
INVENT	DEVOUT	+OSWALD	NEWEST	GEYSER
+IRVING	FAVOUR	SAW-FLY	NOWISE	HOYDEN
JIVING	SAVOUR.	+SEWELL	UNWISE.	KAYOED
LEVANT	REVIVE	UNWELL.	LAWFUL.	+KEYNES
LIVING		BOWING	INWOVE.	*KHYBER
LOVING	BOWMAN	COWING	ALWAYS	*LEYDEN
MOVING	BOW-SAW	+EDWINA	NOWAYS	MAYHEM

179

OXYGEN	BOYISH	HAZARD	DOTARD	BERATE
RHYMED	DRYISH	LIZARD	+EDWARD	BETAKE
RHYMER	MAYEST.	+MOZART	ERRAND	BEWARE
STYLED.	COYOTE	WIZARD.	EXPAND	BINATE
LAY-OFF.	PEYOTE.	NAZISM	+GERALD	BORAGE
VOYAGE.	ADYTUM		HAZARD	BORATE
+PSYCHE	ASYLUM		HERALD	BOVATE
PSYCHO	JOYFUL	ALBATA	+HOWARD	BUTANE
RHYTHM	JOYOUS	ALPACA	INBAND	BYNAME
SCYTHE.	LAYOUT	*ANKARA	INLAID	CARAFE
*GDYNIA	MAYBUG	ARCANA	INLAND	CERATE
PAYNIM	PHYLUM	ARGALA	INWARD	CETANE
PHYSIC	STYLUS	ARMADA	ISLAND	CLEAVE
STYMIE.	TRY-OUT	*BAHAMA	LIZARD	CREASE
UNYOKE.	VOYEUR	BÁLATA	MARAUD	CREATE
DRY-FLY	WAY-OUT	BANANA	ONWARD	CUBAGE
MAYFLY.		CABALA	+OSWALD	CURARE
ANYONE	BAZAAR.	*CANADA	*POLAND	CURATE
BAYING	GAZEBO.	CICADA	REGARD	DAMAGE
BEYOND	BUZZER	CICALA	RELAID	DEBASE
+BRYONY	FIZZED	CLOACA	REMAND	DEBATE
BUYING	FIZZER	ERRATA	REPAID	DECADE
CRYING	JAZZED	*GUYANA	RETARD	DEFACE
DRYING	VIZIER.	*HAVANA	REWARD	DEFAME
FLYING	SYZYGY.	IGUANA	RIBALD	DELATE
*GUYANA	FIZGIG	INDABA	RIBAND	DERATE
GUYING	RAZZIA.	*ITHACA	+ROLAND	DILATE
HAYING	DAZZLE	KANAKA	+RONALD	DOGATE
KEYING	FIZZLE	*MALAGA	STRAND	DONATE
LAYING	GUZZLE	*MALAYA	TABARD	DOSAGE
MAYING	HAZILY	*NEVADA	TOWARD	DOTAGE
PAYING	LAZILY	*OTTAWA	UNHAND	DOUANE
PLYING	MIZZLE	*PANAMA	UNLAID	EFFACE
PRYING	MUZZLE	PYJAMA	UNSAID	ENCAGE
RAYING	NOZZLE	*SAHARA	UPLAND	ENCASE
SAYING	NUZZLE	SONATA	UPWARD	ENFACE
SHYING	OOZILY	SQUAMA	VISARD	ENGAGE
SKYING	PUZZLE	STRATA	WIZARD.	ENLACE
SPYING	SIZZLE.	+ZAPATA	ABLAZE	ENRAGE
TOYING	ECZEMA	ZENANA.	ABRADE	EQUATE
TRYING.	ENZYME.	BEDAUB.	AERATE	ESCAPE
ANYHOW	BEZANT	EDDAIC	AFLAME	ESTATE
*CEYLON	DAZING	JUDAIC	AGNATE	ETHANE
DAY-BOY	DOZING	MOSAIC.	ALKANE	EXHALE
DRY-ROT	GAZING	ABOARD	ARCADE	FACADE
ETYMON	HAZING	AFRAID	ARCANE	FEMALE
GLYCOL	LAZING	CANARD	AUBADE	FINALE
HAYBOX	OOZING	COWARD	AVIATE	FIXATE
THYMOL.	RAZING	DEMAND	BECAME	FORAGE
+SAYERS.	SIZING.	+DONALD	BEHAVE	FUMADE

GARAGE	POT-ALE	ATTACH	ENTAIL	ALWAYS
GREASE	PUPATE	BLEACH	*ISRAEL	BY-PASS
GYRATE	RAVAGE	BREACH	NO-BALL	*CALAIS
+HECATE	REBATE	BREATH	ONFALL	+CASALS
HEXANE	REFACE	BROACH	RECALL	HARASS
HOMAGE	REGALE	BYPATH	RETAIL	MORASS
+HORACE	RELATE	CALASH	SCRAWL	NOWAYS
HUMANE	REMADE	DETACH	SPRAWL	PALAIS
ICE-AXE	REMAKE	ENCASH	SQUALL	SHEARS
IMPALE	RETAKE	PARAPH	THRALL.	VITALS.
INHALE	ROTATE	POTASH	BECALM	ABLAUT
INMATE	SAVAGE	PREACH	DISARM	AGHAST
INNATE	SAVATE	REHASH	EMBALM	ARRANT
INSANE	SCRAPE	SERAPH	NAPALM	ASLANT
INTAKE	SEDATE	SHEATH	ORGASM	BASALT
INVADE	SENATE	SPLASH	SALAAM.	BEZANT
JUGATE	SERAPE	SQUASH	ATTAIN	BREAST
KARATE	SESAME	STRATH	DETAIN	COBALT
LANATE	SEWAGE	THRASH	DOMAIN	DECANT
LEGATE	SILAGE	UNLASH	IMPAWN	DEPART
LINAGE	SOCAGE	WREATH.	OBTAIN	DREAMT
LOBATE	SOLACE	ALKALI	ORDAIN	DYNAST
LOCALE	SQUARE	*HAWAII	PAPAIN	ENRAPT
LOCATE	STRAFE	*MALAWI	REGAIN	ERRANT
LUNATE	STRAKE	SAFARI	REMAIN	EXTANT
LUXATE	TIRADE	SALAMI	RETAIN	GO-CART
MADAME	TISANE	*SOMALI.	SPRAIN	GO-KART
MANAGE	TOWAGE	ATTACK	STRAIN.	*HOBART
MENACE	ULLAGE	DAMASK	DORADO	IMPACT
MIRAGE	UNCASE	DEBARK	DYNAMO	IMPART
MORALE	UNCATE	EMBANK	LEGATO	INFANT
MUTATE	UNLADE	EMBARK	MIKADO	INTACT
NEGATE	UNMADE	HIJACK	*MONACO	*KUWAIT
NONAGE	UNMAKE	MOHAWK	OCTAVO	LEVANT
OBLATE	UNSAFE	*NEWARK	PEDALO	+MOZART
OCTANE	UP-DATE	POLACK	POTATO	MUTANT
OCTAVE	UPTAKE	REMARK	RUBATO	NATANT
OPIATE	URBANE	SHRANK	*TOBAGO	OPTANT
ORNATE	VACATE	SQUAWK	TOMATO	PEDANT
PALACE	VISAGE	THWACK	VIRAGO.	PLIANT
PALATE	VIVACE	UNMASK	DECAMP	RECANT
PARADE	VOYAGE	UNPACK	ENCAMP	RECAST
PAVANE	ZONATE	UNTACK.	UNHASP.	REDACT
PHRASE	ZOUAVE	AGNAIL	AFFAIR	REPAST
+PILATE	ZYMASE.	ASSAIL	BAZAAR	SAVANT
PIRATE	BEHALF	BEFALL	ECLAIR	SECANT
PLEASE	PILAFF.	BEWAIL	IMPAIR	SONANT
POMACE	GOBANG	DERAIL	MOHAIR	STRAIT
POMADE	SPRANG.	DETAIL	REPAIR	+STUART
POTAGE	*ARMAGH	END-ALL	UNFAIR.	TENANT

THWART	TELARY	LOBBED	RUBBLE	BAMBOO
TRUANT	TREATY	MOBBED	RUMBLE	*BILBAO
TYRANT	UNEASY	MORBID	SOMBRE	PUEBLO.
UMLAUT	UNWARY	NABBED	STABLE	BARBER
UPCAST	VAGARY	NOBBED	TIMBRE	BERBER
VACANT.	VOTARY	NUMBED	TREBLE	BOMBER
XANADU.	ZONARY.	OUTBID	TUMBLE	CAMBER
ABBACY	ERSATZ	PROBED	UNABLE	COBBER
*ALBANY		RIBBED	USABLE	COMBER
ANGARY	*ARABIA	ROBBED	VIABLE	CUMBER
APIARY	*BALBOA	RUBBED	WARBLE	DABBER
AVIARY	*GAMBIA	SOBBED	WOBBLE	DIBBER
AWEARY	JERBOA	TABBED	ZOMBIE.	DISBAR
BIGAMY	LAMBDA	TUBBED	GAS-BAG	*DUNBAR
BINARY	PHOBIA	TURBID	HUMBUG	DURBAR
BLEARY	*ZAMBIA.	WEBBED.	KIT-BAG	FIBBER
BOTANY	BAOBAB	ARABLE	+LIEBIG	GIBBER
CANARY	HUBBUB.	BABBLE	MAYBUG	*HUMBER
CREAMY	ARABIC	BAUBLE	RAG-BAG	ISOBAR
CROAKY	BOMBIC	BUBBLE	TEA-BAG.	JABBER
CURACY	IAMBIC	BURBLE	CHIBUK	JOBBER
DENARY	NIOBIC	COBBLE	DYBBUK	*KHYBER
DREAMY	PHOBIC	CORBIE	JAMBOK.	LIMBER
DREARY	*QUEBEC.	DABBLE	BARBEL	LUBBER
FRIARY	AIR-BED	+DEBBIE	BULBIL	LUMBAR
GALAXY	BARBED	DIBBLE	BULBUL	LUMBER
GREASY	BOBBED	DOUBLE	CORBEL	MEMBER
+HILARY	BOMBED	EDIBLE	CYMBAL	NUMBER
HORARY	BRIBED	ENABLE	GAMBOL	ROBBER
INFAMY	BULBED	FEEBLE	GLOBAL	RUBBER
LEGACY	COMBED	FOIBLE	HERBAL	TIMBER
LITANY	CUBBED	FUMBLE	+ISABEL	+WILBUR
LUNACY	CURBED	GABBLE	JUMBAL	YABBER.
MALADY	DABBED	GAMBLE	SYMBOL	ANABAS
MILADY	DAUBED	GARBLE	TIMBAL	+ANUBIS
NONARY	DAY-BED	GOBBLE	TRIBAL	*EREBUS
NOTARY	DISBUD	HOBBLE	VERBAL.	IAMBUS
PAPACY	DUBBED	HUMBLE	BOBBIN	*LESBOS
PIRACY	FIBBED	JUMBLE	BONBON	NIMBUS
QUEASY	FOBBED	KIBBLE	CARBON	+STUBBS
ROMANY	FORBID	LIABLE	CORBAN	*THEBES.
ROSARY	GABBED	MARBLE	DOBBIN	BARBET
ROTARY	GARBED	MUMBLE	DUBBIN	BURBOT
SALARY	HOTBED	NIBBLE	*DURBAN	COMBAT
SLEAZY	JABBED	NIMBLE	GIBBON	GAMBIT
STEADY	JIBBED	NOBBLE	*LISBON	GIBBET
STEAMY	JOBBED	PEBBLE	RABBIN	GOBBET
STRAWY	KERBED	RABBLE	+REUBEN	RABBET
SUGARY	LAMBED	RAMBLE	RIBBON	RABBIT
SWEATY	LIMBED	ROUBLE	TURBAN.	SORBET

TITBIT	RANCID	TALCUM.	CROCUS	TUNDRA.
TURBOT	SAUCED	ASH-CAN	CUSCUS	ACIDIC
WOMBAT.	SLICED	BEACON	DISCUS	BARDIC
HAYBOX	SPACED	*BRECON	FAECES	DYADIC
ICEBOX.	SPICED	CAN-CAN	FASCES	NORDIC
*BOMBAY	TRACED	DEACON	FRACAS	SYNDIC.
BUBBLY	TRICED	+DUNCAN	GLACIS	ABIDED
CARBOY	VISCID	FALCON	PISCES	BANDED
CHUBBY	VOICED	OIL-CAN	PRECIS	BEDDED
COBBLY	WINCED.	TIN-CAN	SLACKS	BENDED
COWBOY	APACHE	TOUCAN	YOICKS.	BLADED
CRABBY	BROCHE	+VULCAN	AVOCET	BONDED
DAY-BOY	CHICLE	ZIRCON.	BOBCAT	BUDDED
DOUBLY	CIRCLE	GAUCHO	+BRECHT	CANDID
DRABLY	CLICHE	NUNCIO	*DIDCOT	CHIDED
DUMBLY	CLOCHE	PONCHO	DULCET	CORDED
FEEBLY	CRECHE	PSYCHO	ELICIT	CURDED
FLABBY	DOUCHE	STUCCO.	FAUCET	ELIDED
GLIBLY	FESCUE	EGG-CUP	LANCET	ELUDED
GRUBBY	FIACRE	HICCUP	MASCOT	ERODED
HUMBLY	FLECHE	ICE-CAP	*MUSCAT	EVADED
KNOBBY	GAUCHE	MADCAP	PLACET	EXUDED
NIMBLY	ICICLE	REDCAP	TERCET	FENDED
NUMBLY	MUSCLE	*SIDCUP	TIPCAT	FEUDED
PEBBLY	ORACLE	TEACUP	TOM-CAT	FOLDED
PLEBBY	+PSYCHE	TOE-CAP.	TRICOT.	FORDED
SCABBY	RESCUE	BRACER	SEA-COW.	FUNDED
SHABBY	SPECIE	CALCAR	COCCYX.	GADDED
SNOBBY	STACTE	CANCER	BEECHY	GELDED
STABLY	TOUCHE.	CONCUR	BITCHY	GILDED
STUBBY	CHICHI	DANCER	BOTCHY	GIRDED
TOMBOY	LITCHI.	DE-ICER	BUNCHY	GOADED
WOBBLY	APICAL	FENCER	CATCHY	GRADED
	BUCCAL	GROCER	CHICLY	GRIDED
ACACIA	CANCEL	LANCER	CROCKY	GUIDED
+ALICIA	DISCAL	LASCAR	DESCRY	HANDED
CONCHA	EPICAL	MERCER	OUTCRY	HEADED
FASCIA	FAECAL	MINCER	PATCHY	HEEDED
+MARCIA.	FAUCAL	PLACER	PITCHY	HERDED
DEUCED	FISCAL	PLACER	PLUCKY	HOODED
EDUCED	GLYCOL	SAUCER	STICKY	HORDED
FENCED	LAICAL	SLICER	STOCKY	KIDDED
FORCED	MESCAL	SOCCER	TETCHY	LANDED
GRACED	PARCEL	SPACER	TOUCHY	LARDED
LANCED	+PASCAL	TRACER	TRICKY	LAUDED
MINCED	PENCIL	TRICAR.		LEADED
PIECED	RASCAL.	ABACUS		LIDDED
PLACED	CAECUM	APICES	*ACADIA	LOADED
PLACID	CIRCUM	CAUCUS	+BUDDHA	LORDED
PRICED	DRACHM	CIRCUS	*CANDIA	MADDED
		COCCUS	+SANDRA	

MELDED	GRUDGE	*KENDAL	WARDEN	REDDER
MENDED	HANDLE	+MENDEL	WOODEN.	RENDER
MINDED	HEDDLE	SANDAL	HOODOO	RUDDER
NEEDED	HUDDLE	SENDAL	STUDIO	SADDER
NODDED	HURDLE	VANDAL.	VOODOO.	SENDER
OUTDID	KIDDIE	ANADEM	HOLD-UP	SOLDER
PADDED	KIDDLE	BELDAM	*MENDIP	SPIDER
PODDED	KINDLE	CONDOM	WIND-UP.	SUNDER
PRIDED	KOEDOE	DIADEM	+BALDER	TEDDER
REEDED	LADDIE	DUMDUM	BIDDER	TENDER
SANDED	MEDDLE	GODDAM	BINDER	TINDER
SEEDED	MIDDLE	IBIDEM	BOLDER	TRADER
SHADED	MUDDLE	RANDOM	BONDER	VENDER
SORDID	NEEDLE	SELDOM	BORDER	VENDOR
TENDED	NODDLE	TANDEM	CINDER	WANDER
TRADED	NOODLE	WISDOM.	CODDER	WARDER
VOIDED	*OUNDLE	*ABADAN	COLDER	WELDER
WADDED	PADDLE	BURDEN	CONDOR	WILDER
WARDED	PEDDLE	*CAMDEN	DANDER	WINDER
WEDDED	PLEDGE	CORDON	DEODAR	WONDER
WEEDED	POODLE	DEADEN	DODDER	YONDER.
WENDED	PUDDLE	GARDEN	FEEDER	CADDIS
WINDED	RADDLE	GOLDEN	FENDER	EXODUS
WOODED	REDDLE	+GORDON	FINDER	+GLADYS
WORDED.	RIDDLE	GRADIN	FODDER	GRADUS
BEADLE	RUDDLE	GUIDON	FOLDER	LANDES
BIRDIE	SADDLE	HARDEN	GANDER	*RHODES.
BOODLE	SLEDGE	*HENDON	GENDER	AMIDST
BRIDGE	SLUDGE	HIDDEN	GIRDER	BANDIT
BRIDLE	SMUDGE.	HODDEN	GLIDER	CREDIT
BUNDLE	STODGE	HOYDEN	HARDER	+DAUDET
CANDLE	SUBDUE	*IBADAN	HEADER	PUNDIT
CAUDLE	SUNDAE	*JORDAN	HINDER	RE-EDIT
CODDLE	TODDLE	LEADEN	HOLDER	LANDAU.
CRADLE	TRUDGE	LEAD-IN	KINDER	MEADOW
CUDDLE	VENDEE	*LEYDEN	LADDER	MILDEW
CURDLE	WADDLE.	LINDEN	LARDER	SHADOW
DANDLE	LAPDOG	*LONDON	LEADER	SUNDEW
DAWDLE	SEA-DOG.	MADDEN	LENDER	WINDOW.
DIDDLE	HOWDAH	MAIDEN	LOADER	ACIDLY
DOODLE	PURDAH.	MIDDEN	LOUDER	ARIDLY
DREDGE	+GANDHI.	PARDON	MADDER	AVIDLY
DRUDGE	DIK-DIK.	RANDAN	MILDER	BALDLY
*DUNDEE	APODAL	REDDEN	MURDER	BOLDLY
FIDDLE	BRIDAL	RIDDEN	PANDER	COLDLY
FLEDGE	CAUDAL	SADDEN	POLDER	CUDDLY
FONDLE	CREDAL	SODDEN	PONDER	DEADLY
FRIDGE	DAEDAL	SUDDEN	POWDER	FONDLY
FUDDLE	FEUDAL	*SWEDEN	RAIDER	FRIDAY
GIRDLE	+HANDEL	TENDON	READER	GLADLY

GOODLY	DEPEND	+PHOEBE	ESTEEM	UPKEEP.
HARDLY	EXCEED	RACEME	LYCEUM	APPEAR
HEYDAY	EXPEND	RECEDE	MUSEUM	ARREAR
KINDLY	EXTEND	REVERE	PHLEGM	CAREER
LEWDLY	FAG-END	SCHEME	REDEEM	COHEIR
LORDLY	FRIEND	SECEDE	SCREAM	DISEUR
LOUDLY	IMPEND	SERENE	STREAM.	ENDEAR
MIDDAY	INDEED	SEVERE	*AEGEAN	LINEAR
MILDLY	INTEND	SLEEVE	+AILEEN	METEOR
MONDAY	LEGEND	SNEEZE	ASTERN	POSEUR
OFF-DAY	NEREID	SPHERE	AUGEAN	VENEER
RAG-DAY	OFFEND	THIEVE	BALEEN	VOYEUR.
SHODDY	*OSTEND	WHEEZE	+BOLEYN	ABBESS
SMUDGY	SCREED	XYLENE.	CAREEN	ACCESS
STODGY	SHIELD	HEREOF	CASEIN	+AEGEUS
SUNDAY	SHREWD	ITSELF	CAVERN	+AENEAS
SUNDRY	SPREAD	MYSELF.	DEMEAN	*AMIENS
TAWDRY	THREAD	AFRESH	+DOREEN	ASSESS
WILDLY	UNBEND	BREECH	+EILEEN	ASSETS
	UNREAD	ENMESH	+GIDEON	*ATHENS
AMOEBA	UPHELD.	IMMESH	GOVERN	+ATREUS
+ANGELA	ACCEDE	+JOSEPH	HEREIN	BICEPS
+ATHENA	ACHENE	SPEECH	INTERN	BOWELS
BODEGA	ADHERE	THRESH.	LATEEN	BREEKS
CAMERA	ALKENE	BEDECK	LOVE-IN	CARESS
CINEMA	ALLEGE	COPECK	MODERN	DIVERS
ECZEMA	AMPERE	KOPECK	PIGEON	DURESS
EUREKA	ANNEXE	REBECK	POTEEN	EGRESS
GALENA	APIECE	SQUEAK	SATEEN	EXCESS
GENERA	+ATHENE	STREAK.	SCREEN	HABEAS
*GENEVA	BIREME	ANNEAL	*SEVERN	JEWESS
+HYGEIA	BREEZE	APPEAL	SOLEMN	OBSESS
NOVENA	CHEESE	AWHEEL	SPLEEN	OGRESS
OEDEMA	COHERE	BEFELL	STREWN	PLIERS
OEPEMA	+CYBELE	BOREAL	TAVERN	RECESS
+PAMELA	DELETE	LINEAL	TUREEN	REVERS
PESETA	EFFETE	ORDEAL	UNHEWN	+RUBENS
+ROWENA	EOCENE	*ORWELL	WYVERN.	+SAYERS
SCHEMA	+EUGENE	PINEAL	BOLERO	STRESS
VELETA.	FLEECE	REPEAL	+CICERO	UNLESS
ADVERB	FREEZE	REVEAL	FOREGO	URAEUS.
SUPERB.	FRIEZE	ROSEAL	GAZEBO	ABJECT
AFIELD	GAMETE	+SEWELL	HERETO	ABSENT
AGREED	*GREECE	SQUEAL	TEREDO	ACCENT
APPEND	+GREENE	UNREAL	TORERO	ACCEPT
ASCEND	GRIEVE	UNREEL	TUXEDO.	ADJECT
ATTEND	IMPEDE	UNSEAL	ASLEEP	ADVENT
BEHEAD	INHERE	UNVEIL	LINE-UP	ADVERT
BEHELD	MISERE	UNWELL.	MAKE-UP	AFFECT
DEFEND	NICENE	BESEEM	PILE-UP	ALBEIT

+ALBERT	INCEST	SANEST	HUGELY	
ARDENT	INDENT	SELECT	+JEREMY	*BIAFRA
ARGENT	INFECT	SILENT	LAMELY	RAFFIA
ARREST	INFEST	*SOLENT	LATELY	*STAFFA.
ASCENT	INGEST	SOREST	LIKELY	CONFAB
ASPECT	INJECT	STREET	LIVELY	PREFAB.
ASSENT	INSECT	SUREST	LIVERY	CHAFED
ASSERT	INSERT	TALENT	LONELY	CUFFED
ATTEST	INTENT	THREAT	LOVELY	DOFFED
BASEST	INVENT	TRUEST	MERELY	DUFFED
BEHEST	INVERT	UNBENT	MISERY	GAFFED
BEREFT	INVEST	UNMEET	MOIETY	HOOFED
BISECT	LAMENT	UNREST	NAMELY	HUFFED
CAVEAT	LATENT	UNSEAT	NICELY	KNIFED
CEMENT	LATEST	UNWEPT	NICETY	LEAFED
CLIENT	LOWEST	UPBEAT	NINETY	MUFFED
COGENT	LUCENT	URGENT	ORRERY	PUFFED
COVERT	MAYEST	VILEST	PALELY	ROOFED
DECEIT	MODEST	WERENT	POPERY	RUFFED
DECENT	MOLEST	WIDEST	PURELY	TRIFID
DEFEAT	MOMENT	WISEST.	RAREFY	TURFED
DEFECT	NEWEST	BUREAU	RARELY	WOLFED.
DEJECT	NICEST	GATEAU	REMEDY	BAFFLE
DEMENT	OBJECT	TELEDU.	RIPELY	COFFEE
DESERT	ODDEST	ARTERY	RUDELY	COFFLE
DETECT	OLDEST	BAKERY	SAFELY	DUFFLE
DETENT	ORIENT	BARELY	SAFETY	MUFFLE
DETEST	+OSBERT	BASELY	SAGELY	PIFFLE
DIGEST	PALEST	BOWERY	SANELY	RAFFLE
DIRECT	PARENT	BREEZY	SCREWY	RIFFLE
DIVERT	PATENT	CELERY	SHEENY	RUFFLE
DIVEST	POTENT	CHEEKY	SINEWY	STIFLE
DRIEST	PRIEST	CHEERY	SLEEPY	TOFFEE
EFFECT	PUREST	CHEESY	SOLELY	TRIFLE
ELDEST	RAREST	CICELY	SORELY	WAFFLE
+ERNEST	RECENT	COMEDY	SPEEDY	YAFFLE
EXCEPT	REGENT	COMELY	STEELY	ZAFFRE.
EXPECT	REJECT	CREEPY	SURELY	LOOFAH
EXPERT	RELENT	CUTELY	SURETY	ARMFUL
EXTENT	REPEAT	DIRELY	SWEENY	ARTFUL
FEWEST	REPENT	FINELY	TAMELY	CUPFUL
FINEST	RESEAT	FINERY	TIMELY	DUFFEL
FLUENT	RESENT	FLEECY	TUMEFY	+EIFFEL
FOMENT	REVERT	FREELY	VILELY	EYEFUL
FOREST	RIPEST	GAIETY	VINERY	FITFUL
HAVENT	+ROBERT	GAMELY	WATERY	FULFIL
HEREAT	RODENT	GREEDY	WHEEZY	IREFUL
HONEST	RUDEST	HEREBY	WIDELY	JOYFUL
+HUBERT	+RUPERT	HERESY	WIFELY	JUGFUL
INCEPT	SAFEST	HOMELY	WISELY	LAWFUL

MANFUL	BOTFLY	JUDGED	CINGLE	RED-GUM
RUEFUL	CHAFFY	JUGGED	DAGGLE	AIR-GUN
SINFUL	CRAFTY	KEDGED	DANGLE	*BERGEN
USEFUL	DRAFFY	KINGED	DENGUE	DRAGON
WILFUL	DRY-FLY	LAGGED	DINGLE	FLAGON
WOEFUL.	FLUFFY	LEGGED	DROGUE	+GORGON
*BAFFIN	GADFLY	LODGED	EMIGRE	+IMOGEN
BIFFIN	MAYFLY	LOGGED	GAGGLE	JARGON
BOFFIN	SAW-FLY	LONGED	GANGUE	MARGIN
COFFIN	SHIFTY	LUGGED	GARGLE	+MORGAN
DEAFEN	STUFFY	LUNGED	GIGGLE	NOGGIN
MUFFIN		MERGED	GOGGLE	*OREGAN
OLEFIN	ENIGMA	MUGGED	GURGLE	ORIGIN
PUFFIN	+FRIGGA	NAGGED	HAGGLE	OXYGEN
TIFFIN.	LINGUA	NUDGED	HIGGLE	PIDGIN
BUFFER	LOGGIA	PEGGED	JANGLE	PLUG-IN
COFFER	QUAGGA	PIGGED	JIGGLE	POPGUN
CONFER	STIGMA	PUGGED	JINGLE	*SAIGON
DIFFER	ZEUGMA.	PURGED	JOGGLE	SLOGAN
DUFFER	TRAGIC.	RAGGED	JUGGLE	TROGON
FURFUR	BAGGED	RANGED	JUNGLE	*VIRGIN
GAFFER	BANGED	RIDGED	LEAGUE	WAGGON.
GOFFER	BEGGED	RIGGED	MANGLE	ADAGIO
GOLFER	BOGGED	RINGED	MEAGRE	GINGKO.
HEIFER	BUDGED	ROUGED	MINGLE	HANG-UP
KAFFIR	BUGGED	RUGGED	MORGUE	BADGER
LOAFER	BUNGED	SAGGED	NIGGLE	*BANGOR
PILFER	COGGED	SINGED	PLAGUE	BEGGAR
PREFER	DIGGED	SUN-GOD	PONGEE	BIGGER
PUFFER	DODGED	SURGED	POOGYE	BUGGER
REEFER	DOGGED	TAGGED	*PRAGUE	BULGER
SUFFER	FAGGED	TANGED	SINGLE	CADGER
SURFER	FANGED	TINGED	TANGLE	CODGER
TELFER	FOGGED	TUGGED	TINGLE	CONGER
TITFER	FORGED	TURGID	TOGGLE	COUGAR
WOOFER.	FRIGID	VERGED	TONGUE	DAGGER
BUFFET	GAGGED	WAGGED	WAGGLE	DANGER
COMFIT	GANGED	WEDGED	WANGLE	DIGGER
FYLFOT	GAUGED	WINGED.	WIGGLE.	DODGER
MISFIT	GORGED	APOGEE	FIZGIG.	DOGGER
OUTFIT	GOUGED	BANGLE	LENGTH.	FINGER
PROFIT	HAGGED	BARGEE	NILGAI.	FORGER
TUFFET.	HANGED	BEAGLE	*BENGAL	GANGER
CURFEW	HINGED	BLAGUE	CUDGEL	GAUGER
GUFFAW.	HOGGED	BOGGLE	+DOUGAL	GEIGER
CARFAX	HUGGED	BOUGIE	FRUGAL	GINGER
DOG-FOX	IMAGED	BROGUE	MONGOL	HANGAR
PREFIX	JAGGED	BUNGLE	TERGAL	HANGER
SUFFIX.	JIGGED	BURGEE	+VIRGIL.	HEDGER
BELFRY	JOGGED	BURGLE	LINGAM	HUNGER

JIGGER	NAUGHT	ITCHED	BISHOP	PATHOS
LAAGER	NOUGAT	JOSHED	MISHAP	TIGHTS
LANGUR	NOUGHT	LASHED	UNSHIP.	TYPHUS.
LARGER	NUGGET	MASHED	AETHER	CACHET
LEDGER	PARGET	MESHED	ANCHOR	CUSHAT
LINGER	PLIGHT	METHOD	ANTHER	ROCHET
LODGER	SLIGHT	NOSHED	ARCHER	SACHET
LOGGER	SOUGHT	ORCHID	+ARTHUR	SUN-HAT
LONGER	SPIGOT	PUSHED	AUTHOR	TOP-HAT
LUGGER	TARGET	RUSHED	BATHER	UPSHOT.
MANGER	TAUGHT	SIGHED	BOTHER	CACHOU
MERGER	WEIGHT.	UNSHOD	CIPHER	PUSHTU.
MONGER	GEWGAW.	WASHED	COSHER	ANYHOW
NAGGER	CRAGGY	WISHED.	CYPHER	CASHEW
NIGGER	DINGHY	+ARCHIE	DASHER	ESCHEW
ONAGER	DOUGHY	+DAPHNE	DITHER	HAW-HAW
RANGER	FLAGGY	EUCHRE	EITHER	NEPHEW.
RINGER	GOOGLY	MASHIE.	ESCHAR	ARCHLY
RUGGER	GROGGY	EIGHTH.	+ESTHER	*BUSHEY
SAGGAR	HUNGRY	ARCHIL	FATHER	EIGHTY
SINGER	JINGLY	BETHEL	FISHER	HIGHLY
STAGER	JUNGLY	BUSHEL	GATHER	MIGHTY
VERGER	KINGLY	LETHAL	GOPHER	NIGHTY
VULGAR.	QUAGGY	METHYL	GUSHER	POSHLY
FUNGUS	SHAGGY	+RACHEL	HIGHER	RASHLY
*GANGES	SINGLY	+WARHOL	HITHER	RICHLY
HAGGIS.	SMUGLY	WITHAL.	KOSHER	
ALIGHT	SNUGLY	ANTHEM	LASHER	ACRITA
ARIGHT	TANGLY	*DURHAM	LATHER	*AFRICA
BLIGHT	TWIGGY	FATHOM	LECHER	ANGINA
BOUGHT		+GRAHAM	LUTHER	ARNICA
BRIGHT	ASTHMA	*LYTHAM	+LUTHER	+ATTILA
BUDGET	*ISCHIA	MAYHEM	MENHIR	COAITA
CATGUT	+JOSHUA	*OLDHAM.	MOTHER	+EDWINA
CAUGHT	+SOPHIA.	*AACHEN	NETHER	FARINA
+DWIGHT	GOTHIC	ARCHON	PUSHER	+GODIVA
FAGGOT	MYTHIC	*BUCHAN	RASHER	+JEMIMA
FIDGET	ORPHIC	*COCHIN	RATHER	LAMINA
FLIGHT	PATHIC.	HYPHEN	RICHER	+LOLITA
FORGET	ARCHED	LICHEN	TETHER	*MANILA
FORGOT	BASHED	+NATHAN	TOTHER	+MARINA
FOUGHT	BUSHED	ORPHAN	WASHER	MAXIMA
FRIGHT	CASHED	PATHAN	WETHER	MINIMA
GADGET	DASHED	PEAHEN	WITHER	+MONICA
GORGET	DISHED	PYTHON	ZEPHYR	PATINA
HEIGHT	ETCHED	RUSHEN	ZITHER.	+REGINA
HOGGET	GASHED	SIPHON	ALPHOS	RETINA
KNIGHT	HASHED	SYPHON	BATHOS	+SABINA
MAGGOT	HUSHED	URCHIN	+BRAHMS	SALIVA
MIDGET	INCHED	WITHIN.	LACHES	SILICA
			ORCHIS	

TROIKA	BESIDE	FUTILE	REFINE	RELIEF
ULTIMA	BETIDE	GUNITE	REGIME	TARIFF.
VAGINA	BODICE	HALIDE	RELINE	ACHING
VESICA	BOLIDE	HAMITE	RELIVE	ACTING
ZARIBA.	BOVINE	IGNITE	REPINE	ADDING
MANIAC	BRAISE	IMBIBE	RESIDE	AIDING
MANIOC	BRUISE	INCISE	RESILE	AILING
ZODIAC.	BY-LINE	INCITE	RETIRE	AIRING
ALLIED	CANINE	INDITE	REVILE	ARCING
BEHIND	CERISE	INSIDE	REVISE	ARMING
BODIED	CHAISE	INVITE	REVIVE	ASKING
BURIED	CHOICE	IODIDE	RUTILE	AWNING
BUSIED	CILICE	IODINE	SALINE	BAKING
COPIED	+CLAIRE	IODIZE	SAMITE	BALING
DEFIED	COSINE	IOLITE	SATIRE	BARING
DENIED	CRUISE	IONIZE	SCRIBE	BATING
EDDIED	DATIVE	+JANICE	SEMITE	BAYING
ENVIED	DECIDE	LABILE	SENILE	*BERING
ESPIED	DEFILE	LEVITE	SHRIKE	BIDING
LEVIED	DEFINE	LIAISE	SHRINE	BITING
MYRIAD	DEMISE	+LOUISE	SHRIVE	BODING
PERIOD	+DENISE	MALICE	SIMILE	BONING
PITIED	DERIDE	MARINE	SLUICE	BORING
RELIED	DERIVE	+MAXINE	SPLICE	BOWING
REMIND	DESIRE	MOBILE	SPLINE	BOXING
SCRIED	DEVICE	MOTIVE	SPRITE	BUYING
TAXIED	DEVISE	MURINE	SQUIRE	CAGING
UNBIND	DIVIDE	+NADINE	STRIDE	CAKING
UNGIRD	DIVINE	NATIVE	STRIFE	CANING
UNKIND	DOCILE	NOTICE	STRIKE	CARING
UNTIED	DRY-ICE	NOVICE	STRIPE	CASING
UNWIND	+ELAINE	NOWISE	STRIVE	CAVING
VARIED.	EMPIRE	NUBILE	SUPINE	CEDING
ACTIVE	ENDIVE	OBLIGE	THRICE	CITING
ADMIRE	ENGINE	OFFICE	THRIVE	CODING
ADVICE	ENSILE	ON-LINE	TONITE	COMING
ADVISE	ENTICE	OOLITE	UMPIRE	COOING
AEDILE	ENTIRE	OREIDE	+UNDINE	COPING
ALBITE	EQUINE	ORPINE	UNLIKE	CORING
ALPINE	ERMINE	OX-HIDE	UNRIPE	COVING
ALVINE	+EUNICE	PETITE	UNWISE	COWING
ARGIVE	EXCISE	PLAICE	+UPDIKE	CRYING
ARRIVE	EXCITE	POLICE	UPSIDE	CUBING
ARSINE	EXPIRE	POLITE	URSINE	CURING
ASPIRE	FACILE	PRAISE	VALISE	DARING
ASSIZE	FAMINE	PUMICE	*VENICE	DATING
ATTIRE	FELINE	RAPINE	VIRILE	DAZING
AUDILE	FERINE	RAVINE	VOTIVE	DICING
AWHILE	FINITE	RECIPE	XYLITE.	DINING
BELIKE	FRAISE	RECITE	BELIEF	DIVING

DOPING	HIRING	NAMING	SAVING	WILING
DOTING	HIVING	NOSING	SAWING	WINING
DOZING	HOEING	NOTING	SAYING	WIPING
DRYING	HOLING	OARING	SEEING	WIRING
DUPING	HOMING	OFFING	SEWING	*WOKING
DURING	HONING	OGLING	SEXING	WOOING
DYEING	HOPING	OILING	SHYING	YAWING
*EALING	HOSING	OOZING	SIDING	YOKING
EARING	IDLING	OPTING	SIRING	ZONING.
EASING	IMPING	ORBING	SITING	AGUISH
EATING	INKING	OUTING	SIZING	AWEIGH
EBBING	IRKING	OWNING	SKIING	BANISH
EDGING	IRVING	PACING	SKYING	BLUISH
EKEING	JADING	PAGING	SOLING	BOYISH
ENDING	JAPING	PALING	SOWING	CALIPH
*EPPING	JAWING	PARING	SPRING	CERIPH
ERRING	JIBING	PAWING	SPYING	DANISH
EYEING	JIVING	PAYING	STRING	DRYISH
FACING	JOKING	*PEKING	TAKING	EDDISH
FADING	KEYING	PILING	TAMING	ELFISH
FAKING	LACING	PINING	TAPING	ENRICH
FARING	LADING	PIPING	TAWING	EOLITH
FILING	LAMING	PLYING	TAXING	FAMISH
FINING	LAYING	POKING	TEEING	FETISH
FIRING	LAZING	POLING	TIDING	FINISH
FIXING	LIKING	PORING	TILING	GARISH
FLYING	LIMING	POSING	TIMING	IMPISH
FOXING	LINING	PRYING	TIRING	+ISAIAH
FUMING	LIVING	PUKING	TOEING	JEWISH
FUSING	LOPING	PULING	TONING	+JOSIAH
GAMING	LOSING	PYXING	TOPING	+JUDITH
GAPING	LOVING	RACING	TOTING	LAVISH
GATING	LOWING	RAGING	TOYING	MODISH
GAZING	LURING	RAKING	TRYING	MULISH
GIBING	LUTING	RAPING	TUBING	OAFISH
GIVING	MAKING	RATING	TUNING	OFFISH
GORING	MATING	RAVING	TYPING	OGRISH
GUYING	MAYING	RAYING	URGING	OWLISH
GYBING	METING	RAZING	VEXING	PARIAH
GYVING	MEWING	RIDING	VIKING	PARISH
HALING	MIMING	RILING	VOLING	PERISH
HARING	MINING	RISING	VOTING	POLISH
HATING	MIRING	RIVING	VOWING	POPISH
HAVING	MIXING	ROBING	WADING	PUNISH
HAWING	*MOOING	ROPING	WAGING	RADISH
HAYING	MOPING	ROVING	WAKING	RAKISH
HAZING	MOVING	ROWING	WALING	RAVISH
HEWING	MOWING	RUEING	WANING	RELISH
HIDING	MUSING	RULING	WAVING	ROMISH
HIKING	MUTING	SATING	WAXING	SHEIKH

SLEIGH	AFFIRM	GABION	EASIER	+JULIET
SQUISH	AUTISM	INDIAN	FOLIAR	JURIST
STAITH	BARIUM	IONIAN	HOLIER	LARIAT
UPPISH	CERIUM	JOVIAN	HOSIER	LEGIST
VANISH	CHRISM	+JULIAN	INLIER	LYRIST
WRAITH	CILIUM	LEGION	JUNIOR	MONIST
ZENITH	CORIUM	LESION	RACIER	NUDIST
*ZURICH.	CUBISM	+LILIAN	RAPIER	PAPIST
*ASSISI	CURIUM	LOTION	ROSIER	PLAINT
BIKINI	EGOISM	MALIGN	SENIOR	QUAINT
GEMINI	ERBIUM	+MARIAN	SEXIER	RACIST
+MEDICI	HELIUM	MEDIAN	TIDIER	RAPIST
*TAHITI	HOLISM	MINION	TINIER	RELICT
WAPITI.	INDIUM	MOTION	UGLIER	RESIST
*KODIAK	INFIRM	NATION	VIZIER	SADIST
SHRIEK	IODISM	NOTION	WARIER	SCHIST
SHRINK	MEDIUM	OPTION	+XAVIER.	SCRIPT
UNPICK	+MIRIAM	PARIAN	ALLIES	SHRIFT
+YORICK.	MONISM	PINION	AUXINS	SOVIET
AERIAL	MUTISM	POTION	CARIES	SPLINT
BASIAL	NAZISM	RADIAN	GENIUS	SPRINT
BELIAL	NUDISM	RATION	GNEISS	SQUINT
BURIAL	OMNIUM	REGION	+HELIOS	SQUIRT
+DANIEL	PODIUM	RESIGN	+JULIUS	STRICT
DENIAL	PURISM	SIMIAN	+LUCIUS	TANIST
ESPIAL	RACISM	TALION	MATINS	THEIST
FACIAL	RADIUM	+TITIAN	OPTICS	THRIFT
FERIAL	SADISM	TYRIAN	RABIES	TYPIST
FETIAL	SCHISM	VISION	RADIUS	UNGIRT
FILIAL	SODIUM	+VIVIAN.	REGIUS	UPLIFT.
FINIAL	SQUIRM	ALBINO	REMISS	JABIRU
GENIAL	TAOISM	BONITO	SERIES	MILIEU.
JOVIAL	TEDIUM	CALICO	SIRIUS	REVIEW.
LABIAL	THEISM	CASINO	THRIPS	SPHINX
MEDIAL	TRUISM.	DOMINO	UNDIES.	SYRINX.
MENIAL	ACTION	ESKIMO	ADDICT	ACUITY
+MURIEL	+ADRIAN	INDIGO	ADRIFT	AERIFY
PENIAL	AMNION	LIBIDO	ANOINT	AIRILY
RACIAL	ASSIGN	LOLIGO	AORIST	ARTILY
RADIAL	BANIAN	MEDICO	ARTIST	BODILY
REFILL	BENIGN	MERINO	ASSIST	BRAINY
SERIAL	BUNION	*MEXICO	AURIST	BUSILY
SHRILL	CAMION	SCHIZO	+CHRIST	CAGILY
SOCIAL	CATION	ULTIMO.	DEPICT	CAVITY
SQUILL	DESIGN	SCRIMP	DESIST	CECITY
THRILL	DORIAN	SHRIMP.	EGOIST	CODIFY
UNCIAL	ENSIGN	ANTIAR	ENLIST	COMITY
UPHILL	FABIAN	CAVIAR	HERIOT	COSILY
VENIAL	FENIAN	COPIER	INDICT	DIMITY
XENIAL.	FUSION	DENIER	INSIST	EASILY

EERILY	UNTIDY	JINKED	TICKED	FIRKIN
EFFIGY	UPPITY	JUNKED	TUCKED	HARKEN
ENMITY	VANITY	KECKED	TUSKED	JERKIN
ENTITY	VERIFY	KICKED	WICKED	KRAKEN
EQUITY	VERILY	KINKED	WINKED	LOOK-IN
EXPIRY	VERITY	LACKED	WORKED	NAPKIN
FAMILY	VILIFY	LARKED	YAKKED	PARKIN
FERITY	VIVIFY	LEAKED	YANKED.	PIPKIN
FIXITY	WARILY	LICKED	BOOKIE	RECKON
FRUITY	WILILY	LINKED	BUCKLE	+RUSKIN
GASIFY	WIRILY	LOCKED	CACKLE	SHAKEN
GRAINY		LOOKED	COCKLE	SICKEN
HAZILY	ODD-JOB	HARKED	COOKIE	SILKEN
HOLILY	*PUNJAB.	MASKED	DECKLE	SISKIN
HOMILY	DONJON	MILKED	FICKLE	SPOKEN
HOMINY	TROJAN.	MOCKED	HACKLE	SUNKEN
HUMIFY	JAM-JAR.	MUCKED	HECKLE	WEAKEN
JIMINY	FAN-JET	NARKED	KECKLE	WELKIN.
LAXITY	GAS-JET	NECKED	KINKLE	CUCKOO.
LAZILY	RAMJET.	NICKED	MACKLE	COCK-UP
LENITY	ACAJOU	NOCKED	MICKLE	HOOKUP
LEVITY		PACKED	MUCKLE	LOCK-UP
MODIFY	BUCKRA.	PARKED	PICKLE	MOCK-UP
MUTINY	BACKED	PEAKED	RANKLE	BACKER
NOTIFY	BALKED	PECKED	ROOKLE	BANKER
NUDITY	BANKED	PEEKED	SICKLE	BARKER
ODDITY	BASKED	PERKED	SUCKLE	BEAKER
OOZILY	BEAKED	PICKED	TACKLE	BICKER
OSSIFY	BOOKED	PINKED	TALKIE	BILKER
PACIFY	BRAKED	QUAKED	TICKLE	BROKER
PARITY	CHOKED	RACKED	TINKLE	BUNKER
POLICY	COCKED	RANKED	WINKLE	BUSKER
POLITY	CONKED	REEKED	YANKEE.	CANKER
PUNILY	COOKED	RICKED	HOOKAH.	CHOKER
PURIFY	CORKED	RINKED	JACKAL	COCKER
PURITY	DECKED	RISKED	NICKEL	CONKER
RACILY	DOCKED	ROCKED	SHEKEL.	COOKER
RAMIFY	DUCKED	ROOKED	BUNKUM	CORKER
RARITY	DUNKED	RUCKED	DINKUM	DARKER
RATIFY	EVOKED	SACKED	*SIKKIM.	DECKER
ROSILY	FLAKED	SLAKED	AWAKEN	DICKER
SALIFY	FLUKED	SMOKED	AWOKEN	DOCKER
SANITY	FORKED	SNAKED	*BALKAN	DUCKER
SEXILY	HACKED	SOAKED	BECKON	DUIKER
*SICILY	HOCKED	SPIKED	BODKIN	HANKER
STRIPY	HONKED	STAKED	BROKEN	HAWKER
TIDILY	HOOKED	SUCKED	BUSKIN	HOOKER
TINILY	HUSKED	TACKED	CALKIN	JUNKER
TYPIFY	JACKED	TALKED	CATKIN	LOCKER
UGLIFY	JERKED	TASKED	DARKEN	LOOKER

LURKER	TICKET	COOLED	REELED	CHILLI
MARKER	TUCKET	CULLED	RIFLED	NUCLEI
MASKER	WICKET.	CURLED	ROLLED	OCELLI.
MEEKER	*RYUKYU.	CYCLED	SAILED	ASYLUM
MILKER	MUSK-OX	DOLLED	SCALED	BEDLAM
MOCKER	PICKAX.	DULLED	SEALED	EMBLEM
NICKER	CRIKEY	+EUCLID	SIDLED	IDOLUM
PACKER	DARKLY	EXILED	SMILED	MOSLEM
PECKER	DICKEY	EYELID	SOILED	MUSLIM
PICKER	DONKEY	FABLED	STOLID	PEPLUM
PORKER	FOLKSY	FAILED	STYLED	PHYLUM
PUCKER	HOCKEY	FILLED	TABLED	PRELIM
QUAKER	HOOKEY	FOALED	TAILED	VALLUM
RANKER	JOCKEY	FOILED	TILLED	VELLUM.
ROCKER	LACKEY	FOOLED	TITLED	*BERLIN
SEEKER	MEEKLY	FOULED	TOLLED	*CEYLON
SHAKER	MICKEY	FURLED	VEILED	*DUBLIN
SICKER	MONKEY	GABLED	WAILED	DUNLIN
SINKER	RANKLY	GALLED	WALLED	+EVELYN
SMOKER	SICKLY	GELLED	WELLED	FALLEN
SOAKER	*TURKEY	GULLED	WHILED	FILL-IN
STOKER	WEAKLY	HAILED	WILLED	GALLON
SUCKER	WEEKLY	HAULED	YELLED	GOBLIN
TALKER		HEALED	YOWLED.	KAOLIN
TANKER	ALALIA	HEELED	+ATTLEE	+MERLIN
TICKER	+AMELIA	HOWLED	BAILEE	MUSLIN
TINKER	AZALEA	HULLED	COLLIE	POLLEN
TUCKER	DAHLIA	JAILED	COOLIE	POPLIN
TUSKER	+STELLA	JELLED	EVOLVE	PULL-IN
WALKER	+THALIA	KEELED	FAILLE	PURLIN
WEAKER	+THELMA.	KILLED	FELLOE	RAGLAN
WICKER	+BELLOC	LADLED	+GAULLE	+STALIN
WORKER	CYCLIC	LOLLED	GILLIE	STOLEN
YORKER.	EXILIC	LULLED	GOALIE	SULLEN
BASKET	FROLIC	MAILED	GRILLE	VIOLIN.
BUCKET	GAELIC	MARLED	GRILSE	+APOLLO
CASKET	GALLIC	MAULED	+ISOLDE	*CALLAO
DOCKET	GARLIC	MILLED	MEALIE	HALLOO
GASKET	ITALIC	MISLED	+NOELLE	NIELLO.
JACKET	OXALIC	MULLED	SHELVE	BURLAP
JUNKET	PUBLIC.	NAILED	SVELTE	CALL-UP
LOCKET	ADDLED	PALLED	TWELVE.	COLLOP
MARKET	AMBLED	PALLID	BOW-LEG	DEWLAP
MUSKET	ANGLED	PEALED	PEG-LEG	DOLLOP
PACKET	BALLAD	PEELED	PUTLOG	FILLIP
PICKET	BAWLED	POLLED	UNPLUG.	GALLOP
POCKET	BILLED	POOLED	FELLAH	GALLUP
RACKET	BOILED	PULLED	HEALTH	LOLLOP
ROCKET	CALLED	PURLED	KIBLAH	+PHILIP
SOCKET	COILED	RAILED	WEALTH.	ROLL-UP

WALLOP.	SAILER	HARLOT	HALLUX	
ANGLER	SAILOR	MALLET	INFLUX	ANOMIA
ANTLER	SCALAR	MILLET	POLLEX	*CRIMEA
ASHLAR	SEALER	MULLET	PROLIX	KALMIA.
BAILER	SELLER	OCELOT	REFLEX	AGAMIC
BOILER	STALER	OMELET	REFLUX.	ATOMIC
BOWLER	SUTLER	OUTLET	BAILEY	BROMIC
BUGLER	TAILOR	PALLET	BARLEY	COSMIC
BUTLER	TALLER	PELLET	BROLLY	FILMIC
CALLER	TELLER	PIGLET	CHALKY	FORMIC
CELLAR	THALER	PIOLET	CHILLY	GNOMIC
CHOLER	TILLER	PULLET	COOLLY	TARMAC.
COALER	TOILER	SCULPT	DEPLOY	BEAMED
COLLAR	TOOLER	SUBLET	*DUDLEY	BLAMED
COOLER	UVULAR	SUNLIT	EMPLOY	BOOMED
CURLER	WHALER.	TABLET	EVILLY	CALMED
CUTLER	+AEOLUS	TOILET	FAULTY	CHIMED
DEALER	CALLUS	TWILIT	*FAWLEY	DAMMED
DOLLAR	*DALLAS	VARLET	FEALTY	DEEMED
DULLER	DOWLAS	+VIOLET	FOULLY	DIMMED
FEELER	+DULLES	WALLET	FRILLY	DOOMED
FELLER	*ECCLES	WHILST	GALLEY	FILMED
FILLER	*NAPLES	ZEALOT.	GUILTY	FLAMED
FOWLER	OBELUS	+PAVLOV.	*HENLEY	FOAMED
FULLER	OODLES	+BELLOW	HURLEY	FORMED
GAOLER	STYLUS	BILLOW	+HUXLEY	FRAMED
HEALER	UMBLES	CALLOW	*ILKLEY	GAMMED
+HITLER	VILLUS	*CARLOW	+LESLEY	GEMMED
HOLLER	+WALLIS.	CURLEW	MEDLEY	GUMMED
HOWLER	AMULET	FALLOW	MISLAY	HAMMED
HURLER	ANKLET	FELLOW	MOTLEY	HARMED
JAILER	ARMLET	FOLLOW	MOULDY	HELMED
+KEPLER	BALLET	HALLOW	ORALLY	HEMMED
KILLER	BALLOT	*HARLOW	OUTLAY	HUMMED
+MAHLER	BILLET	HOLLOW	PARLEY	JAMMED
+MAILER	BULLET	INFLOW	PULLEY	LAMMED
MEDLAR	CHALET	*LUDLOW	REALLY	LOAMED
+MILLER	COLLET	MALLOW	REALTY	LOOMED
NOBLER	CUTLET	*MARLOW	REPLAY	MAIMED
OCULAR	DIGLOT	MELLOW	*SCILLY	MUMMED
OSTLER	DUPLET	OUTLAW	SKILLY	PALMED
PALLOR	EAGLET	PILLOW	SMELLY	PERMED
PEDLAR	EYELET	SALLOW	STILLY	PLUMED
PEELER	FILLET	TALLOW	TRILBY	PRIMED
PILLAR	GIBLET	WALLOW	VALLEY	RAMMED
POPLAR	GIMLET	WILLOW	VOLLEY	RHYMED
PULLER	GOBLET	YELLOW.	WAYLAY	RIMMED
PURLER	GOGLET	AFFLUX	+WESLEY	ROOMED
RIFLER	GULLET	DUPLEX	WHOLLY	SEAMED
ROLLER	HAMLET	EFFLUX	WOOLLY	SEEMED

SHAMED	DOLMEN	HAMMER	CRUMBY	FINNOC
SPUMED	ETYMON	ISOMER	CRUMMY	ICONIC
SUMMED	FIRMAN	+MESMER	DISMAY	IRENIC
TALMUD	FLAMEN	MUMMER	FIRMLY	IRONIC
TEAMED	FLYMAN	MURMUR	FLIMSY	PHONIC
TEEMED	FOEMAN	PALMAR	FRUMPY	PICNIC
TERMED	GAMMON	PALMER	GLUMLY	SCENIC
WARMED	GASMAN	PRIMER	GRIMLY	TANNIC.
WORMED	GERMAN	RAMMER	GRUMPY	ATONED
ZOOMED.	GERMEN	REAMER	PLUMMY	BANNED
COMMIE	GERMON	RHYMER	PRIMLY	BURNED
GRAMME	GNOMON	ROAMER	SCUMMY	CANNED
STYMIE.	GUNMAN	SIMMER	SEEMLY	CONNED
NUTMEG.	HETMAN	SUMMER	SHAMMY	CORNED
WARMTH.	HODMAN	TREMOR	SHIMMY	CRANED
ALUMNI	ICEMAN	WARMER.	SKIMPY	DAMNED
SCAMPI.	LAYMAN	ANIMUS	SLIMLY	DARNED
ANIMAL	MADMAN	+CADMUS	SLUMMY	DAWNED
BRUMAL	MAMMON	COSMOS	STUMPY	DINNED
*CARMEL	MERMAN	DERMIS	SWAMPY	DONNED
DISMAL	MORMON	*GLAMIS	TRIMLY	DOWNED
ENAMEL	+NORMAN	+HERMES	WARMLY	DRONED
FORMAL	PITMAN	KERMES	WHIMSY	DUNNED
HAEMAL	POTMAN	KERMIS		EARNED
KUMMEL	RAGMAN	LAMMAS	AGENDA	EVENED
MAMMAL	SALMON	LITMUS	+AMANDA	FANNED
NORMAL	SEAMAN	PRIMUS	+BRENDA	FAWNED
POMMEL	SEAMEN	*THAMES	CORNEA	GAINED
PRIMAL	SERMON	+THOMAS.	DUENNA	GUNNED
PUMMEL	SHAMAN	CERMET	*GDYNIA	HORNED
+ROMMEL	STAMEN	COMMIT	*GUINEA	IRONED
THYMOL.	SUMMON	EXEMPT	HERNIA	JOINED
ACUMEN	+TRUMAN	FORMAT	+JOANNA	KEENED
AIRMAN	VERMIN	HELMET	QUANTA	KENNED
APE-MAN	YEOMAN	HERMIT	*RWANDA	LEANED
BAGMAN	YES-MAN.	KISMET	SIENNA	LOANED
BARMAN	AKIMBO	MARMOT	STANZA	MAENAD
BATMAN	CRAMBO.	PELMET	*UGANDA	MANNED
*BODMIN	BOOMER	PERMIT	*VIENNA	MOANED
BOWMAN	CALMER	PROMPT	ZINNIA.	MOONED
BUSMAN	*CROMER	SUBMIT	HOBNOB.	OPINED
CABMAN	DAMMAR	SUMMIT.	AGONIC	PAINED
CARMAN	DIMMER	+ASIMOV.	ATONIC	PANNED
+CARMEN	DORMER	CLIMAX.	CLINIC	PAWNED
*CAYMAN	FARMER	BLIMEY	COGNAC	PENNED
COMMON	FIRMER	CALMLY	CYANIC	PHONED
CON-MAN	FORMER	CHUMMY	EDENIC	PINNED
COWMAN	FRAMER	CLAMMY	ETHNIC	PLANED
DAEMON	FULMAR	CLUMSY	FENNEC	PRUNED
DOLMAN	GAMMER	CRIMPY	FINNIC	PUNNED

RAINED	THENCE	SIMNEL	SINNER	AGENCY
REINED	TRANCE	SPINAL	SOONER	BOUNCY
RUINED	TWINGE	TERNAL	TANNER	BOUNTY
SHINED	USANCE	TUNNEL	+TURNER	BRANDY
SIGNED	WHENCE	URINAL	VAINER	CHANCY
SINNED	+YVONNE.	VERNAL.	+WAGNER	CHUNKY
STONED	EGG-NOG.	ANONYM	WINNER.	CLINGY
SUNNED	ACANTH	EPONYM	ACINUS	COUNTY
TANNED	BLANCH	LIGNUM	+ADONIS	CRANKY
TINNED	BLENCH	MAGNUM	AMENDS	CRANNY
TURNED	BRANCH	PAYNIM	ANANAS	DAINTY
TWINED	BRUNCH	PLENUM.	*CANNES	+DISNEY
VEINED	CLENCH	CANNON	+CRONOS	EVENLY
WARNED	CLINCH	FINNAN	+ERINYS	FLINTY
WEANED	CRUNCH	PENNON	+KEYNES	FRENZY
WHINED	DRENCH	PHANON	PRUNUS	GRANNY
YAWNED	FLANCH	TANNIN.	TENNIS	JAUNTY
YENNED.	FLENCH	BAGNIO	THANKS	KEENLY
AVENGE	FLINCH	*BORNEO	*TOTNES	KIDNEY
AVENUE	FRENCH	BRONCO	+URANUS	MAINLY
BLENDE	+HANNAH	LEAN-TO	VIANDS	MAUNDY
BLONDE	HAUNCH	PRONTO	*WIDNES	MOUNTY
BOUNCE	LAUNCH	SHINTO.	ZOUNDS.	OPENLY
+BRONTE	PAUNCH	CAT-NAP	*BARNET	*ORKNEY
BRONZE	PLANCH	KIDNAP	BONNET	PHONEY
CHANCE	PLINTH	TURNIP	+BRANDT	PLENTY
CHANGE	QUENCH	TURN-UP.	BURNET	QUINSY
CRINGE	STANCH	BANNER	CANNOT	+RODNEY
EVINCE	STENCH	BURNER	COBNUT	*ROMNEY
FIANCE	TRENCH	CANNER	CORNET	SAWNEY
FLANGE	WRENCH.	COINER	CYGNET	SCANTY
*FRANCE	*BRUNEI.	CORNER	GANNET	SHANDY
FRINGE	*GDANSK.	DARNER	GARNET	SHANTY
GLANCE	ATONAL	DINNER	HORNET	SHINDY
GRANGE	+BRUNEL	+ELINOR	JENNET	SKINNY
JINNEE	CARNAL	FAWNER	LINNET	SLANGY
JOUNCE	CORNEL	FINNER	MAGNET	SLINKY
LAUNCE	DARNEL	GARNER	PEANUT	SPONGY
LOUNGE	DIRNDL	GUNNER	PIGNUT	STINGY
NUANCE	FENNEL	JOINER	PLANET	SWANKY
ORANGE	FUNNEL	KEENER	PUNNET	*SYDNEY
PLUNGE	HYMNAL	LANNER	RENNET	THINLY
POUNCE	KENNEL	LIMNER	SIGNET	TRENDY
PRANCE	KERNEL	MANNER	SONNET	TWENTY
PRINCE	+LIONEL	OPENER	SPINET	VAINLY
QUINCE	PHENOL	*PINNER	UNKNIT	*VYRNWY
SCONCE	REGNAL	*RADNOR	WALNUT.	WHINNY.
SEANCE	RHINAL	RUNNER	MINNOW	CHINTZ
SPONGE	RUNNEL	SHINER	WINNOW.	
STANCE	SIGNAL	SIGNOR	MAGNOX.	*ANGOLA

ANGORA	NO-GOOD	FURORE	UNROBE	DISOWN
AREOLA	*ORFORD	GALORE	UNYOKE	ENJOIN
AURORA	*OXFORD	GROOVE	VAMOSE	HEROIN
*BOGOTA	RECORD	HAMOSE	VENOSE	INBORN
CORONA	SECOND	HEXOSE	XYLOSE	LAGOON
CUPOLA	SHOOED	IGNORE	ZYGOTE.	MAROON
*DAKOTA	SHROUD	IMPOSE	CUT-OFF	MINOAN
+EUROPA	*STROUD	INCOME	FAR-OFF	RACOON
FEDORA	TOROID	IN-JOKE	LAY-OFF	REBORN
MIMOSA	UNCORD	INSOLE	ONE-OFF	REJOIN
PAGODA	UNFOLD	INTONE	SET-OFF	RENOWN
PELOTA	UNLOAD	INVOKE	TIP-OFF.	SALOON
REMORA	UNTOLD	INWOVE	BELONG	SUBORN
SCROTA	UPHOLD	+JEROME	DUGONG	THROWN
SENORA	VETOED	JOCOSE	OBLONG	TYCOON
STROMA	XYLOID	KETONE	SARONG	UNBORN
*VERONA	ZEROED.	*LAHORE	STRONG	UNWORN
ZYGOMA.	ALCOVE	MOHOLE	THRONG.	UPTOWN.
ABSORB	ANYONE	MOROSE	BROOCH	ARIOSO
ADSORB	ASHORE	+NICOLE	GALOSH	ARROYO
APLOMB	ASLOPE	NODOSE	GOLOSH	COROZO
ENTOMB	BECOME	OPPOSE	MOLOCH	GIGOLO
RESORB.	BEFORE	ORIOLE	SMOOCH	KIMONO
ECHOIC	BEGONE	OTIOSE	SMOOTH	ROCOCO.
HEROIC.	BEHOVE	PAROLE	WHOOSH.	RECOUP.
ABROAD	+BROOKE	PEYOTE	BETOOK	ARBOUR
ACCORD	BYGONE	PILOSE	BOG-OAK	ARDOUR
AFFORD	CAJOLE	PINOLE	OCLOCK	ARMOUR
AGE-OLD	+CAPONE	PYROPE	RETOOK	COLOUR
ALGOID	+CAPOTE	REBORE	UNCORK	DETOUR
ALMOND	CHOOSE	REMOTE	UNHOOK	DEVOUR
+ARNOLD	CHROME	REMOVE	UNLOCK.	DOLOUR
BEHOLD	COMOSE	REPOSE	BEFOOL	FAVOUR
BEYOND	COYOTE	REVOKE	BEFOUL	GIAOUR
BY-ROAD	CREOLE	RIBOSE	RECOIL	HONOUR
BYWORD	DECODE	RIMOSE	SCHOOL	HUMOUR
CONOID	DECOKE	+SALOME	SCROLL	INDOOR
CUBOID	DEMODE	SETOSE	STROLL	LABOUR
DEVOID	DEMOTE	SHROVE	UNCOIL	MEMOIR
ECHOED	DENOTE	SNOOZE	UNROLL.	+RENOIR
ENFOLD	DEPONE	STOOGE	DEFORM	RIGOUR
GANOID	DEPOSE	STROBE	INFORM	RUMOUR
HALOED	DEVOTE	STRODE	PHLOEM	SAVOUR
HALOID	DIPOLE	STROKE	REFORM	TUMOUR
+HAROLD	DITONE	STROVE	SIMOOM.	UNMOOR
*ILFORD	DOLOSE	THRONE	ADJOIN	UPROAR
INROAD	ENCORE	THROVE	ADNOUN	VALOUR
KAYOED	ENROBE	TRIODE	BABOON	VAPOUR
KOBOLD	*EUROPE	*TYRONE	BEMOAN	VIGOUR.
*LOMOND	EXPOSE	UNDONE	COCOON	ACROSS

197

+ALDOUS	REPORT	THEORY	PALPED	PIMPLE
ALGOUS	RESORT	UNHOLY	PEPPED	PURPLE
AUROUS	RETORT		PIMPED	RIPPLE
BOFORS	REVOLT	HOOP-LA	PIPPED	RUMPLE
EMBOSS	SET-OUT	MYOPIA	POPPED	SAMPLE
FAMOUS	SPROUT	UTOPIA.	PUMPED	SIMPLE
FUMOUS	THROAT	MYOPIC	PUPPED	*SKOPJE
JOYOUS	TRY-OUT	TROPIC.	RAMPED	STAPLE
MUCOUS	UNBOLT	BUMPED	RAPPED	STEPPE
ODIOUS	UPMOST	BURPED	RASPED	SUPPLE
PATOIS	UPROOT	CAMPED	RIPPED	TEMPLE
+PELOPS	UTMOST	CAPPED	ROMPED	TIPPLE
PILOUS	WAY-OUT.	CARPED	SAPPED	TOPPLE
POROUS	ORMOLU.	COOPED	SEEPED	TOUPEE
RIMOUS	+ANTONY	COPPED	SHAPED	TRAPSE
RUFOUS	APHONY	CUPPED	SIPPED	TRIPLE
SEROUS	ARGOSY	CUSPED	SLOPED	WIMPLE.
VENOUS	ARROWY	DIPPED	SOAPED	*DELPHI.
VINOUS.	BACONY	DRAPED	SOPPED	CARPAL
ACCOST	BARONY	DUMPED	SOUPED	CARPEL
ADROIT	BETONY	ELOPED	STUPID	CHAPEL
AFLOAT	BLOODY	GASPED	SUPPED	COMPEL
+ALCOTT	BROODY	GRIPED	SWIPED	DISPEL
ALL-OUT	+BRYONY	GROPED	TAMPED	DRUPEL
ALMOST	CANOPY	GULPED	TAPPED	GOSPEL
APPORT	CHOOSY	HAPPED	TIPPED	PROPEL.
ASSORT	COLONY	HARPED	TOPPED	POMPOM.
CAHOOT	EMBODY	HASPED	TORPID	BED-PAN
CAVORT	EULOGY	HEAPED	TRIPOD	+CHOPIN
COHORT	FELONY	HELPED	UNIPED	COUPON
COP-OUT	FLOOZY	HIPPED	VAMPED	DAMPEN
CUT-OUT	GLOOMY	HISPID	VESPID	DEEPEN
DACOIT	GROOVY	HOOPED	WARPED	HAPPEN
DECOCT	IDIOCY	HOPPED	YAPPED	HATPIN
DEPORT	JALOPY	HUMPED	YELPED	HEMPEN
DEVOUT	MELODY	ISOPOD	ZIPPED.	INSPAN
DUGOUT	MEMORY	JUMPED	CORPSE	PIPPIN
EFFORT	MONODY	KIPPED	COUPLE	POMPON
ESCORT	NOBODY	LAPPED	DAPPLE	REOPEN
EXHORT	ONIONY	LEAPED	*DIEPPE	SAMPAN
EXPORT	PAEONY	LIMPED	DIMPLE	TAMPON
EXTORT	PARODY	LIMPID	ELAPSE	TARPAN
IMPORT	POLONY	LIPPED	FRAPPE	TIE-PIN
IMPOST	PRIORY	LISPED	GRIPPE	TREPAN
INMOST	SAVORY	LOOPED	HOOPOE	WEAPON.
LAYOUT	*SAXONY	LOPPED	HOPPLE	NYMPHO
MAHOUT	SIMONY	MAPPED	KELPIE	TROPPO.
ONCOST	SNOOTY	MOPPED	MAGPIE	SLAP-UP
RAGOUT	SODOMY	NAPPED	NIPPLE	*BELPAR
REFOOT	SPOOKY	NIPPED	PEOPLE	BUMPER

CAMPER	ARMPIT	CASQUE	HATRED	COARSE
COOPER	CARPET	CHEQUE	HORRID	COERCE
COPPER	DESPOT	CINQUE	HOT-ROD	CORRIE
CUPPER	HOTPOT	CIRQUE	HYBRID	COURSE
DAMP,ER	INK-POT	CLAQUE	INBRED	COWRIE
DAPPER	LAPPET	CLIQUE	+INGRID	DECREE
DEEPER	LIMPET	MANQUE	INURED	DEGREE
DIAPER	MOPPET	MASQUE	JARRED	ECARTE
DIPPER	OUTPUT	MOSQUE	JEERED	EMERGE
DRAPER	POPPET	OPAQUE	LEERED	ENTREE
DUMPER	PULPIT	PLAQUE	*MADRID	FAERIE
GASPER	PUPPET	PULQUE	MARRED	*FAEROE
HAMPER	RAJPUT	RISQUE	MITRED	FIERCE
HARPER	SEXPOT	TORQUE	MOORED	+GEORGE
HELPER	SIPPET	UNIQUE	NEARED	HEARSE
HOPPER	TAPPET		PAIRED	HOARSE
+JASPER	TEAPOT	CHOREA	PEERED	IMBRUE
JUMPER	TINPOT	DHARMA	PURRED	KERRIE
KEEPER	TIPPET.	+GLORIA	PUTRID	+LAURIE
KIPPER	COW-POX.	NUTRIA	RAMROD	+MONROE
LOOPER	APEPSY	SCORIA	REARED	PIERCE
NIPPER	BIOPSY	SIERRA	RETROD	SCARCE
PAMPER	CHIPPY	*SPARTA.	ROARED	SOIREE
PAUPER	CHOPPY	CHERUB	SACRED	SOURCE
PEEPER	COMPLY	SCARAB.	SCARED	SPARSE
PEPPER	DAMPLY	ACERIC	SCORED	SPURGE
PROPER	DEEPLY	AGARIC	SEARED	STARVE
PULPER	DIMPLY	CHORIC	SHARED	SWERVE
REAPER	DROPSY	CITRIC	SHORED	THORPE
SAPPER	DUMPTY	CLERIC	SNARED	TIERCE
SIMPER	FLOPPY	CUPRIC	SNORED	UNTRUE.
SNIPER	HUMPTY	CYMRIC	SOARED	CHURCH
STUPOR	LIMPLY	FABRIC	SOURED	DEARTH
SUPPER	PIMPLY	FERRIC	SPARED	EXARCH
TAMPER	PREPAY	HYDRIC	SPIRED	FOURTH
TEMPER	RIPPLY	MATRIC	STARED	HEARTH
TIPPER	SIMPLY	METRIC	STORED	HURRAH
TOPPER	SLOPPY	NITRIC	TARRED	INARCH
TORPOR	SNAPPY	RUBRIC.	TETRAD	SCORCH
+VESPER	SUPPLY	+ALFRED	TORRID	SEARCH
WEEPER	TEAPOY	+ASTRID	TOURED	SMIRCH
ZIPPER.	TROPHY	BARRED	VEERED	STARCH.
CAMPUS	TWO-PLY	BLARED	WARRED	ANORAK
CARPUS	WHIPPY	+CONRAD	WHORED.	+DVORAK.
CORPUS		FEARED	ACCRUE	AMORAL
HERPES	BARQUE	FLARED	AMERCE	ASTRAL
PAMPAS	BASQUE	FLORID	AVERSE	BARREL
RUMPUS	BISQUE	FURRED	+BARRIE	CARREL
STAPES	+BRAQUE	GEARED	BOURSE	CHORAL
TRIPOS.	CAIQUE	GLARED	CHARGE	CORRAL

CRURAL	BEARER	BORROW	SPORTY	LIASED
FIBRIL	DEARER	BURROW	STARRY	LOOSED
FLORAL	FUHRER	FARROW	STOREY	MASSED
LAUREL	HEARER	FURROW	STORMY	MESSED
NEURAL	HORROR	*HARROW	STURDY	MISSED
PATROL	MIRROR	HEBREW	*SURREY	NOOSED
PETREL	NEARER	+JARROW	THIRTY	NURSED
PETROL	POORER	MARROW	THORNY	PARSED
PLURAL	POURER	MORROW	WHERRY	PASSED
SACRAL	ROARER	NARROW	YEARLY.	PAUSED
SORREL	SCORER	SORROW	QUARTZ	PHASED
SPIRAL	TERROR	YARROW.		POISED
UMBRAL.	TOURER	IMBREX	*ALASKA	PULSED
ALARUM	USURER.	MATRIX	CASSIA	PURSED
*ANTRIM	*AZORES	THORAX.	FIESTA	RAISED
ANTRUM	CHORUS	AFFRAY	GEISHA	RINSED
MEGRIM	CIRRUS	ASTRAY	MIASMA	SEISED
POGROM	CITRUS	+AUDREY	NAUSEA	SENSED
QUORUM	*CYPRUS	BETRAY	*ODESSA	SOUSED
SACRUM.	DEBRIS	+CHERRY	PLASMA	SUSSED
BARREN	DERRIS	CHIRPY	*RUSSIA	TEASED
+CHARON	FERRIS	CLERGY	SIESTA	TENSED
+CHIRON	*HARRIS	DEARLY	TARSIA.	TOSSED
CITRON	HUBRIS	DEFRAY	AIR-SAC	UNUSED
DACRON	+ICARUS	DOURLY	PARSEC	VERSED.
FIBRIN	*MADRAS	ENERGY	PHASIC	CHASSE
FLORIN	+MORRIS	FAIRLY	PHYSIC.	CHASTE
MACRON	+OSIRIS	FLIRTY	ABASED	CROSSE
MATRON	PHAROS	FLURRY	ABUSED	+JESSIE
MICRON	TAURUS	HEARTY	AMUSED	LASSIE
NEURON	*TIGRIS	HOORAY	BIASED	LESSEE
+OBERON	UTERUS	HOURLY	CAUSED	MOUSSE
OUTRAN	WALRUS.	HURRAY	CEASED	PARSEE
OUTRUN	*ARARAT	*MURRAY	CHASED	PUISNE
PATRON	*BEIRUT	NEARBY	CLOSED	PURSUE
PERRON	CARROT	NEARLY	CURSED	TASSIE
+WARREN.	CLARET	OSPREY	CUSSED	+THISBE
EMBRYO	DRY-ROT	OVERLY	DOSSED	TISSUE
HAIR-DO	FERRET	PEARLY	DOUSED	TOUSLE
*OPORTO	FLORET	POORLY	DOWSED	TUSSLE.
OVERDO	GARRET	QUARRY	ERASED	MASSIF.
QUARTO	LEARNT	SCURFY	FUSSED	BORSCH
STEREO	PARROT	SCURRY	GASSED	KIRSCH
*THURSO.	REGRET	SCURVY	HISSED	PUTSCH.
ENTRAP	SECRET	SHERRY	HORSED	CAUSAL
ENWRAP	SPIRIT	SHIRTY	HOUSED	CHESIL
LARRUP	THIRST	SKERRY	IRISED	CHISEL
SATRAP	TURRET.	SLURRY	KISSED	CONSUL
UNWRAP.	+ANDREW	SMARMY	LAPSED	CRESOL
ADORER	*BARROW	SOURLY	LEASED	DAMSEL

DIESEL	SARSEN	MISSUS	*JERSEY	POETIC
DORSAL	SEASON	RHESUS	KERSEY	RUSTIC
DOSSAL	SEISIN	SEPSIS	MARSHY	SEPTIC
DOSSIL	TOCSIN	STASIS	MEASLY	STATIC
FOSSIL	UNISON	TARSUS	*MERSEY	URETIC.
MISSAL	+WILSON	THESIS	PIGSTY	ABATED
MISSEL	WORSEN.	VERSUS.	PLASHY	BAITED
MORSEL	FIASCO	AVOSET	PLUSHY	BASTED
MUSSEL	FRESCO	BASSET	PRISSY	BATTED
TARSAL	PRESTO.	BED-SIT	*RAASAY	BELTED
TASSEL	GOSSIP	CLOSET	SLUSHY	BESTED
TEASEL	HYSSOP.	CORSET	THUSLY	BETTED
TINSEL	BURSAR	COSSET	TRASHY	BOLTED
TONSIL	+CAESAR	DOESNT	TRUSTY	BOOTED
VASSAL	CENSOR	*DORSET	TWISTY	CANTED
VESSEL	CHASER	GUSSET	WHISKY	CARTED
WEASEL.	CURSOR	OFFSET	YEASTY	COSTED
BALSAM	DENSER	OUTSET		CRATED
DORSUM	DOSSER	POSSET	+AGATHA	DARTED
GYPSUM	DOWSER	PROSIT	APHTHA	DENTED
HANSOM	GEYSER	RUSSET	+BERTHA	DIETED
JETSAM	GUISER	SUNSET	CONTRA	DOITED
LISSOM	HAWSER	TEA-SET	*GRETNA	DOTTED
PASSIM	HUSSAR	VERSET.	MALTHA	DUSTED
POSSUM	KAISER	*NASSAU.	+MARTHA	EDITED
RANSOM.	KISSER	BOW-SAW	QUOTHA	ELATED
+ALISON	LESSER	JIGSAW	ROSTRA.	EXITED
ARISEN	LESSOR	RIP-SAW	CANTAB.	FATTED
BUNSEN	LOOSER	*WARSAW.	ACETIC	FELTED
CHOSEN	MAUSER	*SUSSEX	*ARCTIC	FISTED
COUSIN	MOUSER	UNISEX.	*BALTIC	FITTED
DAMSON	PASSER	BRASHY	BIOTIC	FLUTED
+EDISON	PROSER	BRASSY	CELTIC	FOETID
GODSON	PULSAR	BRUSHY	COPTIC	FOOTED
GRISON	PURSER	CHESTY	CRITIC	GIFTED
*HUDSON	QUASAR	CLASSY	CYSTIC	GUTTED
KELSON	ROUSER	CRISPY	EMETIC	HAFTED
LESSEN	SENSOR	CRUSTY	EROTIC	HALTED
LESSON	TEASER	DRESSY	EXOTIC	HASTED
LOOSEN	TENSOR.	DROSSY	FISTIC	HATTED
+NELSON	BYSSUS	FLASHY	FUSTIC	HEATED
ODDS-ON	CENSUS	FLESHY	HECTIC	HEFTED
ORISON	CRASIS	FLOSSY	KELTIC	HEPTAD
PARSON	CRISIS	FRISKY	LACTIC	HINTED
PEPSIN	DIESIS	FROSTY	LUETIC	HOOTED
PERSON	ENOSIS	GLASSY	MANTIC	HOTTED
POISON	GNOSIS	GLOSSY	MASTIC	HUNTED
PRISON	*KANSAS	GRASSY	MYSTIC	HUTTED
RAISIN	MENSES	GRISLY	PECTIC	JESTED
REASON	MESSRS	GUN-SHY	PEPTIC	JETTED

---T-D			---T-N	
JILTED	SALTED	DOTTLE	WRITHE.	RENTAL
JOLTED	SEATED	FETTLE	TAUTOG.	SEPTAL
JOTTED	SILTED	GENTLE	BLOTCH	VESTAL.
JUTTED	SLATED	GOATEE	CLUTCH	ADYTUM
KILTED	SORTED	+GOETHE	CRATCH	BANTAM
KITTED	SPITED	GOITRE	CROTCH	BOTTOM
LASTED	STATED	HURTLE	CRUTCH	CUSTOM
LIFTED	SUITED	HUSTLE	FLETCH	DIATOM
LILTED	TARTED	JOSTLE	FLITCH	DICTUM
LISTED	TASTED	KETTLE	NAUTCH	FACTUM
LOFTED	TATTED	KIRTLE	QUITCH	RECTUM
LUSTED	TENTED	KITTLE	SCOTCH	RHYTHM
MALTED	TESTED	LITTLE	SKETCH	SEPTUM
MASTED	TILTED	LOATHE	SMUTCH	SPUTUM
MATTED	TOOTED	LUSTRE	SNATCH	SYSTEM
MELTED	TOTTED	MANTLE	STITCH	TOMTOM
MILTED	TOUTED	METTLE	SWITCH	VICTIM.
MINTED	TUFTED	MISTLE	THATCH	+AUSTEN
MISTED	TUTTED	MOTTLE	TWITCH	*AUSTIN
MOATED	UNITED	+MYRTLE	WRETCH.	BARTON
MOOTED	VENTED	NESTLE	+BARTOK.	BATTEN
NESTED	VESTED	NETTLE	AMATOL	BEATEN
NETTED	VETTED	+ODETTE	BRUTAL	*BHUTAN
ORATED	VOLTED	PESTLE	CARTEL	BIOTIN
OUSTED	WAFTED	PINTLE	CENTAL	BITTEN
PANTED	WAITED	PRATIE	COITAL	*BOLTON
PARTED	WANTED	PUTTEE	COSTAL	*BOSTON
PASTED	WASTED	RATTLE	DACTYL	BRETON
PATTED	WELTED	ROOTLE	DENTAL	BRITON
PELTED	WETTED	RUSTLE	DENTIL	*BURTON
PENTAD	WILTED	+SARTRE	DIETAL	BUTTON
PETTED	WONTED.	SCATHE	DISTAL	*BUXTON
PITTED	AUNTIE	SCYTHE	DISTIL	CAFTAN
PLATED	BATTLE	SEETHE	FESTAL	*CANTON
PORTED	BATTUE	SETTEE	FOETAL	CARTON
POSTED	BEETLE	SETTLE	FONTAL	+CAXTON
POTTED	BISTRE	SOOTHE	+GRETEL	CHITIN
POUTED	BLITHE	SORTIE	HOSTEL	CHITON
PRATED	BOOTEE	STATUE	INSTIL	COTTON
PUNTED	*BOOTLE	SUBTLE	LENTIL	CRETIN
RAFTED	BOTTLE	SUTTEE	LINTEL	CRETON
RATTED	BOW-TIE	SWATHE	MANTEL	+DALTON
RENTED	BUSTLE	TATTLE	MENTAL	FASTEN
RESTED	CASTLE	TIPTOE	MORTAL	FATTEN
RIFTED	CATTLE	TITTLE	PASTEL	GLUTEN
ROOTED	CENTRE	TOOTLE	PISTIL	GOTTEN
ROTTED	CLOTHE	TSETSE	PISTOL	GRATIN
ROUTED	COATEE	TURTLE	PORTAL	HASTEN
RUSTED	CUP-TIE	VIRTUE	POSTAL	ISATIN
RUTTED	DOPTRE	WATTLE	RECTAL	JETTON

+JUSTIN	BARTER	HELTER	RATTER	COITUS
KAFTAN	BATTER	HITTER	RECTOR	CULTUS
KITTEN	BEATER	HOOTER	RENTER	FLATUS
LATTEN	BESTIR	HOTTER	RIOTER	FOETUS
LENTEN	BETTER	HUNTER	ROSTER	GRATIS
LEPTON	BITTER	JESTER	ROTTER	HIATUS
LISTEN	BOATER	JITTER	SALTER	IRITIS
MARTEN	BUTTER	JOTTER	SCOTER	MANTIS
+MARTIN	CANTER	LATTER	SECTOR	OTITIS
+MILTON	CANTOR	+LESTER	SETTER	RICTUS
MITTEN	CAPTOR	LETTER	SIFTER	STATUS
MOLTEN	CASTER	LICTOR	SINTER	TESTES.
MUTTON	CASTOR	LIFTER	SISTER	MUSTNT
NEATEN	CAUTER	+LISTER	SITTER	SEPTET
+NEWTON	CO-STAR	LITTER	SKATER	SESTET
PATTEN	COSTER	LOFTER	SLATER	SEXTET.
PECTEN	COTTAR	LOITER	SOFTER	BESTOW
PECTIN	COTTER	LOOTER	SORTER	KOWTOW.
PHOTON	CRATER	MARTYR	STATER	CORTEX
PISTON	CRATUR	MASTER	STATOR	FRUTEX
PLATAN	CUTTER	MATTER	SUITOR	SURTAX
PLATEN	DEBTOR	MENTOR	TARTAR	SYNTAX
PROTON	DEXTER	MISTER	TASTER	VERTEX
RATTAN	DOCTOR	MORTAR	TATTER	VORTEX.
ROTTEN	DUSTER	MUSTER	TAUTER	APATHY
SEXTON	*EASTER	MUTTER	TEETER	CHATTY
SOFTEN	EDITOR	NATTER	TENTER	COSTLY
SULTAN	ELATER	NECTAR	TESTER	CURTLY
SUN-TAN	*EXETER	NEUTER	TETTER	CURTSY
*SUTTON	FACTOR	NUTTER	TITTER	DEFTLY
TARTAN	FALTER	OBITER	TOTTER	EARTHY
TAUTEN	FASTER	ORATOR	*ULSTER	FILTHY
TEUTON	FATTER	OYSTER	URETER	FLATLY
+TRITON	FESTER	PALTER	VASTER	FROTHY
+WALTON	FETTER	PASTOR	VECTOR	GANTRY
WANTON	FILTER	PATTER	+VICTOR	GENTLY
WHITEN	FITTER	PESTER	WAITER	GENTRY
*WILTON.	FOOTER	PEWTER	+WALTER	GRITTY
+CASTRO	FOSTER	+PINTER	WASTER	GROTTY
+CLOTHO	GAITER	PLATER	WELTER	HEATHY
DEXTRO	GARTER	PORTER	WETTER	JUSTLY
GHETTO	GETTER	POSTER	WHITER	KNOTTY
GROTTO	GRATER	POTTER	WINTER	LASTLY
TATTOO.	GUITAR	POUTER	WRITER	NEATLY
INSTEP	GUNTER	PUNTER	XYSTER.	PALTRY
TIPTOP	GUTTER	PUTTER	ABATIS	PANTRY
TITTUP	HALTER	QUOTER	+BRUTUS	PARTLY
UNSTOP.	HATTER	RAFTER	CACTUS	PASTRY
AVATAR	HEATER	RAPTOR	CERTES	PERTLY
BANTER	+HECTOR	RASTER	CISTUS	POETRY

PORTLY	JOCUND	IMPUTE	STRUNG	SEQUIN
PRETTY	LIQUID	INCUSE	UNSUNG.	TEA-URN
RAPTLY	PIQUED	INDUCE	AMBUSH	UPTURN.
SCATTY	QUEUED	INFUSE	AVOUCH	+CARUSO
SENTRY	REFUND	INHUME	CHOUGH	ESCUDO
SMITHY	ROGUED	INJURE	CLOUGH	PSEUDO
SMUTTY	ROTUND	INSURE	CROUCH	TENUTO.
SNOTTY	SHOULD	JEJUNE	DROUTH	JAGUAR
SOFTLY	TWOULD	JUJUBE	ENOUGH	LIQUOR
SPOTTY	VALUED.	LEGUME	EUNUCH	VAGUER
SUBTLY	ABJURE	LOBULE	GROUCH	VALUER.
SULTRY	ACCUSE	MANURE	INRUSH	MAQUIS.
TARTLY	ADDUCE	MATURE	ONRUSH	ABDUCT
TAUTLY	ADJURE	MINUTE	PLOUGH	ABRUPT
VASTLY	ALLUDE	MISUSE	SLEUTH	ACQUIT
VESTRY	ALLURE	MODULE	SLOUCH	ADJUST
*WHITBY	AROUSE	NATURE	*SLOUGH	AMOUNT
WINTRY	ASSUME	NODULE	THOUGH	AUGUST
WORTHY.	ASSURE	OBTUSE	THRUSH	AVAUNT
+CORTEZ	ASTUTE	ORDURE	TROUGH	COQUET
	ATTUNE	PERUKE	UPRUSH.	DEDUCT
COPULA	*BEAUNE	PERUSE	AGOUTI	EXEUNT
FACULA	BEMUSE	PILULE	SALUKI	FLAUNT
FERULA	BLOUSE	REBUKE	TUMULI	INDUCT
FIBULA	+CANUTE	REDUCE	+YEHUDI.	INDULT
LACUNA	+CLAUDE	REFUGE	DEBUNK	INSULT
MACULA	CLAUSE	REFUSE	SHRUNK	JESUIT
+MEDUSA	*DANUBE	REFUTE	STRUCK.	LOCUST
NEBULA	DEDUCE	REPUTE	ACTUAL	LOQUAT
+PETULA	DEFUSE	RESUME	ANNUAL	MINUET
PLEURA	DELUDE	SALUTE	CASUAL	OCCULT
ROTULA	DELUGE	SCOUSE	MANUAL	PIQUET
TRAUMA	DEMURE	SECURE	+MANUEL	+PROUST
UNGULA	DENUDE	SEDUCE	MUTUAL	RESULT
+URSULA	DEPUTE	SOLUTE	REFUEL	ROBUST
VALUTA	DILUTE	SPOUSE	RITUAL	ROQUET
VICUNA.	DISUSE	SPRUCE	+SAMUEL	THRUST
BENUMB	EFFUSE	SUTURE	SEQUEL	TUMULT
SUBURB.	ENDURE	TENURE	SEXUAL	UNHURT
ABOUND	ENSURE	TRIUNE	UNFURL	UNJUST
ABSURD	EXCUSE	TROUPE	UNGUAL	YAOURT
ARGUED	EXHUME	UNSURE	VIDUAL	YOGURT.
AROUND	FERULE	VELURE	VISUAL.	AUGURY
+EDMUND	FIGURE	VOLUME	VACUUM.	BEAUTY
ENSUED	FUTURE	VOLUTE.	AUBURN	CLOUDY
FECUND	GROUSE	ENGULF	AUTUMN	CROUPY
GERUND	ILL-USE	REBUFF	COLUMN	DEPUTY
GROUND	IMMUNE	SCRUFF.	IMPUGN	FLOURY
IMBUED	IMMURE	COBURG	RETURN	INJURY
ISSUED	IMPURE	SPRUNG	+SATURN	LUXURY

OCCUPY	SWIVEL	TROVER	SNOWED	LEEWAY
PENURY	TRAVEL	VULVAR	SPEWED	*MEDWAY
RHEUMY	WEEVIL	WAIVER	STEWED	MIDWAY
SYRUPY	*YEOVIL.	WEAVER.	STOWED	*NORWAY
UNDULY	ALEVIN	CALVES	THAWED	ONE-WAY
UNRULY	+CALVIN	CANVAS	THEWED.	RUNWAY
	CHEVIN	CLEVIS	BROWSE	SEA-WAY
SALVIA	CLOVEN	CORVES	DRAWEE	SLOWLY
+SYLVIA	CRAVEN	+GRAVES	DROWSE.	SUBWAY
TRIVIA.	DRIVEN	HOOVES	BIGWIG	TWO-WAY
PELVIC	ELEVEN	KNIVES	EARWIG.	
SLAVIC.	FLAVIN	LEAVES	GROWTH	ALEXIA
BRAVED	HEAVEN	LOAVES	YAHWEH.	ATAXIA.
CALVED	LEAVEN	PARVIS	AVOWAL	COAXED
CRAVED	+MELVYN	PELVIS	CREWEL	FLEXED.
CURVED	PROVEN	SELVES	TROWEL.	FLAXEN
DELVED	SHAVEN	TURVES	WIGWAM.	KLAXON.
FERVID	SLOVEN	WOLVES.	*DARWIN	ELIXIR
GLOVED	SPAVIN	BREVET	+SELWYN	FLEXOR
GRAVID	+STEVEN	CRAVAT	*WELWYN.	HOAXER.
HALVED	SYLVAN	CURVET	BLOW-UP.	+ALEXIS
HEAVED	UNEVEN.	PRIVET	ANSWER	PLEXUS
HOOVED	BEAVER	TRIVET	BLOWER	PRAXIS
LEAVED	BRAVER	VELVET	BREWER	
NERVED	CLEVER	VERVET.	DRAWER	BARYTA
PEEVED	CLOVER	CERVIX	FLOWER	CORYZA.
PROVED	CULVER	CONVEX.	GLOWER	CORYMB.
REEVED	*DENVER	*CANVEY	GNAWER	BRAYED
REVVED	DRIVER	CHEVVY	GROWER	BUOYED
SALVED	DROVER	CHIVVY	PRE-WAR	CLOYED
SERVED	GLOVER	CONVEY	SHOWER	FLAYED
SHAVED	GRAVER	CONVOY	SKEWER	FRAYED
SHOVED	HEAVER	+HARVEY	SLOWER	OBEYED
SIEVED	+HOOVER	PURVEY	VIEWER.	OX-EYED
SOLVED	LOUVER	SKIVVY	DIMWIT	PLAYED
STAVED	+OLIVER	SURVEY	FROWST	PRAYED
VALVED	PLOVER		GODWIT	PREYED
WAIVED.	QUAVER	COBWEB.	NITWIT	SPAYED
LARVAE	QUIVER	AVOWED	OUTWIT	STAYED
LOUVRE.	SALVER	CHEWED	PEEWIT.	SWAYED
COEVAL	SALVOR	CLAWED	BOW-WOW	X-RAYED
DRIVEL	SERVER	CLEWED	POW-WOW.	ECTYPE
FRIVOL	SHAVER	CROWED	EARWAX.	ENZYME
GRAVEL	SHIVER	FLAWED	AIRWAY	GROYNE
GROVEL	SILVER	FLOWED	BRAWNY	OOCYTE.
LARVAL	SKIVER	GLOWED	*CONWAY	*ARGYLL.
MARVEL	SLAVER	GNAWED	CRAWLY	BANYAN
OGIVAL	SLIVER	SHOWED	DROWSY	BARYON
SHOVEL	STIVER	SKEWED	FROWZY	+BUNYAN
SNIVEL	+TREVOR	SLEWED	*GALWAY	CANYON

205

CRAYON.	BUZZER	BANTAM	CAT-NAP	DORSAL
BUNYIP.	FIZZER	BANYAN	CAUDAL	DOSSAL
LAWYER	GEEZER	BAOBAB	CAUSAL	+DOUGAL
MAGYAR	GLAZER	BARMAN	CAVEAT	DOWLAS
PLAYER	PANZER.	BASIAL	CAVIAR	*DUNBAR
PRAYER	FRIZZY	BATMAN	*CAYMAN	+DUNCAN
SAWYER	SNAZZY	BAZAAR	CELLAR	*DURBAN
SLAYER		BEDLAM	CENTAL	DURBAR
STAYER.		BED-PAN	CHORAL	*DURHAM
ENCYST.	*ABADAN	BEGGAR	CLIMAX	+DVORAK.
LARYNX.	ABROAD	BEHEAD	COEVAL	EARWAX
CLAYEY	ACTUAL	BELDAM	COGNAC	ENDEAR
SYZYGY	+ADRIAN	BELIAL	COITAL	ENTRAP
	*AEGEAN	*BELPAR	COLLAR	ENWRAP
PIAZZA	+AENEAS	BEMOAN	COMBAT	EPICAL
RAZZIA.	AERIAL	*BENGAL	CONFAB	ESCHAR
+BALZAC	AFFRAY	BETRAY	CON-MAN	ESPIAL.
RHIZIC.	AFLOAT	*BHUTAN	+CONRAD	FABIAN
AMAZED	AIRMAN	*BILBAO	*CONWAY	FACIAL
BLAZED	AIR-SAC	BOBCAT	CORBAN	FAECAL
BOOZED	AIRWAY	BOG-OAK	CORRAL	FAUCAL
CRAZED	AMORAL	*BOMBAY	COSTAL	FELLAH
FIZZED	ANABAS	BOREAL	CO-STAR	FENIAN
GLAZED	ANANAS	BOWMAN	COTTAR	FERIAL
GRAZED	ANIMAL	BOW-SAW	COUGAR	FESTAL
JAZZED	ANNEAL	BRIDAL	COWMAN	FETIAL
PRIZED	ANNUAL	BRUMAL	CRAVAT	FEUDAL
SEIZED.	ANORAK	BRUTAL	CREDAL	FILIAL
DAZZLE	ANTIAR	BUCCAL	CRURAL	FINIAL
FIZZLE	APE-MAN	*BUCHAN	CUSHAT	FINNAN
FOOZLE	APICAL	+BUNYAN	CYMBAL.	FIRMAN
GUZZLE	APODAL	BUREAU	DAEDAL	FISCAL
MIZZLE	APPEAL	BURIAL	*DALLAS	FLORAL
MUZZLE*	APPEAR	BURLAP	DAMMAR	FLYMAN
NOZZLE	*ARARAT	BURSAR	DEFEAT	FOEMAN
NUZZLE	ARREAR	BUSMAN	DEFRAY	FOETAL
PUZZLE	ASH-CAN	BY-ROAD.	DEMEAN	FOLIAR
SIZZLE.	ASHLAR	CABMAN	DENIAL	FONTAL
*DANZIG	ASTRAL	+CAESAR	DENTAL	FORMAL
ZIGZAG.	ASTRAY	CAFTAN	DEODAR	FORMAT
BORZOI.	ATONAL	CALCAR	DEWLAP	FRACAS
BENZOL	AUGEAN	*CALLAO	DIETAL	FRIDAY
*BRAZIL	AVATAR	CAN-CAN	DISBAR	FRUGAL
FRAZIL.	AVOWAL.	CANTAB	DISCAL	FULMAR.
AMAZON	BAGMAN	CANVAS	DISMAL	*GALWAY
BLAZON	*BALKAN	CARFAX	DISMAY	GAS-BAG
BRAZEN	BALLAD	CARMAN	DISTAL	GASMAN
FROZEN.	BALSAM	CARNAL	DOLLAR	GATEAU
BLAZER	+BALZAC	CARPAL	DOLMAN	GENIAL
BOOZER	BANIAN	CASUAL	DORIAN	GERMAN

GEWGAW	KIT-BAG	*MUSCAT	QUASAR.	SQUEAL
GLOBAL	*KODIAK.	MUTUAL	*RAASAY	STREAK
GODDAM	LABIAL	MYRIAD.	RACIAL	STREAM
+GRAHAM	LAICAL	*NASSAU	RADIAL	SUBWAY
GUFFAW	LAMMAS	+NATHAN	RADIAN	SULTAN
GUITAR	LANDAU	NECTAR	RAG-BAG	SUNDAE
GUNMAN.	LARIAT	NEURAL	RAG-DAY	SUNDAY
HABEAS	LARVAE	NILGAI	RAGLAN	SUN-HAT
HAEMAL	LARVAL	NORMAL	RAGMAN	SUN-TAN
HANGAR	LASCAR	+NORMAN	RANDAN	SURTAX
+HANNAH	LAYMAN	*NORWAY	RASCAL	SYLVAN
HAW-HAW	LEEWAY	NOUGAT.	RATTAN	SYNTAX.
HEPTAD	LETHAL	OCULAR	RECTAL	TARMAC
HERBAL	+LILIAN	OFF-DAY	REDCAP	TARPAN
HEREAT	LINEAL	OGIVAL	REGNAL	TARSAL
HETMAN	LINEAR	OIL-CAN	RENTAL	TARTAN
HEYDAY	LINGAM	*OLDHAM	REPEAL	TARTAR
HODMAN	LOOFAH	ONE-WAY	REPEAT	TEA-BAG
HOOKAH	LOQUAT	ORDEAL	REPLAY	TERGAL
HOORAY	LUMBAR	*OREGAN	RESEAT	TERNAL
HOWDAH	*LYTHAM.	ORPHAN	REVEAL	TETRAD
HURRAH	MADCAP	OUTLAW	RHINAL	+THOMAS
HURRAY	MADMAN	OUTLAY	RIP-SAW	THORAX
HUSSAR	*MADRAS	OUTRAN.	RITUAL	THREAD
HYMNAL.	MAENAD	PALMAR	ROSEAL	THREAT
*IBADAN	MAGYAR	PAMPAS	RUNWAY.	THROAT
ICE-CAP	MAMMAL	PARIAH	SACRAL	TIMBAL
ICEMAN	MANIAC	PARIAN	SAGGAR	TIN-CAN
INDIAN	MANUAL	+PASCAL	SALAAM	TIPCAT
INROAD	+MARIAN	PATHAN	SAMPAN	+TITIAN
INSPAN	MEDIAL	PEDLAR	SANDAL	TOE-CAP
IONIAN	MEDIAN	PENIAL	SATRAP	TOM-CAT
+ISAIAH	MEDLAR	PENTAD	SCALAR	TOP-HAT
ISOBAR.	*MEDWAY	PICKAX	SCARAB	TOUCAN
JACKAL	MENIAL	PILLAR	SCREAM	TREPAN
JAGUAR	MENTAL	PINEAL	SEAMAN	TRIBAL
JAM-JAR	MERMAN	PITMAN	SEA-WAY	TRICAR
JETSAM	MESCAL	PLATAN	SENDAL	TROJAN
JIGSAW	MIDDAY	PLURAL	SEPTAL	+TRUMAN
*JORDAN	MIDWAY	POPLAR	SERIAL	TURBAN
+JOSIAH	MINOAN	PORTAL	SEXUAL	TWO-WAY
JOVIAL	+MIRIAM	POSTAL	SHAMAN	TYRIAN.
JOVIAN	MISHAP	POTMAN	SIGNAL	UMBRAL
+JULIAN	MISLAY	PREFAB	SIMIAN	UNCIAL
JUMBAL.	MISSAL	PREPAY	SLOGAN	UNGUAL
KAFTAN	MONDAY	PRE-WAR	SOCIAL	UNLOAD
*KANSAS	+MORGAN	PRIMAL	SPINAL	UNREAD
*KENDAL	MORTAL	PULSAR	SPIRAL	UNREAL
KIBLAH	MORTAR	*PUNJAB	SPREAD	UNSEAL
KIDNAP	*MURRAY	PURDAH.	SQUEAK	UNSEAT

UNWRAP	SNOBBY	CILICE	GLANCE	POLICY
UPBEAT	STROBE	CLENCH	*GREECE	POMACE
UPROAR	+STUBBS	CLINCH	GROUCH.	POUNCE
URINAL	STUBBY.	CLOACA	HAUNCH	PRANCE
UVULAR.	+THISBE	CLUTCH	HIJACK	PREACH
VANDAL	TRILBY.	COERCE	+HORACE.	PRINCE
VASSAL	UNROBE.	COPECK	IDIOCY	PUMICE
VENIAL	*WHITBY.	CRATCH	IMPACT	PUTSCH.
VERBAL	ZARIBA	CROTCH	INARCH	QUENCH
VERNAL		CROUCH	INDICT	QUINCE
VESTAL	ABBACY	CRUNCH	INDUCE	QUITCH.
VIDUAL	ABDUCT	CRUTCH	INDUCT	REBECK
VISUAL	ABJECT	CURACY.	INFECT	REDACT
+VIVIAN	ADDICT	DECOCT	INJECT	REDUCE
+VULCAN	ADDUCE	DEDUCE	INSECT	REFACE
VULGAR	ADJECT	DEDUCT	INTACT	REJECT
VULVAR.	ADVICE	DEFACE	*ITHACA.	RELICT
*WARSAW	AFFECT	DEFECT	+JANICE	ROCOCO.
WAYLAY	*AFRICA	DEJECT	JOUNCE.	SCARCE
WIGWAM	AGENCY	DEPICT	KIRSCH	SCONCE
WITHAL	ALPACA	DETACH	KOPECK.	SCORCH
WOMBAT.	AMERCE	DETECT	LAUNCE	SCOTCH
XENIAL.	APIECE	DEVICE	LAUNCH	SEANCE
YEOMAN	ARNICA	DIRECT	LEGACY	SEARCH
YES-MAN.	ASPECT	DRENCH	LUNACY.	SEDUCE
ZIGZAG	ATTACH	DRY-ICE.	MALICE	SELECT
ZODIAC	ATTACK	EFFACE	+MEDICI	SILICA
	AVOUCH.	EFFECT	MEDICO	SKETCH
AKIMBO	BEDECK	ENFACE	MENACE	SLOUCH
AMOEBA.	BISECT	ENLACE	*MEXICO	SLUICE
CHUBBY	BLANCH	ENRICH	MOLOCH	SMIRCH
CRABBY	BLEACH	ENTICE	*MONACO	SMOOCH
CRAMBO	BLENCH	EUNICE	+MONICA.	SMUTCH
CRUMBY.	BLOTCH	EUNUCH	NAUTCH	SNATCH
*DANUBE.	BODICE	EVINCE	NOTICE	SOLACE
ENROBE.	BORSCH	EXARCH	NOVICE	SOURCE
FLABBY.	BOUNCE	EXPECT.	NUANCE.	SPEECH
GAZEBO	BOUNCY	FIANCE	OBJECT	SPLICE
GRUBBY.	BRANCH	FIASCO	OCLOCK	SPRUCE
HEREBY.	BREACH	FIERCE	OFFICE	STANCE
IMBIBE	BREECH	FLANCH	OPTICS.	STANCH
INDABA.	BROACH	FLEECE	PALACE	STARCH
JUJUBE.	BRONCO	FLEECY	PAPACY	STENCH
KNOBBY.	BRONCO	FLENCH	PAUNCH	STITCH
NEARBY.	BRUNCH	FLETCH	PIERCE	STRICT
+PHOEBE	CALICO	FLINCH	PIRACY	STRUCK
PLEBBY.	CHANCE	FLITCH	PLAICE	STUCCO
SCABBY	CHANCY	*FRANCE	PLANCH	SWITCH.
SCRIBE	CHOICE	FRENCH	POLACK	THATCH
SHABBY	CHURCH	FRESCO.	POLICE	THENCE

THRICE	DERIDE	TEREDO	ASLEEP	BATTED
THWACK	DIRNDL	TIRADE	ATONED	BATTEN
TIERCE	DIVIDE	TRENDY	+ATTLEE	BATTER
TRANCE	DORADO.	TRIODE	+AUDREY	BAWLED
TRENCH	EMBODY	TUXEDO.	+AUSTEN	BEAKED
TWITCH.	ESCUDO.	*UGANDA	AVOCET	BEAKER
UNLOCK	FACADE	UNLADE	AVOSET	BEAMED
UNPACK	FUMADE.	UNMADE	AVOWED	BEARER
UNPICK	GREEDY.	UNTIDY	AWAKEN	BEATEN
UNTACK	HAIR-DO	UPSIDE.	AWHEEL	BEATER
USANCE.	HALIDE.	VIANDS.	AWOKEN	BEAVER
*VENICE	IMPEDE	XANADU.	AZALEA	BEDDED
VESICA	INSIDE	+YEHUDI.	*AZORES.	BEGGED
VIVACE.	INVADE	ZOUNDS	BACKED	BELIEF
WHENCE	IODIDE		BACKER	BELTED
WRENCH	+ISOLDE.	*AACHEN	BADGER	BENDED
WRETCH.	LAMBDA	ABASED	BAGGED	BERBER
+YORICK.	LIBIDO.	ABATED	BAILEE	*BERGEN
*ZURICH	MALADY	ABIDED.	BAILER	BESEEM
	MAUNDY	ABUSED	BAILEY	BESTED
ABRADE	MELODY	ACUMEN	BAITED	BETHEL
ACCEDE	MIKADO	ADDLED	+BALDER.	BETTED
AGENDA	MILADY	ADORER	BALEEN	BETTER
ALLUDE	MONODY	AETHER	BALKED	BIASED
+AMANDA	MOULDY.	AGREED	BALLET	BICKER
AMENDS	*NEVADA	+AILEEN	BANDED	BIDDER
ARCADE	NOBODY.	AIR-BED	BANGED	BIGGER
ARMADA	OREIDE	+ALFRED	BANKED	BILKER
AUBADE.	OVERDO	ALLIED	BANKER	BILLED
BESIDE	OX-HIDE.	ALLIES	BANNED	BILLET
BETIDE	PAGODA	AMAZED	BANNER	BINDER
BLENDE	PARADE	AMBLED	BANTER	BITTEN
BLONDE	PARODY	AMULET	BARBED	BITTER
BLOODY	POMADE	AMUSED	BARBEL	BLADED
BOLIDE	PSEUDO.	ANADEM	BARBER	BLAMED
+BRANDT	RECEDE	+ANDREW	BARBET	BLARED
BRANDY	REMADE	ANGLED	BARGEE	BLAZED
+BRENDA	REMEDY	ANGLER	BARKER	BLAZER
BROODY.	RESIDE	ANKLET	BARLEY	BLIMEY
*CANADA	*RWANDA.	ANSWER	*BARNET	BLOWER
CICADA	SECEDE	ANTHEM	BARRED	BOATER
+CLAUDE	SHANDY	ANTHER	BARREL	BOBBED
CLOUDY	SHINDY	ANTLER	BARREN	BODIED
COMEDY.	SHODDY	APICES	BARTER	BOGGED
DECADE	SPEEDY	APOGEE	BASHED	BOILED
DECIDE	STEADY	ARCHED	BASKED	BOILER
DECODE	STRIDE	ARCHER	BASKET	BOLDER
DELUDE	STRODE	ARGUED	BASSET	BOLTED
DEMODE	STURDY.	ARISEN	BASTED	BOMBED
DENUDE	TELEDU	ARMLET	BATHER	BOMBER

BONDED	BURNER	CEASED	CONKED	CUMBER
BONDER	BURNET	CERMET	CONKER	CUPPED
BONNET	BURPED	CERTES	CONNED	CUPPER
BOOKED	BUSHED	CHAFED	CONVEX	CURBED
BOOMED	BUSHEL	CHALET	CONVEY	CURDED
BOOMER	*BUSHEY	CHAPEL	COOKED	CURFEW
BOOTED	BUSIED	CHASED	COOKER	CURLED
BOOTEE	BUSKER	CHASER	COOLED	CURLER
BOOZED	BUTLER	CHEWED	COOLER	CURLEW
BOOZER	BUTTER	CHIDED	COOPED	CURSED
BORDER	BUZZER.	CHIMED	COOPER	CURVED
*BORNEO	CACHET	CHISEL	COPIED	CURVET
BOTHER	CADGER	CHOKED	COPIER	CUSPED
BOW-LEG	CALLED	CHOKER	COPPED	CUSSED
BOWLER	CALLER	CHOLER	COPPER	CUTLER
BRACER	CALMED	CHOREA	COQUET	CUTLET
BRAKED	CALMER	CHOSEN	CORBEL	CUTTER
BRAVED	CALVED	CINDER	CORDED	CYCLED
BRAVER	CALVES	CIPHER	CORKED	CYGNET
BRAYED	CAMBER	CLARET	CORKER	CYPHER.
BRAZEN	*CAMDEN	CLAWED	CORNEA	DABBED
BREVET	CAMPED	CLAYEY	CORNED	DABBER
BREWER	CAMPER	CLEVER	CORNEL	DAGGER
BRIBED	CANCEL	CLEWED	CORNER	DAMMED
BROKEN	CANCER	CLOSED	CORNET	DAMNED
BROKER	CANKER	CLOSET	CORSET	DAMPEN
*BRUNEI	CANNED	CLOVEN	CORTEX	DAMPER
+BRUNEL	CANNER	CLOVER	+CORTEZ	DAMSEL
BUCKET	*CANNES	CLOYED	CORVES	DANCER
BUDDED	CANTED	COALER	COSHER	DANDER
BUDGED	CANTER	COATEE	COSSET	DANGER
BUDGET	*CANVEY	COAXED	COSTED	+DANIEL
BUFFER	CAPPED	COBBER	COSTER	DAPPER
BUFFET	CAREEN	COBWEB	COTTER	DARKEN
BUGGED	CAREER	COCKED	CRANED	DARKER
BUGGER	CARIES	COCKER	CRATED	DARNED
BUGLER	*CARMEL	CODDER	CRATER	DARNEL
BULBED	+CARMEN	CODGER	CRAVED	DARNER
BULGER	CARPED	COFFEE	CRAVEN	DARTED
BULLET	CARPEL	COFFER	CRAZED	DASHED
BUMPED	CARPET	COGGED	CREWEL	DASHER
BUMPER	CARREL	COILED	CRIKEY	DAUBED
BUNGED	CARTED	COINER	*CRIMEA	+DAUDET
BUNKER	CARTEL	COLDER	*CROMER	DAWNED
BUNSEN	CASHED	COLLET	CROWED	DAY-BED
BUOYED	CASHEW	COMBED	CUBBED	DEADEN
BURDEN	CASKET	COMBER	CUDGEL	DEAFEN
BURGEE	CASTER	COMPEL	CUFFED	DEALER
BURIED	CAUSED	CONFER	CULLED	DEARER
BURNED	CAUTER	CONGER	CULVER	DECKED

DECKER	DOOMED	EDUCED	FAWNED	FOBBED
DECREE	+DOREEN	+EIFFEL	FAWNER	FODDER
DEEMED	DORMER	+EILEEN	FEARED	FOGGED
DEEPEN	*DORSET	EITHER	FEEDER	FOILED
DEEPER	DOSSED	ELATED	FEELER	FOLDED
DEFIED	DOSSER	ELATER	FELLER	FOLDER
DEGREE	DOTTED	ELEVEN	FELTED	FOOLED
DE-ICER	DOUSED	ELIDED	FENCED	FOOTED
DELVED	DOWNED	ELOPED	FENCER	FOOTER
DENIED	DOWSED	ELUDED	FENDED	FORCED
DENIER	DOWSER	EMBLEM	FENDER	FORDED
DENSER	DRAPED	ENAMEL	FENNEC	FORGED
DENTED	DRAPER	ENSUED	FENNEL	FORGER
*DENVER	DRAWEE	ENTREE	FERRET	FORGET
DEUCED	DRAWER	ENVIED	FESTER	FORKED
DEXTER	DRIVEL	ERASED	FETTER	FORMED
DIADEM	DRIVEN	ERODED	FEUDED	FORMER
DIAPER	DRIVER	ESCHEW	FIBBED	FOSTER
DIBBER	DRONED	ESPIED	FIBBER	FOULED
DICKER	DROVER	ESTEEM	FIDGET	FOWLER
DICKEY	DRUPEL	+ESTHER	FILLED	FRAMED
DIESEL	DUBBED	ETCHED	FILLER	FRAMER
DIETED	DUCKED	EVADED	FILLET	FRAYED
DIFFER	DUCKER	EVENED	FILMED	FROZEN
DIGGED	*DUDLEY	EVOKED	FILTER	FRUTEX
DIGGER	DUFFED	EXCEED	FINDER	FUHRER
DIMMED	DUFFEL	*EXETER	FINGER	FULLER
DIMMER	DUFFER	EXILED	FINNER	FUNDED
DINNED	DUIKER	EXITED	FIRMER	FUNNEL
DINNER	DULCET	EXUDED	FISHER	FURLED
DIPPED	DULLED	EYELET.	FISTED	FURRED
DIPPER	DULLER	FABLED	FITTED	FUSSED.
DISHED	+DULLES	FAECES	FITTER	GABBED
+DISNEY	DUMPED	FAGGED	FIZZED	GABLED
DISPEL	DUMPER	FAILED	FIZZER	GADDED
DITHER	*DUNDEE	FALLEN	FLAKED	GADGET
DOCKED	DUNKED	FALTER	FLAMED	GAFFED
DOCKER	DUNNED	FANGED	FLAMEN	GAFFER
DOCKET	DUPLET	FAN-JET	FLARED	GAGGED
DODDER	DUPLEX	FANNED	FLAWED	GAINED
DODGED	DUSTED	FARMER	FLAXEN	GAITER
DODGER	DUSTER.	FASCES	FLAYED	GALLED
DOFFED	EAGLET	FASTEN	FLEXED	GALLEY
DOGGED	EARNED	FASTER	FLORET	GAMMED
DOGGER	EASIER	FATHER	FLOWED	GAMMER
DOITED	*EASTER	FATTED	FLOWER	GANDER
DOLLED	*ECCLES	FATTEN	FLUKED	GANGED
DOLMEN	ECHOED	FATTER	FLUTED	GANGER
DONKEY	EDDIED	FAUCET	FOALED	*GANGES
DONNED	EDITED	*FAWLEY	FOAMED	GANNET

GAOLER	GOFFER	HANDED	+HERMES	HULLED
GARBED	GOGLET	+HANDEL	HERPES	*HUMBER
GARDEN	GOLDEN	HANGED	HIDDEN	HUMMED
GARNER	GOLFER	HANGER	HIGHER	HUMPED
GARNET	GOPHER	HANKER	HINDER	HUNGER
GARRET	GORGED	HAPPED	HINGED	HUNTED
GARTER	GORGET	HAPPEN	HINTED	HUNTER
GASHED	GOSPEL	HARDEN	HIPPED	HURLER
GAS-JET	GOTTEN	HARDER	HISSED	HURLEY
GASKET	GOUGED	HARKEN	HITHER	HUSHED
GASPED	GRACED	HARMED	+HITLER	HUSKED
GASPER	GRADED	HARPED	HITTER	HUTTED
GASSED	GRATER	HARPER	HOAXER	+HUXLEY
GATHER	GRAVEL	+HARVEY	HOCKED	HYPHEN.
GAUGED	GRAVER	HASHED	HOCKEY	IBIDEM
GAUGER	+GRAVES	HASPED	HODDEN	*ILKLEY
GEARED	GRAZED	HASTED	HOGGED	IMAGED
GEEZER	+GRETEL	HASTEN	HOGGET	IMBREX
GEIGER	GRIDED	HATRED	HOLDER	IMBUED
GELDED	GRIPED	HATTED	HOLIER	+IMOGEN
GELLED	GROCER	HATTER	HOLLER	INBRED
GEMMED	GROPED	HAULED	HONKED	INCHED
GENDER	GROVEL	HAWKER	HOODED	INDEED
GERMEN	GROWER	HAWSER	HOOFED	INLIER
GETTER	GUIDED	HEADED	HOOKED	INSTEP
GEYSER	*GUINEA	HEADER	HOOKER	INURED
GIBBER	GUISER	HEALED	HOOKEY	IRISED
GIBBET	GULLED	HEALER	HOOPED	IRONED
GIBLET	GULLET	HEAPED	HOOTED	+ISABEL
GIFTED	GULPED	HEARER	HOOTER	ISOMER
GILDED	GUMMED	HEATED	HOOVED	*ISRAEL
GIMLET	GUNNED	HEATER	+HOOVER	ISSUED
GINGER	GUNNER	HEAVED	HOOVES	ITCHED.
GIRDED	GUNTER	HEAVEN	HOPPED	JABBED
GIRDER	GUSHER	HEAVER	HOPPER	JABBER
GLARED	GUSSET	HEBREW	HORDED	JACKED
GLAZED	GUTTED	HEDGER	HORNED	JACKET
GLAZER	GUTTER.	HEEDED	HORNET	JAGGED
GLIDER	HACKED	HEELED	HORSED	JAILED
GLOVED	HAFTED	HEFTED	HOSIER	JAILER
GLOVER	HAGGED	HEIFER	HOSTEL	JAMMED
GLOWED	HAILED	HELMED	HOTBED	JARRED
GLOWER	HALOED	HELMET	HOTTED	+JASPER
GLUTEN	HALTED	HELPED	HOTTER	JAZZED
GNAWED	HALTER	HELPER	HOUSED	JEERED
GNAWER	HALVED	HELTER	HOWLED	JELLED
GOADED	HAMLET	HEMMED	HOWLER	JENNET
GOATEE	HAMMED	HEMPEN	HOYDEN	JERKED
GOBBET	HAMMER	*HENLEY	HUFFED	*JERSEY
GOBLET	HAMPER	HERDED	HUGGED	JESTED

JESTER	KILTED	LEADER	LOAMED	MANGER
JETTED	KINDER	LEAFED	LOANED	MANNED
JIBBED	KINGED	LEAKED	LOAVES	MANNER
JIGGED	KINKED	LEANED	LOBBED	MANTEL
JIGGER	KIPPED	LEAPED	LOCKED	+MANUEL
JILTED	KIPPER	LEASED	LOCKER	MAPPED
JINKED	KISMET	LEAVED	LOCKET	MARKED
JINNEE	KISSED	LEAVEN	LODGED	MARKER
JITTER	KISSER	LEAVES	LODGER	MARKET
JOBBED	KITTED	LECHER	LOFTED	MARLED
JOBBER	KITTEN	LEDGER	LOFTER	MARRED
JOCKEY	KNIFED	LEERED	LOGGED	MARTEN
JOGGED	KNIVES	LEGGED	LOGGER	MARVEL
JOINED	KOSHER	LENDER	LOITER	MASHED
JOINER	KRAKEN	LENTEN	LOLLED	MASKED
JOLTED	KUMMEL.	+LESLEY	LONGED	MASKER
JOSHED	LAAGER	LESSEE	LONGER	MASSED
JOTTED	LACHES	LESSEN	LOOKED	MASTED
JOTTER	LACKED	LESSER	LOOKER	MASTER
JUDGED	LACKEY	+LESTER	LOOMED	MATTED
JUGGED	LADDER	LETTER	LOOPED	MATTER
+JULIET	LADLED	LEVIED	LOOPER	MAULED
JUMPED	LAGGED	*LEYDEN	LOOSED	MAUSER
JUMPER	LAMBED	LIASED	LOOSEN	MAYHEM
JUNKED	LAMMED	LICHEN	LOOSER	MEDLEY
JUNKER	LANCED	LICKED	LOOTER	MEEKER
JUNKET	LANCER	LIDDED	LOPPED	MELDED
JUTTED.	LANCET	LIFTED	LORDED	MELTED
KAISER	LANDED	LIFTER	LOUDER	MEMBER
KAYOED	LANDES	LILTED	LOUVER	MENDED
KECKED	LANNER	LIMBED	LUBBER	+MENDEL
KEDGED	LAPPED	LIMBER	LUGGED	MENSES
KEELED	LAPPET	LIMNER	LUGGER	MERCER
KEENED	LAPSED	LIMPED	LULLED	MERGED
KEENER	LARDED	LIMPET	LUMBER	MERGER
KEEPER	LARDER	LINDEN	LUNGED	*MERSEY
KENNED	LARGER	LINGER	LURKER	MESHED
KENNEL	LARKED	LINKED	LUSTED	+MESMER
+KEPLER	LASHED	LINNET	+LUTHER.	MESSED
KERBED	LASHER	LINTEL	MADDED	MICKEY
KERMES	LASTED	+LIONEL	MADDEN	MIDDEN
KERNEL	LATEEN	LIPPED	MADDER	MIDGET
KERSEY	LATHER	LISPED	MAGNET	MILDER
+KEYNES	LATTEN	LISTED	+MAHLER	MILDEW
*KHYBER	LATTER	LISTEN	MAIDEN	MILIEU
KICKED	LAUDED	+LISTER	MAILED	MILKED
KIDDED	LAUREL	LITTER	+MAILER	MILKER
KIDNEY	LAWYER	LOADED	MAIMED	MILLED
KILLED	LEADED	LOADER	MALLET	+MILLER
KILLER	LEADEN	LOAFER	MALTED	MILLET

MILTED	NARKED	OX-EYED	PEGGED	PODDED
MINCED	NATTER	OXYGEN	PEG-LEG	POISED
MINCER	NAUSEA	OYSTER.	PELLET	POLDER
MINDED	NEARED	PACKED	PELMET	POLLED
MINTED	NEARER	PACKER	PELTED	POLLEN
MINUET	NEATEN	PACKET	PENNED	POLLEX
MISLED	NECKED	PADDED	PEPPED	POMMEL
MISSED	NEEDED	PAINED	PEPPER	PONDER
MISSEL	NEPHEW	PAIRED	PERKED	PONGEE
MISTED	NERVED	PALLED	PERMED	POOLED
MISTER	NESTED	PALLET	PESTER	POORER
MITRED	NETHER	PALMED	PETREL	POPPED
MITTEN	NETTED	PALMER	PETTED	POPPET
MOANED	NEUTER	PALPED	PEWTER	PORKER
MOATED	NICKED	PALTER	PHASED	PORTED
MOBBED	NICKEL	PAMPER	PHLOEM	PORTER
MOCKED	NICKER	PANDER	PHONED	POSSET
MOCKER	NIGGER	PANNED	PHONEY	POSTED
MOLTEN	NIPPED	PANTED	PICKED	POSTER
MONGER	NIPPER	PANZER	PICKER	POTEEN
MONKEY	NOBBED	PARCEL	PICKET	POTTED
MOONED	NOBLER	PARGET	PIECED	POTTER
MOORED	NOCKED	PARKED	PIGGED	POURER
MOOTED	NODDED	PARLEY	PIGLET	POUTED
MOPPED	NOOSED	PARSEC	PILFER	POUTER
MOPPET	NOSHED	PARSED	PIMPED	POWDER
MORSEL	NUCLEI	PARSEE	PINKED	PRATED
MOSLEM	NUDGED	PARTED	PINNED	PRAYED
MOTHER	NUGGET	PASSED	*PINNER	PRAYER
MOTLEY	NUMBED	PASSER	+PINTER	PREFER
MOUSER	NUMBER	PASTED	PIOLET	PREYED
MUCKED	NURSED	PASTEL	PIPPED	PRICED
MUFFED	NUTMEG	PATTED	PIQUED	PRIDED
MUGGED	NUTTER.	PATTEN	PIQUET	PRIMED
MULLED	OBEYED	PATTER	PISCES	PRIMER
MULLET	OBITER	PAUPER	PITIED	PRIVET
MUMMED	OFFSET	PAUSED	PITTED	PRIZED
MUMMER	+OLIVER	PAWNED	PLACED	PROBED
MURDER	OMELET	PEAHEN	PLACER	PROPEL
+MURIEL	ONAGER	PEAKED	PLACET	PROPER
MUSKET	OODLES	PEALED	PLANED	PROSER
MUSSEL	OPENER	PECKED	PLANET	PROVED
MUSTER	OPINED	PECKER	PLATED	PROVEN
MUTTER.	ORATED	PECTEN	PLATEN	PRUNED
NABBED	*ORKNEY	PEEKED	PLATER	PUCKER
NAGGED	OSPREY	PEELED	PLAYED	PUFFED
NAGGER	OSTLER	PEELER	PLAYER	PUFFER
NAILED	OUSTED	PEEPER	PLOVER	PUGGED
*NAPLES	OUTLET	PEERED	PLUMED	PULLED
NAPPED	OUTSET	PEEVED	POCKET	PULLER

PULLET	RANKER	RINGER	SACHET	SERVED
PULLEY	RAPIER	RINKED	SACKED	SERVER
PULPER	RAPPED	RINSED	SACRED	SESTET
PULSED	RASHER	RIOTER	SADDEN	SETTEE
PUMMEL	RASPED	RIPPED	SADDER	SETTER
PUMPED	RASTER	RISKED	SAGGED	SEXIER
PUNNED	RATHER	ROAMER	SAILED	SEXTET
PUNNET	RATTED	ROARED	SAILER	SHADED
PUNTED	RATTER	ROARER	SALTED	SHAKEN
PUNTER	READER	ROBBED	SALTER	SHAKER
PUPPED	REAMER	ROBBER	SALVED	SHAMED
PUPPET	REAPER	ROCHET	SALVER	SHAPED
PURGED	REARED	ROCKED	+SAMUEL	SHARED
PURLED	REDDEN	ROCKER	SANDED	SHAVED
PURLER	REDDER	ROCKET	SAPPED	SHAVEN
PURRED	REDEEM	+RODNEY	SAPPER	SHAVER
PURSED	REEDED	ROGUED	SARSEN	SHEKEL
PURSER	REEFER	ROLLED	SATEEN	SHINED
PURVEY	REEKED	ROLLER	SAUCED	SHINER
PUSHED	REELED	+ROMMEL	SAUCER	SHIVER
PUSHER	REEVED	*ROMNEY	SAWNEY	SHODED
PUTTEE	REFLEX	ROMPED	SAWYER	SHORED
PUTTER.	REFUEL	ROOFED	SCALED	SHOVED
QUAKED	REGRET	ROOKED	SCARED	SHOVEL
QUAKER	REINED	ROOMED	SCORED	SHOWED
QUAVER	RELIED	ROOTED	SCORER	SHOWER
*QUEBEC	RELIEF	ROQUET	SCOTER	SHRIEK
QUEUED	RENDER	ROSIER	SCREED	SICKEN
QUIVER	RENNET	ROSTER	SCREEN	SICKER
QUOTER.	RENTED	ROTTED	SCRIED	SIDLED
RABBET	RENTER	ROTTEN	SEALED	SIEVED
RABIES	REOPEN	ROTTER	SEALER	SIFTER
+RACHEL	RESTED	ROUGED	SEAMED	SIGHED
RACIER	+REUBEN	ROUSER	SEAMEN	SIGNED
RACKED	REVIEW	ROUTED	SEARED	SIGNET
RACKET	REVVED	RUBBED	SEATED	SILKEN
RAFTED	*RHODES	RUBBER	SECRET	SILTED
RAFTER	RHYMED	RUCKED	SEEDED	SILVER
RAGGED	RHYMER	RUDDER	SEEKER	SIMMER
RAIDER	RIBBED	RUFFED	SEEMED	SIMNEL
RAILED	RICHER	RUGGED	SEEPED	SIMPER
RAINED	RICKED	RUGGER	SEISED	SINGED
RAISED	RIDDEN	RUINED	SEIZED	SINGER
RAMJET	RIDGED	RUNNEL	SELLER	SINKER
RAMMED	RIFLED	RUNNER	SELVES	SINNED
RAMMER	RIFLER	RUSHED	SENDER	SINNER
RAMPED	RIFTED	RUSHEN	SENSED	SINTER
RANGED	RIGGED	RUSSET	SEPTET	SIPPED
RANGER	RIMMED	RUSTED	SEQUEL	SIPPET
RANKED	RINGED	RUTTED.	SERIES	SISTER

SITTER	SOVIET	SUNNED	TEASEL	TOOLER
SKATER	SPACED	SUNSET	TEASER	TOOTED
SKEWED	SPACER	SUPPED	TEA-SET	TOPPED
SKEWER	SPARED	SUPPER	TEDDER	TOPPER
SKIVER	SPAYED	SURFER	TEEMED	TOSSED
SLAKED	SPEWED	SURGED	TEETER	TOTHER
SLATED	SPICED	*SURREY	TELFER	*TOTNES
SLATER	SPIDER	SURVEY	TELLER	TOTTED
SLAVER	SPIKED	SUSSED	TEMPER	TOTTER
SLAYER	SPINET	*SUSSEX	TENDED	TOUPEE
SLEWED	SPIRED	SUTLER	TENDER	TOURED
SLICED	SPITED	SUTTEE	TENSED	TOURER
SLICER	SPLEEN	SWAYED	TENTED	TOUTED
SLIVER	SPOKEN	*SWEDEN	TENTER	TRACED
SLOPED	SPUMED	SWIPED	TERCET	TRACER
SLOVEN	STAGER	SWIVEL	TERMED	TRADED
SLOWER	STAKED	*SYDNEY	TESTED	TRADER
SMILED	STALER	SYSTEM.	TESTER	TRAVEL
SMOKED	STAMEN	TABBED	TESTES	TRICED
SMOKER	STAPES	TABLED	TETHER	TRIVET
SNAKED	STARED	TABLET	TETTER	TROVER
SNARED	STATED	TACKED	THALER	TROWEL
SNIPER	STATER	TAGGED	*THAMES	TUBBED
SNIVEL	STAVED	TAILED	THAWED	TUCKED
SNORED	STAYED	TALKED	*THEBES	TUCKER
SNOWED	STAYER	TALKER	THEWED	TUCKET
SOAKED	STEREO	TALLER	TICKED	TUFFET
SOAKER	+STEVEN	TAMPED	TICKER	TUFTED
SOAPED	STEWED	TAMPER	TICKET	TUGGED
SOARED	STIVER	TANDEM	TIDIER	TUNNEL
SOBBED	STOKER	TANGED	TILLED	TUREEN
SOCCER	STOLEN	TANKER	TILLER	TURFED
SOCKET	STONED	TANNED	TILTED	*TURKEY
SODDEN	STORED	TANNER	TIMBER	TURNED
SOFTEN	STOREY	TAPPED	TINDER	+TURNER
SOFTER	STOWED	TAPPET	TINGED	TURRET
SOILED	STREET	TARGET	TINIER	TURVES
SOIREE	STYLED	TARRED	TINKER	TUSKED
SOLDER	SUBLET	TARTED	TINNED	TUSKER
SOLVED	SUCKED	TASKED	TINSEL	TUTTED
SONNET	SUCKER	TASSEL	TIPPED	TWINED.
SOONER	SUDDEN	TASTED	TIPPER	UGLIER
SOPPED	SUFFER	TASTER	TIPPET	*ULSTER
SORBET	SUITED	TATTED	TITFER	UMBLES
SORREL	SULLEN	TATTER	TITLED	UNDIES
SORTED	SUMMED	TAUTEN	TITTER	UNEVEN
SORTER	SUMMER	TAUTER	TOFFEE	UNIPED
SOUPED	SUNDER	TAXIED	TOILER	UNISEX
SOURED	SUNDEW	TEAMED	TOILET	UNITED
SOUSED	SUNKEN	TEASED	TOLLED	UNMEET

UNREEL	WAIVED	*WIDNES	BEREFT.	BORAGE
UNTIED	WAIVER	WILDER	CARAFE	BRIDGE.
UNUSED	WALKER	WILLED	CHAFFY	CHANGE
UPKEEP	WALLED	WILTED	CODIFY	CHARGE
URETER	WALLET	WINCED	CUT-OFF.	CHOUGH
USURER.	+WALTER	WINDED	DRAFFY.	CLERGY
VAGUER	WANDER	WINDER	FAR-OFF	CLINGY
VAINER	WANTED	WINGED	FLUFFY.	CLOUGH
VALLEY	WARDED	WINKED	GASIFY.	CRAGGY
VALUED	WARDEN	WINNER	HUMIFY.	CRINGE
VALUER	WARDER	WINTER	LAY-OFF.	CUBAGE.
VALVED	WARIER	WISHED	MODIFY.	DAMAGE
VAMPED	WARMED	WITHER	NOTIFY.	DELUGE
VARIED	WARMER	WOLFED	ONE-OFF	DESIGN
VARLET	WARNED	WOLVES	OSSIFY.	DOSAGE
VASTER	WARPED	WONDER	PACIFY	DOTAGE
VEERED	WARRED	WONTED	PILAFF	DREDGE
VEILED	+WARREN	WOODED	PURIFY.	DRUDGE.
VEINED	WASHED	WOODEN	RAMIFY	EFFIGY
VELVET	WASHER	WOOFER	RAREFY	EMERGE
VENDEE	WASTED	WORDED	RATIFY	ENCAGE
VENDER	WASTER	WORKED	REBUFF.	ENERGY
VENEER	WEAKEN	WORKER	SALIFY	ENGAGE
VENTED	WEAKER	WORMED	SCRUFF	ENOUGH
VERGED	WEANED	WORSEN	SCURFY	ENRAGE
VERGER	WEASEL	WRITER.	SET-OFF	ENSIGN
VERSED	WEAVER	+XAVIER	SHRIFT	EULOGY.
VERSET	WEBBED	X-RAYED	*STAFFA	FLAGGY
VERTEX	WEDDED	XYSTER.	STRAFE	FLANGE
VERVET	WEDGED	YABBER	STRIFE	FLEDGE
+VESPER	WEEDED	YAHWEH	STUFFY.	FORAGE
VESSEL	WEEPER	YAKKED	TARIFF	FOREGO
VESTED	WELDER	YANKED	THRIFT	FRIDGE
VETOED	WELLED	YANKEE	TIP-UFF	+FRIGGA
VETTED	WELTED	YAPPED	TUMEFY	FRINGE.
VIEWER	WELTER	YAWNED	TYPIFY.	GARAGE
+VIOLET	WENDED	YELLED	UGLIFY	+GEORGE
VIZIER	+WESLEY	YELPED	UNSAFE	GRANGE
VOICED	WETHER	YENNED	UPLIFT.	GROGGY
VOIDED	WETTED	YONDER	VERIFY	GRUDGE.
VOLLEY	WETTER	YORKER	VILIFY	HOMAGE.
VOLTED	WHALER	YOWLED.	VIVIFY	IMPUGN
VORTEX.	WHILED	ZEROED		INDIGO.
WADDED	WHINED	ZIPPED	ALLEGE	LINAGE
WAFTED	WHITEN	ZIPPER	*ARMAGH	LOLIGO
WAGGED	WHITER	ZITHER	ASSIGN	LOUNGE.
+WAGNER	WHORED	ZOOMED	AVENGE	*MALAGA
WAILED	WICKED		AWEIGH.	MALIGN
WAITED	WICKER	ADRIFT	BENIGN	MANAGE
WAITER	WICKET	AERIFY.	BODEGA	MIRAGE

NONAGE.	ARIGHT.	MALTHA	AGNAIL	*BRAZIL
OBLIGE	BEECHY	MARSHY	AGONIC	BROMIC
ORANGE.	+BERTHA	+MARTHA.	ALALIA	BULBIL
PHLEGM	BITCHY	NAUGHT	ALBEIT	BUNYIP
PLEDGE	BLIGHT	NOUGHT	ALEVIN	BUSKIN.
PLOUGH	BLITHE	NYMPHO.	ALEXIA	CADDIS
PLUNGE	BOTCHY	PATCHY	+ALEXIS	*CALAIS
POTAGE.	BOUGHT	PITCHY	ALGOID	CALKIN
QUAGGA	BRASHY	PLASHY	+ALICIA	+CALVIN
QUAGGY.	+BRECHT	PLIGHT	+AMELIA	*CANDIA
RAVAGE	BRIGHT	PLUSHY	ANOMIA	CANDID
REFUGE	BROCHE	PONCHO	*ANTRIM	CASEIN
RESIGN.	BRUSHY	+PSYCHE	+ANUBIS	CASSIA
SAVAGE	+BUDDHA	PSYCHO.	*ARABIA	CATKIN
SEWAGE	BUNCHY.	QUOTHA.	ARABIC	CELTIC
SHAGGY	CATCHY	RHYTHM.	+ARCHIE	CERVIX
SILAGE	CAUGHT	SCATHE	ARCHIL	CHESIL
SLANGY	CHICHI	SCYTHE	*ARCTIC	CHEVIN
SLEDGE	CLICHE	SEETHE	ARMPIT	CHITIN
SLEIGH	CLOCHE	SLIGHT	ASSAIL	+CHOPIN
*SLOUGH	CLOTHE	SLUSHY	+ASTRID	CHORIC
SLUDGE	+CLOTHO	SMITHY	ATAXIA	CITRIC
SMUDGE	CONCHA	SOOTHE	ATOMIC	CLERIC
SMUDGY	CRECHE.	SOUGHT	ATONIC	CLEVIS
SOCAGE	*DELPHI	SWATHE.	ATTAIN	CLINIC
SPONGE	DINGHY	TAUGHT	AUNTIE	*COCHIN
SPONGY	DOUCHE	TETCHY	+AUSTIN.	COFFIN
SPURGE	DOUGHY	TOUCHE	*BAFFIN	COHEIR
STINGY	DRACHM	TOUCHY	BAGNIO	COLLIE
STODGE	+DWIGHT.	TRASHY	*BALTIC	COMFIT
STODGY	EARTHY.	TROPHY.	BANDIT	COMMIE
STOOGE	FILTHY	WEIGHT	BARDIC	COMMIT
SYZYGY.	FLASHY	WORTHY	+BARRIE	CONOID
THOUGH	FLECHE	WRITHE	BED-SIT	COOKIE
*TOBAGO	FLESHY		*BERLIN	COOLIE
TOWAGE	FLIGHT	ABATIS	BESTIR	COPTIC
TROUGH	FOUGHT	ACACIA	BEWAIL	CORBIE
TRUDGE	FRIGHT	*ACADIA	BIFFIN	CORRIE
TWIGGY	FROTHY.	ACERIC	BIGWIG	COSMIC
TWINGE.	+GANDHI	ACETIC	BIOTIC	COUSIN
ULLAGE.	GAUCHE	ACIDIC	BIOTIN	COWRIE
VIRAGO	GAUCHO	ACQUIT	BIRDIE	CRASIS
VISAGE	GEISHA	ADAGIO	BOBBIN	CREDIT
VOYAGE	+GOETHE	ADJOIN	BODKIN	CRETIN
	GUN-SHY.	+ADONIS	*BOODMIN	CRISIS
+AGATHA	HEATHY	ADROIT	BOFFIN	CRITIC
ALIGHT	HEIGHT.	AFFAIR	BOMBIC	CUBOID
APACHE	KNIGHT.	AFRAID	BOOKIE	CUPRIC
APATHY	LITCHI	AGAMIC	BOUGIE	CUP-TIE
APHTHA	LOATHE.	AGARIC	BOW-TIE	CYANIC

CYCLIC	FERVID	HEREIN	*MADRID	OUTBID
CYMRIC	FIBRIL	HERMIT	MAGPIE	OUTDID
CYSTIC.	FIBRIN	HERNIA	MANTIC	OUTFIT
DACOIT	FILL-IN	HEROIC	MANTIS	OUTWIT
DAHLIA	FILLIP	HEROIN	MAQUIS	OXALIC.
*DANZIG	FILMIC	HISPID	+MARCIA	PALAIS
*DARWIN	FINNIC	HORRID	MARGIN	PALLID
+DEBBIE	FIRKIN	HUBRIS	+MARTIN	PAPAIN
DEBRIS	FISTIC	HYBRID	MASHIE	PARKIN
DECEIT	FIZGIG	HYDRIC	MASSIF	PARVIS
DENTIL	FLAVIN	+HYGEIA.	MASTIC	PASSIM
DERAIL	FLORID	IAMBIC	MATRIC	PATHIC
DERMIS	FLORIN	ICONIC	MATRIX	PATOIS
DERRIS	FOETID	IMPAIR	MEALIE	PAYNIM
DETAIL	FORBID	+INGRID	MEGRIM	PECTIC
DETAIN	FORMIC	INLAID	MEMOIR	PECTIN
DEVOID	FOSSIL	INSTIL	*MENDIP	PEEWIT
DIESIS	FRAZIL	IRENIC	MENHIR	PELVIC
DIK-DIK	FRIGID	IRITIS	+MERLIN	PELVIS
DIMWIT	FROLIC	IRONIC	METRIC	PENCIL
DISTIL	FULFIL	ISATIN	MISFIT	PEPSIN
DOBBIN	FUSTIC.	*ISCHIA	MOHAIR	PEPTIC
DOMAIN	GAELIC	ITALIC.	MORBID	PERMIT
DOSSIL	GALLIC	JERKIN	+MORRIS	PHASIC
DUBBIN	*GAMBIA	+JESSIE	MOSAIC	+PHILIP
*DUBLIN	GAMBIT	JESUIT	MUFFIN	PHOBIA
DUNLIN	GANOID	JUDAIC	MUSLIM	PHOBIC
DYADIC.	GARLIC	+JUSTIN.	MUSLIN	PHONIC
EARWIG	*GDYNIA	KAFFIR	MYOPIA	PHYSIC
ECHOIC	GILLIE	KALMIA	MYOPIC	PICNIC
ECLAIR	GLACIS	KAOLIN	MYSTIC	PIDGIN
EDDAIC	*GLAMIS	KELPIE	MYTHIC.	PIPKIN
EDENIC	+GLORIA	KELTIC	NAPKIN	PIPPIN
ELICIT	GNOMIC	KERMIS	NEREID	PISTIL
ELIXIR	GNOSIS	KERRIE	NIOBIC	PLACID
EMETIC	GOALIE	KIDDIE	NITRIC	PLUG-IN
ENJOIN	GOBLIN	*KUWAIT.	NITWIT	POETIC
ENOSIS	GODWIT	LACTIC	NOGGIN	POPLIN
ENTAIL	GOSSIP	LADDIE	NORDIC	PRATIE
EROTIC	GOTHIC	LASSIE	NUNCIO	PRAXIS
ETHNIC	GRADIN	+LAURIE	NUTRIA.	PRECIS
+EUCLID	GRATIN	LEAD-IN	OBTAIN	PREFIX
EXILIC	GRATIS	LENTIL	OLEFIN	PRELIM
EXOTIC	GRAVID.	+LIEBIG	ORCHID	PROFIT
EYELID.	HAGGIS	LIMPID	ORCHIS	PROLIX
FABRIC	HALOID	LIQUID	ORDAIN	PROSIT
FAERIE	*HARRIS	LOGGIA	ORIGIN	PUBLIC
FASCIA	HATPIN	LOOK-IN	ORPHIC	PUFFIN
FERRIC	*HAWAII	LOVE-IN	+OSIRIS	PULL-IN
FERRIS	HECTIC	LUETIC.	OTITIS	PULPIT

219

PUNDIT	STUPID	+WALLIS	TRICKY	BOGGLE
PURLIN	STYMIE	WEEVIL	TROIKA.	BOLDLY
PUTRID.	SUBMIT	WELKIN	UNLIKE	BOODLE
RABBIN	SUFFIX	WITHIN.	UNMAKE	*BOOTLE
RABBIT	SUMMIT	XYLOID.	UNYOKE	BOTFLY
RAFFIA	SUNLIT	*YEOVIL.	UPDIKE	BOTTLE
RAISIN	+SYLVIA	*ZAMBIA	UPTAKE.	BOWELS
RANCID	SYNDIC.	ZINNIA	WHISKY.	BRIDLE
RAZZIA	TALKIE	ZOMBIE	YOICKS	BROLLY
RECOIL	TANNIC			BUBBLE
RE-EDIT	TANNIN	*SKOPJE	ACIDLY	BUBBLY
REGAIN	TARSIA		AEDILE	BUCKLE
REJOIN	TASSIE	*ALASKA.	AFIELD	BUNDLE
RELAID	TENNIS	BELIKE	AGE-OLD	BUNGLE
REMAIN	+THALIA	BETAKE	AIRILY	BURBLE
+RENOIR	THESIS	BREEKS	ALKALI	BURGLE
REPAID	TIE-PIN	+BROOKE.	+ANGELA	BUSILY
REPAIR	TIFFIN	CHALKY	*ANGOLA	BUSTLE.
RETAIL	*TIGRIS	CHEEKY	+APOLLO	CABALA
RETAIN	TITBIT	CHUNKY	ARABLE	CACKLE
RHIZIC	TOCSIN	CRANKY	ARCHLY	CAGILY
ROOKIE	TONSIL	CROAKY	AREOLA	CAJOLE
RUBRIC	TOROID	CROCKY.	ARGALA	CALMLY
+RUSKIN	TORPID	DECOKE.	*ARGYLL	CANDLE
*RUSSIA	TORRID	EUREKA.	ARIDLY	+CASALS
RUSTIC.	TRAGIC	FRISKY.	+ARNOLD	CASTLE
SALVIA	TRIFID	GINGKO.	ARTILY	CATTLE
SCENIC	TRIVIA	IN-JOKE	+ATTILA	CAUDLE
SCORIA	TROPIC	INTAKE	AUDILE	CHICLE
SEISIN	TURBID	INVOKE.	AVIDLY	CHICLY
SEPSIS	TURGID	KANAKA.	AWHILE.	CHILLI
SEPTIC	TURNIP	PERUKE	BABBLE	CHILLY
SEQUIN	TWILIT.	PLUCKY.	BAFFLE	CICALA
*SIKKIM	UNCOIL	REBUKE	BALDLY	CICELY
SISKIN	UNFAIR	REMAKE	BANGLE	CINGLE
SLAVIC	UNKNIT	RETAKE	BARELY	CIRCLE
+SOPHIA	UNLAID	REVOKE.	BASALT	COBALT
SORDID	UNSAID	SALUKI	BASELY	COBBLE
SORTIE	UNSHIP	SHEIKH	BATTLE	COCKLE
SPAVIN	UNVEIL	SHRIKE	BAUBLE	CODDLE
SPECIE	URCHIN	SLACKS	BEADLE	COFFLE
SPIRIT	URETIC	SLINKY	BEAGLE	COLDLY
SPRAIN	UTOPIA.	SPOOKY	BECALM	COMELY
+STALIN	VERMIN	STICKY	BEETLE	COMPLY
STASIS	VESPID	STOCKY	BEFALL	COOLLY
STATIC	VICTIM	STRAKE	BEFELL	COPULA
STOLID	VIOLIN	STRIKE	BEHALF	COSILY
STRAIN	+VIRGIL	STROKE	BEHELD	COSTLY
STRAIT	*VIRGIN	SWANKY.	BEHOLD	COUPLE
STUDIO	VISCID.	THANKS	BODILY	

220

CRADLE	ENGULF	GLUMLY	JUNGLE	MIZZLE
CRAWLY	ENSILE	GOBBLE	JUNGLY	MOBILE
CREOLE	EVENLY	GOGGLE	JUSTLY.	MODULE
CUDDLE	EVILLY	GOODLY	KECKLE	MOHOLE
CUDDLY	EXHALE.	GOOGLY	KEENLY	MORALE
CUPOLA	FACILE	GRILLE	KETTLE	MOTTLE
CURDLE	FACULA	GRIMLY	KIBBLE	MUCKLE
CURTLY	FAILLE	GRISLY	KIDDLE	MUDDLE
CUTELY	FAIRLY	GURGLE	KINDLE	MUFFLE
+CYBELE.	FAMILY	GUZZLE.	KINDLY	MUMBLE
DABBLE	FEEBLE	HACKLE	KINGLY	MUSCLE
DAGGLE	FEEBLY	HAGGLE	KINKLE	MUZZLE
DAMPLY	FEMALE	HANDLE	KIRTLE	+MYRTLE
DANDLE	FERULA	HARDLY	KITTLE	MYSELF.
DANGLE	FERULE	+HAROLD	KOBOLD.	NAMELY
DAPPLE	FETTLE	HAZILY	LABILE	NAPALM
DARKLY	FIBULA	HECKLE	LAMELY	NEARLY
DAWDLE	FICKLE	HEDDLE	LASTLY	NEATLY
DAZZLE	FIDDLE	HERALD	LATELY	NEBULA
DEADLY	FINALE	HIGGLE	LAZILY	NEEDLE
DEARLY	FINELY	HIGHLY	LEWDLY	NESTLE
DECKLE	FIRMLY	HOBBLE	LIABLE	NETTLE
DEEPLY	FIZZLE	HOLILY	LIKELY	NIBBLE
DEFILE	FLATLY	HOMELY	LIMPLY	NICELY
DEFTLY	FOIBLE	HOMILY	LITTLE	+NICOLE
DIBBLE	FONDLE	HOOP-LA	LIVELY	NIELLO
DIDDLE	FONDLY	HOPPLE	LOBULE	NIGGLE
DIMPLE	FOOZLE	HOURLY	LOCALE	NIMBLE
DIMPLY	FOULLY	HUDDLE	LONELY	NIMBLY
DINGLE	FREELY	HUGELY	LORDLY	NIPPLE
DIPOLE	FRILLY	HUMBLE	LOUDLY	NO-BALL
DIRELY	FUDDLE	HUMBLY	LOVELY.	NOBBLE
DOCILE	FUMBLE	HURDLE	MACKLE	NODDLE
+DONALD	FUTILE.	HURTLE	MACULA	NODULE
DOODLE	GABBLE	HUSTLE.	MAINLY	+NOELLE
DOTTLE	GADFLY	ICICLE	MANGLE	NOODLE
DOUBLE	GAGGLE	IMPALE	*MANILA	NOZZLE
DOUBLY	GAMBLE	INDULT	MANTLE	NUBILE
DOURLY	GAMELY	INHALE	MARBLE	NUMBLY
DRABLY	GARBLE	INSOLE	MAYFLY	NUZZLE.
DRY-FLY	GARGLE	INSULT	MEASLY	OCCULT
DUFFLE	+GAULLE	ITSELF.	MEDDLE	OCELLI
DUMBLY.	GENTLE	JANGLE	MEEKLY	ONFALL
EASILY	GENTLY	JIGGLE	MERELY	OOZILY
EDIBLE	+GERALD	JINGLE	METTLE	OPENLY
EERILY	GIGGLE	JINGLY	MICKLE	ORACLE
EMBALM	GIGOLO	JOGGLE	MIDDLE	ORALLY
ENABLE	GIRDLE	JOSTLE	MILDLY	ORIOLE
END-ALL	GLADLY	JUGGLE	MINGLE	ORMOLU
ENFOLD	GLIBLY	JUMBLE	MISTLE	*ORWELL

+OSWALD	REFILL	SIZZLE	TOOTLE	WILDLY
*OUNDLE	REGALE	SKILLY	TOPPLE	WILILY
OVERLY.	RESILE	SLIMLY	TOUSLE	WIMPLE
PADDLE	RESULT	SLOWLY	TREBLE	WINKLE
PALELY	REVILE	SMELLY	TRIFLE	WIRILY
+PAMELA	REVOLT	SMUGLY	TRIMLY	WISELY
PAROLE	RIBALD	SNUGLY	TRIPLE	WOBBLE
PARTLY	RICHLY	SOFTLY	TUMBLE	WOBBLY
PEARLY	RIDDLE	SOLELY	TUMULI	WOOLLY.
PEBBLE	RIFFLE	*SOMALI	TUMULT	YAFFLE
PEBBLY	RIPELY	SORELY	TURTLE	YEARLY
PEDALO	RIPPLE	SOURLY	TUSSLE	
PEDDLE	RIPPLY	SQUALL	TWO-PLY	AFLAME
PEOPLE	+RONALD	SQUILL	TWOULD.	APLOMB
PERTLY	ROOTLE	STABLE	UNABLE	ASSUME
PESTLE	ROSILY	STABLY	UNBOLT	ASTHMA
+PETULA	ROTULA	STAPLE	UNDULY	AUTUMN.
PICKLE	ROUBLE	STEELY	UNFOLD	*BAHAMA
PIFFLE	RUBBLE	*STELLA	UNGULA	BECAME
PILULE	RUDDLE	STIFLE	UNHOLY	BECOME
PIMPLE	RUDELY	STILLY	UNROLL	BENUMB
PIMPLY	RUFFLE	STROLL	UNRULY	BIGAMY
PINOLE	RUMBLE	SUBTLE	UNTOLD	BIREME
PINTLE	RUMPLE	SUBTLY	UNWELL	+BRAHMS
POODLE	RUSTLE	SUCKLE	UPHELD	BYNAME.
POORLY	RUTILE.	SUPPLE	UPHILL	CHROME
PORTLY	SADDLE	SUPPLY	UPHOLD	CHUMMY
POSHLY	SAFELY	SURELY.	+URSULA	CINEMA
POT-ALE	SAGELY	TACKLE	USABLE.	CLAMMY
PRIMLY	SAMPLE	TAMELY	VAINLY	COLUMN
PUDDLE	SANELY	TANGLE	VASTLY	CORYMB
PUEBLO	SAW-FLY	TANGLY	VERILY	CREAMY
PUNILY	*SCILLY	TARTLY	VIABLE	CRUMMY.
PURELY	SCROLL	TATTLE	VILELY	DECAMP
PURPLE	SEEMLY	TAUTLY	VIRILE	DEFAME
PUZZLE.	SENILE	TEMPLE	VITALS.	DHARMA
RABBLE	SETTLE	THINLY	WADDLE	DREAMT
RACILY	+SEWELL	THRALL	WAFFLE	DREAMY
RADDLE	SEXILY	THRILL	WAGGLE	DYNAMO.
RAFFLE	SHIELD	THUSLY	WANGLE	ECZEMA
RAMBLE	SHOULD	TICKLE	WARBLE	ENCAMP
RANKLE	SHRILL	TIDILY	WARILY	ENIGMA
RANKLY	*SICILY	TIMELY	WARMLY	ENTOMB
RAPTLY	SICKLE	TINGLE	WATTLE	ENZYME
RARELY	SICKLY	TINILY	WEAKLY	ESKIMO
RASHLY	SIMILE	TINKLE	WEEKLY	EXHUME.
RATTLE	SIMPLE	TIPPLE	WHOLLY	GLOOMY
REALLY	SIMPLY	TITTLE	WIDELY	GRAMME.
RECALL	SINGLE	TODDLE	WIFELY	INCOME
REDDLE	SINGLY	TOGGLE	WIGGLE	INFAMY

INHUME.	ACHING	BARONY	COSINE	ENGINE
+JEMIMA	ACTING	BATING	COVING	EOCENE
+JEREMY	ADDING	BAYING	COWING	*EPPING
+JEROME.	ADVENT	*BEAUNE	CRANNY	EQUINE
LEGUME.	AIDING	BEGONE	CRYING	ERMINE
MADAME	AILING	BEHIND	CUBING	ERRAND
MAXIMA	AIRING	BELONG	CURING.	ERRANT
MIASMA	*ALBANY	*BERING	+DAPHNE	ERRING
MINIMA.	ALBINO	BETONY	DARING	ETHANE
OEDEMA	ALKANE	BEYOND	DATING	+EUGENE
OEPEMA.	ALKENE	BEZANT	DAZING	EXEUNT
*PANAMA	ALMOND	BIDING	DEBUNK	EXPAND
PLASMA	ALPINE	BIKINI	DECANT	EXPEND
PLUMMY	ALUMNI	BITING	DECENT	EXTANT
PYJAMA.	ALVINE	BODING	DEFEND	EXTEND
RACEME	*AMIENS	BONING	DEFINE	EXTENT
REGIME	AMOUNT	BORING	DEMAND	EYEING.
RESUME	ANGINA	BOTANY	DEMENT	FACING
RHEUMY.	ANOINT	BOVINE	DEPEND	FADING
SALAMI	+ANTONY	BOWING	DEPONE	FAG-END
+SALOME	ANYONE	BOXING	DETENT	FAKING
SCHEMA	APHONY	BRAINY	DICING	FAMINE
SCHEME	APPEND	BRAWNY	DINING	FARINA
SCRIMP	ARCANA	+BRYONY	DITONE	FARING
SCUMMY	ARCANE	BUTANE	DIVINE	FECUND
SESAME	ARCING	BUYING	DIVING	FELINE
SHAMMY	ARDENT	BYGONE	DOESNT	FELONY
SHIMMY	ARGENT	BY-LINE.	DOMINO	FERINE
SHRIMP	ARMING	CAGING	DOPING	FILING
SLUMMY	AROUND	CAKING	DOTING	FINING
SMARMY	ARRANT	CANINE	DOUANE	FIRING
SODOMY	ARSINE	CANING	DOZING	FIXING
SOLEMN	ASCEND	+CAPONE	DRYING	FLAUNT
SQUAMA	ASCENT	CARING	DUENNA	FLUENT
STEAMY	ASKING	CASING	DUGONG	FLYING
STIGMA	ASLANT	CASINO	DUPING	FOMENT
STORMY	ASSENT	CAVING	DURING	FOXING
STROMA.	+ATHENA	CEDING	DYEING.	FRIEND
+THELMA	+ATHENE	CEMENT	*EALING	FUMING
TRAUMA.	*ATHENS	CETANE	EARING	FUSING.
ULTIMA	ATTEND	CITING	EASING	GALENA
ULTIMO.	ATTUNE	CLIENT	EATING	GAMING
VOLUME.	AUXINS	CODING	EBBING	GAPING
ZEUGMA	AVAUNT	COGENT	EDGING	GATING
ZYGOMA	AWNING.	COLONY	+EDMUND	GAZING
	BACONY	COMING	+EDWINA	GEMINI
ABOUND	BAKING	COOING	EKEING	GERUND
ABSENT	BALING	COPING	+ELAINE	GIBING
ACCENT	BANANA	CORING	EMBANK	GIVING
ACHENE	BARING	CORONA	ENDING	GOBANG

GORING	IRKING	METING	PAVANE	RILING
GRAINY	+IRVING	MEWING	PAWING	RISING
GRANNY	ISLAND.	MIMING	PAYING	RIVING
+GREENE	JADING	MINING	PEDANT	ROBING
*GRETNA	JAPING	MIRING	*PEKING	RODENT
GROUND	JAWING	MIXING	PILING	+ROLAND
GROYNE	JEJUNE	MOMENT	PINING	ROMANY
*GUYANA	JIBING	MOOING	PIPING	ROPING
GUYING	JIMINY	MOPING	PLAINT	ROTUND
GYBING	JIVING	MOVING	PLIANT	ROVING
GYVING.	+JOANNA	MOWING	PLYING	+ROWENA
HALING	JOCUND	MURINE	POKING	ROWING
HARING	JOKING.	MUSING	*POLAND	+RUBENS
HATING	KETONE	MUSTNT	POLING	RUEING
*HAVANA	KEYING	MUTANT	POLONY	RULING.
HAVENT	KIMONO.	MUTING	PORING	+SABINA
HAVING	LACING	MUTINY.	POSING	SALINE
HAWING	LACUNA	+NADINE	POTENT	SARONG
HAYING	LADING	NAMING	PRYING	SATING
HAZING	LAMENT	NATANT	PUISNE	SAVANT
HEWING	LAMINA	NICENE	PUKING	SAVING
HEXANE	LAMING	NOSING	PULING	SAWING
HIDING	LARYNX	NOTING	PYXING.	*SAXONY
HIKING	LATENT	NOVENA.	QUAINT.	SAYING
HIRING	LAYING	OARING	RACING	SECANT
HIVING	LAZING	OBLONG	RAGING	SECOND
HOEING	LEARNT	OCTANE	RAKING	SEEING
HOLING	LEGEND	OFFEND	RAPINE	SERENE
HOMING	LEVANT	OFFING	RAPING	SEWING
HOMINY	LIKING	OGLING	RATING	SEXING
HONING	LIMING	OILING	RAVINE	SHEENY
HOPING	LINING	ONIONY	RAVING	SHRANK
HOSING	LITANY	ON-LINE	RAYING	SHRINE
HUMANE.	LIVING	OOZING	RAZING	SHRINK
IDLING	*LOMOND	OPTANT	RECANT	SHRUNK
IGUANA	LOPING	OPTING	RECENT	SHYING
IMMUNE	LOSING	ORBING	REFINE	SIDING
IMPEND	LOVING	ORIENT	REFUND	SIENNA
IMPING	LOWING	ORPINE	REGENT	SILENT
INBAND	LUCENT	*OSTEND	+REGINA	SIMONY
INDENT	LURING	OUTING	RELENT	SIRING
INFANT	LUTING.	OWNING.	RELINE	SITING
INKING	MAKING	PACING	REMAND	SIZING
INLAND	+MARINA	PAEONY	REMIND	SKIING
INSANE	MARINE	PAGING	REPENT	SKINNY
INTEND	MATING	PALING	REPINE	SKYING
INTENT	MATINS	PARENT	RESENT	*SOLENT
INTONE	+MAXINE	PARING	RETINA	SOLING
INVENT	MAYING	PATENT	RIBAND	SONANT
IODINE	MERINO	PATINA	RIDING	SOWING

S---N-				H---O-
SPHINX	UNHAND	ARCHON	CARBON	DRY-ROT
SPLINE	UNKIND	+ASIMOV	CARBOY	+EDISON
SPLINT	UNSUNG	AUTHOR.	*CARLOW	EDITOR
SPRANG	UNWIND	BABOON	CARROT	EGG-NOG
SPRING	UPLAND	*BALBOA	CARTON	+ELINOR
SPRINT	URBANE	BALLOT	CASTOR	EMPLOY
SPRUNG	URGENT	BAMBOO	CATION	ETYMON.
SPYING	URGING	*BANGOR	+CAXTON	FACTOR
SQUINT	URSINE.	*BARROW	CENSOR	*FAEROE
STRAND	VACANT	+BARTOK	*CEYLON	FAGGOT
STRING	VAGINA	BARTON	+CHARON	FALCON
STRONG	*VERONA	BARYON	+CHIRON	FALLOW
STRUNG	VEXING	BATHOS	CHITON	FARROW
SUPINE	VICUNA	BEACON	CITRON	FATHOM
SWEENY	*VIENNA	BECKON	COCOON	FELLOE
SYRINX.	VIKING	BEFOOL	COLLOP	FELLOW
TAKING	VOLING	+BELLOC	COMMON	FINNOC
TALENT	VOTING	+BELLOW	CONDOM	FLAGON
TAMING	VOWING.	BENZOL	CONDOR	FLEXOR
TAPING	WADING	BESTOW	CONVOY	FOLLOW
TAWING	WAGING	BETOOK	CORDON	FORGOT
TAXING	WAKING	BILLOW	COSMOS	FRIVOL
TEEING	WALING	BISHOP	COTTON	FURROW
TENANT	WANING	BLAZON	COUPON	FUSION
THORNY	WAVING	*BOLTON	COWBOY	FYLFOT.
THRONE	WAXING	BONBON	COW-POX	GABION
THRONG	WERENT	BORROW	CRAYON	GALLON
TIDING	WHINNY	BORZOI	CRESOL	GALLOP
TILING	WILING	*BOSTON	CRETON	GAMBOL
TIMING	WINING	BOTTOM	+CRONOS	GAMMON
TIRING	WIPING	BOW-WOW	CUCKOO	GERMON
TISANE	WIRING	*BRECON	CURSOR	GIBBON
TOEING	*WOKING	BRETON	CUSTOM.	+GIDEON
TONING	WOOING.	BRITON	DACRON	GLYCOL
TOPING	XYLENE.	BUNION	DAEMON	GNOMON
TOTING	YAWING	BURBOT	+DALTON	GODSON
TOYING	YOKING	BURROW	DAMSON	+GORDON
TRIUNE	+YVONNE.	*BURTON	DAY-BOY	+GORGON
TRUANT	ZENANA	BUTTON	DEACON	GRISON
TRYING	ZONING	*BUXTON.	DEBTOR	GUIDON.
TUBING		CACHOU	DEPLOY	HALLOO
TUNING	ACAJOU	CAHOOT	DESPOT	HALLOW
TYPING	ACTION	CALLOW	DIATOM	HANSOM
TYRANT	+ALISON	CAMION	*DIDCOT	HARLOT
*TYRONE.	ALPHOS	CANNON	DIGLOT	*HARLOW
UNBEND	AMATOL	CANNOT	DOCTOR	*HARROW
UNBENT	AMAZON	*CANTON	DOG-FOX	HAYBOX
UNBIND	AMNION	CANTOR	DOLLOP	+HECTOR
+UNDINE	ANCHOR	CANYON	DONJON	+HELIOS
UNDONE	ANYHOW	CAPTOR	DRAGON	*HENDON

HEREOF	MAROON	PHAROS	SHADOW	VENDOR	
HERIOT	MARROW	PHENOL	SIGNOR	+VICTOR	
HOBNOB	MASCOT	PHOTON	SIMOOM	VISION	
HOLLOW	MATRON	PIGEON	SIPHON	VOODOO.	
HOODOO	MEADOW	PILLOW	SORROW	WAGGON	
HOOPOE	MELLOW	PINION	SPIGOT	WALLOP	
HORROR	MENTOR	PISTOL	STATOR	WALLOW	
HOTPOT	METEOR	PISTON	STUPOR	+WALTON	
HOT-ROD	METHOD	POGROM	SUITOR	WANTON	
*HUDSON	MICRON	POISON	SUMMON	+WARHOL	
HYSSOP.	+MILTON	POMPOM	SUN-GOD	WEAPON	
ICEBOX	MINION	POMPON	*SUTTON	WILLOW	
INDOOR	MINNOW	POTION	SYMBOL	+WILSON	
INFLOW	MIRROR	POW-WOW	SYPHON.	*WILTON	
INK-POT	MONGOL	PRISON	TAILOR	WINDOW	
ISOPOD.	+MONROE	PROTON	TALION	WINNOW	
JAMBOK	MORMON	PUTLOG	TALLOW	WISDOM.	
JARGON	MORROW	PYTHON.	TAMPON	YARROW	
*JARROW	MOTION	RACOON	TATTOO	YELLOW	
JERBOA	MUSK-OX	*RADNOR	TAUTOG	ZEALOT	
JETTON	MUTTON.	RAMROD	TEAPOT	ZIRCON	
JUNIOR.	NARROW	RANDOM	TEAPOY		
KELSON	NATION	RANSOM	TENDON	ABRUPT	
KLAXON	+NELSON	RAPTOR	TENSOR	ACCEPT	
KOEDOE	NEURON	RATION	TERROR	ASLOPE.	
KOWTOW.	+NEWTON	REASON	TEUTON	BICEPS.	
LAGOON	NO-GOOD	RECKON	THYMOL	CALIPH	
LAPDOG	NOTION.	RECTOR	TINPOT	CANOPY	
LEGION	+OBERON	REFOOT	TIPTOE	CERIPH	
LEPTON	OCELOT	REGION	TIPTOP	CHIPPY	
*LESBOS	ODD-JOB	RETOOK	TOMBOY	CHIRPY	
LESION	ODDS-ON	RETROD	TOMTOM	CHOPPY	
LESSON	OPTION	RIBBON.	TORPOR	CREEPY	
LESSOR	ORATOR	*SAIGON	TREMOR	CRIMPY	
LICTOR	ORISON.	SAILOR	+TREVOR	CRISPY	
LIQUOR	PALLOR	SALLOW	TRICOT	CROUPY.	
*LISBON	PARDON	SALMON	TRIPOD	*DIEPPE.	
LISSOM	PARROT	SALOON	TRIPOS	ECTYPE	
LOLLOP	PARSON	SALVOR	+TRITON	ENRAPT	
*LONDON	PASTOR	SCHOOL	TROGON	ESCAPE	
LOTION	PATHOS	SEA-COW	TURBOT	+EUROPA	
*LUDLOW.	PATROL	SEA-DOG	TYCOON.	*EUROPE	
MACRON	PATRON	SEASON	UNHOOK	EXCEPT	
MAGGOT	+PAVLOV	SECTOR	UNISON	EXEMPT.	
MAGNOX	PENNON	SELDOM	UNMOOR	FLOPPY	
MALLOW	PERIOD	SENIOR	UNSHOD	FRAPPE	
MAMMON	PERRON	SENSOR	UNSTOP	FRUMPY.	
MANIOC	PERSON	SERMON	UPROOT	GRIPPE	
*MARLOW	PETROL	SEXPOT	UPSHOT.	GRUMPY.	
MARMOT	PHANON	SEXTON	VECTOR	INCEPT	

JALOPY	*ANKARA	DEMURE	*HOBART	PANTRY
+JOSEPH.	APIARY	DENARY	HORARY	PASTRY
OCCUPY.	APPORT	DEPART	+HOWARD	PENURY
PARAPH	ARTERY	DEPORT	+HUBERT	PLEURA
+PELOPS	ASHORE	DESCRY	HUNGRY.	PLIERS
PROMPT	ASPIRE	DESERT	IGNORE	POETRY
PYROPE.	ASSERT	DESIRE	*ILFORD	POPERY
RECIPE.	ASSORT	DEXTRO	IMMURE	PRIORY.
SCAMPI	ASSURE	DISARM	IMPART	QUARRY.
SCRAPE	ASTERN	DIVERS	IMPORT	REBORE
SCRIPT	ATTIRE	DIVERT	IMPURE	REBORN
SCULPT	AUBURN	DOPTRE	INBORN	RECORD
SERAPE	AUGURY	DOTARD	INFIRM	REFORM
SERAPH	AURORA	DREARY.	INFORM	REGARD
SKIMPY	AVIARY	+EDWARD	INHERE	REMARK
SLEEPY	AWEARY.	EFFORT	INJURE	REMORA
SLOPPY	BAKERY	EMBARK	INJURY	REPORT
SNAPPY	BEFORE	EMIGRE	INSERT	RESORB
STEPPE	BELFRY	EMPIRE	INSURE	RESORT
STRIPE	BEWARE	ENCORE	INTERN	RETARD
STRIPY	*BIAFRA	ENDURE	INVERT	RETIRE
STUMPY	BINARY	ENSURE	INWARD.	RETORT
SWAMPY	BISTRE	ENTIRE	JABIRU.	RETURN
SYRUPY.	BLEARY	ESCORT	*LAHORE	REVERE
THORPE	BOFORS	EUCHRE	LIVERY	REVERS
THRIPS	BOLERO	EXHORT	LIZARD	REVERT
TROPPO	BOWERY	EXPERT	LOUVRE	REWARD
TROUPE.	BUCKRA	EXPIRE	LUSTRE	+ROBERT
UNRIPE	BYWORD.	EXPIRY	LUXURY.	ROSARY
UNWEPT.	CAMERA	EXPORT	MANURE	ROSTRA
WHIPPY	CANARD	EXTORT.	MATURE	ROTARY
	CANARY	FEDORA	MEAGRE	+RUPERT.
ABJURE	+CASTRO	FIACRE	MEMORY	SAFARI
ABOARD	CAVERN	FIGURE	MESSRS	*SAHARA
ABSORB	CAVORT	FINERY	MISERE	SALARY
ABSURD	CELERY	FLOURY	MISERY	+SANDRA
ACCORD	CENTRE	FLURRY	MODERN	+SARTRE
ADHERE	CHEERY	FRIARY	+MOZART.	SATIRE
ADJURE	+CHERRY	FURORE	NATURE	+SATURN
ADMIRE	+CICERO	FUTURE.	*NEWARK	SAVORY
ADSORB	+CLAIRE	GALORE	NONARY	+SAYERS
ADVERB	COBURG	GANTRY	NOTARY.	SCURRY
ADVERT	COHERE	GENERA	ONWARD	SECURE
AFFIRM	COHORT	GENTRY	ORDURE	SENORA
AFFORD	CONTRA	GO-CART	*ORFORD	SENTRY
+ALBERT	COVERT	GOITRE	ORRERY	SEVERE
ALLURE	COWARD	GO-KART	+OSBERT	*SEVERN
AMPERE	CURARE.	GOVERN.	OUTCRY	SHEARS
ANGARY	DEBARK	HAZARD	*OXFORD.	SHERRY
ANGORA	DEFORM	+HILARY	PALTRY	SIERRA

SKERRY	WINTRY	BY-PASS.	EGOISM	IMPISH
SLURRY	WIZARD	CALASH	EGOIST	IMPOSE
SOMBRE	WYVERN.	CARESS	EGRESS	IMPOST
SPHERE	YAOURT	+CARUSO	ELAPSE	INCEST
SQUARE	YOGURT.	CERISE	ELDEST†	INCISE
SQUIRE	ZAFFRE	CHAISE	ELFISH	INCUSE
SQUIRM	ZONARY	CHASSE	EMBOSS	INFEST
SQUIRT		CHEESE	ENCASE	INFUSE
STARRY	ABBESS	CHEESY	ENCASH	INGEST
+STUART	ACCESS	CHOOSE	ENCYST	INMOST
SUBORN	ACCOST	CHOOSY	ENLIST	INRUSH
SUBURB	ACCUSE	CHRISM	ENMESH	INSIST
SUGARY	ACROSS	+CHRIST	+ERNEST	INVEST
SULTRY	ADJUST	CLASSY	EXCESS	IODISM.
SUNDRY	ADVISE	CLAUSE	EXCISE	JEWESS
SUPERB	AFRESH	CLUMSY	EXCUSE	JEWISH
SUTURE.	AGHAST	COARSE	EXPOSE.	JOCOSE
TABARD	AGUISH	COMOSE	FAMISH	JURIST.
TAVERN	ALMOST	CORPSE	FETISH	LATEST
TAWDRY	AMBUSH	COURSE	FEWEST	LAVISH
TEA-URN	AMIDST	CREASE	FINEST	LEGIST
TELARY	AORIST	CROSSE	FINISH	LIAISE
TENURE	APEPSY	CRUISE	FLIMSY	LOCUST
THEORY	ARGOSY	CUBISM	FLOSSY	+LOUISE
THWART	ARIOSO	CURTSY.	FOLKSY	LOWEST
TIMBRE	AROUSE	DAMASK	FOREST	LYRIST.
TORERO	ARREST	DANISH	FRAISE	MAYEST
TOWARD	ARTIST	DEBASE	FROWST.	+MEDUSA
TUNDRA.	ASSESS	DEFUSE	GALOSH	MIMOSA
UMPIRE	*ASSISI	DEMISE	GARISH	MISUSE
UNBORN	ASSIST	+DENISE	*GDANSK	MODEST
UNCORD	ATTEST	DEPOSE	GLASSY	MODISH
UNCORK	AUGUST	DESIST	GLOSSY	MOLEST
UNFURL	AURIST	DETEST	GNEISS	MONISM
UNGIRD	AUTISM	DEVISE	GOLOSH	MONIST
UNGIRT	AVERSE.	DIGEST	GRASSY	MORASS
UNHURT	BANISH	DISUSE	GREASE	MOROSE
UNSURE	BASEST	DIVEST	GREASY	MOUSSE
UNWARY	BEHEST	DOLOSE	GRILSE	MULISH
UNWORN	BEMUSE	DRESSY	GROUSE.	MUTISM.
UPTURN	BIOPSY	DRIEST	HAMOSE	NAZISM
UPWARD.	BLOUSE	DROPSY	HARASS	NEWEST
VAGARY	BLUISH	DROSSY	HEARSE	NICEST
VELURE	BOURSE	DROWSE	HERESY	NODOSE
VESTRY	BOYISH	DROWSY	HEXOSE	NOWISE
VINERY	BRAISE	DRYISH	HOARSE	NUDISM
VISARD	BRASSY	DURESS	HOLISM	NUDIST.
VOTARY.	BREAST	DYNAST.	HONEST.	OAFISH
WATERY	BROWSE	EDDISH	ILL-USE	OBSESS
WHERRY	BRUISE	EFFUSE	IMMESH	OBTUSE

ODDEST	RIMOSE	VALISE	COYOTE	GAMETE
*ODESSA	RIPEST	VAMOSE	CRAFTY	GHETTO
OFFISH	ROBUST	VANISH	CREATE	GRITTY
OGRESS	ROMISH	VENOSE	CRUSTY	GROTTO
OGRISH	RUDEST.	VILEST.	CURATE.	GROTTY
OLDEST	SADISM	WHILST	DAINTY	GROWTH
ONCOST	SADIST	WHIMSY	*DAKOTA	GUILTY
ONRUSH	SAFEST	WHOOSH	DEARTH	GUNITE
OPPOSE	SANEST	WIDEST	DEBATE	GYRATE.
ORGASM	SCHISM	WISEST.	DELATE	HAMITE
OTIOSE	SCHIST	XYLOSE.	DELETE	HEALTH
OWLISH.	SCOUSE	ZYMASE	DEMOTE	HEARTH
PALEST	SETOSE		DENOTE	HEARTY
PAPIST	SOREST	ACANTH	DEPUTE	+HECATE
PARISH	SPARSE	ACRITA	DEPUTY	HERETO
PERISH	SPLASH	ACUITY	DERATE	HUMPTY.
PERUSE	SPOUSE	AERATE	DEVOTE	IGNITE
PHRASE	SQUASH	AGNATE	DILATE	IMPUTE
PILOSE	SQUISH	AGOUTI	DILUTE	INCITE
PLEASE	STRESS	ALBATA	DIMITY	INDITE
POLISH	SUREST.	ALBITE	DOGATE	INMATE
POPISH	TANIST	+ALCOTT	DONATE	INNATE
POTASH	TAOISM	ASSETS	DROUTH	INVITE
PRAISE	THEISM	ASTUTE	DUMPTY.	IOLITE.
PRIEST	THEIST	AVIATE.	ECARTE	JAUNTY
PRISSY	THIRST	BALATA	EFFETE	+JUDITH
+PROUST	THRASH	BARYTA	EIGHTH	JUGATE.
PUNISH	THRESH	BEAUTY	EIGHTY	KARATE
PUREST	THRUSH	BERATE	ENMITY	KNOTTY.
PURISM.	THRUST	BINATE	ENTITY	LANATE
QUEASY	*THURSO	*BOGOTA	EOLITH	LAXITY
QUINSY.	TRAPSE	BONITO	EQUATE	LEAN-TO
RACISM	TRUEST	BORATE	EQUITY	LEGATE
RACIST	TRUISM	BOUNTY	ERRATA	LEGATO
RADISH	TSETSE	BOVATE	ERSATZ	LENGTH
RAKISH	TYPIST.	BREATH	ESTATE	LENITY
RAPIST	UNCASE	BYPATH.	EXCITE.	LEVITE
RAREST	UNEASY	+CANUTE	FAULTY	LEVITY
RAVISH	UNHASP	+CAPOTE	FEALTY	LOBATE
RECAST	UNJUST	CAVITY	FERITY	LOCATE
RECESS	UNLASH	CECITY	FIESTA	+LOLITA
REFUSE	UNLESS	CERATE	FINITE	LUNATE
REHASH	UNMASK	CHASTE	FIXATE	LUXATE.
RELISH	UNREST	CHATTY	FIXITY	MIGHTY
REMISS	UNWISE	CHESTY	FLINTY	MINUTE
REPAST	UPCAST	CHINTZ	FLIRTY	MOIETY
REPOSE	UPMOST	COAITA	FOURTH	MOUNTY
RESIST	UPPISH	COMITY	FROSTY	MUTATE.
REVISE	UPRUSH	COUNTY	FRUITY.	NEGATE
RIBOSE	UTMOST.		GAIETY	NICETY

NIGHTY	SCATTY	WEALTH	BUNKUM	DEVOUT
NINETY	SCROTA	WRAITH	BYSSUS.	DICTUM
NUDITY.	SEDATE	WREATH.	CACTUS	DINKUM
OBLATE	SEMITE	XYLITE.	+CADMUS	DISBUD
ODDITY	SENATE	YEASTY.	CAECUM	DISCUS
+ODETTE	SHANTY	+ZAPATA	CAIQUE	DISEUR
OOCYTE	SHEATH	ZENITH	CALL-UP	DOLOUR
OOLITE	SHIFTY	ZONATE	CALLUS	DORSUM
OPIATE	SHINTO	ZYGOTE	CAMPUS	DROGUE
*OPORTO	SHIRTY		CARPUS	DUGOUT
ORNATE.	SIESTA	ABACUS	CASQUE	DUMDUM
PALATE	SLEUTH	ABLAUT	CATGUT	DYBBUK.
PARITY	SMOOTH	ACCRUE	CAUCUS	EFFLUX
PELOTA	SMUTTY	ACINUS	CENSUS	EGG-CUP
PESETA	SNOOTY	ADNOUN	CERIUM	ERBIUM
PETITE	SNOTTY	ADYTUM	CHEQUE	*EREBUS
PEYOTE	SOLUTE	+AEGEUS	CHERUB	EXODUS
PIGSTY	SONATA	+AEOLUS	CHIBUK	EYEFUL.
+PILATE	*SPARTA	AFFLUX	CHORUS	FACTUM
PIRATE	SPORTY	AIR-GUN	CILIUM	FAMOUS
PLENTY	SPOTTY	ALARUM	CINQUE	FAVOUR
PLINTH	SPRITE	+ALDOUS	CIRCUM	FESCUE
POLITE	STACTE	ALGOUS	CIRCUS	FITFUL
POLITY	STAITH	ALL-OUT	CIRQUE	FLATUS
POTATO	STRATA	ANIMUS	CIRRUS	FOETUS
PRESTO	STRATH	ANTRUM	CISTUS	FUMOUS
PRETTY	SURETY	ARBOUR	CITRUS	FUNGUS
PRONTO	SVELTE	ARDOUR	CLAQUE	FURFUR.
PUPATE	SWEATY.	ARMFUL	CLIQUE	GALLUP
PURITY	*TAHITI	ARMOUR	COBNUT	GANGUE
PUSHTU.	TENUTO	ARTFUL	COCCUS	GENIUS
QUANTA	THIRTY	+ARTHUR	COCK-UP	GIAOUR
QUARTO	TIGHTS	ASYLUM	COITUS	GRADUS
QUARTZ.	TOMATO	+ATREUS	COLOUR	GYPSUM.
RARITY	TONITE	AUROUS	CONCUR	HALLUX
REALTY	TREATY	AVENUE.	CONSUL	HANG-UP
REBATE	TRUSTY	BARIUM	COP-OUT	HELIUM
RECITE	TWENTY	BARQUE	CORIUM	HIATUS
REFUTE	TWISTY.	BASQUE	CORPUS	HICCUP
RELATE	UNCATE	BATTUE	CRATUR	HOLD-UP
REMOTE	UP-DATE	BEDAUB	CROCUS	HONOUR
REPUTE	UPPITY.	BEFOUL	CULTUS	HOOKUP
ROTATE	VACATE	*BEIRUT	CUPFUL	HUBBUB
RUBATO.	VALUTA	BISQUE	CURIUM	HUMBUG
SAFETY	VANITY	BLAGUE	CUSCUS	HUMOUR.
SALUTE	VELETA	BLOW-UP	CUT-OUT	IAMBUS
SAMITE	VERITY	+BRAQUE	*CYPRUS.	+ICARUS
SANITY	VOLUTE.	BROGUE	DENGUE	IDOLUM
SAVATE	WAPITI	+BRUTUS	DETOUR	IMBRUE
SCANTY	WARMTH	BULBUL	DEVOUR	INDIUM

INFLUX	PLAQUE	STYLUS	CHEVVY	SQUAWK
IREFUL.	PLENUM	SUBDUE.	CHIVVY	STRAWY
+JOSHUA	PLEXUS	TALCUM	CLEAVE.	STREWN.
JOYFUL	PODIUM	TALMUD	DATIVE	THROWN.
JOYOUS	POPGUN	TARSUS	DERIVE.	UNHEWN
JUGFUL	POROUS	TAURUS	ENDIVE	UPTOWN.
+JULIUS.	POSEUR	TEACUP	EVOLVE.	*VYRNWY
LABOUR	POSSUM	TEDIUM	*GENEVA	
LANGUR	*PRAGUE	TISSUE	+GODIVA	ANNEXE.
LARRUP	PRIMUS	TITTUP	GRIEVE	GALAXY.
LAWFUL	PRUNUS	TONGUE	GROOVE	ICE-AXE
LAYOUT	PULQUE	TORQUE	GROOVY.	
LEAGUE	PURSUE.	TRY-OUT	INWOVE.	ALWAYS
LIGNUM	QUORUM.	TUMOUR	MOTIVE	ANONYM
LINE-UP	RADIUM	TURN-UP	NATIVE.	ARROYO.
LINGUA	RADIUS	TYPHUS.	OCTAVE	+BOLEYN.
LITMUS	RAGOUT	UMLAUT	OCTAVO.	COCCYX.
LOCK-UP	RAJPUT	UNIQUE	RELIVE	DACTYL.
+LUCIUS.	RECOUP	UNPLUG	REMOVE	EMBRYO
LYCEUM.	RECTUM	UNTRUE	REVIVE.	EPONYM
MAGNUM	RED-GUM	URAEUS	SALIVA	+ERINYS
MAHOUT	REFLUX	+URANUS	SCURVY	+EVELYN.
MAKE-UP	REGIUS	USEFUL	SHELVE	+GLADYS.
MANFUL	RESCUE	UTERUS.	SHRIVE	*MALAYA
MANQUE	RHESUS	VACUUM	SHROVE	MARTYR
MARAUD	RICTUS	VALLUM	SKIVVY	+MELVYN
MASQUE	RIGOUR	VALOUR	SLEEVE	METHYL.
MAYBUG	RIMOUS	VAPOUR	STARVE	NOWAYS
MEDIUM	RISQUE	VELLUM	STRIVE	POOGYE.
MISSUS	ROLL-UP	VENOUS	STROVE	*RYUKYU.
MOCK-UP	RUEFUL	VERSUS	SWERVE.	+SELWYN.
MORGUE	RUFOUS	VIGOUR	THIEVE	*WELWYN.
MOSQUE	RUMOUR	VILLUS	THRIVE	ZEPHYR
MUCOUS	RUMPUS.	VINOUS	THROVE	
MURMUR	SACRUM	VIRTUE	TWELVE.	ABLAZE
MUSEUM.	SAVOUR	VOYEUR.	VOTIVE.	ASSIZE.
NIMBUS.	SEPTUM	WALNUT	ZOUAVE	BREEZE
OBELUS	SEROUS	WALRUS		BREEZY
ODIOUS	SET-OUT	WAY-OUT	ARROWY.	BRONZE.
OMNIUM	SHROUD	+WILBUR	DISOWN.	COROZO
OPAQUE	*SIDCUP	WILFUL	IMPAWN.	CORYZA.
OUTPUT	SINFUL	WIND-UP	*MALAWI	FLOOZY
OUTRUN.	SIRIUS	WOEFUL	MOHAWK.	FREEZE
PEANUT	SLAP-UP		*OTTAWA.	FRENZY
PEPLUM	SODIUM	ACTIVE	RENOWN.	FRIEZE
PHYLUM	SPROUT	ALCOVE	SCRAWL	FRIZZY
PIGNUT	SPUTUM	ARGIVE	SCREWY	FROWZY.
PILE-UP	STATUE	ARRIVE.	SHREWD	IODIZE
PILOUS	STATUS	BEHAVE	SINEWY	IONIZE.
PLAGUE	*STROUD	BEHOVE.	SPRAWL	PIAZZA

SCHIZO	*SAHARA	*UGANDA.	CONCHA	UTOPIA.
SLEAZY	SALIVA	CHOREA	CONTRA	AURORA
SNAZZY	SALVIA	DHARMA	COPULA	BUCKRA
SNEEZE	+SANDRA	PHOBIA	CORNEA	+BUDDHA
SNOOZE	TARSIA	+THALIA	CORONA	CUPOLA
STANZA.	VAGINA	+THELMA.	CORYZA	DUENNA
WHEEZE	VALUTA	*BIAFRA	+GODIVA	EUREKA
WHEEZY	*ZAMBIA	CICADA	HOOP-LA	+EUROPA
	+ZAPATA	CICALA	+JOANNA	*GUINEA
	ZARIBA.	CINEMA	+JOSHUA	*GUYANA
*BAHAMA	ACACIA	FIBULA	LOGGIA	NUTRIA
BALATA	*ACADIA	FIESTA	+LOLITA	QUAGGA
*BALBOA	ACRITA	LINGUA	+MONICA	QUANTA
BANANA	ECZEMA	MIASMA	NOVENA	QUOTHA
BARYTA	SCHEMA	MIMOSA	ROSTRA	*RUSSIA
CABALA	SCORIA	MINIMA	ROTULA	TUNDRA.
CAMERA	SCROTA.	PIAZZA	+ROWENA	*RWANDA.
*CANADA	+EDWINA	SIENNA	SONATA	+HYGEIA
*CANDIA	*GDYNIA	SIERRA	+SOPHIA.	MYOPIA
CASSIA	*ODESSA.	SIESTA	APHTHA	PYJAMA
DAHLIA	+BERTHA	SILICA	*SPARTA.	*SYLVIA
*DAKOTA	FEDORA	VICUNA	SQUAMA.	ZYGOMA.
FACULA	FERULA	*VIENNA	*ARABIA	AZALEA
FARINA	GEISHA	ZINNIA.	ARCANA	
FASCIA	GENERA	ALALIA	AREOLA	BAOBAB
GALENA	*GENEVA	*ALASKA	ARGALA	CANTAB.
*GAMBIA	HERNIA	ALBATA	ARMADA	ABSORB.
*HAVANA	+JEMIMA	ALEXIA	ARNICA	SCARAB.
KALMIA	JERBOA	*ALICIA	+BRENDA	ADSORB
KANAKA	+MEDUSA	ALPACA	*CRIMEA	ADVERB
LACUNA	NEBULA	CLOACA	ERRATA	ODD-JOB
LAMBDA	*NEVADA	+GLORIA	+FRIGGA	BEDAUB
LAMINA	OEDEMA	PLASMA	*GRETNA	BENUMB
MACULA	OEPEMA	PLEURA	TRAUMA	RESORB.
*MALAGA	PELOTA	ULTIMA.	TRIVIA	CHERUB.
*MALAYA	PESETA	+AMANDA	TROIKA	ENTOMB.
MALTHA	+PETULA	+AMELIA	+URSULA.	COBWEB
*MANILA	+REGINA	AMOEBA.	ASTHMA	CONFAB
+MARCIA	REMORA	+ANGELA	*ISCHIA.	CORYMB
+MARINA	RETINA	ANGINA	ATAXIA	HOBNOB.
+MARTHA	SENORA	*ANGOLA	+ATHENA	APLOMB.
MAXIMA	VELETA	ANGORA	+ATTILA	PREFAB.
NAUSEA	*VERONA	*ANKARA	*ITHACA	HUBBUB
PAGODA	VESICA	ANOMIA	*OTTAWA	*PUNJAB
+PAMELA	ZENANA	ENIGMA	*STAFFA	SUBURB
*PANAMA	ZEUGMA.	INDABA	STANZA	SUPERB
PATINA	*AFRICA.	UNGULA.	+STELLA	
RAFFIA	+AGATHA	BODEGA	STIGMA	*BALTIC
RAZZIA	AGENDA	*BOGOTA	STRATA	+BALZAC
+SABINA	IGUANA	COAITA	STROMA	BARDIC

FABRIC	FISTIC	CYSTIC	FAILED	LACKED
GAELIC	NIOBIC	DYADIC	FANGED	LADLED
GALLIC	NITRIC	HYDRIC	FANNED	LAGGED
GARLIC	PICNIC.	MYOPIC	FATTED	LAMBED
IAMBIC	CLERIC	MYSTIC	FAWNED	LAMMED
LACTIC	CLINIC	MYTHIC	GABBED	LANCED
MANIAC	SLAVIC.	SYNDIC	GABLED	LANDED
MANIOC	EMETIC.		GADDED	LAPPED
MANTIC	GNOMIC.	BACKED	GAFFED	LAPSED
MASTIC	BOMBIC	BAGGED	GAGGED	LARDED
MATRIC	COGNAC	BAITED	GAINED	LARKED
PARSEC	COPTIC	BALKED	GALLED	LASHED
PATHIC	COSMIC	BALLAD	GAMMED	LASTED
TANNIC	FORMIC	BANDED	GANGED	LAUDED
TARMAC.	GOTHIC	BANGED	GANOID	MADDED
ACERIC	MOSAIC	BANKED	GARBED	*MADRID
ACETIC	NORDIC	BANNED	GASHED	MAENAD
ACIDIC	POETIC	BARBED	GASPED	MAILED
ECHOIC	ZODIAC.	BARRED	GASSED	MAIMED
ICONIC	ARABIC	BASHED	GAUGED	MALTED
SCENIC.	*ARCTIC	BASKED	HACKED	MANNED
EDDAIC	BROMIC	BASTED	HAFTED	MAPPED
EDENIC.	CRITIC	BATTED	HAGGED	MARAUD
+BELLOC	EROTIC	BAWLED	HAILED	MARKED
CELTIC	FROLIC	CALLED	HALOED	MARLED
FENNEC	IRENIC	CALMED	HALOID	MARRED
FERRIC	IRONIC	CALVED	HALTED	MASHED
HECTIC	ORPHIC	CAMPED	HALVED	MASKED
HEROIC	TRAGIC	CANARD	HAMMED	MASSED
KELTIC	TROPIC	CANDID	HANDED	MASTED
METRIC	URETIC.	CANNED	HANGED	MATTED
PECTIC	ATOMIC	CANTED	HAPPED	MAULED
PELVIC	ATONIC	CAPPED	HARMED	NABBED
PEPTIC	ETHNIC	CARPED	+HAROLD	NAGGED
SEPTIC.	ITALIC	CARTED	HARPED	NAILED
AGAMIC	STATIC.	CASHED	HASHED	NAPPED
AGARIC	CUPRIC	CAUSED	HASPED	NARKED
AGONIC.	FUSTIC	DABBED	HASTED	PACKED
CHORIC	JUDAIC	DAMMED	HATRED	PADDED
PHASIC	LUETIC	DAMNED	HATTED	PAINED
PHOBIC	PUBLIC	DARNED	HAULED	PAIRED
PHONIC	*QUEBEC	DARTED	HAZARD	PALLED
PHYSIC	RUBRIC	DASHED	JABBED	PALLID
RHIZIC.	RUSTIC.	DAUBED	JACKED	PALMED
AIR-SAC	EXILIC	DAWNED	JAGGED	PALPED
BIOTIC	EXOTIC	DAY-BED	JAILED	PANNED
CITRIC	OXALIC.	EARNED	JAMMED	PANTED
FILMIC	CYANIC	FABLED	JARRED	PARKED
FINNIC	CYCLIC	FAG-END	JAZZED	PARSED
FINNOC	CYMRIC	FAGGED	KAYOED	PARTED

233

PASSED	VARIED	BELTED	KEDGED	REELED
PASTED	WADDED	BENDED	KEELED	REEVED
PATTED	WAFTED	BESTED	KEENED	REFUND
PAUSED	WAGGED	BETTED	KENNED	REGARD
PAWNED	WAILED	BEYOND	KERBED	REINED
RACKED	WAITED	CEASED	LEADED	RELAID
RAFTED	WAIVED	DECKED	LEAFED	RELIED
RAGGED	WALLED	DEEMED	LEAKED	REMAND
RAILED	WANTED	DEFEND	LEANED	REMIND
RAINED	WARDED	DEFIED	LEAPED	RENTED
RAISED	WARMED	DELVED	LEASED	REPAID
RAMMED	WARNED	DEMAND	LEAVED	RESTED
RAMPED	WARPED	DENIED	LEERED	RETARD
RAMROD	WARRED	DENTED	LEGEND	RETROD
RANCID	WASHED	DEPEND	LEGGED	REVVED
RANGED	WASTED	DEUCED	LEVIED	REWARD
RANKED	YAKKED	DEVOID	MELDED	SEALED
RAPPED	YANKED	FEARED	MELTED	SEAMED
RASPED	YAPPED	FECUND	MENDED	SEARED
RATTED	YAWNED.	FELTED	MERGED	SEATED
SACKED	ABASED	FENCED	MESHED	SECOND
SACRED	ABATED	FENDED	MESSED	SEEDED
SAGGED	ABIDED	FERVID	METHOD	SEEMED
SAILED	ABOARD	FEUDED	NEARED	SEEPED
SALTED	ABOUND	GEARED	NECKED	SEISED
SALVED	ABROAD	GELDED	NEEDED	SEIZED
SANDED	ABSURD	GELLED	NEREID	SENSED
SAPPED	ABUSED	GEMMED	NERVED	SERVED
SAUCED	OBEYED.	+GERALD	NESTED	TEAMED
TABARD	ACCORD	GERUND	NETTED	TEASED
TABBED	ECHOED	HEADED	PEAKED	TEEMED
TABLED	SCALED	HEALED	PEALED	TENDED
TACKED	SCARED	HEAPED	PECKED	TENSED
TAGGED	SCORED	HEATED	PEEKED	TENTED
TAILED	SCREED	HEAVED	PEELED	TERMED
TALKED	SCRIED.	HEEDED	PEERED	TESTED
TALMUD	ADDLED	HEELED	PEEVED	TETRAD
TAMPED	EDDIED	HEFTED	PEGGED	VEERED
TANGED	EDITED	HELMED	PELTED	VEILED
TANNED	+EDMUND	HELPED	PENNED	VEINED
TAPPED	EDUCED	HEMMED	PENTAD	VENTED
TARRED	+EDWARD.	HEPTAD	PEPPED	VERGED
TARTED	BEAKED	HERALD	PERIOD	VERSED
TASKED	BEAMED	HERDED	PERKED	VESPID
TASTED	BEDDED	JEERED	PERMED	VESTED
TATTED	BEGGED	JELLED	PETTED	VETOED
TAXIED	BEHEAD	JERKED	REARED	VETTED
VALUED	BEHELD	JESTED	RECORD	WEANED
VALVED	BEHIND	JETTED	REEDED	WEBBED
VAMPED	BEHOLD	KECKED	REELED	WEDDED

234

WEDGED	DIMMED	MINDED	WILLED	SLICED
WEEDED	DINNED	MINTED	WILTED	SLOPED.
WELLED	DIPPED	MISLED	WINCED	AMAZED
WELTED	DISBUD	MISSED	WINDED	AMBLED
WENDED	DISHED	MISTED	WINGED	AMUSED
WETTED	FIBBED	MITRED	WINKED	IMAGED
YELLED	FILLED	NICKED	WISHED	IMBUED
YELPED	FILMED	NIPPED	WIZARD	IMPEND
YENNED	FISTED	PICKED	ZIPPED.	SMILED
ZEROED.	FITTED	PIECED	SKEWED.	SMOKED.
AFFORD	FIZZED	PIGGED	+ALFRED	ANGLED
AFIELD	GIFTED	PIMPED	ALGOID	ENFOLD
AFRAID	GILDED	PINKED	ALLIED	ENSUED
OFFEND.	GIRDED	PINNED	ALMOND	ENVIED
AGE-OLD	HINGED	PIPPED	BLADED	GNAWED
AGREED.	HINTED	PIQUED	BLAMED	INBAND
CHAFED	HIPPED	PITIED	BLARED	INBRED
CHASED	HISPID	PITTED	BLAZED	INCHED
CHEWED	HISSED	RIBALD	CLAWED	INDEED
CHIDED	JIBBED	RIBAND	CLEWED	+INGRID
CHIMED	JIGGED	RIBBED	CLOSED	INLAID
CHOKED	JILTED	RICKED	CLOYED	INLAND
PHASED	JINKED	RIDGED	ELATED	INROAD
PHONED	KICKED	RIFLED	ELIDED	INTEND
RHYMED	KIDDED	RIFTED	ELOPED	INURED
SHADED	KILLED	RIGGED	ELUDED	INWARD
SHAMED	KILTED	RIMMED	FLAKED	KNIFED
SHAPED	KINGED	RINGED	FLAMED	ONWARD
SHARED	KINKED	RINKED	FLARED	SNAKED
SHAVED	KIPPED	RINSED	FLAWED	SNARED
SHIELD	KISSED	RIPPED	FLAYED	SNORED
SHINED	KITTED	RISKED	FLEXED	SNOWED
SHOOED	LIASED	SIDLED	FLORID	UNBEND
SHORED	LICKED	SIEVED	FLOWED	UNBIND
SHOULD	LIDDED	SIGHED	FLUKED	UNCORD
SHOVED	LIFTED	SIGNED	FLUTED	UNFOLD
SHOWED	LILTED	SILTED	GLARED	UNGIRD
SHREWD	LIMBED	SINGED	GLAZED	UNHAND
SHROUD	LIMPED	SINNED	GLOVED	UNIPED
THAWED	LIMPID	SIPPED	GLOWED	UNITED
THEWED	LINKED	TICKED	*ILFORD	UNKIND
THREAD	LIPPED	TILLED	PLACED	UNLAID
WHILED	LIQUID	TILTED	PLACID	UNLOAD
WHINED	LISPED	TINGED	PLANED	UNREAD
WHORED.	LISTED	TINNED	PLATED	UNSAID
AIR-BED	LIZARD	TIPPED	PLAYED	UNSHOD
BIASED	MILKED	TITLED	PLUMED	UNTIED
BILLED	MILLED	VISARD	SLAKED	UNTOLD
DIETED	MILTED	VISCID	SLATED	UNUSED
DIGGED	MINCED	WICKED	SLEWED	UNWIND

BOBBED	FOILED	LOLLED	SOAKED	ARCHED
BODIED	FOLDED	*LOMOND	SOAPED	ARGUED
BOGGED	FOOLED	LONGED	SOARED	+ARNOLD
BOILED	FOOTED	LOOKED	SOBBED	AROUND
BOLTED	FORBID	LOOMED	SOILED	BRAKED
BOMBED	FORCED	LOOPED	SOLVED	BRAVED
BONDED	FORDED	LOOSED	SOPPED	BRAYED
BOOKED	FORGED	LOPPED	SORDID	BRIBED
BOOMED	FORKED	LORDED	SORTED	CRANED
BOOTED	FORMED	MOANED	SOUPED	CRATED
BOOZED	FOULED	MOATED	SOURED	CRAVED
COAXED	GOADED	MOBBED	SOUSED	CRAZED
COCKED	GORGED	MOCKED	TOLLED	CROWED
COGGED	GOUGED	MOONED	TOOTED	DRAPED
COILED	HOCKED	MOORED	TOPPED	DRONED
COMBED	HOGGED	MOOTED	TOROID	ERASED
CONKED	HONKED	MOPPED	TORPID	ERODED
CONNED	HOODED	MORBID	TORRID	ERRAND
CONOID	HOOFED	NOBBED	TOSSED	FRAMED
+CONRAD	HOOKED	NOCKED	TOTTED	FRAYED
COOKED	HOOPED	NODDED	TOURED	FRIEND
COOLED	HOOTED	NO-GOOD	TOUTED	FRIGID
COOPED	HOOVED	NOOSED	TOWARD	GRACED
COPIED	HOPPED	NOSHED	VOICED	GRADED
COPPED	HORDED	PODDED	VOIDED	GRAVID
CORDED	HORNED	POISED	VOLTED	GRAZED
CORKED	HORRID	*POLAND	WOLFED	GRIDED
CORNED	HORSED	POLLED	WONTED	GRIPED
COSTED	HOTBED	POOLED	WOODED	GROPED
COWARD	HOT-ROD	POPPED	WORDED	GROUND
DOCKED	HOTTED	PORTED	WORKED	IRISED
DODGED	HOUSED	POSTED	WORMED	IRONED
DOFFED	+HOWARD	POTTED	YOWLED	ORATED
DOGGED	HOWLED	POUTED	ZOOMED.	ORCHID
DOITED	JOBBED	ROARED	APPEND	*ORFORD
DOLLED	JOCUND	ROBBED	OPINED	PRATED
+DONALD	JOGGED	ROCKED	SPACED	PRAYED
DONNED	JOINED	ROGUED	SPARED	PREYED
DOOMED	JOLTED	+ROLAND	SPAYED	PRICED
DOSSED	JOSHED	ROLLED	SPEWED	PRIDED
DOTARD	JOTTED	ROMPED	SPICED	PRIMED
DOTTED	KOBOLD	+RONALD	SPIKED	PRIZED
DOUSED	LOADED	ROOFED	SPIRED	PROBED
DOWNED	LOAMED	ROOKED	SPITED	PROVED
DOWSED	LOANED	ROOMED	SPREAD	PRUNED
FOALED	LOBBED	ROOTED	SPUMED	TRACED
FOAMED	LOCKED	ROTTED	UPHELD	TRADED
FOBBED	LODGED	ROTUND	UPHOLD	TRICED
FOETID	LOFTED	ROUGED	UPLAND	TRIFID
FOGGED	LOGGED	ROUTED	UPWARD.	TRIPOD

236

X-RAYED.	CUSSED	PUGGED	EXILED	DAZZLE
ASCEND	DUBBED	PULLED	EXITED	FACADE
+ASTRID	DUCKED	PULSED	EXPAND	FACILE
ESPIED	DUFFED	PUMPED	EXPEND	FAERIE
ISLAND	DULLED	PUNNED	EXTEND	*FAERDE
ISOPOD	DUMPED	PUNTED	EXUDED	FAILLE
ISSUED	DUNKED	PUPPED	OX-EYED	FAMINE
*OSTEND	DUNNED	PURGED	*OXFORD.	GABBLE
+OSWALD.	DUSTED	PURLED	BY-ROAD	GAGGLE
ATONED	+EUCLID	PURRED	BYWORD	GALORE
ATTEND	FUNDED	PURSED	CYCLED	GAMBLE
ETCHED	FURLED	PUSHED	EYELID	GAMETE
ITCHED	FURRED	PUTRID	HYBRID	GANGUE
STAKED	FUSSED	QUAKED	MYRIAD	GARAGE
STARED	GUIDED	QUEUED	XYLOID	GARBLE
STATED	GULLED	RUBBED		GARGLE
STAVED	GULPED	RUCKED	BABBLE	GAUCHE
STAYED	GUMMED	RUFFED	BAFFLE	+GAULLE
STEWED	GUNNED	RUGGED	BAILEE	HACKLE
STOLID	GUTTED	RUINED	BANGLE	HAGGLE
STONED	HUFFED	RUSHED	BARGEE	HALIDE
STORED	HUGGED	RUSTED	BARQUE	HAMITE
STOWED	HULLED	RUTTED	+BARRIE	HAMOSE
STRAND	HUMMED	SUCKED	BASQUE	HANDLE
*STROUD	HUMPED	SUITED	BATTLE	JANGLE
STUPID	HUNTED	SUMMED	BATTUE	+JANICE
STYLED.	HUSHED	SUN-GOD	BAUBLE	KARATE
BUDDED	HUSKED	SUNNED	CACKLE	LABILE
BUDGED	HUTTED	SUPPED	CAIQUE	LADDIE
BUGGED	JUDGED	SURGED	CAJOLE	*LAHORE
BULBED	JUGGED	SUSSED	CANDLE	LANATE
BUMPED	JUMPED	TUBBED	CANINE	LARVAE
BUNGED	JUNKED	TUCKED	+CANUTE	LASSIE
BUOYED	JUTTED	TUFTED	+CAPONE	LAUNCE
BURIED	LUGGED	TUGGED	+CAPOTE	+LAURIE
BURNED	LULLED	TURBID	CARAFE	MACKLE
BURPED	LUNGED	TURFED	CASQUE	MADAME
BUSHED	LUSTED	TURGID	CASTLE	MAGPIE
BUSIED	MUCKED	TURNED	CATTLE	MALICE
CUBBED	MUFFED	TUSKED	CAUDLE	MANAGE
CUBOID	MUGGED	TUTTED.	DABBLE	MANGLE
CUFFED	MULLED	AVOWED	DAGGLE	MANQUE
CULLED	MUMMED	EVADED	DAMAGE	MANTLE
CUPPED	NUDGED	EVENED	DANDLE	MANURE
CURBED	NUMBED	EVOKED.	DANGLE	MARBLE
CURDED	NURSED	SWAYED	*DANUBE	MARINE
CURLED	OUSTED	SWIPED	+DAPHNE	MASHIE
CURSED	OUTBID	TWINED	DAPPLE	MASQUE
CURVED	OUTDID	TWOULD.	DATIVE	MATURE
CUSPED	PUFFED	EXCEED	DAWDLE	+MAXINE

237

+NADINE	OBLATE	CERATE	+GEORGE	REGALE
NATIVE	OBLIGE	CERISE	HEARSE	REGIME
NATURE	OBTUSE.	CETANE	+HECATE	RELATE
PADDLE	ACCEDE	DEBASE	HECKLE	RELINE
PALACE	ACCRUE	DEBATE	HEDDLE	RELIVE
PALATE	ACCUSE	DECADE	HEXANE	REMADE
PARADE	ACHENE	DECIDE	HEXOSE	REMAKE
PAROLE	ACTIVE	DECKLE	JEJUNE	REMOTE
PARSEE	ECARTE	DECODE	+JEROME	REMOVE
PAVANE	ECTYPE	DECOKE	+JESSIE	REPINE
RABBLE	ICE-AXE	DECREE	KECKLE	REPOSE
RACEME	ICICLE	DEDUCE	KELPIE	REPUTE
RADDLE	OCTANE	DEFACE	KERRIE	RESCUE
RAFFLE	OCTAVE	DEFAME	KETONE	RESIDE
RAMBLE	SCARCE	DEFILE	KETTLE	RESILE
RANKLE	SCATHE	DEFINE	LEAGUE	RESUME
RAPINE	SCHEME	DEFUSE	LEGATE	RETAKE
RATTLE	SCONCE	DEGREE	LEGUME	RETIRE
RAVAGE	SCOUSE	DELATE	LESSEE	REVERE
RAVINE	SCRAPE	DELETE	LEVITE	REVILE
SADDLE	SCRIBE	DELUDE	MEAGRE	REVISE
SALINE	SCYTHE.	DELUGE	MEALIE	REVIVE
+SALOME	ADDUCE	DEMISE	MEDDLE	REVOKE
SALUTE	ADHERE	DEMODE	MENACE	SEANCE
SAMITE	ADJURE	DEMOTE	METTLE	SECEDE
SAMPLE	ADMIRE	DEMURE	NEEDLE	SECURE
+SARTRE	ADVICE	DENGUE	NEGATE	SEDATE
SATIRE	ADVISE	+DENISE	NESTLE	SEDUCE
SAVAGE	EDIBLE	DENOTE	NETTLE	SEETHE
SAVATE	+ODETTE.	DENUDE	PEBBLE	SEMITE
TACKLE	AEDILE	DEPONE	PEDDLE	SENATE
TALKIE	AERATE	DEPOSE	PEOPLE	SENILE
TANGLE	BEADLE	DEPUTE	PERUKE	SERAPE
TASSIE	BEAGLE	DERATE	PERUSE	SERENE
TATTLE	*BEAUNE	DERIDE	PESTLE	SESAME
VACATE	BECAME	DERIVE	PETITE	SETOSE
VALISE	BECOME	DESIRE	PEYOTE	SETTEE
VAMOSE	BEETLE	DEVICE	REBATE	SETTLE
WADDLE	BEFORE	DEVISE	REBORE	SEVERE
WAFFLE	BEGONE	DEVOTE	REBUKE	SEWAGE
WAGGLE	BEHAVE	FEEBLE	RECEDE	TEMPLE
WANGLE	BEHOVE	FELINE	RECIPE	TENURE
WARBLE	BELIKE	FELLOE	RECITE	VELURE
WATTLE	BEMUSE	FEMALE	REDDLE	VENDEE
YAFFLE	BERATE	FERINE	REDUCE	*VENICE
YANKEE	BESIDE	FERULE	REFACE	VENOSE.
ZAFFRE.	BETAKE	FESCUE	REFINE	AFLAME
ABJURE	BETIDE	FETTLE	REFUGE	EFFACE
ABLAZE	BEWARE	GENTLE	REFUSE	EFFETE
ABRADE	CENTRE		REFUTE	EFFUSE

OFFICE.	DIPOLE	PIFFLE	BLENDE	ENABLE
AGNATE	DISUSE	+PILATE	BLITHE	ENCAGE
IGNITE	DITONE	PILOSE	BLONDE	ENCASE
IGNORE.	DIVIDE	PILULE	BLOUSE	ENCORE
CHAISE	DIVINE	PIMPLE	+CLAIRE	ENDIVE
CHANCE	FIACRE	PINULE	CLAQUE	ENDURE
CHANGE	FIANCE	PINTLE	+CLAUDE	ENFACE
CHARGE	FICKLE	PIRATE	CLAUSE	ENGAGE
CHASSE	FIDDLE	RIBOSE	CLEAVE	ENGINE
CHASTE	FIERCE	RIDDLE	CLICHE	ENLACE
CHEESE	FIGURE	RIFFLE	CLIQUE	ENRAGE
CHEQUE	FINALE	RIMOSE	CLOCHE	ENROBE
CHICLE	FINITE	RIPPLE	CLOTHE	ENSILE
CHOICE	FIXATE	RISQUE	+ELAINE	ENSURE
CHOOSE	FIZZLE	SICKLE	ELAPSE	ENTICE
CHROME	GIGGLE	SILAGE	FLANGE	ENTIRE
+PHOEBE	GILLIE	SIMILE	FLECHE	ENTREE
PHRASE	GIRDLE	SIMPLE	FLEDGE	ENZYME
SHELVE	HIGGLE	SINGLE	FLEECE	INCISE
SHRIKE	JIGGLE	SIZZLE	GLANCE	INCITE
SHRINE	JINGLE	TICKLE	ILL-USE	INCOME
SHRIVE	JINNEE	TIERCE	PLAGUE	INCUSE
SHROVE	KIBBLE	TIMBRE	PLAICE	INDITE
THENCE	KIDDIE	TINGLE	PLAQUE	INDUCE
THIEVE	KIDDLE	TINKLE	PLEASE	INFUSE
+THISBE	KINDLE	TIPPLE	PLEDGE	INHALE
THORPE	KINKLE	TIPTOE	PLUNGE	INHERE
THRICE	KIRTLE	TIRADE	SLEDGE	INHUME
THRIVE	KITTLE	TISANE	SLEEVE	IN-JOKE
THRONE	LIABLE	TISSUE	SLUDGE	INJURE
THROVE	LIAISE	TITTLE	SLUICE	INMATE
WHEEZE	LINAGE	VIABLE	ULLAGE.	INNATE
WHENCE.	LITTLE	VIRILE	AMERCE	INSANE
BINATE	MICKLE	VIRTUE	AMPERE	INSIDE
BIRDIE	MIDDLE	VISAGE	EMERGE	INSOLE
BIREME	MINGLE	VIVACE	EMIGRE	INSURE
BISQUE	MINUTE	WIGGLE	EMPIRE	INTAKE
BISTRE	MIRAGE	WIMPLE	IMBIBE	INTONE
CILICE	MISERE	WINKLE.	IMBRUE	INVADE
CINGLE	MISTLE	*SKOPJE.	IMMUNE	INVITE
CINQUE	MISUSE	ALBITE	IMMURE	INVOKE
CIRCLE	MIZZLE	ALCOVE	IMPALE	INWOVE
CIRQUE	NIBBLE	ALKANE	IMPEDE	ON-LINE
DIBBLE	NICENE	ALKENE	IMPOSE	SNEEZE
DIDDLE	+NICOLE	ALLEGE	IMPURE	SNOOZE
+DIEPPE	NIGGLE	ALLUDE	IMPUTE	UNABLE
DILATE	NIMBLE	ALLURE	SMUDGE	UNCASE
DILUTE	NIPPLE	ALPINE	UMPIRE.	UNCATE
DIMPLE	PICKLE	ALVINE	ANNEXE	+UNDINE
DINGLE	PIERCE	BLAGUE	ANYONE	UNDONE

UNIQUE	DOCILE	+MONROE	TORQUE	BROCHE
UNLADE	DOGATE	MORALE	TOUCHE	BROGUE
UNLIKE	DOLOSE	MORGUE	TOUPEE	+BRONTE
UNMADE	DONATE	MOROSE	TOUSLE	BRONZE
UNMAKE	DOODLE	MOSQUE	TOWAGE	+BROOKE
UNRIPE	DOPTRE	MOTIVE	VOLUME	BROWSE
UNROBE	DOSAGE	MOTTLE	VOLUTE	BRUISE
UNSAFE	DOTAGE	MOUSSE	VOTIVE	CRADLE
UNSURE	DOTTLE	NOBBLE	VOYAGE	CREASE
UNTRUE	DOUANE	NOODLE	WOBBLE	CREATE
UNWISE	DOUBLE	NODOSE	ZOMBIE	CRECHE
UNYOKE.	DOUCHE	NODULE	ZONATE	CREOLE
BODICE	EOCENE	+NOELLE	ZOUAVE.	CRINGE
BOGGLE	FOIBLE	NONAGE	APACHE	CROSSE
BOLIDE	FONDLE	NOODLE	APIECE	CRUISE
BOODLE	FOOZLE	NOTICE	APOGEE	DRAWEE
BOOKIE	FORAGE	NOVICE	OPAQUE	DREDGE
BOOTEE	GOALIE	NOWISE	OPIATE	DROGUE
*BOOTLE	GOATEE	NOZZLE	OPPOSE	DROWSE
BORAGE	GOBBLE	OOCYTE	SPARSE	DRUDGE
BORATE	+GOETHE	OOLITE	SPECIE	DRY-ICE
BOTTLE	GOGGLE	POLICE	SPHERE	ERMINE
BOUGIE	GOITRE	POLITE	SPLICE	FRAISE
BOUNCE	HOARSE	POMACE	SPLINE	*FRANCE
BOURSE	HOBBLE	POMADE	SPONGE	FRAPPE
BOVATE	HOMAGE	PONGEE	SPOUSE	FREEZE
BOVINE	HOOPOE	POODLE	SPRITE	FRIDGE
BOW-TIE	HOPPLE	POOGYE	SPRUCE	FRIEZE
COARSE	+HORACE	POTAGE	SPURGE	FRINGE
COATEE	IODIDE	POT-ALE	UP-DATE	GRAMME
COBBLE	IODINE	POUNCE	+UPDIKE	GRANGE
COCKLE	IODIZE	ROOKIE	UPSIDE	GREASE
CODDLE	IOLITE	ROOTLE	UPTAKE.	*GREECE
COERCE	IONIZE	ROTATE	EQUATE	+GREENE
COFFEE	JOCOSE	ROUBLE	EQUINE	GRIEVE
COFFLE	JOGGLE	SOCAGE	SQUARE	GRILLE
COHERE	JOSTLE	SOIREE	SQUIRE.	GRILSE
COLLIE	JOUNCE	SOLACE	ARABLE	GRIPPE
COMMIE	KOEDOE	SOLUTE	ARCADE	GROOVE
COMOSE	LOATHE	SOMBRE	ARCANE	GROUSE
COOKIE	LOBATE	SOOTHE	+ARCHIE	GROYNE
COOLIE	LOBULE	SORTIE	ARGIVE	GRUDGE
CORBIE	LOCALE	SOURCE	AROUSE	ORACLE
CORPSE	LOCATE	TODDLE	ARRIVE	ORANGE
CORRIE	+LOUISE	TOFFEE	ARSINE	ORDURE
COSINE	LOUNGE	TOGGLE	BRAISE	OREIDE
COUPLE	LOUVRE	TONGUE	+BRAQUE	ORIOLE
COURSE	MOBILE	TONITE	BREEZE	ORNATE
COWRIE	MODULE	TOOTLE	BRIDGE	ORPINE
COYOTE	MOHOLE	TOPPLE	BRIDLE	*PRAGUE

PRAISE	STRIKE	JUMBLE	EVOLVE	BALING
PRANCE	STRIPE	JUNGLE	SVELTE	BARING
PRATIE	STRIVE	LUNATE	+YVONNE.	BATING
PRINCE	STROBE	LUSTRE	AWHILE	BAYING
TRANCE	STRODE	LUXATE	SWATHE	CAGING
TRAPSE	STROKE	MUCKLE	SWERVE	CAKING
TREBLE	STROVE	MUDDLE	TWELVE	CANING
TRIFLE	STYMIE.	MUFFLE	TWINGE.	CARING
TRIODE	AUBADE	MUMBLE	EXCISE	CASING
TRIPLE	AUDILE	MURINE	EXCITE	CAVING
TRIUNE	AUNTIE	MUSCLE	EXCUSE	*DANZIG
TROUPE	BUBBLE	MUTATE	EXHALE	DARING
TRUDGE	BUCKLE	MUZZLE	EXHUME	DATING
URBANE	BUNDLE	NUANCE	EXPIRE	DAZING
URSINE	BUNGLE	NUBILE	EXPOSE	*EALING
WRITHE.	BURBLE	NUZZLE	OX-HIDE.	EARING
ASHORE	BURGEE	*OUNDLE	BYGONE	EARWIG
ASLOPE	BURGLE	PUDDLE	BY-LINE	EASING
ASPIRE	BUSTLE	PUISNE	BYNAME	EATING
ASSIZE	BUTANE	PULQUE	+CYBELE	FACING
ASSUME	CUBAGE	PUMICE	GYRATE	FADING
ASSURE	CUDDLE	PUPATE	+MYRTLE	FAKING
ASTUTE	CUP-TIE	PURPLE	PYROPE	FARING
ESCAPE	CURARE	PURSUE	*TYRONE	GAMING
ESTATE	CURATE	PUTTEE	XYLENE	GAPING
+ISOLDE	CURDLE	PUZZLE	XYLITE	GAS-BAG
+PSYCHE	DUFFLE	QUINCE	XYLOSE	GATING
TSETSE	*DUNDEE	RUBBLE	ZYGOTE	GAZING
USABLE	EUCHRE	RUDDLE	ZYMASE	HALING
USANCE.	+EUGENE	RUFFLE		HARING
+ATHENE	+EUNICE	RUMBLE	FAR-OFF	HATING
ATTIRE	*EUROPE	RUMPLE	LAY-OFF	HAVING
+ATTLEE	FUDDLE	RUSTLE	MASSIF	HAWING
ATTUNE	FUMADE	RUTILE	TARIFF.	HAYING
ETHANE	FUMBLE	SUBDUE	SCRUFF.	HAZING
OTIOSE	FURORE	SUBTLE	BEHALF	JADING
STABLE	FUTILE	SUCKLE	BELIEF	JAPING
STACTE	FUTURE	SUNDAE	HEREOF	JAWING
STANCE	GUNITE	SUPINE	REBUFF	LACING
STAPLE	GURGLE	SUPPLE	RELIEF	LADING
STARVE	GUZZLE	SUTTEE	SET-OFF.	LAMING
STATUE	HUDDLE	SUTURE	PILAFF	LAPDOG
STEPPE	HUMANE	TUMBLE	TIP-OFF.	LAYING
STIFLE	HUMBLE	TURTLE	ENGULF	LAZING
STODGE	HURDLE	TUSSLE.	ONE-OFF.	MAKING
STOOGE	HURTLE	AVENGE	ITSELF.	MATING
STRAFE	HUSTLE	AVENUE	CUT-OFF.	MAYBUG
STRAKE	JUGATE	AVERSE	MYSELF	MAYING
STRIDE	JUGGLE	AVIATE		NAMING
STRIFE	JUJUBE	EVINCE	BAKING	OARING

PACING	SEA-DOG	RILING	HONING	ORBING
PAGING	SEEING	RISING	HOPING	PRYING
PALING	SEWING	RIVING	HOSING	TRYING
PARING	SEXING	SIDING	JOKING	URGING.
PAWING	TEA-BAG	SIRING	LOPING	ASKING.
PAYING	TEEING	SITING	LOSING	STRING
RACING	VEXING.	SIZING	LOVING	STRONG
RAG-BAG	OFFING.	TIDING	LOWING	STRUNG.
RAGING	EGG-NOG	TILING	MOOING	BUYING
RAKING	OGLING.	TIMING	MOPING	CUBING
RAPING	SHYING	TIRING	MOVING	CURING
RATING	THRONG.	VIKING	MOWING	DUGONG
RAVING	AIDING	WILING	NOSING	DUPING
RAYING	AILING	WINING	NOTING	DURING
RAZING	AIRING	WIPING	OOZING	FUMING
SARONG	BIDING	WIRING	POKING	FUSING
SATING	BIGWIG	ZIGZAG.	POLING	GUYING
SAVING	BITING	EKEING	PORING	HUMBUG
SAWING	CITING	SKIING	POSING	LURING
SAYING	DICING	SKYING.	ROBING	LUTING
TAKING	DINING	FLYING	ROPING	MUSING
TAMING	DIVING	PLYING.	ROVING	MUTING
TAPING	FILING	IMPING.	ROWING	NUTMEG
TAUTOG	FINING	ENDING	SOLING	OUTING
TAWING	FIRING	INKING	SOWING	PUKING
TAXING	FIXING	UNPLUG	TOEING	PULING
WADING	FIZGIG	UNSUNG.	TONING	PUTLOG
WAGING	GIBING	BODING	TOPING	RUEING
WAKING	GIVING	BONING	TOTING	RULING
WALING	HIDING	BORING	TOYING	TUBING
WANING	HIKING	BOWING	VOLING	TUNING.
WAVING	HIVING	BOW-LEG	VOTING	AWNING
WAXING	JIBING	BOXING	VOWING	OWNING.
YAWING.	JIVING	COBURG	*WOKING	DYEING
EBBING	KIT-BAG	CODING	WOOING	EYEING
OBLONG.	+LIEBIG	COMING	YOKING	GYBING
ACHING	LIKING	COOING	ZONING.	GYVING
ACTING.	LIMING	COPING	*EPPING	PYXING
ADDING	LINING	CORING	OPTING	TYPING
EDGING	LIVING	COVING	SPRANG	
IDLING.	MIMING	COWING	SPRING	BANISH
BELONG	MINING	DOPING	SPRUNG	CALASH
*BERING	MIRING	DOTING	SPYING.	CALIPH
CEDING	MIXING	DOZING	ARCING	DANISH
HEWING	OILING	FOXING	ARMING	FAMISH
KEYING	PILING	GOBANG	CRYING	GALOSH
METING	PINING	GORING	DRYING	GARISH
MEWING	PIPING	HOEING	ERRING	+HANNAH
PEG-LEG	RIDING	HOLING	IRKING	HAUNCH
*PEKING		HOMING	+IRVING	LAUNCH

242

LAVISH	KIRSCH.	MODISH	PUNISH	DEBARK
NAUTCH	SKETCH.	MOLOCH	PURDAH	DEBUNK
OAFISH	BLANCH	POLISH	PUTSCH	*NEWARK
PARAPH	BLEACH	POPISH	QUENCH	REBECK
PARIAH	BLENCH	POTASH	QUITCH	REMARK
PARISH	BLOTCH	ROMISH.	*ZURICH.	RETOOK.
PAUNCH	BLUISH	SPEECH	AVOUCH.	CHIBUK
RADISH	CLENCH	SPLASH	AWEIGH	SHRANK
RAKISH	CLINCH	UPPISH	OWLISH	SHRIEK
RAVISH	CLOUGH	UPRUSH.	SWITCH	SHRINK
VANISH	CLUTCH	SQUASH	TWITCH	SHRUNK
WARMTH	ELFISH	SQUISH.	EXARCH.	THWACK.
YAHWEH.	FLANCH	*ARMAGH	BYPATH	DIK-DIK
ACANTH	FLENCH	BRANCH		HIJACK.
SCORCH	FLETCH	BREACH	+GANDHI	EMBANK
SCOTCH.	FLINCH	BREATH	*HAWAII	EMBARK.
EDDISH.	FLITCH	BREECH	*MALAWI	ANORAK
CERIPH	PLANCH	BROACH	SAFARI	UNCORK
DEARTH	PLINTH	BROOCH	SALAMI	UNHOOK
DETACH	PLOUGH	BRUNCH	SALUKI	UNLOCK
FELLAH	SLEIGH	CRATCH	*TAHITI	UNMASK
FETISH	SLEUTH	CROTCH	WAPITI.	UNPACK
HEALTH	SLOUCH	CROUCH	OCELLI	UNPICK
HEARTH	*SLOUGH.	CRUNCH	SCAMPI.	UNTACK.
JEWISH	AMBUSH	CRUTCH	*DELPHI	BOG-OAK
LENGTH	IMMESH	DRENCH	GEMINI	COPECK
PERISH	IMPISH	DROUTH	+MEDICI	*KODIAK
REHASH	SMIRCH	DRYISH	+YEHUDI.	KOPECK
RELISH	SMOOCH	FRENCH	AGOUTI.	MOHAWK
SEARCH	SMOOTH	GROUCH	CHICHI	POLACK
SERAPH	SMUTCH.	GROWTH	CHILLI.	+YORICK.
WEALTH	ENCASH	PREACH	BIKINI	SQUAWK
ZENITH.	ENMESH	TRENCH	LITCHI	SQUEAK.
AFRESH	ENOUGH	TROUGH	NILGAI.	ATTACK
OFFISH.	ENRICH	WRAITH	ALKALI	STREAK
AGUISH	INARCH	WREATH	ALUMNI.	STRUCK.
OGRISH.	INRUSH	WRENCH	BORZOI	+DVORAK.
CHOUGH	ONRUSH	WRETCH.	*SOMALI.	DYBBUK
CHURCH	SNATCH	+ISAIAH.	*BRUNEI.	
SHEATH	UNLASH.	ATTACH	*ASSISI.	BARBEL
SHEIKH	BORSCH	STAITH	NUCLEI	BARREL
THATCH	BOYISH	STANCH	TUMULI	BASIAL
THOUGH	EOLITH	STARCH		CANCEL
THRASH	FOURTH	STENCH	+BARTOK	*CARMEL
THRESH	GOLOSH	STITCH	DAMASK	CARNAL
THRUSH	HOOKAH	STRATH.	JAMBOK.	CARPAL
WHOOSH.	HOWDAH	EUNUCH	OCLOCK.	CARPEL
EIGHTH	+JOSEPH	HURRAH	*GDANSK.	CARREL
FINISH	+JOSIAH	+JUDITH	BEDECK	CARTEL
KIBLAH	LOOFAH	MULISH	BETOOK	CASUAL

CAUDAL	BELIAL	TEASEL	SIGNAL	FONTAL
CAUSAL	*BENGAL	TERGAL	SIMNEL	FORMAL
DACTYL	BENZOL	TERNAL	SINFUL	FOSSIL
DAEDAL	BETHEL	VENIAL	TIMBAL	GOSPEL
DAMSEL	BEWAIL	VERBAL	TINSEL	HOSTEL
+DANIEL	CENTAL	VERNAL	VIDUAL	JOVIAL
DARNEL	DENIAL	VESSEL	+VIRGIL	JOYFUL
FACIAL	DENTAL	VESTAL	VISUAL	MONGOL
FAECAL	DENTIL	WEASEL	WILFUL	MORSEL
FAUCAL	DERAIL	WEEVIL	WITHAL.	MORTAL
GAMBOL	DETAIL	XENIAL	FLORAL	NO-BALL
HAEMAL	FENNEL	*YEOVIL.	GLOBAL	NORMAL
+HANDEL	FERIAL	AGNAIL	GLYCOL	POMMEL
JACKAL	FESTAL	OGIVAL.	PLURAL.	PORTAL
LABIAL	FETIAL	CHAPEL	AMATOL	POSTAL
LAICAL	FEUDAL	CHESIL	AMORAL	+ROMMEL
LARVAL	GENIAL	CHISEL	UMBRAL.	ROSEAL
LAUREL	HERBAL	CHORAL	ANIMAL	SOCIAL
LAWFUL	*KENDAL	PHENOL	ANNEAL	SORREL
MAMMAL	KENNEL	RHINAL	ANNUAL	TONSIL
MANFUL	KERNEL	SHEKEL	ENAMEL	WOEFUL.
MANTEL	LENTIL	SHOVEL	END-ALL	APICAL
MANUAL	LETHAL	SHRILL	ENTAIL	APODAL
+MANUEL	MEDIAL	THRALL	INSTIL	APPEAL
MARVEL	+MENDEL	THRILL	ONFALL	EPICAL
PARCEL	MENIAL	THYMOL.	SNIVEL	SPINAL
+PASCAL	MENTAL	DIESEL	UNCIAL	SPIRAL
PASTEL	MESCAL	DIETAL	UNCOIL	SPRAWL
PATROL	METHYL	DIRNDL	UNFURL	UPHILL.
+RACHEL	NEURAL	DISCAL	UNGUAL	SQUALL
RACIAL	PENCIL	DISMAL	UNREAL	SQUEAL
RADIAL	PENIAL	DISPEL	UNREEL	SQUILL.
RASCAL	PETREL	DISTAL	UNROLL	ARCHIL
SACRAL	PETROL	DISTIL	UNSEAL	*ARGYLL
+SAMUEL	RECALL	+EIFFEL	UNVEIL	ARMFUL
SANDAL	RECOIL	FIBRIL	UNWELL.	ARTFUL
TARSAL	RECTAL	FILIAL	BOREAL	*BRAZIL
TASSEL	REFILL	FINIAL	COEVAL	BRIDAL
VANDAL	REFUEL	FISCAL	COITAL	BRUMAL
VASSAL	REGNAL	FITFUL	COMPEL	+BRUNEL
+WARHOL.	RENTAL	LINEAL	CONSUL	BRUTAL
ACTUAL	REPEAL	LINTEL	CORBEL	CREDAL
SCHOOL	RETAIL	+LIONEL	CORNEL	CRESOL
SCRAWL	REVEAL	MISSAL	CORRAL	CREWEL
SCROLL.	SENDAL	MISSEL	COSTAL	CRURAL
AERIAL	SEPTAL	NICKEL	DORSAL	DRIVEL
BEFALL	SEQUEL	PINEAL	DOSSAL	DRUPEL
BEFELL	SERIAL	PISTIL	DOSSIL	FRAZIL
BEFOOL	+SEWELL	PISTOL	+DOUGAL	FRIVOL
BEFOUL	SEXUAL	RITUAL	FOETAL	FRUGAL

244

GRAVEL	BARIUM	PHLEGM	EPONYM	CAN-CAN
+GRETEL	CAECUM	PHLOEM	SPUTUM.	CANNON
GROVEL	FACTUM	PHYLUM	SQUIRM.	*CANTON
IREFUL	FATHOM	RHYTHM	DRACHM	CANYON
ORDEAL	HANSOM	THEISM.	ERBIUM	CARBON
*ORWELL	MAGNUM	CILIUM	+GRAHAM	CAREEN
PRIMAL	MAYHEM	CIRCUM	ORGASM	CARMAN
PROPEL	NAPALM	DIADEM	PRELIM	+CARMEN
TRAVEL	NAZISM	DIATOM	TRUISM.	CARTON
TRIBAL	PASSIM	DICTUM	ASYLUM	CASEIN
TROWEL	PAYNIM	DINKUM	ESTEEM.	CATION
URINAL.	RACISM	DISARM	STREAM.	CATKIN
ASSAIL	RADIUM	LIGNUM	AUTISM	CAVERN
ASTRAL	RANDOM	LINGAM	BUNKUM	+CAXTON
ESPIAL	RANSOM	LISSOM	CUBISM	*CAYMAN
+ISABEL	SACRUM	+MIRIAM	CURIUM	DACRON
*ISRAEL	SADISM	*SIKKIM	CUSTOM	DAEMON
USEFUL.	SALAAM	SIMOOM	DUMDUM	+DALTON
ATONAL	TALCUM	VICTIM	*DURHAM	DAMPEN
STROLL.	TANDEM	WIGWAM	MUSEUM	DAMSON
BUCCAL	TAOISM	WISDOM.	MUSLIM	DARKEN
BULBIL	VACUUM	ALARUM	MUTISM	*DARWIN
BULBUL	VALLUM.	*OLDHAM	NUDISM	FABIAN
BURIAL	IBIDEM.	PLENUM.	PURISM	FALCON
BUSHEL	SCHISM	EMBALM	QUORUM.	FALLEN
CUDGEL	SCREAM.	EMBLEM	GYPSUM	FASTEN
CUPFUL	ADYTUM	OMNIUM.	LYCEUM	FATTEN
DUFFEL	IDOLUM.	ANADEM	*LYTHAM	GABION
FULFIL	BECALM	ANONYM	SYSTEM	GALLON
FUNNEL	BEDLAM	ANTHEM		GAMMON
JUGFUL	BELDAM	*ANTRIM	*AACHEN	GARDEN
JUMBAL	BESEEM	ANTRUM	BABOON	GASMAN
KUMMEL	CERIUM	INDIUM	*BAFFIN	HAPPEN
+MURIEL	DEFORM	INFIRM	BAGMAN	HARDEN
MUSSEL	HELIUM	INFORM	BALEEN	HARKEN
MUTUAL	JETSAM	BOTTOM	*BALKAN	HASTEN
PUMMEL	MEDIUM	CONDOM	BANIAN	HATPIN
RUEFUL	MEGRIM	CORIUM	BANYAN	JARGON
RUNNEL	PEPLUM	DORSUM	BARMAN	KAFTAN
TUNNEL.	RECTUM	GODDAM	BARREN	KAOLIN
AVOWAL.	REDEEM	HOLISM	BARTON	LAGOON
AWHEEL	RED-GUM	IODISM	BARYON	LATEEN
SWIVEL.	REFORM	MONISM	BATMAN	LATTEN
CYMBAL	SELDOM	MOSLEM	BATTEN	LAYMAN
EYEFUL	SEPTUM	PODIUM	CABMAN	MACRON
HYMNAL	TEDIUM	POGROM	CAFTAN	MADDEN
SYMBOL	VELLUM.	POMPOM	CALKIN	MADMAN
	AFFIRM.	POSSUM	+CALVIN	MAIDEN
BALSAM	EGOISM.	SODIUM	*CAMDEN	MALIGN
BANTAM	CHRISM	TOMTOM.	CAMION	MAMMON

245

MARGIN	ACTION	+MELVYN	+CHIRON	RIDDEN
+MARIAN	ACUMEN	+MERLIN	CHITIN	SICKEN
MAROON	ICEMAN	MERMAN	CHITON	SILKEN
MARTEN	SCREEN.	NEATEN	+CHOPIN	SIMIAN
+MARTIN	ADJOIN	+NELSON	CHOSEN	SIPHON
MATRON	ADNOUN	NEURON	PHANON	SISKIN
NAPKIN	+ADRIAN	+NEWTON	PHOTON	TIE-PIN
+NATHAN	+EDISON	PEAHEN	SHAKEN	TIFFIN
NATION	ODDS-ON.	PECTEN	SHAMAN	TIN-CAN
PAPAIN	*AEGEAN	PECTIN	SHAVEN	+TITIAN
PARDON	BEACON	PENNON	THROWN	VIOLIN
PARIAN	BEATEN	PEPSIN	WHITEN.	*VIRGIN
PARKIN	BECKON	PERRON	+AILEEN	.VISION
PARSON	BED-PAN	PERSON	AIR-GUN	+VIVIAN
PATHAN	BEMOAN	REASON	AIRMAN	+WILSON
PATRON	BENIGN	REBORN	BIFFIN	*WILTON
PATTEN	*BERGEN	RECKON	BIOTIN	WITHIN
RABBIN	*BERLIN	REDDEN	BITTEN	ZIRCON.
RACOON	*CEYLON	REGAIN	CITRON	ALEVIN
RADIAN	DEACON	REGION	DISOWN	+ALISON
RAGLAN	DEADEN	REJOIN	+EILEEN	BLAZON
RAGMAN	DEAFEN	REMAIN	FIBRIN	CLOVEN
RAISIN	DEEPEN	RENOWN	FILL-IN	ELEVEN
RANDAN	DEMEAN	REOPEN	FINNAN	FLAGON
RATION	DESIGN	RESIGN	FIRKIN	FLAMEN
RATTAN	DETAIN	RETAIN	FIRMAN	FLAVIN
SADDEN	FENIAN	RETURN	GIBBON	FLAXEN
*SAIGON	GERMAN	+REUBEN	+GIDEON	FLORIN
SALMON	GERMEN	SEAMAN	HIDDEN	FLYMAN
SALOON	GERMON	SEAMEN	KITTEN	GLUTEN
SAMPAN	HEAVEN	SEASON	LICHEN	KLAXON
SARSEN	HEMPEN	SEISIN	LINDEN	OLEFIN
SATEEN	*HENDON	+SELWYN	LISTEN	PLATAN
+SATURN	HEREIN	SEQUIN	MICRON	PLATEN
TALION	HEROIN	SERMON	MIDDEN	PLUG-IN
TAMPON	HETMAN	*SEVERN	+MILTON	SLOGAN
TANNIN	JERKIN	SEXTON	MINION	SLOVEN.
TARPAN	JETTON	TEA-URN	MINOAN	AMAZON
TARTAN	KELSON	TENDON	MITTEN	AMNION
TAUTEN	LEADEN	TEUTON	OIL-CAN	+IMOGEN
TAVERN	LEAD-IN	VERMIN	PIDGIN	IMPAWN
WAGGON	LEAVEN	WEAKEN	PIGEON	IMPUGN.
+WALTON	LEGION	WEAPON	PINION	ENJOIN
WANTON	LENTEN	WELKIN	PIPKIN	ENSIGN
WARDEN	LEPTON	*WELWYN	PIPPIN	GNOMON
+WARREN.	LESION	YEOMAN	PISTON	INBORN
*ABADAN	LESSEN	YES-MAN.	PITMAN	INDIAN
*IBADAN	LESSON	*BHUTAN	RIBBON	INSPAN
+OBERON	*LEYDEN	+CHARON		INTERN
OBTAIN.	MEDIAN	CHEVIN		UNBORN

UNEVEN	LOVE-IN	KRAKEN	*HUDSON	SCHIZO.
UNHEWN	MODERN	ORDAIN	+JULIAN	ADAGIO.
UNISON	MOLTEN	*OREGAN	+JUSTIN	DEXTRO
UNWORN.	+MORGAN	ORIGIN	MUFFIN	HERETO
BOBBIN	MORMON	ORISON	MUSLIN	LEAN-TO
BODKIN	MOTION	ORPHAN	MUTTON	LEGATO
*BODMIN	NOGGIN	PRISON	OUTRAN	MEDICO
BOFFIN	+NORMAN	PROTON	OUTRUN	MERINO
+BOLEYN	NOTION	PROVEN	PUFFIN	*MEXICO
*BOLTON	POISON	TREPAN	PULL-IN	PEDALO
BONBON	POLLEN	+TRITON	PURLIN	TENUTO
*BOSTON	POMPON	TROGON	RUSHEN	TEREDO.
BOWMAN	POPGUN	TROJAN	+RUSKIN	GHETTO
*COCHIN	POPLIN	+TRUMAN	SUBORN	SHINTO
COCOON	POTEEN	URCHIN.	SUDDEN	*THURSO.
COFFIN	POTION	ASH-CAN	SULLEN	*BILBAO
COLUMN	POTMAN	ASSIGN	SULTAN	+CICERO
COMMON	ROTTEN	ASTERN	SUMMON	FIASCO
CON-MAN	SODDEN	ISATIN.	SUNKEN	GIGOLO
CORBAN	SOFTEN	ATTAIN	SUN-TAN	GINGKO
CORDON	SOLEMN	ETYMON	*SUTTON	KIMONO
COTTON	TOCSIN	+STALIN	TURBAN	LIBIDO
COUPON	TOUCAN	STAMEN	TUREEN	MIKADO
COUSIN	WOODEN	+STEVEN	+VULCAN.	NIELLO
COWMAN	WORSEN.	STOLEN	+EVELYN.	VIRAGO.
DOBBIN	APE-MAN	STRAIN	AWAKEN	AKIMBO.
DOLMAN	OPTION	STREWN.	AWOKEN	ALBINO
DOLMEN	SPAVIN	AUBURN	*SWEDEN.	+CLOTHO
DOMAIN	SPLEEN	AUGEAN	OXYGEN.	ULTIMO.
DONJON	SPOKEN	+AUSTEN	HYPHEN	EMBRYO.
+DOREEN	SPRAIN	*AUSTIN	PYTHON	INDIGO.
DORIAN	UPTOWN	AUTUMN	SYLVAN	BOLERO
FOEMAN	UPTURN.	*BUCHAN	SYPHON	BONITO
GOBLIN	ARCHON	BUNION	TYCOON	*BURNEO
GODSON	ARISEN	BUNSEN	TYRIAN	COROZO
GOLDEN	BRAZEN	+BUNYAN	WYVERN	DOMINO
+GORDON	*BRECON	BURDEN		DORADO
+GORGON	BRETON	*BURTON	BAGNIO	FOREGO
GOTTEN	BRITON	BUSKIN	BAMBOO	HOODOO
GOVERN	BROKEN	BUSMAN	CALICO	LOLIGO
HODDEN	CRAVEN	BUTTON	*CALLAO	*MONACO
HODMAN	CRAYON	*BUXTON	+CARUSO	PONCHO
HOYDEN	CRETIN	DUBBIN	CASINO	POTATO
IONIAN	CRETON	+DUBLIN	+CASTRO	ROCOCO
*JORDAN	DRAGON	+DUNCAN	GAUCHO	*TOBAGO
JOVIAN	DRIVEN	DUNLIN	GAZEBO	TOMATO
*LONDON	FROZEN	*DURBAN	HAIR-DO	TORERO
LOOK-IN	GRADIN	FUSION	HALLOO	VOODOO.
LOOSEN	GRATIN	GUIDON	TATTOO.	+APOLLO
LOTION	GRISON	GUNMAN	OCTAVO	*OPORTO

ARIOSO	KIDNAP	BAZAAR	GAUGER	PALTER
ARROYO	LINE-UP	CADGER	HALTER	PAMPER
BRONCO	MISHAP	+CAESAR	HAMMER	PANDER
CRAMBO	PILE-UP	CALCAR	HAMPER	PANZER
FRESCO	*SIDCUP	CALLER	HANGAR	PASSER
GROTTO	TIPTOP	CALMER	HANGER	PASTOR
PRESTO	TITTUP	CAMBER	HANKER	PATTER
PRONTO	WIND-UP.	CAMPER	HARDER	PAUPER
TROPPO.	BLOW-UP	CANCER	HARPER	RACIER
ESCUDO	SLAP-UP.	CANKER	HATTER	*RADNOR
ESKIMO	ENCAMP	CANNER	HAWKER	RAFTER
PSEUDO	ENTRAP	CANTER	HAWSER	RAIDER
PSYCHO.	ENWRAP	CANTOR	JABBER	RAMMER
STEREO	INSTEP	CAPTOR	JAGUAR	RANGER
STUCCO	UNHASP	CAREER	JAILER	RANKER
STUDIO.	UNSHIP	CASTER	JAM-JAR	RAPIER
CUCKOO	UNSTOP	CASTOR	+JASPER	RAPTOR
NUNCIO	UNWRAP.	CAUTER	KAFFIR	RASHER
PUEBLO	COCK-UP	CAVIAR	KAISER	RASTER
QUARTO	COLLOP	DABBER	LAAGER	RATHER
RUBATO	DOLLOP	DAGGER	LABOUR	RATTER
TUXEDO.	GOSSIP	DAMMAR	LADDER	SADDER
OVERDO.	HOLD-UP	DAMPER	LANCER	SAGGAR
DYNAMO	HOOKUP	DANCER	LANGUR	SAILER
NYMPHO	LOCK-UP	DANDER	LANNER	SAILOR
	LOLLOP	DANGER	LARDER	SALTER
CALL-UP	MOCK-UP	DAPPER	LARGER	SALVER
CAT-NAP	ROLL-UP	DARKER	LASCAR	SALVOR
GALLOP	TOE-CAP.	DARNER	LASHER	SAPPER
GALLUP	UPKEEP.	DASHER	LATHER	SAUCER
HANG-UP	ASLEEP.	EASIER	LATTER	SAVOUR
LARRUP	BUNYIP	*EASTER	LAWYER	SAWYER
MADCAP	BURLAP	FACTOR	MADDER	TAILOR
MAKE-UP	TURNIP	FALTER	MAGYAR	TALKER
SATRAP	TURN-UP.	FARMER	+MAHLER	TALLER
WALLOP.	HYSSOP	FASTER	+MAILER	TAMPER
ICE-CAP		FATHER	MANGER	TANKER
SCRIMP.	BACKER	FATTER	MANNER	TANNER
DECAMP	BADGER	FAVOUR	MARKER	TARTAR
DEWLAP	BAILER	FAWNER	MARTYR	TASTER
*MENDIP	+BALDER	GAFFER	MASKER	TATTER
RECOUP	*BANGOR	GAITER	MASTER	TAUTER
REDCAP	BANKER	GAMMER	MATTER	VAGUER
TEACUP	BANNER	GANDER	MAUSER	VAINER
EGG-CUP.	BANTER	GANGER	NAGGER	VALOUR
+PHILIP	BARBER	GAOLER	NATTER	VALUER
SHRIMP.	BARKER	GARNER	PACKER	VAPOUR
BISHOP	BARTER	GARTER	PALLOR	VASTER
FILLIP	BATHER	GASPER	PALMAR	+WAGNER
HICCUP	BATTER	GATHER	PALMER	WAITER

WAIVER	FETTER	REAMER	CHOLER	JIGGER
WALKER	GEEZER	REAPER	*KHYBER	JITTER
+WALTER	GEIGER	RECTOR	RHYMER	KILLER
WANDER	GENDER	REDDER	SHAKER	KINDER
WARDER	GETTER	REEFER	SHAVER	KIPPER
WARIER	GEYSER	RENDER	SHINER	KISSER
WARMER	HEADER	+RENOIR	SHIVER	LICTOR
WASHER	HEALER	RENTER	SHOWER	LIFTER
WASTER	HEARER	REPAIR	THALER	LIMBER
+XAVIER	HEATER	SEALER	WHALER	LIMNER
YABBER.	HEAVER	SECTOR	WHITER.	LINEAR
OBITER.	+HECTOR	SEEKER	BICKER	LINGER
ECLAIR	HEDGER	SELLER	BIDDER	LIQUOR
OCULAR	HEIFER	SENDER	BIGGER	+LISTER
SCALAR	HELPER	SENIOR	BILKER	LITTER
SCORER	HELTER	SENSOR	BINDER	MILDER
SCOTER.	JESTER	SERVER	BITTER	MILKER
ADORER	KEENER	SETTER	CINDER	+MILLER
EDITOR.	KEEPER	SEXIER	CIPHER	MINCER
AETHER	+KEPLER	TEASER	DIAPER	MIRROR
BEAKER	LEADER	TEDDER	DIBBER	MISTER
BEARER	LECHER	TEETER	DICKER	NICKER
BEATER	LEDGER	TELFER	DIFFER	NIGGER
BEAVER	LENDER	TELLER	DIGGER	NIPPER
BEGGAR	LESSER	TEMPER	DIMMER	PICKER
*BELPAR	LESSOR	TENDER	DINNER	PILFER
BERBER	+LESTER	TENSOR	DIPPER	PILLAR
BESTIR	LETTER	TENTER	DISBAR	*PINNER
BETTER	MEDLAR	TERROR	DISEUR	+PINTER
CELLAR	MEEKER	TESTER	DITHER	RICHER
CENSOR	MEMBER	TETHER	EITHER	RIFLER
DEALER	MEMOIR	TETTER	FIBBER	RIGOUR
DEARER	MENHIR	VECTOR	FILLER	RINGER
DEBTOR	MENTOR	VENDER	FILTER	RIOTER
DECKER	MERCER	VENDOR	FINDER	SICKER
DEEPER	MERGER	VENEER	FINGER	SIFTER
DE-ICER	+MESMER	VERGER	FINNER	SIGNOR
DENIER	METEOR	+VESPER	FIRMER	SILVER
DENSER	NEARER	WEAKER	FISHER	SIMMER
*DENVER	NECTAR	WEAVER	FITTER	SIMPER
DEODAR	NETHER	WEEPER	FIZZER	SINGER
DETOUR	NEUTER	WELDER	GIAOUR	SINKER
DEVOUR	PECKER	WELTER	GIBBER	SINNER
DEXTER	PEDLAR	WETHER	GINGER	SINTER
FEEDER	PEELER	WETTER	GIRDER	SISTER
FEELER	PEEPER	ZEPHYR.	HIGHER	SITTER
FELLER	PEPPER	AFFAIR.	HINDER	TICKER
FENCER	PESTER	UGLIER.	HITHER	TIDIER
FENDER	PEWTER	CHASER	+HITLER	TILLER
FESTER	READER	CHOKER	HITTER	TIMBER

TINDER	ANGLER	COTTAR	LOOPER	YONDER
TINIER	ANSWER	COTTER	LOOSER	YORKER.
TINKER	ANTHER	COUGAR	LOOTER	APPEAR
TIPPER	ANTIAR	DOCKER	LOUDER	OPENER
TITFER	ANTLER	DOCTOR	LOUVER	SPACER
TITTER	ENDEAR	DODDER	MOCKER	SPIDER
+VICTOR	GNAWER	DODGER	MOHAIR	UPROAR.
VIEWER	INDOOR	DOGGER	MONGER	ARBOUR
VIGOUR	INLIER	DOLLAR	MORTAR	ARCHER
VIZIER	ONAGER	DOLOUR	MOTHER	ARDOUR
WICKER	SNIPER	DORMER	MOUSER	ARMOUR
+WILBUR	UNFAIR	DOSSER	NOBLER	ARREAR
WILDER	UNMOOR.	DOWSER	POLDER	+ARTHUR
WINDER	BOATER	FODDER	PONDER	BRACER
WINNER	BOILER	FOLDER	POORER	BRAVER
WINTER	BOLDER	FOLIAR	POPLAR	BREWER
WITHER	BOMBER	FOOTER	PORKER	BROKER
ZIPPER	BONDER	FORGER	PORTER	CRATER
ZITHER.	BOOMER	FORMER	POSEUR	CRATUR
SKATER	BOOZER	FOSTER	POSTER	*CROMER
SKEWER	BORDER	FOWLER	POTTER	DRAPER
SKIVER.	BOTHER	GOFFER	POURER	DRAWER
BLAZER	BOWLER	GOLFER	POUTER	DRIVER
BLOWER	COALER	GOPHER	POWDER	DROVER
CLEVER	COBBER	HOAXER	ROAMER	FRAMER
CLOVER	COCKER	HOLDER	ROARER	GRATER
ELATER	CODDER	HOLIER	ROBBER	GRAVER
+ELINOR	CODGER	HOLLER	ROCKER	GROCER
ELIXIR	COFFER	HONOUR	ROLLER	GROWER
FLEXOR	COHEIR	HOOKER	ROSIER	ORATOR
FLOWER	COINER	HOOTER	ROSTER	PRAYER
GLAZER	COLDER	+HOOVER	ROTTER	PREFER
GLIDER	COLLAR	HOPPER	ROUSER	PRE-WAR
GLOVER	COLOUR	HORROR	SOAKER	PRIMER
GLOWER	COMBER	HOSIER	SOCCER	PROPER
+OLIVER	CONCUR	HOTTER	SOFTER	PROSER
PLACER	CONDOR	HOWLER	SOLDER	TRACER
PLATER	CONFER	JOBBER	SOONER	TRADER
PLAYER	CONGER	JOINER	SORTER	TREMOR
PLOVER	CONKER	JOTTER	TOILER	+TREVOR
SLATER	COOKER	KOSHER	TOOLER	TRICAR
SLAVER	COOLER	LOADER	TOPPER	TROVER
SLAYER	COOPER	LOAFER	TORPOR	URETER
SLICER	COPIER	LOCKER	TOTHER	WRITER.
SLIVER	COPPER	LODGER	TOTTER	ASHLAR
SLOWER	CORKER	LOFTER	TOURER	ESCHAR
*ULSTER.	CORNER	LOGGER	VOYEUR	+ESTHER
IMPAIR	COSHER	LOITER	WONDER	ISOBAR
SMOKER.	CO-STAR	LONGER	WOOFER	ISOMER
ANCHOR	COSTER	LOOKER	WORKER	OSTLER

USURER.	HUNTER	TUSKER	RADIUS	TESTES
STAGER	HURLER	VULGAR	+SAYERS	VENOUS
STALER	HUSSAR	VULVAR.	TARSUS	VERSUS.
STATER	JUMPER	AVATAR	TAURUS	EGRESS
STATOR	JUNIOR	UVULAR.	+WALLIS	OGRESS.
STAYER	JUNKER	*EXETER.	WALRUS.	CHORUS
STIVER	LUBBER	CYPHER	ABACUS	PHAROS
STOKER	LUGGER	OYSTER	ABATIS	RHESUS
STUPOR.	LUMBAR	XYSTER	ABBESS	*RHODES
AUTHOR	LUMBER		OBELUS	SHEARS
BUFFER	LURKER	BATHOS	OBSESS.	*THAMES
BUGGER	+LUTHER	CACTUS	ACCESS	THANKS
BUGLER	MUMMER	CADDIS	ACINUS	*THEBES
BULGER	MURDER	+CADMUS	ACROSS	THESIS
BUMPER	MURMUR	*CALAIS	*ECCLES	+THOMAS
BUNKER	MUSTER	CALLUS	+ICARUS.	THRIPS.
BURNER	MUTTER	CALVES	+ADONIS	BICEPS
BURSAR	NUMBER	CAMPUS	ODIOUS.	CIRCUS
BUSKER	NUTTER	*CANNES	+AEGEUS	CIRRUS
BUTLER	PUCKER	CANVAS	+AENEAS	CISTUS
BUTTER	PUFFER	CARESS	+AEOLUS	CITRUS
BUZZER	PULLER	CARIES	CENSUS	DIESIS
CULVER	PULPER	CARPUS	CERTES	DISCUS
CUMBER	PULSAR	+CASALS	DEBRIS	DIVERS
CUPPER	PUNTER	CAUCUS	DERMIS	HIATUS
CURLER	PURLER	*DALLAS	DERRIS	LITMUS
CURSOR	PURSER	FAECES	FERRIS	MISSUS
CUTLER	PUSHER	FAMOUS	GENIUS	NIMBUS
CUTTER	PUTTER	FASCES	+HELIOS	PILOUS
DUCKER	QUAKER	*GANGES	+HERMES	PISCES
DUFFER	QUASAR	HABEAS	HERPES	RICTUS
DUIKER	QUAVER	HAGGIS	JEWESS	RIMOUS
DULLER	QUIVER	HARASS	KERMES	SIRIUS
DUMPER	QUOTER	*HARRIS	KERMIS	TIGHTS
*DUNBAR	RUBBER	IAMBUS	+KEYNES	*TIGRIS
DURBAR	RUDDER	*KANSAS	LEAVES	VIANDS
DUSTER	RUGGER	LACHES	*LESBOS	VILLUS
FUHRER	RUMOUR	LAMMAS	MENSES	VINOUS
FULLER	RUNNER	LANDES	MESSRS	VITALS
FULMAR	SUCKER	*MADRAS	+PELOPS	*WIDNES.
FURFUR	SUFFER	MANTIS	PELVIS	+ALDOUS
GUISER	SUITOR	MAQUIS	RECESS	+ALEXIS
GUITAR	SUMMER	MATINS	REGIUS	ALGOUS
GUNNER	SUNDER	*NAPLES	REMISS	ALLIES
GUNTER	SUPPER	PALAIS	REVERS	ALPHOS
GUSHER	SURFER	PAMPAS	SELVES	ALWAYS
GUTTER	SUTLER	PARVIS	SEPSIS	CLEVIS
*HUMBER	TUCKER	PATHOS	SERIES	FLATUS
HUMOUR	TUMOUR	PATOIS	SEROUS	GLACIS
HUNGER	+TURNER	RABIES	TENNIS	+GLADYS

*GLAMIS	FRACAS	BALLET	MAYEST	SCRIPT
PLEXUS	GRADUS	BALLOT	NATANT	SCULPT.
PLIERS	GRATIS	BANDIT	NAUGHT	ADDICT
SLACKS.	+GRAVES	BARBET	PACKET	ADJECT
AMENDS	IRITIS	*BARNET	PALEST	ADJUST
*AMIENS	ORCHIS	BASALT	PALLET	ADRIFT
EMBOSS	PRAXIS	BASEST	PAPIST	ADROIT
UMBLES.	PRECIS	BASKET	PARENT	ADVENT
ANABAS	PRIMUS	BASSET	PARGET	ADVERT
ANANAS	PRUNUS	CACHET	PARROT	ODDEST.
ANIMUS	TRIPOS	CAHOOT	PATENT	BED-SIT
*ANUBIS	URAEUS	CANNOT	RABBET	BEHEST
ENOSIS	+URANUS.	CARPET	RABBIT	*BEIRUT.
GNEISS	ASSESS	CARROT	RACIST	BEREFT
GNOSIS	ASSETS	CASKET	RACKET	BEZANT
KNIVES	+OSIRIS.	CATGUT	RAGOUT	CEMENT
UNDIES	*ATHENS	CAUGHT	RAJPUT	CERMET
UNLESS.	+ATREUS	CAVEAT	RAMJET	DECANT
BOFORS	OTITIS	CAVORT	RAPIST	DECEIT
BOWELS	STAPES	DACOIT	RAREST	DECENT
COCCUS	STASIS	*DAUDET	SACHET	DECOCT
COITUS	STATUS	EAGLET	SADIST	DEDUCT
CORPUS	STRESS	FAGGOT	SAFEST	DEFEAT
CORVES	+STUBBS	FAN-JET	SANEST	DEFECT
COSMOS	STYLUS	FAUCET	SAVANT	DEJECT
DOWLAS	UTERUS.	GADGET	TABLET	DEMENT
FOETUS	AUROUS	GAMBIT	TALENT	DEPART
HOOVES	AUXINS	GANNET	TANIST	DEPICT
JOYOUS	CULTUS	GARNET	TAPPET	DEPORT
LOAVES	CUSCUS	GARRET	TARGET	DESERT
MORASS	+DULLES	GAS-JET	TAUGHT	DESIST
*MORRIS	DURESS	GASKET	VACANT	DESPOT
NOWAYS	FUMOUS	HAMLET	VARLET	DETECT
OODLES	FUNGUS	HARLOT	WALLET	DETENT
POROUS	HUBRIS	HAVENT	WALNUT	DETEST
*TOTNES	+JULIUS	JACKET	WAY-OUT	DEVOUT
WOLVES	+LUCIUS	LAMENT	YAOURT.	FERRET
YOICKS	MUCOUS	LANCET	ABDUCT	FEWEST
ZOUNDS.	+RUBENS	LAPPET	ABJECT	HEIGHT
APICES	RUFOUS	LARIAT	ABLAUT	HELMET
OPTICS.	RUMPUS	LATENT	ABRUPT	HEREAT
+BRAHMS	TURVES.	LATEST	ABSENT	HERIOT
BREEKS	EXCESS	LAYOUT	OBJECT.	HERMIT
+BRUTUS	EXODUS.	MAGGOT	ACCENT	JENNET
CRASIS	BY-PASS	MAGNET	ACCEPT	JESUIT
CRISIS	BYSSUS	MAHOUT	ACCOST	LEARNT
CROCUS	*CYPRUS	MALLET	ACQUIT	LEGIST
+CRONOS	TYPHUS.	MARKET	OCCULT	LEVANT
*EREBUS	*AZORES	MARMOT	OCELOT	NEWEST
+ERINYS		MASCOT	SCHIST	PEANUT

PEDANT	EFFORT	TIPCAT	INDULT	FOMENT
PEEWIT	OFFSET.	TIPPET	INFANT	FOREST
PELLET	AGHAST	TITBIT	INFECT	FORGET
PELMET	EGOIST.	VILEST	INFEST	FORGOT
PERMIT	CHALET	+VIOLET	INGEST	FORMAT
RECANT	+CHRIST	WICKET	INJECT	FOUGHT
RECAST	SHRIFT	WIDEST	INK-POT	GOBBET
RECENT	THEIST	WISEST.	INMOST	GOBLET
REDACT	THIRST	ALBEIT	INSECT	GO-CART
RE-EDIT	THREAT	+ALBERT	INSERT	GODWIT
REFOOT	THRIFT	+ALCOTT	INSIST	GOGLET
REGENT	THROAT	ALIGHT	INSULT	GO-KART
REGRET	THRUST	ALL-OUT	INTACT	GORGET
REJECT	THWART	ALMOST	INTENT	*HOBART
RELENT	WHILST.	BLIGHT	INVENT	HOGGET
RELICT	BILLET	CLARET	INVERT	HONEST
RENNET	BISECT	CLIENT	INVEST	HORNET
REPAST	*DIDCOT	CLOSET	KNIGHT	HOTPOT
REPEAT	DIGEST	ELDEST	ONCOST	LOCKET
REPENT	DIGLOT	ELICIT	UNBENT	LOCUST
REPORT	DIMWIT	FLAUNT	UNBOLT	LOQUAT
RESEAT	DIRECT	FLIGHT	UNGIRT	LOWEST
RESENT	DIVERT	FLORET	UNHURT	MODEST
RESIST	DIVEST	FLUENT	UNJUST	MOLEST
RESORT	FIDGET	OLDEST	UNKNIT	MOMENT
RESULT	FILLET	PLACET	UNMEET	MONIST
RETORT	FINEST	PLAINT	UNREST	MOPPET
REVERT	GIBBET	PLANET	UNSEAT	+MOZART
REVOLT	GIBLET	PLIANT	UNWEPT.	NOUGAT
SECANT	GIMLET	PLIGHT	AORIST	NOUGHT
SECRET	KISMET	SLIGHT.	BOBCAT	POCKET
SELECT	LIMPET	AMIDST	BONNET	POPPET
SEPTET	LINNET	AMOUNT	BOUGHT	POSSET
SESTET	MIDGET	AMULET	COBALT	POTENT
SET-OUT	MILLET	IMPACT	COBNUT	+ROBERT
SEXPOT	MINUET	IMPART	COGENT	ROBUST
SEXTET	MISFIT	IMPORT	COHORT	ROCHET
TEAPOT	NICEST	IMPOST	COLLET.	ROCKET
TEA-SET	NITWIT	OMELET	COMBAT	RODENT
TENANT	PICKET	UMLAUT.	COMFIT	ROQUET
TERCET	PIGLET	ANKLET	COMMIT	SOCKET
VELVET	PIGNUT	ANOINT	COP-OUT	*SOLENT
VERSET	PIOLET	ENCYST	COQUET	SONANT
VERVET	PIQUET	ENLIST	CORNET	SONNET
WEIGHT	RIPEST	ENRAPT	CORSET	SORBET
WERENT	SIGNET	INCEPT	COSSET	SOREST
ZEALOT.	SILENT	INCEST	COVERT	SOUGHT
AFFECT	SIPPET	INDENT	DOCKET	SOVIET
AFLOAT	TICKET	INDICT	DOESNT	TOILET
EFFECT	TINPOT	INDUCT	*DORSET	TOM-CAT

253

TOP-HAT	TRIVET	OUTFIT	CACHOU	JIGSAW
WOMBAT	TRUANT	OUTLET	GATEAU	MILDEW
YOGURT.	TRUEST	OUTPUT	JABIRU	MINNOW
APPORT	TRY-OUT	OUTSET	LANDAU	PILLOW
OPTANT	URGENT.	OUTWIT	*NASSAU	RIP-SAW
SPIGOT	ASCENT	PULLET	XANADU.	WILLOW
SPINET	ASLANT	PULPIT	ACAJOU.	WINDOW
SPIRIT	ASPECT	PUNDIT	TELEDU.	WINNOW.
SPLINT	ASSENT	PUNNET	MILIEU.	+ANDREW
SPRINT	ASSERT	PUPPET	ORMOLU.	ANYHOW
SPROUT	ASSIST	PUREST	BUREAU	INFLOW.
UPBEAT	ASSORT	QUAINT	PUSHTU.	BORROW
UPCAST	ESCORT	RUDEST	*RYUKYU	BOW-SAW
UPLIFT	+OSBERT.	+RUPERT		BOW-WOW
UPMOST	ATTEST	RUSSET	+PAVLOV.	FOLLOW
UPROOT	STRAIT	SUBLET	+ASIMOV	HOLLOW
UPSHOT.	STREET	SUBMIT		KOWTOW
SQUINT	STRICT	SUMMIT	*BARROW	MORROW
SQUIRT.	+STUART	SUN-HAT	CALLOW	POW-WOW
*ARARAT	UTMOST.	SUNLIT	*CARLOW	SORROW.
ARDENT	AUGUST	SUNSET	CASHEW	ESCHEW.
ARGENT	AURIST	SUREST	FALLOW	BURROW
ARIGHT	BUCKET	TUCKET	FARROW	CURFEW
ARMLET	BUDGET	TUFFET	HALLOW	CURLEW
ARMPIT	BUFFET	TUMULT	*HARLOW	FURROW
ARRANT	BULLET	TURBOT	*HARROW	GUFFAW
ARREST	BURBOT	TURRET.	HAW-HAW	*LUDLOW
ARTIST	BURNET	AVAUNT	*JARROW	OUTLAW
+BRANDT	CURVET	AVOCET	MALLOW	SUNDEW
BREAST	CUSHAT	AVOSET.	*MARLOW	
+BRECHT	CUTLET	+DWIGHT	MARROW	CARFAX
BREVET	CUT-OUT	TWILIT.	NARROW	EARWAX
BRIGHT	DUGOUT	EXCEPT	SALLOW	HALLUX
CRAVAT	DULCET	EXEMPT	TALLOW	HAYBOX
CREDIT	DUPLET	EXEUNT	WALLOW	LARYNX
DREAMT	GULLET	EXHORT	*WARSAW	MAGNOX
DRIEST	GUSSET	EXPECT	YARROW.	MATRIX.
DRY-ROT	+HUBERT	EXPERT	+BELLOW	ICEBOX.
+ERNEST	+JULIET	EXPORT	BESTOW	CERVIX
ERRANT	JUNKET	EXTANT	FELLOW	REFLEX
FRIGHT	JURIST	EXTENT	GEWGAW	REFLUX
FROWST	*KUWAIT	EXTORT.	HEBREW	VERTEX.
ORIENT	LUCENT	CYGNET	MEADOW	AFFLUX
PRIEST	MULLET	DYNAST	MELLOW	EFFLUX.
PRIVET	*MUSCAT	EYELET	NEPHEW	THORAX.
PROFIT	MUSKET	FYLFOT	REVIEW	PICKAX.
PROMPT	MUSTNT	LYRIST	SEA-COW	CLIMAX.
PROSIT	MUTANT	TYPIST	YELLOW.	IMBREX.
+PROUST	NUDIST	TYRANT	SHADOW.	INFLUX
TRICOT	NUGGET		BILLOW	UNISEX

254

COCCYX	GAMELY	SAVORY	EERILY	VERILY
CONVEX	GANTRY	SAW-FLY	FEALTY	VERITY
CORTEX	GASIFY	SAWNEY	FEEBLY	VESTRY
COW-POX	HARDLY	*SAXONY	FELONY	WEAKLY
DOG-FOX	+HARVEY	TAMELY	FERITY	WEEKLY
POLLEX	HAZILY	TANGLY	GENTLY	+WESLEY
VORTEX.	JALOPY	TARTLY	GENTRY	YEARLY
SPHINX.	JAUNTY	TAUTLY	HEARTY	YEASTY.
FRUTEX	LACKEY	TAWDRY	HEATHY	AFFRAY
PREFIX	LAMELY	VAGARY	*HENLEY	EFFIGY
PROLIX.	LASTLY	VAINLY	HEREBY	OFF-DAY
DUPLEX	LATELY	VALLEY	HERESY	AGENCY
MUSK-OX	LAXITY	VANITY	HEYDAY	UGLIFY.
SUFFIX	LAZILY	VASTLY	+JEREMY	CHAFFY
SURTAX	MAINLY	WARILY	*JERSEY	CHALKY
*SUSSEX.	MALADY	WARMLY	KEENLY	CHANCY
SYNTAX	MARSHY	WATERY	KERSEY	CHATTY
SYRINX	MAUNDY	WAYLAY.	LEEWAY	CHEEKY
	MAYFLY	ABBACY.	LEGACY	CHEERY
BACONY	NAMELY	ACIDLY	LENITY	CHEESY
BAILEY	PACIFY	ACUITY	+LESLEY	+CHERRY
BAKERY	PAEONY	OCCUPY	LEVITY	CHESTY
BALDLY	PALELY	SCABBY	LEWDLY	CHEVVY
BARELY	PALTRY	SCANTY	MEASLY	CHICLY
BARLEY	PANTRY	SCATTY	MEDLEY	CHILLY
BARONY	PAPACY	*SCILLY	*MEDWAY	CHIPPY
BASELY	PARITY	SCREWY	MEEKLY	CHIRPY
CAGILY	PARLEY	SCUMMY	MELODY	CHIVVY
CALMLY	PARODY	SCURFY	MEMORY	CHOOSY
CANARY	PARTLY	SCURRY	MERELY	CHOPPY
CANOPY	PASTRY	SCURVY.	*MERSEY	CHUBBY
*CANVEY	PATCHY	IDIOCY	NEARBY	CHUMMY
CARBOY	*RAASAY	ODDITY.	NEARLY	CHUNKY
CATCHY	RACILY	AERIFY	NEATLY	PHONEY
CAVITY	RAG-DAY	BEAUTY	PEARLY	RHEUMY
DAINTY	RAMIFY	BEECHY	PEBBLY	SHABBY
DAMPLY	RANKLY	BELFRY	?ENURY	SHAGGY
DARKLY	RAPTLY	BETONY	PERTLY	SHAMMY
DAY-BOY	RAREFY	BETRAY	REALLY	SHANDY
EARTHY	RARELY	CECITY	REALTY	SHANTY
EASILY	RARITY	CELERY	REMEDY	SHEENY
FAIRLY	RASHLY	DEADLY	REPLAY	SHERRY
FAMILY	RATIFY	DEARLY	SEA-WAY	SHIFTY
FAULTY	SAFELY	DEEPLY	SEEMLY	SHIMMY
*FAWLEY	SAFETY	DEFRAY	SENTRY	SHINDY
GADFLY	SAGELY	DEFTLY	SEXILY	SHIRTY
GAIETY	SALARY	DENARY	TEAPOY	SHODDY
GALAXY	SALIFY	DEPLOY	TELARY	THEORY
GALLEY	SANELY	DEPUTY	TETCHY	THINLY
*GALWAY	SANITY	DESCRY	VERIFY	THIRTY

THORNY	NICELY	FLASHY	INJURY	GOOGLY
THUSLY	NICETY	FLATLY	KNOBBY	HOCKEY
WHEEZY	NIGHTY	FLEECY	KNOTTY	HOLILY
WHERRY	NIMBLY	FLESHY	ONE-WAY	HOMELY
WHIMSY	NINETY	FLIMSY	ONIONY	HOMILY
WHINNY	PIGSTY	FLINTY	SNAPPY	HOMINY
WHIPPY	PIMPLY	FLIRTY	SNAZZY	HOOKEY
WHISKY	PIRACY	FLOOZY	SNOBBY	HOORAY
*WHITBY	PITCHY	FLOPPY	SNOOTY	HORARY
WHOLLY.	RICHLY	FLOSSY	SNOTTY	HOURLY
AIRILY	RIPELY	FLOURY	SNUGLY	JOCKEY
AIRWAY	RIPPLY	FLUFFY	UNDULY	LONELY
BIGAMY	*SICILY	FLURRY	UNEASY	LORDLY
BINARY	SICKLY	GLADLY	UNHOLY	LOUDLY
BIOPSY	SIMONY	GLASSY	UNRULY	LOVELY
BITCHY	SIMPLY	GLIBLY	UNTIDY	MODIFY
CICELY	SINEWY	GLOOMY	UNWARY.	MOIETY
DICKEY	SINGLY	GLOSSY	BODILY	MONDAY
DIMITY	TIDILY	GLUMLY	BOLDLY	MONKEY
DIMPLY	TIMELY	*ILKLEY	*BOMBAY	MONODY
DINGHY	TINILY	PLASHY	BOTANY	MOTLEY
DIRELY	VILELY	PLEBBY	BOTCHY	MOULDY
DISMAY	VILIFY	PLENTY	BOTFLY	MOUNTY
+DISNEY	VINERY	PLUCKY	BOUNCY	NOBODY
EIGHTY	VIVIFY	PLUMMY	BOUNTY	NONARY
FILTHY	WIDELY	PLUSHY	BOWERY	*NORWAY
FINELY	WIFELY	SLANGY	COBBLY	NOTARY
FINERY	WILDLY	SLEAZY	CODIFY	NOTIFY
FIRMLY	WILILY	SLEEPY	COLDLY	OOZILY
FIXITY	WINTRY	SLIMLY	COLONY	POETRY
HIGHLY	WIRILY	SLINKY	COMEDY	POLICY
+HILARY	WISELY.	SLOPPY	COMELY	POLITY
JIMINY	SKERRY	SLOWLY	COMITY	POLONY
JINGLY	SKILLY	SLUMMY	COMPLY	POORLY
KIDNEY	SKIMPY	SLURRY	CONVEY	POPERY
KINDLY	SKINNY	SLUSHY.	CONVOY	PORTLY
KINGLY	SKIVVY.	EMBODY	*CONWAY	POSHLY
LIKELY	*ALBANY	EMPLOY	COOLLY	+RODNEY
LIMPLY	BLEAPY	SMARMY	COSILY	ROMANY
LITANY	BLIMEY	SMELLY	COSTLY	*ROMNEY
LIVELY	BLOODY	SMITHY	COUNTY	ROSARY
LIVERY	CLAMMY	SMUDGY	COWBOY	ROSILY
MICKEY	CLASSY	SMUGLY	DONKEY	ROTARY
MIDDAY	CLAYEY	SMUTTY.	DOUBLY	SODOMY
MIDWAY	CLERGY	ANGARY	DOUGHY	SOFTLY
MIGHTY	CLINGY	+ANTONY	DOURLY	SOLELY
MILADY	CLOUDY	ENERGY	FOLKSY	SORELY
MILDLY	CLUMSY	ENMITY	FONDLY	SOURLY
MISERY	FLABBY	ENTITY	FOULLY	TOMBOY
MISLAY	FLAGGY	INFAMY	GOODLY	TOUCHY

256

VOLLEY	CRUSTY	TRUSTY.	LUXURY	SYZYGY
VOTARY	DRABLY	ASTRAY	*MURRAY	TYPIFY
WOBBLY	DRAFFY	OSPREY	MUTINY	*VYRNWY
WOOLLY	DREAMY	OSSIFY.	NUDITY	
WORTHY	DREARY	STABLY	NUMBLY	CHINTZ.
ZONARY.	DRESSY	STARRY	OUTCRY	+CORTEZ.
APATHY	DROPSY	STEADY	OUTLAY	ERSATZ.
APEPSY	DROSSY	STEAMY	PULLEY	QUARTZ
APHONY	DROWSY	STEELY	PUNILY	
APIARY	DRY-FLY	STICKY	PURELY	
OPENLY	FREELY	STILLY	PURIFY	
SPEEDY	FRENZY	STINGY	PURITY	
SPONGY	FRIARY	STOCKY	PURVEY	
SPOOKY	FRIDAY	STODGY	QUAGGY	
SPORTY	FRILLY	STOREY	QUARRY	
SPOTTY	FRISKY	STORMY	QUEASY	
UPPITY.	FRIZZY	STRAWY	QUINSY	
EQUITY.	FROSTY	STRIPY	RUDELY	
ARCHLY	FROTHY	STUBBY	RUNWAY	
ARGOSY	FROWZY	STUFFY	SUBTLY	
ARIDLY	FRUITY	STUMPY	SUBWAY	
ARROWY	FRUMPY	STURDY.	SUGARY	
ARTERY	GRAINY	+AUDREY	SULTRY	
ARTILY	GRANNY	AUGURY	SUNDAY	
BRAINY	GRASSY	BUBBLY	SUNDRY	
BRANDY	GREASY	BUNCHY	SUPPLY	
BRASHY	GREEDY	*BUSHEY	SURELY	
BRASSY	GRIMLY	BUSILY	SURETY	
BRAWNY	GRISLY	CUDDLY	*SURREY	
BREEZY	GRITTY	CURACY	SURVEY	
BROLLY	GROGGY	CURTLY	TUMEFY	
BROODY	GROOVY	CURTSY	*TURKEY.	
BRUSHY	GROTTY	CUTELY	AVIARY	
+BRYONY	GRUBBY	*DUDLEY	AVIDLY	
CRABBY	GRUMPY	DUMBLY	EVENLY	
CRAFTY	ORALLY	DUMPTY	EVILLY	
CRAGGY	*ORKNEY	EULOGY	OVERLY.	
CRANKY	ORRERY	GUILTY	AWEARY	
CRANNY	PREPAY	GUN-SHY	SWAMPY	
CRAWLY	PRETTY	HUGELY	SWANKY	
CREAMY	PRIMLY	HUMBLY	SWEATY	
CREEPY	PRIORY	HUMIFY	SWEENY	
CRIKEY	PRISSY	HUMPTY	TWENTY	
CRIMPY	TRASHY	HUNGRY	TWIGGY	
CRISPY	TREATY	HURLEY	TWISTY	
CROAKY	TRENDY	HURRAY	TWO-PLY	
CROCKY	TRICKY	+HUXLEY	TWO-WAY.	
CROUPY	TRILBY	JUNGLY	EXPIRY.	
CRUMBY	TRIMLY	JUSTLY	*SYDNEY	
CRUMMY	TROPHY	LUNACY	SYRUPY	

ABALONE	ALCAZAR	ATELIER	*ABIDJAN	ALLUDED
ABANDON	ALCHEMY	*AVEBURY	+ABIGAIL	ALLURED
ACADEMY	ALCOHOL	AVENGER	ABILITY	*ATLANTA
ACALEPH	ALCORAN	AVERAGE	ABIOTIC	AXLE-BOX
ADAMANT	ANCHOVY	AVERRED	ACIDIFY	AXLE-PIN
ADAPTED	ANCIENT	AVERTED	ACIDITY	ADMIRAL
ADAPTER	ARCHAIC	AWESOME.	ACINOSE	ADMIRER
AGAINST	ARCHERY	AFFABLE	ADIPOSE	ADMIXED
*AJACCIO	ARCHING	AFFINAL	AGILELY	AIMLESS
*ALABAMA	ARCHWAY	AFFINED	AGILITY	ALMANAC
AMALGAM	ARCUATE	AFFIXED	AGITATE	ALMONER
AMANITA	ASCETIC	AFFLICT	AGITATO	ALMSMAN
AMASSED	ASCRIBE	AFFRONT	ALIDADE	AMMETER
AMATEUR	AUCTION.	ALFALFA	ALIENEE	AMMONIA
AMATIVE	ABDOMEN	AWFULLY.	ALIFORM	ARM-BAND
AMATORY	ADDENDA	AGGRESS	ALIMENT	ARMIGER
AMAZING	ADDRESS	ALGEBRA	ALIMONY	ARMLESS
ANAEMIA	ANDANTE	*ALGERIA	ALIQUOT	ARMOURY.
ANAEMIC	ANDIRON	*ALGIERS	AMIABLE	*AINTREE
ANAGRAM	*ANDORRA	ANGELIC	ANILINE	AMNESIA
ANALECT	*ANDOVER	ANGELUS	ANIMATE	AMNESTY
ANALOGY	ARDENCY	ANGERED	ANIMISM	+ANNABEL
ANALYSE	ARDUOUS	ANGLICE	ANISEED	+ANNETTE
ANALYST	AUDIBLE	ANGLING	+ARIADNE	ANNEXED
ANARCHY	AUDITED	ANGRIER	ARIDITY	ANNOYED
ANATOMY	AUDITOR.	ANGRILY	ARISING	ANNUITY
APANAGE	ABETTED	ANGUINE	*ARIZONA	ANNULAR
ARABIAN	ABETTOR	ANGUISH	ASIATIC	ANNULET.
+ARACHNE	ACERBIC	ANGULAR	ASININE	ABOLISH
ARAMAIC	ACETATE	ARGUING	AVIATOR	ABORTED
ATARAXY	ACETIFY	AUGMENT	AVIDITY	ABOULIA
ATAVISM	ACETONE	AUGURED.	*AVIGNON	ACOLYTE
AVAILED	ACETOUS	+ACHATES	AXIALLY	ACONITE
AVARICE	ADENOID	ACHIEVE	AZIMUTH.	ADORING
AWAITED	ADENOSE	ADHERED	ABJURED	AEOLIAN
AWARDED.	ADENOUS	ADHIBIT	ADJOURN	AGONIZE
*ALBANIA	AGELESS	AMHARIC	ADJUDGE	ALOOFLY
ALBUMEN	ALEMBIC	APHASIA	ADJUNCT.	AMOEBIC
AMBIENT	ALERTED	APHELIA	ASKANCE	AMONGST
AMBLING	AMENDED	APHESIS	AWKWARD.	AMORIST
ARBITER	AMENITY	APHIDES	ACLINIC	AMOROUS
ARBUTUS	AMENTIA	APHONIC	AILERON	ANODIZE
AUBAINE.	AMERCED	ASHAMED	AILMENT	ANODYNE
ACCEDED	*AMERICA	*ASHFORD	ALLAYED	ANOESIS
ACCLAIM	ANEMONE	ASHTRAY	ALLEGED	ANOETIC
ACCOUNT	ANEROID	ATHEISM	ALLEGRO	ANOMALY
ACCRETE	AREOLAR	ATHIRST	ALLERGY	ANOSMIA
ACCURST	ASEPSIS	ATHLETE	ALLOWED	ANOTHER
ACCUSAL	ASEPTIC	ATHWART.	ALLOYED	+ANQUILH
ACCUSED	ASEXUAL	ABIDING	ALL-TIME	APOLOGY

258

APOSTLE	AIRPORT	+ANTHONY	ABYSSAL	BRAMBLE
AROUSED	AIR-RAID	ANTHRAX	ALYSSUM	BRANDED
ATOMIZE	AIRSHIP	ANTIGEN	AMYLOID	BRASHLY
ATONING	ALREADY	*ANTIGUA	ANYBODY	BRASSIE
AVOCADO	APRICOT	ANTILOG	ANYWISE	BRAVADO
AVOWING	APROPOS	ANTIQUE	AZYMOUS	BRAVELY
AXOLOTL.	ARRAIGN	ANTONYM		BRAVERY
+AMPHION	ARRANGE	APTERAL	BEACHED	BRAVEST
AMPHORA	ARRIVAL	APTERYX	BEADING	BRAVING
AMPLIFY	ARRIVED	APTNESS	BEAMING	BRAVURA
AMPOULE	ATROPHY	+ARTEMIS	BEARING	BRAWLER
AMPULLA	+ATROPOS	ARTICLE	BEARISH	BRAYING
AMPUTEE	AUREATE	ARTISAN	BEAR-PIT	BRAZIER
APPAREL	AUREOLA	ARTISTE	BEASTLY	BRAZING.
APPEASE	AURICLE	ARTLESS	BEATIFY	BABBLER
APPLAUD	AUROCHS	+ASTARTE	BEATING	BABYISH
APPLIED	AURORAL.	ASTATIC	+BEATLES	*BABYLON
APPOINT	ABSCESS	ASTOUND	BEATNIK	BABY-SIT
APPRISE	ABSCIND	+ASTRAEA	BLABBED	BIBELOT
APPROVE	ABSCOND	ASTRIDE	BLACKEN	BOBBERY
ASPERSE	ABSENCE	ATTACHE	BLACKER	BOBBING
ASPHALT	ABSINTH	ATTAINT	BLADDER	BOBTAIL
ASPIRED	ABSOLVE	ATTEMPT	BLAMING	BUBBLED
ASPIRIN.	ABSTAIN	ATTIRED	+BLANCHE	BUBONIC.
ACQUIRE	ALSO-RAN	ATTRACT	BLANDLY	BACCHIC
ASQUINT.	ARSENAL	ATTUNED	BLANKED	+BACCHUS
ABRADED	ARSENIC	AUTOCAR	BLANKET	BACILLI
+ABRAHAM	ASSAGAI	AUTOMAT	BLANKLY	BACKING
ABREACT	ASSAULT	AUTOPSY.	BLARING	BACKLOG
ABREAST	ASSAYED	ABUSIVE	BLARNEY	BECAUSE
ABRIDGE	ASSIZES	ABUTTER	BLASTED	+BECKETT
ABROACH	ASSUAGE	ACUTELY	BLASTIN	BECLOUD
ACREAGE	ASSUMED	ADULATE	BLATANT	BICYCLE
ACROBAT	ASSURED	ALUMINA	BLAZING	BUCKING
ACRONYM	AUSPICE	ALUMNUS	BOARDER	BUCKISH
ACRYLIC	AUSSIES	AMUSING	BOASTER	BUCKLED
ADRENAL	AUSTERE	AQUATIC	BOATFUL	BUCKRAM
AERATED	AUSTRAL	AQUEOUS	BOATING	BUCOLIC.
AERATOR	*AUSTRIA.	*ARUNDEL	BOATMAN	BADDISH
AEROBIC	ACTABLE	ASUNDER	BRACING	BEDDING
AEROSOL	+ACTAEON	AZURINE.	BRACKEN	BEDEVIL
AGRAFFE	ACTINIC	ADVANCE	BRACKET	*BEDFORD
AGROUND	ACTRESS	ADVERSE	BRADAWL	BEDIZEN
AIRFLOW	ACTUARY	ADVISED	*BRAEMAR	BEDOUIN
AIR-HOLE	ACTUATE	ADVISER	BRAGGED	BEDPOST
AIRLESS	ALTERED	ALVEOLE.	BRAHMIN	BED-ROCK
AIRLIFT	ANTACID	ANXIETY	BRAIDED	BEDSIDE
AIRLINE	+ANTAEUS	ANXIOUS.	BRAILLE	BEDSORE
AIR-LOCK	ANTENNA	ABYSMAL	BRAINED	BEDTIME
AIRMAIL	ANT-HILL		BRAISED	BIDDING

259

BODEFUL	BUGGING	BALLADE	BEMUSED	BLOATED
BUDDING	BUGLING	BALLAST	BOMBARD	BLOATER
BUDGING.	BUGLOSS.	BALLOON	BOMBAST	BLOCKED
BEECHEN	*BAHRAIN	BELATED	BOMBING	BLOODED
BEEHIVE	BEHAVED	BELAYED	BUMMALO	BLOOMED
BEE-LINE	*BOHEMIA.	BELCHER	BUMPING	BLOOMER
BEES-WAX	BAILIFF	*BELFAST	BUMPKIN.	BLOSSOM
BLEAKLY	BAILING	BELGIAN	*BANBURY	BLOTCHY
BLEATED	BAITING	*BELGIUM	BANDAGE	BLOTTED
BLEEPED	BLINDED	BELIEVE	BANDBOX	BLOTTER
BLEMISH	BLINDLY	+BELINDA	BANDEAU	BLOW-FLY
BLENDED	BLINKED	BELISHA	BANDIED	BLOWING
BLESBOK	BLISTER	BELL-BOY	BANDING	BLOW-OUT
BLESSED	BOILING	BELL-HOP	BAND-SAW	BOOKING
BREADED	BRIBERY	BELLIED	BANEFUL	BOOKISH
BREADTH	BRIBING	*BELLINI	BANGING	BOOKLET
BREAKER	BRICKED	+BELLONA	*BANGKOK	BOOKMAN
BREAK-UP	BRICOLE	BELLOWS	BANKING	BOOMING
BREATHE	BRIDGED	BELOVED	BANKSIA	BOORISH
BRECCIA	+BRIDGET	BELTANE	BANNING	BOOSTER
BREEDER	BRIDLED	BELTING	BANNOCK	BOOTLEG
+BRENDAN	BRIDOON	BELYING	BANQUET	BROADEN
BREVIER	BRIEFLY	BILIARY	BANSHEE	BROADER
BREVITY	BRIGADE	BILIOUS	BANTING	BROADLY
BREWAGE	BRIGAND	BILKING	BENCHER	BROCADE
BREWERY	BRIMFUL	BILLING	BENDING	BROCKET
BREWING.	BRIMMER	BILLION	BENEATH	BROILER
BAFFLED	BRINDLE	BILTONG	BENEFIT	BROKING
BIFOCAL	BRIOCHE	BOLDEST	*BENELUX	BROMATE
BUFFALO	BRIQUET	BOLIVAR	BENGALI	BROMIDE
BUFFING	BRISKET	*BOLIVIA	BENISON	BROMINE
BUFFOON.	BRISKLY	BOLLARD	BENTHOS	BRONCHI
BAGASSE	BRISTLE	*BOLOGNA	BENZENE	+BRONWEN
BAGGAGE	BRISTLY	BOLONEY	BENZOIN	BROODED
BAGGING	*BRISTOL	BOLSTER	BINDING	BROTHEL
*BAGHDAD	*BRITAIN	BOLTING	BONDAGE	BROTHER
BAGPIPE	BRITISH	BULBOUS	BONDING	BROUGHT
BEGGARY	BRITTLE	BULGING	BONDMAN	BROWNED
BEGGING	*BRIXHAM	BULIMIA	BONE-ASH	BROWNIE
BEGONIA	BUILDER	BULLACE	BONFIRE	BROWSED
BEGUILE	BUILT-IN	BULLATE	BONKERS	BUOYAGE
BIGGEST	BUILT-UP.	BULLDOG	BONNILY	BUOYANT.
BIG-HEAD	+BAKUNIN.	BULLIED	BUNCHED	BAPTISM
BIGOTED	BALANCE	BULLION	BUNDLED	BAPTIST
BIGOTRY	BALCONY	BULLISH	BUNGLER	BAPTIZE
BOGGING	BALDEST	BULLOCK	BUNKING	BIPLANE
BOGGLER	BALDRIC	BULRUSH	BUNTING.	BIPOLAR.
BUGABOO	+BALDWIN	BULWARK.	+BEOWULF	BEQUEST.
BUGBEAR	BALEFUL	BAMBINO	BIOLOGY	+BARBARA
BUGGERY	BALKING	*BAMPTON	BIOTYPE	BARBATE

BARBOLA	BASILIC	BAUXITE	CEASING	CLAMBER
BARGAIN	BASINET	BLUBBER	CHABLIS	CLAMOUR
BARGING	BASKING	BLUEING	CHAFFER	CLAMPED
*BARKING	BASSOON	BLUFFER	CHAFING	CLAMPER
BARMAID	BASTARD	BLUFFLY	+CHAGALL	CLANGED
+BARNABY	BASTING	BLUNDER	CHAGRIN	CLANGER
BARN-OWL	BASTION	BLUNTED	CHAINED	CLANKED
BARONET	BESEECH	BLUNTLY	CHAIRED	CLAP-NET
BAROQUE	BESIDES	BLURRED	CHALICE	CLAPPED
BARRACK	BESIEGE	BLURTED	CHAMBER	CLAPPER
BARRAGE	BESMEAR	BLUSHED	CHAMFER	CLARIFY
BARRIER	B'ESPEAK	BLUSTER	CHAMOIS	CLARION
BARRING	BESPOKE	BOUDOIR	CHANCED	CLARITY
BARYTES	BESTEAD	*BOULDER	CHANCEL	CLARKIA
BERATED	BESTIAL	BOULTER	CHANCRE	CLASHED
BEREAVE	BESTREW	BOUNCER	CHANGED	CLASPED
BERHYME	BISCUIT	BOUNDER	CHANNEL	CLASSED
+BERLIOZ	BISMUTH	BOUQUET	CHANTED	CLASSIC
*BERMUDA	BOSCAGE	BOURBON	CHANTRY	CLASTIC
+BERNARD	+BOSWELL	BOURDON	CHAOTIC	CLATTER
BERSERK	BUSHIDO	BOURREE	CHAPLET	+CLAUDIA
BERTHED	BUSHMAN	BRUISED	+CHAPLIN	CLAUSAL
+BERTRAM	BUSKING	BRUMOUS	CHAPMAN	CLAVIER
BIRCHED	BUSTARD	BRUSHED	CHAPPED	CLAWING
BIRETTA	BUSTING	BRUSQUE	CHAPTER	COACHED
BORACIC	BUSTLED.	BRUTISH.	CHARADE	COAL-BED
BOREDOM	BATHING	BIVALVE	CHARGED	COAL-GAS
+BORODIN	+BATISTA	BIVOUAC.	CHARGER	COALING
BOROUGH	BATISTE	BAWDILY	CHARILY	COAL-PIT
BORSTAL	BATTERY	BAWLING	CHARIOT	COAL-TAR
BURBLED	BATTING	BEWITCH	CHARITY	COAL-TIT
BURDOCK	BATTLED	BOWLFUL	+CHARLES	COAMING
BUREAUX	BETAKEN	BOWLINE	CHARMER	COARSEN
BURETTE	BETHINK	BOWLING	CHARNEL	COASTAL
BURGEON	BETIMES	BOWSHOT.	CHARRED	COASTED
BURGESS	BETOKEN	BOXHAUL	CHARTED	COASTER
BURGHER	BETROTH	BOX-KITE	CHARTER	COATING
BURGLAR	BETTING	BOX-TREE	CHASING	COAXING
BURGLED	BETWEEN	BOXWOOD.	CHASSIS	CRABBED
BURNING	BETWIXT	BAYONET	CHASTEN	CRACKED
BURNISH	BITTERN	BOYCOTT	CHATEAU	CRACKER
*BURNLEY	BITUMEN	BOYHOOD	*CHATHAM	CRACKLE
BURNOUS	BOTANIC	BRYOZOA	CHATTED	CRACK-UP
BURPING	BOTARGO	BUYABLE.	CHATTEL	CRAMMED
BURSARY.	BOTCHER	BAZOOKA	CHATTER	CRAMMER
BASALLY	BOTTLED	BEZIQUE	+CHAUCER	CRAMPED
BASCULE	BUTCHER	BIZARRE	CLACKED	CRAMPON
BASHFUL	BUTTERY	BUZZARD	*CLACTON	CRANAGE
BASHING	BUTTOCK	BUZZING	CLAIMED	CRANIAL
BASILAR	BUTYRIC.		CLAMANT	CRANING

CRANIUM	CODEINE	CREATOR	CRIBBED	CHLORIC
CRANKED	CODFISH	CREEPER	CRIBBER	+CHLORIS
CRASHED	CODICIL	CREMATE	CRICKED	CILIARY
CRASSLY	COOLING	CRENATE	CRICKET	CILIATE
CRAVING	CUDDLED.	CRESSET	CRIMPED	COLDEST
CRAWLER	CAESIUM	CRESTED	CRIMSON	COLDISH
CRAZIER	CHEAPEN	CREVICE.	CRINGED	COLICKY
CRAZILY	CHEAPLY	CUFFING.	CRINGLE	COLITIS
CRAZING	CHEATED	COGENCY	CRINKLE	COLLAGE
CYANIDE	CHECKED	COGNATE	CRINKLY	COLLATE
CZARDAS	CHECKER	COGNIZE.	CRINOID	COLLECT
CZARINA.	CHECK-UP	COHABIT	CRIPPLE	COLLEEN
CABARET	*CHEDDAR	COHERER.	CRISPER	COLLEGE
CABBAGE	CHEEPER	CAISSON	CRITTER	COLLIDE
CABINET	CHEERED	CAITIFF	*CUILLIN	COLLIER
CABLING	CHEERIO	CEILING	CUIRASS	COLLOID
CABOOSE	CHEESED	CHIANTI	CUISINE.	COLLUDE
CAB-RANK	CHEETAH	CHIASMA	CAJOLED.	COLOGNE
COBBLER	+CHEKHOV	*CHICAGO	CALAMUS	COLONEL
CUBBING	CHELATE	CHICANE	+CALCHAS	COLTISH
CUBICLE.	*CHELSEA	CHICKEN	CALCIFY	CULLING
CACIQUE	CHEMISE	CHICORY	CALCINE	CULPRIT
CACKLED	CHEMIST	CHIDING	CALCITE	CULTURE
CACODYL	CHEQUER	CHIEFLY	CALCIUM	CULVERT.
+CECILIA	CHERISH	CHIFFON	CALENDS	CAMBIST
COCAINE	CHEROOT	CHIGNON	*CALGARY	CAMBIUM
COCHLEA	CHERVIL	CHILLED	CALIBRE	CAMBRIC
COCKADE	*CHESTER	CHIMERA	CALL-BOX	CAMP-BED
COCKILY	*CHEVIOT	CHIMING	CALLING	CAMPHOR
COCKING	CHEVRON	CHIMNEY	CALLOUS	CAMPING
COCKNEY	CHEWING	CHINESE	CALMEST	CAMPION
COCKPIT	CLEANED	CHINKED	CALMING	CEMBALO
COCONUT	CLEANER	CHINNED	CALOMEL	COMBINE
COCOTTE	CLEANLY	CHINWAG	CALORIC	COMBING
+COCTEAU	CLEANSE	CHIPPED	CALORIE	COMFORT
CUCKOLD	CLEARED	CHIRPED	CALOTTE	COMFREY
CYCLING	CLEARER	CHIRRUP	CALTROP	COMICAL
CYCLIST	CLEARLY	CLICKED	CALUMET	COMMAND
CYCLOID	CLEAVED	CLICKER	CALUMNY	COMMEND
CYCLONE	CLEAVER	CLIMATE	CALVARY	COMMENT
CYCLOPS.	+CLEMENT	CLIMBER	CALVING	COMMODE
CADAVER	COELIAC	CLINGER	CALYCES	COMMONS
CADDISH	COEQUAL	CLINKER	+CALYPSO	COMMUNE
CADENCE	COERCED	CLIPPED	CELADON	COMMUTE
CADENCY	COEXIST	CLIPPER	*CELEBES	COMPACT
CADENZA	CREAKED	CLIPPIE	CELESTA	COMPANY
CADGING	CREAMED	CLIQUEY	+CELESTE	COMPARE
CADMIUM	CREAMER	COILING	CELLIST	COMPASS
CEDILLA	CREASED	COINAGE	CELLULE	COMPEER
CODDLED	CREATED	COINING	CHLORAL	COMPERE

COMPETE	CONDYLE	CHOPINE	CAPPING	+CARROLL
COMPILE	CONFESS	CHOPPED	CAPRICE	CARROTY
COMPLEX	CONFIDE	CHOPPER	CAPROIC	CARTAGE
COMPORT	CONFINE	CHORALE	CAPSIZE	CARTING
COMPOSE	CONFIRM	CHORION	CAPSTAN	CARTOON
COMPOST	CONFLUX	CHORTLE	CAPSULE	CARVING
COMPOTE	CONFORM	CHOWDER	CAPTAIN	CERAMIC
COMPUTE	CONFUSE	CLOACAL	CAPTION	CEREOUS
COMRADE	CONFUTE	CLOAKED	CAPTIVE	CERESIN
CUMQUAT	CONGEAL	CLOBBER	CAPTURE	CERTAIN
CUMULUS	CONGEST	CLOCKED	COPAIBA	CERTIFY
CYMBALO.	CONIFER	CLOGGED	CO-PILOT	CERVINE
CANASTA	CONJOIN	CLOSELY	COPIOUS	CHRISOM
CANDELA	CONJURE	CLOSE-UP	COPPERY	+CHRISTI
CANDIED	CONKING	CLOSING	COPPICE	CHROMIC
CANDOUR	CONNATE	CLOSURE	COPPING	CHRONIC
CANNERY	CONNECT	CLOTHED	COPY-CAT	CIRCLED
CANNILY	CONNING	CLOTHES	COPYIST	CIRCLET
CANNING	CONNIVE	CLOTTED	CUPPING	CIRCUIT
*CANNOCK	CONNOTE	CLOUDED	CUPRITE	CIRROSE
CANONRY	CONQUER	CLOUTED	CUPROUS	CORACLE
CANTATA	CONSENT	CLOWNED	CYPRESS	CORANTO
CANTEEN	CONSIGN	CLOYING	CYPRIOT.	CORDAGE
CANTING	CONSIST	COOKERY	CARACUL	CORDATE
CANVASS	CONSOLE	COOKING	*CARACUS	CORDIAL
CENSURE	CONSORT	COOLANT	CARAMEL	CORDITE
CENTAUR	CONSULT	COOLEST	CARAVAN	*CORINTH
CENTIME	CONSUME	COOLING	CARAWAY	CORKAGE
CENTNER	CONTACT	CROAKER	CARBIDE	CORKING
CENTRAL	CONTAIN	CROCHET	CARBINE	CORN-COB
CENTRIC	CONTEMN	CROCKET	CARCASS	CORNICE
CENTURY	CONTEND	+CROESUS	CARDIAC	CORNILY
CINDERY	CONTENT	CROFTER	*CARDIFF	CORNISH
CONCAVE	CONTEST	CROOKED	CARDOON	COROLLA
CONCEAL	CONTEXT	CROONER	CAREFUL	CORONAL
CONCEDE	CONTORT	CROPPED	CARIBOU	CORONER
CONCEIT	CONTOUR	CROPPER	CARIOUS	CORONET
CONCEPT	CONTROL	CROQUET	CARKING	CORPORA
CONCERN	CONVENE	CROSIER	CARLINE	CORRECT
CONCERT	CONVENT	CROSSED	CARMINE	CORRODE
CONCISE	CONVERT	CROSSLY	CARNAGE	CORRUPT
CONCOCT	CONVICT	CROUTON	+CAROLYN	CORSAGE
CONCORD	CONVOKE	CROWBAR	CAROTID	CORSAIR
CONCUSS	CUNNING	CROWDED	CAROTIN	CORSLET
CONDEMN	CYNICAL	CROWING	CAROUSE	CORTEGE
CONDIGN	+CYNTHIA.	CROWNED	CARPING	CORVINE
CONDOLE	CHOCTAW	*CROYDEN.	CARRACK	*CURACAO
CONDONE	CHOKING	CAPABLE	CARRIED	CURATOR
CONDUCE	CHOLERA	CAPITAL	CARRIER	CURBING
CONDUIT	CHOLINE	CAPITOL	CARRION	CURCUMA

CURDING	CATBOAT	CLUSTER	CAYENNE	DEBATED
CURDLED	CATCALL	CLUTTER	CLYSTER	DEBAUCH
CURETTE	CATCHER	COUCHED	COYNESS	DEBITED
CURIOUS	CATECHU	COUGHED	CRY-BABY	+DEBORAH
CURLING	CATERER	COULDST	CRYOGEN	DEBOUCH
CURRACH	CAT-EYED	COULOMB	CRYPTIC	+DEBUSSY
CURRANT	CATFALL	COULTER	CRYSTAL.	DIBASIC
CURRENT	CATFISH	COUNCIL	+CEZANNE	DIBBLED
CURRIED	CATHEAD	COUNSEL	COZENER	DUBBING
CURRISH	CATHODE	COUNTED		DUBIETY
CURSING	CATLING	COUNTER	DEAD-END	DUBIOUS.
CURSIVE	CATMINT	COUNTRY	DEADPAN	DECADAL
CURSORY	CATS-EYE	COUPLER	DEALING	DECAGON
CURTAIL	CATS-PAW	COUPLET	DEANERY	DECANAL
CURTAIN	CATTILY	COURAGE	DEAREST	DECAPOD
CURTSEY	CATTISH	COURIER	DEATHLY	DECAYED
CURVATE	CATWALK	COURSER	DIABASE	DECEASE
CURVING.	CITADEL	COURTLY	DIABOLO	DECEIVE
CASCADE	CITHARA	COUVADE	DIAGRAM	DECENCY
CASCARA	CITIZEN	CRUCIAL	DIALECT	DECIBEL
CASE-LAW	CITRATE	CRUCIFY	DIALLED	DECIDED
CASEOUS	CITRINE	CRUDELY	DIAMOND	DECIMAL
CASHIER	CITROUS	CRUDITY	DIARCHY	DECKING
CASHING	COTERIE	CRUELLY	DIARIST	DECLAIM
*CASPIAN	CO-TIDAL	CRUELTY	DRABBLE	DECLARE
CASSAVA	COTTAGE	CRUISED	DRACHMA	DECLINE
CASSOCK	COTTIER	CRUISER	DRAFTED	DECODED
CASTILE	COTTONY	CRUMBLE	DRAFTEE	DECODER
CASTING	CUTAWAY	CRUMBLY	DRAGGED	DECOLOR
CASTLED	CUT-BACK	CRUMPET	DRAGGLE	DECORUM
CAST-OFF	CUTICLE	CRUMPLE	DRAG-NET	DECOYED
CASUIST	CUTLASS	CRUNCHY	DRAGOON	DECRIAL
CESSION	CUTLERY	CRUPPER	DRAINED	DECRIER
CESSPIT	CUTTING.	CRUSADE	DRAINER	DECUPLE
CESTOID	CAUDATE	CRUSHED	DRAPERY	DICE-BOX
CISTERN	CAUSING	CRUSTED.	DRAPING	+DICKENS
COSSACK	CAUSTIC	CAVALRY	DRASTIC	DICTATE
COSTARD	CAUTERY	CAVE-MAN	DRATTED	DICTION
COSTATE	CAUTION	CIVILLY	DRAUGHT	DOCKAGE
COSTEAN	CHUCKED	CIVVIES	DRAWING	DOCKING
COSTING	CHUCKLE	COVERED	DRAWLED	DUCHESS
COSTIVE	CHUFFED	COVETED.	DRAYMAN	DUCKING
COSTUME	CHUGGED	COWBANE	DUALISM	DUCTILE.
CUSHION	CHUKKER	COWERED	DUALITY	DADAISM
CUSPATE	CHURCHY	COWHERD	DUALIZE	DEDUCED
CUSSING	CHURNED	COWHIDE	DWARFED.	DIDDLER
CUSTARD	CHUTNEY	COWLICK	DABBING	DODGING
CUSTODY.	CLUBBED	COWLING	DABBLED	DUDGEON.
CATALPA	CLUBMAN	COWSLIP.	DEBACLE	DEEMING
CATARRH	CLUMPED	COXCOMB.	DEBASED	DEEPEST

DEEP-FRY	DEHISCE.	DAMFOOL	DIOCESE	DERIVED
DEEP-SEA	DAISIED	DAMMING	DIOPSIS	+DERRICK
DIEHARD	DEICIDE	DAMNIFY	DIOPTER	DERVISH
DIETARY	DEIFIED	DAMNING	DIOPTRE	DIREFUL
DIETING	DEIFORM	DAMPING	DIORAMA	DIRTIED
DIETIST	DEIGNED	DAMPISH	DIORITE	DIRTILY
DOESKIN	+DEIRDRE	DEMERIT	DIOXIDE	*DORKING
DREADED	DEISTIC	DEMESNE	DOODLED	DORMANT
DREAMER	DRIBBLE	DEMIGOD	DOORMAN	+DOROTHY
DREDGER	DRIBLET	DEMISED	DOORMAT	DURABLE
*DRESDEN	DRIFTER	DEMONIC	DOORWAY	DURABLY
+DRESFUS	DRILLED	DEMOTED	DROMOND	DURAMEN
DRESSED	DRINKER	DEMOTIC	DRONING	DURANCE
DRESSER	DRIP-DRY	DEMOUNT	DROOLED	+DURRELL.
DUELLED	DRIPPED	DIMMING	DROOPED	DASHING
DUELLER	DRIVE-IN	DIMNESS	DROPLET	DASTARD
DWELLER.	DRIVING	DIMPLED	DROP-OUT	DESCALE
DEFACED	DRIZZLE	DUMPING.	DROPPED	DESCANT
DEFAMED	DRIZZLY	DANCING	DROPPER	DESCEND
DEFAULT	DWINDLE.	DANDIFY	DROSERA	DESCENT
DEFENCE	DUKEDOM.	DANELAW	DROSHKY	DESERVE
DEFIANT	DALLIED	DANGLED	DROUGHT	DESIRED
DEFICIT	DELAINE	DANKISH	DROUTHY	+DESMOND
DEFILED	DELATED	DENIZEN	DROWNED	DESPAIR
DEFINED	DELATOR	*DENMARK	DROWSED	DESPISE
DEFLATE	DELAYED	DENOTED.	DUOTONE.	DESPITE
DEFLECT	DELETED	DENSELY	DAPPLED	DESPOIL
DEFRAUD	DELIGHT	DENSEST	DEPLETE	DESPOND
DEFROCK	DELIMIT	DENSITY	DEPLORE	DESSERT
DEFROST	DELIVER	DENTARY	DEPOSED	DESTINE
DEFUNCT	DELOUSE	DENTATE	DEPOSIT	DESTINY
DEFUSED	DELPHIC	DENTINE	DEPRAVE	DESTROY
DIFFUSE	DELTOID	DENTIST	DEPRESS	DISABLE
DUFFING.	DELUDED	DENTURE	DEPRIVE	DISAVOW
DEGAUSS	DELUGED	DENUDED	DIPHASE	DISBAND
DEGRADE	DELVING	DENYING	DIPLOID	DISCARD
DIGGING	DILATED	DINGING	DIPLOMA	DISCERN
DIGITAL	DILATOR	DINNING	DIPNOAN	DISCOID
DIGNIFY	DILEMMA	DONATED	DIPOLAR	DISCORD
DIGNITY	DILUENT	DONATOR	DIPPING	DISCUSS
DIGRAPH	DILUTED	*DONEGAL	DIPTERA	DISDAIN
DIGRESS	DILUTER	DONNING	DIPTYCH	DISEASE
DOGFISH	DOLEFUL	DONNISH	DUPABLE.	DISGUST
DOGGART	+DOLORES	*DUNDALK	DARKEST	DISHFUL
DOGGING	DOLPHIN	DUNGEON	DARKISH	DISHING
DOGGONE	DOLTISH	DUNKING	DARLING	DISHMAT
DOG-ROSE	DULCIFY	DUNNAGE	DARNING	DISJOIN
DOGSKIN	DULLARD	DUNNING	DARTING	DISLIKE
DOGTROT	DULLEST	DYNAMIC	DERANGE	DISLIMN
DOGWOOD.	DULLING.	DYNASTY.	DERIDED	DISMAST

DISMISS	*DOUGLAS	DAZZLED	ESCAPEE	EVENING
DISOBEY	DOUSING	DIZZILY	ESCHEAT	*EVEREST
DISPLAY	DRUBBED		ETCHING	EVERTED
DISPORT	DRUDGED	EDACITY	EUCHRED	EXECUTE
DISPOSE	DRUGGED	EGALITY	EXCERPT	EXERTED
DISPUTE	DRUGGET	ELAPSED	EXCISED	EYEBALL
DISROBE	DRUIDIC	ELASTIC	EXCITED	EYE-BATH
DISRUPT	DRUMLIN	ELASTIN	EXCLAIM	EYE-BOLT
DISSECT	DRUMMED	ELATING	EXCLUDE	EYEBROW
DISSENT	DRUMMER	ELATION	EXCRETA	EYEHOLE
DISTAFF	DRUNKEN.	EMANATE	EXCRETE	EYELASH
DISTANT	DEVALUE	+EMANUEL	EXCUSED.	EYELESS
DISTEND	DEVELOP	ENABLED	ECDYSIS	EYESHOT
DISTICH	DEVIATE	ENACTED	EIDETIC	EYESORE
DISTORT	DEVILRY	ENAMOUR	EIDOLON	EYEWASH
DISTURB	DEVIOUS	EPAULET	ELDERLY	+EZEKIEL.
DISTYLE	DEVISED	ERASING	ENDEMIC	EFFASED
DOSSIER	*DEVIZES	ERASION	END-GAME	EFFENDI
DOSSING	DEVOLVE	+ERASMUS	ENDLESS	EFFUSED
DUSKIER	DEVOTED	ERASURE	ENDLONG	ENFACED
DUSKILY	DEVOTEE	EVACUEE	ENDMOST	ENFEOFF
DUSTBIN	DIVERGE	EVADING	ENDORSE	*ENFIELD
DUSTIER	DIVERSE	EVASION	ENDOWED	ENFORCE.
DUSTILY	DIVIDED	EVASIVE	ENDURED	EAGERLY
DUSTING	DIVINED	EXACTED	ENDWAYS	EGG-FLIP
DUSTMAN	DIVINER	EXACTLY	ENDWISE.	EGGHEAD
DUSTPAN.	DIVISOR	EXACTOR	EGESTED	ENGAGED
DATABLE	DIVORCE	EXALTED	EJECTED	*ENGLAND
DETENTE	DIVULGE	EXAMINE	EJECTOR	ENGLISH
DETERED	DOVECOT	EXAMPLE.	+ELEANOR	ENGORGE
DETRACT	DOVEKIE.	EBB-TIDE	ELECTED	ENGRAFT
DETRAIN	DAWDLER	ECBOLIC	ELECTOR	ENGRAIN
*DETROIT	DAWNING	ELBOWED	+ELECTRA	ENGRAVE
DETRUDE	DEW-CLAW	EMBARGO	ELEGANT	ENGROSS
DITCHED	DEWDROP	EMBASSY	ELEGIAC	EUGENIC.
DITCHER	DEWPOND	EMBAYED	ELEGIST	ECHELON
DOTTING	DOWAGER	EMBOLUS	ELEGIZE	ECHIDNA
DUTEOUS	DOWDILY	EMBOSOM	ELEMENT	ECHINUS
DUTIFUL.	DOWNING	EMBOWER	ELEVATE	ECHOING
DAUBING	DOWSING.	EMBRACE	EMENDED	ECHOISM
DAUNTED	DEXTRAL	EMBROIL.	EMERALD	ENHANCE
DAUPHIN	DEXTRAN	ENCAGED	EMERGED	ETHANOL
DIURNAL	DEXTRIN.	ENCASED	EMETINE	ETHICAL
DOUBLED	DAYBOOK	ENCHAIN	EPERGNE	EXHALED
DOUBLET	DAY-GIRL	ENCHANT	ERECTED	EXHAUST
DOUBTED	DAYLONG	ENCHASE	ERECTLY	EXHIBIT
DOUBTER	DAY-TIME	ENCLAVE	ERECTOR	EXHUMED.
DOUCEUR	DRY-DOCK	ENCLOSE	EREMITE	EDICTAL
DOUCHED	DRY-SHOD.	ENCRUST	ETERNAL	EDIFICE
DOUGHTY	DAZEDLY	ESCAPED	ETESIAN	EDIFIED

EDITING	EROSIVE	ERRATUM.	EQUALLY	FRAILTY
EDITION	EROTICA	EASEFUL	EQUATED	FRAMING
ELIDING	ETONIAN	EASTERN	EQUATOR	+FRANCIS
ELISION	EVOKING	EASTING	EQUERRY	FRANKLY
EMINENT	EVOLVED	ECSTASY	EQUINOX	FRANTIC
EMITTED	EXOGAMY.	ENSILED	ERUDITE	FRAUGHT
EMITTER	EMPANEL	ENSLAVE	ERUPTED	FRAYING
EPICENE	EMPATHY	ENSNARE	EXUDING	FRAZZLE.
EPICURE	EMPEROR	ENSURED	EXULTED.	FABLIAU
EPIGRAM	EMPIRIC	EPSILON	ENVELOP	FEBRILE
EPISODE	EMPOWER	ESSAYED	ENVENOM	FIBBING
EPISTLE	EMPRESS	ESSENCE	ENVIOUS	FIBROID
EPITAPH	EMPTIER	ESSENES	ENVIRON	FIBROUS
EPITHET	EMPTILY	EXSCIND.	ENVYING.	FIBSTER
EPITOME	ESPARTO	EATABLE	ELYSIAN	FOBBING.
EPIZOON	ESPOUSE	ENTENTE	ELYSIUM	FACTION
EVICTED	ESPYING	ENTERIC		FACTORY
EVIDENT	EUPHONY	ENTHRAL	FEARFUL	FACTUAL
EVINCED	EXPANSE	ENTHUSE	FEARING	FACTURE
EXIGENT	EXPENSE	ENTICED	FEASTED	FACULTY
EXILIAN	EXPIATE	ENTITLE	FEATHER	FICTILE
EXILING	EXPIRED	ENTOMIC	FEATURE	FICTION
EXISTED	EXPLAIN	ENTRAIN	FLACCID	FICTIVE
EXITING.	EXPLODE	ENTRANT	FLAG-DAY	FOCUSED
ENJOYED.	EXPLOIT	ENTREAT	FLAGGED	FUCHSIA.
*ESKDALE.	EXPLORE	ENTROPY	FLAGMAN	FADDIST
ECLIPSE	EXPOSAL	ENTRUST	FLAILED	FEDERAL
ECLOGUE	EXPOSED	ENTWINE	FLAKILY	FIDDLED
EEL-FARE	EXPRESS	+ESTELLA	FLAKING	FIDDLER
EEL-WORM	EXPUNGE.	ESTHETE	FLAMING	FUDDLED.
ELLIPSE	ENQUIRE	ESTRIOL	FLANEUR	FEEDING
ENLACED	ENQUIRY	ESTRONE	FLANGED	FEELING
ENLARGE	ESQUIRE.	ESTUARY	FLANKER	FIELDED
ENLIVEN.	EAR-ACHE	+EUTERPE	FLANNEL	FIELDER
ENNOBLE.	EAR-DRUM	EXTINCT	FLAPPED	FIERILY
EBONIST	EARLDOM	EXTRACT	FLAPPER	FLECKED
EBONITE	EARLIER	EXTREME	FLARING	FLEDGED
EBONIZE	EARMARK	EXTRUDE.	FLASHED	FLEEING
ECOLOGY	EARNEST	*ECUADOR	FLASHER	FLEETED
ECONOMY	EARNING	EDUCATE	FLATLET	+FLEMING
EGOTISM·	EARRING	EDUCING	FLATTEN	FLEMISH
EGOTIST	EARSHOT	ELUDING	FLATTER	FLESHED
ELOPING	EARTHED	ELUSION	FLAVOUR	FLESHLY
EMOTION	EARTHEN	ELUSIVE	FLAWING	FLEXILE
EMOTIVE	EARTHLY	ELUSORY	FLAYING	FLEXING
ENOUNCE	EIRENIC	ELUVIAL	FOALING	FLEXION
EPOCHAL	ENRAGED	EMULATE	FOAMING	FLEXURE
ERODENT	ENROBED	EMULOUS	FRAGILE	FREAKED
ERODING	ERRANCY	EQUABLE	FRAIBLE	FRECKLE
EROSION	ERRATIC	EQUABLY	FRAILLY	FRECKLY

FREEDOM	FRISKED	FINALLY	FROWSTY.	FORFEIT
FREEING	FRISKET	FINANCE	FOPPERY	FORGAVE
FREEMAN	FRITTED	FINBACK	FOPPISH.	FORGERY
FREESIA	FRITTER	FINDING	FARADAY	FORGING
FREEZER	FRIZZED	FINESSE	FARAWAY	FORGIVE
FREIGHT	FRIZZLE.	FINICAL	FARCEUR	FORGONE
FRESHEN	FALANGE	FINICKY	FARCING	FORKFUL
FRESHER	FALCATE	*FINLAND	FARMING	FORKING
FRESHET	FALLACY	FINNISH	*FARNHAM	FORLORN
FRESHLY	FALL-GUY	FONDLED	FARRAGO	FORMATE
FRETFUL	FALLING	+FONTEYN	FARRIER	FORMING
FRET-SAW	FALL-OUT	FUNDING	FARTHER	*FORMOSA
FRETTED	FALSELY	FUNERAL	FERMENT	FORMULA
FUELLED.	FALSIES	FUN-FAIR	FERMION	FORRARD
FIFTEEN	FALSIFY	FUNGOID	FERMIUM	FORSAKE
FIFTHLY.	FALSITY	FUNGOUS	FERNERY	FORSOOK
FAGGING	+FELLINI	FUNNILY.	FERN-OWL	+FORSTER
FIGHTER	FELONRY	FEOFFEE	FERRATE	FORTIFY
FIG-LEAF	FELSITE	FEOFFOR	FERRETY	FORTUNE
FIGMENT	FELSPAR	FLOATER	FERRIED	FORWARD
FIGURAL	FELTING	FLOCKED	FERRITE	FORWENT
FIGURED	FELUCCA	FLOGGED	FERROUS	FURBALL
FOGBANK	FILARIA	FLOODED	FERRULE	FURBISH
FOGGIER	FILBERT	FLOORED	FERTILE	FURCATE
FOGGILY	FILCHED	FLOPPED	FERVENT	FURIOUS
FOGGING	FILLING	*FLORIDA	FERVOUR	FURLING
FOGHORN	FILMING	FLORIST	FIRE-ARM	FURLONG
FUGUIST.	FOLDING	FLORUIT	FIREBOX	FURNACE
FAIENCE	FOLIAGE	FLOTSAM	FIRE-BUG	FURNISH
FAILING	FOLIATE	FLOUNCE	FIREDOG	FURRIER
FAILURE	FULCRUM	FLOURED	FIREFLY	FURRING
FAINTED	FULLEST	FLOUTED	FIREMAN	FURTHER
FAINTLY	FULSOME	FLOWERY	FIRMING	FURTIVE.
FAIRILY	FULVOUS.	FLOWING	FIRSTLY	FASCINE
FAIRING	FAMULUS	FOOLERY	FORAGER	FASCISM
FAIRWAY	FEMORAL	FOOLING	FORAMEN	FASCIST
FEIGNED	FUMBLER.	FOOLISH	FORAYED	FASHION
FLICKED	FANATIC	FOOTAGE	FORBADE	FAST-DAY
FLICKER	FANCIED	FOOTING	FORBEAR	FASTEST
FLIGHTY	FANCIER	FOOTPAD	FORBORE	FASTING
FLIPPER	FANFARE	FOOTWAY	FORCING	FESTIVE
FLIRTED	FANNING	FROCKED	FORDING	FESTOON
FLITTED	FANTAIL	FROGGED	FOREARM	FISHERY
FLITTER	FANTAST	FROGMAN	FOREIGN	FISHILY
FOILING	FANTASY	•FRONTAL	FORELEG	FISHING
FOISTED	FENCING	FRONTED	FORESAW	FISSILE
FRIBBLE	FENDING	FROSTED	FORESEE	FISSION
FRIGATE	+FENELLA	FROTHED	FORETOP	FISSURE
FRILLED	FINABLE	FROWARD	FOREVER	FISTFUL
FRINGED	FINAGLE	FROWNED	FOREVER	FISTULA

FOSSICK	FOXHUNT	GRANDER	GRECISM	+GALAHAD
FUSCOUS	FOX-TROT.	GRANDLY	GREENER	+GALILEO
FUSIBLE	FLYAWAY	GRANDMA	GREETED	GALLANT
FUSSING	FLY-BOAT	GRANDPA	+GREGORY	GALLEON
FUSS-POT	FLY-BOOK	GRANITE	GREMLIN	GALLERY
FUSTIAN	FLY-HALF	GRANTED	*GRENADA	GALLING
FUSTILY.	FLYLEAF	GRANTEE	GRENADE	GALLIOT
FATALLY	FLY-OVER	GRANTOR	GREYISH	GALLIUM
FATEFUL	FLY-PAST	GRANULE	GREYLAG	GALLOON
FAT-HEAD	FLY-TRAP.	GRAPERY	GUELDER	GALLOWS
FATIGUE	FIZZING	GRAPHIC	GUERDON	GALUMPH
FATLING	FIZZLED	GRAPNEL	GUESSED.	GELATIN
FATNESS		GRAPPLE	GAFFING.	GELDING
FATTEST	GEAR-BOX	GRASPER	GAGGING	GELLING
FATUOUS	GEARING	GRASSED	GAGGLED	+GILBERT
FETCHED	GHASTLY	GRATIFY	GAGSMAN	GILDING
FETIDLY	GLACIAL	GRATING	GIGGLER	+GILLIAN
FETLOCK	GLACIER	GRAVELY	GOGGLED.	GILLION
FITCHEW	GLADDEN	GRAVEST	GEHENNA.	+GOLDING
FITMENT	GLAMOUR	GRAVING	GAINFUL	GOLIARD
FITNESS	GLANCED	GRAVITY	GAINING	GULLING
FITTEST	GLARING	GRAVURE	GAINSAY	GULPING.
FITTING	*GLASGOW	GRAZING	GLIDING	GAMBLER
FUTHORC.	GLAZIER	GUARDED.	GLIMMER	GAMBOGE
FAULTED	GLAZING	GABBING	GLIMPSE	GAMETIC
FEUDING	GNARLED	GABBLED	GLINTED	GAMMING
FLUENCY	GNASHED	+GABRIEL	GLISTEN	GEMMATE
FLUMMOX	GNATHIC	GIBBOUS	GLISTER	GEMMING
FLUNKEY	GNAWING	GOBBLER	GLITTER	GIMBALS
FLUSHED	GOADING	GOBELIN.	GRIDDLE	GIMMICK
FLUSTER	GO-AHEAD	GADDING	GRIDING	GUMBOIL
FLUTING	GOATISH	GIDDILY	GRIEVED	GUMMING
FLUTIST	GRABBED	GODDAMN	GRIFFIN	GYMNAST.
FLUTTER	GRABBER	GODDESS	GRILLED	GANGING
FLUVIAL	GRABBLE	+GODFREY	GRIMACE	GANGLIA
FLUXION	GRACILE	GODHEAD	GRIMMER	GANGWAY
FOULARD	GRACING	GODLESS	*GRIMSBY	GENERAL
FOULING	GRADATE	GODSEND	GRINDER	GENERIC
FOUMART	GRADELY	GODSHIP	GRINNED	GENESIS
FOUNDER	GRADING	GUDGEON.	GRIPING	GENETIC
FOUNDRY	GRADUAL	GHERKIN	GRIPPED	GENISTA
FOURGON	GRAFTED	GLEAMED	GRISKIN	GENITAL
FRUITER	GRAFTER	GLEANER	GRISTLE	GENTIAN
FRUSTUM.	+GRAHAME	GLEEFUL	GRISTLY	GENTILE
FAWNING	GRAINED	GREASED	GRITTED	GENUINE
FOWLING.	GRAMMAR	GREASER	GRIZZLE	GINGERY
FIXABLE	GRAMPUS	GREATER	GRIZZLY	GINGHAM
FIXATED	GRANARY	GREATLY	GUIDING	GONDOLA
FIXTURE	GRANDAD	GREAVES	GUILDER	GUNBOAT
FOXHOLE	GRANDEE	GRECIAN	GUIPURE.	GUNFIRE

GUNLOCK	GARFISH	GLUTTED	HEBETIC	HOGGISH
GUNNAGE	GARGLED	GLUTTON	HEBRAIC	HOGSKIN
GUNNERY	GARLAND	GOUACHE	HOBBLED	HOGWASH
GUNNING	GARMENT	GOUGING	HOBNAIL.	HUGGING
GUNROOM	GARNISH	GOULASH	HACKING	HYGIENE.
GUNSHOT	GAROTTE	GOURMET	HACKLET	HAILING
GUNWALE.	GERMANE	GRUBBED	*HACKNEY	HAIR-CUT
GEODESY	*GERMANY	GRUBBER	HACKSAW	HAIRILY
GEOLOGY	GIRAFFE	GRUDGED	HECKLER	HAIRNET
GEORDIE	GIRASOL	GRUFFLY	HECTARE	HAIRPIN
*GEORGIA	GIRLISH	GRUMBLE	HICKORY	HEINOUS
GEORGIC	GORDIAN	GRUMMET	HOCKING.	HEIRDOM
GHOSTED	GORGING	GRUNTED	HADDOCK	HEIRESS
GHOSTLY	GORILLA	GRUYERE.	+HADRIAN	HEISTED
GLOATED	GURGLED	GAVOTTE.	HEDDLES	HOICKED
GLOBOSE	GYRATED.	GLYPHIC	HEDGING	HOISTED.
GLOBULE	GASEITY	GLYPTIC	HEDONIC	HIJINKS.
GLORIED	GASEOUS	GRYPHON.	HIDALGO	HALBERD
GLORIFY	GASHING	GAZELLE	HIDEOUS	HALCYON
GLOSSED	GAS-MAIN	GAZETTE	HIDEOUT	HALF-PAY
GLOTTAL	GAS-MASK	GIZZARD	HUDDLED	HALFWAY
GLOTTIS	GASPING	GUZZLER	HYDATID	HALF-WIT
GLOWING	GAS-RING		HYDRANT	HALIBUT
GLOZING	GASSING	HEADING	HYDRATE	*HALIFAX
GNOMISH	GASTRIC	HEADMAN	HYDRIDE	HALOGEN
GNOSTIC	GESTALT	HEAD-SET	HYDROUS.	HALTING
GOOD-BYE	GESTAPO	HEADWAY	HEEDFUL	HALVING
GOODISH	GESTURE	HEALING	HEEDING	HALYARD
GOODMAN	+GISELLE	HEALTHY	HEELING.	HELICAL
*GOODWIN	GOSHAWK	HEAPING	HAFNIUM	HELICES
GROANED	GOSLING	HEARDIN	HAFTING	HELLCAT
GROCERY	*GOSPORT	HEARING	HEFTILY	HELLENE
GROGRAM	GOSSIPY	HEARKEN	HEFTING	HELLISH
GROINED	GOSSOON	HEARSAY	HUFFILY	HELPFUL
GROMMET	GUSHING.	HEARTED	HUFFING	HELPING
GROOMED	GATEMAN	HEARTEN	HUFFISH.	+HILLARY
GROOVER	GATEWAY	HEATHEN	HAGFISH	HILLOCK
GROPING	GATLING	+HEATHER	HAGGADA	+HOLBEIN
GROSSED	*GATWICK	HEATING	+HAGGARD	HOLDALL
GROSSLY	GETAWAY	HEAVIER	HAGGING	HOLDING
GROUCHY	GETTING	HEAVILY	HAGGISH	HOLIDAY
GROUPED	GOTHICK	HEAVING	HAGGLER	HOLIEST
GROUSER	G-STRING	HOARDER	HIGGLER	*HOLLAND
GROUTED	GUTTATE	HOAXING	HIGHDAY	HOLMIUM
GROWLER	GUTTING.	HYALINE	HIGHEST	HOLM-OAK
GROWN-UP.	GAUDILY	HYALITE	HIGH-HAT	HOLSTER
GARAGED	GAUGING	HYALOID.	HIGHWAY	HULKING
GARBAGE	GAUNTLY	HABITAT	+HOGARTH	HULLING.
GARBING	GLUCOSE	HABITED	HOGBACK	*HAMBURG
GARBLED	GLUEING	HABITUE	HOGGING	HAMITIC

270

HAMMING	HOOKING	HEROINE	*HITCHIN	IMBIBED
HAMMOCK	HOOPING	HEROISM	HITTING	IMBRUED
*HAMPTON	HOOSGOW	HERONRY	HOTFOOT	IMBURSE
HAMSTER	HOOTING	HERRING	HOT-HEAD	INBEING
HEMATIN	HYOSCIN.	HERSELF	HOTTEST	INBOARD
HEMLOCK	HAPENNY	HIRCINE	HOTTING	INBREED.
HEMMING	HAPLESS	HIRSUTE	HUTCHED	INCENSE
HIMSELF	HAPLOID	HORALLY	HUTMENT	INCHING
HOMBURG	HAPPIER	+HORATIO	HUTTING.	INCISED
HOMERIC	HAPPILY	HORDING	HAUBERK	INCISOR
HOMINID	HAPPING	HORIZON	HAUGHTY	INCITED
HOMONYM	HEPATIC	HORMONE	HAULAGE	INCLINE
HUMANLY	HEPTANE	HORNING	HAULIER	INCLOSE
HUMBLED	HIPPING	*HORNSEA	HAULING	INCLUDE
HUMDRUM	HIPSTER	HORRIFY	HAUNTED	INCOMER
HUMERAL	HOP-BINE	HORSING	HAUTBOY	INCRUST
HUMERUS	HOPEFUL	HURDLER	HAUTEUR	INCUBUS
HUMIDOR	HOPLITE	HURLING	+HOUDINI	INCUSED
HUMMING	HOPPING	HURRIED	HOUNDED	ISCHIAL
HUMMOCK	HOPPLED	HURTFUL	HOUSING	ISCHIUM
HUMPING	HYPERON	HURTING	+HOUSMAN	ITCHING.
HYMNIST	HYPNOID.	HURTLED.	*HOUSTON.	*INDIANA
HYMNODY.	HARBOUR	HAS-BEEN	HAVENER	INDICES
HANDBAG	HARDEST	HASHING	HOVERED.	INDICIA
HANDFUL	HARDIER	HASHISH	HAWKING	INDITED
HANDILY	HARDILY	HASLETS	HAWK-OWL	INDOORS
HANDING	HARDPAN	HASPING	HOWBEIT	INDORSE
HANDLER	HARD-SET	HASSOCK	HOWEVER	INDRAWN
HANDOUT	HARDTOP	HASTATE	HOWLING.	INDUCED
HANDSEL	HARE-LIP	HASTILY	HEXAGON	INDULGE
HANGDOG	HARICOT	HESSIAN	HEXAPOD.	IODIZED.
HANGING	HARKING	HISSING	HAYCOCK	IBERIAN
HANGMAN	HARMFUL	HISTORY	HAYFORK	ICEBERG
*HANOVER	HARMING	HOSANNA	*HAYLING	ICE-FLOE
HANSARD	HARMONY	HOSIERY	HAYRICK	*ICELAND
HENBANE	HARNESS	HOSPICE	HAYSEED	ICE-PACK
HENNERY	HARPING	HOSTAGE	HAYWARD	IDEALLY
HENPECK	HARPIST	HOSTESS	HAYWIRE	INEPTLY
HINTING	HARPOON	HOSTILE		INERTIA
HONESTY	HARRIED	HUSBAND	IMAGERY	INERTLY
HONEYED	HARRIER	HUSHING	IMAGINE	INEXACT
*HONITON	+HARRIET	HUSKING	IMAGING	*IRELAND
HONKING	HARSHLY	HUSTLER.	IMAGISM	ITEMIZE
HUNCHED	HARVEST	HATBAND	INANELY	ITERATE.
HUNDRED	*HARWICH	HATCHER	INANITY	INFANCY
*HUNGARY	HERBAGE	HATCHET	INAPTLY	INFANTA
HUNKERS	+HERBERT	HATEFUL	IRANIAN	INFANTE
HUNTING.	HERETIC	HATRACK	IRATELY	INFERNO
HOODING	HERITOR	HETAERA	ISATINE	INFIDEL
HOODLUM	HERNIAL	HITCHED	ITALIAN.	INFIELD

INFIXED	IRONING	INSURED	JIGGING	JUSTICE
INFLAME	IRONIST	INSURER	JIGGLED	JUSTIFY
INFLATE	ISOBATH	*IPSWICH.	JOGGING	+JUSTINE.
INFLECT	ISODONT	ICTERUS	JOGGLED	JETTING
INFLICT	ISOLATE	INTEGER	JOG-TROT	JITTERY
INFUSED.	ISOTONE	INTENSE	JUGGING	JOTTING
INGENUE	ISOTOPE.	INTERIM	JUGGLED	*JUTLAND
INGOING	IMPALED	INTONED	JUGGLER	JUTTING.
INGRAIN	IMPANEL	INTRANT	JUGULAR.	JAUNTED
INGRATE	IMPASSE	INTROIT	+JEHOVAH	JOUNCED
INGRESS.	IMPASTE	INTRUDE	+JOHNSON.	JOURNAL
ICHABOD	IMPASTO	INTRUST	JOINDER	JOURNEY
ICHTHYS	IMPEACH	ISTHMUS.	JOINING	JOUSTED.
INHABIT	IMPEDED	INURING	JOINTED	JAVELIN.
INHALER	IMPERIL	INURNED.	JOINTER	JAW-BONE
INHERED	IMPETUS	INVADER	JOINTLY.	JEWELRY.
INHERIT	IMPFING	INVALID	JEJUNUM	JOYLESS
INHIBIT	IMPIETY	INVEIGH	JUJITSU.	JOY-RIDE
INHUMAN	IMPINGE	INVERSE	JUKEBOX.	JAZZILY
INHUMED	IMPIOUS	INVITED	JELLIED	JAZZING
+ISHMAEL.	IMPLANT	INVOICE	JELLING	+JEZEBEL
IDIOTIC	IMPLIED	INVOKED	JILTING	
IMITATE	IMPLODE	INVOLVE.	JOLLIER	KHALIFA
INITIAL	IMPLORE	INWEAVE	JOLLIFY	KHAMSIN
IRIDIUM	IMPOSED	INWOVEN.	JOLLITY	+KHAYYAM
IRIDIZE.	IMPOUND	IDYLLIC	JOLTING	KNACKER
INJURED.	IMPRESS		+JULIANA.	KNAPPED
INKHORN	IMPREST	JEALOUS.	*JAMAICA	KNAVERY
INKLING	IMPRINT	JABBING	JAMMING	KNAVISH
INKWELL	IMPROVE	JIBBING	JUMBLED	KRAALED.
IRKSOME.	IMPULSE	JIB-DOOR	JUMPING.	KABBALA
ILL-BRED	IMPUTED.	JOBBERY	JANGLED	KIBBUTZ.
ILLEGAL	INQUEST	JOBBING	JANITOR	KECKING
ILLICIT	INQUIRE	JOBLESS	JANUARY	KECKLED
ILLNESS	INQUIRY.	JUBILEE.	JINGLED	KICKING
ILL-WILL	ISRAELI.	JACINTH	JINKING	KICK-OFF
ISLAMIC.	INSCAPE	JACKASS	+JONQUIL	KEDGING
IMMENSE	INSHORE	JACKDAW	JUNIPER	KIDDING
IMMERSE	INSIDER	JACKING	JUNKING.	KIDSKIN.
IMMORAL	INSIGHT	JACKPOT	+JUPITER.	KEELING
IMMURED.	INSIPID	JACOBIN	JARRING	KEELMAN
IGNEOUS	INSOFAR	JACONET	JERKILY	KEELSON
IGNITED	INSPECT	+JOCASTA	JERKING	KEENEST
IGNOBLE	INSPIRE	+JOCELYN	JURYMAN.	KEENING
IGNORAL	INSTALL	JOCULAR.	+JASMINE	KEEPING
IGNORED	INSTANT	JUDAISM	+JESSICA	KNEADED
INNARDS	INSTATE	JUDAIZE.	JESTING	KNEE-CAP
INNINGS	INSTEAD	JEERING.	JOSHING	KNEELED
IONIZED.	INSULAR	+JEFFREY.	JOSTLED	KNEELER
IDOLIZE	INSULIN	JAGGING	JUSSIVE	KNELLED

KREMLIN.	KERBING.	LOBWORM.	LEGIBLY	LAND-TAX
KAINITE	KESTREL	LACE-UPS	LEGLESS	LANGUID
KNIFING	*KESWICK	LACKING	LEG-PULL	LANGUOR
KNITTED	KISSING.	LACONIC	LEGUMIN	LANOLIN
KNITTER	*KATANGA	LACQUER	LIGHTEN	LANTERN
KRIMMER.	KATYDID	LACTASE	LIGHTER	LANYARD
KALMUCK	KETCHUP	LACTEAL	LIGHTLY	LENDING
*KILDARE	KITCHEN	LACTOSE	LIGNITE	LENGTHY
KILLICK	KITTING.	LACUNAL	LOG-BOOK	LENIENT
KILLING	KNUCKLE	LECHERY	LOGGING	LENTISK
KILLJOY	KNURLED.	LECTERN	LOGICAL	LENTOID
KILOTON	KEYHOLE	LECTURE	LOG-ROLL	*LINCOLN
KOLKHOZ.	KEYNOTE	LICENCE	LOGWOOD	LINCTUS
KUMQUAT.	KEY-RING	LICENSE	LUGGAGE	+LINDSEY
KANTIAN	KRYPTOL	LICITLY	LUGGING.	LINEAGE
+KENNEDY	KRYPTON	LICKING	LAICIZE	LINEATE
+KENNETH		LOCALLY	LEISTER	LINEMAN
KENNING	LEACHED	LOCATED	LEISURE	LINGUAL
KENOSIS	LEADING	LOCKING	LYING-IN	LINKAGE
KENOTIC	LEAFAGE	LOCKJAW	LYINGLY.	LINKING
KENTISH	LEAFING	LOCK-OUT	LALLANS	LINOCUT
KINDEST	LEAFLET	LUCARNE	LALLING	LINSANG
KINDLER	LEAKAGE	*LUCERNE	LILTING	LINSEED
KINDRED	LEAKILY	LUCIDLY	LOLLARD	LONGBOW
KINETIC	LEAKING	+LUCILLE	LOLLING	LONGEST
KINGCUP	+LEANDER	LUCKIER	LULLABY	LONGING
KINGDOM	LEANING	LUCKILY.	LULLING.	LUNATIC
KINGING	LEAPING	LADLING	LAMAISM	LUNCHED
KINGLET	LEARNED	LODGING	LAMBENT	LUNETTE
KINGPIN	LEASHED	LUDDITE	LAMBERT	LUNGING
KINKILY	LEASING	LYDDITE.	LAMBING	LYNCHED.
KINKING	LEATHER	+LAERTES	LAMBKIN	LEONINE
KINKLED	LEAVING	LEERING	LAMELLA	+LEONORA
*KINROSS	LIAISON	LEEWARD.	LAMINAL	LEOPARD
KINSHIP	LOADING	LEFTIST	LAMMING	*LEOPOLD
KINSMAN.	LOAFING	LIFTBOY	LAMPION	LEOTARD
KNOBBED	LOAMING	LIFTING	LAMP-OIL	LIONCEL
KNOBBLE	LOANING	LIFTMAN	LAMPOON	LIONESS
KNOBBLY	LOATHED	LIFT-OFF	LAMPREY	LIONIZE
KNOCKED	LOATHLY.	LOFTIER	LEMMING	LOOKING
KNOCKER	*LEBANON	LOFTILY	LEMURES	LOOK-OUT
KNOCK-ON	LIBERAL	LOFTING.	LIMBATE	LOOK-SEE
*KNOSSOS	*LIBERIA	LAGGARD	LIMBECK	LOOMING
KNOTTED	LIBERTY	LAGGING	LIMITED	LOOPING
KNOW-ALL	LIBRARY	LEGALLY	LIMNING	LOOSELY
KNOW-HOW	LIBRATE	LEGATED	LIMPING	LOOSEST
KNOWING.	LOBBIED	LEGATEE	LUMBAGO	LOOTING.
KIPPING.	LOBBING	LEGGING	LUMPISH.	LAPPING
*KARACHI	LOBELIA	LEGHORN	LANCING	LAPPISH
KERATIN	LOBSTER	LEGIBLE	LANDING	LAPSING

LAPWING	LAUNDER	MUCKILY	MAH-JONG	MULLION.
LEPROSY	LAUNDRY	MUCKING	MOHICAN.	MAMILLA
LIPPING	LOUDEST	MYCOSIS.	MAILBAG	MAMMARY
LOPPING.	LOUNGER	MADDEST	MAILING	MAMMOTH
LIQUATE	LOURING	MADDING	MAILLOT	MEMENTO
LIQUEFY	LOUSILY	*MADEIRA	MAIMING	MIMESIS
LIQUEUR.	LOUTISH.	MADNESS	MEIOSIS	MIMETIC
LARCENY	+LAVINIA	MADONNA	MOIDORE	MIMICRY
LARDING	LEVERED	MEDDLED	MOISTEN.	MUMBLED
LARGELY	LEVERET	MEDIATE	MAJESTY	MUMMERY
LARGESS	LEVYING	MEDICAL	*MAJORCA	MUMMIFY
LARGEST	LIVABLE	MEDULLA	MAJORED	MUMMING.
LARGISH	LIVIDLY	MIDDLED	MUJITSA.	MANACLE
LARKING	LOVABLE	MIDLAND	MALACCA	MANAGED
LORDING	LOVABLY.	MIDMOST	MALAISE	MANAGER
+LORELEI	LAWLESS	MIDRIFF	MALARIA	MANATEE
LURCHED	LAWSUIT	MIDSHIP	+MALCOLM	MANDALA
LURIDLY	LOW-BORN	MIDWIFE	MALEFIC	MANDATE
LURKING	LOW-BRED	MODESTY	MALLARD	MANDREL
LYRICAL.	LOWBROW	MODICUM	MALMSEY	MANGLED
LASHING	LOW-DOWN	MODISTE	+MALTHUS	MANHOLE
LASSOED	LOWLAND.	MUD-BATH	MALTING	MANHOOD
LASTING	LAXNESS	MUDDIED	MALTOSE	MAN-HOUR
LESBIAN	LEXICAL	MUDDLED	*MALVERN	MANHUNT
*LESOTHO	LEXICON	MUDFISH	+MELANIE	MANIKIN
LISPING	LUXATED.	MUDFLAP	MELANIN	MANILLA
LISTING	LAYETTE	MUDFLAT	MELDING	MANIPLE
LUSTFUL	LOYALLY	MUDLARK.	MELISMA	MANKIND
LUSTILY	LOYALTY.	*MAESTEG	+MELISSA	MANLIER
LUSTING	LOZENGE	MAESTRO	MELODIC	MANLIKE
LUSTRAL.		MEEKEST	MELTING	MANNING
LATCHED	MEANDER	MEETING	MILDEST	MANNISH
LATENCY	MEANING	MUEZZIN.	MILDEWY	MANSARD
LATERAL	MEASLES	MAFFICK	+MILDRED	MANSION
LATHERY	MEASURE	MUFFING	MILEAGE	MANTLED
LATRINE	MIAOWED	MUFFLED	*MILFORD	MANTRUM
LATTICE	MIASMAL	MUFFLER.	MILITIA	MANUMIT
LETHEAN	MOANING.	MAGENTA	MILK-BAR	MANURED
LETTING	MOBBING	MAGGOTY	MILKING	MENACED
LETTUCE	MOBSTER.	MAGICAL	MILKMAN	MENDING
LITERAL	MACABRE	MAGNATE	MILKSOP	MENFOLK
LITHIUM	MACADAM	MAGNETO	MILLING	MENTHOL
LITOTES	+MACBETH	MAGNIFY	MILLION	MENTION
LITTLER	*MACDUFF	MEGATON	MILTING	+MENUHIN
LITURGY	MACHETE	MIGRANT	+MOLIERE	MINARET
*LOTHIAN	MACHINE	MIGRATE	MOLLIFY	MINCING
LOTTERY	+MICHAEL	MUGGING	MOLLUSC	MINDFUL
LUTEOUS.	MICROBE	MUGGINS	MULATTO	MINDING
LAUDING	MOCKERY	MUGWUMP.	MULCHED	MINERAL
LAUGHED	MOCKING	MAHATMA	MULLING	+MINERVA

MINGLED	MARLING	MESSILY	MOTIVED	NOCTURN
MINIBUS	+MARLOWE	MESSING	MOTORED	NUCLEAR
MINICAB	MARMITE	MESTIZO	MOTTLED	NUCLEIC
MINIMAL	MARQUEE	MISCALL	MUTABLE	NUCLEON
MINIMUM	MARQUIS	MISCAST	MUTAGEN	NUCLEUS
MINIVER	MARRIED	MISDEAL	MUTATED.	NUCLIDE.
MINSTER	MARRING	MISDEED	MAUDLIN	NODDING
MINTAGE	MARSHAL	MISERLY	MAULING	NODICAL
MINTING	MARTIAL	MISFIRE	MAUNDER	NODULAR
MINUTED	MARTIAN	MISGAVE	+MAUREEN	NUDGING.
MONADIC	MARTINI	MISGIVE	+MAURICE	NEEDFUL
MONARCH	MARTLET	MISLAID	MOULDED	NEEDILY
MONEYED	MARXISM	MISLEAD	MOULDER	NEEDING
MONGREL	+MERCURY	MISLIKE	MOULTED	NEEDLED.
MONITOR	MERGING	MISREAD	MOUNDED	NAGGING
MONKISH	MERITED	MISRULE	MOUNTED	NEGATED
MONOCLE	MERMAID	MISSILE	MOURNER	NEGLECT
MONOMER	MERRILY	MISSING	MOUTHED.	NEGLIGE
MONSOON	MIRACLE	MISSION	MOVABLE.	NEGRESS
MONSTER	+MIRANDA	MISSIVE	MAWKISH.	NEGRITO
MONTAGE	MORAINE	MISTAKE	MAXILLA	NEGROID
+MONTAGU	MORALLY	MISTILY	MAXIMAL	*NIGERIA
*MONTANA	MORDANT	MISTING	MAXIMUM	NIGGARD
MONTHLY	MORELLO	MISTOOK	+MAXWELL	NIGGLED
MUNCHED	MORNING	MISTRAL	MIXTURE.	NIGHTLY
MUNDANE.	*MOROCCO	MISUSED	MAYBUSH	NOGGING.
MIOCENE	MORONIC	MUSCLED	MAYPOLE.	NAILING
MOOCHED	MORPHIA	MUSICAL	MAZURKA	*NAIROBI
MOODILY	MORTIFY	MUSK-RAT	MIZZLED	NAIVELY
MOONBUG	MORTISE	MUSTANG	MUZZLED	NAIVETE
MOONING	+MURILLO	MUSTARD		NAIVETY
MOONLIT	MURKILY	MYSTERY	NEAREST	NEIGHED
MOORAGE	MURRAIN.	MYSTIFY.	NEARING.	NEITHER
MOORHEN	MASCARA	MATADOR	NABBING	NOISIER
MOORING	MASHING	MATCHED	+NABOKOV	NOISILY
MOORISH	MASKING	MATCHET	NEBULAR	NOISOME.
MOOTING.	MASONIC	+MATILDA	NIBBLED	NAKEDLY.
MAPPING	MASONRY	MATINEE	NIBLICK	NULLIFY
MOPPING.	MASSAGE	+MATISSE	NOBBING	NULLITY
MARBLED	MASSEUR	*MATLOCK	NOBBLER	NYLGHAU.
MARCHED	MASSING	+MATTHEW	NOBLEST.	NAMABLE
+MARCUSE	MASSIVE	MATTING	NACELLE	NEMESIS
*MARGATE	MASTERY	MATTOCK	NECKING	NOMADIC
+MARGERY	MASTIFF	MATURED	NECKLET	NOMINAL
+MARILYN	MASTOID	METAZOA	NECK-TIE	NOMINEE
MARIMBA	MESEEMS	METCAST	NECTARY	NUMBING
MARINER	MESHING	METHANE	NICKING	NUMERAL
MARITAL	MESSAGE	METRICS	*NICOSIA	NYMPHAL
MARKING	MESSIAH	METRIST	NOCKING	NYMPHET.
MARLINE	MESSIER	MITOSIS	NOCTULE	NANKEEN

*NINEVEH	NETWORK	OBEYING	ORIFICE	*ONTARIO
NINTHLY	NITRATE	*OCEANIA	OVIDUCT	OPTICAL
NONPLUS	NITROUS	OCEANIC	OVIFORM	OPTIMUM
NON-STOP	NOTABLE	OCELLUS	OXIDANT	ORTOLAN
NONSUCH	NOTABLY	OLEFINE	OXIDASE	OSTRICH
NONSUIT	NOTCHED	ONE-EYED	OXIDIZE.	OTTOMAN
NON-USER	NOTEPAD	ONENESS	OAK-GALL.	OUTBACK
NUNNERY.	NOTHING	ONEROUS	OBLIGED	OUTCAST
NEOLOGY	NOTICED	ONESELF	OBLIQUE	OUTCOME
NIOBIUM	NUT-CASE	OPENING	OBLOQUY	OUTCROP
NOONDAY	NUTTING.	OPERATE	OILCAKE	OUTDONE
NOOSING.	NAUGHTY	OVERACT	OILLESS	OUTDOOR
NAPHTHA	NEUTRAL	OVERALL	OILMEAL	OUTFACE
NAPPING	NEUTRON	OVERARM	OIL-SILK	OUTFALL
NEPOTIC	NOURISH.	OVERAWE	OILSKIN	OUTFLOW
+NEPTUNE	NAVY-CUT	OVERDID	OIL-WELL.	OUTGONE
NIPPING	+NEVILLE	OVERDUE	OSMOSIS	OUTGREW
NUPTIAL.	NOVELTY.	OVERLAP	OSMOTIC.	OUTGROW
NARRATE	NEW-LAID	OVERLAY	OMNIBUS.	OUTLAST
NARTHEX	*NEWPORT	OVERRAN	ODOROUS	OUTLIER
NARWHAL	*NEWTOWN	OVERRUN	OPOSSUM	OUTLINE
NERVINE	NOWHERE.	OVERSAW	OROTUND	OUTLIVE
NERVING	NOXIOUS.	OVERSEA	OTOLOGY	OUTLOOK
NERVOUS	NUZZLED	OVERSEE	OXONIAN.	OUTMOST
NERVURE		OVERSET	OPPIDAN	OUTPLAY
NIRVANA	OCARINA	OVERSEW	OPPOSER	OUTPOST
*NORFOLK	ONANISM	OVERTAX	OPPRESS	OUTRAGE
NORLAND	ONANIST	OVERTLY	ORPHEAN	OUTRIDE
NORTHER	OPACITY	OVERTOP.	+ORPHEUS	OUTRODE
*NORWICH	OPALINE	OFFBEAT	ORPHREY.	OUTSAIL
NURSERY	ORATING	OFFENCE	OARSMAN	OUTSIDE
NURSING	ORATION	OFFERED	OERSTED	OUTSIZE
NURTURE.	ORATORY	OFF-HAND	OGREISH	OUTSPAN
NASALLY	OVARIAN	OFFICER	OURSELF.	OUTSTAY
NASCENT	OVATION.	OFF-LINE	OBSCENE	OUTTALK
NASTIER	ORBITAL	OFF-PEAK	OBSCURE	OUTVOTE
NASTILY	ORBITED	OFF-SIDE	OBSERVE	OUTWARD
NESTING	+OSBORNE.	OFFWARD.	OESTRUS	OUTWEAR
NESTLED	OCCIPUT	ORGANIC	OSSEOUS	OUTWENT
NOSEBAG	OCCLUDE	ORGANON.	OSSICLE	OUTWORE
NOSEGAY	ORCHARD.	OCHROUS	OSSUARY	OUTWORK
NOSHING	ODDMENT	OGHAMIC	OUSTING.	OUTWORN.
NOSTRIL	ODDNESS	+OPHELIA	OATCAKE	OCULATE
NOSTRUM.	+OEDIPUS	OPHIDIA.	OATMEAL	OCULIST
+NATALIE	OLDSTER	OLIVARY	OBTRUDE	OPULENT.
NATURAL	ORDERED	+OLIVIER	OCTAGON	OBVERSE
NETBALL	ORDERLY	OMINOUS	OCTOBER	OBVIATE
NETSUKE	ORDINAL.	OMITTED	OCTOPOD	OBVIOUS.
NETTING	OBELISK	OPINING	OCTOPUS	ONWARDS.
NETTLED	OBELIZE	OPINION	OCTUPLE	ODYSSEY

*OLYMPIA	PLAUDIT	PADDLED	PREMIER	POINTER
OLYMPIC	PLAY-ACT	PADDOCK	PREMISE	POISING
*OLYMPUS	PLAYBOY	PADLOCK	PREMIUM	PRICING
	PLAYFUL	PEDDLED	PREPAID	PRICKER
PEACOCK	PLAYING	PEDICEL	PREPARE	PRICKET
PEAKING	PLAYLET	PEDICLE	PREPUCE	PRICKLE
PEALING	PLAY-OFF	PIDDOCK	PRESAGE	PRICKLY
PEARLED	PLAYPEN	PODAGRA	PRESENT	PRIDING
PEARLER	POACHED	PODDING	PRESIDE	PRIGGED
+PEARSON	POACHER	PUDDING	PRESSED	PRIMACY
PEASANT	PRAETOR	PUDDLER	PRESSER	PRIMARY
PEA-SOUP	PRAIRIE	PUDENDA.	*PRESTON	PRIMATE
PEAT-BOG	PRAISED	PEEKING	PRESUME	PRIMELY
+PHAEDRA	PRAKRIT	PEELING	PRETEND	PRIMING
PHAETON	PRALINE	PEEPING	PRETEXT	PRIMMED
PHALANX	PRANCED	PEERAGE	PREVAIL	PRIMULA
PHALLIC	PRANKED	PEERESS	PREVENT	PRINTED
PHALLUS	PRATING	PEERING	PREVIEW	PRINTER
PHANTOM	PRATTLE	PEEVING	PREYING	PRITHEE
PHARAOH	PRAWNED	PEEVISH	PUERILE.	PRIVACY
PHARYNX	PRAYING	PFENNIG	PUFFING.	PRIVATE
PHASING	PSALTER.	PIEBALD	PAGEANT	PRIVILY
PIANIST	PABULUM	PIECING	PAGINAL	PRIVITY
PIANOLA	PEBBLED	PIE-EYED	+PEGASUS	PRIZING.
PIASTRE	PIBROCH	PIERAGE	PEGGING	PYJAMAS.
PLACARD	PUBERTY	PIERCED	PIGGERY	PIKELET.
PLACATE	PUBLISH.	PIERROT	PIGGING	PALADIN
PLACEBO	*PACIFIC	PIETISM	PIGGISH	PALATAL
PLACING	PACKAGE	PLEADER	PIG-IRON	PALAVER
PLACKET	PACKING	PLEASED	PIGLING	PALETTE
PLAGUED	PACKMAN	PLEATED	PIGMENT	PALFREY
PLAINER	PECCANT	PLEDGED	PIGSKIN	PALLING
PLAINLY	PECCARY	PLEDGEE	PIGTAIL	PALLIUM
PLAITED	PECCAVI	PLEDGET	PIGWASH	PALMARY
PLANING	PECKING	PLENARY	PUGGING	PALMATE
PLANISH	PECKISH	POETESS	PUG-MILL	PALMING
PLANKED	PICADOR	POETIZE	PUG-NOSE	PALMIST
PLANNED	PICAMAR	PREBEND	PYGMEAN.	PALM-OIL
PLANNER	PICCOLO	PRECEDE	PAILFUL	*PALMYRA
PLANTAR	PICKAXE	PRECEPT	PAINFUL	PALPATE
PLANTED	PICKING	PRECESS	PAINING	PALPING
PLANTER	PICKLED	PRECISE	PAINTED	PALSIED
PLASMIC	PICOTEE	PREDICT	PAINTER	PALUDAL
PLASTER	PICQUET	PRE-EMPT	PAIRING	PELAGIC
PLASTIC	PICTISH	PREENED	*PAISLEY	PELICAN
PLATEAU	PICTURE	PREFACE	PHILTRE	PELISSE
PLATING	POCHARD	PREFECT	PLIABLE	PELTING
PLATOON	+PUCCINI	PRELACY	PLIANCY	PHLEGMY
PLATTED	PUCKISH.	PRELATE	PLICATE	PILCHER
PLATTER	PADDING	PRELUDE	POINTED	PILGRIM

PILLAGE	PANTILE	PHONATE	PROTEAN	PARQUET
PILL-BOX	PANTING	PHONING	PROTECT	PARRIED
PILLION	PENALLY	PIONEER	PROTEGE	PARSING
PILLORY	PENALTY	PIOUSLY	PROTEID	PARSLEY
PILOTED	PENANCE	PLODDER	PROTEIN	PARSNIP
PILULAR	PENATES	PLONKED	PROTEST	PARTAKE
PÓLACCA	PENDANT	PLOPPED	+PROTEUS	PARTIAL
POLE-AXE	PENDENT	PLOSIVE	PROUDER	PARTIED
POLECAT	PENDING	PLOTTER	PROUDLY	PARTING
POLEMIC	PENGUIN	POOLING	PROVERB	PARTITE
POLENTA	PENNANT	POOR-BOX	PROVIDE	PARTNER
POLICED	PENNILL	POOREST	PROVING	PARTOOK
POLITIC	PENNING	PROBANG	PROVISO	PARVENU
POLLACK	*PENRITH	PROBATE	PROVOKE	PERCALE
POLLARD	PENSILE	PROBING	PROVOST	PERCEPT
POLLING	PENSION	PROBITY	PROWESS	PERCHED
+POLLOCK	PENSIVE	PROBLEM	PROWLER	PERCUSS
POLL-TAX	PENTANE	PROCEED	PROXIMO	PERFECT
POLLUTE	PENTODE	PROCESS	+PTOLEMY.	PERFIDY
POLYGON	PENTOSE	PROCTOR	PAPILLA	PERFORM
POLYMER	PINBALL	PROCURE	PAPOOSE	PERFUME
POLYNIA	PINCERS	PRODDED	PAPRIKA	PERGOLA
POLYPOD	PINCHED	PRODDER	PAPYRUS	PERHAPS
POLYPUS	PINETUM	PRODIGY	PEPPERY	PERIGEE
PULLING	PINFOLD	PRODUCE	PEPPING	PERIWIG
PULLMAN	PINGUID	PRODUCT	PEPTIDE	PERJURE
PULPIFY	PINGUIN	PROFANE	PIPEFUL	PERJURY
PULPING	PINHEAD	PROFESS	PIPETTE	PERKILY
PULSATE	PINHOLE	PROFFER	PIPPING	PERKING
PULSING	PINK-EYE	PROFILE	POPCORN	PERLITE
PYLORUS.	PINKING	PROFUSE	POP-EYED	PERMIAN
PIMENTO	PINKISH	PROGENY	POPPING	PERMING
PIMPING	PINNACE	PROGRAM	POPULAR	PERMUTE
POMATUM	PINNATE	PROJECT	PUPPING.	PERPEND
POMPANO	PINNING	PROLATE	PIQUANT.	PERPLEX
*POMPEII	PINTADO	PROLONG	PARABLE	+PERSEUS
POMPOUS	PONIARD	PROMISE	PARADED	PERSIAN
PUMPING	PONTIFF	PROMOTE	PARADOS	PERSIST
PUMPKIN.	PONTIFY	PRONGED	PARADOX	PERSONA
PANACEA	PONTOON	PRONOUN	PARAGON	PERTAIN
PANACHE	PUNCHED	PROOFED	PARAPET	PERTURB
PANCAKE	PUNCH-UP	PROPANE	PARASOL	PERUSAL
+PANDORA	PUNGENT	PROPHET	PARBOIL	PERUSED
PANICKY	PUNNING	PROPOSE	PARCHED	PERVADE
PANNIER	PUNSTER	PROPPED	PARESIS	PERVERT
PANNING	PUNTING.	PROSAIC	PARKING	PHRASED
PANOPLY	PEONAGE	PROSILY	PARLOUR	PHRENIC
PAN-PIPE	PEOPLED	PROSING	PARLOUS	PIRAGUA
PANTHER	+PHOEBUS	PROSODY	PAROLED	PIRATED
PANTIES	*PHOENIX	PROSPER	PAROTID	PIROGUE

278

PORCINE	POSTERN	PLUCKED	QUACKED	*READING
PORK-PIE	POSTING	PLUGGED	QUADRAT	READMIT
PORRECT	POSTMAN	PLUMAGE	QUADREL	REAGENT
PORTAGE	POSTURE	PLUMBER	QUAFFED	REALGAR
PORTEND	POST-WAR	PLUMBIC	QUAILED	REALISM
PORTENT	PUSHING	PLUMING	QUAKING	REALIST
PORTICO	+PUSHKIN	PLUMMET	QUALIFY	REALITY
PORTING	PUSHPIN	PLUMOSE	QUALITY	REALIZE
PORTION	PUSTULE.	PLUMPER	QUANTUM	REALTOR
PORTRAY	PATCHED	PLUMPLY	QUARREL	REAMING
PURBECK	PATELLA	PLUNDER	QUARTAN	REAPING
+PURCELL	PATHWAY	PLUNGED	QUARTER	REARING
PURGING	PATIENT	PLUNGER	QUARTET	REARMED
PURITAN	+PATRICK	PLUNKED	QUASHED	REAUMUR
PURLIEU	PATRIOT	PLUSHER	QUASSIA.	ROAD-HOG
PURLING	PATTERN	PLUVIAL	QUEENED	ROADMAN
PURLOIN	PATTING	POUCHED	QUEENLY	ROADWAY
PURPLED	PETERED	+POULENC	QUEERER	ROAMING
PURPORT	PETIOLE	POULTRY	QUEERLY	ROARING
PURPOSE	PETRIFY	POUNCED	QUELLED	ROASTED
PURRING	PETTILY	POUNDAL	+QUENTIN	ROASTER.
PURSING	PETTING	POUNDER	QUERIED	RABBITY
PURSUER	PETTISH	POURING	QUERIST	RABIDLY
PURSUIT	PETUNIA	POUTING	QUESTED.	REBATED
PURVIEW	PITCHED	PRUDENT	QUIBBLE	+REBECCA
PYRAMID	PITCHER	PRUDERY	QUICKEN	REBIRTH
PYRETIC	PITEOUS	PRUDISH	QUICKER	REBORED
PYREXIA	PITFALL	PRUNING	QUICKIE	REBOUND
PYRITES	PIT-HEAD	PRURIGO	QUICKLY	REBUKED
PYRRHIC.	PITHILY	PRUSSIC.	QUIETEN	RIBBING
PASCHAL	PITIFUL	+PAVLOVA	QUIETER	ROBBERY
PASSAGE	PITTING	PIVOTAL	QUIETLY	ROBBING
PASSANT	PITYING	PIVOTED	QUIETUS	+ROBERTA
PASSING	POTABLE	POVERTY.	QUILLED	RUBBERY
PASSION	POTENCE	PAWKILY	QUILTED	RUBBING
PASSIVE	POTENCY	PAWNING	QUINARY	RUBBISH
PASSMAN	POT-HERB	POWDERY	QUININE	RUB-DOWN
PASTERN	POTHOLE	POWERED.	QUINTAN	RUBELLA
+PASTEUR	POTHOOK	PAYABLE	QUINTET	RUBEOLA.
PASTIME	POTLUCK	PAY-LOAD	QUIPPED	RACCOON
PASTING	POT-SHOT	PAYMENT	QUITTED	RACEMIC
PASTURE	POTTERY	PAY-ROLL	QUITTER	RACKING
PESSARY	POTTING	+PHYLLIS	+QUIXOTE	RACQUET
PISCINA	PUTREFY	PHYSICS	QUIZZED.	RECEDED
PISCINE	PUTTIER	PLYWOOD	QUONDAM	RECEIPT
PISTOLE	PUTTING.	PSYCHIC	QUOTING	RECEIVE
POSITED	PAUCITY	PTYALIN.		RECITAL
POSSESS	+PAULINE	PUZZLER	REACHED	RECITER
POSTAGE	PAUNCHY		REACTOR	RECLAIM
POSTBAG	PAUSING	QUABIRD	READILY	RECLINE

RECLUSE	ROEBUCK.	REINING	RUMMILY	REPLACE
RECOUNT	RAFFISH	REISSUE	RUMNESS	REPLANT
RECOVER	RAFFLED	RHIZOID	RUMPLED.	REPLETE
RECRUIT	RAFTING	RHIZOME	RANCHER	REPLICA
RECTIFY	REFACED	ROISTER	RANCOUR	REPLIED
RECTORY	REFEREE	RUINATE	RANGING	REPOINT
+RICHARD	REFINED	RUINING	RANKEST	REPOSED
RICHEST	REFLECT	RUINOUS	RANKING	REPRESS
RICKETS	REFLOAT	*RUISLIP.	RANKLED	REPRINT
RICKETY	REFRACT	RAJPOOT	RANSACK	REPROOF
RICKING	REFRAIN	REJOICE.	RANTING	REPROVE
ROCKERY	REFRAME	RAKE-OFF.	RENDING	REPTILE
ROCKIER	REFRESH	+RALEIGH	RENEGUE	REPULSE
ROCKILY	REFUGEE	RALLIED	RENEWAL	REPUTED
ROCKING	REFUSAL	RELAPSE	RENEWED	RIP-CORD
RUCKING.	REFUSED	RELATED	*RENFREW	RIPOSTE
RADDLED	REFUTED	RELAXED	RENTIER	RIPPING
RADIANT	RIFFLER	RELEASE	RENTING	RIPPLED
RADIATE	RIFLING	RELIANT	RINGING	RIP-TIDE
RADICAL	RIFTING	RELIEVE	RINGLET	RUPTION
RADICEL	RUFFIAN	RELINED	*RINGWAY	RUPTURE.
RADICES	RUFFING	RELIVED	RINKING	REQUEST
RADICLE	RUFFLED.	ROLLING.	RINSING	REQUIEM
RED-COAT	RAGGING	RAMADAN	RONDEAU	REQUIRE
REDDEST	RAGTIME	RAMBLED	RUNAWAY	REQUITE.
REDDISH	REGALED	RAMBLER	RUN-BACK	RAREBIT
RED-HEAD	REGALIA	RAMMING	RUN-DOWN	REREDOS
*REDHILL	REGALLY	RAMPAGE	RUNNING.	RORQUAL.
REDOUBT	REGATTA	RAMPANT	RHODIUM	RASPING
REDOUND	REGENCY	RAMPART	RHOMBIC	RESCIND
REDPOLL	REGIMEN	RAMPING	RHOMBUS	RESCUER
REDRESS	REGNANT	REMARRY	RIOTING	RESERVE
*REDRUTH	REGRESS	REMNANT	RIOTOUS	RESIDED
REDSKIN	REGROUP	REMORSE	ROOFING	RESIDUA
REDUCED	REGULAR	REMOULD	ROOKERY	RESIDUE
REDWOOD	RIGGING	REMOUNT	ROOKING	RESILED
RIDABLE	RIGHTED	REMOVAL	ROOMFUL	RESINED
RIDDING	RIGHTLY	REMOVED	ROOMIER	RESOLVE
RIDDLED	RIGIDLY	REMOVER	ROOMING	RESOUND
RUDDIER	ROGUERY	+RIMBAUD	ROOSTER	RESPECT
RUDDILY	ROGUISH.	RIMMING	ROOTAGE	RESPIRE
RUDDLED	RAIDING	ROMANCE	ROOTING	RESPITE
+RUDOLPH.	RAILING	ROMANIC	ROOTLED.	RESPOND
REEDING	RAILWAY	*ROMFORD	+RAPHAEL	RESTATE
REEFING	RAIMENT	ROMPERS	RAPIDLY	RESTFUL
REEKING	RAINBOW	ROMPING	RAPPING	RESTING
REELING	RAINING	+ROMULUS	RAPPORT	RESTIVE
RE-ENTER	RAISING	*RUMANIA	RAPTURE	RESTORE
RE-ENTRY	*REIGATE	RUMBLED	REPAPER	RESUMED
RHENIUM	REIGNED	RUMMAGE	REPINED	RISIBLE

RISKIER	RUTTISH.	+RAYMOND	SEA-SALT	SLAVING
RISKILY	RAUCOUS	REYNARD	SEA-SICK	SLAVISH
RISKING	*REUNION	RHYMING	SEASIDE	SLAYING
RISOTTO	REUNITE	ROYALLY	SEATING	SMACKED
RISSOLE	RHUBARB	ROYALTY.	*SEATTLE	SMACKER
ROSEATE	+ROUAULT	RAZORED	SEA-WALL	SMALLER
ROSEBUD	ROUGHEN		SEAWARD	SMARTED
ROSE-CUT	ROUGHER	SCABBED	SEAWEED	SMARTEN
ROSEOLA	ROUGHLY	SCABIES	SEA-WOLF	SMARTLY
ROSETTE	ROUGING	*SCAFELL	SHACKED	SMASHED
ROSINED	ROULADE	SCAFFED	SHACKLE	SMASHER
+ROSSINI	ROUNDEL	SCALDED	SHADIER	SMASH-UP
ROSTRAL	ROUNDER	SCALENE	SHADILY	SNAFFLE
ROSTRUM	ROUNDLY	SCALING	SHADING	SNAGGED
RUSHING	ROUND-UP	SCALLOP	SHADOWY	SNAKILY
+RUSSELL	ROUSING	SCALPED	SHAGGED	SNAKING
RUSSIAN	ROUSTED	SCALPEL	SHAKILY	SNAPPER
RUSSIFY	ROUTINE	SCALPER	SHAKING	SNARING
RUSTIER	ROUTING.	SCAMPED	SHALLOP	SNARLED
RUSTILY	RAVAGED	SCAMPER	SHALLOT	SNATCHY
RUSTING	RAVELIN	SCANDAL	SHALLOW	SOAKING
RUSTLED	RAVIOLI	SCANNED	SHAMBLE	SOAP-BOX
RUSTLER.	REVELRY	SCANTLE	SHAMING	SOAPILY
RATABLE	REVENGE	SCAPULA	SHAMMED	SOAPING
RATAFIA	REVENUE	SCARCER	SHAMPOO	SOARING
RATCHET	REVERED	SCARIFY	SHAPELY	SPACING
RATFINK	REVERIE	SCARING	SHAPING	SPANCEL
RAT-RACE	REVERSE	SCARLET	SHARING	SPANGLE
RAT-TAIL	REVERSO	SCARPED	SHARKED	SPANIEL
RATTING	REVILED	SCARRED	SHARPEN	SPANISH
RATTLER	REVISAL	SCARVES	SHARPER	SPANKED
RAT-TRAP	REVISED	SCATHED	SHATTER	SPANKER
RETAKEN	REVIVAL	SCATTER	SHAVING	SPANNED
RETCHED	REVIVER	SEA-BANK	SIAMESE	SPANNER
RETHINK	REVOKED	SEABIRD	SJAMBOK	SPARELY
RETIARY	REVOLVE	SEA-COAL	SKALDIC	SPARING
RETICLE	REVVING	SEA-FOWL	SKATING	SPARKED
RETINUE	RIVALRY	SEAGULL	SLACKEN	SPARKLE
RETIRED	RIVETER	SEA-KALE	SLACKER	SPARRED
RETOUCH	RIVIERE	SEA-LEGS	SLACKLY	SPARROW
RETRACE	RIVULET.	SEA-LINE	SLAKING	SPARTAN
RETRACT	RAWHIDE	SEALING	SLAMMED	SPASTIC
RETREAD	RAWNESS	SEA-LION	SLANDER	SPATIAL
RETRIED	REWRITE	SEA-MARK	SLANGED	SPATTER
ROTATED	REWROTE	SEA-MILE	SLANTED	SPATULA
ROTATOR	ROWDIER	SEAMING	SLAPPED	SPAWNED
ROTTING	ROWDILY	SEA-PINK	SLASHED	SPAYING
ROTUNDA	ROWELED	SEAPORT	SLATING	STABBED
*RUTLAND	ROWLOCK.	SEARING	SLATTED	STABLED
RUTTING	RAYLESS	SEA-ROOM	SLAVERY	STACKED

STADIUM	SWAGGER	SECRETE	SHELLAC	STEELED
STAFFED	SWAGMAN	SECTARY	SHELLED	STEEPED
STAGGER	SWAHILI	SECTILE	+SHELLEY	STEEPEN
STAGING	SWALLOW	SECTION	SHELTER	STEEPER
STAIDLY	SWAMPED	SECULAR	SHELTIE	STEEPLE
STAINED	*SWANAGE	SECURED	SHELVED	STEERER
*STAINES	SWANKED	SICK-BAY	*SHEPPEY	STELLAR
STAKING	*SWANSEA	SICK-BED	SHERBET	STEMMED
STALEST	SWAPPED	SICKEST	SHEREEF	STENCIL
STALKED	SWARMED	SICK-PAY	SHERIFF	STEN-GUN
STALKER	SWARTHY	SOCIETY	SIEVING	+STEPHEN
STALLED	SWASHED	SUCCADE	SKEPTIC	STEPPED
STAMINA	SWATHED	SUCCEED	SKETCHY	STEPSON
STAMMER	SWATTED	SUCCESS	SKEWING	STERILE
STAMPED	SWATTER	SUCCOSE	SLEDDED	STERNAL
+STANLEY	SWAYING.	SUCCOUR	SLEDGED	STERNER
STANNEL	SABAOTH	SUCCUMB	SLEEKER	STERNLY
STANNIC	SABBATH	SUCKING	SLEEKLY	STERNUM
STANNUM	+SABRINA	SUCKLED	SLEEPER	STEROID
STAPLER	SIBLING	SUCROSE	SLEETED	STETSON
STARCHY	SOBBING	SUCTION.	SLEEVED	STEWARD
STARDOM	SOBERED	SADDEST	SLEIGHT	+STEWART
STARING	SOBERLY	SADDLER	SLENDER	STEWING
STARKLY	SUBACID	SADNESS	SLEWING	SWEARER
STARLET	SUBDEAN	SEDATED	SMEARED	SWEATED
STARLIT	SUBDUAL	SEDILIA	SNEAKED	SWEATER
STARRED	SUBDUED	SEDUCER	SNEERED	SWEDISH
STARTED	SUB-EDIT	SIDECAR	SNEEZED	SWEEPER
STARTER	SUBERIN	SIDLING	SPEAKER	SWEETEN
STARTLE	SUBFUSC	*SUDBURY.	SPEARED	SWEETER
STARVED	SUBJECT	SCENERY	SPECIAL	SWEETIE
STASHED	SUBJOIN	SCENTED	SPECIES	SWEETLY
STATELY	SUBLIME	SCEPSIS	SPECIFY	SWELLED
STATICE	SUBPLOT	SCEPTIC	SPECKED	SWELTER
STATICS	SUBSIDE	SCEPTRE	SPECKLE	SWERVED.
STATING	SUBSIDY	SEEDBED	SPECTRA	SAFFRON
STATION	SUBSIST	SEEDILY	SPECTRE	SIFTING
STATISM	SUBSOIL	SEEDING	SPECULA	SOFTEST
STATURE	SUBSUME	SEEKING	SPEEDED	SUFFICE
STATUTE	SUBTEND	SEEMING	SPEEDER	*SUFFOLK
STAUNCH	SUBVERT.	SEEPAGE	SPELLED	SUFFUSE.
STAVING	SACCATE	SEEPING	SPELLER	SAGGING
STAYING	SACCULE	SEETHED	SPELTER	SEGMENT
SUASION	SACKBUT	SHEARED	+SPENCER	+SEGOVIA
SUASIVE	SACKING	SHEATHE	SPENDER	SIGHING
SUAVELY	SACRING	SHEAVES	SPEWING	SIGHTED
SUAVITY	SACRIST	SHEBANG	STEALTH	SIGHTLY
SWABBED	SECEDED	SHEBEEN	STEAMED	SIGNIFY
SWABBER	SECLUDE	SHEERED	STEAMER	SIGNING
SWADDLE	SECRECY	SHEETED	STEARIN	SIGNORA

SOGGILY	SKITTLE	*STILTON	SILTING	SANDIER
SUGARED	SLICING	STIMULI	SILVERY	SANDING
SUGGEST.	SLICKER	STINKER	SOLACED	SANDMAN
SCHEMER	SLICKLY	STINTED	SOLDIER	SENATOR
SCHERZO	SLIDING	STIPEND	SOLICIT	SENATUS
SCHOLAR	SLIMMER	STIPPLE	SOLIDLY	SENDING
SPHERIC.	SLIPPED	STIRRED	SOLOIST	SEND-OFF
SAILING	SLIPPER	STIRRUP	+SOLOMON	*SENEGAL
SAINTED	SLIPWAY	SUICIDE	SOLUBLE	SENSING
SAINTLY	SLITHER	SUITING	SOLVENT	SENSORY
SCIATIC	SMILING	SWIFTER	SOLVING	SENSUAL
SCIENCE	SMIRKED	SWIFTLY	SPLASHY	SINCERE
SCISSOR	SMITTEN	SWIGGED	SPLAYED	SINGING
SEISING	SNICKER	SWILLED	SPLENIC	SINGLED
SEISMAL	SNIFFED	SWIMMER	SPLICED	SINGLET
SEISMIC	SNIGGER	SWINDLE	SPLINED	SINKING
SEIZING	SNIPING	*SWINDON	SPLODGE	SINLESS
SEIZURE	SNIPPED	SWINGER	SPLOTCH	SINNING
SHIFTER	SNIPPET	SWINGLE	SPLURGE	SINUOUS
SHIMMER	SOILING	SWINISH	SULKILY	SONSHIP
SHINDIG	SPICIER	SWIPING	SULLIED	SUNBEAM
SHINGLE	SPICILY	SWIRLED	SULPHUR	SUNBURN
SHINILY	SPICING	SWISHED	SULTANA	SUNDIAL
SHINING	SPIDERY	SWIZZLE.	SYLVINE.	SUNDOWN
SHINNED	SPIELER	SOJOURN.	SAMISEN	SUNLESS
SHIPPED	SPIKING	SALABLE	SAMOVAR	SUNNIER
SHIPPEN	SPILLED	*SALFORD	SAMOYED	SUNNING
SHIPPER	SPINACH	SALICIN	SAMPLED	SUNRISE
SHIP-WAY	SPINDLE	SALIENT	SAMPLER	SUNSPOT
SHIRKER	SPINDLY	SALLIED	SAMURAI	SUN-TRAP
+SHIRLEY	SPINNER	SALSIFY	SEMINAL	SUNWARD
SHIVERY	SPINNEY	SALTERN	SEMINAR	SUNWISE
SKIDDED	SPIN-OFF	SALTING	SEMITIC	SYNAPSE
SKID-LID	SPINOUS	SALTIRE	SIMILAR	SYNCARP
SKID-PAN	+SPINOZA	SALT-PAN	SOMATIC	SYNCOPE
SKIFFLE	SPIRANT	SALUTED	SOMEHOW	SYNERGY
SKI-JUMP	SPIRING	SALVAGE	SOMEONE	SYNODAL
SKILFUL	SPIRTED	SALVING	*SUMATRA	SYNODIC
SKI-LIFT	SPITING	SELFISH	SUMMARY	SYNONYM
SKILLED	SPITTED	*SELKIRK	SUMMERY	SYNOVIA.
SKILLET	SPITTLE	SELLING	SUMMING	SCOLDED
SKIMMER	STICKED	SELL-OUT	SUMMONS	SCOLLOP
SKIMPED	STICKER	SELTZER	SYMBION	SCONCED
SKINFUL	STIFFEN	SILENCE	SYMPTOM.	SCOOPED
SKINNED	STIFFER	*SILESIA	SANCTUM	SCOOTER
SKIPPED	STIFFLY	SILICIC	SANCTUS	SCORIFY
SKIPPER	STIFLED	SILICON	SANDBAG	SCORING
SKIRLED	STILLED	SILKILY	SAND-BAR	SCORNED
SKIRTED	STILLER	SILLIER	SANDBOY	SCORPIO
SKITTER	STILTED	SILLILY	SAND-FLY	SCOTISM

283

SCOTOMA	SPOILED	SOPHIST	SORDINE	SUSSING
SCOURER	SPONDEE	SOPPILY	SORGHUM	SUSTAIN
SCOURGE	SPONDYL	SOPPING	SORTING	SYSTOLE
SCOUTED	SPONGER	SOPRANO	SPRAYER	SYSTYLE.
SCOWLED	SPONSOR	SUPPING	SPRIGHT	SATANIC
SHOALED	SPOOFED	SUPPLED	SPRINGY	SATCHEL
SHOCKER	SPOOLED	SUPPORT	SPRUCED	SATIATE
SHOEING	SPOONED	SUPPOSE	STRAFED	SATIETY
SHOOING	SPORRAN	SUPREME.	STRANGE	SATIRIC
SHOOTER	SPORTED	SEQUENT	STRATUM	SATISFY
SHOPMAN	SPOTTED	SEQUOIA.	STRATUS	*SATSUMA
SHOPPED	SPOTTER	SARACEN	+STRAUSS	SATYRIC
SHOPPER	SPOUTED	*SARAWAK	STRAYED	SETBACK
SHORING	STOCKED	SARCASM	STREAKY	SET-DOWN
SHORTED	STOICAL	SARCODE	STRETCH	SET-FAIR
SHORTEN	STOKING	SARCOMA	STREWED	SETTING
SHORTER	STOMACH	SARDINE	STRIATE	SETTLED
SHORTLY	STOMATA	SARKING	STRIKER	SETTLER
SHOTGUN	STONIER	SCRAGGY	STRINGY	SETTLOR
SHOUTED	STONING	SCRAPER	STRIPED	SIT-DOWN
SHOVING	STOOGED	SCRAPPY	STRIVEN	SITTING
SHOWBIZ	STOOKED	SCRATCH	STROKED	SITUATE
SHOWERY	STOOPED	SCRAWNY	STROPHE	SOTTISH
SHOWILY	STOPGAP	SCREECH	SURCOAT	SUTURAL
SHOWING	STOPPED	SCREWED	SURDITY	SUTURED.
SHOWMAN	STOPPER	SCRIBAL	SURFACE	SAUCILY
SHOW-OFF	STOPPLE	SCRIBER	SURFEIT	SAUCING
SLOBBER	STORAGE	SCROTUM	SURFING	SAUNTER
•SLOGGER	STORIED	SCRUBBY	SURGEON	SAURIAN
SLOPING	STORING	SCRUFFY	SURGERY	SAUSAGE
SLOPPED	STORMED	SCRUNCH	SURGING	SCUDDED
SLOSHED	STOUTER	SCRUPLE	*SURINAM	SCUFFED
SLOTTED	STOUTLY	SCRYING	SURLIER	SCUFFLE
SLOWEST	STOWAGE	+SERAPIS	SURLILY	SCULLER
SMOKILY	STOWING	SERIATE	SURLOIN	SCULPED
SMOKING	SWOLLEN	SERIOUS	SURMISE	SCUMBLE
SMOOCHY	SWOONED	SERPENT	SURNAME	SCUMMED
SMOTHER	SWOOPED	SERRATE	SURPASS	SCUPPER
SNOGGED	SWOPPED	SERRIED	SURPLUS	SCUTAGE
SNOOKER	SWOTTED.	SERVANT	SURVIVE	SCUTTER
SNOOPER	SAPIENT	SERVERY	SYRINGA	SCUTTLE
SNOOZED	SAPLESS	+SERVICE	SYRINGE.	SHUCKED
SNORING	SAPLING	SERVILE	+SASSOON	SHUDDER
SNORTER	SAPPHIC	SERVING	SESSION	SHUFFLE
*SNOWDON	SAPPING	SHRILLY	SESTINA	SHUNNED
SNOWILY	SAPSAGO	SHRIVEL	SISTRUM	SHUNTED
SNOWING	SAPWOOD	SHRUBBY	+SUSANNA	SHUSHED
SNOWMAN	SEPTATE	SIRLOIN	SUSPECT	SHUT-EYE
SOOTHED	SIPPING	SIROCCO	SUSPEND	SHUT-OUT
SOOTILY	SOPHISM	SORCERY	SUSPIRE	SHUTTER

284

SHUTTLE	STUDIED	STYMIED	TRAPPED	+THERESA
SKULKED	STUFFED	STYPTIC	TRAPPER	THERETO
SLUBBED	STUMBLE	STYRENE.	TRAPSED	THERMAL
SLUGGED	STUMPED	SIZABLE	TRASHED	THERMIC
SLUICED	STUNNER	SIZZLED	TRAVAIL	THERMIT
SLUMBER	STUNTED	SOZZLED	TRAWLER	THERMOS
SLUMMED	STUPEFY		TWADDLE	+THESEUS
SLUMPED	STUTTER.	TEACAKE	TWANGED.	THEURGY
SLURRED	SAVABLE	TEACHER	TABBING	TIERCEL
SMUDGED	SAVAGED	TEACH-IN	TABETIC	TIERCET
SMUGGLE	SAVANNA	TEA-COSY	TABLEAU	TOEHOLD
SMUTTED	SAVE-ALL	TEA-LEAF	TABLING	TOENAIL
SNUBBED	SAVELOY	TEAMING	TABLOID	TREACLE
SNUFFED	SAVIOUR	TEARFUL	TABOOED	TREACLY
SNUFFLE	SAVOURY	TEAR-GAS	TOBACCO	TREADLE
SNUGGED	SEVENTH	TEARING	TOBY-JUG	TREASON
SNUGGLE	SEVENTY	TEA-ROOM	TUBBING	TREATED
SOUFFLE	SEVERAL	TEA-ROSE	TUBULAR.	TREBLED
SOUGHED	SEVERED	TEA-SHOP	TACITLY	TREDDLE
SOULFUL	*SEVILLE.	TEASING	TACKING	TREEING
SOUNDED	SAWBILL	TEA-TRAY	TACKLER	TREFOIL
SOUNDLY	SAWDUST	THANKED	TACTFUL	TREKKED
SOUPCON	SAWFISH	THAWING	TACTICS	TRELLIS
SOUREST	SAW-MILL	TOASTER	TACTILE	TREMBLE
SOURING	SEWERED.	TRACERY	TACTUAL	TREMBLY
SOUSING	SAXHORN	TRACHEA	TECHNIC	TREMOLO
SOUTANE	SEXIEST	TRACING	TICKING	TRENDED
SPUMING	SEXLESS	TRACKED	TICKLER	TREPANG
SPURNED	SEXTAIN	TRACKER	TOCCATA	TRESSED
SPURRED	SEXTANT	TRACTOR	TUCK-BOX	TRESTLE
SPURTED	SIXFOLD	TRADE-IN	TUCKING.	TUESDAY
SPUTNIK	SIXTEEN.	TRADING	TADPOLE	TWEAKED
SPUTTER	SCYTHED	TRADUCE	TEDDING	TWEEZER
SQUAILS	+SEYMOUR	TRAFFIC	TEDIOUS	TWELFTH.
SQUALID	SHYNESS	TRAGEDY	TIDDLER	TAFFETA
SQUALLY	SHYSTER	TRAILED	TIDDLEY	TIFFANY
SQUALOR	SKY-BLUE	TRAILER	TIDEWAY	TUFTING.
SQUARED	SKY-HIGH	TRAINEE	TIDIEST	TAGGING
SQUASHY	SKYLARK	TRAINER	TIDINGS	TIGHTEN
SQUEAKY	SKYLINE	TRAIPSE	TODDLER.	TIGHTER
SQUEEZE	SKYSAIL	TRAITOR	TEEMING	TIGHTLY
SQUELCH	SKYWARD	TRAM-CAR	TEENAGE	TIGRESS
SQUIFFY	SLYNESS	TRAMMED	THEATRE	TUGGING.
SQUINCH	SPY-HOLE	TRAMMEL	THEOREM	TAIL-END
STUBBED	STYGIAN	TRAMPED	THERAPY	TAILING
STUBBLE	STYLING	TRAMPLE	THEREAT	TAINTED
STUBBLY	STYLISH	TRAMWAY	THEREBY	THIAMIN
STUCK-UP	STYLIST	TRANSIT	THEREIN	THICKEN
STUDDED	STYLITE	TRANSOM	THEREOF	THICKER
STUDENT	STYLIZE	TRAPEZE	THEREON	THICKET

THICKLY	TWILLED	TOMPION	TUNABLE	TOPSAIL
THIEVED	TWINGED	TUMBLED	TUNEFUL	TOPSIDE
THIMBLE	TWINING	TUMBLER	*TUNISIA.	TYPHOID
THINKER	TWINKLE	TUMBREL	THOMISM	TYPHOON
THINNED	TWINNED	TUMULUS.	+THOREAU	TYPHOUS
THINNER	TWIN-SET	TANAGRA	THORIDE	TYPICAL.
THIRDLY	TWIRLED	TANGENT	THORIUM	TARDILY
THIRSTY	TWISTER	*TANGIER	THOUGHT	TARNISH
THISTLE	TWITTED	TANGING	TOOLING	TARRIED
THISTLY	TWITTER	TANGLED	TOOTHED	TARRING
THITHER	TZIGANE.	TANGOED	*TOOTING	TARTING
TRIABLE	TAKE-OFF	TANKAGE	TOOTLED	TARTLET
TRIBUNE	TEKTITE.	TANKARD	TROCHEE	TERBIUM
TRIBUTE	TALIPED	TANNAGE	TRODDEN	+TERENCE
TRICEPS	TALKING	TANNATE	TROLLED	TERMING
TRICING	TALLBOY	TANNERY	TROLLEY	TERMINI
TRICKED	TALLEST	TANNING	TROLLOP	TERMITE
TRICKLE	TALLIED	TANTRUM	TROMMEL	TERPENE
TRICKSY	TALLNES	TENABLE	TROOPER	TERRACE
TRIDENT	TALLY-HO	TENABLY	TROPISM	TERRAIN
TRIFLED	TALONED	TENANCY	+TROTSKY	TERRENE
TRIFLER	TELEXED	TENDING	TROTTER	TERRIER
TRIFORM	TELLING	TENDRIL	TROUBLE	TERRIFY
TRIGGER	TELPHER	TENFOLD	TROUNCE	TERRINE
TRIGLOT	*TILBURY	TENONED	TROUPER	TERSELY
TRILITH	TILLAGE	TENPINS	TWOFOLD	TERTIAN
TRILLED	TILLING	TENSELY	TWOSOME	THRIFTY
TRILOGY	TILTING	TENSEST	TWO-STEP	THRIVED
TRIMMED	+TOLKIEN	TENSILE	TWO-TIME.	THRIVEN
TRIMMER	TOLLAGE	TENSING	TAPERED	THROATY
TRINGLE	TOLLING	TENSION	TAPIOCA	THRONED
TRINITY	+TOLSTOY	TENTHLY	TAPPING	THROUGH
TRINKET	TOLUENE.	TENTING	TAP-ROOM	THROWER
TRIOLET	TAMABLE	TENT-PEG	TAP-ROOT	TORMENT
TRIPLED	TAMBOUR	TENUITY	TAPSTER	TORNADO
TRIPLET	TAMPING	TENUOUS	TEPIDLY	*TORONTO
TRIPLEX	TAMPION	TINFOIL	TIPPING	TORPEDO
*TRIPOLI	TEMPERA	TINGING	TIPPLER	*TORQUAY
TRIPPER	TEMPEST	TINGLED	TIPSILY	TORRENT
TRIREME	TEMPLAR	TINIEST	TIPSTER	TORSION
TRISECT	TEMPLET	TINNILY	TIPTOED	TORTILE
*TRISTAN	TEMPTER	TINNING	TOP-BOOT	TORTURE
TRITELY	TIMBREL	TINTACK	TOP-COAT	TURBINE
TRITIUM	TIME-LAG	*TINTERN	TOPIARY	TURFING
TRIUMPH	TIMIDLY	TINWARE	TOPICAL	TURKISH
TRIVIAL	+TIMOTHY	TONGUED	TOPKNOT	TURMOIL
TRIVIUM	TIMPANI	TONIGHT	TOPMAST	TURNERY
TUITION	TIMPANO	TONNAGE	TOPMOST	TURNING
TWIDDLE	TOMBOLA	TONSURE	TOPPING	TURNKEY
TWIGGED	TOMFOOL	TONTINE	TOPPLED	TURN-OUT

TYRANNY.	TOURISM	UNBLOWN	UNITIVE	UPTHROW
TASKING	TOURIST	UNBOSOM	URINARY	UPTIGHT
TASTIER	TOURNEY	UNBOUND	UTILITY	UTTERED
TASTILY	TOUSLED	UNBOWED	UTILIZE.	UTTERLY.
TASTING	TOUTING	UNBRACE	UNKEMPT	UKULELE
TESSERA	TRUANCY	UNBUILT	UNKNOWN.	ULULATE
TESTACY	TRUCKED	UPBRAID.	UGLIEST	UNUSUAL
TESTATE	TRUCKLE	UNCANNY	UNLADEN	*URUGUAY
TESTIFY	+TRUDEAU	UNCARED	UNLEARN	USUALLY
TESTILY	TRUDGED	UNCASED	UNLEASH	USURPER.
TESTING	TRUFFLE	UNCHAIN	UNLOOSE	UNWOUND
TESTUDO	TRUMPED	UNCIVIL	UNLUCKY.	UNWRUNG
TISSUED	TRUMPET	UNCLASP	UNMANLY	UPWARDS.
TOSSING	TRUNDLE	UNCLEAN	UNMEANT	+ULYSSES
TUSSLED	TRUSSED	UNCLOAK	UNMORAL	UNYOKED.
TUSSOCK	TRUSTED	UNCLOSE	UNMOVED.	UNZONED
TUSSORE.	TRUSTEE.	UNCOUTH	UNNAMED	
TATTILY	TAWNILY	UNCOVER	UNNERVE.	VIADUCT.
TATTING	TOWARDS	UNCTION.	UTOPIAN.	VIBRANT
TATTLER	TOWLINE	UNDERGO	UMPIRED	VIBRATE
TETANIC	TOWPATH	UNDOING	UMPTEEN.	VIBRATO.
TETANUS	TOW-ROPE.	UNDRESS	UNQUIET	VACANCY
TETRODE	TAXABLE	UNDYING.	UNQUOTE.	VACATED
+TITANIA	TAX-FREE	UNEARTH	UNRAVEL	VACCINE
TITANIC	TAXI-CAB	UNEQUAL	UNREADY	VACUITY
TITLARK	TAXIING	URETHRA	UNRISEN	VACUOLE
TITLING	TAXIMAN	USELESS	UNROBED	VACUOUS
TITRATE	TEXTILE	UTENSIL	UPRIGHT	VICEROY
TITULAR	TEXTUAL	UTERINE.	UTRICLE	VICINAL
TOTALLY	TEXTURE.	UNFIXED	+UTRILLO.	VICIOUS
TOTEMIC	THYROID	UNFROCK	UNSCREW	VICTORY
TOTTERY	THYRSUS	UNFROZE.	UNSEXED	VICTUAL
TOTTING	THYSELF	UNGODLY	UNSLING	VOCABLE
TUTELAR	TOYSHOP	UNGUENT	UNSOUND	VOCALIC
TUTORED	TRYPSIN	UP-GRADE	UNSPENT	VOCALLY.
TUTTING.	TRYSAIL	URGENCY.	UNSTICK	VEDANTA
TAUNTED	TRYSTED	UNHANDY	UNSTRAP	VEDETTE
*TAUNTON		UNHAPPY	UNSTUCK	VIDUITY.
TAURINE	UNACTED	UNHEARD	UPSTAGE	VEERING
TAUTEST	UNAIDED	UNHINGE	UPSTAIR	*VIETNAM
THUDDED	UNAIRED	UNHITCH	UPSTART	VIEWING.
THULIUM	UNARMED	UNHOPED	UPSURGE	VAGINAL
THUMBED	UNASKED	UNHORSE	UPSWEPT.	VAGRANT
THUMPED	UNAWARE	UPHEAVE	UNTAMED	VAGUELY
THUNDER	URAEMIA	USHERED.	UNTAXED	VEGETAL.
TOUCHED	URANIAN	UNICORN	UNTRIED	VEHICLE.
TOUGHEN	URANISM	UNIFIED	UNTRUSS	VAINEST
TOUGHER	URANIUM	UNIFORM	UNTRUTH	VEILING
TOUGHLY	URANOUS.	UNITARY	UNTWINE	VEINING
TOURING	UMBRAGE	UNITING	UNTWIST	VOICING

VOIDING.	VAPIDLY	VETERAN	WHEEDLE	WHIRRED
VALANCE	VAPOURY.	VETOING	WHEELED	WHISKED
VALENCE	VAQUERO.	VETTING	WHEEZED	WHISKER
VALENCY	VARIANT	VITALLY	WHELPED	WHISKEY
+VALERIE	VARICES	VITAMIN	WHENEER	WHISPER
VALETED	VARIETY	VITIATE	WHEREAS	WHISTLE
VALIANT	VARIOLA	VITRIFY	WHEREAT	WHITEST
VALIDLY	VARIOUS	VITRIOL.	WHEREBY	WHITHER
VELOURS	VARMINT	+VAUGHAN	WHEREER	WHITING
VELVETY	VARNISH	VAULTED	WHEREIN	WHITISH
VILLAGE	VARSITY	VAULTER	WHEREOF	WHITLOW
VILLAIN	VARYING	VAUNTED	WHEREON	+WHITMAN
VILLEIN	VERANDA	VOUCHER.	WHERETO	WHITSUN
VILLOUS	VERBENA	+VIVALDI	WHETHER	WHITTLE
VOLCANO	VERBOSE	VIVIDLY.	WHETTED	WHIZZED
VOLTAGE	VERDANT	VOYAGER	WIELDED	WRIGGLE
VOLTAIC	VERDICT		WREAKED	WRINGER
VOLTING	VERDURE	WEAKEST	WREATHE	WRINKLE
VOLUBLE	VERGING	WEALTHY	WRECKED	WRITE-UP
VOLUTED	VERIEST	WEANING	WRECKER	WRITHED
VULGATE	+VERMEER	WEARIER	WRESTED	WRITING
VULPINE	VERMEIL	WEARILY	WRESTLE.	WRITTEN.
VULTURE.	*VERMONT	WEARING	WAFFLED	WALKING
VAMOOSE	VERNIER	WEATHER	WAFTING.	WALK-OUT
VAMPING	VERONAL	WEAVING	WAGERED	WALLABY
VAMPIRE	VERRUCA	WHACKED	WAGGERY	+WALLACE
VOMITED.	VERSIFY	WHALING	WAGGING	WALLING
+VANDYKE	VERSING	WHARFED	WAGGISH	WALLOON
+VANESSA	VERSION	WHARVES	WAGGLED	+WALPOLE
VANILLA	VERTIGO	WHATEER	WAGONER	*WALSALL
VANNING	VERVAIN	WHATNOT	WAGTAIL	WALTZED
VANTAGE	VIRELAY	WRANGLE	WIGGLED	WELCOME
VANWARD	VIRGATE	WRAPPED	*WIGTOWN.	WELDING
VENALLY	VIRGULE	WRAPPER.	WAILING	WELFARE
VENDACE	VIRTUAL.	WEBBING	WAISTED	WELLING
VENDING	VASCULA	WOBBLED.	WAITING	WELL-OFF
VENISON	VASTEST	*WICKLOW.	WAIVING	WELSHER
VENOMED	VESICLE	WADABLE	WEIGHED	WELTING
VENTAGE	VESPERS	WADDING	WEIGH-IN	WILDCAT
VENTING	VESTIGE	WADDLED	WEIGHTY	WILDEST
*VENTNOR	VESTING	WEDDING	WEIRDLY	+WILFRED
VENTRAL	VESTURE	WEDGING	WHIFFED	+WILLIAM
VENTURE	VISCERA	WEDLOCK	WHIFFLE	WILLING
+VINCENT	VISCOSE	WIDGEON	WHILING	WILLOWY
VINEGAR	VISCOUS	WIDOWER.	WHIMPER	WILTING
VINTAGE	VISIBLE	WEEDING	WHIMSEY	WOLFING
VINTNER.	VISITED	WEEKDAY	WHINING	WOLFISH
VIOLATE	VISITOR	WEEK-END	WHIPPED	WOLFRAM.
VIOLENT	*VISTULA.	WEEPING	WHIPPET	*WEMBLEY
VIOLIST.	*VATICAN	WHEATEN	WHIRLED	WIMPLED

WOMANLY.	*WARWICK	WAXBILL	ZOOMING	NAMABLE
WANGLED	WERWOLF	WAXWORK.	ZOOTOMY.	NASALLY
WANNESS	WIRABLE	WAY-BILL	ZIPPING.	+NATALIE
WANTING	WORDILY	WAYSIDE	ZEROING.	PALADIN
WENCHED	WORDING	WAYWARD	ZESTFUL.	PALATAL
WENDING	WORKDAY	WRYNECK	*ZETLAND	PALAVER
WINCHED	WORKING	WRYNESS.		PANACEA
WINDBAG	WORKMAN	WIZENED		PANACHE
WINDIER	WORK-OUT		BAGASSE	PARABLE
WINDING	WORK-SHY	X-RAYING.	BALANCE	PARADED
WINDROW	*WORKSOP	XIPHOID.	BASALLY	PARADOS
*WINDSOR	WORLDLY	XERASIA	CABARET	PARADOX
WINGING	WORMING		CADAVER	PARAGON
WINKERS	WORRIED	YEARNED.	CALAMUS	PARAPET
WINKING	WORRIER	YACHTED	CANASTA	PARASOL
WINKLED	WORSHIP	*YUCATAN.	CAPABLE	PAYABLE
WINNING	WORSTED.	YIDDISH.	CARACUL	RAMADAN
WINSOME	WASH-DAY	YIELDED.	*CARACUS	RATABLE
+WINSTON	WASHING	YOGHURT.	CARAMEL	RATAFIA
+WYNDHAM.	WASH-OUT	YAKKING.	CARAVAN	RAVAGED
WHOEVER	WASPISH	YELLING	CARAWAY	SABAOTH
WHOOPED	WASSAIL	YELLOWY	CATALPA	SALABLE
WHOPPER	WASTAGE	YELPING	CATARRH	SARACEN
WHORING	WASTING	YULE-LOG.	CAVALRY	*SARAWAK
WOODCUT	WASTREL	*YANGTZE	DADAISM	SATANIC
WOODIER	WEST-END	YANKING	DATABLE	SAVABLE
WOODMAN	WESTERN	YENNING	EAR-ACHE	SAVAGED
WOOLLEN	WESTING	YAPPING.	EATABLE	SAVANNA
*WOOMERA	*WISBECH	YARDAGE	FALANGE	TAMABLE
WRONGLY	WISHFUL	YORKING	FANATIC	TANAGRA
WROUGHT	WISHING	YORKIST.	FARADAY	TAXABLE
*WYOMING.	WISTFUL.	YASHMAK.	FARAWAY	VACANCY
WARBLER	WATCHED	YTTRIUM.	FATALLY	VACATED
WARDING	WATERED	YOUNGER.	+GALAHAD	VALANCE
WARFARE	*WATFORD	YAWNING	GARAGED	WADABLE.
WARHEAD	WATTAGE	YOWLING	*JAMAICA	BABBLER
WARLIKE	WATTLED		*KARACHI	BAMBINO
WARLOCK	WETNESS	ZEALOUS.	*KATANGA	*BANBURY
WAR-LORD	WETTEST	ZEBRINE.	LAMAISM	+BARBARA
WARMEST	WETTING	ZEDOARY.	MACABRE	BARBATE
WARMING	WITCHED	*ZEELAND.	MACADAM	BARBOLA
WARNING	WITHERS	*ZAMBESI	MAHATMA	CABBAGE
WARPATH	WITHOUT	ZYMOTIC	MALACCA	CAMBIST
WARPING	WITLESS	ZYMURGY.	MALAISE	CAMBIUM
WARRANT	WITNESS	ZONALLY.	MALARIA	CAMBRIC
WARRING	WITTIER	ZEOLITE	MANACLE	CARBIDE
WARRIOR	WITTILY	ZIONISM	MANAGED	CARBINE
WARSHIP	WITTING.	ZIONIST	MANAGER	CATBOAT
WART-HOG	WOUNDED.	ZOOGAMY	MANATEE	DABBING
WARTIME	WAVERED.	ZOOLOGY	MATADOR	DABBLED

DAUBING	CATCALL	BADDISH	PADDING	HAPENNY
DAYBOOK	CATCHER	BALDEST	PADDLED	HARE-LIP
GABBING	DANCING	BALDRIC	PADDOCK	HATEFUL
GABBLED	FALCATE	+BALDWIN	+PANDORA	HAVENER
GAMBLER	FANCIED	BANDAGE	RADDLED	JAVELIN
GAMBOGE	FANCIER	BANDBOX	RAIDING	LACE-UPS
GARBAGE	FARCEUR	BANDEAU	SADDEST	LAMELLA
GARBING	FARCING	BANDIED	SADDLER	LATENCY
GARBLED	FASCINE	BANDING	SANDBAG	LATERAL
HALBERD	FASCISM	BAND-SAW	SAND-BAR	LAYETTE
*HAMBURG	FASCIST	BAWDILY	SANDBOY	*MADEIRA
HARBOUR	HALCYON	CADDISH	SAND-FLY	MAGENTA
HAS-BEEN	HATCHER	CANDELA	SANDIER	MAJESTY
HATBAND	HATCHET	CANDIED	SANDING	MALEFIC
HAUBERK	HAYCOCK	CANDOUR	SANDMAN	NACELLE
JABBING	LAICIZE	CARDIAC	SARDINE	NAKEDLY
JAW-BONE	LANCING	*CARDIFF	SAWDUST	PAGEANT
KABBALA	LARCENY	CARDOON	TARDILY	PALETTE
LAMBENT	LATCHED	CAUDATE	+VANDYKE	PARESIS
LAMBERT	+MALCOLM	DANDIFY	WADDING	PATELLA
LAMBING	MARCHED	DAWDLER	WADDLED	RACEMIC
LAMBKIN	+MARCUSE	EAR-DRUM	WARDING	RAKE-OFF
+MACBETH	MASCARA	FADDIST	YARDAGE.	+RALEIGH
MARBLED	MATCHED	GADDING	BALEFUL	RAREBIT
MAYBUSH	MATCHET	GAUDILY	BANEFUL	RAVELIN
NABBING	NASCENT	HADDOCK	CADENCE	,SAVE-ALL
PARBOIL	OATCAKE	HANDBAG	CADENCY	SAVELOY
RABBITY	PANCAKE	HANDFUL	CADENZA	TABETIC
RAMBLED	PARCHED	HANDILY	CALENDS	TAKE-OFF
RAMBLER	PASCHAL	HANDING	CAREFUL	TAPERED
SABBATH	PATCHED	HANDLER	CASE-LAW	VALENCE
SAWBILL	PAUCITY	HANDOUT	CASEOUS	VALENCY
TABBING	RACCOON	HANDSEL	CATECHU	+VALERIE
TAMBOUR	RANCHER	HARDEST	CATERER	VALETED
WARBLER	RANCOUR	HARDIER	CAT-EYED	+VANESSA
WAXBILL	RATCHET	HARDILY	CAVE-MAN	WAGERED
WAY-BILL	RAUCOUS	HARDPAN	CAYENNE	WATERED
*ZAMBESI.	SACCATE	HARD-SET	DANELAW	WAVERED.
BACCHIC	SACCULE	HARDTOP	DAZEDLY	BAFFLED
+BACCHUS	SANCTUM	LANDING	EAGERLY	CATFALL
BALCONY	SANCTUS	LAND-TAX	EASEFUL	CATFISH
BASCULE	SARCASM	LARDING	FAIENCE	DAMFOOL
+CALCHAS	SARCODE	LAUDING	FATEFUL	FANFARE
CALCIFY	SARCOMA	*MACDUFF	GAMETIC	GAFFING
CALCINE	SATCHEL	MADDEST	GASEITY	GARFISH
CALCITE	SAUCILY	MADDING	GASEOUS	HAGFISH
CALCIUM	SAUCING	MANDALA	GATEMAN	HALF-PAY
CARCASS	VACCINE	MANDATE	GATEWAY	HALFWAY
CASCADE	VASCULA	MANDREL	GAZELLE	HALF-WIT
CASCARA	WATCHED.	MAUDLIN	GAZETTE	HAYFORK

MAFFICK	LAUGHED	RAWHIDE	PAGINAL	DARKEST
PALFREY	MAGGOTY	SAXHORN	PANICKY	DARKISH
RAFFISH	MANGLED	WARHEAD	PAPILLA	HACKING
RAFFLED	*MARGATE	WASH-DAY	PATIENT	HACKLET
RATFINK	+MARGERY	WASHING	RABIDLY	*HACKNEY
SAFFRON	NAGGING	WASH-OUT	RADIANT	HACKSAW
*SALFORD	NAUGHTY	YACHTED	RADIATE	HARKING
SAWFISH	OAK-GALL	YASHMAK.	RADICAL	HAWKING
TAFFETA	RAGGING	BACILLI	RADICEL	HAWK-OWL
TAX-FREE	RANGING	BASILAR	RADICES	JACKASS
WAFFLED	SAGGING	BASILIC	RADICLE	JACKDAW
WARFARE	TAGGING	BASINET	RAPIDLY	JACKING
*WATFORD.	TANGENT	+BATISTA	RAVIOLI	JACKPOT
BAGGAGE	*TANGIER	BATISTE	SALICIN	LACKING
BAGGING	TANGING	CABINET	SALIENT	LARKING
BANGING	TANGLED	CACIQUE	SAMISEN	MANKIND
*BANGKOK	TANGOED	CALIBRE	SAPIENT	MARKING
BARGAIN	+VAUGHAN	CAPITAL	SATIATE	MASKING
BARGING	WAGGERY	CAPITOL	SATIETY	MAWKISH
CADGING	WAGGING	CARIBOU	SATIRIC	NANKEEN
*CALGARY	WAGGISH	CARIOUS	SATISFY	PACKAGE
DANGLED	WAGGLED	FATIGUE	SAVIOUR	PACKING
DAY-GIRL	WANGLED	+GALILEO	TACITLY	PACKMAN
FAGGING	*YANGTZE.	HABITAT	TALIPED	PARKING
GAGGING	*BAGHDAD	HABITED	TAPIOCA	PAWKILY
GAGGLED	BASHFUL	HABITUE	TAXI-CAB	RACKING
GANGING	BASHING	HALIBUT	TAXIING	RANKEST
GANGLIA	BATHING	*HALIFAX	TAXIMAN	RANKING
GANGWAY	CASHIER	HAMITIC	VAGINAL	RANKLED
GARGLED	CASHING	HARICOT	VALIANT	SACKBUT
GAUGING	CATHEAD	JACINTH	VALIDLY	SACKING
HAGGADA	CATHODE	JANITOR	VANILLA	SARKING
+HAGGARD	DASHING	LAMINAL	VAPIDLY	TACKING
HAGGING	FASHION	+LAVINIA	VARIANT	TACKLER
HAGGISH	FAT-HEAD	MAGICAL	VARICES	TALKING
HAGGLER	GASHING	MAMILLA	VARIETY	TANKAGE
HANGDOG	HASHING	MANIKIN	VARIOLA	TANKARD
HANGING	HASHISH	MANILLA	VARIOUS	TASKING
HANGMAN	LASHING	MANIPLE	*VATICAN.	WALKING
HAUGHTY	LATHERY	+MARILYN	MAH-JONG.	WALK-OUT
JAGGING	MACHETE	MARIMBA	BACKING	YAKKING
JANGLED	MACHINE	MARINER	BACKLOG	YANKING.
LAGGARD	MANHOLE	MARITAL	BALKING	BAILIFF
LAGGING	MANHOOD	+MATILDA	BANKING	BAILING
LANGUID	MAN-HOUR	MATINEE	BANKSIA	BALLADE
LANGUOR	MANHUNT	+MATISSE	*BARKING	BALLAST
LARGELY	MASHING	MAXILLA	BASKING	BALLOON
LARGESS	NAPHTHA	MAXIMAL	CACKLED	BAWLING
LARGEST	PATHWAY	MAXIMUM	CARKING	CABLING
LARGISH	+RAPHAEL	*PACIFIC	DANKISH	CALL-BOX

CALLING	MAULING	GAS-MAIN	*FARNHAM	VAUNTED
CALLOUS	NAILING	GAS-MASK	FATNESS	WANNESS
CARLINE	PADLOCK	HAMMING	FAWNING	WARNING
CATLING	PAILFUL	HAMMOCK	GAINFUL	YAWNING.
DALLIED	PALLING	HARMFUL	GAINING	BARONET
DARLING	PALLIUM	HARMING	GAINSAY	BAROQUE
DAYLONG	PARLOUR	HARMONY	GARNISH	BAYONET
EARLDOM	PARLOUS	JAMMING	GAUNTLY	BAZOOKA
EARLIER	+PAULINE	+JASMINE	HAFNIUM	CABOOSE
FABLIAU	+PAVLOVA	KALMUCK	HARNESS	CACODYL
FAILING	PAY-LOAD	LAMMING	HAUNTED	CAJOLED
FAILURE	RAILING	MAIMING	JAUNTED	CALOMEL
FALLACY	RAILWAY	MALMSEY	KAINITE	CALORIC
FALL-GUY	RALLIED	MAMMARY	LAUNDER	CALORIE
FALLING	RAYLESS	MAMMOTH	LAUNDRY	CALOTTE
FALL-OUT	SAILING	MARMITE	LAXNESS	CANONRY
FATLING	SALLIED	OATMEAL	MADNESS	+CAROLYN
FAULTED	SAPLESS	PALMARY	MAGNATE	CAROTID
GALLANT	SAPLING	PALMATE	MAGNETO	CAROTIN
GALLEON	TABLEAU	PALMING	MAGNIFY	CAROUSE
GALLERY	TABLING	PALMIST	MANNING	GAROTTE
GALLING	TABLOID	PALM-OIL	MANNISH	GAVOTTE
GALLIOT	TAIL-END	*PALMYRA	MAUNDER	HALOGEN
GALLIUM	TAILING	PAYMENT	PAINFUL	*HANOVER
GALLOON	TALLBOY	RAIMENT	PAINING	JACOBIN
GALLOWS	TALLEST	RAMMING	PAINTED	JACONET
GARLAND	TALLIED	+RAYMOND	PAINTER	LACONIC
GATLING	TALLNES	SAW-MILL	PANNIER	LANOLIN
HAILING	TALLY-HO	VARMINT	PANNING	MADONNA
HAPLESS	VAULTED	WARMEST	PAUNCHY	*MAJORCA
HAPLOID	VAULTER	WARMING.	PAWNING	MAJORED
HASLETS	WAILING	BANNING	RAINBOW	MASONIC
HAULAGE	WALLABY	BANNOCK	RAINING	MASONRY
HAULIER	+WALLACE	+BARNABY	RAWNESS	+NABOKOV
HAULING	WALLING	BARN-OWL	SADNESS	PANOPLY
*HAYLING	WALLOON	CANNERY	SAINTED	PAPOOSE
LADLING	WARLIKE	CANNILY	SAINTLY	PAROLED
LALLANS	WARLOCK	CANNING	SAUNTER	PAROTID
LALLING	WAR-LORD.	*CANNOCK	TAINTED	RAZORED
LAWLESS	BARMAID	CARNAGE	TANNAGE	SAMOVAR
MAILBAG	CADMIUM	DAMNIFY	TANNATE	SAMOYED
MAILING	CALMEST	DAMNING	TANNERY	SAVOURY
MAILLOT	CALMING	DARNING	TANNING	TABOOED
MALLARD	CARMINE	DAUNTED	TARNISH	TALONED
MANLIER	CATMINT	DAWNING	TAUNTED	VAMOOSE
MANLIKE	DAMMING	EARNEST	*TAUNTON	VAPOURY
MARLINE	EARMARK	EARNING	TAWNILY	WAGONER.
MARLING	FARMING	FAINTED	VAINEST	BAGPIPE
+MARLOWE	GAMMING	FAINTLY	VANNING	*BAMPTON
*MATLOCK	GARMENT	FANNING	VARNISH	CAMP-BED

292

CAMPHOR	WARPATH	NARRATE	*MAESTEG	CANTEEN
CAMPING	WARPING	PAIRING	MAESTRO	CANTING
CAMPION	WASPISH	PAPRIKA	MANSARD	CAPTAIN
CAPPING	YAPPING.	PARRIED	MANSION	CAPTION
CARPING	BANQUET	+PATRICK	MARSHAL	CAPTIVE
*CASPIAN	LACQUER	PATRIOT	MASSAGE	CAPTURE
DAMPING	MARQUEE	PAY-ROLL	MASSEUR	CARTAGE
DAMPISH	MARQUIS	RAT-RACE	MASSING	CARTING
DAPPLED	PARQUET	+SABRINA	MASSIVE	CARTOON
DAUPHIN	RACQUET.	SACRING	OARSMAN	CASTILE
GASPING	*BAHRAIN	SACRIST	*PAISLEY	CASTING
*HAMPTON	BARRACK	SAURIAN	PALSIED	CASTLED
HAPPIER	BARRAGE	TAP-ROOM	PARSING	CAST-OFF
HAPPILY	BARRIER	TAP-ROOT	PARSLEY	CATTILY
HAPPING	BARRING	TARRIED	PARSNIP	CATTISH
HARPING	CAB-RANK	TARRING	PASSAGE	CAUTERY
HARPIST	CAPRICE	TAURINE	PASSANT	CAUTION
HARPOON	CAPROIC	VAGRANT	PASSING	DARTING
HASPING	CARRACK	WARRANT	PASSION	DASTARD
LAMPION	CARRIED	WARRING	PASSIVE	DAY-TIME
LAMP-OIL	CARRIER	WARRIOR.	PASSMAN	EARTHED
LAMPOON	CARRION	BANSHEE	PAUSING	EARTHEN
LAMPREY	+CARROLL	BASSOON	RAISING	EARTHLY
LAPPING	CARROTY	CAESIUM	RANSACK	EASTERN
LAPPISH	EARRING	CAISSON	SALSIFY	EASTING
MAPPING	FAIRILY	CAPSIZE	SAPSAGO	FACTION
MAYPOLE	FAIRING	CAPSTAN	+SASSOON	FACTORY
NAPPING	FAIRWAY	CAPSULE	*SATSUMA	FACTUAL
PALPATE	FARRAGO	CASSAVA	SAUSAGE	FACTURE
PALPING	FARRIER	CASSOCK	TAPSTER	FANTAIL
PAN-PIPE	+GABRIEL	CATS-EYE	VARSITY	FANTAST
RAJPOOT	GAS-RING	CATS-PAW	WAISTED	FANTASY
RAMPAGE	+HADRIAN	CAUSING	*WALSALL	FARTHER
RAMPANT	HAIR-CUT	CAUSTIC	WARSHIP	FAST-DAY
RAMPART	HAIRILY	DAISIED	WASSAIL	FASTEST
RAMPING	HAIRNET	EARSHOT	WAYSIDE.	FASTING
RAPPING	HAIRPIN	FALSELY	BAITING	FATTEST
RAPPORT	HARRIED	FALSIES	BANTING	GASTRIC
RASPING	HARRIER	FALSIFY	BAPTISM	HAFTING
SAMPLED	+HARRIET	FALSITY	BAPTIST	HALTING
SAMPLER	HATRACK	GAGSMAN	BAPTIZE	HASTATE
SAPPHIC	HAYRICK	GASSING	BASTARD	HASTILY
SAPPING	JARRING	HAMSTER	BASTING	HAUTBOY
TADPOLE	+LAERTES	HANSARD	BASTION	HAUTEUR
TAMPING	LATRINE	HARSHLY	BATTERY	KANTIAN
TAMPION	MARRIED	HASSOCK	BATTING	LACTASE
TAPPING	MARRING	HAYSEED	BATTLED	LACTEAL
VAMPING	+MAUREEN	LAPSING	CAITIFF	LACTOSE
VAMPIRE	+MAURICE	LASSOED	CALTROP	LANTERN
+WALPOLE	*NAIROBI	LAWSUIT	CANTATA	LASTING

293

LATTICE	TACTICS	VAQUERO.	ABSCIND	*ECUADOR
+MALTHUS	TACTILE	CALVARY	ABSCOND	ICHABOD
MALTING	TACTUAL	CALVING	OBSCENE	*OCEANIA
MALTOSE	TANTRUM	CANVASS	OBSCURE.	OCEANIC
MANTLED	TARTING	CARVING	ABIDING	OCTAGON
MANTRUM	TARTLET	HALVING	*ABIDJAN.	SCIATIC
MARTIAL	TASTIER	HARVEST	ABREACT	SCRAGGY
MARTIAN	TASTILY	*MALVERN	ABREAST	SCRAPER
MARTINI	TASTING	NAIVELY	ABSENCE	SCRAPPY
MARTLET	TATTILY	NAIVETE	OBSERVE	SCRATCH
MASTERY	TATTING	NAIVETY	OBVERSE.	SCRAWNY.
MASTIFF	TATTLER	PARVENU	+ABIGAIL.	ICEBERG
MASTOID	TAUTEST	SALVAGE	ABRIDGE	SCABBED
+MATTHEW	VANTAGE	SALVING	ABSINTH	SCABIES.
MATTING	VASTEST	WAIVING.	OBLIGED	ACADEMY
MATTOCK	WAFTING	CATWALK	OBLIQUE	ACIDIFY
NARTHEX	WAGTAIL	*GATWICK	OBVIATE	ACIDITY
NASTIER	WAITING	*HARWICH	OBVIOUS.	SCUDDED.
NASTILY	WALTZED	HAYWARD	ABALONE	ACCEDED
PANTHER	WANTING	HAYWIRE	ABILITY	ACREAGE
PANTIES	WART-HOG	LAPWING	ABOLISH	ECHELON
PANTILE	WARTIME	+MAXWELL	OBELISK	ICTERUS
PANTING	WASTAGE	NARWHAL	OBELIZE.	SCHEMER
PARTAKE	WASTING	SAPWOOD	ABANDON	SCHERZO
PARTIAL	WASTREL	VANWARD	EBONIST	SCIENCE
PARTIED	WATTAGE	*WARWICK	EBONITE	SCREECH
PARTING	WATTLED.	WAXWORK	EBONIZE.	SCREWED.
PARTITE	+BAKUNIN	WAYWARD.	ABDOMEN	ICE-FLOE
PARTNER	CALUMET	BAUXITE	ABIOTIC	*SCAFELL
PARTOOK	CALUMNY	MARXISM.	ABROACH	SCAFFED
PASTERN	CASUIST	BABYISH	ABSOLVE	SCUFFED
+PASTEUR	FACULTY	*BABYLON	OBLOQUY.	SCUFFLE.
PASTIME	FAMULUS	BABY-SIT	ABORTED	ACHIEVE
PASTING	FATUOUS	BARYTES	IBERIAN	ACLINIC
PASTURE	GALUMPH	CALYCES	OBTRUDE.	ACTINIC
PATTERN	JANUARY	+CALYPSO	ABUSIVE	ECHIDNA
PATTING	LACUNAL	HALYARD	ABYSMAL	ECHINUS
RAFTING	MANUMIT	KATYDID	ABYSSAL.	ECLIPSE
RAGTIME	MANURED	LANYARD	ABETTED	OCCIPUT
RANTING	MATURED	NAVY-CUT	ABETTOR	SCRIBAL
RAPTURE	MAZURKA	PAPYRUS	ABSTAIN	SCRIBER.
RAT-TAIL	NATURAL	SATYRIC	ABUTTER	ACALEPH
RATTING	PABULUM	VARYING.	EBB-TIDE.	ACCLAIM
RATTLER	PALUDAL	DAZZLED	ABJURED	ACOLYTE
RAT-TRAP	SALUTED	JAZZILY	ABOULIA.	ECOLOGY
SALTERN	SAMURAI	JAZZING	OBEYING	*ICELAND
SALTING	VACUITY			OCCLUDE
SALTIRE	VACUOLE	ABRADED	+ACHATES	OCELLUS
SALT-PAN	VACUOUS	+ABRAHAM.	ACTABLE	OCULATE
TACTFUL	VAGUELY	ABSCESS	+ACTAEON	OCULIST

SCALDED	SCARIFY	EDUCING.	DEBAUCH	REPAPER
SCALENE	SCARING	ADDENDA	DECADAL	RETAKEN
SCALING	SCARLET	ADHERED	DECAGON	SEDATED
SCALLOP	SCARPED	ADRENAL	DECANAL	SENATOR
SCALPED	SCARRED	ADVERSE.	DECAPOD	SENATUS
SCALPEL	SCARVES	EDIFICE	DECAYED	+SERAPIS
SCALPER	SCORIFY	EDIFIED.	DEFACED	TENABLE
SCOLDED	SCORING	ADHIBIT	DEFAMED	TENABLY
SCOLLOP	SCORNED	ADMIRAL	DEFAULT	TENANCY
SCULLER	SCORPIO.	ADMIRER	DEGAUSS	TETANIC
SCULPED.	SCISSOR.	ADMIXED	DELAINE	TETANUS
SCAMPED	ACETATE	ADVISED	DELATED	VEDANTA
SCAMPER	ACETIFY	ADVISER.	DELATOR	VENALLY
SCUMBLE	ACETONE	ADULATE	DELAYED	VERANDA
SCUMMED.	ACETOUS	IDOLIZE	DERANGE	XERASIA.
ACINOSE	ACUTELY	IDYLLIC.	DEVALUE	CEMBALO
ACONITE	ECSTASY	ADAMANT	GELATIN	HENBANE
ECONOMY	ICHTHYS	ODDMENT.	GETAWAY	HERBAGE
SCANDAL	SCATHED	ADENOID	HEMATIN	+HERBERT
SCANNED	SCATTER	ADENOSE	HEPATIC	KERBING
SCANTLE	SCOTISM	ADENOUS	HETAERA	LESBIAN
SCENERY	SCOTOMA	ODDNESS.	HEXAGON	NETBALL
SCENTED	SCUTAGE	ADJOURN	HEXAPOD	PEBBLED
SCONCED.	SCUTTER	IDIOTIC.	KERATIN	SEA-BANK
ACCOUNT	SCUTTLE	ADAPTED	*LEBANON	SEABIRD
ACROBAT	SCYTHED.	ADAPTER	LEGALLY	SETBACK
ACRONYM	ACCURST	ADIPOSE.	LEGATED	TERBIUM
ECBOLIC	ACCUSAL	ADDRESS	LEGATEE	VERBENA
ECHOING	ACCUSED	ADORING	MEGATON	VERBOSE
ECHOISM	ACQUIRE	ODOROUS.	+MELANIE	WEBBING
ECLOGUE	ACTUARY	ODYSSEY.	MELANIN	*WEMBLEY.
OCTOBER	ACTUATE	EDITING	MENACED	BEACHED
OCTOPOD	OCTUPLE	EDITION.	METAZOA	BEECHEN
OCTOPUS	SCOURER	ADJUDGE	NEGATED	BELCHER
SCHOLAR	SCOURGE	ADJUNCT	+PEGASUS	BENCHER
SCOOPED	SCOUTED		PELAGIC	DEICIDE
SCOOTER	SCRUBBY	AERATED	PENALLY	DESCALE
SCROTUM.	SCRUFFY	AERATOR	PENALTY	DESCANT
ICE-PACK	SCRUNCH	BECAUSE	PENANCE	DESCEND
SCAPULA	SCRUPLE.	BEHAVED	PENATES	DESCENT
SCEPSIS	SCOWLED.	BELATED	REBATED	DEW-CLAW
SCEPTIC	ACRYLIC	BELAYED	REFACED	FENCING
SCEPTRE	ECDYSIS	BERATED	REGALED	FETCHED
SCUPPER.	SCRYING	BETAKEN	REGALIA	KETCHUP
ACCRETE		CELADON	REGALLY	LEACHED
ACERBIC	ADVANCE	CERAMIC	REGATTA	+MERCURY
ACTRESS	IDEALLY.	+CEZANNE	RELAPSE	METCAST
OCARINA	EDACITY	DEBACLE	RELATED	PEACOCK
OCHROUS	EDICTAL	DEBASED	RELAXED	PECCANT
SCARCER	EDUCATE	DEBATED	REMARRY	PECCARY

PECCAVI	*READING	GENERIC	FEOFFOR	METHANE
PERCALE	READMIT	GENESIS	+JEFFREY	PERHAPS
PERCEPT	REDDEST	GENETIC	LEAFAGE	RED-HEAD
PERCHED	REDDISH	HEBETIC	LEAFING	*REDHILL
PERCUSS	REEDING	HERETIC	LEAFLET	RETHINK
REACHED	RENDING	JEWELRY	MENFOLK	TECHNIC.
REACTOR	SEEDBED	+JEZEBEL	PERFECT	BEDIZEN
RED-COAT	SEEDILY	LEVERED	PERFIDY	BELIEVE
RESCIND	SEEDING	LEVERET	PERFORM	+BELINDA
RESCUER	SENDING	MEMENTO	PERFUME	BELISHA
RETCHED	SEND-OFF	MESEEMS	REEFING	BENISON
SEA-COAL	SET-DOWN	NEMESIS	*RENFREW	BESIDES
TEACAKE	TEDDING	PETERED	SEA-FOWL	BESIEGE
TEACHER	TENDING	+REBECCA	SELFISH	BETIMES
TEACH-IN	TENDRIL	RECEDED	SET-FAIR	BEWITCH
TEA-COSY	VENDACE	RECEIPT	TENFOLD	BEZIQUE
WELCOME	VENDING	RECEIVE	WELFARE.	+CECILIA
WENCHED.	VERDANT	REFEREE	BEGGARY	CEDILLA
BEADING	VERDICT	REGENCY	BEGGING	DEBITED
BEDDING	VERDURE	RELEASE	BELGIAN	DECIBEL
BENDING	WEDDING	RENEGUE	*BELGIUM	DECIDED
DEAD-END	WEEDING	RENEWAL	BENGALI	DECIMAL
DEADPAN	WELDING	RENEWED	DEIGNED	DEFIANT
DEWDROP	WENDING.	REREDOS	FEIGNED	DEFICIT
FEEDING	BEDEVIL	RESERVE	HEDGING	DEFILED
FENDING	BENEATH	REVELRY	KEDGING	DEFINED
FEUDING	BENEFIT	REVENGE	LEGGING	DEHISCE
GELDING	*BENELUX	REVENUE	LENGTHY	DELIGHT
GEODESY	BEREAVE	REVERED	MERGING	DELIMIT
HEADING	BESEECH	REVERIE	NEIGHED	DELIVER
HEADMAN	*CELEBES	REVERSE	PEGGING	DEMIGOD
HEAD-SET	CELESTA	REVERSO	PENGUIN	DEMISED
HEADWAY	+CELESTE	SECEDED	PERGOLA	DENIZEN
HEDDLES	CEREOUS	*SENEGAL	REAGENT	DERIDED
HEEDFUL	CERESIN	SEVENTH	*REIGATE	DERIVED
HEEDING	DECEASE	SEVENTY	REIGNED	DESIRED
LEADING	DECEIVE	SEVERAL	SEAGULL	DEVIATE
LENDING	DECENCY	SEVERED	VERGING	DEVILRY
MEDDLED	DEFENCE	SEWERED	WEDGING	DEVIOUS
MELDING	DELETED	TELEXED	WEIGHED	DEVISED
MENDING	DEMERIT	+TERENCE	WEIGH-IN	*DEVIZES
NEEDFUL	DEMESNE	VEDETTE	WEIGHTY.	FETIDLY
NEEDILY	DESERVE	VEGETAL	BEEHIVE	GENISTA
NEEDING	DETENTE	VETERAN.	BERHYME	GENITAL
NEEDLED	DETERED	*BEDFORD	BETHINK	HELICAL
PEDDLED	DEVELOP	*BELFAST	KEYHOLE	HELICES
PENDANT	FEDERAL	DEIFIED	LECHERY	HERITOR
PENDENT	+FENELLA	DEIFORM	LEGHORN	LEGIBLE
PENDING	GEHENNA	EEL-FARE	LETHEAN	LEGIBLY
READILY	GENERAL	FEOFFEE	MESHING	LENIENT

LEXICAL	VEHICLE	DEFLATE	SEA-LION	VERMEIL
LEXICON	VENISON	DEFLECT	SECLUDE	*VERMONT.
MEDIATE	VERIEST	DEPLETE	SELLING	+BERNARD
MEDICAL	VESICLE.	DEPLORE	SELL-OUT	DEANERY
MELISMA	PERJURE	FEELING	SEXLESS	FERNERY
+MELISSA	PERJURY.	+FELLINI	TEA-LEAF	FERN-OWL
MERITED	+BECKETT	FETLOCK	TELLING	HEINOUS
+NEVILLE	DECKING	GELLING	VEILING	HENNERY
+OEDIPUS	HECKLER	GEOLOGY	WEALTHY	HERNIAL
PEDICEL	JERKILY	HEALING	WEDLOCK	KEENEST
PEDICLE	JERKING	HEALTHY	WELLING	KEENING
PELICAN	KECKING	HEELING	WELL-OFF	+KENNEDY
PELISSE	KECKLED	HELLCAT	YELLING	+KENNETH
PERIGEE	LEAKAGE	HELLENE	YELLOWY	KENNING
PERIWIG	LEAKILY	HELLISH	ZEALOUS	KEYNOTE
PETIOLE	LEAKING	HEMLOCK	*ZEELAND	+LEANDER
REBIRTH	MEEKEST	JEALOUS	ZEOLITE	LEANING
RECITAL	NECKING	JELLIED	*ZETLAND.	LEONINE
RECITER	NECKLET	JELLING	BEAMING	+LEONORA
REFINED	NECK-TIE	KEELING	*BERMUDA	MEANDER
REGIMEN	PEAKING	KEELMAN	BESMEAR	MEANING
RELIANT	PECKING	KEELSON	DEEMING	PENNANT
RELIEVE	PECKISH	LEGLESS	*DENMARK	PENNILL
RELINED	PEEKING	NEGLECT	+DESMOND	PENNING
RELIVED	PERKILY	NEGLIGE	FERMENT	PEONAGE
REPINED	PERKING	NEOLOGY	FERMION	RE-ENTER
RESIDED	REEKING	NEW-LAID	FERMIUM	RE-ENTRY
RESIDUA	SEA-KALE	PEALING	GEMMATE	REGNANT
RESIDUE	SEEKING	PEELING	GEMMING	REINING
RESILED	*SELKIRK	PERLITE	GERMANE	REMNANT
RESINED	WEAKEST	REALGAR	*GERMANY	*REUNION
RETIARY	WEEKDAY	REALISM	HEMMING	REUNITE
RETICLE	WEEK-END	REALIST	LEMMING	REYNARD
RETINUE	AEOLIAN	REALITY	MERMAID	TEENAGE
RETIRED	BECLOUD	REALIZE	PERMIAN	VEINING
REVILED	BEE-LINE	REALTOR	PERMING	VERNIER
REVISAL	BELL-BOY	RECLAIM	PERMUTE	WEANING
REVISED	BELL-HOP	RECLINE	REAMING	WETNESS
REVIVAL	BELLIED	RECLUSE	SEA-MARK	YENNING.
REVIVER	+BELLINI	REELING	SEA-MILE	AEROBIC
SEDILIA	+BELLONA	REFLECT	SEAMING	AEROSOL
SEMINAL	BELLOWS	REFLOAT	SEEMING	BEDOUIN
SEMINAR	+BERLIOZ	REPLACE	SEGMENT	BEGONIA
SEMITIC	CEILING	REPLANT	+SEYMOUR	BELOVED
SERIATE	CELLIST	REPLETE	TEAMING	BETOKEN
SERIOUS	CELLULE	REPLICA	TEEMING	+DEBORAH
*SEVILLE	DEALING	REPLIED	TERMING	DEBOUCH
SEXIEST	DECLAIM	SEA-LEGS	TERMINI	DECODED
TEDIOUS	DECLARE	SEA-LINE	TERMITE	DECODER
TEPIDLY	DECLINE	SEALING	+VERMEER	DECOLOR

DECORUM	VERONAL	TENPINS	JEERING	TEARING
DECOYED	VETOING	TERPENE	KEY-RING	TEA-ROOM
DELOUSE	ZEDOARY	VESPERS	LEARNED	TEA-ROSE
DEMONIC	ZEROING.	WEEPING	LEERING	TERRACE
DEMOTED	BEDPOST	YELPING.	LEPROSY	TERRAIN
DEMOTIC	BESPEAK	BEARING	MERRILY	TERRENE
DEMOUNT	BESPOKE	BEARISH	METRICS	TERRIER
DENOTED	DEEPEST	BEAR-PIT	METRIST	TERRIFY
DEPOSED	DEEP-FRY	BED-ROCK	NEAREST	TERRINE
DEPOSIT	DEEP-SEA	BETROTH	NEARING	TETRODE
DEVOLVE	DELPHIC	DEAREST	NEGRESS	VEERING
DEVOTED	DESPAIR	DECRIAL	NEGRITO	VERRUCA
DEVOTEE	DESPISE	DECRIER	NEGROID	WEARIER
FELONRY	DESPITE	DEFRAUD	PEARLED	WEARILY
FEMORAL	DESPOIL	DEFROCK	PEARLER	WEARING
HEDONIC	DESPOND	DEFROST	+PEARSON	WEIRDLY
HEROINE	DEWPOND	DEGRADE	PEERAGE	YEARNED
HEROISM	HEAPING	+DEIRDRE	PEERESS	ZEBRINE.
HERONRY	HELPFUL	DEPRAVE	PEERING	BEASTLY
+JEHOVAH	HELPING	DEPRESS	*PENRITH	BEDSIDE
KENOSIS	HENPECK	DEPRIVE	PETRIFY	BEDSORE
KENOTIC	KEEPING	+DERRICK	REARING	BEES-WAX
*LESOTHO	LEAPING	DETRACT	REARMED	BERSERK
MEIOSIS	LEG-PULL	DETRAIN	RECRUIT	CEASING
MELODIC	LEOPARD	*DETROIT	REDRESS	CENSURE
NEPOTIC	+LEOPOLD	DETRUDE	*REDRUTH	CESSION
REBORED	*NEWPORT	FEARFUL	REFRACT	CESSPIT
REBOUND	PEEPING	FEARING	REFRAIN	DEISTIC
RECOUNT	PEOPLED	FEBRILE	REFRAME	DENSELY
RECOVER	PEPPERY	FERRATE	REFRESH	DENSEST
REDOUBT	PEPPING	FERRETY	REGRESS	DENSITY
REDOUND	PERPEND	FERRIED	REGROUP	DESSERT
REJOICE	PERPLEX	FERRITE	REPRESS	FEASTED
REMORSE	REAPING	FERROUS	REPRINT	FELSITE
REMOULD	REDPOLL	FERRULE	REPROOF	FELSPAR
REMOUNT	RESPECT	GEAR-BOX	REPROVE	HEISTED
REMOVAL	RESPIRE	GEARING	RETRACE	HERSELF
REMOVED	RESPITE	GEORDIE	RETRACT	HESSIAN
REMOVER	RESPOND	*GEORGIA	RETREAD	+JESSICA
REPOINT	SEA-PINK	GEORGIC	RETRIED	LEASHED
REPOSED	SEAPORT	HEARDIN	REWRITE	LEASING
RESOLVE	SEEPAGE	HEARING	REWROTE	LEISTER
RESOUND	SEEPING	HEARKEN	SEARING	LEISURE
RETOUCH	SERPENT	HEARSAY	SEA-ROOM	MEASLES
REVOKED	TELPHER	HEARTED	SECRECY	MEASURE
REVOLVE	TEMPERA	HEARTEN	SECRETE	MESSAGE
+SEGOVIA	TEMPEST	HEBRAIC	SERRATE	MESSIAH
TENONED	TEMPLAR	HEIRDOM	SERRIED	MESSIER
VELOURS	TEMPLET	HEIRESS	TEARFUL	MESSILY
VENOMED	TEMPTER	HERRING	TEAR-GAS	MESSING

NETSUKE	BETTING	LENTISK	SESTINA	DENUDED
OERSTED	CENTAUR	LENTOID	SETTING	FELUCCA
PEASANT	CENTIME	LEOTARD	SETTLED	GENUINE
PEA-SOUP	CENTNER	LETTING	SETTLER	JEJUNUM
PENSILE	CENTRAL	LETTUCE	SETTLOR	LEGUMIN
PENSION	CENTRIC	MEETING	SEXTAIN	LEMURES
PENSIVE	CENTURY	MELTING	SEXTANT	MEDULLA
+PERSEUS	CERTAIN	MENTHOL	TEA-TRAY	+MENUHIN
PERSIAN	CERTIFY	MENTION	TEKTITE	NEBULAR
PERSIST	CESTOID	MESTIZO	TENTHLY	PERUSAL
PERSONA	DEATHLY	NECTARY	TENTING	PERUSED
PESSARY	DELTOID	NEITHER	TENT-PEG	PETUNIA
REDSKIN	DENTARY	+NEPTUNE	TERTIAN	REAUMUR
REISSUE	DENTATE	NESTING	TESTACY	REBUKED
SEA-SALT	DENTINE	NESTLED	TESTATE	REDUCED
SEA-SICK	DENTIST	NETTING	TESTIFY	REFUGEE
SEASIDE	DENTURE	NETTLED	TESTILY	REFUSAL
SEISING	DESTINE	NEUTRAL	TESTING	REFUSED
SEISMAL	DESTINY	NEUTRON	TESTUDO	REFUTED
SEISMIC	DESTROY	*NEWTOWN	TEXTILE	REGULAR
SENSING	DEXTRAL	OESTRUS	TEXTUAL	REPULSE
SENSORY	DEXTRAN	PEAT-BOG	TEXTURE	REPUTED
SENSUAL	DEXTRIN	PELTING	VENTAGE	REQUEST
SESSION	FEATHER	PENTANE	VENTING	REQUIEM
TEA-SHOP	FEATURE	PENTODE	*VENTNOR	REQUIRE
TEASING	FELTING	PENTOSE	VENTRAL	REQUITE
TENSELY	FERTILE	PEPTIDE	VENTURE	RESUMED
TENSEST	FESTIVE	PERTAIN	VERTIGO	SECULAR
TENSILE	FESTOON	PERTURB	VESTIGE	SECURED
TENSING	GENTIAN	PETTILY	VESTING	SEDUCER
TENSION	GENTILE	PETTING	VESTURE	SEQUENT
TERSELY	GESTALT	PETTISH	VETTING	SEQUOIA
TESSERA	GESTAPO	RECTIFY	WEATHER	TENUITY
VERSIFY	GESTURE	RECTORY	WELTING	TENUOUS.
VERSING	GETTING	RENTIER	WEST-END	CERVINE
VERSION	HEATHEN	RENTING	WESTERN	DELVING
WELSHER.	+HEATHER	REPTILE	WESTING	DERVISH
BEATIFY	HEATING	RESTATE	WETTEST	FERVENT
BEATING	HECTARE	RESTFUL	WETTING	FERVOUR
+BEATLES	HEFTILY	RESTING	ZESTFUL.	HEAVIER
BEATNIK	HEFTING	RESTIVE	BEGUILE	HEAVILY
BEDTIME	HEPTANE	RESTORE	BEMUSED	HEAVING
BELTANE	JESTING	SEATING	BEQUEST	LEAVING
BELTING	JETTING	*SEATTLE	+DEBUSSY	NERVINE
BENTHOS	KENTISH	SECTARY	DECUPLE	NERVING
BERTHED	KESTREL	SECTILE	DEDUCED	NERVOUS
+BERTRAM	LEATHER	SECTION	DEFUNCT	NERVURE
BESTEAD	LECTERN	SEETHED	DEFUSED	PEEVING
BESTIAL	LECTURE	SELTZER	DELUDED	PEEVISH
BESTREW	LEFTIST	SEPTATE	DELUGED	PERVADE

PERVERT		CHOCTAW	CHAGRIN	CHIMNEY
REVVING	AGRAFFE	CHUCKED	CHIGNON	KHAMSIN
SERVANT	OGHAMIC.	CHUCKLE	CHUGGED	RHOMBIC
SERVERY	IGNEOUS	SHACKED	SHAGGED.	RHOMBUS
+SERVICE	OGREISH.	SHACKLE	CHAINED	RHYMING
SERVILE	EGG-FLIP.	SHOCKER	CHAIRED	SHAMBLE
SERVING	EGGHEAD.	SHUCKED	CHRISOM	SHAMING
VELVETY	AGAINST	THICKEN	+CHRISTI	SHAMMED
VERVAIN	IGNITED	THICKER	SHRILLY	SHAMPOO
WEAVING.	UGLIEST.	THICKET	SHRIVEL	SHIMMER
+BEOWULF	AGELESS	THICKLY	THRIFTY	THIMBLE
BETWEEN	AGILELY	WHACKED.	THRIVED	THOMISM
BETWIXT	AGILITY	*CHEDDAR	THRIVEN.	THUMBED
EEL-WORM	EGALITY.	CHIDING	+CHEKHOV	THUMPED
*KESWICK	AGONIZE.	RHODIUM	CHOKING	WHIMPER
LEEWARD	AGROUND	SHADIER	CHUKKER	WHIMSEY.
NETWORK	IGNOBLE	SHADILY	SHAKILY	CHANCED
REDWOOD	IGNORAL	SHADING	SHAKING.	CHANCEL
SEA-WALL	IGNORED.	SHADOWY	CHALICE	CHANCRE
SEAWARD	AGGRESS.	SHUDDER	CHELATE	CHANGED
SEAWEED	EGESTED.	THUDDED.	*CHELSEA	CHANNEL
SEA-WOLF	AGITATE	CHEEPER	CHILLED	CHANTED
WERWOLF.	AGITATO	CHEERED	CHOLERA	CHANTRY
BELYING	EGOTISM	CHEERIO	CHOLINE	CHINESE
DENYING	EGOTIST	CHEESED	KHALIFA	CHINKED
LEVYING.		CHEETAH	PHALANX	CHINNED
BENZENE		CHIEFLY	PHALLIC	CHINWAG
BENZOIN	CHEAPEN	CHIEFLY	PHALLUS	PHANTOM
SEIZING	CHEAPLY	+PHAEDRA	PHILTRE	PHONATE
SEIZURE	CHEATED	PHAETON	+PHYLLIS	PHONING
	CHIANTI	PHLEGMY	SHALLOP	RHENIUM
	CHIASMA	+PHOEBUS	SHALLOT	SHINDIG
AFFABLE	PHRASED	*PHOENIX	SHALLOW	SHINGLE
EFFASED.	SHEARED	PHRENIC	SHELLAC	SHINILY
OFFBEAT.	SHEATHE	SHEERED	SHELLED	SHINING
EFFENDI	SHEAVES	SHEETED	+SHELLEY	SHINNED
OFFENCE	SHOALED	SHOEING	SHELTER	SHUNNED
OFFERED.	THEATRE	THIEVED	SHELTIE	SHUNTED
OFF-HAND.	THIAMIN	WHEEDLE	SHELVED	SHYNESS
AFFINAL	WHEATEN.	WHEELED	THULIUM	THANKED
AFFINED	CHABLIS	WHEEZED	WHALING	THINKER
AFFIXED	RHUBARB	WHOEVER.	WHELPED	THINNED
OFFICER.	SHEBANG	CHAFFER	WHILING.	THINNER
AFFLICT	SHEBEEN.	CHAFING	CHAMBER	THUNDER
OFF-LINE.	CHECKED	CHIFFON	CHAMFER	WHENEER
PFENNIG.	CHECKER	CHUFFED	CHAMOIS	WHINING.
OFF-PEAK.	CHECK-UP	SHIFTER	CHEMISE	CHAOTIC
AFFRONT.	*CHICAGO	SHUFFLE	CHEMIST	CHLORAL
OFF-SIDE.	CHICANE	WHIFFED	CHIMERA	CHLORIC
EFFUSED.	CHICKEN	WHIFFLE.	CHIMING	+CHLORIS
OFFWARD	CHICORY	+CHAGALL		

CHROMIC	CHORALE	WHERETO	SHOUTED	RIVALRY
CHRONIC	CHORION	WHIRLED	SHRUBBY	SIZABLE
SHODING	CHORTLE	WHIRRED	THEURGY	+TITANIA
SHOOTER	CHURCHY	WHORING.	THOUGHT.	TITANIC
THEOREM	CHURNED	CHASING	*CHEVIOT	VITALLY
THROATY	GHERKIN	CHASSIS	CHEVRON	VITAMIN
THRONED	PHARAOH	CHASTEN	SHAVING	+VIVALDI
THROUGH	PHARYNX	*CHESTER	SHIVERY	WIRABLE.
THROWER	SHARING	GHASTLY	SHOVING.	DIABASE
WHOOPED.	SHARKED	GHOSTED	CHEWING	DIABOLO
CHAPLET	SHARPEN	GHOSTLY	CHOWDER	DIBBLED
+CHAPLIN	SHARPER	PHASING	SHOWBIZ	DISBAND
CHAPMAN	SHERBET	PHYSICS	SHOWERY	FIBBING
CHAPPED	SHEREEF	SHUSHED	SHOWILY	FILBERT
CHAPTER	SHERIFF	SHYSTER	SHOWING	FINBACK
CHIPPED	SHIRKER	+THESEUS	SHOWMAN	GIBBOUS
CHOPINE	+SHIRLEY	THISTLE	SHOW-OFF	+GILBERT
CHOPPED	SHORING	THISTLY	SHOWMAN	GIMBALS
CHOPPER	SHORTED	THYSELF	+KHAYYAM.	JIBBING
SHAPELY	SHORTEN	WHISKED	RHIZOID	KIBBUTZ
SHAPING	SHORTER	WHISKER	RHIZOME	LIMBATE
*SHEPPEY	SHORTLY	WHISKEY	WHIZZED	LIMBECK
SHIPPED	THERAPY	WHISPER		NIBBLED
SHIPPEN	THEREAT	WHISTLE.	BIVALVE	NIOBIUM
SHIPPER	THEREBY	CHATEAU	BIZARRE	PIEBALD
SHIP-WAY	THEREIN	*CHATHAM	CITADEL	PINBALL
SHOPMAN	THEREOF	CHATTED	DIBASIC	RIBBING
SHOPPED	THEREON	CHATTEL	DILATED	+RIMBAUD
SHOPPER	+THERESA	CHATTER	DILATOR	*TILBURY
WHIPPED	THERETO	CHUTNEY	DISABLE	TIMBREL
WHIPPET	THERMAL	SHATTER	DISAVOW	*WISBECH.
WHOPPER.	THERMIC	SHOTGUN	FILARIA	BIRCHED
CHEQUER.	THERMIT	SHUT-EYE	FINABLE	BISCUIT
CHARADE	THERMOS	SHUT-OUT	FINAGLE	CIRCLED
CHARGED	THIRDLY	SHUTTER	FINALLY	CIRCLET
CHARGER	THIRSTY	SHUTTLE	FINANCE	CIRCUIT
CHARILY	+THOREAU	THITHER	FIXABLE	DIOCESE
CHARIOT	THORIDE	WHATEER	FIXATED	DISCARD
CHARITY	THORIUM	WHATNOT	GIRAFFE	DISCERN
+CHARLES	THYROID	WHETHER	GIRASOL	DISCOID
CHARMER	THYRSUS	WHETTED	HIDALGO	DISCORD
CHARNEL	WHARFED	WHITEST	LIVABLE	DISCUSS
CHARRED	WHARVES	WHITHER	MINARET	DITCHED
CHARTED	WHEREAS	WHITING	MIRACLE	DITCHER
CHARTER	WHEREAT	WHITISH	+MIRANDA	FILCHED
CHERISH	WHEREBY	WHITLOW	PICADOR	FITCHEW
CHEROOT	WHEREER	+WHITMAN	PICAMAR	HIRCINE
CHERVIL	WHEREIN	WHITSUN	PIRAGUA	HITCHED
CHIRPED	WHEREOF	WHITTLE.	PIRATED	*HITCHIN
CHIRRUP	WHEREON	+CHAUCER	RIDABLE	KITCHEN

*LINCOLN	RIDDING	MISERLY	MISGAVE	+RICHARD
LINCTUS	RIDDLED	*NIGERIA	MISGIVE	RICHEST
MINCING	SIT-DOWN	*NINEVEH	NIGGARD	RIGHTED
MIOCENE	TIDDLER	PIE-EYED	NIGGLED	RIGHTLY
MISCALL	TIDDLEY	PIKELET	PIGGERY	SIGHING
MISCAST	VIADUCT	PIMENTO	PIGGING	SIGHTED
OILCAKE	WILDCAT	PINETUM	PIGGISH	SIGHTLY
PICCOLO	WILDEST	PIPEFUL	PILGRIM	TIGHTEN
PIECING	WINDBAG	PIPETTE	PINGUID	TIGHTER
PILCHER	WINDIER	PITEOUS	PINGUIN	TIGHTLY
PINCERS	WINDING	RIVETER	RIGGING	WISHFUL
PINCHED	WINDROW	SIDECAR	RINGING	WISHING
PISCINA	*WINDSOR	SILENCE	RINGLET	WITHERS
PISCINE	YIDDISH.	*SILESIA	*RINGWAY	WITHOUT
PITCHED	AILERON	TIDEWAY	SINGING	XIPHOID.
PITCHER	BIBELOT	TIME-LAG	SINGLED	BILIARY
RIP-CORD	BIRETTA	VICEROY	SINGLET	BILIOUS
SINCERE	DICE-BOX	VINEGAR	TINGING	CILIARY
+VINCENT	DILEMMA	VIRELAY	TINGLED	CILIATE
VISCERA	DIREFUL	WIZENED.	VIRGATE	CITIZEN
VISCOSE	DISEASE	AIRFLOW	VIRGULE	CIVILLY
VISCOUS	DIVERGE	DIFFUSE	WIDGEON	DIGITAL
WINCHED	DIVERSE	*MILFORD	WIGGLED	DIVIDED
WITCHED.	EIDETIC	MISFIRE	WINGING.	DIVINED
BIDDING	EIRENIC	PINFOLD	AIR-HOLE	DIVINER
BINDING	FINESSE	PITFALL	BIG-HEAD	DIVISOR
CINDERY	FIRE-ARM	RIFFLER	CITHARA	FINICAL
DIDDLER	FIREBOX	SIXFOLD	DIEHARD	FINICKY
DISDAIN	FIRE-BUG	TIFFANY	DIPHASE	HIJINKS
FIDDLED	FIREDOG	TINFOIL	DISHFUL	LIAISON
FIDDLER	FIREFLY	+WILFRED.	DISHING	LICITLY
FINDING	FIREMAN	BIGGEST	DISHMAT	LIMITED
GIDDILY	+GISELLE	DIAGRAM	FIGHTER	LIVIDLY
GILDING	HIDEOUS	DIGGING	FISHERY	MILITIA
JIB-DOOR	HIDEOUT	DINGING	FISHILY	MIMICRY
KIDDING	KINETIC	DISGUST	FISHING	MINIBUS
*KILDARE	LIBERAL	GIGGLER	HIGHDAY	MINICAB
KINDEST	*LIBERIA	GINGERY	HIGHEST	MINIMAL
KINDLER	LIBERTY	GINGHAM	HIGH-HAT	MINIMUM
KINDRED	LICENCE	HIGGLER	HIGHWAY	MINIVER
+LINDSEY	LICENSE	JIGGING	LIGHTEN	PIG-IRON
MIDDLED	LINEAGE	JIGGLED	LIGHTER	PITIFUL
MILDEST	LINEATE	JINGLED	LIGHTLY	RIGIDLY
MILDEWY	LINEMAN	KINGCUP	LITHIUM	RISIBLE
+MILDRED	LITERAL	KINGDOM	+MICHAEL	RIVIERE
MINDFUL	MILEAGE	KINGING	NIGHTLY	SILICIC
MINDING	MIMESIS	KINGLET	PINHEAD	SILICON
MISDEAL	MIMETIC	KINGPIN	PINHOLE	SIMILAR
MISDEED	MINERAL	LINGUAL	PIT-HEAD	TIDIEST
PIDDOCK	+MINERVA	MINGLED	PITHILY	TIDINGS

TIMIDLY	WINKING	TILLAGE	PINNING	LIPPING
TINIEST	WINKLED.	TILLING	PIONEER	LISPING
VICINAL	AIMLESS	TITLARK	SIGNIFY	NIPPING
VICIOUS	AIRLESS	TITLING	SIGNING	PIMPING
VISIBLE	AIRLIFT	VILLAGE	SIGNORA	PIPPING
VISITED	AIRLINE	VILLAIN	SINNING	RIPPING
VISITOR	AIR-LOCK	VILLEIN	TINNILY	RIPPLED
VITIATE	BILLING	VILLOUS	TINNING	SIPPING
VIVIDLY.	BILLION	VIOLATE	WINNING	TIMPANI
DISJOIN.	BIOLOGY	VIOLENT	WITNESS	TIMPANO
BILKING	BIPLANE	VIOLIST	ZIONISM	TIPPING
+DICKENS	DIALECT	WIELDED	ZIONIST.	TIPPLER
HICKORY	DIALLED	+WILLIAM	BIFOCAL	WIMPLED
JINKING	DIPLOID	WILLING	BIGOTED	ZIPPING.
KICKING	DIPLOMA	WILLOWY	BIGOTRY	PICQUET.
KICK-OFF	DISLIKE	WITLESS	BIPOLAR	AIR-RAID
KINKILY	DISLIMN	YIELDED.	BIVOUAC	CIRROSE
KINKING	FIELDED	AILMENT	DIPOLAR	CITRATE
KINKLED	FIELDER	AIRMAIL	DISOBEY	CITRINE
LICKING	FIG-LEAF	BISMUTH	DIVORCE	CITROUS
LINKAGE	FILLING	DIAMOND	EIDOLON	DIARCHY
LINKING	*FINLAND	DIMMING	KILOTON	DIARIST
MILK-BAR	+GILLIAN	DISMAST	LINOCUT	DIGRAPH
MILKING	GILLION	DISMISS	LITOTES	DIGRESS
MILKMAN	GIRLISH	FIGMENT	MIAOWED	DIORAMA
MILKSOP	+HILLARY	FILMING	MITOSIS	DIORITE
NICKING	HILLOCK	FIRMING	*NICOSIA	DISROBE
PICKAXE	KILLICK	FITMENT	PICOTEE	DISRUPT
PICKING	KILLING	GIMMICK	PILOTED	DIURNAL
PICKLED	KILLJOY	MIDMOST	PIROGUE	FIBROID
PINK-EYE	MIDLAND	OILMEAL	PIVOTAL	FIBROUS
PINKING	MILLING	PIGMENT	PIVOTED	FIERILY
PINKISH	MILLION	RIMMING	RIPOSTE	*KINROSS
RICKETS	MISLAID	SIAMESE.	RISOTTO	LIBRARY
RICKETY	MISLEAD	DIGNIFY	SIROCCO	LIBRATE
RICKING	MISLIKE	DIGNITY	+TIMOTHY	MICROBE
RINKING	NIBLICK	DIMNESS	WIDOWER.	MIDRIFF
RISKIER	OILLESS	DINNING	AIRPORT	MIGRANT
RISKILY	PIGLING	DIPNOAN	DIMPLED	MIGRATE
RISKING	PILLAGE	FINNISH	DIOPSIS	MISREAD
SICK-BAY	PILL-BOX	FITNESS	DIOPTER	MISRULE
SICK-BED	PILLION	LIGNITE	DIOPTRE	NITRATE
SICKEST	PILLORY	LIMNING	DIPPING	NITROUS
SICK-PAY	RIFLING	LIONCEL	DISPLAY	PIBROCH
SILKILY	SIBLING	LIONESS	DISPORT	PIERAGE
SINKING	SIDLING	LIONIZE	DISPOSE	PIERCED
TICKING	SILLIER	PIANIST	DISPUTE	PIERCED
TICKLER	SILLILY	PIANOLA	HIPPING	PIERROT
*WICKLOW	SINLESS	PINNACE	KIPPING	TIERCEL
WINKERS	SIRLOIN	PINNATE	LIMPING	TIERCET
				TIGRESS

TITRATE	DIETING	PINTADO	CIVVIES	SKATING
VIBRANT	DIETIST	PISTOLE	NIRVANA	SKETCHY
VIBRATE	DIPTERA	PITTING	SIEVING	SKITTER
VIBRATO	DIPTYCH	RIFTING	SILVERY.	SKITTLE.
VITRIFY	DIRTIED	RIOTING	MIDWIFE	SKEWING
VITRIOL.	DIRTILY	RIOTOUS	OIL-WELL	SKYWARD
AIRSHIP	DISTAFF	RIP-TIDE	PIGWASH	
DISSECT	DISTANT	SIFTING	TINWARE	*ALBANIA
DISSENT	DISTEND	SILTING	VIEWING.	ALCAZAR
FIBSTER	DISTICH	SISTRUM	DIOXIDE.	ALFALFA
FIRSTLY	DISTORT	SITTING	BICYCLE	ALLAYED
FISSILE	DISTURB	SIXTEEN	PITYING.	ALMANAC
FISSION	DISTYLE	TILTING	DIZZILY	BLEAKLY
FISSURE	FICTILE	TINTACK	FIZZING	BLEATED
HIMSELF	FICTION	*TINTERN	FIZZLED	BLOATED
HIPSTER	FICTIVE	TIPTOED	GIZZARD	BLOATER
HIRSUTE	FIFTEEN	VICTORY	MIZZLED	CLEANED
HISSING	FIFTHLY	VICTUAL	SIZZLED	CLEANER
KIDSKIN	FISTFUL	*VIETNAM		CLEANLY
KINSHIP	FISTULA	VINTAGE	*AJACCIO	CLEANSE
KINSMAN	FITTEST	VINTNER	EJECTED	CLEARED
KISSING	FITTING	VIRTUAL	EJECTOR.	CLEARER
LINSANG	FIXTURE	*VISTULA	SJAMBOK	CLEARLY
LINSEED	HINTING	*WIGTOWN		CLEAVED
MIASMAL	HISTORY	WILTING	SKY-BLUE.	CLEAVER
MIDSHIP	HITTING	WISTFUL	SKIDDED	CLOACAL
MINSTER	JILTING	WITTIER	SKID-LID	CLOAKED
MISSILE	JITTERY	WITTILY	SKID-PAN.	+ELEANOR
MISSING	KITTING	WITTING.	SKIFFLE.	FLOATER
MISSION	LIFTBOY	BITUMEN	SKY-HIGH.	FLYAWAY
MISSIVE	LIFTING	DILUENT	SKI-JUMP.	GLEAMED
OIL-SILK	LIFTMAN	DILUTED	SKALDIC	GLEANER
OILSKIN	LIFT-OFF	DILUTER	SKILFUL	GLOATED
PIASTRE	LILTING	DIVULGE	SKI-LIFT	PLEADER
PIGSKIN	LISTING	FIGURAL	SKILLED	PLEASED
RINSING	LITTLER	FIGURED	SKILLET	PLEATED
RISSOLE	MILTING	LIQUATE	SKULKED	PLIABLE
TIPSILY	MINTAGE	LIQUEFY	SKYLARK	PLIANCY.
TIPSTER	MINTING	LIQUEUR	SKYLINE	*ALABAMA
TISSUED	MISTAKE	LITURGY	UKULELE.	BLABBED
WINSOME	MISTILY	MINUTED	SKIMMER	BLUBBER
+WINSTON.	MISTING	MISUSED	SKIMPED.	CLOBBER
*AINTREE	MISTOOK	PILULAR	SKINFUL	CLUBBED
BILTONG	MISTRAL	PIOUSLY	SKINNED.	CLUBMAN
BIOTYPE	MIXTURE	PIQUANT	SKEPTIC	FLY-BOAT
BITTERN	NINTHLY	RIVULET	SKIPPED	FLY-BOOK
CISTERN	PICTISH	SINUOUS	SKIPPER.	GLOBOSE
DICTATE	PICTURE	SITUATE	SKIRLED	GLOBULE
DICTION	PIETISM	TITULAR	SKIRTED.	ILL-BRED
DIETARY	PIGTAIL	VIDUITY.	SKYSAIL.	SLOBBER

SLUBBED.	ALLEGED	FLAKILY	BLENDED	FLOODED
BLACKEN	ALLEGRO	FLAKING	BLINDED	FLOORED
BLACKER	ALLERGY	SLAKING.	BLINDLY	FLY-OVER.
BLOCKED	ALREADY	FLYLEAF	BLINKED	CLAP-NET
CLACKED	ALTERED	ULULATE.	BLUNDER	CLAPPED
*CLACTON	ALVEOLE	ALEMBIC	BLUNTED	CLAPPER
CLICKED	BLEEPED	ALIMENT	BLUNTLY	CLIPPED
CLICKER	BLUEING	ALIMONY	CLANGED	CLIPPER
CLOCKED	ELDERLY	ALUMINA	CLANGER	CLIPPIE
ELECTED	FLEEING	ALUMNUS	CLANKED	ELAPSED
ELECTOR	FLEETED	BLAMING	CLINGER	ELOPING
+ELECTRA	FLUENCY	BLEMISH	CLINKER	FLAPPED
FLACCID	GLEEFUL	CLAMANT	FLANEUR	FLAPPER
FLECKED	GLUEING	CLAMBER	FLANGED	FLIPPER
FLICKED	ILLEGAL	CLAMOUR	FLANKER	FLOPPED
FLICKER	SLEEKER	CLAMPED	FLANNEL	FLY-PAST
FLOCKED	SLEEKLY	CLAMPER	FLUNKEY	GLYPHIC
GLACIAL	SLEEPER	+CLEMENT	GLANCED	GLYPTIC
GLACIER	SLEETED	CLIMATE	GLINTED	PLOPPED
GLUCOSE	SLEEVED.	CLIMBER	ILLNESS	SLAPPED
PLACARD	ALIFORM	CLUMPED	PLANING	SLIPPED
PLACATE	BLUFFER	ELEMENT	PLANISH	SLIPPER
PLACEBO	BLUFFLY	FLAMING	PLANKED	SLIPWAY
PLACING	OLEFINE.	+FLEMING	PLANNED	SLOPING
PLACKET	CLOGGED	FLEMISH	PLANNER	SLOPPED.
PLICATE	ELEGANT	FLUMMOX	PLANTAR	ALIQUOT
PLUCKED	ELEGIAC	GLAMOUR	PLANTED	CLIQUEY.
SLACKEN	ELEGIST	GLIMMER	PLANTER	ALERTED
SLACKER	ELEGIZE	GLIMPSE	PLENARY	BLARING
SLACKLY	FLAG-DAY	*OLYMPIA	PLONKED	BLARNEY
SLICING	FLAGGED	OLYMPIC	PLUNDER	BLURRED
SLICKER	FLAGMAN	*OLYMPUS	PLUNGED	BLURTED
SLICKLY.	FLIGHTY	PLUMAGE	PLUNGER	CLARIFY
ALIDADE	FLOGGED	PLUMBER	PLUNKED	CLARION
BLADDER	PLAGUED	PLUMBIC	SLANDER	CLARITY
ELIDING	PLUGGED	PLUMING	SLANGED	CLARKIA
ELUDING	SLOGGER	PLUMMET	SLANTED	FLARING
FLEDGED	SLUGGED.	PLUMOSE	SLENDER	FLIRTED
GLADDEN	ALCHEMY	PLUMPER	SLYNESS.	*FLORIDA
GLIDING	FLY-HALF.	PLUMPLY	ALCOHOL	FLORIST
PLEDGED	*ALGIERS	SLAMMED	ALCORAN	FLORUIT
PLEDGEE	CLAIMED	SLIMMER	ALLOWED	GLARING
PLEDGET	ELLIPSE	SLUMBER	ALLOYED	GLORIED
PLODDER	FLAILED	SLUMMED	ALMONER	GLORIFY
SLEDDED	ILLICIT	SLUMPED.	ALOOFLY	SLURRED.
SLEDGED	PLAINER	+BLANCHE	ALSO-RAN	ALMSMAN
SLIDING.	PLAINLY	BLANDLY	BLOODED	ALYSSUM
ALGEBRA	PLAITED	BLANKED	BLOOMED	BLASTED
*ALGERIA	SLEIGHT	BLANKET	BLOOMER	BLASTIN
ALIENEE	SLUICED.	BLANKLY	ELBOWED	BLESBOK

BLESSED	CLOTHES	SLAVING	SMUDGED.	EMINENT
BLISTER	CLOTTED	SLAVISH.	AMMETER	OMINOUS.
BLOSSOM	CLUTTER	BLOW-FLY	AMNESIA	AMMONIA
BLUSHED	ELATING	BLOWING	AMNESTY	AMPOULE
BLUSTER	ELATION	BLOW-OUT	AMOEBIC	EMBOLUS
CLASHED	FLATLET	CLAWING	EMPEROR	EMBOSOM
CLASPED	FLATTEN	CLOWNED	IMMENSE	EMBOWER
CLASSED	FLATTER	FLAWING	IMMERSE	EMPOWER
CLASSIC	FLITTED	FLOWERY	IMPEACH	IMMORAL
CLASTIC	FLITTER	FLOWING	IMPEDED	IMPOSED
CLOSELY	FLOTSAM	GLOWING	IMPERIL	IMPOUND
CLOSE-UP	FLUTING	ILL-WILL	IMPETUS.	SMOOCHY.
CLOSING	FLUTIST	PLYWOOD	IMPFING.	AMERCED
CLOSURE	FLUTTER	SLEWING	IMAGERY	*AMERICA
CLUSTER	FLY-TRAP	SLOWEST.	IMAGINE	AMORIST
CLYSTER	GLITTER	FLEXILE	IMAGING	AMOROUS
ELASTIC	GLOTTAL	FLEXING	IMAGISM	EMBRACE
ELASTIN	GLOTTIS	FLEXION	SMUGGLE.	EMBROIL
ELISION	GLUTTED	FLEXURE	+AMPHION	EMERALD
ELUSION	GLUTTON	FLUXION.	AMPHORA.	EMERGED
ELUSIVE	PLATEAU	CLOYING	AMBIENT	EMPRESS
ELUSORY	PLATING	FLAYING	EMPIRIC	IMBRUED
ELYSIAN	PLATOON	PLAY-ACT	IMBIBED	IMPRESS
ELYSIUM	PLATTED	PLAYBOY	IMPIETY	IMPREST
FLASHED	PLATTER	PLAYFUL	IMPINGE	IMPRINT
FLASHER	PLOTTER	PLAYING	IMPIOUS	IMPROVE
FLESHED	SLATING	PLAYLET	OMNIBUS	SMARTED
FLESHLY	SLATTED	PLAY-OFF	UMPIRED.	SMARTEN
FLUSHED	SLITHER	PLAYPEN	SMOKILY	SMARTLY
FLUSTER	SLOTTED.	SLAYING.	SMOKING.	SMIRKED
*GLASGOW	ALBUMEN	BLAZING	AMALGAM	UMBRAGE.
GLISTEN	ALLUDED	GLAZIER	AMBLING	AMASSED
GLISTER	ALLURED	GLAZING	AMPLIFY	AMUSING
GLOSSED	+CLAUDIA	GLOZING	AMYLOID	SMASHED
OLDSTER	CLAUSAL		EMULATE	SMASHER
PLASMIC	CLOUDED	AMHARIC	EMULOUS	SMASH-UP
PLASTER	CLOUTED	AMIABLE	IMPLANT	AMATEUR
PLASTIC	FLOUNCE	EMBARGO	IMPLIED	AMATIVE
PLOSIVE	FLOURED	EMBASSY	IMPLODE	AMATORY
PLUSHER	FLOUTED	EMBAYED	IMPLORE	EMETINE
SLASHED	PLAUDIT.	EMPANEL	SMALLER	EMITTED
SLOSHED	CLAVIER	EMPATHY	SMILING.	EMITTER
+ULYSSES.	ELEVATE	IMPALED	AMANITA	EMOTION
ALL-TIME	ELUVIAL	IMPANEL	AMENDED	EMOTIVE
BLATANT	FLAVOUR	IMPASSE	AMENITY	EMPTIER
BLOTCHY	FLUVIAL	IMPASTE	AMENTIA	EMPTILY
BLOTTED	OLIVARY	IMPASTO	AMONGST	IMITATE
BLOTTER	+OLIVIER	SMEARED.	EMANATE	OMITTED
CLATTER	PLUVIAL	SMACKED	+EMANUEL	SMITTEN
CLOTHED	SLAVERY	SMACKER.	EMENDED	SMOTHER

SMUTTED	KNOBBLY	UNHEARD	INCISED	UNCLEAN
UMPTEEN.	SNUBBED.	UNKEMPT	INCISOR	UNCLOAK
AMPULLA	ENACTED	UNLEARN	INCITED	UNCLOSE
AMPUTEE	INSCAPE	UNLEASH	*INDIANA	UNSLING.
IMBURSE	KNACKER	UNMEANT	INDICES	ANEMONE
IMMURED	KNOCKED	UNNERVE	INDICIA	ANIMATE
IMPULSE	KNOCKER	UNREADY	INDITED	ANIMISM
IMPUTED.	KNOCK-ON	UNSEXED.	INFIDEL	ANOMALY
.AMAZING	KNUCKLE	KNIFING	INFIELD	ENAMOUR
	SNICKER	SNAFFLE	INFIXED	ENDMOST
ANDANTE	UNACTED	SNIFFED	INHIBIT	GNOMISH.
+ANNABEL	UNICORN	SNUFFED	INNINGS	ENSNARE
ANTACID	UNSCREW.	SNUFFLE	INSIDER	INANELY
+ANTAEUS	ANODIZE	UNIFIED	INSIGHT	INANITY
ENCAGED	ANODYNE.	UNIFORM.	INSIPID	ONANISM
ENCASED	ANAEMIA	ANAGRAM	INVITED	ONANIST
ENFACED	ANAEMIC	END-GAME	UNAIDED	ONENESS
ENGAGED	ANGELIC	SNAGGED	UNAIRED	UNKNOWN.
ENHANCE	ANGELUS	SNIGGER	UNCIVIL	*ANDORRA
ENLACED	ANGERED	SNOGGED	UNFIXED	*ANDOVER
ENLARGE	+ANNETTE	SNUGGED	UNHINGE	ANNOYED
ENRAGED	ANNEXED	SNUGGLE.	UNHITCH	ANTONYM
INFANCY	ANOESIS	ANCHOVY	UNRISEN.	ENDORSE
INFANTA	ANOETIC	ANT-HILL	SNAKILY	ENDOWED
INFANTE	ANTENNA	+ANTHONY	SNAKING.	ENFORCE
INHABIT	ENDEMIC	ANTHRAX	ANALECT	ENGORGE
INHALER	ENFEOFF	ENCHAIN	ANALOGY	ENJOYED
INNARDS	ENTENTE	ENCHANT	ANALYSE	ENNOBLE
INVADER	ENTERIC	ENCHASE	ANALYST	ENROBED
INVALID	ENVELOP	ENTHRAL	ANGLICE	ENTOMIC
KNEADED	ENVENOM	ENTHUSE	ANGLING	INBOARD
*ONTARIO	INBEING	INCHING	ANILINE	INCOMER
ONWARDS	INCENSE	INKHORN	ENCLAVE	INDOORS
SNEAKED	INFERNO	INSHORE	ENCLOSE	INDORSE
UNCANNY	INGENUE	UNCHAIN.	ENDLESS	INGOING
UNCARED	INHERED	ANCIENT	ENDLONG	INSOFAR
UNCASED	INHERIT	ANDIRON	*ENGLAND	INTONED
UNEARTH	INTEGER	ANTIGEN	ENGLISH	INVOICE
UNHANDY	INTENSE	*ANTIGUA	ENSLAVE	INVOKED
UNHAPPY	INTERIM	ANTILOG	INCLINE	INVOLVE
UNLADEN	INVEIGH	ANTIQUE	INCLOSE	INWOVEN
UNMANLY	INVERSE	ANXIETY	INCLUDE	SNOOKER
UNNAMED	INWEAVE	ANXIOUS	INFLAME	SNOOPER
UNRAVEL	KNEE-CAP	*ENFIELD	INFLATE	SNOOZED
UNTAMED	KNEELED	ENLIVEN	INFLECT	UNBOSOM
UNTAXED.	KNEELER	ENSILED	INFLICT	UNBOUND
ANYBODY	ONE-EYED	ENTICED	INKLING	UNBOWED
ENABLED	SNEERED	ENTITLE	KNELLED	UNCOUTH
KNOBBED	SNEEZED	ENVIOUS	UNBLOWN	UNCOVER
KNOBBLE	UNDERGO	ENVIRON	UNCLASP	UNDOING

UNGODLY	INURNED	ENDURED	BOTARGO	VOCALLY
UNHOPED	KNURLED	ENOUNCE	COCAINE	VOYAGER
UNHORSE	ONEROUS	ENQUIRE	COHABIT	WOMANLY
UNLOOSE	SNARING	ENQUIRY	COPAIBA	ZONALLY.
UNMORAL	SNARLED	ENSURED	CORACLE	BOBBERY
UNMOVED	SNORING	INCUBUS	CORANTO	BOBBING
UNROBED	SNORTER	INCUSED	DONATED	BOMBARD
UNSOUND	UNARMED	INDUCED	DONATOR	BOMBAST
UNWOUND	UNBRACE	INDULGE	DOWAGER	BOMBING
UNYOKED	UNDRESS	INFUSED	FORAGER	COBBLER
UNZONED.	UNFROCK	INHUMAN	FORAMEN	COMBINE
INAPTLY	UNFROZE	INHUMED	FORAYED	COMBING
INEPTLY	UNTRIED	INJURED	GOUACHE	COWBANE
INSPECT	UNTRUSS	INQUEST	+HOGARTH	DOUBLED
INSPIRE	UNTRUTH	INQUIRE	HORALLY	DOUBLET
KNAPPED	UNWRUNG.	INQUIRY	+HORATIO	DOUBTED
SNAPPER	ANISEED	INSULAR	HOSANNA	DOUBTER
SNIPING	ANOSMIA	INSULIN	+JOCASTA	FOBBING
SNIPPED	GNASHED	INSURED	LOCALLY	FOGBANK
SNIPPET	GNOSTIC	INSURER	LOCATED	FORBADE
UNSPENT.	*KNOSSOS	UNBUILT	LOVABLE	FORBEAR
UNEQUAL.	ONESELF	UNGUENT	LOVABLY	FORBORE
ANARCHY	UNASKED	UNLUCKY	LOYALLY	GOBBLER
ANEROID	UNUSUAL.	UNQUIET	LOYALTY	HOBBLED
ANGRIER	ANATOMY	UNQUOTE.	MONADIC	HOGBACK
ANGRILY	ANOTHER	KNAVERY	MONARCH	+HOLBEIN
ENCRUST	GNATHIC	KNAVISH.	MORAINE	HOMBURG
ENGRAFT	INITIAL	*ANTWERP	MORALLY	HOP-BINE
ENGRAIN	INSTALL	ANYWISE	MOVABLE	HOWBEIT
ENGRAVE	INSTANT	ENDWAYS	NOMADIC	JOBBERY
ENGROSS	INSTATE	ENDWISE	NOTABLE	JOBBING
ENTRAIN	INSTEAD	ENTWINE	NOTABLY	LOBBIED
ENTRANT	KNITTED	GNAWING	PODAGRA	LOBBING
ENTREAT	KNITTER	INKWELL	POLACCA	LOG-BOOK
ENTROPY	KNOTTED	KNOW-ALL	POMATUM	LOW-BORN
ENTRUST	SNATCHY	KNOW-HOW	POTABLE	LOW-BRED
GNARLED	UNCTION	KNOWING	ROMANCE	LOWBROW
INBREED	UNITARY	*SNOWDON	ROMANIC	MOBBING
INCRUST	UNITING	SNOWILY	ROTATED	NOBBING
INDRAWN	UNITIVE	SNOWING	ROTATOR	NOBBLER
INERTIA	UNSTICK	SNOWMAN	+ROUAULT	ROBBERY
INERTLY	UNSTRAP	UNAWARE	ROYALLY	ROBBING
INGRAIN	UNSTUCK.	UNTWINE	ROYALTY	ROEBUCK
INGRATE	ANGUINE	UNTWIST.	SOLACED	SOBBING
INGRESS	ANGUISH	INEXACT.	SOMATIC	TOMBOLA
INTRANT	ANGULAR	ENVYING	TOBACCO	TOP-BOOT
INTROIT	ANNUITY	UNDYING	TOTALLY	WOBBLED.
INTRUDE	ANNULAR		TOWARDS	BOSCAGE
INTRUST	ANNULET	BORACIC	VOCABLE	BOTCHER
INURING	+ANQUILH	BOTANIC	VOCALIC	BOYCOTT

COACHED	CORDITE	BOREDOM	ROSEBUD	FORGERY
CONCAVE	DOODLED	CODEINE	ROSE-CUT	FORGING
CONCEAL	DOWDILY	COGENCY	ROSEOLA	FORGIVE
CONCEDE	FOLDING	COHERER	ROSETTE	FORGONE
CONCEIT	FONDLED	COTERIE	ROWELED	GOGGLED
CONCEPT	FORDING	COVERED	SOBERED	GORGING
CONCERN	GOADING	COVETED	SOBERLY	GOUGING
CONCERT	GODDAMN	COWERED	SOMEHOW	HOGGING
CONCISE	GODDESS	COZENER	SOMEONE	HOGGISH
CONCOCT	+GOLDING	DOLEFUL	TOTEMIC.	JOGGING
CONCORD	GONDOLA	*DONEGAL	BONFIRE	JOGGLED
CONCUSS	GOOD-BYE	DOVECOT	CODFISH	LODGING
COUCHED	GOODISH	DOVEKIE	COMFORT	LOGGING
COXCOMB	GOODMAN	FOREARM	COMFREY	LONGBOW
DOUCEUR	*GOODWIN	FOREIGN	CONFESS	LONGEST
DOUCHED	GORDIAN	FORELEG	CONFIDE	LONGING
FORCING	HOLDALL	FOREMAN	CONFINE	MONGREL
HOICKED	HOLDING	FORESAW	CONFIRM	NOGGING
MOOCHED	HOODING	FORESEE	CONFLUX	ROUGHEN
NOTCHED	HOODLUM	FORETOP	CONFORM	ROUGHER
POACHED	HORDING	FOREVER	CONFUSE	ROUGHLY
POACHER	+HOUDINI	GOBELIN	CONFUTE	ROUGING
POPCORN	LOADING	HOMERIC	DOGFISH	SOGGILY
PORCINE	LORDING	HONESTY	FORFEIT	SORGHUM
POUCHED	LOUDEST	HONEYED	+GODFREY	SOUGHED
SORCERY	LOW-DOWN	HOPEFUL	HOTFOOT	TONGUED
TOCCATA	MOIDORE	HOVERED	LOAFING	TOUGHEN
TOP-COAT	MOODILY	HOWEVER	*NORFOLK	TOUGHER
TOUCHED	MORDANT	+JOCELYN	*ROMFORD	TOUGHLY
VOICING	NODDING	LOBELIA	ROOFING	ZOOGAMY.
VOLCANO	PODDING	+LORELEI	SOUFFLE	BOXHAUL
VOUCHER.	POWDERY	LOZENGE	TOMFOOL	BOYHOOD
BOLDEST	ROAD-HOG	MODESTY	WOLFING	COCHLEA
BONDAGE	ROADMAN	MONEYED	WOLFISH	COWHERD
BONDING	ROADWAY	MORELLO	WOLFRAM.	COWHIDE
BONDMAN	RONDEAU	NOSEBAG	BOGGING	FOGHORN
BOUDOIR	ROWDIER	NOSEGAY	BOGGLER	FOXHOLE
CODDLED	ROWDILY	NOTEPAD	CONGEAL	FOXHUNT
COLDEST	SOLDIER	NOVELTY	CONGEST	GO-AHEAD
COLDISH	SORDINE	POLE-AXE	COUGHED	GODHEAD
CONDEMN	TODDLER	POLECAT	DODGING	GOSHAWK
CONDIGN	VOIDING	POLEMIC	DOGGART	GOTHICK
CONDOLE	WOODCUT	POLENTA	DOGGING	HOT-HEAD
CONDONE	WOODIER	POP-EYED	DOGGONE	JOSHING
CONDUCE	WOODMAN	POTENCE	DOUGHTY	*LOTHIAN
CONDUIT	WORDILY	POTENCY	*DOUGLAS	NOSHING
CONDYLE	WORDING.	POVERTY	FOGGIER	NOTHING
CORDAGE	BODEFUL	POWERED	FOGGILY	NOWHERE
CORDATE	*BOHEMIA	+ROBERTA	FOGGING	POCHARD
CORDIAL	BONE-ASH	ROSEATE	FORGAVE	POT-HERB

-O-H---			-O-N---	
POTHOLE	TOPIARY	WORKDAY	GODLESS	COMMONS
POTHOOK	TOPICAL	WORKING	GOSLING	COMMUNE
SOPHISM	VOMITED.	WORKMAN	GOULASH	COMMUTE
SOPHIST	CONJOIN	WORK-OUT	*HOLLAND	DORMANT
TOEHOLD	CONJURE.	WORK-SHY	HOPLITE	FOAMING
YOGHURT.	BONKERS	*WORKSOP	HOWLING	FORMATE
BOLIVAR	BOOKING	YORKING	JOBLESS	FORMING
*BOLIVIA	BOOKISH	YORKIST.	JOLLIER	*FORMOSA
CODICIL	BOOKLET	BOILING	JOLLIFY	FORMULA
COLICKY	BOOKMAN	BOLLARD	JOLLITY	FOUMART
COLITIS	BOX-KITE	*BOULDER	JOYLESS	HOLMIUM
COMICAL	COCKADE	BOULTER	LOLLARD	HOLM-OAK
CONIFER	COCKILY	BOWLFUL	LOLLING	HORMONE
CO-PILOT	COCKING	BOWLINE	LOWLAND	LOAMING
COPIOUS	COCKNEY	BOWLING	MOLLIFY	LOOMING
*CORINTH	COCKPIT	COAL-BED	MOLLUSC	ROAMING
CO-TIDAL	CONKING	COAL-GAS	MOULDED	ROOMFUL
FOLIAGE	COOKERY	COALING	MOULDER	ROOMIER
FOLIATE	COOKING	COAL-PIT	MOULTED	ROOMING
GOLIARD	CORKAGE	COAL-TAR	NOBLEST	TOPMAST
GORILLA	CORKING	COAL-TIT	NORLAND	TOPMOST
HOLIDAY	DOCKAGE	CODLING	POLLACK	TORMENT
HOLIEST	DOCKING	COELIAC	POLLARD	*WOOMERA
HOMINID	*DORKING	COILING	POLLING	WORMING
*HONITON	FORKFUL	COLLAGE	+POLLOCK	ZOOMING.
HORIZON	FORKING	COLLATE	POLL-TAX	BONNILY
HOSIERY	HOCKING	COLLECT	POLLUTE	BOUNCER
IODIZED	HONKING	COLLEEN	POOLING	BOUNDER
IONIZED	HOOKING	COLLEGE	POTLUCK	COGNATE
LOGICAL	KOLKHOZ	COLLIDE	+POULENC	COGNIZE
MODICUM	LOCKING	COLLIER	POULTRY	COINAGE
MODISTE	LOCKJAW	COLLOID	ROLLING	COINING
MOHICAN	LOCK-OUT	COLLUDE	ROULADE	CONNATE
+MOLIERE	LOOKING	COOLANT	ROWLOCK	CONNECT
MONITOR	LOOK-OUT	COOLEST	SOILING	CONNING
MOTIVED	LOOK-SEE	COOLING	SOULFUL	CONNIVE
NODICAL	MOCKERY	COULDST	TOLLAGE	CONNOTE
NOMINAL	MOCKING	COULOMB	TOLLING	CORN-COB
NOMINEE	MONKISH	COULTER	TOOLING	CORNICE
NOTICED	NOCKING	COWLICK	TOWLINE	CORNILY
NOXIOUS	PORK-PIE	COWLING	WOOLLEN	CORNISH
POLICED	ROCKERY	FOALING	WORLDLY	COUNCIL
POLITIC	ROCKIER	FOILING	YOWLING	COUNSEL
PONIARD	ROCKILY	FOOLERY	ZOOLOGY.	COUNTED
POSITED	ROCKING	FOOLING	BOOMING	COUNTER
ROSINED	ROOKERY	FOOLISH	COAMING	COUNTRY
SOCIETY	ROOKING	FORLORN	COMMAND	COYNESS
SOLICIT	SOAKING	FOULARD	COMMEND	DONNING
SOLIDLY	+TOLKIEN	FOULING	COMMENT	DONNISH
TONIGHT	TOPKNOT	FOWLING	COMMODE	DOWNING

FOUNDER	CORONET	ROMPERS	MOORING	+FORSTER
FOUNDRY	+DOLORES	ROMPING	MOORISH	FOSSICK
HOBNAIL	+DOROTHY	SOAP-BOX	MOURNER	GODSEND
HORNING	HOMONYM	SOAPILY	NOURISH	GODSHIP
*HORNSEA	MONOCLE	SOAPING	POOR-BOX	GOSSIPY
HOUNDED	MONOMER	SOPPILY	POOREST	GOSSOON
+JOHNSON	*MOROCCO	SOPPING	PORRECT	HOGSKIN
JOINDER	MORONIC	SOUPCON	POURING	HOISTED
JOINING	MOTORED	TOMPION	ROARING	HOLSTER
JOINTED	SOJOURN	TOPPING	SOARING	HOOSGOW
JOINTER	SOLOIST	TOPPLED	SOPRANO	HORSING
JOINTLY	+SOLOMON	TORPEDO	SOUREST	HOUSING
JOUNCED	*TORONTO.	TOWPATH.	SOURING	+HOUSMAN
LOANING	COMPACT	BOUQUET	TORRENT	*HOUSTON
LOUNGER	COMPANY	COEQUAL	TOURING	JOUSTED
MOANING	COMPARE	CONQUER	TOURISM	LOBSTER
MOONBUG	COMPASS	+JONQUIL	TOURIST	LOOSELY
MOONING	COMPEER	RORQUAL	TOURNEY	LOOSEST
MOONLIT	COMPERE	*TORQUAY.	TOW-ROPE	LOUSILY
MORNING	COMPETE	BOARDER	WORRIED	MOBSTER
MOUNDED	COMPILE	BOORISH	WORRIER.	MOISTEN
MOUNTED	COMPLEX	BOURBON	BOASTER	MONSOON
NOONDAY	COMPORT	BOURDON	BOLSTER	MONSTER
POINTED	COMPOSE	BOURREE	BOOSTER	NOISIER
POINTER	COMPOST	COARSEN	BORSTAL	NOISILY
POUNCED	COMPOTE	COERCED	BOWSHOT	NOISOME
POUNDAL	COMPUTE	COMRADE	COASTAL	NON-STOP
POUNDER	COPPERY	CORRECT	COASTED	NONSUCH
ROUNDEL	COPPICE	CORRODE	COASTER	NONSUIT
ROUNDER	COPPING	CORRUPT	CONSENT	NOOSING
ROUNDLY	CORPORA	COURAGE	CONSIGN	POISING
ROUND-UP	COUPLER	COURIER	CONSIST	POSSESS
SOUNDED	COUPLET	COURSER	CONSOLE	POT-SHOT
SOUNDLY	DOLPHIN	COURTLY	CONSORT	ROASTED
TOENAIL	FOPPERY	DOG-ROSE	CONSULT	ROASTER
TONNAGE	FOPPISH	DOORMAN	CONSUME	ROISTER
TORNADO	*GOSPORT	DOORMAT	CORSAGE	ROOSTER
WOUNDED	HOOPING	DOORWAY	CORSAIR	+ROSSINI
YOUNGER.	HOPPING	FORRARD	CORSLET	ROUSING
*BOLOGNA	HOPPLED	FOURGON	COSSACK	ROUSTED
BOLONEY	HOSPICE	GOURMET	COWSLIP	SONSHIP
BORODIN	LOOPING	HOARDER	DOESKIN	SOUSING
BOROUGH	LOPPING	HORRIFY	DOGSKIN	TOASTER
COCONUT	MOPPING	JOURNAL	DOSSIER	+TOLSTOY
COCOTTE	MORPHIA	JOURNEY	DOSSING	TONSURE
COLOGNE	NONPLUS	JOY-RIDE	DOUSING	TOPSAIL
COLONEL	POMPANO	LOG-ROLL	DOWSING	TOPSIDE
COROLLA	*POMPEII	LOURING	FOISTED	TORSION
CORONAL	POMPOUS	MOORAGE	FORSAKE	TOSSING
CORONER	POPPING	MOORHEN	FORSOOK	TOUSLED

311

TOYSHOP	HOTTEST	ROOTAGE	BOXWOOD	APTERYX
WORSHIP	HOTTING	ROOTING	DOGWOOD	+OPHELIA
WORSTED.	JOG-TROT	ROOTLED	FORWARD	SPEEDED
BOATFUL	JOLTING	ROSTRAL	FORWENT	SPEEDER
BOATING	JOSTLED	ROSTRUM	HOGWASH	SPHERIC
BOATMAN	JOTTING	ROTTING	LOBWORM	SPIELER
BOBTAIL	LOATHED	ROUTINE	LOGWOOD	SPLENIC
BOLTING	LOATHLY	ROUTING	*NORWICH.	UPHEAVE.
BOOTLEG	LOFTIER	SOFTEST	COAXING	EPIGRAM.
BOTTLED	LOFTILY	SOOTHED	COEXIST	SPY-HOLE
BOX-TREE	LOFTING	SOOTILY	HOAXING.	UPTHROW.
COATING	LOOTING	SORTING	COPY-CAT	APHIDES
+COCTEAU	LOTTERY	SOTTISH	COPYIST	APRICOT
COLTISH	LOUTISH	SOUTANE	POLYGON	EPSILON
CONTACT	MONTAGE	TONTINE	POLYMER	OPHIDIA
CONTAIN	+MONTAGU	TOOTHED	POLYNIA	OPPIDAN
CONTEMN	*MONTANA	*TOOTING	POLYPOD	OPTICAL
CONTEND	MONTHLY	TOOTLED	POLYPUS	OPTIMUM
CONTENT	MOOTING	TORTILE	TOBY-JUG.	SPLICED
CONTEST	MORTIFY	TORTURE	SOZZLED	SPLINED
CONTEXT	MORTISE	TOTTERY		SPOILED
CONTORT	MOTTLED	TOTTING	APHASIA	SPRIGHT
CONTOUR	MOUTHED	TOUTING	APPAREL	SPRINGY
CONTROL	NOCTULE	VOLTAGE	SPEAKER	UPRIGHT
CORTEGE	NOCTURN	VOLTAIC	SPEARED	UPTIGHT.
COSTARD	NORTHER	VOLTING	SPLASHY	SPIKING.
COSTATE	NOSTRIL	ZOOTOMY.	SPLAYED	APOLOGY
COSTEAN	NOSTRUM	FOCUSED	SPRAYER	APPLAUD
COSTING	POETESS	JOCULAR	UPWARDS.	APPLIED
COSTIVE	POETIZE	NODULAR	EPICENE	OPALINE
COSTUME	PONTIFF	NON-USER	EPICURE	OPULENT
COTTAGE	PONTIFY	POPULAR	EPOCHAL	SPELLED
COTTIER	PONTOON	ROGUERY	OPACITY	SPELLER
COTTONY	PORTAGE	ROGUISH	SPACING	SPELTER
DOGTROT	PORTEND	+ROMULUS	SPECIAL	SPILLED.
DOLTISH	PORTENT	ROTUNDA	SPECIES	SPUMING.
DOTTING	PORTICO	SOLUBLE	SPECIFY	APANAGE
+FONTEYN	PORTING	TOLUENE	SPECKED	APTNESS
FOOTAGE	PORTION	VOLUBLE	SPECKLE	OPENING
FOOTING	PORTRAY	VOLUTED.	SPECTRA	OPINING
FOOTPAD	POSTAGE	CONVENE	SPECTRE	OPINION
FOOTWAY	POSTBAG	CONVENT	SPECULA	SPANCEL
FORTIFY	POSTERN	CONVERT	SPICIER	SPANGLE
FORTUNE	POSTING	CONVICT	SPICILY	SPANIEL
FOX-TROT	POSTMAN	CONVOKE	SPICING.	SPANISH
GOATISH	POSTURE	CORVINE	SPIDERY.	SPANKED
HOOTING	POST-WAR	COUVADE	APHELIA	SPANKER
HOSTAGE	POTTERY	SOLVENT	APHESIS	SPANNED
HOSTESS	POTTING	SOLVING.	APPEASE	SPANNER
HOSTILE	POUTING	+BOSWELL	APTERAL	+SPENCER

312

SPENDER	EPITHET	ARRANGE	DRIBLET	PRECESS
SPINACH	EPITOME	BREADED	DRUBBED	PRECISE
SPINDLE	SPATIAL	BREADTH	FRIBBLE	PRICING
SPINDLY	SPATTER	BREAKER	GRABBED	PRICKER
SPINNER	SPATULA	BREAK-UP	GRABBER	PRICKET
SPINNEY	SPITING	BREATHE	GRABBLE	PRICKLE
SPIN-OFF	SPITTED	BROADEN	GRUBBED	PRICKLY
SPINOUS	SPITTLE	BROADER	GRUBBER	PROCEED
+SPINOZA	SPOTTED	BROADLY	PREBEND	PROCESS
SPONDEE	SPOTTER	CREAKED	PROBANG	PROCTOR
SPONDYL	SPUTNIK	CREAMED	PROBATE	PROCURE
SPONGER	SPUTTER	CREAMER	PROBING	TRACERY
SPONSOR.	UPSTAGE	CREASED	PROBITY	TRACHEA
APHONIC	UPSTAIR	CREATED	PROBLEM	TRACING
APPOINT	UPSTART.	CREATOR	TREBLED	TRACKED
APROPOS	EPAULET	CROAKER	TRIBUNE	TRACKER
OPPOSER	SPLURGE	DREADED	TRIBUTE.	TRACTOR
SPLODGE	SPOUTED	DREAMER	+ARACHNE	TRICEPS
SPLOTCH	SPRUCED	ERRANCY	BRACING	TRICING
SPOOFED	UPSURGE.	ERRATIC	BRACKEN	TRICKED
SPOOLED	*IPSWICH	ERRATUM	BRACKET	TRICKLE
SPOONED.	SPAWNED	FREAKED	BRECCIA	TRICKSY
APPRISE	SPEWING	GREASED	BRICKED	TROCHEE
APPROVE	UPSWEPT.	GREASER	BRICOLE	TRUCKED
EPERGNE	SPAYING.	GREATER	BROCADE	TRUCKLE
OPERATE	EPIZOON	GREATLY	BROCKET	WRECKED
OPPRESS		GREAVES	CRACKED	WRECKER.
		GROANED	CRACKER	ARIDITY
SPARELY	AQUATIC	KRAALED	CRACKLE	BRADAWL
SPARING	EQUABLE	ORGANIC	CRACK-UP	BRIDGED
SPARKED	EQUABLY	ORGANON	CRICKED	+BRIDGET
SPARKLE	EQUALLY	TREACLE	CRICKET	BRIDLED
SPARRED	EQUATED	TREACLY	CROCHET	BRIDOON
SPARROW	EQUATOR	TREADLE	CROCKET	CRUDELY
SPARTAN	SQUAILS	TREASON	CRUCIAL	CRUDITY
SPIRANT	SQUALID	TREATED	CRUCIFY	DREDGER
SPIRING	SQUALLY	TRIABLE	DRACHMA	DRUDGED
SPIRTED	SQUALOR	TRUANCY	ERECTED	DRY-DOCK
SPORRAN	SQUARED	WREAKED	ERECTLY	ERODENT
SPORTED	SQUASHY.	WREATHE.	ERECTOR	ERODING
SPURNED	AQUEOUS	ARABIAN	FRECKLE	ERUDITE
SPURRED	EQUERRY	ARM-BAND	FRECKLY	GRADATE
SPURTED	SQUEAKY	BRIBERY	FROCKED	GRADELY
UPBRAID	SQUEEZE	BRIBING	GRACILE	GRADING
UP-GRADE.	SQUELCH.	CRABBED	GRACING	GRADUAL
APOSTLE	EQUINOX	CRIBBED	GRECIAN	GRIDDLE
EPISODE	SQUIFFY	CRIBBER	GRECISM	GRIDING
EPISTLE	SQUINCH	CRY-BABY	GROCERY	GRUDGED
OPOSSUM		DRABBLE	PRECEDE	IRIDIUM
SPASTIC.	+ARIADNE	DRIBBLE	PRECEPT	IRIDIZE
EPITAPH	ARRAIGN			

313

PREDICT	GRAFTER	ARBITER	PROLATE	PRIMATE
PRIDING	GRIFFIN	ARMIGER	PROLONG	PRIMELY
PRODDED	GRUFFLY	ARRIVAL	TRELLIS	PRIMING
PRODDER	ORIFICE	ARRIVED	TRILITH	PRIMMED
PRODIGY	PREFACE	ARTICLE	TRILLED	PRIMULA
PRODUCE	PREFECT	ARTISAN	TRILOGY	PROMISE
PRODUCT	PROFANE	ARTISTE	TROLLED	PROMOTE
PRUDENT	PROFESS	BRAIDED	TROLLEY	TRAM-CAR
PRUDERY	PROFFER	BRAILLE	TROLLOP.	TRAMMED
PRUDISH	PROFILE	BRAINED	ARAMAIC	TRAMMEL
TRADE-IN	PROFUSE	BRAISED	BRAMBLE	TRAMPED
TRADING	TRAFFIC	BROILER	BRIMFUL	TRAMPLE
TRADUCE	TREFOIL	BRUISED	BRIMMER	TRAMWAY
TREDDLE	TRIFLED	CRUISED	BROMATE	TREMBLE
TRIDENT	TRIFLER	CRUISER	BROMIDE	TREMBLY
TRODDEN	TRIFORM	DRAINED	BROMINE	TREMOLO
+TRUDEAU	TRUFFLE.	DRAINER	BRUMOUS	TRIMMED
TRUDGED.	BRAGGED	DRUIDIC	CRAMMED	TRIMMER
ARDENCY	BRIGADE	FRAIBLE	CRAMMER	TROMMEL
ARSENAL	BRIGAND	FRAILLY	CRAMPED	TRUMPED
ARSENIC	DRAGGED	FRAILTY	CRAMPON	TRUMPET.
+ARTEMIS	DRAGGLE	FREIGHT	CREMATE	*ARUNDEL
*BRAEMAR	DRAG-NET	FRUITER	CRIMPED	BRANDED
BREEDER	DRAGOON	GRAINED	CRIMSON	+BRENDAN
BRIEFLY	DRUGGED	GROINED	CRUMBLE	BRINDLE
CREEPER	DRUGGET	ORBITAL	CRUMBLY	BRONCHI
+CROESUS	FRAGILE	ORBITED	CRUMPET	+BRONWEN
CRUELLY	FRIGATE	ORDINAL	CRUMPLE	CRANAGE
CRUELTY	FROGGED	PRAIRIE	DROMOND	CRANIAL
FREEDOM	FROGMAN	PRAISED	DRUMLIN	CRANING
FREEING	+GREGORY	TRAILED	DRUMMED	CRANIUM
FREEMAN	GROGRAM	TRAILER	DRUMMER	CRANKED
FREESIA	PRIGGED	TRAINEE	EREMITE	CRENATE
FREEZER	PROGENY	TRAINER	FRAMING	CRINGED
GREENER	PROGRAM	TRAIPSE	GRAMMAR	CRINGLE
GREETED	TRAGEDY	TRAITOR.	GRAMPUS	CRINKLE
GRIEVED	TRIGGER	PROJECT.	GREMLIN	CRINKLY
ORDERED	TRIGLOT	BROKING	GRIMACE	CRINOID
ORDERLY	*URUGUAY	PRAKRIT	GRIMMER	CRUNCHY
PRAETOR	WRIGGLE.	TREKKED.	*GRIMSBY	DRINKER
PRE-EMPT	ARCHAIC	ARMLESS	GROMMET	DRONING
PREENED	ARCHERY	ARTLESS	GRUMBLE	DRUNKEN
TREEING	ARCHING	DRILLED	GRUMMET	+FRANCIS
URAEMIA	ARCHWAY	FRILLED	KREMLIN	FRANKLY
URGENCY.	BRAHMIN	GRILLED	KRIMMER	FRANTIC
CROFTER	+GRAHAME	*IRELAND	PREMIER	FRINGED
DRAFTED	ORCHARD	PRALINE	PREMISE	FRONTAL
DRAFTEE	ORPHEAN	PRELACY	PREMIUM	FRONTED
DRIFTER	+ORPHEUS	PRELATE	PRIMACY	GRANARY
GRAFTED	ORPHREY.	PRELUDE	PRIMARY	GRANDAD

GRANDEE	CRYOGEN	TROPISM	FROSTED	GRATIFY
GRANDER	DROOLED	TRYPSIN	FRUSTUM	GRATING
GRANDLY	DROOPED	WRAPPED	GRASPER	GRITTED
GRANDMA	GROOMED	WRAPPER.	GRASSED	IRATELY
GRANDPA	GROOVER	BRIQUET	GRISKIN	ORATING
GRANITE	ORTOLAN	CROQUET.	GRISTLE	ORATION
GRANTED	PROOFED	PRURIGO	GRISTLY	ORATORY
GRANTEE	TRIOLET	TRIREME.	GROSSED	OROTUND
GRANTOR	TROOPER.	ARISING	GROSSLY	PRATING
GRANULE	CRIPPLE	BRASHLY	IRKSOME	PRATTLE
*GRENADA	CROPPED	BRASSIE	PRESAGE	PRETEND
GRENADE	CROPPER	BRISKET	PRESENT	PRETEXT
GRINDER	CRUPPER	BRISKLY	PRESIDE	PRITHEE
GRINNED	CRYPTIC	BRISTLE	PRESSED	PROTEAN
GRUNTED	DRAPERY	BRISTLY	PRESSER	PROTECT
IRANIAN	DRAPING	*BRISTOL	*PRESTON	PROTEGE
IRONING	DRIP-DRY	BRUSHED	PRESUME	PROTEID
IRONIST	DRIPPED	BRUSQUE	PROSAIC	PROTEIN
PRANCED	DROPLET	CRASHED	PROSILY	PROTEST
PRANKED	DROP-OUT	CRASSLY	PROSING	+PROTEUS
PRINTED	DROPPED	CRESSET	PROSODY	TRITELY
PRINTER	DROPPER	CRESTED	PROSPER	TRITIUM
PRONGED	ERUPTED	CRISPER	PRUSSIC	+TROTSKY
PRONOUN	GRAPERY	CROSIER	TRASHED	TROTTER
PRUNING	GRAPHIC	CROSSED	TRESSED	URETHRA
TRANSIT	GRAPNEL	CROSSLY	TRESTLE	WRITE-UP
TRANSOM	GRAPPLE	CRUSADE	TRISECT	WRITHED
TRENDED	GRIPING	CRUSHED	*TRISTAN	WRITING
TRINGLE	GRIPPED	CRUSTED	TRUSSED	WRITTEN.
TRINITY	GROPING	CRYSTAL	TRUSTED	ARBUTUS
TRINKET	GRYPHON	DRASTIC	TRUSTEE	ARCUATE
TRUNDLE	KRYPTOL	*DRESDEN	TRYSAIL	ARDUOUS
URANIAN	KRYPTON	+DRESFUS	TRYSTED	ARGUING
URANISM	PREPAID	DRESSED	WRESTED	AROUSED
URANIUM	PREPARE	DRESSER	WRESTLE.	BROUGHT
URANOUS	PREPUCE	DROSERA	*BRITAIN	CROUTON
URINARY	PROPANE	DROSHKY	BRITISH	DRAUGHT
WRANGLE	PROPHET	DRY-SHOD	BRITTLE	DROUGHT
WRINGER	PROPOSE	ERASING	BROTHEL	DROUTHY
WRINKLE	PROPPED	ERASION	BROTHER	FRAUGHT
WRONGLY	TRAPEZE	+ERASMUS	BRUTISH	GROUCHY
WRYNECK	TRAPPED	ERASURE	CRITTER	GROUPED
WRYNESS.	TRAPPER	EROSION	DRATTED	GROUSER
AREOLAR	TRAPSED	EROSIVE	EROTICA	GROUTED
ARMOURY	TREPANG	FRESHEN	FRETFUL	PROUDER
BRIOCHE	TRIPLED	FRESHER	FRET-SAW	PROUDLY
BROODED	TRIPLET	FRESHET	FRETTED	TRIUMPH
BRYOZOA	TRIPLEX	FRESHLY	FRITTED	TROUBLE
CROOKED	*TRIPOLI	FRISKED	FRITTER	TROUNCE
CROONER	TRIPPER	FRISKET	FROTHED	TROUPER

315

WROUGHT.	FROWARD	ISRAELI	ASSUAGE	UTTERLY.
BRAVADO	FROWNED	USUALLY.	ASSUMED	STAFFED
BRAVELY	FROWSTY	ISOBATH.	ASSURED	STIFFEN
BRAVERY	GROWLER	PSYCHIC.	ESQUIRE	STIFFER
BRAVEST	GROWN-UP	*ESKDALE	ESTUARY	STIFFLY
BRAVING	PRAWNED	ISODONT.	OSSUARY.	STIFLED
BRAVURA	PROWESS	ASCETIC	ASEXUAL.	STUFFED.
BREVIER	PROWLER	ASPERSE	ESPYING	STAGGER
BREVITY	TRAWLER.	ESSENCE		STAGING
CRAVING	*BRIXHAM	ESSENES	*ATLANTA	STYGIAN.
CREVICE	PROXIMO.	+ESTELLA	ATTACHE	ETCHING
DRIVE-IN	BRAYING	OSSEOUS	ATTAINT	ITCHING.
DRIVING	*CROYDEN	USHERED.	ETHANOL	ATHIRST
GRAVELY	DRAYMAN	*ASHFORD.	PTYALIN	ATTIRED
GRAVEST	FRAYING	ASPHALT	STEALTH	ETHICAL
GRAVING	GREYISH	ESCHEAT	STEAMED	STAIDLY
GRAVITY	GREYLAG	ESTHETE	STEAMER	STAINED
GRAVURE	GRUYERE	ISCHIAL	STEARIN	*STAINES
PREVAIL	PRAYING	ISCHIUM	STRAFED	STOICAL
PREVENT	PREYING	ISTHMUS.	STRANGE	STRIATE
PREVIEW	X-RAYING.	ASPIRED	STRATUM	STRIKER
PRIVACY	*ARIZONA	ASPIRIN	STRATUS	STRINGY
PRIVATE	BRAZIER	ASSIZES	+STRAUSS	STRIPED
PRIVILY	BRAZING	OSSICLE.	STRAYED.	STRIVEN
PRIVITY	CRAZIER	ISOLATE	STABBED	UTRICLE
PROVERB	CRAZILY	PSALTER	STABLED	+UTRILLO.
PROVIDE	CRAZING	USELESS.	STUBBED	STAKING
PROVING	DRIZZLE	+ISHMAEL.	STUBBLE	STOKING.
PROVISO	DRIZZLY	ASININE	STUBBLY.	ATELIER
PROVOKE	FRAZZLE	ASUNDER.	STACKED	ATHLETE
PROVOST	FRIZZED	ASTOUND	STICKED	ITALIAN
TRAVAIL	FRIZZLE	ESPOUSE	-STICKER	OTOLOGY
TRIVIAL	GRAZING	+OSBORNE	STOCKED	+PTOLEMY
TRIVIUM.	GRIZZLE	OSMOSIS	STUCK-UP.	STALEST
BRAWLER	GRIZZLY	OSMOTIC.	STADIUM	STALKED
BREWAGE	PRIZING	ASEPSIS	STUDDED	STALKER
BREWERY		ASEPTIC.	STUDENT	STALLED
BREWING	ASHAMED	ASCRIBE	STUDIED.	STELLAR
BROWNED	ASIATIC	+ASTRAEA	ATHEISM	STILLED
BROWNIE	ASKANCE	ASTRIDE	ATTEMPT	STILLER
BROWSED	ASSAGAI	ESTRIOL	STEELED	STILTED
CRAWLER	ASSAULT	ESTRONE	STEEPED	*STILTON
CROWBAR	ASSAYED	G-STRING	STEEPEN	STYLING
CROWDED	+ASTARTE	OSTRICH	STEEPER	STYLISH
CROWING	ASTATIC	USURPER.	STEEPLE	STYLIST
CROWNED	ESCAPED	ASHTRAY	STEERER	STYLITE
DRAWING	ESCAPEE	ISATINE	STREAKY	STYLIZE
DRAWLED	ESPARTO	ISOTONE	STRETCH	UTILITY
DROWNED	ESSAYED	ISOTOPE.	STREWED	UTILIZE.
DROWSED	ISLAMIC	ASQUINT	UTTERED	ATOMIZE

316

ITEMIZE	ITERATE	STOWING.	MUMBLED	SUCCOUR
STAMINA	STARCHY	STAYING	NUMBING	SUCCUMB
STAMMER	STARDOM		OUTBACK	SUICIDE
STAMPED	STARING	AUBAINE	PURBECK	SURCOAT.
STEMMED	STARKLY	BUGABOO	QUABIRD	BUDDING
STIMULI	STARLET	BUYABLE	QUIBBLE	BUNDLED
STOMACH	STARLIT	*CURACAO	RUBBERY	BURDOCK
STOMATA	STARRED	CURATOR	RUBBING	CUDDLED
STUMBLE	STARTED	CUTAWAY	RUBBISH	CURDING
STUMPED	STARTER	DUPABLE	RUMBLED	CURDLED
STYMIED.	STARTLE	DURABLE	RUN-BACK	*DUNDALK
ATONING	STARVED	DURABLY	*SUDBURY	FUDDLED
ETONIAN	STERILE	DURAMEN	SUNBEAM	FUNDING
+STANLEY	STERNAL	DURANCE	SUNBURN	GUIDING
STANNEL	STERNER	HUMANLY	TUBBING	HUDDLED
STANNIC	STERNLY	JUDAISM	TUMBLED	HUMDRUM
STANNUM	STERNUM	JUDAIZE	TUMBLER	HUNDRED
STENCIL	STEROID	LUCARNE	TUMBREL	HURDLER
STEN-GUN	STIRRED	LUNATIC	TURBINE.	LUDDITE
STINKER	STIRRUP	LUXATED	BUNCHED	MUDDIED
STINTED	STORAGE	MULATTO	BUTCHER	MUDDLED
STONIER	STORIED	MUTABLE	CURCUMA	MUNDANE
STONING	STORING	MUTAGEN	DULCIFY	OUTDONE
STUNNER	STORMED	MUTATED	FULCRUM	OUTDOOR
STUNTED	STYRENE	*RUMANIA	FURCATE	PUDDING
UTENSIL.	UTERINE	RUNAWAY	FUSCOUS	PUDDLER
ATROPHY	YTTRIUM.	SUBACID	HUNCHED	QUADRAT
+ATROPOS	ETESIAN	SUGARED	HUTCHED	QUADREL
OTTOMAN	STASHED.	*SUMATRA	LUNCHED	RUB-DOWN
STOOGED	STATELY	+SUSANNA	LURCHED	RUDDIER
STOOKED	STATICE	TUNABLE	MULCHED	RUDDILY
STOOPED	STATICS	*YUCATAN.	MUNCHED	RUDDLED
STROKED	STATING	BUBBLED	MUSCLED	RUN-DOWN
STROPHE.	STATION	BUGBEAR	NUT-CASE	SUBDEAN
STAPLER	STATISM	BULBOUS	OUTCAST	SUBDUAL
+STEPHEN	STATURE	BURBLED	OUTCOME	SUBDUED
STEPPED	STATUTE	CUBBING	OUTCROP	SUNDIAL
STEPSON	STETSON	CURBING	+PUCCINI	SUNDOWN
STIPEND	STUTTER.	CUT-BACK	PUNCHED	SURDITY.
STIPPLE	ATTUNED	DUBBING	PUNCH-UP	AUREATE
STOPGAP	STAUNCH	FUMBLER	+PURCELL	AUREOLA
STOPPED	STOUTER	FURBALL	QUACKED	BUREAUX
STOPPER	STOUTLY.	FURBISH	QUICKEN	BURETTE
STOPPLE	ATAVISM	GUMBOIL	QUICKER	CURETTE
STUPEFY	STAVING.	GUNBOAT	QUICKIE	DUKEDOM
•STYPTIC	ATHWART	HUMBLED	QUICKLY	DUTEOUS
UTOPIAN.	STEWARD	HUSBAND	SUCCADE	EUGENIC
ATARAXY	+STEWART	JUMBLED	SUCCEED	+EUTERPE
ATTRACT	STEWING	LUMBAGO	SUCCESS	FUNERAL
ETERNAL	STOWAGE	MUD-BATH	SUCCOSE	HUMERAL

HUMERUS	SUFFUSE	FUCHSIA	HULKING	GUILDER
JUKEBOX	SURFACE	FUTHORC	HUNKERS	GULLING
*LUCERNE	SURFEIT	GUSHING	HUSKING	GUNLOCK
LUNETTE	SURFING	HUSHING	JUNKING	HULLING
LUTEOUS	TURFING.	PUSHING	LUCKIER	HURLING
NUMERAL	BUDGING	+PUSHKIN	LUCKILY	*JUTLAND
PUBERTY	BUGGERY	PUSHPIN	LURKING	LULLABY
PUDENDA	BUGGING	RUSHING	MUCKILY	LULLING
QUEENED	BULGING	AUDIBLE	MUCKING	MUDLARK
QUEENLY	BUNGLER	AUDITED	MURKILY	MULLING
QUEERER	BURGEON	AUDITOR	MUSK-RAT	MULLION
QUEERLY	BURGESS	AURICLE	PUCKISH	NUCLEAR
QUIETEN	BURGHER	BULIMIA	QUAKING	NUCLEIC
QUIETER	BURGLAR	CUBICLE	RUCKING	NUCLEON
QUIETLY	BURGLED	CURIOUS	SUCKING	NUCLEUS
QUIETUS	DUDGEON	CUTICLE	SUCKLED	NUCLIDE
RUBELLA	DUNGEON	DUBIETY	SULKILY	NULLIFY
RUBEOLA	FUNGOID	DUBIOUS	TUCK-BOX	NULLITY
SUB-EDIT	FUNGOUS	DUTIFUL	TUCKING	OUTLAST
SUBERIN	GUDGEON	FURIOUS	TURKISH.	OUTLIER
TUNEFUL	GURGLED	FUSIBLE	BUGLING	OUTLINE
TUTELAR	HUGGING	HUMIDOR	BUGLOSS	OUTLIVE
YULE-LOG.	*HUNGARY	JUBILEE	BUILDER	OUTLOOK
BUFFALO	JUGGING	JUJITSU	BUILT-IN	PUBLISH
BUFFING	JUGGLED	+JULIANA	BUILT-UP	PULLING
BUFFOON	JUGGLER	JUNIPER	BULLACE	PULLMAN
CUFFING	LUGGAGE	+JUPITER	BULLATE	PURLIEU
DUFFING	LUGGING	LUCIDLY	BULLDOG	PURLING
FUN-FAIR	LUNGING	LURIDLY	BULLIED	PURLOIN
GUNFIRE	MUGGING	MUJITSA	BULLION	QUALIFY
HUFFILY	MUGGINS	+MURILLO	BULLISH	QUALITY
HUFFING	NUDGING	MUSICAL	BULLOCK	QUELLED
HUFFISH	OUTGONE	PURITAN	*CUILLIN	QUILLED
MUDFISH	OUTGREW	QUAILED	CULLING	QUILTED
MUDFLAP	OUTGROW	*SURINAM	CURLING	*RUTLAND
MUDFLAT	PUGGING	*TUNISIA.	CUTLASS	SUBLIME
MUFFING	PUNGENT	SUBJECT	CUTLERY	SULLIED
MUFFLED	PURGING	SUBJOIN.	DUALISM	SUNLESS
MUFFLER	SUGGEST	BUCKING	DUALITY	SURLIER
OUTFACE	SURGEON	BUCKISH	DUALIZE	SURLILY
OUTFALL	SURGERY	BUCKLED	DUELLED	SURLOIN.
OUTFLOW	SURGING	BUCKRAM	DUELLER	AUGMENT
PUFFING	TUGGING	BUNKING	DULLARD	BUMMALO
QUAFFED	VULGATE.	BUSKING	DULLEST	GUMMING
RUFFIAN	BUSHIDO	CUCKOLD	DULLING	HUMMING
RUFFING	BUSHMAN	DUCKING	DULLING	HUMMOCK
RUFFLED	CUSHION	DUNKING	FUELLED	HUTMENT
SUBFUSC	DUCHESS	DUSKIER	FULLEST	MUMMERY
SUFFICE	EUCHRED	DUSKILY	FURLING	MUMMIFY
*SUFFOLK	EUPHONY		FURLONG	MUMMING
			GUELDER	

OUTMOST	BUBONIC	CURRIED	PURSUER	FUSTILY
PUG-MILL	BUCOLIC	CURRISH	PURSUIT	GUTTATE
RUMMAGE	+RUDOLPH	+DURRELL	QUASHED	GUTTING
RUMMILY	TUTORED.	FURRIER	QUASSIA	HUNTING
SUMMARY	AUSPICE	FURRING	QUESTED	HURTFUL
SUMMERY	BUMPING	GUARDED	*RUISLIP	HURTING
SUMMING	BUMPKIN	GUERDON	+RUSSELL	HURTLED
SUMMONS	BURPING	GUNROOM	RUSSIAN	HUSTLER
SURMISE	CULPRIT	HURRIED	RUSSIFY	HUTTING
TURMOIL.	CUPPING	MURRAIN	SUASION	JUSTICE
BURNING	CUSPATE	OUTRAGE	SUASIVE	JUSTIFY
BURNISH	DUMPING	OUTRIDE	SUBSIDE	+JUSTINE
*BURNLEY	GUIPURE	OUTRODE	SUBSIDY	JUTTING
BURNOUS	GULPING	PUERILE	SUBSIST	LUSTFUL
CUNNING	HUMPING	PURRING	SUBSOIL	LUSTILY
DUNNAGE	JUMPING	PUTREFY	SUBSUME	LUSTING
DUNNING	LUMPISH	QUARREL	SUNSPOT	LUSTRAL
FUNNILY	OUTPLAY	QUARTAN	SUSSING	MUSTANG
FURNACE	OUTPOST	QUARTER	TUESDAY	MUSTARD
FURNISH	PULPIFY	QUARTET	TUSSLED	NUPTIAL
GUNNAGE	PULPING	QUERIED	TUSSOCK	NURTURE
GUNNERY	PUMPING	QUERIST	TUSSORE.	NUTTING
GUNNING	PUMPKIN	SUCROSE	AUCTION	OUSTING
NUNNERY	PUPPING	SUNRISE	AUSTERE	OUTTALK
PUG-NOSE	PURPLED	SUPREME.	AUSTRAL	PUNTING
PUNNING	PURPORT	AUSSIES	*AUSTRIA	PUSTULE
QUANTUM	PURPOSE	BURSARY	BUNTING	PUTTIER
+QUENTIN	QUIPPED	CUISINE	BUSTARD	PUTTING
QUINARY	RUMPLED	CURSING	BUSTING	QUITTED
QUININE	SUBPLOT	CURSIVE	BUSTLED	QUITTER
QUINTAN	SULPHUR	CURSORY	BUTTERY	QUOTING
QUINTET	SUPPING	CUSSING	BUTTOCK	RUPTION
QUONDAM	SUPPLED	FULSOME	CULTURE	RUPTURE
RUINATE	SUPPORT	FUSSING	CURTAIL	RUSTIER
RUINING	SUPPOSE	FUSS-POT	CURTAIN	RUSTILY
RUINOUS	SURPASS	GUESSED	CURTSEY	RUSTING
RUMNESS	SURPLUS	GUNSHOT	CUSTARD	RUSTLED
RUNNING	SUSPECT	JUSSIVE	CUSTODY	RUSTLER
SUNNIER	SUSPEND	NURSERY	CUTTING	RUTTING
SUNNING	SUSPIRE	NURSING	DUCTILE	RUTTISH
SURNAME	VULPINE.	OURSELF	DUOTONE	SUBTEND
TURNERY	CUMQUAT	OUTSAIL	DUSTBIN	SUCTION
TURNING	KUMQUAT.	OUTSIDE	DUSTIER	SUITING
TURNKEY	BULRUSH	OUTSIZE	DUSTILY	SULTANA
TURN-OUT.	CUIRASS	OUTSPAN	DUSTING	SUN-TRAP
AUROCHS	CUPRITE	OUTSTAY	DUSTMAN	SUSTAIN
AURORAL	CUPROUS	PULSATE	DUSTPAN	TUFTING
AUTOCAR	CURRACH	PULSING	FURTHER	TUITION
AUTOMAT	CURRANT	PUNSTER	FURTIVE	TUTTING
AUTOPSY	CURRENT	PURSING	FUSTIAN	VULTURE

AUGURED	EVIDENT	SWEEPER	SWIRLED	EXILING
CUMULUS	OVIDUCT.	SWEETEN	TWIRLED.	EXPLAIN
FUGUIST	OVIFORM.	SWEETER	AWESOME	EXPLODE
JUGULAR	*AVIGNON.	SWEETIE	SWASHED	EXPLOIT
SUTURAL	AVAILED.	SWEETLY	SWISHED	EXPLORE
SUTURED	EVOKING.	TWEEZER.	TWISTER	EXULTED.
TUBULAR	EVOLVED.	SWIFTER	TWOSOME	EXAMINE
TUMULUS.	AVENGER	SWIFTLY	TWO-STEP.	EXAMPLE.
CULVERT	EVENING	TWOFOLD.	SWATHED	OXONIAN.
CURVATE	EVINCED.	SWAGGER	SWATTED	EXPOSAL
CURVING	AVARICE	SWAGMAN	SWATTER	EXPOSED.
FULVOUS	AVERAGE	SWIGGED	SWOTTED	EXCRETA
OUTVOTE	AVERRED	TWIGGED.	TWITTED	EXCRETE
PURVIEW	AVERTED	SWAHILI.	TWITTER	EXERTED
SUAVELY	*EVEREST	AWAITED.	TWO-TIME.	EXPRESS
SUAVITY	EVERTED	DWELLER	AWFULLY.	EXTRACT
SUBVERT	OVARIAN	SWALLOW	AWKWARD.	EXTREME
SURVIVE.	OVERACT	SWELLED	SWAYING.	EXTRUDE.
BULWARK	OVERALL	SWELTER	SWIZZLE	EXISTED.
GUNWALE	OVERARM	SWILLED		EXITING.
MUGWUMP	OVERAWE	SWOLLEN	AXIALLY	EXCUSED
OUTWARD	OVERDID	TWELFTH	EXHALED	EXHUMED
OUTWEAR	OVERDUE	TWILLED.	EXHAUST	EXPUNGE
OUTWENT	OVERLAP	SWAMPED	EXPANSE.	
OUTWORE	OVERLAY	SWIMMER.	EXACTED	DYNAMIC
OUTWORK	OVERRAN	DWINDLE	EXACTLY	DYNASTY
OUTWORN	OVERRUN	*SWANAGE	EXACTOR	GYRATED
SUNWARD	OVERSAW	SWANKED	EXECUTE	HYDATID
SUNWISE.	OVERSEA	*SWANSEA	EXSCIND.	PYJAMAS
+QUIXOTE.	OVERSEE	SWINDLE	EXUDING	PYRAMID
BUOYAGE	OVERSET	*SWINDON	OXIDANT	SYNAPSE
BUOYANT	OVERSEW	SWINGER	OXIDASE	TYRANNY.
BUTYRIC	OVERTAX	SWINGLE	OXIDIZE.	CYMBALO
JURYMAN.	OVERTLY	SWINISH	AXLE-BOX	EYEBALL
BUZZARD	OVERTOP.	TWANGED	AXLE-PIN	EYE-BATH
BUZZING	EVASION	TWINGED	EXCERPT	EYE-BOLT
GUZZLER	EVASIVE.	TWINING	EXPENSE.	EYEBROW
MUEZZIN	OVATION.	TWINKLE	EXIGENT	SYMBION.
MUZZLED	AVOWING	TWINNED	EXOGAMY.	LYNCHED
NUZZLED		TWIN-SET.	EXCISED	SYNCARP
PUZZLER	SWEARER	SWOONED	EXCITED	SYNCOPE.
QUIZZED	SWEATED	SWOOPED.	EXHIBIT	LYDDITE
	SWEATER	SWAPPED	EXPIATE	+WYNDHAM.
AVIATOR.	TWEAKED.	SWIPING	EXPIRED	HYPERON
*AVEBURY.	SWABBED	SWOPPED.	EXTINCT.	PYRETIC
AVOCADO	SWABBER.	AWARDED	AXOLOTL	PYREXIA
EVACUEE	SWADDLE	DWARFED	EXALTED	SYNERGY.
EVICTED.	SWEDISH	SWARMED	EXCLAIM	NYLGHAU.
AVIDITY	TWADDLE	SWARTHY	EXCLUDE	EYEHOLE
EVADING	TWIDDLE.	SWERVED	EXILIAN	TYPHOID

TYPHOON	MYSTIFY	UNAWARE.	GRANDAD	SCALENE
TYPHOUS.	SYSTOLE	BLABBED	GRANDEE	SEA-LEGS
CYNICAL	SYSTYLE.	BRAMBLE	GRANDER	SEAWEED
HYGIENE	ZYMURGY.	CHAMBER	GRANDLY	SHAPELY
LYRICAL	SYLVINE.	CLAMBER	GRANDMA	SIAMESE
PYRITES	EYEWASH	COAL-BED	GRANDPA	SLAVERY
SYRINGA		CRABBED	GUARDED	SPARELY
SYRINGE	TZIGANE.	DRABBLE	HEARDIN	STALEST
TYPICAL.	+EZEKIEL.	FRAIBLE	HOARDER	STATELY
CYCLING	AZIMUTH	GEAR-BOX	+LEANDER	SUAVELY
CYCLIST	AZYMOUS.	GRABBED	MEANDER	TEA-LEAF
CYCLOID	AZURINE	GRABBER	+PHAEDRA	TRACERY
CYCLONE	CZARDAS	GRABBLE	PLAUDIT	TRADE-IN
CYCLOPS	CZARINA	PEAT-BOG	SCALDED	TRAGEDY
EYELASH		PLAYBOY	SCANDAL	TRAPEZE
EYELESS		SCABBED	SKALDIC	WEAKEST
HYALINE	ADAMANT	SHAMBLE	SLANDER	WHATEER.
HYALITE	*ALABAMA	SJAMBOK	STAIDLY	BOATFUL
HYALOID.	APANAGE	SOAP-BOX	STARDOM	CHAFFER
PYGMEAN	ARAMAIC	STABBED	SWADDLE	CHAMFER
*WYOMING.	ATARAXY	SWABBED	TWADDLE	DWARFED
CYANIDE	BLATANT	SWABBER.	UNAIDED.	FEARFUL
GYMNAST	BRADAWL	*AJACCIO	ACADEMY	PLAYFUL
HYMNIST	BRAVADO	ANARCHY	ACALEPH	QUAFFED
HYMNODY	+CHAGALL	+BLANCHE	AMATEUR	SCAFFED
HYPNOID	CHARADE	CHANCED	ANALECT	SNAFFLE
LYING-IN	CLAMANT	CHANCEL	BRAVELY	STAFFED
LYINGLY.	CRANAGE	CHANCRE	BRAVERY	TEARFUL
MYCOSIS	DIABASE	+CHAUCER	BRAVEST	TRAFFIC
PYLORUS	EMANATE	DIARCHY	CHATEAU	WHARFED.
SYNODAL	GRADATE	FLACCID	DEAD-END	AMALGAM
SYNODIC	+GRAHAME	+FRANCIS	DEANERY	BRAGGED
SYNONYM	GRANARY	GLANCED	DEAREST	CHANGED
SYNOVIA	LEAFAGE	PRANCED	DIALECT	CHARGED
ZYMOTIC.	LEAKAGE	SCARCER	DRAPERY	CHARGER
NYMPHAL	PEASANT	SNATCHY	FLANEUR	CLANGED
NYMPHET	PHALANX	SPANCEL	GO-AHEAD	CLANGER
SYMPTOM.	PHARAOH	STARCHY	GRADELY	COAL-GAS
CYPRESS	PLACARD	TRAM-CAR.	GRAPERY	DRAGGED
CYPRIOT	PLACATE	ABANDON	GRAVELY	DRAGGLE
HYDRANT	PLAY-ACT	AWARDED	GRAVEST	DRAUGHT
HYDRATE	SEA-BANK	BLADDER	IMAGERY	FLAGGED
HYDRIDE	SEA-KALE	BLANDLY	INANELY	FLANGED
HYDROUS	SEA-MARK	BOARDER	IRATELY	FRAUGHT
PYRRHIC.	SEA-SALT	BRAIDED	KNAVERY	*GLASGOW
EYESHOT	SEA-WALL	BRANDED	NEAREST	REALGAR
EYESORE	SEAWARD	+CLAUDIA	PLACEBO	SHAGGED
HYOSCIN.	*SWANAGE	CZARDAS	PLATEAU	SLANGED
+CYNTHIA	TEACAKE	FLAG-DAY	REAGENT	SNAGGED
MYSTERY	TRAVAIL	GLADDEN	*SCAFELL	SPANGLE

STAGGER	ATAVISM	EGALITY	IMAGINE	*READING
SWAGGER	AVARICE	ELATING	IMAGING	REALISM
TEAR-GAS	BEADING	ELATION	IMAGISM	REALIST
TWANGED	BEAMING	ERASING	INANITY	REALITY
WRANGLE.	BEARING	ERASION	IRANIAN	REALIZE
+ARACHNE	BEARISH	EVADING	ISATINE	REAMING
BEACHED	BEATIFY	EVASION	ITALIAN	REAPING
BRASHLY	BEATING	EVASIVE	KHALIFA	REARING
*CHATHAM	BLAMING	EXAMINE	KNAVISH	ROAMING
CLASHED	BLARING	FEARING	LEADING	ROARING
COACHED	BLAZING	FLAKILY	LEAFING	SCABIES
CRASHED	BOATING	FLAKING	LEAKILY	SCALING
DEATHLY	BRACING	FLAMING	LEAKING	SCARIFY
DRACHMA	BRAVING	FLARING	LEANING	SCARING
FEATHER	BRAYING	FLAWING	LEAPING	SEABIRD
FLASHED	BRAZIER	FLAYING	LEASING	SEA-LINE
FLASHER	BRAZING	FOALING	LEAVING	SEALING
GNASHED	CEASING	FOAMING	LOADING	SEA-LION
GNATHIC	CHAFING	FRAGILE	LOAFING	SEA-MILE
GRAPHIC	CHALICE	FRAMING	LOAMING	SEAMING
HEATHEN	CHARILY	FRAYING	LOANING	SEA-PINK
+HEATHER	CHARIOT	GEARING	MEANING	SEARING
LEACHED	CHARITY	GLACIAL	MOANING	SEA-SICK
LEASHED	CHASING	GLACIER	NEARING	SEASIDE
LEATHER	CLARIFY	GLARING	OCARINA	SEATING
LOATHED	CLARION	GLAZIER	ONANISM	SHADIER
LOATHLY	CLARITY	GLAZING	ONANIST	SHADILY
POACHED	CLAVIER	GNAWING	OPACITY	SHADING
POACHER	CLAWING	GOADING	OPALINE	SHAKILY
QUASHED	COALING	GOATISH	ORATING	SHAKING
REACHED	COAMING	GRACILE	ORATION	SHAMING
ROAD-HOG	COATING	GRACING	OVARIAN	SHAPING
SCATHED	COAXING	GRADING	OVATION	SHARING
SLASHED	CRANIAL	GRANITE	PEAKING	SHAVING
SMASHED	CRANING	GRATIFY	PEALING	SKATING
SMASHER	CRANIUM	GRATING	PHASING	SLAKING
SMASH-UP	CRAVING	GRAVING	PIANIST	SLATING
STASHED	CRAZIER	GRAVITY	PLACING	SLAVING
SWASHED	CRAZILY	GRAZING	PLANING	SLAVISH
SWATHED	CRAZING	HEADING	PLANISH	SLAYING
TEACHER	CYANIDE	HEALING	PLATING	SNAKILY
TEACH-IN	CZARINA	HEAPING	PLAYING	SNAKING
TEA-SHOP	DEALING	HEARING	PRALINE	SNARING
TRACHEA	DIARIST	HEATING	PRATING	SOAKING
TRASHED	DRAPING	HEAVIER	PRAYING	SOAPILY
WEATHER.	DRAWING	HEAVILY	QUABIRD	SOAPING
AMANITA	DUALISM	HEAVING	QUAKING	SOARING
AMATIVE	DUALITY	HOAXING	QUALIFY	SPACING
AMAZING	DUALIZE	HYALINE	QUALITY	SPANIEL
ARABIAN	EDACITY	HYALITE	READILY	SPANISH

SPARING	CRANKED	LEAFLET	SWARMED	GLAMOUR
SPATIAL	FLANKER	MEASLES	TRAMMED	HYALOID
SPAYING	FRANKLY	PEARLED	TRAMMEL	JEALOUS
STADIUM	HEARKEN	PEARLER	UNARMED	ORATORY
STAGING	KNACKER	PHALLIC	URAEMIA.	PEACOCK
STAKING	PLACKET	PHALLUS	AGAINST	PEA-SOUP
STAMINA	PLANKED	PLAYLET	BEATNIK	PIANOLA
STARING	PRANKED	QUAILED	BLARNEY	PLATOON
STATICE	QUACKED	SCALLOP	BRAINED	PLAY-OFF
STATICS	SHACKED	SCARLET	CHAINED	SEA-COAL
STATING	SHACKLE	SHALLOP	CHANNEL	SEA-FOWL
STATION	SHARKED	SHALLOT	CHARNEL	SEAPORT
STATISM	SLACKEN	SHALLOW	CLAP-NET	SEA-ROOM
STAVING	SLACKER	SMALLER	DRAG-NET	SEA-WOLF
STAYING	SLACKLY	SNARLED	DRAINED	SHADOWY
SUASION	SMACKED	STABLED	DRAINER	TEA-COSY
SUASIVE	SMACKER	STALLED	FLANNEL	TEA-ROOM
SUAVITY	SPANKED	+STANLEY	GRAINED	TEA-ROSE
SWAHILI	SPANKER	STAPLER	GRAPNEL	URANOUS
SWAYING	SPARKED	STARLET	LEARNED	ZEALOUS.
TEAMING	SPARKLE	STARLIT	PLAINER	BEAR-PIT
TEARING	STACKED	SWALLOW	PLAINLY	CHAPPED
TEASING	STALKED	TRAILED	PLANNED	CLAMPED
THAWING	STALKER	TRAILER	PLANNER	CLAMPER
TRACING	STARKLY	TRAWLER.	PRAWNED	CLAPPED
TRADING	SWANKED	ANAEMIA	SCANNED	CLAPPER
URANIAN	THANKED	ANAEMIC	SPANNED	CLASPED
URANISM	TRACKED	BOATMAN	SPANNER	COAL-PIT
URANIUM	TRACKER	*BRAEMAR	SPAWNED	CRAMPED
WEANING	UNASKED	BRAHMIN	STAINED	CRAMPON
WEARIER	WHACKED.	CHAPMAN	*STAINES	DEADPAN
WEARILY	AVAILED	CHARMER	STANNEL	EXAMPLE
WEARING	+BEATLES	CLAIMED	STANNIC	FLAPPED
WEAVING	BRAILLE	CRAMMED	STANNUM	FLAPPER
WHALING	BRAWLER	CRAMMER	STAUNCH	GRAMPUS
X-RAYING.	CHABLIS	DRAYMAN	TRAINEE	GRAPPLE
BLACKEN	CHAPLET	+ERASMUS	TRAINER	GRASPER
BLACKER	+CHAPLIN	FLAGMAN	WHATNOT	KNAPPED
BLANKED	+CHARLES	GRAMMAR	YEARNED.	PLAYPEN
BLANKET	CRAWLER	HEADMAN	ABALONE	SCALPED
BLANKLY	DIALLED	MIASMAL	AMATORY	SCALPEL
BRACKEN	DRAWLED	PLASMIC	ANALOGY	SCALPER
BRACKET	ENABLED	READMIT	ANATOMY	SCAMPED
CLACKED	EPAULET	REARMED	CHAMOIS	SCAMPER
CLANKED	FLAILED	REAUMUR	CLAMOUR	SCARPED
CLARKIA	FLATLET	ROADMAN	DIABOLO	SHAMPOO
CRACKED	FRAILLY	SHAMMED	DIAMOND	SHARPEN
CRACKER	FRAILTY	SLAMMED	DRAGOON	SHARPER
CRACKLE	GNARLED	STAMMER	ENAMOUR	SLAPPED
CRACK-UP	KRAALED	SWAGMAN	FLAVOUR	SNAPPER

STAMPED	AWAITED	PIASTRE	GRAVURE	DUBIETY
SWAMPED	BEASTLY	PLAITED	MEASURE	INBREED
SWAPPED	BLASTED	PLANTAR	PLAGUED	JOBBERY
TRAIPSE	BLASTIN	PLANTED	SCAPULA	JOBLESS
TRAMPED	BOASTER	PLANTER	SEAGULL	NOBLEST
TRAMPLE	CHANTED	PLASTER	SPATULA	ROBBERY
TRAPPED	CHANTRY	PLASTIC	STATURE	RUBBERY
TRAPPER	CHAOTIC	PLATTED	STATUTE	SUBDEAN
WRAPPED	CHAPTER	PLATTER	TRADUCE	SUBJECT
WRAPPER.	CHARTED	PRAETOR	VIADUCT.	SUBTEND
ANAGRAM	CHARTER	PRATTLE	SCARVES	SUBVERT
CHAGRIN	CHASTEN	PSALTER	STARVED	TABLEAU.
CHAIRED	CHATTED	QUANTUM	WHARVES.	AMBLING
CHARRED	CHATTEL	QUARTAN	HEADWAY	AUBAINE
DIAGRAM	CHATTER	QUARTER	MIAOWED	BABYISH
PRAIRIE	*CLACTON	QUARTET	ROADWAY	BOBBING
PRAKRIT	CLASTIC	REACTOR	TRAMWAY.	CABLING
QUADRAT	CLATTER	REALTOR	ANALYSE	CUBBING
QUADREL	COAL-TAR	ROASTED	ANALYST	DABBING
QUARREL	COAL-TIT	ROASTER	+KHAYYAM	DUBBING
SCARRED	COASTAL	SCANTLE	PHARYNX.	EBB-TIDE
SPARRED	COASTED	SCATTER	FRAZZLE	FABLIAU
SPARROW	COASTER	*SEATTLE		FEBRILE
STARRED	DRAFTED	SHATTER	BOBTAIL	FIBBING
TEA-TRAY	DRAFTEE	SLANTED	CABBAGE	FOBBING
UNAIRED.	DRASTIC	SLATTED	CAB-RANK	GABBING
AMASSED	DRATTED	SMARTED	EMBRACE	+GABRIEL
BRAISED	ELASTIC	SMARTEN	HEBRAIC	INBEING
BRASSIE	ELASTIN	SMARTLY	HOBNAIL	JABBING
CHASSIS	ENACTED	SPARTAN	INBOARD	JIBBING
CLASSED	EXACTED	SPASTIC	KABBALA	JOBBING
CLASSIC	EXACTLY	SPATTER	LIBRARY	LOBBIED
CLAUSAL	EXACTOR	STARTED	LIBRATE	LOBBING
COARSEN	EXALTED	STARTER	SABBATH	MOBBING
CRASSLY	FEASTED	STARTLE	UMBRAGE	NABBING
ELAPSED	FLATTEN	SWARTHY	UNBRACE	NIBLICK
GRASSED	FLATTER	SWATTED	UPBRAID	NOBBING
HEAD-SET	FRANTIC	SWATTER	VIBRANT	PUBLISH
HEARSAY	GHASTLY	TOASTER	VIBRATE	RABBITY
KHAMSIN	GRAFTED	TRACTOR	VIBRATO.	RIBBING
LIAISON	GRAFTER	TRAITOR	IMBIBED.	ROBBING
+PEARSON	GRANTED	UNACTED	CUBICLE	RUBBING
PRAISED	GRANTEE	WEALTHY.	DEBACLE	RUBBISH
QUASSIA	GRANTOR	BRAVURA	+REBECCA	+SABRINA
*SWANSEA	HEALTHY	+EMANUEL	SUBACID	SIBLING
TRANSIT	HEARTED	ERASURE	TOBACCO.	SOBBING
TRANSOM	HEARTEN	EVACUEE	RABIDLY	SUBLIME
TRAPSED.	INAPTLY	FEATURE	SUB-EDIT.	SUBSIDE
ADAPTED	PHAETON	GRADUAL	AMBIENT	SUBSIDY
ADAPTER	PHANTOM	GRANULE	BOBBERY	SUBSIST

TABBING	SUBJOIN	SUBSUME	VOCABLE.	ALCOHOL
TABLING	SUBSOIL	UNBOUND.	BICYCLE.	BACCHIC
TUBBING	TABLOID	ELBOWED	ACCEDED	+BACCHUS
UNBUILT	TABOOED	EMBOWER	CACODYL	ARCHING
WEBBING	UNBLOWN.	UNBOWED.	DECADAL	ASCRIBE
ZEBRINE.	CABARET	EMBAYED	DECIDED	AUCTION
TOBY-JUG.	+DEBORAH		DECODED	BACKING
+NABOKOV	EMBARGO	ACCLAIM	DECODER	BUCKING
REBUKED.	IMBURSE	ARCHAIC	DECODER	BUCKISH
BABBLER	LIBERAL	ARCUATE	JACKDAW	COCAINE
*BABYLON	*LIBERIA	COCKADE	LUCIDLY	COCKILY
BIBELOT	LIBERTY	DECEASE	MACADAM	COCKING
BUBBLED	+OSBORNE	DECLAIM	PICADOR	CYCLING
COBBLER	PUBERTY	DECLARE	RECEDED	CYCLIST
DABBLED	REBIRTH	DICTATE	SECEDED.	DECEIVE
DIBBLED	REBORED	DOCKAGE	ACCRETE	DECKING
ECBOLIC	+ROBERTA	ENCHAIN	ALCHEMY	DECLINE
EMBOLUS	SOBERED	ENCHANT	ANCIENT	DECRIAL
GABBLED	SOBERLY	ENCHASE	ARCHERY	DECRIER
GOBBLER	SUBERIN.	ENCLAVE	+BECKETT	DICTION
GOBELIN	BABY-SIT	EXCLAIM	+COCTEAU	DOCKING
HOBBLED	DEBASED	HECTARE	+DICKENS	DUCKING
JUBILEE	+DEBUSSY	JACKASS	DUCHESS	DUCTILE
LOBELIA	DIBASIC	LACTASE	ESCHEAT	ETCHING
NEBULAR	EMBASSY	+MICHAEL	EXCRETA	FACTION
NIBBLED	EMBOSOM	NECTARY	EXCRETE	FICTILE
NOBBLER	UNBOSOM.	ORCHARD	LACTEAL	FICTION
PABULUM	ARBITER	PACKAGE	LECHERY	FICTIVE
PEBBLED	ARBUTUS	PECCANT	LECTERN	HACKING
RUBELLA	DEBATED	PECCARY	+MACBETH	HOCKING
SUBPLOT	DEBITED	PECCAVI	MACHETE	INCHING
TUBULAR	FIBSTER	PICKAXE	MOCKERY	INCLINE
WOBBLED.	HABITAT	POCHARD	NUCLEAR	ISCHIAL
ALBUMEN.	HABITED	RECLAIM	NUCLEIC	ISCHIUM
*ALBANIA	HABITUE	+RICHARD	NUCLEON	ITCHING
BUBONIC	HEBETIC	SACCATE	NUCLEUS	JACKING
CABINET	LOBSTER	SECTARY	RICHEST	KECKING
*LEBANON.	MOBSTER	SUCCADE	RICKETS	KICKING
CABOOSE	ORBITAL	TOCCATA	RICKETY	LACKING
DUBIOUS	ORBITED	UNCHAIN	ROCKERY	LICKING
EMBROIL	REBATED	UNCLASP.	SECRECY	LOCKING
FIBROID	TABETIC.	DECIBEL	SECRETE	LUCKIER
FIBROUS	DEBAUCH	DICE-BOX	SICKEST	LUCKILY
GIBBOUS	DEBOUCH	INCUBUS	SOCIETY	MACHINE
JIB-DOOR	IMBRUED	JACOBIN	SUCCEED	MOCKING
LOBWORM	KIBBUTZ	MACABRE	SUCCESS	MUCKILY
PIBROCH	REBOUND	SACKBUT	UNCLEAN.	MUCKING
RUB-DOWN	SUBDUAL	SICK-BAY	*PACIFIC	NECKING
RUBEOLA	SUBDUED	SICK-BED	TACTFUL.	NICKING
SABAOTH	SUBFUSC	TUCK-BOX	DECAGON	NOCKING
			ENCAGED.	

NUCLIDE	NACELLE	SUCROSE	RECITAL	MUD-BATH
PACKING	NECKLET	UNCLOAK	RECITER	MUDLARK
PECKING	PICKLED	UNCLOSE	TACITLY	RADIANT
PECKISH	SECULAR	VACUOLE	VACATED	RADIATE
PICKING	SUCKLED	VACUOUS	YACHTED	ZEDOARY.
PICTISH	TACKLER	VICIOUS	*YUCATAN.	AUDIBLE
+PUCCINI	TICKLER	VICTORY.	ACCOUNT	RIDABLE
PUCKISH	VOCALIC	COCKPIT	BECAUSE	WADABLE.
RACKING	VOCALLY	DECAPOD	ENCRUST	CODICIL
RECEIPT	*WICKLOW.	DECUPLE	EXCLUDE	DEDUCED
RECEIVE	DECIMAL	ESCAPED	FACTUAL	INDICES
RECLINE	INCOMER	ESCAPEE	FACTURE	INDICIA
RECTIFY	PACKMAN	JACKPOT	INCLUDE	INDUCED
RICKING	PICAMAR	OCCIPUT	INCRUST	MEDICAL
ROCKIER	RACEMIC.	SICK-PAY.	LACE-UPS	MODICUM
ROCKILY	COCKNEY	CACIQUE.	LACQUER	NODICAL
ROCKING	COCONUT	ACCURST	LECTURE	PEDICEL
RUCKING	DECANAL	ALCORAN	*MACDUFF	PEDICLE
SACKING	DECENCY	BUCKRAM	NOCTULE	RADICAL
SACRING	*HACKNEY	DECORUM	NOCTURN	RADICEL
SACRIST	INCENSE	EUCHRED	OCCLUDE	RADICES
SECTILE	JACINTH	EXCERPT	PICQUET	RADICLE
SECTION	JACONET	LUCARNE	PICTURE	REDUCED
SUCKING	LACONIC	*LUCERNE	RACQUET	SEDUCER
SUCTION	LACUNAL	SECURED	RECLUSE	SIDECAR.
TACKING	LICENCE	UNCARED	RECOUNT	ADDRESS
TACTICS	LICENSE	VICEROY.	RECRUIT	DUDGEON
TACTILE	TECHNIC	ACCUSAL	SACCULE	ENDLESS
TICKING	UNCANNY	ACCUSED	SECLUDE	GODDESS
TUCKING	VACANCY	ENCASED	SUCCUMB	GODHEAD
UNCTION	VICINAL.	EXCISED	TACTUAL	GODLESS
VACCINE	ANCHOVY	EXCUSED	UNCOUTH	GODSEND
VACUITY.	BECLOUD	FOCUSED	VICTUAL.	GUDGEON
LOCKJAW.	CUCKOLD	FUCHSIA	RECOVER	MADDEST
BACILLI	CYCLOID	HACKSAW	UNCIVIL	MADNESS
BACKLOG	CYCLONE	INCISED	UNCOVER.	ODDMENT
BUCKLED	CYCLOPS	INCISOR	ARCHWAY.	ODDNESS
BUCOLIC	ENCLOSE	INCUSED	DECAYED	REDDEST
CACKLED	FACTORY	+JOCASTA	DECOYED.	RED-HEAD
+CECILIA	HICKORY	MYCOSIS	ALCAZAR	REDRESS
COCHLEA	INCLOSE	*NICOSIA		SADDEST
DECOLOR	KICK-OFF	UNCASED.	END-GAME	SADNESS
FACULTY	LACTOSE	ASCETIC	ENDWAYS	TIDIEST
HACKLET	LOCK-OUT	COCOTTE	GODDAMN	UNDRESS
HECKLER	MICROBE	EXCITED	HYDRANT	WIDGEON.
+JOCELYN	PICCOLO	INCITED	HYDRATE	BODEFUL.
JOCULAR	RACCOON	LICITLY	*INDIANA	PODAGRA.
KECKLED	RECTORY	LOCATED	INDRAWN	GODSHIP
LOCALLY	SUCCOSE	NECK-TIE	MEDIATE	MIDSHIP.
+LUCILLE	SUCCOUR	PICOTEE	MIDLAND	BADDISH

BEDDING	WADDING	TIDINGS	*REDRUTH	SEEPAGE
BEDSIDE	WEDDING	VEDANTA.	*SUDBURY.	SHEBANG
BEDTIME	WEDGING	ARDUOUS	*ANDOVER	STEWARD
BIDDING	YIDDISH.	*BEDFORD	BEDEVIL	+STEWART
BUDDING	KIDSKIN	BEDPOST	CADAVER.	TEENAGE
BUDGING	REDSKIN.	BED-ROCK	ENDOWED	THERAPY
CADDISH	CEDILLA	BEDSORE	TIDEWAY	TOENAIL
CADGING	CODDLED	ENDLONG	WIDOWER.	TREPANG
CADMIUM	CUDDLED	ENDMOST	BEDIZEN	*ZEELAND.
CODEINE	DIDDLER	HADDOCK	IODIZED	ACERBIC
CODFISH	EIDOLON	HIDEOUS		ALEMBIC
COOLING	FIDDLED	HIDEOUT	ACETATE	BLESBOK
DADAISM	FIDDLER	HYDROUS	AVERAGE	SEEDBED
DODGING	FUDDLED	INDOORS	BREWAGE	SHERBET
ENDWISE	HEDDLES	MIDMOST	CHELATE	TREMBLE
FADDIST	HIDALGO	PADDOCK	CREMATE	TREMBLY.
GADDING	HUDDLED	PADLOCK	CRENATE	AMERCED
GIDDILY	INDULGE	PIDDOCK	DIEHARD	BRECCIA
+HADRIAN	MEDDLED	RED-COAT	DIETARY	COERCED
HEDGING	MEDULLA	REDPOLL	ELEGANT	KNEE-CAP
HYDRIDE	MIDDLED	REDWOOD	ELEVATE	PIERCED
JUDAISM	MUDDLED	TADPOLE	EMERALD	SKETCHY
JUDAIZE	MUDFLAP	TEDIOUS	EYEBALL	+SPENCER
KEDGING	MUDFLAT	WEDLOCK.	EYE-BATH	STENCIL
KIDDING	NODULAR	+OEDIPUS.	EYELASH	TIERCEL
LADLING	PADDLED	ANDIRON	EYEWASH	TIERCET
LODGING	PEDDLED	*ANDORRA	*GRENADA	TREACLE
LUDDITE	PUDDLER	ELDERLY	GRENADE	TREACLY.
LYDDITE	RADDLED	ENDORSE	*ICELAND	AMENDED
MADDING	RIDDLED	ENDURED	ICE-PACK	BLENDED
*MADEIRA	RUDDLED	FEDERAL	INEXACT	BREADED
MIDRIFF	+RUDOLPH	+GODFREY	*IRELAND	BREADTH
MIDWIFE	SADDLER	INDORSE	ITERATE	BREEDER
MUDDIED	SEDILIA	ORDERED	LEEWARD	+BRENDAN
MUDFISH	TIDDLER	ORDERLY	OPERATE	*CHEDDAR
NODDING	TIDDLEY	UNDERGO.	OVERACT	DREADED
NUDGING	TODDLER	ECDYSIS	OVERALL	*DRESDEN
PADDING	WADDLED.	MODESTY	OVERARM	EMENDED
PODDING	ABDOMEN	MODISTE.	OVERAWE	FIELDED
PUDDING	ENDEMIC.	AUDITED	PEERAGE	FIELDER
REDDISH	ADDENDA	AUDITOR	PIEBALD	FREEDOM
*REDHILL	ANDANTE	EIDETIC	PIERAGE	GUELDER
RIDDING	ARDENCY	HYDATID	PLENARY	GUERDON
RUDDIER	CADENCE	INDITED	PREFACE	KNEADED
RUDDILY	CADENCY	OLDSTER	PRELACY	OVERDID
SIDLING	CADENZA	SEDATED	PRELATE	OVERDUE
TEDDING	HEDONIC	VEDETTE.	PREPAID	PLEADER
UNDOING	MADONNA	BEDOUIN	PREPARE	SLEDDED
UNDYING	ORDINAL	REDOUBT	PRESAGE	SLENDER
VIDUITY	PUDENDA	REDOUND	PREVAIL	SPEEDED

SPEEDER	WHEREER	CHERISH	PEERING	CHECK-UP
SPENDER	WHEREIN	*CHEVIOT	PEEVING	CREAKED
TREADLE	WHEREOF	CHEWING	PEEVISH	DOESKIN
TREDDLE	WHEREON	COELIAC	PIECING	FLECKED
TRENDED	WHERETO.	COEXIST	PIETISM	FREAKED
TUESDAY	DEEP-FRY	CREVICE	POETIZE	FRECKLE
WEEKDAY	+DRESFUS	DEEMING	PRECISE	FRECKLY
WHEEDLE	FRETFUL	DIETING	PREDICT	GHERKIN
WIELDED	GLEEFUL	DIETIST	PREMIER	SLEEKER
YIELDED.	HEEDFUL	ELEGIAC	PREMISE	SLEEKLY
AGELESS	NEEDFUL	ELEGIST	PREMIUM	SNEAKED
BREWERY	TWELFTH.	ELEGIZE	PRESIDE	SPEAKER
✦CLEMENT	AVENGER	EMETINE	PREVIEW	SPECKED
DEEPEST	DREDGER	EREMITE	PREYING	SPECKLE
ELEMENT	EMERGED	ETESIAN	PUERILE	TREKKED
*EVEREST	EPERGNE	EVENING	QUERIED	TWEAKED
EYELESS	FLEDGED	+EZEKIEL	QUERIST	WREAKED
ICEBERG	FREIGHT	FEEDING	REEDING	WRECKED
KEENEST	PLEDGED	FEELING	REEFING	WRECKER.
MEEKEST	PLEDGEE	FIERILY	REEKING	AREOLAR
ONENESS	PLEDGET	FLEEING	REELING	DUELLED
ONESELF	SLEDGED	+FLEMING	RHENIUM	DUELLER
PEERESS	SLEIGHT	FLEMISH	SEEDILY	DWELLER
POETESS	STEN-GUN.	FLEXILE	SEEDING	FUELLED
PREBEND	BEECHEN	FLEXING	SEEKING	GREMLIN
PRECEDE	+CHEKHOV	FLEXION	SEEMING	GREYLAG
PRECEPT	EYESHOT	FREEING	SEEPING	ICE-FLOE
PRECESS	FLESHED	GRECIAN	SHERIFF	IDEALLY
PREFECT	FLESHLY	GRECISM	SIEVING	KNEELED
PRESENT	FRESHEN	GREYISH	SKEWING	KNEELER
PRETEND	FRESHER	HEEDING	SLEWING	KNELLED
PRETEXT	FRESHET	HEELING	SPECIAL	KREMLIN
PREVENT	FRESHLY	IBERIAN	SPECIES	NEEDLED
SCENERY	SEETHED	ITEMIZE	SPECIFY	OCELLUS
SHEBEEN	+STEPHEN	JEERING	SPEWING	OVERLAP
SHEREEF	URETHRA	KEELING	STERILE	OVERLAY
THEREAT	WHETHER.	KEENING	STEWING	QUELLED
THEREBY	ACETIFY	KEEPING	SWEDISH	SHELLAC
THEREIN	AMENITY	LEERING	TEEMING	SHELLED
THEREOF	*AMERICA	MEETING	TREEING	+SHELLEY
THEREON	ATELIER	NEEDILY	UTERINE	SPELLED
+THERESA	BEEHIVE	NEEDING	VEERING	SPELLER
THERETO	BEE-LINE	OBELISK	VIEWING	STEALTH
+THESEUS	BLEMISH	OBELIZE	WEEDING	STEELED
USELESS	BREVIER	OBEYING	WEEPING.	STELLAR
WEEK-END	BREVITY	OLEFINE	BLEAKLY	SWELLED
WHENEER	BREWING	OPENING	BREAKER	TREBLED
WHEREAS	CAESIUM	PEEKING	BREAK-UP	TRELLIS
WHEREAT	CHEMISE	PEELING	CHECKED	WHEELED.
WHEREBY	CHEMIST	PEEPING	CHECKER	CREAMED

328

CREAMER	BLEEPED	GREASER	+LAERTES	UNEQUAL.
DREAMER	CHEAPEN	GUESSED	*MAESTEG	CHERVIL
FREEMAN	CHEAPLY	KEELSON	MAESTRO	CLEAVED
GLEAMED	CHEEPER	OVERSAW	OVERTAX	CLEAVER
KEELMAN	CREEPER	OVERSEA	OVERTLY	GREAVES
PRE-EMPT	*SHEPPEY	OVERSEE	OVERTOP	SHEAVES
STEAMED	SLEEPER	OVERSET	PLEATED	SHELVED
STEAMER	STEEPED	OVERSEW	*PRESTON	SLEEVED
STEMMED	STEEPEN	PLEASED	+QUENTIN	SWERVED.
THERMAL	STEEPER	PRESSED	QUESTED	BEES-WAX.
THERMIC	STEEPLE	PRESSER	RE-ENTER	ONE-EYED
T.HERMIT	STEPPED	SCEPSIS	RE-ENTRY	PIE-EYED.
THERMOS.	SWEEPER	STEPSON	SCENTED	FREEZER
CLEANED	WHELPED.	STETSON	SCEPTIC	MUEZZIN
CLEANER	AVERRED	TREASON	SCEPTRE	SNEEZED
CLEANLY	CHEERED	TRESSED	SHEATHE	TWEEZER
CLEANSE	CHEERIO	UTENSIL.	SHEETED	WHEEZED
+ELEANOR	CHEVRON	ABETTED	SHELTER	
ETERNAL	CLEARED	ABETTOR	SHELTIE	BUFFALO
GLEANER	CLEARER	ALERTED	SKEPTIC	DEFIANT
GREENER	CLEARLY	AMENTIA	SLEETED	DEFLATE
*OCEANIA	EYEBROW	ASEPTIC	SPECTRA	DEFRAUD
OCEANIC	OVERRAN	AVERTED	SPECTRE	INFLAME
PFENNIG	OVERRUN	BLEATED	SPELTER	INFLATE
PREENED	PIERROT	BREATHE	SWEATED	OFF-HAND
QUEENED	QUEERER	CHEATED	SWEATER	OFFWARD
QUEENLY	QUEERLY	CHEETAH	SWEETEN	REFRACT
STERNAL	SHEARED	*CHESTER	SWEETER	REFRAIN
STERNER	SHEERED	CREATED	SWEETIE	REFRAME
STERNLY	SMEARED	CREATOR	SWEETLY	TIFFANY.
STERNUM	SNEERED	CRESTED	SWELTER	AFFABLE
*VIETNAM.	SPEARED	EGESTED	THEATRE	LIFTBOY.
ACETONE	STEARIN	EJECTED	TREATED	BIFOCAL
ACETOUS	STEERER	EJECTOR	TRESTLE	DEFACED
ADENOID	SWEARER	ELECTED	WHEATEN	DEFICIT
ADENOSE	THEOREM	ELECTOR	WHETTED	ENFACED
ADENOUS	THEURGY	+ELECTRA	WREATHE	OFFICER
ANEMONE	UNEARTH.	ERECTED	WRESTED	REFACED.
ANEROID	ASEPSIS	ERECTLY	WRESTLE.	INFIDEL.
AWESOME	BLESSED	ERECTOR	ASEXUAL	DEFLECT
CHEROOT	CHEESED	EVERTED	*AVEBURY	*ENFIELD
EYE-BOLT	*CHELSEA	EXERTED	CHEQUER	FIFTEEN
EYEHOLE	CREASED	FLEETED	COEQUAL	INFIELD
EYESORE	CRESSET	FRETTED	EXECUTE	INFLECT
+GREGORY	DEEP-SEA	GREATER	FLEXURE	OFFBEAT
ONEROUS	DRESSED	GREATLY	PRELUDE	OFF-PEAK
STEROID	DRESSER	GREETED	PREPUCE	REFLECT
TOEHOLD	FREESIA	INEPTLY	PRESUME	REFRESH
TREFOIL	FRET-SAW	INERTIA	ROEBUCK	SOFTEST
TREMOLO.	GREASED	INERTLY	SPECULA	TAFFETA

REFUGEE.	DEFINED	+HAGGARD	ROGUERY	LOGGING
FIFTHLY.	DEFUNCT	HOGBACK	SEGMENT	LUGGING
AFFLICT	EFFENDI	HOGWASH	SUGGEST	MAGNIFY
BUFFING	INFANCY	INGRAIN	TIGRESS	MUGGING
CUFFING	INFANTA	INGRATE	UNGUENT	MUGGINS
DUFFING	INFANTE	LAGGARD	VAGUELY	NAGGING
GAFFING	OFFENCE	LUGGAGE	WAGGERY.	NEGLIGE
HAFNIUM	REFINED.	MAGNATE	ENGAGED.	NEGRITO
HAFTING	AFFRONT	MIGRANT	HIGH-HAT.	NOGGING
HEFTILY	BUFFOON	MIGRATE	ANGLICE	PEGGING
HEFTING	DEFROCK	NIGGARD	ANGLING	PIGGING
HUFFILY	DEFROST	PAGEANT	ANGRIER	PIGGISH
HUFFING	ENFEOFF	PIGTAIL	ANGRILY	PIGLING
HUFFISH	LIFT-OFF	PIGWASH	ANGUINE	PUGGING
INFLICT	REFLOAT	REGNANT	ANGUISH	PUG-MILL
LEFTIST	*SUFFOLK	UP-GRADE	ARGUING	RAGGING
LIFTING	UNFROCK	VAGRANT	BAGGING	RAGTIME
LOFTIER	UNFROZE.	WAGTAIL.	BAGPIPE	RIGGING
LOFTILY	ENFORCE	ALGEBRA	BEGGING	ROGUISH
LOFTING	INFERNO	BUGABOO	BEGUILE	SAGGING
MAFFICK	+JEFFREY	LEGIBLE	BOGGING	SIGHING
MUFFING	OFFERED	LEGIBLY.	BUGGING	SIGNIFY
OFF-LINE	REFEREE	LOGICAL	BUGLING	SIGNING
OFF-SIDE	SAFFRON.	MAGICAL.	COGNIZE	SOGGILY
PUFFING	DEFUSED	*BAGHDAD	DIGGING	TAGGING
RAFFISH	EFFASED	HIGHDAY	DIGNIFY	TUGGING
RAFTING	EFFUSED	RIGIDLY	DIGNITY	WAGGING
RIFLING	INFUSED	UNGODLY.	DOGFISH	WAGGISH.
RIFTING	REFUSAL	AGGRESS	DOGGING	DOGSKIN
RUFFIAN	REFUSED.	*ALGIERS	ENGLISH	HOGSKIN
RUFFING	REFUTED.	AUGMENT	FAGGING	PIGSKIN.
SIFTING	DEFAULT	BIGGEST	FOGGIER	ANGELIC
SUFFICE	DIFFUSE	BIG-HEAD	⊤FOGGILY	ANGELUS
TUFTING	SUFFUSE.	BUGBEAR	FOGGING	ANGULAR
WAFTING.	AFFIXED	BUGGERY	FUGUIST	BOGGLER
ALFALFA	INFIXED	DIGRESS	GAGGING	EGG-FLIP
AWFULLY	UNFIXED	EGGHEAD	HAGFISH	GAGGLED
BAFFLED		FIG-LEAF	HAGGING	GIGGLER
DEFILED	BAGGAGE	FIGMENT	HAGGISH	GOGGLED
MUFFLED	BEGGARY	HIGHEST	HOGGING	HAGGLER
MUFFLER	COGNATE	HYGIENE	HOGGISH	HIGGLER
RAFFLED	DEGRADE	INGRESS	HUGGING	JIGGLED
RIFFLER	DIGRAPH	LEGLESS	INGOING	JOGGLED
RUFFLED	DOGGART	MAGNETO	JAGGING	JUGGLED
WAFFLED.	*ENGLAND	NEGLECT	JIGGING	JUGGLER
DEFAMED	ENGRAFT	NEGRESS	JOGGING	JUGULAR
LIFTMAN.	ENGRAIN	PIGGERY	JUGGING	LEGALLY
AFFINAL	ENGRAVE	PIGMENT	LAGGING	NIGGLED
AFFINED	FOGBANK	PYGMEAN	LEGGING	REGALED
DEFENCE	HAGGADA	REGRESS	LIGNITE	REGALIA

REGALLY	+PEGASUS.	ECHOING	AGITATE	BLINDLY
REGULAR	BIGOTED	ECHOISM.	AGITATO	BRINDLE
WAGGLED	BIGOTRY	APHELIA	ALIDADE	BUILDER
WIGGLED.	DIGITAL	ECHELON	ANIMATE	+DEIRDRE
GAGSMAN	FIGHTER	EXHALED	BRIGADE	DRIP-DRY
LEGUMIN	LEGATED	INHALER	BRIGAND	DWINDLE
REGIMEN.	LEGATEE	+OPHELIA	*BRITAIN	GRIDDLE
BEGONIA	LIGHTEN	SCHOLAR.	*CHICAGO	GRINDER
COGENCY	LIGHTER	ASHAMED	CHICANE	GUILDER
EUGENIC	LIGHTLY	*BOHEMIA	CLIMATE	HEIRDOM
INGENUE	MEGATON	EXHUMED	COINAGE	JOINDER
MAGENTA	NEGATED	INHUMAN	CUIRASS	SHINDIG
ORGANIC	NIGHTLY	INHUMED	EPITAPH	SKIDDED
ORGANON	REGATTA	OGHAMIC	FRIGATE	SPINDLE
PAGINAL	RIGHTED	SCHEMER.	GRIMACE	SPINDLY
REGENCY	RIGHTLY	APHONIC	IMITATE	SWINDLE
URGENCY	SIGHTED	ECHINUS	OLIVARY	*SWINDON
VAGINAL	SIGHTLY	ENHANCE	OXIDANT	THIRDLY
WAGONER.	TIGHTEN	ETHANOL	OXIDASE	TWIDDLE
BUGLOSS	TIGHTER	GEHENNA	PLICATE	WEIRDLY.
DOGGONE	TIGHTLY	UNHANDY	PRIMACY	AGILELY
DOG-ROSE	VEGETAL.	UNHINGE.	PRIMARY	ALIMENT
DOGWOOD	DEGAUSS	*ASHFORD	PRIMATE	ANISEED
ENGROSS	LEG-PULL	MAH-JONG	PRIVACY	BRIBERY
FOGHORN	MUGWUMP	OCHROUS.	PRIVATE	CHIMERA
LEGHORN	YOGHURT.	UNHAPPY	QUINARY	CHINESE
LOG-BOOK	+SEGOVIA.	UNHOPED.	*REIGATE	DRIVE-IN
LOG-ROLL	HIGHWAY	ADHERED	RUINATE	EMINENT
LOGWOOD		AMHARIC	SPINACH	EPICENE
MAGGOTY	ATHWART	ASHTRAY	SPIRANT	EVIDENT
NEGROID	*BAHRAIN	ATHIRST	TZIGANE	EXIGENT
PUG-NOSE	+ISHMAEL	COHERER	UNITARY	HEIRESS
REGROUP	UNHEARD	INHERED	URINARY.	NAIVELY
SIGNORA	UPHEAVE.	INHERIT	AMIABLE	NAIVETE
*WIGTOWN.	ADHIBIT	SCHERZO	CLIMBER	NAIVETY
*ALGERIA	COHABIT	SPHERIC	CRIBBED	PRIMELY
ANGERED	EXHIBIT	UNHORSE	CRIBBER	RAIMENT
AUGURED	ICHABOD	USHERED.	DRIBBLE	SHIVERY
DOGTROT	INHABIT	APHASIA	FRIBBLE	SPIDERY
EAGERLY	INHIBIT.	APHESIS	MAILBAG	STIPEND
ENGORGE	ETHICAL	DEHISCE	PLIABLE	TAIL-END
FIGURAL	MOHICAN	+JOHNSON.	QUIBBLE	TRICEPS
FIGURED	VEHICLE.	+ACHATES	RAINBOW	TRIDENT
+HOGARTH	APHIDES	MAHATMA	THIMBLE	TRIREME
JOG-TROT	ECHIDNA	UNHITCH.	TRIABLE.	TRISECT
*NIGERIA	OPHIDIA.	EXHAUST.	BRIOCHE	TRITELY
PIG-IRON	ACHIEVE	BEHAVED	EVINCED	VAINEST
SUGARED	ATHLETE.	+JEHOVAH	HAIR-CUT.	WHITEST
WAGERED.	ICHTHYS.	+ARIADNE		WRITE-UP
BAGASSE	ATHEISM	+ABIGAIL	BLINDED	BRIEFLY

BRIMFUL	ABIDING	IRIDIZE	SWINISH	PRICKET
CHIEFLY	ABILITY	JOINING	SWIPING	PRICKLE
CHIFFON	ACIDIFY	KAINITE	TAILING	PRICKLY
GAINFUL	ACIDITY	KNIFING	TRICING	QUICKEN
GRIFFIN	AGILITY	LAICIZE	TRILITH	QUICKER
PAILFUL	ANILINE	MAILING	TRINITY	QUICKIE
PAINFUL	ANIMISM	MAIMING	TRITIUM	QUICKLY
SKIFFLE	ARIDITY	NAILING	TRIVIAL	SHIRKER
SKILFUL	ARISING	NOISIER	TRIVIUM	SLICKER
SKINFUL	ASININE	NOISILY	TUITION	SLICKLY
SNIFFED	AVIDITY	+OLIVIER	TWINING	SMIRKED
STIFFEN	BAILIFF	OPINING	UNIFIED	SNICKER
STIFFER	BAILING	OPINION	UNITING	STICKED
STIFFLY	BAITING	ORIFICE	UNITIVE	STICKER
WHIFFED	BOILING	OXIDIZE	UTILITY	-STINKER
WHIFFLE.	BRIBING	PAINING	UTILIZE	THICKEN
BRIDGED	BRITISH	PAIRING	VEILING	THICKER
+BRIDGET	CAITIFF	POISING	VEINING	THICKET
CLINGER	CEILING	PRICING	VOICING	THICKLY
CRINGED	CHIDING	PRIDING	VOIDING	THINKER
CRINGLE	CHIMING	PRIMING	WAILING	TRICKED
FRINGED	COILING	PRIVILY	WAITING	TRICKLE
LYING-IN	COINING	PRIVITY	WAIVING	TRICKSY
LYINGLY	CUISINE	PRIZING	WHILING	TRINKET
PRIGGED	DAISIED	QUININE	WHINING	TWINKLE
SHINGLE	DEICIDE	RAIDING	WHITING	WHISKED
SNIGGER	DEIFIED	RAILING	WHITISH	WHISKER
SWIGGED	DRIVING	RAINING	WRITING.	WHISKEY
SWINGER	EDIFICE	RAISING	*ABIDJAN.	WRINKLE.
SWINGLE	EDIFIED	REINING	BLINKED	AXIALLY
TRIGGER	EDITING	RUINING	BRICKED	BRIDLED
TRINGLE	EDITION	SAILING	BRISKET	CHILLED
TWIGGED	ELIDING	SEISING	BRISKLY	*CUILLIN
TWINGED	ELISION	SEIZING	CHICKEN	DRIBLET
WRIGGLE	EXILIAN	SHINILY	CHINKED	DRILLED
WRINGER.	EXILING	SHINING	CLICKED	FRILLED
*BRIXHAM	EXITING	SKI-LIFT	CLICKER	GRILLED
EPITHET	FAILING	SLICING	CRICKED	MAILLOT
FLIGHTY	FAIRILY	SLIDING	CRICKET	*PAISLEY
NEIGHED	FAIRING	SMILING	CRINKLE	QUILLED
NEITHER	FOILING	SNIPING	CRINKLY	*RUISLIP
PRITHEE	GAINING	SOILING	DRINKER	+SHIRLEY
SLITHER	GLIDING	SPICIER	FLICKED	SKID-LID
SWISHED	GRIDING	SPICILY	FLICKER	SKILLED
THITHER	GRIPING	SPICING	FRISKED	SKILLET
WEIGHED	GUIDING	SPIKING	FRISKET	SKIRLED
WEIGH-IN	HAILING	SPIRING	FRISKIN	SPIELER
WEIGHTY	HAIRILY	SPITING	GRISKIN	SPILLED
WHITHER	INITIAL	SUICIDE	HOICKED	STIFLED
WRITHED.	IRIDIUM	SUITING	PRICKER	STILLED

STILLER	THINNER	SKID-PAN	FAINTED	SMITTEN
SWILLED	TWINNED.	SKIMPED	FAINTLY	SPIRTED
SWIRLED	ACINOSE	SKIPPED	FLIRTED	SPITTED
TRIFLED	ADIPOSE	SKIPPER	FLITTED	SPITTLE
TRIFLER	ALIFORM	SLIPPED	FLITTER	STILTED
TRIGLOT	ALIMONY	SLIPPER	FOISTED	*STILTON
TRILLED	*ARIZONA	SNIPPED	FRITTED	STINTED
TRIOLET	BRICOLE	SNIPPET	FRITTER	SWIFTER
TRIPLED	BRIDOON	STIPPLE	GLINTED	SWIFTLY
TRIPLET	CHICORY	TRIPPER	GLISTEN	TAINTED
TRIPLEX	CRINOID	WHIMPER	GLISTER	THISTLE
TWILLED	DEIFORM	WHIPPED	GLITTER	THISTLY
TWIRLED	EPISODE	WHIPPET	GRISTLE	*TRISTAN
WHIRLED	EPITOME	WHISPER.	GRISTLY	TWISTER
WHITLOW.	EPIZOON	CHIRRUP	GRITTED	TWITTED
BRIMMER	HEINOUS	EPIGRAM	HEISTED	TWITTER
GLIMMER	MOIDORE	STIRRED	HOISTED	WAISTED
GRIMMER	*NAIROBI	STIRRUP	IDIOTIC	WHISTLE
KRIMMER	NOISOME	WHIRRED.	JOINTED	WHITTLE
PRIMMED	OMINOUS	CAISSON	JOINTER	WRITTEN.
SEISMAL	OVIFORM	CHIASMA	JOINTLY	ALIQUOT
SEISMIC	+QUIXOTE	CRIMSON	KNITTED	AZIMUTH
SHIMMER	RHIZOID	GAINSAY	KNITTER	BRIQUET
SKIMMER	RHIZOME	*GRIMSBY	LEISTER	CLIQUEY
SLIMMER	RUINOUS	MEIOSIS	MOISTEN	EPICURE
SWIMMER	SPIN-OFF	REISSUE	OMITTED	FAILURE
THIAMIN	SPINOUS	SCISSOR	PAINTED	GUIPURE
TRIMMED	+SPINOZA	THIRSTY	PAINTER	LEISURE
TRIMMER	TRIFORM	TWIN-SET	PHILTRE	OVIDUCT
TRIUMPH	TRILOGY	WHIMSEY	POINTED	PRIMULA
+WHITMAN.	*TRIPOLI	WHITSUN.	POINTER	SEIZURE
ALIENEE	UNICORN	ABIOTIC	PRINTED	SKI-JUMP
*AVIGNON	UNIFORM.	ASIATIC	PRINTER	STIMULI
CHIANTI	CHIPPED	AVIATOR	QUIETEN	TRIBUNE
CHIGNON	CHIRPED	BLISTER	QUIETER	TRIBUTE.
CHIMNEY	CLIPPED	BRISTLE	QUIETLY	GRIEVED
CHINNED	CLIPPER	BRISTLY	QUIETUS	THIEVED.
DEIGNED	CLIPPIE	*BRISTOL	QUILTED	CHINWAG
FAIENCE	CRIMPED	BRITTLE	QUINTAN	FAIRWAY
FEIGNED	CRIPPLE	BUILT-IN	QUINTET	RAILWAY
GRINNED	CRISPER	BUILT-UP	QUITTED	SHIP-WAY
HAIRNET	DRIPPED	CRITTER	QUITTER	SLIPWAY.
PLIANCY	FLIPPER	DEISTIC	ROISTER	DRIZZLE
REIGNED	GLIMPSE	DRIFTER	SAINTED	DRIZZLY
SCIENCE	GRIPPED	EDICTAL	SAINTLY	FRIZZED
SHINNED	HAIRPIN	EMITTED	SCIATIC	FRIZZLE
SKINNED	QUIPPED	EMITTER	SHIFTER	GRIZZLE
SPINNER	SHIPPED	EPISTLE	SKIRTED	GRIZZLY
SPINNEY	SHIPPEN	EVICTED	SKITTER	QUIZZED
THINNED	SHIPPER	EXISTED	SKITTLE	SWIZZLE

WHIZZED	*CALGARY	+WALLACE	BELIEVE	EC OGUE
	CALVARY	*WALSALL	BOLDEST	FALL-GU
ADJUDGE.	CILIARY	WELFARE.	CALMEST	HALOGEN
REJOICE.	CILIATE	AXLE-BOX	COLDEST	ILLEGAL
CAJOLED.	COLLAGE	BELL-BOY	COLLECT	OBLIGED
PYJAMAS.	COLLATE	CALIBRE	COLLEEN	PELAGIC
ADJUNCT	DULLARD	CALL-BOX	COLLEGE	PHLEGMY
HIJINKS	EEL-FARE	*CELEBES	CULVERT	POLYGON.
JEJUNUM.	FALCATE	HALIBUT	DILUENT	BELCHER
RAJPOOT.	FALLACY	MILK-BAR	DULLEST	BELL-HOP
ABJURED	FOLIAGE	PILL-BOX	FALSELY	+CALCHAS
INJURED	FOLIATE	SALABLE	FILBERT	DELPHIC
*MAJORCA	GALLANT	SOLUBLE	FULLEST	DOLPHIN
MAJORED.	GOLIARD	TALLBOY	GALLEON	FILCHED
MAJESTY.	HALYARD	VOLUBLE.	GALLERY	+GALAHAD
JUJITSU	+HILLARY	CALYCES	+GILBERT	KOLKHOZ
MUJITSA.	HOLDALL	COLICKY	HALBERD	+MALTHUS
ADJOURN	*HOLLAND	ENLACED	HELLENE	MULCHED
SOJOURN.	+JULIANA	FELUCCA	+HOLBEIN	NYLGHAU
ENJOYED	*KILDARE	HELICAL	HOLIEST	PILCHER
	LALLANS	HELICES	ILLNESS	SULPHUR
AWKWARD	LOLLARD	HELLCAT	*MALVERN	TELPHER
*ESKDALE	LULLABY	ILLICIT	MILDEST	WELSHER.
OAK-GALL.	MALLARD	MALACCA	MILDEWY	ALL-TIME
JUKEBOX.	MILEAGE	PELICAN	+MOLIERE	BALKING
DUKEDOM	OILCAKE	POLACCA	OILLESS	BELGIAN
NAKEDLY.	PALMARY	POLECAT	OILMEAL	*BELGIUM
INKWELL.	PALMATE	POLICED	OIL-WELL	BELLIED
INKLING	PALPATE	SALICIN	RELIEVE	+BELLINI
TEKTITE	PILLAGE	SILICIC	SALIENT	BELTING
YAKKING.	POLE-AXE	SILICON	SALTERN	BELYING
PIKELET.	POLLACK	SOLACED	SILVERY	BILKING
UNKEMPT.	POLLARD	SOLICIT	SOLVENT	BILLING
ASKANCE	PULSATE	SPLICED	TALLEST	BILLION
+BAKUNIN.	RELEASE	UNLUCKY	TOLUENE	BOLTING
INKHORN	RELIANT	WILDCAT.	UGLIEST	BULGING
IRKSOME	SALVAGE	ALLUDED	VELVETY	BULLIED
RAKE-OFF	SULTANA	BULLDOG	VILLEIN	BULLION
TAKE-OFF	TILLAGE	CELADON	WILDEST.	BULLISH
UNKNOWN	TOLLAGE	DELUDED	BALEFUL	CALCIFY
	UNLEARN	HOLIDAY	DOLEFUL	CALCINE
BALLADE	UNLEASH	MELODIC	*HALIFAX	CALCITE
BALLAST	VALIANT	PALADIN	HELPFUL	CALCIUM
*BELFAST	VILLAGE	PALUDAL	MALEFIC.	CALLING
BELTANE	VILLAIN	SOLIDLY	ALLEGED	CALMING
BILIARY	VOLCANO	SPLODGE	ALLEGRO	CALVING
BOLLARD	VOLTAGE	UNLADEN	*BOLOGNA	CELLIST
BULLACE	VOLTAIC	VALIDLY.	COLOGNE	COLDISH
BULLATE	VULGATE	AILMENT	DELIGHT	COLLIDE
BULWARK	WALLABY	BALDEST	DELUGED	COLLIER

COLTISH	LULLING	TALLIED	POLENTA	ELLIPSE
CULLING	MALAISE	TELLING	POLYNIA	FELSPAR
DALLIED	MALTING	TILLING	RELINED	HALF-PAY
DELAINE	MELDING	TILTING	SILENCE	POLYPOD
DELVING	MELTING	+TOLKIEN	SPLENIC	POLYPUS
DOLTISH	MILKING	TOLLING	SPLINED	RELAPSE
DULCIFY	MILLING	VOLTING	TALLNES	SALT-PAN
DULLING	MILLION	VULPINE	TALONED	TALIPED.
FALLING	MILTING	WALKING	VALANCE	OBLIQUE
FALSIES	MOLLIFY	WALLING	VALENCE	OBLOQUY.
FALSIFY	MULLING	WELDING	VALENCY.	AILERON
FALSITY	MULLION	WELLING	BALCONY	ALLERGY
+FELLINI	NULLIFY	WELTING	BALLOON	ALLURED
FELSITE	NULLITY	+WILLIAM	+BELLONA	BALDRIC
FELTING	OIL-SILK	WILLING	BELLOWS	CALORIC
FILLING	PALLING	WILTING	BILIOUS	CALORIE
FILMING	PALLIUM	WOLFING	BILTONG	CALTROP
FOLDING	PALMING	WOLFISH	BULBOUS	CHLORAL
GALLING	PALMIST	YELLING	BULLOCK	CHLORIC
GALLIOT	PALPING	YELPING.	CALLOUS	+CHLORIS
GALLIUM	PALSIED	KILLJOY.	COLLOID	CULPRIT
GELDING	PELTING	OILSKIN.	DELTOID	+DOLORES
GELLING	PILLION	+GALILEO	EEL-WORM	ENLARGE
GILDING	POLLING	PILULAR	FALL-OUT	FILARIA
+GILLIAN	PULLING	YULE-LOG.	FULSOME	FULCRUM
GILLION	PULPIFY	BULIMIA	FULVOUS	ILL-BRED
+GOLDING	PULPING	CALAMUS	GALLEON	MALARIA
GULLING	PULSING	CALOMEL	GALLOWS	+MILDRED
GULPING	+RALEIGH	CALUMET	HILLOCK	PALFREY
HALTING	RALLIED	CALUMNY	HOLM-OAK	PILGRIM
HALVING	ROLLING	DELIMIT	+MALCOLM	PYLORUS
HELLISH	SALLIED	DILEMMA	MALTOSE	SPLURGE
HELPING	SALSIFY	GALUMPH	PALM-OIL	+VALERIE
HOLDING	SALTING	ISLAMIC	+MILFORD	+WILFRED
HOLMIUM	SALTIRE	MILKMAN	PILLORY	WOLFRAM.
HULKING	SALVING	POLEMIC	+POLLOCK	BELISHA
HULLING	SELFISH	POLYMER	*SALFORD	CELESTA
ILL-WILL	*SELKIRK	PULLMAN	SELL-OUT	+CELESTE
JELLIED	SELLING	+SOLOMON.	UNLOOSE	MALMSEY
JELLING	SILKILY	ACLINIC	VILLOUS	MELISMA
JILTING	SILLIER	*ATLANTA	WALK-OUT	MELISSA
JOLLIER	SILLILY	BALANCE	WALLCON	+MELISSA
JOLLIFY	SILTING	+BELINDA	+WALPOLE	MILKSOP
JOLLITY	SOLDIER	BOLONEY	WELCOME	PELISSE
JOLTING	SOLOIST	CALENDS	WELL-OFF	*SILESIA
KILLICK	SOLVING	COLONEL	WILLOWY	SPLASHY.
KILLING	SULKILY	FALANGE	YELLOWY.	BELATED
LALLING	SULLIED	FELONRY	AXLE-PIN	BOLSTER
LILTING	SYLVINE	+MELANIE	+CALYPSO	CALOTTE
LOLLING	TALKING	MELANIN	ECLIPSE	COLITIS
				DELATED

335

DELATOR	HALCYON	COMPERE	LAMAISM	TUMBLED
DELETED	*PALMYRA	COMPETE	LAMBING	TUMBLER
DILATED	SPLAYED	DIMNESS	LAMMING	TUMULUS
DILATOR	TALLY-HO.	HIMSELF	LAMPION	*WEMBLEY
DILUTED	SELTZER	LAMBENT	LEMMING	WIMPLED.
DILUTER	WALTZED	LAMBERT	LIMNING	ALMSMAN.
GELATIN		LIMBECK	LIMPING	ALMANAC
HOLSTER	ARM-BAND	MUMMERY	LUMPISH	ALMONER
KILOTON	BOMBARD	*POMPEII	MUMMIFY	AMMONIA
MILITIA	BOMBAST	ROMPERS	MUMMING	DEMONIC
MULATTO	BUMMALO	RUMNESS	NUMBING	HOMINID
PALATAL	CEMBALO	SUMMERY	PIMPING	HOMONYM
PALETTE	COMMAND	TEMPERA	PUMPING	HUMANLY
PILOTED	COMPACT	TEMPEST	RAMMING	IMMENSE
POLITIC	COMPANY	*ZAMBESI.	RAMPING	LAMINAL
POLL-TAX	COMPARE	ARMIGER	RIMMING	MEMENTO
RELATED	COMPASS	DEMIGOD.	ROMPING	NOMINAL
SALUTED	COMRADE	CAMPHOR	RUMMILY	NOMINEE
SPLOTCH	CYMBALO	NYMPHAL	SUMMING	PIMENTO
+TOLSTOY	GEMMATE	NYMPHET	SYMBION	ROMANCE
VALETED	GIMBALS	SOMEHOW.	TAMPING	ROMANIC
VOLUTED.	GYMNAST	BAMBINO	TAMPION	*RUMANIA
BULRUSH	LIMBATE	BOMBING	TOMPION	SEMINAL
CELLULE	LUMBAGO	BUMPING	VAMPING	SEMINAR
COLLUDE	MAMMARY	CAMBIST	VAMPIRE.	UNMANLY
CULTURE	POMPANO	CAMBIUM	BUMPKIN	WOMANLY.
DELOUSE	RAMPAGE	CAMPING	LAMBKIN	COMFORT
KALMUCK	RAMPANT	CAMPION	PUMPKIN.	COMMODE
MOLLUSC	RAMPART	COMBINE	COMPLEX	COMMONS
POLLUTE	REMNANT	COMBING	CUMULUS	COMPORT
*TILBURY	+RIMBAUD	COMPILE	DIMPLED	COMPOSE
VELOURS	RUMMAGE	DAMMING	FAMULUS	COMPOST
VULTURE.	SUMMARY	DAMNIFY	FUMBLER	COMPOTE
BELOVED	TIMPANI	DAMNING	GAMBLER	DAMFOOL
BOLIVAR	TIMPANO	DAMPING	HUMBLED	GAMBOGE
*BOLIVIA	UNMEANT.	DAMPISH	JUMBLED	GUMBOIL
DELIVER	CAMP-BED	DIMMING	LAMELLA	HAMMOCK
ENLIVEN	NAMABLE	DUMPING	MAMILLA	HEMLOCK
PALAVER	TAMABLE.	GAMMING	MUMBLED	HUMMOCK
RELIVED.	COMICAL	GEMMING	RAMBLED	HYMNODY
ALLOWED	MIMICRY.	GIMMICK	RAMBLER	LAMP-OIL
+BALDWIN	HUMIDOR	GUMMING	+ROMULUS	LAMPOON
HALFWAY	NOMADIC	HAMMING	RUMBLED	MAMMOTH
HALF-WIT.	RAMADAN	HEMMING	RUMPLED	POMPOUS
RELAXED	TIMIDLY.	HUMMING	SAMPLED	*ROMFORD
TELEXED.	AIMLESS	HUMPING	SAMPLER	SOMEONE
ALLAYED	ARMLESS	HYMNIST	SIMILAR	SUMMONS
ALLOYED	COMMEND	*JAMAICA	TEMPLAR	TAMBOUR
BELAYED	COMMENT	JAMMING	TEMPLET	TOMBOLA
DELAYED	COMPEER	JUMPING	TIME-LAG	TOMFOOL

VAMOOSE.	VOMITED	JANUARY	SANDBOY	DENSELY
ADMIRAL	ZYMOTIC.	LANYARD	TENABLE	DENSEST
ADMIRER	ARMOURY	LINEAGE	TENABLY	DUNGEON
CAMBRIC	COMMUNE	LINEATE	TUNABLE	+FONTEYN
COMFREY	COMMUTE	LINKAGE	WINDBAG.	GINGERY
DEMERIT	COMPUTE	LINSANG	CYNICAL	GUNNERY
FEMORAL	CUMQUAT	MANDALA	FINICAL	HENNERY
HOMERIC	DEMOUNT	MANDATE	FINICKY	HENPECK
HUMDRUM	*HAMBURG	MANSARD	KINGCUP	HUNKERS
HUMERAL	HOMBURG	MINTAGE	LINOCUT	+KENNEDY
HUMERUS	KUMQUAT	MONTAGE	MANACLE	+KENNETH
IMMERSE	REMOULD	+MONTAGU	MENACED	KINDEST
IMMORAL	REMOUNT.	*MONTANA	MINICAB	LANTERN
IMMURED	REMOVAL	MUNDANE	MONOCLE	LENIENT
LAMPREY	REMOVED	PANCAKE	PANACEA	LINSEED
LEMURES	REMOVER	PENDANT	PANACHE	LONGEST
NUMERAL	SAMOVAR	PENNANT	PANICKY.	NANKEEN
REMARRY	UNMOVED.	PENTANE	DENUDED	NUNNERY
REMORSE	ADMIXED.	PINBALL	HANGDOG	PENDENT
SAMURAI	SAMOYED	PINNACE	KINGDOM	PINCERS
TIMBREL		PINNATE	MONADIC	PINHEAD
TUMBREL	BANDAGE	PINTADO	SYNODAL	PINK-EYE
UNMORAL	BENEATH	PONIARD	SYNODIC.	PUNGENT
ZYMURGY.	BENGALI	RANSACK	BANDEAU	RANKEST
BEMUSED	BONDAGE	RUN-BACK	BENZENE	RONDEAU
DEMESNE	BONE-ASH	SUNWARD	BONKERS	SINCERE
DEMISED	CANTATA	SYNCARP	CANDELA	SINLESS
MIMESIS	CANVASS	TANKAGE	CANNERY	SUNBEAM
NEMESIS	CENTAUR	TANKARD	CANTEEN	SUNLESS
OSMOSIS	CONCAVE	TANNAGE	CINDERY	TANGENT
SAMISEN.	CONNATE	TANNATE	CONCEAL	TANNERY
AMMETER	CONTACT	TINTACK	CONCEDE	TENSELY
*BAMPTON	CONTAIN	TINWARE	CONCEIT	TENSEST
DEMOTED	*DENMARK	TONNAGE	CONCEPT	TINIEST
DEMOTIC	DENTARY	VANTAGE	CONCERN	*TINTERN
GAMETIC	DENTATE	VANWARD	CONCERT	+VINCENT
HAMITIC	*DUNDALK	VENDACE	CONDEMN	WANNESS
*HAMPTON	DUNNAGE	VENTAGE	CONFESS	WINKERS.
HAMSTER	FANFARE	VINTAGE.	CONGEAL	BANEFUL
HEMATIN	FANTAIL	+ANNABEL	CONGEST	BENEFIT
LIMITED	FANTAST	BANDBOX	CONNECT	CONIFER
MIMETIC	FANTASY	ENNOBLE	CONSENT	HANDFUL
OSMOTIC	FINBACK	FINABLE	CONTEMN	MINDFUL
POMATUM	*FINLAND	HANDBAG	CONTEND	SAND-FLY
SEMITIC	FUN-FAIR	IGNOBLE	CONTENT	TUNEFUL.
SOMATIC	GUNNAGE	LONGBOW	CONTEST	*DONEGAL
*SUMATRA	GUNWALE	MINIBUS	CONTEXT	FINAGLE
SYMPTOM	HANSARD	OMNIBUS	CONVENE	MANAGED
TEMPTER	HENBANE	SANDBAG	CONVENT	MANAGER
+TIMOTHY	*HUNGARY	SAND-BAR	CONVERT	RENEGUE

337

*SENEGAL	CONDIGN	KINGING	RINSING	+FENELLA
TANAGRA	CONFIDE	KINKILY	RUNNING	FINALLY
TONIGHT	CONFINE	KINKING	SANDIER	FONDLED
VINEGAR.	CONFIRM	LANCING	SANDING	GANGLIA
BANSHEE	CONKING	LANDING	SENDING	HANDLER
BENCHER	CONNING	LENDING	SENSING	JANGLED
BENTHOS	CONNIVE	LENTISK	SINGING	JINGLED
BUNCHED	CONSIGN	LINKING	SINKING	KINDLER
+CYNTHIA	CONSIST	LONGING	SINNING	KINGLET
GINGHAM	CONVICT	LUNGING	SUNDIAL	KINKLED
GUNSHOT	CUNNING	MANKIND	SUNNIER	LANOLIN
HUNCHED	DANCING	MANLIER	SUNNING	MANGLED
KINSHIP	DANDIFY	MANLIKE	SUNRISE	MANILLA
LUNCHED	DANKISH	MANNING	SUNWISE	MANTLED
LYNCHED	DENSITY	MANNISH	*TANGIER	MINGLED
MENTHOL	DENTINE	MANSION	TANGING	NONPLÜS
+MENUHIN	DENTIST	MENDING	TANNING	PENALLY
MONTHLY	DENYING	MENTION	TENDING	PENALTY
MUNCHED	DINGING	MINCING	TENPINS	RANKLED
NINTHLY	DINNING	MINDING	TENSILE	RINGLET
PANTHER	DONNING	MINTING	TENSING	SINGLED
PINCHED	DONNISH	MONKISH	TENSION	SINGLET
PUNCHED	DUNKING	PANNIER	TENTING	TANGLED
PUNCH-UP	DUNNING	PANNING	TENUITY	TINGLED
RANCHER	FANCIED	PAN-PIPE	TINGING	VANILLA
SONSHIP	FANCIER	PANTIES	TINNILY	VENALLY
TENTHLY	FANNING	PANTILE	TINNING	WANGLED
WENCHED	FENCING	PANTING	TONTINE	WINKLED
WINCHED	FENDING	PENDING	VANNING	ZONALLY.
+WYNDHAM.	FINDING	PENNILL	VENDING	BONDMAN
ANNUITY	FINNISH	PENNING	VENTING	DYNAMIC
BANDIED	FUNDING	*PENRITH	WANTING	HANGMAN
BANDING	FUNNILY	PENSILE	WENDING	KINSMAN
BANGING	GANGING	PENSION	WINDIER	LINEMAN
BANKING	GENTIAN	PENSIVE	WINDING	MANUMIT
BANNING	GENTILE	PINKING	WINGING	MINIMAL
BANTING	GENUINE	PINKISH	WINKING	MINIMUM
BENDING	GUNFIRE	PINNING	WINNING	MONOMER
BINDING	GUNNING	PONTIFF	YANKING	SANDMAN
BONDING	HANDILY	PONTIFY	YENNING.	UNNAMED
BONFIRE	HANDING	PUNNING	*BANGKOK	VENOMED.
BONNILY	HANGING	PUNTING	MANIKIN.	CANONRY
BUNKING	HINTING	RANGING	ANNULAR	CENTNER
BUNTING	HONKING	RANKING	ANNULET	FINANCE
CANDIED	HUNTING	RANTING	*BENELUX	INNINGS
CANNILY	JINKING	RENDING	BUNDLED	PENANCE
CANNING	JUNKING	RENTIER	BUNGLER	SYNONYM
CANTING	KANTIAN	RENTING	CONFLUX	TENANCY
CENTIME	KENNING	RINGING	DANELAW	TENONED
CONCISE	KENTISH	RINKING	DANGLED	*VENTNOR

338

VINTNER.	WINSOME.	NON-USER	DENTURE	LEOTARD
BANNOCK	JUNIPER	*TUNISIA	+JONQUIL	MOORAGE
BENZOIN	KINGPIN	+VANESSA	LANGUID	PEONAGE
CANDOUR	MANIPLE	VENISON	LANGUOR	PHONATE
*CANNOCK	PANOPLY	*WINDSOR.	LINGUAL	PROBANG
CONCOCT	SUNSPOT	+ANNETTE	MANHUNT	PROBATE
CONCORD	SYNAPSE	DENOTED	NONSUCH	PROFANE
CONDOLE	TENT-PEG.	DONATED	NONSUIT	PROLATE
CONDONE	*AINTREE	DONATOR	PENGUIN	PROPANE
CONFORM	CENTRAL	FANATIC	PINGUID	PROSAIC
CONJOIN	CENTRIC	GENETIC	PINGUIN	ROOTAGE
CONNOTE	CONTROL	GENITAL	SENSUAL	STOMACH
CONSOLE	FUNERAL	*HONITON	SUNBURN	STOMATA
CONSORT	GENERAL	IGNITED	TONGUED	STORAGE
CONTORT	GENERIC	JANITOR	TONSURE	STOWAGE
CONTOUR	HUNDRED	KENOTIC	VENTURE.	VIOLATE
CONVOKE	IGNORAL	KINETIC	*HANOVER	ZOOGAMY.
FUNGOID	IGNORED	LAND-TAX	MINIVER	AMOEBIC
FUNGOUS	INNARDS	LENGTHY	*NINEVEH	CLOBBER
GONDOLA	KINDRED	LINCTUS	SYNOVIA.	CROWBAR
GUNBOAT	MANDREL	LUNATIC	GANGWAY	GOOD-BYE
GUNLOCK	MANTRUM	LUNETTE	RENEWAL	KNOBBED
GUNROOM	MANURED	MANATEE	RENEWED	KNOBBLE
HANDOUT	MINARET	MINSTER	*RINGWAY	KNOBBLY
IGNEOUS	MINERAL	MINUTED	RUNAWAY.	MOONBUG
*KINROSS	+MINERVA	MONITOR	ANNEXED.	+PHOEBUS
LENTOID	MONARCH	MONSTER	ANNOYED	POOR-BOX
*LINCOLN	MONGREL	NON-STOP	CONDYLE	RHOMBIC
MANHOLE	*RENFREW	PENATES	HONEYED	RHOMBUS
MANHOOD	SUN-TRAP	PINETUM	MONEYED	SHOWBIZ
MAN-HOUR	SYNERGY	PUNSTER	+VANDYKE.	SLOBBER
MENFOLK	TANTRUM	SANCTUM	DENIZEN	TROUBLE.
MONSOON	TENDRIL	SANCTUS	IONIZED	BLOTCHY
+PANDORA	UNNERVE	SENATOR		BRONCHI
PENTODE	VENTRAL	SENATUS	ANOMALY	CLOACAL
PENTOSE	WINDROW.	+WINSTON	AVOCADO	GROUCHY
PINFOLD	AMNESIA	*YANGTZE.	BROCADE	HYOSCIN
PINHOLE	AMNESTY	*BANBURY	BROMATE	LIONCEL
PONTOON	BAND-SAW	BANQUET	BUOYAGE	SCONCED
RANCOUR	BANKSIA	CENSURE	BUOYANT	SMOOCHY
RUN-DOWN	BENISON	CENTURY	CHORALE	STOICAL
SEND-OFF	CANASTA	CONCUSS	COOLANT	WOODCUT.
SENSORY	DYNASTY	CONDUCE	DIORAMA	BLOODED
SINUOUS	FINESSE	CONDUIT	EXOGAMY	BROADEN
SUNDOWN	GENESIS	CONFUSE	FOOTAGE	BROADER
SYNCOPE	GENISTA	CONFUTE	FROWARD	BROADLY
TANGOED	HANDSEL	CONJURE	ISOBATH	BROODED
TENFOLD	HONESTY	CONQUER	ISOLATE	CHOWDER
TENUOUS	KENOSIS	CONSULT	KNOW-ALL	CLOUDED
TINFOIL	+LINDSEY	CONSUME	LEOPARD	CROWDED

*CROYDEN	SLOWEST	ACONITE	FOOTING	ROOMING
FLOODED	+THOREAU	ADORING	GLORIED	ROOTING
GEORDIE	VIOLENT	AEOLIAN	GLORIFY	SCORIFY
NOONDAY	*WOOMERA.	AGONIZE	GLOWING	SCORING
PLODDER	ALOOFLY	AMORIST	GLOZING	SCOTISM
PRODDED	BLOW-FLY	ANODIZE	GNOMISH	SHOEING
PRODDER	FEOFFEE	+ANOUILH	GOODISH	SHOOING
PROUDER	FEOFFOR	ATOMIZE	GROPING	SHORING
PROUDLY	PROFFER	ATONING	HOODING	SHOVING
QUONDAM	PROOFED	AVOWING	HOOKING	SHOWILY
SCOLDED	ROOMFUL	BLOWING	HOOPING	SHOWING
*SNOWDON	SPOOFED.	BOOKING	HOOTING	SLOPING
SPONDEE	AMONGST	BOOKISH	IDOLIZE	SMOKILY
SPONDYL	BROUGHT	BOOMING	IRONING	SMOKING
TRODDEN.	DROUGHT	BOORISH	IRONIST	SNORING
CHOLERA	FLOGGED	BROKING	KNOWING	SNOWILY
CLOSELY	FROGGED	BROMIDE	LEONINE	SNOWING
CLOSE-UP	*GEORGIA	BROMINE	LIONIZE	SOOTILY
COOKERY	GEORGIC	CHOKING	LOOKING	STOKING
COOLEST	HOOSGOW	CHOLINE	LOOMING	STONIER
DIOCESE	PRONGED	CHOPINE	LOOPING	STONING
DRÓSERA	SHOTGUN	CHORION	LOOTING	STORIED
ERODENT	SLOGGER	CLOSING	MOODILY	STORING
FLOWERY	SNOGGED	CLOYING	MOONING	STOWING
FOOLERY	SPONGER	COOKING	MOORING	THOMISM
GEODESY	STOOGED	COOLING	MOORISH	THORIDE
GROCERY	STOPGAP	CROSIER	MOOTING	THORIUM
LIONESS	THOUGHT	CROWING	NIOBIUM	TOOLING
LOOSELY	WRONGLY	DIORITE	NOOSING	*TOOTING
LOOSEST	WROUGHT.	DIOXIDE	OXONIAN	TROPISM
MIOCENE	ANOTHER	DRONING	PHONING	TWO-TIME
PIONEER	BROTHEL	EBONIST	PLOSIVE	UTOPIAN
POOREST	BROTHER	EBONITE	POOLING	VIOLIST
PROCEED	CLOTHED	EBONIZE	PROBING	WHORING
PROCESS	CLOTHES	EGOTISM	PROBITY	WOODIER
PROFESS	CROCHET	EGOTIST	PRODIGY	*WYOMING
PROGENY	DROSHKY	ELOPING	PROFILE	ZEOLITE
PROJECT	EPOCHAL	EMOTION	PROMISE	ZIONISM
PROTEAN	FROTHED	EMOTIVE	PROSILY	ZIONIST
PROTECT	KNOW-HOW	ERODING	PROSING	ZOOMING.
PROTEGE	MOOCHED	EROSION	PROVIDE	BLOCKED
PROTEID	MOORHEN	EROSIVE	PROVING	BROCKET
PROTEIN	PROPHET	EROTICA	PROVISO	CLOAKED
PROTEST	SLOSHED	ETONIAN	PROXIMO	CLOCKED
+PROTEUS	SMOTHER	EVOKING	QUOTING	CROAKER
PROVERB	SOOTHED	*FLORIDA	RHODIUM	CROCKET
PROWESS	TOOTHED	FLORIST	RIOTING	CROOKED
+PTOLEMY	TROCHEE.	FLOWING	ROOFING	FLOCKED
ROOKERY	ABOLISH	FOOLING	ROOKING	FROCKED
SHOWERY		FOOLISH	ROOMIER	KNOCKED

KNOCKER	CLOWNED	CHOPPED	GROUSER	SPORTED
KNOCK-ON	CROONER	CHOPPER	*KNOSSOS	SPOTTED
PLONKED	CROWNED	CROPPED	LOOK-SEE	SPOTTER
SHOCKER	DROWNED	CROPPER	OPOSSUM	SPOUTED
SNOOKER	ENOUNCE	DROOPED	PIOUSLY	STOUTER
STOCKED	FLOUNCE	DROPPED	SPONSOR	STOUTLY
STOOKED.	FROWNED	DROPPER	+TROTSKY.	SWOTTED
ABOULIA	GROANED	FLOPPED	ABORTED	TROTTER
BOOKLET	GROINED	FOOTPAD	ANOETIC	TWO-STEP
BOOTLEG	GROWN-UP	GROUPED	APOSTLE	+BEOWULF
BROILER	*PHOENIX	PLOPPED	BLOATED	CLOSURE
DOODLED	SCORNED	PROPPED	BLOATER	CROQUET
DROOLED	SPOONED	PROSPER	BLOTTED	FLORUIT
DROPLET	SWOONED	SCOOPED	BLOTTER	GLOBULE
GROWLER	TROUNCE.	SCORPIO	BOOSTER	OROTUND
HOODLUM	AMOROUS	SHOPPED	CHOCTAW	PROCURE
MOONLIT	APOLOGY	SHOPPER	CHORTLE	PRODUCE
PEOPLED	AXOLOTL	SLOPPED	CLOTTED	PRODUCT
PROBLEM	BIOLOGY	SNOOPER	CLOUTED	PROFUSE.
PROWLER	BLOW-OUT	STOOPED	CROFTER	EVOLVED
ROOTLED	DROMOND	STOPPED	CROUTON	GROOVER
SCOLLOP	DROP-OUT	STOPPER	DIOPTER	WHOEVER.
SCOWLED	DUOTONE	STOPPLE	DIOPTRE	+BRONWEN
SHOALED	ECOLOGY	SWOOPED	DROUTHY	DOORWAY
SPOILED	ECONOMY	SWOPPED	FLOATER	FOOTWAY
SPOOLED	GEOLOGY	TROOPER	FLOUTED	*GOODWIN.
SWOLLEN	GLOBOSE	TROUPER	FRONTAL	ACOLYTE
TOOTLED	ISODONT	WHOOPED	FRONTED	ANODYNE
TROLLED	ISOTONE	WHOPPER.	FROSTED	BIOTYPE.
TROLLEY	ISOTOPE	FLOORED	GHOSTED	SNOOZED
TROLLOP	+LEONORA	FLOURED	GHOSTLY	
WOOLLEN.	+LEOPOLD	GROGRAM	GLOATED	APPEASE
ANOSMIA	LOOK-OUT	PROGRAM	GLOTTAL	APPLAUD
BLOOMED	NEOLOGY	SCOURER	GLOTTIS	ASPHALT
BLOOMER	ODOROUS	SCOURGE	GNOSTIC	BIPLANE
BOOKMAN	OTOLOGY	SPORRAN.	GROUTED	CAPTAIN
DOORMAN	PROLONG	ANDESIS	KNOTTED	DEPRAVE
DOORMAT	PROMOTE	AROUSED	PLOTTER	DIPHASE
FROGMAN	PRONOUN	BLOSSOM	PROCTOR	EXPIATE
GOODMAN	PROPOSE	BROWSED	ROOSTER	EXPLAIN
GROMMET	PROSODY	+CROESUS	SCOOTER	HEPTANE
GROOMED	PROVOKE	CROSSED	SCOUTED	IMPEACH
SHOPMAN	PROVOST	CROSSLY	SHOOTER	IMPLANT
SHOWMAN	RIOTOUS	DIOPSIS	SHORTED	+RAPHAEL
SNOWMAN	SCOTOMA	DROWSED	SHORTEN	REPLACE
STORMED	SHOW-OFF	FLOTSAM	SHORTER	REPLANT
TROMMEL	TWOFOLD	FROWSTY	SHORTLY	SAPSAGO
WOODMAN.	TWOSOME	GLOSSED	SHOUTED	SEPTATE
BROWNED	ZOOLOGY	GROSSED	SLOTTED	SOPRANO
BROWNIE	ZOOTOMY.	GROSSLY	SNORTER	TOPIARY

341

TOPMAST	COPAIBA	SAPLING	EXPLOIT	IMPASTO
TOPSAIL.	COPPICE	SAPPING	EXPLORE	IMPOSED
CAPABLE	COPPING	SIPPING	HAPLOID	OPPOSER
DUPABLE.	COPYIST	SOPHISM	HYPNOID	REPOSED
COPY-CAT	CUPPING	SOPHIST	IMPIOUS	RIPOSTE.
TOPICAL	CUPRITE	SOPPILY	IMPLODE	AMPUTEE
TYPICAL.	CYPRIOT	SOPPING	IMPLORE	CAPITAL
IMPEDED	DEPRIVE	SUPPING	IMPROVE	CAPITOL
OPPIDAN	DIPPING	TAPPING	LEPROSY	CAPSTAN
RAPIDLY	EMPTIER	TIPPING	PAPOOSE	EMPATHY
TEPIDLY	EMPTILY	TIPSILY	POPCORN	HEPATIC
VAPIDLY.	ESPYING	TOPPING	RAPPORT	HIPSTER
COPPERY	FOPPISH	TOPSIDE	REPROOF	IMPETUS
CYPRESS	HAPPIER	YAPPING	REPROVE	IMPUTED
DEPLETE	HAPPILY	ZIPPING.	RIP-CORD	+JUPITER
DEPRESS	HAPPING	AMPULLA	SAPWOOD	NAPHTHA
DIPTERA	HIPPING	BIPOLAR	SUPPORT	NEPOTIC
EMPRESS	HOP-BINE	CO-PILOT	SUPPOSE	PIPETTE
EXPRESS	HOPLITE	DAPPLED	TAPIOCA	REPUTED
FOPPERY	HOPPING	DIPOLAR	TAP-ROOM	TAPSTER
HAPLESS	IMPFING	HOPPLED	TAP-ROOT	TIPSTER.
IMPIETY	IMPLIED	IMPALED	TIPTOED	AMPOULE
IMPRESS	IMPRINT	IMPULSE	TOP-BOOT	CAPSULE
IMPREST	KIPPING	PAPILLA	TOP-COAT	CAPTURE
OPPRESS	LAPPING	POPULAR	TOPMOST	ESPOUSE
ORPHEAN	LAPPISH	REPULSE	TYPHOID	IMPOUND
+ORPHEUS	LAPSING	RIPPLED	TYPHOON	+NEPTUNE
PEPPERY	LAPWING	SUPPLED	TYPHOUS	RAPTURE
REPLETE	LIPPING	TIPPLER	XIPHOID.	RUPTURE
REPRESS	LOPPING	TOPPLED.	REPAPER.	VAPOURY.
SAPIENT	MAPPING	EMPANEL	APPAREL	EMPOWER.
SAPLESS	MOPPING	EXPANSE	ASPERSE	DIPTYCH
SUPREME	NAPPING	EXPENSE	ASPIRED	POP-EYED
UMPTEEN.	NIPPING	EXPUNGE	ASPIRIN	
HOPEFUL	NUPTIAL	HAPENNY	EMPEROR	LIQUATE
PIPEFUL.	PAPRIKA	IMPANEL	EMPIRIC	PIQUANT.
SAPPHIC.	PEPPING	IMPINGE	ESPARTO	BEQUEST
+AMPHION	PEPTIDE	REPINED	EXPIRED	INQUEST
AMPLIFY	PIPPING	TOPKNOT.	HYPERON	LIQUEFY
APPLIED	POPPING	AMPHORA	IMPERIL	LIQUEUR
APPOINT	PUPPING	APPROVE	ORPHREY	REQUEST
APPRISE	RAPPING	CAPROIC	PAPYRUS	SEQUENT
BAPTISM	REPLICA	COPIOUS	TAPERED	VAQUERO.
BAPTIST	REPLIED	CUPROUS	UMPIRED.	ACQUIRE
BAPTIZE	REPOINT	DEPLORE	DEPOSED	ASQUINT
CAPPING	REPRINT	DIPLOID	DEPOSIT	ENQUIRE
CAPRICE	REPTILE	DIPLOMA	EXPOSAL	ENQUIRY
CAPSIZE	RIPPING	DIPNOAN	EXPOSED	ESQUIRE
CAPTION	RIP-TIDE	EUPHONY	IMPASSE	INQUIRE
CAPTIVE	RUPTION	EXPLODE	IMPASTE	INQUIRY

REQUIEM	FORRARD	DURABLY	BURGESS	TERSELY
REQUIRE	FORSAKE	ENROBED	CORRECT	TORMENT
REQUITE	FORWARD	FIREBOX	CORTEGE	TORPEDO
UNQUIET.	FURBALL	FIRE-BUG	CURRENT	TORRENT
SEQUOIA	FURCATE	PARABLE	DARKEST	TURNERY
UNQUOTE	FURNACE	RAREBIT	+DURRELL	VARIETY
	GARBAGE	SCRIBAL	EARNEST	VERBENA
ABREACT	GARLAND	SCRIBER	FARCEUR	VERIEST
ABREAST	GERMANE	SCRUBBY	FERMENT	+VERMEER
ABROACH	*GERMANY	SHRUBBY	FERNERY	VERMEIL
ACREAGE	HERBAGE	UNROBED	FERRETY	WARHEAD
AIRMAIL	*MARGATE	WIRABLE.	FERVENT	WARMEST.
AIR-RAID	MERMAID	APRICOT	FORBEAR	AGRAFFE
ALREADY	MORDANT	AURICLE	FORFEIT	CAREFUL
AUREATE	MURRAIN	AUROCHS	FORGERY	DIREFUL
+BARBARA	NARRATE	BORACIC	FORWENT	FIREFLY
BARBATE	NIRVANA	CARACUL	GARMENT	FORKFUL
BARGAIN	NORLAND	*CARACUS	HARDEST	GIRAFFE
BARMAID	PARTAKE	CORACLE	HARNESS	HARMFUL
+BARNABY	PERCALE	CORN-COB	HARVEST	HURTFUL
BARRACK	PERHAPS	*CURACAO	+HERBERT	SCRUFFY
BARRAGE	PERTAIN	EAR-ACHE	HERSELF	STRAFED
BEREAVE	PERVADE	HARICOT	ISRAELI	THRIFTY.
+BERNARD	PORTAGE	*KARACHI	LARCENY	ENRAGED
BUREAUX	SARCASM	LYRICAL	LARGELY	FORAGER
BURSARY	SERIATE	MIRACLE	LARGESS	GARAGED
CARCASS	SERRATE	*MOROCCO	LARGEST	PARAGON
CARNAGE	SERVANT	SARACEN	+MARGERY	PERIGEE
CARRACK	STREAKY	SIROCCO	NURSERY	PIRAGUA
CARTAGE	STRIATE	SPRUCED	OURSELF	PIROGUE
CERTAIN	SURFACE	UTRICLE	PARVENU	SCRAGGY
CORDAGE	SURNAME	VARICES.	PERCEPT	SPRIGHT
CORDATE	SURPASS	ABRADED	PERFECT	UPRIGHT.
CORKAGE	TERRACE	ABRIDGE	PERPEND	+ABRAHAM
CORSAGE	TERRAIN	BOREDOM	+PERSEUS	AIRSHIP
CORSAIR	THROATY	+BORODIN	PERVERT	BERTHED
CURRACH	TORNADO	DERIDED	PORRECT	BIRCHED
CURRANT	UNREADY	EARLDOM	PORTEND	BURGHER
CURTAIL	VARIANT	FARADAY	PORTENT	EARSHOT
CURTAIN	VERDANT	FIREDOG	PURBECK	EARTHED
CURVATE	VERVAIN	LURIDLY	+PURCELL	EARTHEN
DORMANT	VIRGATE	PARADED	SCREECH	EARTHLY
EARMARK	WARFARE	PARADOS	SERPENT	*FARNHAM
FARRAGO	WARPATH	PARADOX	SERVERY	FARTHER
FERRATE	WARRANT	REREDOS	SORCERY	FURTHER
FIRE-ARM	YARDAGE.	WORKDAY	SURFEIT	HARSHLY
FORBADE	ACROBAT	WORLDLY.	SURGEON	LURCHED
FOREARM	AEROBIC	AIRLESS	SURGERY	MARCHED
FORGAVE	CARIBOU	BERSERK	TERPENE	MARSHAL
FORMATE	DURABLE	BURGEON	TERRENE	MORPHIA

343

NARTHEX	CURVING	+HARRIET	PARTING	TORTILE
NARWHAL	DARKISH	*HARWICH	PARTITE	TURBINE
NORTHER	DARLING	HERNIAL	PERFIDY	TURFING
PARCHED	DARNING	HEROINE	PERKILY	TURKISH
PERCHED	DARTING	HEROISM	PERKING	TURNING
PYRRHIC	+DERRICK	HERRING	PERLITE	VARMINT
SORGHUM	DERVISH	HIRCINE	PERMIAN	VARNISH
WARSHIP	DIRTIED	HORDING	PERMING	VARSITY
WART-HOG	DIRTILY	HORNING	PERSIAN	VARYING
WORSHIP.	*DORKING	HORRIFY	PERSIST	VERDICT
AIRLIFT	EARLIER	HORSING	PORCINE	VERGING
AIRLINE	EARNING	HURLING	PORTICO	VERNIER
ARRAIGN	EARRING	HURRIED	PORTING	VERSIFY
BARGING	FARCING	HURTING	PORTION	VERSING
*BARKING	FARMING	JARRING	PURGING	VERSION
BARRIER	FARRIER	JERKILY	PURLIEU	VERTIGO
BARRING	FERMION	JERKING	PURLING	WARDING
+BERLIOZ	FERMIUM	KERBING	PURRING	WARLIKE
BURNING	FERRIED	LARDING	PURSING	WARMING
BURNISH	FERRITE	LARGISH	PURVIEW	WARNING
BURPING	FERTILE	LARKING	SARDINE	WARPING
CARBIDE	FIRMING	LORDING	SARKING	WARRING
CARBINE	FORCING	LURKING	SCRYING	WARRIOR
CARDIAC	FORDING	MARKING	SERRIED	WARTIME
*CARDIFF	FOREIGN	MARLINE	+SERVICE	*WARWICK
CARKING	FORGING	MARLING	SERVILE	WORDILY
CARLINE	FORGIVE	MARMITE	SERVING	WORDING
CARMINE	FORKING	MARRIED	SORDINE	WORKING
CARPING	FORMING	MARRING	SORTING	WORMING
CARRIED	FORTIFY	MARTIAL	SURDITY	WORRIED
CARRIER	FURBISH	MARTIAN	SURFING	WORRIER
CARRION	FURLING	MARTINI	SURGING	YORKING
CARTING	FURNISH	MARXISM	SURLIER	YORKIST
CARVING	FURRIER	MERGING	SURLILY	ZEROING.
CERTIFY	FURRING	MERRILY	SURMISE	STRIKER
CERVINE	FURTIVE	MORAINE	SURVIVE	STROKED
CORDIAL	GARBING	MORNING	TARDILY	TURNKEY.
CORDITE	GARFISH	MORTIFY	TARNISH	ACRYLIC
CORKING	GARNISH	MORTISE	TARRIED	AIRFLOW
CORNICE	GIRLISH	MURKILY	TARRING	BURBLED
CORNILY	GORDIAN	NERVINE	TARTING	BURGLAR
CORNISH	GORGING	NERVING	TERBIUM	BURGLED
CORVINE	HARDIER	*NORWICH	TERMING	*BURNLEY
CURBING	HARDILY	NURSING	TERMINI	+CAROLYN
CURDING	HARKING	OGREISH	TERMITE	CIRCLED
CURLING	HARMING	PARKING	TERRIER	CIRCLET
CURRIED	HARPING	PARRIED	TERRIFY	COROLLA
CURRISH	HARPIST	PARSING	TERRINE	CORSLET
CURSING	HARRIED	PARTIAL	TERTIAN	CURDLED
CURSIVE	HARRIER	PARTIED	TORSION	FORELEG

GARBLED	ERRANCY	HARBOUR	AEROSOL	PYRITES
GARGLED	HERONRY	HARMONY	CERESIN	SCRATCH
GORILLA	MARINER	HARPOON	CHRISOM	SCROTUM
GURGLED	+MIRANDA	HORMONE	+CHRISTI	STRATUM
HARE-LIP	MORONIC	+MARLOWE	CURTSEY	STRATUS
HORALLY	PARSNIP	NERVOUS	FORESAW	STRETCH
HURDLER	PARTNER	*NORFOLK	FORESEE	WORSTED.
HURTLED	PHRENIC	PARBOIL	GIRASOL	AGROUND
+LORELEI	SCRUNCH	PARLOUR	HARD-SET	*BERMUDA
MARBLED	SPRINGY	PARLOUS	*HORNSEA	BOROUGH
+MARILYN	STRANGE	PARTOOK	PARASOL	CAROUSE
MARTLET	STRINGY	PERFORM	PARESIS	CIRCUIT
MORALLY	*SURINAM	PERGOLA	PERUSAL	CORRUPT
MORELLO	SYRINGA	PERSONA	PERUSED	CURCUMA
+MURILLO	SYRINGE	PURLOIN	PHRASED	FERRULE
PAROLED	+TERENCE	PURPORT	UNRISEN	FORMULA
¡PARSLEY	THRONED	PURPOSE	WORK-SHY	FORTUNE
PERPLEX	*TORONTO	SARCODE	*WORKSOP	HIRSUTE
PURPLED	TYRANNY	SARCOMA	XERASIA.	+MARCUSE
SHRILLY	VERANDA	SERIOUS	AERATED	MARQUEE
SURPLUS	VERONAL.	SIRLOIN	AERATOR	MARQUIS
TARTLET	AIR-HOLE	SURCOAT	BARYTES	+MERCURY
+UTRILLO	AIR-LOCK	SURLOIN	BERATED	NERVURE
VIRELAY	AIRPORT	TURMOIL	BIRETTA	NURTURE
WARBLER.	AUREOLA	TURN-OUT	BORSTAL	PARQUET
CARAMEL	BARBOLA	VARIOLA	BURETTE	PERCUSS
CERAMIC	BARN-OWL	VARIOUS	CAROTID	PERFUME
CHROMIC	BURDOCK	VERBOSE	CAROTIN	PERJURE
DURAMEN	BURNOUS	*VERMONT	CURATOR	PERJURY
FIREMAN	CARDOON	WARLOCK	CURETTE	PERMUTE
FORAMEN	CARIOUS	WAR-LORD	+DOROTHY	PERTURB
FOREMAN	+CARROLL	WERWOLF	ERRATIC	PURSUER
JURYMAN	CARROTY	WORK-OUT.	ERRATUM	PURSUIT
MARIMBA	CARTOON	APROPOS	FIRSTLY	RORQUAL
OARSMAN	CEREOUS	ATROPHY	FORETOP	+STRAUSS
PYRAMID	CIRROSE	+ATROPOS	+FORSTER	THROUGH
WORKMAN.	CORPORA	HARDPAN	GAROTTE	*TORQUAY
ACRONYM	CORRODE	PARAPET	GYRATED	TORTURE
ADRENAL	CURIOUS	PORK-PIE	HARDTOP	VERDURE
ARRANGE	CURSORY	SCRAPER	HERETIC	VERRUCA
BARONET	FERN-OWL	SCRAPPY	HERITOR	VIRGULE
CHRONIC	FERROUS	SCRUPLE	+HORATIO	VIRTUAL.
CORANTO	FERVOUR	+SERAPIS	KERATIN	ARRIVAL
*CORINTH	FORBORE	STRIPED	MARITAL	ARRIVED
CORONAL	FORGONE	STROPHE.	MERITED	CARAVAN
CORONER	FORLORN	BAROQUE.	OERSTED	DERIVED
CORONET	*FORMOSA	AURORAL	PAROTID	FOREVER
DERANGE	FORSOOK	+BERTRAM	PIRATED	SHRIVEL
DURANCE	FURIOUS	EAR-DRUM	PURITAN	STRIVEN
EIRENIC	FURLONG	PORTRAY.	PYRETIC	THRIVED

THRIVEN	HOSTAGE	WASH-DAY.	VISCERA	DOSSIER
UNRAVEL.	HUSBAND	ABSCESS	WEST-END	DOSSING
CARAWAY	INSCAPE	AUSTERE	WESTERN	DUSKIER
FARAWAY	INSTALL	BESEECH	*WISBECH.	DUSKILY
PERIWIG	INSTANT	BESIEGE	BASHFUL	DUSTIER
*SARAWAK	INSTATE	BESMEAR	DISHFUL	DUSTILY
SCRAWNY	MASCARA	BESPEAK	EASEFUL	DUSTING
SCREWED	MASSAGE	BESTEAD	FISTFUL	EASTING
STREWED	MESSAGE	+BOSWELL	INSOFAR	EXSCIND
THROWER.	MISCALL	CISTERN	LUSTFUL	FASCINE
PYREXIA.	MISCAST	COSTEAN	RESTFUL	FASCISM
BERHYME	MISGAVE	DESCEND	WISHFUL	FASCIST
FORAYED	MISLAID	DESCENT	WISTFUL	FASHION
SPRAYER	MISTAKE	DESSERT	ZESTFUL.	FASTING
STRAYED.	MUSTANG	DISCERN	ASSAGAI	FESTIVE
HORIZON	MUSTARD	DISSECT	INSIGHT	FISHILY
	OSSUARY	DISSENT	NOSEGAY.	FISHING
ABSTAIN	PASSAGE	DISTEND	PASCHAL.	FISSILE
ASSUAGE	PASSANT	EASTERN	ABSCIND	FISSION
BASTARD	PESSARY	FASTEST	AUSPICE	FOSSICK
BOSCAGE	POSTAGE	FISHERY	AUSSIES	FUSSING
BUSTARD	RESTATE	HAS-BEEN	BASHING	FUSTIAN
CASCADE	ROSEATE	HASLETS	BASKING	FUSTILY
CASCARA	SUSTAIN	HOSIERY	BASTING	GASEITY
CASSAVA	TESTACY	HOSTESS	BASTION	GASHING
COSSACK	TESTATE	INSPECT	BESTIAL	GASPING
COSTARD	UPSTAGE	INSTEAD	BUSHIDO	GAS-RING
COSTATE	UPSTAIR	MASSEUR	BUSKING	GASSING
CUSPATE	UPSTART	MASTERY	BUSTING	GOSLING
CUSTARD	WASSAIL	MESEEMS	CASHIER	GOSSIPY
DASTARD	WASTAGE.	MISDEAL	CASHING	GUSHING
DESCALE	DISABLE	MISDEED	*CASPIAN	HASHING
DESCANT	DISOBEY	MISLEAD	CASTILE	HASHISH
DESPAIR	DUSTBIN	MISREAD	CASTING	HASPING
DISBAND	FUSIBLE	MYSTERY	CASUIST	HASTILY
DISCARD	NOSEBAG	NASCENT	CESSION	HESSIAN
DISDAIN	POSTBAG	OBSCENE	COSTING	HISSING
DISEASE	RISIBLE	PASTERN	COSTIVE	HOSPICE
DISMAST	ROSEBUD	+PASTEUR	CUSHION	HOSTILE
DISTAFF	VISIBLE.	POSSESS	CUSSING	HUSHING
DISTANT	MUSICAL	POSTERN	DASHING	HUSKING
ECSTASY	OSSICLE	RESPECT	DESPISE	INSPIRE
ENSLAVE	ROSE-CUT	+RUSSELL	DESPITE	*IPSWICH
ENSNARE	VESICLE.	SUSPECT	DESTINE	+JASMINE
GAS-MAIN	BESIDES	SUSPEND	DESTINY	+JESSICA
GAS-MASK	FAST-DAY	TESSERA	DISHING	JESTING
GESTALT	INSIDER	UNSPENT	DISLIKE	JOSHING
GESTAPO	RESIDED	UPSWEPT	DISLIMN	JUSSIVE
GOSHAWK	RESIDUA	VASTEST	DISMISS	JUSTICE
HASTATE	RESIDUE	VESPERS	DISTICH	JUSTIFY

+JUSTINE	RESTIVE	NESTLED	HASSOCK	UNSTRAP
*KESWICK	RISKIER	RESILED	HISTORY	UPSURGE
KISSING	RISKILY	RESOLVE	INSHORE	WASTREL
LASHING	RISKING	RUSTLED	LASSOED	MISUSED.
LASTING	+ROSSINI	RUSTLER	MASTOID	*LESOTHO
LESBIAN	RUSHING	TUSSLED.	MISTOOK	POSITED
LISPING	RUSSIAN	ASSUMED	OSSEOUS	RISOTTO
LISTING	RUSSIFY	BUSHMAN	PISTOLE	ROSETTE
LUSTILY	RUSTIER	DISHMAT	RESPOND	VISITED
LUSTING	RUSTILY	DUSTMAN	RESTORE	VISITOR.
MASHING	RUSTING	PASSMAN	RISSOLE	ASSAULT
MASKING	SESSION	POSTMAN	ROSEOLA	BASCULE
MASSING	SESTINA	RESUMED	+SASSCON	BISCUIT
MASSIVE	SUSPIRE	YASHMAK.	SYSTOLE	BISMUTH
MASTIFF	SUSSING	ABSENCE	TUSSOCK	COSTUME
MESHING	TASKING	ABSINTH	TUSSORE	DISCUSS
MESSIAH	TASTIER	ARSENAL	VISCOSE	DISGUST
MESSIER	TASTILY	ARSENIC	VISCOUS	DISPUTE
MESSILY	TASTING	BASINET	WASH-OUT.	DISRUPT
MESSING	TESTIFY	ESSENCE	CESSPIT	DISTURB
MESTIZO	TESTILY	ESSENES	DUSTPAN	FISSURE
MISFIRE	TESTING	HOSANNA	FUSS-POT	FISTULA
MISGIVE	TOSSING	MASONIC	INSIPID	GESTURE
MISLIKE	UNSLING	MASONRY	PUSHPIN.	MISRULE
MISSILE	UNSTICK	RESINED	ALSO-RAN	OBSCURE
MISSING	VESTIGE	ROSINED	ASSURED	PASTURE
MISSION	VESTING	+SUSANNA.	AUSTRAL	POSTURE
MISSIVE	WASHING	ABSCOND	*AUSTRIA	PUSTULE
MISTILY	WASPISH	BASSOON	BESTREW	RESCUER
MISTING	WASTING	BESPOKE	DESERVE	RESOUND
MYSTIFY	WESTING	CASEOUS	DESIRED	TESTUDO
NASTIER	WISHING.	CASSOCK	DESTROY	TISSUED
NASTILY	+PUSHKIN.	CAST-OFF	ENSURED	UNSOUND
NESTING	ABSOLVE	CESTOID	GASTRIC	UNSTUCK
NOSHING	BASALLY	CUSTODY	INSURED	VASCULA
OUSTING	BASILAR	+DESMOND	INSURER	VESTURE
PASSING	BASILIC	DESPOIL	KESTREL	*VISTULA.
PASSION	BUSTLED	DESPOND	LUSTRAL	DISAVOW.
PASSIVE	CASE-LAW	DISCOID	MISERLY	POST-WAR
PASTIME	CASTLED	DISCORD	MISTRAL	UNSEXED.
PASTING	DISPLAY	DISJOIN	MUSK-RAT	ASSAYED
PISCINA	ENSILED	DISPORT	NOSTRIL	DISTYLE
PISCINE	EPSILON	DISPOSE	NOSTRUM	ESSAYED
POSTING	+GISELLE	DISROBE	OBSERVE	SYSTYLE.
PUSHING	HUSTLER	DISTORT	OESTRUS	ASSIZES
RASPING	INSULAR	FESTOON	RESERVE	
RESCIND	INSULIN	FUSCOUS	ROSTRAL	ACTUARY
RESPIRE	JOSTLED	GASEOUS	ROSTRUM	ACTUATE
RESPITE	MUSCLED	*GOSPORT	SISTRUM	+ASTRAEA
RESTING	NASALLY	GOSSOON	UNSCREW	ATTRACT

CATCALL	ACTABLE	HUTMENT	MATCHET	*LOTHIAN
CATFALL	DATABLE	JITTERY	+MATTHEW	MATTING
CATWALK	EATABLE	LATHERY	NOTCHED	METRICS
CITHARA	MUTABLE	LETHEAN	PATCHED	METRIST
CITRATE	NOTABLE	LOTTERY	PITCHED	NETTING
COTTAGE	NOTABLY	OATMEAL	PITCHER	NOTHING
CUT-BACK	OCTOBER	OUTWEAR	POT-SHOT	NUTTING
CUTLASS	POTABLE	OUTWENT	RATCHET	OSTRICH
DETRACT	RATABLE.	PATIENT	RETCHED	OUTLIER
DETRAIN	ANTACID	PATTERN	SATCHEL	OUTLINE
ENTRAIN	ARTICLE	PIT-HEAD	WATCHED	OUTLIVE
ENTRANT	ATTACHE	POT-HERB	WITCHED.	OUTRIDE
ESTUARY	AUTOCAR	POTTERY	ANT-HILL	OUTSIDE
EXTRACT	CATECHU	PUTREFY	ASTRIDE	OUTSIZE
GUTTATE	CUTICLE	RETREAD	ATTAINT	+PATRICK
HATBAND	ENTICED	SATIETY	BATHING	PATRIOT
HATRACK	NOTICED	TOTTERY	BATTING	PATTING
INTRANT	OPTICAL	WETNESS	BETHINK	PETRIFY
*JUTLAND	RETICLE	WETTEST	BETTING	PETTILY
METCAST	*VATICAN.	WITHERS	BETWIXT	PETTING
METHANE	CITADEL	WITLESS	CATFISH	PETTISH
NETBALL	CO-TIDAL	WITNESS.	CATLING	PITHILY
NITRATE	FETIDLY	DUTIFUL	CATMINT	PITTING
NUT-CASE	KATYDID	FATEFUL	CATTILY	PITYING
OATCAKE	MATADOR.	HATEFUL	CATTISH	POTTING
OUTBACK	+ACTAEON	PITIFUL	CITRINE	PUTTIER
OUTCAST	ACTRESS	RATAFIA.	COTTIER	PUTTING
OUTFACE	+ANTAEUS	ANTIGEN	CUTTING	RATFINK
OUTFALL	*ANTWERP	*ANTIGUA	DOTTING	RATTING
OUTLAST	APTNESS	FATIGUE	ENTWINE	RETHINK
OUTRAGE	ARTLESS	INTEGER	ESTRIOL	RETRIED
OUTSAIL	BATTERY	MUTAGEN	FATLING	ROTTING
OUTTALK	BETWEEN	OCTAGON	FITTING	RUTTING
OUTWARD	BITTERN	UPTIGHT.	GATLING	RUTTISH
PITFALL	BUTTERY	BOTCHER	*GATWICK	SETTING
RAT-RACE	CATHEAD	BUTCHER	GETTING	SITTING
RAT-TAIL	CATS-EYE	CATCHER	GOTHICK	SOTTISH
RETIARY	CUTLERY	DITCHED	G-STRING	TATTILY
RETRACE	ENTREAT	DITCHER	GUTTING	TATTING
RETRACT	ESTHETE	FETCHED	HITTING	TITLING
*RUTLAND	EXTREME	FITCHEW	HOTTING	TOTTING
SATIATE	FAT-HEAD	HATCHER	HUTTING	TUTTING
SETBACK	FATNESS	HATCHET	JETTING	UNTRIED
SET-FAIR	FATTEST	HITCHED	JOTTING	UNTWINE
SITUATE	FITMENT	*HITCHIN	JUTTING	UNTWIST
TITLARK	FITNESS	HUTCHED	KITTING	VETOING
TITRATE	FITTEST	KETCHUP	LATRINE	VETTING
VITIATE	HETAERA	KITCHEN	LATTICE	VITRIFY
WATTAGE	HOT-HEAD	LATCHED	LETTING	VITRIOL
*ZETLAND.	HOTTEST	MATCHED	LITHIUM	WETTING

WITTIER	DETENTE	OUTWORN	SUTURAL	COUVADE
WITTILY	ENTENTE	PETIOLE	SUTURED	CRUSADE
WITTING	EXTINCT	PITEOUS	TUTORED	EDUCATE
YTTRIUM.	INTENSE	POTHOLE	UPTHROW	EMULATE
BETAKEN	INTONED	POTHOOK	UTTERED	FOULARD
BETOKEN	*KATANGA	SET-DOWN	UTTERLY	FOUMART
RETAKEN.	LATENCY	SIT-DOWN	VETERAN	GOULASH
ANTILOG	MATINEE	TETRODE	WATERED.	HAULAGE
BATTLED	PETUNIA	*WATFORD	ARTISAN	OCULATE
BOTTLED	POTENCE	WITHOUT.	ARTISTE	PLUMAGE
CATALPA	POTENCY	AUTOPSY	+BATISTA	RHUBARB
+ESTELLA	RETINUE	CATS-PAW	BATISTE	ROULADE
FATALLY	ROTUNDA	NOTEPAD	+MATISSE	SAUSAGE
LITTLER	SATANIC	OCTOPOD	MITOSIS	SCUTAGE
+MATILDA	TETANIC	OCTOPUS	SATISFY.	SOUTANE
MOTTLED	TETANUS	OCTUPLE	ASTATIC	SQUEAKY
+NATALIE	+TITANIA	OUTSPAN.	ENTITLE	ULULATE.
NETTLED	TITANIC.	ANTIQUE.	LITOTES	BLUBBER
ORTOLAN	+ANTHONY	ALTERED	MUTATED	BOURBON
OUTFLOW	BETROTH	ANTHRAX	OUTSTAY	CLUBBED
OUTPLAY	BUTTOCK	APTERAL	ROTATED	CRUMBLE
PATELLA	CATBOAT	APTERYX	ROTATOR.	CRUMBLY
RATTLER	CATHODE	+ASTARTE	ASTOUND	DRUBBED
SETTLED	CITROUS	ATTIRED	DETRUDE	EQUABLE
SETTLER	COTTONY	BOTARGO	ENTHUSE	EQUABLY
SETTLOR	*DETROIT	BUTYRIC	ENTRUST	GRUBBED
TATTLER	DUTEOUS	CATARRH	EXTRUDE	GRUBBER
TITULAR	ENTROPY	CATERER	INTRUDE	GRUMBLE
TOTALLY	ESTRONE	COTERIE	INTRUST	HAUTBOY
TUTELAR	FATUOUS	DETERED	LETTUCE	PLUMBER
VITALLY	FETLOCK	ENTERIC	NETSUKE	PLUMBIC
WATTLED.	FUTHORC	ENTHRAL	OBTRUDE	SCUMBLE
+ARTEMIS	HOTFOOT	+EUTERPE	POTLUCK	SLUBBED
ATTEMPT	INTROIT	ICTERUS	RETOUCH	SLUMBER
AUTOMAT	LUTEOUS	INTERIM	*SATSUMA	SNUBBED
BETIMES	*MATLOCK	LATERAL	UNTRUSS	STUBBED
BITUMEN	MATTOCK	LITERAL	UNTRUTH.	STUBBLE
ENTOMIC	NETWORK	LITURGY	MOTIVED.	STUBBLY
GATEMAN	NITROUS	MATURED	CUTAWAY	STUMBLE
ISTHMUS	OUTCOME	MOTORED	GATEWAY	THUMBED.
OPTIMUM	OUTDONE	NATURAL	GETAWAY	BOUNCER
OTTOMAN	OUTDOOR	*ONTARIO	PATHWAY.	CHURCHY
TOTEMIC	OUTGONE	OUTCROP	UNTAXED.	COUNCIL
UNTAMED	OUTLOOK	OUTGREW	CAT-EYED.	CRUNCHY
VITAMIN.	OUTMOST	OUTGROW	CITIZEN	GOUACHE
ACTINIC	OUTPOST	PETERED	METAZOA	JOUNCED
ANTENNA	OUTRODE	RAT-TRAP		PAUNCHY
ANTONYM	OUTVOTE	RETIRED	ADULATE	POUNCED
ATTUNED	OUTWORE	SATIRIC	CAUDATE	SLUICED
BOTANIC	OUTWORK	SATYRIC	COURAGE	SOUPCON

*ARUNDEL	STUDENT	POUCHED	LOURING	COUPLER
ASUNDER	STUPEFY	ROUGHEN	LOUSILY	COUPLET
BLUNDER	TAUTEST	ROUGHER	LOUTISH	CRUELLY
*BOULDER	+TRUDEAU	ROUGHLY	MAULING	CRUELTY
BOUNDER	UKULELE.	SHUSHED	+MAURICE	DOUBLED
BOURDON	BLUFFER	SOUGHED	NOURISH	DOUBLET
COULDST	BLUFFLY	TOUCHED	OCULIST	*DOUGLAS
DRUIDIC	CHUFFED	TOUGHEN	PAUCITY	DRUMLIN
*ECUADOR	GRUFFLY	TOUGHER	+PAULINE	EQUALLY
FOUNDER	SCUFFED	TOUGHLY	PAUSING	KNURLED
FOUNDRY	SCUFFLE	+VAUGHAN	PLUMING	MAUDLIN
HOUNDED	SHUFFLE	VOUCHER.	PLUVIAL	SCULLER
LAUNDER	SNUFFED	ABUSIVE	POURING	SQUALID
LAUNDRY	SNUFFLE	ALUMINA	POUTING	SQUALLY
MAUNDER	SOUFFLE	AMUSING	PRUDISH	SQUALOR
MOULDED	SOULFUL	AZURINE	PRUNING	SQUELCH
MOULDER	SQUIFFY	BAUXITE	PRURIGO	TOUSLED
MOUNDED	STUFFED	BLUEING	*REUNION	USUALLY.
PLUNDER	TRUFFLE.	BRUTISH	REUNITE	CLUBMAN
POUNDAL	CHUGGED	CAUSING	ROUGING	DRUMMED
POUNDER	DRUDGED	CAUTION	ROUSING	DRUMMER
ROUNDEL	DRUGGED	COURIER	ROUTINE	FLUMMOX
ROUNDER	DRUGGET	CRUCIAL	ROUTING	GOURMET
ROUNDLY	FOURGON	CRUCIFY	SAUCILY	GRUMMET
ROUND-UP	GRUDGED	CRUDITY	SAUCING	+HOUSMAN
SCUDDED	LOUNGER	DAUBING	SAURIAN	PLUMMET
SHUDDER	PLUGGED	DOUSING	SOURING	SCUMMED
SOUNDED	PLUNGED	EDUCING	SOUSING	SLUMMED.
SOUNDLY	PLUNGER	ELUDING	SPUMING	ALUMNUS
STUDDED	SLUGGED	ELUSION	SQUAILS	CHURNED
THUDDED	SMUDGED	ELUSIVE	STUDIED	CHUTNEY
THUNDER	SMUGGLE	ELUVIAL	TAURINE	DIURNAL
TRUNDLE	SNUGGED	ERUDITE	THULIUM	EQUINOX
WOUNDED.	SNUGGLE	EXUDING	TOURING	FLUENCY
ACUTELY	TRUDGED	FEUDING	TOURISM	INURNED
CAUTERY	YOUNGER.	FLUTING	TOURIST	JOURNAL
CRUDELY	BLUSHED	FLUTIST	TOUTING.	JOURNEY
DOUCEUR	BRUSHED	FLUVIAL	CHUCKED	MOURNER
GRUYERE	COUCHED	FLUXION	CHUCKLE	SHUNNED
HAUBERK	COUGHED	FOULING	CHUKKER	SPURNED
HAUTEUR	CRUSHED	GAUDILY	DRUNKEN	SPUTNIK
LOUDEST	DAUPHIN	GAUGING	FLUNKEY	SQUINCH
+MAUREEN	DOUCHED	GLUEING	KNUCKLE	STUNNER
OPULENT	DOUGHTY	GOUGING	PLUCKED	TOURNEY
+POULENC	FLUSHED	HAULIER	PLUNKED	TRUANCY.
PRUDENT	HAUGHTY	HAULING	SHUCKED	AQUEOUS
PRUDERY	LAUGHED	+HOUDINI	.SKULKED	BOUDOIR
SHUT-EYE	MOUTHED	HOUSING	STUCK-UP	BRUMOUS
SOUREST	NAUGHTY	INURING	TRUCKED	COULOMB
SQUEEZE	PLUSHER	LAUDING	TRUCKLE.	ELUSORY

EMULOUS	COURTLY	OBVIATE	DIVINED	BIVOUAC
GLUCOSE	CRUSTED	SAVE-ALL.	DIVINER	SAVOURY.
PLUMOSE	DAUNTED	LIVABLE	ENVENOM	REVIVAL
RAUCOUS	DOUBTED	LOVABLE	HAVENER	REVIVER.
SHUT-OUT.	DOUBTER	LOVABLY	+LAVINIA	*DEVIZES
CLUMPED	EQUATED	MOVABLE	REVENGE	
CRUMPET	EQUATOR	SAVABLE.	REVENUE	COWBANE
CRUMPLE	ERUPTED	DOVECOT	SAVANNA	INWEAVE
CRUPPER	EXULTED	NAVY-CUT.	SEVENTH	LOWLAND
PLUMPER	FAULTED	DIVIDED	SEVENTY.	NEW-LAID
PLUMPLY	FLUSTER	INVADER	ALVEOLE	TOWPATH.
SCULPED	FLUTTER	LIVIDLY	DEVIOUS	COWHERD
SCUPPER	FRUITER	VIVIDLY.	ENVIOUS	HOWBEIT
SLUMPED	FRUSTUM	RIVIERE.	OBVIOUS	LAWLESS
STUMPED	GAUNTLY	RAVAGED	+PAVLOVA	NOWHERE
THUMPED	GLUTTED	SAVAGED.	RAVIOLI	POWDERY
TRUMPED	GLUTTON	CIVVIES	SAVIOUR.	RAWNESS.
TRUMPET	GRUNTED	ENVYING	ADVERSE	BOWLFUL.
USURPER.	HAUNTED	INVEIGH	COVERED	DOWAGER.
BRUSQUE.	*HOUSTON	INVOICE	DIVERGE	BOWSHOT.
BLURRED	JAUNTED	LEVYING	DIVERSE	BAWDILY
BOURREE	JOUSTED	REVVING.	DIVORCE	BAWLING
EQUERRY	MOULTED	DOVEKIE	ENVIRON	BOWLINE
NEUTRAL	MOUNTED	INVOKED	HOVERED	BOWLING
NEUTRON	POULTRY	REVOKED.	INVERSE	COWHIDE
SLURRED	ROUSTED	BIVALVE	LEVERED	COWLICK
SPURRED	SAUNTER	CAVALRY	LEVERET	COWLING
SQUARED.	SCUTTER	CIVILLY	OBVERSE	DAWNING
BRUISED	SCUTTLE	DEVALUE	POVERTY	DOWDILY
COUNSEL	SHUNTED	DEVELOP	REVERED	DOWNING
COURSER	SHUTTER	DEVILRY	REVERIE	DOWSING
CRUISED	SHUTTLE	DEVOLVE	REVERSE	FAWNING
CRUISER	SMUTTED	DIVULGE	REVERSO	FOWLING
PRUSSIC	SPURTED	ENVELOP	SEVERAL	HAWKING
SQUASHY	SPUTTER	INVALID	SEVERED	HOWLING
TRUSSED.	STUNTED	INVOLVE	WAVERED.	MAWKISH
ABUTTER	STUTTER	JAVELIN	ADVISED	PAWKILY
AQUATIC	TAUNTED	+NEVILLE	ADVISER	PAWNING
BLUNTED	*TAUNTON	NOVELTY	DEVISED	RAWHIDE
BLUNTLY	TRUSTED	RAVELIN	DIVISOR	REWRITE
BLURTED	TRUSTEE	REVELRY	REVISAL	ROWDIER
BLUSTER	VAULTED	REVILED	REVISED.	ROWDILY
BOULTER	VAULTER	REVOLVE	COVETED	SAWBILL
CAUSTIC	VAUNTED.	RIVALRY	DEVOTED	SAWFISH
CLUSTER	BOUQUET	RIVULET	DEVOTEE	SAW-MILL
CLUTTER	+ROUAULT	SAVELOY	GAVOTTE	TAWNILY
COULTER	UNUSUAL	*SEVILLE	INVITED	TOWLINE
COUNTED	*URUGUAY	+VIVALDI.	PIVOTAL	YAWNING
COUNTER		CAVE-MAN.	PIVOTED	YOWLING.
COUNTRY	DEVIATE	ADVANCE	RIVETER.	COWSLIP

DAWDLER	MAXILLA.	WRYNESS.	DAYLONG	JAZZING.
DEW-CLAW	MAXIMAL	CRYOGEN	DRY-DOCK	DAZZLED
JEWELRY	MAXIMUM	VOYAGER.	FLY-BOAT	FIZZLED
ROWELED.	TAXIMAN.	DRY-SHOD	FLY-BOOK	GAZELLE
DEWPOND	ANXIOUS	GLYPHIC	HAYCOCK	GUZZLER
HAWK-OWL	BOXWOOD	GRYPHON	HAYFORK	MIZZLED
JAW-BONE	COXCOMB	PSYCHIC	KEYHOLE	MUZZLED
LOW-BORN	FOXHOLE	SCYTHED	KEYNOTE	NUZZLED
LOW-DOWN	NOXIOUS	TOYSHOP.	MAYPOLE	PUZZLER
*NEWPORT	SAXHORN	ANYWISE	PAY-LOAD	SIZZLED
*NEWTOWN	SIXFOLD	DAY-GIRL	PAY-ROLL	SOZZLED.
REWROTE	WAXWORK.	DAY-TIME	PLYWOOD	+CEZANNE
ROWLOCK	HEXAPOD.	ELYSIAN	+RAYMOND	COZENER
TOW-ROPE.	BOX-TREE	ELYSIUM	+SEYMOUR	LOZENGE
COWERED	DEXTRAL	*HAYLING	SPY-HOLE	UNZONED
DEWDROP	DEXTRAN	HAYRICK	THYROID.	WIZENED.
LOW-BRED	DEXTRIN	HAYWIRE	*OLYMPIA	BAZOOKA.
LOWBROW	FOX-TROT	JOY-RIDE	OLYMPIC	BEZIQUE.
ONWARDS	TAX-FREE.	KEY-RING	*OLYMPUS.	BIZARRE
POWERED	FIXATED	PHYSICS	FLY-TRAP.	MAZURKA
SEWERED	LUXATED.	RHYMING	ABYSSAL	RAZORED.
TOWARDS	FIXTURE	SKY-HIGH	ALYSSUM	GAZETTE
UPWARDS.	FOXHUNT	SKYLINE	ODYSSEY	
BEWITCH.	MIXTURE	STYGIAN	THYRSUS	
LAWSUIT	TEXTUAL	STYLING	TRYPSIN	+ABRAHAM
SAWDUST	TEXTURE	STYLISH	+ULYSSES.	ALCAZAR
UNWOUND		STYLIST	CLYSTER	ALMANAC
UNWRUNG.	CRY-BABY	STYLITE	CRYPTIC	ASSAGAI
HOWEVER	FLY-HALF	STYLIZE	CRYSTAL	CARAVAN
INWOVEN	FLY-PAST	STYMIED	GLYPTIC	CARAWAY
	HAYWARD	WAY-BILL	KRYPTOL	CLOACAL
BOXHAUL	REYNARD	WAYSIDE.	KRYPTON	*CURACAO
SEXTAIN	SKYLARK	UNYOKED.	LAYETTE	CUTAWAY
SEXTANT.	SKYSAIL	IDYLLIC	SHYSTER	DECADAL
FIXABLE	SKYWARD	LOYALLY	STYPTIC	DECANAL
TAXABLE.	TRYSAIL	LOYALTY	TRYSTED.	FARADAY
LEXICAL	WAYWARD.	+PHYLLIS	MAYBUSH.	FARAWAY
LEXICON	BUYABLE	PTYALIN	FLY-OVER.	FLYAWAY
TAXI-CAB.	PAYABLE.	ROYALLY	FLYAWAY.	+GALAHAD
ANXIETY	COYNESS	ROYALTY	BRYOZOA	GETAWAY
LAXNESS	FLYLEAF	SKY-BLUE.		MACADAM
+MAXWELL	HAYSEED	ABYSMAL.	BUZZARD	PALATAL
SEXIEST	JOYLESS	BAYONET	GIZZARD.	PICAMAR
SEXLESS	PAYMENT	CAYENNE.	+JEZEBEL	PYJAMAS
SIXTEEN.	RAYLESS	AMYLOID	SIZABLE.	RAMADAN
HEXAGON.	SHYNESS	ANYBODY	DAZEDLY.	RUNAWAY
BOX-KITE	SLYNESS	AZYMOUS	BUZZING	*SARAWAK
TAXIING	STYRENE	BOYCOTT	DIZZILY	*YUCATAN.
TEXTILE	THYSELF	BOYHOOD	FIZZING	COPAIBA.
WAXBILL.	WRYNECK	DAYBOOK	JAZZILY	ADVANCE

ASKANCE	CADAVER	FREAKED	SCRAPER	EAR-ACHE
BALANCE	CARAMEL	GARAGED	SEDATED	EMPATHY
DEBAUCH	CHEAPEN	GLEAMED	SHEARED	GOUACHE
DURANCE	CHEATED	GLEANER	SHEAVES	*KARACHI
ENHANCE	CITADEL	GLOATED	SHOALED	PANACHE
ERRANCY	CLEANED	GREASED	SMEARED	SHEATHE
FINANCE	CLEANER	GREASER	SNEAKED	SPLASHY
INFANCY	CLEARED	GREATER	SOLACED	SQUASHY
*JAMAICA	CLEARER	GREAVES	SPEAKER	WREATHE.
MALACCA	CLEAVED	GROANED	SPEARED	*ALBANIA
MONARCH	CLEAVER	GYRATED	SPLAYED	AMHARIC
PENANCE	CLOAKED	IMPALED	SPRAYER	ANTACID
PLIANCY	CREAKED	IMPANEL	SQUARED	APHASIA
POLACCA	CREAMED	INHALER	STEAMED	AQUATIC
ROMANCE	CREAMER	INVADER	STEAMER	ASIATIC
SCRATCH	CREASED	KNEADED	STRAFED	ASTATIC
TENANCY	CREATED	KRAALED	STRAYED	BORACIC
TOBACCO	CROAKER	LEGATED	SUGARED	BOTANIC
TRUANCY	DEBASED	LEGATEE	SWEARER	CERAMIC
VACANCY	DEBATED	LOCATED	SWEATED	COHABIT
VALANCE.	DECAYED	LUXATED	SWEATER	DIBASIC
INNARDS	DEFACED	MANAGED	TREATED	DYNAMIC
+MIRANDA	DEFAMED	MANAGER	TWEAKED	ERRATIC
ONWARDS	DELATED	MANATEE	UNCARED	FANATIC
TOWARDS	DELAYED	MENACED	UNCASED	FILARIA
UNHANDY	DILATED	MINARET	UNLADEN	GELATIN
UPWARDS	DONATED	MUTAGEN	UNNAMED	HEMATIN
VERANDA	DOWAGER	MUTATED	UNRAVEL	HEPATIC
+VIVALDI.	DREADED	NEGATED	UNTAMED	+HORATIO
ABRADED	DREAMER	PALAVER	UNTAXED	HYDATID
+ACHATES	DURAMEN	PANACEA	VACATED	INHABIT
AERATED	EFFASED	PARADED	VOYAGER	INVALID
ALLAYED	EMBAYED	PARAPET	WHEATEN	ISLAMIC
+ANNABEL	EMPANEL	PENATES	WREAKED.	KERATIN
APPAREL	ENCAGED	PHRASED	AGRAFFE	LUNATIC
ASHAMED	ENCASED	PIRATED	ALFALFA	MALARIA
ASSAYED	ENFACED	PLEADER	GIRAFFE.	+MELANIE
BEHAVED	ENGAGED	PLEASED	ARRAIGN	MELANIN
BELATED	ENLACED	PLEATED	ARRANGE	MONADIC
BELAYED	ENRAGED	RAVAGED	BOTARGO	+NATALIE
BERATED	EQUATED	REBATED	DERANGE	NOMADIC
BETAKEN	ESCAPED	REFACED	EMBARGO	*OCEANIA
BLEATED	ESCAPEE	REGALED	ENLARGE	OCEANIC
BLOATED	ESSAYED	RELATED	FALANGE	OGHAMIC
BLOATER	EXHALED	RELAXED	HIDALGO	*ONTARIO
BREADED	FIXATED	REPAPER	*KATANGA	ORGANIC
BREAKER	FLOATER	RETAKEN	SCRAGGY	PALADIN
BROADEN	FORAGER	ROTATED	STRANGE.	PELAGIC
BROADER	FORAMEN	SARACEN	ATTACHE	PTYALIN
CABARET	FORAYED	SAVAGED	BREATHE	PYRAMID

353

RATAFIA	HUMANLY	WIRABLE	PICADOR	MULATTO
REGALIA	IDEALLY	WOMANLY	ROTATOR	PENALTY
ROMANIC	ISRAELI	ZONALLY.	SENATOR	REGATTA
*RUMANIA	LEGALLY	CHIASMA	SQUALOR	ROYALTY
SATANIC	LIVABLE	MAHATMA.	TREASON.	SABAOTH
SCIATIC	LOCALLY	+ARIADNE	CATALPA	STEALTH
+SERAPIS	LOVABLE	ATTAINT	SCRAPPY	UNEARTH
SOMATIC	LOVABLY	AUBAINE	UNHAPPY.	VEDANTA.
SQUALID	LOYALLY	+CEZANNE	BIZARRE	+ANTAEUS
STEARIN	MANACLE	COCAINE	CATARRH	BREAK-UP
SUBACID	MIRACLE	DELAINE	CAVALRY	CALAMUS
TETANIC	MORALLY	HOSANNA	HETAERA	CARACUL
THIAMIN	MOVABLE	LUCARNE	MACABRE	*CARACUS
+TITANIA	MUTABLE	MORAINE	PODAGRA	DEVALUE
TITANIC	NAMABLE	SAVANNA	REMARRY	ERRATUM
VITAMIN	NASALLY	SCRAWNY	RIVALRY	+PEGASUS
VOCALIC	NOTABLE	+SUSANNA	*SUMATRA	PIRAGUA
XERASIA.	NOTABLY	TYRANNY	TANAGRA	POMATUM
ACTABLE	PARABLE	UNCANNY.	THEATRE.	SENATUS
AFFABLE	PAYABLE	+ACTAEON	BAGASSE	STRATUM
AMIABLE	PENALLY	AERATOR	BECAUSE	STRATUS
ASSAULT	PLIABLE	AVIATOR	CLEANSE	TETANUS.
AXIALLY	POTABLE	BUGABOO	DADAISM	BIVALVE.
BASALLY	RATABLE	CELADON	DEGAUSS	JUDAIZE
BLEAKLY	REGALLY	CREATOR	EMBASSY	
BROADLY	RIDABLE	CURATOR	EXHAUST	
BUYABLE	+ROUAULT	DECAGON	EXPANSE	ARABIAN
CAPABLE	ROYALLY	DECAPOD	IMPASSE	BUGBEAR
CHEAPLY	SALABLE	DELATOR	JUDAISM	CATBOAT
CLEANLY	SAVABLE	DILATOR	LAMAISM	CLUBMAN
CLEARLY	SIZABLE	DISAVOW	MALAISE	FLY-BOAT
CORACLE	SQUAILS	DONATOR	RELAPSE	FORBEAR
DATABLE	SQUALLY	*ECUADOR	+STRAUSS	GUNBOAT
DEBACLE	TAMABLE	+ELEANOR	SYNAPSE.	LESBIAN
DEFAULT	TAXABLE	EQUATOR	ANDANTE	OFFBEAT
DISABLE	TENABLE	ETHANOL	+ASTARTE	SUNBEAM.
DUPABLE	TENABLY	GIRASOL	*ATLANTA	CRY-BABY
DURABLE	TOTALLY	HEXAGON	BREADTH	CUT-BACK
DURABLY	TREACLE	HEXAPOD	CANASTA	FINBACK
EATABLE	TREACLY	ICHABOD	CHIANTI	HOGBACK
EQUABLE	TREADLE	*LEBANON	CORANTO	LIMBECK
EQUABLY	TRIABLE	MATADOR	DYNASTY	OUTBACK
EQUALLY	TUNABLE	MEGATON	ESPARTO	PURBECK
FATALLY	UNMANLY	METAZOA	+HOGARTH	ROEBUCK
FINABLE	USUALLY	OCTAGON	IMPASTE	RUN-BACK
FINAGLE	VENALLY	ORGANON	IMPASTO	SETBACK
FINALLY	VITALLY	PARADOS	INFANTA	*WISBECH.
FIXABLE	VOCABLE	PARADOX	INFANTE	ANYBODY
GREATLY	VOCALLY	PARAGON	+JOCASTA	CARBIDE
HORALLY	WADABLE	PARASOL	LOYALTY	FORBADE.
				BABBLER

BLABBED	SNUBBED	WAXBILL	TUBBING	LIMBATE
BLUBBER	STABBED	WAY-BILL.	TURBINE	+MACBETH
BUBBLED	STABLED	*ALABAMA.	VERBENA	MUD-BATH
BURBLED	STUBBED	ARM-BAND	WEBBING.	PROBATE
CLOBBER	SWABBED	BAMBINO	DAYBOOK	PROBITY
CLUBBED	SWABBER	BOBBING	EYEBROW	RABBITY
COBBLER	TIMBREL	BOMBING	FLY-BOOK	SABBATH
CRABBED	TREBLED	BRIBING	LOG-BOOK	TRIBUTE.
CRIBBED	TUMBLED	CARBINE	LOWBROW	BULBOUS
CRIBBER	TUMBLER	COMBINE	SYMBION	CAMBIUM
DABBLED	TUMBREL	COMBING	TOP-BOOT.	GIBBOUS
DIBBLED	WARBLER	COWBANE	*AVEBURY	HARBOUR
DOUBLED	*WEMBLEY	CUBBING	*BANBURY	NIOBIUM
DOUBLET	WOBBLED.	CURBING	+BARBARA	+RIMBAUD
DOUBTED	CABBAGE	DABBING	BOBBERY	SKY-BLUE
DOUBTER	GAMBOGE	DAUBING	BOMBARD	TAMBOUR
DRIBLET	GARBAGE	DISBAND	BRIBERY	TERBIUM
DRUBBED	HERBAGE	DUBBING	FILBERT	
ENABLED	LUMBAGO.	FIBBING	FORBORE	+CALCHAS
FUMBLER	CAMBRIC	FOBBING	+GILBERT	CHOCTAW
GABBLED	CHABLIS	FOGBANK	HALBERD	CONCEAL
GAMBLER	GUMBOIL	GABBING	*HAMBURG	CRUCIAL
GARBLED	+HOLBEIN	GARBING	HAUBERK	DEW-CLAW
GOBBLER	HOWBEIT	HATBAND	+HERBERT	EDICTAL
GRABBED	LAMBKIN	HENBANE	HOMBURG	EPOCHAL
GRABBER	PARBOIL.	HOP-BINE	ICEBERG	GLACIAL
GRUBBED	BARBOLA	HUSBAND	JOBBERY	GRECIAN
GRUBBER	CEMBALO	JABBING	LAMBERT	PASCHAL.
HAS-BEEN	CYMBALO	JAW-BONE	LOW-BORN	RED-COAT
HOBBLED	DIABOLO	JIBBING	QUABIRD	SEA-COAL
HUMBLED	DRABBLE	JOBBING	RHUBARB	SPECIAL
ILL-BRED	DRIBBLE	KERBING	ROBBERY	SURCOAT
JUMBLED	EYEBALL	LAMBENT	RUBBERY	TOP-COAT
KNOBBED	EYE-BOLT	LAMBING	SEABIRD	PLACEBO.
LOBBIED	FRIBBLE	LOBBING	*SUDBURY	CONCOCT
LOW-BRED	FURBALL	MOBBING	SUNBURN	HAYCOCK
MARBLED	GIMBALS	NABBING	*TILBURY.	PEACOCK.
MUMBLED	GLOBULE	NOBBING	BOMBAST	AVOCADO
NIBBLED	GRABBLE	NUMBING	CAMBIST	BROCADE
NOBBLER	KABBALA	PREBEND	DIABASE	CASCADE
PEBBLED	KNOBBLE	PROBANG	FURBISH	CONCEDE
PROBLEM	KNOBBLY	PROBING	GLOBOSE	DEICIDE
RAMBLED	NETBALL	RIBBING	MAYBUSH	PRECEDE
RAMBLER	PIEBALD	ROBBING	RUBBISH	SARCODE
RUMBLED	PINBALL	RUBBING	VERBOSE	SUCCADE
SCABBED	QUIBBLE	SEA-BANK	*ZAMBESI.	SUICIDE.
SCABIES	SAWBILL	SHEBANG	BARBATE	BEACHED
SHEBEEN	STUBBLE	SOBBING	EYE-BATH	BEECHEN
SLOBBER	STUBBLY	TABBING	ISOBATH	BELCHER
SLUBBED	TOMBOLA	TRIBUNE	KIBBUTZ	BENCHER

355

BIRCHED	GLACIER	SHOCKER	FLACCID	ABSCOND
BLACKEN	HATCHER	SHUCKED	*HITCHIN	+ARACHNE
BLACKER	HATCHET	SLACKEN	PSYCHIC	BALCONY
BLOCKED	HITCHED	SLACKER	QUICKIE	BRACING
BOTCHER	HOICKED	SLICKER	TEACH-IN.	CALCINE
BRACKEN	HUNCHED	SMACKED	OATCAKE	CHICANE
BRACKET	HUTCHED	SMACKER	OILCAKE	DANCING
BRICKED	KITCHEN	SNICKER	PANCAKE	DESCANT
BROCKET	KNACKER	SPECIES	TEACAKE.	DESCEND
BUNCHED	KNOCKED	SPECKED	BASCULE	DESCENT
BUTCHER	KNOCKER	SPICIER	BRICOLE	EDUCING
CATCHER	LATCHED	STACKED	CATCALL	EPICENE
CHECKED	LEACHED	STICKED	CHUCKLE	EXSCIND
CHECKER	LUNCHED	STICKER	CRACKLE	FARCING
CHICKEN	LURCHED	STOCKED	DESCALE	FASCINE
CHUCKED	LYNCHED	SUCCEED	ERECTLY	FENCING
CIRCLED	MARCHED	TEACHER	EXACTLY	FORCING
CIRCLET	MATCHED	THICKEN	FRECKLE	GRACING
CLACKED	MATCHET	THICKER	FRECKLY	HIRCINE
CLICKED	MOOCHED	THICKET	GRACILE	LANCING
CLICKER	MULCHED	TOUCHED	KNUCKLE	LARCENY
CLOCKED	MUNCHED	TRACHEA	*LINCOLN	MINCING
COACHED	MUSCLED	TRACKED	+MALCOLM	MIOCENE
COUCHED	NOTCHED	TRACKER	MISCALL	NASCENT
CRACKED	PARCHED	TRICKED	PERCALE	OBSCENE
CRACKER	PATCHED	TROCHEE	PICCOLO	PECCANT
CRICKED	PERCHED	TRUCKED	PRICKLE	PIECING
CRICKET	PILCHER	UNACTED	PRICKLY	PISCINA
CROCHET	PINCHED	UNSCREW	+PURCELL	PISCINE
CROCKET	PITCHED	VOUCHER	QUICKLY	PLACING
DITCHED	PITCHER	WATCHED	SACCULE	PORCINE
DITCHER	PLACKET	WENCHED	SAUCILY	PRICING
DOUCHED	PLUCKED	WHACKED	SHACKLE_	+PUCCINI
EJECTED	POACHED	WINCHED	SLACKLY	RESCIND
ELECTED	POACHER	WITCHED	SLICKLY	SAUCING
ENACTED	POUCHED	WRECKED	SPECKLE	SLICING
ERECTED	PRICKER	WRECKER.	SPECULA	SPACING
EVACUEE	PRICKET	CALCIFY	SPICILY	SPICING
EVICTED	PROCEED	CRUCIFY	THICKLY	TRACING
EXACTED	PUNCHED	DULCIFY	TRICKLE	TRICING
FANCIED	QUACKED	SPECIFY.	TRUCKLE	VACCINE
FANCIER	QUICKEN	BOSCAGE	VASCULA.	+VINCENT
FETCHED	QUICKER	*CHICAGO.	COXCOMB	VOICING
FILCHED	RANCHER	*AJACCIO	CURCUMA	VOLCANO.
FITCHEW	RATCHET	BACCHIC	DRACHMA	*CLACTON
FLECKED	REACHED	BISCUIT	OUTCOME	EJECTOR
FLICKED	RESCUER	BRECCIA	SARCOMA	ELECTOR
FLICKER	RETCHED	CIRCUIT	SUCCUMB	ERECTOR
FLOCKED	SATCHEL	CONCEIT	WELCOME.	EXACTOR
FROCKED	SHACKED	DISCOID	ABSCIND	HALCYON

KNOCK-ON	+MARCUSE	*ABIDJAN	BRIDGED	RADDLED
OUTCROP	METCAST	BANDEAU	+BRIDGET	RIDDLED
PROCTOR	MISCAST	BAND-SAW	BRIDLED	ROWDIER
RACCOON	NUT-CASE	BONDMAN	BUNDLED	RUDDIER
REACTOR	OUTCAST	CARDIAC	CANDIED	RUDDLED
TRACTOR.	PERCUSS	*CHEDDAR	CODDLED	SADDLER
CONCEPT	PRECESS	CORDIAL	CUDDLED	SANDIER
INSCAPE	PRECISE	DEADPAN	CURDLED	SCUDDED
PERCEPT	PROCESS	GOODMAN	DAWDLER	SEEDBED
PRECEPT	SARCASM	GORDIAN	DIDDLER	SHADIER
SYNCOPE	SUCCESS	GRADUAL	DOODLED	SHUDDER
TRICEPS.	SUCCOSE	HANDBAG	DREDGER	SKIDDED
CASCARA	TEA-COSY	HARDPAN	DRUDGED	SLEDDED
CHICORY	TRICKSY	HEADMAN	FIDDLED	SLEDGED
CONCERN	VISCOSE.	HEADWAY	FIDDLER	SMUDGED
CONCERT	BOYCOTT	LAND-TAX	FLEDGED	SOLDIER
CONCORD	CALCITE	MISDEAL	FONDLED	STUDDED
DISCARD	EDACITY	QUADRAT	FUDDLED	STUDIED
DISCERN	EDUCATE	ROADMAN	GLADDEN	SUBDUED
DISCORD	EXECUTE	ROADWAY	GRUDGED	THUDDED
+ELECTRA	FALCATE	RONDEAU	HANDLER	TIDDLER
EPICURE	FURCATE	SANDBAG	HANDSEL	TIDDLEY
GROCERY	OPACITY	SAND-BAR	HARDIER	TODDLER
MASCARA	PAUCITY	SANDMAN	HARD-SET	TRODDEN
+MERCURY	PLACATE	SKID-PAN	HEAD-SET	TRUDGED
OBSCURE	PLICATE	SUBDEAN	HEDDLES	WADDLED
PECCARY	SACCATE	SUBDUAL	HUDDLED	WINDIER
PINCERS	TOCCATA.	SUNDIAL	HUNDRED	WOODIER.
PLACARD	+BACCHUS	+TRUDEAU	HURDLER	ACIDIFY
POPCORN	CALCIUM	WILDCAT	KINDLER	*CARDIFF
PROCURE	CHECK-UP	WINDBAG	KINDRED	DANDIFY
RIP-CORD	CRACK-UP	WOODMAN	+LINDSEY	*MACDUFF
SINCERE	DOUCEUR	+WYNDHAM.	MANDREL	SEND-OFF
SORCERY	FARCEUR	BURDOCK	MEDDLED	BANDAGE
SPECTRA	FULCRUM	CONDUCE	MIDDLED	BONDAGE
SPECTRE	FUSCOUS	DRY-DOCK	+MILDRED	CONDIGN
SYNCARP	KETCHUP	HADDOCK	MISDEED	CORDAGE
TRACERY	LINCTUS	OVIDUCT	MUDDIED	PRODIGY
UNICORN	PUNCH-UP	PADDOCK	MUDDLED	YARDAGE.
VISCERA.	RANCOUR	PIDDOCK	NEEDLED	BALDRIC
ABSCESS	RAUCOUS	PREDICT	PADDLED	+BALDWIN
CARCASS	SANCTUM	PRODUCE	PEDDLED	BOUDOIR
CONCISE	SANCTUS	PRODUCT	PLEDGED	CONDUIT
CONCUSS	STUCK-UP	TRADUCE	PLEDGEE	DISDAIN
DIOCESE	SUCCOUR	VENDACE	PLEDGET	*GOODWIN
DISCUSS	VISCOUS.	VERDICT	PLODDER	MAUDLIN
FASCISM	CONCAVE	VIADUCT.	PRODDED	READMIT
FASCIST	PECCAVI.	ALIDADE.	PRODDER	SKID-LID
GLUCOSE	LAICIZE	BANDIED	PUDDLER	TENDRIL
GRECISM		BLADDER	QUADREL	TRADE-IN

+VANDYKE.	ELUDING	PENDENT	PRUDERY	RHODIUM
BAWDILY	ERODENT	PENDING	SPIDERY	STADIUM
CANDELA	ERODING	PODDING	VERDURE.	WOODCUT.
CONDOLE	EVADING	PRIDING	BADDISH	BRADAWL
CONDYLE	EVIDENT	PRUDENT	BALDEST	LOW-DOWN
CRUDELY	EXUDING	PUDDING	BOLDEST	MILDEWY
DOWDILY	FEEDING	RAIDING	CADDISH	RUB-DOWN
*DUNDALK	FENDING	*READING	COLDEST	RUN-DOWN
*ESKDALE	FEUDING	REEDING	COLDISH	SET-DOWN
GAUDILY	FINDING	RENDING	FADDIST	SHADOWY
GIDDILY	FOLDING	RIDDING	GEODESY	SIT-DOWN
GONDOLA	FORDING	SANDING	GODDESS	SUNDOWN.
GRADELY	FUNDING	SARDINE	GOODISH	GOOD-BYE
GRIDDLE	GADDING	SEEDING	HARDEST	ANODIZE
HANDILY	GELDING	SENDING	KINDEST	IRIDIZE
HARDILY	GILDING	SHADING	LOUDEST	OXIDIZE
HOLDALL	GLIDING	SLIDING	MADDEST	
MANDALA	GOADING	SORDINE	MILDEST	ADRENAL
MOODILY	+GOLDING	STUDENT	OXIDASE	APTERAL
NEEDILY	GRADING	TEDDING	PRUDISH	ARSENAL
READILY	GRIDING	TENDING	REDDEST	*BRAEMAR
ROWDILY	GUIDING	TRADING	REDDISH	CASE-LAW
RUDDILY	HANDING	TRIDENT	SADDEST	CAVE-MAN
SAND-FLY	HEADING	VENDING	SAWDUST	CHEETAH
SEEDILY	HEEDING	VERDANT	SWEDISH	DANELAW
SHADILY	HOLDING	VOIDING	WILDEST	*DONEGAL
SWADDLE	HOODING	WADDING	YIDDISH.	FEDERAL
TARDILY	HORDING	WARDING	ACIDITY	FIREMAN
TREDDLE	+HOUDINI	WEDDING	ARIDITY	FOREMAN
TWADDLE	ISODONT	WEEDING	AVIDITY	FORESAW
TWIDDLE	KIDDING	WELDING	CAUDATE	FREEMAN
WORDILY.	LANDING	WENDING	CORDATE	FUNERAL
ACADEMY	LARDING	WINDING	CORDITE	GATEMAN
CONDEMN	LAUDING	WORDING.	CRUDITY	GATEWAY
GODDAMN.	LEADING	BANDBOX	ERUDITE	GENERAL
ABIDING	LENDING	BRIDOON	GRADATE	HUMERAL
ANODYNE	LOADING	CARDOON	LUDDITE	ILLEGAL
BANDING	LORDING	DEWDROP	LYDDITE	KNEE-CAP
BEADING	MADDING	HARDTOP	MANDATE	LATERAL
BEDDING	MELDING	JIB-DOOR	SURDITY.	LIBERAL
BENDING	MENDING	OUTDOOR	CANDOUR	LINEMAN
BIDDING	MINDING	ROAD-HOG	EAR-DRUM	LITERAL
BINDING	MORDANT	SANDBOY	HANDFUL	MINERAL
BONDING	MUNDANE	WINDROW	HANDOUT	NOSEBAG
BUDDING	NEEDING	*WINDSOR.	HEEDFUL	NOSEGAY
CHIDING	NODDING	CINDERY	HOODLUM	NOTEPAD
CONDONE	OUTDONE	*KILDARE	HUMDRUM	NUMERAL
CURDING	OXIDANT	MOIDORE	IRIDIUM	POLECAT
DEAD-END	PADDING	+PANDORA	MINDFUL	RENEWAL
ELIDING	PENDANT	POWDERY	NEEDFUL	*SENEGAL

SEVERAL	ANGERED	PREENED	WHOEVER	GOBELIN
SIDECAR	ANNEXED	QUEENED	WIZENED.	HARE-LIP
TIDEWAY	BLEEPED	QUEERER	ENFEOFF	HEBETIC
TIME-LAG	BREEDER	QUIETEN	RAKE-OFF	HERETIC
TUTELAR	CATERER	QUIETER	TAKE-OFF.	HOMERIC
VEGETAL	CAT-EYED	RECEDED	ACREAGE	IMPERIL
VETERAN	*CELEBES	REFEREE	ALLERGY	INHERIT
VINEGAR	CHEEPER	RENEWED	DIVERGE	INTERIM
VIRELAY.	CHEERED	REVERED	FOREIGN	JAVELIN
ABREACT	CHEESED	RIVETER	INVEIGH	KINETIC
ABSENCE	COHERER	ROWELED	LINEAGE	*LIBERIA
ARDENCY	COVERED	SCHEMER	LOZENGE	LOBELIA
BESEECH	COVETED	SCREWED	MILEAGE	MALEFIC
CADENCE	COWERED	SECEDED	+RALEIGH	MIMESIS
CADENCY	COZENER	SEVERED	REVENGE	MIMETIC
COGENCY	CREEPER	SEWERED	SYNERGY	NEMESIS
DECENCY	DELETED	SHEERED	UNDERGO.	*NIGERIA
DEFENCE	DETERED	SHEETED	CATECHU.	+OPHELIA
ESSENCE	ESSENES	SLEEKER	*ALGERIA	PARESIS
FAIENCE	FLEETED	SLEEPER	AMNESIA	*PHOENIX
FLUENCY	FORELEG	SLEETED	AMOEBIC	PHRENIC
IMPEACH	FORESEE	SLEEVED	ANAEMIA	POLEMIC
LATENCY	FOREVER	SNEERED	ANAEMIC	PYRETIC
LICENCE	FREEZER	SNEEZED	ANGELIC	PYREXIA
OFFENCE	GREENER	SOBERED	ANOESIS	RACEMIC
POTENCE	GREETED	SPEEDED	ANOETIC	RAREBIT
POTENCY	GRIEVED	SPEEDER	APHELIA	RAVELIN
+REBECCA	HAVENER	SPIELER	APHESIS	REVERIE
REGENCY	HONEYED	STEELED	ARSENIC	*SILESIA
SCIENCE	HOVERED	STEEPED	+ARTEMIS	SPHERIC
SCREECH	HOWEVER	STEEPEN	ASCETIC	SPLENIC
SILENCE	IMPEDED	STEEPER	AXLE-PIN	SUB-EDIT
SQUELCH	INHERED	STEERER	BEDEVIL	SUBERIN
STRETCH	INTEGER	STREWED	BENEFIT	SWEETIE
+TERENCE	+JEZEBEL	SWEEPER	*BOHEMIA	TABETIC
URGENCY	KNEELED	SWEETEN	CERESIN	TOTEMIC
VALENCE	KNEELER	SWEETER	CHEERIO	URAEMIA
VALENCY.	LEVERED	TAPERED	COTERIE	+VALERIE.
ADDENDA	LEVERET	TELEXED	DEMERIT	SQUEAKY
ALREADY	+LORELEI	THIEVED	DOVEKIE	STREAKY.
CALENDS	MONEYED	TWEEZER	EIDETIC	ALVEOLE
EFFENDI	*NINEVEH	UNSEXED	EIRENIC	AUREOLA
PUDENDA	OFFERED	USHERED	ENDEMIC	BRIEFLY
UNREADY.	ONE-EYED	UTTERED	ENTERIC	CHIEFLY
ACCEDED	ORDERED	VALETED	EUGENIC	CRUELLY
ADHERED	PETERED	WAGERED	FREESIA	DAZEDLY
ALIENEE	PIE-EYED	WATERED	GAMETIC	EAGERLY
ALLEGED	PIKELET	WAVERED	GENERIC	ELDERLY
ALTERED	POP-EYED	WHEELED	GENESIS	+ESTELLA
AMMETER	POWERED	WHEEZED	GENETIC	+FENELLA

FIREFLY	DOVECOT	INCENSE	BANEFUL	CADENZA
GAZELLE	DUKEDOM	INTENSE	*BENELUX	SCHERZO
+GISELLE	ECHELON	INVERSE	BODEFUL	SQUEEZE
LAMELLA	EMPEROR	LICENSE	BUREAUX	
MISERLY	ENVELOP	OBVERSE	CAREFUL	HALF-PAY
MORELLO	ENVENOM	OGREISH	CASEOUS	HALFWAY
NACELLE	FIREBOX	RELEASE	CEREOUS	MUDFLAP
NAKEDLY	FIREDOG	REVERSE	+CROESUS	MUDFLAT
ORDERLY	FORETOP	REVERSO	DIREFUL	RUFFIAN
PATELLA	FREEDOM	UNLEASH	DOLEFUL	WOLFRAM.
QUEENLY	HYPERON	+VANESSA.	DUTEOUS	EDIFICE
QUEERLY	JUKEBOX	AMNESTY	EASEFUL	MAFFICK
QUIETLY	PHAETON	+ANNETTE	FATEFUL	ORIFICE
ROSEOLA	PRAETOR	AUREATE	FIRE-BUG	OUTFACE
RUBELLA	REREDOS	BENEATH	GASEOUS	PERFECT
RUBEOLA	SAVELOY	BIRETTA	GLEEFUL	PREFACE
SAVE-ALL	SOMEHOW	BURETTE	HATEFUL	PREFECT
SLEEKLY	VICEROY	CELESTA	HIDEOUS	SUFFICE
SOBERLY	YULE-LOG.	+CELESTE	HIDEOUT	SURFACE.
STEEPLE	ATTEMPT	CRUELTY	HOPEFUL	CONFIDE
SWEETLY	+EUTERPE	CURETTE	HUMERUS	PERFIDY.
UTTERLY	EXCERPT	DETENTE	ICTERUS	BAFFLED
WHEEDLE.	LACE-UPS	ENTENTE	IGNEOUS	BLUFFER
DILEMMA	PRE-EMPT	GASEITY	IMPETUS	CHAFFER
MESEEMS	RECEIPT	GAZETTE	INGENUE	CHUFFED
PHLEGMY.	UNKEMPT.	HONESTY	LUTEOUS	COMFREY
ANTENNA	ALGEBRA	LAYETTE	OSSEOUS	CROFTER
BLUEING	ALLEGRO	LIBERTY	+PHOEBUS	DEIFIED
CAYENNE	EQUERRY	LINEATE	PINETUM	DRAFTED
CODEINE	FIRE-ARM	LUNETTE	PIPEFUL	DRAFTEE
DEMESNE	FOREARM	MAGENTA	PITEOUS	DRIFTER
FLEEING	JEWELRY	MAJESTY	QUIETUS	EDIFIED
FREEING	*MADEIRA	MEMENTO	RENEGUE	FEOFFEE
GEHENNA	+PHAEDRA	MODESTY	REVENUE	+GODFREY
GLUEING	REVELRY	NOVELTY	ROSEBUD	GRAFTED
HAPENNY	UNHEARD	PALETTE	ROSE-CUT	GRAFTER
INBEING	UNLEARN.	PIMENTO	TUNEFUL.	+JEFFREY
INFERNO	ABREAST	PIPETTE	BEREAVE	LEAFLET
*LUCERNE	ADVERSE	POLENTA	DECEIVE	MUFFLED
PAGEANT	APPEASE	POVERTY	DESERVE	MUFFLER
SHOEING	ASPERSE	PUBERTY	INWEAVE	PALFREY
SOMEONE	ATHEISM	+ROBERTA	+MINERVA	PROFFER
TREEING	BONE-ASH	ROSEATE	OBSERVE	QUAFFED
UNMEANT.	DECEASE	ROSETTE	RECEIVE	RAFFLED
AILERON	DISEASE	SEVENTH	RESERVE	*RENFREW
AXLE-BOX	DIVERSE	SEVENTY	UNNERVE	RIFFLER
BIBELOT	EXPENSE	VEDETTE.	UPHEAVE.	RUFFLED
BOREDOM	FINESSE	ANGELUS	POLE-AXE.	SCAFFED
DEVELOP	IMMENSE	AQUEOUS	APTERYX	SCUFFED
DICE-BOX	IMMERSE	BALEFUL	+JOCELYN.	SHIFTER

SNIFFED	TWOFOLD	OVIFORM	PROGRAM	PLUGGED
SNUFFED	WHIFFLE.	PERFORM	*RINGWAY	PRIGGED
STAFFED	PERFUME.	*ROMFORD	STYGIAN	REIGNED
STIFFEN	BUFFING	*SALFORD	SWAGMAN	RINGLET
STIFFER	CHAFING	TRIFORM	*URUGUAY	ROUGHEN
STIFLED	CONFINE	UNIFORM	+VAUGHAN.	ROUGHER
STUFFED	CUFFING	WARFARE	BRIGADE	SHAGGED
SWIFTER	DUFFING	*WATFORD	HAGGADA	SINGLED
TAX-FREE	GAFFING	WELFARE.	TRAGEDY.	SINGLET
TRIFLED	HUFFING	*BELFAST	BOGGLER	SLOGGER
TRIFLER	IMPFING	CATFISH	BRAGGED	SLUGGED
UNIFIED	KNIFING	CODFISH	BUNGLER	SNAGGED
WAFFLED	LEAFING	CONFESS	BURGHER	SNIGGER
WHIFFED	LOAFING	CONFUSE	BURGLED	SNOGGED
+WILFRED.	MUFFING	DIFFUSE	CHUGGED	SNUGGED
LEAFAGE.	OLEFINE	DOGFISH	CLOGGED	SOUGHED
EGG-FLIP	PROFANE	GARFISH	COUGHED	STAGGER
FORFEIT	PUFFING	HAGFISH	DANGLED	SWAGGER
FUN-FAIR	RATFINK	HUFFISH	DEIGNED	SWIGGED
GRIFFIN	REEFING	MUDFISH	DRAGGED	*TANGIER
HALF-WIT	ROOFING	PROFESS	DRAG-NET	TANGLED
SET-FAIR	RUFFING	PROFUSE	DRUGGED	TANGOED
SURFEIT	SURFING	RAFFISH	DRUGGET	TINGLED
TINFOIL	TIFFANY	SAWFISH	FEIGNED	TONGUED
TRAFFIC	TURFING	SELFISH	FLAGGED	TOUGHEN
TREFOIL.	WOLFING.	SUBFUSC	FLOGGED	TOUGHER
BLUFFLY	AIRFLOW	SUFFUSE	FOGGIER	TRIGGER
BUFFALO	BUFFOON	WOLFISH.	FROGGED	TWIGGED
CATFALL	CHIFFON	CONFUTE	GAGGLED	WAGGLED
GRUFFLY	DAMFOOL	TAFFETA.	GARGLED	WANGLED
HUFFILY	FEOFFOR	CONFLUX.	GIGGLER	WEIGHED
MENFOLK	HOTFOOT	SEA-FOWL	GOGGLED	WIGGLED.
*NORFOLK	ICE-FLOE		GURGLED	BAGGAGE
OUTFALL	OUTFLOW	ANAGRAM	HAGGLER	LUGGAGE.
PINFOLD	SAFFRON	BELGIAN	HIGGLER	LENGTHY.
PITFALL	TOMFOOL.	BURGLAR	JANGLED	+ABIGAIL
PROFILE	ALIFORM	CONGEAL	JIGGLED	BARGAIN
*SCAFELL	*ASHFORD	DIAGRAM	JINGLED	CHAGRIN
SCUFFLE	*BEDFORD	ELEGIAC	JOGGLED	FUNGOID
SHUFFLE	BONFIRE	EPIGRAM	JUGGLED	GANGLIA
SIXFOLD	COMFORT	FLAG-DAY	JUGGLER	KINGPIN
SKIFFLE	CONFIRM	FLAGMAN	KINGLET	LANGUID
SNAFFLE	CONFORM	FROGMAN	LAUGHED	PENGUIN
SNUFFLE	DEIFORM	GANGWAY	MANGLED	PILGRIM
SOUFFLE	EEL-FARE	GINGHAM	MINGLED	PINGUID
STIFFLY	FANFARE	GROGRAM	MONGREL	PINGUIN
*SUFFOLK	GUNFIRE	HANGMAN	NEIGHED	WEIGH-IN
SWIFTLY	HAYFORK	LINGUAL	NIGGLED	BENGALI
TENFOLD	*MILFORD	NYLGHAU	OUTGREW	+CHAGALL
TRUFFLE	MISFIRE		PLAGUED	DRAGGLE

FOGGILY	JIGGING	DUDGEON	*REIGATE	EUCHRED
FRAGILE	JOGGING	DUNGEON	VIRGATE	FIGHTER
LARGELY	JUGGING	GUDGEON	VULGATE	LIGHTEN
OAK-GALL	KEDGING	HANGDOG	WEIGHTY.	LIGHTER
PERGOLA	KINGING	KINGDOM	*BELGIUM	+MICHAEL
ROUGHLY	LAGGING	LANGUOR	FUNGOUS	ORPHREY
SEAGULL	LEGGING	LONGBOW	KINGCUP	+RAPHAEL
SMUGGLE	LODGING	OUTGROW	SORGHUM.	RIGHTED
SNUGGLE	LOGGING	SURGEON	FORGAVE	SIGHTED
SOGGILY	LONGING	TRIGLOT	FORGIVE	TIGHTEN
TOUGHLY	LUGGING	WIDGEON.	MISGAVE	TIGHTER
VIRGULE	LUNGING	BEGGARY	MISGIVE.	YACHTED.
WRIGGLE.	MERGING	BUGGERY	ELEGIZE	SKY-HIGH
END-GAME	MUGGING	*CALGARY	*YANGTZE	NAPHTHA.
EXOGAMY	MUGGINS	DAY-GIRL		ARCHAIC
ZOOGAMY.	NAGGING	DOGGART	ANTHRAX	BRAHMIN
BAGGING	NOGGING	FORGERY	ARCHWAY	ENCHAIN
BANGING	NUDGING	GINGERY	*BAGHDAD	FUCHSIA
BARGING	OUTGONE	+GREGORY	BIG-HEAD	+PUSHKIN
BEGGING	PEGGING	+HAGGARD	BUSHMAN	PUSHPIN
BOGGING	PIGGING	*HUNGARY	CATHEAD	TECHNIC
BRIGAND	PROGENY	IMAGERY	DISHMAT	TYPHOID
BUDGING	PUGGING	LAGGARD	EGGHEAD	UNCHAIN
BUGGING	PUNGENT	NIGGARD	ENTHRAL	XIPHOID.
BULGING	PURGING	PIGGERY	ESCHEAT	AIR-HOLE
CADGING	RAGGING	SURGERY	FAT-HEAD	ANT-HILL
DIGGING	RANGING	WAGGERY.	GO-AHEAD	ASPHALT
DINGING	REAGENT	BIGGEST	GODHEAD	EYEHOLE
DODGING	RIGGING	BURGESS	HIGHDAY	FISHILY
DOGGING	RINGING	CONGEST	HIGH-HAT	FLY-HALF
DOGGONE	ROUGING	DISGUST	HIGHWAY	FOXHOLE
ELEGANT	SAGGING	ELEGIST	HOT-HEAD	KEYHOLE
EXIGENT	SINGING	HAGGISH	ISCHIAL	LIGHTLY
FAGGING	STAGING	HOGGISH	LETHEAN	MANHOLE
FOGGING	SURGING	IMAGISM	*LOTHIAN	NIGHTLY
FORGING	TAGGING	LARGESS	ORPHEAN	PINHOLE
FORGONE	TANGENT	LARGEST	PATHWAY	PITHILY
GAGGING	TANGING	LARGISH	PINHEAD	POTHOLE
GANGING	TINGING	LONGEST	PIT-HEAD	*REDHILL
GAUGING	TUGGING	PIGGISH	RED-HEAD	RIGHTLY
GORGING	TZIGANE	SUGGEST	WARHEAD	SIGHTLY
GOUGING	VERGING	WAGGISH.	WASH-DAY	SPY-HOLE
HAGGING	WAGGING	DOUGHTY	YASHMAK.	SWAHILI
HANGING	WEDGING	FLIGHTY	GOTHICK.	TIGHTLY
HEDGING	WINGING.	FRIGATE	BUSHIDO	TOEHOLD.
HOGGING	*AVIGNON	HAUGHTY	CATHODE	ALCHEMY
HUGGING	*BANGKOK	MAGGOTY	COWHIDE	BERHYME
IMAGINE	BURGEON	*MARGATE	RAWHIDE.	+GRAHAME.
IMAGING	CHIGNON	NAUGHTY	CASHIER	+ANTHONY
JAGGING	DRAGOON		COCHLEA	ARCHING

BASHING	INKHORN	DECIMAL	EXTINCT	DESIRED
BATHING	INSHORE	DIGITAL	SQUINCH	DEVISED
BETHINK	LATHERY	ETHICAL	TAPIOCA	*DEVIZES
CASHING	LECHERY	FINICAL	UNHITCH.	DIVIDED
DASHING	LEGHORN	GENITAL	+BELINDA	DIVINED
DISHING	NOWHERE	HABITAT	+MATILDA.	DIVINER
ENCHANT	ORCHARD	*HALIFAX	ADMIRER	DRAINED
ETCHING	POCHARD	HELICAL	ADMIXED	DRAINER
EUPHONY	POT-HERB	HOLIDAY	ADVISED	ENLIVEN
FISHING	+RICHARD	LAMINAL	ADVISER	ENSILED
FOXHUNT	SAXHORN	LEXICAL	AFFINED	ENTICED
GASHING	WITHERS	LOGICAL	AFFIXED	EXCISED
GUSHING	YOGHURT.	LYRICAL	ANTIGEN	EXCITED
HASHING	DIPHASE	MAGICAL	APHIDES	EXPIRED
HUSHING	DUCHESS	MARITAL	ARBITER	FLAILED
INCHING	ENCHASE	MAXIMAL	ARMIGER	FRUITER
ITCHING	ENTHUSE	MEDICAL	ARRIVED	+GALILEO
JOSHING	HASHISH	MINICAB	ASPIRED	GRAINED
LASHING	HIGHEST	MINIMAL	ASSIZES	GROINED
MACHINE	RICHEST	MOHICAN	ATTIRED	HABITED
MANHUNT	SOPHISM	MUSICAL	AUDITED	HELICES
MASHING	SOPHIST.	NODICAL	AVAILED	IGNITED
MESHING	ESTHETE	NOMINAL	AWAITED	IMBIBED
METHANE	MACHETE.	OPPIDAN	BASINET	INCISED
NOSHING	BASHFUL	OPTICAL	BEDIZEN	INCITED
NOTHING	BOXHAUL	ORBITAL	BESIDES	INDICES
OFF-HAND	DISHFUL	ORDINAL	BETIMES	INDITED
PUSHING	ISCHIUM	PAGINAL	BRAIDED	INFIDEL
RETHINK	ISTHMUS	PELICAN	BRAINED	INFIXED
RUSHING	LITHIUM	PURITAN	BRAISED	INSIDER
SIGHING	MAN-HOUR	RADICAL	BROILER	INVITED
WASHING	+ORPHEUS	RECITAL	BRUISED	IODIZED
WISHING.	TYPHOUS	REVISAL	CABINET	IONIZED
+AMPHION	WASH-OUT	REVIVAL	CHAINED	JUBILEE
BOYHOOD	WISHFUL	SCRIBAL	CHAIRED	JUNIPER
CUSHION	WITHOUT.	SEMINAL	CITIZEN	+JUPITER
FASHION	ANCHOVY	SEMINAR	CLAIMED	LIMITED
MANHOOD	BEEHIVE.	SIMILAR	CONIFER	MARINER
POTHOOK	GOSHAWK	STOICAL	CRUISED	MATINEE
TYPHOON		*SURINAM	CRUISER	MERITED
UPTHROW.	ADMIRAL	TAXI-CAB	DEBITED	MINIVER
PERHAPS.	AFFINAL	TAXIMAN	DECIBEL	MOTIVED
AMPHORA	ARRIVAL	TOPICAL	DECIDED	NOMINEE
ARCHERY	ARTISAN	TYPICAL	DEFILED	NOTICED
CITHARA	BASILAR	VAGINAL	DEFINED	OBLIGED
COWHERD	BOLIVAR	*VATICAN	DELIVER	OFFICER
DIEHARD	CAPITAL	VICINAL.	DEMISED	ORBITED
FISHERY	COMICAL	MARIMBA.	DENIZEN	PEDICEL
FOGHORN	CO-TIDAL	BEWITCH	DERIDED	PERIGEE
FUTHORC	CYNICAL	DEHISCE	DERIVED	PLAINER

PLAITED	SQUIFFY.	SALICIN	RAVIOLI	EPSILON
POLICED	ABRIDGE	SATIRIC	RETICLE	EQUINOX
POSITED	BESIEGE	SEDILIA	RIGIDLY	HARICOT
PRAISED	FOLIAGE	SEMITIC	RISIBLE	HERITOR
PYRITES	IMPINGE	SILICIC	*SEVILLE	*HONITON
QUAILED	INNINGS	SOLICIT	SHRILLY	HORIZON
RADICEL	SPRINGY	*TUNISIA	SOLIDLY	HUMIDOR
RADICES	STRINGY	UNCIVIL.	STAIDLY	INCISOR
RECITER	SYRINGA	COLICKY	TACITLY	JANITOR
REFINED	SYRINGE	FINICKY	TEPIDLY	LEXICON
REGIMEN	TIDINGS	HIJINKS	TIMIDLY	LIAISON
RELINED	UNHINGE.	PANICKY.	UTRICLE	MONITOR
RELIVED	BELISHA	ARTICLE	+UTRILLO	PIG-IRON
REPINED	DELIGHT	AUDIBLE	VALIDLY	SILICON
RESIDED	FREIGHT	AURICLE	VANILLA	TRAITOR
RESILED	INSIGHT	BACILLI	VAPIDLY	VENISON
RESINED	SLEIGHT	BRAILLE	VARIOLA	VISITOR.
RETIRED	SPRIGHT	CEDILLA	VEHICLE	*ALGIERS
REVILED	TONIGHT	CIVILLY	VESICLE	BILIARY
REVISED	UPRIGHT	CUBICLE	VISIBLE	CALIBRE
REVIVER	UPTIGHT.	CUTICLE	VIVIDLY.	CILIARY
ROSINED	ACLINIC	*ENFIELD	MELISMA.	DEVILRY
SAMISEN	ACTINIC	ENTITLE	AMBIENT	GOLIARD
SCRIBER	ADHIBIT	FETIDLY	ANCIENT	HOSIERY
SHRIVEL	ASPIRIN	FRAIBLE	DEFIANT	MIMICRY
SLUICED	BASILIC	FRAILLY	ECHIDNA	+MOLIERE
SPLICED	*BOLIVIA	FUSIBLE	HYGIENE	PONIARD
SPLINED	BULIMIA	GORILLA	*INDIANA	RETIARY
SPOILED	+CECILIA	INFIELD	+JULIANA	RIVIERE
STAINED	CODICIL	LEGIBLE	LENIENT	TOPIARY.
*STAINES	COLITIS	LEGIBLY	PATIENT	AGAINST
STRIKER	DEFICIT	LICITLY	RADIANT	ATHIRST
STRIPED	DELIMIT	LIVIDLY	RELIANT	ECLIPSE
STRIVEN	DRUIDIC	LUCIDLY	SALIENT	ELLIPSE
TALIPED	EMPIRIC	+LUCILLE	SAPIENT	HOLIEST
THRIVED	EXHIBIT	LURIDLY	TAXIING	JUJITSU
THRIVEN	HAMITIC	MAMILLA	VALIANT	+MATISSE
TRAILED	HOMINID	MANILLA	VARIANT.	+MELISSA
TRAILER	ILLICIT	MANIPLE	ANDIRON	MUJITSA
TRAINEE	INDICIA	MAXILLA	ANTILOG	PELISSE
TRAINER	INHIBIT	+MURILLO	APRICOT	SEXIEST
UMPIRED	INSIPID	+NEVILLE	AUDITOR	TIDIEST
UNAIDED	+LAVINIA	OSSICLE	BENISON	TINIEST
UNAIRED	MANIKIN	PAPILLA	CAPITOL	TRAIPSE
UNFIXED	MILITIA	PEDICLE	CARIBOU	UGLIEST
UNRISEN	OPHIDIA	PETIOLE	CHRISOM	VERIEST.
VARICES	*PACIFIC	PLAINLY	CO-PILOT	ABSINTH
VISITED	PERIWIG	RABIDLY	DEMIGOD	ANXIETY
VOMITED.	POLITIC	RADICLE	DIVISOR	ARTISTE
SATISFY	PRAIRIE	RAPIDLY	ENVIRON	+BATISTA

BATISTE	OBVIOUS	DUSKIER	SHAKILY	LINKING
+CHRISTI	OCCIPUT	+EZEKIEL	SILKILY	LOCKING
CILIATE	+OEDIPUS	HACKLET	SMOKILY	LOOKING
*CORINTH	OMNIBUS	*HACKNEY	SNAKILY	LURKING
DEVIATE	OPTIMUM	HECKLER	SULKILY.	MANKIND
DUBIETY	PITIFUL	KECKLED	BACKING	MARKING
EXPIATE	RESIDUA	KINKLED	BALKING	MASKING
FOLIATE	RESIDUE	LOOK-SEE	BANKING	MILKING
FRAILTY	RETINUE	LUCKIER	*BARKING	MOCKING
GENISTA	SAVIOUR	NANKEEN	BASKING	MUCKING
IMPIETY	SERIOUS	NECKLET	BILKING	NECKING
JACINTH	TEDIOUS	PICKLED	BOOKING	NICKING
MEDIATE	VARIOUS	RANKLED	BROKING	NOCKING
MODISTE	VICIOUS.	RISKIER	BUCKING	PACKING
OBVIATE	ACHIEVE	ROCKIER	BUNKING	PARKING
RADIATE	BELIEVE	SICK-BED	BUSKING	PEAKING
REBIRTH	RELIEVE.	SUCKLED	CARKING	PECKING
SATIATE	+MARILYN	TACKLER	CHOKING	PEEKING
SATIETY		TICKLER	COCKING	PERKING
SERIATE	PROJECT	TREKKED	CONKING	PICKING
SOCIETY	SUBJECT.	WINKLED.	COOKING	PINKING
STRIATE	CONJOIN	KICK-OFF.	CORKING	QUAKING
THRIFTY	DISJOIN	CORKAGE	DECKING	RACKING
VARIETY	SUBJOIN.	DOCKAGE	+DICKENS	RANKING
VITIATE.	SKI-JUMP.	LEAKAGE	DOCKING	REEKING
*ANTIGUA	MAH-JONG.	LINKAGE	*DORKING	RICKING
ANTIQUE	CONJURE	PACKAGE	DUCKING	RINKING
ANXIOUS	PERJURE	TANKAGE.	DUNKING	RISKING
BEZIQUE	PERJURY	WORK-SHY.	EVOKING	ROCKING
BILIOUS		BANKSIA	FLAKING	ROOKING
CACIQUE	BOOKMAN	COCKPIT	FORKING	RUCKING
CARIOUS	BUCKRAM	NECK-TIE	HACKING	SACKING
COPIOUS	HACKSAW	PORK-PIE	HARKING	SARKING
CURIOUS	JACKDAW	PRAKRIT.	HAWKING	SEEKING
DEVIOUS	LOCKJAW	COCKILY	HOCKING	SHAKING
DUBIOUS	MILK-BAR	CUCKOLD	HONKING	SINKING
DUTIFUL	MILKMAN	DUSKILY	HOOKING	SLAKING
ECHINUS	MUSK-RAT	FLAKILY	HULKING	SMOKING
ENVIOUS	PACKMAN	JERKILY	HUSKING	SNAKING
FATIGUE	SICK-BAY	KINKILY	JACKING	SOAKING
FURIOUS	SICK-PAY	LEAKILY	JERKING	SPIKING
HABITUE	WEEKDAY	LUCKILY	JINKING	STAKING
HALIBUT	WORKDAY	MUCKILY	JUNKING	STOKING
IMPIOUS	WORKMAN.	MURKILY	KECKING	SUCKING
MAXIMUM	COCKADE.	PAWKILY	KICKING	TACKING
MINIBUS	BOOKLET	PERKILY	KINKING	TALKING
MINIMUM	BUCKLED	RISKILY	LACKING	TASKING
MODICUM	CACKLED	ROCKILY	LARKING	TICKING
NOXIOUS	CHUKKER	SEA-KALE	LEAKING	TUCKING
OBLIQUE	COCKNEY		LICKING	WALKING

WEEK-END	WALK-OUT	GUNLOCK	DUELLER	SPELTER
WINKING	WORK-OUT.	HEMLOCK	DWELLER	SPILLED
WORKING	HAWK-OWL.	HILLOCK	EARLIER	STALKED
YAKKING	PICKAXE.	INFLECT	EVOLVED	STALKER
YANKING	PINK-EYE	INFLICT	EXALTED	STALLED
YORKING.		KILLICK	EXULTED	STILLED
BACKLOG	AEOLIAN	*MATLOCK	FAULTED	STILLER
+CHEKHOV	AMALGAM	NEGLECT	FIELDED	STILTED
JACKPOT	COAL-GAS	NIBLICK	FIELDER	SULLIED
KOLKHOZ	COAL-TAR	PADLOCK	FRILLED	SURLIER
MILKSOP	COELIAC	POLLACK	FUELLED	SWELLED
TOPKNOT	EXILIAN	+POLLOCK	GRILLED	SWELTER
TUCK-BOX	FABLIAU	POTLUCK	GUELDER	SWILLED
*WICKLOW	FIG-LEAF	PRELACY	GUILDER	SWOLLEN
*WORKSOP.	FLYLEAF	REFLECT	HAULIER	TALLIED
BONKERS	+GILLIAN	REPLACE	IMPLIED	TALLNES
COOKERY	HELLCAT	REPLICA	JELLIED	TRILLED
HICKORY	ITALIAN	ROWLOCK	JOLLIER	TROLLED
HUNKERS	KEELMAN	+WALLACE	KNELLED	TROLLEY
MOCKERY	MAILBAG	WARLOCK	MANLIER	TWILLED
ROCKERY	MISLEAD	WEDLOCK.	MOULDED	VAULTED
ROOKERY	NUCLEAR	BALLADE	MOULDER	VAULTER
*SELKIRK	PAY-LOAD	COLLIDE	MOULTED	WHELPED
TANKARD	POLL-TAX	COLLUDE	OUTLIER	WIELDED
WINKERS.	PULLMAN	EXCLUDE	PSALTER	WOOLLEN
BOOKISH	RAILWAY	EXPLODE	PURLIEU	YIELDED.
BUCKISH	REALGAR	IMPLODE	QUELLED	AIRLIFT
DANKISH	REFLOAT	INCLUDE	QUILLED	AMPLIFY
DARKEST	SHELLAC	NUCLIDE	QUILTED	BAILIFF
DARKISH	STELLAR	OCCLUDE	RALLIED	JOLLIFY
JACKASS	TABLEAU	PRELUDE	REPLIED	KHALIFA
MAWKISH	TEA-LEAF	ROULADE	SALLIED	MOLLIFY
MEEKEST	UNCLEAN	SECLUDE.	SCALDED	NULLIFY
MONKISH	UNCLOAK	APPLIED	SCALPED	QUALIFY
PECKISH	+WILLIAM.	ATELIER	SCALPEL	SKI-LIFT
PINKISH	LULLABY.	BELLIED	SCALPER	WELL-OFF
PUCKISH	WALLABY.	*BOULDER	SCOLDED	ANALOGY
RANKEST	AFFLICT	BOULTER	SCULLER	APOLOGY
SICKEST	AIR-LOCK	BUILDER	SCULPED	BIOLOGY
TURKISH	ANALECT	BULLIED	SHELLED	COLLAGE
WEAKEST	ANGLICE	*CHELSEA	+SHELLEY	COLLEGE
YORKIST.	BULLACE	CHILLED	SHELTER	ECOLOGY
+BECKETT	BULLOCK	COAL-BED	SHELVED	GEOLOGY
BOX-KITE	CHALICE	COLLEEN	SILLIER	HAULAGE
RICKETS	COLLECT	COLLIER	SKILLED	NEGLIGE
RICKETY.	COWLICK	COULTER	SKILLET	NEOLOGY
FORKFUL	DEFLECT	DALLIED	SKULKED	OTOLOGY
LOCK-OUT	DIALECT	DIALLED	SMALLER	PILLAGE
LOOK-OUT	FALLACY	DRILLED	SPELLED	SEA-LEGS
SACKBUT	FETLOCK	DUELLED	SPELLER	TILLAGE

TOLLAGE	DISLIMN	*FINLAND	OFF-LINE	WALLING
TRILOGY	INFLAME	FOALING	OPALINE	WELLING
VILLAGE	+PTOLEMY	FOILING	OPULENT	WHALING
ZOOLOGY.	SUBLIME.	FOOLING	OUTLINE	WHILING
HEALTHY	ABALONE	FOULING	PALLING	WILLING
TALLY-HO	AIRLINE	FOWLING	+PAULINE	YELLING
WEALTHY.	AMBLING	FURLING	PEALING	YOWLING
ACCLAIM	ANGLING	FURLONG	PEELING	*ZEELAND
AMYLOID	ANILINE	GALLANT	PHALANX	*ZETLAND.
BUILT-IN	BAILING	GALLING	PIGLING	BALLOON
COAL-PIT	BAWLING	GARLAND	POLLING	BELL-BOY
COAL-TIT	BEE-LINE	GATLING	POOLING	BELL-HOP
COLLOID	+BELLINI	GELLING	+POULENC	+BERLIOZ
*CUILLIN	+BELLONA	GOSLING	PRALINE	BILLION
CYCLOID	BILLING	GULLING	PROLONG	BULLDOG
DECLAIM	BIPLANE	HAILING	PULLING	BULLION
DIPLOID	BOILING	HAULING	PURLING	CALL-BOX
EXCLAIM	BOWLINE	*HAYLING	RAILING	EARLDOM
EXPLAIN	BOWLING	HEALING	RECLINE	GALLEON
EXPLOIT	BUGLING	HEELING	REELING	GALLIOT
HAPLOID	CABLING	HELLENE	REPLANT	GALLOON
HYALOID	CALLING	*HOLLAND	RIFLING	GILLION
IDYLLIC	CARLINE	HOWLING	ROLLING	KEELSON
MISLAID	CATLING	HULLING	*RUTLAND	KILLJOY
NEW-LAID	CEILING	HURLING	SAILING	MAILLOT
NUCLEIC	CHOLINE	HYALINE	SAPLING	MILLION
PHALLIC	COALING	*ICELAND	SCALENE	MULLION
+PHYLLIS	CODLING	IMPLANT	SCALING	NUCLEON
PURLOIN	COILING	INCLINE	SEA-LINE	OUTLOOK
RECLAIM	COOLANT	INKLING	SEALING	PILL-BOX
SHELTIE	COOLING	*IRELAND	SELLING	PILLION
SIRLOIN	COWLING	JELLING	SIBLING	REALTOR
SKALDIC	CULLING	*JUTLAND	SIDLING	SCALLOP
SURLOIN	CURLING	KEELING	SKYLINE	SCOLLOP
TABLOID	CYCLING	KILLING	SMILING	SEA-LION
TRELLIS	CYCLONE	LADLING	SOILING	SHALLOP
VILLAIN	DARLING	LALLANS	STYLING	SHALLOT
VILLEIN.	DAYLONG	LALLING	TABLING	SHALLOW
DISLIKE	DEALING	LOLLING	TAIL-END	*STILTON
MANLIKE	DECLINE	LOWLAND	TAILING	SWALLOW
MISLIKE	DULLING	LULLING	TELLING	TALLBOY
WARLIKE.	ENDLONG	MAILING	TILLING	TROLLOP
AGILELY	*ENGLAND	MARLINE	TITLING	WALLOON.
CELLULE	EXILING	MARLING	TOLLING	ACALEPH
SILLILY	FAILING	MAULING	TOOLING	CYCLOPS.
SURLILY	FALLING	MIDLAND	TOWLINE	BOLLARD
UKULELE	FATLING	MILLING	UNSLING	CHOLERA
WORLDLY.	FEELING	MULLING	VEILING	CUTLERY
COULOMB	+FELLINI	NAILING	VIOLENT	DECLARE
DIPLOMA	FILLING	NORLAND	WAILING	DEPLORE

367

DULLARD	JOBLESS	PERLITE	REALIZE	PREMIER
EXPLORE	JOYLESS	POLLUTE	STYLIZE	PRIMMED
FAILURE	LAWLESS	PRELATE	UTILIZE	ROOMIER
FOOLERY	LEGLESS	PROLATE		SCAMPED
FORLORN	MOLLUSC	QUALITY	BESMEAR	SCAMPER
FOULARD	NOBLEST	REALITY	GRAMMAR	SCUMMED
GALLERY	OBELISK	REPLETE	HOLM-OAK	SHAMMED
+HILLARY	OCULIST	STYLITE	OATMEAL	SHIMMER
IMPLORE	OILLESS	TRILITH	OILMEAL	SKIMMER
LOLLARD	OUTLAST	TWELFTH	PERMIAN	SKIMPED
MALLARD	PUBLISH	ULULATE	PYGMEAN	SLAMMED
MUDLARK	RAYLESS	UTILITY	TRAM-CAR	SLIMMER
PHILTRE	REALISM	VIOLATE	TRAMWAY.	SLUMBER
PILLORY	REALIST	ZEOLITE.	*GRIMSBY.	SLUMMED
POLLARD	RECLUSE	APPLAUD	GIMMICK	SLUMPED
POULTRY	SAPLESS	BECLOUD	GRIMACE	STAMMER
SKYLARK	SEXLESS	BOWLFUL	HAMMOCK	STAMPED
TITLARK	SINLESS	BUILT-UP	HUMMOCK	STEMMED
WAR-LORD.	STALEST	CALLOUS	KALMUCK	STUMPED
ABOLISH	STYLISH	EMULOUS	PRIMACY	STYMIED
AGELESS	STYLIST	FALL-GUY	STOMACH.	SWAMPED
AIMLESS	SUNLESS	FALL-OUT	*BERMUDA	SWIMMER
AIRLESS	TALLEST	GALLIUM	BROMIDE	THUMBED
ANALYSE	UNCLASP	JEALOUS	COMMODE.	THUMPED
ANALYST	UNCLOSE	NUCLEUS	BRIMMER	TRAMMED
ARMLESS	USELESS	OCELLUS	CHAMBER	TRAMMEL
ARTLESS	VIOLIST	PAILFUL	CHAMFER	TRAMPED
BALLAST	WITLESS.	PALLIUM	CHIMNEY	TRIMMED
BUGLOSS	ABILITY	PARLOUR	CLAMBER	TRIMMER
BULLISH	ACOLYTE	PARLOUS	CLAMPED	TROMMEL
CELLIST	ADULATE	PHALLUS	CLAMPER	TRUMPED
COOLEST	AGILITY	SELL-OUT	CLIMBER	TRUMPET
COULDST	ATHLETE	SKILFUL	CLUMPED	+VERMEER
CUTLASS	AXOLOTL	SOULFUL	CRAMMED	WHIMPER
CYCLIST	BULLATE	THULIUM	CRAMMER	WHIMSEY.
DUALISM	CHELATE	VILLOUS	CRAMPED	MUMMIFY.
DULLEST	COLLATE	ZEALOUS.	CRIMPED	PLUMAGE
ENCLOSE	DEFLATE	ENCLAVE	CRUMPET	RUMMAGE.
ENDLESS	DEPLETE	ENSLAVE	DRUMMED	AIRMAIL
ENGLISH	DUALITY	OUTLIVE	DRUMMER	ALEMBIC
EYELASH	EGALITY	+PAVLOVA.	GLIMMER	ARAMAIC
EYELESS	EMULATE	BELLOWS	GRIMMER	BARMAID
FOOLISH	HASLETS	GALLOWS	GROMMET	CHAMOIS
FULLEST	HOPLITE	+MARLOWE	GRUMMET	DRUMLIN
GIRLISH	HYALITE	UNBLOWN	+ISHMAEL	GAS-MAIN
GODLESS	INFLATE	WILLOWY	KRIMMER	GREMLIN
GOULASH	ISOLATE	YELLOWY.	MALMSEY	KHAMSIN
HAPLESS	JOLLITY	DUALIZE	PLUMBER	KREMLIN
HELLISH	NULLITY	IDOLIZE	PLUMMET	MERMAID
INCLOSE	OCULATE	OBELIZE	PLUMPER	*OLYMPIA

OLYMPIC	COMMEND	PLUMING	CALMEST	GRAMPUS
PALM-OIL	COMMENT	PRIMING	CHEMISE	HARMFUL
PLUMBIC	COMMONS	RAIMENT	CHEMIST	HOLMIUM
RHOMBIC	COMMUNE	RAMMING	DISMAST	*OLYMPUS
TURMOIL	DAMMING	+RAYMOND	DISMISS	PREMIUM
VERMEIL.	DEEMING	REAMING	ENDMOST	RHOMBUS
ANOMALY	+DESMOND	RHYMING	FLEMISH	ROOMFUL
BRAMBLE	DIAMOND	RIMMING	*FORMOSA	+SEYMOUR.
BUMMALO	DIMMING	ROAMING	GAS-MASK	ATOMIZE
CRUMBLE	DORMANT	ROOMING	GLIMPSE	ITEMIZE
CRUMBLY	DROMOND	SEAMING	GNOMISH	
CRUMPLE	ELEMENT	SEEMING	MIDMOST	+BRENDAN
EXAMPLE	EXAMINE	SEGMENT	OUTMOST	CHINWAG
FORMULA	FARMING	SHAMING	PALMIST	CRANIAL
GRUMBLE	FERMENT	SPUMING	PLUMOSE	DIPNOAN
PLUMPLY	FIGMENT	STAMINA	PREMISE	ETONIAN
PRIMELY	FILMING	SUMMING	PROMISE	*FARNHAM
PRIMULA	FIRMING	SUMMONS	SIAMESE	FRONTAL
PUG-MILL	FITMENT	TEAMING	SURMISE	GAINSAY
RUMMILY	FLAMING	TEEMING	THOMISM	GRANDAD
SAW-MILL	+FLEMING	TERMING	TOPMAST	HERNIAL
SCUMBLE	FOAMING	TERMINI	TOPMOST	IRANIAN
SEA-MILE	FORMING	TORMENT	WARMEST.	NOONDAY
SHAMBLE	FRAMING	VARMINT	ANIMATE	OXONIAN
STIMULI	GAMMING	*VERMONT	AZIMUTH	PLANTAR
STUMBLE	GARMENT	WARMING	BISMUTH	POUNDAL
THIMBLE	GEMMING	WORMING	BROMATE	QUINTAN
TRAMPLE	GERMANE	*WYOMING	CLIMATE	QUONDAM
TREMBLE	*GERMANY	ZOOMING.	COMMUTE	SCANDAL
TREMBLY	GUMMING	CRAMPON	CREMATE	URANIAN.
TREMOLO.	HAMMING	CRIMSON	EREMITE	+BARNABY.
ADAMANT	HARMING	FERMION	FORMATE	BANNOCK
AILMENT	HARMONY	FLUMMOX	GEMMATE	*CANNOCK
ALIMENT	HEMMING	SHAMPOO	MAMMOTH	CONNECT
ALIMONY	HORMONE	SJAMBOK.	MARMITE	CORNICE
ALUMINA	HUMMING	CHIMERA	PALMATE	FURNACE
ANEMONE	HUTMENT	*DENMARK	PERMUTE	PINNACE
AUGMENT	JAMMING	EARMARK	PRIMATE	SPINACH
BEAMING	+JASMINE	FOUMART	PROMOTE	WRYNECK.
BLAMING	LAMMING	MAMMARY	STOMATA	CYANIDE
BOOMING	LEMMING	MUMMERY	TERMITE.	*GRENADA
BROMINE	LOAMING	PALMARY	ALUMNUS	GRENADE
CALMING	LOOMING	*PALMYRA	AZYMOUS	HYMNODY
CARMINE	MAIMING	PRIMARY	BRIMFUL	+KENNEDY
CATMINT	MUMMING	SEA-MARK	BRUMOUS	TORNADO.
CHIMING	ODDMENT	SUMMARY	CADMIUM	AMENDED
CLAMANT	PALMING	SUMMERY	CLAMOUR	*ARUNDEL
+CLEMENT	PAYMENT	*WOOMERA.	ENAMOUR	ASUNDER
COAMING	PERMING	ANIMISM	FERMIUM	AVENGER
COMMAND	PIGMENT	BLEMISH	GLAMOUR	BLANKED

BLANKET	GRUNTED	SHUNNED	YOUNGER.	DWINDLE
BLENDED	HAUNTED	SHUNTED	DAMNIFY	FAINTLY
BLINDED	*HORNSEA	SKINNED	DIGNIFY	FRANKLY
BLINKED	HOUNDED	SLANDER	MAGNIFY	FUNNILY
BLUNDER	JAUNTED	SLANGED	SIGNIFY	GAUNTLY
BLUNTED	JOINDER	SLANTED	SPIN-OFF.	GRANDLY
BOUNCER	JOINTED	SLENDER	APANAGE	GRANULE
BOUNDER	JOINTER	SOUNDED	CARNAGE	INANELY
BRANDED	JOUNCED	SPANCEL	COINAGE	JOINTLY
+BRONWEN	LAUNDER	SPANIEL	CRANAGE	LYINGLY
*BURNLEY	+LEANDER	SPANKED	DUNNAGE	PENNILL
CHANCED	LIONCEL	SPANKER	GUNNAGE	PIANOLA
CHANCEL	LOUNGER	SPANNED	PEONAGE	ROUNDLY
CHANGED	MAUNDER	SPANNER	*SWANAGE	SAINTLY
CHANNEL	MEANDER	+SPENCER	TANNAGE	SCANTLE
CHANTED	MOUNDED	SPENDER	TEENAGE	SHINGLE
CHINKED	MOUNTED	SPINNER	TONNAGE.	SHINILY
CHINNED	PAINTED	SPINNEY	+BLANCHE	SOUNDLY
CLANGED	PAINTER	SPONDEE	BRONCHI	SPANGLE
CLANGER	PANNIER	SPONGER	CRUNCHY	SPINDLE
CLANKED	PIONEER	+STANLEY	PAUNCHY.	SPINDLY
CLINGER	PLANKED	STANNEL	ADENOID	SWINDLE
CLINKER	PLANNED	STINKER	AMENTIA	SWINGLE
COUNSEL	PLANNER	STINTED	COUNCIL	TAWNILY
COUNTED	PLANTED	STONIER	CRINOID	TINNILY
COUNTER	PLANTER	STUNNER	+FRANCIS	TRINGLE
CRANKED	PLONKED	STUNTED	FRANTIC	TRUNDLE
CRINGED	PLUNDER	SUNNIER	HOBNAIL	TWINKLE
DAUNTED	PLUNGED	SWANKED	HYPNOID	WRANGLE
DRINKER	PLUNGER	*SWANSEA	LYING-IN	WRINKLE
DRUNKEN	PLUNKED	SWINGER	MOONLIT	WRONGLY.
+EMANUEL	POINTED	TAINTED	PFENNIG	ECONOMY
EMENDED	POINTER	TAUNTED	+QUENTIN	GRANDMA
EVINCED	POUNCED	THANKED	SHINDIG	SURNAME.
FAINTED	POUNDER	THINKER	STANNIC	ASININE
FLANGED	PRANCED	THINNED	STENCIL	ATONING
FLANKER	PRANKED	THINNER	TOENAIL	BANNING
FLANNEL	PRINTED	THUNDER	TRANSIT	BURNING
FLUNKEY	PRINTER	TRENDED	UTENSIL.	CANNING
FOUNDER	PRONGED	TRINKET	BLANDLY	COINING
FRINGED	QUINTET	TURNKEY	BLANKLY	CONNING
FRONTED	RE-ENTER	TWANGED	BLINDLY	CRANING
GLANCED	ROUNDEL	TWINGED	BLUNTLY	CUNNING
GLINTED	ROUNDER	TWINNED	BONNILY	DAMNING
GRANDEE	SAINTED	TWIN-SET	BRINDLE	DARNING
GRANDER	SAUNTER	VAUNTED	CANNILY	DAWNING
GRANTED	SCANNED	VERNIER	CORNILY	DINNING
GRANTEE	SCENTED	WHENEER	CRINGLE	DONNING
GRINDER	SCONCED	WOUNDED	CRINKLE	DOWNING
GRINNED	SHINNED	WRINGER	CRINKLY	DRONING

DUNNING	VANNING	CHINESE	CONNATE	LIONIZE
EARNING	VEINING	CORNISH	CONNOTE	+SPINOZA
EMINENT	WARNING	COYNESS	CRENATE	
EVENING	WEANING	DIMNESS	DIGNITY	ACROBAT
FANNING	WHINING	DONNISH	EBONITE	ALCORAN
FAWNING	WINNING	EARNEST	EMANATE	ALSO-RAN
GAINING	YAWNING	EBONIST	GRANITE	AREOLAR
GUNNING	YENNING.	FATNESS	INANITY	AURORAL
HORNING	ABANDON	FINNISH	KAINITE	AUTOCAR
IRONING	CORN-COB	FITNESS	+KENNETH	AUTOMAT
JOINING	GRANTOR	FURNISH	KEYNOTE	BIFOCAL
KEENING	+JOHNSON	GARNISH	LIGNITE	BIPOLAR
KENNING	OPINION	GYMNAST	MAGNATE	BIVOUAC
LEANING	PHANTOM	HARNESS	MAGNETO	CHLORAL
LEONINE	RAINBOW	HYMNIST	PHONATE	CORONAL
LIMNING	*REUNION	ILLNESS	PINNATE	+DEBORAH
LOANING	SPONSOR	IRONIST	REUNITE	DIPOLAR
MANNING	*SWINDON	KEENEST	RUINATE	EXPOSAL
MEANING	*TAUNTON	LAXNESS	TANNATE	FEMORAL
MOANING	TRANSOM.	LIONESS	TRINITY.	IGNORAL
MOONING	GRANDPA.	MADNESS	ADENOUS	IMMORAL
MORNING	+BERNARD	MANNISH	BURNOUS	INSOFAR
OPENING	CANNERY	ODDNESS	CRANIUM	+JEHOVAH
OPINING	CHANCRE	ONANISM	FLANEUR	ORTOLAN
PAINING	CHANTRY	ONANIST	GAINFUL	OTTOMAN
PANNING	COUNTRY	ONENESS	HAFNIUM	PIVOTAL
PAWNING	DEANERY	PIANIST	HEINOUS	REMOVAL
PENNANT	ENSNARE	PLANISH	MOONBUG	SAMOVAR
PENNING	FERNERY	PUG-NOSE	OMINOUS	SCHOLAR
PHONING	FOUNDRY	RAWNESS	PAINFUL	SYNODAL
PINNING	GRANARY	RUMNESS	PRONOUN	UNMORAL
PLANING	GUNNERY	SADNESS	QUANTUM	VERONAL.
PRUNING	HENNERY	SHYNESS	RHENIUM	REDOUBT.
PUNNING	LAUNDRY	SLYNESS	ROUND-UP	ABROACH
QUININE	+LEONORA	SPANISH	RUINOUS	DEBOUCH
RAINING	NUNNERY	SWINISH	SKINFUL	DIVORCE
REGNANT	PLENARY	TARNISH	SPINOUS	ENFORCE
REINING	QUINARY	URANISM	STANNUM	INVOICE
REMNANT	RE-ENTRY	VAINEST	STEN-GUN	*MAJORCA
RUINING	REYNARD	VARNISH	TURN-OUT	*MOROCCO
RUNNING	SCENERY	WANNESS	URANIUM	REJOICE
SHINING	SIGNORA	WETNESS	URANOUS.	RETOUCH
SIGNING	TANNERY	WITNESS	CONNIVE.	SIROCCO
SINNING	TURNERY	WRYNESS	BARN-OWL	SPLOTCH.
STONING	URINARY.	ZIONISM	FERN-OWL	ABDOMEN
SUNNING	ACINOSE	ZIONIST.	UNKNOWN.	ALLOWED
TANNING	ADENOSE	ACONITE	SPONDYL.	ALLOYED
TINNING	AMONGST	AMANITA	AGONIZE	ALMONER
TURNING	APTNESS	AMENITY	COGNIZE	*ANDOVER
TWINING	BURNISH	COGNATE	EBONIZE	ANNOYED

BARONET	JACONET	UNYOKED	MELODIC	ALCOHOL
BAYONET	LITOTES	UNZONED	MITOSIS	APROPOS
BELOVED	MAJORED	VENOMED	MORONIC	+ATROPOS
BETOKEN	MIAOWED	WAGONER	MYCOSIS	BRYOZOA
BIGOTED	MONOMER	WHOOPED	NEPOTIC	DECOLOR
BLOODED	MOTORED	WIDOWER.	*NICOSIA	EIDOLON
BLOOMED	OCTOBER	BOROUGH	OSMOSIS	EMBOSOM
BLOOMER	OPPOSER	ENGORGE	OSMOTIC	KILOTON
BOLONEY	PAROLED	SPLODGE	PAROTID	+NABOKOV
BROODED	PICOTEE	THROUGH.	+SEGOVIA	OCTOPOD
CAJOLED	PILOTED	ATROPHY	SYNODIC	+SOLOMON
CALOMEL	PIVOTED	AUROCHS	SYNOVIA	UNBOSOM.
COLONEL	PROOFED	BRIOCHE	ZYMOTIC.	+RUDOLPH.
CORONER	RAZORED	+DOROTHY	BAZOOKA.	ADJOURN
CORONET	REBORED	*LESOTHO	ALOOFLY	*ANDORRA
CROOKED	RECOVER	SMOOCHY	AMPOULE·	ARMOURY
CROONER	REMOVED	STROPHE	COROLLA	BIGOTRY
CRYOGEN	REMOVER	+TIMOTHY.	ENNOBLE	CANONRY
DECODED	REPOSED	ABIOTIC	IGNOBLE	FELONRY
DECODER	REVOKED	AEROBIC	MONOCLE	HERONRY
DECOYED	SAMOYED	AMMONIA	PANOPLY	INBOARD
DEMOTED	SCOOPED	APHONIC	REMOULD	INDOORS
DENOTED	SCOOTER	BEDOUIN	UNGODLY.	MASONRY
DEPOSED	SHOOTER	BEGONIA	ACCOUNT	SAVOURY
DEVOTED	SNOOKER	+BORODIN	AGROUND	SOJOURN
DEVOTEE	SNOOPER	BUBONIC	APPOINT	VAPOURY
DISOBEY	SNOOZED	BUCOLIC	ASTOUND	VELOURS
+DOLORES	SPOOFED	CALORIC	*BOLOGNA	ZEDOARY.
DROOLED	SPOOLED	CALORIE	COLOGNE	AUTOPSY
DROOPED	SPOONED	CAROTID	DEMOUNT	CABOOSE
ELBOWED	STOOGED	CAROTIN	ECHOING	CAROUSE
EMBOWER	STOOKED	CHAOTIC	HEROINE	DELOUSE
EMPOWER	STOOPED	CHLORIC	IMPOUND	ECHOISM
ENDOWED	STROKED	+CHLORIS	INGOING	ENDORSE
ENJOYED	SWOONED	CHROMIC	MADONNA	ESPOUSE
ENROBED	SWOOPED	CHRONIC	+OSBORNE	HEROISM
EXPOSED	TABOOED	DEMONIC	REBOUND	INDORSE
FLOODED	TALONED	DEMOTIC	RECOUNT	PAPOOSE
FLOORED	TENONED	DEPOSIT	REDOUND	REMORSE
FLY-OVER	THEOREM	ECBOLIC	REMOUNT	SOLOIST
GROOMED	THRONED	ENTOMIC	REPOINT	UNHORSE
GROOVER	THROWER	HEDONIC	RESOUND	UNLOOSE
HALOGEN	TRIOLET	IDIOTIC	SHOOING	VAMOOSE.
*HANOVER	TROOPER	JACOBIN	UNBOUND	CALOTTE
IGNORED	TUTORED	KENOSIS	UNDOING	COCOTTE
IMPOSED	UNBOWED	KENOTIC	UNSOUND	GAROTTE
INCOMER	UNCOVER	LACONIC	UNWOUND	GAVOTTE
INTONED	UNHOPED	LANOLIN	VETOING	RIPOSTE ·
INVOKED	UNMOVED	MASONIC	ZEROING.	RISOTTO
INWOVEN	UNROBED	MEIOSIS	AEROSOL	THROATY

*TORONTO	ADAPTER	SAMPLED	BUMPKIN	CHOPINE
UNCOUTH.	CAMP-BED	SAMPLER	+CHAPLIN	COMPANY
BAROQUE	CHAPLET	SCUPPER	CLIPPIE	COPPING
COCONUT	CHAPPED	*SHEPPEY	CRYPTIC	CUPPING
DECORUM	CHAPTER	SHIPPED	CULPRIT	DAMPING
ECLOGUE	CHIPPED	SHIPPEN	DAUPHIN	DESPOND
EMBOLUS	CHOPPED	SHIPPER	DELPHIC	DEWPOND
LINOCUT	CHOPPER	SHOPPED	DESPAIR	DIPPING
OBLOQUY	CLAP-NET	SHOPPER	DESPOIL	DRAPING
OCTOPUS	CLAPPED	SKIPPED	DIOPSIS	DUMPING
PIROGUE	CLAPPER	SKIPPER	DOLPHIN	ELOPING
PYLORUS	CLIPPED	SLAPPED	GLYPHIC	GASPING
SCROTUM.	CLIPPER	SLIPPED	GLYPTIC	GRIPING
ABSOLVE	COMPEER	SLIPPER	GRAPHIC	GROPING
DEVOLVE	COMPLEX	SLOPPED	LAMP-OIL	GULPING
INVOLVE	COUPLER	SNAPPER	MORPHIA	HAPPING
RESOLVE	COUPLET	SNIPPED	*POMPEII	HARPING
REVOLVE.	CROPPED	SNIPPET	PREPAID	HASPING
ACRONYM	CROPPER	STAPLER	PUMPKIN	HEAPING
ANTONYM	CRUPPER	STEPPED	SAPPHIC	HELPING
CACODYL	DAPPLED	+STEPHEN	SCEPSIS	HIPPING
+CAROLYN	DEEP-SEA	STEPPED	SCEPTIC	HOOPING
HOMONYM	DIMPLED	STOPPED	SKEPTIC	HOPPING
SYNONYM	DIOPTER	STOPPER	STYPTIC	HUMPING
	DRIPPED	SUPPLED	TRYPSIN.	JUMPING
BESPEAK	DROPLET	SWAPPED	GESPOKE.	KEEPING
*CASPIAN	DROPPED	SWOPPED	COMPILE	KIPPING
CHAPMAN	DROPPER	TELPHER	CRIPPLE	LAPPING
DISPLAY	ELAPSED	TEMPLET	GRAPPLE	LEAPING
NYMPHAL	ERUPTED	TEMPTER	HAPPILY	LIMPING
OFF-PEAK	FLAPPED	TIPPLER	INAPTLY	LIPPING
OUTPLAY	FLAPPER	TOPPLED	INEPTLY	LISPING
SHIP-WAY	FLIPPER	TRAPPED	LEG-PULL	LOOPING
SHOPMAN	FLOPPED	TRAPPER	+LEOPOLD	LOPPING
SLIPWAY	GRAPNEL	TRAPSED	MAYPOLE	MAPPING
STOPGAP	GRIPPED	TRIPLED	REDPOLL	MOPPING
TEMPLAR	HAPPIER	TRIPLET	SCAPULA	NAPPING
UTOPIAN.	HOPPLED	TRIPLEX	SHAPELY	NIPPING
AUSPICE	KNAPPED	TRIPPER	SOAPILY	PALPING
COMPACT	LAMPREY	WHIPPED	SOPPILY	PEEPING
COPPICE	NYMPHET	WHIPPET	STIPPLE	PEPPING
HENPECK	PEOPLED	WHOPPER	STOPPLE	PERPEND
HOSPICE	PERPLEX	WIMPLED	TADPOLE	PIMPING
ICE-PACK	PLOPPED	WRAPPED	*TRIPOLI	PIPPING
INSPECT	PROPHET	WRAPPER.	+WALPOLE.	POMPANO
PREPUCE	PROPPED	PULPIFY	BUMPING	POPPING
RESPECT	PURPLED	STUPEFY.	BURPING	PROPANE
SUSPECT.	QUIPPED	RAMPAGE	CAMPING	PULPING
TORPEDO.	RIPPLED	SEEPAGE.	CAPPING	PUMPING
ADAPTED	RUMPLED	ASEPSIS	CAPPING	PUPPING
		ASEPTIC	CARPING	

RAMPANT	SOAP-BOX	FLY-PAST	MARQUIS.	DEFROCK
RAMPING	SOUPCON	FOPPISH	ALIQUOT	+DERRICK
RAPPING	STEPSON	HARPIST		DETRACT
RASPING	SUBPLOT	LAPPISH	CZARDAS	EMBRACE
REAPING	SYMPTOM	LUMPISH	DECRIAL	EXTRACT
RESPOND	TAMPION	OUTPOST	DIURNAL	HATRACK
RIPPING	TOMPION.	PROPOSE	DOORMAN	HAYRICK
ROMPING	BAGPIPE	PURPOSE	DOORMAT	+MAURICE
SAPPING	PAN-PIPE.	SUPPOSE	DOORWAY	METRICS
SEA-PINK	AIRPORT	SURPASS	ENTREAT	OSTRICH
SEEPING	COMPARE	TEMPEST	ETERNAL	OVERACT
SERPENT	COMPERE	TROPISM	FAIRWAY	+PATRICK
SHAPING	COMPORT	WASPISH.	+HADRIAN	PIBROCH
SIPPING	COPPERY	COMPETE	HEARSAY	PORRECT
SLOPING	CORPORA	COMPOTE	IBERIAN	RAT-RACE
SNIPING	DEEP-FRY	COMPUTE	JOURNAL	REFRACT
SOAPING	DIOPTRE	CUSPATE	MISREAD	RETRACE
SOPPING	DISPORT	DESPITE	OVARIAN	RETRACT
STIPEND	DRAPERY	DISPUTE	OVERLAP	SECRECY
SUPPING	DRIP-DRY	PALPATE	OVERLAY	TERRACE
SUSPEND	FOPPERY	RESPITE	OVERRAN	UNBRACE
SWIPING	*GOSPORT	TOWPATH	OVERSAW	UNFROCK
TAMPING	GRAPERY	WARPATH.	OVERTAX	VERRUCA.
TAPPING	GUIPURE	DROP-OUT	QUARTAN	ASTRIDE
TENPINS	INSPIRE	HELPFUL	RETREAD	CHARADE
TERPENE	LEOPARD	NONPLUS	SAURIAN	COMRADE
TIMPANI	*NEWPORT	POMPOUS	SPARTAN	CORRODE
TIMPANO	PEPPERY	SULPHUR	SPORRAN	DEGRADE
TIPPING	PREPARE	SURPLUS.	STERNAL	DETRUDE
TOPPING	PURPORT	TRAPEZE	TEAR-GAS	EXTRUDE
TREPANG	RAMPART		THEREAT	*FLORIDA
UNSPENT	RAPPORT	COEQUAL	THERMAL	HYDRIDE
VAMPING	RESPIRE	CUMQUAT	+THOREAU	INTRUDE
VULPINE	ROMPERS	KUMQUAT	WHEREAS	JOY-RIDE
WARPING	SCEPTRE	RORQUAL	WHEREAT.	OBTRUDE
WEEPING	SEAPORT	*TORQUAY	ASCRIBE	OUTRIDE
YAPPING	SUPPORT	UNEQUAL.	DISROBE	OUTRODE
YELPING	SUSPIRE	BANQUET	MICROBE	TETRODE
ZIPPING.	TEMPERA	BOUQUET	*NAIROBI	THORIDE
*BAMPTON	VAMPIRE	BRIQUET	THEREBY	UP-GRADE
CAMPHOR	VESPERS.	CHEQUER	WHEREBY.	ABORTED
CAMPION	ADIPOSE	CLIQUEY	*AMERICA	ALERTED
GRYPHON	BEDPOST	CONQUER	ATTRACT	AMERCED
*HAMPTON	COMPASS	CROQUET	AVARICE	ANGRIER
HARPOON	COMPOSE	LACQUER	BARRACK	+ASTRAEA
KRYPTOL	COMPOST	MARQUEE	BED-ROCK	AVERRED
KRYPTON	DAMPISH	PARQUET	CAPRICE	AVERTED
LAMPION	DEEPEST	PICQUET	CARRACK	AWARDED
LAMPOON	DESPISE	RACQUET.	CORRECT	BARRIER
RAJPOOT	DISPOSE	+JONQUIL	CURRACH	BLARNEY

BLURRED	LEARNED	SPURTED	PIERAGE	PAPRIKA.
BLURTED	MARRIED	STARLET	PRURIGO	ANGRILY
BOARDER	+MAUREEN	STARRED	STORAGE	+CARROLL
BOURREE	MOORHEN	STARTED	UMBRAGE.	CHARILY
CARRIED	MOURNER	STARTER	ANARCHY	CHORALE
CARRIER	OVERSEA	STARVED	CHURCHY	CHORTLE
CHARGED	OVERSEE	STERNER	DIARCHY	COURTLY
CHARGER	OVERSET	STIRRED	STARCHY	+DURRELL
+CHARLES	OVERSEW	STORIED	SWARTHY.	EMERALD
CHARMER	PARRIED	STORMED	ACERBIC	FAIRILY
CHARNEL	PEARLED	SWARMED	AIR-RAID	FEBRILE
CHARRED	PEARLER	SWERVED	ANEROID	FERRULE
CHARTED	PIERCED	SWIRLED	*BAHRAIN	FIERILY
CHARTER	QUARREL	TARRIED	BEAR-PIT	HAIRILY
CHIRPED	QUARTER	TERRIER	CAPROIC	INERTLY
CHURNED	QUARTET	TIERCEL	CHERVIL	LOG-ROLL
COARSEN	QUERIED	TIERCET	CLARKIA	MERRILY
COERCED	REARMED	TOURNEY	DETRAIN	MISRULE
COURIER	RETRIED	TWIRLED	*DETROIT	OVERALL
COURSER	SCARCER	UNARMED	EMBROIL	OVERTLY
CURRIED	SCARLET	UNTRIED	ENGRAIN	PAY-ROLL
DECRIER	SCARPED	USURPER	ENTRAIN	PUERILE
DWARFED	SCARRED	WEARIER	FIBROID	SHORTLY
EMERGED	SCARVES	WHARFED	FLORUIT	SMARTLY
EVERTED	SCORNED	WHARVES	GEORDIE	SPARELY
EXERTED	SERRIED	WHEREER	*GEORGIA	SPARKLE
FARRIER	SHARKED	WHIRLED	GEORGIC	STARKLY
FERRIED	SHARPEN	WHIRRED	GHERKIN	STARTLE
FLIRTED	SHARPER	WORRIED	HAIRPIN	STERILE
FURRIER	SHERBET	WORRIER	HEARDIN	STERNLY
+GABRIEL	SHEREEF	YEARNED.	HEBRAIC	THIRDLY
GLORIED	SHIRKER	CLARIFY	INERTIA	WEARILY
GNARLED	+SHIRLEY	ENGRAFT	INGRAIN	WEIRDLY.
GOURMET	SHORTED	GLORIFY	INTROIT	DIORAMA
GUARDED	SHORTEN	HORRIFY	MURRAIN	EXTREME
HAIRNET	SHORTER	MIDRIFF	NEGROID	REFRAME
HARRIED	SKIRLED	PETRIFY	OVERDID	SUPREME
HARRIER	SKIRTED	PUTREFY	PYRRHIC	TRIREME.
+HARRIET	SLURRED	SCARIFY	RECRUIT	ADORING
HEARKEN	SMARTED	SCORIFY	REFRAIN	AFFRONT
HEARTED	SMARTEN	SHERIFF	SCORPIO	AZURINE
HEARTEN	SMIRKED	TERRIFY	STARLIT	BARRING
HOARDER	SNARLED	VITRIFY.	STEROID	BEARING
HURRIED	SNORTER	AVERAGE	TERRAIN	BLARING
IMBRUED	SPARKED	BARRAGE	THEREIN	CAB-RANK
INBREED	SPARRED	COURAGE	THERMIC	CITRINE
INURNED	SPIRTED	FARRAGO	THERMIT	CURRANT
JOURNEY	SPORTED	MOORAGE	THYROID	CURRENT
KNURLED	SPURNED	OUTRAGE	UPBRAID	CZARINA
+LAERTES	SPURRED	PEERAGE	WHEREIN.	EARRING

ENTRANT	SPIRING	THERMOS	MOORISH	SERRATE
EPERGNE	STARING	VITRIOL	NEAREST	THERETO
ESTRONE	STORING	WARRIOR	NEGRESS	THIRSTY
FAIRING	STYRENE	WHEREOF	NOURISH	TITRATE
FEARING	TARRING	WHEREON.	OPPRESS	UNTRUTH
FLARING	TAURINE	CORRUPT	PEERESS	VIBRATE
FURRING	TEARING	DIGRAPH	POOREST	VIBRATO
GAS-RING	TERRENE	DISRUPT	QUERIST	WHERETO.
GEARING	TERRINE	ENTROPY	REDRESS	AMOROUS
GLARING	TORRENT	THERAPY	REFRESH	CHIRRUP
G-STRING	TOURING	TOW-ROPE.	REGRESS	CITROUS
HEARING	UNWRUNG	+DEIRDRE	REPRESS	CUPROUS
HERRING	UTERINE	FORRARD	SACRIST	DEFRAUD
HYDRANT	VAGRANT	LIBRARY	SOUREST	FEARFUL
IMPRINT	VEERING	OVERARM.	SUCROSE	FERROUS
INTRANT	VIBRANT	ACTRESS	SUNRISE	FIBROUS
INURING	WARRANT	ADDRESS	TEA-ROSE	HAIR-CUT
JARRING	WARRING	AGGRESS	+THERESA	HYDROUS
JEERING	WEARING	AMORIST	TIGRESS	NITROUS
KEY-RING	WHORING	APPRISE	TOURISM	OCHROUS
LATRINE	ZEBRINE.	BEARISH	TOURIST	ODOROUS
LEERING	BOURBON	BOORISH	UNDRESS	ONEROUS
LOURING	BOURDON	BULRUSH	UNTRUSS.	OVERDUE
MARRING	CARRION	CHERISH	ACCRETE	OVERRUN
MIGRANT	CHARIOT	CIRROSE	BETROTH	REGROUP
MOORING	CHEROOT	CUIRASS	CARROTY	STERNUM
NEARING	CHORION	CURRISH	CHARITY	STIRRUP
OCARINA	CLARION	CYPRESS	CITRATE	TEARFUL
PAIRING	CYPRIOT	DEAREST	CLARITY	THORIUM
PEERING	ESTRIOL	DEFROST	CUPRITE	THYRSUS
PHARYNX	FOURGON	DEPRESS	DIORITE	YTTRIUM.
POURING	GEAR-BOX	DIARIST	EXCRETA	APPROVE
PURRING	GUERDON	DIGRESS	EXCRETE	DEPRAVE
REARING	GUNROOM	DOG-ROSE	FERRATE	DEPRIVE
REPRINT	HEIRDOM	EMPRESS	FERRETY	ENGRAVE
ROARING	OVERTOP	ENCRUST	FERRITE	IMPROVE
+SABRINA	PATRIOT	ENGROSS	HYDRATE	REPROVE.
SACRING	+PEARSON	ENTRUST	INGRATE	INDRAWN
SCARING	PHARAOH	*EVEREST	ITERATE	OVERAWE.
SCORING	PIERROT	EXPRESS	LIBRATE	ATARAXY.
SEARING	POOR-BOX	FLORIST	MIGRATE	UNFROZE
SHARING	REPROOF	HEIRESS	NARRATE	
SHORING	SEA-ROOM	IMPRESS	NEGRITO	ABYSMAL
SNARING	SPARROW	IMPREST	NITRATE	ABYSSAL
SNORING	STARDOM	INCRUST	OPERATE	ALMSMAN
SOARING	TAP-ROOM	INGRESS	*PENRITH	BEES-WAX
SOPRANO	TAP-ROOT	INTRUST	*REDRUTH	BORSTAL
SOURING	TEA-ROOM	LEPROSY	REWRITE	CAPSTAN
SPARING	THEREOF	METRIST	REWROTE	CATS-PAW
SPIRANT	THEREON		SECRETE	COASTAL

CRYSTAL	BLASTED	FROSTED	SHUSHED	CESSPIT
ELYSIAN	BLESSED	GHOSTED	SHYSTER	CHASSIS
ETESIAN	BLISTER	GLISTEN	SLASHED	CLASSIC
FELSPAR	BLUSHED	GLISTER	SLOSHED	CLASTIC
GAGSMAN	BLUSTER	GLOSSED	SMASHED	CORSAIR
HESSIAN	BOASTER	GNASHED	SMASHER	COWSLIP
+HOUSMAN	BOLSTER	GRASPER	STASHED	DEISTIC
KINSMAN	BOOSTER	GRASSED	SWASHED	DOESKIN
MARSHAL	BRISKET	GROSSED	SWISHED	DOGSKIN
MESSIAH	BRUSHED	GUESSED	TAPSTER	DRASTIC
MIASMAL	CHASTEN	HAMSTER	TIPSTER	ELASTIC
OARSMAN	*CHESTER	HAYSEED	TISSUED	ELASTIN
OUTSPAN	CLASHED	HEISTED	TOASTER	GNOSTIC
OUTSTAY	CLASPED	HIPSTER	TOUSLED	GODSHIP
PASSMAN	CLASSED	HOISTED	TRASHED	GRISKIN
PERSIAN	CLUSTER	HOLSTER	TRESSED	HOGSKIN
RUSSIAN	CLYSTER	JOUSTED	TRUSSED	HYOSCIN
SEISMAL	COASTED	LASSOED	TRUSTED	KIDSKIN
SENSUAL	COASTER	LEASHED	TRUSTEE	KINSHIP
*TRISTAN	CORSLET	LEISTER	TRYSTED	LAWSUIT
TUESDAY	CRASHED	LINSEED	TUSSLED	MIDSHIP
UNUSUAL.	CRESSET	LOBSTER	TWISTER	NONSUIT
CASSOCK	CRESTED	*MAESTEG	TWO-STEP	OILSKIN
COSSACK	CRISPER	MEASLES	+ULYSSES	OUTSAIL
DISSECT	CROSIER	MESSIER	UNASKED	PARSNIP
FOSSICK	CROSSED	MINSTER	WAISTED	PIGSKIN
HASSOCK	CRUSHED	MOBSTER	WELSHER	PLASMIC
+JESSICA	CRUSTED	MOISTEN	WHISKED	PLASTIC
NONSUCH	DAISIED	MONSTER	WHISKER	PROSAIC
PHYSICS	DOSSIER	NOISIER	WHISKEY	PRUSSIC
RANSACK	*DRESDEN	ODYSSEY	WHISPER	PURSUIT
SEA-SICK	DRESSED	OERSTED	WORSTED	QUASSIA
TRISECT	DRESSER	OLDSTER	WRESTED.	REDSKIN
TUSSOCK.	EGESTED	*PAISLEY	FALSIFY	*RUISLIP
BEDSIDE	EXISTED	PALSIED	RUSSIFY	SEISMIC
CRUSADE	FALSIES	PARSLEY	SALSIFY	SKYSAIL
EPISODE	FEASTED	PLASTER	VERSIFY.	SONSHIP
OFF-SIDE	FIBSTER	PLUSHER	CONSIGN	SPASTIC
OUTSIDE	FLASHED	PRESSED	CORSAGE	SUBSOIL
PRESIDE	FLASHER	PRESSER	MASSAGE	TOPSAIL
PROSODY	FLESHED	PROSPER	MESSAGE	TRYSAIL
SEASIDE	FLUSHED	PUNSTER	PASSAGE	WARSHIP
SUBSIDE	FLUSTER	PURSUER	PRESAGE	WASSAIL
SUBSIDY	FOISTED	QUASHED	SAPSAGO	WORSHIP.
TOPSIDE	+FORSTER	QUESTED	SAUSAGE.	DROSHKY
WAYSIDE.	FRESHEN	ROASTED	AIRSHIP	FORSAKE
AMASSED	FRESHER	ROASTER	ANOSMIA	NETSUKE.
ANISEED	FRESHET	ROISTER	BLASTIN	APOSTLE
AUSSIES	FRISKED	ROOSTER	BRASSIE	BEASTLY
BANSHEE	FRISKET	ROUSTED	CAUSTIC	BRASHLY

BRISKLY	FULSOME	RAISING	TENSION	ELYSIUM
BRISTLE	IRKSOME	RINSING	+TOLSTOY	+ERASMUS
BRISTLY	NOISOME	+ROSSINI	TORSION	FRUSTUM
CAPSULE	PRESUME	ROUSING	TOYSHOP	MASSEUR
CLOSELY	*SATSUMA	SEISING	VERSION	OPOSSUM
CONSOLE	SUBSUME	SENSING	+WINSTON.	PEA-SOUP
CONSULT	TWOSOME	SOUSING	GOSSIPY.	+PERSEUS
CRASSLY	WINSOME.	SUSSING	BEDSORE	REISSUE
CROSSLY	AMUSING	TEASING	BERSERK	SMASH-UP
DENSELY	ARISING	TENSING	BURSARY	+THESEUS.
EPISTLE	CAUSING	TOSSING	CENSURE	ABUSIVE
FALSELY	CEASING	VERSING.	CLOSURE	CASSAVA
FIRSTLY	CHASING	BASSOON	CONSORT	CURSIVE
FISSILE	CLOSING	BLESBOK	CURSORY	ELUSIVE
FLESHLY	CONSENT	BLOSSOM	DESSERT	EROSIVE
FRESHLY	CUISINE	BOWSHOT	DROSERA	EVASIVE
GHASTLY	CURSING	*BRISTOL	ELUSORY	JUSSIVE
GHOSTLY	CUSSING	CAISSON	ERASURE	MASSIVE
GRISTLE	DISSENT	CESSION	EYESORE	MISSiVE
GRISTLY	DOSSING	DRY-SHOD	FISSURE	PASSIVE
GROSSLY	DOUSING	EARSHOT	HANSARD	PENSIVE
HARSHLY	DOWSING	ELISION	LEISURE	PLOSIVE
HERSELF	ERASING	ELUSION	MAESTRO	SUASIVE.
HIMSELF	FUSSING	ERASION	MANSARD	CATS-EYE
LOOSELY	GASSING	EROSION	MEASURE	CAPSIZE
LOUSILY	GODSEND	EVASION	NURSERY	OUTSIZE
MESSILY	HISSING	EYESHOT	PESSARY	
MISSILE	HORSING	FISSION	PIASTRE	ASHTRAY
NOISILY	HOUSING	FORSOOK	SENSORY	AUSTRAL
OIL-SILK	KISSING	FUSS-POT	TESSERA	+BERTRAM
ONESELF	LAPSING	*GLASGOW	TONSURE	BESTEAD
OURSELF	LEASING	GOSSOON	TUSSORE.	BESTIAL
PENSILE	LINSANG	GUNSHOT	CONSIST	BOATMAN
PROSILY	MASSING	HOOSGOW	DENSEST	CENTRAL
RISSOLE	MESSING	*HOUSTON	LOOSEST	CHATEAU
+RUSSELL	MISSING	*KNOSSOS	PERSIST	*CHATHAM
SEA-SALT	NOOSING	MANSION	POSSESS	+COCTEAU
TENSELY	NURSING	MISSION	SUBSIST	COSTEAN
TENSILE	PARSING	MONSOON	TENSEST.	DEXTRAL
TERSELY	PASSANT	NON-STOP	DENSITY	DEXTRAN
THISTLE	PASSING	PASSION	FALSITY	DUSTMAN
THISTLY	PAUSING	PENSION	FELSITE	DUSTPAN
THYSELF	PEASANT	POT-SHOT	HIRSUTE	FACTUAL
TIPSILY	PERSONA	*PRESTON	PULSATE	FAST-DAY
TRESTLE	PHASING	+SASSOON	VARSITY.	FLOTSAM
*WALSALL	POISING	SCISSOR	ALYSSUM	FLY-TRAP
WHISTLE	PRESENT	SESSION	BRUSQUE	FOOTPAD
WRESTLE.	PROSING	SUASION	CAESIUM	FOOTWAY
AWESOME	PULSING	SUNSPOT	CLOSE-UP	FRET-SAW
CONSUME	PURSING	TEA-SHOP	+DRESFUS	FUSTIAN

378

GENTIAN	TINTACK	FARTHER	PUTTIER	VINTNER
GLOTTAL	UNSTICK	FEATHER	QUITTED	WALTZED
INITIAL	UNSTUCK.	FIFTEEN	QUITTER	WASTREL
INSTEAD	CUSTODY	FLATLET	RATTLER	WATTLED
KANTIAN	EBB-TIDE	FLATTEN	RENTIER	WEATHER
LACTEAL	PENTODE	FLATTER	ROOTLED	WHATEER
LIFTMAN	PEPTIDE	FLITTED	RUSTIER	WHETHER
LUSTRAL	PINTADO	FLITTER	RUSTLED	WHETTED
MARTIAL	RIP-TIDE	FLUTTER	RUSTLER	WHITHER
MARTIAN	TESTUDO.	FRETTED	SCATHED	WITTIER
MISTRAL	ABETTED	FRITTED	SCATTER	WRITHED
NEUTRAL	ABUTTER	FRITTER	SCUTTER	WRITTEN.
NUPTIAL	*AINTREE	FROTHED	SCYTHED	ACETIFY
PARTIAL	ANOTHER	FURTHER	SEETHED	BEATIFY
PLATEAU	BATTLED	GLITTER	SELTZER	CAITIFF
PORTRAY	+BEATLES	GLUTTED	SETTLED	CAST-OFF
POSTBAG	BERTHED	GRITTED	SETTLER	CERTIFY
POSTMAN	BESTREW	HEATHEN	SHATTER	DISTAFF
POST-WAR	BLOTTED	+HEATHER	SHUTTER	FORTIFY
PROTEAN	BLOTTER	HURTLED	SIXTEEN	GRATIFY
RAT-TRAP	BOOTLEG	HUSTLER	SKITTER	JUSTIFY
ROSTRAL	BOTTLED	JOSTLED	SLATTED	LIFT-OFF
SALT-PAN	BOX-TREE	KESTREL	SLITHER	MASTIFF
SPATIAL	BROTHEL	KNITTED	SLOTTED	MORTIFY
SUN-TRAP	BROTHER	KNITTER	SMITTEN	MYSTIFY
TACTUAL	BUSTLED	KNOTTED	SMOTHER	PONTIFF
TEA-TRAY	CANTEEN	LEATHER	SMUTTED	PONTIFY
TERTIAN	CASTLED	LITTLER	SOOTHED	RECTIFY
TEXTUAL	CENTNER	LOATHED	SPATTER	TESTIFY.
UNSTRAP	CHATTED	LOFTIER	SPITTED	CARTAGE
VENTRAL	CHATTEL	MANTLED	SPOTTED	CORTEGE
VICTUAL	CHATTER	MARTLET	SPOTTER	COTTAGE
*VIETNAM	CHUTNEY	+MATTHEW	SPUTTER	FOOTAGE
VIRTUAL	CLATTER	MOTTLED	STUTTER	HOSTAGE
+WHITMAN.	CLOTHED	MOUTHED	SWATHED	MINTAGE
BUTTOCK	CLOTHES	NARTHEX	SWATTED	MONTAGE
CONTACT	CLOTTED	NASTIER	SWATTER	+MONTAGU
DIPTYCH	CLUTTER	NEITHER	SWOTTED	PORTAGE
DISTICH	COTTIER	NESTLED	TARTLET	POSTAGE
EROTICA	CRITTER	NETTLED	TASTIER	PROTEGE
JUSTICE	CURTSEY	NORTHER	TATTLER	ROOTAGE
LATTICE	DIRTIED	OMITTED	TENT-PEG	SCUTAGE
LETTUCE	DRATTED	PANTHER	THITHER	UPSTAGE
MATTOCK	DUSTIER	PANTIES	TIPTOED	VANTAGE
PORTICO	EARTHED	PARTIED	TOOTHED	VENTAGE
PROTECT	EARTHEN	PARTNER	TOOTLED	VERTIGO
STATICE	EMITTED	PLATTED	TROTTER	VESTIGE
STATICS	EMITTER	PLATTER	TWITTED	VINTAGE
TACTICS	EMPTIER	PLOTTER	TWITTER	VOLTAGE
TESTACY	EPITHET	PRITHEE	UMPTEEN	WASTAGE

WATTAGE.	EARTHLY	WHITTLE	EASTING	MILTING
BLOTCHY	EMPTILY	WITTILY.	EDITING	MINTING
SKETCHY	FERTILE	ALL-TIME	ELATING	MISTING
SNATCHY.	FICTILE	ANATOMY	EMETINE	*MONTANA
ABSTAIN	FIFTHLY	BEDTIME	EXITING	MOOTING
*AUSTRIA	FISTULA	CENTIME	FASTING	MUSTANG
BEATNIK	FUSTILY	CONTEMN	FELTING	+NEPTUNE
BOBTAIL	GENTILE	COSTUME	FITTING	NESTING
*BRITAIN	GESTALT	DAY-TIME	FLUTING	NETTING
CAPTAIN	HASTILY	EPITOME	FOOTING	NUTTING
CENTRIC	HEFTILY	PASTIME	FORTUNE	ORATING
CERTAIN	HOSTILE	RAGTIME	GETTING	OROTUND
CESTOID	INSTALL	SCOTOMA	GRATING	OUSTING
CONTAIN	IRATELY	TWO-TIME	GUTTING	PANTING
CURTAIL	LOATHLY	WARTIME	HAFTING	PARTING
CURTAIN	LOFTILY	ZOOTOMY.	HALTING	PASTING
+CYNTHIA	LUSTILY	ACETONE	HEATING	PATTING
DELTOID	MISTILY	BAITING	HEFTING	PELTING
DEXTRIN	MONTHLY	BANTING	HEPTANE	PENTANE
DUSTBIN	NASTILY	BASTING	HINTING	PETTING
FANTAIL	NINTHLY	BATTING	HITTING	PITTING
GASTRIC	NOCTULE	BEATING	HOOTING	PLATING
GLOTTIS	OUTTALK	BELTANE	HOTTING	PORTEND
GNATHIC	PANTILE	BELTING	HUNTING	PORTENT
LENTOID	PETTILY	BETTING	HURTING	PORTING
MASTOID	PISTOLE	BILTONG	HUTTING	POSTING
NOSTRIL	PRATTLE	BLATANT	INSTANT	POTTING
PERTAIN	PUSTULE	BOATING	ISATINE	POUTING
PIGTAIL	REPTILE	BOLTING	ISOTONE	PRATING
PROTEID	RUSTILY	BUNTING	JESTING	PRETEND
PROTEIN	SCUTTLE	BUSTING	JETTING	PUNTING
RAT-TAIL	*SEATTLE	CANTING	JILTING	PUTTING
SEXTAIN	SECTILE	CARTING	JOLTING	QUOTING
SPUTNIK	SHUTTLE	CASTING	JOTTING	RAFTING
SUSTAIN	SKITTLE	COATING	+JUSTINE	RANTING
UPSTAIR	SOOTILY	CONTEND	JUTTING	RATTING
VOLTAIC	SPATULA	CONTENT	KITTING	RENTING
WAGTAIL.	SPITTLE	COSTING	LASTING	RESTING
MISTAKE	STATELY	COTTONY	LETTING	RIFTING
PARTAKE	SYSTOLE	CUTTING	LIFTING	RIOTING
+TROTSKY.	SYSTYLE	DARTING	LILTING	ROOTING
ACUTELY	TACTILE	DENTINE	LISTING	ROTTING
BRITTLE	TASTILY	DESTINE	LOFTING	ROUTINE
CASTILE	TATTILY	DESTINY	LOOTING	ROUTING
CATTILY	TENTHLY	DIETING	LUSTING	RUSTING
DEATHLY	TESTILY	DISTANT	MALTING	RUTTING
DIRTILY	TEXTILE	DISTEND	MARTINI	SALTING
DISTYLE	TORTILE	DOTTING	MATTING	SEATING
DUCTILE	TRITELY	DUOTONE	MEETING	SESTINA
DUSTILY	*VISTULA	DUSTING	MELTING	SETTING

SEXTANT	CONTROL	CAUTERY	SECTARY	RUTTISH
SIFTING	DESTROY	CENTURY	STATURE	SCOTISM
SILTING	DICTION	CISTERN	TEXTURE	SOFTEST
SITTING	DOGTROT	CONTORT	*TINTERN	SOTTISH
SKATING	EDITION	COSTARD	TORTURE	STATISM
SLATING	ELATION	CULTURE	TOTTERY	TAUTEST
SORTING	EMOTION	CUSTARD	UNITARY	VASTEST
SOUTANE	FACTION	DASTARD	UPSTART	WETTEST
SPITING	FESTOON	DENTARY	URETHRA	WHITEST
STATING	FICTION	DENTURE	VENTURE	WHITISH.
SUBTEND	FOX-TROT	DIETARY	VESTURE	ACETATE
SUITING	GLUTTON	DIPTERA	VICTORY	AGITATE
SULTANA	HAUTBOY	DISTORT	VULTURE	AGITATO
TARTING	JOG-TROT	DISTURB	WESTERN.	CANTATA
TASTING	LIFTBOY	EASTERN	BAPTISM	COSTATE
TATTING	MENTHOL	FACTORY	BAPTIST	DENTATE
TENTING	MENTION	FACTURE	BRITISH	DICTATE
TESTING	MISTOOK	FEATURE	BRUTISH	GUTTATE
TILTING	NEUTRON	FIXTURE	CATTISH	HASTATE
TONTINE	ORATION	GESTURE	COLTISH	IMITATE
*TOOTING	OVATION	HECTARE	CONTEST	INSTATE
TOTTING	PARTOOK	HISTORY	DENTIST	PARTITE
TOUTING	PEAT-BOG	JITTERY	DIETIST	RESTATE
TUFTING	PLATOON	LANTERN	DOLTISH	SEPTATE
TUTTING	PONTOON	LECTERN	ECSTASY	STATUTE
UNITING	PORTION	LECTURE	EGOTISM	TEKTITE
VENTING	RUPTION	LEOTARD	EGOTIST	TESTATE.
VESTING	SECTION	LOTTERY	FANTAST	ACETOUS
VETTING	SETTLOR	MASTERY	FANTASY	AMATEUR
VOLTING	STATION	MIXTURE	FASTEST	BOATFUL
WAFTING	STETSON	MUSTARD	FATTEST	CENTAUR
WAITING	SUCTION	MYSTERY	FITTEST	CONTOUR
WANTING	TUITION	NECTARY	FLUTIST	FISTFUL
WASTING	UNCTION	NOCTURN	GOATISH	FRETFUL
WELTING	*VENTNOR	NURTURE	HOSTESS	HAUTEUR
WEST-END	WART-HOG	ORATORY	HOTTEST	HURTFUL
WESTING	WHATNOT	PASTERN	KENTISH	LUSTFUL
WETTING	WHITLOW.	PASTURE	LACTASE	+MALTHUS
WHITING	BIOTYPE	PATTERN	LACTOSE	MANTRUM
WILTING	EPITAPH	PERTURB	LEFTIST	NOSTRUM
WITTING	GESTAPO	PICTURE	LENTISK	OESTRUS
WRITING.	ISOTOPE.	POSTERN	LOUTISH	+PASTEUR
ABETTOR	AMATORY	POSTURE	MALTOSE	+PROTEUS
AUCTION	AUSTERE	POTTERY	MORTISE	RESTFUL
BASTION	BASTARD	RAPTURE	PENTOSE	RIOTOUS
BENTHOS	BATTERY	RECTORY	PETTISH	ROSTRUM
CALTROP	BITTERN	RESTORE	PICTISH	SHOTGUN
CAPTION	BUSTARD	RUPTURE	PIETISM	SHUT-OUT
CARTOON	BUTTERY	SALTERN	POETESS	SISTRUM
CAUTION	CAPTURE	SALTIRE	PROTEST	TACTFUL

TANTRUM	SCRUBBY	IMPUTED	ZYMURGY.	TRIUMPH.
TRITIUM	SHRUBBY.	INCUSED	BROUGHT	ACQUIRE
WHITSUN	ADJUNCT	INDUCED	DRAUGHT	ACTUARY
WISTFUL	DEFUNCT	INFUSED	DROUGHT	ENQUIRE
WRITE-UP	ENOUNCE	INHUMED	DROUTHY	ENQUIRY
ZESTFUL.	FELUCCA	INJURED	FRAUGHT	ESQUIRE
AMATIVE	FLOUNCE	INSURED	GROUCHY	ESTUARY
CAPTIVE	SCRUNCH	INSURER	THOUGHT	INQUIRE
COSTIVE	STAUNCH	LEMURES	WROUGHT.	INQUIRY
EMOTIVE	TROUNCE.	MANURED	ABOULIA	JANUARY
FESTIVE	ROTUNDA.	MATURED	+BAKUNIN	OSSUARY
FICTIVE	ABJURED	MINUTED	+CLAUDIA	REQUIRE
FURTIVE	ACCUSED	MISUSED	INSULIN	ROGUERY
RESTIVE	ALBUMEN	NON-USER	LEGUMIN	VAQUERO.
UNITIVE.	ALLUDED	PERUSED	MANUMIT	ACCURST
*NEWTOWN	ALLURED	PROUDER	+MENUHIN	ANGUISH
*WIGTOWN.	AMPUTEE	REBUKED	PETUNIA	BEQUEST
CONTEXT	ANNULET	REDUCED	PLAUDIT	CASUIST
PRETEXT.	AROUSED	REFUGEE	SEQUOIA.	+DEBUSSY
+FONTEYN	ASSUMED	REFUSED	MAZURKA	FUGUIST
ICHTHYS	ASSURED	REFUTED	UNLUCKY.	IMBURSE
SHUT-EYE.	ATTUNED	REPUTED	AMPULLA	IMPULSE
BAPTIZE	AUGURED	REQUIEM	+ANOUILH	INQUEST
MESTIZO	BEMUSED	RESUMED	AWFULLY	REPULSE
POETIZE	BITUMEN	RIVULET	BEGUILE	REQUEST
	CALUMET	SALUTED	DECUPLE	ROGUISH.
ACCUSAL	+CHAUCER	SCOURER	MEDULLA	ACTUATE
ANGULAR	CLOUDED	SCOUTED	OCTUPLE	ANNUITY
ANNULAR	CLOUTED	SECURED	PIOUSLY	ARCUATE
CLAUSAL	DEDUCED	SEDUCER	PROUDLY	FACULTY
FIGURAL	DEFUSED	SHOUTED	SCRUPLE	LIQUATE
INHUMAN	DELUDED	SPOUTED	SOLUBLE	REQUITE
INSULAR	DELUGED	SPRUCED	STOUTLY	SITUATE
JOCULAR	DENUDED	STOUTER	TROUBLE	TENUITY
JUGULAR	DILUTED	SUTURED	UNBUILT	UNQUOTE
LACUNAL	DILUTER	TROUPER	VACUOLE	VACUITY
NATURAL	EFFUSED	UNQUIET	VAGUELY	VIDUITY.
NEBULAR	ENDURED	VOLUTED.	VOLUBLE.	ARBUTUS
NODULAR	ENSURED	LIQUEFY	ANGUINE	ARDUOUS
PALUDAL	EPAULET	SCRUFFY.	ARGUING	CUMULUS
PERUSAL	EXCUSED	ADJUDGE	ASQUINT	FAMULUS
PILULAR	EXHUMED	ASSUAGE	CALUMNY	FATUOUS
POPULAR	FIGURED	DIVULGE	DILUENT	INCUBUS
REFUSAL	FLOURED	EXPUNGE	GENUINE	JEJUNUM
REGULAR	FLOUTED	INDULGE	PIQUANT	LIQUEUR
SAMURAI	FOCUSED	LITURGY	SEQUENT	PABULUM
SECULAR	GROUPED	SCOURGE	TOLUENE	REAUMUR
SUTURAL	GROUSER	SPLURGE	UNGUENT.	+ROMULUS
TITULAR	GROUTED	THEURGY	CROUTON.	SINUOUS
TUBULAR.	IMMURED	UPSURGE	GALUMPH	TENUOUS

TUMULUS	HEAVING	PROVISO	SPAWNED	BOXWOOD
VACUOUS	LEAVING	PROVOST	TRAWLER.	DOGWOOD
	NERVINE	SLAVISH.	MIDWIFE	KNOW-HOW
ELUVIAL	NERVING	BREVITY	SHOW-OFF.	LOGWOOD
FLUVIAL	NIRVANA	CURVATE	BREWAGE	PLYWOOD
PLUVIAL	PARVENU	ELEVATE	STOWAGE.	REDWOOD
TRIVIAL.	PEEVING	GRAVITY	BROWNIE	SAPWOOD
CONVICT	PREVENT	NAIVETE	SHOWBIZ.	*SNOWDON.
CREVICE	PROVING	NAIVETY	+BEOWULF	UPSWEPT.
PRIVACY	REVVING	OUTVOTE	BLOW-FLY	*ANTWERP
+SERVICE.	SALVING	PRIVATE	+BOSWELL	ATHWART
BRAVADO	SERVANT	PRIVITY	CATWALK	AWKWARD
COUVADE	SERVING	SUAVITY	GUNWALE	BREWERY
PERVADE	SHAVING	VELVETY.	ILL-WILL	BULWARK
PROVIDE.	SHOVING	FERVOUR	INKWELL	EEL-WORM
BREVIER	SIEVING	FLAVOUR	KNOW-ALL	FLOWERY
CIVVIES	SLAVING	FULVOUS	+MAXWELL	FORWARD
CLAVIER	SOLVENT	NERVOUS	OIL-WELL	FROWARD
HEAVIER	SOLVING	TRIVIUM.	SEA-WALL	HAYWARD
+OLIVIER	STAVING	SURVIVE	SEA-WOLF	HAYWIRE
PREVIEW	SYLVINE		SHOWILY	LEEWARD
PURVIEW.	WAIVING	CROWBAR	SNOWILY	LOBWORM
SALVAGE.	WEAVING.	NARWHAL	WERWOLF.	NETWORK
DRIVE-IN	*CHEVIOT	OUTWEAR	MUGWUMP.	OFFWARD
PREVAIL	CHEVRON.	SHOWMAN	AVOWING	OUTWARD
TRAVAIL	BRAVERY	SNOWMAN.	BLOWING	OUTWORE
VERVAIN.	BRAVURA	*GATWICK	BREWING	OUTWORK
CONVOKE	CALVARY	*HARWICH	CHEWING	OUTWORN
PROVOKE.	CONVERT	*IPSWICH	CLAWING	SEAWARD
BRAVELY	CULVERT	*KESWICK	CROWING	SHOWERY
GRAVELY	GRAVURE	*NORWICH	DRAWING	SKYWARD
HEAVILY	KNAVERY	*WARWICK.	ENTWINE	STEWARD
NAIVELY	*MALVERN	BETWEEN	FLAWING	+STEWART
PRIVILY	NERVURE	BRAWLER	FLOWING	SUNWARD
SERVILE	OLIVARY	BROWNED	FORWENT	TINWARE
SUAVELY.	PERVERT	BROWSED	GLOWING	UNAWARE
BRAVING	PROVERB	CHOWDER	GNAWING	VANWARD
CALVING	SERVERY	CLOWNED	KNOWING	WAXWORK
CARVING	SHIVERY	CRAWLER	LAPWING	WAYWARD.
CERVINE	SILVERY	CROWDED	OUTWENT	ANYWISE
CONVENE	SLAVERY	CROWNED	SHOWING	ENDWISE
CONVENT	SUBVERT.	DRAWLED	SKEWING	EYEWASH
CORVINE	ATAVISM	DROWNED	SLEWING	HOGWASH
CRAVING	BRAVEST	DROWSED	SNOWING	PIGWASH
CURVING	CANVASS	FROWNED	SPEWING	PROWESS
DELVING	DERVISH	GROWLER	STEWING	SLOWEST
DRIVING	GRAVEST	PRAWNED	STOWING	SUNWISE
FERVENT	HARVEST	PROWLER	THAWING	UNTWIST.
GRAVING	KNAVISH	SCOWLED	UNTWINE	FROWSTY.
HALVING	PEEVISH	SEAWEED	VIEWING.	BLOW-OUT

GROWN-UP.	FLAYING	RHIZOID.	ALREADY	BOXHAUL
BETWIXT.	FRAYING	CRAZILY	ANIMATE	BRADAWL
ENDWAYS	LEVYING	DIZZILY	ANOMALY	BRAVADO
	OBEYING	DRIZZLE	APANAGE	BREWAGE
ASEXUAL	PITYING	DRIZZLY	APPEASE	BRIGADE
*BRIXHAM.	PLAYING	FRAZZLE	APPLAUD	BRIGAND
INEXACT.	PRAYING	FRIZZLE	ARAMAIC	*BRITAIN
DIOXIDE.	PREYING	GRIZZLE	ARCHAIC	BROCADE
FLEXILE.	SCRYING	GRIZZLY	ARCUATE	BROMATE
PROXIMO.	SLAYING	JAZZILY	ARM-BAND	BUFFALO
COAXING	SPAYING	SWIZZLE.	ASPHALT	BULLACE
FLEXING	STAYING	RHIZOME.	ASSUAGE	BULLATE
HOAXING.	SWAYING	AMAZING	+ASTRAEA	BULWARK
FLEXION	UNDYING	*ARIZONA	ATARAXY	BUMMALO
FLUXION.	VARYING	BENZENE	ATHWART	BUOYAGE
FLEXURE.	X-RAYING.	BLAZING	ATTRACT	BUOYANT
COEXIST	*BABYLON	BRAZING	AUREATE	BUREAUX
MARXISM.	PLAYBOY	BUZZING	AVERAGE	BURSARY
BAUXITE	POLYGON	CRAZING	AVOCADO	BUSTARD
+QUIXOTE	POLYPOD.	FIZZING	AWKWARD.	BUZZARD.
	GRUYERE	GLAZING	BAGGAGE	CABBAGE
COPY-CAT	HALYARD	GLOZING	*BAHRAIN	CAB-RANK
DRAYMAN	LANYARD.	GRAZING	BALLADE	*CALGARY
GREYLAG	BABYISH	JAZZING	BALLAST	CALVARY
JURYMAN	+CALYPSO	PRIZING	BANDAGE	CANTATA
+KHAYYAM.	COPYIST	SEIZING.	+BARBARA	CANVASS
PLAY-ACT.	GREYISH.	EPIZOON.	BARBATE	CAPTAIN
BARYTES	NAVY-CUT	BUZZARD	BARGAIN	CARCASS
CALYCES	PAPYRUS	GIZZARD	BARMAID	CARNAGE
*CROYDEN	PLAYFUL	SEIZURE	+BARNABY	CARRACK
PLAYLET	POLYPUS		BARRACK	CARTAGE
PLAYPEN	TOBY-JUG		BARRAGE	CASCADE
POLYMER.		+ABIGAIL	BASTARD	CASCARA
PLAY-OFF.	BRAZIER	ABREACT	BEGGARY	CASSAVA
BUOYAGE.	CRAZIER	ABREAST	*BELFAST	CATCALL
ACRYLIC	DAZZLED	ABROACH	BELTANE	CATFALL
BABY-SIT	FIZZLED	ABSTAIN	BENEATH	CATWALK
BUTYRIC	FRIZZED	ACCLAIM	BENGALI	CAUDATE
ECDYSIS	GLAZIER	ACETATE	BEREAVE	CEMBALO
KATYDID	GUZZLER	ACREAGE	+BERNARD	CENTAUR
POLYNIA	MIZZLED	ACTUARY	BILIARY	CERTAIN
SATYRIC.	MUZZLED	ACTUATE	BIPLANE	+CHAGALL
BICYCLE.	NUZZLED	ADAMANT	BLATANT	CHARADE
BELYING	PUZZLER	ADULATE	BOBTAIL	CHELATE
BRAYING	QUIZZED	AGITATE	BOLLARD	CHICAGO
BUOYANT	SIZZLED	AGITATO	BOMBARD	*CHICANE
CLOYING	SOZZLED	AIRMAIL	BOMBAST	CHORALE
DENYING	WHIZZED.	AIR-RAID	BONDAGE	CILIARY
ENVYING	BENZOIN	*ALABAMA	BONE-ASH	CILIATE
ESPYING	MUEZZIN	ALIDADE	BOSCAGE	CITHARA.

CITRATE	DECLARE	ENDWAYS	FURBALL	*HUNGARY
CLAMANT	DEFIANT	*ENGLAND	FURCATE	HUSBAND
CLIMATE	DEFLATE	ENGRAFT	FURNACE.	HYDRANT
COCKADE	DEFRAUD	ENGRAIN	GALLANT	HYDRATE.
COGNATE	DEGRADE	ENGRAVE	GARBAGE	*ICELAND
COINAGE	*DENMARK	ENSLAVE	GARLAND	ICE-PACK
COLLAGE	DENTARY	ENSNARE	GAS-MAIN	IMITATE
COLLATE	DENTATE	ENTRAIN	GAS-MASK	IMPEACH
COMMAND	DEPRAVE	ENTRANT	GEMMATE	IMPLANT
COMPACT	DESCALE	EPITAPH	GERMANE	INBOARD
COMPANY	DESCANT	*ESKDALE	*GERMANY	*INDIANA
COMPARE	DESPAIR	ESTUARY	GESTALT	INDRAWN
COMPASS	DETRACT	EXCLAIM	GESTAPO	INEXACT
COMRADE	DETRAIN	EXOGAMY	GIMBALS	INFLAME
CONCAVE	DEVIATE	EXPIATE	GIZZARD	INFLATE
CONNATE	DIABASE	EXPLAIN	GODDAMN	INGRAIN
CONTACT	DICTATE	EXTRACT	GOLIARD	INGRATE
CONTAIN	DIEHARD	EYEBALL	GOSHAWK	INSCAPE
COOLANT	DIETARY	EYE-BATH	GOULASH	INSTALL
CORDAGE	DIGRAPH	EYELASH	GRADATE	INSTANT
CORDATE	DIORAMA	EYEWASH.	+GRAHAME	INSTATE
CORKAGE	DIPHASE	FALCATE	GRANARY	INTRANT
CORSAGE	DISBAND	FALLACY	*GRENADA	INWEAVE
CORSAIR	DISCARD	FANFARE	GRENADE	*IRELAND
COSSACK	DISDAIN	FANTAIL	GRIMACE	+ISHMAEL
COSTARD	DISEASE	FANTAST	GUNNAGE	ISOBATH
COSTATE	DISMAST	FANTASY	GUNWALE	ISOLATE
COTTAGE	DISTAFF	FARRAGO	GUTTATE	ITERATE.
COURAGE	DISTANT	FERRATE	GYMNAST.	JACKASS
COUVADE	DOCKAGE	FINBACK	HAGGADA	JANUARY
COWBANE	DOGGART	*FINLAND	+HAGGARD	+JULIANA .
CRANAGE	DORMANT	FIRE-ARM	HALYARD	*JUTLAND.
CREMATE	DULLARD	FLY-HALF	HANSARD	KABBALA
CRENATE	*DUNDALK	FLY-PAST	HASTATE	*KILDARE
CRUSADE	DUNNAGE.	FOGBANK	HATBAND	KNOW-ALL
CRY-BABY	EARMARK	FOLIAGE	HATRACK	LACTASE
CUIRASS	ECSTASY	FOLIATE	HAULAGE	LAGGARD
CURRACH	EDUCATE	FOOTAGE	HAYWARD	LALLANS
CURRANT	EEL-FARE	FORBADE	HEBRAIC	LANYARD
CURTAIL	ELEGANT	FOREARM	HECTARE	LEAFAGE
CURTAIN	ELEVATE	FORGAVE	HENBANE	LEAKAGE
CURVATE	EMANATE	FORMATE	HEPTANE	LEEWARD
CUSPATE	EMBRACE	FORRARD	HERBAGE	LEOPARD
CUSTARD	EMERALD	FORSAKE	+HILLARY	LEOTARD
CUT-BACK	EMULATE	FORWARD	HOBNAIL	LIBRARY
CUTLASS	ENCHAIN	FOULARD	HOGBACK	LIBRATE
CYMBALO.	ENCHANT	FOUMART	HOGWASH	LIMBATE
DASTARD	ENCHASE	FRIGATE	HOLDALL	LINEAGE
DECEASE	ENCLAVE	FROWARD	*HOLLAND	LINEATE
DECLAIM	END-GAME	FUN-FAIR	HOSTAGE	LINKAGE

LINSANG	NORLAND	PESSARY	RADIANT	SECTARY
LIQUATE	NUT-CASE.	PHALANX	RADIATE	SEEPAGE
LOLLARD	OAK-GALL	PHARAOH	RAMPAGE	SEPTATE
LOWLAND	OATCAKE	PHONATE	RAMPANT	SERIATE
LUGGAGE	OBVIATE	PICKAXE	RAMPART	SERRATE
LULLABY	OCULATE	PIEBALD	RANSACK	SERVANT
LUMBAGO.	OFF-HAND	PIERAGE	+RAPHAEL	SETBACK
MAGNATE	OFFWARD	PIGTAIL	RAT-RACE	SET-FAIR
MALLARD	OILCAKE	PIGWASH	RAT-TAIL	SEXTAIN
MAMMARY	OLIVARY	PILLAGE	RECLAIM	SEXTANT
MANDALA	OPERATE	PINBALL	REFRACT	SHEBANG
MANDATE	ORCHARD	PINNACE	REFRAIN	SITUATE
MANSARD	OSSUARY	PINNATE	REFRAME	SKYLARK
*MARGATE	OUTBACK	PINTADO	REGNANT	SKYSAIL
MASCARA	OUTCAST	PIQUANT	*REIGATE	SKYWARD
MASSAGE	OUTFACE	PITFALL	RELEASE	SOPRANO
MEDIATE	OUTFALL	PLACARD	RELIANT	SOUTANE
MERMAID	OUTLAST	PLACATE	REMNANT	SPINACH
MESSAGE	OUTRAGE	PLAY-ACT	REPLACE	SPIRANT
METCAST	OUTSAIL	PLENARY	REPLANT	SQUEAKY
METHANE	OUTTALK	PLICATE	RESTATE	STEWARD
+MICHAEL	OUTWARD	PLUMAGE	RETIARY	+STEWART
MIDLAND	OVERACT	POCHARD	RETRACE	STOMACH
MIGRANT	OVERALL	POLE-AXE	RETRACT	STOMATA
MIGRATE	OVERARM	POLLACK	REYNARD	STORAGE
MILEAGE	OVERAWE	POLLARD	RHUBARB	STOWAGE
MINTAGE	OXIDANT	POMPANO	+RICHARD	STREAKY
MISCALL	OXIDASE.	PONIARD	+RIMBAUD	STRIATE
MISCAST	PACKAGE	PORTAGE	ROOTAGE	SUCCADE
MISGAVE	PAGEANT	POSTAGE	ROSEATE	SULTANA
MISLAID	PALMARY	PREFACE	ROULADE	SUMMARY
MISTAKE	PALMATE	PRELACY	RUINATE	SUNWARD
MONTAGE	PALPATE	PRELATE	RUMMAGE	SURFACE
+MONTAGU	PANCAKE	PREPAID	RUN-BACK	SURNAME
*MONTANA	PARTAKE	PREPARE	*RUTLAND.	SURPASS
MOORAGE	PASSAGE	PRESAGE	SABBATH	SUSTAIN
MORDANT	PASSANT	PREVAIL	SACCATE	*SWANAGE
MUD-BATH	PEASANT	PRIMACY	SALVAGE	SYNCARP.
MUDLARK	PECCANT	PRIMARY	SAPSAGO	TANKAGE
MUNDANE	PECCARY	PRIMATE	SARCASM	TANKARD
MURRAIN	PECCAVI	PRIVACY	SATIATE	TANNAGE
MUSTANG	PEERAGE	PRIVATE	SAUSAGE	TANNATE
MUSTARD.	PENDANT	PROBANG	SAVE-ALL	TEACAKE
NARRATE	PENNANT	PROBATE	SCUTAGE	TEENAGE
NECTARY	PENTANE	PROFANE	SEA-BANK	TERRACE
NETBALL	PEONAGE	PROLATE	SEA-KALE	TERRAIN
NEW-LAID	PERCALE	PROPANE	SEA-MARK	TESTACY
NIGGARD	PERHAPS	PROSAIC	SEA-SALT	TESTATE
NIRVANA	PERTAIN	PULSATE.	SEA-WALL	THERAPY
NITRATE	PERVADE	QUINARY.	SEAWARD	THROATY

TIFFANY	VIBRATE	BUGABOO	GRABBLE	POTABLE.
TILLAGE	VIBRATO	BUYABLE.	GRUBBED	QUIBBLE.
TIMPANI	VILLAGE	CALIBRE	GRUBBER	RAINBOW
TIMPANO	VILLAIN	CALL-BOX	GRUMBLE.	RAREBIT
TINTACK	VINTAGE	CAMP-BED	HALIBUT	RATABLE
TINWARE	VIOLATE	CAPABLE	HANDBAG	RHOMBIC
TITLARK	VIRGATE	CARIBOU	HAUTBOY.	RHOMBUS
TITRATE	VITIATE	*CELEBES	ICHABOD	RIDABLE
TOCCATA	VOLCANO	CHAMBER	IGNOBLE	RISIBLE
TOENAIL	VOLTAGE	CLAMBER	IMBIBED	ROSEBUD.
TOLLAGE	VOLTAIC	CLIMBER	INCUBUS	SACKBUT
TONNAGE	VULGATE.	CLOBBER	INHABIT	SALABLE
TOPIARY	WAGTAIL	CLUBBED	INHIBIT.	SANDBAG
TOPMAST	WALLABY	COAL-BED	JACOBIN	SAND-BAR
TOPSAIL	+WALLACE	COHABIT	+JEZEBEL	SANDBOY
TORNADO	*WALSALL	CRABBED	JUKEBOX.	SAVABLE
TOWPATH	WARFARE	CRIBBED	KNOBBED	SCABBED
TRAVAIL	WARPATH	CRIBBER	KNOBBLE	SCRIBAL
TREPANG	WARRANT	CROWBAR	KNOBBLY.	SCRIBER
TRYSAIL	WASSAIL	CRUMBLE	LEGIBLE	SCRUBBY
TZIGANE.	WASTAGE	CRUMBLY.	LEGIBLY	SCUMBLE
ULULATE	WATTAGE	DATABLE	LIFTBOY	SEEDBED
UMBRAGE	WAYWARD	DECIBEL	LIVABLE	SHAMBLE
UNAWARE	WELFARE.	DICE-BOX	LONGBOW	SHERBET
UNBRACE	YARDAGE.	DISABLE	LOVABLE	SHOWBIZ
UNCHAIN	ZEDOARY	DISOBEY	LOVABLY.	SHRUBBY
UNCLASP	*ZEELAND	DRABBLE	MACABRE	SICK-BAY
UNHEARD	*ZETLAND	DRIBBLE	MAILBAG	SICK-BED
UNITARY	ZOOGAMY	DRUBBED	MILK-BAR	SIZABLE
UNLEARN		DUPABLE	MINIBUS	SJAMBOK
UNLEASH	ACERBIC	DURABLE	MOONBUG	SLOBBER
UNMEANT	ACROBAT	DURABLY	MOVABLE	SLUBBED
UNREADY	ACTABLE	DUSTBIN.	MUTABLE.	SLUMBER
UPBRAID	ADHIBIT	EATABLE	NAMABLE	SNUBBED
UP-GRADE	AEROBIC	ENNOBLE	NOSEBAG	SOAP-BOX
UPHEAVE	AFFABLE	ENROBED	NOTABLE	SOLUBLE
UPSTAGE	ALEMBIC	EQUABLE	NOTABLY.	STABBED
UPSTAIR	ALGEBRA	EQUABLY	OCTOBER	STUBBED
UPSTART	AMIABLE	EXHIBIT.	OMNIBUS.	STUBBLE
URINARY.	AMOEBIC	FINABLE	PARABLE	STUBBLY
VAGRANT	+ANNABEL	FIREBOX	PAYABLE	STUMBLE
VALIANT	AUDIBLE	FIRE-BUG	PEAT-BOG	SWABBED
VANTAGE	AXLE-BOX.	FIXABLE	+PHOEBUS	SWABBER.
VANWARD	BANDBOX	FRAIBLE	PILL-BOX	TALLBOY
VARIANT	BELL-BOY	FRIBBLE	PLAYBOY	TAMABLE
VENDACE	BLABBED	FUSIBLE.	PLIABLE	TAXABLE
VENTAGE	BLESBOK	GEAR-BOX	PLUMBER	TENABLE
VERDANT	BLUBBER	GOOD-BYE	PLUMBIC	TENABLY
VERVAIN	BOURBON	GRABBED	POOR-BOX	THIMBLE
VIBRANT	BRAMBLE	GRABBER	POSTBAG	THUMBED

387

TREMBLE	COUNCIL	MENACED	SOLACED	BOARDER
TREMBLY	CRUNCHY	MIMICRY	SOLICIT	BOREDOM
TRIABLE	CUBICLE	MINICAB	SOUPCON	+BORODIN
TROUBLE	*CURACAO	MIRACLE	SPANCEL	*BOULDER
TUCK-BOX	CUTICLE	MODICUM	+SPENCER	BOUNDER
TUNABLE.	CYNICAL.	MOHICAN	SPLICED	BOURDON
UNROBED.	DEBACLE	MONOCLE	SPRUCED	BRAIDED
VISIBLE	DEDUCED	*MOROCCO	STARCHY	BRANDED
VOCABLE	DEFACED	MUSICAL.	STENCIL	BREADED
VOLUBLE.	DEFICIT	NAVY-CUT	STOICAL	BREADTH
WADABLE	DIARCHY	NODICAL	SUBACID.	BREEDER
WINDBAG	DOVECOT.	NOTICED.	TAXI-CAB	+BRENDAN
WIRABLE	EAR-ACHE	OFFICER	TIERCEL	BRINDLE
	ENFACED	OPTICAL	TIERCET	BROADEN
*AJACCIO	ENLACED	OSSICLE.	TOBACCO	BROADER
AMERCED	ENTICED	PANACEA	TOPICAL	BROADLY
ANARCHY	ETHICAL	PANACHE	TRAM-CAR	BROODED
ANTACID	EVINCED.	PANICKY	TREACLE	BUILDER
APRICOT	FELUCCA	PAUNCHY	TREACLY	BULLDOG.
ARTICLE	FINICAL	PEDICEL	TYPICAL.	CACODYL
ATTACHE	FINICKY	PEDICLE	UNLUCKY	CELADON
AURICLE	FLACCID	PELICAN	UTRICLE.	*CHEDDAR
AUROCHS	+FRANCIS.	PIERCED	VARICES	CHOWDER
AUTOCAR.	GLANCED	POLACCA	*VATICAN	CITADEL
BICYCLE	GOUACHE	POLECAT	VEHICLE	+CLAUDIA
BIFOCAL	GROUCHY.	POLICED	VESICLE.	CLOUDED
+BLANCHE	HAIR-CUT	POUNCED	WILDCAT	CO-TIDAL
BLOTCHY	HARICOT	PRANCED.	WOODCUT	COULDST
BORACIC	HELICAL	RADICAL		CROWDED
BOUNCER	HELICES	RADICEL	ABANDON	*CROYDEN
BRECCIA	HELLCAT	RADICES	ABRADED	CZARDAS.
BRIOCHE	HYOSCIN.	RADICLE	ABRIDGE	DAZEDLY
BRONCHI.	ILLICIT	+REBECCA	ACCEDED	DECADAL
CALYCES	INDICES	REDUCED	ADJUDGE	DECIDED
CARACUL	INDICIA	REFACED	ALLUDED	DECODED
*CARACUS	INDUCED.	RETICLE	AMENDED	DECODER
CATECHU	JOUNCED.	RUSE-CUT.	APHIDES	+DEIRDRE
CHANCED	*KARACHI	SALICIN	+ARIADNE	DELUDED
CHANCEL	KINGCUP	SARACEN	*ARUNDEL	DENUDED
CHANCRE	KNEE-CAP.	SCARCER	ASUNDER	DERIDED
+CHAUCER	LEXICAL	SCONCED	AWARDED.	DIVIDED
CHURCHY	LEXICON	SEDUCER	*BAGHDAD	DREADED
CLOACAL	LINOCUT	SIDECAR	BESIDES	*DRESDEN
CODICIL	LIONCEL	SILICIC	BLADDER	DRIP-DRY
COERCED	LOGICAL	SILICON	BLANDLY	DRUIDIC
COLICKY	LYRICAL.	SIROCCO	BLENDED	DUKEDOM
COMICAL	MAGICAL	SKETCHY	BLINDED	DWINDLE.
COPY-CAT	MALACCA	SLUICED	BLINDLY	EARLDOM
CORACLE	MANACLE	SMOOCHY	BLOODED	ECHIDNA
CORN-COB	MEDICAL	SNATCHY	BLUNDER	*ECUADOR

EMENDED.	MATADOR	SECEDED	WEIRDLY	BESIEGE
FARADAY	MAUNDER	SHINDIG	WHEEDLE	BESMEAR
FAST-DAY	MEANDER	SHUDDER	WIELDED	BESPEAK
FETIDLY	MELODIC	SKALDIC	WORKDAY	BESTEAD
FIELDED	MONADIC	SKIDDED	WORLDLY	BETWEEN
FIELDER	MOULDED	SLANDER	WOUNDED.	BIGGEST
FIREDOG	MOULDER	SLEDDED	YIELDED	BIG-HEAD
FLAG-DAY	MOUNDED.	SLENDER		BITTERN
FLOODED	NAKEDLY	*SNOWDON	ABSCESS	BOBBERY
FOUNDER	NOMADIC	SOLIDLY	ACADEMY	BOLDEST
FOUNDRY	NOONDAY.	SOUNDED	ACALEPH	BONKERS
FREEDOM.	OPHIDIA	SOUNDLY	ACCRETE	+BOSWELL
GEORDIE	OPPIDAN	SPEEDED	ACHIEVE	BRAVELY
GLADDEN	OVERDID	SPEEDER	+ACTAEON	BRAVERY
GRANDAD	OVERDUE.	SPENDER	ACTRESS	BRAVEST
GRANDEE	PALADIN	SPINDLE	ACUTELY	BREWERY
GRANDER	PALUDAL	SPINDLY	ADDRESS	BRIBERY
GRANDLY	PARADED	SPLODGE	AGELESS	BUGBEAR
GRANDMA	PARADOS	SPONDEE	AGGRESS	BUGGERY
GRANDPA	PARADOX	SPONDYL	AGILELY	BURGEON
GRIDDLE	+PHAEDRA	STAIDLY	AILMENT	BURGESS
GRINDER	PICADOR	STARDOM	AIMLESS	BUTTERY.
GUARDED	PLAUDIT	STUDDED	AIRLESS	CALMEST
GUELDER	PLEADER	SUB-EDIT	ALCHEMY	CANDELA
GUERDON	PLODDER	SWADDLE	*ALGIERS	CANNERY
GUILDER.	PLUNDER	SWINDLE	ALIMENT	CANTEEN
HANGDOG	POUNDAL	*SWINDON	AMATEUR	CATHEAD
HEARDIN	POUNDER	SYNODAL	AMBIENT	CATS-EYE
HEIRDOM	PRODDED	SYNODIC.	ANALECT	CAUTERY
HIGHDAY	PRODDER	TEPIDLY	ANCIENT	CHATEAU
HOARDER	PROUDER	THIRDLY	ANISEED	CHIMERA
HOLIDAY	PROUDLY.	THUDDED	+ANTAEUS	CHINESE
HOUNDED	QUONDAM.	THUNDER	*ANTWERP	CHOLERA
HUMIDOR.	RABIDLY	TIMIDLY	ANXIETY	CINDERY
IMPEDED	RAMADAN	TREADLE	APTNESS	CISTERN
INFIDEL	RAPIDLY	TREDDLE	ARCHERY	+CLEMENT
INSIDER	RECEDED	TRENDED	ARMLESS	CLOSELY
INVADER.	REREDOS	TRODDEN	ARTLESS	CLOSE-UP
JACKDAW	RESIDED	TRUNDLE	ATHLETE	+COCTEAU
JOINDER.	RESIDUA	TUESDAY	AUGMENT	COLDEST
KATYDID	RESIDUE	TWADDLE	AUSTERE.	COLLECT
KINGDOM	RIGIDLY	TWIDDLE.	BALDEST	COLLEEN
KNEADED.	ROUNDEL	UNAIDED	BANDEAU	COLLEGE
LAUNDER	ROUNDER	UNGODLY	BATTERY	COMMEND
LAUNDRY	ROUNDLY	UNLADEN.	+BECKETT	COMMENT
+LEANDER	ROUND-UP.	VALIDLY	BELIEVE	COMPEER
LIVIDLY	SCALDED	VAPIDLY	BENZENE	COMPERE
LUCIDLY	SCANDAL	VIVIDLY.	BEQUEST	COMPETE
LURIDLY.	SCOLDED	WASH-DAY	BERSERK	CONCEAL
MACADAM	SCUDDED	WEEKDAY	BESEECH	CONCEDE

CONCEIT	DIPTERA	FISHERY	HETAERA	LECHERY
CONCEPT	DISCERN	FITMENT	HIGHEST	LECTERN
CONCERN	DISSECT	FITNESS	HIMSELF	LEGLESS
CONCERT	DISSENT	FITTEST	+HOLBEIN	LENIENT
CONDEMN	DISTEND	FLANEUR	HOLIEST	LETHEAN
CONFESS	DOUCEUR	FLOWERY	HOSIERY	LIMBECK
CONGEAL	DRAPERY	FLYLEAF	HOSTESS	LINSEED
CONGEST	DRIVE-IN	+FONTEYN	HOT-HEAD	LIONESS
CONNECT	DROSERA	FOOLERY	HOTTEST	LIQUEFY
CONSENT	DUBIETY	FOPPERY	HOWBEIT	LIQUEUR
CONTEMN	DUCHESS	FORBEAR	HUNKERS	LONGEST
CONTEND	DUDGEON	FORFEIT	HUTMENT	LOOSELY
CONTENT	DULLEST	FORGERY	HYGIENE.	LOOSEST
CONTEST	DUNGEON	FORWENT	ICEBERG	LOTTERY
CONTEXT	+DURRELL.	FULLEST.	ILLNESS	LOUDEST.
CONVENE	EARNEST	GALLEON	IMAGERY	+MACBETH
CONVENT	EASTERN	GALLERY	IMPIETY	MACHETE
CONVERT	EGGHEAD	GARMENT	IMPRESS	MADDEST
COOKERY	ELEMENT	GEODESY	IMPREST	MADNESS
COOLEST	EMINENT	+GILBERT	INANELY	MAGNETO
COPPERY	EMPRESS	GINGERY	INBREED	+MALVERN
CORRECT	ENDLESS	GO-AHEAD	INFIELD	+MARGERY
CORTEGE	*ENFIELD	GODDESS	INFLECT	MASSEUR
COSTEAN	ENTREAT	GODHEAD	INGRESS	MASTERY
COWHERD	EPICENE	GODLESS	INKWELL	+MAUREEN
COYNESS	ERODENT	GODSEND	INQUEST	+MAXWELL
CRUDELY	ESCHEAT	GRADELY	INSPECT	MEEKEST
CULVERT	ESTHETE	GRAPERY	INSTEAD	MESEEMS
CURRENT	*EVEREST	GRAVELY	IRATELY	MILDEST
CUTLERY	EVIDENT	GRAVEST	ISRAELI.	MILDEWY
CYPRESS.	EXCRETA	GROCERY	JITTERY	MIOCENE
DARKEST	EXCRETE	GRUYERE	JOBBERY	MISDEAL
DEAD-END	EXIGENT	GUDGEON	JOBLESS	MISDEED
DEANERY	EXPRESS	GUNNERY.	JOYLESS.	MISLEAD
DEAREST	EXTREME	HALBERD	KEENEST	MISREAD
DEEPEST	EYELESS.	HAPLESS	+KENNEDY	MOCKERY
DEFLECT	FALSELY	HARDEST	+KENNETH	+MOLIERE
DENSELY	FARCEUR	HARNESS	KINDEST	MUMMERY
DENSEST	FASTEST	HARVEST	KNAVERY.	MYSTERY.
DEPLETE	FAT-HEAD	HAS-BEEN	LACTEAL	NAIVELY
DEPRESS	FATNESS	HASLETS	LAMBENT	NAIVETE
DESCEND	FATTEST	HAUBERK	LAMBERT	NAIVETY
DESCENT	FERMENT	HAUTEUR	LANTERN	NANKEEN
DESSERT	FERNERY	HAYSEED	LARCENY	NASCENT
DIALECT	FERRETY	HEIRESS	LARGELY	NEAREST
+DICKENS	FERVENT	HELLENE	LARGESS	NEGLECT
DIGRESS	FIFTEEN	HENNERY	LARGEST	NEGRESS
DILUENT	FIG-LEAF	HENPECK	LATHERY	NOBLEST
DIMNESS	FIGMENT	+HERBERT	LAWLESS	NOWHERE
DIOCESE	FILBERT	HERSELF	LAXNESS	NUCLEAR

NUCLEIC	PORTEND	REGRESS	SILVERY	TERPENE
NUCLEON	PORTENT	RELIEVE	SINCERE	TERRENE
NUCLEUS	POSSESS	REPLETE	SINLESS	TERSELY
NUNNERY	POSTERN	REPRESS	SIXTEEN	TESSERA
NURSERY.	POT-HERB	REQUEST	SLAVERY	THEREAT
OATMEAL	POTTERY	RESPECT	SLOWEST	THEREBY
OBSCENE	+POULENC	RETREAD	SLYNESS	THEREIN
ODDMENT	POWDERY	RICHEST	SOCIETY	THEREOF
ODDNESS	PREBEND	RICKETS	SOFTEST	THEREON
OFFBEAT	PRECEDE	RICKETY	SOLVENT	+THERESA
OFF-PEAK	PRECEPT	RIVIERE	SORCERY	THERETO
OILLESS	PRECESS	ROBBERY	SOUREST	+THESEUS
OILMEAL	PREFECT	ROCKERY	SPARELY	+THOREAU
OIL-WELL	PRESENT	ROGUERY	SPIDERY	THYSELF
ONENESS	PRETEND	ROMPERS	SQUEEZE	TIDIEST
ONESELF	PRETEXT	RONDEAU	STALEST	TIGRESS
OPPRESS	PREVENT	ROOKERY	STATELY	TINIEST
OPULENT	PRIMELY	RUBBERY	STIPEND	+TINTERN
ORPHEAN	PROCEED	RUMNESS	STUDENT	TOLUENE
+ORPHEUS	PROCESS	+RUSSELL.	STUPEFY	TORMENT
OURSELF	PROFESS	SADDEST	STYRENE	TORPEDO
OUTWEAR	PROGENY	SADNESS	SUAVELY	TORRENT
OUTWENT.	PROJECT	SALIENT	SUBDEAN	TOTTERY
PARVENU	PROTEAN	SALTERN	SUBJECT	TRACERY
PASTERN	PROTECT	SAPIENT	SUBTEND	TRADE-IN
+PASTEUR	PROTEGE	SAPLESS	SUBVERT	TRAGEDY
PATIENT	PROTEID	SATIETY	SUCCEED	TRAPEZE
PATTERN	PROTEIN	*SCAFELL	SUCCESS	TRICEPS
PAYMENT	PROTEST	SCALENE	SUGGEST	TRIDENT
PEERESS	+PROTEUS	SCENERY	SUMMERY	TRIREME
PENDENT	PROVERB	SCREECH	SUNBEAM	TRISECT
PEPPERY	PROWESS	SEA-LEGS	SUNLESS	TRITELY
PERCEPT	PRUDENT	SEAWEED	SUPREME	+TRUDEAU
PERFECT	PRUDERY	SECRECY	SURFEIT	TURNERY.
PERPEND	+PTOLEMY	SECRETE	SURGEON	UGLIEST
+PERSEUS	PUNGENT	SEGMENT	SURGERY	UKULELE
PERVERT	PURBECK	SEQUENT	SUSPECT	UMPTEEN
PIGGERY	+PURCELL	SERPENT	SUSPEND.	UNCLEAN
PIGMENT	PUTREFY	SERVERY	TABLEAU	UNDRESS
PINCERS	PYGMEAN.	SEXIEST	TAFFETA	UNGUENT
PINHEAD	RAIMENT	SEXLESS	TAIL-END	UNSPENT
PINK-EYE	RANKEST	SHAPELY	TALLEST	UPSWEPT
PIONEER	RAWNESS	SHEBEEN	TANGENT	USELESS.
PIT-HEAD	RAYLESS	SHEREEF	TANNERY	VAGUELY
PLACEBO	REAGENT	SHIVERY	TAUTEST	VAINEST
PLATEAU	REDDEST	SHOWERY	TEA-LEAF	VAQUERO
POETESS	RED-HEAD	SHUT-EYE	TEMPERA	VARIETY
*POMPEII	REDRESS	SHYNESS	TEMPEST	VASTEST
POOREST	REFLECT	SIAMESE	TENSELY	VELVETY
PORRECT	REFRESH	SICKEST	TENSEST	VERBENA

VERIEST	BLUFFLY	PIPEFUL	ANTIGEN	FORAGER
+VERMEER	BOATFUL	PITIFUL	*ANTIGUA	FOURGON
VERMEIL	BODEFUL	PLAYFUL	ARMIGER	FRAUGHT
VESPERS	BOWLFUL	PROFFER	ASSAGAI	FREIGHT
VILLEIN	BRIEFLY	PROOFED.	AVENGER.	FRINGED
+VINCENT	BRIMFUL.	QUAFFED.	*BOLOGNA	FROGGED.
VIOLENT	CAREFUL	RATAFIA	BRAGGED	GARAGED
VISCERA.	CHAFFER	RESTFUL	BRIDGED	*GEORGIA
WAGGERY	CHAMFER	ROOMFUL.	+BRIDGET	GEORGIC
WANNESS	CHIEFLY	SAND-FLY	BROUGHT.	*GLASGOW
WARHEAD	CHIFFON	SCAFFED	CHANGED	GRUDGED.
WARMEST	CHUFFED	SCRUFFY	CHARGED	HALOGEN
WEAKEST	CONIFER.	SCUFFED	CHARGER	HEXAGON
WEEK-END	DEEP-FRY	SCUFFLE	CHUGGED	HOOSGOW.
WEST-END	DIREFUL	SHUFFLE	CLANGED	ILLEGAL
WESTERN	DISHFUL	SKIFFLE	CLANGER	INSIGHT
WETNESS	DOLEFUL	SKILFUL	CLINGER	INTEGER.
WETTEST	+DRESFUS	SKINFUL	CLOGGED	LOUNGER
WHATEER	DUTIFUL	SNAFFLE	COAL-GAS	LYING-IN
WHENEER	DWARFED.	SNIFFED	COLOGNE	LYINGLY.
WHEREAS	EASEFUL.	SNUFFED	CRINGED	MANAGED
WHEREAT	FATEFUL	SNUFFLE	CRINGLE	MANAGER
WHEREBY	FEARFUL	SOUFFLE	CRYOGEN.	MUTAGEN.
WHEREER	FEOFFEE	SOULFUL	DECAGON	NOSEGAY.
WHEREIN	FEOFFOR	SPOOFED	DELIGHT	OBLIGED
WHEREOF	FIREFLY	SQUIFFY	DELUGED	OCTAGON.
WHEREON	FISTFUL	STAFFED	DEMIGOD	PARAGON
WHERETO	FORKFUL	STIFFEN	*DONEGAL	PELAGIC
WHITEST	FRETFUL.	STIFFER	DOWAGER	PERIGEE
WIDGEON	GAINFUL	STIFFLY	DRAGGED	PHLEGMY
WILDEST	GIRAFFE	STRAFED	DRAGGLE	PIRAGUA
WINKERS	GLEEFUL	STUFFED.	DRAUGHT	PIROGUE
*WISBECH	GRIFFIN	TACTFUL	DREDGER	PLEDGED
WITHERS	GRUFFLY.	TEARFUL	DROUGHT	PLEDGEE
WITLESS	*HALIFAX	THRIFTY	DRUDGED	PLEDGET
WITNESS	HANDFUL	TRAFFIC	DRUGGED	PLUGGED
*WOOMERA	HARMFUL	TRUFFLE	DRUGGET.	PLUNGED
WRITE-UP	HATEFUL	TUNEFUL	ECLOGUE	PLUNGER
WRYNECK	HEEDFUL	TWELFTH.	EMERGED	PODAGRA
WRYNESS.	HELPFUL	WHARFED	ENCAGED	POLYGON
*ZAMBESI	HOPEFUL	WHIFFED	ENGAGED	PRIGGED
	HURTFUL.	WHIFFLE	ENRAGED	PRONGED.
AGRAFFE	INSOFAR.	WISHFUL	EPERGNE.	RAVAGED
ALOOFLY.	LUSTFUL.	WISTFUL.	FALL-GUY	REALGAR
BALEFUL	MALEFIC	ZESTFUL	FATIGUE	REFUGEE
BANEFUL	MINDFUL.		FINAGLE	RENEGUE.
BASHFUL	NEEDFUL.		FLAGGED	SAVAGED
BENEFIT	*PACIFIC	ALLEGED	FLANGED	SCRAGGY
BLOW-FLY	PAILFUL	ALLEGRO	FLEDGED	*SENEGAL
BLUFFER	PAINFUL	AMALGAM	FLOGGED	SHAGGED
		AMONGST		

SHINGLE	+ARACHNE.	EARTHED	KOLKHOZ.	POT-SHOT
SHOTGUN	BACCHIC	EARTHEN	LATCHED	POUCHED
SLANGED	+BACCHUS	EARTHLY	LAUGHED	PRITHEE
SLEDGED	BANSHEE	EPITHET	LEACHED	PROPHET
SLEIGHT	BEACHED	EPOCHAL	LEASHED	PSYCHIC
SLOGGER	BEECHEN	EYESHOT.	LEATHER	PUNCHED
SLUGGED	BELCHER	*FARNHAM	LOATHED	PUNCH-UP
SMUDGED	BELL-HOP	FARTHER	LOATHLY	PYRRHIC.
SMUGGLE	BENCHER	FEATHER	LUNCHED	QUASHED
SNAGGED	BENTHOS	FETCHED	LURCHED	RANCHER
SNIGGER	BERTHED	FIFTHLY	LYNCHED.	RATCHET
SNOGGED	BIRCHED	FILCHED	+MALTHUS	REACHED
SNUGGED	BLUSHED	FITCHEW	MARCHED	RETCHED
SNUGGLE	BOTCHER	FLASHED	MARSHAL	ROAD-HOG
SPANGLE	BOWSHOT	FLASHER	MATCHED	ROUGHEN
SPONGER	BRASHLY	FLESHED	MATCHET	ROUGHER
SPRIGHT	*BRIXHAM	FLESHLY	+MATTHEW	ROUGHLY.
STAGGER	BROTHEL	FLIGHTY	MENTHOL	SAPPHIC
STEN-GUN	BROTHER	FLUSHED	+MENUHIN	SATCHEL
STOOGED	BRUSHED	FRESHEN	MIDSHIP	SCATHED
STOPGAP	BUNCHED	FRESHER	MONTHLY	SCYTHED
SWAGGER	BURGHER	FRESHET	MOOCHED	SEETHED
SWIGGED	BUTCHER.	FRESHLY	MOORHEN	SHUSHED
SWINGER	+CALCHAS	FROTHED	MORPHIA	SLASHED
SWINGLE.	CAMPHOR	FURTHER.	MOUTHED	SLITHER
TANAGRA	CATCHER	+GALAHAD	MULCHED	SLOSHED
TEAR-GAS	*CHATHAM	GINGHAM	MUNCHED.	SMASHED
THOUGHT	+CHEKHOV	GLYPHIC	NARTHEX	SMASHER
TONIGHT	CLASHED	GNASHED	NARWHAL	SMASH-UP
TRIGGER	CLOTHED	GNATHIC	NAUGHTY	SMOTHER
TRINGLE	CLOTHES	GODSHIP	NEIGHED	SOMEHOW
TRUDGED	COACHED	GRAPHIC	NEITHER	SONSHIP
TWANGED	COUCHED	GRYPHON	NINTHLY	SOOTHED
TWIGGED	COUGHED	GUNSHOT.	NORTHER	SORGHUM
TWINGED.	CRASHED	HARSHLY	NOTCHED	SOUGHED
UPRIGHT	CROCHET	HATCHER	NYLGHAU	STASHED
UPTIGHT.	CRUSHED	HATCHET	NYMPHAL	+STEPHEN
VINEGAR	+CYNTHIA.	HAUGHTY	NYMPHET.	SULPHUR
VOYAGER.	DAUPHIN	HEATHEN	PANTHER	SWASHED
WRANGLE	DEATHLY	+HEATHER	PARCHED	SWATHED
WRIGGLE	DELPHIC	HIGH-HAT	PASCHAL	SWISHED.
WRINGER	DITCHED	HITCHED	PATCHED	TEACHER
WRONGLY	DITCHER	*HITCHIN	PERCHED	TEACH-IN
WROUGHT.	DOLPHIN	HUNCHED	PILCHER	TEA-SHOP
YOUNGER	DOUCHED	HUTCHED.	PINCHED	TELPHER
	DOUGHTY	ICHTHYS.	PITCHED	TENTHLY
+ABRAHAM	DRACHMA	KETCHUP	PITCHER	THITHER
AIRSHIP	DROSHKY	KINSHIP	PLUSHER	TOOTHED
ALCOHOL	DRY-SHOD.	KITCHEN	POACHED	TOUCHED
ANOTHER	EARSHOT	KNOW-HOW	POACHER	TOUGHEN

TOUGHER	*AMERICA	BAILIFF	BETTING	BULGING
TOUGHLY	AMORIST	BAILING	BETWIXT	BULLIED
TOYSHOP	+AMPHION	BAITING	BIDDING	BULLION
TRACHEA	AMPLIFY	BALKING	BILKING	BULLISH
TRASHED	AMUSING	BAMBINO	BILLING	BUMPING
TROCHEE.	ANGLICE	BANDIED	BILLION	BUNKING
URETHRA.	ANGLING	BANDING	BINDING	BUNTING
+VAUGHAN	ANGRIER	BANGING	BLAMING	BURNING
VOUCHER.	ANGRILY	BANKING	BLARING	BURNISH
WARSHIP	ANGUINE	BANNING	BLAZING	BURPING
WART-HOG	ANGUISH	BANTING	BLEMISH	BUSHIDO
WATCHED	ANILINE	BAPTISM	BLOWING	BUSKING
WEATHER	ANIMISM	BAPTIST	BLUEING	BUSTING
WEIGHED	ANNUITY	BAPTIZE	BOATING	BUZZING.
WEIGH-IN	ANODIZE	BARGING	BOBBING	CABLING
WEIGHTY	+ANQUILH	*BARKING	BOGGING	CADDISH
WELSHER	ANT-HILL	BARRIER	BOILING	CADGING
WENCHED	ANYWISE	BARRING	BOLTING	CADMIUM
WHETHER	APPLIED	BASHING	BOMBING	CAESIUM
WHITHER	APPOINT	BASKING	BONDING	CAITIFF
WINCHED	APPRISE	BASTING	BONFIRE	CALCIFY
WITCHED	ARABIAN	BASTION	BONNILY	CALCINE
WORSHIP	ARCHING	BATHING	BOOKING	CALCITE
WRITHED	ARGUING	BATTING	BOOKISH	CALCIUM
+WYNDHAM	ARIDITY	BAUXITE	BOOMING	CALLING
	ARISING	BAWDILY	BOORISH	CALMING
ABIDING	ARRAIGN	BAWLING	BOWLINE	CALVING
ABILITY	ASCRIBE	BEADING	BOWLING	CAMBIST
ABOLISH	ASININE	BEAMING	BOX-KITE	CAMBIUM
ABSCIND	ASQUINT	BEARING	BRACING	CAMPING
ABUSIVE	ASTRIDE	BEARISH	BRAVING	CAMPION
ACETIFY	ATAVISM	BEATIFY	BRAYING	CANDIED
ACIDIFY	ATELIER	BEATING	BRAZIER	CANNILY
ACIDITY	ATHEISM	BEDDING	BRAZING	CANNING
ACONITE	ATOMIZE	BEDSIDE	BREVIER	CANTING
ACQUIRE	ATONING	BEDTIME	BREVITY	CAPPING
ADORING	ATTAINT	BEEHIVE	BREWING	CAPRICE
AEOLIAN	AUBAINE	BEE-LINE	BRIBING	CAPSIZE
AFFLICT	AUCTION	BEGGING	BRITISH	CAPTION
AGILITY	AUSPICE	BEGUILE	BROKING	CAPTIVE
AGONIZE	AUSSIES	BELGIAN	BROMIDE	CARBIDE
AIRLIFT	AVARICE	*BELGIUM	BROMINE	CARBINE
AIRLINE	AVIDITY	BELLIED	BRUTISH	CARDIAC
ALL-TIME	AVOWING	+BELLINI	BUCKING	*CARDIFF
ALUMINA	AZURINE.	BELTING	BUCKISH	CARKING
AMANITA	BABYISH	BELYING	BUDDING	CARLINE
AMATIVE	BACKING	BENDING	BUDGING	CARMINE
AMAZING	BADDISH	+BERLIOZ	BUFFING	CARPING
AMBLING	BAGGING	BESTIAL	BUGGING	CARRIED
AMENITY	BAGPIPE	BETHINK	BUGLING	CARRIER

CARRION	COAMING	COWLICK	DARKISH	DISTICH
CARTING	COATING	COWLING	DARLING	DIZZILY
CARVING	COAXING	CRANIAL	DARNING	DOCKING
CASHIER	COCAINE	CRANING	DARTING	DODGING
CASHING	COCKILY	CRANIUM	DASHING	DOGFISH
*CASPIAN	COCKING	CRAVING	DAUBING	DOGGING
CASTILE	CODEINE	CRAZIER	DAWNING	DOLTISH
CASTING	CODFISH	CRAZILY	DAY-GIRL	DONNING
CASUIST	CODLING	CRAZING	DAY-TIME	DONNISH
CATFISH	COELIAC	CREVICE	DEALING	*DORKING
CATLING	COEXIST	CROSIER	DECEIVE	DOSSIER
CATMINT	COGNIZE	CROWING	DECKING	DOSSING
CATTILY	COILING	CRUCIAL	DECLINE	DOTTING
CATTISH	COINING	CRUCIFY	DECRIAL	DOUSING
CAUSING	COLDISH	CRUDITY	DECRIER	DOWDILY
CAUTION	COLLIDE	CUBBING	DEEMING	DOWNING
CEASING	COLLIER	CUFFING	DEICIDE	DOWSING
CEILING	COLTISH	CUISINE	DEIFIED	DRAPING
CELLIST	COMBINE	CULLING	DELAINE	DRAWING
CENTIME	COMBING	CUNNING	DELVING	DRIVING
CERTIFY	COMPILE	CUPPING	DENSITY	DRONING
CERVINE	CONCISE	CUPRITE	DENTINE	DUALISM
CESSION	CONDIGN	CURBING	DENTIST	DUALITY
CHAFING	CONFIDE	CURDING	DENYING	DUALIZE
CHALICE	CONFINE	CURLING	DEPRIVE	DUBBING
CHARILY	CONFIRM	CURRIED	+DERRICK	DUCKING
CHARIOT	CONKING	CURRISH	DERVISH	DUCTILE
CHARITY	CONNING	CURSING	DESPISE	DUFFING
CHASING	CONNIVE	CURSIVE	DESPITE	DULCIFY
CHEMISE	CONSIGN	CURVING	DESTINE	DULLING
CHEMIST	CONSIST	CUSHION	DESTINY	DUMPING
CHERISH	CONVICT	CUSSING	DIARIST	DUNKING
*CHEVIOT	COOKING	CUTTING	DICTION	DUNNING
CHEWING	COOLING	CYANIDE	DIETING	DUSKIER
CHIDING	COPAIBA	CYCLING	DIETIST	DUSKILY
CHIMING	COPPICE	CYCLIST	DIGGING	DUSTIER
CHOKING	COPPING	CYPRIOT	DIGNIFY	DUSTILY
CHOLINE	COPYIST	CZARINA.	DIGNITY	DUSTING.
CHOPINE	CORDIAL	DABBING	DIMMING	EARLIER
CHORION	CORDITE	DADAISM	DINGING	EARNING
CITRINE	CORKING	DAISIED	DINNING	EARRING
CIVVIES	CORNICE	DALLIED	DIORITE	EASTING
CLARIFY	CORNILY	DAMMING	DIOXIDE	EBB-TIDE
CLARION	CORNISH	DAMNIFY	DIPPING	EBONIST
CLARITY	CORVINE	DAMNING	DIRTIED	EBONITE
CLAVIER	COSTING	DAMPING	DIRTILY	EBONIZE
CLAWING	COSTIVE	DAMPISH	DISHING	ECHOING
CLOSING	COTTIER	DANCING	DISLIKE	ECHOISM
CLOYING	COURIER	DANDIFY	DISLIMN	EDACITY
COALING	COWHIDE	DANKISH	DISMISS	EDIFICE

EDIFIED	EVOKING	FICTION	FORKING	GENTILE
EDITING	EXAMINE	FICTIVE	FORMING	GENUINE
EDITION	EXILIAN	FIERILY	FORTIFY	GETTING
EDUCING	EXILING	FILLING	FOSSICK	GIDDILY
EGALITY	EXITING	FILMING	FOULING	GILDING
EGOTISM	EXSCIND	FINDING	FOWLING	+GILLIAN
EGOTIST	EXUDING	FINNISH	FRAGILE	GILLION
ELATING	+EZEKIEL.	FIRMING	FRAMING	GIMMICK
ELATION	FABLIAU	FISHILY	FRAYING	GIRLISH
ELEGIAC	FACTION	FISHING	FREEING	GLACIAL
ELEGIST	FADDIST	FISSILE	FUGUIST	GLACIER
ELEGIZE	FAGGING	FISSION	FUNDING	GLARING
ELIDING	FAILING	FITTING	FUNNILY	GLAZIER
ELISION	FAIRILY	FIZZING	FURBISH	GLAZING
ELOPING	FAIRING	FLAKILY	FURLING	GLIDING
ELUDING	FALLING	FLAKING	FURNISH	GLORIED
ELUSION	FALSIES	FLAMING	FURRIER	GLORIFY
ELUSIVE	FALSIFY	FLARING	FURRING	GLOWING
ELUVIAL	FALSITY	FLAWING	FURTIVE	GLOZING
ELYSIAN	FANCIED	FLAYING	FUSSING	GLUEING
ELYSIUM	FANCIER	FLEEING	FUSTIAN	GNAWING
EMETINE	FANNING	+FLEMING	FUSTILY.	GNOMISH
EMOTION	FARCING	FLEMISH	GABBING	GOADING
EMOTIVE	FARMING	FLEXILE	+GABRIEL	GOATISH
EMPTIER	FARRIER	FLEXING	GADDING	+GOLDING
EMPTILY	FASCINE	FLEXION	GAFFING	GOODISH
ENDWISE	FASCISM	*FLORIDA	GAGGING	GORDIAN
ENGLISH	FASCIST	FLORIST	GAINING	GORGING
ENQUIRE	FASHION	FLOWING	GALLING	GOSLING
ENQUIRY	FASTING	FLUTING	GALLIOT	GOSSIPY
ENTWINE	FATLING	FLUTIST	GALLIUM	GOTHICK
ENVYING	FAWNING	FLUVIAL	GAMMING	GOUGING
ERASING	FEARING	FLUXION	GANGING	GRACILE
ERASION	FEBRILE	FOALING	GARBING	GRACING
EREMITE	FEEDING	FOAMING	GARFISH	GRADING
ERODING	FEELING	FOBBING	GARNISH	GRANITE
EROSION	+FELLINI	FOGGIER	GASEITY	GRATIFY
EROSIVE	FELSITE	FOGGILY	GASHING	GRATING
EROTICA	FELTING	FOGGING	GASPING	GRAVING
ERUDITE	FENCING	FOILING	GAS-RING	GRAVITY
ESPYING	FENDING	FOLDING	GASSING	GRAZING
ESQUIRE	FERMION	FOOLING	GATLING	GRECIAN
ESTRIOL	FERMIUM	FOOLISH	*GATWICK	GRECISM
ETCHING	FERRIED	FOOTING	GAUDILY	GREYISH
ETESIAN	FERRITE	FOPPISH	GAUGING	GRIDING
ETONIAN	FERTILE	FORCING	GEARING	GRIPING
EVADING	FESTIVE	FORDING	GELDING	GROPING
EVASION	FEUDING	FOREIGN	GELLING	G-STRING.
EVASIVE	FIBBING	FORGING	GEMMING	GUIDING
EVENING	FICTILE	FORGIVE	GENTIAN	GULLING

GULPING	HEAVILY	HUMMING	JAGGING	KEY-RING
GUMMING	HEAVING	HUMPING	*JAMAICA	KHALIFA
GUNFIRE	HEDGING	HUNTING	JAMMING	KICKING
GUNNING	HEEDING	HURLING	JARRING	KIDDING
GUSHING	HEELING	HURRIED	+JASMINE	KILLICK
GUTTING.	HEFTILY	HURTING	JAZZILY	KILLING
HACKING	HEFTING	HUSHING	JAZZING	KINGING
+HADRIAN	HELLISH	HUSKING	JEERING	KINKILY
HAFNIUM	HELPING	HUTTING	JELLIED	KINKING
HAFTING	HEMMING	HYALINE	JELLING	KIPPING
HAGFISH	HERNIAL	HYALITE	JERKILY	KISSING
HAGGING	HEROINE	HYDRIDE	JERKING	KITTING
HAGGISH	HEROISM	HYMNIST.	+JESSICA	KNAVISH
HAILING	HERRING	IBERIAN	JESTING	KNIFING
HAIRILY	HESSIAN	IDOLIZE	JETTING	KNOWING.
HALTING	HINTING	ILL-WILL	JIBBING	LACKING
HALVING	HIPPING	IMAGINE	JIGGING	LADLING
HAMMING	HIRCINE	IMAGING	JILTING	LAGGING
HANDILY	HISSING	IMAGISM	JINKING	LAICIZE
HANDING	HITTING	IMPFING	JOBBING	LALLING
HANGING	HOAXING	IMPLIED	JOGGING	LAMAISM
HAPPIER	HOCKING	IMPRINT	JOINING	LAMBING
HAPPILY	HOGGING	INANITY	JOLLIER	LAMMING
HAPPING	HOGGISH	INBEING	JOLLIFY	LAMPION
HARDIER	HOLDING	INCHING	JOLLITY	LANCING
HARDILY	HOLMIUM	INCLINE	JOLTING	LANDING
HARKING	HONKING	INFLICT	JOSHING	LAPPING
HARMING	HOODING	INGOING	JOTTING	LAPPISH
HARPING	HOOKING	INITIAL	JOY-RIDE	LAPSING
HARPIST	HOOPING	INKLING	JUDAISM	LAPWING
HARRIED	HOOTING	INQUIRE	JUDAIZE	LARDING
HARRIER	HOP-BINE	INQUIRY	JUGGING	LARGISH
+HARRIET	HOPLITE	INSPIRE	JUMPING	LARKING
*HARWICH	HOPPING	INURING	JUNKING	LASHING
HASHING	HORDING	INVEIGH	JUSSIVE	LASTING
HASHISH	HORNING	INVOICE	JUSTICE	LATRINE
HASPING	HORRIFY	*IPSWICH	JUSTIFY	LATTICE
HASTILY	HORSING	IRANIAN	+JUSTINE	LAUDING
HAULIER	HOSPICE	IRIDIUM	JUTTING.	LEADING
HAULING	HOSTILE	IRIDIZE	KAINITE	LEAFING
HAWKING	HOTTING	IRONING	KANTIAN	LEAKILY
*HAYLING	+HOUDINI	IRONIST	KECKING	LEAKING
HAYRICK	HOUSING	ISATINE	KEDGING	LEANING
HAYWIRE	HOWLING	ISCHIAL	KEELING	LEAPING
HEADING	HUFFILY	ISCHIUM	KEENING	LEASING
HEALING	HUFFING	ITALIAN	KEEPING	LEAVING
HEAPING	HUFFISH	ITCHING	KENNING	LEERING
HEARING	HUGGING	ITEMIZE.	KENTISH	LEFTIST
HEATING	HULKING	JABBING	KERBING	LEGGING
HEAVIER	HULLING	JACKING	*KESWICK	LEMMING

LENDING	LUSTILY	MESSING	NABBING	ONANISM
LENTISK	LUSTING	MESTIZO	NAGGING	ONANIST
LEONINE	LYDDITE.	METRICS	NAILING	OPACITY
LESBIAN	MACHINE	METRIST	NAPPING	OPALINE
LETTING	MADDING	MIDRIFF	NASTIER	OPENING
LEVYING	*MADEIRA	MIDWIFE	NASTILY	OPINING
LICKING	MAFFICK	MILKING	NEARING	OPINION
LIFTING	MAGNIFY	MILLING	NECKING	ORATING
LIGNITE	MAILING	MILLION	NEEDILY	ORATION
LILTING	MAIMING	MILTING	NEEDING	ORIFICE
LIMNING	MALAISE	MINCING	NEGLIGE	OSTRICH
LIMPING	MALTING	MINDING	NEGRITO	OUSTING
LINKING	MANKIND	MINTING	NERVINE	OUTLIER
LIONIZE	MANLIER	MISFIRE	NERVING	OUTLINE
LIPPING	MANLIKE	MISGIVE	NESTING	OUTLIVE
LISPING	MANNING	MISLIKE	NETTING	OUTRIDE
LISTING	MANNISH	MISSILE	NIBLICK	OUTSIDE
LITHIUM	MANSION	MISSING	NICKING	OUTSIZE
LOADING	MAPPING	MISSION	NIOBIUM	OVARIAN
LOAFING	MARKING	MISSIVE	NIPPING	OVATION
LOAMING	MARLINE	MISTILY	NOBBING	OXIDIZE
LOANING	MARLING	MISTING	NOCKING	OXONIAN.
LOBBIED	MARMITE	MOANING	NODDING	PACKING
LOBBING	MARRIED	MOBBING	NOGGING	PADDING
LOCKING	MARRING	MOCKING	NOISIER	PAINING
LODGING	MARTIAL	MOLLIFY	NOISILY	PAIRING
LOFTIER	MARTIAN	MONKISH	NOOSING	PALLING
LOFTILY	MARTINI	MOODILY	*NORWICH	PALLIUM
LOFTING	MARXISM	MOONING	NOSHING	PALMING
LOGGING	MASHING	MOORING	NOTHING	PALMIST
LOLLING	MASKING	MOORISH	NOURISH	PALPING
LONGING	MASSING	MOOTING	NUCLIDE	PALSIED
LOOKING	MASSIVE	MOPPING	NUDGING	PANNIER
LOOMING	MASTIFF	MORAINE	NULLIFY	PANNING
LOOPING	MATTING	MORNING	NULLITY	PAN-PIPE
LOOTING	MAULING	MORTIFY	NUMBING	PANTIES
LOPPING	+MAURICE	MORTISE	NUPTIAL	PANTILE
LORDING	MAWKISH	MUCKILY	NURSING	PANTING
*LOTHIAN	MEANING	MUCKING	NUTTING.	PAPRIKA
LOURING	MEETING	MUDDIED	OBELISK	PARKING
LOUSILY	MELDING	MUDFISH	OBELIZE	PARRIED
LOUTISH	MELTING	MUFFING	OBEYING	PARSING
LUCKIER	MENDING	MUGGING	OCARINA	PARTIAL
LUCKILY	MENTION	MUGGINS	OCULIST	PARTIED
LUDDITE	MERGING	MULLING	OFF-LINE	PARTING
LUGGING	MERRILY	MULLION	OFF-SIDE	PARTITE
LULLING	MESHING	MUMMIFY	OGREISH	PASSING
LUMPISH	MESSIAH	MUMMING	OIL-SILK	PASSION
LUNGING	MESSIER	MURKILY	OLEFINE	PASSIVE
LURKING	MESSILY	MYSTIFY.	+OLIVIER	PASTIME

PASTING	PIGGING	PRIDING	QUININE	REPOINT
+PATRICK	PIGGISH	PRIMING	QUOTING.	REPRINT
PATRIOT	PIGLING	PRIVILY	RABBITY	REPTILE
PATTING	PILLION	PRIVITY	RACKING	REQUIEM
PAUCITY	PIMPING	PRIZING	RAFFISH	REQUIRE
+PAULINE	PINKING	PROBING	RAFTING	REQUITE
PAUSING	PINKISH	PROBITY	RAGGING	RESCIND
PAWKILY	PINNING	PRODIGY	RAGTIME	RESPIRE
PAWNING	PIPPING	PROFILE	RAIDING	RESPITE
PEAKING	PISCINA	PROMISE	RAILING	RESTING
PEALING	PISCINE	PROSILY	RAINING	RESTIVE
PECKING	PITHILY	PROSING	RAISING	RETHINK
PECKISH	PITTING	PROVIDE	+RALEIGH	RETRIED
PEEKING	PITYING	PROVING	RALLIED	*REUNION
PEELING	PLACING	PROVISO	RAMMING	REUNITE
PEEPING	PLANING	PROXIMO	RAMPING	REVVING
PEERING	PLANISH	PRUDISH	RANGING	REWRITE
PEEVING	PLATING	PRUNING	RANKING	RHENIUM
PEEVISH	PLAYING	PRURIGO	RANTING	RHODIUM
PEGGING	PLOSIVE	PUBLISH	RAPPING	RHYMING
PELTING	PLUMING	+PUCCINI	RASPING	RIBBING
PENDING	PLUVIAL	PUCKISH	RATFINK	RICKING
PENNILL	PODDING	PUDDING	RATTING	RIDDING
PENNING	POETIZE	PUERILE	RAWHIDE	RIFLING
*PENRITH	POISING	PUFFING	READILY	RIFTING
PENSILE	POLLING	PUGGING	*READING	RIGGING
PENSION	PONTIFF	PUG-MILL	REALISM	RIMMING
PENSIVE	PONTIFY	PULLING	REALIST	RINGING
PEPPING	POOLING	PULPIFY	REALITY	RINKING
PEPTIDE	POPPING	PULPING	REALIZE	RINSING
PERFIDY	PORCINE	PULSING	REAMING	RIOTING
PERKILY	PORTICO	PUMPING	REAPING	RIPPING
PERKING	PORTING	PUNNING	REARING	RIP-TIDE
PERLITE	PORTION	PUNTING	RECEIPT	RISKIER
PERMIAN	POSTING	PUPPING	RECEIVE	RISKILY
PERMING	POTTING	PURGING	RECLINE	RISKING
PERSIAN	POURING	PURLIEU	RECTIFY	ROAMING
PERSIST	POUTING	PURLING	REDDISH	ROARING
PETRIFY	PRALINE	PURRING	*REDHILL	ROBBING
PETTILY	PRATING	PURSING	REEDING	ROCKIER
PETTING	PRAYING	PURVIEW	REEFING	ROCKILY
PETTISH	PRECISE	PUSHING	REEKING	ROCKING
PHASING	PREDICT	PUTTIER	REELING	ROGUISH
PHONING	PREMIER	PUTTING.	REINING	ROLLING
PHYSICS	PREMISE	QUABIRD	REJOICE	ROMPING
PIANIST	PREMIUM	QUAKING	RENDING	ROOFING
PICKING	PRESIDE	QUALIFY	RENTIER	ROOKING
PICTISH	PREVIEW	QUALITY	RENTING	ROOMIER
PIECING	PREYING	QUERIED	REPLICA	ROOMING
PIETISM	PRICING	QUERIST	REPLIED	ROOTING

+ROSSINI	SCABIES	SHINILY	SOAPING	STOKING
ROTTING	SCALING	SHINING	SOARING	STONIER
ROUGING	SCARIFY	SHOEING	SOBBING	STONING
ROUSING	SCARING	SHOOING	SOGGILY	STORIED
ROUTINE	SCORIFY	SHORING	SOILING	STORING
ROUTING	SCORING	SHOVING	SOLDIER	STOWING
ROWDIER	SCOTISM	SHOWILY	SOLOIST	STUDIED
ROWDILY	SCRYING	SHOWING	SOLVING	STYGIAN
RUBBING	SEABIRD	SIBLING	SOOTILY	STYLING
RUBBISH	SEA-LINE	SIDLING	SOPHISM	STYLISH
RUCKING	SEALING	SIEVING	SOPHIST	STYLIST
RUDDIER	SEA-LION	SIFTING	SOPPILY	STYLITE
RUDDILY	SEA-MILE	SIGHING	SOPPING	STYLIZE
RUFFIAN	SEAMING	SIGNIFY	SORDINE	STYMIED
RUFFING	SEA-PINK	SIGNING	SORTING	SUASION
RUINING	SEARING	SILKILY	SOTTISH	SUASIVE
RUMMILY	SEA-SICK	SILLIER	SOURING	SUAVITY
RUNNING	SEASIDE	SILLILY	SOUSING	SUBLIME
RUPTION	SEATING	SILTING	SPACING	SUBSIDE
RUSHING	SECTILE	SINGING	SPANIEL	SUBSIDY
RUSSIAN	SECTION	SINKING	SPANISH	SUBSIST
RUSSIFY	SEEDILY	SINNING	SPARING	SUCKING
RUSTIER	SEEDING	SIPPING	SPATIAL	SUCTION
RUSTILY	SEEKING	SITTING	SPAYING	SUFFICE
RUSTING	SEEMING	SKATING	SPECIAL	SUICIDE
RUTTING	SEEPING	SKEWING	SPECIES	SUITING
RUTTISH.	SEISING	SKI-LIFT	SPECIFY	SULKILY
+SABRINA	SEIZING	SKY-HIGH	SPEWING	SULLIED
SACKING	SELFISH	SKYLINE	SPICIER	SUMMING
SACRING	*SELKIRK	SLAKING	SPICILY	SUNDIAL
SACRIST	SELLING	SLATING	SPICING	SUNNIER
SAGGING	SENDING	SLAVING	SPIKING	SUNNING
SAILING	SENSING	SLAVISH	SPIRING	SUNRISE
SALLIED	SERRIED	SLAYING	SPITING	SUNWISE
SALSIFY	+SERVICE	SLEWING	SPUMING	SUPPING
SALTING	SERVILE	SLICING	SQUAILS	SURDITY
SALTIRE	SERVING	SLIDING	STADIUM	SURFING
SALVING	SESSION	SLOPING	STAGING	SURGING
SANDIER	SESTINA	SMILING	STAKING	SURLIER
SANDING	SETTING	SMOKILY	STAMINA	SURLILY
SAPLING	SHADIER	SMOKING	STARING	SURMISE
SAPPING	SHADILY	SNAKILY	STATICE	SURVIVE
SARDINE	SHADING	SNAKING	STATICS	SUSPIRE
SARKING	SHAKILY	SNARING	STATING	SUSSING
SAUCILY	SHAKING	SNIPING	STATION	SWAHILI
SAUCING	SHAMING	SNORING	STATISM	SWAYING
SAURIAN	SHAPING	SNOWILY	STAVING	SWEDISH
SAWBILL	SHARING	SNOWING	STAYING	SWINISH
SAWFISH	SHAVING	SOAKING	STERILE	SWIPING
SAW-MILL	SHERIFF	SOAPILY	STEWING	SYLVINE

SYMBION.	TERRINE	TUGGING	VESTIGE	WELTING
TABBING	TERTIAN	TUITION	VESTING	WENDING
TABLING	TESTIFY	TURBINE	VETOING	WESTING
TACKING	TESTILY	TURFING	VETTING	WETTING
TACTICS	TESTING	TURKISH	VIDUITY	WHALING
TACTILE	TEXTILE	TURNING	VIEWING	WHILING
TAGGING	THAWING	TUTTING	VIOLIST	WHINING
TAILING	THOMISM	TWINING	VITRIFY	WHITING
TALKING	THORIDE	TWO-TIME.	VITRIOL	WHITISH
TALLIED	THORIUM	UNBUILT	VOICING	WHORING
TAMPING	THULIUM	UNCTION	VOIDING	+WILLIAM
TAMPION	TICKING	UNDOING	VOLTING	WILLING
*TANGIER	TILLING	UNDYING	VULPINE.	WILTING
TANGING	TILTING	UNIFIED	WADDING	WINDIER
TANNING	TINGING	UNITING	WAFTING	WINDING
TAPPING	TINNILY	UNITIVE	WAGGING	WINGING
TARDILY	TINNING	UNQUIET	WAGGISH	WINKING
TARNISH	TIPPING	UNSLING	WAILING	WINNING
TARRIED	TIPSILY	UNSTICK	WAITING	WISHING
TARRING	TITLING	UNTRIED	WAIVING	WITTIER
TARTING	+TOLKIEN	UNTWINE	WALKING	WITTILY
TASKING	TOLLING	UNTWIST	WALLING	WITTING
TASTIER	TOMPION	URANIAN	WANTING	WOLFING
TASTILY	TONTINE	URANISM	WARDING	WOLFISH
TASTING	TOOLING	URANIUM	WARLIKE	WOODIER
TATTILY	*TOOTING	UTERINE	WARMING	WORDILY
TATTING	TOPPING	UTILITY	WARNING	WORDING
TAURINE	TOPSIDE	UTILIZE	WARPING	WORKING
TAWNILY	TORSION	UTOPIAN.	WARRING	WORMING
TAXIING	TORTILE	VACCINE	WARRIOR	WORRIED
TEAMING	TOSSING	VACUITY	WARTIME	WORRIER
TEARING	TOTTING	VAMPING	*WARWICK	WRITING
TEASING	TOURING	VAMPIRE	WASHING	*WYOMING.
TEDDING	TOURISM	VANNING	WASPISH	X-RAYING
TEEMING	TOURIST	VARMINT	WASTING	YAKKING
TEKTITE	TOUTING	VARNISH	WAXBILL	YANKING
TELLING	TOWLINE	VARSITY	WAY-BILL	YAPPING
TENDING	TRACING	VARYING	WAYSIDE	YAWNING
TENPINS	TRADING	VEERING	WEANING	YELLING
TENSILE	TREEING	VEILING	WEARIER	YELPING
TENSING	TRICING	VEINING	WEARILY	YENNING
TENSION	TRILITH	VENDING	WEARING	YIDDISH
TENTING	TRINITY	VENTING	WEAVING	YORKING
TENUITY	TRITIUM	VERDICT	WEBBING	YORKIST
TERBIUM	TRIVIAL	VERGING	WEDDING	YOWLING
TERMING	TRIVIUM	VERNIER	WEDGING	YTTRIUM.
TERMINI	TROPISM	VERSIFY	WEEDING	ZEBRINE
TERMITE	TUBBING	VERSING	WEEPING	ZEOLITE
TERRIER	TUCKING	VERSION	WELDING	ZEROING
TERRIFY	TUFTING	VERTIGO	WELLING	ZIONISM

ZIONIST	CREAKED	PRICKET	STRIKER	BABBLER
ZIPPING	CRICKED	PRICKLE	STROKED	*BABYLON
ZOOMING	CRICKET	PRICKLY	STUCK-UP	BACILLI
	CRINKLE	PUMPKIN	SWANKED.	BACKLOG
*ABIDJAN.	CRINKLY	+PUSHKIN.	THANKED	BAFFLED
KILLJOY.	CROAKER	QUACKED	THICKEN	BASALLY
LOCKJAW.	CROCKET	QUICKEN	THICKER	BASILAR
TOBY-JUG	CROOKED.	QUICKER	THICKET	BASILIC
	DOESKIN	QUICKIE	THICKLY	BATTLED
*BANGKOK	DOGSKIN	QUICKLY.	THINKER	+BEATLES
BETAKEN	DOVEKIE	REBUKED	TRACKED	*BENELUX
BETOKEN	DRINKER	REDSKIN	TRACKER	BIBELOT
BLACKEN	DRUNKEN.	RETAKEN	TREKKED	BIPOLAR
BLACKER	FLANKER	REVOKED.	TRICKED	BIVALVE
BLANKED	FLECKED	SHACKED	TRICKLE	BOGGLER
BLANKET	FLICKED	SHACKLE	TRICKSY	BOOKLET
BLANKLY	FLICKER	SHARKED	TRINKET	BOOTLEG
BLEAKLY	FLOCKED	SHIRKER	TRUCKED	BOTTLED
BLINKED	FLUNKEY	SHOCKER	TRUCKLE	BRAILLE
BLOCKED	FRANKLY	SHUCKED	TURNKEY	BRAWLER
BRACKEN	FREAKED	SKULKED	TWEAKED	BRIDLED
BRACKET	FRECKLE	SLACKEN	TWINKLE.	BROILER
BREAKER	FRECKLY	SLACKER	UNASKED	BUBBLED
BREAK-UP	FRISKED	SLACKLY	UNYOKED.	BUCKLED
BRICKED	FRISKET	SLEEKER	WHACKED	BUCOLIC
BRISKET	FROCKED.	SLEEKLY	WHISKED	BUNDLED
BRISKLY	GHERKIN	SLICKER	WHISKER	BUNGLER
BROCKET	GRISKIN.	SLICKLY	WHISKEY	BURBLED
BUMPKIN.	HEARKEN	SMACKED	WREAKED	BURGLAR
CHECKED	HOGSKIN	SMACKER	WRECKED	BURGLED
CHECKER	HOICKED.	SMIRKED	WRECKER	*BURNLEY
CHECK-UP	INVOKED.	SNEAKED	WRINKLE	BUSTLED.
CHICKEN	KIDSKIN	SNICKER		CACKLED
CHINKED	KNACKER	SNOOKER	ABOULIA	CAJOLED
CHUCKED	KNOCKED	SPANKED	ABSOLVE	+CAROLYN
CHUCKLE	KNOCKER	SPANKER	ACRYLIC	CASE-LAW
CHUKKER	KNOCK-ON	SPARKED	AIRFLOW	CASTLED
CLACKED	KNUCKLE.	SPARKLE	ALFALFA	CATALPA
CLANKED	LAMBKIN.	SPEAKER	AMPULLA	CAVALRY
CLARKIA	MANIKIN.	SPECKED	ANGELIC	+CECILIA
CLICKED	+NABOKOV.	SPECKLE	ANGELUS	CEDILLA
CLICKER	OILSKIN.	STACKED	ANGULAR	CHABLIS
CLINKER	PIGSKIN	STALKED	ANNULAR	CHAPLET
CLOAKED	PLACKET	STALKER	ANNULET	+CHAPLIN
CLOCKED	PLANKED	STARKLY	ANTILOG	+CHARLES
CRACKED	PLONKED	STICKED	APHELIA	CHILLED
CRACKER	PLUCKED	STICKER	AREOLAR	CIRCLED
CRACKLE	PLUNKED	STINKER	AVAILED	CIRCLET
CRACK-UP	PRANKED	STOCKED	AWFULLY	CIVILLY
CRANKED	PRICKER	STOOKED	AXIALLY.	COBBLER

COCHLEA	ECBOLIC	GURGLED	KNELLED	NEEDLED
CODDLED	ECHELON	GUZZLER.	KNURLED	NESTLED
COMPLEX	EGG-FLIP	HACKLET	KRAALED	NETTLED
CONFLUX	EIDOLON	HAGGLER	KREMLIN.	+NEVILLE
CO-PILOT	EMBOLUS	HANDLER	LAMELLA	NIBBLED
COROLLA	ENABLED	HARE-LIP	LANOLIN	NIGGLED
CORSLET	ENSILED	HECKLER	LEAFLET	NOBBLER
COUPLER	ENVELOP	HEDDLES	LEGALLY	NODULAR
COUPLET	EPAULET	HIDALGO	LITTLER	NONPLUS
COWSLIP	EPSILON	HIGGLER	LOBELIA	NOVELTY
CRAWLER	EQUALLY	HOBBLED	LOCALLY	NUZZLED.
CRUELLY	+ESTELLA	HOODLUM	+LORELEI	OCELLUS
CRUELTY	EXHALED.	HOPPLED	LOYALLY	+OPHELIA
CUDDLED	FACULTY	HORALLY	LOYALTY	ORTOLAN
*CUILLIN	FAMULUS	HUDDLED	+LUCILLE.	OUTFLOW
CUMULUS	FATALLY	HUMBLED	MAILLOT	OUTPLAY
CURDLED.	+FENELLA	HURDLER	MAMILLA	OVERLAP
DABBLED	FIDDLED	HURTLED	MANGLED	OVERLAY.
DANELAW	FIDDLER	HUSTLER.	MANILLA	PABULUM
DANGLED	FINALLY	ICE-FLOE	MANTLED	PADDLED
DAPPLED	FIZZLED	IDEALLY	MARBLED	*PAISLEY
DAWDLER	FLAILED	IDYLLIC	+MARILYN	PAPILLA
DAZZLED	FLATLET	IMPALED	MARTLET	PAROLED
DECOLOR	FONDLED	IMPULSE	+MATILDA	PARSLEY
DEFILED	FORELEG	INDULGE	MAUDLIN	PATELLA
DEVALUE	FRAILLY	INHALER	MAXILLA	PEARLED
DEVELOP	FRAILTY	INSULAR	MEASLES	PEARLER
DEVILRY	FRILLED	INSULIN	MEDDLED	PEBBLED
DEVOLVE	FUDDLED	INVALID	MEDULLA	PEDDLED
DEW-CLAW	FUELLED	INVOLVE.	MIDDLED	PENALLY
DIALLED	FUMBLER.	JANGLED	MINGLED	PENALTY
DIBBLED	GABBLED	JAVELIN	MIZZLED	PEOPLED
DIDDLER	GAGGLED	JEWELRY	MOONLIT	PERPLEX
DIMPLED	+GALILEO	JIGGLED	MORALLY	PHALLIC
DIPOLAR	GAMBLER	JINGLED	MORELLO	PHALLUS
DISPLAY	GANGLIA	+JOCELYN	MOTTLED	+PHYLLIS
DIVULGE	GARBLED	JOCULAR	MUDDLED	PICKLED
DOODLED	GARGLED	JOGGLED	MUDFLAP	PIKELET
DOUBLED	GAZELLE	JOSTLED	MUDFLAT	PILULAR
DOUBLET	GIGGLER	JUBILEE	MUFFLED	PLAYLET
*DOUGLAS	+GISELLE	JUGGLED	MUFFLER	POPULAR
DRAWLED	GNARLED	JUGGLER	MUMBLED	PROBLEM
DRIBLET	GOBBLER	JUGULAR	+MURILLO	PROWLER
DRILLED	GOBELIN	JUMBLED.	MUSCLED	PTYALIN
DROOLED	GOGGLED	KECKLED	MUZZLED.	PUDDLER
DROPLET	GORILLA	KINDLER	NACELLE	PURPLED
DRUMLIN	GREMLIN	KINGLET	NASALLY	PUZZLER.
DUELLED	GREYLAG	KINKLED	NEBULAR	QUAILED
DUELLER	GRILLED	KNEELED	NECKLET	QUELLED
DWELLER.	GROWLER	KNEELER	NEEDLED	QUILLED

RADDLED	SETTLER	SWALLOW	VENALLY	CALAMUS
RAFFLED	SETTLOR	SWELLED	VIRELAY	CALOMEL
RAMBLED	*SEVILLE	SWILLED	VITALLY	CALUMET
RAMBLER	SHALLOP	SWIRLED	+VIVALDI	CALUMNY
RANKLED	SHALLOT	SWOLLEN.	VOCALIC	CARAMEL
RATTLER	SHALLOW	TACKLER	VOCALLY.	CAVE-MAN
RAVELIN	SHELLAC	TANGLED	WADDLED	CERAMIC
REGALED	SHELLED	TARTLET	WAFFLED	CHAPMAN
REGALIA	+SHELLEY	TATTLER	WAGGLED	CHARMER
REGALLY	+SHIRLEY	TEMPLAR	WANGLED	CHROMIC
REGULAR	SHOALED	TEMPLET	WARBLER	CLAIMED
REPULSE	SHRILLY	TICKLER	WATTLED	CLUBMAN
RESILED	SIMILAR	TIDDLER	*WEMBLEY	CRAMMED
RESOLVE	SINGLED	TIDDLEY	WHEELED	CRAMMER
REVELRY	SINGLET	TIME-LAG	WHIRLED	CREAMED
REVILED	SIZZLED	TINGLED	WHITLOW	CREAMER.
REVOLVE	SKID-LID	TIPPLER	*WICKLOW	DECIMAL
RIDDLED	SKILLED	TITULAR	WIGGLED	DEFAMED
RIFFLER	SKILLET	TODDLER	WIMPLED	DELIMIT
RINGLET	SKIRLED	TOOTLED	WINKLED	DILEMMA
RIPPLED	SKY-BLUE	TOPPLED	WOBBLED	DISHMAT
RIVALRY	SMALLER	TOTALLY	WOOLLEN.	DOORMAN
RIVULET	SNARLED	TOUSLED	YULE-LOG.	DOORMAT
+ROMULUS	SOZZLED	TRAILED	ZONALLY	DRAYMAN
ROOTLED	SPELLED	TRAILER		DREAMER
ROWELED	SPELLER	TRAWLER	ABDOMEN	DRUMMED
ROYALLY	SPIELER	TREBLED	ABYSMAL	DRUMMER
ROYALTY	SPILLED	TRELLIS	ALBUMEN	DURAMEN
RUBELLA	SPOILED	TRIFLED	ALMSMAN	DUSTMAN
RUDDLED	SPOOLED	TRIFLER	ANAEMIA	DYNAMIC.
+RUDOLPH	SQUALID	TRIGLOT	ANAEMIC	ENDEMIC
RUFFLED	SQUALLY	TRILLED	ANOSMIA	ENTOMIC
*RUISLIP	SQUALOR	TRIOLET	+ARTEMIS	+ERASMUS
RUMBLED	SQUELCH	TRIPLED	ASHAMED	EXHUMED.
RUMPLED	STABLED	TRIPLET	ASSUMED	FIREMAN
RUSTLED	STALLED	TRIPLEX	ATTEMPT	FLAGMAN
RUSTLER.	+STANLEY	TROLLED	AUTOMAT.	FLUMMOX
SADDLER	STAPLER	TROLLEY	BETIMES	FORAMEN
SAMPLED	STARLET	TROLLOP	BITUMEN	FOREMAN
SAMPLER	STARLIT	TUBULAR	BLOOMED	FREEMAN
SAVELOY	STEALTH	TUMBLED	BLOOMER	FROGMAN.
SCALLOP	STEELED	TUMBLER	BOATMAN	GAGSMAN
SCARLET	STELLAR	TUMULUS	*BOHEMIA	GALUMPH
SCHOLAR	STIFLED	TUSSLED	BONDMAN	GATEMAN
SCOLLOP	STILLED	TUTELAR	BOOKMAN	GLEAMED
SCOWLED	STILLER	TWILLED	*BRAEMAR	GLIMMER
SCULLER	SUBPLOT	TWIRLED.	BRAHMIN	GOODMAN
SECULAR	SUCKLED	USUALLY	BRIMMER	GOURMET
SEDILIA	SUPPLED	+UTRILLO.	BULIMIA	GRAMMAR
SETTLED	SURPLUS	VANILLA	BUSHMAN.	GRIMMER

GROMMET	ROADMAN.	ABSINTH	CAYENNE	EIRENIC
GROOMED	SANDMAN	ACLINIC	CENTNER	+ELEANOR
GRUMMET.	SCHEMER	ACRONYM	+CEZANNE	EMPANEL
HANGMAN	SCUMMED	ACTINIC	CHAINED	ENHANCE
HEADMAN	SEISMAL	ADDENDA	CHANNEL	ENOUNCE
+HOUSMAN.	SEISMIC	ADJUNCT	CHARNEL	ENTENTE
INCOMER	SHAMMED	ADRENAL	CHIANTI	ENVENOM
INHUMAN	SHIMMER	ADVANCE	CHIGNON	EQUINOX
INHUMED	SHOPMAN	AFFINAL	CHIMNEY	ERRANCY
ISLAMIC	SHOWMAN	AFFINED	CHINNED	ESSENCE
ISTHMUS.	SKIMMER	AGAINST	CHRONIC	ESSENES
JURYMAN.	SLAMMED	*ALBANIA	CHURNED	ETERNAL
KEELMAN	SLIMMER	ALIENEE	CHUTNEY	ETHANOL
KINSMAN	SLUMMED	ALMANAC	CLAP-NET	EUGENIC
KRIMMER.	SNOWMAN	ALMONER	CLEANED	EXPANSE
LEGUMIN	+SOLOMON	ALUMNUS	CLEANER	EXPENSE
LIFTMAN	STAMMER	AMMONIA	CLEANLY	EXPUNGE
LINEMAN.	STEAMED	ANDANTE	CLEANSE	EXTINCT.
MANUMIT	STEAMER	ANTENNA	CLOWNED	FAIENCE
MARIMBA	STEMMED	ANTONYM	COCKNEY	FALANGE
MAXIMAL	STORMED	APHONIC	COCONUT	FEIGNED
MAXIMUM	SWAGMAN	ARDENCY	COGENCY	FELONRY
MIASMAL	SWARMED	ARRANGE	COLONEL	FINANCE
MILKMAN	SWIMMER.	ARSENAL	CORANTO	FLANNEL
MINIMAL	TAXIMAN	ARSENIC	*CORINTH	FLOUNCE
MINIMUM	THERMAL	ASKANCE	CORONAL	FLUENCY
MONOMER.	THERMIC	*ATLANTA	CORONER	FROWNED.
OARSMAN	THERMIT	ATTUNED	CORONET	GEHENNA
OGHAMIC	THERMOS	*AVIGNON.	COZENER	GLEANER
OPTIMUM	THIAMIN	+BAKUNIN	CROONER	GRAINED
OTTOMAN.	TOTEMIC	BALANCE	CROWNED.	GRAPNEL
PACKMAN	TRAMMED	BARONET	DECANAL	GREENER
PASSMAN	TRAMMEL	BASINET	DECENCY	GRINNED
PICAMAR	TRIMMED	BAYONET	DEFENCE	GROANED
PLASMIC	TRIMMER	BEATNIK	DEFINED	GROINED
PLUMMET	TRIUMPH	BEGONIA	DEFUNCT	GROWN-UP
POLEMIC	TROMMEL.	+BELINDA	DEIGNED	*HACKNEY
POLYMER	UNARMED	BLARNEY	DEMONIC	HAIRNET
POSTMAN	UNKEMPT	BOLONEY	DERANGE	HAPENNY
PRE-EMPT	UNNAMED	BOTANIC	DETENTE	HAVENER
PRIMMED	UNTAMED	BRAINED	DIURNAL	HEDONIC
PULLMAN	URAEMIA.	BROWNED	DIVINED	HERONRY
PYJAMAS	VENOMED	BROWNIE	DIVINER	HIJINKS
PYRAMID.	VITAMIN.	BUBONIC.	DRAG-NET	HOMINID
RACEMIC	+WHITMAN	CABINET	DRAINED	HOMONYM
READMIT	WOODMAN	CADENCE	DRAINER	HOSANNA
REARMED	WORKMAN.	CADENCY	DROWNED	HUMANLY.
REAUMUR	YASHMAK	CADENZA	DURANCE.	IMMENSE
REGIMEN		CALENDS	ECHINUS	IMPANEL
RESUMED	ABSENCE	CANONRY	EFFENDI	IMPINGE

405

INCENSE	PFENNIG	SPINNEY	UNCANNY	ANXIOUS
INFANCY	*PHOENIX	SPLENIC	UNHANDY	ANYBODY
INFANTA	PHRENIC	SPLINED	UNHINGE	APOLOGY
INFANTE	PIMENTO	SPOONED	UNMANLY	APPROVE
INGENUE	PLAINER	SPRINGY	UNZONED	AQUEOUS
INNINGS	PLAINLY	SPURNED	URGENCY.	ARDUOUS
INTENSE	PLANNED	SPUTNIK	VACANCY	*ARIZONA
INTONED	PLANNER	SQUINCH	VAGINAL	*ASHFORD
INURNED.	PLIANCY	STAINED	VALANCE	AUREOLA
JACINTH	POLENTA	*STAINES	VALENCE	AWESOME
JACONET	POLYNIA	STANNEL	VALENCY	AXOLOTL
JEJUNUM	POTENCE	STANNIC	VEDANTA	AZYMOUS.
JOURNAL	POTENCY	STANNUM	*VENTNOR	BALCONY
JOURNEY.	PRAWNED	STAUNCH	VERANDA	BALLOON
*KATANGA.	PREENED	STERNAL	VERONAL	BANNOCK
LACONIC	PUDENDA.	STERNER	VICINAL	BARBOLA
LACUNAL	QUEENED	STERNLY	*VIETNAM	BARN-OWL
LAMINAL	QUEENLY.	STERNUM	VINTNER.	BASSOON
LATENCY	REFINED	STRANGE	WAGONER	BAZOOKA
+LAVINIA	REGENCY	STRINGY	WHATNOT	BECLOUD
LEARNED	REIGNED	STUNNER	WIZENED	*BEDFORD
*LEBANON	RELINED	*SURINAM	WOMANLY.	BEDPOST
LICENCE	REPINED	+SUSANNA	YEARNED	BED-ROCK
LICENSE	RESINED	SWOONED		BEDSORE
LOZENGE.	RETINUE	SYNONYM	ABALONE	+BELLONA
MADONNA	REVENGE	SYRINGA	ABSCOND	BELLOWS
MAGENTA	REVENUE	SYRINGE.	ACETONE	BENZOIN
MARINER	ROMANCE	TALLNES	ACETOUS	BESPOKE
MASONIC	ROMANIC	TALONED	ACINOSE	BETROTH
MASONRY	ROSINED	TECHNIC	ADENOID	BILIOUS
MATINEE	ROTUNDA	TENANCY	ADENOSE	BILTONG
+MELANIE	*RUMANIA.	TENONED	ADENOUS	BIOLOGY
MELANIN	SATANIC	+TERENCE	ADIPOSE	BLOW-OUT
MEMENTO	SAVANNA	TETANIC	AFFRONT	BOUDOIR
+MIRANDA	SCANNED	TETANUS	AIR-HOLE	BOXWOOD
MORONIC	SCIENCE	THINNED	AIR-LOCK	BOYCOTT
MOURNER.	SCORNED	THINNER	AIRPORT	BOYHOOD
NOMINAL	SCRUNCH	THRONED	ALIFORM	BRICOLE
NOMINEE.	SEMINAL	TIDINGS	ALIMONY	BRIDOON
*OCEANIA	SEMINAR	+TITANIA	ALVEOLE	BRUMOUS
OCEANIC	SEVENTH	TITANIC	AMATORY	BUFFOON
OFFENCE	SEVENTY	TOPKNOT	AMOROUS	BUGLOSS
ORDINAL	SHINNED	*TORONTO	AMPHORA	BULBOUS
ORGANIC	SHUNNED	TOURNEY	AMYLOID	BULLOCK
ORGANON.	SILENCE	TRAINEE	ANALOGY	BURDOCK
PAGINAL	SKINNED	TRAINER	ANATOMY	BURNOUS
PARSNIP	SPANNED	TROUNCE	ANCHOVY	BUTTOCK.
PARTNER	SPANNER	TRUANCY	ANEMONE	CABOOSE
PENANCE	SPAWNED	TWINNED	ANEROID	CALLOUS
PETUNIA	SPINNER	TYRANNY.	+ANTHONY	CANDOUR

*CANNOCK	CURSORY	ENDMOST	GLAMOUR	ISOTOPE.
CAPROIC	CUSTODY	ENFEOFF	GLOBOSE	JAW-BONE
CARDOON	CYCLOID	ENGROSS	GLUCOSE	JEALOUS
CARIOUS	CYCLONE	ENTROPY	GONDOLA	JIB-DOOR
+CARROLL	CYCLOPS.	ENVIOUS	*GOSPORT	KEYHOLE
CARROTY	DAMFOOL	EPISODE	GOSSOON	KEYNOTE
CARTOON	DAYBOOK	EPITOME	+GREGORY	KICK-OFF
CASEOUS	DAYLONG	EPIZOON	GUMBOIL	*KINROSS.
CASSOCK	DEFROCK	ESTRONE	GUNBOAT	LACTOSE
CAST-OFF	DEFROST	EUPHONY	GUNLOCK	LAMP-OIL
CATBOAT	DEIFORM	EXPLODE	GUNROOM.	LAMPOON
CATHODE	DELTOID	EXPLOIT	HADDOCK	LASSOED
CEREOUS	DEPLORE	EXPLORE	HAMMOCK	LEGHORN
CESTOID	+DESMOND	EYE-BOLT	HANDOUT	LENTOID
CHAMOIS	DESPOIL	EYEHOLE	HAPLOID	+LEONORA
CHEROOT	DESPOND	EYESORE.	HARBOUR	+LEOPOLD
CHICORY	*DETROIT	FACTORY	HARMONY	LEPROSY
CIRROSE	DEVIOUS	FALL-OUT	HARPOON	LIFT-OFF
CITROUS	DEWPOND	FATUOUS	HASSOCK	*LINCOLN
CLAMOUR	DIABOLO	FERN-OWL	HAWK-OWL	LOBWORM
COLLOID	DIAMOND	FERROUS	HAYCOCK	LOCK-OUT
COMFORT	DIPLOID	FERVOUR	HAYFORK	LOG-BOOK
COMMODE	DIPLOMA	FESTOON	HEINOUS	LOG-ROLL
COMMONS	DIPNOAN	FETLOCK	HEMLOCK	LOGWOOD
COMPORT	DISCOID	FIBROID	HICKORY	LOOK-OUT
COMPOSE	DISCORD	FIBROUS	HIDEOUS	LOW-BORN
COMPOST	DISJOIN	FLAVOUR	HIDEOUT	LOW-DOWN
COMPOTE	DISPORT	FLY-BOAT	HILLOCK	LUTEOUS.
CONCOCT	DISPOSE	FLY-BOOK	HISTORY	MAGGOTY
CONCORD	DISROBE	FOGHORN	HOLM-OAK	MAH-JONG
CONDOLE	DISTORT	FORBORE	HORMONE	+MALCOLM
CONDONE	DOGGONE	FORGONE	HOTFOOT	MALTOSE
CONFORM	DOG-ROSE	FORLORN	HUMMOCK	MAMMOTH
CONJOIN	DOGWOOD	*FORMOSA	HYALOID	MANHOLE
CONNOTE	DRAGOON	FORSOOK	HYDROUS	MANHOOD
CONSOLE	DROMOND	FOXHOLE	HYMNODY	MAN-HOUR
CONSORT	DROP-OUT	FULSOME	HYPNOID.	+MARLOWE
CONTORT	DRY-DOCK	FULVOUS	IGNEOUS	MASTOID
CONTOUR	DUBIOUS	FUNGOID	IMPIOUS	*MATLOCK
CONVOKE	DUOTONE	FUNGOUS	IMPLODE	MATTOCK
COPIOUS	DUTEOUS.	FURIOUS	IMPLORE	MAYPOLE
CORPORA	ECOLOGY	FURLONG	IMPROVE	MENFOLK
CORRODE	ECONOMY	FUSCOUS	INCLOSE	MICROBE
COTTONY	EEL-WORM	FUTHORC.	INDOORS	MIDMOST
COULOMB	ELUSORY	GALLOON	INKHORN	*MILFORD
COXCOMB	EMBROIL	GALLOWS	INSHORE	MISTOOK
CRINOID	EMULOUS	GAMBOGE	INTROIT	MOIDORE
CUCKOLD	ENAMOUR	GASEOUS	IRKSOME	MONSOON.
CUPROUS	ENCLOSE	GEOLOGY	ISODONT	*NAIROBI
CURIOUS	ENDLONG	GIBBOUS	ISOTONE	NEGROID

NEOLOGY	PIANOLA	RHIZOID	SUCCOUR	TYPHOUS.
NERVOUS	PIBROCH	RHIZOME	SUCROSE	UNBLOWN
NETWORK	PICCOLO	RIOTOUS	*SUFFOLK	UNCLOAK
*NEWPORT	PIDDOCK	RIP-CORD	SUMMONS	UNCLOSE
*NEWTOWN	PILLORY	RISSOLE	SUNDOWN	UNFROCK
NITROUS	PINFOLD	*ROMFORD	SUPPORT	UNFROZE
NOISOME	PINHOLE	ROSEOLA	SUPPOSE	UNICORN
*NORFOLK	PISTOLE	ROWLOCK	SURCOAT	UNIFORM
NOXIOUS.	PITEOUS	RUB-DOWN	SURLOIN	UNKNOWN
OBVIOUS	PLATOON	RUBEOLA	SYNCOPE	UNLOOSE
OCHROUS	PLAY-OFF	RUINOUS	SYSTOLE.	UNQUOTE
ODOROUS	PLUMOSE	RUN-DOWN.	TABLOID	URANOUS.
OMINOUS	PLYWOOD	SABAOTH	TABOOED	VACUOLE
ONEROUS	+POLLOCK	*SALFORD	TADPOLE	VACUOUS
ORATORY	POMPOUS	SAPWOOD	TAKE-OFF	VAMOOSE
OSSEOUS	PONTOON	SARCODE	TAMBOUR	VARIOLA
OTOLOGY	POPCORN	SARCOMA	TANGOED	VARIOUS
OUTCOME	POTHOLE	SAVIOUR	TAPIOCA	VERBOSE
OUTDONE	POTHOOK	SAXHORN	TAP-ROOM	*VERMONT
OUTDOOR	PROLONG	SCOTOMA	TAP-ROOT	VICIOUS
OUTGONE	PROMOTE	SEA-COAL	TEA-COSY	VICTORY
OUTLOOK	PRONOUN	SEA-FOWL	TEA-RCOM	VILLOUS
OUTMOST	PROPOSE	SEAPORT	TEA-ROSE	VISCOSE
OUTPOST	PROSODY	SEA-ROOM	TEDIOUS	VISCOUS.
OUTRODE	PROVOKE	SEA-WOLF	TENFOLD	WALK-OUT
OUTVOTE	PROVOST	SELL-OUT	TENUOUS	WALLOON
OUTWORE	PUG-NOSE	SEND-OFF	TETRODE	+WALPOLE
OUTWORK	PURLOIN	SENSORY	THYROID	WARLOCK
OUTWORN	PURPORT	SEQUOIA	TINFOIL	WAR-LORD
OVIFORM.	PURPOSE.	SERIOUS	TIPTOED	WASH-OUT
PADDOCK	+QUIXOTE.	SET-DOWN	TOEHOLD	*WATFORD
PADLOCK	RACCOON	*SEYMOUR	TOMBOLA	WAXWORK
PALM-OIL	RAJPOOT	+SEYMOUR	TOMFOOL	WEDLOCK
+PANDORA	RAKE-OFF	SHADOWY	TOP-BOOT	WELCOME
PAPOOSE	RANCOUR	SHOW-OFF	TOP-COAT	WELL-OFF
PARBOIL	RAPPORT	SHUT-OUT	TOPMOST	WERWOLF
PARLOUR	RAUCOUS	SIGNORA	TOW-ROPE	*WIGTOWN
PARLOUS	RAVIOLI	SINUOUS	TREFOIL	WILLOWY
PARTOOK	+RAYMOND	SIRLOIN	TREMOLO	WINSOME
+PAVLOVA	RECTORY	SIT-DOWN	TRIFORM	WITHOUT
PAY-LOAD	RED-COAT	SIXFOLD	TRILOGY	WORK-OUT
PAY-ROLL	REDPOLL	SOMEONE	*TRIPOLI	XIPHOID.
PEACOCK	REDWOOD	SPIN-OFF	TURMOIL	YELLOWY.
PEA-SOUP	REFLOAT	SPINOUS	TURN-OUT	ZEALOUS
PENTODE	REGROUP	+SPINOZA	TUSSOCK	ZOOLOGY
PENTOSE	REPROOF	SPY-HOLE	TUSSORE	ZOOTOMY
PERFORM	REPROVE	STEROID	TWOFOLD	
PERGOLA	RESPOND	SUBJOIN	TWOSOME	APROPOS.
PERSONA	RESTORE	SUBSOIL	TYPHOID	ATROPHY
PETIOLE	REWROTE	SUCCOSE	TYPHOON	+ATROPOS

AUTOPSY	FELSPAR	SCALPEL	STUMPED	ALCORAN
AXLE-PIN.	FLAPPED	SCALPER	SUNSPOT	*ALGERIA
BEAR-PIT	FLAPPER	SCAMPED	SWAMPED	ALLERGY
BLEEPED.	FLIPPER	SCAMPER	SWAPPED	ALLURED
+CALYPSO	FLOPPED	SCARPED	SWEEPER	ALSO-RAN
CATS-PAW	FOOTPAD	SCOOPED	SWOOPED	ALTERED
CESSPIT	FUSS-POT.	SCORPIO	SWOPPED	AMHARIC
CHAPPED	GLIMPSE	SCRAPER	SYNAPSE.	ANAGRAM
CHEAPEN	GRAMPUS	SCRAPPY	TALIPED	ANDIRON
CHEAPLY	GRAPPLE	SCRUPLE	TENT-PEG	*ANDORRA
CHEEPER	GRASPER	SCULPED	THUMPED	ANGERED
CHIPPED	GRIPPED	SCUPPER	TRAIPSE	ANTHRAX
CHIRPED	GROUPED.	+SERAPIS	TRAMPED	APPAREL
CHOPPED	HAIRPIN	SHAMPOO	TRAMPLE	APTERAL
CHOPPER	HALF-PAY	SHARPEN	TRAPPED	APTERYX
CLAMPED	HARDPAN	SHARPER	TRAPPER	ASHTRAY
CLAMPER	HEXAPOD.	*SHEPPEY	TRIPPER	ASPERSE
CLAPPED	INSIPID.	SHIPPED	TROOPER	ASPIRED
CLAPPER	JACKPOT	SHIPPEN	TROUPER	ASPIRIN
CLASPED	JUNIPER.	SHIPPER	TRUMPED	ASSURED
CLIPPED	KINGPIN	SHOPPED	TRUMPET.	+ASTARTE
CLIPPER	KNAPPED.	SHOPPER	UNHAPPY	ATHIRST
CLIPPIE	MANIPLE.	SICK-PAY	UNHOPED	ATTIRED
CLUMPED	NOTEPAD.	SKID-PAN	USURPER.	AUGURED
COAL-PIT	OCCIPUT	SKIMPED	WHELPED	AURORAL
COCKPIT	OCTOPOD	SKIPPED	WHIMPER	AUSTRAL
CRAMPED	OCTOPUS	SKIPPER	WHIPPED	*AUSTRIA
CRAMPON	OCTUPLE	SLAPPED	WHIPPET	AVERRED.
CREEPER	+OEDIPUS	SLEEPER	WHISPER	BALDRIC
CRIMPED	*OLYMPIA	SLIPPED	WHOOPED	+BERTRAM
CRIPPLE	OLYMPIC	SLIPPER	WHOPPER	BESTREW
CRISPER	*OLYMPUS	SLOPPED	WRAPPED	BIZARRE
CROPPED	OUTSPAN.	SLUMPED	WRAPPER	BLURRED
CROPPER	PANOPLY	SNAPPER		BOTARGO
CRUMPET	PARAPET	SNIPPED	ANTIQUE.	BOURREE
CRUMPLE.	PLAYPEN	SNIPPET	BAROQUE	BOX-TREE
CRUPPER.	PLOPPED	SNOOPER	BEZIQUE	BUCKRAM
DEADPAN	PLUMPER	STAMPED	BRUSQUE.	BUTYRIC.
DECAPOD	PLUMPLY	STEEPED	CACIQUE.	CABARET
DECUPLE	POLYPOD	STEEPEN	OBLIQUE	CALORIC
DRIPPED	POLYPUS	STEEPER	OBLOQUY	CALORIE
DROOPED	PORK-PIE	STEEPLE		CALTROP
DROPPED	PROPPED	STEPPED	ABJURED	CAMBRIC
DROPPER	PROSPER	STIPPLE	ACCURST	CATARRH
DUSTPAN.	PUSHPIN.	STOOPED	ADHERED	CATERER
ECLIPSE	QUIPPED	STOPPED	ADMIRAL	CENTRAL
ELLIPSE	RELAPSE	STOPPER	ADMIRER	CENTRIC
ESCAPED	REPAPER.	STOPPLE	ADVERSE	CHAGRIN
ESCAPEE	SALT-PAN	STRIPED	AILERON	CHAIRED
EXAMPLE.	SCALPED	STROPHE	*AINTREE	CHARRED

CHEERED	EQUERRY	+JEFFREY	ORDERED	SCHERZO
CHEERIO	ESPARTO	JOG-TROT.	ORDERLY	SCOURER
CHEVRON	EUCHRED	KESTREL	ORPHREY	SCOURGE
CHIRRUP	+EUTERPE	KINDRED.	+OSBORNE	SECURED
CHLORAL	EXCERPT	LAMPREY	OUTCROP	SEVERAL
CHLORIC	EXPIRED	LATERAL	OUTGREW	SEVERED
+CHLORIS	EYEBROW.	LEMURES	OUTGROW	SEWERED
CLEARED	FEDERAL	LEVERED	OVERRAN	SHEARED
CLEARER	FEMORAL	LEVERET	OVERRUN.	SHEERED
CLEARLY	FIGURAL	LIBERAL	PALFREY	SISTRUM
COHERER	FIGURED	*LIBERIA	PAPYRUS	SLURRED
COMFREY	FILARIA	LIBERTY	PETERED	SMEARED
CONTROL	FLOORED	LITERAL	PIERROT	SNEERED
COTERIE	FLOURED	LITURGY	PIG-IRON	SOBERED
COVERED	FLY-TRAP	LOW-BRED	PILGRIM	SOBERLY
COWERED	FOX-TROT	LOWBROW	PORTRAY	SPARRED
CULPRIT.	FULCRUM	LUCARNE	POVERTY	SPARROW
+DEBORAH	FUNERAL.	*LUCERNE	POWERED	SPEARED
DECORUM	GASTRIC	LUSTRAL.	PRAIRIE	SPHERIC
DEMERIT	GENERAL	*MAJORCA	PRAKRIT	SPLURGE
DESERVE	GENERIC	MAJORED	PROGRAM	SPORRAN
DESIRED	+GODFREY	MALARIA	PUBERTY	SPURRED
DESTROY	GROGRAM.	MANDREL	PYLORUS.	SQUARED
DETERED	+HOGARTH	MANTRUM	QUADRAT	STARRED
DEWDROP	HOMERIC	MANURED	QUADREL	STEARIN
DEXTRAL	HOVERED	MATURED	QUARREL	STEERER
DEXTRAN	HUMDRUM	MAZURKA	QUEERER	STIRRED
DEXTRIN	HUMERAL	+MILDRED	QUEERLY.	STIRRUP
DIAGRAM	HUMERUS	MINARET	RAT-TRAP	SUBERIN
DIVERGE	HUNDRED	MINERAL	RAZORED	SUGARED
DIVERSE	HYPERON.	+MINERVA	REBIRTH	SUN-TRAP
DIVORCE	ICTERUS	MISERLY	REBORED	SUTURAL
DOGTROT	IGNORAL	MISTRAL	REFEREE	SUTURED
+DOLORES.	IGNORED	MONARCH	REMARRY	SWEARER
EAGERLY	ILL-BRED	MONGREL	REMORSE	SYNERGY.
EAR-DRUM	IMBURSE	MOTORED	+ROBERTA	TANTRUM
ELDERLY	IMMERSE	MUSK-RAT.	ROSTRAL	TAPERED
EMBARGO	IMMORAL	NATURAL	ROSTRUM.	TAX-FREE
EMPEROR	IMMURED	NEUTRAL	SAFFRON	TEA-TRAY
EMPIRIC	IMPERIL	NEUTRON	SAMURAI	TENDRIL
ENDORSE	INDORSE	*NIGERIA	SATIRIC	THEOREM
ENDURED	INFERNO	NOSTRIL	SATYRIC	THEURGY
ENFORCE	INHERED	NOSTRUM	SCARRED	TIMBREL
ENGORGE	INHERIT	NUMERAL.	ROSTRAL	TOWARDS
ENLARGE	INJURED	OBSERVE		TUMBREL
ENSURED	INNARDS	OBVERSE		TUTORED.
ENTERIC	INSURED	OESTRUS		UMPIRED
ENTHRAL	INSURER	OFFERED		UNAIRED
ENVIRON	INTERIM	*ONTARIO		UNCARED
EPIGRAM	INVERSE.	ONWARDS		UNDERGO

UNEARTH	BEMUSED	DROWSED	+JOCASTA	REFUSED
UNHORSE	BENISON	DYNASTY.	+JOHNSON.	REISSUE
UNMORAL	BLESSED	ECDYSIS	KEELSON	REPOSED
UNNERVE	BLOSSOM	EFFASED	KENOSIS	REVISAL
UNSCREW	BRAISED	EFFUSED	KHAMSIN	REVISED
UNSTRAP	BRASSIE	ELAPSED	*KNOSSOS.	RIPOSTE.
UPSURGE	BROWSED	EMBASSY	LIAISON	SAMISEN
UPTHROW	BRUISED.	EMBOSOM	+LINDSEY	SATISFY
UPWARDS	CAISSON	ENCASED	LOOK-SEE.	SCEPSIS
USHERED	CANASTA	EXCISED	MAJESTY	SCISSOR
UTTERED	CELESTA	EXCUSED	MALMSEY	*SILESIA
UTTERLY.	+CELESTE	EXPOSAL	+MATISSE	SPLASHY
+VALERIE	CERESIN	EXPOSED.	MEIOSIS	SPONSOR
VENTRAL	CHASSIS	FINESSE	MELISMA	SQUASHY
VETERAN	CHEESED	FLOTSAM	+MELISSA	STEPSON
VICEROY.	*CHELSEA	FOCUSED	MILKSOP	STETSON
WAGERED	CHIASMA	FORESAW	MIMESIS	*SWANSEA.
WASTREL	CHRISOM	FORESEE	MISUSED	THIRSTY
WATERED	+CHRISTI	FREESIA	MITOSIS	THYRSUS
WAVERED	CLASSED	FRET-SAW	MODESTY	TRANSIT
WHIRRED	CLASSIC	FROWSTY	MODISTE	TRANSOM
+WILFRED	CLAUSAL	FUCHSIA.	MYCOSIS.	TRAPSED
WINDROW	COARSEN	GAINSAY	NEMESIS	TREASON
WOLFRAM.	COUNSEL	GENESIS	*NICOSIA	TRESSED
ZYMURGY	COURSER	GENISTA	NON-USER.	+TROTSKY
	CRASSLY	GIRASOL	ODYSSEY	TRUSSED
ABYSSAL	CREASED	GLOSSED	OPOSSUM	TRYPSIN
ACCUSAL	CRESSET	GRASSED	OPPOSER	*TUNISIA
ACCUSED	CRIMSON	GREASED	OSMOSIS	TWIN-SET
ADVISED	+CROESUS	GREASER	OVERSAW	+ULYSSES
ADVISER	CROSSED	*GRIMSBY	OVERSEA	UNBOSOM
AEROSOL	CROSSLY	GROSSED	OVERSEE	UNCASED
ALYSSUM	CRUISED	GROSSLY	OVERSET	UNRISEN
AMASSED	CRUISER	GROUSER	OVERSEW.	UTENSIL.
AMNESIA	CURTSEY.	GUESSED.	PARASOL	+VANESSA
AMNESTY	DEBASED	HACKSAW	PARESIS	VENISON.
ANOESIS	+DEBUSSY	HANDSEL	+PEARSON	WHIMSEY
APHASIA	DEEP-SEA	HARD-SET	+PEGASUS	WHITSUN
APHESIS	DEFUSED	HEAD-SET	PELISSE	*WINDSOR
AROUSED	DEHISCE	HEARSAY	PERUSAL	WORK-SHY
ARTISAN	DEMESNE	HONESTY	PERUSED	*WORKSOP.
ARTISTE	DEMISED	*HORNSEA.	PHRASED	XERASIA
ASEPSIS.	DEPOSED	IMPASSE	PIOUSLY	
BABY-SIT	DEPOSIT	IMPASTE	PLEASED	ABETTED
BAGASSE	DEVISED	IMPASTO	PRAISED	ABETTOR
BAND-SAW	DIBASIC	IMPOSED	PRESSED	ABIOTIC
BANKSIA	DIOPSIS	INCISED	PRESSER	ABORTED
+BATISTA	DIVISOR	INCISOR	PRUSSIC.	ABUTTER
BATISTE	DRESSED	INCUSED	QUASSIA.	+ACHATES
BELISHA	DRESSER	INFUSED.	REFUSAL	ADAPTED

411

ADAPTER	BRISTLY	CREATOR	EMITTED	FRONTAL
AERATED	*BRISTOL	CRESTED	EMITTER	FRONTED
AERATOR	BRITTLE	CRITTER	EMPATHY	FROSTED
ALERTED	BUILT-IN	CROFTER	ENACTED	FRUITER
AMENTIA	BUILT-UP	CROUTON	ENTITLE	FRUSTUM.
AMMETER	BURETTE.	CRUSTED	EPISTLE	GAMETIC
AMPUTEE	CALOTTE	CRYPTIC	EQUATED	GAROTTE
+ANNETTE	CAPITAL	CRYSTAL	EQUATOR	GAUNTLY
ANOETIC	CAPITOL	CURATOR	ERECTED	GAVOTTE
APOSTLE	CAPSTAN	CURETTE.	ERECTLY	GAZETTE
AQUATIC	CAROTID	DAUNTED	ERECTOR	GELATIN
ARBITER	CAROTIN	DEBATED	ERRATIC	GENETIC
ARBUTUS	CAUSTIC	DEBITED	ERRATUM	GENITAL
ASCETIC	CHANTED	DEISTIC	ERUPTED	GHASTLY
ASEPTIC	CHANTRY	DELATED	EVERTED	GHOSTED
ASIATIC	CHAOTIC	DELATOR	EVICTED	GHOSTLY
ASTATIC	CHAPTER	DELETED	EXACTED	GLINTED
AUDITED	CHARTED	DEMOTED	EXACTLY	GLISTEN
AUDITOR	CHARTER	DEMOTIC	EXACTOR	GLISTER
AVERTED	CHASTEN	DENOTED	EXALTED	GLITTER
AVIATOR	CHATTED	DEVOTED	EXCITED	GLOATED
AWAITED.	CHATTEL	DEVOTEE	EXERTED	GLOTTAL
*BAMPTON	CHATTER	DIGITAL	EXISTED	GLOTTIS
BARYTES	CHEATED	DILATED	EXULTED.	GLUTTED
BEASTLY	CHEETAH	DILATOR	FAINTED	GLUTTON
BELATED	*CHESTER	DILUTED	FAINTLY	GLYPTIC
BERATED	CHOCTAW	DILUTER	FANATIC	GNOSTIC
BEWITCH	CHORTLE	DIOPTER	FAULTED	GRAFTED
BIGOTED	*CLACTON	DIOPTRE	FEASTED	GRAFTER
BIGOTRY	CLASTIC	DONATED	FIBSTER	GRANTED
BIRETTA	CLATTER	DONATOR	FIGHTER	GRANTEE
BLASTED	CLOTTED	+DOROTHY	FIRSTLY	GRANTOR
BLASTIN	CLOUTED	DOUBTED	FIXATED	GREATER
BLEATED	CLUSTER	DOUBTER	FLATTEN	GREATLY
BLISTER	CLUTTER	DRAFTED	FLATTER	GREETED
BLOATED	CLYSTER	DRAFTEE	FLEETED	GRISTLE
BLOATER	COAL-TAR	DRASTIC	FLIRTED	GRISTLY
BLOTTED	COAL-TIT	DRATTED	FLITTED	GRITTED
BLOTTER	COASTAL	DRIFTER	FLITTER	GROUTED
BLUNTED	COASTED	DROUTHY.	FLOATER	GRUNTED
BLUNTLY	COASTER	EDICTAL	FLOUTED	GYRATED.
BLURTED	COCOTTE	EGESTED	FLUSTER	HABITAT
BLUSTER	COLITIS	EIDETIC	FLUTTER	HABITED
BOASTER	COULTER	EJECTED	FOISTED	HABITUE
BOLSTER	COUNTED	EJECTOR	FORETOP	HAMITIC
BOOSTER	COUNTER	ELASTIC	+FORSTER	*HAMPTON
BORSTAL	COUNTRY	ELASTIN	FRANTIC	HAMSTER
BOULTER	COURTLY	ELECTED	FRETTED	HARDTOP
BREATHE	COVETED	ELECTOR	FRITTED	HAUNTED
BRISTLE	CREATED	+ELECTRA	FRITTER	HEALTHY

HEARTED	*LESOTHO	PAINTER	QUIETEN	*SEATTLE
HEARTEN	LICITLY	PALATAL	QUIETER	SEDATED
HEBETIC	LIGHTEN	PALETTE	QUIETLY	SEMITIC
HEISTED	LIGHTER	PAROTID	QUIETUS	SENATOR
HEMATIN	LIGHTLY	PENATES	QUILTED	SENATUS
HEPATIC	LIMITED	PHAETON	QUINTAN	SHATTER
HERETIC	LINCTUS	PHANTOM	QUINTET	SHEATHE
HERITOR	LITOTES	PHILTRE	QUITTED	SHEETED
HIPSTER	LOBSTER	PIASTRE	QUITTER.	SHELTER
HOISTED	LOCATED	PICOTEE	REACTOR	SHELTIE
HOLSTER	LUNATIC	PILOTED	REALTOR	SHIFTER
*HONITON	LUNETTE	PINETUM	REBATED	SHOOTER
+HORATIO	LUXATED.	PIPETTE	RECITAL	SHORTED
*HOUSTON	*MAESTEG	PIRATED	RECITER	SHORTEN
HYDATID.	MAESTRO	PIVOTAL	RE-ENTER	SHORTER
IDIOTIC	MAHATMA	PIVOTED	RE-ENTRY	SHORTLY
IGNITED	MANATEE	PLAITED	REFUTED	SHOUTED
IMPETUS	MARITAL	PLANTAR	REGATTA	SHUNTED
IMPUTED	MEGATON	PLANTED	RELATED	SHUTTER
INAPTLY	MERITED	PLANTER	REPUTED	SHUTTLE
INCITED	MILITIA	PLASTER	RIGHTED	SHYSTER
INDITED	MIMETIC	PLASTIC	RIGHTLY	SIGHTED
INEPTLY	MINSTER	PLATTED	RISOTTO	SIGHTLY
INERTIA	MINUTED	PLATTER	RIVETER	SKEPTIC
INERTLY	MOBSTER	PLEATED	ROASTED	SKIRTED
INVITED.	MOISTEN	PLOTTER	ROASTER	SKITTER
JANITOR	MONITOR	POINTED	ROISTER	SKITTLE
JAUNTED	MONSTER	POINTER	ROOSTER	SLANTED
JOINTED	MOULTED	POLITIC	ROSETTE	SLATTED
JOINTER	MOUNTED	POLL-TAX	ROTATED	SLEETED
JOINTLY	MUJITSA	POMATUM	ROTATOR	SLOTTED
JOUSTED	MULATTO	POSITED	ROUSTED.	SMARTED
JUJITSU	MUTATED.	POULTRY	SAINTED	SMARTEN
+JUPITER.	NAPHTHA	PRAETOR	SAINTLY	SMARTLY
KENOTIC	NECK-TIE	PRATTLE	SALUTED	SMITTEN
KERATIN	NEGATED	*PRESTON	SANCTUM	SMUTTED
KILOTON	NEPOTIC	PRINTED	SANCTUS	SNORTER
KINETIC	NIGHTLY	PRINTER	SAUNTER	SOMATIC
KNITTED	NON-STOP.	PROCTOR	SCANTLE	SPARTAN
KNITTER	OERSTED	PSALTER	SCATTER	SPASTIC
KNOTTED	OLOSTER	PUNSTER	SCENTED	SPATTER
KRYPTOL	OMITTED	PURITAN	SCEPTIC	SPECTRA
KRYPTON.	ORBITAL	PYRETIC	SCEPTRE	SPECTRE
+LAERTES	ORBITED	PYRITES.	SCIATIC	SPELTER
LAND-TAX	OSMOTIC	QUANTUM	SCOOTER	SPIRTED
LAYETTE	OUTSTAY	QUARTAN	SCOUTED	SPITTED
LEGATED	OVERTAX	QUARTER	SCRATCH	SPITTLE
LEGATEE	OVERTLY	QUARTET	SCROTUM	SPLOTCH
LEISTER	OVERTOP.	+QUENTIN	SCUTTER	SPORTED
LENGTHY	PAINTED	QUESTED	SCUTTLE	SPOTTED

413

SPOTTER	TRACTOR	ASSAULT	DEBOUCH	INCRUST
SPOUTED	TRAITOR	ASTOUND	DEFAULT	INTRUDE
SPURTED	TREATED	*AVEBURY	DEGAUSS	INTRUST.
SPUTTER	TRESTLE	AZIMUTH.	DELOUSE	+JONQUIL.
STARTED	*TRISTAN	*BANBURY	DEMOUNT	KALMUCK
STARTER	TROTTER	BANQUET	DENTURE	KIBBUTZ
STARTLE	TRUSTED	BASCULE	DETRUDE	KUMQUAT.
STILTED	TRUSTEE	BECAUSE	DIFFUSE	LACE-UPS
*STILTON	TRYSTED	BEDOUIN	DISCUSS	LACQUER
STINTED	TWISTER	+BEOWULF	DISGUST	LANGUID
STOUTER	TWITTED	*BERMUDA	DISPUTE	LANGUOR
STOUTLY	TWITTER	BISCUIT	DISRUPT	LAWSUIT
STRATUM	TWO-STEP.	BISMUTH	DISTURB.	LECTURE
STRATUS	UNACTED	BIVOUAC	+EMANUEL	LEG-PULL
STRETCH	UNHITCH.	BOROUGH	ENCRUST	LEISURE
STUNTED	VACATED	BOUQUET	ENTHUSE	LETTUCE
STUTTER	VALETED	BRAVURA	ENTRUST	LINGUAL.
STYPTIC	VAULTED	BRIQUET	EPICURE	*MACDUFF
*SUMATRA	VAULTER	BULRUSH.	ERASURE	MANHUNT
SWARTHY	VAUNTED	CAPSULE	ESPOUSE	+MARCUSE
SWATTED	VEDETTE	CAPTURE	EVACUEE	MARQUEE
SWATTER	VEGETAL	CAROUSE	EXCLUDE	MARQUIS
SWEATED	VISITED	CELLULE	EXECUTE	MAYBUSH
SWEATER	VISITOR	CENSURE	EXHAUST	MEASURE
SWEETEN	VOLUTED	CENTURY	EXTRUDE.	+MERCURY
SWEETER	VOMITED.	CHEQUER	FACTUAL	MISRULE
SWEETIE	WAISTED	CIRCUIT	FACTURE	MIXTURE
SWEETLY	WEALTHY	CLIQUEY	FAILURE	MOLLUSC
SWELTER	WHEATEN	CLOSURE	FEATURE	MUGWUMP.
SWIFTER	WHETTED	COEQUAL	FERRULE	+NEPTUNE
SWIFTLY	WHISTLE	COLLUDE	FISSURE	NERVURE
SWOTTED	WHITTLE	COMMUNE	FISTULA	NETSUKE
SYMPTOM.	+WINSTON	COMMUTE	FIXTURE	NOCTULE
TABETIC	WORSTED	COMPUTE	FLEXURE	NOCTURN
TACITLY	WREATHE	CONCUSS	FLORUIT	NONSUCH
TAINTED	WRESTED	CONDUCE	FORMULA	NONSUIT
TAPSTER	WRESTLE	CONDUIT	FORTUNE	NURTURE.
TAUNTED	WRITTEN.	CONFUSE	FOXHUNT.	OBSCURE
*TAUNTON	YACHTED	CONFUTE	GESTURE	OBTRUDE
TEMPTER	*YANGTZE	CONJURE	GLOBULE	OCCLUDE
THEATRE	*YUCATAN.	CONQUER	GRADUAL	OROTUND
THISTLE	ZYMOTIC	CONSULT	GRANULE	OVIDUCT.
THISTLY		CONSUME	GRAVURE	PARQUET
TIGHTEN	ACCOUNT	CORRUPT	GUIPURE.	PASTURE
TIGHTER	ADJOURN	COSTUME	*HAMBURG	PENGUIN
TIGHTLY	AGROUND	CROQUET	HIRSUTE	PERCUSS
+TIMOTHY	ALIQUOT	CULTURE	HOMBURG.	PERFUME
TIPSTER	AMPOULE	CUMQUAT	IMBRUED	PERJURE
TOASTER	ARMOURY	CURCUMA.	IMPOUND	PERJURY
+TOLSTOY	ASEXUAL	DEBAUCH	INCLUDE	PERMUTE

PERTURB	SPECULA	VULTURE.	SWERVED	SHIP-WAY
PICQUET	STATURE	YOGHURT	SYNOVIA.	SLIPWAY
PICTURE	STATUTE		THIEVED	STREWED.
PINGUID	STIMULI	*ANDOVER	THRIVED	THROWER
PINGUIN	+STRAUSS	ARRIVAL	THRIVEN.	TIDEWAY
PLAGUED	SUBDUAL	ARRIVED.	UNCIVIL	TRAMWAY.
POLLUTE	SUBDUED	BEDEVIL	UNCOVER	UNBOWED.
POSTURE	SUBFUSC	BEHAVED	UNMOVED	WIDOWER
POTLUCK	SUBSUME	BELOVED	UNRAVEL.	
PRELUDE	SUCCUMB	BOLIVAR	WHARVES	ADMIXED
PREPUCE	*SUDBURY	*BOLIVIA.	WHOEVER	AFFIXED
PRESUME	SUFFUSE	CADAVER		ANNEXED.
PRIMULA	SUNBURN.	CARAVAN	ALLOWED	INFIXED.
PROCURE	TACTUAL	CHERVIL	ARCHWAY.	PYREXIA.
PRODUCE	TESTUDO	CLEAVED	+BALDWIN	RELAXED.
PRODUCT	TEXTUAL	CLEAVER.	BEES-WAX	TELEXED
PROFUSE	TEXTURE	DELIVER	+BRONWEN.	UNFIXED
PURSUER	THROUGH	DERIVED	CARAWAY	UNSEXED
PURSUIT	*TILBURY	DISAVOW.	CHINWAG	UNTAXED
PUSTULE.	TISSUED	ENLIVEN	CUTAWAY.	
RACQUET	TONGUED	EVOLVED.	DOORWAY.	ACOLYTE
RAPTURE	TONSURE	FLY-OVER	ELBOWED	ALLAYED
REBOUND	*TORQUAY	FOREVER.	EMBOWER	ALLOYED
RECLUSE	TORTURE	GREAVES	EMPOWER	ANALYSE
RECOUNT	TRADUCE	GRIEVED	ENDOWED.	ANALYST
RECRUIT	TRIBUNE	GROOVER.	FAIRWAY	ANNOYED
REDOUBT	TRIBUTE.	*HANOVER	FARAWAY	ANODYNE
REDOUND	UNBOUND	HOWEVER.	FLYAWAY	ASSAYED.
*REDRUTH	UNCOUTH	INWOVEN.	FOOTWAY.	BELAYED
REMOULD	UNEQUAL	+JEHOVAH.	GANGWAY	BERHYME
REMOUNT	UNSOUND	MINIVER	GATEWAY	BIOTYPE.
RESCUER	UNSTUCK	MOTIVED.	GETAWAY	CAT-EYED
RESOUND	UNTRUSS	*NINEVEH.	*GOODWIN.	CONDYLE.
RETOUCH	UNTRUTH	PALAVER.	HALFWAY	DECAYED
ROEBUCK	UNUSUAL	RECOVER	HALF-WIT	DECOYED
RORQUAL	UNWOUND	RELIVED	HEADWAY	DELAYED
+ROUAULT	UNWRUNG	REMOVAL	HIGHWAY.	DIPTYCH
RUPTURE.	*URUGUAY.	REMOVED	MIAOWED.	DISTYLE.
SACCULE	VAPOURY	REMOVER	PATHWAY	EMBAYED
*SATSUMA	VASCULA	REVIVAL	PERIWIG	ENJOYED
SAVOURY	VELOURS	REVIVER.	POST-WAR.	ESSAYED.
SAWDUST	VENTURE	SAMOVAR	RAILWAY	FORAYED.
SCAPULA	VERDURE	SCARVES	RENEWAL	HALCYON
SEAGULL	VERRUCA	+SEGOVIA	RENEWED	HONEY.ED.
SECLUDE	VESTURE	SHEAVES	*RINGWAY	+KHAYYAM.
SEIZURE	VIADUCT	SHELVED	ROADWAY	MONEYED.
SENSUAL	VICTUAL	SHRIVEL	RUNAWAY.	ONE-EYED
SKI-JUMP	VIRGULE	SLEEVED	*SARAWAK	*PALMYRA
SOJOURN	VIRTUAL	STARVED	SCRAWNY	PHARYNX
SPATULA	*VISTULA	STRIVEN	SCREWED	PIE-EYED

415

POP-EYED.	CASE-LAW	PAGINAL	BESTIAL	SEA-COAL
SAMOYED	*CASPIAN	PALATAL	CENTRAL	SECULAR
SPLAYED	CATBOAT	PALUDAL	DEADPAN	SEISMAL
SPRAYER	CATHEAD	PARTIAL	+DEBORAH	SEMINAL
STRAYED	CATS-PAW	PASCHAL	DECADAL	SEMINAR
SYSTYLE.	CAVE-MAN	PASSMAN	DECANAL	*SENEGAL
TALLY-HO.	DANELAW	PATHWAY	DECIMAL	SENSUAL
+VANDYKE	FABLIAU	PAY-LOAD	DECRIAL	SEVERAL
	FACTUAL	RADICAL	DEW-CLAW	TEA-LEAF
ALCAZAR	FAIRWAY	RAILWAY	DEXTRAL	TEAR-GAS
ASSIZES.	FARADAY	RAMADAN	DEXTRAN	TEA-TRAY
BEDIZEN	FARAWAY	RAT-TRAP	FEDERAL	TEMPLAR
BRYOZOA.	*FARNHAM	SALT-PAN	FELSPAR	TERTIAN
CITIZEN.	FAST-DAY	SAMOVAR	FEMORAL	TEXTUAL
DENIZEN	FAT-HEAD	SAMURAI	GENERAL	VEGETAL
*DEVIZES	GAGSMAN	SANDBAG	GENITAL	VENTRAL
DRIZZLE	GAINSAY	SAND-BAR	GENTIAN	VERONAL
DRIZZLY.	+GALAHAD	SANDMAN	GETAWAY	VETERAN
FRAZZLE	GANGWAY	*SARAWAK	HEADMAN	WEEKDAY.
FREEZER	GATEMAN	SAURIAN	HEADWAY	AFFINAL
FRIZZED	GATEWAY	TABLEAU	HEARSAY	OFFBEAT
FRIZZLE.	HABITAT	TACTUAL	HELICAL	OFF-PEAK
GRIZZLE	HACKSAW	TAXI-CAB	HELLCAT	EGGHEAD
GRIZZLY.	+HADRIAN	TAXIMAN	HERNIAL	IGNORAL.
HORIZON.	HALF-PAY	VAGINAL	HESSIAN	CHAPMAN
IODIZED	HALFWAY	*VATICAN	+JEHOVAH	CHATEAU
IONIZED.	*HALIFAX	+VAUGHAN	KEELMAN	*CHATHAM
METAZOA	HANDBAG	WARHEAD	LESBIAN	*CHEDDAR
MUEZZIN.	HANGMAN	WASH-DAY	LETHEAN	CHEETAH
QUIZZED.	HARDPAN	YASHMAK.	LEXICAL	CHINWAG
SELTZER	JACKDAW	*ABIDJAN	MEDICAL	CHLORAL
SNEEZED	KANTIAN	+ABRAHAM	MESSIAH	CHOCTAW
SNOOZED	LACTEAL	ABYSMAL	NEBULAR	+KHAYYAM
SWIZZLE.	LACUNAL	ABYSSAL	NEUTRAL	SHELLAC
TWEEZER.	LAMINAL	IBERIAN.	PELICAN	SHIP-WAY
WALTZED	LAND-TAX	ACCUSAL	PERMIAN	SHOPMAN
WHEEZED	LATERAL	ACROBAT	PERSIAN	SHOWMAN
WHIZZED	MACADAM	SCANDAL	PERUSAL	THEREAT
	MAGICAL	SCHOLAR	REALGAR	THERMAL
	MAILBAG	SCRIBAL.	RECITAL	+THOREAU
*BAGHDAD	MARITAL	ADMIRAL	RED-COAT	WHEREAS
BANDEAU	MARSHAL	ADRENAL	RED-HEAD	WHEREAT
BAND-SAW	MARTIAL	EDICTAL.	REFLOAT	+WHITMAN.
BASILAR	MARTIAN	AEOLIAN	REFUSAL	BIFOCAL
+CALCHAS	MAXIMAL	BEES-WAX	REGULAR	BIG-HEAD
CAPITAL	NARWHAL	BELGIAN	REMOVAL	BIPOLAR
CAPSTAN	NATURAL	+BERTRAM	RENEWAL	BIVOUAC
CARAVAN	OARSMAN	BESMEAR	RETREAD	DIAGRAM
CARAWAY	OATMEAL	BESPEAK	REVISAL	DIGITAL
CARDIAC	PACKMAN	BESTEAD	REVIVAL	DIPNOAN

DIPOLAR	+WILLIAM	BOATMAN	POLECAT	GRECIAN
DISHMAT	WINDBAG.	BOLIVAR	POLL-TAX	GREYLAG
DISPLAY	SKID-PAN.	BONDMAN	POPULAR	GROGRAM
DIURNAL	ALCAZAR	BOOKMAN	PORTRAY	IRANIAN
FIG-LEAF	ALCORAN	BORSTAL	POSTBAG	ORBITAL
FIGURAL	ALMANAC	COAL-GAS	POSTMAN	ORDINAL
FINICAL	ALMSMAN	COAL-TAR	POST-WAR	ORPHEAN
FIREMAN	ALSO-RAN	COASTAL	POUNDAL	ORTOLAN
+GILLIAN	CLAUSAL	+COCTEAU	ROADMAN	PROGRAM
GINGHAM	CLOACAL	COELIAC	ROADWAY	PROTEAN
HIGHDAY	CLUBMAN	COEQUAL	RONDEAU	TRAM-CAR
HIGH-HAT	ELEGIAC	COMICAL	RORQUAL	TRAMWAY
HIGHWAY	ELUVIAL	CONCEAL	ROSTRAL	*TRISTAN
KINSMAN	ELYSIAN	CONGEAL	TOP-COAT	TRIVIAL
LIBERAL	FLAG-DAY	COPY-CAT	TOPICAL	+TRUDEAU
LIFTMAN	FLAGMAN	CORDIAL	*TORQUAY	URANIAN
LINEMAN	FLOTSAM	CORONAL	WOLFRAM	*URUGUAY.
LINGUAL	FLUVIAL	COSTEAN	WOODMAN	ASEXUAL
LITERAL	FLYAWAY	CO-TIDAL	WORKDAY	ASHTRAY
MIASMAL	FLY-BOAT	*DONEGAL	WORKMAN.	ASSAGAI
MILK-BAR	FLYLEAF	DOORMAN	APTERAL	ESCHEAT
MILKMAN	FLY-TRAP	DOORMAT	EPIGRAM	ISCHIAL.
MINERAL	GLACIAL	DOORWAY	EPOCHAL	ETERNAL
MINICAB	GLOTTAL	*DOUGLAS	OPPIDAN	ETESIAN
MINIMAL	ILLEGAL	FOOTPAD	OPTICAL	ETHICAL
MISDEAL	PLANTAR	FOOTWAY	SPARTAN	ETONIAN
MISLEAD	PLATEAU	FORBEAR	SPATIAL	ITALIAN
MISREAD	PLUVIAL	FOREMAN	SPECIAL	OTTOMAN
MISTRAL	SLIPWAY.	FORESAW	SPORRAN.	STELLAR
OILMEAL	AMALGAM	GO-AHEAD	ARABIAN	STERNAL
PICAMAR	IMMORAL.	GODHEAD	ARCHWAY	STOICAL
PILULAR	ANAGRAM	GOODMAN	AREOLAR	STOPGAP
PINHEAD	ANGULAR	GORDIAN	ARRIVAL	STYGIAN
PIT-HEAD	ANNULAR	HOLIDAY	ARSENAL	UTOPIAN.
PIVOTAL	ANTHRAX	HOLM-OAK	ARTISAN	AURORAL
*RINGWAY	ENTHRAL	HOT-HEAD	*BRAEMAR	AUSTRAL
SICK-BAY	ENTREAT	+HOUSMAN	+BRENDAN	AUTOCAR
SICK-PAY	INHUMAN	JOCULAR	*BRIXHAM	AUTOMAT
SIDECAR	INITIAL	JOURNAL	CRANIAL	BUCKRAM
SIMILAR	INSOFAR	LOCKJAW	CROWBAR	BUGBEAR
TIDEWAY	INSTEAD	LOGICAL	CRUCIAL	BURGLAR
TIME-LAG	INSULAR	*LOTHIAN	CRYSTAL	BUSHMAN
TITULAR	KNEE-CAP	MOHICAN	DRAYMAN	CUMQUAT
VICINAL	SNOWMAN	NODICAL	FREEMAN	*CURACAO
VICTUAL	UNCLEAN	NODULAR	FRET-SAW	CUTAWAY
*VIETNAM	UNCLOAK	NOMINAL	FROGMAN	DUSTMAN
VINEGAR	UNEQUAL	NOONDAY	FRONTAL	DUSTPAN
VIRELAY	UNMORAL	NOSEBAG	GRADUAL	FUNERAL
VIRTUAL	UNSTRAP	NOSEGAY	GRAMMAR	FUSTIAN
WILDCAT	UNUSUAL.	NOTEPAD	GRANDAD	GUNBOAT

HUMERAL	NYMPHAL	*MAJORCA	METRICS	SIROCCO
JUGULAR	PYGMEAN	MALACCA	NEGLECT	TINTACK
JURYMAN	PYJAMAS	*MATLOCK	PEACOCK	VIADUCT
KUMQUAT	SYNODAL	MATTOCK	PENANCE	*WISBECH.
LUSTRAL	TYPICAL	+MAURICE	PERFECT	FLOUNCE
MUDFLAP	+WYNDHAM.	PADDOCK	+REBECCA	FLUENCY
MUDFLAT	CZARDAS	PADLOCK	REFLECT	PLAY-ACT
MUSICAL		+PATRICK	REFRACT	PLIANCY.
MUSK-RAT	+BARNABY	RANSACK	REGENCY	*AMERICA
NUCLEAR	MARIMBA	RAT-RACE	REJOICE	EMBRACE
NUMERAL	*NAIROBI	TACTICS	REPLACE	IMPEACH.
NUPTIAL	WALLABY.	TAPIOCA	REPLICA	ANALECT
OUTPLAY	SCRUBBY	VACANCY	RESPECT	ANGLICE
OUTSPAN	REDOUBT.	VALANCE	RETOUCH	ENFORCE
OUTSTAY	SHRUBBY	VALENCE	RETRACE	ENHANCE
OUTWEAR	THEREBY	VALENCY	RETRACT	ENOUNCE
PULLMAN	WHEREBY.	+WALLACE	SEA-SICK	INEXACT
PURITAN	DISROBE	WARLOCK	SECRECY	INFANCY
QUADRAT	MICROBE.	*WARWICK.	+SERVICE	INFLECT
QUARTAN	PLACEBO.	ABREACT	SETBACK	INFLICT
QUINTAN	COPAIBA.	ABROACH	TENANCY	INSPECT
QUONDAM	CRY-BABY	ABSENCE.	+TERENCE	INVOICE
RUFFIAN	*GRIMSBY.	ICE-PACK	TERRACE	UNBRACE
RUNAWAY	ASCRIBE.	SCIENCE	TESTACY	UNFROCK
RUSSIAN	LULLABY	SCRATCH	VENDACE	UNHITCH
SUBDEAN		SCREECH	VERDICT	UNSTICK
SUBDUAL	BALANCE	SCRUNCH.	VERRUCA	UNSTUCK.
SUNBEAM	BANNOCK	ADJUNCT	WEDLOCK.	COGENCY
SUNDIAL	BARRACK	ADVANCE	AFFLICT	COLLECT
SUN-TRAP	CADENCE	EDIFICE.	OFFENCE.	COMPACT
SURCOAT	CADENCY	BED-ROCK	CHALICE	CONCOCT
*SURINAM	*CANNOCK	BESEECH	PHYSICS.	CONDUCE
SUTURAL	CAPRICE	BEWITCH	AIR-LOCK	CONNECT
TUBULAR	CARRACK	DEBAUCH	DIALECT	CONTACT
TUESDAY	CASSOCK	DEBOUCH	DIPTYCH	CONVICT
TUTELAR	FAIENCE	DECENCY	DISSECT	COPPICE
*YUCATAN.	FALLACY	DEFENCE	DISTICH	CORNICE
OVARIAN	*GATWICK	DEFLECT	DIVORCE	CORRECT
OVERLAP	HADDOCK	DEFROCK	FINANCE	COSSACK
OVERLAY	HAMMOCK	DEFUNCT	FINBACK	COWLICK
OVERRAN	*HARWICH	DEHISCE	GIMMICK	FOSSICK
OVERSAW	HASSOCK	+DERRICK	HILLOCK	GOTHICK
OVERTAX.	HATRACK	DETRACT	KILLICK	HOGBACK
SWAGMAN.	HAYCOCK	FELUCCA	LICENCE	HOSPICE
EXILIAN	HAYRICK	FETLOCK	LIMBECK	MONARCH
EXPOSAL	*JAMAICA	HEMLOCK	NIBLICK	*MOROCCO
OXONIAN.	KALMUCK	HENPECK	PIBROCH	NONSUCH
CYNICAL	LATENCY	+JESSICA	PIDDOCK	*NORWICH
LYRICAL	LATTICE	*KESWICK	PINNACE	POLACCA
NYLGHAU	MAFFICK	LETTUCE	SILENCE	POLLACK

+POLLOCK	BULLOCK	SEASIDE	CRUSADE	CANTEEN
PORRECT	BURDOCK	SECLUDE	*GRENADA	CARAMEL
PORTICO	BUTTOCK	TESTUDO	GRENADE	CARRIED
POTENCE	CURRACH	TETRODE	PRECEDE	CARRIER
POTENCY	CUT-BACK	VERANDA.	PRELUDE	CASHIER
POTLUCK	DURANCE	EFFENDI	PRESIDE	CASTLED
ROEBUCK	FURNACE	OFF-SIDE.	PROSODY	CATCHER
ROMANCE	GUNLOCK	CHARADE	PROVIDE	CATERER
ROWLOCK	HUMMOCK	THORIDE.	TRAGEDY.	CAT-EYED
TOBACCO.	JUSTICE	DIOXIDE	ASTRIDE.	DABBLED
*IPSWICH	OUTBACK	+MIRANDA	BUSHIDO	DAISIED
SPINACH	OUTFACE	PINTADO	CUSTODY	DALLIED
SPLOTCH.	PURBECK	RIP-TIDE	NUCLIDE	DANGLED
SQUELCH	RUN-BACK	+VIVALDI.	OUTRIDE	DAPPLED
SQUINCH.	SUBJECT	ALIDADE	OUTRODE	DAUNTED
ARDENCY	SUFFICE	ALREADY	OUTSIDE	DAWDLER
CREVICE	SURFACE	*FLORIDA.	PUDENDA	DAZZLED
DRY-DOCK	SUSPECT	IMPLODE.	SUBSIDE	EARLIER
EROTICA	TUSSUCK.	ANYBODY	SUBSIDY	EARTHED
ERRANCY	AVARICE	INCLUDE	SUCCADE	EARTHEN
GRIMACE	OVERACT	INNARDS	SUICIDE.	FAINTED
ORIFICE	OVIDUCT.	INTRUDE	AVOCADO.	FALSIES
PREDICT	EXTINCT	ONWARDS	EXCLUDE	FANCIED
PREFACE	EXTRACT	UNHANDY	EXPLODE	FANCIER
PREFECT		UNREADY.	EXTRUDE.	FARRIER
PRELACY	BALLADE	COCKADE	CYANIDE	FARTHER
PREPUCE	CALENDS	COLLIDE	HYDRIDE	FAULTED
PRIMACY	CARBIDE	COLLUDE	HYMNODY	GABBLED
PRIVACY	CASCADE	COMMODE		+GABRIEL
PRODUCE	CATHODE	COMRADE	BABBLER	GAGGLED
PRODUCT	HAGGADA	CONCEDE	BAFFLED	+GALILEO
PROJECT	+MATILDA	CONFIDE	BANDIED	GAMBLER
PROTECT	RAWHIDE	CORRODE	BANQUET	GARAGED
TRADUCE	SARCODE	COUVADE	BANSHEE	GARBLED
TRISECT	WAYSIDE.	COWHIDE	BARONET	GARGLED
TROUNCE	EBB-TIDE	FORBADE	BARRIER	HABITED
TRUANCY	OBTRUDE.	JOY-RIDE	BARYTES	HACKLET
URGENCY	OCCLUDE.	ROTUNDA	BASINET	*HACKNEY
WRYNECK.	ADDENDA.	ROULADE	BATTLED	HAGGLER
ASKANCE	BEDSIDE	TOPSIDE	BAYONET	HAIRNET
ESSENCE	+BELINDA	TORNADO	CABARET	HALOGEN
OSTRICH.	*BERMUDA	TORPEDO	CABINET	HAMSTER
ATTRACT	DEGRADE	TOWARDS.	CACKLED	HANDLER
STATICE	DEICIDE	EPISODE	CADAVER	HANDSEL
STATICS	DETRUDE	UP-GRADE	CAJOLED	*HANOVER
STAUNCH	+KENNEDY	UPWARDS.	CALOMEL	HAPPIER
STOMACH	PENTODE	BRAVADO	CALUMET	HARDIER
STRETCH.	PEPTIDE	BRIGADE	CALYCES	HARD-SET
AUSPICE	PERFIDY	BROCADE	CAMP-BED	HARRIED
BULLACE	PERVADE	BROMIDE	CANDIED	HARRIER

+HARRIET	PALFREY	TALUNED	SCALPER	BELLIED
HAS-BEEN	PALSIED	*TANGIER	SCAMPED	BELOVED
HATCHER	PANACEA	TANGLED	SCAMPER	BEMUSED
HATCHET	PANNIER	TANGOED	SCANNED	BENCHER
HAULIER	PANTHER	TAPERED	SCARCER	BERATED
HAUNTED	PANTIES	TAPSTER	SCARLET	BERTHED
HAVENER	PARADED	TARRIED	SCARPED	BESIDES
HAYSEED	PARAPET	TARTLET	SCARRED	BESTREW
JACONET	PARCHED	TASTIER	SCARVES	BETAKEN
JANGLED	PAROLED	TATTLER	SCATHED	BETIMES
JAUNTED	PARQUET	TAUNTED	SCATTER	BETOKEN
LACQUER	PARRIED	TAX-FREE	SCENTED	BETWEEN
+LAERTES	PARSLEY	VACATED	SCHEMER	*CELEBES
LAMPREY	PARTIED	VALETED	SCOLDED	CENTNER
LASSOED	PARTNER	VARICES	SCONCED	DEBASED
LATCHED	PATCHED	VAULTED	SCOOPED	DEBATED
LAUGHED	RACQUET	VAULTER	SCOOTER	DEBITED
LAUNDER	RADDLED	VAUNTED	SCORNED	DECAYED
*MAESTEG	RADICEL	WADDLED	SCOURER	DECIBEL
MAJORED	RADICES	WAFFLED	SCOUTED	DECIDED
MALMSEY	RAFFLED	WAGERED	SCOWLED	DECODED
MANAGED	RALLIED	WAGGLED	SCRAPER	DECODER
MANAGER	RAMBLED	WAGONER	SCREWED	DECOYED
MANATEE	RAMBLER	WAISTED	SCRIBER	DECRIER
MANDREL	RANCHER	WALTZED	SCUDDED	DEDUCED
MANGLED	RANKLED	WANGLED	SCUFFED	DEEP-SEA
MANLIER	+RAPHAEL	WARBLER	SCULLER	DEFACED
MANTLED	RATCHET	WASTREL	SCULPED	DEFAMED
MANURED	RATTLER	WATCHED	SCUMMED	DEFILED
MARBLED	RAVAGED	WATERED	SCUPPER	DEFINED
MARCHED	RAZORED	WATTLED	SCUTTER	DEFUSED
MARINER	SADDLER	WAVERED	SCYTHED.	DEIFIED
MARQUEE	SAINTED	YACHTED.	ADAPTED	DEIGNED
MARRIED	SALLIED	ABDOMEN	ADAPTER	DELATED
MARTLET	SALUTED	ABETTED	ADHERED	DELAYED
MATCHED	SAMISEN	ABJURED	ADMIRER	DELETED
MATCHET	SAMOYED	ABORTED	ADMIXED	DELIVER
MATINEE	SAMPLED	ABRADED	ADVISED	DELUDED
+MATTHEW	SAMPLER	ABUTTER	ADVISER	DELUGED
MATURED	SANDIER	OBLIGED.	EDIFIED	DEMISED
MAUNDER	SARACEN	ACCEDED	ODYSSEY.	DEMOTED
+MAUREEN	SATCHEL	ACCUSED	AERATED	DENIZEN
NANKEEN	SAUNTER	+ACHATES	BEACHED	DENOTED
NARTHEX	SAVAGED	OCTOBER	+BEATLES	DENUDED
NASTIER	TABOOED	SCABBED	BEDIZEN	DEPOSED
PADDLED	TACKLER	SCABIES	BEECHEN	DERIDED
PAINTED	TAINTED	SCAFFED	BEHAVED	DERIVED
PAINTER	TALIPED	SCALDED	BELATED	DESIRED
*PAISLEY	TALLIED	SCALPED	BELAYED	DETERED
PALAVER	TALLNES	SCALPEL	BELCHER	DEVISED

420

*DEVIZES	OERSTED	RESINED	IGNORED.	CHUKKER
DEVOTED	PEARLED	RESUMED	CHAFFER	CHURNED
DEVOTEE	PEARLER	RETAKEN	CHAINED	CHUTNEY
FEASTED	PEBBLED	RETCHED	CHAIRED	GHOSTED
FEATHER	PEDDLED	RETIRED	CHAMBER	PHRASED
FEIGNED	PEDICEL	RETRIED	CHAMFER	SHACKED
FEOFFEE	PENATES	REVERED	CHANCED	SHADIER
FERRIED	PEOPLED	REVILED	CHANCEL	SHAGGED
FETCHED	PERCHED	REVISED	CHANGED	SHAMMED
HEAD-SET	PERIGEE	REVIVER	CHANNEL	SHARKED
HEARKEN	PERPLEX	REVOKED	CHANTED	SHARPEN
HEARTED	PERUSED	SEAWEED	CHAPLET	SHARPER
HEARTEN	PETERED	SECEDED	CHAPPED	SHATTER
HEATHEN	REACHED	SECURED	CHAPTER	SHEARED
+HEATHER	REARMED	SEDATED	CHARGED	SHEAVES
HEAVIER	REBATED	SEDUCER	CHARGER	SHEBEEN
HECKLER	REBORED	SEEDBED	+CHARLES	SHEERED
HEDDLES	REBUKED	SEETHED	CHARMER	SHEETED
HEISTED	RECEDED	SELTZER	CHARNEL	SHELLED
HELICES	RECITER	SERRIED	CHARRED	+SHELLEY
+JEFFREY	RECOVER	SETTLED	CHARTED	SHELTER
JELLIED	REDUCED	SETTLER	CHARTER	SHELVED
+JEZEBEL	RE-ENTER	SEVERED	CHASTEN	*SHEPPEY
KECKLED	REFACED	SEWERED	CHATTED	SHERBET
KESTREL	REFEREE	TEACHER	CHATTEL	SHEREEF
LEACHED	REFINED	TELEXED	CHATTER	SHIFTER
LEAFLET	REFUGEE	TELPHER	+CHAUCER	SHIMMER
+LEANDER	REFUSED	TEMPLET	CHEAPEN	SHINNED
LEARNED	REFUTED	TEMPTER	CHEATED	SHIPPED
LEASHED	REGALED	TENONED	CHECKED	SHIPPEN
LEATHER	REGIMEN	TENT-PEG	CHECKER	SHIPPER
LEGATED	REIGNED	TERRIER	CHEEPER	SHIRKER
LEGATEE	RELATED	VENOMED	CHEERED	+SHIRLEY
LEISTER	RELAXED	+VERMEER	CHEESED	SHOALED
LEMURES	RELINED	VERNIER	*CHELSEA	SHOCKER
LEVERED	RELIVED	WEARIER	CHEQUER	SHOOTER
LEVERET	REMOVED	WEATHER	*CHESTER	SHOPPED
MEANDER	REMOVER	WEIGHED	CHICKEN	SHOPPER
MEASLES	RENEWED	WELSHER	CHILLED	SHORTED
MEDDLED	*RENFREW	*WEMBLEY	CHIMNEY	SHORTEN
MENACED	RENTIER	WENCHED	CHINKED	SHORTER
MERITED	REPAPER	YEARNED.	CHINNED	SHOUTED
MESSIER	REPINED	AFFINED	CHIPPED	SHRIVEL
NECKLET	REPLIED	AFFIXED	CHIRPED	SHUCKED
NEEDLED	REPOSED	EFFASED	CHOPPED	SHUDDER
NEGATED	REPUTED	EFFUSED	CHOPPER	SHUNNED
NEIGHED	REQUIEM	OFFERED	CHOWDER	SHUNTED
NEITHER	RESCUER	OFFICER.	CHUCKED	SHUSHED
NESTLED	RESIDED	EGESTED	CHUFFED	SHUTTER
NETTLED	RESILED	IGNITED	CHUGGED	SHYSTER

THANKED	CIRCLED	LITTLER	TIGHTEN	BLANKED
THEOREM	CIRCLET	MIAOWED	TIGHTER	BLANKET
THICKEN	CITADEL	+MICHAEL	TIMBREL	BLARNEY
THICKER	CITIZEN	MIDDLED	TINGLED	BLASTED
THICKET	CIVVIES	+MILDRED	TIPPLER	BLEATED
THIEVED	DIALLED	MINARET	TIPSTER	BLEEPED
THINKER	DIBBLED	MINGLED	TIPTOED	BLENDED
THINNED	DIDDLER	MINIVER	TISSUED	BLESSED
THINNER	DILATED	MINSTER	VINTNER	BLINDED
THITHER	DILUTED	MINUTED	VISITED	BLINKED
THRIVED	DILUTER	MISDEED	WIDOWER	BLISTER
THRIVEN	DIMPLED	MISUSED	WIELDED	BLOATED
THRONED	DIOPTER	MIZZLED	WIGGLED	BLOATER
THROWER	DIRTIED	NIBBLED	+WILFRED	BLOCKED
THUDDED	DISOBEY	NIGGLED	WIMPLED	BLOODED
THUMBED	DITCHED	*NINEVEH	WINCHED	BLOOMED
THUMPED	DITCHER	PICKLED	WINDIER	BLOOMER
THUNDER	DIVIDED	PICOTEE	WINKLED	BLOTTED
WHACKED	DIVINED	PICQUET	WITCHED	BLOTTER
WHARFED	DIVINER	PIE-EYED	WITTIER	BLUBBER
WHARVES	FIBSTER	PIERCED	WIZENED	BLUFFER
WHATEER	FIDDLED	PIKELET	YIELDED.	BLUNDER
WHEATEN	FIDDLER	PILCHER	EJECTED.	BLUNTED
WHEELED	FIELDED	PILOTED	SKIDDED	BLURRED
WHEEZED	FIELDER	PINCHED	SKILLED	BLURTED
WHELPED	FIFTEEN	PIONEER	SKILLET	BLUSHED
WHENEER	FIGHTER	PIRATED	SKIMMER	BLUSTER
WHEREER	FIGURED	PITCHED .	SKIMPED	CLACKED
WHETHER	FILCHED	PITCHER	SKINNED	CLAIMED
WHETTED	FITCHEW	PIVOTED	SKIPPED	CLAMBER
WHIFFED	FIXATED	RIDDLED	SKIPPER	CLAMPED
WHIMPER	FIZZLED	RIFFLER	SKIRLED	CLAMPER
WHIMSEY	GIGGLER	RIGHTED	SKIRTED	CLANGED
WHIPPED	HIGGLER	RINGLET	SKITTER	CLANGER
WHIPPET	HIPSTER	RIPPLED	SKULKED.	CLANKED
WHIRLED	HITCHED	RISKIER	ALBUMEN	CLAP-NET
WHIRRED	JIGGLED	RIVETER	ALERTED	CLAPPED
WHISKED	JINGLED	RIVULET	ALIENEE	CLAPPER
WHISKER	KINDLER	SICK-BED	ALLAYED	CLASHED
WHISKEY	KINDRED	SIGHTED	ALLEGED	CLASPED
WHISPER	KINGLET	SILLIER	ALLOWED	CLASSED
WHITHER	KINKLED	SINGLED	ALLOYED	CLATTER
WHIZZED	KITCHEN	SINGLET	ALLUDED	CLAVIER
WHOEVER	LIGHTEN	SIXTEEN	ALLURED	CLEANED
WHOOPED	LIGHTER	SIZZLED	ALMONER	CLEANER
WHOPPER.	LIMITED	TICKLER	ALTERED	CLEARED
*AINTREE	+LINDSEY	TIDDLER	BLABBED	CLEARER
BIGOTED	LINSEED	TIDDLEY	BLACKEN	CLEAVED
BIRCHED	LIONCEL	TIERCEL	BLACKER	CLEAVER
BITUMEN	LITOTES	TIERCET	BLADDER	CLICKED

422

CLICKER	FLOODED	PLOPPED	AMPUTEE	ENDOWED
CLIMBER	FLOORED	PLOTTER	+EMANUEL	ENDURED
CLINGER	FLOPPED	PLUCKED	EMBAYED	ENFACED
CLINKER	FLOURED	PLUGGED	EMBOWER	ENGAGED
CLIPPED	FLOUTED	PLUMBER	EMENDED	ENJOYED
CLIPPER	FLUNKEY	PLUMMET	EMERGED	ENLACED
CLIQUEY	FLUSHED	PLUMPER	EMITTED	ENLIVEN
CLOAKED	FLUSTER	PLUNDER	EMITTER	ENRAGED
CLOBBER	FLUTTER	PLUNGED	EMPANEL	ENROBED
CLOCKED	FLY-OVER	PLUNGER	EMPOWER	ENSILED
CLOGGED	GLACIER	PLUNKED	EMPTIER	ENSURED
CLOTHED	GLADDEN	PLUSHER	IMBIBED	ENTICED
CLOTHES	GLANCED	SLACKEN	IMBRUED	GNARLED
CLOTTED	GLAZIER	SLACKER	IMMURED	GNASHED
CLOUDED	GLEAMED	SLAMMED	IMPALED	INBREED
CLOUTED	GLEANER	SLANDER	IMPANEL	INCISED
CLOWNED	GLIMMER	SLANGED	IMPEDED	INCITED
CLUBBED	GLINTED	SLANTED	IMPLIED	INCOMER
CLUMPED	GLISTEN	SLAPPED	IMPOSED	INCUSED
CLUSTER	GLISTER	SLASHED	IMPUTED	INDICES
CLUTTER	GLITTER	SLATTED	OMITTED	INDITED
CLYSTER	GLOATED	SLEDDED	SMACKED	INDUCED
ELAPSED	GLORIED	SLEDGED	SMACKER	INFIDEL
ELBOWED	GLOSSED	SLEEKER	SMALLER	INFIXED
ELECTED	GLUTTED	SLEEPER	SMARTED	INFUSED
FLAGGED	ILL-BRED	SLEETED	SMARTEN	INHALER
FLAILED	OLDSTER	SLEEVED	SMASHED	INHERED
FLANGED	+OLIVIER	SLENDER	SMASHER	INHUMED
FLANKER	PLACKET	SLICKER	SMEARED	INJURED
FLANNEL	PLAGUED	SLIMMER	SMIRKED	INSIDER
FLAPPED	PLAINER	SLIPPED	SMITTEN	INSURED
FLAPPER	PLAITED	SLIPPER	SMOTHER	INSURER
FLASHED	PLANKED	SLITHER	SMUDGED	INTEGER
FLASHER	PLANNED	SLOBBER	SMUTTED	INTONED
FLATLET	PLANNER	SLOGGER	UMPIRED	INURNED
FLATTEN	PLANTED	SLOPPED	UMPTEEN.	INVADER
FLATTER	PLANTER	SLOSHED	*ANDOVER	INVITED
FLECKED	PLASTER	SLOTTED	ANGERED	INVOKED
FLEDGED	PLATTED	SLUBBED	ANGRIER	INWOVEN
FLEETED	PLATTER	SLUGGED	ANISEED	KNACKER
FLESHED	PLAYLET	SLUICED	+ANNABEL	KNAPPED
FLICKED	PLAYPEN	SLUMBER	ANNEXED	KNEADED
FLICKER	PLEADER	SLUMMED	ANNOYED	KNEELED
FLIPPER	PLEASED	SLUMPED	ANNULET	KNEELER
FLIRTED	PLEATED	SLURRED	ANOTHER	KNELLED
FLITTED	PLEDGED	+ULYSSES.	ANTIGEN	KNITTED
FLITTER	PLEDGEE	AMASSED	ENABLED	KNITTER
FLOATER	PLEDGET	AMENDED	ENACTED	KNOBBED
FLOCKED	PLODDER	AMERCED	ENCAGED	KNOCKED
FLOGGED	PLONKED	AMMETER	ENCASED	KNOCKER

KNOTTED	BOGGLER	COWERED	LOATHED	ROOMIER
KNURLED	BOLONEY	COZENER	LOBBIED	ROOSTER
ONE-EYED	BOLSTER	+DOLORES	LOBSTER	ROOTLED
SNAGGED	BOOKLET	DONATED	LOCATED	ROSINED
SNAPPER	BOOSTER	DOODLED	LOFTIER	ROTATED
SNARLED	BOOTLEG	DOSSIER	LOOK-SEE	ROUGHEN
SNEAKED	BOTCHER	DOUBLED	+LORELEI	ROUGHER
SNEERED	BOTTLED	DOUBLET	LOUNGER	ROUNDEL
SNEEZED	*BOULDER	DOUBTED	LOW-BRED	ROUNDER
SNICKER	BOULTER	DOUBTER	MOBSTER	ROUSTED
SNIFFED	BOUNCER	DOUCHED	MOISTEN	ROWDIER
SNIGGER	BOUNDER	DOWAGER	MONEYED	ROWELED
SNIPPED	BOUQUET	FOCUSED	MONGREL	SOBERED
SNIPPET	BOURREE	FOGGIER	MONOMER	SOLACED
SNOGGED	BOX-TREE	FOISTED	MONSTER	SOLDIER
SNOOKER	COACHED	FONDLED	MOOCHED	SOOTHED
SNOOPER	COAL-BED	FORAGER	MOORHEN	SOUGHED
SNOOZED	COARSEN	FORAMEN	MOTIVED	SOUNDED
SNORTER	COASTED	FORAYED	MOTORED	SOZZLED
SNUBBED	COASTER	FORELEG	MOTTLED	TOASTER
SNUFFED	COBBLER	FORESEE	MOULDED	TODDLER
SNUGGED	COCHLEA	FOREVER	MOULDER	+TOLKIEN
UNACTED	COCKNEY	+FORSTER	MOULTED	TONGUED
UNAIDED	CODDLED	FOUNDER	MOUNDED	TOOTHED
UNAIRED	COERCED	GOBBLER	MOUNTED	TOOTLED
UNARMED	COHERER	+GODFREY	MOURNER	TOPPLED
UNASKED	COLLEEN	GOGGLED	MOUTHED	TOUCHED
UNBOWED	COLLIER	GOURMET	NOBBLER	TOUGHEN
UNCARED	COLONEL	HOARDER	NOISIER	TOUGHER
UNCASED	COMFREY	HOBBLED	NOMINEE	TOURNEY
UNCOVER	COMPEER	HOICKED	NON-USER	TOUSLED
UNFIXED	COMPLEX	HOISTED	NORTHER	VOLUTED
UNHOPED	CONIFER	HOLSTER	NOTCHED	VOMITED
UNIFIED	CONQUER	HONEYED	NOTICED	VOUCHER
UNLADEN	CORONER	HOPPLED	POACHED	VOYAGER
UNMOVED	CORONET	*HORNSEA	POACHER	WOBBLED
UNNAMED	CORSLET	HOUNDED	POINTED	WOODIER
UNQUIET	COTTIER	HOVERED	POINTER	WOOLLEN
UNRAVEL	COUCHED	HOWEVER	POLICED	WORRIED
UNRISEN	COUGHED	IODIZED	POLYMER	WORRIER
UNROBED	COULTER	IONIZED	POP-EYED	WORSTED
UNSCREW	COUNSEL	JOGGLED	POSITED	WOUNDED
UNSEXED	COUNTED	JOINDER	POUCHED	YOUNGER.
UNTAMED	COUNTER	JOINTED	POUNCED	APHIDES
UNTAXED	COUPLER	JOINTER	POUNDER	APPAREL
UNTRIED	COUPLET	JOLLIER	POWERED	APPLIED
UNYOKED	COURIER	JOSTLED	ROASTED	EPAULET
UNZONED.	COURSER	JOUNCED	ROASTER	EPITHET
BOARDER	COVERED	JOURNEY	ROCKIER	OPPOSER
BOASTER	COVETED	JOUSTED	ROISTER	SPANCEL

424

SPANIEL	AROUSED	CREEPER	DRIPPED	GREASER
SPANKED	ARRIVED	CRESSET	DROOLED	GREATER
SPANKER	*ARUNDEL	CRESTED	DROOPED	GREAVES
SPANNED	BRACKEN	CRIBBED	DROPLET	GREENER
SPANNER	BRACKET	CRIBBER	DROPPED	GREETED
SPARKED	BRAGGED	CRICKED	DROPPER	GRIEVED
SPARRED	BRAIDED	CRICKET	DROWNED	GRILLED
SPATTER	BRAINED	CRIMPED	DROWSED	GRIMMER
SPAWNED	BRAISED	CRINGED	DRUBBED	GRINDER
SPEAKER	BRANDED	CRISPER	DRUDGED	GRINNED
SPEARED	BRAWLER	CRITTER	DRUGGED	GRIPPED
SPECIES	BRAZIER	CROAKER	DRUGGET	GRITTED
SPECKED	BREADED	CROCHET	DRUMMED	GROANED
SPEEDED	BREAKER	CROCKET	DRUMMER	GROINED
SPEEDER	BREEDER	CROFTER	DRUNKEN	GROMMET
SPELLED	BREVIER	CROOKED	ERECTED	GROOMED
SPELLER	BRICKED	CROONER	ERUPTED	GROOVER
SPELTER	BRIDGED	CROPPED	FREAKED	GROSSED
+SPENCER	+BRIDGET	CROPPER	FREEZER	GROUPED
SPENDER	BRIDLED	CROQUET	FRESHEN	GROUSER
SPICIER	BRIMMER	CROSIER	FRESHER	GROUTED
SPIELER	BRIQUET	CROSSED	FRESHET	GROWLER
SPILLED	BRISKET	CROWDED	FRETTED	GRUBBED
SPINNER	BROADEN	CROWNED	FRILLED	GRUBBER
SPINNEY	BROADER	*CROYDEN	FRINGED	GRUDGED
SPIRTED	BROCKET	CRUISED	FRISKED	GRUMMET
SPITTED	BROILER	CRUISER	FRISKET	GRUNTED
SPLAYED	+BRONWEN	CRUMPET	FRITTED	KRAALED
SPLICED	BROODED	CRUPPER	FRITTER	KRIMMER
SPLINED	BROTHEL	CRUSHED	FRIZZED	ORBITED
SPOILED	BROTHER	CRUSTED	FROCKED	ORDERED
SPONDEE	BROWNED	CRYOGEN	FROGGED	ORPHREY
SPONGER	BROWSED	DRAFTED	FRONTED	PRAISED
SPOOFED	BRUISED	DRAFTEE	FROSTED	PRANCED
SPOOLED	BRUSHED	DRAGGED	FROTHED	PRANKED
SPOONED	CRABBED	DRAG-NET	FROWNED	PRAWNED
SPORTED	CRACKED	DRAINED	FRUITER	PREENED
SPOTTED	CRACKER	DRAINER	GRABBED	PREMIER
SPOTTER	CRAMMED	DRATTED	GRABBER	PRESSED
SPOUTED	CRAMMER	DRAWLED	GRAFTED	PRESSER
SPRAYER	CRAMPED	DREADED	GRAFTER	PREVIEW
SPRUCED	CRANKED	DREAMER	GRAINED	PRICKER
SPURNED	CRASHED	DREDGER	GRANDEE	PRICKET
SPURRED	CRAWLER	*DRESDEN	GRANDER	PRIGGED
SPURTED	CRAZIER	DRESSED	GRANTED	PRIMMED
SPUTTER.	CREAKED	DRESSER	GRANTEE	PRINTED
EQUATED	CREAMED	DRIBLET	GRAPNEL	PRINTER
SQUARED.	CREAMER	DRIFTER	GRASPER	PRITHEE
ARBITER	CREASED	DRILLED	GRASSED	PROBLEM
ARMIGER	CREATED	DRINKER	GREASED	PROCEED

425

PRODDED	TROUPER	STANNEL	STUFFED	HURTLED
PRODDER	TRUCKED	STAPLER	STUMPED	HUSTLER
PROFFER	TRUDGED	STARLET	STUNNER	HUTCHED
PRONGED	TRUMPED	STARRED	STUNTED	JUBILEE
PROOFED	TRUMPET	STARTED	STUTTER	JUGGLED
PROPHET	TRUSSED	STARTER	STYMIED	JUGGLER
PROPPED	TRUSTED	STARVED	UTTERED.	JUMBLED
PROSPER	TRUSTEE	STASHED	AUDITED	JUNIPER
PROUDER	TRYSTED	STEAMED	AUGURED	+JUPITER
PROWLER	WRAPPED	STEAMER	AUSSIES	LUCKIER
TRACHEA	WRAPPER	STEELED	BUBBLED	LUNCHED
TRACKED	WREAKED	STEEPED	BUCKLED	LURCHED
TRACKER	WRECKED	STEEPEN	BUILDER	LUXATED
TRAILED	WRECKER	STEEPER	BULLIED	MUDDIED
TRAILER	WRESTED	STEERER	BUNCHED	MUDDLED
TRAINEE	WRINGER	STEMMED	BUNDLED	MUFFLED
TRAINER	WRITHED	+STEPHEN	BUNGLER	MUFFLER
TRAMMED	WRITTEN.	STEPPED	BURBLED	MULCHED
TRAMMEL	ASHAMED	STERNER	BURGHER	MUMBLED
TRAMPED	ASPIRED	STICKED	BURGLED	MUNCHED
TRAPPED	ASSAYED	STICKER	*BURNLEY	MUSCLED
TRAPPER	ASSIZES	STIFFEN	BUSTLED	MUTAGEN
TRAPSED	ASSUMED	STIFFER	BUTCHER	MUTATED
TRASHED	ASSURED	STIFLED	CUDDLED	MUZZLED
TRAWLER	+ASTRAEA	STILLED	CURDLED	NUZZLED
TREATED	ASUNDER	STILLER	CURRIED	OUTGREW
TREBLED	ESCAPED	STILTED	CURTSEY	OUTLIER
TREKKED	ESCAPEE	STINKER	DUELLED	PUDDLER
TRENDED	ESSAYED	STINTED	DUELLER	PUNCHED
TRESSED	ESSENES	STIRRED	DURAMEN	PUNSTER
TRICKED	+ISHMAEL	STOCKED	DUSKIER	PURLIEU
TRIFLED	PSALTER	STONIER	DUSTIER	PURPLED
TRIFLER	USHERED	STOOGED	EUCHRED	PURSUER
TRIGGER	USURPER.	STOOKED	FUDDLED	PURVIEW
TRILLED	ATELIER	STOOPED	FUELLED	PUTTIER
TRIMMED	ATTIRED	STOPPED	FUMBLER	PUZZLER
TRIMMER	ATTUNED	STOPPER	FURRIER	QUACKED
TRINKET	STABBED	STORIED	FURTHER	QUADREL
TRIOLET	STABLED	STORMED	GUARDED	QUAFFED
TRIPLED	STACKED	STOUTER	GUELDER	QUAILED
TRIPLET	STAFFED	STRAFED	GUESSED	QUARREL
TRIPLEX	STAGGER	STRAYED	GUILDER	QUARTER
TRIPPER	STAINED	STREWED	GURGLED	QUARTET
TROCHEE	*STAINES	STRIKER	GUZZLER	QUASHED
TRODDEN	STALKED	STRIPED	HUDDLED	QUEENED
TROLLED	STALKER	STRIVEN	HUMBLED	QUEERER
TROLLEY	STALLED	STROKED	HUNCHED	QUELLED
TROMMEL	STAMMER	STUBBED	HUNDRED	QUERIED
TROOPER	STAMPED	STUDDED	HURDLER	QUESTED
TROTTER	+STANLEY	STUDIED	HURRIED	QUICKEN

QUICKER	SWABBED	EXCUSED	GIRAFFE	*KATANGA
QUIETEN	SWABBER	EXERTED	KICK-OFF	MASSAGE
QUIETER	SWAGGER	EXHALED	LIFT-OFF	PACKAGE
QUILLED	SWAMPED	EXHUMED	LIQUEFY	PASSAGE
QUILTED	SWANKED	EXISTED	MIDRIFF	+RALEIGH
QUINTET	*SWANSEA	EXPIRED	MIDWIFE	RAMPAGE
QUIPPED	SWAPPED	EXPOSED	SIGNIFY	SALVAGE
QUITTED	SWARMED	EXULTED.	VITRIFY.	SAPSAGO
QUITTER	SWASHED	GYRATED	SKI-LIFT.	SAUSAGE
QUIZZED	SWATHED	LYNCHED	ALFALFA	TANKAGE
RUDDIER	SWATTED	NYMPHET	CLARIFY	TANNAGE
RUDDLED	SWATTER	PYRITES.	GLORIFY	VANTAGE
RUFFLED	SWEARER	+EZEKIEL	PLAY-OFF.	WASTAGE
RUMBLED	SWEATED		AMPLIFY.	WATTAGE
RUMPLED	SWEATER	BAILIFF	ENFEOFF	YARDAGE.
RUSTIER	SWEEPER	CAITIFF	ENGRAFT.	ABRIDGE.
RUSTLED	SWEETEN	CALCIFY	FORTIFY	ACREAGE
RUSTLER	SWEETER	*CARDIFF	HORRIFY	ECOLOGY
SUBDUED	SWELLED	CAST-OFF	JOLLIFY	SCOURGE
SUCCEED	SWELTER	DAMNIFY	MOLLIFY	SCRAGGY
SUCKLED	SWERVED	DANDIFY	MORTIFY	SCUTAGE.
SUGARED	SWIFTER	FALSIFY	PONTIFF	ADJUDGE.
SULLIED	SWIGGED	*MACDUFF	PONTIFY.	BESIEGE
SUNNIER	SWILLED	MAGNIFY	SPECIFY	DERANGE
SUPPLED	SWIMMER	MASTIFF	SPIN-OFF.	GEOLOGY
SURLIER	SWINGER	RAKE-OFF	SQUIFFY.	HERBAGE
SUTURED	SWIRLED	SALSIFY	CRUCIFY	LEAFAGE
TUMBLED	SWISHED	SATISFY	GRATIFY.	LEAKAGE
TUMBLER	SWOLLEN	TAKE-OFF.	STUPEFY.	MESSAGE
TUMBREL	SWOONED	ACETIFY	DULCIFY	NEGLIGE
TURNKEY	SWOOPED	ACIDIFY	JUSTIFY	NEOLOGY
TUSSLED	SWOPPED	SCARIFY	MUMMIFY	PEERAGE
TUTORED.	SWOTTED	SCORIFY	NULLIFY	PEONAGE
AVAILED	TWANGED	SCRUFFY.	PULPIFY	REVENGE
AVENGER	TWEAKED	BEATIFY	PUTREFY	SEA-LEGS
AVERRED	TWEEZER	CERTIFY	QUALIFY	SEEPAGE
AVERTED	TWIGGED	PETRIFY	RUSSIFY.	TEENAGE
EVACUEE	TWILLED	RECTIFY	MYSTIFY	VENTAGE
EVERTED	TWINGED	SEND-OFF		VERTIGO
EVICTED	TWINNED	TERRIFY	BAGGAGE	VESTIGE.
EVINCED	TWIN-SET	TESTIFY	BANDAGE	*CHICAGO
EVOLVED	TWIRLED	VERSIFY	BARRAGE	THEURGY
OVERSEA	TWISTER	WELL-OFF.	CABBAGE	THROUGH.
OVERSEE	TWITTED	AGRAFFE.	CARNAGE	BIOLOGY
OVERSET	TWITTER	KHALIFA	CARTAGE	DIVERGE
OVERSEW.	TWO-STEP.	SHERIFF	FALANGE	DIVULGE
AWAITED	EXACTED	SHOW-OFF.	FARRAGO	HIDALGO
AWARDED	EXALTED	AIRLIFT	GAMBOGE	LINEAGE
DWARFED	EXCISED	DIGNIFY	GARBAGE	LINKAGE
DWELLER	EXCITED	DISTAFF	HAULAGE	LITURGY

MILEAGE	TONNAGE	LENGTHY	BALDRIC	PAROTID
MINTAGE	VOLTAGE	*LESOTHO	+BALDWIN	PARSNIP
PIERAGE	ZOOLOGY.	WEALTHY.	BANKSIA	RACEMIC
PILLAGE	APANAGE	CHURCHY	BARGAIN	RAREBIT
TIDINGS	APOLOGY	SHEATHE	BARMAID	RATAFIA
TILLAGE	SPLODGE	THOUGHT.	BASILIC	RAT-TAIL
VILLAGE	SPLURGE	DIARCHY	CALORIC	RAVELIN
VINTAGE.	SPRINGY.	+TIMOTHY.	CALORIE	SALICIN
SKY-HIGH.	UPSTAGE	SKETCHY.	CAMBRIC	SAPPHIC
ALLERGY	UPSURGE.	+BLANCHE	CAPROIC	SATANIC
PLUMAGE.	ARRAIGN	BLOTCHY	CAPTAIN	SATIRIC
EMBARGO	ARRANGE	SLEIGHT.	CAROTID	SATYRIC
IMPINGE	BREWAGE	EMPATHY	CAROTIN	TABETIC
UMBRAGE.	CRANAGE	SMOOCHY.	CAUSTIC	TABLOID
ANALOGY	PRESAGE	ANARCHY	DAUPHIN	+VALERIE
ENGORGE	PRODIGY	INSIGHT	FANATIC	WAGTAIL
ENLARGE	PROTEGE	SNATCHY.	FANTAIL	WARSHIP
INDULGE	PRURIGO	+DOROTHY	GAMETIC	WASSAIL.
INNINGS	TRILOGY.	GOUACHE	GANGLIA	+ABIGAIL
INVEIGH	ASSUAGE.	TONIGHT	GAS-MAIN	ABIOTIC
UNDERGO	OTOLOGY.	WORK-SHY.	GASTRIC	ABOULIA
UNHINGE.	STORAGE	SPLASHY	HAIRPIN	ABSTAIN.
BONDAGE	STOWAGE	SPRIGHT	HALF-WIT	ACCLAIM
BOROUGH	STRANGE	UPRIGHT	HAMITIC	ACERBIC
BOSCAGE	STRINGY.	UPTIGHT.	HAPLOID	ACLINIC
BOTARGO	BUOYAGE	SQUASHY.	HARE-LIP	ACRYLIC
COINAGE	DUNNAGE	BREATHE	JACOBIN	ACTINIC
COLLAGE	GUNNAGE	BRIOCHE	JAVELIN	ECBOLIC
COLLEGE	LUGGAGE	BRONCHI	KATYDID	ECDYSIS
CONDIGN	LUMBAGO	BROUGHT	LACONIC	*OCEANIA
CONSIGN	OUTRAGE	CRUNCHY	LAMBKIN	OCEANIC
CORDAGE	RUMMAGE.	DRAUGHT	LAMP-OIL	SCEPSIS
CORKAGE	AVERAGE.	DROUGHT	LANGUID	SCEPTIC
CORSAGE	*SWANAGE.	DROUTHY	LANOLIN	SCIATIC
CORTEGE	EXPUNGE.	FRAUGHT	+LAVINIA	SCORPIO.
COTTAGE	SYNERGY	FREIGHT	LAWSUIT	ADENOID
COURAGE	SYRINGA	GROUCHY	MALARIA	ADHIBIT
DOCKAGE	SYRINGE	WREATHE	MALEFIC	IDIOTIC
FOLIAGE	ZYMURGY	WROUGHT.	MANIKIN	IDYLLIC.
FOOTAGE		ATROPHY	MANUMIT	AEROBIC
FOREIGN	CATECHU	ATTACHE	MARQUIS	BEAR-PIT
HOSTAGE	EAR-ACHE	STARCHY	MASONIC	BEATNIK
LOZENGE	*KARACHI	STROPHE.	MASTOID	BEDEVIL
MONTAGE	NAPHTHA	AUROCHS.	MAUDLIN	BEDOUIN
+MONTAGU	PANACHE	SWARTHY	+NATALIE	BEGONIA
MOORAGE	PAUNCHY		*PACIFIC	BENEFIT
PORTAGE	TALLY-HO.	BABY-SIT	PALADIN	BENZOIN
POSTAGE	BELISHA	BACCHIC	PALM-OIL	+CECILIA
ROOTAGE	DELIGHT	*BAHRAIN	PARBOIL	CENTRIC
TOLLAGE	HEALTHY	+BAKUNIN	PARESIS	CERAMIC

428

CERESIN	PENGUIN	RHOMBIC	TITANIC	ENCHAIN
CERTAIN	PERIWIG	SHELTIE	VILLAIN	ENDEMIC
CESSPIT	PERTAIN	SHINDIG	VILLEIN	ENGRAIN
CESTOID	PETUNIA	SHOWBIZ	VITAMIN	ENTERIC
DECLAIM	READMIT	THEREIN	XIPHOID.	ENTOMIC
DEFICIT	RECLAIM	THERMIC	*AJACCIO.	ENTRAIN
DEISTIC	RECRUIT	THERMIT	SKALDIC	GNATHIC
DELIMIT	REDSKIN	THIAMIN	SKEPTIC	GNOSTIC
DELPHIC	REFRAIN	THYROID	SKID-LID	INDICIA
DELTOID	REGALIA	WHEREIN.	SKYSAIL.	INERTIA
DEMERIT	REVERIE	AIRMAIL	*ALBANIA	INGRAIN
DEMONIC	SEDILIA	AIR-RAID	ALEMBIC	INHABIT
DEMOTIC	+SEGOVIA	AIRSHIP	*ALGERIA	INHERIT
DEPOSIT	SEISMIC	BISCUIT	BLASTIN	INHIBIT
DESPAIR	SEMITIC	CIRCUIT	CLARKIA	INSIPID
DESPOIL	SEQUOIA	DIBASIC	CLASSIC	INSULIN
DETRAIN	+SERAPIS	DIOPSIS	CLASTIC	INTERIM
*DETROIT	SET-FAIR	DIPLOID	+CLAUDIA	INTROIT
DEXTRIN	SEXTAIN	DISCOID	CLIPPIE	INVALID
GELATIN	TEACH-IN	DISDAIN	ELASTIC	*ONTARIO
GENERIC	TECHNIC	DISJOIN	ELASTIN	UNCHAIN
GENESIS	TENDRIL	EIDETIC	FLACCID	UNCIVIL.
GENETIC	TERRAIN	EIRENIC	FLORUIT	BOBTAIL
GEORDIE	TETANIC	FIBROID	GLOTTIS	*BOHEMIA
*GEORGIA	VERMEIL	FILARIA	GLYPHIC	*BOLIVIA
GEORGIC	VERVAIN	*HITCHIN	GLYPTIC	BORACIC
HEARDIN	WEIGH-IN	KIDSKIN	ILLICIT	+BORODIN
HEBETIC	XERASIA.	KINETIC	*OLYMPIA	BOTANIC
HEBRAIC	PFENNIG.	KINGPIN	OLYMPIC	BOUDOIR
HEDONIC	EGG-FLIP	KINSHIP	PLASMIC	COAL-PIT
HEMATIN	OGHAMIC.	*LIBERIA	PLASTIC	COAL-TIT
HEPATIC	CHABLIS	MIDSHIP	PLAUDIT	COCKPIT
HERETIC	CHAGRIN	MILITIA	PLUMBIC.	CODICIL
KENOSIS	CHAMOIS	MIMESIS	AMENTIA	COHABIT
KENOTIC	CHAOTIC	MIMETIC	AMHARIC	COLITIS
KERATIN	+CHAPLIN	MISLAID	AMMONIA	COLLOID
LEGUMIN	CHASSIS	MITOSIS	AMNESIA	CONCEIT
LENTOID	CHEERIO	*NICOSIA	AMOEBIC	CONDUIT
MEIOSIS	CHERVIL	*NIGERIA	AMYLOID	CONJOIN
+MELANIE	CHLORIC	OILSKIN	EMBROIL	CONTAIN
MELANIN	+CHLORIS	PIGSKIN	EMPIRIC	CORSAIR
MELODIC	CHROMIC	PIGTAIL	IMPERIL.	COTERIE
+MENUHIN	CHRONIC	PILGRIM	ANAEMIA	COUNCIL
MERMAID	GHERKIN	PINGUID	ANAEMIC	COWSLIP
NECK-TIE	KHAMSIN	PINGUIN	ANEROID	DOESKIN
NEGROID	PHALLIC	*SILESIA	ANGELIC	DOGSKIN
NEMESIS	*PHOENIX	SILICIC	ANOESIS	DOLPHIN
NEPOTIC	PHRENIC	SIRLOIN	ANOETIC	DOVEKIE
NEW-LAID	+PHYLLIS	TINFOIL	ANOSMIA	FORFEIT
PELAGIC	RHIZOID	+TITANIA	ANTACID	GOBELIN

GODSHIP	+ARTEMIS	STANNIC	SWEETIE.	+TROTSKY.
*GOODWIN	BRAHMIN	STARLIT	AXLE-PIN	STREAKY
HOBNAIL	BRASSIE	STEARIN	EXCLAIM	
HOGSKIN	BRECCIA	STENCIL	EXHIBIT	BACILLI
+HOLBEIN	*BRITAIN	STEROID	EXPLAIN	BARBOLA
HOMERIC	BROWNIE	STYPTIC	EXPLOIT.	BASALLY
HOMINID	CRINOID	UTENSIL.	CYCLOID	BASCULE
+HORATIO	CRYPTIC	*AUSTRIA	+CYNTHIA	BAWDILY
HOWBEIT	DRASTIC	BUBONIC	DYNAMIC	CANDELA
+JONQUIL	DRIVE-IN	BUCOLIC	HYALOID	CANNILY
LOBELIA	DRUIDIC	BUILT-IN	HYDATID	CAPABLE
MONADIC	DRUMLIN	BULIMIA	HYOSCIN	CAPSULE
MOONLIT	ERRATIC	BUMPKIN	HYPNOID	+CARROLL
MORONIC	+FRANCIS	BUTYRIC	LYING-IN	CASTILE
MORPHIA	FRANTIC	*CUILLIN	MYCOSIS	CATCALL
NOMADIC	FREESIA	CULPRIT	PYRAMID	CATFALL
NONSUIT	GRAPHIC	CURTAIL	PYRETIC	CATTILY
NOSTRIL	GREMLIN	CURTAIN	PYREXIA	CATWALK
POLEMIC	GRIFFIN	DUSTBIN	PYRRHIC	DATABLE
POLITIC	GRISKIN	EUGENIC	SYNODIC	DAZEDLY
POLYNIA	KREMLIN	FUCHSIA	SYNOVIA	EAGERLY
*POMPEII	ORGANIC	FUN-FAIR	TYPHOID	EARTHLY
PORK-PIE	PRAIRIE	FUNGOID	ZYMOTIC	EATABLE
ROMANIC	PRAKRIT	GUMBOIL		FAINTLY
SOLICIT	PREPAID	LUNATIC	BAZOOKA	FAIRILY
SOMATIC	PREVAIL	MUEZZIN	MANLIKE	FALSELY
SONSHIP	PROSAIC	MURRAIN	MAZURKA	FATALLY
TOENAIL	PROTEID	NUCLEIC	OATCAKE	GAUDILY
TOPSAIL	PROTEIN	OUTSAIL	PANCAKE	GAUNTLY
TOTEMIC	PRUSSIC	PUMPKIN	PANICKY	GAZELLE
VOCALIC	TRADE-IN	PURLOIN	PAPRIKA	HAIRILY
VOLTAIC	TRAFFIC	PURSUIT	PARTAKE	HANDILY
WORSHIP.	TRANSIT	+PUSHKIN	+VANDYKE	HAPPILY
APHASIA	TRAVAIL	PUSHPIN	WARLIKE.	HARDILY
APHELIA	TREFOIL	QUASSIA	BESPOKE	HARSHLY
APHESIS	TRELLIS	+QUENTIN	NETSUKE	HASTILY
APHONIC	TRYPSIN	QUICKIE	TEACAKE.	JAZZILY
+OPHELIA	TRYSAIL	*RUISLIP	DISLIKE	KABBALA
OPHIDIA	URAEMIA.	*RUMANIA	FINICKY	LAMELLA
SPASTIC	ASCETIC	SUBACID	HIJINKS	LARGELY
SPHERIC	ASEPSIS	SUB-EDIT	MISLIKE	+MALCOLM
SPLENIC	ASEPTIC	SUBERIN	MISTAKE	MAMILLA
SPUTNIK	ASIATIC	SUBJOIN	OILCAKE.	MANACLE
UPBRAID	ASPIRIN	SUBSOIL	UNLUCKY.	MANDALA
UPSTAIR.	ASTATIC	SURFEIT	COLICKY	MANHOLE
AQUATIC	ISLAMIC	SURLOIN	CONVOKE	MANILLA
SQUALID.	OSMOSIS	SUSTAIN	FORSAKE.	MANIPLE
ARAMAIC	OSMOTIC	*TUNISIA	SQUEAKY.	MAXILLA
ARCHAIC	PSYCHIC.	TURMOIL.	DROSHKY	+MAXWELL
ARSENIC	PTYALIN	OVERDID.	PROVOKE	MAYPOLE

430

NACELLE	ACTABLE	PENALLY	CHORTLE	KINKILY
NAIVELY	ACUTELY	PENNILL	CHUCKLE	LICITLY
NAKEDLY	OCTUPLE	PENSILE	GHASTLY	LIGHTLY
NAMABLE	*SCAFELL	PERCALE	GHOSTLY	*LINCOLN
NASALLY	SCANTLE	PERGOLA	SHACKLE	LIVABLE
NASTILY	SCAPULA	PERKILY	SHADILY	LIVIDLY
OAK-GALL	SCRUPLE	PETIOLE	SHAKILY	MIRACLE
PANOPLY	SCUFFLE	PETTILY	SHAMBLE	MISCALL
PANTILE	SCUMBLE	READILY	SHAPELY	MISERLY
PAPILLA	SCUTTLE.	*REDHILL	SHINGLE	MISRULE
PARABLE	IDEALLY.	REDPOLL	SHINILY	MISSILE
PATELLA	BEASTLY	REGALLY	SHORTLY	MISTILY
PAWKILY	BEGUILE	REMOULD	SHOWILY	NIGHTLY
PAYABLE	BENGALI	REPTILE	SHRILLY	NINTHLY
PAY-ROLL	+BEOWULF	RETICLE	SHUFFLE	OIL-SILK
RABIDLY	CEDILLA	SEAGULL	SHUTTLE	OIL-WELL
RADICLE	CELLULE	SEA-KALE	THICKLY	PIANOLA
RAPIDLY	CEMBALO	SEA-MILE	THIMBLE	PICCOLO
RATABLE	DEATHLY	SEA-SALT	THIRDLY	PIEBALD
RAVIOLI	DEBACLE	*SEATTLE	THISTLE	PINBALL
SACCULE	DECUPLE	SEA-WALL	THISTLY	PINFOLD
SAINTLY	DEFAULT	SEA-WOLF	THYSELF	PINHOLE
SALABLE	DENSELY	SECTILE	WHEEDLE	PIOUSLY
SAND-FLY	DESCALE	SEEDILY	WHIFFLE	PISTOLE
SAUCILY	FEBRILE	SERVILE	WHISTLE	PITFALL
SAVABLE	+FENELLA	*SEVILLE	WHITTLE.	PITHILY
SAVE-ALL	FERRULE	TENABLE	AIR-HOLE	RIDABLE
SAWBILL	FERTILE	TENABLY	BICYCLE	RIGHTLY
SAW-MILL	FETIDLY	TENFOLD	CIVILLY	RIGIDLY
TACITLY	GENTILE	TENSELY	DIABOLO	RISIBLE
TACTILE	GESTALT	TENSILE	DIRTILY	RISKILY
TADPOLE	HEAVILY	TENTHLY	DISABLE	RISSOLE
TAMABLE	HEFTILY	TEPIDLY	DISTYLE	SIGHTLY
TARDILY	HERSELF	TERSELY	DIZZILY	SILKILY
TASTILY	JERKILY	TESTILY	FICTILE	SILLILY
TATTILY	KEYHOLE	TEXTILE	FIERILY	SIXFOLD
TAWNILY	LEAKILY	VEHICLE	FIFTHLY	SIZABLE
TAXABLE	LEGALLY	VENALLY	FINABLE	TIGHTLY
VACUOLE	LEGIBLE	VESICLE	FINAGLE	TIMIDLY
VAGUELY	LEGIBLY	WEARILY	FINALLY	TINNILY
VALIDLY	LEG-PULL	WEIRDLY	FIREFLY	TIPSILY
VANILLA	+LEOPOLD	WERWOLF.	FIRSTLY	VIRGULE
VAPIDLY	MEDULLA	AFFABLE.	FISHILY	VISIBLE
VARIOLA	MENFOLK	AGILELY.	FISSILE	*VISTULA
VASCULA	MERRILY	IGNOBLE.	FISTULA	VITALLY
WADABLE	MESSILY	+CHAGALL	FIXABLE	VIVIDLY
+WALPOLE	NEEDILY	CHARILY	GIDDILY	WIRABLE
*WALSALL	NETBALL	CHEAPLY	GIMBALS	WITTILY.
WAXBILL	+NEVILLE	CHIEFLY	+GISELLE	SKIFFLE
WAY-BILL.	PEDICLE	CHORALE	HIMSELF	SKITTLE

431

UKULELE.	KNOW-ALL	*NORFOLK	SQUALLY.	GREATLY
ALOOFLY	KNUCKLE	NOTABLE	ARTICLE	GRIDDLE
ALVEOLE	ONESELF	NOTABLY	BRAILLE	GRISTLE
BLANDLY	SNAFFLE	POTABLE	BRAMBLE	GRISTLY
BLANKLY	SNAKILY	POTHOLE	BRASHLY	GRIZZLE
BLEAKLY	SNOWILY	ROCKILY	BRAVELY	GRIZZLY
BLINDLY	SNUFFLE	ROSEOLA	BRICOLE	GROSSLY
BLOW-FLY	SNUGGLE	+ROUAULT	BRIEFLY	GRUFFLY
BLUFFLY	UNBUILT	ROUGHLY	BRINDLE	GRUMBLE
BLUNTLY	UNGODLY	ROUNDLY	BRISKLY	IRATELY
CLEANLY	UNMANLY.	ROWDILY	BRISTLE	ORDERLY
CLEARLY	BONNILY	ROYALLY	BRISTLY	PRATTLE
CLOSELY	+BOSWELL	SOAPILY	BRITTLE	PRICKLE
ELDERLY	COCKILY	SOBERLY	BROADLY	PRICKLY
FLAKILY	COMPILE	SOGGILY	CRACKLE	PRIMELY
FLESHLY	CONDOLE	SOLIDLY	CRASSLY	PRIMULA
FLEXILE	CONDYLE	SOLUBLE	CRAZILY	PRIVILY
FLY-HALF	CONSOLE	SOOTILY	CRINGLE	PROFILE
GLOBULE	CONSULT	SOPPILY	CRINKLE	PROSILY
ILL-WILL	CORACLE	SOUFFLE	CRINKLY	PROUDLY
PLAINLY	CORNILY	SOUNDLY	CRIPPLE	TRAMPLE
PLIABLE	COROLLA	TOEHOLD	CROSSLY	TREACLE
PLUMPLY	COURTLY	TOMBOLA	CRUDELY	TREACLY
SLACKLY	DOWDILY	TORTILE	CRUELLY	TREADLE
SLEEKLY	FOGGILY	TOTALLY	CRUMBLE	TREDDLE
SLICKLY.	FORMULA	TOUGHLY	CRUMBLY	TREMBLE
AMIABLE	FOXHOLE	VOCABLE	CRUMPLE	TREMBLY
AMPOULE	GONDOLA	VOCALLY	DRABBLE	TREMOLO
AMPULLA	GORILLA	VOLUBLE	DRAGGLE	TRESTLE
EMERALD	HOLDALL	WOMANLY	DRIBBLE	TRIABLE
EMPTILY	HORALLY	WORDILY	DRIZZLE	TRICKLE
SMARTLY	HOSTILE	WORLDLY	DRIZZLY	TRINGLE
SMOKILY	JOINTLY	ZONALLY.	ERECTLY	*TRIPOLI
SMUGGLE.	LOATHLY	APOSTLE	FRAGILE	TRITELY
ANGRILY	LOCALLY	EPISTLE	FRAIBLE	TROUBLE
ANOMALY	LOFTILY	SPANGLE	FRAILLY	TRUCKLE
+ANQUILH	LOG-ROLL	SPARELY	FRANKLY	TRUFFLE
ANT-HILL	LOOSELY	SPARKLE	FRAZZLE	TRUNDLE
*ENFIELD	LOUSILY	SPATULA	FRECKLE	WRANGLE
ENNOBLE	LOVABLE	SPECKLE	FRECKLY	WRESTLE
ENTITLE	LOVABLY	SPECULA	FRESHLY	WRIGGLE
INANELY	LOYALLY	SPICILY	FRIBBLE	WRINKLE
INAPTLY	MONOCLE	SPINDLE	FRIZZLE	WRONGLY.
INEPTLY	MONTHLY	SPINDLY	GRABBLE	ASPHALT
INERTLY	MOODILY	SPITTLE	GRACILE	ASSAULT
INFIELD	MORALLY	SPY-HOLE.	GRADELY	*ESKDALE
INKWELL	MORELLO	EQUABLE	GRANDLY	+ESTELLA
INSTALL	MOVABLE	EQUABLY	GRANULE	ISRAELI
KNOBBLE	NOCTULE	EQUALLY	GRAPPLE	OSSICLE
KNOBBLY	NOISILY	SQUAILS	GRAVELY	USUALLY·

STAIDLY	MUTABLE	DAY-TIME	TRIREME.	CARBINE
STARKLY	OURSELF	MAHATMA	+PTOLEMY.	CARKING
STARTLE	OUTFALL	PASTIME	CURCUMA	CARLINE
STATELY	OUTTALK	RAGTIME	FULSOME	CARMINE
STEEPLE	PUERILE	SARCOMA	MUGWUMP	CARPING
STERILE	PUG-MILL	*SATSUMA	OUTCOME	CARTING
STERNLY	+PURCELL	WARTIME.	SUBLIME	CARVING
STIFFLY	PUSTULE	ACADEMY	SUBSUME	CASHING
STIMULI	QUEENLY	ECONOMY	SUCCUMB	CASTING
STIPPLE	QUEERLY	SCOTOMA.	SUPREME	CATLING
STOPPLE	QUIBBLE	BEDTIME	SURNAME.	CATMINT
STOUTLY	QUICKLY	BERHYME	AWESOME	CAUSING
STUBBLE	QUIETLY	CENTIME	TWOSOME	CAYENNE
STUBBLY	RUBELLA	MELISMA	TWO-TIME.	DABBING
STUMBLE	RUBEOLA	MESEEMS	EXOGAMY	DAMMING
UTRICLE	RUDDILY	PERFUME	EXTREME	DAMNING
+UTRILLO	RUMMILY	REFRAME		DAMPING
UTTERLY.	+RUSSELL	WELCOME.	BACKING	DANCING
AUDIBLE	RUSTILY	CHIASMA	BAGGING	DARLING
AUREOLA	SUAVELY	PHLEGMY	BAILING	DARNING
AURICLE	*SUFFOLK	RHIZOME.	BAITING	DARTING
BUFFALO	SULKILY	DILEMMA	BALCONY	DASHING
BUMMALO	SURLILY	DIORAMA	BALKING	DAUBING
BUYABLE	TUNABLE.	DIPLOMA	BAMBINO	DAWNING
CUBICLE	OVERALL	DISLIMN	BANDING	DAYLONG
CUCKOLD	OVERTLY.	WINSOME.	BANGING	EARNING
CUTICLE	AWFULLY	SKI-JUMP.	BANKING	EARRING
DUCTILE	DWINDLE	*ALABAMA	BANNING	EASTING
*DUNDALK	SWADDLE	ALCHEMY	BANTING	FAGGING
DUPABLE	SWAHILI	ALL-TIME.	BARGING	FAILING
DURABLE	SWEETLY	ANATOMY	*BARKING	FAIRING
DURABLY	SWIFTLY	END-GAME	BARRING	FALLING
+DURRELL	SWINDLE	INFLAME.	BASHING	FANNING
DUSKILY	SWINGLE	CONDEMN	BASKING	FARCING
DUSTILY	SWIZZLE	CONSUME	BASTING	FARMING
FUNNILY	TWADDLE	CONTEMN	BATHING	FASCINE
FURBALL	TWIDDLE	COSTUME	BATTING	FASTING
FUSIBLE	TWINKLE	COULOMB	BAWLING	FATLING
FUSTILY	TWOFOLD.	COXCOMB	CABLING	FAWNING
GUNWALE	AXIALLY	GODDAMN	CAB-RANK	GABBING
HUFFILY	EXACTLY	NOISOME	CADGING	GADDING
HUMANLY	EXAMPLE.	ZOOGAMY	CALCINE	GAFFING
LUCIDLY	CYMBALO	ZOOTOMY.	CALLING	GAGGING
+LUCILLE	EYEBALL	EPITOME.	CALMING	GAINING
LUCKILY	EYE-BOLT	DRACHMA	CALUMNY	GALLANT
LURIDLY	EYEHOLE	+GRAHAME	CALVING	GALLING
LUSTILY	LYINGLY	GRANDMA	CAMPING	GAMMING
MUCKILY	SYSTOLE	IRKSOME	CANNING	GANGING
+MURILLO	SYSTYLE	PRESUME	CANTING	GARBING
MURKILY		PROXIMO	CAPPING	GARLAND

433

GARMENT	LARDING	PATTING	TANGING	OCARINA
GASHING	LARKING	+PAULINE	TANNING	SCALENE
GASPING	LASHING	PAUSING	TAPPING	SCALING
GAS-RING	LASTING	PAWNING	TARRING	SCARING
GASSING	LATRINE	PAYMENT	TARTING	SCORING
GATLING	LAUDING	RACKING	TASKING	SCRAWNY
GAUGING	MACHINE	RADIANT	TASTING	SCRYING.
HACKING	MADDING	RAFTING	TATTING	ADAMANT
HAFTING	MADONNA	RAGGING	TAURINE	ADORING
HAGGING	MAH-JONG	RAIDING	TAXIING	EDITING
HAILING	MAILING	RAILING	VACCINE	EDUCING
HALTING	MAIMING	RAIMENT	VAGRANT	ODDMENT.
HALVING	MALTING	RAINING	VALIANT	BEADING
HAMMING	MANHUNT	RAISING	VAMPING	BEAMING
HANDING	MANKIND	RAMMING	VANNING	BEARING
HANGING	MANNING	RAMPANT	VARIANT	BEATING
HAPENNY	MAPPING	RAMPING	VARMINT	BEDDING
HAPPING	MARKING	RANGING	VARYING	BEE-LINE
HARKING	MARLINE	RANKING	WADDING	BEGGING
HARMING	MARLING	RANTING	WAFTING	+BELLINI
HARMONY	MARRING	RAPPING	WAGGING	+BELLONA
HARPING	MARTINI	RASPING	WAILING	BELTANE
HASHING	MASHING	RATFINK	WAITING	BELTING
HASPING	MASKING	RATTING	WAIVING	BELYING
HATBAND	MASSING	+RAYMOND	WALKING	BENDING
HAULING	MATTING	+SABRINA	WALLING	BENZENE
HAWKING	MAULING	SACKING	WANTING	BETHINK
*HAYLING	NABBING	SACRING	WARDING	BETTING
JABBING	NAGGING	SAGGING	WARMING	CEASING
JACKING	NAILING	SAILING	WARNING	CEILING
JAGGING	NAPPING	SALIENT	WARPING	CERVINE
JAMMING	NASCENT	SALTING	WARRANT	+CEZANNE
JARRING	PACKING	SALVING	WARRING	DEAD-END
+JASMINE	PADDING	SANDING	WASHING	DEALING
JAW-BONE	PAGEANT	SAPIENT	WASTING	DECKING
JAZZING	PAINING	SAPLING	YAKKING	DECLINE
LACKING	PAIRING	SAPPING	YANKING	DEEMING
LADLING	PALLING	SARDINE	YAPPING	DEFIANT
LAGGING	PALMING	SARKING	YAWNING.	DELAINE
LALLANS	PALPING	SAUCING	ABALONE	DELVING
LALLING	PANNING	SAVANNA	ABIDING	DEMESNE
LAMBENT	PANTING	TABBING	ABSCIND	DEMOUNT
LAMBING	PARKING	TABLING	ABSCOND	DENTINE
LAMMING	PARSING	TACKING	OBEYING	DENYING
LANCING	PARTING	TAGGING	OBSCENE.	DESCANT
LANDING	PARVENU	TAIL-END	ACCOUNT	DESCEND
LAPPING	PASSANT	TAILING	ACETONE	DESCENT
LAPSING	PASSING	TALKING	ECHIDNA	+DESMOND
LAPWING	PASTING	TAMPING	ECHOING	DESPOND
LARCENY	PATIENT	TANGENT	*ICELAND	DESTINE

DESTINY	KEY-RING	PENTANE	SELLING	WELTING
DEWPOND	LEADING	PEPPING	SENDING	WENDING
FEARING	LEAFING	PERKING	SENSING	WEST-END
FEEDING	LEAKING	PERMING	SEQUENT	WESTING
FEELING	LEANING	PERPEND	SERPENT	WETTING
+FELLINI	LEAPING	PERSONA	SERVANT	YELLING
FELTING	LEASING	PETTING	SERVING	YELPING
FENCING	LEAVING	*READING	SESTINA	YENNING
FENDING	LEERING	REAGENT	SETTING	ZEBRINE
FERMENT	LEGGING	REAMING	SEXTANT	*ZEELAND
FERVENT	LEMMING	REAPING	TEAMING	ZEROING
FEUDING	LENDING	REARING	TEARING	*ZETLAND.
GEARING	LENIENT	REBOUND	TEASING	AFFRONT
GEHENNA	LEONINE	RECLINE	TEDDING	OFF-HAND
GELDING	LETTING	RECOUNT	TEEMING	OFF-LINE
GELLING	LEVYING	REDOUND	TELLING	AGROUND.
GEMMING	MEANING	REEDING	TENDING	CHAFING
GENUINE	MEETING	REEFING	TENPINS	CHASING
GERMANE	MELDING	REEKING	TENSING	CHEWING
*GERMANY	MELTING	REELING	TENTING	CHICANE
GETTING	MENDING	REGNANT	TERMING	CHIDING
HEADING	MERGING	REINING	TERMINI	CHIMING
HEALING	MESHING	RELIANT	TERPENE	CHOKING
HEAPING	MESSING	REMNANT	TERRENE	CHOLINE
HEARING	METHANE	REMOUNT	TERRINE	CHOPINE
HEATING	NEARING	RENDING	TESTING	PHALANX
HEAVING	NECKING	RENTING	VEERING	PHARYNX
HEDGING	NEEDING	REPLANT	VEILING	PHASING
HEEDING	+NEPTUNE	REPOINT	VEINING	PHONING
HEELING	NERVINE	REPRINT	VENDING	RHYMING
HEFTING	NERVING	RESCIND	VENTING	SHADING
HELLENE	NESTING	RESOUND	VERBENA	SHAKING
HELPING	NETTING	RESPOND	VERDANT	SHAMING
HEMMING	PEAKING	RESTING	VERGING	SHAPING
HENBANE	PEALING	RETHINK	*VERMONT	SHARING
HEPTANE	PEASANT	REVVING	VERSING	SHAVING
HEROINE	PECCANT	SEA-BANK	VESTING	SHEBANG
HERRING	PECKING	SEA-LINE	VETOING	SHINING
JEERING	PEEKING	SEALING	VETTING	SHOEING
JELLING	PEELING	SEAMING	WEANING	SHOOING
JERKING	PEEPING	SEA-PINK	WEARING	SHORING
JESTING	PEERING	SEARING	WEAVING	SHOVING
JETTING	PEEVING	SEATING	WEBBING	SHOWING
KECKING	PEGGING	SEEDING	WEDDING	THAWING
KEDGING	PELTING	SEEKING	WEDGING	WHALING
KEELING	PENDANT	SEEMING	WEEDING	WHILING
KEENING	PENDENT	SEEPING	WEEK-END	WHINING
KEEPING	PENDING	SEGMENT	WEEPING	WHITING
KENNING	PENNANT	SEISING	WELDING	WHORING.
KERBING	PENNING	SEIZING	WELLING	AILMENT

AIRLINE	KITTING	RIPPING	CLAWING	IMPOUND
BIDDING	LICKING	RISKING	+CLEMENT	IMPRINT
BILKING	LIFTING	SIBLING	CLOSING	SMILING
BILLING	LILTING	SIDLING	CLOYING	SMOKING.
BILTONG	LIMNING	SIEVING	ELATING	ANCIENT
BINDING	LIMPING	SIFTING	ELEGANT	ANEMONE
BIPLANE	LINKING	SIGHING	ELEMENT	ANGLING
CITRINE	LINSANG	SIGNING	ELIDING	ANGUINE
DIAMOND	LIPPING	SILTING	ELOPING	ANILINE
+DICKENS	LISPING	SINGING	ELUDING	ANODYNE
DIETING	LISTING	SINKING	FLAKING	ANTENNA
DIGGING	MIDLAND	SINNING	FLAMING	+ANTHONY
DILUENT	MIGRANT	SIPPING	FLARING	ENCHANT
DIMMING	MILKING	SITTING	FLAWING	ENDLONG
DINGING	MILLING	TICKING	FLAYING	*ENGLAND
DINNING	MILTING	TIFFANY	FLEEING	ENTRANT
DIPPING	MINCING	TILLING	+FLEMING	ENTWINE
DISBAND	MINDING	TILTING	FLEXING	ENVYING
DISHING	MINTING	TIMPANI	FLOWING	GNAWING
DISSENT	MIOCENE	TIMPANO	FLUTING	INBEING
DISTANT	MISSING	TINGING	GLARING	INCHING
DISTEND	MISTING	TINNING	GLAZING	INCLINE
FIBBING	NICKING	TIPPING	GLIDING	*INDIANA
FIGMENT	NIPPING	TITLING	GLOWING	INFERNO
FILLING	NIRVANA	VIBRANT	GLOZING	INGOING
FILMING	PICKING	VIEWING	GLUEING	INKLING
FINDING	PIECING	+VINCENT	OLEFINE	INSTANT
*FINLAND	PIGGING	VIOLENT	PLACING	INTRANT
FIRMING	PIGLING	WILLING	PLANING	INURING
FISHING	PIGMENT	WILTING	PLATING	KNIFING
FITMENT	PIMPING	WINDING	PLAYING	KNOWING
FITTING	PINKING	WINGING	PLUMING	SNAKING
FIZZING	PINNING	WINKING	SLAKING	SNARING
GILDING	PIPPING	WINNING	SLATING	SNIPING
HINTING	PIQUANT	WISHING	SLAVING	SNORING
HIPPING	PISCINA	WITTING	SLAYING	SNOWING
HIRCINE	PISCINE	ZIPPING.	SLEWING	UNBOUND
HISSING	PITTING	SKATING	SLICING	UNCANNY
HITTING	PITYING	SKEWING	SLIDING	UNDOING
JIBBING	RIBBING	SKYLINE.	SLOPING.	UNDYING
JIGGING	RICKING	ALIMENT	AMAZING	UNGUENT
JILTING	RIDDING	ALIMONY	AMBIENT	UNITING
JINKING	RIFLING	ALUMINA	AMBLING	UNMEANT
KICKING	RIFTING	BLAMING	AMUSING	UNSLING
KIDDING	RIGGING	BLARING	EMETINE	UNSOUND
KILLING	RIMMING	BLATANT	EMINENT	UNSPENT
KINGING	RINGING	BLAZING	IMAGINE	UNTWINE
KINKING	RINKING	BLOWING	IMAGING	UNWOUND
KIPPING	RINSING	BLUEING	IMPFING	UNWRUNG.
KISSING	RIOTING	CLAMANT	IMPLANT	BOATING

436

BOBBING	DODGING	HORMONE	NOSHING	TONTINE
BOGGING	DOGGING	HORNING	NOTHING	TOOLING
BOILING	DOGGONE	HORSING	PODDING	*TOOTING
*BOLOGNA	DONNING	HOSANNA	POISING	TOPPING
BOLTING	*DORKING	HOTTING	POLLING	TORMENT
BOMBING	DORMANT	+HOUDINI	POMPANO	TORRENT
BONDING	DOSSING	HOUSING	POOLING	TOSSING
BOOKING	DOTTING	HOWLING	POPPING	TOTTING
BOOMING	DOUSING	JOBBING	PORCINE	TOURING
BOWLINE	DOWNING	JOGGING	PORTEND	TOUTING
BOWLING	DOWSING	JOINING	PORTENT	TOWLINE
COALING	FOALING	JOLTING	PORTING	VOICING
COAMING	FOAMING	JOSHING	POSTING	VOIDING
COATING	FOBBING	JOTTING	POTTING	VOLCANO
COAXING	FOGBANK	LOADING	+POULENC	VOLTING
COCAINE	FOGGING	LOAFING	POURING	WOLFING
COCKING	FOILING	LOAMING	POUTING	WORDING
CODEINE	FOLDING	LOANING	ROAMING	WORKING
CODLING	FOOLING	LOBBING	ROARING	WORMING
COILING	FOOTING	LOCKING	ROBBING	YORKING
COINING	FORCING	LODGING	ROCKING	YOWLING
COLOGNE	FORDING	LOFTING	ROLLING	ZOOMING.
COMBINE	FORGING	LOGGING	ROMPING	APPOINT
COMBING	FORGONE	LOLLING	ROOFING	EPERGNE
COMMAND	FORKING	LONGING	ROOKING	EPICENE
COMMEND	FORMING	LOOKING	ROOMING	OPALINE
COMMENT	FORTUNE	LOOMING	ROOTING	OPENING
COMMONS	FORWENT	LOOPING	+ROSSINI	OPINING
COMMUNE	FOULING	LOOTING	ROTTING	OPULENT
COMPANY	FOWLING	LOPPING	ROUGING	SPACING
CONDONE	FOXHUNT	LORDING	ROUSING	SPARING
CONFINE	GOADING	LOURING	ROUTINE	SPAYING
CONKING	GODSEND	LOWLAND	ROUTING	SPEWING
CONNING	+GOLDING	MOANING	SOAKING	SPICING
CONSENT	GORGING	MOBBING	SOAPING	SPIKING
CONTEND	GOSLING	MOCKING	SOARING	SPIRANT
CONTENT	GOUGING	*MONTANA	SOBBING	SPIRING
CONVENE	HOAXING	MOONING	SOILING	SPITING
CONVENT	HOCKING	MOORING	SOLVENT	SPUMING.
COOKING	HOGGING	MOOTING	SOLVING	+ARACHNE
COOLANT	HOLDING	MOPPING	SOMEONE	ARCHING
COOLING	*HOLLAND	MORAINE	SOPPING	ARGUING
COPPING	HONKING	MORDANT	SOPRANO	+ARIADNE
CORKING	HOODING	MORNING	SORDINE	ARISING
CORVINE	HOOKING	NOBBING	SORTING	*ARIZONA
COSTING	HOOPING	NOCKING	SOURING	ARM-BAND
COTTONY	HOOTING	NODDING	SOUSING	BRACING
COWBANE	HOP-BINE	NOGGING	SOUTANE	BRAVING
COWLING	HOPPING	NOOSING	TOLLING	BRAYING
DOCKING	HORDING	NORLAND	TOLUENE	BRAZING

437

BREWING	PROSING	BUGGING	HUGGING	PULSING
BRIBING	PROVING	BUGLING	HULKING	PUMPING
BRIGAND	PRUDENT	BULGING	HULLING	PUNGENT
BROKING	PRUNING	BUMPING	HUMMING	PUNNING
BROMINE	TRACING	BUNKING	HUMPING	PUNTING
CRANING	TRADING	BUNTING	HUNTING	PUPPING
CRAVING	TREEING	BUOYANT	HURLING	PURGING
CRAZING	TREPANG	BURNING	HURTING	PURLING
CROWING	TRIBUNE	BURPING	HUSBAND	PURRING
DRAPING	TRICING	BUSKING	HUSHING	PURSING
DRAWING	TRIDENT	BUSTING	HUSKING	PUSHING
DRIVING	WRITING	BUZZING	HUTMENT	PUTTING
DROMOND	X-RAYING.	CUBBING	HUTTING	QUAKING
DRONING	ASININE	CUFFING	JUGGING	QUININE
ERASING	ASQUINT	CUISINE	+JULIANA	QUOTING
ERODENT	ASTOUND	CULLING	JUMPING	RUBBING
ERODING	ESPYING	CUNNING	JUNKING	RUCKING
FRAMING	ESTRONE	CUPPING	+JUSTINE	RUFFING
FRAYING	G-STRING	CURBING	*JUTLAND	RUINING
FREEING	ISATINE	CURDING	JUTTING	RUNNING
GRACING	ISODONT	CURLING	LUCARNE	RUSHING
GRADING	ISOTONE	CURRANT	*LUCERNE	RUSTING
GRATING	+OSBORNE.	CURRENT	LUGGING	*RUTLAND
GRAVING	ATONING	CURSING	LULLING	RUTTING
GRAZING	ATTAINT	CURVING	LUNGING	SUBTEND
GRIDING	ETCHING	CUSSING	LURKING	SUCKING
GRIPING	ITCHING	CUTTING	LUSTING	SUITING
GROPING	STAGING	DUBBING	MUCKING	SULTANA
*IRELAND	STAKING	DUCKING	MUFFING	SUMMING
IRONING	STAMINA	DUFFING	MUGGING	SUMMONS
ORATING	STARING	DULLING	MUGGINS	SUNNING
OROTUND	STATING	DUMPING	MULLING	SUPPING
PRALINE	STAVING	DUNKING	MUMMING	SURFING
PRATING	STAYING	DUNNING	MUNDANE	SURGING
PRAYING	STEWING	DUOTONE	MUSTANG	+SUSANNA
PREBEND	STIPEND	DUSTING	NUDGING	SUSPEND
PRESENT	STOKING	EUPHONY	NUMBING	SUSSING
PRETEND	STONING	FUNDING	NURSING	TUBBING
PREVENT	STORING	FURLING	NUTTING	TUCKING
PREYING	STOWING	FURLONG	OUSTING	TUFTING
PRICING	STUDENT	FURRING	OUTDONE	TUGGING
PRIDING	STYLING	FUSSING	OUTGONE	TURBINE
PRIMING	STYRENE	GUIDING	OUTLINE	TURFING
PRIZING	UTERINE.	GULLING	OUTWENT	TURNING
PROBANG	AUBAINE	GULPING	+PUCCINI	TUTTING
PROBING	AUGMENT	GUMMING	PUDDING	VULPINE.
PROFANE	BUCKING	GUNNING	PUFFING	AVOWING
PROGENY	BUDDING	GUSHING	PUGGING	EVADING
PROLONG	BUDGING	GUTTING	PULLING	EVENING
PROPANE	BUFFING	HUFFING	PULPING	EVIDENT

438

EVOKING.	GALLIOT	OCTOPOD	SENATOR	KILOTON
SWAYING	GALLOON	SCALLOP	SESSION	KINGDOM
SWIPING	HALCYON	SCISSOR	SETTLOR	LIAISON
TWINING.	*HAMPTON	SCOLLOP.	TEA-ROOM	LIFTBOY
EXAMINE	HANGDOG	EDITION.	TEA-SHOP	MILKSOP
EXIGENT	HARDTOP	AERATOR	TENSION	MILLION
EXILING	HARICOT	AEROSOL	VENISON	MISSION
EXITING	HARPOON	BELL-BOY	*VENTNOR	MISTOOK
EXSCIND	HAUTBOY	BELL-HOP	VERSION.	PICADOR
EXUDING	JACKPOT	BENISON	CHARIOT	PIERROT
OXIDANT.	JANITOR	BENTHOS	+CHEKHOV	PIG-IRON
CYCLING	LAMPION	+BERLIOZ	CHEROOT	PILL-BOX
CYCLONE	LAMPOON	CELADON	*CHEVIOT	PILLION
HYALINE	LANGUOR	CESSION	CHEVRON	SILICON
HYDRANT	MAILLOT	DECAGON	CHIFFON	VICEROY
HYGIENE	MANHOOD	DECAPOD	CHIGNON	VISITOR
SYLVINE	MANSION	DECOLOR	CHORION	VITRIOL
TYRANNY	MATADOR	DELATOR	CHRISOM	*WICKLOW
*WYOMING.	+NABOKOV	DEMIGOD	PHAETON	WIDGEON
AZURINE	PARADOS	DESTROY	PHANTOM	WINDROW
CZARINA	PARADOX	DEVELOP	PHARAOH	*WINDSOR
TZIGANE	PARAGON	DEWCROP	SHALLOP	+WINSTON.
	PARASOL	FEOFFOR	SHALLOT	EJECTOR
*BABYLON	PARTOOK	FERMION	SHALLOW	SJAMBOK.
BACKLOG	PASSION	FESTOON	SHAMPOO	ALCOHOL
BALLOON	PATRIOT	GEAR-BOX	THEREOF	ALIQUOT
*BAMPTON	RACCOON	HEIRDOM	THEREON	BLESBOK
BANDBOX	RAINBOW	HERITOR	THERMOS	BLOSSOM
*BANGKOK	RAJPOOT	HEXAGON	WHATNOT	*CLACTON
BASSOON	SAFFRON	HEXAPOD	WHEREOF	CLARION
BASTION	SANDBOY	KEELSON	WHEREON	ELATION
CAISSON	SAPWOOD	*LEBANON	WHITLOW.	+ELEANOR
CALL-BOX	+SASSOON	LEXICON	AILERON	ELECTOR
CALTROP	SAVELOY	MEGATON	AIRFLOW	ELISION
CAMPHOR	TALLBOY	MENTHOL	BIBELOT	ELUSION
CAMPION	TAMPION	MENTION	BILLION	FLEXION
CAPITOL	TAP-ROOM	METAZOA	DICE-BOX	FLUMMOX
CAPTION	TAP-ROOT	NEUTRON	DICTION	FLUXION
CARDOON	*TAUNTON	+PEARSON	DILATOR	FLY-BOOK
CARIBOU	WALLOON	PEAT-BOG	DISAVOW	*GLASGOW
CARRION	WARRIOR	PENSION	DIVISOR	GLUTTON
CARTOON	WART-HOG.	REACTOR	EIDOLON	PLATOON
CAUTION	ABANDON	REALTOR	FICTION	PLAYBOY
DAMFOOL	ABETTOR.	REDWOOD	FIREBOX	PLYWOOD.
DAYBOOK	+ACTAEON	REPROOF	FIREDOG	+AMPHION
EARLDOM	ECHELON	REREDOS	FISSION	EMBOSOM
EARSHOT	*ECUADOR	*REUNION	GILLION	EMOTION
FACTION	ICE-FLOE	SEA-LION	GIRASOL	EMPEROR.
FASHION	ICHABOD	SEA-ROOM	JIB-DOOR	ANDIRON
GALLEON	OCTAGON	SECTION	KILLJOY	ANTILOG

ENVELOP	ROAD-HOG	TREASON	OVERTOP.	
ENVENOM	ROTATOR	TRIGLOT	SWALLOW	*BANBURY
ENVIRON	SOAP-BOX	TROLLOP.	*SWINDON.	+BARBARA
INCISOR	+SOLOMON	ESTRIOL.	AXLE-BOX	BASTARD
KNOCK-ON	SOMEHOW	+ATROPOS	EXACTOR.	BATTERY
*KNOSSOS	SOUPCON	ETHANOL	CYPRIOT	*CALGARY
KNOW-HOW	+TOLSTOY	STARDOM	EYEBROW	CALIBRE
*SNOWDON	TOMFOOL	STATION	EYESHOT	CALVARY
UNBOSOM	TOMPION	STEPSON	HYPERON	CANNERY
UNCTION.	TOP-BOOT	STETSON	SYMBION	CANONRY
BOREDOM	TOPKNOT	*STILTON.	SYMPTOM	CAPTURE
BOURBON	TORSION	AUCTION	TYPHOON	CASCARA
BOURDON	TOYSHOP	AUDITOR		CATARRH
BOWSHOT	*WORKSOP.	BUFFOON	BAGPIPE	CAUTERY
BOXWOOD	APRICOT	BUGABOO	CATALPA	CAVALRY
BOYHOOD	APROPOS	BULLDOG	GALUMPH	DASTARD
CONTROL	EPIZOON	BULLION	LACE-UPS	DAY-GIRL
CO-PILOT	EPSILON	BURGEON	PAN-PIPE.	EARMARK
CORN-COB	OPINION	CURATOR	ACALEPH	EASTERN
DOGTROT	SPARROW	CUSHION	SCRAPPY.	FACTORY
DOGWOOD	SPONSOR	DUDGEON	GESTAPO	FACTURE
DONATOR	UPTHROW.	DUKEDOM	PERCEPT	FAILURE
DOVECOT	EQUATOR	DUNGEON	PERHAPS	FANFARE
FORETOP	EQUINOX	FUSS-POT	RECEIPT	GALLERY
FORSOOK	SQUALOR.	GUDGEON	THERAPY.	+HAGGARD
FOURGON	BRIDOON	GUERDON	BIOTYPE	HALBERD
FOX-TROT	*BRISTOL	GUNROOM	DIGRAPH	HALYARD
GOSSOON	BRYOZOA	GUNSHOT	DISRUPT.	*HAMBURG
*HONITON	CRAMPON	HUMIDOR	ENTROPY	HANSARD
HOOSGOW	CREATOR	JUKEBOX	INSCAPE	HAUBERK
HORIZON	CRIMSON	MULLION	UNHAPPY	HAYFORK
HOTFOOT	CROUTON	NUCLEON	UNKEMPT.	HAYWARD
*HOUSTON	DRAGOON	OUTCROP	CONCEPT	HAYWIRE
JOG-TROT	DRY-SHOD	OUTDOOR	CORRUPT	JANUARY
+JOHNSON	ERASION	OUTFLOW	GOSSIPY	LAGGARD
KOLKHOZ	ERECTOR	OUTGROW	TOW-ROPE.	LAMBERT
LOG-BOOK	EROSION	OUTLOOK	EPITAPH	LANTERN
LOGWOOD	FREEDOM	RUPTION	UPSWEPT.	LANYARD
LONGBOW	GRANTOR	SUASION	GRANDPA	LATHERY
LOWBROW	GRYPHON	SUBPLOT	PRECEPT	LAUNDRY
MONITOR	KRYPTOL	SUCTION	PRE-EMPT	MACABRE
MONSOON	KRYPTON	SUNSPOT	TRICEPS	*MADEIRA
NON-STOP	ORATION	SURGEON	TRIUMPH.	MAESTRO
POLYGON	ORGANON	TUCK-BOX	ISOTOPE.	MALLARD
POLYPOD	PRAETOR	TUITION	ATTEMPT.	*MALVERN
PONTOON	*PRESTON	YULE-LOG.	+EUTERPE	MAMMARY
POOR-BOX	PROCTOR	AVIATOR	+RUDOLPH.	MANSARD
PORTION	TRACTOR	*AVIGNON	EXCERPT.	+MARGERY
POTHOOK	TRAITOR	EVASION	CYCLOPS	MASCARA
POT-SHOT	TRANSOM	OVATION	SYNCOPE	MASONRY

MASTERY	DEPLORE	SEAWARD	FISHERY	PLENARY
PALMARY	DESSERT	SECTARY	FISSURE	SLAVERY.
*PALMYRA	DEVILRY	SEIZURE	FIXTURE	AMATORY
+PANDORA	EEL-FARE	*SELKIRK	+GILBERT	AMPHORA
PASTERN	EEL-WORM	SENSORY	GINGERY	IMAGERY
PASTURE	FEATURE	SERVERY	GIZZARD	IMPLORE.
PATTERN	FELONRY	TEMPERA	HICKORY	*ANDORRA
RAMPART	FERNERY	TESSERA	+HILLARY	*ANTWERP
RAPPORT	GESTURE	TEXTURE	HISTORY	ENQUIRE
RAPTURE	HECTARE	VELOURS	JITTERY	ENQUIRY
*SALFORD	HENNERY	VENTURE	LIBRARY	ENSNARE
SALTERN	+HERBERT	VERDURE	*MILFORD	INBOARD
SALTIRE	HERONRY	VESPERS	MIMICRY	INDOORS
SAVOURY	HETAERA	VESTURE	MISFIRE	INKHORN
SAXHORN	JEWELRY	WELFARE	MIXTURE	INQUIRE,
TANAGRA	LECHERY	WESTERN	NIGGARD	INQUIRY
TANKARD	LECTERN	ZEDOARY.	PIASTRE	INSHORE
TANNERY	LECTURE	OFFWARD.	PICTURE	INSPIRE
VAMPIRE	LEEWARD	CHANCRE	PIGGERY	KNAVERY
VANWARD	LEGHORN	CHANTRY	PILLORY	UNAWARE
VAPOURY	LEISURE	CHICORY	PINCERS	UNHEARD
VAQUERO	+LEONORA	CHIMERA	+RICHARD	UNICORN
WAGGERY	LEOPARD	CHOLERA	RIP-CORD	UNIFORM
WARFARE	LEOTARD	+PHAEDRA	RIVALRY	UNITARY
WAR-LORD	MEASURE	PHILTRE	RIVIERE	UNLEARN.
*WATFORD	+MERCURY	RHUBARB	SIGNORA	BOBBERY
WAXWORK	NECTARY	SHIVERY	SILVERY	BOLLARD
WAYWARD.	NERVURE	SHOWERY	SINCERE	BOMBARD
OBSCURE.	NETWORK	THEATRE.	*TILBURY	BONFIRE
ACQUIRE	*NEWPORT	AIRPORT	*TINTERN	BONKERS
ACTUARY	PECCARY	BIGOTRY	TINWARE	COMFORT
ICEBERG	PEPPERY	BILIARY	TITLARK	COMPARE
SCENERY	PERFORM	BITTERN	VICTORY	COMPERE
SCEPTRE.	PERJURE	BIZARRE	VISCERA	COMPORT
ADJOURN.	PERJURY	CILIARY	WINKERS	CONCERN
*BEDFORD	PERTURB	CINDERY	WITHERS.	CONCERT
BEDSORE	PERVERT	CISTERN	SKYLARK	CONCORD
BEGGARY	PESSARY	CITHARA	SKYWARD.	CONFIRM
+BERNARD	RECTORY	DIEHARD	ALGEBRA	CONFORM
BERSERK	RE-ENTRY	DIETARY	*ALGIERS	CONJURE
CENSURE	REMARRY	DIOPTRE	ALIFORM	CONSORT
CENTURY	REQUIRE	DIPTERA	ALLEGRO	CONTORT
DEANERY	RESPIRE	DISCARD	CLOSURE	CONVERT
DECLARE	RESTORE	DISCERN	+ELECTRA	COOKERY
DEEP-FRY	RETIARY	DISCORD	ELUSORY	COPPERY
DEIFORM	REVELRY	DISPORT	FLEXURE	CORPORA
+DEIRDRE	REYNARD	DISTORT	FLOWERY	COSTARD
*DENMARK	SEABIRD	DISTURB	OLIVARY	COUNTRY
DENTARY	SEA-MARK	FILBERT	PLACARD	COWHERD
DENTURE	SEAPORT	FIRE-ARM		DOGGART

441

-O---R-		-C---S-		
FOGHORN	YOGHURT.	CULTURE	BADDISH	LAWLESS
FOOLERY	EPICURE	CULVERT	BAGASSE	LAXNESS
FOPPERY	SPECTRA	CURSORY	BALDEST	MADDEST
FORBORE	SPECTRE	CUSTARD	BALLAST	MADNESS
FOREARM	SPIDERY	CUTLERY	BAPTISM	MALAISE
FORGERY	UPSTART.	DULLARD	BAPTIST	MALTOSE
FORLORN	EQUERRY.	FUTHORC	CABOOSE	MANNISH
FORRARD	ARCHERY	GUIPURE	CADDISH	+MARCUSE
FORWARD	ARMOURY	GUNFIRE	CALMEST	MARXISM
FOULARD	BRAVERY	GUNNERY	+CALYPSO	+MATISSE
FOUMART	BRAVURA	*HUNGARY	CAMBIST	MAWKISH
FOUNDRY	BREWERY	HUNKERS	CANVASS	MAYBUSH
GOLIARD	BRIBERY	MUDLARK	CARCASS	PALMIST
*GOSPORT	DRAPERY	MUMMERY	CAROUSE	PAPOOSE
HOMBURG	DRIP-DRY	MUSTARD	CASUIST	RAFFISH
HOSIERY	DROSERA	NUNNERY	CATFISH	RANKEST
JOBBERY	ERASURE	NURSERY	CATTISH	RAWNESS
LOBWORM	FROWARD	NURTURE	DADAISM	RAYLESS
LOLLARD	GRANARY	OUTWARD	DAMPISH	SACRIST
LOTTERY	GRAPERY	OUTWORE	DANKISH	SADDEST
LOW-BORN	GRAVURE	OUTWORK	DARKEST	SADNESS
MOCKERY	+GREGORY	OUTWORN	DARKISH	SAPLESS
MOIDORE	GROCERY	PURPORT	EARNEST	SARCASM
+MOLIERE	GRUYERE	QUABIRD	FADDIST	SAWDUST
NOCTURN	ORATORY	QUINARY	FANTAST	SAWFISH
NOWHERE	ORCHARD	RUBBERY	FANTASY	TALLEST
POCHARD	PREPARE	RUPTURE	FASCISM	TARNISH
PODAGRA	PRIMARY	SUBVERT	FASCIST	TAUTEST
POLLARD	PROCURE	*SUDBURY	FASTEST	VAINEST
PONIARD	PROVERB	*SUMATRA	FATNESS	VAMOOSE
POPCORN	PRUDERY	SUMMARY	FATTEST	+VANESSA
POSTERN	TRACERY	SUMMERY	GARFISH	VARNISH
POSTURE	TRIFORM	SUNBURN	GARNISH	VASTEST
POT-HERB	URETHRA	SUNWARD	GAS-MASK	WAGGISH
POTTERY	URINARY.	SUPPORT	HAGFISH	WANNESS
POULTRY	*ASHFORD	SURGERY	HAGGISH	WARMEST
POWDERY	ESQUIRE	SUSPIRE	HAPLESS	WASPISH
ROBBERY	ESTUARY	TURNERY	HARDEST	*ZAMBESI.
ROCKERY	OSSUARY.	TUSSORE	HARNESS	ABOLISH
ROGUERY	ATHWART	VULTURE.	HARPIST	ABREAST
*ROMFORD	STÁTURE	*AVEBURY	HARVEST	ABSCESS
ROMPERS	STEWARD	OVERARM	HASHISH	EBONIST
ROOKERY	+STEWART.	OVIFORM.	JACKASS	OBELISK
SOJOURN	AUSTERE	AWKWARD.	LACTASE	OBVERSE.
SORCERY	BUGGERY	EXPLORE.	LACTOSE	ACCURST
TONSURE	BULWARK	EYESORE	LAMAISM	ACINOSE
TOPIARY	BURSARY	MYSTERY	LAPPISH	ACTRESS
TORTURE	BUSTARD	SYNCARP	LARGESS	ECHOISM
TOTTERY	BUTTERY		LARGEST	ECLIPSE
*WOOMERA	BUZZARD	BABYISH	LARGISH	ECSTASY

442

OCULIST	REALIST	DIFFUSE	ELLIPSE	INTRUST
SCOTISM.	RECLUSE	DIGRESS	FLEMISH	INVERSE
ADDRESS	REDDEST	DIMNESS	FLORIST	KNAVISH
ADENOSE	REDDISH	DIOCESE	FLUTIST	ONANISM
ADIPOSE	REDRESS	DIPHASE	FLY-PAST	ONANIST
ADVERSE	REFRESH	DISCUSS	GLIMPSE	ONENESS
ODDNESS.	REGRESS	DISEASE	GLOBOSE	UNCLASP
BEARISH	RELAPSE	DISGUST	GLUCOSE	UNCLOSE
BECAUSE	RELEASE	DISMAST	ILLNESS	UNDRESS
BEDPOST	REMORSE	DISMISS	PLANISH	UNHORSE
*BELFAST	REPRESS	DISPOSE	PLUMOSE	UNLEASH
BEQUEST	REPULSE	DIVERSE	SLAVISH	UNLOOSE
CELLIST	REQUEST	FINESSE	SLOWEST	UNTRUSS
DEAREST	REVERSE	FINNISH	SLYNESS.	UNTWIST.
+DEBUSSY	REVERSO	FITNESS	AMONGST	BOLDEST
DECEASE	SELFISH	FITTEST	AMORIST	BOMBAST
DEEPEST	SEXIEST	GIRLISH	EMBASSY	BONE-ASH
DEFROST	SEXLESS	HIGHEST	EMPRESS	BOOKISH
DEGAUSS	TEA-COSY	KINDEST	IMAGISM	BOORISH
DELOUSE	TEA-ROSE	*KINROSS	IMBURSE	CODFISH
DENSEST	TEMPEST	LICENSE	IMMENSE	COEXIST
DENTIST	TENSEST	LIONESS	IMMERSE	COLDEST
DEPRESS	VERBOSE	MIDMOST	IMPASSE	COLDISH
DERVISH	VERIEST	MILDEST	IMPRESS	COLTISH
DESPISE	WEAKEST	MISCAST	IMPREST	COMPASS
GEODESY	WETNESS	OILLESS	IMPULSE.	COMPOSE
HEIRESS	WETTEST.	PIANIST	ANALYSE	COMPOST
HELLISH	AGAINST	PICTISH	ANALYST	CONCISE
HEROISM	AGELESS	PIETISM	ANGUISH	CONCUSS
KEENEST	AGGRESS	PIGGISH	ANIMISM	CONFESS
KENTISH	EGOTISM	PIGWASH	ANYWISE	CONFUSE
LEFTIST	EGOTIST	PINKISH	ENCHASE	CONGEST
LEGLESS	OGREISH	RICHEST	ENCLOSE	CONSIST
LENTISK	UGLIEST.	SIAMESE	ENCRUST	CONTEST
LEPROSY	CHEMISE	SICKEST	ENDLESS	COOLEST
MEEKEST	CHEMIST	SINLESS	ENDMOST	COPYIST
+MELISSA	CHERISH	TIDIEST	ENDORSE	CORNISH
METCAST	CHINESE	TIGRESS	ENDWISE	COULDST
METRIST	SHYNESS	TINIEST	ENGLISH	COYNESS
NEAREST	+THERESA	VIOLIST	ENGROSS	DOGFISH
NEGRESS	THOMISM	VISCOSE	ENTHUSE	DOG-ROSE
PECKISH	WHITEST	WILDEST	ENTRUST	DOLTISH
PEERESS	WHITISH.	WITLESS	GNOMISH	DONNISH
PEEVISH	AIMLESS	WITNESS	INCENSE	FOOLISH
PELISSE	AIRLESS	YIDDISH	INCLOSE	FOPPISH
PENTOSE	BIGGEST	ZIONISM	INCRUST	*FORMOSA
PERCUSS	CIRROSE	ZIONIST.	INDORSE	GOATISH
PERSIST	DIABASE	BLEMISH	INGRESS	GODDESS
PETTISH	DIARIST	CLEANSE	INQUEST	GODLESS
REALISM	DIETIST	ELEGIST	INTENSE	GOODISH

443

-O---S-			-E---T-	
GOULASH	PREMISE	NUT-CASE	CANASTA	ABILITY
HOGGISH	PROCESS	OUTCAST	CANTATA	ABSINTH
HOGWASH	PROFESS	OUTLAST	CARROTY	EBONITE
HOLIEST	PROFUSE	OUTMOST	CAUDATE	OBVIATE.
HOSTESS	PROMISE	OUTPOST	FACULTY	ACCRETE
HOTTEST	PROPOSE	PUBLISH	FALCATE	ACETATE
JOBLESS	PROTEST	PUCKISH	FALSITY	ACIDITY
JOYLESS	PROVISO	PUG-NOSE	GAROTTE	ACOLYTE
LONGEST	PROVOST	PURPOSE	GASEITY	ACONITE
LOOSEST	PROWESS	QUERIST	GAVOTTE	ACTUATE
LOUDEST	PRUDISH	RUBBISH	GAZETTE	OCULATE.
LOUTISH	TRAIPSE	RUMNESS	HASLETS	ADULATE
MOLLUSC	TRICKSY	RUTTISH	HASTATE	EDACITY
MONKISH	TROPISM	SUBFUSC	HAUGHTY	EDUCATE.
MOORISH	URANISM	SUBSIST	JACINTH	+BECKETT
MORTISE	WRYNESS.	SUCCESS	KAINITE	BENEATH
NOBLEST	ASPERSE	SUCCOSE	LAYETTE	BETROTH
NOURISH	ESPOUSE	SUCROSE	+MACBETH	CELESTA
POETESS	USELESS.	SUFFUSE.	MACHETE	+CELESTE
POOREST	ATAVISM	SUGGEST	MAGENTA	DEFLATE
POSSESS	ATHEISM	SUNLESS	MAGGOTY	DENSITY
ROGUISH	ATHIRST	SUNRISE	MAGNATE	DENTATE
SOFTEST	STALEST	SUNWISE	MAGNETO	DEPLETE
SOLOIST	STATISM	SUPPOSE	MAJESTY	DESPITE
SOPHISM	+STRAUSS	SURMISE	MAMMOTH	DETENTE
SOPHIST	STYLISH	SURPASS	MANDATE	DEVIATE
SOTTISH	STYLIST.	TURKISH.	*MARGATE	FELSITE
SOUREST	AUTOPSY	*EVEREST.	MARMITE	FERRATE
TOPMAST	BUCKISH	SWEDISH	NAIVETE	FERRETY
TOPMOST	BUGLOSS	SWINISH.	NAIVETY	FERRITE
TOURISM	BULLISH	EXHAUST	NARRATE	GEMMATE
TOURIST	BULRUSH	EXPANSE	NAUGHTY	GENISTA
WOLFISH	BURGESS	EXPENSE	PALETTE	+KENNETH
YORKIST.	BURNISH	EXPRESS	PALMATE	KEYNOTE
APPEASE	CUIRASS	OXIDASE.	PALPATE	MEDIATE
APPRISE	CURRISH	CYCLIST	PARTITE	MEMENTO
APTNESS	CUTLASS	CYPRESS	PAUCITY	NEGRITO
OPPRESS	DUALISM	EYELASH	RABBITY	PENALTY
SPANISH.	DUCHESS	EYELESS	RADIATE	*PENRITH
ARMLESS	DULLEST	EYEWASH	SABAOTH	PERLITE
ARTLESS	FUGUIST	GYMNAST	SABBATH	PERMUTE
BRAVEST	FULLEST	HYMNIST	SACCATE	REALITY
BRITISH	FURBISH	SYNAPSE	SATIATE	REBIRTH
BRUTISH	FURNISH		SATIETY	*REDRUTH
GRAVEST	HUFFISH	BARBATE	TAFFETA	REGATTA
GRECISM.	JUDAISM	+BATISTA	TANNATE	*REIGATE
GREYISH	JUJITSU	BATISTE	VACUITY	REPLETE
IRONIST	LUMPISH	BAUXITE	VARIETY	REQUITE
PRECESS	MUDFISH	CALCITE	VARSITY	RESPITE
PRECISE	MUJITSA	CALOTTE	WARPATH.	RESTATE·

REUNITE	PIMENTO	COGNATE	ERUDITE	PULSATE
REWRITE	PINNATE	COLLATE	FRAILTY	QUALITY
REWROTE	PIPETTE	COMMUTE	FRIGATE	+QUIXOTE
SECRETE	RICKETS	COMPETE	FROWSTY	RUINATE
SEPTATE	RICKETY	COMPOTE	GRADATE	SUAVITY
SERIATE	RIPOSTE	COMPUTE	GRANITE	SURDITY
SERRATE	RISOTTO	CONFUTE	GRAVITY	VULGATE.
SEVENTH	SITUATE	CONNATE	PRELATE	AVIDITY.
SEVENTY	TITRATE	CONNOTE	PRIMATE	TWELFTH.
TEKTITE	VIBRATE	CORANTO	PRIVATE	AXOLOTL
TENUITY	VIBRATO	CORDATE	PRIVITY	EXCRETA
TERMITE	VIDUITY	CORDITE	PROBATE	EXCRETE
TESTATE	VIOLATE	*CORINTH	PROBITY	EXECUTE
VEDANTA	VIRGATE	COSTATE	PROLATE	EXPIATE.
VEDETTE	VITIATE.	DOUGHTY	PROMOTE	DYNASTY
VELVETY	CLARITY	FOLIATE	TRIBUTE	EYE-BATH
WEIGHTY	CLIMATE	FORMATE	TRILITH	HYALITE
ZEOLITE.	ELEVATE	+HOGARTH	TRINITY.	HYDRATE
AGILITY	FLIGHTY	HONESTY	+ASTARTE	LYDDITE.
AGITATE	PLACATE	HOPLITE	ESPARTO	AZIMUTH
AGITATO	PLICATE	+JOCASTA	ESTHETE	+BACCHUS
EGALITY.	ULULATE.	JOLLITY	ISOBATH	BALEFUL
CHARITY	AMANITA	LOYALTY	ISOLATE.	BANEFUL
CHELATE	AMENITY	MODESTY	ATHLETE	BAROQUE
CHIANTI	AMNESTY	MODISTE	*ATLANTA	BASHFUL
+CHRISTI	EMANATE	NOVELTY	ITERATE	CACIQUE
PHONATE	EMULATE	POLENTA	STATUTE	CADMIUM
THERETO	IMITATE	POLLUTE	STEALTH	CAESIUM
THIRSTY	IMPASTE	POVERTY	STOMATA	CALAMUS
THRIFTY	IMPASTO	+ROBERTA	STRIATE	CALCIUM
THROATY	IMPIETY.	ROSEATE	STYLITE	CALLOUS
WHERETO.	ANDANTE	ROSETTE	UTILITY.	CAMBIUM
BIRETTA	ANIMATE	ROYALTY	AUREATE	CANDOUR
BISMUTH	+ANNETTE	SOCIETY	BULLATE	CARACUL
CILIATE	ANNUITY	TOCCATA	BURETTE	*CARACUS
CITRATE	ANXIETY	*TORONTO	CUPRITE	CAREFUL
DICTATE	ENTENTE	TOWPATH.	CURETTE	CARIOUS
DIGNITY	INANITY	OPACITY	CURVATE	CASEOUS
DIORITE	INFANTA	OPERATE.	CUSPATE	EAR-DRUM
DISPUTE	INFANTE	ARCUATE	DUALITY	EASEFUL
HIRSUTE	INFLATE	ARIDITY	DUBIETY	FALL-GUY
KIBBUTZ	INGRATE	ARTISTE	FURCATE	FALL-OUT
LIBERTY	INSTATE	BREADTH	GUTTATE	FAMULUS
LIBRATE	UNCOUTH	BREVITY	LUDDITE	FARCEUR
LIGNITE	UNEARTH	BROMATE	LUNETTE	FATEFUL
LIMBATE	UNQUOTE	CREMATE	MUD-BATH	FATIGUE
LINEATE	UNTRUTH.	CRENATE	MULATTO	FATUOUS
LIQUATE	BOX-KITE	CRUDITY	NULLITY	GAINFUL
MIGRATE	BOYCOTT	CRUELTY	OUTVOTE	GALLIUM
NITRATE	COCOTTE	EREMITE	PUBERTY	

445

GASEOUS	ADENOUS	CHECK-UP	SKILFUL	MODICUM
HABITUE	ODOROUS.	CHIRRUP	SKINFUL	MOONBUG
HAFNIUM	BECLOUD	PHALLUS	SKY-BLUE.	NONPLUS
HAIR-CUT	*BELGIUM	+PHOEBUS	ALUMNUS	NOSTRUM
HALIBUT	*BENELUX	RHENIUM	ALYSSUM	NOXIOUS
HANDFUL	BEZIQUE	RHODIUM	BLOW-OUT	POLYPUS
HANDOUT	CENTAUR	RHOMBUS	CLAMOUR	POMATUM
HARBOUR	CEREOUS	SHOTGUN	CLOSE-UP	POMPOUS
HARMFUL	DECORUM	SHUT-OUT	ELYSIUM	+ROMULUS
HATEFUL	DEFRAUD	+THESEUS	FLANEUR	ROOMFUL
HAUTEUR	DEVALUE	THORIUM	FLAVOUR	ROSEBUD
+MALTHUS	DEVIOUS	THULIUM	GLAMOUR	ROSE-CUT
MAN-HOUR	FEARFUL	THYRSUS	GLEEFUL	ROSTRUM
MANTRUM	FERMIUM	WHITSUN.	*OLYMPUS	ROUND-UP
MASSEUR	FERROUS	BILIOUS	PLAYFUL.	SORGHUM
MAXIMUM	FERVOUR	CITROUS	AMATEUR	SOULFUL
NAVY-CUT	HEEDFUL	DIREFUL	AMOROUS	TOBY-JUG
PABULUM	HEINOUS	DISHFUL	EMBOLUS	WOODCUT
PAILFUL	HELPFUL	FIBROUS	EMULOUS	WORK-OUT
PAINFUL	JEALOUS	FIRE-BUG	IMPETUS	APPLAUD
PALLIUM	JEJUNUM	FISTFUL	IMPIOUS	OPOSSUM
PAPYRUS	KETCHUP	GIBBOUS	OMINOUS	OPTIMUM
PARLOUR	NEEDFUL	HIDEOUS	OMNIBUS	SPINOUS.
PARLOUS	NERVOUS	HIDEOUT	SMASH-UP.	AQUEOUS.
+PASTEUR	+OEDIPUS	KINGCUP	ANGELUS	ARBUTUS
RANCOUR	OESTRUS	LINCTUS	+ANTAEUS	ARDUOUS
RAUCOUS	PEA-SOUP	LINOCUT	*ANTIGUA	BREAK-UP
SACKBUT	+PEGASUS	LIQUEUR	ANTIQUE	BRIMFUL
SANCTUM	+PERSEUS	LITHIUM	ANXIOUS	BRUMOUS
SANCTUS	REAUMUR	MINDFUL	ENAMOUR	BRUSQUE
SAVIOUR	REGROUP	MINIBUS	ENVIOUS	CRACK-UP
TACTFUL	REISSUE	MINIMUM	INCUBUS	CRANIUM
TAMBOUR	RENEGUE	NIOBIUM	INGENUE	+CROESUS
TANTRUM	RESIDUA	NITROUS	ONEROUS.	+DRESFUS
VACUOUS	RESIDUE	PINETUM	BOATFUL	DROP-OUT
VARIOUS	RESTFUL	PIPEFUL	BODEFUL	+ERASMUS
WALK-OUT	RETINUE	PIRAGUA	BOWLFUL	ERRATUM
WASH-OUT.	REVENUE	PIROGUE	BOXHAUL	FRETFUL
OBLIQUE	SELL-OUT	PITEOUS	COCONUT	FRUSTUM
OBLOQUY	SENATUS	PITIFUL	CONFLUX	GRAMPUS
OBVIOUS.	SERIOUS	+RIMBAUD	CONTOUR	GROWN-UP
ACETOUS	+SEYMOUR	RIOTOUS	COPIOUS	IRIDIUM
ECHINUS	TEARFUL	SINUOUS	DOLEFUL	+ORPHEUS
ECLOGUE	TEDIOUS	SISTRUM	DOUCEUR	PREMIUM
ICTERUS	TENUOUS	VICIOUS	FORKFUL	PRONOUN
OCCIPUT	TERBIUM	VILLOUS	HOLMIUM	+PROTEUS
OCELLUS	TETANUS	VISCOUS	HOODLUM	TRITIUM
OCHROUS	ZEALOUS	WISHFUL	HOPEFUL	TRIVIUM
OCTOPUS	ZESTFUL.	WISTFUL	LOCK-OUT	URANIUM
SCROTUM.	IGNEOUS.	WITHOUT.	LOOK-OUT	URANOUS

WRITE-UP.		FORGAVE	ACRONYM	CLARKIA
ISCHIUM	CAPTIVE	FORGIVE.	ICHTHYS.	+CLAUDIA
ISTHMUS	CASSAVA	APPROVE	SHUT-EYE.	CZARINA
OSSEOUS.	MASSIVE	UPHEAVE.	PINK-EYE.	DRACHMA
STADIUM	PASSIVE	EROSIVE.	ANTONYM	GRANDMA
STANNUM	+PAVLOVA.	CURSIVE	ENDWAYS.	GRANDPA
STEN-GUN	ABSOLVE	FURTIVE	+FONTEYN	KHALIFA
STERNUM	ABUSIVE	JUSSIVE	GOOD-BYE	OCARINA
STIRRUP	OBSERVE.	OUTLIVE	HOMONYM	+PHAEDRA
STRATUM	ACHIEVE.	SUASIVE	+JOCELYN.	PIANOLA
STRATUS	BEEHIVE	SURVIVE.	APTERYX	QUASSIA
STUCK-UP	BELIEVE	EVASIVE	SPONDYL.	SCAPULA
YTTRIUM.	BEREAVE		SYNONYM	SPATULA
BUILT-UP	DECEIVE			STAMINA
BULBOUS	DEPRAVE	BARN-OWL		*SWANSEA
BUREAUX	DEPRIVE	GALLOWS	BAPTIZE	TRACHEA
BURNOUS	DESERVE	HAWK-OWL	CADENZA	URAEMIA.
CUMULUS	DEVOLVE	+MARLOWE.	CAPSIZE	*ALBANIA
CUPROUS	FESTIVE	BELLOWS	LAICIZE	KABBALA
CURIOUS	PECCAVI	FERN-OWL	*YANGTZE.	*LIBERIA
DUBIOUS	PENSIVE	*NEWTOWN	EBONIZE	LOBELIA
DUTEOUS	RECEIVE	SEA-FOWL	OBELIZE.	+REBECCA
DUTIFUL	RELIEVE	SET-DOWN	SCHERZO.	+ROBERTA
FULCRUM	REPROVE	YELLOWY.	IDOLIZE.	RUBELLA
FULVOUS	RESERVE	SHADOWY.	MESTIZO	RUBEOLA
FUNGOUS	RESOLVE	MILDEWY	REALIZE.	+SABRINA.
FURIOUS	RESTIVE	SIT-DOWN	AGONIZE.	+CECILIA
FUSCOUS	REVOLVE.	*WIGTOWN	LIONIZE.	COCHLEA
HUMDRUM	BIVALVE	WILLOWY.	ELEGIZE.	EXCRETA
HUMERUS	FICTIVE	INDRAWN	ANODIZE	FUCHSIA
HURTFUL	+MINERVA	UNBLOWN	UNFROZE.	+JOCASTA
LUSTFUL	MISGAVE	UNKNOWN.	COGNIZE	*NICOSIA
LUTEOUS	MISGIVE	GOSHAWK	POETIZE.	TOCCATA.
NUCLEUS	MISSIVE.	LOW-DOWN.	+SPINOZA.	ADDENDA
PUNCH-UP	ELUSIVE	BRADAWL.	SQUEEZE.	*ANDORRA
QUANTUM	PLOSIVE.	RUB-DOWN	IRIDIZE	CADENZA
QUIETUS	AMATIVE	RUN-DOWN	TRAPEZE.	CEDILLA
RUINOUS	EMOTIVE	SUNDOWN.	ATOMIZE	*INDIANA
SUCCOUR	IMPROVE.	OVERAWE	ITEMIZE	INDICIA
SULPHUR	ANCHOVY		STYLIZE	*MADEIRA
SURPLUS	ENCLAVE	BETWIXT.	UTILIZE.	MADONNA
TUMULUS	ENGRAVE	PICKAXE.	DUALIZE	MEDULLA
TUNEFUL	ENSLAVE	CONTEXT	JUDAIZE	PODAGRA
TURN-OUT.	INVOLVE	POLE-AXE.	OUTSIZE.	PUDENDA
OVERDUE	INWEAVE	PRETEXT.	OXIDIZE	SEDILIA
OVERRUN.	UNITIVE	ATARAXY		VEDANTA.
HYDROUS	UNNERVE.	CACODYL	*ALABAMA	AMENTIA
PYLORUS	CONCAVE	+CAROLYN	AMANITA	*AMERICA
TYPHOUS.	CONNIVE	CATS-EYE	ANAEMIA	BRECCIA
AZYMOUS	COSTIVE	+MARILYN.	BRAVURA	*CHELSEA

447

DEEP-SEA	+JULIANA	SCOTOMA	ROSEOLA	CLASTIC
+ELECTRA	MALACCA	STOMATA	SESTINA	DRASTIC
FREESIA	MALARIA	*WOOMERA.	+SUSANNA	ELASTIC
*GRENADA	MELISMA	AMPHORA	TESSERA	FRANTIC
INERTIA	+MELISSA	AMPULLA	VASCULA	GNATHIC
*OCEANIA	MILITIA	COPAIBA	VISCERA	GRAPHIC
OVERSEA	*PALMYRA	DIPLOMA	*VISTULA.	PHALLIC
SPECTRA	POLACCA	DIPTERA	ANTENNA	PLASMIC
SPECULA	POLENTA	NAPHTHA	*ANTIGUA	PLASTIC
+THERESA	POLYNIA	PAPILLA	+ASTRAEA	SKALDIC
URETHRA.	*SILESIA	PAPRIKA	+BATISTA	SPASTIC
ALFALFA	SULTANA.	REPLICA	CATALPA	STANNIC
INFANTA	AMMONIA	TAPIOCA.	CITHARA	TRAFFIC.
TAFFETA.	+JAMAICA	SEQUOIA.	*ESTELLA	BUBONIC
ALGEBRA	LAMELLA	AUREOLA	HETAERA	DIBASIC
*ALGERIA	MAMILLA	+BARBARA	*KATANGA	ECBOLIC
BEGONIA	*RUMANIA	BARBOLA	+MATILDA	HEBETIC
HAGGADA	*SUMATRA	*BERMUDA	METAZOA	HEBRAIC
MAGENTA	TEMPERA	BIRETTA	PATELLA	SUBFUSC
*NIGERIA	TOMBOLA.	COROLLA	PETUNIA	TABETIC.
REGALIA	AMNESIA	CORPORA	RATAFIA	ARCHAIC
REGATTA	BANKSIA	CURCUMA	ROTUNDA	ASCETIC
+SEGOVIA	CANASTA	*FORMOSA	*SATSUMA	BACCHIC
SIGNORA.	CANDELA	FORMULA	+TITANIA.	BUCOLIC
APHASIA	CANTATA	GORILLA	ALUMINA.	LACONIC
APHELIA	+CYNTHIA	*HORNSEA	+LAVINIA	NUCLEIC
*BOHEMIA	+FENELLA	MARIMBA	+PAVLOVA	*PACIFIC
ECHIDNA	GANGLIA	+MIRANDA	SAVANNA.	RACEMIC
GEHENNA	GENISTA	MORPHIA	MAXILLA.	TECHNIC
MAHATMA	GONDOLA	NIRVANA	BRYOZOA	VOCALIC.
+OPHELIA	MANDALA	PERGOLA	*OLYMPIA.	EIDETIC
OPHIDIA.	MANILLA	PERSONA	BAZOOKA	ENDEMIC
*ARIZONA	+MINERVA	PIRAGUA	MAZURKA	HEDONIC.
CHIASMA	*MONTANA	PYREXIA		ACERBIC
CHIMERA	PANACEA	SARCOMA	SUCCUMB.	ALEMBIC
PRIMULA	+PANDORA	SYRINGA	MINICAB.	ASEPTIC
+SPINOZA.	SYNOVIA	VARIOLA	PROVERB.	COELIAC
*MAJORCA	TANAGRA	VERANDA	CORN-COB	ELEGIAC
MUJITSA.	*TUNISIA	VERBENA	PERTURB.	OCEANIC
*ATLANTA	+VANESSA	VERRUCA	DISTURB.	SCEPTIC
+BELINDA	VANILLA.	XERASIA.	POT-HERB.	SHELLAC
BELISHA	ABOULIA	*AUSTRIA	COULOMB	SKEPTIC
+BELLONA	ANOSMIA	CASCARA	RHUBARB.	THERMIC.
*BOLIVIA	CHOLERA	CASSAVA	COXCOMB	ANGELIC
*BOLOGNA	DIORAMA	FISTULA	TAXI-CAB	EUGENIC
BULIMIA	DROSERA	HOSANNA		ORGANIC.
CELESTA	EROTICA	+JESSICA	ANAEMIC	AMHARIC
DILEMMA	*FLORIDA	MASCARA	ARAMAIC	APHONIC
FELUCCA	*GEORGIA	PISCINA	CHAOTIC	OGHAMIC
FILARIA	+LEONORA	RESIDUA	CLASSIC	SPHERIC

ABIOTIC	RHOMBIC.	STYPTIC	DRATTED	QUAFFED
ASIATIC	CAPROIC		DRAWLED	QUAILED
DEISTIC	EMPIRIC	ADAPTED	DWARFED	QUASHED
IDIOTIC	HEPATIC	AMASSED	ELAPSED	REACHED
SCIATIC	NEPOTIC	AVAILED	ENABLED	REARMED
SEISMIC.	SAPPHIC.	AWAITED	ENACTED	ROASTED
ACLINIC	ACRYLIC	AWARDED	EXACTED	SCABBED
BALDRIC	AEROBIC	BEACHED	EXALTED	SCAFFED
CALORIC	BORACIC	BLABBED	FEASTED	SCALDED
CHLORIC	CARDIAC	BLANKED	FLACCID	SCALPED
DELPHIC	CERAMIC	BLASTED	FLAGGED	SCAMPED
ISLAMIC	CHROMIC	BRAGGED	FLAILED	SCANNED
MALEFIC	CHRONIC	BRAIDED	FLANGED	SCARPED
MELODIC	EIRENIC	BRAINED	FLAPPED	SCARRED
MOLLUSC	ERRATIC	BRAISED	FLASHED	SCATHED
PELAGIC	HERETIC	BRANDED	GLANCED	SEABIRD
POLEMIC	MORONIC	CHAINED	GNARLED	SEAWARD
POLITIC	PHRENIC	CHAIRED	GNASHED	SEAWEED
SILICIC	PYRETIC	CHANCED	GO-AHEAD	SHACKED
SPLENIC	PYRRHIC.	CHANGED	GRABBED	SHAGGED
VOLTAIC.	ARSENIC	CHANTED	GRAFTED	SHAMMED
ALMANAC	BASILIC	CHAPPED	GRAINED	SHARKED
CAMBRIC	GASTRIC	CHARGED	GRANDAD	SLAMMED
DEMONIC	MASONIC.	CHARRED	GRANTED	SLANGED
DEMOTIC	ACTINIC	CHARTED	GRASSED	SLANTED
GAMETIC	ASTATIC	CHATTED	GUARDED	SLAPPED
HAMITIC	BOTANIC	CLACKED	HEARTED	SLASHED
HOMERIC	BUTYRIC	CLAIMED	HYALOID	SLATTED
MIMETIC	ENTERIC	CLAMPED	KNAPPED	SMACKED
NOMADIC	ENTOMIC	CLANGED	KRAALED	SMARTED
OSMOTIC	FUTHORC	CLANKED	LEACHED	SMASHED
ROMANIC	SATANIC	CLAPPED	LEARNED	SNAGGED
SEMITIC	SATIRIC	CLASHED	LEASHED	SNARLED
SOMATIC	SATYRIC	CLASPED	LOATHED	SPANKED
ZYMOTIC.	TETANIC	CLASSED	MIAOWED	SPANNED
CENTRIC	TITANIC	COACHED	PEARLED	SPARKED
DYNAMIC	TOTEMIC.	COAL-BED	PLACARD	SPARRED
FANATIC	AQUATIC	COASTED	PLAGUED	SPAWNED
GENERIC	CAUSTIC	CRABBED	PLAITED	STABBED
GENETIC	DRUIDIC	CRACKED	PLANKED	STABLED
KENOTIC	PLUMBIC	CRAMMED	PLANNED	STACKED
KINETIC	+POULENC	CRAMPED	PLANTED	STAFFED
LUNATIC	PRUSSIC.	CRANKED	PLATTED	STAINED
MONADIC	BIVOUAC.	CRASHED	POACHED	STALKED
SYNODIC.	CRYPTIC	DEAD-END	PRAISED	STALLED
AMOEBIC	GLYPHIC	DIALLED	PRANCED	STAMPED
ANOETIC	GLYPTIC	DIAMOND	PRANKED	STARRED
GEORGIC	IDYLLIC	DRAFTED	PRAWNED	STARTED
GNOSTIC	OLYMPIC	DRAGGED	QUABIRD	STARVED
PROSAIC	PSYCHIC	DRAINED	QUACKED	STASHED

SWABBED	SOBERED	*BEDFORD	CLEARED	PREPAID
SWAMPED	SUBACID	CODDLED	CLEAVED	PRESSED
SWANKED	SUBDUED	CUDDLED	COERCED	PRETEND
SWAPPED	SUBTEND	DEDUCED	CREAKED	QUEENED
SWARMED	TABLOID	ENDOWED	CREAMED	QUELLED
SWASHED	TABOOED	ENDURED	CREASED	QUERIED
SWATHED	UNBOUND	FIDDLED	CREATED	QUESTED
SWATTED	UNBOWED	FUDDLED	CRESTED	SCENTED
THANKED	UPBRAID	GODHEAD	DIEHARD	SEEDBED
TRACKED	WOBBLED.	GODSEND	DREADED	SEETHED
TRAILED	ACCEDED	HUDDLED	DRESSED	SHEARED
TRAMMED	ACCUSED	HYDATID	DUELLED	SHEERED
TRAMPED	BECLOUD	INDITED	EGESTED	SHEETED
TRAPPED	BUCKLED	INDUCED	EJECTED	SHELLED
TRAPSED	CACKLED	IODIZED	ELECTED	SHELVED
TRASHED	CUCKOLD	MEDDLED	EMENDED	SLEDDED
TWANGED	CYCLOID	MIDDLED	EMERALD	SLEDGED
UNACTED	DECAPOD	MIDLAND	EMERGED	SLEETED
UNAIDED	DECAYED	MUDDIED	ERECTED	SLEEVED
UNAIRED	DECIDED	MUDDLED	EVERTED	SMEARED
UNARMED	DECODED	ORDERED	EXERTED	SNEAKED
UNASKED	DECOYED	PADDLED	FIELDED	SNEERED
WHACKED	ENCAGED	PEDDLED	FLECKED	SNEEZED
WHARFED	ENCASED	RADDLED	FLEDGED	SPEARED
WRAPPED	ESCAPED	RED-HEAD	FLEETED	SPECKED
YEARNED.	EUCHRED	REDOUND	FLESHED	SPEEDED
BUBBLED	EXCISED	REDUCED	FREAKED	SPELLED
DABBLED	EXCITED	REDWOOD	FRETTED	STEAMED
DEBASED	EXCUSED	RIDDLED	FUELLED	STEELED
DEBATED	FOCUSED	RUDDLED	GLEAMED	STEEPED
DEBITED	INCISED	SEDATED	GREASED	STEMMED
DIBBLED	INCITED	WADDLED.	GREETED	STEPPED
ELBOWED	INCUSED	ABETTED	GUESSED	STEROID
EMBAYED	KECKLED	ADENOID	*ICELAND	STEWARD
FIBROID	LOCATED	ALERTED	*IRELAND	SWEATED
GABBLED	ORCHARD	AMENDED	KNEADED	SWELLED
HABITED	PICKLED	AMERCED	KNEELED	SWERVED
HOBBLED	POCHARD	ANEROID	KNELLED	TOEHOLD
IMBIBED	RECEDED	AVERRED	LEEWARD	TREATED
IMBRUED	+RICHARD	AVERTED	NEEDLED	TREBLED
INBOARD	SECEDED	BLEATED	ONE-EYED	TREKKED
INBREED	SECURED	BLEEPED	OVERDID	TRENDED
LOBBIED	SICK-BED	BLENDED	PIEBALD	TRESSED
NIBBLED	SUCCEED	BLESSED	PIE-EYED	TWEAKED
ORBITED	SUCKLED	BREADED	PIERCED	WEEK-END
PEBBLED	UNCARED	CHEATED	PLEASED	WHEELED
REBATED	UNCASED	CHECKED	PLEATED	WHEEZED
REBORED	VACATED	CHEERED	PLEDGED	WHELPED
REBOUND	YACHTED.	CHEESED	PREBEND	WHETTED
REBUKED	AUDITED	CLEANED	PREENED	WIELDED

WREAKED	LEGATED	EMITTED	SKIRTED	ALLAYED
WRECKED	LOGWOOD	EVICTED	SLIPPED	ALLEGED
WRESTED	NEGATED	EVINCED	SMIRKED	ALLOWED
YIELDED	NEGROID	EXISTED	SNIFFED	ALLOYED
*ZEELAND.	NIGGARD	FAINTED	SNIPPED	ALLUDED
AFFINED	NIGGLED	FEIGNED	SPILLED	ALLURED
AFFIXED	REGALED	FLICKED	SPIRTED	BELATED
BAFFLED	RIGHTED	FLIRTED	SPITTED	BELAYED
DEFACED	SIGHTED	FLITTED	STICKED	BELLIED
DEFAMED	SUGARED	FOISTED	STIFLED	BELOVED
DEFILED	WAGERED	FRILLED	STILLED	BOLLARD
DEFINED	WAGGLED	FRINGED	STILTED	BULLIED
DEFRAUD	WIGGLED.	FRISKED	STINTED	COLLOID
DEFUSED	ADHERED	FRITTED	STIPEND	DALLIED
EFFASED	ASHAMED	FRIZZED	STIRRED	DELATED
EFFUSED	*ASHFORD	GLINTED	SWIGGED	DELAYED
ENFACED	BEHAVED	GRIEVED	SWILLED	DELETED
*ENFIELD	EXHALED	GRILLED	SWIRLED	DELTOID
INFIELD	EXHUMED	GRINNED	SWISHED	DELUDED
INFIXED	ICHABOD	GRIPPED	TAIL-END	DELUGED
INFUSED	INHERED	GRITTED	TAINTED	DILATED
MUFFLED	INHUMED	HEISTED	THIEVED	DILUTED
OFFERED	UNHEARD	HOICKED	THINNED	DULLARD
OFF-HAND	UNHOPED	HOISTED	TRICKED	ENLACED
OFFWARD	USHERED.	JOINTED	TRIFLED	FILCHED
RAFFLED	ANISEED	KNITTED	TRILLED	+GALAHAD
REFACED	BLINDED	NEIGHED	TRIMMED	GOLIARD
REFINED	BLINKED	OMITTED	TRIPLED	HALBERD
REFUSED	BRICKED	PAINTED	TWIGGED	HALYARD
REFUTED	BRIDGED	POINTED	TWILLED	*HOLLAND
RUFFLED	BRIDLED	PRIGGED	TWINGED	ILL-BRED
UNFIXED	BRIGAND	PRIMMED	TWINNED	JELLIED
WAFFLED.	CHILLED	PRINTED	TWIRLED	LOLLARD
ANGERED	CHINKED	QUILLED	TWITTED	MALLARD
AUGURED	CHINNED	QUILTED	UNIFIED	+MILDRED
*BAGHDAD	CHIPPED	QUIPPED	WAISTED	*MILFORD
BIG-HEAD	CHIRPED	QUITTED	WEIGHED	MULCHED
BIGOTED	CLICKED	QUIZZED	WHIFFED	OBLIGED
DOGWOOD	CLIPPED	REIGNED	WHIPPED	PALSIED
EGGHEAD	CRIBBED	RHIZOID	WHIRLED	PILOTED
ENGAGED	CRICKED	SAINTED	WHIRRED	POLICED
*ENGLAND	CRIMPED	SHINNED	WHISKED	POLLARD
FIGURED	CRINGED	SHIPPED	WHIZZED	POLYPOD
GAGGLED	CRINOID	SKIDDED	WRITHED.	RALLIED
GOGGLED	DAISIED	SKID-LID	ABJURED	RELATED
+HAGGARD	DEIFIED	SKILLED	CAJOLED	RELAXED
JIGGLED	DEIGNED	SKIMPED	ENJOYED	RELINED
JOGGLED	DRILLED	SKINNED	INJURED	RELIVED
JUGGLED	DRIPPED	SKIPPED	MAJORED.	*SALFORD
LAGGARD	EDIFIED	SKIRLED	AWKWARD.	SALLIED

SALUTED	CONCORD	TANGOED	FLOURED	SLOTTED
SOLACED	CONTEND	TANKARD	FLOUTED	SNOGGED
SPLAYED	DANGLED	TENFOLD	FOOTPAD	SNOOZED
SPLICED	DENOTED	TENONED	FROCKED	SOOTHED
SPLINED	DENUDED	TINGLED	FROGGED	SPOILED
SULLIED	DONATED	TONGUED	FRONTED	SPOOFED
TALIPED	FANCIED	UNNAMED	FROSTED	SPOOLED
TALLIED	*FINLAND	VANWARD	FROTHED	SPOONED
TALONED	FONDLED	VENOMED	FROWARD	SPORTED
TELEXED	FUNGOID	WANGLED	FROWNED	SPOTTED
VALETED	HANSARD	WENCHED	GHOSTED	SPOUTED
VOLUTED	HONEYED	WINCHED	GLOATED	STOCKED
WALTZED	HUNCHED	WINKLED.	GLORIED	STOOGED
+WILFRED.	HUNDRED	ABORTED	GLOSSED	STOOKED
ADMIXED	IGNITED	AROUSED	GROANED	STOOPED
ARM-BAND	IGNORED	BLOATED	GROINED	STOPPED
BEMUSED	IONIZED	BLOCKED	GROOMED	STORIED
BOMBARD	JANGLED	BLOODED	GROSSED	STORMED
CAMP-BED	JINGLED	BLOOMED	GROUPED	SWOONED
COMMAND	KINDRED	BLOTTED	GROUTED	SWOOPED
COMMEND	KINKLED	BROODED	KNOBBED	SWOPPED
DEMIGOD	LANGUID	BROWNED	KNOCKED	SWOTTED
DEMISED	LANYARD	BROWSED	KNOTTED	TOOTHED
DEMOTED	LENTOID	CHOPPED	LEOPARD	TOOTLED
DIMPLED	LINSEED	CLOAKED	+LEOPOLD	TROLLED
HOMINID	LUNCHED	CLOCKED	LEOTARD	TWOFOLD
HUMBLED	LYNCHED	CLOGGED	MOOCHED	WHOOPED.
IMMURED	MANAGED	CLOTHED	OROTUND	APPLAUD
JUMBLED	MANGLED	CLOTTED	PEOPLED	APPLIED
LIMITED	MANHOOD	CLOUDED	PLONKED	ASPIRED
MUMBLED	MANKIND	CLOUTED	PLOPPED	DAPPLED
RAMBLED	MANSARD	CLOWNED	PROCEED	DEPOSED
REMOULD	MANTLED	CROOKED	PRODDED	DIPLOID
REMOVED	MANURED	CROPPED	PRONGED	EXPIRED
+RIMBAUD	MENACED	CROSSED	PROOFED	EXPOSED
*ROMFORD	MINGLED	CROWDED	PROPPED	HAPLOID
RUMBLED	MINUTED	CROWNED	PROTEID	HOPPLED
RUMPLED	MONEYED	DOODLED	ROOTLED	HYPNOID
SAMOYED	MUNCHED	DROMOND	SCOLDED	IMPALED
SAMPLED	PINCHED	DROOLED	SCONCED	IMPEDED
TUMBLED	PINFOLD	DROOPED	SCOOPED	IMPLIED
UNMOVED	PINGUID	DROPPED	SCORNED	IMPOSED
VOMITED	PINHEAD	DROWNED	SCOUTED	IMPOUND
WIMPLED.	PONIARD	DROWSED	SCOWLED	IMPUTED
ANNEXED	PUNCHED	EVOLVED	SHOALED	POP-EYED
ANNOYED	RANKLED	FLOCKED	SHOPPED	REPINED
BANDIED	RENEWED	FLOGGED	SHORTED	REPLIED
BUNCHED	SINGLED	FLOODED	SHOUTED	REPOSED
BUNDLED	SUNWARD	FLOORED	SLOPPED	REPUTED
CANDIED	TANGLED	FLOPPED	SLOSHED	RIP-CORD

452

RIPPLED	MERMAID	DESPOND	CAT-EYED	BLUNTED
SAPWOOD	NORLAND	DISBAND	CATHEAD	BLURRED
SUPPLED	OERSTED	DISCARD	DETERED	BLURTED
TAPERED	PARADED	DISCOID	DITCHED	BLUSHED
TIPTOED	PARCHED	DISCORD	ENTICED	BRUISED
TOPPLED	PAROLED	DISTEND	FAT-HEAD	BRUSHED
TYPHOID	PAROTID	ENSILED	FETCHED	CHUCKED
UMPIRED	PARRIED	ENSURED	HATBAND	CHUFFED
XIPHOID.	PARTIED	ESSAYED	HITCHED	CHUGGED
ABRADED	PERCHED	EXSCIND	HOT-HEAD	CHURNED
AERATED	PERPEND	HUSBAND	HUTCHED	CLUBBED
AGROUND	PERUSED	INSIPID	INTONED	CLUMPED
AIR-RAID	PHRASED	INSTEAD	*JUTLAND	COUCHED
ARRIVED	PIRATED	INSURED	KATYDID	COUGHED
BARMAID	PORTEND	JOSTLED	LATCHED	COUNTED
BERATED	PURPLED	LASSOED	MATCHED	CRUISED
+BERNARD	PYRAMID	MASTOID	MATURED	CRUSHED
BERTHED	SCREWED	MISDEED	MOTIVED	CRUSTED
BIRCHED	SERRIED	MISLAID	MOTORED	DAUNTED
BURBLED	SPRUCED	MISLEAD	MOTTLED	DOUBLED
BURGLED	STRAFED	MISREAD	MUTATED	DOUBTED
CAROTID	STRAYED	MISUSED	NETTLED	DOUCHED
CARRIED	STREWED	MUSCLED	NOTCHED	DRUBBED
CIRCLED	STRIPED	MUSTARD	NOTEPAD	DRUDGED
CURDLED	STROKED	NESTLED	NOTICED	DRUGGED
CURRIED	TARRIED	POSITED	OCTOPOD	DRUMMED
DERIDED	THRIVED	RESCIND	OUTWARD	EQUATED
DERIVED	THRONED	RESIDED	PATCHED	ERUPTED
DIRTIED	UNROBED	RESILED	PETERED	EXULTED
EARTHED	WARHEAD	RESINED	PITCHED	FAULTED
ENRAGED	WAR-LORD	RESOUND	PIT-HEAD	FLUSHED
ENROBED	WORRIED	RESPOND	RETCHED	FOULARD
FERRIED	WORSTED.	RESUMED	RETIRED	GLUTTED
FORAYED	ABSCIND	ROSEBUD	RETREAD	GRUBBED
FORRARD	ABSCOND	ROSINED	RETRIED	GRUDGED
FORWARD	ASSAYED	RUSTLED	ROTATED	GRUNTED
GARAGED	ASSUMED	SUSPEND	*RUTLAND	HAUNTED
GARBLED	ASSURED	TISSUED	SETTLED	HOUNDED
GARGLED	BASTARD	TUSSLED	SUTURED	INURNED
GARLAND	BESTEAD	UNSEXED	TUTORED	JAUNTED
GURGLED	BUSTARD	UNSOUND	UNTAMED	JOUNCED
GYRATED	BUSTLED	VISITED	UNTAXED	JOUSTED
HARRIED	CASTLED	WEST-END.	UNTRIED	KNURLED
HURRIED	CESTOID	ALTERED	UTTERED	LAUGHED
HURTLED	COSTARD	ANTACID	WATCHED	MOULDED
LURCHED	CUSTARD	ASTOUND	WATERED	MOULTED
MARBLED	DASTARD	ATTIRED	*WATFORD	MOUNDED
MARCHED	DESCEND	ATTUNED	WATTLED	MOUNTED
MARRIED	DESIRED	BATTLED	WITCHED	MOUTHED
MERITED	+DESMOND	BOTTLED	*ZETLAND.	PLUCKED

453

PLUGGED	VAULTED	STYMIED	GRACILE	TWADDLE
PLUNGED	VAUNTED	THYROID	GRADATE	UNAWARE
PLUNKED	WOUNDED.	TRYSTED	+GRAHAME	WRANGLE.
POUCHED	ADVISED	UNYOKED	GRANDEE	AUBAINE
POUNCED	COVERED	WAYWARD.	GRANITE	CABBAGE
ROUSTED	COVETED	BUZZARD	GRANTEE	CABOOSE
SCUDDED	DEVISED	DAZZLED	GRANULE	CUBICLE
SCUFFED	DEVOTED	FIZZLED	GRAPPLE	DEBACLE
SCULPED	DIVIDED	GIZZARD	GRAVURE	EBB-TIDE
SCUMMED	DIVINED	MIZZLED	HYALINE	EMBRACE
SHUCKED	HOVERED	MUZZLED	HYALITE	FEBRILE
SHUNNED	INVALID	NUZZLED	IMAGINE	HABITUE
SHUNTED	INVITED	RAZORED	ISATINE	IMBURSE
SHUSHED	INVOKED	SIZZLED	LEAFAGE	JUBILEE
SKULKED	LEVERED	SOZZLED	LEAKAGE	LIBRATE
SLUBBED	PIVOTED	UNZONED	MEASURE	+OSBORNE
SLUGGED	RAVAGED	WIZENED	OPALINE	SUBLIME
SLUICED	REVERED		PIASTRE	SUBSIDE
SLUMMED	REVILED	ABALONE	PLACATE	SUBSUME
SLUMPED	REVISED	AMATIVE	PRAIRIE	UMBRAGE
SLURRED	REVOKED	ANALYSE	PRALINE	UNBRACE
SMUDGED	SAVAGED	APANAGE	PRATTLE	VIBRATE
SMUTTED	SEVERED	+ARACHNE	REALIZE	ZEBRINE.
SNUBBED	WAVERED.	AVARICE	SCALENE	ACCRETE
SNUFFED	COWERED	+BLANCHE	SCANTLE	ARCUATE
SNUGGED	COWHERD	BRAILLE	SEA-KALE	ASCRIBE
SOUGHED	DEWPOND	BRAMBLE	SEA-LINE	BECAUSE
SOUNDED	LOW-BRED	BRASSIE	SEA-MILE	BICYCLE
SPURNED	LOWLAND	CHALICE	SEASIDE	CACIQUE
SPURRED	NEW-LAID	CHANCRE	*SEATTLE	COCAINE
SPURTED	POWERED	CHARADE	SHACKLE	COCKADE
SQUALID	ROWELED	CRACKLE	SHAMBLE	COCOTTE
SQUARED	SEWERED	CRANAGE	SIAMESE	CYCLONE
STUBBED	UNWOUND.	CYANIDE	SNAFFLE	DECEASE
STUDDED	BOXWOOD	DIABASE	SPANGLE	DECEIVE
STUDIED	FIXATED	DRABBLE	SPARKLE	DECLARE
STUFFED	HEXAPOD	DRAFTEE	STARTLE	DECLINE
STUMPED	LUXATED	DRAGGLE	STATICE	DECUPLE
STUNTED	SIXFOLD.	DUALIZE	STATURE	DICTATE
TAUNTED	AMYLOID	EMANATE	STATUTE	DOCKAGE
THUDDED	BOYHOOD	ERASURE	SUASIVE	DUCTILE
THUMBED	DRY-SHOD	EVACUEE	SWADDLE	ENCHASE
THUMPED	HAYSEED	EVASIVE	*SWANAGE	ENCLAVE
TOUCHED	HAYWARD	EXAMINE	TEACAKE	ENCLOSE
TOUSLED	PAY-LOAD	EXAMPLE	TÉA-ROSE	ESCAPEE
TRUCKED	PLYWOOD	FEATURE	TRADUCE	EXCLUDE
TRUDGED	+RAYMOND	FRAGILE	TRAINEE	EXCRETE
TRUMPED	REYNARD	FRAIBLE	TRAIPSE	FACTURE
TRUSSED	SCYTHED	FRAZZLE	TRAMPLE	FICTILE
TRUSTED	SKYWARD	GRABBLE	TRAPEZE	FICTIVE

HECTARE	ENDORSE	OBELIZE	OFFENCE	ANIMATE
INCENSE	ENDWISE	OLEFINE	OFF-LINE	+ARIADNE
INCLINE	HYDRATE	OPERATE	OFF-SIDE	ASININE
INCLOSE	HYDRIDE	OVERAWE	REFEREE	BRICOLE
INCLUDE	INDORSE	OVERDUE	REFRAME	BRIGADE
LACTASE	INDULGE	OVERSEE	REFUGEE	BRINDLE
LACTOSE	JUDAIZE	PEERAGE	SUFFICE	BRIOCHE
LECTURE	LUDDITE	PIERAGE	SUFFUSE	BRISTLE
LICENCE	LYDDITE	PLEDGEE	UNFROZE.	BRITTLE
LICENSE	MEDIATE	POETIZE	ANGLICE	CHICANE
LUCARNE	MIDWIFE	PRECEDE	ANGUINE	CHINESE
*LUCERNE	MODISTE	PRECISE	BAGASSE	CLIMATE
+LUCILLE	PEDICLE	PREFACE	BAGGAGE	CLIPPIE
MACABRE	RADIATE	PRELATE	BAGPIPE	COINAGE
MACHETE	RADICLE	PRELUDE	BEGUILE	CRINGLE
MACHINE	RIDABLE	PREMISE	COGNATE	CRINKLE
MICROBE	TADPOLE	PREPARE	COGNIZE	CRIPPLE
NACELLE	VEDETTE	PREPUCE	DEGRADE	CUISINE
NECK-TIE	WADABLE.	PRESAGE	DOGGONE	DEICIDE
NOCTULE	ACETATE	PRESIDE	DOG-ROSE	+DEIRDRE
NUCLIDE	ACETONE	PRESUME	ENGORGE	DRIBBLE
OCCLUDE	ADENOSE	PUERILE	ENGRAVE	DRIZZLE
PACKAGE	ANEMONE	SCEPTRE	HYGIENE	DWINDLE
PICKAXE	AVERAGE	SEEPAGE	INGENUE	EDIFICE
PICOTEE	AWESOME	SHEATHE	INGRATE	EPICENE
PICTURE	BEEHIVE	SHELTIE	LEGATEE	EPICURE
RECEIVE	BEE-LINE	SPECKLE	LEGIBLE	EPISODE
RECLINE	BREATHE	SPECTRE	LIGNITE	EPISTLE
RECLUSE	BREWAGE	STEEPLE	LUGGAGE	EPITOME
SACCATE	CHELATE	STERILE	MAGNATE	FAIENCE
SACCULE	CHEMISE	SWEETIE	MIGRATE	FAILURE
SECLUDE	CLEANSE	TEENAGE	NEGLIGE	FRIBBLE
SECRETE	CREMATE	THEATRE	PUG-NOSE	FRIGATE
SECTILE	CRENATE	TREACLE	RAGTIME	FRIZZLE
SUCCADE	CREVICE	TREADLE	UP-GRADE.	GLIMPSE
SUCCOSE	ELEGIZE	TREDDLE	ACHIEVE	GRIDDLE
SUCROSE	ELEVATE	TREMBLE	ATHLETE	GRIMACE
TACTILE	EMETINE	TRESTLE	DEHISCE	GRISTLE
UNCLOSE	EPERGNE	UTERINE	ENHANCE	GRIZZLE
VACCINE	EREMITE	WHEEDLE	UNHINGE	GUIPURE
VACUOLE	EXECUTE	WREATHE	UNHORSE	IMITATE
VOCABLE.	EYEHOLE	WRESTLE.	UPHEAVE	IRIDIZE
ANDANTE	EYESORE	AFFABLE	VEHICLE.	KAINITE
AUDIBLE	FLEXILE	DEFENCE	ACINOSE	LAICIZE
BEDSIDE	FLEXURE	DEFLATE	ADIPOSE	LEISURE
BEDSORE	FRECKLE	DIFFUSE	AGITATE	MOIDORE
BEDTIME	GRENADE	ENFORCE	ALIDADE	NAIVETE
CADENCE	ICE-FLOE	INFANTE	ALIENEE	NOISOME
CODEINE	ITEMIZE	INFLAME	AMIABLE	ORIFICE
END-GAME	ITERATE	INFLATE	ANILINE	OXIDASE

455

OXIDIZE	IRKSOME	PILLAGE	NAMABLE	GUNFIRE
PHILTRE	TEKTITE.	POLE-AXE	NOMINEE	GUNNAGE
PLIABLE	ALL-TIME	POLLUTE	RAMPAGE	GUNWALE
PLICATE	BALANCE	PULSATE	REMORSE	HENBANE
PRICKLE	BALLADE	RELAPSE	ROMANCE	IGNOBLE
PRIMATE	BELIEVE	RELEASE	RUMMAGE	LINEAGE
PRITHEE	BELTANE	RELIEVE	SOMEONE	LINEATE
PRIVATE	BULLACE	SALABLE	TAMABLE	LINKAGE
QUIBBLE	BULLATE	SALTIRE	VAMOOSE	LUNETTE
QUICKIE	CALCINE	SALVAGE	VAMPIRE.	MANACLE
QUININE	CALCITE	SILENCE	*AINTREE	MANATEE
+QUIXOTE	CALIBRE	SOLUBLE	+ANNETTE	MANDATE
*REIGATE	CALORIE	SPLODGE	BANDAGE	MANHOLE
REISSUE	CALOTTE	SPLURGE	BANSHEE	MANIPLE
RHIZOME	+CELESTE	SYLVINE	BENZENE	MANLIKE
RUINATE	CELLULE	TILLAGE	BONDAGE	MINTAGE
SCIENCE	CILIATE	TOLLAGE	BONFIRE	MONOCLE
SEIZURE	COLLAGE	TOLUENE	CENSURE	MONTAGE
SHINGLE	COLLATE	UNLOOSE	CENTIME	MUNDANE
SKIFFLE	COLLEGE	VALANCE	CONCAVE	PANACHE
SKITTLE	COLLIDE	VALENCE	CONCEDE	PANCAKE
SPINDLE	COLLUDE	+VALERIE	CONCISE	PAN-PIPE
SPITTLE	COLOGNE	VILLAGE	CONDOLE	PANTILE
STIPPLE	CULTURE	VOLTAGE	CONDONE	PENANCE
SUICIDE	DELAINE	VOLUBLE	CONDUCE	PENSILE
SWINDLE	DELOUSE	VULGATE	CONDYLE	PENSIVE
SWINGLE	ECLIPSE	VULPINE	CONFIDE	PENTANE
SWIZZLE	ECLOGUE	VULTURE	CONFINE	PENTODE
THIMBLE	EEL-FARE	+WALLACE	CONFUSE	PENTOSE
THISTLE	ELLIPSE	+WALPOLE	CONFUTE	PINHOLE
TRIABLE	ENLARGE	WELCOME	CONJURE	PINK-EYE
TRIBUNE	FALANGE	WELFARE.	CONNATE	PINNACE
TRIBUTE	FALCATE	COMBINE	CONNIVE	PINNATE
TRICKLE	FELSITE	COMMODE	CONNOTE	RENEGUE
TRINGLE	FOLIAGE	COMMUNE	CONSOLE	SINCERE
TRIREME	FOLIATE	COMMUTE	CONSUME	SUNRISE
TWIDDLE	FULSOME	COMPARE	CONVENE	SUNWISE
TWINKLE	HELLENE	COMPERE	CONVOKE	SYNAPSE
TZIGANE	*KILDARE	COMPETE	DENTATE	SYNCOPE
UNITIVE	MALAISE	COMPILE	DENTINE	TANKAGE
UTILIZE	MALTOSE	COMPOSE	DENTURE	TANNAGE
WHIFFLE	+MELANIE	COMPOTE	DUNNAGE	TANNATE
WHISTLE	MILEAGE	COMPUTE	ENNOBLE	TENABLE
WHITTLE	+MOLIERE	COMRADE	FANFARE	TENSILE
WRIGGLE	OBLIQUE	DEMESNE	FINABLE	TINWARE
WRINKLE.	OILCAKE	GAMBOGE	FINAGLE	TONNAGE
ADJUDGE	PALETTE	GEMMATE	FINANCE	TONSURE
REJOICE.	PALMATE	IMMENSE	FINESSE	TONTINE
ASKANCE	PALPATE	IMMERSE	GENTILE	TUNABLE
*ESKDALE	PELISSE	LIMBATE	GENUINE	UNNERVE

+VANDYKE	LIONIZE	CUPRITE	ACREAGE	FORSAKE
VANTAGE	LOOK-SEE	DEPLETE	AGRAFFE	FORTUNE
VENDACE	MIOCENE	DEPLORE	AIR-HOLE	FURCATE
VENTAGE	MOORAGE	DEPRAVE	AIRLINE	FURNACE
VENTURE	PEONAGE	DEPRIVE	ARRANGE	FURTIVE
VINTAGE	PHONATE	DIPHASE	AUREATE	GARBAGE
WINSOME	PLOSIVE	DUPABLE	AURICLE	GAROTTE
*YANGTZE.	PROBATE	ESPOUSE	BARBATE	GERMANE
ACOLYTE	PROCURE	EXPANSE	BAROQUE	GIRAFFE
ACONITE	PRODUCE	EXPENSE	BARRAGE	HERBAGE
AGONIZE	PROFANE	EXPIATE	BEREAVE	HEROINE
ANODIZE	PROFILE	EXPLODE	BERHYME	HIRCINE
ANODYNE	PROFUSE	EXPLORE	BURETTE	HIRSUTE
APOSTLE	PROLATE	EXPUNGE	CARBIDE	HORMONE
ATOMIZE	PROMISE	HEPTANE	CARBINE	+MARCUSE
BIOTYPE	PROMOTE	HOP-BINE	CARLINE	*MARGATE
BROCADE	PROPANE	HOPLITE	CARMINE	MARLINE
BROMATE	PROPOSE	IMPASSE	CARNAGE	+MARLOWE
BROMIDE	PROTEGE	IMPASTE	CAROUSE	MARMITE
BROMINE	PROVIDE	IMPINGE	CARTAGE	MARQUEE
BROWNIE	PROVOKE	IMPLODE	CERVINE	MIRACLE
BUOYAGE	ROOTAGE	IMPLORE	CIRROSE	MORAINE
CHOLINE	SCOURGE	IMPROVE	CORACLE	MORTISE
CHOPINE	SPONDEE	IMPULSE	CORDAGE	NARRATE
CHORALE	STOPPLE	+NEPTUNE	CORDATE	NERVINE
CHORTLE	STORAGE	PAPOOSE	CORDITE	NERVURE
CLOSURE	STOWAGE	PEPTIDE	CORKAGE	NURTURE
DIOCESE	THORIDE	PIPETTE	CORNICE	PARABLE
DIOPTRE	TROCHEE	RAPTURE	CORRODE	PARTAKE
DIORITE	TROUBLE	REPLACE	CORSAGE	PARTITE
DIOXIDE	TROUNCE	REPLETE	CORTEGE	PERCALE
DUOTONE	TWOSOME	REPROVE	CORVINE	PERFUME
EBONITE	TWO-TIME	REPTILE	CURETTE	PERIGEE
EBONIZE	VIOLATE	REPULSE	CURSIVE	PERJURE
EMOTIVE	ZEOLITE.	RIPOSTE	CURVATE	PERLITE
ENOUNCE	AMPOULE	RIP-TIDE	DERANGE	PERMUTE
EROSIVE	AMPUTEE	RUPTURE	DURABLE	PERVADE
FEOFFEE	APPEASE	SEPTATE	DURANCE	PIROGUE
FLOUNCE	APPRISE	SUPPOSE	EAR-ACHE	PORCINE
FOOTAGE	APPROVE	SUPREME	FERRATE	PORK-PIE
GEORDIE	ASPERSE	TOPSIDE.	FERRITE	PORTAGE
GLOBOSE	BAPTIZE	ACQUIRE	FERRULE	PURPOSE
GLOBULE	BIPLANE	ENQUIRE	FERTILE	SARCODE
GOOD-BYE	CAPABLE	ESQUIRE	FORBADE	SARDINE
IDOLIZE	CAPRICE	INQUIRE	FORBORE	SCRUPLE
ISOLATE	CAPSIZE	LIQUATE	FORESEE	SERIATE
ISOTONE	CAPSULE	REQUIRE	FORGAVE	SERRATE
ISOTOPE	CAPTIVE	REQUITE	FORGIVE	+SERVICE
KNOBBLE	CAPTURE	UNQUOTE.	FORGONE	SERVILE
LEONINE	COPPICE	ABRIDGE	FORMATE	SORDINE

STRANGE	DISPOSE	RESERVE	ESTRONE	VITIATE
STRIATE	DISPUTE	RESIDUE	+EUTERPE	WATTAGE.
STROPHE	DISROBE	RESOLVE	EXTREME	ABUSIVE
SURFACE	DISTYLE	RESPIRE	EXTRUDE	ADULATE
SURMISE	ENSLAVE	RESPITE	FATIGUE	AZURINE
SURNAME	ENSNARE	RESTATE	GUTTATE	BAUXITE
SURVIVE	ESSENCE	RESTIVE	INTENSE	BOURREE
SYRINGE	FASCINE	RESTORE	INTRUDE	BRUSQUE
+TERENCE	FESTIVE	RISIBLE	LATRINE	CAUDATE
TERMITE	FISSILE	RISSOLE	LATTICE	CHUCKLE
TERPENE	FISSURE	ROSEATE	LETTUCE	COURAGE
TERRACE	FUSIBLE	ROSETTE	MATINEE	COUVADE
TERRENE	GESTURE	SUSPIRE	+MATISSE	CRUMBLE
TERRINE	+GISELLE	SYSTOLE	METHANE	CRUMPLE
TORTILE	HASTATE	SYSTYLE	MUTABLE	CRUSADE
TORTURE	HOSPICE	TESTATE	+NATALIE	EDUCATE
TURBINE	HOSTAGE	TUSSORE	NETSUKE	ELUSIVE
UTRICLE	HOSTILE	UPSTAGE	NITRATE	EMULATE
VERBOSE	INSCAPE	UPSURGE	NOTABLE	EQUABLE
VERDURE	INSHORE	VESICLE	NUT-CASE	ERUDITE
VIRGATE	INSPIRE	VESTIGE	OATCAKE	GLUCOSE
VIRGULE	INSTATE	VESTURE	OBTRUDE	GOUACHE
WARFARE	+JASMINE	VISCOSE	OCTUPLE	GRUMBLE
WARLIKE	JUSSIVE	VISIBLE	OUTCOME	GRUYERE
WARTIME	JUSTICE	WASTAGE.	OUTDONE	HAULAGE
WIRABLE	+JUSTINE	ACTABLE	OUTFACE	KNUCKLE
YARDAGE.	MASSAGE	ACTUATE	OUTGONE	+MAURICE
ABSENCE	MASSIVE	ANTIQUE	OUTLINE	OCULATE
ABSOLVE	MESSAGE	ARTICLE	OUTLIVE	+PAULINE
ASSUAGE	MISFIRE	ARTISTE	OUTRAGE	PLUMAGE
AUSPICE	MISGAVE	+ASTARTE	OUTRIDE	PLUMOSE
AUSTERE	MISGIVE	ASTRIDE	OUTRODE	REUNITE
BASCULE	MISLIKE	ATTACHE	OUTSIDE	ROULADE
BESIEGE	MISRULE	BATISTE	OUTSIZE	ROUTINE
BESPOKE	MISSILE	CATHODE	OUTVOTE	SAUSAGE
BOSCAGE	MISSIVE	CATS-EYE	OUTWORE	SCUFFLE
CASCADE	MISTAKE	CITRATE	PETIOLE	SCUMBLE
CASTILE	OBSCENE	CITRINE	POTABLE	SCUTAGE
COSTATE	OBSCURE	COTERIE	POTENCE	SCUTTLE
COSTIVE	OBSERVE	COTTAGE	POTHOLE	SHUFFLE
COSTUME	OSSICLE	CUTICLE	RATABLE	SHUT-EYE
CUSPATE	PASSAGE	DATABLE	RAT-RACE	SHUTTLE
DESCALE	PASSIVE	DETENTE	RETICLE	SMUGGLE
DESERVE	PASTIME	DETRUDE	RETINUE	SNUFFLE
DESPISE	PASTURE	EATABLE	RETRACE	SNUGGLE
DESPITE	PISCINE	ENTENTE	SATIATE	SOUFFLE
DESTINE	PISTOLE	ENTHUSE	SITUATE	SOUTANE
DISABLE	POSTAGE	ENTITLE	TETRODE	SQUEEZE
DISEASE	POSTURE	ENTWINE	TITRATE	STUBBLE
DISLIKE	PUSTULE	ESTHETE	UNTWINE	STUMBLE

TAURINE	BOX-TREE	CAITIFF	ERASING	PLANING
TRUCKLE	FIXABLE	SPIN-OFF.	EVADING	PLATING
TRUFFLE	FIXTURE	RAKE-OFF	FEARING	PLAYING
TRUNDLE	FOXHOLE	TAKE-OFF.	FLAKING	PRATING
TRUSTEE	MIXTURE	WELL-OFF.	FLAMING	PRAYING
UKULELE	TAXABLE	HIMSELF.	FLARING	QUAKING
ULULATE.	TAX-FREE	PONTIFF	FLAWING	*READING
ADVANCE	TEXTILE	SEND-OFF.	FLAYING	REAMING
ADVERSE	TEXTURE.	+BEOWULF	FOALING	REAPING
ALVEOLE	ANYWISE	SHOW-OFF.	FOAMING	REARING
BIVALVE	BUYABLE	REPROOF.	FRAMING	ROAD-HOG
DEVALUE	CAYENNE	*CARDIFF	FRAYING	ROAMING
DEVIATE	DAY-TIME	HERSELF	GEARING	ROARING
DEVOLVE	HAYWIRE	OURSELF	GLARING	SCALING
DEVOTEE	JOY-RIDE	WERWOLF.	GLAZING	SCARING
DIVERGE	KEYHOLE	CAST-OFF	GNAWING	SEALING
DIVERSE	KEYNOTE	DISTAFF	GOADING	SEAMING
DIVORCE	LAYETTE	MASTIFF.	GRACING	SEARING
DIVULGE	MAYPOLE	FLY-HALF	GRADING	SEATING
DOVEKIE	PAYABLE	FLYLEAF	GRATING	SHADING
GAVOTTE	SKY-BLUE	THYSELF	GRAVING	SHAKING
INVERSE	SKYLINE		GRAZING	SHAMING
INVOICE	SPY-HOLE	AMAZING	HEADING	SHAPING
INVOLVE	STYLITE	BEADING	HEALING	SHARING
LIVABLE	STYLIZE	BEAMING	HEAPING	SHAVING
LOVABLE	STYRENE	BEARING	HEARING	SKATING
MOVABLE	WAYSIDE.	BEATING	HEATING	SLAKING
+NEVILLE	BEZIQUE	BLAMING	HEAVING	SLATING
OBVERSE	BIZARRE	BLARING	HOAXING	SLAVING
OBVIATE	+CEZANNE	BLAZING	IMAGING	SLAYING
REVENGE	GAZELLE	BOATING	LEADING	SNAKING
REVENUE	GAZETTE	BRACING	LEAFING	SNARING
REVERIE	LOZENGE	BRAVING	LEAKING	SOAKING
REVERSE	SIZABLE	BRAYING	LEANING	SOAPING
REVOLVE		BRAZING	LEAPING	SOARING
RIVIERE	PLAY-OFF	CEASING	LEASING	SPACING
SAVABLE	SEA-WOLF	CHAFING	LEAVING	SPARING
*SEVILLE.	TEA-LEAF.	CHASING	LOADING	SPAYING
BOWLINE	KICK-OFF	CLAWING	LOAFING	STAGING
COWBANE	*MACDUFF.	COALING	LOAMING	STAKING
COWHIDE	MIDRIFF.	COAMING	LOANING	STARING
INWEAVE	ONESELF	COATING	MEANING	STATING
JAW-BONE	SHEREEF	COAXING	MOANING	STAVING
NOWHERE	SHERIFF	CRANING	NEARING	STAYING
RAWHIDE	THEREOF	CRAVING	ORATING	SWAYING
REWRITE	WHEREOF.	CRAZING	PEAKING	TEAMING
REWROTE	ENFEOFF	DEALING	PEALING	TEARING
TOWLINE	LIFT-OFF.	DRAPING	PEAT-BOG	TEASING
TOW-ROPE.	FIG-LEAF.	DRAWING	PHASING	THAWING
BOX-KITE	BAILIFF	ELATING	PLACING	TRACING

TRADING	LACKING	CHEWING	VIEWING	PIGLING
WEANING	LICKING	DEEMING	WEEDING	PUGGING
WEARING	LOCKING	DIETING	WEEPING.	RAGGING
WEAVING	MOCKING	EVENING	BUFFING	RIGGING
WHALING	MUCKING	FEEDING	CUFFING	SAGGING
X-RAYING.	NECKING	FEELING	DUFFING	SIGHING
AMBLING	NICKING	FLEEING	GAFFING	SIGNING
BOBBING	NOCKING	+FLEMING	HAFTING	TAGGING
CABLING	PACKING	FLEXING	HEFTING	TUGGING
CUBBING	PECKING	FREEING	HUFFING	WAGGING.
DABBING	PICKING	GREYLAG	LIFTING	ECHOING
DUBBING	RACKING	HEEDING	LOFTING	MAH-JONG
FIBBING	RICKING	HEELING	MUFFING	ABIDING
FOBBING	ROCKING	ICEBERG	PUFFING	ARISING
GABBING	RUCKING	JEERING	RAFTING	BAILING
INBEING	SACKING	KEELING	RIFLING	BAITING
JABBING	SACRING	KEENING	RIFTING	BOILING
JIBBING	SUCKING	KEEPING	RUFFING	BRIBING
JOBBING	TACKING	LEERING	SIFTING	CEILING
LOBBING	TICKING	*MAESTEG	TUFTING	CHIDING
MOBBING	TUCKING.	MEETING	WAFTING.	CHIMING
NABBING	BEDDING	NEEDING	ANGLING	CHINWAG
NOBBING	BIDDING	OBEYING	ARGUING	COILING
RIBBING	BUDDING	OPENING	BAGGING	COINING
ROBBING	BUDGING	PEEKING	BEGGING	DRIVING
RUBBING	CADGING	PEELING	BOGGING	EDITING
SIBLING	CODLING	PEEPING	BUGGING	ELIDING
SOBBING	DODGING	PEERING	BUGLING	EXILING
TABBING	ENDLONG	PEEVING	DIGGING	EXITING
TABLING	GADDING	PFENNIG	DOGGING	FAILING
TOBY-JUG	HEDGING	PIECING	FAGGING	FAIRING
TUBBING	KEDGING	PREYING	FOGGING	FOILING
WEBBING.	KIDDING	REEDING	GAGGING	GAINING
ARCHING	LADLING	REEFING	HAGGING	GLIDING
BACKING	LODGING	REEKING	HOGGING	GRIDING
BACKLOG	MADDING	REELING	HUGGING	GRIPING
BUCKING	NODDING	SEEDING	INGOING	GUIDING
COCKING	NUDGING	SEEKING	JAGGING	HAILING
CYCLING	PADDING	SEEMING	JIGGING	JOINING
DECKING	PODDING	SEEPING	JOGGING	KNIFING
DOCKING	PUDDING	SHEBANG	JUGGING	MAILBAG
DUCKING	RIDDING	SIEVING	LAGGING	MAILING
ETCHING	SIDLING	SKEWING	LEGGING	MAIMING
HACKING	TEDDING	SLEWING	LOGGING	NAILING
HOCKING	UNDOING	SPEWING	LUGGING	OPINING
INCHING	UNDYING	STEWING	MUGGING	PAINING
ITCHING	WADDING	TEEMING	NAGGING	PAIRING
JACKING	WEDDING	TREEING	NOGGING	POISING
KECKING	WEDGING.	TREPANG	PEGGING	PRICING
KICKING	BREWING	VEERING	PIGGING	PRIDING

460

PRIMING	CALLING	SELLING	RAMPING	LENDING
PRIZING	CALMING	SILTING	RIMMING	LINKING
RAIDING	CALVING	SOLVING	ROMPING	LINSANG
RAILING	CULLING	TALKING	SUMMING	LONGING
RAINING	DELVING	TELLING	TAMPING	LUNGING
RAISING	DULLING	TILLING	TIME-LAG	MANNING
REINING	FALLING	TILTING	VAMPING.	MENDING
RUINING	FELTING	TOLLING	BANDING	MINCING
SAILING	FILLING	VOLTING	BANGING	MINDING
SEISING	FILMING	WALKING	BANKING	MINTING
SEIZING	FOLDING	WALLING	BANNING	PANNING
SHINDIG	GALLING	WELDING	BANTING	PANTING
SHINING	GELDING	WELLING	BENDING	PENDING
SLICING	GELLING	WELTING	BINDING	PENNING
SLIDING	GILDING	WILLING	BONDING	PINKING
SMILING	+GOLDING	WILTING	BUNKING	PINNING
SNIPING	GULLING	WOLFING	BUNTING	PUNNING
SOILING	GULPING	YELLING	CANNING	PUNTING
SPICING	HALTING	YELPING	CANTING	RANGING
SPIKING	HALVING	YULE-LOG.	CONKING	RANKING
SPIRING	HELPING	BOMBING	CONNING	RANTING
SPITING	HOLDING	BUMPING	CUNNING	RENDING
SUITING	HULKING	CAMPING	DANCING	RENTING
SWIPING	HULLING	COMBING	DENYING	RINGING
TAILING	JELLING	DAMMING	DINGING	RINKING
TRICING	JILTING	DAMNING	DINNING	RINSING
TWINING	JOLTING	DAMPING	DONNING	RUNNING
UNITING	KILLING	DIMMING	DUNKING	SANDBAG
VEILING	LALLING	DUMPING	DUNNING	SANDING
VEINING	LILTING	GAMMING	FANNING	SENDING
VOICING	LOLLING	GEMMING	FENCING	SENSING
VOIDING	LULLING	GUMMING	FENDING	SINGING
WAILING	MALTING	*HAMBURG	FINDING	SINKING
WAITING	MELDING	HAMMING	FUNDING	SINNING
WAIVING	MELTING	HEMMING	GANGING	SUNNING
WHILING	MILKING	HOMBURG	GUNNING	TANGING
WHINING	MILLING	HUMMING	HANDBAG	TANNING
WHITING	MILTING	HUMPING	HANDING	TENDING
WRITING.	MULLING	JAMMING	HANGDOG	TENSING
INKLING	PALLING	JUMPING	HANGING	TENTING
YAKKING.	PALMING	LAMBING	HINTING	TENT-PEG
BALKING	PALPING	LAMMING	HONKING	TINGING
BELTING	PELTING	LEMMING	HUNTING	TINNING
BELYING	POLLING	LIMNING	JINKING	VANNING
BILKING	PULLING	LIMPING	JUNKING	VENDING
BILLING	PULPING	MUMMING	KENNING	VENTING
BILTONG	PULSING	NUMBING	KINGING	WANTING
BOLTING	ROLLING	PIMPING	KINKING	WENDING
BULGING	SALTING	PUMPING	KINKING	WINDBAG
BULLDOG	SALVING	RAMMING	LANCING	WINDING
			LANDING	

WINGING	PROVING	RIPPING	HARPING	WARRING
WINKING	QUOTING	SAPLING	HERRING	WART-HOG
WINNING	RIOTING	SAPPING	HORDING	WORDING
YANKING	ROOFING	SIPPING	HORNING	WORKING
YENNING.	ROOKING	SOPPING	HORSING	WORMING
ADORING	ROOMING	SUPPING	HURLING	YORKING
ATONING	ROOTING	TAPPING	HURTING	ZEROING.
AVOWING	SCORING	TIPPING	JARRING	BASHING
BLOWING	SHOEING	TOPPING	JERKING	BASKING
BOOKING	SHOOING	YAPPING	KERBING	BASTING
BOOMING	SHORING	ZIPPING.	LARDING	BUSKING
BOOTLEG	SHOVING	BARGING	LARKING	BUSTING
BROKING	SHOWING	*BARKING	LORDING	CASHING
CHOKING	SLOPING	BARRING	LURKING	CASTING
CLOSING	SMOKING	BURNING	MARKING	COSTING
CLOYING	SNORING	BURPING	MARLING	CUSSING
COOKING	SNOWING	CARKING	MARRING	DASHING
COOLING	STOKING	CARPING	MERGING	DISHING
CROWING	STONING	CARTING	MORNING	DOSSING
DRONING	STORING	CARVING	NERVING	DUSTING
ELOPING	STOWING	CORKING	NURSING	EASTING
ERODING	TOOLING	CURBING	PARKING	FASTING
EVOKING	*TOOTING	CURDING	PARSING	FISHING
FLOWING	WHORING	CURLING	PARTING	FUSSING
FOOLING	*WYOMING	CURSING	PERIWIG	GASHING
FOOTING	ZOOMING.	CURVING	PERKING	GASPING
GLOWING	CAPPING	DARLING	PERMING	GAS-RING
GLOZING	COPPING	DARNING	PORTING	GASSING
GROPING	CUPPING	DARTING	PURGING	GOSLING
HOODING	DIPPING	*DORKING	PURLING	GUSHING
HOOKING	ESPYING	EARNING	PURRING	HASHING
HOOPING	HAPPING	EARRING	PURSING	HASPING
HOOTING	HIPPING	FARCING	SARKING	HISSING
IRONING	HOPPING	FARMING	SCRYING	HUSHING
KNOWING	IMPFING	FIRE-BUG	SERVING	HUSKING
LOOKING	KIPPING	FIREDOG	SORTING	JESTING
LOOMING	LAPPING	FIRMING	SURFING	JOSHING
LOOPING	LAPSING	FORCING	SURGING	KISSING
LOOTING	LAPWING	FORDING	TARRING	LASHING
MOONBUG	LIPPING	FORELEG	TARTING	LASTING
MOONING	LOPPING	FORGING	TERMING	LISPING
MOORING	MAPPING	FORKING	TURFING.	LISTING
MOOTING	MOPPING	FORMING	TURNING	LUSTING
NOOSING	NAPPING	FURLING	VARYING	MASHING
PHONING	NIPPING	FURLONG	VERGING	MASKING
POOLING	PEPPING	FURRING	VERSING	MASSING
PROBANG	PIPPING	GARBING	WARDING	MESHING
PROBING	POPPING	GORGING	WARMING	MESSING
PROLONG	PUPPING	HARKING	WARNING	MISSING
PROSING	RAPPING	HARMING	WARPING	MISTING

MUSTANG	NUTTING	SOUSING	BUCKISH	EPITAPH
NESTING	PATTING	SPUMING	JACINTH	SPINACH
NOSEBAG	PETTING	TOURING	+MACBETH	SWINISH
NOSHING	PITTING	TOUTING.	PECKISH	TRILITH
OUSTING	PITYING	ENVYING	PICTISH	TRIUMPH
PASSING	POTTING	LEVYING	PUCKISH	WHITISH.
PASTING	PUTTING	REVVING.	UNCOUTH.	BULLISH
POSTBAG	RATTING	BAWLING	BADDISH	BULRUSH
POSTING	ROTTING	BOWLING	CADDISH	COLDISH
PUSHING	RUTTING	COWLING	CODFISH	COLTISH
RASPING	SETTING	DAWNING	MUD-BATH	DOLTISH
RESTING	SITTING	DOWNING	MUDFISH	GALUMPH
RISKING	TATTING	DOWSING	REDDISH	HELLISH
RUSHING	TITLING	FAWNING	*REDRUTH	+RALEIGH
RUSTING	TOTTING	FOWLING	+RUDOLPH	SELFISH
SUSSING	TUTTING	HAWKING	YIDDISH.	SPLOTCH
TASKING	VETOING	HOWLING	BLEMISH	UNLEASH
TASTING	VETTING	PAWNING	BREADTH	WOLFISH.
TESTING	WETTING	UNWRUNG	CHEETAH	DAMPISH
TOSSING	WITTING.	YAWNING	CHERISH	LUMPISH
UNSLING	AMUSING	YOWLING.	EYE-BATH	MAMMOTH.
VESTING	BLUEING	TAXIING.	EYELASH	BENEATH
WASHING	CAUSING	DAYLONG	EYEWASH	BONE-ASH
WASTING	DAUBING	*HAYLING	FLEMISH	DANKISH
WESTING	DOUSING	KEY-RING	GREYISH	DONNISH
WISHING.	EDUCING	RHYMING	PEEVISH	FINNISH
ANTILOG	ELUDING	STYLING.	STEALTH	+KENNETH
BATHING	EXUDING	BUZZING	SWEDISH	KENTISH
BATTING	FEUDING	FIZZING	TWELFTH	MANNISH
BETTING	FLUTING	JAZZING	UNEARTH.	MONARCH
CATLING	FOULING		HUFFISH	MONKISH
CUTTING	GAUGING	ACALEPH	RAFFISH	*NINEVEH
DOTTING	GLUEING	BEARISH	REFRESH.	NONSUCH
FATLING	GOUGING	GOATISH	ANGUISH	*PENRITH
FITTING	HAULING	KNAVISH	DIGRAPH	PINKISH.
GATLING	HOUSING	PHARAOH	DOGFISH	ABOLISH
GETTING	INURING	PLANISH	ENGLISH	+ANOUILH
G-STRING	LAUDING	SLAVISH	HAGFISH	BOOKISH
GUTTING	LOURING	SPANISH	HAGGISH	BOORISH
HITTING	MAULING	STAUNCH.	+HOGARTH	FOOLISH
HOTTING	PAUSING	BABYISH	HOGGISH	GNOMISH
HUTTING	PLUMING	DEBAUCH	HOGWASH	GOODISH
JETTING	POURING	+DEBORAH	PIGGISH	ISOBATH
JOTTING	POUTING	DEBOUCH	PIGWASH	MOORISH
JUTTING	PRUNING	PIBROCH	ROGUISH	STOMACH.
KITTING	ROUGING	PUBLISH	WAGGISH.	DIPTYCH
LETTING	ROUSING	REBIRTH	+JEHOVAH	FOPPISH
MATTING	ROUTING	RUBBISH	UNHITCH.	IMPEACH
NETTING	SAUCING	SABAOTH	AZIMUTH	LAPPISH.
NOTHING	SOURING	SABBATH.	BRITISH	ABROACH

BOROUGH	SQUELCH	UNCLOAK.	BERSERK	ROWLOCK.
BURNISH	SQUINCH.	BED-ROCK	BURDOCK	WAXWORK.
*CORINTH	INVEIGH	HADDOCK	CARRACK	DAYBOOK
CORNISH	SEVENTH.	MUDLARK	+DERRICK	DRY-DOCK
CURRACH	BEWITCH	PADDOCK	EARMARK	FLY-BOOK
CURRISH	MAWKISH	PADLOCK	FORSOOK	HAYCOCK
DARKISH	SAWFISH	PIDDOCK	*NORFOLK	HAYFORK
DERVISH	TOWPATH.	WEDLOCK.	PARTOOK	HAYRICK
FURBISH	MAYBUSH	BLESBOK	PURBECK	SKYLARK
FURNISH	SKY-HIGH	ICE-PACK	*SARAWAK	WRYNECK
GARFISH	STYLISH	OBELISK	WARLOCK	
GARNISH		ROEBUCK.	*WARWICK.	BOATFUL
GIRLISH	SWAHILI.	DEFROCK	BESPEAK	BRADAWL
*HARWICH	BACILLI	MAFFICK	CASSOCK	+CHAGALL
LARGISH	PECCAVI	OFF-PEAK	COSSACK	CHANCEL
*NORWICH	+PUCCINI.	*SUFFOLK	FOSSICK	CHANNEL
OGREISH	EFFENDI.	UNFROCK.	GAS-MASK	CHARNEL
SCRATCH	CHIANTI	FOGBANK	GOSHAWK	CHATTEL
SCREECH	*NAIROBI	HOGBACK	HASSOCK	CLAUSAL
SCRUNCH	STIMULI	LOG-BOOK.	*KESWICK	COASTAL
STRETCH	*TRIPOLI.	BULLOCK	MISTOOK	CRANIAL
TARNISH	+BELLINI	BULWARK	TUSSOCK	+EMANUEL
THROUGH	+FELLINI.	HILLOCK	UNSTICK	FEARFUL
TURKISH	*POMPEII	HOLM-OAK	UNSTUCK	FLANNEL
VARNISH	SAMURAI	KALMUCK	YASHMAK.	GLACIAL
WARPATH.	TIMPANI	KILLICK	BETHINK	GRADUAL
ABSINTH	*ZAMBESI.	OIL-SILK	BUTTOCK	GRAPNEL
BESEECH	BENGALI.	POLLACK	CATWALK	MIASMAL
BISMUTH	BRONCHI.	+POLLOCK	CUT-BACK	PLAYFUL
DISTICH	+CHRISTI	*SELKIRK.	FETLOCK	QUADREL
HASHISH	ISRAELI	GIMMICK	*GATWICK	QUARREL
*IPSWICH	*KARACHI	HAMMOCK	GOTHICK	*SCAFELL
MESSIAH	+LORELEI	HEMLOCK	HATRACK	SCALPEL
WASPISH	MARTINI	HUMMOCK	*MATLOCK	SCANDAL
*WISBECH.	TERMINI.	LIMBECK.	MATTOCK	SEA-COAL
BETROTH	ASSAGAI	*BANGKOK	NETWORK	SEA-FOWL
CATARRH	+ROSSINI.	BANNOCK	OUTBACK	SEAGULL
CATFISH	+HOUDINI.	*CANNOCK	OUTLOOK	SEA-WALL
CATTISH	RAVIOLI	*DENMARK	OUTTALK	SPANCEL
OSTRICH	+VIVALDI	*DUNDALK	OUTWORK	SPANIEL
PETTISH		FINBACK	+PATRICK	SPATIAL
RETOUCH	BEATNIK	GUNLOCK	POTHOOK	STANNEL
RUTTISH	PEACOCK	HENPECK	POTLUCK	TEARFUL
SOTTISH	SEA-BANK	LENTISK	RATFINK	TRAMMEL
UNTRUTH.	SEA-MARK	MENFOLK	RETHINK	TRAVAIL.
BRUTISH	SEA-PINK	RANSACK	SETBACK	BOBTAIL
GOULASH	SEA-SICK	RUN-BACK	TITLARK.	EMBROIL
LOUTISH	SJAMBOK.	TINTACK.	HAUBERK	+GABRIEL
NOURISH	CAB-RANK	AIR-LOCK	SPUTNIK.	HOBNAIL
PRUDISH	NIBLICK.	BARRACK	COWLICK	LIBERAL

464

--B---L			--S---L	
ORBITAL	TIERCEL	PALATAL	SENSUAL	FORKFUL
SUBDUAL	TOENAIL	PALM-OIL	SUNDIAL	FURBALL
SUBSOIL.	TREFOIL	PALUDAL	SYNODAL	GIRASOL
ACCUSAL	UNEQUAL	*WALSALL.	TENDRIL	HARMFUL
ALCOHOL	UTENSIL.	ADMIRAL	TINFOIL	HERNIAL
CACODYL	AFFINAL	COMICAL	TUNEFUL	HURTFUL
DECADAL	BIFOCAL	DAMFOOL	VENTRAL.	LYRICAL
DECANAL	INFIDEL	FEMORAL	AXOLOTL	MARITAL
DECIBEL	REFUSAL.	GUMBOIL	BROTHEL	MARSHAL
DECIMAL	DIGITAL	HUMERAL	CLOACAL	MARTIAL
DECRIAL	FIGURAL	IMMORAL	EPOCHAL	NARWHAL
FACTUAL	LEG-PULL	LAMINAL	FRONTAL	PARASOL
ISCHIAL	LOGICAL	LAMP-OIL	GLOTTAL	PARBOIL
LACTEAL	LOG-ROLL	NOMINAL	KNOW-ALL	PARTIAL
LACUNAL	MAGICAL	NUMERAL	LIONCEL	PERUSAL
+MICHAEL	PAGINAL	NYMPHAL	ROOMFUL	+PURCELL
RECITAL	PIGTAIL	REMOVAL	SPONDYL	RORQUAL
TACTFUL	PUG-MILL	SEMINAL	STOICAL	SCRIBAL
TACTUAL	VAGINAL	TIMBREL	TROMMEL.	SHRIVEL
UNCIVIL	VEGETAL	TOMFOOL	APPAREL	TURMOIL
VICINAL	WAGTAIL.	TUMBREL	CAPITAL	UNRAVEL
VICTUAL.	ETHANOL	UNMORAL.	CAPITOL	VERMEIL
BEDEVIL	ETHICAL	+ANNABEL	EMPANEL	VERONAL
BODEFUL	+ISHMAEL.	BANEFUL	EXPOSAL	VIRTUAL.
CODICIL	+ABIGAIL	CENTRAL	HOPEFUL	ARSENAL
FEDERAL	BRIMFUL	CONCEAL	IMPANEL	AUSTRAL
MEDICAL	*BRISTOL	CONGEAL	IMPERIL	BASHFUL
NODICAL	EDICTAL	CONTROL	NUPTIAL	BESTIAL
ORDINAL	GAINFUL	CYNICAL	PIPEFUL	+BOSWELL
PEDICEL	INITIAL	*DONEGAL	+RAPHAEL	DESPOIL
RADICAL	PAILFUL	FANTAIL	TOPICAL	DISHFUL
RADICEL	PAINFUL	FINICAL	TOPSAIL	EASEFUL
*REDHILL	SEISMAL	FUNERAL	TYPICAL.	FISTFUL
REDPOLL.	SKILFUL	GENERAL	ADRENAL	INSTALL
ASEXUAL	SKINFUL	GENITAL	AEROSOL	KESTREL
CHERVIL	TRIVIAL.	HANDFUL	AIRMAIL	LUSTFUL
COEQUAL	INKWELL	HANDSEL	ARRIVAL	LUSTRAL
ETERNAL	OAK-GALL.	IGNORAL	AURORAL	MISCALL
EYEBALL	BALEFUL	+JONQUIL	BARN-OWL	MISDEAL
+EZEKIEL	CALOMEL	LINGUAL	BORSTAL	MISTRAL
FRETFUL	CHLORAL	MANDREL	CARACUL	MUSICAL
GLEEFUL	COLONEL	MENTHOL	CARAMEL	NOSTRIL
HEEDFUL	DOLEFUL	MINDFUL	CAREFUL	PASCHAL
NEEDFUL	HELICAL	MINERAL	+CARROLL	RESTFUL
OVERALL	HELPFUL	MINIMAL	CORDIAL	ROSTRAL
PREVAIL	HOLDALL	MONGREL	CORONAL	+RUSSELL
SPECIAL	ILLEGAL	PENNILL	CURTAIL	WASSAIL
STENCIL	ILL-WILL	PINBALL	DIREFUL	WASTREL
STERNAL	OILMEAL	RENEWAL	+DURRELL	WISHFUL
THERMAL	OIL-WELL	*SENEGAL	FERN-OWL	WISTFUL

--S---L		--A---N		
ZESTFUL.	DEXTRAL	RECLAIM.	CONFORM	STRATUM
ANT-HILL	LEXICAL	CADMIUM	GINGHAM	*SURINAM
APTERAL	MAXIMAL	DADAISM	GUNROOM	TERBIUM.
CATCALL	+MAXWELL	JUDAISM	KINGDOM	FASCISM
CATFALL	TEXTUAL	MODICUM.	MANTRUM	NOSTRUM
CITADEL	WAXBILL.	CAESIUM	MINIMUM	ROSTRUM
CO-TIDAL	ABYSMAL	FREEDOM	PINETUM	SISTRUM.
DUTIFUL	ABYSSAL	GRECISM	SANCTUM	ANTONYM
ENTHRAL	CRYSTAL	OVERARM	SUNBEAM	INTERIM
ESTRIOL	DAY-GIRL	PIETISM	SYNONYM	LITHIUM
FATEFUL	KRYPTOL	PREMIUM	TANTRUM	OPTIMUM
HATEFUL	PAY-ROLL	RHENIUM	+WYNDHAM.	YTTRIUM.
LATERAL	SKYSAIL	STERNUM	BLOSSOM	FRUSTUM
LITERAL	TRYSAIL	THEOREM	EGOTISM	THULIUM
NATURAL	WAY-BILL.	*VIETNAM.	FLOTSAM	TOURISM.
NETBALL	+JEZEBEL	HAFNIUM.	GROGRAM	ENVENOM.
OATMEAL		ATHEISM	HOODLUM	MAXIMUM.
OPTICAL	AMALGAM	ECHOISM.	NIOBIUM	ALYSSUM
OUTFALL	ANAGRAM	ALIFORM	OPOSSUM	ELYSIUM
OUTSAIL	ATAVISM	ANIMISM	PROBLEM	
PITFALL	*CHATHAM	*BRIXHAM	PROGRAM	ABANDON
PITIFUL	CRANIUM	DEIFORM	QUONDAM	ARABIAN
RAT-TAIL	DIAGRAM	EPIGRAM	RHODIUM	BLACKEN
SATCHEL	DUALISM	HEIRDOM	SCOTISM	BLASTIN
SUTURAL	IMAGISM	IRIDIUM	THOMISM	BOATMAN
VITRIOL.	+KHAYYAM	OVIFORM	THORIUM	BRACKEN
*ARUNDEL	ONANISM	TRIFORM	TROPISM	BRAHMIN
COUNCIL	PHANTOM	TRITIUM	ZIONISM.	CHAGRIN
COUNSEL	QUANTUM	TRIVIUM	BAPTISM	+CHAPLIN
CRUCIAL	REALISM	UNIFORM.	SOPHISM	CHAPMAN
DIURNAL	SEA-ROOM	JEJUNUM.	TAP-ROOM.	CHASTEN
ELUVIAL	STADIUM	DUKEDOM.	REQUIEM.	*CLACTON
FLUVIAL	STANNUM	*BELGIUM	+ABRAHAM	CLARION
JOURNAL	STARDOM	CALCIUM	ACRONYM	COARSEN
NEUTRAL	STATISM	EEL-WORM	+BERTRAM	CRAMPON
PLUVIAL	TEA-ROOM	FULCRUM	BOREDOM	DEADPAN
POUNDAL	TRANSOM	GALLIUM	CHRISOM	DRAGOON
ROUNDEL	URANISM	HOLMIUM	EAR-DRUM	DRAYMAN
SOULFUL	URANIUM.	+MALCOLM	EARLDOM	ELASTIN
UNUSUAL.	EMBOSOM	PALLIUM	ERRATUM	ELATION
PIVOTAL	LOBWORM	PILGRIM	*FARNHAM	ERASION
REVISAL	PABULUM	+WILLIAM	FERMIUM	EVASION
REVIVAL	UNBOSOM.	WOLFRAM.	FIRE-ARM	FLAGMAN
SAVE-ALL	ACCLAIM	CAMBIUM	FOREARM	FLATTEN
SEVERAL.	BUCKRAM	HOMONYM	HEROISM	GLADDEN
BOWLFUL	DECLAIM	HUMDRUM	MARXISM	HEADMAN
HAWK-OWL	DECORUM	LAMAISM	PERFORM	HEARDIN
SAWBILL	EXCLAIM	POMATUM	SARCASM	HEARKEN
SAW-MILL.	ISCHIUM	SYMPTOM.	SCROTUM	HEARTEN
BOXHAUL	MACADAM	CONFIRM	SORGHUM	HEATHEN

IRANIAN	UNCLEAN	WHEATEN	HAIRPIN	MILLION
ITALIAN	UNCTION	WHEREIN	LYING-IN	MULLION
KHAMSIN	*YUCATAN.	WHEREON.	MOISTEN	OILSKIN
LIAISON	ABDOMEN	BUFFOON	OPINION	PALADIN
ORATION	ANDIRON	FIFTEEN	QUICKEN	PELICAN
OVARIAN	BEDIZEN	LIFTMAN	QUIETEN	PILLION
OVATION	BEDOUIN	REFRAIN	QUINTAN	POLYGON
+PEARSON	DUDGEON	RUFFIAN	SHIPPEN	PULLMAN
PHAETON	EIDOLON	SAFFRON.	SKID-PAN	SALICIN
PLATOON	GODDAMN	DOGSKIN	SMITTEN	SALTERN
PLAYPEN	GUDGEON	ENGRAIN	STIFFEN	SALT-PAN
QUARTAN	+HADRIAN	FOGHORN	*STILTON	SILICON
ROADMAN	INDRAWN	GAGSMAN	*SWINDON	+SOLOMON
SEA-LION	KIDSKIN	HOGSKIN	THIAMIN	+TOLKIEN
SHARPEN	REDSKIN	INGRAIN	THICKEN	UNLADEN
SLACKEN	WIDGEON.	LEGHORN	*TRISTAN	UNLEARN
SMARTEN	BEECHEN	LEGUMIN	TUITION	VILLAIN
SPARTAN	+BRENDAN	LIGHTEN	UNICORN	VILLEIN
STATION	CHEAPEN	MEGATON	WEIGH-IN	WALLOON.
SUASION	CHEVRON	ORGANON	+WHITMAN	ALMSMAN
SWAGMAN	DOESKIN	PIG-IRON	WHITSUN	*BAMPTON
TEACH-IN	*DRESDEN	PIGSKIN	WRITTEN.	BUMPKIN
TRADE-IN	ETESIAN	PYGMEAN	ADJOURN	CAMPION
URANIAN.	FLEXION	REGIMEN	SOJOURN.	*HAMPTON
ALBUMEN	FREEMAN	TIGHTEN	+BAKUNIN	HEMATIN
*BABYLON	FRESHEN	*WIGTOWN.	INKHORN	LAMBKIN
GOBELIN	GHERKIN	*BAHRAIN	UNKNOWN.	LAMPION
*LEBANON	GRECIAN	ECHELON	AILERON	LAMPOON
RUB-DOWN	GREMLIN	INHUMAN	AXLE-PIN	PUMPKIN
SUBDEAN	GUERDON	+JOHNSON	+BALDWIN	RAMADAN
SUBERIN	IBERIAN	MOHICAN.	BALLOON	SAMISEN
SUBJOIN	KEELMAN	*ABIDJAN	BELGIAN	SYMBION
UNBLOWN.	KEELSON	*AVIGNON	BILLION	TAMPION
ALCORAN	KREMLIN	BRIDOON	BULLION	TOMPION.
AUCTION	MUEZZIN	*BRITAIN	CELADON	BENISON
DECAGON	OVERRAN	BUILT-IN	COLLEEN	BENZOIN
DICTION	OVERRUN	CAISSON	DOLPHIN	BONDMAN
ENCHAIN	*PRESTON	CHICKEN	ENLIVEN	CANTEEN
FACTION	+QUENTIN	CHIFFON	GALLEON	CONCERN
FICTION	SHEBEEN	CHIGNON	GALLCON	CONDEMN
JACOBIN	STEARIN	CRIMSON	GELATIN	CONDIGN
+JOCELYN	STEEPEN	*CUILLIN	+GILLIAN	CONJOIN
LECTERN	STEN-GUN	DRIVE-IN	GILLION	CONSIGN
NOCTURN	+STEPHEN	EDITION	HALCYON	CONTAIN
NUCLEON	STEPSON	ELISION	HALOGEN	CONTEMN
PACKMAN	STETSON	EPIZOON	+HOLBEIN	DENIZEN
RACCOON	SWEETEN	EXILIAN	KILOTON	DUNGEON
SECTION	THEREIN	GLISTEN	*MALVERN	+FONTEYN
SUCTION	THEREON	GRIFFIN	MELANIN	GENTIAN
UNCHAIN	TREASON	GRISKIN	MILKMAN	HANGMAN

*HONITON	SHOWMAN	+MARILYN	HESSIAN	DRUMLIN
KANTIAN	*SNOWDON	MARTIAN	INSULIN	DRUNKEN
KINGPIN	SNOWMAN	MURRAIN	LESBIAN	ELUSION
KINSMAN	SPORRAN	OARSMAN	MISSION	FLUXION
LANOLIN	SWOLLEN	PARAGON	PASSION	FOURGON
LANTERN	TRODDEN	PERMIAN	PASSMAN	GLUTTON
*LINCOLN	UTOPIAN	PERSIAN	PASTERN	+HOUSMAN
LINEMAN	WOODMAN	PERTAIN	POSTERN	*HOUSTON
MANIKIN	WOOLLEN.	PORTION	POSTMAN	MAUDLIN
MANSION	+AMPHION	PURITAN	+PUSHKIN	+MAUREEN
MENTION	ASPIRIN	PURLOIN	PUSHPIN	NEUTRON
+MENUHIN	CAPSTAN	SARACEN	RUSSIAN	*REUNION
MONSOON	CAPTAIN	SIRLOIN	+SASSOON	ROUGHEN
NANKEEN	CAPTION	STRIVEN	SESSION	SAURIAN
PENGUIN	DIPNOAN	SURGEON	SUSTAIN	SOUPCON
PENSION	EXPLAIN	SURLOIN	WESTERN.	*TAUNTON
PINGUIN	HYPERON	TERRAIN	+ACTAEON	TOUGHEN
PONTOON	OPPIDAN	TERTIAN	ANTIGEN	+VAUGHAN.
RUN-DOWN	ORPHEAN	THRIVEN	ARTISAN	CAVE-MAN
SANDMAN	POPCORN	TORSION	BETAKEN	ENVIRON
SUNBURN	RUPTION	UNRISEN	BETOKEN	JAVELIN
SUNDOWN	TYPHOON	VERSION	BETWEEN	RAVELIN.
TENSION	UMPTEEN.	VERVAIN	BITTERN	INWOVEN
*TINTERN	ARRAIGN	WORKMAN.	BITUMEN	LOW-BORN
VENISON	BARGAIN	ABSTAIN	CITIZEN	LOW-DOWN
+WINSTON.	+BORODIN	ALSO-RAN	DETRAIN	*NEWTOWN.
AEOLIAN	BURGEON	BASSOON	ENTRAIN	DEXTRAN
BOOKMAN	CARAVAN	BASTION	GATEMAN	DEXTRIN
BROADEN	CARDOON	BUSHMAN	*HITCHIN	HEXAGON
+BRONWEN	+CAROLYN	*CASPIAN	KITCHEN	LEXICON
CHORION	CAROTIN	CESSION	LETHEAN	SAXHORN
CROUTON	CARRION	CISTERN	*LOTHIAN	SEXTAIN
*CROYDEN	CARTOON	COSTEAN	MUTAGEN	SIXTEEN
DOORMAN	CERESIN	CUSHION	OCTAGON	TAXIMAN.
EMOTION	CERTAIN	DISCERN	ORTOLAN	CRYOGEN
EROSION	CURTAIN	DISDAIN	OTTOMAN	ELYSIAN
ETONIAN	DURAMEN	DISJOIN	OUTSPAN	GRYPHON
FROGMAN	EARTHEN	DISLIMN	OUTWORN	KRYPTON
GOODMAN	FERMION	DUSTBIN	PATTERN	PTYALIN
*GOODWIN	FIREMAN	DUSTMAN	RETAKEN	STYGIAN
HYOSCIN	FORAMEN	DUSTPAN	SET-DOWN	TRYPSIN
KNOCK-ON	FOREIGN	EASTERN	SIT-DOWN	
MOORHEN	FOREMAN	EPSILON	*VATICAN	*AJACCIO
OXONIAN	FORLORN	FASHION	VETERAN	BRAVADO
PRONOUN	GORDIAN	FESTOON	VITAMIN.	DIABOLO
PROTEAN	HARDPAN	FISSION	BOURBON	PLACEBO
PROTEIN	HARPOON	FUSTIAN	BOURDON	SHAMPOO.
SHOPMAN	HORIZON	GAS-MAIN	CAUTION	EMBARGO
SHORTEN	JURYMAN	GOSSOON	CLUBMAN	TOBACCO
SHOTGUN	KERATIN	HAS-BEEN	DAUPHIN	VIBRATO

PICCOLO.	TORNADO	CLOSE-UP	CLAPPER	ROASTER
HIDALGO	*TORONTO	GROWN-UP	CLATTER	SCALPER
UNDERGO.	TORPEDO	SCOLLOP	CLAVIER	SCAMPER
CHEERIO	+UTRILLO	STOPGAP	COAL-TAR	SCARCER
MAESTRO	VERTIGO.	TROLLOP	COASTER	SCATTER
THERETO	BUSHIDO	TWO-STEP.	CRACKER	SHADIER
TREMOLO	GESTAPO	AIRSHIP	CRAMMER	SHARPER
WHERETO.	*LESOTHO	FORETOP	CRAWLER	SHATTER
BUFFALO	MESTIZO	HARDTOP	CRAZIER	SLACKER
INFERNO.	RISOTTO	HARE-LIP	DRAINER	SLANDER
BUGABOO	TESTUDO.	PARSNIP	ENAMOUR	SMACKER
MAGNETO	BOTARGO	WARSHIP	EXACTOR	SMALLER
NEGRITO.	*ONTARIO.	*WORKSOP	FEATHER	SMASHER
SCHERZO.	PRURIGO.	WORSHIP.	FLANEUR	SNAPPER
AGITATO	REVERSO	UNSTRAP.	FLANKER	SPANKER
*CHICAGO.		*ANTWERP	FLAPPER	SPANNER
ALLEGRO	CRACK-UP	KETCHUP	FLASHER	SPATTER
+CALYPSO	PEA-SOUP	OUTCROP	FLATTER	STAGGER
+GALILEO	SCALLOP	RAT-TRAP.	FLAVOUR	STALKER
MULATTO	SHALLOP	ROUND-UP	GLACIER	STAMMER
TALLY-HO	SMASH-UP	STUCK-UP.	GLAMOUR	STAPLER
VOLCANO.	TEA-SHOP.	DEVELOP	GLAZIER	STARTER
BAMBINO	UNCLASP.	ENVELOP.	GRABBER	SWABBER
BUMMALO	GODSHIP	COWSLIP	GRAFTER	SWAGGER
CEMBALO	MIDSHIP	DEWDROP.	GRAMMAR	SWATTER
CYMBALO	MUDFLAP.	FLY-TRAP	GRANDER	TEACHER
LUMBAGO	BREAK-UP	TOYSHOP	GRANTOR	TOASTER
MEMENTO	CHECK-UP		GRASPER	TRACKER
PIMENTO	KNEE-CAP	ADAPTER	+HEATHER	TRACTOR
POMPANO	OVERLAP	AMATEUR	HEAVIER	TRAILER
TIMPANO.	OVERTOP.	BLACKER	HOARDER	TRAINER
PINTADO.	EGG-FLIP	BLADDER	KNACKER	TRAITOR
AVOCADO	MUGWUMP	BOARDER	+LEANDER	TRAM-CAR
PROVISO	REGROUP.	BOASTER	LEATHER	TRAPPER
PROXIMO	BUILT-UP	*BRAEMAR	MEANDER	TRAWLER
SCORPIO.	CHIRRUP	BRAWLER	PEARLER	WEARIER
ESPARTO	*RUISLIP	BRAZIER	PLAINER	WEATHER
IMPASTO	SKI-JUMP	CHAFFER	PLANNER	WHATEER
SAPSAGO	STIRRUP	CHAMBER	PLANTAR	WRAPPER.
SOPRANO.	WRITE-UP	CHAMFER	PLANTER	ARBITER
VAQUERO.	BELL-HOP	CHAPTER	PLASTER	BABBLER
CORANTO	CALTROP	CHARGER	PLATTER	COBBLER
*CURACAO	MILKSOP.	CHARMER	POACHER	EMBOWER
FARRAGO	KINGCUP	CHARTER	PRAETOR	FIBSTER
+HORATIO	KINSHIP	CHATTER	PSALTER	GOBBLER
MORELLO	NON-STOP	+CHAUCER	QUARTER	JIB-DOOR
*MOROCCO	PUNCH-UP	CLAMBER	REACTOR	LOBSTER
+MURILLO	SONSHIP	CLAMOUR	REALGAR	MOBSTER
PORTICO	SUN-TRAP	CLAMPER	REALTOR	NEBULAR
SIROCCO	SYNCARP.	CLANGER	REAUMUR	NOBBLER

TUBULAR.	CLEARER	WHEREER	GUILDER	TWITTER
ALCAZAR	CLEAVER	WHETHER	JOINDER	WHIMPER
DECODER	CREAMER	WRECKER.	JOINTER	WHISKER
DECOLOR	CREATOR	LOFTIER	KNITTER	WHISPER
DECRIER	CREEPER	MUFFLER	KRIMMER	WHITHER
HECKLER	DREAMER	OFFICER	LEISTER	WRINGER.
INCISOR	DREDGER	RIFFLER.	NEITHER	BELCHER
INCOMER	DRESSER	ANGRIER	NOISIER	BOLIVAR
JOCULAR	DUELLER	ANGULAR	+OLIVIER	BOLSTER
LACQUER	DWELLER	BOGGLER	PAINTER	COLLIER
LUCKIER	EJECTOR	BUGBEAR	POINTER	DELATOR
NUCLEAR	+ELEANOR	FIGHTER	PRICKER	DELIVER
PICADOR	ELECTOR	FOGGIER	PRINTER	DILATOR
PICAMAR	ERECTOR	GIGGLER	QUICKER	DILUTER
RECITER	FIELDER	HAGGLER	QUIETER	FELSPAR
RECOVER	FREEZER	HIGGLER	QUITTER	HOLSTER
ROCKIER	FRESHER	JUGGLER	ROISTER	JOLLIER
SECULAR	GLEANER	JUGULAR	SCISSOR	MILK-BAR
SUCCOUR	GREASER	LIGHTER	SHIFTER	PALAVER
TACKLER	GREATER	REGULAR	SHIMMER	PILCHER
TICKLER	GREENER	TIGHTER	SHIPPER	PILULAR
UNCOVER.	GUELDER	WAGONER.	SHIRKER	POLYMER
*ANDOVER	KNEELER	COHERER	SKIMMER	SELTZER
AUDITOR	PLEADER	INHALER	SKIPPER	SILLIER
CADAVER	PREMIER	SCHEMER	SKITTER	SOLDIER
DIDDLER	PRESSER	SCHOLAR.	SLICKER	SULPHUR
FIDDLER	QUEERER	AVIATOR	SLIMMER	TELPHER
NODULAR	RE-ENTER	BLISTER	SLIPPER	WELSHER.
OLDSTER	SHELTER	BRIMMER	SLITHER	ADMIRER
PUDDLER	SLEEKER	BUILDER	SNICKER	ALMONER
RUDDIER	SLEEPER	CLICKER	SNIGGER	AMMETER
SADDLER	SLENDER	CLIMBER	SPICIER	ARMIGER
SEDUCER	SPEAKER	CLINGER	SPIELER	CAMPHOR
SIDECAR	SPEEDER	CLINKER	SPINNER	COMPEER
TIDDLER	SPELLER	CLIPPER	STICKER	FUMBLER
TODDLER	SPELTER	CRIBBER	STIFFER	GAMBLER
WIDOWER.	+SPENCER	CRISPER	STILLER	HAMSTER
ABETTOR	SPENDER	CRITTER	STINKER	HUMIDOR
AREOLAR	STEAMER	DRIFTER	SWIFTER	RAMBLER
ATELIER	STEEPER	DRINKER	SWIMMER	REMOVER
AVENGER	STEERER	EMITTER	SWINGER	SAMOVAR
BREAKER	STELLAR	FLICKER	THICKER	SAMPLER
BREEDER	STERNER	FLIPPER	THINKER	SEMINAR
BREVIER	SWEARER	FLITTER	THINNER	SIMILAR
CHECKER	SWEATER	FRITTER	THITHER	TAMBOUR
*CHEDDAR	SWEEPER	GLIMMER	TRIFLER	TEMPLAR
CHEEPER	SWEETER	GLISTER	TRIGGER	TEMPTER
CHEQUER	SWELTER	GLITTER	TRIMMER	TUMBLER.
*CHESTER	TWEEZER	GRIMMER	TRIPPER	ANNULAR
CLEANER	WHENEER	GRINDER	TWISTER	BENCHER

BUNGLER	CHOWDER	WOODIER.	TERRIER	SET-FAIR
CANDOUR	CLOBBER	BIPOLAR	THROWER	SETTLER
CENTAUR	CROAKER	DIPOLAR	+VERMEER	SETTLOR
CENTNER	CROFTER	EMPEROR	VERNIER	TATTLER
CONIFER	CROONER	EMPOWER	WARBLER	TITULAR
CONQUER	CROPPER	EMPTIER	WARRIOR	TUTELAR
CONTOUR	CROSIER	HAPPIER	WORRIER.	WITTIER.
DONATOR	CROWBAR	HIPSTER	BASILAR	ABUTTER
FANCIER	DIOPTER	+JUPITER	BESMEAR	ASUNDER
FUN-FAIR	DROPPER	OPPOSER	CASHIER	BLUBBER
HANDLER	FEOFFOR	POPULAR	DESPAIR	BLUFFER
*HANOVER	FLOATER	REPAPER	DOSSIER	BLUNDER
JANITOR	GROOVER	TAPSTER	DUSKIER	BLUSTER
JUNIPER	GROUSER	TIPPLER	DUSTIER	BOUDOIR
KINDLER	GROWLER	TIPSTER.	HUSTLER	*BOULDER
LANGUOR	KNOCKER	LIQUEUR.	INSIDER	BOULTER
MANAGER	PIONEER	AERATOR	INSOFAR	BOUNCER
MAN-HOUR	PLODDER	BARRIER	INSULAR	BOUNDER
MANLIER	PLOTTER	BURGHER	INSURER	CHUKKER
MINIVER	PROCTOR	BURGLAR	MASSEUR	CLUSTER
MINSTER	PRODDER	CARRIER	MESSIER	CLUTTER
MONITOR	PROFFER	CORONER	NASTIER	COULTER
MONOMER	PROSPER	CORSAIR	+PASTEUR	COUNTER
MONSTER	PROUDER	CURATOR	POST-WAR	COUPLER
NON-USER	PROWLER	EARLIER	RESCUER	COURIER
PANNIER	ROOMIER	FARCEUR	RISKIER	COURSER
PANTHER	ROOSTER	FARRIER	RUSTIER	CRUISER
PUNSTER	SCOOTER	FARTHER	RUSTLER	CRUPPER
RANCHER	SCOURER	FERVOUR	TASTIER	DOUBTER
RANCOUR	SHOCKER	FORAGER	UPSTAIR	DOUCEUR
RENTIER	SHOOTER	FORBEAR	VISITOR.	DRUMMER
SAND-BAR	SHOPPER	FOREVER	AUTOCAR	*ECUADOR
SANDIER	SHORTER	+FORSTER	BOTCHER	EQUATOR
SENATOR	SLOBBER	FURRIER	BUTCHER	FLUSTER
SUNNIER	SLOGGER	FURTHER	CATCHER	FLUTTER
*TANGIER	SMOTHER	HARBOUR	CATERER	FOUNDER
*VENTNOR	SNOOKER	HARDIER	COTTIER	FRUITER
VINEGAR	SNOOPER	HARRIER	DITCHER	GRUBBER
VINTNER	SNORTER	HERITOR	HATCHER	HAULIER
WINDIER	SPONGER	HURDLER	INTEGER	HAUTEUR
*WINDSOR.	SPONSOR	MARINER	LITTLER	LAUNDER
ANOTHER	SPOTTER	NORTHER	MATADOR	LOUNGER
BLOATER	STONIER	PARLOUR	OCTOBER	MAUNDER
BLOOMER	STOPPER	PARTNER	OUTDOOR	MOULDER
BLOTTER	STOUTER	PURSUER	OUTLIER	MOURNER
BOOSTER	TROOPER	SCRAPER	OUTWEAR	PLUMBER
BROADER	TROTTER	SCRIBER	PITCHER	PLUMPER
BROILER	TROUPER	SPRAYER	PUTTIER	PLUNDER
BROTHER	WHOEVER	STRIKER	RATTLER	PLUNGER
CHOPPER	WHOPPER	SURLIER	ROTATOR	PLUSHER

471

POUNDER	GRAMPUS	SADNESS	OMINOUS	TUMULUS.
ROUGHER	JEALOUS	TEDIOUS	QUIETUS	BENTHOS
ROUNDER	MEASLES	TIDINGS	RUINOUS	BONKERS
SAUNTER	PHALLUS	UNDRESS.	SPINOUS	CANVASS
SCULLER	SCABIES	ACETOUS	TRICEPS.	CONCUSS
SCUPPER	SCARVES	ADENOUS	HIJINKS	CONFESS
SCUTTER	SEA-LEGS	AGELESS	PYJAMAS.	FUNGOUS
SHUDDER	*STAINES	ASEPSIS	BELLOWS	GENESIS
SHUTTER	STATICS	+DRESFUS	BILIOUS	HUNKERS
SLUMBER	TEAR-GAS	EYELESS	BULBOUS	IGNEOUS
SPUTTER	URANOUS	GREAVES	CALAMUS	INNARDS
SQUALOR	WHARVES	+LAERTES	+CALCHAS	INNINGS
STUNNER	ZEALOUS.	OCELLUS	CALENDS	KENOSIS
STUTTER	ARBUTUS	ONENESS	CALLOUS	*KINROSS
THUNDER	DUBIOUS	ONEROUS	CALYCES	LINCTUS
TOUGHER	EMBOLUS	PEERESS	*CELEBES	MINIBUS
USURPER	FIBROUS	POETESS	+CHLORIS	NONPLUS
VAULTER	GIBBOUS	PRECESS	COLITIS	OMNIBUS
VOUCHER	JOBLESS.	SCEPSIS	+DOLORES	PANTIES
YOUNGER.	+BACCHUS	SHEAVES	FALSIES	PENATES
ADVISER	CYCLOPS	SPECIES	FULVOUS	PINCERS
DIVINER	+DICKENS	THERMOS	GALLOWS	SANCTUS
DIVISOR	DUCHESS	+THESEUS	HELICES	SENATUS
HAVENER	INCUBUS	TRELLIS	ILLNESS	SINLESS
INVADER	JACKASS	USELESS	LALLANS	SINUOUS
REVIVER	LACE-UPS	WHEREAS.	+MALTHUS	SUNLESS
RIVETER	MYCOSIS	AGGRESS	OILLESS	TENPINS
SAVIOUR.	NUCLEUS	*ALGIERS	POLYPUS	TENUOUS
DAWDLER	RICKETS	ANGELUS	PYLORUS	WANNESS
DOWAGER	SUCCESS	BUGLOSS	TALLNES	WINKERS.
HOWEVER	TACTICS	DEGAUSS	VELOURS	AMOROUS
ROWDIER.	VACUOUS	DIGRESS	VILLOUS.	ANOESIS
CLYSTER	VICIOUS.	ENGROSS	AIMLESS	CLOTHES
FLY-OVER	ADDRESS	INGRESS	ARMLESS	+CROESUS
+SEYMOUR	ARDUOUS	LEGLESS	COMMONS	DIOPSIS
SHYSTER	ECDYSIS	MUGGINS	COMPASS	GLOTTIS
VOYAGER.	ENDLESS	NEGRESS	CUMULUS	*KNOSSOS
COZENER	ENDWAYS	+PEGASUS	DIMNESS	LIONESS
GUZZLER	GODDESS	REGRESS	FAMULUS	ODOROUS
PUZZLER	GODLESS	TIGRESS.	GIMBALS	+PHOEBUS
	HEDDLES	+ACHATES	HUMERUS	PROCESS
+BEATLES	HIDEOUS	APHESIS	LEMURES	PROFESS
CHABLIS	HYDROUS	APHIDES	MIMESIS	+PROTEUS
CHAMOIS	INDICES	ECHINUS	NEMESIS	PROWESS
+CHARLES	INDOORS	ICHTHYS	OSMOSIS	RHOMBUS
CHASSIS	MADNESS	OCHROUS.	POMPOUS	RIOTOUS.
COAL-GAS	ODDNESS	CUIRASS	ROMPERS	COPIOUS
CZARDAS	+OEDIPUS	HEINOUS	+ROMULUS	CUPROUS
+ERASMUS	RADICES	HEIRESS	RUMNESS	CYPRESS
+FRANCIS	REDRESS	MEIOSIS	SUMMONS	DEPRESS

EMPRESS	CASEOUS	*DEVIZES	LEAFLET	EXCERPT
EXPRESS	DISCUSS	ENVIOUS	NEAREST	HACKLET
HAPLESS	DISMISS	OBVIOUS.	ONANIST	INCRUST
IMPETUS	ESSENES	LAWLESS	PEASANT	JACKPOT
IMPIOUS	FUSCOUS	ONWARDS	PIANIST	JACONET
IMPRESS	GASEOUS	RAWNESS	PLACKET	LOCK-OUT
OPPRESS	HASLETS	TOWARDS	PLAUDIT	NECKLET
+ORPHEUS	HOSTESS	UPWARDS.	PLAY-ACT	OCCIPUT
PAPYRUS	MESEEMS	ANXIOUS	PLAYLET	PECCANT
REPRESS	OESTRUS	LAXNESS	PRAKRIT	PICQUET
SAPLESS	OSSEOUS	NOXIOUS	QUADRAT	RACQUET
TYPHOUS.	POSSESS	SEXLESS.	QUARTET	RECEIPT
AIRLESS	VESPERS	AZYMOUS	READMIT	RECOUNT
APROPOS	VISCOUS.	COYNESS	REAGENT	RECRUIT
+ATROPOS	ACTRESS	JOYLESS	REALIST	RICHEST
AUROCHS	+ANTAEUS	*OLYMPUS	SCARLET	SACKBUT
BARYTES	APTNESS	+PHYLLIS	SEAPORT	SACRIST
BURGESS	+ARTEMIS	PHYSICS	SEA-SALT	SICKEST.
BURNOUS	ARTLESS	RAYLESS	SHALLOT	BEDPOST
*CARACUS	BETIMES	SHYNESS	STALEST	ENDMOST
CARCASS	CITROUS	SLYNESS	STARLET	FADDIST
CARIOUS	CUTLASS	THYRSUS	STARLIT	HIDEOUT
CEREOUS	OUTEOUS	+ULYSSES	TRANSIT	HYDRANT
CURIOUS	FATNESS	WRYNESS	VIADUCT	MADDEST
FERROUS	FATUOUS		WEAKEST	MIDMOST
FURIOUS	FITNESS	ADAMANT	WHATNOT.	MUDFLAT
HARNESS	ICTERUS	AGAINST	AMBIENT	ODDMENT
LARGESS	ISTHMUS	ANALECT	BABY-SIT	RADIANT
MARQUIS	LITOTES	ANALYST	BIBELOT	RED-COAT
NERVOUS	LUTEOUS	BEAR-PIT	CABARET	REDDEST
PARADOS	METRICS	BLANKET	CABINET	REDOUBT
PARESIS	MITOSIS	BLATANT	HABITAT	SADDEST
PARLOUS	NITROUS	BRACKET	NOBLEST	TIDIEST.
PERCUSS	OCTOPUS	BRAVEST	SUB-EDIT	CHEMIST
PERHAPS	PITEOUS	CHAPLET	SUBJECT	CHEROOT
+PERSEUS	TETANUS	CHARIOT	SUBPLOT	*CHEVIOT
PYRITES	UNTRUSS	CLAMANT	SUBSIST	+CLEMENT
REREDOS	WETNESS	CLAP-NET	SUBVERT	COEXIST
+SERAPIS	WITHERS	COAL-PIT	UNBUILT	CRESSET
SERIOUS	WITLESS	COAL-TIT	VIBRANT.	DEEPEST
STRATUS	WITNESS.	DEAREST	ACCOUNT	DIETIST
+STRAUSS	ALUMNUS	DIALECT	ACCURST	ELEGANT
SURPASS	AQUEOUS	DIARIST	ANCIENT	ELEGIST
SURPLUS	BRUMOUS	DRAG-NET	+BECKETT	ELEMENT
VARICES	*DOUGLAS	DRAUGHT	COCKPIT	*EVEREST
VARIOUS.	EMULOUS	EPAULET	COCONUT	EYE-BOLT
ABSCESS	RAUCOUS	FLATLET	CYCLIST	EYESHOT
ASSIZES	SQUAILS.	FRAUGHT	ENCHANT	FREIGHT
AUSSIES	CIVVIES	GRAVEST	ENCRUST	FRESHET
BESIDES	DEVIOUS	HEAD-SET	ESCHEAT	INEXACT

--E---T			--O---T	
KEENEST	PIGMENT	WHITEST.	COMMENT	LENIENT
MEEKEST	REGNANT	ADJUNCT	COMPACT	LINOCUT
OVERACT	SEGMENT	RAJPOOT.	COMPORT	LONGEST
OVERSET	SUGGEST	PIKELET	COMPOST	MANHUNT
PIERROT	UNGUENT	UNKEMPT.	CUMQUAT	MANUMIT
PLEDGET	VAGRANT	AILMENT	DEMERIT	MINARET
PRECEPT	YOGHURT.	BALDEST	DEMOUNT	NONSUIT
PREDICT	ADHIBIT	BALLAST	GYMNAST	PENDANT
PRE-EMPT	ATHIRST	*BELFAST	HYMNIST	PENDENT
PREFECT	ATHWART	BOLDEST	KUMQUAT	PENNANT
PRESENT	COHABIT	CALMEST	LAMBENT	PUNGENT
PRETEXT	EXHAUST	CALUMET	LAMBERT	RANKEST
PREVENT	EXHIBIT	CELLIST	NYMPHET	RINGLET
QUERIST	INHABIT	COLDEST	RAMPANT	SINGLET
SHERBET	INHERIT	COLLECT	RAMPART	SUNSPOT
SLEIGHT	INHIBIT.	CULPRIT	REMNANT	TANGENT
+STEWART	ALIMENT	CULVERT	REMOUNT	TENSEST
THEREAT	ALIQUOT	DELIGHT	TEMPEST	TINIEST
THERMIT	+BRIDGET	DELIMIT	TEMPLET	TONIGHT
TIERCET	BRIQUET	DILUENT	UNMEANT.	+VINCENT.
WHEREAT.	BRISKET	DULLEST	ANNULET	AMONGST
AFFLICT	CRICKET	FALL-OUT	BANQUET	AMORIST
AFFRONT	DRIBLET	FILBERT	BENEFIT	BLOW-OUT
DEFAULT	EMINENT	FULLEST	CONCEIT	BOOKLET
DEFIANT	EPITHET	GALLANT	CONCEPT	BROCKET
DEFICIT	EVIDENT	GALLIOT	CONCERT	BROUGHT
DEFLECT	EXIGENT	+GILBERT	CONCOCT	BUOYANT
DEFROST	FRISKET	HALF-WIT	CONDUIT	COOLANT
DEFUNCT	HAIR-CUT	HALIBUT	CONGEST	COOLEST
INFLECT	HAIRNET	HELLCAT	CONNECT	CROCHET
INFLICT	MAILLOT	HOLIEST	CONSENT	CROCKET
LEFTIST	OVIDUCT	ILLICIT	CONSIST	CROQUET
OFFBEAT	OXIDANT	MILDEST	CONSORT	DOORMAT
REFLECT	PRICKET	PALMIST	CONSULT	DROPLET
REFLOAT	QUINTET	POLECAT	CONTACT	DROP-OUT
REFRACT	RAIMENT	RELIANT	CONTENT	DROUGHT
SOFTEST.	SKI-LIFT	SALIENT	CONTEST	EBONIST
AUGMENT	SKILLET	SELL-OUT	CONTEXT	EGOTIST
BIGGEST	SNIPPET	SOLICIT	CONTORT	ERODENT
DOGGART	SPIRANT	SOLOIST	CONVENT	FLORIST
DOGTROT	THICKET	SOLVENT	CONVERT	FLORUIT
ENGRAFT	TRIDENT	TALLEST	CONVICT	GROMMET
FIGMENT	TRIGLOT	UGLIEST	DENSEST	IRONIST
FUGUIST	TRINKET	VALIANT	DENTIST	ISODONT
HIGHEST	TRIOLET	WALK-OUT	FANTAST	LOOK-OUT
HIGH-HAT	TRIPLET	WILDCAT	GUNBOAT	LOOSEST
JOG-TROT	TRISECT	WILDEST.	GUNSHOT	MOONLIT
MIGRANT	TWIN-SET	BOMBAST	HANDOUT	POOREST
NEGLECT	VAINEST	CAMBIST	KINDEST	PRODUCT
PAGEANT	WHIPPET	COMFORT	KINGLET	PROJECT

PROPHET	CIRCLET	VERDANT	CATBOAT	PRUDENT
PROTECT	CIRCUIT	VERDICT	CATMINT	+ROUAULT
PROTEST	CORONET	VERIEST	DETRACT	SHUT-OUT
PROVOST	CORRECT	*VERMONT	*DETROIT	SOUREST
SLOWEST	CORRUPT	WARMEST	ENTRANT	STUDENT
THOUGHT	CORSLET	WARRANT	ENTREAT	TAUTEST
VIOLENT	CURRANT	WORK-OUT	ENTRUST	TOURIST
VIOLIST	CURRENT	YORKIST.	EXTINCT	TRUMPET.
WOODCUT	DARKEST	ASSAULT	EXTRACT	DOVECOT
WROUGHT	DORMANT	BASINET	FATTEST	LEVERET
ZIONIST.	EARNEST	BISCUIT	FITMENT	NAVY-CUT
APPOINT	EARSHOT	CASUIST	FITTEST	RIVULET.
ASPHALT	FERMENT	CESSPIT	HATCHET	BOWSHOT
BAPTIST	FERVENT	DESCANT	HOTFOOT	HOWBEIT
CO-PILOT	FORFEIT	DESCENT	HOTTEST	LAWSUIT
COPY-CAT	FORWENT	DESSERT	HUTMENT	*NEWPORT
COPYIST	GARMENT	DISGUST	INTRANT	SAWDUST.
CYPRIOT	HARDEST	DISHMAT	INTROIT	FOXHUNT
DEPOSIT	HARD-SET	DISMAST	INTRUST	FOX-TROT
EXPLOIT	HARICOT	DISPORT	MATCHET	SEXIEST
IMPLANT	HARPIST	DISRUPT	METCAST	SEXTANT.
IMPREST	+HARRIET	DISSECT	METRIST	BAYONET
IMPRINT	HARVEST	DISSENT	OUTCAST	BOYCOTT
RAPPORT	+HERBERT	DISTANT	OUTLAST	FLY-BOAT
REPLANT	LARGEST	DISTORT	OUTMOST	FLY-PAST
REPOINT	MARTLET	FASCIST	OUTPOST	PAYMENT
REPRINT	MORDANT	FASTEST	OUTWENT	STYLIST
SAPIENT	PARAPET	FUSS-POT	PATIENT	
SOPHIST	PARQUET	GESTALT	PATRIOT	CHATEAU
SUPPORT	PERCEPT	*GOSPORT	POT-SHOT	PLATEAU.
TAP-ROOT	PERFECT	INSIGHT	RATCHET	FABLIAU
TOP-BOOT	PERSIST	INSPECT	RETRACT	TABLEAU.
TOP-COAT	PERVERT	INSTANT	UNTWIST	+COCTEAU.
TOPKNOT	PORRECT	MISCAST	UPTIGHT	JUJITSU.
TOPMAST	PORTENT	MUSK-RAT	WETTEST	NYLGHAU.
TOPMOST.	PURPORT	NASCENT	WITHOUT.	BANDEAU
ASQUINT	PURSUIT	PASSANT	BOUQUET	+MONTAGU
BEQUEST	RAREBIT	RESPECT	COULDST	RONDEAU.
INQUEST	SERPENT	ROSE-CUT	COUPLET	+THOREAU.
PIQUANT	SERVANT	SUSPECT	CRUMPET	CARIBOU
REQUEST	SPRIGHT	UNSPENT	DOUBLET	PARVENU
SEQUENT	SURCOAT	UPSTART	DRUGGET	PURLIEU.
UNQUIET.	SURFEIT	UPSWEPT	FLUTIST	CATECHU.
ABREACT	TARTLET	VASTEST	FOUMART	+TRUDEAU
ABREAST	TORMENT	WASH-OUT.	GOURMET	
ACROBAT	TORRENT	ATTAINT	GRUMMET	+NABOKOV.
AIRLIFT	TURN-OUT	ATTEMPT	LOUDEST	+CHEKHOV
AIRPORT	UPRIGHT	ATTRACT	OCULIST	
APRICOT	VARIANT	AUTOMAT	OPULENT	*GLASGOW
BARONET	VARMINT	BETWIXT	PLUMMET	SHALLOW

SPARROW	CALL-BOX	FLAG-DAY	STATELY	SECRECY
SWALLOW.	*HALIFAX	FLAKILY	SUAVELY	SECTARY
HACKSAW	PILL-BOX	FRAILLY	SUAVITY	SICK-BAY
JACKDAW	POLL-TAX.	FRAILTY	SWARTHY	SICK-PAY
LOCKJAW	COMPLEX.	FRANKLY	TEA-COSY	SOCIETY
*WICKLOW.	BANDBOX	GHASTLY	TEA-TRAY	TACITLY
EYEBROW	*BENELUX	GRADELY	TRACERY	UNCANNY
FRET-SAW	CONFLUX	GRANARY	TRAGEDY	VACANCY
OVERSAW	LAND-TAX.	GRANDLY	TRAMWAY	VACUITY
OVERSEW	*PHOENIX	GRAPERY	WEALTHY	VICEROY
PREVIEW.	POOR-BOX.	GRATIFY	WEARILY.	VICTORY
RAINBOW	BUREAUX	GRAVELY	BOBBERY	VOCALLY.
WHITLOW.	FIREBOX	GRAVITY	+DEBUSSY	ARDENCY
SOMEHOW.	NARTHEX	HEADWAY	DUBIETY	CADENCY
BAND-SAW	PARADOX	HEALTHY	EMBASSY	ELDERLY
DANELAW	PERPLEX.	HEARSAY	JOBBERY	GIDDILY
LONGBOW	ANTHRAX	HEAVILY	LIBERTY	+GODFREY
*RENFREW	APTERYX.	IMAGERY	LIBRARY	MODESTY
WINDROW.	EQUINOX	INANELY	PUBERTY	ORDERLY
CHOCTAW	FLUMMOX	INANITY	RABBITY	RUDDILY
HOOSGOW		INAPTLY	RABIDLY	*SUDBURY
KNOW-HOW.	ACADEMY	IRATELY	ROBBERY	TIDDLEY
AIRFLOW	AMATORY	KNAVERY	RUBBERY	TIDEWAY
FORESAW	ANALOGY	LEAKILY	SOBERLY	VIDUITY
PURVIEW.	ANARCHY	LOATHLY	SUBSIDY.	ZEDOARY.
BESTREW	ANATOMY	OPACITY	ALCHEMY	ACETIFY
CASE-LAW	ATARAXY	ORATORY	ANCHOVY	AMENITY
DISAVOW	BEASTLY	PLAINLY	ARCHERY	*AVEBURY
UNSCREW.	BEATIFY	PLAYBOY	ARCHWAY	BLEAKLY
CATS-PAW	BLANDLY	QUALIFY	COCKILY	BREVITY
FITCHEW	BLANKLY	QUALITY	COCKNEY	BREWERY
+MATTHEW	BLARNEY	READILY	DECENCY	CHEAPLY
OUTFLOW	BRASHLY	REALITY	FACTORY	CLEANLY
OUTGREW	BRAVELY	ROADWAY	FACULTY	CLEARLY
OUTGROW	BRAVERY	SCARIFY	*HACKNEY	DEEP-FRY
UPTHROW.	CHANTRY	SHADILY	HICKORY	DIETARY
DEW-CLAW	CHARILY	SHADOWY	LECHERY	ERECTLY
LOWBROW	CHARITY	SHAKILY	LICITLY	FIERILY
	CLARIFY	SHAPELY	LOCALLY	FLESHLY
GEAR-BOX	CLARITY	SLACKLY	LUCIDLY	FRECKLY
PHALANX	CRASSLY	SLAVERY	LUCKILY	FRESHLY
PHARYNX	CRAZILY	SMARTLY	MOCKERY	GREATLY
SOAP-BOX.	DEANERY	SNAKILY	MUCKILY	+GREGORY
DICE-BOX	DEATHLY	SOAPILY	NECTARY	IDEALLY
TUCK-BOX.	DIARCHY	SPARELY	PECCARY	INEPTLY
BEES-WAX	DRAPERY	STAIDLY	RECTIFY	INERTLY
OVERTAX.	DUALITY	+STANLEY	RECTORY	NEEDILY
TRIPLEX.	EDACITY	STARCHY	RICKETY	OVERLAY
JUKEBOX.	EGALITY	STARKLY	ROCKERY	OVERTLY
AXLE-BOX	EXACTLY		ROCKILY	PLENARY

PRELACY	RIGHTLY	*PAISLEY	CALUMNY	COMPANY
QUEENLY	RIGIDLY	PLIANCY	CALVARY	DAMNIFY
QUEERLY	ROGUERY	PRICKLY	CILIARY	HUMANLY
RE-ENTRY	SIGHTLY	PRIMACY	COLICKY	HYMNODY
SCENERY	SIGNIFY	PRIMARY	DULCIFY	LAMPREY
SEEDILY	SOGGILY	PRIMELY	FALLACY	MAMMARY
+SHELLEY	TIGHTLY	PRIVACY	FALL-GUY	MIMICRY
*SHEPPEY	UNGODLY	PRIVILY	FALSELY	MUMMERY
SKETCHY	URGENCY	PRIVITY	FALSIFY	MUMMIFY
SLEEKLY	VAGUELY	QUICKLY	FALSITY	REMARRY
SPECIFY	WAGGERY.	QUIETLY	FELONRY	RUMMILY
STERNLY	ASHTRAY	QUINARY	GALLERY	SUMMARY
SWEETLY	UNHANDY	RAILWAY	HALF-PAY	SUMMERY
THERAPY	UNHAPPY.	SAINTLY	HALFWAY	TIMIDLY
THEREBY	ABILITY	SHINILY	+HILLARY	+TIMOTHY
THEURGY	ACIDIFY	SHIP-WAY	HOLIDAY	UNMANLY
TREACLY	ACIDITY	+SHIRLEY	JOLLIFY	*WEMBLEY
TREMBLY	AGILELY	SHIVERY	JOLLITY	WOMANLY
TUESDAY	AGILITY	SLICKLY	KILLJOY	ZYMURGY.
WEEKDAY	ALIMONY	SLIPWAY	LULLABY	AMNESTY
WHEREBY.	ARIDITY	SPICILY	MALMSEY	ANNUITY
AWFULLY	AVIDITY	SPIDERY	MILDEWY	*BANBURY
FIFTHLY	AXIALLY	SPINDLY	MOLLIFY	BONNILY
HEFTILY	BLINDLY	SPINNEY	NULLIFY	CANNERY
HUFFILY	BRIBERY	STIFFLY	NULLITY	CANNILY
INFANCY	BRIEFLY	SWIFTLY	OBLOQUY	CANONRY
+JEFFREY	BRISKLY	THICKLY	PALFREY	CENTURY
LIFTBOY	BRISTLY	THIRDLY	PALMARY	CINDERY
LOFTILY	CHICORY	THIRSTY	PHLEGMY	DANDIFY
TIFFANY.	CHIEFLY	THISTLY	PILLORY	DENSELY
ANGRILY	CHIMNEY	TRICKSY	PULPIFY	DENSITY
BEGGARY	CLIQUEY	TRILOGY	SALSIFY	DENTARY
BIGOTRY	CRINKLY	TRINITY	SILKILY	DYNASTY
BUGGERY	DRIP-DRY	TRITELY	SILLILY	FANTASY
COGENCY	DRIZZLY	UNITARY	SILVERY	FINALLY
DIGNIFY	FAINTLY	URINARY	SOLIDLY	FINICKY
DIGNITY	FAIRILY	UTILITY	SPLASHY	FUNNILY
EAGERLY	FAIRWAY	WEIGHTY	SULKILY	GANGWAY
FOGGILY	FLIGHTY	WEIRDLY	TALLBOY	GINGERY
HIGHDAY	GAINSAY	WHIMSEY	*TILBURY	GUNNERY
HIGHWAY	*GRIMSBY	WHISKEY.	+TOLSTOY	HANDILY
LEGALLY	GRISTLY	MAJESTY.	UNLUCKY	HENNERY
LEGIBLY	GRIZZLY	NAKEDLY.	VALENCY	HONESTY
LIGHTLY	HAIRILY	ALLERGY	VALIDLY	*HUNGARY
MAGGOTY	JOINTLY	BALCONY	VELVETY	JANUARY
MAGNIFY	LYINGLY	BELL-BOY	WALLABY	+KENNEDY
NIGHTLY	NAIVELY	BILIARY	WILLOWY	KINKILY
PIGGERY	NAIVETY	BOLONEY	YELLOWY.	LENGTHY
REGALLY	NOISILY	CALCIFY	ARMOURY	+LINDSEY
REGENCY	OLIVARY	*CALGARY	COMFREY	MONTHLY

NINTHLY	LOOSELY	LIQUEFY.	SCRAWNY	LUSTILY
NUNNERY	MOODILY	ALREADY	SCRUBBY	MASONRY
PANICKY	NEOLOGY	ATROPHY	SCRUFFY	MASTERY
PANOPLY	NOONDAY	+BARNABY	SERVERY	MESSILY
PENALLY	OTOLOGY	*BURNLEY	SHRILLY	MISERLY
PENALTY	PIOUSLY	BURSARY	SHRUBBY	MISTILY
PONTIFY	PROBITY	CARAWAY	SORCERY	MYSTERY
*RINGWAY	PRODIGY	CARROTY	SPRINGY	MYSTIFY
RUNAWAY	PROGENY	CERTIFY	STREAKY	NASALLY
SANDBOY	PROSILY	CORNILY	STRINGY	NASTILY
SAND-FLY	PROSODY	CURSORY	SURDITY	NOSEGAY
SENSORY	PROUDLY	CURTSEY	SURGERY	OSSUARY
SYNERGY	+PTOLEMY	DIRTILY	SURLILY	PESSARY
TANNERY	ROOKERY	+DOROTHY	TARDILY	RISKILY
TENABLY	SCORIFY	DURABLY	TERRIFY	RUSSIFY
TENANCY	SHORTLY	EARTHLY	TERSELY	RUSTILY
TENSELY	SHOWERY	ERRANCY	THRIFTY	TASTILY
TENTHLY	SHOWILY	FARADAY	THROATY	TESTACY
TENUITY	SMOKILY	FARAWAY	*TORQUAY	TESTIFY
TINNILY	SMOOCHY	FERNERY	TURNERY	TESTILY
VENALLY	SNOWILY	FERRETY	TURNKEY	WASH-DAY.
ZONALLY.	SOOTILY	FIREFLY	TYRANNY	ACTUARY
ALOOFLY	STOUTLY	FIRSTLY	UNREADY	+ANTHONY
ANOMALY	TROLLEY	FORGERY	VARIETY	AUTOPSY
APOLOGY	+TROTSKY	FORTIFY	VARSITY	BATTERY
BIOLOGY	WRONGLY	*GERMANY	VERSIFY	BUTTERY
BLOTCHY	ZOOGAMY	HARDILY	VIRELAY	CATTILY
BLOW-FLY	ZOOLOGY	HARMONY	WORDILY	COTTONY
BROADLY	ZOOTOMY.	HARSHLY	WORKDAY	CUTAWAY
CLOSELY	AMPLIFY	HERONRY	WORK-SHY	CUTLERY
COOKERY	COPPERY	HORALLY	WORLDLY.	ENTROPY
CROSSLY	EMPATHY	HORRIFY	BASALLY	ESTUARY
DOORWAY	EMPTILY	JERKILY	CUSTODY	FATALLY
DROSHKY	EUPHONY	LARCENY	DESTINY	FETIDLY
DROUTHY	FOPPERY	LARGELY	DESTROY	GATEWAY
ECOLOGY	HAPENNY	LURIDLY	DISOBEY	GETAWAY
ECONOMY	HAPPILY	+MARGERY	DISPLAY	JITTERY
EXOGAMY	IMPIETY	+MERCURY	DUSKILY	LATENCY
FLOWERY	LEPROSY	MERRILY	DUSTILY	LATHERY
FOOLERY	ORPHREY	MORALLY	ECSTASY	LITURGY
FOOTWAY	PEPPERY	MORTIFY	FAST-DAY	LOTTERY
FROWSTY	RAPIDLY	MURKILY	FISHERY	NOTABLY
GEODESY	SOPPILY	NURSERY	FISHILY	OUTPLAY
GEOLOGY	TEPIDLY	PARSLEY	FUSTILY	OUTSTAY
GHOSTLY	TIPSILY	PERFIDY	GASEITY	PATHWAY
GLORIFY	TOPIARY	PERJURY	GOSSIPY	PETRIFY
GROCERY	VAPIDLY	PERKILY	HASTILY	PETTILY
GROSSLY	VAPOURY.	PORTRAY	HISTORY	PITHILY
GROUCHY	ENQUIRY	SCRAGGY	HOSIERY	POTENCY
KNOBBLY	INQUIRY	SCRAPPY	JUSTIFY	POTTERY

478

PUTREFY	SAUCILY
RETIARY	SOUNDLY
SATIETY	SQUALLY
SATISFY	SQUASHY
TATTILY	SQUEAKY
TOTALLY	SQUIFFY
TOTTERY	STUBBLY
UTTERLY	STUPEFY
VITALLY	TOUGHLY
VITRIFY	TOURNEY
WITTILY.	TRUANCY
ACUTELY	*URUGUAY
BLUFFLY	USUALLY.
BLUNTLY	CAVALRY
CAUTERY	CIVILLY
CHURCHY	DEVILRY
CHUTNEY	LIVIDLY
COUNTRY	LOVABLY
COURTLY	NOVELTY
CRUCIFY	POVERTY
CRUDELY	REVELRY
CRUDITY	RIVALRY
CRUELLY	SAVELOY
CRUELTY	SAVOURY
CRUMBLY	SEVENTY
CRUNCHY	VIVIDLY.
DOUGHTY	BAWDILY
ELUSORY	DOWDILY
EQUABLY	JEWELRY
EQUALLY	PAWKILY
EQUERRY	POWDERY
FLUENCY	ROWDILY
FLUNKEY	TAWNILY.
FOUNDRY	ANXIETY.
GAUDILY	ANYBODY
GAUNTLY	CRY-BABY
GRUFFLY	FLYAWAY
HAUGHTY	LOYALLY
HAUTBOY	LOYALTY
JOURNEY	ODYSSEY
LAUNDRY	ROYALLY
LOUSILY	ROYALTY.
NAUGHTY	DAZEDLY
PAUCITY	DIZZILY
PAUNCHY	JAZZILY
PLUMPLY	
POULTRY	KIBBUTZ.
PRUDERY	KOLKHOZ.
ROUGHLY	SHOWBIZ.
ROUNDLY	+BERLIOZ

479

Notes

Notes

Notes

Notes

Notes

Notes

Notes